D1343196

⊚Harden's

BEST UK RESTAURANTS

2018

SURVEY DRIVEN REVIEWS OF OVER 2,800 RESTAURANTS

Put us in your client's pocket!

Branded gift books and editions for iPhone
call to discuss the options on 020 7839 4763.

Follow Harden's on Twitter – @hardensbites

© **Harden's Limited 2017**

ISBN 978-0-9929408-2-9

British Library Cataloguing-in-Publication data: a catalogue record for this book is available from the British Library.

Printed in Britain by SRP, Exeter

Client Relations Manager: Clare Burnage
Assistant editors: Karen Moss, Bruce Millar, Clodagh Kinsella
Designers: (text) Paul Smith, (cover) Calverts Coop

Harden's Limited
Beta Space, 25 Holywell Row, London EC2A 4XE

Would restaurateurs (and PRs) please address communications to 'Editorial' at the above address, or ideally by email to: editorial@hardens.com The contents of this book are believed correct at the time of printing. Nevertheless, the publisher can accept no responsibility for errors or changes in or omissions from the details given.

◎Harden's 100

The UK's 100 Best Restaurants for 2018, as dictated by Harden's annual survey of diners

1	The Araki	London
2	Casamia, The General	Bristol
3	The Ledbury	London
4	Restaurant Nathan Outlaw	Port Isaac
5	The Fat Duck	Bray
6	Marianne	London
7	Waterside Inn	Bray
8	Black Swan	Oldstead
9	Restaurant Martin Wishart	Edinburgh
10	The Clove Club	London
11	Gidleigh Park	Chagford
12	Fraiche	Oxton
13	Restaurant Sat Bains	Nottingham
14	Ormer Mayfair	London
15	Gareth Ward at Ynyshir	Eglwys Fach
16	Sushi Tetsu	London
17	Story	London
18	L'Enclume	Cartmel
19	Yorke Arms	Ramsgill-in-Nidderdale
20	The Greenhouse	London
21	Midsummer House	Cambridge
22	Le Gavroche	London

The Araki, London

Casamia, The General, Bristol

Waterside Inn, Bray

Gidleigh Park, Chagford

23	Pied à Terre	*London*
24	Sketch, Lecture Room	*London*
25	Belmond Le Manoir aux Quat' Saisons	*Great Milton*
26	Umu	*London*
27	Bubbledogs, Kitchen Table	*London*
28	The Five Fields	*London*
29	Raby Hunt	*Summerhouse*
30	Moor Hall	*Aughton*
31	Bohemia	*Jersey*
32	Adam's	*Birmingham*
33	Texture	*London*
34	Estiatorio Milos	*London*
35	Andrew Fairlie	*Auchterarder*
36	Morston Hall	*Morston*
37	Hélène Darroze	*London*
38	Tyddyn Llan	*Llandrillo*
39	The Box Tree	*Ilkley*
40	Le Cochon Aveugle	*York*
41	Pétrus	*London*
42	Hedone	*London*
43	Hambleton Hall	*Hambleton*
44	The Neptune	*Old Hunstanton*
45	The Ritz	*London*
46	Roux at Parliament Square	*London*
47	The Kitchin	*Edinburgh*
48	Murano	*London*

◎Harden's **100**

49	Llangoed Hall	*Llyswen*
50	Paul Ainsworth at No. 6	*Padstow*
51	108 Garage	*London*
52	Hakkasan Mayfair	*London*
53	Chez Bruce	*London*
54	Lympstone Manor	*Exmouth*
55	Jamavar	*London*
56	Hunan	*London*
57	The Forest Side	*Grasmere*
58	The Art School	*Liverpool*
59	André Garrett At Cliveden	*Taplow*
60	House of Tides	*Newcastle upon Tyne*
61	Artichoke	*Amersham*
62	5 North Street	*Winchcombe*
63	Goodman City	*London*
64	Trishna	*London*
65	Wilks	*Bristol*
66	Norn	*Edinburgh*
67	One-O-One	*London*
68	The Three Chimneys	*Dunvegan*
69	Elystan Street	*London*
70	Typing Room	*London*
71	La Trompette	*London*
72	Where The Light Gets In	*Stockport*
73	The Man Behind The Curtain	*Leeds*
74	Restaurant James Sommerin	*Penarth*

75	Marcus, The Berkeley	*London*
76	The Whitebrook	*Whitebrook*
77	Pollen Street Social	*London*
78	Gauthier Soho	*London*
79	Zuma	*London*
80	La Petite Maison	*London*
81	Locanda Locatelli	*London*
82	Northcote	*Langho*
83	The Harrow at Little Bedwyn	*Marlborough*
84	The Woodspeen	*Newbury*
85	The Sportsman	*Seasalter*
86	The Glasshouse	*Kew*
87	Wiltons	*London*
88	Purnells	*Birmingham*
89	Coya	*London*
90	La Dame de Pic London	*London*
91	Roka	*London*
92	Seafood Restaurant	*Padstow*
93	The Seahorse	*Dartmouth*
94	The Peat Inn	*Cupar*
95	Scott's	*London*
96	Stovell's	*Chobham*
97	Trinity	*London*
98	Portland	*London*
99	Min Jiang	*London*
100	Medlar	*London*

Restaurants are helping change the way we eat.

North Sea cod is back on the menu, thanks in part to the many restaurants who gave the popular fish a break by taking it off their menus. Tonnes less plastic will be clogging up our oceans after a growing number of restaurants and pubs stopped automatically sticking straws in every drink they served. And, in response to the public's increasing appetite for more vegetable based dishes, chefs are shaking up their menus and offering platefuls of plant-based deliciousness.

These are just three of the myriad of ways in which restaurants are changing, responding positively to the urgent environmental and health demands we all face, by using food as a force for good.

That's why we are proud to partner with the Sustainable Restaurant Association again this year – to include their Food Made Good sustainability stars awarded to restaurants that have demonstrated they are serving food that not only tastes good, but does good too.

At the beginning of the decade food waste was seen in the sector as a dirty, difficult problem, best swept into a dark corner of the kitchen. Now, it's starting to be viewed as a business opportunity with restaurants like Spring creating scratch menus using ingredients otherwise deemed surplus to requirements.

As the issues that affect our food system evolve, so the SRA has moved on, introducing a new means of assessing restaurants.

Now it defines a Good Restaurant as one that will do these ten things:

Support Global Farmers	Source Fish Responsibly
Value Natural Resources	Serve More Veg & Better Meat
Treat People Fairly	Reduce Reuse Recycle
Feed Children Well	Waste no Food
Celebrate Local	Support the Community

Winners at the 2016 Food Made Good Awards included:

Lussmanns Fish and Grill – *People's Favourite Restaurant*

Poco – *Food Made Good Restaurant of the Year*

Captain's Galley – *Food Made Good Scottish Restaurant of the Year*

The Gallery, Barry – *Food Made Good, Welsh Restaurant of the Year*

Arbor Restaurant – *Food Made Good Environment Award*

www.foodmadegood.org · www.thesra.org · @the_sra.org · @foodmadegood.org

CONTENTS

108 Garage W10

Aster SW1

RATINGS & PRICES

Ratings

Our rating system does not tell you – as most guides do – that expensive restaurants are often better than cheap ones! What we do is compare each restaurant's performance – as judged by the average ratings awarded by reporters in the survey – with other similarly-priced restaurants.

This approach has the advantage that it helps you find – whatever your budget for any particular meal – where you will get the best 'bang for your buck'.

The following qualities are assessed:

F	—	Food
S	—	Service
A	—	Ambience

The rating indicates that, *in comparison with other restaurants in the same price-bracket*, performance is...

5	—	Exceptional
4	—	Very good
3	—	Good
2	—	Average
1	—	Poor

> ## NEW SINCE 2015!
> Regular readers remember we've turned our marking system on its head. **5** is the new **1**!

Prices

The price shown for each restaurant is the cost for one (1) person of an average threecourse dinner with half a bottle of house wine and coffee, any cover charge, service and VAT. Lunch is often cheaper. With BYO restaurants, we have assumed that two people share a £7 bottle of off-licence wine.

Telephone number – all numbers are '020' numbers.

Map reference – shown immediately after the telephone number.

Full postcodes – for non-group restaurants, the first entry in the 'small print' at the end of each listing, so you can set your sat-nav.

Website and Twitter – shown in the small print, where applicable.

Last orders time – listed after the website (if applicable); Sunday may be up to 90 minutes earlier.

Opening hours – unless otherwise stated, restaurants are open for lunch and dinner seven days a week.

Credit and debit cards – unless otherwise stated, Mastercard, Visa, Amex and Maestro are accepted.

Dress – where appropriate, the management's preferences concerning patrons' dress are given.

Special menus – if we know of a particularly good value set menu we note this (e.g. "set weekday L"), together with its formula price (FP), calculated exactly as in 'Prices' above. Details change, so always check ahead.

SRA Star Rating – the sustainability index, as calculated by the Sustainable Restaurant Association – see page 10 for more information.

FROM THE EDITORS

Welcome to our 27th anniversary edition of what you users and diners have helped to make the UK's most authoritative restaurant guide.

As ever, Harden's is written 'from the bottom up' based on the results of the survey conducted in late spring 2017. It is completely rewritten each year, with the selection of restaurants based on that unique annual poll of thousands of restaurant-goers, in which you are most welcome to take part. (Further details of this are given overleaf.)

Unlike any other national UK restaurant guide – certainly of a print variety – reviews and ratings in the book are primarily statistically derived and driven from our user-survey. This is a much more direct, and we believe democratic use of user feedback than the processes of some competing publications, particularly those who solicit reader feedback, but where the linkage between such feedback and the reviews and ratings in the guide is much less clear-cut.

The survey methodology is also a very different kettle of fish from the modus operandi of user-review sites such as TripAdvisor. The latter has been put under the spotlight as never before in recent times with questions raised over the veracity of a huge number of reviews. With the Harden's survey however, because we don't publish the raw reviews supplied by the dining public, but only a summary based on the careful curation of those raw reviews, it is a much harder ballot to stuff. Of course, restaurants do still try to stuff the ballot in their favour – or less often to disadvantage their competitors – but the presence of so many diners who have participated in the survey for many years provides a good sanity check on the veracity of reviews from more recent sign-ups.

This guide includes the full content of our separately-published London guide, as well as coverage of cities, towns and villages across the whole of the UK. We recognise that the result is a guide somewhat skewed to London. We urge readers, though, to think of this extensive London coverage as a bonus rather than a defect. After all, our out-of-London coverage alone exceeds the headline number of reviews in the whole of The Good Food Guide including London. Add in our London coverage and there are more than double the number of entries than the rival publication.

It is certainly no longer true, as one could have said as recently as five years ago, that large areas of the UK are pretty much restaurant deserts, devoid of almost anything of interest to the discerning visitor. This ongoing transformation is perhaps most obvious in the great regional centres – even Manchester, a 'second city' which has been a laggard until very recently, seems finally to be getting its act together!

We urge all our readers to help us do even better justice to the restaurant scene outside the capital. If you think your area is under-represented, the answer is largely in your own hands – take part in our annual survey, and make sure your friends do too!

We are very grateful to each of our thousands of reporters, without whose input this guide could not have been written. Many reporters express views about a number of restaurants at some length, knowing full well that – given the concise format of the guide – we can seemingly never 'do justice' to their observations. We must assume that they do so in the confidence that the short – and we hope snappy – summaries we produce are as fair and well-informed as possible.

You, the reader, must judge – restaurant guides are not works of literature, and should be assessed on the basis of utility. This is a case where the proof of the pudding really is in the eating.

All restaurant guides are the subject of continual revision, and the more input we have, the more accurate and comprehensive future editions will be. If you are not already signed up, please do join the www.hardens.com mailing list – we will then ensure that you are invited to take part in future surveys.

Harden's, Shoreditch, November 2017

HOW THIS BOOK IS ORGANISED

The guide begins in London, and contains the full text of the guide already published as *London Restaurants 2018*. Thereafter, the guide is organised strictly alphabetically by location, without regard to national divisions – Beaumaris, Belfast and Birmingham appear together under 'B'.

For *cities and larger towns*, you should therefore be able to turn straight to the relevant section. In addition to the entries for the restaurants themselves, cities which have significant numbers of restaurants also have a brief introductory overview.

In *less densely populated areas*, you will generally find it easiest to start with the relevant map at the back of the book, which will guide you to the appropriate place names.

If you are looking for a specific restaurant, the alphabetical index at the very back of the book lists all of the restaurants – London and UK – in this guide.

YOUR CONTRIBUTION

This book is the result of a research effort involving thousands of 'reporters'. As a group, you are 'ordinary' members of the public who share with us summary reviews of the best and the worst of your annual dining experiences. This year, over 8,500 of you gave us some 50,000 reviews in total.

The density of the feedback on London (where many of the top places attract several hundred reviews each) is such that the ratings for the restaurants in the capital are almost exclusively statistical in derivation. (We have, as it happens, visited almost all the restaurants in the London section, anonymously, and at our own expense, but we use our personal experiences only to inform the standpoint from which to interpret the consensus opinion.)

In the case of the more commented-upon restaurants away from the capital, we have adopted an essentially statistical approach very similar to London. In the case of less visited provincial establishments, however, the interpretation of survey results owes as much to art as it does to science.

In our experience, smaller establishments are – for better or worse – generally quite consistent, and we have therefore felt able to place a relatively high level of confidence in a lower level of commentary. Conservatism on our part, however, may have led to some smaller places being under-rated compared to their more-visited peers.

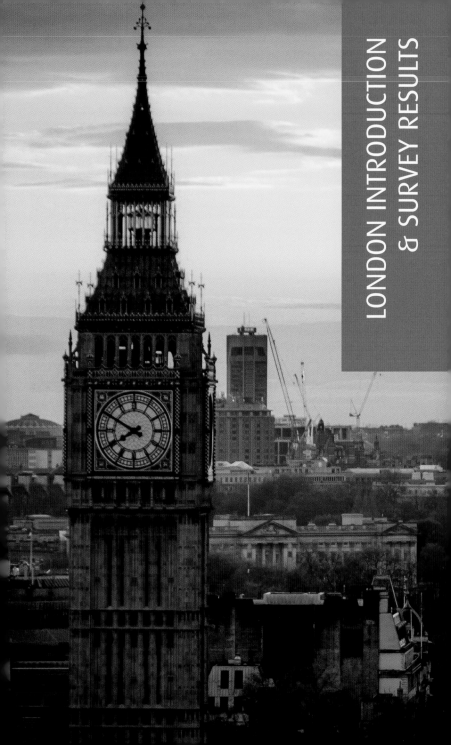

RANKED BY THE NUMBER OF REPORTERS' VOTES

These are the restaurants which were most frequently mentioned by reporters. (Last year's position is given in brackets.) An asterisk* indicates the first appearance in the list of a recently-opened restaurant.

1	J Sheekey (1)
2	Clos Maggiore (2)
3	Chez Bruce (4)
4	Scott's (6)
5	Le Gavroche (3)
6	The Ledbury (5)
7	The Wolseley (8)
8	Gymkhana (7)
9	Gauthier Soho (14)
10	Brasserie Zédel (9)

J Sheekey

11	The Delaunay (11)
12	La Trompette (13)
13	Andrew Edmunds (16)
14	Fera at Claridge's, Claridge's Hotel (12)
15	The River Café (15)
16	The Cinnamon Club (10)
17	Bocca Di Lupo (21)
18	Dinner, Mandarin Oriental (31)
19	Galvin La Chapelle (19)
20	Pollen Street Social (17)

Galvin La Chapelle

21	Benares (23)
22	La Poule au Pot (19)
23	Trinity (-)
24	Gordon Ramsay (24)
25	Sexy Fish (36)
26	Le Caprice (30)
27	Medlar (22)
28	Galvin Bistrot de Luxe (27)
29	Noble Rot (-)
30	The Goring Hotel (-)

Benares

31	Bleeding Heart Restaurant (27)
32	The Five Fields (-)
33	Bentley's (-)
34	A Wong (40)
35	Chutney Mary (-)
36	Fischer's (-)
37	Pied à Terre (26)
38	Moro (32)
39	Hoppers (-)
40	Enoteca Turi (-)

Bentley's

Top gastronomic experience

1   The Ledbury (1)
2   Chez Bruce (3)
3   Le Gavroche (2)
4   Gauthier Soho (5)
5   Clos Maggiore (-)
6   Fera at Claridge's, Claridge's Hotel (4)
7   The Five Fields (-)
8   La Trompette (8)
9   Dinner, Mandarin Oriental (-)
10 Pollen Street Social (6)

Favourite

1   Chez Bruce (1)
2   J Sheekey (4)
3   La Trompette (8)
4   Le Gavroche (2)
5   The River Café (10)
6   The Wolseley (7)
7   Moro (6)
8   The Ledbury (3)
9   Clos Maggiore (-)
10 Gauthier Soho (5)

Best for business

1   The Wolseley (1)
2   The Delaunay (4)
3   Bleeding Heart Restaurant (2)
4   Scott's (5)
5   City Social (6)
6   Coq d'Argent (-)
7   Savoy Grill (-)
8   Galvin La Chapelle (-)
9   Hawksmoor*
10 The Don (7)

Best for romance

1   Clos Maggiore (1)
2   La Poule au Pot (2)
3   Andrew Edmunds (3)
4   Gauthier Soho (7)
5   Bleeding Heart Restaurant (4)
6   Le Caprice (8)
7   Le Gavroche (5)
8   J Sheekey (-)
9   The Ledbury (-)
10 Chez Bruce (9)

Best breakfast/brunch

1   The Wolseley (1)
2   The Delaunay (2)
3   The Ivy Chelsea Garden (-)
4   Riding House Café (9)
5   Caravan King's Cross*
6   Granger & Co*
7   Cecconi's (3)
8   The Ivy Kensington Brasserie (-)
9   Milk (-)
10 Breakfast Club*

Best bar/pub food

1   The Anchor & Hope (1)
2   Harwood Arms (2)
3   Bull & Last (4)
4   The Anglesea Arms (-)
5   The Eagle (-)
6   The Camberwell Arms (5)
6= Pig & Butcher (6)
8   Earl Spencer (-)
9   The Marksman (-)
10 The Ladbroke Arms (3)

Most disappointing cooking

1   Oxo Tower (Restaurant) (1)
2   The Chiltern Firehouse (2)
3   Alain Ducasse at The Dorchester (-)
4   Dinner, Mandarin Oriental (9)
5   The Ivy Café*
6   Le Gavroche (-)
7   The River Café (-)
8   Pollen Street Social (4)
9   Tredwell's (-)
10 1 Chez Bruce (-)

Most overpriced restaurant

1   The River Café (2)
2   Sexy Fish (1)
3   Gordon Ramsay (4)
4   Oxo Tower (Restaurant) (3)
5   Dinner, Mandarin Oriental (-)
6   The Chiltern Firehouse (6)
7   Alain Ducasse at The Dorchester (9)
8   Le Gavroche (8)
9   Aqua Shard (-)
10 Hutong, The Shard (10)

SURVEY HIGHEST RATINGS

FOOD

SERVICE

£100+

	FOOD		SERVICE
1	The Araki	1	The Araki
2	The Ledbury	2	The Ledbury
3	Marianne	3	Le Gavroche
4	The Clove Club	4	Hélène Darroze
5	Ormer Mayfair	5	Marianne

£75-£99

1	Sushi Tetsu	1	Sushi Tetsu
2	The Five Fields	2	The Five Fields
3	Roux at Parliament Sq	3	Club Gascon
4	Chez Bruce	4	Chez Bruce
5	Jamavar	5	L'Autre Pied

£60-£74

1	108 Garage	1	108 Garage
2	HKK	2	Oslo Court
3	Dinings	3	Cabotte
4	Anglo	4	Otto's
5	Tamarind	5	HKK

£45-£59

1	José	1	The Anglesea Arms
2	A Wong	2	Margot
3	Babur	3	The Barbary
4	The Barbary	4	José
5	Jin Kichi	5	Pig & Butcher

£44 or less

1	Santa Maria	1	Paradise Hampstead
2	Barrafina	2	Barrafina x 3
3	Bleecker Burger	3	Brady's
4	Silk Road	4	Kricket
5	Padella	5	Kiln

AMBIENCE

I	Sketch (Lecture Rm)
2	The Ritz
3	Céleste
4	Marianne
5	Galvin at Windows

I	Clos Maggiore
2	The Berners Tavern
3	Bob Bob Ricard
4	Duck & Waffle
5	Sushisamba

I	La Poule au Pot
2	108 Garage
3	Smith's Wapping
4	Oslo Court
5	The Wolseley

I	José
2	The Anglesea Arms
3	The Barbary
4	Andrew Edmunds
5	Margot

I	Barrafina
2	Brasserie Zédel
3	Dishoom
4	temper Soho
5	Blacklock

OVERALL

I	The Ledbury
2	Marianne
3	The Araki
4	The Ritz
5	Le Gavroche

I	Sushi Tetsu
2	The Five Fields
3	Clos Maggiore
4	Chez Bruce
5	Gauthier Soho

I	108 Garage
2	HKK
3	Oslo Court
4	Clarke's
5	Smith's Wapping

I	José
2	The Anglesea Arms
3	The Barbary
4	Margot
5	Pig & Butcher

I	Barrafina
2	Kricket
3	Brady's
4	Paradise Hampstead
5	Kiln

SURVEY BEST BY CUISINE

These are the restaurants which received the best average food ratings (excluding establishments with a small or notably local following).

Where the most common types of cuisine are concerned, we present the results in two price-brackets. For less common cuisines, we list the top three, regardless of price.

For further information about restaurants which are particularly notable for their food, see the cuisine lists starting on page 158. These indicate, using an asterisk*, restaurants which offer exceptional or very good food.

British, Modern

£60 and over		Under £60	
1	The Ledbury	1	The Frog
2	The Five Fields	2	Pig & Butcher
3	Marianne	3	10 Greek Street
4	The Clove Club	4	The Anglesea Arms
5	Ormer Mayfair	5	The Camberwell Arms

French

£60 and over		Under £60	
1	The Greenhouse	1	Cabotte
2	Le Gavroche	2	Blanchette
3	Pied à Terre	3	Casse-Croute
4	La Trompette	4	Café du Marché
5	Gauthier Soho	5	Gazette

Italian/Mediterranean

£60 and over		Under £60	
1	Murano	1	Padella
2	Locanda Locatelli	2	Palatino
3	Assaggi	3	Margot
4	Bocca Di Lupo	4	Ottolenghi
5	L'Anima	5	L'Amorosa

Indian & Pakistani

£60 and over		Under £60	
1	Jamavar	1	Babur
2	Trishna	2	Kricket
3	Tamarind	3	Paradise Hampstead
4	Gymkhana	4	The Painted Heron
5	Amaya	5	Café Spice Namaste

Chinese

£60 and over

1. HKK
2. Hakkasan Mayfair
3. Hunan
4. Min Jiang
5. Yauatcha

Under £60

1. A Wong
2. Silk Road
3. Shikumen
4. Yming
5. Singapore Garden

Japanese

£60 and over

1. The Araki
2. Sushi Tetsu
3. Dinings
4. Roka
5. Umu

Under £60

1. Takahashi
2. Jin Kichi
3. Bone Daddies
4. Pham Sushi
5. Yoshino

British, Traditional

1. Scott's
2. The Ritz
3. St John

Vegetarian

1. Mildreds W1
2. Gate SW6
3. Ganapati

Burgers, etc

1. Bleecker Burger
2. Patty and Bun
3. Honest Burgers

Pizza

1. Santa Maria
2. Pizza Pilgrims
3. Pizza East

Fish & Chips

1. Brady's
2. Toff's
3. North Sea Fish

Thai

1. Som Saa
2. Kiln
3. Sukho Fine Thai Cuisine

Steaks & Grills

1. Zelman Meats
2. Goodman City
3. Blacklock

Fish & Seafood

1. Scott's
2. Outlaw's
3. One-O-One

Fusion

1. 108 Garage
2. Bubbledogs (KT)
3. Providores

Spanish

1. José
2. Barrafina Drury Lane
3. Moro

Turkish

1. Mangal 1
2. Fez Mangal
3. Best Mangal

Lebanese

1. Cedar
2. Maroush
3. Arabica

THE RESTAURANT SCENE

Turning point?

There are 193 newcomers in this year's guide. This is the second largest figure recorded in its 27-year history, but a tad lower than last year's record-breaking 200.

Closings are up a little on last year's 76 to 84: a figure at the upper end of that typically recorded (the third highest), but still well below the record (of 113 in 2004).

Net openings (openings minus closings) slipped to 110: just below the low 120s in the two preceding years. A further sense that the market is no longer 'screaming along' comes from the ratio of openings to closings – at 2.3:1, this is a second year of decline from 2016's high peak.

Is this the dreaded Brexit-effect many fear? It may be in part (see 'So stupid, so short-sighted, so xenophobic' below), but another significant factor is a slight decline in the fully independent restaurant sector in London as chains – and in particular small chains – proliferate.

Indies give way to small chains

Harden's has historically favoured listing indies over multiples, and the declines noted above partly reflect this methodology. We have never sought to track bigger groups, excluding openings from our statistics after a chain becomes more numerous than a couple of spin-offs.

But the proliferation of small groups is one of the big stories of the current restaurant market. Familiar one-offs are all of a sudden 'rolling out'. The Ivy is the most obvious example, but there are other smaller ones (such as Mildreds). Meanwhile, it is taken as read that newer brands will seek to clone themselves at the earliest opportunity.

If branches we have historically excluded are added into our statistics, this would imply another pretty hot year, with the number of previously excluded spin-offs more than doubling from 25 to 53, to give an 'aggregate' newcomers total of 246 this year vs 225 a year earlier.

So, in the 'quality-ish' restaurant sector, this would imply the growth rate is still strong after all. And while there is some shift from indies to small groups, this growth in the small chain market is still good news for restaurant-goers, and undercuts the worst of the Brexit-doom scenarios.

"So stupid, so short-sighted, so xenophobic…"

In accepting his Lifetime Achievement Award at this year's Harden's London Restaurant Awards, Jeremy King chose the above words to describe Brexit. It shows how little things have moved on in the year since Bruce Poole – in accepting the same award twelve months earlier – addressed the same issue more pithily: "Without Europeans, we're f###ked".

Why are top restaurateurs not more sanguine about Brexit?

Could it be anything to do with the fact that according to the British Hospitality Association, 75% of London's waiting staff come from Europe? And also a very high proportion of its chefs, sous-chefs, kitchen porters…

With the post-Brexit uncertainty and the hit to the pound, it has seldom been so hard to recruit staff. Chef Alexis Gauthier recently made catering press headlines describing the current situation as 'toxic' and saying that in 20 years in London restaurants he has never seen such pressures on recruiting people.

London's restaurants nowadays are a superb advertisement for the capital. They are also a fine advertisement for the pluspoints of immigration. When Britons speak proudly of having the greatest restaurant city on earth, it is the diversity of the capital's offering – with restaurants from all points of the globe – which is usually touted as its worldbeating feature. Of really traditional British restaurants, there are vanishingly few. It's not why people want to come!

Where and what's hot

After Central London, East London remains London's prime area for restaurant openings, although almost as popular was South London this year (East had 39 debuts vs South's 36). A particularly weak performance from West London made it the least interesting point on the compass: a distinction traditionally reserved for North London.

Modern British and Italian cuisines remain the most popular for new openings. But meat-based cuisines were less to the fore than last year, with Indian openings pipping them to the post as the third most popular category. Japanese openings, in fourth place, continue to lead other more 'traditional' categories such as French.

The hottest of the hot

Every year, we choose what to us seem to be the most significant openings of the year. This year our selection is as follows:

Core	Lorne
La Dame de Pic	Luca
Honey & Smoke	108 Garage
Ikoyi	Plaquemine Lock
Jamavar	Western's Laundry

Prices

The average price of dinner for one at establishments listed in this guide is £53.20 (compared to £51.37 last year). Prices have risen by 3.6% in the past 12 months (up on 2.1% in the preceding 12 months). This rate compares with a general annual inflation rate of 2.9% for the 12 months to August 2017, accelerating the trend seen last year of restaurant price rises running somewhat higher than inflation generally.

Jamavar W1

OPENINGS AND CLOSURES

Openings (193)

Alcedo
L'Antica Pizzeria da Michele
Arthur Hooper's
Assaggi Bar & Pizzeria
Aster Restaurant
Aviary
Babette
Bala Baya
Baluchi, Lalit Hotel London
Bang Bang Oriental
Bar Douro
Bistro Vadouvan
Bleecker Burger (SW1, EC4)
Bokan
Bon Vivant
La Bonne Bouffe
Bonnie Gull Seafood Shack
The Bothy
Breddos Tacos
Brigadiers
Brookmill
by Chloe
Cabotte
Café Murano Pastificio
  (WC2)
Campania & Jones
Cartel
Ceru
Chai Thali
Chelsea Cellar
Chick 'n' Sours (WC2)
Chik'n
Chin Chin Club
Cinnamon Bazaar
Clarette
The Clifton
Coal Rooms
The Coal Shed
The Colton Arms
Comptoir Café & Wine
Corazón
Core by Clare Smyth
La Dame de Pic London
Dandy
Darjeeling Express
Dastaan
Dean & DeLuca
Dinings (SW3)

Dokke
Duck & Waffle Local
Duckroad
Duddell's
Dum Biryani
Emilia's Crafted Pasta
Fancy Crab
Ferdi
Fiume
Flavour Bastard
The Frog (WC2)
La Fromagerie (WC1)
Fucina
Gabeto Cantina
The Garden Cafe at
  the Garden Museum
The Gate (W1)
GBR
Ginza Onodera
Go-Viet
Greenwood
Gul and Sepoy
Hai Cenato
Henrietta
Honey & Smoke
Hoppers (W1)
Hot Pot
Humble Grape (N1)
Ikoyi
Indian Accent
Isabel
James Cochran EC3 (N1,
  EC3)
Japan Centre Food Hall
Jean-Georges at
The Connaught
Jugemu
Jules
Juniper Tree
Knife
Koya (EC2)
Lady Mildmay
Lao Cafe
Laphet
LASSCO Bar & DIning
The Laughing Heart
Lockhouse
London Shell Co.

Lorne
Louie Louie
Luca
Lupins
Mac & Wild (EC2)
Machiya
Madame D's
Made of Dough (SE15)
Magpie
MAM
Mare Street Market
Mayfair Garden
Megan's by the Green (SW6)
Mei Ume
Meraki
Messapica
Minnow
Monty's Deli
Mother
Nanashi
The Ned
Neo Bistro
Nobu Shoreditch (EC2)
Noizé
Nutbourne
Oak N4
108 Garage
Oree (W8, SW3)
The Other Naughty Piglet
Over Under
The Oystermen Seafood
Kitchen & Bar
Palatino
Pamban
Il Pampero
The Pantechnicon
Parlez
Passione e Tradizione
Pastaio
The Petersham
PF Chang's Asian Table
Piebury Corner (N1)
Pisqu
Pizzastorm
Plaquemine Lock
Plot
Pomaio
Pomona's

Popolo
Quartieri
Radici
Rambla
Red Rooster
Rick Stein
Rigo'
Rola Wala
Sabor
Saiphin's Thai Kitchen
Santo Remedio
Sibarita
Skewd Kitchen
Smoking Goat (E1)
Sophie's Steakhouse (W1)
Southam Street
Sparrow
Spinach

Stagolee's
Stecca
Sticky Mango at RSJ
The Stoke House
Strangers Dining Room,
House of Commons
Street XO
Summers
Sumosan Twiga
Table Du Marche
TAKA
Tamarind Kitchen
Tandoor Chop House
temper City (EC2)
Temple & Sons
Test Kitchen
tibits (SE1)
Timmy Green

Tom Simmons
Tratra
Trawler Trash
Treves & Hyde
The Truscott Arms
Tuyo
The Vincent
VIVI
Waka
Walnut
Westerns Laundry
The Wigmore, The Langham
Winemakers Deptford
XU
Yolk
Zheng

Closures (84)

Almeida
Alquimia
Antico
Atari-Ya (NW4)
L'Autre Pied
Barnyard
Bibo
La Brasserie
Brasserie Gustave
Buoni Amici
Café Pistou
Canvas
The Chancery
Chapters
Chor Bizarre
Le Coq
Cornish Tiger
CURIO + TA TA
Dabbous
The Depot
Les Deux Salons
Dickie Fitz
Emile's
Escocesa
Fields
Fish Club
Foxlow
Grain Store (N1)
Habanera

Hibiscus
Hill & Szrok Pub (N1)
Ho (W1)
Hush (EC4)
Ichiryu
Imli Street
Inaho
Indian Zilla
K10 (EC2)
Kerbisher & Malt (EC1)
Koffmann's, The Berkeley
KOJAWAN, Hilton
Metropole
Kricket, Pop Brixton (SW9)
Kurobuta Harvey Nics (SW1)
The Lady Ottoline
Leong's Legends (W1)
Lobster Pot
Lotus
Magdalen
Market
Masala Grill
Matsuri
Murakami
New Mayflower
The Newman Arms
160 Smokehouse (NW6)
Orso
Osteria 60

Ottolenghi (W8)
Patio
Poco (E2)
Polpo, Harvey Nichols (SW1)
Princess Victoria
The Richmond
Rivington Grill (EC2)
RSJ
Salmontini
Samarkand
San Daniele del Friuli
Shotgun
Smoke and Salt (Residency)
Sophie's Steakhouse (WC2)
Spring Workshop
Sumosan
Tartufo
Toto's
Tsunami (W1)
Vico (WC2)
Vintage Salt (EC2)
Vintage Salt (N1)
Wazen
West Thirty Six
The Woodford
Wormwood
Yumi Izakay

Duck & Waffle Local SW1

Duddell's SE1

FLAVOUR BASTARD

63-64 FRITH STREET

Flavour Bastard W1

LONDON DIRECTORY

A Cena TW1 £50 3️⃣4️⃣4️⃣
418 Richmond Rd 020 8288 0108 1–4A
*This favourite, rather smart St Margaret's Italian
as ever earns consistent praise from satisfied locals:
"a terrific restaurant, with lovely food and attentive
service". It's handy before or after a game at nearby
Twickenham, too. / TW1 2EB; www.acena.co.uk;
@acenarestaurant; 10 pm; closed Mon L & Sun D;
booking max 6 may apply; set weekday L £33 (FP).*

A Wong SW1 £46 5️⃣5️⃣3️⃣
70 Wilton Rd 020 7828 8931 2–4B
*"Andrew Wong is a magician!" – and his "new-
school Chinese" in Pimlico provides not only some
of "the most exhilarating food in London", but also,
contrary to cultural stereotypes, the service here is
"exceptionally graceful and helpful". The setting is
"lively" (if "crowded") too, and in the evening, there's
also the option of a small Chef's Table, or eating in
the "decadent" 'Forbidden City' basement bar. There's
a wide range of eating options too, from "incredibly
inventive dim sum", to a "fabulous 10-course tasting
menu". / SW1V 1DE; www.awong.co.uk; @awongSW1;
10.15 pm; closed Mon L & Sun; credit card required
to book.*

The Abingdon W8 £65 3️⃣3️⃣4️⃣
54 Abingdon Rd 020 7937 3339 6–2A
*In a "quiet backstreet south of High Street Ken",
this posh gastropub stalwart remains "a tremendous
local" for a loyal well-heeled crowd ("it's full of
regulars, so must be doing something right!"). Top
Tip – the best seats are in the booths. / W8 6AP;
www.theabingdon.co.uk; @TheAbingdonW8; 10.30 pm,
Fri & Sat 11 pm, Sun 10 pm.*

About Thyme SW1 £53 2️⃣3️⃣3️⃣
82 Wilton Rd 020 7821 7504 2–4B
*Long-serving manager Issy is a popular host
at this "reliable" Pimlico stalwart, serving
"good, Spanish-orientated" dishes. / SW1V 1DL;
www.aboutthyme.co.uk; 10 pm; closed Sun.*

L'Absinthe NW1 £49 2️⃣4️⃣3️⃣
40 Chalcot Rd 020 7483 4848 9–3B
*Burgundian patron, Jean-Christophe Slowik always
makes this "lively" corner bistro in Primrose Hill
"a fun place to be". There's some question as to
whether its "limited" and "distinctly French" menu
"needs re-inventing", but "it does now offer brunch
and Sunday lunch". / NW1 8LS; www.labsinthe.co.uk;
@absinthe07jc; 10 pm, Sun 9 pm; closed Mon, Tue L,
Wed L & Thu L.*

Abu Zaad W12 £23 3️⃣3️⃣2️⃣
29 Uxbridge Rd 020 8749 5107 8–1C
*"Excellent fresh food prepared to order and in very
generous portions" underpins the appeal of this
"lively" Syrian café at the top of Shepherd's Bush
market, serving a wide array of mezze, wraps,
and juices plus more substantial fare. / W12 8LH;*

*www.abuzaad.co.uk; 11 pm, Sat & Sun midnight; No
Amex.*

Adams Café W12 £33 3️⃣5️⃣3️⃣
77 Askew Rd 020 8743 0572 8–1B
*"Thoughtful, charming service" and "hearty,
uncomplicated dishes" ("delicious tagines and other
Tunisian/Moroccan specialities" like brik à l'oeuf)
mean the folk of 'Askew Village' are lucky to have
this sweet café, which "has maintained excellent
quality for over 25 years", and where "the BYO
policy (£3 corkage) leads to a very modest bill"
(although it is also licensed). By day, it's a British
greasy spoon. / W12 9AH; www.adamscafe.co.uk;
@adamscafe; 10 pm; closed Sun.*

Addie's Thai Café SW5 £33 3️⃣2️⃣2️⃣
121 Earl's Court Rd 020 7259 2620 6–2A
*"The bill's so modest, you wonder if they forgot
something!", at this "wonderful, small and compact"
street food café in Earl's Court. / SW5 9RL;
www.addiesthai.co.uk; 11 pm, Sun 10.30 pm; No Amex.*

Addomme SW2 £41 4️⃣3️⃣2️⃣
17-21 Sternhold
Avenue 020 8678 8496 11–2C
*Next to Streatham Hill station, this "small and
modestly furnished" café and take-away (overseen
by Stefano and Nadia from Capri) is "top of the
pile locally" serving "terrific pizzas from the wood
burning oven, together with a range of specials
changed weekly at very reasonable prices!" / SW2
4PA; www.addomme.co.uk; @PizzAddomme; 11 pm.*

**The Admiral Codrington
SW3** £58 2️⃣3️⃣4️⃣
17 Mossop St 020 7581 0005 6–2C
*An age-old favourite backstreet boozer – albeit
with a touch of "Chelsea elegance" – the 'Cod'
is still "all in all a great place" when it comes to
atmosphere, although its food offer has received
a more mixed billing in recent times. / SW3 2LY;
www.theadmiralcodrington.co.uk; @TheAdCod; 10 pm,
Thu-Sat 11 pm, Sun 9 pm; No trainers.*

Afghan Kitchen N1 £26 4️⃣3️⃣2️⃣
35 Islington Grn 020 7359 8019 9–3D
*"A great little local standby" for a "quick bite" – this
Afghan canteen by Islington Green scores well for
consistency and value with its "small selection" of
simple dishes. The only quibble is that "the menu is
static" – "but you know what you're getting every
time". / N1 8DU; 11 pm; closed Mon & Sun; Cash only;
no booking.*

Aglio e Olio SW10 £48 3️⃣3️⃣3️⃣
194 Fulham Rd 020 7351 0070 6–3B
*"No frills good food" – in particular "perfect pasta"
– fuels the "loud and buzzy" atmosphere ("manic
on Chelsea match days") at this "fun", little café,
near Chelsea & Westminster Hospital. "Still my
firm favourite after over 10 years; the menu is*

reassuringly unchanged and the quality is excellent".
/ SW10 9PN; www.aglioeolio.co.uk; 11.00 pm.

Al Duca SW1 £53 **3****3****2**
4-5 Duke of York St   020 7839 3090   3–3D
"No more expensive than some chains, but with
better and varied Italian staples" – this "slightly
tucked-away", low-key St James's fixture is boosted
by its "attentive and friendly staff", and has for
many years now provided a consistently "pleasant"
and "reasonably priced" experience. / SW1Y 6LA;
www.alduca-restaurant.co.uk; 11 pm; closed Sun.

Al Forno £47 **2****4****4**
349 Upper Richmond Rd, SW15
020 8878 7522   11–2A
2a King's Rd, SW19   020 8540 5710   11–2B
"Service is attentive to just the right level" at this
"friendly" small chain of slightly old-fashioned local
Italians across southwest London. The pizza and
pasta dishes are at "good value" prices, and there's
a "really pleasant atmosphere, be it for dinner with
friends or Sunday lunch with the littlies". / 10 pm-11
pm.

Alain Ducasse at The Dorchester
W1 £134 **2****2****2**
53 Park Ln   020 7629 8866   3–3A
"It seriously makes me doubt the Michelin
rating system" – the world-famous Gallic chef's
Mayfair venture is "not in the same league as the
Waterside Inn or Fat Duck" yet inexplicably retains
its 3-star top billing. Admittedly, many reports
do advocate this hotel dining room's "discreetly
opulent surroundings", its "courteous" staff and
its "awesome" cuisine, but far too many sceptics
say it's "waaaayyyyyyy overpriced" for "muted"
food that's "nice but not a wow", and find the
luxurious interior rather "soulless". / W1K 1QA;
www.alainducasse-dorchester.com; 9.30 pm; closed
Mon, Sat L & Sun; Jacket required; booking essential; set
weekday L £95 (FP).

Albertine W12 £56 **3****3****4**
1 Wood Ln   020 8743 9593   8–1C
"Enhanced rather than revolutionised, so it continues
to feel like an old local favourite" – this veteran
Shepherds Bush wine bar (once the haunt of BBC
types from the former TV Centre nearby) has been
taken over and spruced up by Allegra McEvedy
(whose mother opened it in 1978) leaving it "less
scruffy, while maintaining its informality". There's
"not a huge menu" but the food is "vastly improved"
and there's "interesting wine" too. / W12 7DP;
www.albertinewinebar.co.uk; @AlbertineWine; 11 pm,
Thu-Sat midnight; closed Sat L & Sun; No Amex.

Albion £54 **2****2****2**
NEO Bankside, Holland St, SE1
020 3764 5550   10–3B
2-4 Boundary St, E2   020 7729 1051   13–1B

63 Clerkenwell Rd, EC1
020 3862 0750   10–1A
"Possibly a bit bland" sums up the lukewarm
reactions to Sir Terence Conran's trio of "un-
memorable" all-day pit stops in Bankside,
Clerkenwell and Shoreditch. They are "light,
clean and smart", so make "a good alternative
for business meetings", but it's "difficult to be
fantastically enthusiastic" about the "reasonably
average and slightly expensive" food and "sometimes
erratic" service. / 10 pm-11 pm, Sun-Sat E2 Fri & Sat
1 am, EC1, Fri & Sat midnight, Sun 6 pm-11 pm.

Alcedo N7 NEW £43 **3****4****3**
237 Holloway Rd   020 7998 7672   9–2D
"A new arrival bringing a touch of class and much
needed good bistro food to Holloway". "The menu is
limited, but all carefully prepared, and the proprietor
is very friendly". / N7 8HG.

The Alfred Tennyson
SW1 £61 **3****3****4**
10 Motcomb St   020 7730 6074   6–1D
"There's a good buzz about this place" – a
comfortably converted Belgravia Pub (part of
the Cubitt House Group), formerly known as The
Pantechnicon Dining Rooms (and re-named to
avoid confusion with their forthcoming venture in
the nearby building of the same name). "The food
is simple, but well-cooked" and fair value for such a
prime address. / SW1X 8LA; thealfredtennyson.co.uk;
@TheTennysonSW1; 10 pm, Sun 9.30 pm.

Ali Baba NW1 £25 **3****2****2**
32 Ivor Pl   020 7723 5805   2–1A
This "unique family-run Egyptian café" behind
a Marylebone takeaway owes its "engaging
personality" to its location in the owners' living room.
There's an "interesting" choice, so "order a variety
of starters with one or two main courses", and
remember to BYO. / NW1 6DA; alibabarestaurant.
co.uk; @alibabalondon; midnight; Cash only.

Alounak £27 **3****2****3**
10 Russell Gdns, W14   020 7603 1130   8–1D
44 Westbourne Grove, W2
020 7229 0416   7–1B
These "reliable BYO Persian cafés" have provided
"authentic and cheap" Middle Eastern food for 20
years at two atmospheric venues in Bayswater and
Olympia. / 11.30 pm; no Amex.

Alyn Williams, Westbury Hotel
W1 £96 **3****3****2**
37 Conduit St   020 7183 6426   3–2C
"Top notch cuisine and super service" still secure
many plaudits for Alyn Williams's (windowless)
Mayfair dining room, in the bowels of a hotel
off Bond Street, but it put in a more uneven
performance this year. "As quite often happens with
hotel restaurants, its atmosphere can lack" however,

F S A

and it took significant flak from critics this year for a number of "disappointing" and "unjustifiably expensive" meals. / W1S 2YF; www.alynwilliams.com; @Alyn_Williams; 10.30 pm; closed Mon & Sun; Jacket required; set weekday L £56 (FP).

Amaya SW1 £80 4 2 3
Halkin Arc, 19 Motcomb St
020 7823 1166 6–1D
"Amaya-zing!". "Your taste-buds go pop with delightfully subtle tapas" capturing the "distinctive flavours of Indian grills" at this "chic" modern Belgravia operation, arranged around an open kitchen – perennially one of London's top nouvelle Indians. / SW1X 8JT; www.amaya.biz; @theamaya_; 11.30 pm, Sun 10.30 pm; set weekday L £44 (FP).

The American Bar SW1 £58
16 - 18 Saint James's Place
020 7493 0111 3–4C
"Benoit is the perfect host" at this preppy St James's hideaway, at the end of a cute mews (splendid outside tables in summer), festooned with the ties and hats donated by patrons in decades past. Best known as a drinking den ("the 'White Mouse' is a must"), it also nowadays has a fairly substantial 'club-brasserie-style' menu, served from breakfast on, but – especially if you are having a dram – "bring lots of money". / SW1A 1NJ; thestaffordlondon.com/the-american-bar; @StaffordLondon; 10 pm; booking L only.

Ametsa with Arzak Instruction, Halkin Hotel SW1 £91 3 3 2
5 Halkin St 020 7333 1234 2–3A
"It was like having a magician as a waiter", say fans of the Arzac family's Belgravia outpost, extolling "course after course of treats, from mouthfuls to more substantial dishes, all exploring new tastes". The room itself can seem "as dull as ditchwater" however, and critics are disappointed by food they find "more startling to the eye than agreeable to the palette". / SW1X 7DJ; www.comohotels.com/thehalkin/dining/ametsa; @AmetsaArzak; 10 pm; closed Mon L & Sun; set weekday L £68 (FP).

L'Amorosa W6 £47 4 4 3
278 King St 020 8563 0300 8–2B
"High end cuisine at local prices" has won renown for Andy Needham's "unassuming looking", venture near Ravenscourt Park, whose "smart, but down-to-earth style" gives no hint that it serves "some of the best and best value Italian food in town" ("the pasta is very good, with lots of flavour"). Thoughtful staff" are "charming" too, and although "it's a neighbourhood place, people travel from miles around to eat here". / W6 0SP; www.lamorosa.co.uk; @LamorosaLondon; 9.30 pm, Fri & Sat 10 pm; closed Mon & Sun D.

Anarkali W6 £36
303-305 King St 020 8748 1760 8–2B
"A cut above the after-pub curry house", this "high-quality" Hammersmith Indian of decades standing has been able to thrive "in an area of high competition (Zing, Potli)". In summer 2017 it closed for a total reformat under long-term owner Rafique – when it re-opens we expect it to be good, but we've removed the (very solid) ratings as a sharp break with the past seems to be on the cards. / W6 9NH; www.anarkalifinedining.com; @anarkalidining; midnight; closed Mon L & Sun L; No Amex.

The Anchor & Hope SE1 £52 4 2 2
36 The Cut 020 7928 9898 10–4A
"Sometimes you have to bare-knuckle it for a table" at this "bursting-at-the-seams" boozer, a short walk from the Old Vic – still hanging on to its crown as the survey's No. 1 pub. "It's worth the crush though" for the "simple", yet "sophisticated" pub grub "done oh-so-well", which still "trumps the stretched staff, the slightly chaotic ambience and tired fixtures". "I really wish you could book" ("unfortunately you can only reserve for Sunday lunch"). / SE1 8LP; www.anchorandhopepub.co.uk; @AnchorHopeCut; 10.30 pm, Sun 3.15 pm; closed Mon L & Sun D; No Amex; no booking; set weekday L £32 (FP).

Andi's N16 £43 3 4 4
176 Stoke Newington Church St
020 7241 6919 1–1C
"Amazing brunch and a gorgeous little garden!" are highlights of this "very good addition to Stokey", where La Patronne, 'Great British Menu' judge Andi Oliver, is "exceptionally friendly and jolly", and provides an imaginative, modern British menu. / N16 0JL; www.andis.london; @andisrestaurant; 10.30 pm; closed weekday L.

Andina E2 £51 4 3 3
1 Redchurch St 020 7920 6499 13–1B
"Great ceviche" along with the "authentic cocktails (I know, I have Peruvian friends)" are the star turns at this "noisy and full, but not expensive" South American hotspot in Shoreditch: "raw fish seemed adventurous at first, but it was so well flavoured you just wanted to eat more!". / E2 7DJ; www.andinalondon.com; @AndinaLondon; 10.30 pm; booking max 6 may apply.

The Andover Arms W6 £51 3 5 4
57 Aldensey Rd 020 8748 2155 8–1B
With its "roaring fire in winter" and "good service" this "traditional small pub" in a cute corner of Brackenbury Village is one of London's jollier hostelries. No fireworks on the food front, but its hearty gastropub scoff is very dependable. / W6 0DL; www.theandoverarms.com; @theandoverarms; 10 pm, Sun 9 pm; No Amex.

ANDREW EDMUNDS W1 £56 🟦3🟥4🟥5
46 Lexington St 020 7437 5708 4–2C
"THE place for a date in Soho" – "time stands still"
at this "intriguing" townhouse that wins the hearts
of legions of Londoners with its "dark and Gothic"
Bohemian, candle-lit charm, its "casual yet engaged
staff", and its "splendiferous wine list (without
hefty mark-ups too"). Don't expect great comfort
(although the "cramped quarters do make for
romantic closeness") and while "the no-frills cooking
is very flavoursome it's not haute cuisine". / W1F
0LP; www.andrewedmunds.com; 10.45 pm, Sun 10.30
pm; No Amex; booking max 6 may apply.

Angelus W2 £72 🟦3🟥5🟦3
4 Bathurst St 020 7402 0083 7–2D
"You get looked after like an old friend even if
you've never been before", if you visit Thierry
Tomasin's prettified pub near Lancaster Gate – a
"small and intimate venue" ("you eat in close
quarters") whose star turn is the "fab wine list
you'd expect from Le Gavroche's former head
sommelier". Most (if not quite all) reports are of
"reliably good French cuisine" to match. / W2 2SD;
www.angelusrestaurant.co.uk; @AngelusLondon; 11 pm,
Sun 10 pm.

**Angie's Little Food Shop
W4** £32 🟦3🟦3🟦3
114 Chiswick High Rd 020 8994 3931 8–2A
Angie Steele's cute café is becoming quite the
Chiswick favourite – her super-healthy salads, cakes
and juices are "great for brunch, a quick snack or
coffee". / W4 1PU; www.angieslittlefoodshop.com; 7
pm, Sun 6 pm; L only.

**Angler, South Place Hotel
EC2** £93 🟦3🟥2🟥2
3 South Pl 020 3215 1260 13–2A
"Ultra fresh seafood and superb views" are
undisputed attractions of this rooftop venture near
Moorgate. But while the terrace (heated in winter)
is undoubtedly "lovely", the overall impression of
the venue as a whole can be "pretty soulless", and
fans concede that it's "so expensive" too ("the
bill's only fine if you're a banker"). / EC2M 2AF;
www.anglerrestaurant.com; @southplacehotel; 10 pm;
closed Sat L; May need 8+ to book; set weekday L £66
(FP).

The Anglesea Arms W6 £56 🟥4🟥4🟥4
35 Wingate Rd 020 8749 1291 8–1B
"Back to its former glory. Hurrah!" – This "well-
established pub" in a side street near Ravenscourt
Park is "just what a gastropub should be with a cosy
pubby bit at the front with a roaring fire (offering
some quality ales) and a restaurant bit at the back"
serving "exceptionally well thought-through dishes at
very reasonable prices". / W6 0UR;

www.angleseaarmspub.co.uk; @_AngleseaArmsW6;
10 pm, Fri 11 pm, Sat & Sun 10 pm; closed weekday
L; no booking.

Anglo EC1 £69 🟥5🟥4🟦2
30 St Cross St 020 7430 1503 10–1A
"Light years ahead of some famous names in terms
of quality" – Mark Jarvis and Jack Cashmore's
Hatton Garden yearling has "an unlikely location"
("you squeeze into a little shop") and its "slightly
dull and muted") but "don't let the room put you
off" – "the quality is arguably unbeaten for the price
in Central London" and "to change the menu so
regularly, but with such imagination and high quality
every time takes some serious talent". Top Tip – "the
lunchtime menu with accompanying wines is a real
bargain". / EC1N 8UH; www.anglorestaurant.com; 9.30
pm; closed Sun; booking max 4 may apply.

L'Anima EC2 £71 🟥4🟥4🟦3
1 Snowden St 020 7422 7000 13–2B
"Benissimo!" – "the food is consistently good, even
after Francesco Mazzei's departure" at this well-
known Italian near Liverpool Street. "The price is
quite hefty", but as a business venue it's "perfect
(or would be if it was a little less noisy")", thanks
to its "well-organised" service and "cool, modern,
white interior". / EC2A 2DQ; www.lanima.co.uk;
@lanimalondon; 11 pm, Sat 11.30 pm; closed Sat L
& Sun.

L'Anima Café EC2 £56 🟦3🟦3🟦2
10 Appold St 020 7422 7080 13–2B
"Sustained high levels of Italian fare, and reasonably
strong service" make it worth remembering this
"busy, if slightly cavernous room" near Liverpool
Street – ideal for an informal business bite –
majoring in "excellent pizza", plus pasta. "It's
not cheap though" (although there is a deli
section where you can grab & go, or perch at a
shared table). / EC2A 2AP; www.lanimacafe.co.uk;
@LAnimacafe; 10 pm; closed Sun.

Anima e Cuore NW1 £40 🟥5🟥4🟥1
129 Kentish Town Rd 020 7267 2410 9–2B
"Don't judge a book by its cover – some of the best
Italian food in London hides behind the rundown
exterior" of this tiny Kentish Town BYO, serving a
"long and interesting menu". "'Heart and Soul' is
the absolute truth: the venue is a dump, but the
honest graft put in by the team wins through every
time". Top Tips: "cucumber ice cream is a standout",
and "when there are truffles on the menu,
portions are generous and prices low". / NW1 8PB;
@animaecuoreuk; 9 pm, Sun 2.30 pm.

Annie's £44 🟦2🟦3🟥4
162 Thames Rd, W4 020 8994 9080 1–3A
36-38 White Hart Ln, SW13
020 8878 2020 11–1A
"Happy and relaxed" hangouts in Barnes and

Strand-on-the-Green, Chiswick, drawing a busy mix of locals meeting up for a bite and a drink. "The food, though mostly enjoyable, is not the main event – it's the quaint, charming ambience and friendly waiting staff that make them so appealing". / www.anniesrestaurant.co.uk; 10 pm, Sun 9.30 pm.

The Anthologist EC2   **£54**   2 2 3
58 Gresham St 0845 468 0101 10–2C
"Deservedly busy", attractive bar/restaurant near the Guildhall whose "spacious tables work for meetings, brunch, lunch, dinner…". "It's a lazy option as the food's good not great, but it's close to work and easy to book". / EC2V 7BB; www.theanthologistbar.co.uk; @theanthologist; 11 pm, Thu & Fri 1 am; closed Sat & Sun.

L' Antica Pizzeria NW3   **£40**   4 4 3
66 Heath St 020 7431 8516 9–1A
"Tiny, buzzy and cosy Neapolitan pizzeria" on Hampstead High Street, loved by locals for its "excellent pizza from the wood-fired oven". / NW3 1DN; www.anticapizzeria.co.uk; @AnticaHamp; 10.30 pm; Mon-Thu D only, Fri-Sun open L & D.

**L'Antica Pizzeria da Michele
N16** NEW   **£20**   3 4 3
125 Stoke Newington Church St
020 7687 0009 1–1C
"You can have any pizza you want, provided it's either a margarita or marinara" at this first UK outpost, in Stokey, of the Naples original (est 1870). The occasional report says it "doesn't live up to the hype", but on most accounts "it's everything you could want, with speedy, no-nonsense service and exceptional pizzas straight outta Napoli". / N16 0UH; www.damichele.net; @damichelelondon; May need 6+ to book.

Antidote Wine Bar W1   **£59**   2 2 3
12a Newburgh St   020 7287 8488   4–1B
"Perplexingly refreshing" – the view of one fan of this quirky, Gallic-run wine bar and restaurant, seconds from bustling Carnaby Street, which has an elegant, small upstairs dining room. Its profile is tiny nowadays though, despite its heart-of-Soho location, and critics say "the food's pretty average, at a price that merits better". / W1F 7RR; www.antidotewinebar.com; @AntidoteWineBar; 10.30 pm; closed Mon & Sun.

Anzu SW1   **£43**
Saint James's Market, 1 Norris St
020 7930 8414   4–4D
Press reviews have not been kind to this Japanese brasserie in the luxe but unengaging St James's Market development, and – though it did inspire the odd positive report – the low level of feedback it inspired from reporters gave insufficient confidence for a rating as yet. / SW1Y 4SB; www.anzulondon.com; @anzurestaurant.

Applebee's Fish SE1   **£62**   4 3 2
5 Stoney St   020 7407 5777   10–4C
"Superb!"… "a proper fish restaurant" is how all reporters view this "lovely café", where "sensitive cooking" does real justice to the "simply prepared" dishes. "Prices are a bit high, but that's normal for somewhere on the edge of Borough Market". / SE1 9AA; www.applebeesfish.com; @applebeesfish; 10 pm, Thu-Sat 11 pm; closed Sun; No Amex.

Apulia EC1   **£50**   3 3 3
50 Long Ln   020 7600 8107   10–2B
"Fabulously hearty, rustic Puglian dishes, served with a smile" and at "good-value prices" win numerous very enthusiastic reviews for this "far-from-standard" Italian, beside Smithfield Market; but "it's a great place for supper, rather than 'a destination'". / EC1A 9EJ; www.apuliarestaurant.co.uk; 10 pm; closed Sun D.

Aqua Nueva W1   **£68**   2 2 3
240 Regent Street (entrance 30 Argyll St)
020 7478 0540   4–1A
Part of a ritzy, roof-top complex with terraces above Oxford Circus, this glossy Spanish venue adjoins Aqua Kyoto (its Japanese sibling) and Aqua Spirit (a bar), and is a more low-rise, less famous alternative to its well-known Shard-based siblings, Aqua Shard and Hutong. On limited feedback, its scores aren't bad at all, but it attracts few reports nowadays, and there's a slight feeling that it's (perhaps unjustifiably) been abandoned to out-of-towners. / W1B 3BR; www.aqua-london.com; @aqualondon; 11 pm, Sun 8 pm; set pre theatre £36 (FP).

Aqua Shard SE1   **£104**   1 1 2
Level 31, 31 St Thomas St
020 3011 1256   10–4C
"An utterly disgraceful fleecing of out-of-towners looking for a glamorous 'occasion' meal but getting ripped off!" – that's the gist of too many reports on this 31st-floor chamber which is "so completely disappointing" it "risks giving the Capital a bad name". "You do get a remarkable view of London" and romantics say it's "the perfect place to watch the sunset and the lights coming on over the City"… "but that's it!". Top Tip – "breakfast is the still-not-cheap-but-cheapest way to sample this otherwise extortionate experience: book the earliest slot the ensure a window table and the chance to watch the city awake!!" / SE1 9RY; www.aquashard.co.uk; @aquashard; 10.45 pm; set weekday L £64 (FP), set brunch £78 (FP).

Aquavit SW1   **£77**   3 3 3
St James's Market, 1 Carlton St
020 7024 9848   4–4D
With its "classy and spacious" Manhattan-esque decor, this spin-off from the Big Apple's acclaimed Nordic fine dining stalwart, in the new St James's Market development, is "ideal for people-watching", and – with its "clean-tasting Scandi fare from

exceptional ingredients" – both "a great addition" to the capital, and one that's "perfect for a business lunch". On the downside, the "cavernous space is slightly sterile", and muted ratings overall mean this is "not yet a chip off the NYC block". / SW1Y 4QQ; www.aquavitrestaurants.com; @aquavitlondon; set weekday L £52 (FP), set pre-theatre £53 (FP).

Arabica Bar and Kitchen
SE1   £52 3 2 3
3 Rochester Walk   020 3011 5151   10–4C
"Delicious Middle Eastern-North African food" keeps a "lively and hipsterish crowd" well fed and happy under the arches by Borough Market. "If you want somewhere with character and food with oodles of flavour, this is the place" – "I left with a warm glow and a spring in my step". / SE1 9AF; www.arabicabarandkitchen.com; @ArabicaLondon; 10.30 pm, Sat 11 pm, Sun 8.30 pm; closed Sun D.

The Araki W1   £380 5 5 3
Unit 4 12 New Burlington St
020 7287 2481   4–3A
"Can heaven be far away?" – "If you can afford it, Mitsuhiro Araki's Mayfair restaurant is a unique experience" and a "world class" one that for a second year won the highest food-rating of any restaurant in the UK. "Be one of nine diners enjoying a specially prepared meal from one of Tokyo's top chefs" that's "as close to Japan as you can get in London". "You feel like you are at a theatrical performance, sat in line watching the numerous chefs, and Mr Araki himself, and there are too many amazing dishes to mention". "The price is world class too" of course but "worth every penny for what you get" (in the view of all reporters, including those who are themselves Japanese). "Clients can't fail to be impressed… and at that price so they should be!" STOP PRESS. On October 2, Michelin finally woke up and awarded the Araki the three stars it should have granted last year. / W1S 3BH; www.the-araki.com; seatings only at 6 pm and 8.30 pm; D only, closed Mon; booking essential.

Ariana II NW6   £29 3 2 2
241 Kilburn High Rd   020 3490 6709   1–2B
Family-run Afghani in Kilburn, handily close to the Tricycle Theatre, serving grilled meat or veg with rice and salad – "for the money, it's really, really good… and it's BYO!". / NW6 7JN; www.ariana2restaurant.co.uk; @Ariana2kilburn; midnight.

Ark Fish E18   £39 3 3 2
142 Hermon Hill   020 8989 5345   1–1D
"You can rely on good quality fish" at this popular chippy in South Woodford, run by the Faulkner family (who have in their time managed Lisson Grove's famous Seashell, and Dalston's Faulkners). / E18 1QH; www.arkfishrestaurant.co.uk; 9.45 pm, Fri & Sat 10.15 pm, Sun 8.45 pm; closed Mon; No Amex; no booking.

Arlo's SW12   £49 2 3 2
1 Ramsden Rd   020 3019 6590   11–2C
"It ain't the only restaurant in town offering quality steak at an affordable price" but fans say this Balham yearling "stands out for its simple, limited menu of unusual British-sourced cuts, plus nine or ten sides cooked exactly to order". One or two incidents of poor preparation are also reported however, hence the middling grades. / SW12 8QX; www.arlos.co.uk.

Arthur Hooper's
SE1 NEW   £63
8 Stoney St awaiting tel 10–4C
This stylishly monochrome spot overlooking Borough Market is named after the fruit salesman who once occupied the building. Chef Lale Oztek presents a modern European menu of seasonal fare, much of it sourced from the market and surrounding shops. / SE1 9AA; www.arthurhoopers.co.uk; @arthurhoopers; 10.30 pm, Fri & Sat 11.30 pm; booking max 6 may apply; set weekday L £40 (FP).

Artigiano NW3   £56 3 2 2
12a Belsize Ter   020 7794 4288   9–2A
"A good standard has been maintained" over the years at this "very pleasant" (if "rather squashed") Italian in Belsize Park – no-one hails it as London's best, but it's "dependable". / NW3 4AX; www.etruscarestaurants.com; @artiganoesp; 10 pm; closed Mon L.

L'Artista NW11   £40 3 4 4
917 Finchley Rd   020 8731 7501   1–1B
"Service with a smile" helps ensure this age-old pizza and pasta favourite in the Golders Green railway arches is "always full-to-bursting". "If you have kids, what you want is a big, noisy place full of Italians who love small children" – "what more could you ask for?". / NW11 7PE; www.lartistapizzeria.com; 11.30 pm.

L'Artiste Musclé W1   £48 2 2 5
1 Shepherd Mkt   020 7493 6150   3–4B
This wonderfully named Gallic bistro in quaint Shepherd Market is a "favourite cheap place" that "has not changed" for 40 years or more. "An amazing wine list, too!" / W1J 7PA; @lartistemuscle; 10 pm.

Artusi SE15   £44 4 4 3
161 Bellenden Rd   020 3302 8200   1–4D
This three-year-old, "heart-of-Peckham gem" offers "consistently good Italian cooking with vivid flavours in even the simplest dishes"; and its "good value" makes it "very popular with local hipsters". (There's now also a Deptford spin-off too called Marcella.) / SE15 4DH; www.artusi.co.uk; @artusipeckham; 10.30 pm, Sun 8 pm; closed Mon L.

Asakusa NW I £36 5️⃣2️⃣2️⃣

265 Eversholt St 020 7388 8533 9–3C
"Incongruously, a really good Japanese set in a rather shabby faux-Tudor setting" – this surprising outfit near Mornington Crescent impresses with its "exceptional prices for the quality". / NW1 1BA; 11.30 pm, Sat 11 pm; D only, closed Sun.

Asia de Cuba, St Martin's Lane Hotel WC2 £82 2️⃣2️⃣3️⃣

45 St Martin's Ln 020 7300 5588 5–4C
"Brilliant decor" and "lovely mojitos" have always been highpoints at this "sexy as…"West End boutique hotel, near the Coliseum. The Cuban-inspired fusion cuisine is "expensive", and even fans are "not sure it's authentic", but "the menu always offers something unusual", and won better ratings this year. / WC2N 4HX; www.morganshotelgroup.com; @asiadecuba; 11 pm, Fri & Sat midnight, Sun 10.30 pm; set pre-theatre & Sun L £51 (FP).

Assaggi W2 £76 4️⃣5️⃣2️⃣

39 Chepstow Pl 020 7792 5501 7–1B
"Thank goodness it's back!" – This resurrected, first-floor pub dining room in Bayswater (long renowned as London's top Italian) reopened a couple of years ago under one of its original owners to the ecstatic delight of its long-term fanclub and has "now expanded downstairs" (see Assaggi Bar). As ever, "Nino and his team are superb" in terms of charm, and although the consensus is that the "rather expensive" rustic fare is perhaps "not the best in town" any more, it remains "eternally high achieving". As ever the acoustics of this simple room can be "challenging". / W2 4TS; www.assaggi.co.uk; 11 pm; closed Sun; No Amex.

Assaggi Bar & Pizzeria W2 NEW £57 4️⃣3️⃣2️⃣

39 Chepstow Place 020 7792 5501 7–1B
"A great addition to Notting Hill/Bayswater" – the Assaggi team have taken over the ground floor of the pub they have occupied for so many years to create this "superb", more achievably priced, all-day pizza/pastaria, with tapas "catering to the discerning and top pizza". / W2 4TS; www.assaggi.co.uk; No bookings.

Assunta Madre W I £106 3️⃣3️⃣3️⃣

8-10 Blenheim St 020 3230 3032 3–2B
"Fantastic fresh fish", flown in daily, is the boast of this Mayfair 'Pescheria' – offshoot of a famous seafood restaurant in Rome – which generated consistent (if slightly limited) support this year and escaped the brickbats of former years for its hefty prices (although arguably "Estaitorio Milos is better value for a similar formula"). / W1S 1LJ; www.assuntamadre.com; @assuntamadre; 10 pm.

Aster Restaurant SW I NEW £58 3️⃣3️⃣3️⃣

150 Victoria St 020 3875 5555 2–4B
"A genuinely Nordic addition to Victoria's new concrete canyons!" – D&D London have 'gone for it', with Helena Puolakka's "French/Scandinavian hybrid cuisine" at this Nova-development newcomer, comprising a ground floor café, and more "comfortable" (and business friendly) upstairs space ("with views of the surrounding glass and steel buildings"). On the downside, despite "lovely" design the very urban milieu can seem "sterile" and – given some "bland" dishes – the overall effect can seem "just a bit meh". Most reports though are of "interesting" cooking, and undoubtedly this is "a great plus in what has hitherto been a bit of a desert". / SW1E 5LB; www.aster-restaurant.com; @AsterVictoria; 9.30 pm.

Atari-Ya £31 4️⃣2️⃣1️⃣

20 James St, W1 020 7491 1178 3–1A
7 Station Pde, W3 020 8896 1552 1–2A
1 Station Pde, W5 020 8896 3175 1–3A
595 High Rd, N12 020 8446 6669 9–1B
75 Fairfax Rd, NW6 020 7328 5338 9–2A
"Always packed and rightly so" was the worst report this year on this group of Japanese caffs, run by a food import business, where the dishes ("mostly excellent sushi") can be "divine". The decor, though, is "very simple" and the resulting atmosphere "pretty rubbish". / www.sushibaratariya.co.uk; W1 8 pm, NW6 & W5 9.30 pm, W9 9 pm, N12 & W3 6.30 pm, Sat & Sun 7 pm; NW6 closed Mon, W5 closed Mon & Tue.

L'Atelier de Joel Robuchon WC2 £117 2️⃣1️⃣2️⃣

13-15 West St 020 7010 8600 5–2B
"Astronomical" prices have always been a feature of this star French chef's opulent Covent Garden outpost, where you kick off in the glam, rooftop cocktail bar, and then descend to one of two luxurious dining floors (be it the dark, ground floor, where you perch on high stools near the open kitchen, or the more conventional first floor). But while many fans do find its "theatrical" succession of exquisite ("miniscule") dishes to be "unbelievably enjoyable", others feel its level of achievement nowadays is "a far cry from the heady times when it first opened": "sky high prices are totally justifiable in my book, but only if performance warrants them… but the food was really flat and service careless and terribly slow". / WC2H 9NE; www.joelrobuchon.co.uk; @latelierlondon; 11.30 pm, Sun 10 pm; No trainers; set weekday L £57 (FP).

The Atlas SW6 £50 4️⃣4️⃣4️⃣

16 Seagrave Rd 020 7385 9129 6–3A
"A standard-bearer for the gastropub category" – this "beautiful, traditional pub" is hidden-away near West Brompton tube and offers "gourmet food" with "a nice Italian slant", delivered by "cheery and

charming staff". There's also "a cracking, huge, new terrace garden" (expanding the old one), which is "a real gem". / SW6 1RX; www.theatlaspub.co.uk; @theatlasfulham; 10 pm.

Augustine Kitchen SW11 £51　[3][4][2]
63 Battersea Bridge Rd　020 7978 7085　6–4C
This little Savoyard bistro is "now well established in Battersea after a slow start" and is overseen by "a chef who cares and staff who want to look after you". There were a couple of 'off' reports this year ("don't know what's happened"... "I don't get this place"), but mostly feedback says it's "a really worthwhile local", with "good food" and "great price/performance ratio". / SW11 3AU; www.augustine-kitchen.co.uk; @augustinekitchen; closed Mon & Sun D; set weekday L £28 (FP).

Aurora W1　£58　[3][4][4]
49 Lexington St　020 7494 0514　4–2C
This "really friendly" and supremely "cosy" stalwart (opposite Andrew Edmunds) is little known, but has long been a good option for a "romantic" bite in Soho. It earns consistently solid praise for its modern European cooking, with some "excellent dishes" on the small menu. Top Tip – "sit in the great secret garden" out back. / W1F 9AP; www.aurorasoho.co.uk; 10 pm, Wed-Sat 10.30 pm, Sun 9 pm.

The Avalon SW12　£49　[2][2][3]
16 Balham Hill　020 8675 8613　11–2C
"Big, busy (noisy) Balham gastropub" with an "attractive, large back room" and lovely garden. Fans applaud its "good no-nonsense cooking" but ratings are under-cut by those who find it "too un-memorable". / SW12 9EB; www.theavalonlondon.com; @threecheerspubs; 10.30 pm, Sun 9 pm.

L'Aventure NW8　£67　[3][4][4]
3 Blenheim Terrace　020 7624 6232　9–3A
Catherine Parisot's "charmant" Gallic classic in St John's Wood "provides a thoroughly enjoyable evening" combining a "lovely" superbly "romantic" setting with a "small, expertly executed menu" of archetypal cuisine bourgeoise. La Patronne's occasional stormy outbreaks were not in evidence this year. / NW8 0EH; www.laventure.co.uk; 11 pm; closed Sat L & Sun.

The Avenue SW1　£68　[2][4][3]
7-9 St James's St　020 7321 2111　3–4D
A "lovely, light room", "excellent value set menus" and "impeccable service" all help make D&D London's "vast" Manhattan-style brasserie a useful choice, especially for business diners, aided by its "prestigious" St James's location. The food? – "reliable without ever hitting the heights". / SW1A 1EE; www.avenue-restaurant.co.uk; @avenuestjames; 10.30 pm; closed Sat L & Sun.

Aviary EC2　NEW　£53
10th Floor, 22-25 Finsbury Square
020 3873 4060　13–2A
Overlooking Finsbury Square from the 10th floor, this new ETM-group venture is long on glam' with its big rooftop terrace and marvellous views of the City skyline, and serves a modern British brasserie menu. / EC2A 1DX; aviarylondon.com; @AviaryLDN.

Awesome Thai SW13　£29　[3][4][3]
68 Church Rd　020 8563 7027　11–1A
Opposite the Olympic Studios cinema in Barnes, this very popular family-run local is "permanently packed" due to its "really well-realised, traditional Thai dishes", "service-with-a-smile" and "good value". "It gives more upmarket places a run for their money!" / SW13 0DQ; www.awesomethai.co.uk; 10.30 pm, Sun 10 pm; Mon-Thu D only, Fri-Sun open L & D.

Le Bab W1　£45　[5][4][3]
2nd Floor, Kingly Ct　020 7439 9222　4–2B
A superb gourmet take on the kebab, off Carnaby Street – everything is made from scratch in-house and there's "good cocktails, too". / W1B 5PW; www.eatlebab.com; @EatLeBab; 10 pm, Sun 7 pm; booking max 6 may apply.

Babaji Pide W1　£45　[3][2][2]
73 Shaftesbury Ave　020 3327 3285　5–3A
Two-year-old Turkish concept on Shaftesbury Avenue that's "finally found its stride", with improving food scores this year. Created by Hakkasan founder Alan Yau, it majors on 'pide' – a bit like pizza – and the "freshly made food is better than expected". / W1D 6EX; www.babaji.com.tr; @babajipidesalon; 11 pm, Fri & Sat 11.30 pm, Sun 10 pm.

Babette SE15　NEW　£39　[3][3][4]
57 Nunhead Lane　020 3172 2450　1–4D
Positive initial reports on this revivified Old Truman Pub in Nunhead, where the blackboards on its brick walls mostly offer sharing boards, as well as a few main dishes. / SE15 3TR; www.babettenunhead.com; @babettenunhead; 11 pm, Fri & Sat midnight, Sun 5 pm; closed Mon & Tue, Wed & Thu D only, Fri & Sat L & D, Sun L only.

Babur SE23　£56　[5][5][4]
119 Brockley Rise　020 8291 2400　1–4D
"A stalwart of the Forest Hill dining scene that's worth a trip into SE London!". For over 20 years, this surprisingly "exotic" modern Indian has "had people beating a path to its door" on account of its "delightful service" and some of London's best Indian cooking – "eye-catching", "subtly-spiced and aromatic" dishes "with intense and unique flavours". / SE23 1JP; www.babur.info; @BaburRestaurant; 11.30 pm.

Babylon, Kensington Roof Gardens W8 £75 2️⃣2️⃣4️⃣
99 Kensington High St   020 7368 3993   6–1A
"Stunning views from high up in Kensington", "on a rooftop with lovely gardens and its own lake", make this "moody, night-clubby" venue "unlike any other in London". "The food may not live up to everything else – it's solid if unspectacular – but it's a great choice for a date or Sunday lunch". / W8 5SA; www.virginlimitededition.com/en/the-roof-gardens/b; 10.30 pm; closed Sun D; SRA-Food Made Good – 2 stars.

Bacco TW9 £58 3️⃣2️⃣2️⃣
39-41 Kew Rd   020 8332 0348   1–4A
A "classic Italian menu" consistently well realised ("when it's good it's very good") help make this "an excellent local", and it's particularly "convenient for Richmond theatre-goers". / TW9 2NQ; www.bacco-restaurant.co.uk; @BaccoRichmond; 11 pm; closed Sun D; set pre theatre £39 (FP).

Bageriet WC2 £12 4️⃣4️⃣3️⃣
24 Rose St   020 7240 0000   5–3C
"A little piece of Swedish heaven", "tucked away" down an alleyway in Covent Garden – this "tiny café" serves "excellent coffee" and "fabulous Nordic treats". "The cinnamon buns are even more delicious than any I've tasted in Sweden (and I've tasted a lot by the way!)". / WC2E 9EA; www.bageriet.co.uk; @BagerietLondon; 7 pm; L & early evening only, closed Sun; no booking.

Bala Baya SE1 NEW £67 3️⃣2️⃣3️⃣
Arch 25, Old Union Yard Arches, 229 Union St   020 8001 7015   10–4B
"A bright spark sorely needed in Southwark" – this "Tel Aviv inspired" newcomer from Israeli-born chef Eran Tibi (formerly of Ottolenghi et al) provides "imaginative Middle Eastern fusion" dishes "in an unusual setting under the Waterloo arches". "It could be a tad less expensive, though, "the music could be a bit less loud", and service is "smiley" but not always on the case. / SE1 0LR; balabaya.co.uk; @bala_baya; 11.30 pm, Sun 5 pm; closed Sun D.

The Balcon, Sofitel St James SW1 £67 2️⃣2️⃣2️⃣
8 Pall Mall   020 7968 2900   2–3C
The "pleasingly light and airy dining room" at this former bank off Trafalgar Square, with its bistro-style cooking, perhaps fails to thrill. But it does get a thumbs-up as a business rendezvous, and for a "very good value prix fixe pre-theatre menu". / SW1Y 5NG; www.thebalconlondon.com; @TheBalcon; 10.45 pm, Sat & Sun 9.45 pm.

Balthazar WC2 £70 2️⃣2️⃣4️⃣
4 - 6 Russell St   020 3301 1155   5–3D
"Transport yourself from touristy Covent Garden to an altogether chic and classy world", say fans of Keith McNally's "absolutely heaving" Grand Café, liked particularly for its "enjoyable brunch" and suitability for business entertaining. "For standard brasserie fare, it's very expensive" however – "presumably you're paying for the very stylish interior". / WC2B 5HZ; www.balthazarlondon.com; @balthazarlondon; midnight, Sun 11 pm; set pre theatre £47 (FP).

Baltic SE1 £57 4️⃣4️⃣4️⃣
74 Blackfriars Rd   020 7928 1111   10–4A
"Lovely, gutsy Polish home cooking" washed down with lashings of homemade vodka helps induce good vibes at this "friendly" fixture in an "airy" Georgian factory-conversion near the Cut. "It's good to see east European food being given the gourmet treatment", and the bar "is a good pit stop for drinks" too. / SE1 8HA; www.balticrestaurant.co.uk; @balticlondon; 11.15 pm, Sun 10.30 pm; closed Mon L.

Baluchi, Lalit Hotel London SE1 NEW £77
181 Tooley St   020 3765 0000   10–4D
A former school hall (St Olave's) decorated with a striking midnight blue ceiling houses this new dining room, in a five-star hotel near Tower Bridge (part of a luxury hotel group spanning the subcontinent). Initial feedback is limited, but such as we've had is ecstatic about its stunning cuisine and setting. / SE1 2JR; www.thelalit.com/the-lalit-london/eat-and-drink/baluchi/; @TheLalitLondon; 9.30 pm.

Bandol SW10 £65 3️⃣3️⃣3️⃣
6 Hollywood Road, Kensington
020 7351 1322   6–3B
"Excellent" sharing plates of summery Provençal and Niçoise cuisine shine at this two-year-old, a sibling to nearby Margaux. The location is part of the appeal for Chelsea types – "you can't beat the Hollywood Road scene!" / SW10 9HY; www.barbandol.co.uk; @Margaux_Bandol; 11 pm, Sun 10 pm; set weekday L £39 (FP).

Bang Bang Oriental NW9 NEW £36
399 Edgware Rd   no tel   1–1A
Successor to the food court at the former Yaohan Shopping Plaza – also known as Oriental City – which was demolished in 2014, this gargantuan (30,000 sq ft) Asian food hall in Colindale boasts a restaurant, supermarket and community space with room for 450 diners. / NW9 0AS; www.bangbangoriental.com; @bangbangofh.

Bangalore Express EC3 £39 3️⃣3️⃣3️⃣
1 Corbet Ct   020 7220 9195   10–2C
"Always good tastes and good value" win fans for this "reliable" contemporary-style Indian, right in the heart of the Square Mile. / EC3V 0AT; www.bangaloreuk.com; @bangaloreuk; 11pm.

Bánh Bánh SE15   **£36** 3 4 3
46 Peckham Rye   020 7207 2935   1–4D
*The Nguyen family achieves positive (if not quite
unanimous) support for the "tasty and cheap
Vietnamese fare" at their bare-brick-walled
Peckham Rye yearling. / SE15; www.banhbanh.com;
@BanhBanhHQ; 9.30 pm, Fri & Sat 10 pm; closed
Mon.*

Banners N8   **£46** 3 4 5
21 Park Rd   020 8348 2930   9–1C
*This all-day haven of "hearty, generous, seriously
tasty scoff" is a Crouch End legend, with its epic
brunch being the favoured (some would say
only) time to visit. With its Caribbean flavours
and "ramshackle world music vibe", it's "not at
all refined, but that's why we love it!". / N8 8TE;
www.bannersrestaurant.com; 11 pm, Fri 11.30 pm, Sat
midnight, Sun 10.30 pm; No Amex.*

Bao   **£28** 4 3 2
31 Windmill St, W1   020 3011 1632   5–1A
53 Lexington St, W1   07769 627811 4–2C
13 - 23 Westgate St, E8   no tel   14–2B
*"Heaven in a bun"; "very special steamed bao, with
great fillings", plus other "incredible" street food
dishes – "as good as in Taiwan" – all at "realistic
prices" have made this Soho café (and its more
recent Fitzrovia spin-off) one of the biggest hits of
recent years. You can book in WC1 for the basement,
but in Soho "you have to queue behind a bus-stop-
type sign on the other side of the road" – "the bao
are to die for… so you long as you didn't die of the
wait to get them…" / W1F Mon-Wed 10 pm, Thu-Sat
10.30 pm, W1T Mon-Sat 10 pm, E8 Sat 4 pm; W1F &
W1T closed Sun, E8 open Sat L only; W1 no bookings,
E8 takeout only.*

Baozi Inn WC2   **£24**
26 Newport Ct   020 7287 6877   5–3B
*Just off the main Chinatown drag, this Sichuan
canteen won a name with its bold, street-food-
inspired dishes ("very garlicky and not shy with
the chilli spice") and kitsch Maoist memorabilia.
Mid-survey in May 2017 it emerged with a toned
down look and reduced but pricier menu – we've
removed the ratings for now as change seems to be
afoot. / WC2H 7JS; www.baoziinnlondon.com; 9.30 pm;
Cash only; no booking.*

Le Bar EC1
59 West Smithfield   020 7600 7561   10–2B
*What was 'Cellar Gascon' next to Club Gascon has
recently rebranded and re-launched with a more
modish new look, serving Gascon 'Frapas' (French
tapas) alongside 'hand-crafted' cocktails. / EC1A 9DS;
www.lebarlondon.co.uk; @lebarlondon; midnight.*

**Bar Boulud, Mandarin Oriental
SW1**   **£69** 3 4 4
66 Knightsbridge   020 7201 3899   6–1D
*"Conveniently below street level opposite Harvey
Nick's" this "Knightsbridge-crowd, but friendly"
spin-off from the NYC original is "a den worth the
descent" and particularly popular for a "thoroughly
reliable" business bite thanks to its "smooth service"
and "famous burgers" hailed by many as "London's
best" (although the the menu is primarily "a good
choice of American-influenced French bistro fare").
/ SW1X 7LA; www.barboulud.com; @barbouludlondon;
10.45 pm, Sun 9.45 pm; No trainers; set weekday L &
pre-theatre £41 (FP).*

Bar Douro SE1 NEW   **£53** 4 3 3
Arch 25b Flat Iron Square, Union St
020 7378 0524   10–4B
*"A wonderful additional to London" in Bankside's
new Flat Iron Square, whose pretty blue-and-white
tiled interior with "all bar seating" ("the stools
are a bit uncomfortable") help make it akin to a
Portuguese Barrafina – from your perch you get
"a theatrical view of the immaculate assembly of
brilliant small dishes, served with broad smiles". /
SE1 1TD; www.bardouro.co.uk; @BarDouro; 11.30 pm;
booking max 4 may apply.*

Bar Esteban N8   **£43** 4 4 4
29 Park Rd   020 8340 3090   1–1C
*"Wonderful, every single time" – so say local fans
of this "favourite" Crouch End bar, with its yummy
tapas and fun vibe. / N8 8TE; www.baresteban.com;
@barestebanN8; 9.30 pm, Fri & Sat 10.30 pm, Sun 9
pm; closed weekday L; booking max 8 may apply.*

Bar Italia W1   **£32** 2 3 5
22 Frith St   020 7437 4520   5–2A
*"Legendary", "open-all-hours" haunt redolent of
post-War Soho, whose basic interior is "pleasantly
untouched" by the passage of years. "You don't
go for the food, but for the coffee and the buzz"
and for "an institution that's a one-off. May it
never, ever go!" / W1D 4RF; www.baritaliasoho.co.uk;
@TheBaristas; open 24 hours, Sun 4 am; No Amex; no
booking.*

Bar Termini W1   **£35** 3 3 5
7 Old Compton St   07860 945018   5–2B
*"Simply the best coffee you'll find anywhere"
is part of the resolutely and genuinely Italian
approach at Tony Conigliaro's tiny (expect no great
encouragement to linger) but characterful Soho
bar, known also for its definitive Negronis and
authentic bites. In early summer 2017, a much
larger 'Centrale' branch opened near Selfridges, with
an expanded food offering including salads and
panzerotti (akin to a fried mini-calzone). / W1D 5JE;
www.bar-termini.com; @Bar_Termini; 11.30 pm, Fri &
Sat 1 am, Sun 10.30 pm.*

The Barbary WC2 £49 5 5 4
16 Neal's Yard awaiting tel 5–2C
"Bringing the fun and fizz of the best places in Jerusalem and Tel Aviv to London" – the debut of Palomar's little brother in Neal's Yard fully lives up to its stablemate's trailblazing performance, with "a brilliant selection of totally delicious and vibrant Mediterranean dishes", eaten "in a small plate, counter eating-style format", complete with "loud banging music and chefs dancing along". "Perfect for a drop in and quick bite, but beware of the queues!!" STOP PRESS: The Barbary now takes bookings for lunch and early dinner. / WC2H 9DP; www.thebarbary.co.uk; @barbarylondon; 10 pm, Sun 9 pm; no booking.

Barbecoa £73 2 2 2
Nova, Victoria St, SW1   no tel   2–4C
194-196 Piccadilly, W1   020 3005 9666   4–4C
20 New Change Pas, EC4
020 3005 8555   10–2B
"Good quality meat but SOOOO overpriced" – that's the trade off at Jamie Oliver's good-looking chain of luxury grills, which added a new, swish-looking branch right by Piccadilly this year. So long as you are packing the company's plastic, the City original (in a big mall), which has "great views of St Paul's", can be "perfect for business". / EC4M Mon-Sat 11 pm, Sun 10 pm, W1J Mon-Thu 11 pm, Fri & Sat midnight, Sun 10.30 pm.

Il Baretto W1 £76 2 2 2
43 Blandford St   020 7486 7340   2–1A
"Rather straightforward Italian fare" is on the menu at this "buzzy (or noisy?) basement" venue in Marylebone. As ever, it fails to whip up huge enthusiasm, but does have a dedicated fan club: "it's not everyone's favourite, but I have yet to have a bad meal here". / W1U 7HF; www.ilbaretto.co.uk; @IlBarettoLondon; 10.15 pm, Sun 9.45 pm.

Barrafina £43 5 5 5
26-27 Dean St, W1   020 7813 8016   4–1D
10 Adelaide St, WC2   020 7440 1456   5–4C
43 Drury Ln, WC2   020 7440 1456   5–2D
"The wait can sometimes be twice the time spent at the counter", but no-one seems to mind at the Hart Bros kick-ass small group of Barcelona-inspired tapas haunts in Soho (now relocated to the ground floor of Quo Vadis) and Covent Garden. "The buzz is amazing" and, having nabbed a perch (fewer than 30 in each branch), everyone "loves the open kitchen and watching the keen staff at work", while the dishes themselves are genius – "fresh seafood is amongst the highlights" but "even something as simple as tomato bruschetta is transformed here". (So far, the February 2017 departure of founding group exec head chef, Nieves Barragán Mohacho, to found Sabor, has had zero effect on ratings – the new incumbent is Angel Zapata Martin.) /

www.barrafina.co.uk; 11 pm, Sun 10 pm; no booking, max group 4.

Barrica W1 £55 3 2 2
62 Goodge St   020 7436 9448   2–1B
"A truly wonderful tapas place" near Goodge Street station, where "standards remain really high". "You get a genuinely Spanish experience, with a superb selection of wines that you won't easily find elsewhere". / W1T 4NE; www.barrica.co.uk; @barricatapas; 10.30 pm; closed Sun.

Barshu W1 £58 4 2 2
28 Frith St   020 7287 6688   5–3A
"Less a meal than a dare!" – the "seriously spicy cooking gives way to rich depths of flavour for the strong-hearted and willed" at this "excellent" Soho café. "If you want a Sichuan fix, go!" – there are "some real lip-smackers in there, including some wonderful unusual dishes (smacked cucumber, gung bao chicken, ants climbing trees…)", but "you still suffer Chinatown-style woes – sometimes indifferent service, and poor ambience". / W1D 5LF; www.barshurestaurant.co.uk; @BarshuLondon; 10.30 pm, Fri & Sat 11 pm.

Bbar SW1 £58 3 4 3
43 Buckingham Palace Rd
020 7958 7000   2–4B
A "good pit stop near Victoria" serving "great burgers and steak" and other fare, plus Saffa wines, all "under the South African banner". / SW1W 0PP; www.bbarlondon.com; @bbarlondon; 10 pm; No shorts.

Bea's Cake Boutique WC1 £39 3 3 3
44 Theobalds Rd   020 7242 8330   2–1D
"Delicious cupcakes" have helped this cosy café near Holborn Library blossom into a spin-off chain. It's an "unexpectedly feminine tea room serving wonderful cakes, proper teas and lunchtime sandwiches". / WC1X 8NW; www.beasofbloomsbury.com; @beas_bloomsbury; 7 pm; L & early evening only.

Bean & Hop SW18 £11 3 3 2
424-426 Garratt Lane   020 7998 6584   11–2B
All the key bases are covered at this "good neighbourhood spot" in Earlsfield, serving "varied brunches", "excellent coffee and tempting cakes by day", and "great homemade pizza with a selection of craft beers in the evening". / SW18 4HN; www.beanandhop.co.uk; @beanandhop.

Bears Ice Cream W12 £6 3 3 3
244 Goldhawk Rd   020 3441 4982   8–1B
Just one "wonderful" flavour of Icelandic ice cream blended with a myriad of "tempting toppings" is the winning recipe of this simple parlour (with small garden) on the busy gyratory at the foot of Askew Road – "guaranteed smiles all round!" / W12 9PE; www.bearsicecream.co.uk; @bears_icecream; 8.30 pm; L & early evening only.

Beast W1 £115 ①②②
3 Chapel Pl 020 7495 1816 3–1B
"Ludicrous pricing" ("so crazy I struggle to find
the adjectives") is the unanimous verdict on this
dramatic-looking, candle-lit, Goodman-owned, steak-
and-crab experience off Oxford Street – even from
reporters who applaud the "great fun and good
food". "I've never been so outraged as when I found
out our Norwegian king crab starter for six was
£470!! Bonkers!… Daylight robbery!…". / W1G
0BG; www.beastrestaurant.co.uk; @beastrestaurant;
10.30 pm; closed Mon & Sun; May need 7+ to book.

The Begging Bowl SE15 £45 ④③②
168 Bellenden Rd 020 7635 2627 1–4D
"Wonderful" if tightly packed Thai street-food
café in Peckham that's an "outpost of real
excellence in SE London" thanks to its "short
choice of genuinely spiced dishes". / SE15 4BW;
www.thebeggingbowl.co.uk; @thebeggingbowl; 9.45 pm,
Sun 9.15 pm; no booking.

Beijing Dumpling WC2 £33 ④②②
23 Lisle St 020 7287 6888 5–3A
"Watching the chefs making the dumplings in the
window is an incredibly comforting experience" at
this "very busy", "tightly packed" little Chinatown
pit stop, where "there are regular queues outside"
(although "you can book and walk straight in!"). /
WC2H 7BA; 11.30 pm, Sun 10.30 pm.

Bel Canto, Corus Hotel Hyde Park W2 £95 ②③③
1 Lancaster Gate 020 7262 1678 7–2C
Opera singers appear on the quarter hour at this
long-established Bayswater basement dining room,
where the traditional dishes often feature luxury
ingredients. / W2 3LG; www.belcantolondon.co.uk;
@london@lebelcanto.co.uk; 10.30 pm; D only, closed
Mon & Sun.

Bellamy's W1 £61 ③④③
18-18a Bruton Pl 020 7491 2727 3–2B
Owner Gavin Rankin (ex MD of Annabel's) "keeps a
strict eye" on this art-lined brasserie, whose "classic",
"unchallenging" French cuisine and "competent
and well-oiled" service make it "the very definition
of civilisation" to its "tidily dressed and mostly
besuited" Mayfair clientele. (It's one of a handful of
restaurants ever visited by The Queen). / W1J 6LY;
www.bellamysrestaurant.co.uk; 10.30 pm; closed Sat
L & Sun.

Bellanger N1 £59 ②③③
9 Islington Grn 020 7226 2555 9–3D
"It's the best thing that's happened to Islington for
years", say fans of Corbin & King's "elegant", all-day
brasserie on Islington Green, who say its "clubby,
wood-lined" interior "feels like it's always been
there", and that it's "interesting take on Alsatian
brasserie cooking (with brilliant tartes flambées)"
makes "an excellent choice for breakfast, lunch or
dinner". A sceptical minority however are left cold
by the experience: "it's all too faux, the food's only
passable, service is drilled but charmless, and all-in-
all it's a pretty set, with no actual drama". / N1 2XH;
www.bellanger.co.uk; @BellangerN1; 11 pm, Sun 10.30
pm; set dinner £36 (FP).

Belpassi Bros SW17 £40 ③③③
70 Tooting High St 020 8767 6399 11–2C
For a "fantastic, simple dinner of Italian meatballs
and sides", fans tip this "casual and relaxed", brick-
lined newcomer in Tooting: the work of brothers
Livio and Lorenzo (who used to sell similar fare
from a truck). There are numerous options when it
comes to the balls, sauces and bases. / SW17 0RN;
www.belpassibros.com; @BelpassiBros; 9.30 pm, Thu-
Sat 10 pm, Sun 8.30 pm; booking max 4 may apply.

Belvedere Restaurant W8 £69 ②③④
off Abbotsbury Rd in Holland Park
020 7602 1238 8–1D
"A wonderful location, actually in Holland Park
itself" – and set in a grand 17th-century ballroom
– provides unbeatably "romantic surroundings" for
this well-known destination. The food struggles to
match the setting, but there are nevertheless reports
of "superb celebratory meals" and "excellent-value
Sunday lunches". Top Tip – "best upstairs, or by
the balcony on summer evenings". / W8 6LU;
www.belvedererestaurant.co.uk; 11 pm, Sun 3.30 pm;
closed Sun D; set weekday L £43 (FP).

Benares W1 £108 ②②②
12a Berkeley Square House,
020 7629 8886 3–3B
Opinions again divide on Atul Kochar's acclaimed
contemporary Indian, which occupies a sprawling
and first-floor site on Berkeley Square. Critics
– who accuse it of "going through the motions"
– drag down its overall ratings, but the majority
lavish praise on his "innovative" cuisine's "delicate
spicing", and say a meal is a "wow, how-did-they-
make-it-taste-so-good experience". / W1J 6BS;
www.benaresrestaurant.co.uk; @benaresofficial; 10.45
pm, Sun 9.45 pm; closed Sun L; booking max 10 may
apply; set weekday L & pre-theatre £66 (FP).

Bentley's W1 £84 ③④④
11-15 Swallow St 020 7734 4756 4–4B
"Celebrating over 100 years of serving some of
the best fish and seafood in London" – Richard
Corrigan's "British classic" near Piccadilly Circus
is "expensive", but "utterly reliable" – "it's easy
to forget that this is one of the best restaurants
in the West End". Downstairs "the booths in the
busy oyster bar are best": the "old-fashioned, silver
service" upstairs is more comfortable but "not as
involving" as below. Top Menu Tips – "exceptional
oysters and lobster". / W1B 4DG; www.bentleys.org;
@bentleys_london; 10.30 pm, Sun 10 pm; No shorts;
booking max 8 may apply; set weekday L £57 (FP).

Berber & Q E8 £48 5️⃣2️⃣5️⃣
Arch 338 Acton Mews   020 7923 0829   14–2A
"The best beef short ribs in town… and the chargrilled cauliflower rocks!" – be it meat or vegetarian, all dishes dazzle at this "pretty damn cool" and "very reasonably priced" North African-inspired grill in a Haggerston railway arch – they even have their own collaboration beer with a great local brewery. / E8 4EA; www.berberandq.com; @berberandq; 10.30 pm, Sun 9.30 pm; D only, closed Mon; May need 6+ to book.

Berber & Q Shawarma Bar EC1 £47 4️⃣3️⃣3️⃣
Exmouth Market   020 79230 0829   10–1A
"Perfectly formed Middle Eastern cuisine", revolving around spit-roasted chicken and lamb, is the focus at this new Exmouth Market venue from Hackney's Berber & Q, which "punches well above its weight". "Although it caters to carnivores, it's also a vegetarian paradise". "Shame you can't reserve a table". / EC1R 4QL; www.berberandq.com; @berberandq; 10.30 pm, Sun 9.30 pm; closed Mon; no booking.

Bernardi's W1 £58 3️⃣3️⃣4️⃣
62 Seymour St   020 3826 7940   2–2A
"The beautifully designed room looks like an amazing space from the pages of Elle Decor" and helps instil a "buzzy atmosphere" at this "fun Italian", on the border between Marylebone and Bayswater. "These guys can cook" too… "but you certainly pay for the pleasure". / W1H 5BN; www.bernardis.co.uk; @BernardisLondon; 11 pm, Mon & Sat 10.30 pm, Sun 9.30 pm.

The Berners Tavern W1 £75 2️⃣3️⃣5️⃣
10 Berners St   020 7908 7979   3–1D
"The magnificent room" – "not an intimate affair, but a breathtaking and fun showpiece" that "makes you feel glamorous and special" – underpins the appeal of this "impressively grand" chamber, north of Oxford Street. The modern British cuisine (overseen by Jason Atherton) is "OK", but "unduly expensive" – "you're there for the ambience". Top Tip – "brunch here makes for a perfect Sunday morning". / W1T 3NP; www.bernerstavern.com; @bernersTavern; 11.45 pm, Sun 10.15 pm; set weekday L £53 (FP).

Best Mangal £42 4️⃣3️⃣3️⃣
619 Fulham Rd, SW6   020 7610 0009   6–4A
104 North End Rd, W14
020 7610 1050   8–2D
66 North End Rd, W14   020 7602 0212   8–2D
"Very good charcoal-grilled meat", "super-fresh salads" and "generous portions" have made a name for this Turkish operation that has expanded to three branches in its 21 years in Fulham. / www.bestmangal.com; midnight, Sat 1 am; no Amex.

Bibendum SW3 £104 2️⃣2️⃣3️⃣
81 Fulham Rd   020 7581 5817   6–2C
"You could never tire of the feeling of decadence and class", say fans of this "lovely and refined" dining space within the iconic Michelin Building on Brompton Cross (converted by Sir Terence Conran in the late 1980s), where "a visit is best when the sun is shining and streaming in through the beautiful windows". Claude Bosi took over in early 2017, with a view to restoring it to its former glory, but initial reports are deeply divided. To advocates, "this classic venue has been re-imagined" and "is now better than Hibiscus" (his previous highly regarded venture). Critics though "miss the old Bibendum with its wholesome fare" and feel the new more ambitious culinary régime comes at "ridiculous prices". / SW3 6RD; www.bibendum.co.uk; @bibendumltd; 11 pm, Sun 10.30 pm; booking max 12 may apply; set Sun L £58 (FP), set weekday L £59 (FP).

Bibendum Oyster Bar SW3 £52 3️⃣2️⃣3️⃣
Michelin House, 81 Fulham Rd
020 7581 5817   6–2C
"New menu, new chef, new decor: all very good" – that's the upbeat view on this long-established Chelsea rendezvous, off the foyer of the Michelin Building, where Claude Bosi's new régime has added luxurious hot staples to the bill of fare alongside its traditional cold seafood platters. It still hasn't re-established itself as the local magnet it once was however, and critical reporters say "it's an old favourite that has gone completely downhill". / SW3 6RD; www.bibendum.co.uk; @bibendumrestaurant; 10 pm; closed Sun D; no booking.

Bibimbap Soho £28 3️⃣2️⃣2️⃣
10 Charlotte St, W1   020 7287 3434   2–1C
11 Greek St, W1   020 7287 3434   5–2A
39 Leadenhall Mkt, EC3   020 72839165   10–2D
Fans say these Korean canteens in Soho and Fitzrovia (with a take-away in the City) are "hard to beat compared with other fast-food places". "They do one thing" – the signature mixed rice dish they're named after – "and do it well". / 11pm, EC3 3 pm; W1 Sun, EC3 Sat & Sun; no bookings.

Big Easy £57 2️⃣2️⃣3️⃣
12 Maiden Ln, WC2   020 3728 4888   5–3D
332-334 King's Rd, SW3   020 7352 4071   6–3C
Crossrail Pl, E14   020 3841 8844   12–1C
"The closest you can feel to America in London" conveys much of what need to know – pro or con – about these US-style BBQs in Chelsea, Covent Garden and Canary Wharf. "What's not to like – bottomless beer or margaritas, a constant supply of chicken and ribs with sides of coleslaw, fries and beans, chirpy and attentive staff and great music!", is the friendly view. "Just awful" is the riposte. / www.bigeasy.co.uk; Mon-Thu 11 pm, Fri & Sat 11.30 pm, Sun 10.30 pm.

The Bingham TW10 £64 4|5|4
61-63 Petersham Rd 020 8940 0902 1–4A
"Smart and sophisticated, without being snobby" – the "really comfortable" dining room of this boutique hotel in Richmond on Thames, which boasts "a beautiful setting on the river". Staff ensure you are "well looked after" and its "slickly prepared" food helps make it a logical choice for a special occasion. Top Tip – "the market menu lunch is exceptional value"; eat it on the balcony overlooking the garden. / TW10 6UT; www.thebingham.co.uk; 10 pm; closed Sun D; No trainers.

The Bird in Hand W14 £49 3|3|4
88 Masbro Rd 020 7371 2721 8–1C
"Excellent pizzas" top the bill at this converted pub in the backstreets of Olympia. "Prices are a little high", and "with the rest of the menu they're sometimes trying to be too clever", but overall it's a "great local". Sibling to the Oaks in W2 and W12. / W14 0LR; www.thebirdinhandlondon.com; @TBIHLondon; 10 pm, Sun 9.15 pm; booking weekdays only.

Bird of Smithfield EC1 £59 2|2|2
26 Smithfield St 020 7559 5100 10–2B
Limited but upbeat feedback on this "buzzy" five-storey Georgian townhouse in Smithfield – it's most worth knowing about for its summer roof terrace. / EC1A 9LB; www.birdofsmithfield.com; @BirdoSmithfield; 10 pm; closed Sun.

Bistro Aix N8 £56 4|3|4
54 Topsfield Pde, Tottenham Ln
020 8340 6346 9–1C
The "fine, traditional French cuisine" at chef-proprietor Lynne Sanders's small and smartly turned-out bistro is "worth a trip to Crouch End". "It's a lovely venue with a good vibe", and has become a local fixture after 15 years on the site. / N8 8PT; www.bistroaix.co.uk; @bistroaixlondon; 10 pm, Fri & Sat 11 pm; Mon-Thu D only, Fri-Sun open L & D; No Amex.

Bistro Union SW4 £57 3|3|3
40 Abbeville Rd 020 7042 6400 11–2D
Adam Byatt's "friendly", bistro spin-off from Trinity in Clapham is a "neighbourhood winner", and even if not as accomplished as its sibling provides "plenty of choice" and scores "mostly hits" on the food front. Top Tip – "Sunday supper club with the children – they eat free and you can take your own wine with no corkage -£26 for set 3 courses". / SW4 9NG; www.bistrounion.co.uk; @BistroUnion; 10 pm, Sun 8 pm; booking max 8 may apply.

Bistro Vadouvan
SW15 NEW £55
30 Brewhouse Lane 020 3475 3776 11–2B
Chef-patron Durga Misra (Brasserie Chavot) and co-founder Uttam Tripathy (Potli) both hail from the same town in India (although they only met years later at college). They have realised a long-held dream with this Thames-view Putney Wharf newcomer, which offers French cooking with Asian spicing. / SW15 2JX; bistrovadouvan.co.uk; @BistroVadouvan; 10.30 pm.

Bistrotheque E2 £58 3|2|4
23-27 Wadeson St 020 8983 7900 14–2B
"Its hip heyday is a decade in the past, and it's now a tourist trap for those in search of cool east London" – that's the cynical view on this light and airy warehouse-conversion, but more numerous are fans who still tip it as a fun brunch haunt. / E2 9DR; www.bistrotheque.com; @Bistrotheque; 10.30 pm, Fri & Sat 11 pm; closed weekday L.

Black Axe Mangal N1 £48 5|4|2
156 Canonbury Rd no tel 9–2D
"If you don't mind the noise" ("not everyone's into heavy metal!"), Lee Tiernan's head-banging Highbury Corner yearling is "certainly more than a few notches up from your average kebab house" and practically all reporters "love, love, LOVE" the "varied and meat-heavy" dishes ("lamb offal flatbread was one of the culinary highlights of the year!)". "He's gonna need a bigger restaurant…" / N1; www.blackaxemangal.com; @blackaxemangal; 10.30 pm, Sun 3 pm; D only Mon-Fri, Sat L & D, Sun L only; no booking.

Black Prince SE11 £38 3|3|3
6 Black Prince Rd 020 7582 2818 2–4D
Though it's consistently well-rated, there's nothing overly gastro' about this classic Kennington boozer, serving classic pub grub with the odd bit of gentle 21st-century updating (eg corn & beetroot slaw with your chicken 'n' chips). / SE11 6HS; www.theblackprincepub.co.uk; 11 pm.

Black Roe W1 £68 3|2|2
4 Mill St 020 3794 8448 3–2C
High-fashion, Hawaiian-inspired two-year-old in Mayfair where dishes 'poke' – marinated raw fish – and hot dishes cooked on a kiawe (mesquite wood) grill. The result is "delicious, fresh, healthy food" presented in a "sexy ambience (although the music's a bit loud)" – but it's also "very expensive". / W1S 2AX; www.blackroe.com; @blackroe; 10.45 pm; closed Sun.

Blacklock £39 4|4|4
24 Great Windmill St, W1 020 3441 6996. 4–2D
13 Philpot Lane, EC3 020 7998 7676 10–3D
NEW
"My inner caveman loves this place!" – "Chops, crispy on the outside and juicy in the middle" provide "amazing meat and amazing value" at this "laid back and very cool", "no frills" Soho basement, which is "a case study of picking something you're good at and sticking with it". In Spring 2017 it

opened its second branch – a larger City outlet off Eastcheap. Top Tip – "the amount of food on the 'All In' has to be seen to be believed!"

Blanchette £50 ❹❸❹
9 D'Arblay St, W1   020 7439 8100   4–1C
204 Brick Lane, E1   020 7729 7939   13–1C
"You can imagine you have been whisked away to France", particularly at the "noisy and boisterous" Soho original of this Gallic duo (which "looks like it's been there for years, but is actually only three years old"), whose year-old East End sibling is also providing "a great addition to Brick Lane". Founded on a traditional mix of "cheeses, cut meats and small plates", the arrival of ex Bibendum chef Tam Storrar as chef/director seems to have taken the menu in a "more complicated and increasingly Mediterranean" direction. / 11 pm, Sun 9 pm.

Blandford Comptoir W1 £60 ❸❸❸
1 Blandford St   020 7935 4626   2–1A
"The justly-renowned wine-list" is the key feature of Xavier Rousset's "crowded" yearling, but its "friendly" style and "simple, effective" Italian dishes, all contribute to its very high popularity as "a good addition to Marylebone". / W1U 3DA; blandford-comptoir.co.uk; @BlandfordCompt; 10 pm; No Amex.

Bleecker Burger £22 ❺❷❷
205 Victoria St, SW1   no tel   2–4B **NEW**
Unit B Pavilion Building, Spitalfields Mkt, E1
07712 540501   13–2B
Bloomberg Arcade, Queen Victoria St, EC4
awaiting tel   10–2C **NEW**
"The juiciest, most flavourful burgers blow the socks off competitors". Former NYC corporate lawyer Zan Kaufman launched his burger biz from the back of a truck five years ago. A permanent site in Spitalfields opened two years ago, followed by venues in Victoria and the City's new Bloomberg Arcade. The "street" has been dropped from the branding, but not the quality: fans feel that "If you don't think Bleecker is the best burger in London, you need your taste buds examined".

Bleeding Heart Restaurant EC1 £66 ❸❸❺
Bleeding Heart Yd, Greville St
020 7242 8238   10–2A
"The convivial atmosphere never fails to be stunning, and the Gallic cooking seldom fails to please" at this "unique Dickensian-style" warren, on the fringe of the City: "a perfect place to impress that special someone in your life", be it romantically or on business! The "gorgeous and imaginative wine list" is key to its appeal, as are staff who are "friendly but, hard to understand given the strong French accents!" (It's a big operation, comprising a restaurant, wine bar and tavern, all interlinked, and all with somewhat different price points.) / EC1N 8SJ;

bleedingheart.co.uk/restaurants/the-restaurant; @bleedingheartyd; 10.30 pm; closed Sat & Sun.

Blixen E1 £47 ❸❸❸
65a Brushfield St   020 7101 0093   13–2C
"Relaxed, casual and cool" all-day brasserie, right by Spitalfields Market, whose handsomely decorated, "bustling" quarters "get especially busy for weekend brunch". / E1 6AA; www.blixen.co.uk; @BlixenLondon; 11 pm, Sun 8 pm.

Blue Boat W6 £50 ❷❷❸
Distillery Wharf   020 3092 2090   8–2C
"A very enterprising newcomer on the riverfront in a new development in Hammersmith". The main attraction is its big sun-trap terrace, but "the quality of the modern pub grub is a welcome surprise". / W6 9GD; www.theblueboat.co.uk; @BlueBoatW6; 10 pm, Sun 9 pm.

Bluebird SW3 £74 ❸❸❸
350 King's Rd   020 7559 1000   6–3C
"Like the new look!" – This D&D landmark has just had "lots of work done refurbishing it" and, with its "very spacious and pleasant" interior and contemporary cuisine that's "not cheap but value for money", it seems to be emerging as the "lovely" venue it's always had the potential to be. Can it be that after 20 years, they've finally sorted the place out? / SW3 5UU; www.bluebird-restaurant.co.uk; @bluebirdchelsea; 10.30 pm, Sun 9.30 pm; set weekday L £46 (FP).

Blueprint Café SE1 £48 ❷❷❹
28 Shad Thames, Butler's Wharf
020 7378 7031   10–4D
A "wonderful location" with "great views over the Thames" is reason enough to visit what is now a stand-alone D&D group restaurant since the Design Museum headed west to Kensington. The food here has always tended to be "a bit hit and miss" and "unexciting", and this year is no exception... / SE1 2YD; www.blueprintcafe.co.uk; @BlueprintCafe; 10.30 pm; closed Mon & Tue; no booking.

Bó Drake W1 £52 ❷❷❸
6 Greek St   020 7439 9989   5–2A
Korean and US influences seem most apparent in the spicy tapas of this vibey, small Soho two-year-old, although its performance varies from "exceptional" to "amateurish". / W1D 4DE; www.bodrake.co.uk; @bodrakesoho; 10.30 pm, Sun 8.30 pm; closed Sun; booking max 6 may apply.

Bob Bob Cité EC3
122 Leadenhall St awaiting tel   10–2D
Tomorrow and tomorrow and tomorrow... – we've been billing the arrival of BBC – sibling to Soho's glam Bob Bob Ricard – for over a year now as its opening is pushed back and back, but it is finally slated to appear in January 2018. Set to occupy the entire third floor of 'The Cheesegrater' – more 'press

for champagne' buttons are promised, alongside cooking provided by well-known chef, Eric Chavot. When it finally arrives, one thing is certain: it won't be subtle… / EC3V 4PE; www.bobbobricard.com.

Bob Bob Ricard W1   £85   3 4 5
1 Upper James St   020 3145 1000   4–2C
"Everyone is dazzled by the exotic boothed interior and the press-for-champagne buttons", when visiting this lavish Russian-owned diner in Soho, which is "super for impressing your guest". Sceptics say its comfort food is "poor for the price", but a number of reporters note that it's "miles better than it was" under chef Anna Haugh (appointed in late 2016). / W1F 9DF; www.bobbobricard.com; @BobBobRicard; 11.15 pm, Sat midnight, Sun 11.15 pm; closed Sat L; Jacket required.

The Bobbin SW4   £52   4 4 4
1-3 Lillieshall Rd   020 7738 8953   11–1D
"A cool Clapham crowd underpin this trendy gastropub", drawn by its "way-above-average" food, and it manages to be "romantic and ambient" as well. "Awesome" Sunday roasts rate mention as does the "indulgent Bobbin's burger (it's the spicy mayo that does it")). / SW4 0LN; www.thebobbinclapham.com; @bobbinsw4; 10 pm, Sun 9 pm.

Bobo Social W1   £45   3 3 3
95 Charlotte St   020 7636 9310   2–1C
Fans say "top burgers" (using rare-breed meat) and an extensive cocktail-menu accompaniment are the highlights at this small town-house conversion in Fitzrovia. Survey feedback has its highs and lows, but the best reviews are enthusiastic: "I will be back!" / W1T 4PZ; www.bobosocial.com; @BoboSocial; 10.30 pm; closed Sun.

Bocca Di Lupo W1   £62   4 4 3
12 Archer St   020 7734 2223   4–3D
"Unexpected, distinctive regional dishes" and staff who are "knowledgeable" and "brilliantly friendly" continue to win a major thumbs up for Jacob Kenedy's "energetic" Italian, near Piccadilly Circus. "Noise is a big issue here – it can be hard to hold a conversation". And the "stimulating" setting can feel too "crowded", both in the rear section and at the front counter (which is "hated" by a few, but for most reporters "a favourite place, where you can watch the chefs and see what other people are eating"). "There are two very wise policies – all options come in half/main portions, and many of the interesting wines are available by the glass or in 500cc pichets". / W1D 7BB; www.boccadilupo.com; @boccadilupo; 11 pm, Sun 9.30 pm; booking max 10 may apply.

Bocconcino W1   £88   3 3 3
19 Berkeley St   020 7499 4510   3–3C
"Expensive but good" is actually the least

enthusiastic endorsement of this agreeable, bare-brick-walled, Russian-owned Italian and pizzeria in Mayfair's eurotrashiest of enclaves. / W1J 8ED; www.bocconcinorestaurant.co.uk; @BocconcinoUK; 11.30 pm, Sun 10.30 pm.

Al Boccon di'vino TW9   £66   3 4 5
14 Red Lion St   020 8940 9060   1–4A
"Starve yourself before going!" – "A real 'Venetian wedding'-style feast" greets diners at this "completely different" operation in Richmond. "Beautiful Italian food is made from fresh ingredients, and while there's no choice of menu, there are so many dishes that you walk out with a warm glow, feeling like you've just left Nonna's house". / TW9 1RW; www.nonsolovinoltd.co.uk; 11 pm; closed Mon, Tue L & Wed L; No Amex.

Bodean's   £51   2 2 2
10 Poland St, W1   020 7287 7575   4–1C
25 Catherine St, WC2   020 7257 2790   5–3D
4 Broadway Chambers, SW6
020 7610 0440   6–4A
348 Muswell Hill Broadway, N10
020 8883 3089   1–1C
225 Balham High St, SW17
020 8682 4650   11–2C
169 Clapham High St, SW4
020 7622 4248   11–2D
201 City Rd, EC1   020 7608 7230   13–1A
16 Byward St, EC3   020 7488 3883   10–3D
These Kansas City-style BBQ joints were some of the first to mine the capital's enthusiasm for Americana, and their "cookie-cutter feel" is arguably all part of the "fun". The large, "all-American menu" seems to follow the principle of "pile it high and sell it cheap" – results are "decent, but not great". / www.bodeansbbq.com; 11 pm, Sun 10.30 pm, NW10 10 pm, Fri & Sat 11 pm; booking: min 8.

La Bodega Negra Cafe W1   £48   3 2 4
16 Moor St   020 7758 4100   5–2B
This low-lit Soho basement Mexican wins converts mainly for its "buzzy" atmosphere, but reporters are perfectly satisfied with the food on offer, too. / W1D 5NH; www.labodeganegra.com; midnight, Thu-Sat 1 am, Sun 11 pm.

Boisdale of Belgravia SW1   £65   3 2 4
15 Eccleston St   020 7730 6922   2–4B
With its "plush jockinese decor and fabulous bar", Ranald Macdonald's "always fun" and "very clubbable" Belgravian provides "an excellent all-round experience", bolstered by its "great selection of wines and spirits", regular jazz, and cigar terrace. The "traditional, meaty Scottish fare" is "pricey" but consistently well rated. / SW1W 9LX; www.boisdale.co.uk/belgravia; @boisdale; midnight; closed Sat L & Sun.

Boisdale of Bishopsgate EC2 £72 🗅②🗅
Swedeland Court, 202 Bishopsgate
020 7283 1763 10–2D
"A great atmosphere" (by the standards of City restaurants) helps win fans for this outpost of the Caledonian Victoria original, down an alley near Liverpool Street, which has a ground floor bar and basement dining room, and serves a similar modern Scottish formula, with an emphasis on wines and whiskies. / EC2M 4NR; www.boisdale.co.uk; @Boisdale; 11 pm; closed Sat & Sun; set pre theatre £48 (FP).

Boisdale of Canary Wharf E14 £62 🗅🗅🗅
Cabot Place 020 7715 5818 12–1C
"Good fun" (a rare commodity in Canary Wharf) is to be had at this "surprisingly enjoyable" (including at the weekend) Scottish themed venue, whose meaty fare, "great live music and selection of drinks" follow a similar formula to the Belgravia original. "If you can grab a space on the terrace, it's an ideal place for an after work bevvie too". / E14 4QT; www.boisdale.co.uk/canary-wharf; @boisdaleCW; 11 pm, Wed-Sat midnight, Sun 4 pm; closed Sun D.

Boisdale of Mayfair W1 NEW £77 🗅🗅🗅
12 North Row 020 3873 8888 2–2A
This bistro-style new Mayfair addition to the Boisdale clan is off to a good start, and wins very respectable ratings for its Scottish-slanted cuisine, plus the usual indulgences: wine, whisky and regular jazz. / W1K 7DF; www.boisdale.co.uk/mayfair; @Boisdale; 11 pm, Sun 6 pm; closed Sun D.

Bokan E14 NEW £70
40 Marsh Wall 020 3530 0550 12–2C
Located on the 37th floor of the new Novotel Canary Wharf, this 65-cover restaurant features modern European cuisine from Aurelie Altemaire, formerly of L'Atelier de Joël Robuchon. Limited feedback to-date, but such as there is praises "thoroughly enjoyable cooking without silly prices", but with splendid views. / E14 9TP; bokanlondon.co.uk; 10 pm.

Bombay Brasserie SW7 £65 🗅🗅🗅
Courtfield Rd 020 7370 4040 6–2B
"Excellent food in a somewhat formal setting" – an elegant conservatory with colonial decor – elevates this South Kensington stalwart beyond "run-of-the-mill curry houses". Reports have dwindled in recent years, but consistently high ratings suggest it's worth a second look. / SW7 4QH; www.bombayb.co.uk; @bbsw7; 11 pm, Sun 10.30 pm; closed Mon L.

Bombay Palace W2 £41 🗅🗅②
50 Connaught St 020 7723 8855 7–1D
This long-time Bayswater favourite reopened at long last after a fire closed the doors for over a

year, sparking concern among the many fans of its "fabulous Indian flavours". "After the initial hiccups, they've got it just right", is the relieved verdict shared by most – if not quite all – reporters. The interior, always the weak point at this venue, is "a marked improvement, and the food still of consistent high quality". / W2 2AA; www.bombay-palace.co.uk; @bombaypalaceW2; 10.45 pm; booking essential.

Bombetta E11 £51 🗅🗅②
Station Approach 020 3871 0890 1–1D
This "charming and well-meaning", "cheap 'n' cheerful" Puglian newcomer on the "outer reaches of the Central Line" – near Snaresbrook station in Wanstead – "is no ordinary Italian". For one, there's "no pizza". Instead, "a small-plates menu with lots of meaty and good vegetarian options" followed by the signature "bombetta" (cheesy-meaty bites). / E11 1QE; www.bombettalondon.com; @bombettaLondon.

Bon Vivant WC1 NEW £57 🗅🗅🗅
75-77 Marchmont St 020 7713 6111 9–4C
"A brave and useful addition to an increasingly buzzy corner of Bloomsbury" – this "minimalist" newcomer is "more intimate and grown-up than many offerings in this part of town" with "well-executed and presented" Gallic fare. / WC1N 1AP; www.bonvivantrestaurant.co.uk; set weekday L £33 (FP).

Bone Daddies £42 🗅🗅🗅
Nova, Victoria St, SW1 no tel 2–4B
14a, Old Compton St, W1
020 7734 7492 5–2A
30-31 Peter St, W1 020 7287 8581 4–2D
46-48 James St, W1
020 3019 7140 3–1A NEW
Whole Foods, Kensington High St, W8
020 7287 8581 6–1A
The Bower, Baldwin St, EC1
020 7439 9299 13–1A
"Good lord, that stock they use in the ramen!" – Aussie restaurateur, Ross Shonhan's funky fusion chain offers "noodles served in lovely, rich broths, as well as some fantastic salads and small dishes" to create a "superb all-round experience"; branches are regularly "heaving". / www.bonedaddies.com/restaurant/bermondsey/; 10 pm, Thu-Sat 11 pm, Sun 9.30 pm; W1 no bookings.

Bonhams Restaurant, Bonhams Auction House W1 £75 🗅🗅②
101 New Bond St 020 7468 5868 3–2B
Tom Kemble's "amazing food" won instant renown for this "intimately proportioned, if rather sterilely decorated" three-year-old, at the back of the famous Mayfair auction house (and also with its own, separate entrance). Of equal attraction is the "incredible wine list that leverages the wines at the auction house's disposal" – "the wine markups, or lack thereof, are unheard of in their generosity", with many available by the glass. Top Tip – "wander

round the auction rooms post meal". / W1K 5ES;
www.bonhamsrestaurant.com; @dineatbonhams; 8.30
pm; L only, Fri L & D, closed Sat & Sun.

La Bonne Bouffe
SE22 NEW £53 3️⃣2️⃣3️⃣
49 North Cross Rd 020 3730 2107 1–4D
"New on the block, with French bistro food harking
back to the '70s": this East Dulwich arrival evokes
mostly supportive reviews. There are critics who
feel "more polish is required", but fans – while
acknowledging some "not-quite-knowing-how-things-
work moments" – say "it's not trying anything
too clever", but can be "brilliant". / SE22 9ET;
www.labonnebouffe.co.uk; @laBonneBouffe49.

Bonnie Gull W1 £57 4️⃣3️⃣3️⃣
21a Foley St 020 7436 0921 2–1B
"A wide range of fresh fish is cooked with flair and
skill" in this "bright and cheerful" Fitzrovia dining
room, whose small size is at odds with its huge
following. Conditions are "so cramped", but "it's
compact nature makes it cosy", as does the "very
friendly service". / W1W 6DS; www.bonniegull.com;
@BonnieGull; 9.45 pm, Sun 8.45 pm.

Bonnie Gull Seafood Shack
W1 NEW £52 5️⃣3️⃣3️⃣
22 Bateman St 020 7436 0921 5–2A
For "very fresh fish and seafood from a changing
menu" it's worth discovering this "cosy and slightly
cramped" Fitzrovia dining room – "a quiet corner of
London not far from the bustle of Oxford Street",
with "an enjoyable, familial feel to it". / W1D 3AN;
www.bonniegull.com/seafood-shack/soho; @BonnieGull;
11 pm, Sun 9 pm.

Bonoo NW2 £42 5️⃣4️⃣3️⃣
675 Finchley Rd 020 7794 8899 1–1B
"What a find! Finally a fabulous local restaurant
in NW2!" – "this friendly, neighbourhood tapas-
style Indian in Childs Hill surpasses many swanky
competitors" with "fantastic street food dishes,
plus a few usual old favourites". / NW2 2JP;
www.bonoo.co.uk; @bonoohampstead; 10.30 pm.

The Booking Office, St Pancras
Renaissance Hotel NW1 £67 2️⃣2️⃣4️⃣
Euston Rd 020 7841 3566 9–3C
The hugely characterful, former St Pancras station
ticket office makes a "lovely location" for calm
all-day refuelling (at nights it can be "rocking").
Food reports are a tad uneven, but it's a good
bet for a "quality afternoon tea". / NW1 2AR;
www.bookingofficerestaurant.com; @StPancrasRen;
11 pm.

Boqueria £46 4️⃣4️⃣4️⃣
192 Acre Ln, SW2 020 7733 4408 11–2D
278 Queenstown Rd, SW8
020 7498 8427 11–1C

"Fresh, light tapas dishes, with influences from Asia"
provide a "different take on the usual fare" at these
"stylish", "buzzy and fun" neighbourhood places,
in Battersea and on the Clapham/Brixton border;
"charming service" too.

Il Bordello E1 £56 3️⃣3️⃣4️⃣
81 Wapping High St 020 7481 9950 12–1A
"Love the place!" – a fixture in Wapping, this "very
traditional Italian" is "always thrumming, which gives
it a terrific atmosphere". "Always good value", it's
"unchanged for years – including the waiters...". /
E1W 2YN; www.ilbordello.com; 11 pm, Sun 10.30 pm;
closed Sat L.

Boro Bistro SE1 £44 3️⃣4️⃣3️⃣
Montague Cl, 6-10 Borough High St
020 7378 0788 10–3C
"A hidden gem" in Borough Market worth
remembering as a good "cheap 'n' cheerful" option
and whose "basic" Gallic decor is part of its charm.
It serves "great sharing boards, plus a surprisingly
good cheese and wine selection". #NotReeling / SE1
9QQ; www.borobistro.co.uk; @borobistro; 10.30 pm,
Mon & Sun 9 pm; closed Mon & Sun; booking max 6
may apply.

The Botanist £68 2️⃣2️⃣2️⃣
7 Sloane Sq, SW1 020 7730 0077 6–2D
Broadgate Circle, EC2 020 3058 9888 13–2B
"A Sloaney spot for ladies who lunch" – the well-
known, "very lively" Chelsea branch right on Sloane
Square that's also convenient for "business lunches
or drinks" (no-one talks about its City offshoot). The
food avoided the drubbing of prior surveys and won
consistent support this year. / thebotanist.uk.com;
SW1 breakfast 8, Sat & Sun 9, SW1 & EC2 11 pm.

The Bothy E14 NEW £53
16 Hertsmere Rd 020 3907 0320 12–1C
An enviable waterside location in Canary Wharf
(in the same former warehouse buildings as the
Docklands Museum) provides the setting for
this large new Drake & Morgan's outlet; all-day
dining, Sunday roasts, cocktails, plenty of outside
seating and weekend brunch complete the
picture. / E14 4AX; drakeandmorgan.co.uk/the-bothy;
@TheBothyW1Q; 10 pm, Sun 9 pm.

Boudin Blanc W1 £58 3️⃣3️⃣4️⃣
5 Trebeck St 020 7499 3292 3–4B
"Classic Gallic food and service in a lovely old
building" (with extensive al fresco seating) draws a
steady crowd to this "romantic" and "cosy Mayfair
staple" in picturesque Shepherd Market. / W1J 7LT;
www.boudinblanc.co.uk; 11 pm.

Boulestin SW1 £71 3️⃣3️⃣2️⃣
5 St James's St 020 7930 2030 3–4D
Joel Kissin's three-year-old brasserie (on the site
that was L'Oranger, long RIP) revives the name of a

famous 1920s fine dining Gallic basement in Covent Garden. Perhaps unsurprisingly given its swanky location it seems "slightly pricey" for what it is, but attractions do include "one of the best breakfasts in St James's", plus "a super little courtyard for outdoor dining in summer". / SW1A 1EF; www.boulestin.com; @BoulestinLondon; 10.30 pm; closed Sun; No trainers.

The Brackenbury W6 £56 4️⃣4️⃣3️⃣
129-131 Brackenbury Rd
020 8741 4928 8–1C
The epitome of "an excellent neighbourhood restaurant" – chef/patron Humphrey Fletcher's "lovely local" in the backstreets of Hammersmith provides "frequently changing seasonal fare", very "charming" service and a civilised atmosphere, enhanced by a sizeable terrace in summer. The re-jigged layout – with a bar in one of its two rooms – seems to be working well too. / W6 0BQ; www.brackenburyrestaurant.co.uk; @BrackenburyRest; 9.30 pm; closed Mon & Sun D.

Brackenbury Wine Rooms W6 £57 3️⃣3️⃣4️⃣
Hammersmith Grove 020 3696 8240 8–1C
"A very good range of wine by the glass as well as bottle" is just one attraction at this Hammersmith corner-spot – others include very decent cooking, "friendly" staff, very attractive styling, and a large outside terrace. Inviting neighbouring café/deli too, with "exceptional coffee". / W6 0NQ; winerooms. london/brackenbury; @Wine_Rooms; 11.30 pm, Sun 10.30 pm.

Bradley's NW3 £62 3️⃣2️⃣2️⃣
25 Winchester Rd 020 7722 3457 9–2A
"Convenient for the Hampstead Theatre", this "off-the-beaten-track" Swiss Cottage stalwart serves a modern British menu of some ambition, and offers "especially good value pre-show menus". At other times, prices are "a bit steep", service can lag, and it can seem "curiously unmemorable" even though "objectively the food is good, and the room tastefully restrained". / NW3 3NR; www.bradleysnw3.co.uk; 10 pm; closed Sun D.

Brady's SW18 £39 3️⃣3️⃣3️⃣
39 Jews Row 020 8877 9599 11–2B
"Still loving it after over 20 years" – "The Brady's family-owned fish 'n' chip shop may have changed location a few years ago", but even if "it's not as lively as it used to be" in its "posh" new Thames-side home ("rather hidden away near Wandsworth Bridge") this is "a simple formula that's survived the test of time and the move" – "superb fish 'n' chips" (with "a grand choice of specials alongside old favourites") and "a warm welcome". Top Menu Tip – "Mr Brady's famous desserts are a big draw too". / SW18 1DG; www.bradysfish.co.uk; @Bradyfish; 10 pm; Tue-Thu D only, Fri & Sat L & D, Sun L only, closed Mon; no booking.

Brasserie Blanc £56 1️⃣3️⃣2️⃣
'Brasserie Bland' would unfortunately be a better title for Raymond Blanc's modern brasserie chain. To be sure there are less enjoyable standbys out there, and for an "OK pre-theatre meal" they could be worse, but the fare is "formulaic" and "the ambience AWOL". / www.brasserieblanc.com; most branches close between 10 pm & 11 pm; SE1 closed Sun D, City branches closed Sat & Sun.

Brasserie Toulouse-Lautrec SE11 £56 3️⃣3️⃣3️⃣
140 Newington Butts 020 7582 6800 1–3C
"Surprisingly good" cooking is to be found at this genuinely Gallic brasserie (and popular live music venue) in a thinly-provided corner of Kennington ("convenient for the nearby cinema museum"). / SE11 4RN; www.btlrestaurant.co.uk; @btlrestaurant; 10.30 pm, Sat & Sun 11 pm.

BRASSERIE ZÉDEL W1 £40 1️⃣3️⃣5️⃣
20 Sherwood St 020 7734 4888 4–3C
"Why bother with any restaurant chain when you can actually eat here cheaper and get the Corbin & King experience on a budget!" Their "breathtaking refurbishment of the Regent Palace Hotel's Art Deco basement grill room" provides a "dramatic and unexpected setting in a fantastic location, just off Piccadilly Circus", that's "very evocative of a true Parisian brasserie" ("democratic and wonderful!"). The trade-off is the "conveyor-belt" classic brasserie fare which can utterly "lack spark", but even so "at these prices you can't go wrong". Top Menu Tips – "stick to the classics like steak haché" or the "incredible value set options". / W1F 7ED; www.brasseriezedel.com; @brasseriezedel; 11.45 pm, Sun 10.45 pm.

Bravas E1 £46 3️⃣4️⃣3️⃣
St Katharine Docks 020 7481 1464 10–3D
Prettily located overlooking the marina at St Katharine dock, this "favourite" modern Basque three-year-old provides "excellent high-quality tapas". / E1W 1AT; http://www.bravasrestaurant.com; @Bravas_Tapas; 10 pm.

Brawn E2 £62 4️⃣3️⃣3️⃣
49 Columbia Rd 020 7729 5692 14–2A
"Skilled and seasonal" small plates, plus "a funky and sometimes challenging (in a good way) list of natural wines" have earned exalted foodie status for Ed Wilson's rough-hewn venue in a former Bethnal Green workshop. Scores have slipped off their high peak here though, amidst the odd gripe that "its former zip and precision are missing". / E2 7RG; www.brawn.co; @brawn49; 11 pm; closed Mon L & Sun D; No Amex.

Bread Street Kitchen
EC4 **£64** 222
10 Bread St 020 3030 4050 10–2B
The "great fit-out" of this Gordon Ramsay operation in a City shopping mall makes it "a surprisingly welcoming environment for such a huge space", and its sizeable fan club like its "buzzy atmosphere" and "varied menu" of food that's "good without being great but not bad value". But while it escaped harsh critiques, for some tastes it's all just too "formulaic". / EC4M 9AJ; www.breadstreetkitchen.com; @breadstreet; 11 pm, Sun 8 pm.

Breakfast Club
£43 333
33 D'Arblay St, W1 020 7434 2571 4–1C
2-4 Rufus St, N1 020 7729 5252 13–1B
31 Camden Pas, N1 020 7226 5454 9–3D
12-16 Artillery Ln, E1 020 7078 9633 13–2B
"Delicious breakfasts: English, American, Antipodean (the waffles are a must!), …" supply "food that's worth getting up for" at this growing group of "consistently high-quality" cafés. There is a snag though: "go off-peak to avoid the crowds and long waiting times". Top Menu Tip – the "ever-popular huevos rancheros". / www.thebreakfastclubcafes.com; SRA-Food Made Good – 3 stars.

Breddos Tacos EC1 NEW **£41** 444
82 Goswell Rd 020 3535 8301 10–1B
"Mouthwatering tacos" – an "innovative take on Mexican food in a City with few good Mexicans" – draw a strong fanclub to this "fun and vibrant" Clerkenwell cantina, which started out as a stall in E8, and is about to open a second Soho branch in September 2017 on the former site of Shotgun (RIP). / EC1M 7AH; www.breddostacos.com; @breddostacos; no booking.

Brew House Café, Kenwood House
NW3 **£31** 223
Hampstead Heath 020 8348 1286 9–1A
"If you can just muster enough patience to manage the queues at the check-out, there's nowhere better on a sunny day in North London for a delicious piece of cake and a cup of tea than this stunning garden", which adjoins the self-service café within the stable blocks of this stately home, on Hampstead Heath; "wonderful breakfasts" too. / NW3 7JR; www.english-heritage.org.uk/visit/places/kenwood/facilities; @EHKenwood; 6 pm (summer), 4 pm (winter); L only.

Briciole W1 **£50** 343
20 Homer St 020 7723 0040 7–1D
"Excellent, authentic Italian cooking" wins high popularity for this deli-trattoria favourite in the backwoods of Marylebone (a spin-off from Latium), aided by its "buzzy atmosphere" and "charming staff". It's "a bit pricey" though – at times, "while the quality is there, the quantity isn't". / W1H 4NA; www.briciole.co.uk; @briciolelondon; 10.15 pm.

Brick Lane Beigel Bake
E1 **£6** 411
159 Brick Ln 020 7729 0616 13–1C
"Long waits, hectoring staff" and "imperious queue marshalling" do nothing to diminish the rockstar status of this epic, 24/7 Brick Lane veteran, which sells the "best beigels ever, and they're SO cheap". / E1 6SB; open 24 hours; Cash only; no booking.

Brigadiers EC2 NEW
Bloomberg Arcade, Queen Victoria St awaiting tel 10–2C
JKS Restaurants (AKA the Sethi siblings), the founders of Gymkhana and Hoppers, are behind this Indian BBQ restaurant inspired by traditional Indian Army mess halls. It is slated to open autumn 2017 alongside nine other eateries in the new Bloomberg City HQ. / EC2R; www.jksrestaurants.com.

The Bright Courtyard
W1 **£62** 422
43-45 Baker St 020 7486 6998 2–1A
Consistently high ratings again this year for this comparatively little-known, contemporary Marylebone Chinese, tipped particularly for its dim sum. / W1U 8EW; www.lifefashiongroup.com; @BrightCourtyard; 10.45 pm, Thu-Sat 11.15 pm.

Brilliant UB2 **£46** 443
72-76 Western Rd 020 8574 1928 1–3A
A "Southall institution" that "never disappoints" – this big and bustling 'burbs Punjabi is "certainly not resting on its laurels", providing "finely spiced" food ("with an East African bias as the owners are from Kenya"). "I hesitated for 40 years before coming and it was worth the wait!". / UB2 5DZ; www.brilliantrestaurant.com; @brilliantrst; 11 pm, Fri & Sat 11.30 pm; closed Mon, Sat L & Sun L.

Brinkley's SW10 **£62** 223
47 Hollywood Rd 020 7351 1683 6–3B
"A lively spot, with an excellent wine list" – key selling points of John Brinkley's Chelsea perennial, near the C&W hospital. "The food isn't bad, but it's unlikely to be the main attraction to the twenty-something, local bright-young-things that seem so attracted to the place". / SW10 9HX; www.brinkleys.com; @BrinkleysR; 11.30 pm; closed weekday L.

Bronte WC2 **£69** 234
Grand Buildings, 1-3 Strand
020 7930 8855 2–3C
Even critics of this big and ambitious yearling off Trafalgar Square confess it looks "amazing" ("an Aladdin's cave of to-die-for Tom Dixon design-treasures"). "When fusion food goes wrong, it goes really wrong" however, and even though the "Asian-ish fare" can impress, it can also be "atrocious". Perhaps try it out first for a "lovely cocktail" ("it's a stunning place for a drink, particularly if you grab

the outdoor table with a through-the-arch view of Nelson's Column"), or try the "top notch brunch". / WC2N 5EJ; www.bronte.co.uk; @bronte_london.

Brookmill SE8 NEW £50 333
65 Cranbrook Rd   020 8333 0899   1–4D
Recently-refurbished Deptford gastropub, "definitely worth a visit if you're passing" for its superior cooking and "nice city garden". / SE8 4EJ; www.thebrookmill.co.uk; @thebrookmillpub; 10 pm, Sun & Mon 9 pm.

The Brown Dog SW13 £46 333
28 Cross St   020 8392 2200   11–1A
A "gem" tucked away in the cute backstreets of Barnes's 'Little Chelsea', this "reliable local gastropub" dishes up "the best roasts in the vicinity (based on extensive testing!)". Children and dogs are welcome. / SW13 0AP; www.thebrowndog.co.uk; @browndogbarnes; 10 pm, Sun 9 pm.

Brown's Hotel, The English Tea Room W1 £74 344
Albemarle St   020 7493 6020   3–3C
"A great balance between cosy comfort and formality" – Rocco Forte's "classic" Mayfair hotel lounge haven is renowned for its "memorable afternoon tea", which is one of London's 'greats' in this department. / W1S 4BP; www.roccofortehotels.com; No trainers.

Brown's Hotel, HIX Mayfair W1 £69 223
Albemarle St   020 7518 4004   3–3C
For fans this civilised Mayfair chamber provides "a quintessential London dining experience", and it wins particular praise both as a "power" lunch or "delicious breakfast" spot. Mark Hix's régime here has almost as many detractors as fans however, who feel the traditional cuisine is too "average" and "overpriced". / W1S 4BP; www.thealbemarlerestaurant.com; 11 pm, Sun 10.30 pm.

Brunswick House Café SW8 £56 335
30 Wandsworth Rd   020 7720 2926   11–1D
The "improbable" and "eccentrically wonderful" setting of an architectural salvage and antiques shop inside the former Duke of Brunswick's Georgian mansion on Vauxhall roundabout hosts this modern British dining room. "A regularly changing menu of delicious and innovative food" makes any meal here a "quirky treat". Top Tip – "lunch is a steal". / SW8 2LG; www.brunswickhouse.co; 10 pm; closed Sun D.

Bubbledogs, Kitchen Table W1 £134 534
70 Charlotte St   020 7637 7770   2–1C
"One of the best experiences ever" – James

Knappett's "truly unique" venture, tucked away behind his and his wife's adjoining hot dog place – is as "absolutely fascinating" as it is unexpected. Seated at stools around the 20-seat kitchen table creates "great intimacy with the team" and the daily changing 12-course array of dishes ("on the whole sourced from the UK, and very well explained") are "from another world". "It's cosy, it's unpretentious, it's delicious, it's friendly, it's excellent value". / W1T 4QG; www.kitchentablelondon.co.uk; @bubbledogsKT; seatings only at 6 pm & 7.30 pm; D only, closed Mon & Sun.

Buen Ayre E8 £62 442
50 Broadway Market   020 7275 9900   14–2B
"Top steaks (and a couple of vegetarian BBQ options too)" seal high satisfaction with this well-established and popular Argentinian 'parilla' in the heart of Hackney's happening Broadway Market. / E8 4QJ; www.buenayre.co.uk; 10 pm, Fri & Sat 10.30 pm, Sun 10 pm; No Amex.

The Builders Arms SW3 £54 223
13 Britten St   020 7349 9040   6–2C
"Fun, with reliable, simple grub" – this modernised pub (part of the Geronimo Inns chain) in a cute Chelsea backstreet wins very consistent praise, especially for its "relaxed ambience". / SW3 3TY; www.thebuildersarmschelsea.co.uk; @BuildersChelsea; 10 pm, Thu-Sat 11 pm, Sun 9.30 pm; no booking.

Bukowski Grill £38 332
10-11 D'Arblay St, W1   020 3857 4756   4–1C
Brixton Market, Unit 10 Market Row, SW9
020 7733 4646   11–2D
Boxpark, Unit 61, 4-6 Bethnal Green Rd, E1
020 7033 6601   13–2B
"Good for carnivores", these "friendly", "reasonably priced" American-style grills with branches in Soho, Brixton and Shoreditch max out on burgers and ribs. / W1 10.30 pm, E1 10 pm, Sun 6 pm, SW9 11 pm, Sun 9 pm, Croydon 11 pm, Sun 10 pm; SW9 closed Mon; W1 online bookings.

The Bull N6 £53 344
13 North Hill   020 8341 0510   9–1B
"Homely and welcoming with a very good menu", this microbrewery pub in Highgate has brought its food up a notch in the past year or so. / N6 4AB; thebullhighgate.co.uk; @Bull_Highgate.

Bull & Last NW5 £65 333
168 Highgate Rd   020 7267 3641   9–1B
This "quintessential gastropub" in Kentish Town feels "more like a homely local than a high class place" but remains north London's most popular hostelry – "the food is amazingly consistent" ("lovely for a big Sunday lunch" after a walk on the heath) and "served with infectious enthusiasm". / NW5 1QS; www.thebullandlast.co.uk; @thebullandlast; 10 pm, Sun 9 pm.

Bumpkin £59 ②②②
119 Sydney St, SW3   020 3730 9344   6–3C
102 Old Brompton Rd, SW7
020 7341 0802   6–2B
Westfield Stratford City, The St, E20
020 8221 9900   14–1D
This "comfy and slightly rustic" West London mini-chain featuring British fare is reduced in numbers nowadays and its performance "continues to vary wildly". Fans, though, say the service "may be chaotic but is always cheerful", "love the farm-to-table options", and find it OK value. / www.bumpkinuk.com; 11 pm; closed Mon.

Buona Sera £45 ③③③
289a King's Rd, SW3   020 7352 8827   6–3C
22 Northcote Rd, SW11
020 7228 9925   11–2C
"Basic Italian cooking done to a satisfactory standard" along with a "family-friendly atmosphere" have established this "busy" and incredibly "consistent" café as a Clapham institution; it has a Chelsea spin-off too at the King's Road 'Jam' – an age-old place with fun double-decker booths. / SW11 11.30 pm, Sun 10.30 pm; SW3 11 pm; SW3 closed Mon L.

Burger & Lobster £59 ③②③
Harvey Nichols, 109-125 Knightsbridge, SW1
020 7235 5000   6–1D
26 Binney St, W1   020 3637 5972   3–2A
29 Clarges St, W1   020 7409 1699   3–4B
36 Dean St, W1   020 7432 4800   5–2A
6 Little Portland St, W1   020 7907 7760   3–1C
195-198 High Holborn, WC1
020 7432 4805   2–1D
18 Hertsmere Rd, E14
020 3637 6709   12–1C **NEW**
40 St John St, EC1   020 7490 9230   10–1B
Bow Bells Hs, 1 Bread St, EC4
020 7248 1789   10–2B
"For a straightforward, relaxed meal with a bit of pizzazz", these "buzzy" joints maintain their massive popularity with a "simple" formula executed "with style": "awesome lobster rolls" are "excellent value" – the burgers "are rather expensive, albeit well-executed". / www.burgerandlobster.com; 10.30 pm-11pm, where open Sun 8 pm-10 pm; WC1 & EC2 closed Sun; booking: min 6.

Busaba Eathai £39 ②②③
"Original and unique decor" has always helped distinguish these communal canteens (who share the same founder as Wagamama). Critics feel its cooking has "really gone downhill" over the years, but most reporters still say its "westernised Thai food" provides "a good formula for a quick, cheap meal". / www.busaba.co.uk; 11 pm, Fri & Sat 11.30 pm, Sun 10 pm; W1 no booking; WC1 booking: min 10.

Butler's Restaurant, The Chesterfield Mayfair W1 £83 ②④③
35 Charles St   020 7958 7729   3–3B
Traditional Mayfair dining room, where fans applaud its "relaxed" style and Nathan Hindmarsh's dependable (if, some would say, pricey) British cuisine. The hotel's star turn actually takes place in the adjoining "lovely" 'Conservatory' – "a fun all-you-can-eat afternoon tea themed around Charlie and the Chocolate Factory". / W1J 5EB; www.chesterfieldmayfair.com; @chesterfield_MF; 10 pm; Jacket required; booking max 8 may apply; set pre theatre £54 (FP).

Butlers Wharf Chop House SE1 £65 ②②③
36e Shad Thames   020 7403 3403   10–4D
A "good riverside location" near Tower Bridge is what most qualifies this D&D London venue as "a decent option", as its "high-end comfort food" is "never special, and pricey for what you get". Its better-known stablemate, Le Pont de la Tour, is next door but one. / SE1 2YE; www.chophouse-restaurant.co.uk; @bwchophousetowerbridge/; 11 pm, Sun 10 pm.

La Buvette TW9 £45 ③③③
6 Church Walk   020 8940 6264   1–4A
"Hidden away up an alleyway in a charming location" beside a churchyard in the heart of Richmond, this "good-value French bistro" is "the perfect local". "Good game (duck and venison), with traditional starters (fish soup) and desserts" are highlights of the menu. / TW9 1SN; www.labuvette.co.uk; @labuvettebistro; 10 pm; booking max 8 may apply.

by Chloe WC2 **NEW**
34-43 Russell St awaiting tel 5–2D
The first overseas site from this American, plant-based restaurant brand arrives in Covent Garden. Its London flagship (a roll-out no doubt is on its way) will seat 70 and offers a grab and go service too. / WC2B 5HA; www.eatbychloe.com; @eatbychloe.

Byron £36 ②②②
Supporters say "hats off to an unformulaic formula", but enthusiasm is waning fast for this 'posh patties' group, which seems increasingly "overtaken by the independent burger joints", and whose ratings are heading inexorably south. Supporters do still applaud its "upmarket burgers and good choice of sides", but there are too many former fans who – amidst gripes over "slipping standards" and "soulless" branches – say its "descent to chain-dom" is nearly complete. (Whether Tom Byng its founder stepping down as CEO at the end of the 2016 is causative or symptomatic is hard to read). / www.byronhamburgers.com; most branches 11 pm.

C London W1 £95 ⬜⬜🔳
25 Davies St   020 7399 0500   3–2B
*"Maybe I'm just not the target audience, but that
still doesn't justify the bill!" – this eurotrashy Mayfair
scene (forced to drop the [C]'ipriani' from its name
in a lawsuit a few years ago) continues to live down
to the low expectations formed by former surveys:
"service is slow and condescending", and "prices are
outrageous for ordinary dishes" (think of a number,
then double it). / W1K 3DE; www.crestaurant.co.uk;
11.45 pm.*

C&R Cafe £30 🔳⬜⬜
3-4 Rupert Ct, W1   020 7434 1128   4–3D
52 Westbourne Grove, W2
020 7221 7979   7–1B
*"Ignore the Formica! The flavours and smells
are pure Malaysia" at this "café-style" venue, in
Chinatown (with a glossier offshoot in Bayswater).
"If you like South East Asian food, this is the
place to find it" – "made fresh and brought
quickly" – and it's "fantastic value for money". /
www.cnrrestaurant.com; W1 10 pm, Fri & Sat 11 pm;
W2 10.30 pm, Fri & Sat 11 pm, Sun 10 pm; W2 closed
Tue.*

Cabotte EC2 🆕 £67 🔳🔳🔳
48 Gresham St   020 7600 1616   10–2C
*"Working equally well for a quick bite and business
chat, or a long, slow afternoon of indulgence with
one of London's most astonishing wine lists" – this
"refined" newcomer near the Guildhall is one of
the best restaurants to have hit the Square Mile in
recent years, certainly of a more traditional nature.
"There's a distinct Burgundian feel" to the "elegant
and full flavoured" cuisine which is the counterpoint
to "an exemplary wine list from the region, with
very fair markups headed up by not one but two
Master Sommeliers." The "delightful" atmosphere is
uncharacteristic for the ECs too – "buzzy but not
macho". / EC2V 7AY; www.cabotte.co.uk; @Cabotte_;
9.30 pm.*

Cacio & Pepe SW1 £58 🔳⬜⬜
46 Churton St   020 7630 7588   2–4B
*"There's bar seating upstairs and more tables in
the vaulted cellar" (the former is preferred) at this
year-old Italian, in a Pimlico backwater. A couple of
misfires, particularly on the food front hit its ratings
this year, but fans applaud its "authentic" and
"friendly" style. / SW1V 2LP; www.cacioepepe.co.uk;
10.30 pm, Fri & Sat 11 pm, Sun 10 pm.*

Café Below EC2 £43 🔳⬜🔳
St Mary-le-Bow, Cheapside
020 7329 0789   10–2B
*"Shhh, don't tell anyone", but this "busy, noisy
café in the crypt of St Mary-Le-Bow" (and,
weather permitting, al fresco in the churchyard)
is "surely one of the City's best-kept secrets". The
"good food" includes "decent, reasonably priced*

*breakfasts", "nice salads and hot dishes". / EC2 6AU;
www.cafebelow.co.uk; 2.30 pm; L only.*

Café del Parc N19 £45 🔳🔳🔳
167 Junction Rd   020 7281 5684   9–1C
*"A perfect local" that "never fails to deliver" – this
"charming oasis on the Archway Road" is a "terrific
partnership between the chef and the head waiter"
and "whizzes out" an "inventive" set menu of
Spanish and North African tapas: "there's no choice,
but none is needed as everything is fresh, interesting
and delicious". / N19 5PZ; www.delparc.com; 10.30
pm; open D only, Wed-Sun; No Amex; booking D only.*

Café du Marché EC1 £57 🔳🔳🔳
22 Charterhouse Sq   020 7608 1609   10–1B
*It can feel "magical", especially when the pianist is
playing, at this "romantic, candle-lit and cosy" old
Gallic bistro, just off Charterhouse Square, which
has been a "reassuringly unchanging" feature
of the area since long before the environs of
Smithfield became fashionable, and its "classic (if
perhaps unadventurous) cuisine" is "always a great
pleasure". / EC1M 6DX; www.cafedumarche.co.uk;
@cafedumarche; 10 pm; closed Sat L & Sun.*

Café East SE16 £24 🔳⬜⬜
100 Redriff Rd   020 7252 1212   12–2B
*This Bermondsey canteen is "mostly full of
Vietnamese" for a good reason: "the best pho
in London", according to its devotees. And it's
not just the pho: "everything tastes so fresh" –
"and at bargain-basement prices". / SE16 7LH;
www.cafeeastpho.co.uk/; @cafeeastpho; 10.30 pm, Sun
10 pm; closed Tue; No Amex; no booking.*

**Cafe Football, Westfield Stratford
E20** £47 🔳🔳🔳
The St   020 8702 2590   14–1D
*With its "football-themed menu names and the
multi-screens tuned to Sky Sports", this big Stratford
diner doesn't aim for gastronomy, but wins solid
praise for a "cheap 'n' cheerful" night, especially
in a group. / E20 1EN; www.cafe-football.com;
@cafefootballuk; 10 pm.*

**Café in the Crypt, St Martin in the
Fields WC2** £30 🔳⬜🔳
Duncannon St   020 7766 1158   2–2C
*"Huge" crypt, beneath St Martin-in-the-Fields and
right on Trafalgar Square. To some its self-service
cafeteria style is too "soulless", but fans adore the
setting and that you can get "tasty snacks at really
good prices" so centrally. / WC2N 4JJ; stmartin-in-the-
fields.org/cafe-in-the-crypt; @smitf_london; 8 pm, Wed
10.30 pm, Thu-Sat 9 pm, Sun 6 pm; L & early evening
only; No Amex; no booking.*

Café Monico W1 £62 🔳🔳🔳
39-45 Shaftesbury Avenue
020 3727 6161   5–3A

"At last! A grown-up oasis of pleasure and calm amidst the hustle and bustle of theatreland" – the Soho House group's carefully distressed, retro-vibe brasserie is a welcome "addition to the dining desert that is Shaftesbury Avenue". "A firm favourite for business in the heart of London", it's "great for lunch" and "pre or post theatre", despite food that's no better than "solid". / W1D 6LA; www.cafemonico.com; @cafemonico; midnight, Fri & Sat 1 am; set weekday L £40 (FP).

Cafe Murano £69 🟥2️⃣🟥
33 St James's St, SW1   020 3371 5559   3–3C
34 Tavistock St, WC2
020 3535 7884   5–3D **NEW**
36 Tavistock St, WC2   020 3371 5559   5–3D
"Proper decent Italian food without needless bells and whistles – just as you'd expect from Angela Hartnett, plus some surprisingly good (and well-priced) wines" help win a huge fan club for her "more relaxed" Theatreland and St James's outposts, especially amongst business-lunchers who like their "reliable and low-key" style. The cooking "lacks the magic of the Murano mothership" however, and the "welcoming" staff can be off the case. / www.cafemurano.co.uk; 11 pm, Sun 4 pm, Pastificio 9 pm, Sun closed.

Café Spice Namaste E1 £55 🟥🟥🟥
16 Prescot St   020 7488 9242   12–1A
"Every mouthful is a joy", say fans of Cyrus Todiwala's "airy and bright" (somewhat "eccentrically decorated") City-fringe Indian, where "extremely attentive service" is a hallmark, and where "the man himself usually does the rounds in a clubbable fashion". The "wide variety of unusual Parsi dishes" – "quite different food to standard Indian fare" – "are spicy rather than just hot (though you can have that too)". / E1 8AZ; www.cafespice.co.uk; @cafespicenamast; 10.30 pm; closed Sat L & Sun.

Caffè Caldesi W1 £61 2️⃣🟥🟥
118 Marylebone Ln   020 7487 0754   2–1A
This congenial "old-school Italian" in Marylebone Lane provides antipasti, light meals and wine in the downstairs bar and full-scale dining upstairs. Many reporters praise the "exceptional and good-value" Tuscan cuisine, but marks were hit this year by a couple of "disappointing" reports. / W1U 2QF; www.caldesi.com; 10.30 pm, Sun 9.30 pm.

La Cage Imaginaire NW3 £48 2️⃣2️⃣🟥
16 Flask Walk   020 7794 6674   9–1A
This "tiny and close-packed" old spot on a super-cute Hampstead backstreet knocks out "delightful traditional French cuisine", albeit without pushing back any gastronomic frontiers. Service is not always on-the-ball, but amiable. / NW3 1HE; www.la-cage-imaginaire.co.uk; 11 pm.

Cah-Chi £37 🟥🟥🟥
394 Garratt Ln, SW18   020 8946 8811   11–2B
34 Durham Rd, SW20   020 8947 1081   11–2B
"Brilliant, fresh, full-flavoured Korean food" attracts Asian expats as well as adventurous south west London foodies to these "great value", "busy and friendly" venues in Raynes Park and Earlsfield. "BYO is a bonus". / SW18 midnight, SW20 11 pm; SW18 & SW20 closed Mon; cash only.

The Camberwell Arms SE5 £54 🟥🟥🟥
65 Camberwell Church St
020 7358 4364   1–3C
"They pack in the umami flavour here", with "inspired British cooking" at this Camberwell gastro-boozer that retains the "slightly grubby", "rough-around-the-edges decor" of the traditional pub. There's an argument that "the little sibling is finally outgunning SE1's Anchor & Hope: the food's more interesting and original" – "and you can even get a table!". / SE5 8TR; www.thecamberwellarms.co.uk; @camberwellarms; 10 pm; closed Mon L & Sun D.

Cambio de Tercio SW5 £71 🟥🟥2️⃣
161-163 Old Brompton Rd
020 7244 8970   6–2B
The "superb modern cooking" at Abel Lusa's Earl's Court Hispanic is of a "quality that vies with Barrafina". There's also "an astonishingly broad and interesting range of Spanish wines", although "the wine prices are in nosebleed territory" (hence the "very well-heeled Eurobanker crowd"). / SW5 0LJ; www.cambiodetercio.co.uk; @CambiodTercio; 11.15 pm, Sun 11 pm.

Cambridge Street Kitchen SW1 £56 🟥🟥🟥
52 Cambridge St   020 3262 0501   2–4B
"For a delightful and friendly brunch", this "busy and vibrant" neighbourhood spot is just the ticket – a converted boozer in the side streets of Pimlico that's a key hang-out in the locality. / SW1V 4QQ; www.cambridgestreetcafe.co.uk; @TheCambridgeSt; 9 pm, Sat 9.30 pm, Sun 8 pm.

Camino £50 🟥🟥2️⃣
3 Varnishers Yd, Regent Quarter, N1
020 7841 7330   9–3C
The Blue Fin Building, 5 Canvey St, SE1
020 3617 3169   10–4A
15 Mincing Ln, EC3   020 7841 7335   10–3D
33 Blackfriars Ln, EC4   020 7125 0930   10–2A
"Lovely", "well-sourced" tapas is the straightforward appeal of this Spanish group, much favoured for business lunching. Staff manage to be both "attentive" and "unobtrusive", but branches can get "noisy" at busy times. / www.camino.uk.com; 11pm, EC3 Sat 10 pm, Sun 10pm; EC3 closed Sun, EC4 closed Sat & Sun.

Campania & Jones E2 NEW
23 Ezra St   020 7613 0015   14–2A
*Columbia Road's Campania Gastronomia has
moved around the corner into this idyllic-looking
former cowshed and dairy; it's still serving up
handmade pasta, hearty Italian dishes and
breakfasts to locals and market visitors alike. / E2
7RH; campaniaandjones.com; 10.30 pm.*

**Cannizaro House, Hotel du Vin
SW19**   **£58**   1 2 3
West Side, Wimbledon Common 0871 943 0345
11–2A
*With its "beautiful position on Wimbledon Common"
and "stunning views over Cannizaro Park", this
Hotel du Vin venue should be a winner and "it's
hard to believe you're half an hour from central
London". But eating here is an "unpredictable
experience", with too many complaints: "the
Caesar salad was neither Caesar nor salad"… "the
location is so special, but the food is so average". /
SW19 4UE; www.hotelduvin.com/locations/wimbledon;
@HotelduVinBrand; 10 pm.*

Cannons N8   **£35**   4 4 2
4-6 Park Rd   020 8348 3018   9–1C
*"Cooked to order fish", "brilliant chips" and "helpful
staff" help win a small but very enthusiastic fan
club for this Crouch End chippy; they have one in
Southgate too. / N8 8TD; www.cannons-fish.co.uk;
@CannonsFish; 10 pm, Fri & Sat 11.30 pm, Sun &
Mon 9 pm.*

Cantina Laredo WC2   **£58**   3 2 3
10 Upper St Martin's Lane, St Martin's
Courtyard   020 7420 0630   5–3C
*Limited feedback on this heart-of-Theatreland
outpost of the relatively upmarket US Mexican
chain. For fans, "the guacamole made at the
table is fab" and emblematic of the "good fun
and food", but doubters "don't understand
the crowds, given bland dishes and (perhaps
understandably) under-pressure service". / WC2H
9FB; www.cantinalaredo.co.uk; @CantinaLaredoUK; 10
pm, Fri & Sat 10.30 pm, Sun 9 pm.*

Canto Corvino E1   **£65**   4 3 3
21 Artillery Lane   020 7655 0390   13–2B
*"Very good quality pasta" heads the list at this
"solid" modern Italian by Spitalfields Market, which
serves "a rather limited but good quality menu" of
"interesting dishes". Unusually for an Italian, it's
also "great for an informal business breakfast" or
cocktail-fuelled brunch, when a "full Italian" is on
the menu. / E1 7HA; www.cantocorvino.co.uk; @
cantocorvinoe1.*

Canton Arms SW8   **£51**   4 2 4
177 South Lambeth Rd   020 7582 8710   11–1D
*"Fantastic British produce from a pretty much daily
changing menu" makes this an "excellent", even*

*"ideal" Stockwell gastroboozer (it's sibling to SE1's
stellar Anchor & Hope). "Service can be a bit slow
at busy times, although it doesn't matter for a lazy
Sunday lunch". / SW8 1XP; www.cantonarms.com;
@cantonarms; 10.30 pm; closed Mon L & Sun D; No
Amex; no booking.*

Capote Y Toros SW5   **£50**   3 4 4
157 Old Brompton Rd   020 7373 0567   6–2B
*"Close your eyes and imagine you're in Sevilla"
at Cambio de Tercio's neighbouring bar, where
at times "the great atmosphere is helped by
someone strumming away on a guitar". "It's not
a cheap night out for tapas, but you get the best
croquetas this side of the Pyrenees!" / SW5 OLJ;
www.cambiodetercio.co.uk; @CambiodTercio; 11.30 pm;
D only, closed Mon & Sun; booking D only.*

Capricci SE1   **£55**   4 4 3
NEO Bankside Unit C South, 72 Holland St
020 7021 0703   10–3B
*"Perfect for coffee or lunch while visiting Tate
Modern" – a "tiny space" within an upscale Italian
food store nearby, offering "a great choice of wines"
and small but good (if sometimes expensive) menu.
/ SE1 9NX; www.capricciforlondon.co.uk; 10.30 pm, Fri
& Sat 11 pm.*

Le Caprice SW1   **£81**   2 4 4
20 Arlington St   020 7629 2239   3–4C
*"A very special place" for many of the most blasé of
Londoners – this "slick oasis of sophistication" near
The Ritz owes its enduring success to the "elegance
of the interior with its superb lighting", "the comfort
of the piano playing", and staff under Jesus Adorno
who "make you feel like a million dollars (even if
you're far from it)". "The food is hardly the point
here" and never really has been, but "prices have
gone up under Richard Caring" making what
has always seemed "well executed and unfussy
dishes" now seem "fairly ordinary and expensive for
what they are". / SW1A 1RJ; www.le-caprice.co.uk;
@CapriceHoldings; 11.30 pm, Sun 10.30 pm; May
need 6+ to book; set weekday L £51 (FP).*

Caraffini SW1   **£61**   3 5 3
61-63 Lower Sloane St   020 7259 0235   6–2D
*"You always leave feeling you have been well
looked after", after a visit to this veteran trattoria
near Sloane Square, whose "old school, wonderfully
welcoming staff remember everyone". The food is
"reliable (if unambitious) and even if "the tables
are rather close to each other", "there always seems
to be a happy crowd". "Nice terrace in summer". /
SW1W 8DH; www.caraffini.co.uk; 11 pm; closed Sun.*

Caravaggio EC3   **£62**   3 2 2
107-112 Leadenhall St   020 7626 6206   10–2D
*"The food doesn't let you down, even if it's a
little pricey" at this "smart" City Italian, whose
location right by Leadenhall Market helps earn*

*it strong nominations "for a business lunch".
On the downside, the atmosphere can seem
"slightly dull" and an unusual number of service
glitches were reported this year. / EC3A 4DP;
www.etruscarestaurants.com; 10 pm; closed Sat & Sun.*

Caravan £57 3 3 4
1 Granary Sq, N1   020 7101 7661   9–3C
Metal Box Factory, 30 Great Guildford St, SE1
020 7101 1190   10–4B
11-13 Exmouth Mkt, EC1
020 7833 8115   10–1A
Bloomberg Arcade, Queen Victoria St, EC2   no
tel   10–2C **NEW**
*"London's most interesting brunch dishes" – "light
pastries and wholesome porridge to unusual spicy
and savoury options" (not to mention "fabulous
speciality coffees") – help drive a "vibrant" buzz
at these "funky" hang-outs, with the "bustling
industrial-style" Granary Square outlet vying for
top popularity with the smaller Exmouth Market
original (Bankside has yet to make many waves; and
there's also a new City branch is opening in October
2017, in the new 'Bloomberg Arcade').The eclectic
dishes can seem too "keen to be innovative at the
expense of polish" though, or just plain "weird". /
www.caravanonexmouth.co.uk; 10.30 pm, Sun 8 pm ;
closed Sun.*

Carob Tree NW5 £36 3 4 3
15 Highgate Rd   020 7267 9880   9–1B
*"Grilled fish prepared on charcoal" is the highpoint
of the "reliable, sometimes exceptional" Greek fare
at this Dartmouth Park local, where "they treat
everyone entering as their favourite customer".Top
Tip – "Fish dish of the day is pricey, but will feed two
or three and is usually very well cooked". / NW5
1QX; www.carobtree.in; 10.30 pm, Sun 9 pm; closed
Mon; No Amex.*

Carousel W1 £57 5 4 4
71 Blandford St   020 7487 5564   3–1A
*An "inspiring" programme of guest chefs from
around the world (who take over the kitchen for
two weeks at a time) makes for some "superb"
meals at this unique Marylebone merry-go-round
– a "brilliant" and "laudable concept" ("you eat
some amazing food you wouldn't have come
across otherwise"). Be prepared to be "squashed at
sharing tables" amid "high noise levels". / W1U 8AB;
www.carousel-london.com; @Carousel_LDN; one seating
only, at 7 pm; closed Mon L & Sun L.*

Cartel SW11 **NEW** £39
517-519 Battersea Park Rd
020 8610 9761   11–1C
*You can sample 100 different Mezcals in the
dedicated Mezcaleria room of this new Battersea
Mexican, serving quesadillas and tacos to
accompany the wide range of latino spirits.We're
not sure whether they ran the name past the good*

*taste committee first... / SW11 3BN; cartelbattersea.
co.uk; @cartelbattersea.*

Casa Brindisa SW7 £49 2 2 2
7-9 Exhibition Rd   020 7590 0008   6–2C
*For foodies, the Brindisa name casts a halo around
this South Kensington café (with large outside
terrace) and they salute its "high-quality fresh
tapas". A more realistic view perhaps is that the
food here is "not earth-shattering, but fine" – "ideal
before/after a visit to the Royal Albert Hall or
one of the museums on Exhibition Road". / SW7
2HE; www.brindisatapaskitchens.com/casa-brindisa;
@TapasKitchens; 11 pm, Sun 10 pm; booking max 8
may apply.*

Casa Cruz W11 £80 2 3 4
123 Clarendon Rd   020 3321 5400   7–2A
*"Gaucho-size portions" of "top-quality beef"
("there's even a kilo steak on the menu") and
"extremely stylish decor" make Juan Santa Cruz's
lavish Argentinian pub conversion on the edge of
Notting Hill "a brilliant night out"… "if you can
get a table". But even fans concede it is "extremely
expensive" – "at £36 for a main course this is a
place to go when someone else is paying". / W11
4JG; www.casacruz.london; @CasaCruzrest; 12.30 am,
Sun 5 pm; closed Mon.*

Casita Andina W1 £37 4 3 4
31 Great Windmill St   020 3327 9464   4–3D
*"Unusual, flavoursome small plates" with big
Latino flavours win consistently high ratings for
Martin Morales's year-old 'picanteria' in Soho
– his fourth opening in the capital. / W1F 9UE;
www.andinalondon.com/casita; @CasitaAndina.*

Casse-Croute SE1 £54 4 3 4
109 Bermondsey St   020 7407 2140   10–4D
*"Think of the film 'Amélie'", and you won't be a
million miles off this "cramped", "more-French-than-
France" bistro in Bermondsey (where "you leave
expecting to see the Eiffel Tower, but instead it's
The Shard"). "On the blackboard, a selection of
three starters, mains and desserts" – "the simplicity
of choice means it's modern cuisine grand-mère
is always fresh and well-prepared". / SE1 3XB;
www.cassecroute.co.uk; @CasseCroute109; 10 pm, Sun
4 pm; closed Sun D.*

Catford Constitutional Club SE6 £38 3 4 4
Catford Broadway   020 8613 7188   1–4D
*"This semi-derelict former Conservative Club has
been converted into a popular pub with a garden (of
sorts) by Antic".The food's good and "the local cool
cats are loving it". / SE6 4SP; catfordconstitutionalclub.
com; @CatfordCClub; 10 pm.*

Cau **£54** 2️2️2️
10-12 Royal Pde, SE3   020 8318 4200   1–4D
33 High St, SW19   020 8318 4200   11–2B
1 Commodity Quay, E1
020 7702 0341   10–3D
"Gaucho's little brother chain" offers a stripped down version of the main brand, featuring "reasonably priced steaks" and burgers plus an "interesting range of other Argentinian-derived dishes" and "a good choice of South American wines". Ratings overall are middling however, reflecting a feeling in some quarters that the offer is "pleasant but lacking something". / 11 pm, Sun 10 pm.

Caxton Grill SW1 **£75** 2️3️3️
2 Caxton St   020 7227 7773   2–4C
This hotel dining room, tucked away in Westminster, is still readjusting to Adam Handling's departure in May 2016 and reports tend to include highs and lows. It's a characterful space however, that's worth remembering. / SW1H 0QW; www.caxtongrill.co.uk; 10.30 pm.

Cây Tre **£43** 3️3️2️
42-43 Dean St, W1   020 7317 9118   5–2A
301 Old St, EC1   020 7729 8662   13–1B
"Brilliant value and authentic Vietnamese" venues in Soho and Shoreditch. The interiors might be "inauspicious", but staff are "helpful" and the food is "warming and packed with taste". / www.vietnamesekitchen.co.uk; 11 pm, Fri & Sat 11.30 pm, Sun 10.30 pm; booking: min 8.

Cecconi's W1 **£78** 2️2️3️
5a Burlington Gdns   020 7434 1500   4–4A
Soho House's "vibrant" all-day Venetian-style brasserie near Old Bond Street makes "a great place to relax, take your time, and watch the world go by" and is well liked – except by a few who find it "snotty" and "arrogant" – for its "professional and fun" approach. Even many fans think its food ("pleasant in a simple sort of way") is "expensive", but this place is a particular favourite "for an upmarket business breakfast". / W1S 3EP; www.cecconis.co.uk; @SohoHouse; 11.30 pm, Sun 10.30 pm.

The Cedar **£43** 3️3️3️
65 Fernhead Rd, W9   020 8964 2011   1–2B
202 West End Lane, NW6
020 3602 0862   1–1B
81 Boundary Rd, NW8   020 3204 0030   9–3A
"The variety of Lebanese dishes from mezzes to mains is one of the best in town" (including Lebanese-style breakfasts and pizza) at these agreeable, brick-walled ventures in Hampstead, Maida Vale and St John's Wood.

Céleste, The Lanesborough
SW1 **£107** 2️3️5️
Hyde Park Corner   020 7259 5599   2–3A
In over 25 years of its existence, the incredibly "impressive" dining room of this ultra-swanky Hyde Park Corner hotel has never really hit a full stride, and has been through a succession of incarnations. The management of Paris's Le Bristol are the latest to have a go, and their version is doing better than most to date, with "elegant looks presaging a traditional style of service", and cuisine that "puts an emphasis on British ingredients and French technique". Service is "expert" – perhaps a little "over-attentive" – and other than that it's "generally expensive" most reports are upbeat. Top Tip – "set menus are good value, if with limited choice". / SW1X 7TA; www.lanesborough.com/eng/restaurant-bars/celeste; @TheLanesborough; 10.30 pm; set weekday L £71 (FP).

Cepages W2 **£50** 3️3️3️
69 Westbourne Park Rd   020 3602 8890   7–1B
"Small, noisy (the only drawback), Bayswater bistro with a loyal (partly French) customer-base", of note for its "exceptional wine list, with many fine wines sourced directly from small growers", and backed up by some "consistently accomplished, small, tapas-type dishes". "The place is, unsurprisingly, always full". / W2 5QH; www.cepages.co.uk; @cepagesWPR; 11 pm, Sun 10 pm.

Ceru SW7 NEW **£39** 4️3️2️
7-9 Bute St   020 3195 3001   6–2C
"Excellent Levantine cuisine at very reasonable prices" win consistent praise for this middle eastern newcomer. Some fans "are puzzled at by the decor choices" but for a "cheap and cheerful" option "convenient to South Kensington and the museums" it fits the bill. / SW7 3EY; www.cerurestaurants.com; @cerulondon ; 11 pm, Sun 10 pm.

Ceviche **£55** 4️3️3️
17 Frith St, W1   020 7292 2040   5–2A
Alexandra Trust, Baldwin St, EC1
020 3327 9463   13–1A
"Amazing, seriously tasty dishes, with lots of fresh tastes", and washed down with "perfect Pisco sours" instill high esteem for these "buzzy" (if "rather noisy") Latino ventures, in Soho and near Old Street. / www.cevicheuk.com; W1D 11.30 pm, Sun 10.15 pm, EC1V 10.45 pm, Fri & Sat 11.30 pm, Sun 9.30 pm.

Chai Thali NW1 NEW **£33** 3️3️4️
Centro 3, 19 Mandela St   020 7383 2030   9–3C
"A fun place to have a gathering" with "non-clichéd, fresh-tasting Indian dishes" – a big, "attractive" pan-Indian street food and bar operation, "tucked away" in a new development near Mornington Crescent. / NW1 0DU; chaithali.com; @ChaiThaliCamden.

Honey & Smoke W1

Hoppers Marylebone W1

Ikoyi SW1

Chakra W8　　　£57　3|3|3
33c Holland St　020 7229 2115　7–2B
*"Beautiful cooking with a high-level modern twist"
wins consistent praise for this comfortable Indian,
"in a pretty locale" near High Street Ken tube
– not at all a standard curry house. / W8 4LX;
www.chakralondon.com; @ChakraLondon; 11 pm, Sun
10.30 pm.*

Champor-Champor SE1　£54　4|4|4
62 Weston St　020 7403 4600　10–4C
*Colourful, eclectic decor and distinctive "fresh
tasting" Thai-Malay cuisine (the name means 'mix
and match') still win an enthusiastic, if small fanclub
for this "old-favourite, little oasis, tucked away in
unassuming location", near the Shard. / SE1 3QJ;
www.champor-champor.com; @ChamporChampor; 10
pm; D only.*

Charlotte's　　　£52　3|4|3
6 Turnham Green Ter, W4
020 8742 3590　8–2A
*"An excellent cocktail bar" with "a lovely gin
selection" helps set a "friendly and homely" tone
at the W4 Charlotte's – a "buzzy bistro and bar"
near Turnham Green Tube, whose "tasty" fare suits
an "informal" get-together. In W5, in Ealing's new
Dickens Yard development, its younger sibling is also
"a good local venue" popular with business-lunchers
and families at weekends. (Both are spin-offs
from Charlotte's Place, also in W5 – see also). /
www.charlottes.co.uk; W4 midnight, Sun 11 pm, W5
10 pm, W5 11.30 pm.*

Charlotte's Place W5　£52　3|3|4
16 St Matthew's Rd　020 8567 7541　1–3A
*"You can always find something delicious to
enjoy" at Alex Wrethman's "pleasantly quiet"
long-established (1984) fixture by Ealing Common
– acclaimed by its local fanclub as "the best
restaurant in Ealing by a long way" (although dishes
which are "amazing and creative" to some tastes
are a little "complicated" to others). / W5 3JT;
www.charlottes.co.uk; @CharlottesW5; 10.30 pm, Fri &
Sat 11 pm, Sun 9 pm; booking max 10 may apply.*

**Chelsea Cellar
SW10** NEW　　　£40　4|4|3
9 Park Walk　020 7351 4933　6–3B
*"Charming basement newcomer", in a side street
near the Chelsea & Westminster hospital, which
"features Pugliese cooking (delicious burrata,
antipasti, and pasta) and an excellent, wide selection
of interesting Pugliese wines" (250 bins). "It's not
expensive, service is engaging" and "the room's
reasonably quiet even when full". / SW10 0AJ;
www.thechelseacellar.co.uk; midnight.*

Chettinad W1　　£40　4|3|3
16 Percy St　020 3556 1229　2–1C
"Proper south Indian fare" ("yummy" Tamil

*specialities including dosas and dishes served on
fresh banana leaves) win praise for this busy venue
in Fitzrovia. / W1T 1DT; www.chettinadrestaurant.com;
@chettinadlondon; 11 pm, Sun 10 pm; No Amex.*

**Cheyne Walk Brasserie
SW3**　　　　£74　2|2|3
50 Cheyne Walk　020 7376 8787　6–3C
*Beautiful-people Chelsea brasserie, whose chic
interior is arranged around the central open wood
fire grill. As ever, prices can seem "rather dear",
but the high quality BBQ dishes are consistently
well-rated. / SW3 5LR; www.cheynewalkbrasserie.com;
@CheyneWalkBrass; 10.30 pm, Sun 9.30 pm; closed
Mon L.*

Chez Abir W14　　£39　3|3|2
34 Blythe Rd　020 7603 3241　8–1D
*"High quality, reliable Lebanese food" makes
it worth truffling out this "cheap 'n' cheerful"
backstreet café behind Olympia (that some still
remember as Chez Marcelle... she's retired.) / W14
0HA; www.chezabir.co.uk; 11 pm; closed Mon.*

CHEZ BRUCE SW17　£86　5|5|4
2 Bellevue Rd　020 8672 0114　11–2C
*"So professional, but without any of the
usual nonsense!" – Bruce Poole's "wonderful
neighbourhood restaurant" by Wandsworth Common
is, for the 13th year in a row, the survey's No. 1
favourite destination. It's by no means a flash
place – "the understated atmosphere is of a
comfortable local" – but for legions of Londoners
it provides "perfection where it counts", not least
the "immaculate service", and "inspiring food":
dishes are "fine, but not fussy", and with "enough
innovation to surprise you each time" thanks to their
"exceptional, and deft flavour combinations". "AND,
it's affordable! For once you don't need a second
mortgage..." / SW17 7EG; www.chezbruce.co.uk;
@ChezBruce; 10 pm, Fri & Sat 10.30 pm, Sun 9 pm;
set weekday L £57 (FP), set Sun L £63 (FP).*

Chicama SW10　　£59　2|2|3
383 King's Rd　020 3874 2000　6–3C
*"Outstanding fish comes at a cost in this Peruvian
newcomer" in Chelsea (from the team behind
Marylebone's Pachamama) – an enjoyably "vibrant"
(if "crowded and noisy") place. The approach doesn't
please everyone though: "dishes arrived in any order,
which might suit the kitchen, but resulted in some
not-so-good flavour combinations". / SW10 0LP;
www.chicamalondon.com; @chicamalondon.*

Chick 'n' Sours　　£42　3|3|3
1 Earlham St, WC2　020 3198 4814　5–2B
390 Kingsland Rd, E8　020 3620 8728　14–2D
*"Everything you could wish for in a crunchy-fried,
tender, perfectly cooked chicken" gets a big thumbs
up for this "really fun" Dalston joint (now with a
Covent Garden branch); "accoutrements to die for"*

too ("surprisingly, the outstanding dish didn't involve chicken – the amazing Sichuan aubergine stole the show").

Chicken Shop £34 3|3|3
199-206 High Holborn, WC1
020 7661 3040 2–1D
5 Oak Rd, W5   020 3859 1120   1–3A **NEW**
274-276 Holloway Rd, N7
020 3841 7787   9–2D
46 The Broadway, N8
020 3757 4848   9–1C **NEW**
79 Highgate Rd, NW5   020 3310 2020   9–1B
128 Allitsen Rd, NW8   020 3757 4849   9–3A
7a Chestnut Grove, SW12
020 8102 9300   11–2C
141 Tooting High St, SW17
020 8767 5200   11–2B
Piano House, 9 Brighton Terrace, SW9
020 3859 1130   11–2D **NEW**
27a Mile End Rd, E1   020 3310 2010   13–2D
Arguably they're just "a fancy version of Nandos", but Soho House's "deliciously moreish and quite addictive" pit stops "do one thing, and do it well": "succulent moist chicken, piping hot salty chips, melt in your mouth corn on the cob and the grand finale, the spongy light apple pie". / Mon-Thu 11 pm, Fri & Sat midnight, Sun 10-10.30 pm; WC1V closed Sun.

Chik'n W1 **NEW** £18
134 Baker St   020 7935 6648   2–1A
From the people who brought us Chick 'n' Sours, a new idea along similar, but pared down lines – the first branch appeared in Baker Street in July 2017. It's very fast food style: you grab and go. / W1U 6SH; www.chikn.com; @lovechikn; 11.30 pm; no booking.

Chilli Cool WC1 £34 5|2|1
15 Leigh St   020 7383 3135   2–1D
"Wonderfully spicy" Sichuan cooking is the reason to discover this "brilliant find in Bloomsbury". Forget the "plain" surroundings and the "hit-and-miss service": "you can put up with all that to eat such fantastic dishes!" / WC1H 9EW; www.chillicool.co.uk; 10.15 pm; No Amex.

The Chiltern Firehouse
W1 £96 1|1|3
1 Chiltern St   020 7073 7676   2–1A
"If you're not a C-Z lister, don't go" to this Marylebone haunt – "a stunningly decorated old firehouse" where only "people watching is top of the menu". True, there is a minority of fans who applaud its "imaginative food", but even they can find it "incredibly overpriced" and "there are nowadays far too many sceptics for whom it's a bad case of 'Emperor's New Clothes', providing "very odd food combinations" and "staff who wander around looking fabulous, but not attending on customers". / W1U 7PA; www.chilternfirehouse.com; 10.30 pm.

Chin Chin Club W1 **NEW**
54 Greek St   no tel   5–2A
Camden Town's 'instant' ice cream bar (made on-the-spot with nitrogen and seasonal, sometimes bonkers, ingredients) arrived in Soho in summer 2017, with this white marble and gold outlet. The options here are similarly 'out there', but some flavours are pre-made rather than, as at the original, zapped on the spot. / W1D 3DS; www.chinchinicecream.com; @chinchinicecream; 9 pm, Fri & Sat 10 pm.

China Tang, Dorchester Hotel
W1 £84 4|3|3
53 Park Ln   020 7629 9988   3–3A
The "classy cocktail bar" is a big highlight of Sir David Tang's (RIP) recreation of '30s Shanghai in the basement of a Mayfair hotel, whose main dining room surprisingly can "lack atmosphere", particularly at lunch. The food (with Peking Duck the speciality) has been lacklustre over the years, but was very highly rated in this year's survey. / W1K 1QA; www.chinatanglondon.co.uk; @ChinaTangLondon; 11.45 pm.

The Chipping Forecast
W11 £42 3|3|3
29 All Saints Rd   020 7460 2745   7–1B
"The fish is fab" at this new Notting Hill take on the trad fish 'n' chip shop, using sustainable fish landed in Cornwall less than 48 hours earlier. Having started out as a street stall in Soho's Berwick Street Market, it has a "great supper club feel". "Friendly, quirky and bound to become stupidly expensive, so get there now while it's fresh and fun!" Cute garden too. / W11 1HE; www.chippingforecast.com; @CForecast; 9.30 pm, Fri & Sat 10 pm, Sun 9pm; closed Mon; no booking.

Chisou £56 4|3|2
4 Princes St, W1   020 7629 3931   4–1A
31 Beauchamp Pl, SW3   020 3155 0005   6–1D
"Excellent sushi, sashimi and tempura" are the stars of the show at this "long-established and quite smart – though not unduly expensive – Mayfair Japanese" (with an offshoot near Harrods), which boasts a "great sake list, too". The "quiet" original is "a civilised retreat from the fray of Regent Street", and its chichily-located Knightsbridge branch is in a similar vein. / www.chisourestaurant.com; Mon-Sat 10.30 pm, Sun 9.30 pm.

Chiswell Street Dining Rooms
EC1 £63 2|2|2
56 Chiswell St   020 7614 0177   13–2A
"Usefully placed for City meetings", this outfit near the Barbican is consistently well-rated "reasonably priced" and fairly "convivial", "if perhaps with tables a little close together". / EC1Y 4SA; www.chiswellstreetdining.com; @chiswelldining; 11 pm; closed Sat & Sun; set pre theatre £42 (FP).

Chit Chaat Chai SW18 £45 4 3 2
356 Old York Rd 020 8480 2364 11–2B
"Extremely authentic Indian street food bites" served
"in funky surroundings" draws fans, young and old,
to this local "gem", near Wandsworth Town station.
/ SW18 1SS; chitchaatchai.com; @ChitChaatChai; 10
pm, Sun 9 pm.

Chotto Matte W1 £60 4 3 5
11-13 Frith St 020 7042 7171 5–2A
"The surprising fusion of different cuisines
works very well" at this impressively "buzzy"
and "clubby" Japanese-Peruvian haunt in Soho,
which – aided by "quirky decor" and "excellent
Peruvian-styled cocktails" – "somehow really works",
even if "the final bill is a bit heavy". / W1D 4RB;
www.chotto-matte.com; @ChottoMatteSoho; 1 am, Sun
11 pm; set pre theatre £32 (FP).

Chriskitch £59 4 3 3
7 Tetherdown, N10 020 8411 0051 1–1C
5 Hoxton Market, N1 020 7033 6666 13–1B
The "intense and interesting flavours" of Christian
Honor's "inventive" cuisine have won a record of
admirers for his two-year-old café in a converted
Muswell Hill front room, and his follow-up open-
kitchen venture in Hoxton: "it's a funky experience
but someone here knows how to cook" and "the
welcome is very warm". "Fabulous cakes, too". / N10
6 pm, Sat-Mon 5 pm; N1 10.30pm ; N1 closed L and
Sun & Mon; N10 min 3 people.

Christopher's WC2 £78 2 2 3
18 Wellington St 020 7240 4222 5–3D
"Discreet, classy, American (so 1/3rd like Trump)"
– this stalwart 25-year-old occupies a huge and
particularly beautiful Covent Garden townhouse.
The food on the surf 'n' turf-dominated menu
has always divided views – to fans "fabulous",
to foes "average" and "overpriced". Top Tips –
good brunch and downstairs bar. / WC2E 7DD;
www.christophersgrill.com; @christopherswc2; May
need 6+ to book; set weekday L & pre-theatre £45
(FP).

Chucs £82 3 3 3
30b Dover St, W1 020 3763 2013 3–3C
226 Westbourne Grove, W11
020 7243 9136 7–1B
Owned by an Italian luxury brand of 'resort' wear,
these "cozy and calm" cafés adjoining shops in
Mayfair and Chelsea aim to inspire the yachtie life
of the Riviera in the 1960s. There's "excellent service
and solid food", although some reporters favour
breakfast over lunch. / W1 11.30 pm, Sat midnight,
Sun 4.30 pm; W11 11 pm, Sun 10 pm ; W1 closed
Sun D.

Churchill Arms W8 £35 3 2 5
119 Kensington Church St
020 7792 1246 7–2B

"Unbeatable value for a very good nosh-up" is to
be had at this "quirky-but-real pub", just off Notting
Hill Gate, whose "butterfly-themed conservatory"
makes a feature of "great, simple Thai food", and
provides "a good deal in a normally expensive area".
"Service can be brusque, but the place is so busy it's
hard to see how it could be otherwise". / W8 7LN;
www.churchillarmskensington.co.uk; @ChurchilArmsW8;
10 pm, Sun 9.30 pm.

Chutney Mary SW1 £84 4 4 4
73 St James's St 020 7629 6688 3–4D
In its "lavish and beautifully decorated" St James's
home for over two years now, this "very glam"
relocated stalwart (which for over two decades was
on the fringe of Chelsea) remains one of London's
foremost 'posh' Indians, serving "brilliantly spiced"
contemporary cuisine, plus "fantastic cocktails" ("the
Pukka bar is great for a clandestine drink"). / SW1A
1PH; www.chutneymary.com; @thechutneymary; 10.30
pm; closed Sat L & Sun; booking max 4 may apply; set
weekday L £55 (FP), set brunch £57 (FP).

Chutneys NW1 £27 3 2 2
124 Drummond St 020 7388 0604 9–4C
"A Mecca for veggie Indian cuisine near Euston"
("especially the ridiculously cheap Sunday night and
weekday lunchtime buffet") – "for the money, this
place just can't be beaten". "The decor upstairs is
acceptable, less so the slightly scruffy downstairs". /
NW1 2PA; www.chutneyseuston.co.uk; 11 pm; No Amex;
May need 5+ to book.

Ciao Bella WC1 £45 2 3 4
86-90 Lamb's Conduit St
020 7242 4119 2–1D
"The perfect trat'" is a typically affectionate tribute
to this "merry" Bloomsbury Italian, where "the food
is not spectacular" but "unbelievably good value"
and served in "an ambience reminiscent of 1960s
Fellini and Antonioni films". "It was my staple when
I was poor and first moved to London, then I got
marginally richer and moved on, but I recently went
back and was reminded how great it is". / WC1N
3LZ; www.ciaobellarestaurant.co.uk; @CiaobellaLondon;
11.30 pm, Sun 10.30 pm.

Cibo W14 £58 4 5 3
3 Russell Gdns 020 7371 6271 8–1D
"Lovely, authentic cuisine" ("pasta as it should be"
and other "great, simple dishes") and "an owner
who goes out of his way to make sure you have a
good time" is the recipe for longevity at this "slightly
cramped" Italian stalwart on a side street near
Olympia (a favourite of the late Michael Winner).
Fans feel "it deserves to be busier". / W14 8EZ;
www.ciborestaurant.net; 10.30 pm; closed Sat L &
Sun D.

Cigala WC1 £48 3|3|3
54 Lamb's Conduit St 020 7405 1717 2–1D
"Every neighbourhood should be blessed with
somewhere as friendly and reliable as this", say
happy regulars of this long-serving Bloomsbury
Spaniard. Its "classic tapas and Iberian gastronomy"
make it "the sort of place where you get ideas to
go home and try yourself". On the negative side,
"the surroundings are ordinary". / WC1N 3LW;
www.cigala.co.uk; 10.45 pm, Sun 9.45 pm.

Cigalon WC2 £58 3|4|4
115 Chancery Lane 020 7242 8373 2–2D
"In an area not overstocked with restaurants", this
"airy and charming" fixture on Chancery Lane (built
as a book auction room, and with a "huge rooflight,
which lets in lots of sunshine at lunchtime") really
stands out with its "skilful service", and "excellent,
interesting Provençal cuisine" (from the team
behind Club Gascon). / WC2A 1PP; www.cigalon.co.uk;
@cigalon_london; 10 pm; closed Sat & Sun.

Cinnamon Bazaar
WC2 NEW £40 2|3|3
28 Maiden Lane 020 7395 1400 5–4D
The latest Cinnamon Club spin-off occupies the
"quirky and appealing", two-floor Covent Garden
site that was formerly La Perla (RIP). But while fans
praise its "exciting and tasty fusion food", critics
say "it was well-cooked but bordering on bland
– they need to up the heat/spice!" / WC2E 7NA;
www.cinnamon-bazaar.com; @Cinnamon_Bazaar.

THE CINNAMON CLUB
SW1 £84 3|3|4
Old Westminster Library, Great Smith St
020 7222 2555 2–4C
Vivek Singh's "refined cuisine" served in the
"magnificent" (slightly "cavernous") setting of
the old Westminster Public Library still creates a
winning formula for London's grandest nouvelle
Indian, which is nowadays one of the Top-40
most-mentioned restaurants in town. If it were not
quite so "expensive", its ratings would reach even
loftier heights. / SW1P 3BU; www.cinnamonclub.com;
@cinnamonclub; 10.30 pm; closed Sun; No trainers;
booking max 14 may apply; set weekday L £61 (FP);
SRA-Food Made Good – 2 stars.

Cinnamon Kitchen EC2 £59 4|3|3
9 Devonshire Sq 020 7626 5000 10–2D
"Excellent Indian food that's reasonably priced for
the City" is the mainstay of the Cinnamon Club's
easterly cousin – "a most enjoyable" destination in
an attractive, large covered atrium near Liverpool
Street. / EC2M 4YL; www.cinnamon-kitchen.com;
@cinnamonkitchen; 10.45 pm; closed Sat L & Sun.

Cinnamon Soho W1 £46 3|2|2
5 Kingly St 020 7437 1664 4–2B
The casual operation, behind Regent Street,

"may not be up there with the Cinnamon Club",
but "it has an interesting menu of well-cooked
Indian food" and "is really affordable". / W1B
5PE; www.cinnamon-kitchen.com/soho-home;
@cinnamonsoho; 11 pm, Sun 4.30 pm; closed Sun D.

City Barge W4 £51 3|2|3
27 Strand-on-the-Green 020 8994 2148 1–3A
This is "a great little bistro-pub" in a "lovely spot
on the river" at Strand-on-the-Green, Chiswick, and
where "the food is really rather good". / W4 3PH;
www.citybargechiswick.com; @citybargew4; 11 pm, Fri
& Sat midnight, Sun 10.30 pm.

City Càphê EC2 £18 3|3|2
17 Ironmonger St no tel 10–2C
Limited but enthusiastic reports on this popular
Vietnamese pit stop near Bank – you may have
to queue at lunch. / EC2V 8EY; www.citycaphe.com;
4.30pm; L only, closed Sat & Sun; no booking.

City Social EC2 £86 2|3|5
Tower 42 25 Old Broad St
020 7877 7703 10–2C
"You do pay for the vista", but Jason Atherton's
24th floor perch in the City's Tower 42 boasts
"thrilling views" and "plenty of wow factor", hence
it's often "first choice for a business lunch" ("clients
love it!"). "The food won't take your breath away,
but you won't complain either". / EC2N 1HQ;
www.citysociallondon.com; @CitySocial_T42; 10.30 pm;
closed Sat & Sun; booking max 4 may apply.

Clarette W1 NEW £81
44 Blandford St 020 3019 7750 3–1A
Set in a chicly revamped Tudorbethan pub, this
plush new Marylebone wine bar has an impressive
pedigree – for example, one of the owners is
Alexandra Petit-Mentzelopoulos, daughter of
Corinne Mentzelopoulos, who owns Château
Margaux! The focus is on the wines (with a whole
page of the list dedicated to Margaux), and to offset
them is a menu of Mediterranean small plates. /
W1U 7HS; www.clarettelondon.com; @ClaretteLondon;
set weekday L £51 (FP).

Clarke's W8 £71 5|5|4
124 Kensington Church St
020 7221 9225 7–2B
"Although a classic of the neighbourhood, it doesn't
rest on its laurels" and "how standards have stayed
so high here over all these years is a testament
to the omnipresent and charming Sally Clarke".
"Superb ingredients are cooked with a light touch",
in the Californian style that first inspired her, while
"professional-without-hovering" service is "absolutely
spot on". "If you are under thirty, the only downside
is that it can be full of 'old timers'". / W8 4BH;
www.sallyclarke.com; @SallyClarkeLtd; 10 pm; closed
Sun; booking max 14 may apply.

Claude's Kitchen, Amuse Bouche SW6 £58 444
51 Parsons Green Lane 020 7371 8517 11–1B
Claude Compton's "quirky neighbourhood gem", upstairs from the "heaving" Amuse Bouche fizz bar by Parsons Green station, serves "interesting but tasty food in generous portions". "The cooking is confident and the service charming" – "I went home feeling inspired and satisfied". / SW6 4JA; www.amusebouchelondon.com/claudes-kitchen; @AmuseBoucheLDN; 11 pm; D only, closed Sun.

Clerkenwell Cafe £38 344
80a Mortimer St, W1 020 7253 5754 10–1A
St Christopher's Place, W1
020 7253 5754 3–1A
27 Clerkenwell Rd, EC1
020 7253 5754 10–1A
60a Holborn Viaduct, EC1 no tel 10–2A
Fans hail "by far the best coffee in town" at this small chain with its own roastery – "don't let the lack of comfort put you off!". Along with a "range of different brews to try", they also serve snacks and pastries, while the Clerkenwell original goes a step further, with a full brunch and lunch menu. / workshopcoffee.com/; EC1M 6 pm, Tue-Fri 7 pm; W1U & W1W 7 pm, Sat & Sun 6 pm; EC1A 6 pm; EC1 closed Sat & Sun; no bookings.

The Clifton NW8 NEW
96 Clifton Hill 020 7625 5010 9–3A
This gorgeous, tucked-away St John's Wood pub (famously where Edward VII used to hook up with Lillie Langtry) has re-opened after three years, having been rescued from the developers by brothers Ben and Ed Robson (ex Boopshi's). The menu doesn't attempt culinary fireworks here, but that's never been the point of a visit here. / NW8 0JT; www.thecliftonnw8.com; @thecliftonnw8.

Clipstone W1 £60 443
5 Clipstone St 020 7637 0871 2–1B
"An equally fantastic experience as at Portland (same team)", say the many fans of this Fitzrovia newcomer, lauding its "very inventive, beautifully prepared small plates from the open kitchen" and "really outstanding wine list (full of remarkable, little known options)", all delivered by "a super-friendly and attentive young team". The "buzzy" setting is too "austere" for some tastes however, and there is a minority who feel that "although all the major food critics have eulogised, the cuisine is not quite as cosmic as has been suggested, albeit good". / W1W 6BB; www.clipstonerestaurant.co.uk; @clipstonerestaurant; 11 pm.

CLOS MAGGIORE WC2 £77 345
33 King St 020 7379 9696 5–3C
"You feel that love is in the air!" at this "very special" destination (yet again the survey's No. 1 choice for a romantic occasion), especially in "the inner sanctum" – "the lovely glass-roofed courtyard at the back, hung with blossom, a roof that opens in fine weather, and with an open fire for chilly nights". "Amidst the dross of Covent Garden", not only is it "an oasis of calm", but staff are "charming" and "professional", the French-inspired cuisine is "very enjoyable" and the "daunting" wine bible – one of London's most extensive lists – is "really something else". "Securing one of the courtyard seats is a challenge", but "the experience in the somewhat blander upstairs is still memorable". / WC2E 8JD; www.closmaggiore.com; @closmaggiorewc2; 11 pm, Sun 10 pm; set pre theatre £55 (FP).

THE CLOVE CLUB EC1 £108 544
Shoreditch Town Hall, 380 Old St
020 7729 6496 13–1B
Isaac McHale's temple to "fine dining Shoreditch-style" sits in London's culinary Top-5 nowadays, and his "theatrically presented" 5-course and 10-course menus offer "an absolute balance between sophistication, simplicity, and creativity". The space itself within the fine old town hall is "a bit urban-ascetic" (no table cloths, of course), but is "not too archly hipster" and the "relaxed yet professional service" creates an appropriately "chilled out" yet "truly memorable" experience. Very progressively, there's a "brilliant non-alcoholic drink match" alongside the more conventional wine pairings. / EC1V 9LT; www.thecloveclub.com; @thecloveclub; 9.30 pm; closed Mon & Sun.

Club Gascon EC1 £98
57 West Smithfield 020 7600 6144 10–2B
"Special", "extremely elaborate" Gascon cuisine ("the dish arrives and looks like a Matisse") – famously featuring oodles of foie gras – has carved a huge name for Pascal Aussignac and Vincent Labyrie's ambitious 20-year-old, in a fine Smithfield corner site (a former Lyon's Tea House). Despite consistently maintaining standards, its profile has waned somewhat in recent years and in August 2017 the restaurant closed for a major revamp, prior to an autumn re-launch with a new look and tweaked concept (hence we've removed what were good ratings). / EC1A 9DS; www.clubgascon.com; @club_gascon; 9 pm, Fri & Sat 9.30 pm; closed Sat L & Sun; set weekday L £67 (FP).

Coal Rooms SE15 NEW
11a Station Way 020 7635 6699 1–4D
Meat and fish are grilled in a special coal oven at this newly restored former Grade II listed ticket office at Peckham Rye station, which opens from breakfast on, and serves a flat-bread based lunch menu. / SE15 4RX; www.coalrooms.com; @coalrooms; 10 pm, Sun 6 pm.

The Coal Shed SE1 NEW
One Tower Bridge 01273 322998 10–4D
Overlooking the recently completed public piazza

at the centre of the new One Tower Bridge development, Brighton's favourite steak joint is heading up to the Smoke in autumn 2017. / SE1 2AA; www.coalshed-restaurant.co.uk.

CôBa N7 £40 4 4 3
244 York Way 07495 963336 9–2C
Damon Bui's Vietnamese BBQ dishes come with an Aussie twist at his pub conversion in Barnsbury – a "young and vibrant" joint whose "simple menu" and "great cocktails" earn solid scores across the board. / N7 9AG; www.cobarestaurant.co.uk; @cobafood; 10 pm; booking D only.

Cocotte W2 £48 4 3 4
95 Westbourne Grove 020 3220 0076 7–1B
"Fantastic chicken" is the only option at this year-old rotisserie concept, on the Notting Hill/Bayswater border, with poultry from the French team's own farm in Normandy. Fans say it's "the best roast chicken ever eaten", accompanied by a "delicious" choice of potatoes, salads and sauces. / W2 4UW; www.mycocotte.uk; @cocotte_rotisserie; 10 pm, Fri & Sat 11 pm.

Colbert SW1 £62 2 2 3
51 Sloane Sq 020 7730 2804 6–2D
"There's plenty of buzz" at Corbin & King's "busy" Parisian-style brasserie on a prime Sloane Square corner. A "reliable breakfast" is its highest claim to culinary fame though – otherwise its "competent but unexciting" fodder and "erratic service" make it a handily situated but "underwhelming" destination. / SW1W 8AX; www.colbertchelsea.com; @ColbertChelsea; 11 pm, Fri & Sat 11.30 pm, Sun 10.30 pm.

La Collina NW1 £54 3 4 3
17 Princess Rd 020 7483 0192 9–3B
"Piedmontese cuisine that's unusual and very well executed" and some "very good house wines" have carved a dedicated following for this "traditional Italian with a modern twist", tucked away on the fringes of Primrose Hill – a "romantic" spot, whose "ambience is exceptional in the garden in summer". / NW1 8JR; www.lacollinarestaurant.co.uk; @LacollinaR; 10.15 pm, Sat-Sun 9.15 pm; closed Mon L; booking max 8 may apply.

The Collins Room SW1 £99 2 4 5
Wilton Place 020 7107 8866 6–1D
"Exquisite attention to detail" – particularly the "fabulous miniature-styled cakes" – help create an "elegant, refined and beautiful" experience, when you sample the "fashion-inspired 'Pret-a-Portea'" at the Berkeley hotel in Knightsbridge. "I go twice a year with my mother, and we simply adore the new designs each season (the prices creep up, too, but we are always able to justify it by taking advantage of the unlimited supplies…!)". / SW1X 7RL; www.the-berkeley.co.uk; @TheBerkeley; 10.45 pm, Sun 10.15 pm.

Le Colombier SW3 £69 3 5 4
145 Dovehouse St 020 7351 1155 6–2C
"Totally French, with bags of Gallic charm!" – Didier Garner's "perfect brasserie" on a tucked-away corner near the King's Road, particularly benefits from "wonderfully welcoming" service. "Patrons may not be so young" but the ambience is very "authentique", and "while the menu is unadventurous, it does what it does very well indeed"; "excellent value wine list". / SW3 6LB; www.le-colombier-restaurant.co.uk; 10.30 pm, Sun 10 pm.

Colony Grill Room, Beaumont Hotel W1 £78 3 3 3
The Beaumont, 8 Balderton Street, Brown Hart Gardens 020 7499 9499 3–2A
"You feel like you are stepping onto the set of a Hollywood movie with dim lighting, booths and decadent atmosphere" at Corbin & King's "luxurious" Mayfair dining room: "a proper, traditionally wood-panelled room" which provides "a Gatsby-worthy setting for Alaïa-clad blue-bloods to gorge on classic US comfort food" – "meatloaf and mac 'n' cheese, as well as excellent grills". On the downside, critics feel the menu is "boring" – "fine so far as it goes, but rather overpriced for what it is" – and the setting "a little stuffy". / W1K 6TF; www.colonygrillroom.com; @ColonyGrillRoom; midnight, Sun 11 pm.

The Colton Arms W14 NEW £45 2 3 4
187 Greyhound Rd 020 3757 8050 8–2C
At the rear of Queen's Club, this Baron's Court boozer has been transformed by Hippo Inns from one of London's more quirkily characterful and old-fashioned backstreet pubs into a particularly stylish modern gastro' haunt (with fab back garden). Ratings are undercut by the odd uneven report, but all agree the straightforward cooking here has potential. / W14 9SD; www.thecoltonarms.co.uk; @thecoltonarms; 10 pm, Sun 8 pm.

Como Lario SW1 £70 2 3 2
18-22 Holbein Pl 020 7730 2954 6–2D
This "true neighbourhood Italian near Sloane Square" is, to its loyal (older) fans, a "throwback" of the best sort – "it's so much fun" and "you feel you're in safe hands" with the "friendly and professional" staff and "charmingly unspecial but adequate 'cucina'". / SW1W 8NL; www.comolario.co.uk; 11 pm, Sun 9.30 pm.

Comptoir Café & Wine W1 NEW £55
Weighhouse St 0207 499 9800 3–2B
Xavier Rousset, of the hugely successful Blandford Comptoir and Cabotte, opened a third venue, this time near Bond Street in May 2017; an all-day brasserie, cafe and wine shop (open from breakfast

*on), it features over 2000 wines. / W1K 5AH;
comptoir-cafe-and-wine.co.uk.*

Comptoir Gascon EC1 £51 ❸❸❷
63 Charterhouse St 020 7608 0851 10–1A
*"Duck, duck and more duck, plus BBQ meats and
other delights (the deluxe burger is a joy)" from
southwest France continue to inspire all-round
praise for this "very enjoyable" Smithfield bistro,
including as a business lunch destination. Even
so, a number of fans noted "a slight going off the
boil" this year – the distractions of preparing for
a refurb at its parent, Club Gascon? / EC1M 6HJ;
www.comptoirgascon.com; @ComptoirGascon; 10 pm,
Thu & Fri 10.30 pm; closed Mon & Sun.*

Comptoir Libanais £36 ❷❷❷
*"Choose the right dish and you can have a good
meal" at this Lebanese chain, which "makes you
feel welcome as you arrive, and plies you with free
baklava as you leave". Brightly decorated, perhaps
they "don't seem entirely authentic", but they're
solid standbys. / www.lecomptoir.co.uk; 10 pm (SW
8 pm), W1C & E20 Sun 8 pm; W12 closed Sun D; no
bookings.*

Il Convivio SW1 £70 ❹❸❹
143 Ebury St 020 7730 4099 2–4A
*"Superb, high-quality Italian fare" is served
in a "timelessly attractive room" at this
Belgravia stalwart, which combines "consistent"
favourite dishes with a changing weekly menu.
(There's another space upstairs that is "very
good for business events.") / SW1W 9QN;
www.etruscarestaurants.com/il-convivio; 10.45 pm;
closed Sun.*

Coopers Restaurant & Bar WC2 £49 ❷❸❸
49 Lincoln's Inn Fields 020 7831 6211 2–2D
*"Handy for legal eagles and academics from the
LSE", this understated operation arguably "benefits
from not having much competition nearby", but
by-and-large "does what it says on the tin" and "is
good for clients and business discussions". / WC2A
3PF; www.coopersrestaurant.co.uk; @coopers_bistro;
10.30 pm; closed Sat & Sun; no booking; set weekday
L £30 (FP).*

Coq d'Argent EC2 £86 ❷❷❸
1 Poultry 020 7395 5000 10–2C
*"Whisking up in a lift and having it open onto
a gorgeous rooftop" helps set up good vibes –
especially for expense-accounters – at D&D
London's well-known landmark, "in the heart of the
City" (right by Bank). "You are paying for the view"
to some extent, but its current culinary performance
is "sound – perfectly OK without being exceptional".
/ EC2R 8EJ; www.coqdargent.co.uk; @coqdargent1;
9.45 pm; closed Sun D; booking max 10 may apply; set
brunch £50 (FP), set weekday L & pre-theatre £56 (FP).*

Corazón W1 NEW £41 ❸❹❸
29 Poland St 020 3813 1430 4–1C
*"Away from the increasing chain-ification of
Wahaca", Laura Sheffield's new Soho taqueria
scratches a similar itch with its "fabulously
flavourful", "fluffy light tacos" with "friendly service
in cheerful surroundings at a great price" – "what
more could you ask for in W1?" / W1F 8QN;
www.corazonlondon.co.uk; @corazon_uk.*

Core by Clare Smyth W11 NEW
92 Kensington Park Rd 020 3937 5086 7–2B
*Clare Smyth, former 'chef patron' at Restaurant
Gordon Ramsay – and the first British woman to
hold three Michelin stars – chose this well-known
site (previously Notting Hill Kitchen, RIP, and once
the site of the original Leith's) to launch her first
solo venture in summer 2017! / W11 2PN; www.
corebyclaresmyth.com.*

Cork & Bottle WC2 £58 ❷❸❺
44-46 Cranbourn St 020 7734 7807 5–3B
*"The perfect bolt-hole in the West End" – this
atmospheric, charmingly dated cellar is, for those
who know it, a much-loved haven, just off Leicester
Square. "It's the comprehensive wine list that
shoots it up the scale", but there's some "decent",
if "slightly safe" grub too. Tip Tips: "cheese and ham
pie is super" (but not for slimmers). / WC2H 7AN;
www.thecorkandbottle.co.uk; @corkbottle1971; 11.30
pm, Sun 10.30 pm; no booking D.*

Corner Kitchen E7 £43 ❸❸❸
58 Woodgrange Rd 020 8555 8068 14–1D
*"A great local in up-and-coming Forest Gate" – this
all-day outfit is "not just a pizzeria", but that's
the highlight, with a "genuine Italian pizzaiolo at
the oven serving up pizza using sourdough". / E7;
cornerkitchen.london; @CornerKitchenE7; 10 pm, Fri &
Sat 10.30 pm, Sun 9 pm; no booking.*

Corner Room E2 £53 ❸❹❹
Patriot Sq 020 7871 0461 14–2B
*"Hidden away at the back of the hotel", this
"tiny", "sparse" chamber shares a kitchen with
the better-known Typing Room; for fans, it's "a
wonderful fashionista inside secret" and a "splendid
gastronomic delight", but for sceptics "the food
doesn't taste quite as good as hoped". / E2 9NF;
www.townhallhotel.com/cornerroom; @townhallhotel;
9.30 pm, Thu-Sat 10 pm.*

Corrigan's Mayfair W1 £91 ❸❹❸
28 Upper Grosvenor St 020 7499 9943 3–3A
*"There's just the right balance of fine dining
and a relaxed approach" at Richard Corrigan's
"masculine and clubby", and business-friendly,
Mayfair HQ, "whose honest cooking of first-rate
ingredients avoids the over-elaboration that often
mars restaurants that are trying to win gongs". Top
Tips – "the Sunday set lunch menu stands out as*

good value for the posh location" and the "private dining room experience is outstanding, be it at the Chef's Table or in the Library". / W1K 7EH; www.corrigansmayfair.com; @CorriganMayfair; 10 pm; closed Sat L; booking max 12 may apply; set Sun L £58 (FP), set weekday L £64 (FP).

Côte £48 ②②②
"You know what you're going to get" from this ubiquitous French brasserie chain: a formula that's "classier than Café Rouge's", and whose "easy and convenient, if uninspiring" virtues nowadays make it the survey's most-mentioned multiple. The "classic bistro fare" is "formulaic but edible" (steak-frites is a popular choice) and while service is "hit or miss" and conditions often "noisy", the "sensible pricing" especially of lunch or pre-theatre deals underpins its massive popularity. / www.cote-restaurants.co.uk; 11 pm.

Counter Culture SW4 £54 ④③③
16 The Pavement 020 8191 7960 11–2D
A year-old offshoot from Robin Gill's well-known Dairy next door, this "very little restaurant" (15 seats) knocks out "great-tasting", "well-sourced" small dishes on the Pavement in Clapham; "very friendly" service too. / SW4 0HY; www.countercultureclapham.co.uk; @culturesnax; no booking.

Counter Vauxhall Arches
SW8 £59 ④③④
Arch 50, South Lambeth Pl
020 3693 9600 11–1D
"The new head chef has kicked the kitchen up several levels" at this "rocking" two-year-old in a Vauxhall railway arch (at 60m long, its claim-to-fame is as London's longest restaurant). "From oysters to lobster burger and chateaubriand, this arch now stands shoulder-to-shoulder with the grand brasseries of the West End" (well, nearly!). / SW8 1SP; www.counterrestaurants.com; @eatatcounter; 12.30 am, Fri & Sat 1.30 am.

The Cow W2 £58 ③③④
89 Westbourne Park Rd 020 7221 0021 7–1B
"Exceptional seafood" is the gastronomic draw at Tom Conran's "really relaxed and friendly" Irish pub in the Notting Hill-Bayswater hinterland. "The fish stew is highly recommended", alongside the oysters and Guinness. / W2 5QH; www.thecowlondon.co.uk; @TheCowLondon; 11 pm, Sun 10 pm; No Amex.

Coya W1 £83 ④③⑤
118 Piccadilly 020 7042 7118 3–4B
"Wow! What a lot of fun". This "exciting" Peruvian in Mayfair is "that rare restaurant" which can deliver "a truly spectacular meal", with an "amazing atmosphere (especially when the band starts playing)" and "exquisite flavour combinations" that "set the palette alight". Even fans though say "the

prices are as outstanding as the cuisine". / W1J 7NW; www.coyarestaurant.com; @coyalondon_; 11 pm, Sun-Wed 10.30 pm.

Craft London SE10 £61 ④④②
Peninsula Square 020 8465 5910 12–1D
"Quelle surprise! A real restaurant at the O2" – Stevie Parle has created one of his better places on the Greenwich Peninsular. The first-floor kitchen serves "inspired, locally sourced food in a beautiful room with impeccable service", while the café downstairs makes "top pizza". Top Tip – "try the tester (not taster) menu", served on Tuesdays. / SE10 0SQ; www.craft-london.co.uk; @CraftLDN; 10.30 pm (cafe 6pm); cafe L only; restaurant D only, Sat L & D, closed Mon & Sun.

Crate Brewery and Pizzeria
E9 £27 ③②④
7, The White Building, Queens Yard
020 8533 3331 14–1C
"Our go-to place for pizza, with fantastic atmosphere and great service" – this "cracking", conscientiously grungy hipster craft brewery and pizzeria beside the canal by the Olympic Park is "still as popular as ever with the Hackney Massive". / E9 5EN; www.cratebrewery.com; @cratebrewery; 10 pm, Fri & Sat 11 pm.

Crazy Bear Fitzrovia W1 £71 ③③④
26-28 Whitfield St 020 7631 0088 2–1C
"Quirky and plush" – this idiosyncratic Thai, hidden away off Tottenham Court Road "doesn't stand out from the street", but is "gorgeous once inside". The beautifully presented food was well-rated this year, and no meal here is complete without a visit to the superb, "funky" basement bar. / W1T 2RG; www.crazybeargroup.co.uk/fitzrovia; @CrazyBearGroup; 10.45 pm, Sun 10 pm; closed Mon; No shorts.

Crocker's Folly NW8 £64 ②②④
23-24 Aberdeen Pl 020 7289 9898 9–4A
"This most impressive and original of London's 19th-century pubs" – a monumental pile built by the said Mr Crocker in the misplaced belief that a huge railway terminus would be built in St John's Wood – "could be really wonderful". Its owners of the last few years, Maroush Group, have struggled to make their mark, but – bizarre as it may seem – its recent ditching of a British menu to focus on the Lebanese cuisine that made the group's name seems like a good first step. / NW8 8JR; www.crockersfolly.com; @Crockers_Folly; 10.30 pm; set weekday L £40 (FP).

The Crooked Well SE5 £48 ③②③
16 Grove Ln 020 7252 7798 1–3C
"High-quality cooking in this tucked-away corner of town" sums up the appeal of this "lovely neighbourhood pub" in Camberwell. Plenty of space means it's "really comfortable for all the family", with a "nicely buzzing atmosphere". / SE5 8SY;

www.thecrookedwell.com; @crookedwell; 10.30 pm;
closed Mon L; No Amex; booking max 6 may apply.

The Cross Keys SW3 £54 **3****4****4**
1 Lawrence St 020 7351 0686 6–3C
Chelsea's oldest boozer is nowadays a stablemate
of the Sands End in Fulham, and it wins consistently
good scores with its "friendly local atmosphere"
and some "excellent" pub nosh. / SW3 5NB;
www.thecrosskeyschelsea.co.uk; @CrossKeys_PH; 10
pm, Sun 9 pm.

The Culpeper E1 £51 **2****2****3**
40 Commercial St 020 7247 5371 13–2C
An "inventive" approach helps win fans for this
Spitalfields two-year-old – a wittily updated old
corner boozer, with a more upscale dining room
over the happening bar. However, it's not the fave
rave it was when it first burst on the scene. / E1 6LP;
www.theculpeper.com; @TheCulpeper; midnight, Fri &
Sat 2 am, Sun 11 pm; SRA-Food Made Good – 0 stars.

Cumberland Arms W14 £48 **4****4****3**
29 North End Rd 020 7371 6806 8–2D
"The best pub for food in the area around
Olympia" – this "very friendly" gastropub serves
a "cracking" Med-inspired menu and "makes a
good place to meetup and discuss the world".
"Nice outdoor space" in summer. / W14 8SZ;
www.thecumberlandarmspub.co.uk; @thecumberland;
10 pm, Sun 9.30 pm.

Cut, 45 Park Lane W1 £124 **2****2****2**
45 Park Ln 020 7493 4545 3–4A
US celebrity chef Wolfgang Puck's "very expensive"
London outpost, tucked inside a boutique hotel on
Park Lane, again earnt a mixed rep this year. It does
have its fans, who say that "steaks don't get better
than this", but not that many of them, and almost
as numerous are those who find it "stuffy and rather
disappointing" or even "a total waste of money". /
W1K 1PN; www.45parklane.com; @45ParkLaneUK;
10.30 pm; set pre theatre £87 (FP).

Cut The Mustard SW16 £23 **3****2****3**
68 Moyser Rd 07725 034101 11–2D
The decor's distressed, but customers aren't at this
"little Streatham café", serving "a good selection
of brunches", plus a "great array of breads and
pastries". / SW16 6SQ; cutthemustardcafe.com;
@WeCutTheMustard; 5.30 pm, Sun 4 pm; L only.

Cyprus Mangal SW1 £38 **3****2****2**
45 Warwick Way 020 7828 5940 2–4B
For a "cheap 'n' cheerful" blow out, this well-
established Pimlico café is just the job: "delicious
Turkish barbecue meat and kebabs, with fresh
salads, washed down with a good range of wines
and beers". / SW1V 1QS; www.cyprusmangal.co.uk;
10.45 pm, Fri & Sat 11.45 pm.

Da Mario SW7 £48 **3****3****4**
15 Gloucester Rd 020 7584 9078 6–1B
For "an efficient and cheerful meal, especially before
a visit to the Royal Albert Hall" this "buzzing Italian
pizza-fest" ("there's a wide selection including
vegetarian, gluten-free, halal and per bambini")
is "so good, you can forgive them their kitsch,
Princess Di-themed decor!" "It's not overpriced for
the location and always entertaining". / SW7 4PP;
www.damario.co.uk; 11.30 pm.

Da Mario WC2 £53 **3****4****3**
63 Endell St 020 7240 3632 5–1C
"Superb pasta" tops the bill at this "cosy, traditional
family-run Italian in Covent Garden" ("and there
ain't many of those left in central London"), which
has a big fanclub thanks to its "welcoming" (if
"noisy") style and "excellent value". / WC2H 9AJ;
www.da-mario.co.uk; 11.15 pm; closed Sun.

The Dairy SW4 £49 **4****4****4**
15 The Pavement 020 7622 4165 11–2D
"Wow… double wow!" – Robin Gill's "quirky,
amazing value and ever changing" small plates are
"bursting with flavour", according to most reports on
this "very casual and so popular" Clapham hangout,
which fans cross town for. As it matures though, it's
drawing increasing flak, for seeming "too cool for
school and charging ridiculous prices". / SW4 0HY;
www.the-dairy.co.uk; @thedairyclapham; 9.45 pm;
closed Mon, Tue L & Sun D.

Dalloway Terrace, Bloomsbury Hotel WC1 £56 **3****2****4**
16-22 Great Russell St 020 7347 1221 2–1C
An exceptional al fresco dining space – a leafy
terrace, complete with fully retractable roof – is
the special reason to truffle out this year-old
eatery, whose bucolic nature is utterly at odds with
the grungy environs of Centre Point. Limited but
consistent feedback on its cooking too. / WC1B
3NN; www.dallowayterrace.com; @DallowayTerrace;
10.30 pm.

La Dame de Pic London EC3 NEW £100 **3****3****2**
10 Trinity Square 020 7297 3799 10–3D
An "excellent addition to the City" – this high-
ceilinged arrival occupies the gobsmackingly grand,
ex-HQ of the old Port of London Authority, near the
Tower of London: since January 2017, the second
outpost of Four Seasons Hotels in the capital. The
dining room – run by the Pic family, who run a
much-fêted, Gallic dining empire dating to 1889 in
Valence, SE France – is an instant hit with expense-
accounters, and wins bouquets from most foodies
too for the "sophisticated" and "intense" cuisine
from ex-Apsleys chef Luca Piscazzi. There are niggles
too: the space – "romantic" to fans – can seem
too "blingy" to critics, flavour combinations strike
some reporters as "odd", and, perhaps inevitably,

it can all seem *"way overpriced"*. / EC3N 4AJ; ladamedepiclondon.co.uk; @FSTenTrinity; No shorts; set weekday L £66 (FP).

Dandy N16 NEW £50 4 4 3
20 Newington Green   020 8617 1930   1–1C
"Carrying across the real joy and passion for food to this bigger place in Newington Green" – this Aussie-owned communal canteen (the new incarnation of Hackney's Dandy Café) provides simple, funky (lots of Asian and middle eastern spicing) dishes alongside coffee and breads from their bakery. / N16 9PU; www.dandycafe.co.uk; @DandyCaf; 11 pm, Sun-Tue 5 pm; Sun-Tue L only.

Daphne's SW3 £80 2 2 2
112 Draycott Ave   020 7589 4257   6–2C
Once a favourite of Princess Di's, this *"romantic"* Italian stalwart in Chelsea is *"just about keeping up appearances"* but doesn't delight everyone. To its fans it's *"great fun"* (*"not too noisy but not too silent"*) and with acceptable cuisine, but to detractors service is so so and *"the food has been a disappointment of late"*. / SW3 3AE; www.daphnes-restaurant.co.uk; @DaphnesLondon/; 11 pm, Sun 10 pm; set weekday L £50 (FP).

Daquise SW7 £49 2 3 2
20 Thurloe St   020 7589 6117   6–2C
This 70-year-old South Ken institution *"is a time-warp, but in a good way"*. Old fans as well as one-off visitors love coming here for the *"charming service and good, solid Polish fare"*. *"Excellent stuffed eggs and delicious stuffed cabbage with potato vodka – all without having to travel to Poland"*. / SW7 2LT; www.daquise.co.uk; @GesslerDaquise; 11 pm; No Amex.

Darbaar EC2 £62 4 3 2
1 Snowden St   020 7422 4100   13–2B
"Subtle spicing" is key to ex Cinnamon Kitchen chef, Abdul Yaseen's very superior take on Indian cuisine at this Liverpool Street yearling – a *"fine"*, but slightly cold site inherited from svelte Japanese, Chrysan (Long RIP). / EC2A 2DQ; www.darbaarrestaurants.com; @DarbaarbyAbdul; 10.45 pm.

Darjeeling Express
W1 NEW £48 4 3 3
6-8 Kingly St   020 7287 2828   4–2B
From supper club star, to pop-up favourite (at The Sun and 13 Cantons), Asma Khan's Darjeeling Express has finally found a permanent station atop Kingly Court in Soho, serving an array of north Indian dishes that are *"generous, interesting and so delicious"*. / W1B 5PW; www.darjeeling-express.com; @AsmaKhanCooks; 10 pm, Sun 4 pm.

Dartmouth Arms NW5
35 York Rise   020 7485 3267   9–1B
This well-liked pub in Parliament Hill, was rescued from the developers by Andy Bird and his London Public House Group (Fanny Nelson's, The Chesham Arms in Hackney and co-owner of Happiness Forgets in Hoxton). Now restored, its kitchen is due to reopen in summer 2017. / NW5 1SP; www.dartmoutharms.uk; @dartmoutharms; 10 pm; No Amex.

The Dartmouth Castle
W6 £47 3 4 4
26 Glenthorne Rd   020 8748 3614   8–2C
There's *"always a fun vibe"* at this *"hustling and bustling gastropub"* with cute terrace, a short walk from Hammersmith Broadway. *"The food's always a notch above the rest"*, service is *"super-fast"*, and it's *"a great place to relax and unwind"*. / W6 0LS; www.thedartmouthcastle.co.uk; @DartmouthCastle; 9.30 pm, Sun 9 pm; closed Sat L.

Darwin Brasserie EC3 £69 2 3 4
1 Sky Garden Walk   033 3772 0020   10–3D
"That you can wander among tropical foliage in the Sky Garden all the while surrounded by the most breathtaking views of the capital…" is the big draw to this all-day operation at the top of the Walkie-Talkie. *"Not as bad or overpriced as some restaurants with a view"* is a fair, if slightly grudging summary of its culinary performance this year, with breakfast particularly recommended. / EC3M 8AF; skygarden.london/darwin; @SG_Darwin; 10.30 pm.

Dastaan KT19 NEW £39 5 4 3
447 Kingston Rd   020 8786 8999   1–4A
In the depths of South London 'burbs, this simple newcomer from a duo of ex-Gymkhana chefs leaves early reporters *"blown away"*: *"it's a small menu, but everything was marvellous; the fish was wonderfully hot, spicy and fresh, and lamb chops are a must!"* / KT19 0DB; dastaan.co.uk; @Dastaan447; Booking weekdays only.

Daylesford Organic £51 3 2 3
44b Pimlico Rd, SW1   020 7881 8060   6–2D
Selfridges & Co, 400 Oxford St, W1   0800 123 400 3–1A
6-8 Blandford St, W1   020 3696 6500   2–1A
208-212 Westbourne Grove, W11   020 7313 8050   7–1B
"Great healthy brunches" help draw a busy crowd to Lady Bamford's rus-in-urbis organic cafés. Service can be variable and even *"sniffy"* however, and high prices are a recurring concern: *"the food is nice, but it is SO expensive that I always feel a little bit ripped off"*. / www.daylesfordorganic.com; SW1 & W11 9.30 pm, Mon 7 pm, Sun 4 pm; W1 9 pm, Sun 6.15 pm; W11 no booking L.

Dean & DeLuca W1 NEW
11 Mount St awaiting tel 3–3A
In the former heart-of-Mayfair premises of Allen's the Butchers, this most chichi (and expensive!) of NYC lifestyle brands (a global business now, of which

a chunk is still held by founder Giorgio DeLuca, who opened his first SoHo store in 1977) aims to storm the capital in the second half of 2017. So many US businesses founder on overpricing when they hit London – perhaps having a British chairman (Charles Finch) will help them judge the market better than some of their peers. / W1K 2AP; www.deandeluca.com; @deandeluca.

Dean Street Townhouse W1 £66 ②②④
69-71 Dean St 020 7434 1775 4–1D
"Watching the parade of Soho media types" can make for good sport at this "smooth" operation – an "atmospheric" brasserie with "a great buzz to it". True to form for owners Soho House, "it's a bit variable food and service-wise", but generally it's found "it's an uplifting place to visit", especially for "a great breakfast in cool surroundings". / W1D 3SE; www.deanstreettownhouse.com; @deanstreettownhouse; 11.30 pm, Fri & Sat midnight, Sun 10.30 pm; set weekday L £41 (FP).

Defune W1 £72 ③②①
34 George St 020 7935 8311 3–1A
Even fans of this decades-old veteran have always conceded that the interior feels "barren", and that "it might be cheaper to fly to Tokyo for lunch", but still they acclaim its "fantastic sushi" and other "top, no-fusion-nonsense, Japanese dishes". A couple of reporters sounded a warning note this year though: "it used to be our treat, but we found its quality had gone down". / W1U 7DP; www.defune.com; 10.45 pm, Sun 10.30 pm.

Dehesa W1 £52 ③②③
25 Ganton St 020 7494 4170 4–2B
"Awesome Spanish and Italian tapas" has made this "convivial" dining room with terrace off Carnaby Street a "firm favourite" for many ("I always feel at home here even with the crowds shopping!"). But food scores are down this year, as they are for several Salt Yard group stablemates – not helped by the Spring 2017 departure of chef-director Ben Tish? / W1F 9BP; www.saltyardgroup.co.uk/dehesa; @SaltYardGroup; 10.45 pm, Sun 9.45 pm.

THE DELAUNAY WC2 £58 ②④⑤
55 Aldwych 020 7499 8558 2–2D
"Not as grand as its sibling The Wolseley", Corbin & King's "glamorous" outpost on Aldwych "is in a similar vein, but feels less frantic", and in its own more "intimate" way is "one of the classiest rooms in town". "The cooking, in an Austrian bent, is OK without being fantastic", majoring in "jolly gigantic schnitzel" and other "stodgy" (slightly "complacent and expensive") fare. As with its Piccadilly stablemate, breakfast here is a prime strength – "a very civilised way to start the day" – and its "well-spaced", comfortable and "old-fashioned" style similarly makes it a major

business favourite, being "smart enough to impress, without ever being overbearing". It's "brilliantly convenient for pre-theatre too." Next door, its spin-off, 'The Counter', "serves a great coffee and the pastries are to die for!" / WC2B 4BB; www.thedelaunay.com; @TheDelaunayRest; midnight, Sun 11 pm.

Delfino W1 £53 ④③②
121a Mount St 020 7499 1256 3–3B
"Amazing prices for Mayfair" help evoke the spirit of "Italian-as-they-used-to-be" at this squashed, "really busy and noisy" outfit, just along the road from the Connaught, serving "great pizzas". / W1K 3NW; www.finos.co.uk; 10 pm; closed Sun.

Delhi Grill N1 £25 ③②②
21 Chapel Mkt 020 7278 8100 9–3D
"Still the best simple curries in Islington" – "succulent, spicy" and with "tender meat" – this Chapel Market canteen is "better than most restaurants at double the price" (with lunch particularly good value). / N1 9EZ; www.delhigrill.com; @delhigrill; 10.30 pm; Cash only.

Delisserie NW8 £40 ③②②
87 Allitsen Rd 020 7722 7444 9–3A
"The Temple Fortune branch of this small chain of NYC-style delis is always full of families at lunch". Kids in particular love the "gargantuan portions, of tasty American New York Jewish deli food" ("don't go if you're afraid of calories or cholesterol!") / NW8 7AS; www.delisserie.com/st-johns-wood; 10 pm.

La Delizia Limbara SW3 £44 ③③③
63-65 Chelsea Manor St 020 7376 4111 6–3C
This "little neighbourhood pizza joint", just off the Kings Road – "unchanged in 30+ years" – serves "wonderful thin-crust pizzas" ("I just love this intimate, cheap and cheerful place"). / SW3 5RZ; www.ladelizia.org.uk; @ladelizia; 11 pm, Sun 10.30 pm; No Amex.

Department of Coffee, and Social Affairs EC1 £13 ③④④
14-16 Leather Ln 020 7419 6906 10–2A
"What it claims to be: a good coffee stop!" – the "no frills" but straightforward proposition at this Leather Lane original of what is now a mini-chain of coffee bars. "It's small and not always easy to get a seat, but always good", with "great cakes". / EC1N 7SU; www.departmentofcoffee.co.uk; @DeptOfCoffee; 5.30 pm, Sat 4 pm; L only; no booking.

The Dining Room, The Goring Hotel SW1 £91 ③④④
15 Beeston Pl 020 7396 9000 2–4B
"One of the last bastions of the English style of the old days" – this "time-warp" family-run hotel between Victoria and Buckingham Palace provides "the quintessential country house experience in London", with "smartly dressed staff with many

years of service" and a "hugely traditional, well-spaced interior". It's shot to prominence in recent years – both since the Middletons stayed here prior to the Royal Wedding and since Michelin (slightly bafflingly) awarded the "classic" British cuisine a star, although in truth the top culinary attractions are its superb breakfasts and afternoon tea ("just how it should be – comfy sofas and chairs, endless streams of sandwiches and scones, followed by dainty cakes"). But "oh dear, is it starting to rest on its regal laurels?" It took more flak this year for being "very expensive". / SW1W 0JW; www.thegoring.com; @TheGoring; 9.30 pm; closed Sat L; No jeans; booking max 8 may apply; set brunch £52 (FP), set pre-theatre £61 (FP).

Dinings   **£68**   5 4 2
22 Harcourt St, W1   020 7723 0666   9–4A
Walton House, Walton St, SW3
020 7723 0666   6–2C **NEW**
"Don't be put off by the simplicity of the dining room" – "a noisy concrete basement" (although you can also sit at the ground floor bar): Tomonari Chiba's sushi and other Japanese fare is "genius", albeit "spectacularly expensive" at his original Marylebone venture of over ten years standing. In May 2017 he opened a considerably swankier offshoot in the beautiful and chichi premises vacated by Toto's (RIP) which seem likely to become the dominant member of the duo hereafter. It features a mashup of Japanese and Western ingredients and ideas – early press reviews are mixed. / dinings.co.uk.

**Dinner, Mandarin Oriental
SW1**   **£112**   2 3 2
66 Knightsbridge   020 7201 3833   6–1D
"I am perplexed as to how it achieved a second Michelin Star and made it onto the World's 50 Best!" – verdicts are ever-harsher on Heston's "historically inspired" Knightsbridge dining room, which increasingly "trades on the Blumenthal name". Yes, many reporters do still enjoy "an amazing taste sensation" from its "delicious Olde Worlde English recipes with a twist". And yes it has "stunning views over Hyde Park". But far too many refuseniks nowadays report "terrifying bills" for food that's "simply OK", from a menu that reads like "a marketing con" (and barely changes), in a room with all the ambience of "a plush hotel foyer". "If I want a modern take on 15th century chicken, in future I think I'll go to Chicken Cottage!" Top Menu Tip – "the Meat Fruit is cool". / SW1X 7LA; www.dinnerbyheston.com; 10.30 pm; set weekday L £69 (FP).

Dip & Flip   **£34**   3 3 3
87 Battersea Rise, SW11   no tel   11–2C
115 Tooting High St, SW17   no tel   11–2C
62 The Broadway, SW19   no tel   11–2B
64-68 Atlantic Rd, SW9   no tel   11–2D

For fans – and there are plenty – this burger-'n'-gravy concept with four outlets across southwest London (Battersea, Brixton, Tooting and Wimbledon) offers "the best burgers in town by far!". By no means everyone agrees though: "Maybe I just don't get it, but I wasn't impressed by the quality of the burger or by the messy gravy". / 10 pm, Thu-Sat 11 pm; SW9 & SW17 booking: 8 min.

Dirty Burger   **£33**   3 2 2
78 Highgate Rd, NW5   020 3310 2010   9–2B
Arch 54, 6 South Lambeth Rd, SW8
020 7074 1444   2–4D
13 Bethnal Green Rd, E1
020 7749 4525   13–1B
27a, Mile End Rd, E1   020 3727 6165   13–2D
"Curiously satisfying burgers served in a hipster shed" sums up the appeal of these funky snack-shacks. "When you do something right, there's no need for other options!" / www.eatdirtyburger.com; 10 pm-midnight, Fri & Sat 11pm-2 am, Sun 8 pm-11 pm; no bookings.

Dishoom   **£41**   4 4 5
22 Kingly St, W1   020 7420 9322   4–2B
12 Upper St Martins Ln, WC2
020 7420 9320   5–3B
The Barkers Building, Derry St, W8 awaiting tel
8–1D **NEW**
Stable St, Granary Sq, N1
020 7420 9321   9–3C
7 Boundary St, E2   020 7420 9324   13–1B
"My daughter in law (born in Delhi) says it reminds her so much of Bombay food – and that is really high praise!" These "high energy" replicas of Mumbai's Parsi cantinas are "quite exceptional" for a chain, with Indian reporters feeling "nostalgia for my childhood… the noise, the bustle, the products on display in the loos!" "The evening queues are deeply tedious" ("you can only book for 6 or more") but the payoff is "exceptionally flavoursome Indian street-food with a difference", "a fun cocktail list" and "a real buzz". "Breakfast with a twist" is another option and it's easier to get a table. Top Menu Tips – black dhal, or, for breakfast, their "reinvented bacon butty" – "a bacon naan with spicy ketchup is a great start to the day!" / www.dishoom.com; 11pm, Thu-Sat midnight; breakfast 8, Sat & Sun 9; booking: min 6 at D.

**Diwana Bhel-Poori House
NW1**   **£27**   3 2 1
121-123 Drummond St   020 7387 5556   9–4C
"The best bargain meal in London" – an "incredibly good lunchtime buffet for very little cash" – is to be found at this battered veggie "institution", in the 'Little India' behind Euston station. "You can't beat their de luxe dosas" and the eponymous Bhel-Poori are also well worth a try, but "forget the decor!". "I've been coming since 1972, and it's always a safe bet!" Top Tip – BYO. / NW1 2HL; www.diwanabph.com;

@DiwanaBhelPoori; 11 pm, Sun 10 pm; No Amex; May need 10+ to book.

Diyarbakir Kitchen N4 £37 3️⃣3️⃣3️⃣
52-53 Green Lanes   020 8802 5498   1–1C
"Vast amounts" of "terrific"Turkish scoff "for comparatively little money" win praise for this "busy and atmospheric" Haringey ocakbasi. / N4 1AG; www.diyarbakir.co.uk; @DiyarbakirKtchn; 1 am.

The Dock Kitchen, Portobello Dock W10 £60 2️⃣2️⃣3️⃣
342-344 Ladbroke Grove, Portobello Dock
020 8962 1610   1–2B
Stevie Parle's "creative" and "ever-changing" menu from all points of the globe has earned a loyal following for this Victorian warehouse conversion, by the canal (lovely in summer) at the 'wrong' end of Ladbroke Grove. At its worst though, the end-result is "mundane imitations of a variety of styles of cuisine". / W10 5BU; www.dockkitchen.co.uk/contact.php; @TheDockKitchen; 9.30 pm; closed Sun D.

Dokke E1 🆕 £44
Ivory House, 50 St Katharine's Way
020 7481 3954   10–3D
Healthy small plates and brunch are a focus at Niel Wager's open kitchen, all-day café newcomer, in the heart of St Katharine's Dock. / E1W 1LA; www.dokke.co.uk; @dokkelondon; 10 pm; booking max 10 may apply.

Dominique Ansel Bakery London SW1 £24 5️⃣4️⃣3️⃣
17-21 Elizabeth St   020 7324 7705   2–4B
"The long awaited opening of this globally renowned pâtissier" in Belgravia last year has gone down a storm, bringing London not only his trademarked 'cronut' – a croissant crossed with a doughnut – but other "cakes to die for", such as the Ansel take on Brit classics like Eton mess. / SW1W 9RP; www.dominiqueansellondon.com; @DominiqueAnsel; no booking.

The Don EC4 £67 3️⃣3️⃣2️⃣
The Courtyard, 20 St Swithin's Lane
020 7626 2606   10–3C
"A perfect business venue"; this "well oiled machine", tucked away near the Bank of England, is one of the City's prime choices for entertaining thanks to its "discreet" and "prompt" service, "well-spaced tables", "outstanding wine list" and a cuisine that's "very dependable" – all "minus the bling and over-charging". See also Sign of the Don. / EC4N 8AD; www.thedonrestaurant.com; @thedonlondon; 10 pm; closed Sat & Sun; No shorts.

The Don Bistro and Bar EC4 £55 3️⃣3️⃣4️⃣
21 St Swithin's Ln   020 7626 2606   10–3C
"My go-to place in the Square Mile"; this "reliable" basement brasserie occupies the "atmospheric old cellars" that once housed the Sandeman wine and sherry importers. "Cheerful and relatively cheap", with a "small but perfectly formed menu", it "avoids the style over substance of many City restaurants" and is "less stuffy than The Don next door". / EC4N 8AD; www.thesignofthedon.com; @signofthedon; 10 pm; closed Sat & Sun.

Donostia W1 £53 4️⃣4️⃣4️⃣
10 Seymour Pl   020 3620 1845   2–2A
"Exceptional pintxos and tapas" have earned a cult following for this "buzzy" Basque outfit near Marble Arch, sibling to nearby Lurra. "One of the better Spanish restaurants in the capital" – "sit at the bar around the open kitchen to watch the chefs at work" (or there are a couple of tables in the small rear space). "The wine list is also extensive and intriguing". / W1H 7ND; www.donostia.co.uk; @DonostiaW1; 11 pm; closed Mon L; booking max 8 may apply.

Doppio NW1 £6 3️⃣3️⃣3️⃣
177 Kentish Town Rd   020 7267 5993   9–2B
"Exceptional coffee from experts" who "take real pride in making an outstanding brew" can be sampled at these on-trend espresso bars, operated by a coffee wholesaler in Camden Town, Shoreditch and Battersea. NB they "sell and service coffee machines", but "they don't serve food"! / NW1 8PD; www.doppiocoffee.co.uk; @doppiocoffeeltd; 6 pm; L only; no booking.

Dorchester Grill, Dorchester Hotel W1 £107 3️⃣4️⃣4️⃣
53 Park Lane   020 7629 8888   3–3A
Chapeau! to Alain Ducasse who has successfully turned around this formerly lacklustre traditional dining room in Mayfair, to create "a most enjoyable experience" with "expensive but faultless" modern French cuisine, charmingly served in tasteful, luxurious surroundings. / W1K 1QA; www.thedorchester.com; @TheDorchester; 10.15 pm, Sat 10.45 pm, Sun 10.15 pm; No trainers; set pre-theatre £64 (FP), set Sun L £74 (FP).

Dotori N4 £33 4️⃣3️⃣2️⃣
3a Stroud Green Rd   020 7263 3562   9–1D
Squeezing into this popular East Asian outfit near Finsbury Park station is "a bit like eating in a corridor". But it's worth it: "the sushi is brilliant and the Korean food out of this world". / N4 2DQ; www.dotorirestaurant.wix.com/dotorirestaurant; 10.30 pm, Sun 10pm; closed Mon; No Amex; no booking.

The Dove W6 £50 3|3|4
19 Upper Mall   020 8748 5405   8–2B
*"An atmospheric 18th-century hostelry right by
the river on Chiswick Mall", a short walk from
Hammersmith. There's "excellent pub food" – "true
English fare" – "and local London Pride ale on tap",
but it's really all about the location: "lovely outside
on the terrace in the summer, or cosy by the fire in
winter". / W6 9TA; www.fullers.co.uk; @thedovew6; 11
pm; closed Sun D.*

Dozo W1 £48 3|3|3
32 Old Compton St   020 7434 3219   5–2A
*"The perfect neighbourhood sushi stop" –
"reasonably priced for the location" near South
Kensington tube too. (There's also a branch
in Soho, but no-one reports on it). / W1D 4TP;
www.dozosushi.co.uk; @DozoLondon; 10 pm, Thu-Sat
11 pm.*

Dragon Castle SE17 £48 4|3|3
100 Walworth Rd   020 7277 3388   1–3C
*"Amazing and authentic Chinese cuisine" –
particularly "top dim sum" – wins consistent acclaim
this year for this "barn-like" but "buzzy" Cantonese
venue, stuck out near Elephant & Castle, which is
"full of Chinese families, especially at weekends".
"It's back on song after a dip in recent times,
with some interesting new regional dishes on the
menu". / SE17 1JL; www.dragoncastlelondon.com;
@Dragoncastle100; 11 pm, Sun 10 pm.*

Dragon Palace SW5 £42 4|2|2
207 Earls Court Rd   020 7370 1461   6–2A
*"Plenty of Chinese frequent" this inconspicuous
modern café "right on the Earl's Court Road" near
the tube, where by all accounts the all-day dim sum
is "excellent". / SW5; www.thedragonpalace.com/; 11
pm.*

Drakes Tabanco W1 £49 3|2|2
3 Windmill St   020 7637 9388   2–1C
*"Authentic tapas", "sherries from the cask and good
Spanish wine" draw a steady crowd to this "bustling
Fitzrovia cantina", named after the sherry taverns
of Andalucia. / W1T 2HY; www.drakestabanco.com;
@drakestabanco; 10 pm; booking max 7 may apply.*

The Drapers Arms N1 £53 3|2|3
44 Barnsbury St   020 7619 0348   9–3D
*"A nice balance between pub and restaurant" – this
well-known Islingtonian knocks out an "interesting
seasonal menu", although "service can be patchy".
"The wine list is a real delight, with a huge range
of bottles priced to invite exploration". / N1 1ER;
www.thedrapersarms.com/; @DrapersArms; 10.30 pm;
No Amex.*

The Duck & Rice W1 £59 3|3|4
90 Berwick St   020 3327 7888   4–2C
*Design-wise it looks "really cool", and this Soho two-
year-old is the latest prototype format of restaurant*

*impresario Alan Yau, combining "interesting, small
Chinese dishes" with the great British boozer. It
doesn't yet look like a hit on the scale of Hakkasan
or Wagamama, but the food's "really tasty" and
the place has "a great atmosphere". / W1F 0QB;
www.theduckandrice.com; @theduckandrice; 11 pm, Fri
& Sat 11.30 pm, Sun 10 pm.*

Duck & Waffle Local
SW1 NEW £50
No 2, St. James's Market, 52 Haymarket 0203
900 4444   4–4D
*London's highest restaurant (on the 40th floor of
110 Bishopsgate, alongside SushiSamba) has a
new sibling: one with its feet firmly on the ground
this time, at Haymarket's new St James's Market
development. Although it shares some dishes with
its City namesake, this is a fast-food café operation:
you can't book, you order at the counter, and
food (and cocktails) come quickly. / SW1Y 4RP;
duckandwafflelocal.com; @duckwafflelocal; 1 am.*

Duck & Waffle EC2 £75 2|2|5
110 Bishopsgate, Heron Tower
020 3640 7310   10–2D
*"The view is jaw-dropping" on the 40th floor of
the Heron Tower (next to Sushi Samba) – "an ideal
date spot" that's "worth it for the lift-ride alone"
(the fastest in western Europe). "No doubt this is
factored into the bill", but most reporters feel it's
"not overpriced" all-things-considered. Some of
the combinations are its meaty, calorie-laden menu
sound "insane", and views divide on the end-result:
"unusual and delicious" in most cases, but "really
awful" in a few. Brunch is the best bet. / EC2N 4AY;
www.duckandwaffle.com; @DuckandWaffle; open 24
hours.*

Duckroad SW8 NEW
Battersea Power Station, 188 Riverlight Quay
awaiting tel   11–1C
*Sibling to Soho's Ducksoup and Hackney's Rawduck,
this newcomer is set to open in January 2018, in
the Circus West Village at Battersea Power Station. /
SW8 5BN; www.ducksoupsoho.co.uk.*

Ducksoup W1 £61 3|3|4
41 Dean St   020 7287 4599   5–2A
*"Inventive" dishes with Italian and North African
influences, "friendly (and informative) service"
and "an impressive selection of natural wines (by
the glass on frequent rotation)" are the makings
of a "lovely evening" at this Soho spot. "You have
to relish its super-buzzy crowded spaces", but
most reporters "love every minute". / W1D 4PY;
www.ducksoupsoho.co.uk; @ducksoup; 10.30 pm;
closed Sun D; May need 3+ to book.*

Duddell's SE1 NEW
6 St Thomas St awaiting tel   10–4C
*Hong Kong comes to London in autumn 2017
when this authentic Cantonese/dim sum chain (with*

10 sites across HK) opens its first UK branch, in St Thomas Church in London Bridge. Chef Daren Liew was, until recently, executive sous chef with the Hakkasan Group. / SE1 9RY; www.duddells.co; @DuddellsHK.

Duke of Sussex W4 £49 2️⃣3️⃣4️⃣
75 South Pde 020 8742 8801 8–1A
"Lovely pub food with a Spanish twist" ("there's always something interesting and new on the menu") ensures the grand rear dining room is kept busy at this Victorian tavern beside Acton Common Green. Why are its marks not higher? – even fans say "it can be hit or miss". / W4 5LF; www.metropolitanpubcompany.com; @thedukew4; 10.30 pm, Sun 9.30 pm.

Duke's Brew & Que N1 £51 4️⃣3️⃣4️⃣
33 Downham Rd 020 3006 0795 14–2A
"Amazing beef ribs the size of your forearm and the best burgers around" are real crowd-pleasers at this "loud and hopping"Texan BBQ in Dalston. "An excellent selection of beers on tap" ("but be warned: some of the imports are very pricey") make for a "fantastic evening of meat and ale". / N1 5AA; www.dukesbrewandque.com; @dukesJoint; 10 pm, Sun 9.30 pm.

Dum Biryani W1 NEW £53 4️⃣4️⃣3️⃣
187 Wardour St 020 3638 0974 3–1D
*Limited but positive feedback on this walk-in, late 2016 newcomer in a small Soho basement: fans say it "deserves to be successful, delivering the best biryani in a long time" (cooked in a heavy pot, the 'dum' and with a pastry top). / W1F 8ZB; dumlondon. com; 10.30 pm, Sun 10 pm; May need 5+ to book.

Dynamo SW15 £42 3️⃣3️⃣3️⃣
200-204 Putney Bridge Rd
020 3761 2952 11–2B
"Built for cyclists but cooking for everyone!" – this cycle-themed café in Putney seems "set to last in a funny location that has failed in previous guises". The sense of permanency stems not least from the "consistently good brunches and fabulous sourdough pizzas" and "popularity with MAMILS (middle-aged men in lycra) means excellent coffee!". / SW15; www.the-dynamo.co.uk; @WeAreTheDynamo; 10 pm, Thu-Sat 11 pm.

The Dysart Petersham TW10 £70 3️⃣4️⃣4️⃣
135 Petersham Rd 020 8940 8005 1–4A
A "trusted favourite" to its sizeable fanclub – this "smart and spacious"Arts & Crafts pub between Richmond Park and the Thames serves Kenneth Culhane's "imaginative food in a beautiful setting" and "manager Barney and his team are always very attentive". It provoked a couple of 'off' reports this year however, accusing it of being "prissy, expensive and not that exciting". / TW10 7AA;

www.thedysartarms.co.uk; @dysartpetersham; Mon - Tue closed, Wed - Sat 9.30 pm, Sun 3.30 pm; closed Sun D.

E&O W11 £57 3️⃣3️⃣3️⃣
14 Blenheim Cr 020 7229 5454 7–1A
*It's no longer the A-lister magnet it once was, but Will Ricker's buzzy Notting Hill haunt still "keeps a high standard" of "great cocktails" and "wonderful" pan-Asian tapas. / W11 1NN; www.rickerrestaurants.com; 11 pm, Sun 10.30 pm; booking max 6 may apply.

The Eagle EC1 £37 4️⃣2️⃣5️⃣
159 Farringdon Rd 020 7837 1353 10–1A
*"Loud… crowded… open kitchen… stubbly chefs… short Anglo-Mediterranean menu on the blackboard… good beer"; that's the "dreamy and simple" formula that made London's original gastropub near Exmouth Market "a benchmark", and for its very many fans "it still rocks" – "ace" dishes are "generous and full-flavoured", and enjoyed "in a rough-and-tumble, everyone-having-a-good-time atmosphere". / EC1R 3AL; www.theeaglefarringdon.co.uk; @eaglefarringdon; 10.30 pm; closed Sun D; No Amex; no booking.

Ealing Park Tavern W5 £54 3️⃣4️⃣3️⃣
222 South Ealing Rd 020 8758 1879 1–3A
"A fantastic mix of pub and restaurant" – this spacious former coaching inn in South Ealing has its own on-site microbrewery. Quality has varied in the past, but it's "consistently back on form". / W5 4RL; www.ealingparktavern.com; @Ealingpark; 10 pm, Sun 9 pm.

Earl Spencer SW18 £48 3️⃣2️⃣4️⃣
260-262 Merton Rd 020 8870 9244 11–2B
*This substantial early 20th-century roadhouse on a trafficky route through Wandsworth is a "great local gastropub" with an impressively large following: a "fun place" with "good, daily-changing gastro-fare". / SW18 5JL; www.theearlspencer.co.uk; @TheEarlSpencer; 11 pm; Mon-Thu D only, Fri-Sun open L & D.

Eat 17 £43 3️⃣4️⃣3️⃣
28-30 Orford Rd, E17 020 8521 5279 1–1D
64-66 Brooksbys Walk, E9
020 8986 6242 14–1C
"A lovely spot in Walthamstow Village" – an "enjoyable" British kitchen whose "attentive staff" provide "locally sourced" fare that's "great value for money". Bacon jam was invented here, so take a jar home with you and "check out the Spar next door which is run by Eat 17 and specialises in supplies from interesting small producers". / www.eat17.co.uk; E17 10 pm, Sun 9 pm, E9 9 pm, Fri & Sat 9.30 pm, Sun 8 pm.

Eat Tokyo £29 4 3 2
16 Old Compton St, W1
020 7439 9887 5–2A **NEW**
50 Red Lion St, WC1 020 7242 3490 2–1D
15 Whitcomb St, WC2 020 7930 6117 5–4B
27 Catherine St, WC2
020 3489 1700 5–3D **NEW**
169 King St, W6 020 8741 7916 8–2B
18 Hillgate St, W8 020 7792 9313 7–2B
14 North End Rd, NW11
020 8209 0079 1–1B
628 Finchley Rd, NW11
020 3609 8886 1–1B **NEW**
*"The mostly Japanese clientele speaks volumes" for
the virtues of these "busy and cramped" canteens
("like a typical Tokyo dive"), which serve "excellent
sushi and have plenty of other dishes to choose
from": "portions are generous and the price is good
for the quality". Top Tip – a wide variety of "great
value bento boxes". / www.eattokyo.co.uk; Mon-Sat
11.30 pm, Sun 10.30 pm.*

**Ebury Restaurant & Wine Bar
SW1** £59 2 2 3
139 Ebury St 020 7730 5447 2–4A
*Consistent (if limited) praise for this age-old,
traditional wine bar on a picturesque corner near
Victoria station, whose performance is "as it's always
been", with solid, if not spectacular cooking and wine
that's "fairly priced" for this posh 'hood. / SW1W
9QU; www.eburyrestaurant.co.uk; @EburyRestaurant;
10 pm; closed Sat L & Sun L; booking max 14 may
apply.*

Eco SW4 £36 3 3 3
162 Clapham High St 020 7978 1108 11–2D
*"Consistently good food and cheerful service" keep
this "popular Clapham hangout" impressively busy
("it's usually packed and noisy") after over 20 years
in business. / SW4 7UG; www.ecorestaurants.com;
@ecopizzaLDN; 11 pm, Fri & Sat 11.30 pm.*

Edera W11 £65 3 4 3
148 Holland Park Ave 020 7221 6090 7–2A
*"Authentic" Sardinian cuisine from an "interesting
menu" backed up by "very obliging service" have
long made this "quiet" Holland Park fixture a very
"professional" kind of local (although of course "it's
not cheap"). Top Tip – "go in the truffle season". /
W11 4UE; www.edera.co.uk; 11 pm, Sun 10 pm.*

Edwins SE1 £56 3 4 4
202-206 Borough High St
020 7403 9913 10–4B
*"A hidden gem near Borough tube station", this
bistro upstairs from a mock-Tudor pub has "tasty
grub, excellent cocktails and lovely service". / SE1
1JX; www.edwinsborough.co.uk; @edwinsborough; 10
pm, Sun 4 pm; closed Sun D.*

8 Hoxton Square N1 £52 3 3 3
8-9 Hoxton Sq 020 7729 4232 13–1B
*"Interesting, tasty food" from a menu changing
daily, "friendly service, and tables where you can
talk quietly over lunch" all help make this "highly
recommended" destination a Hoxton favourite. /
N1 6NU; www.8hoxtonsquare.com; @8HoxtonSquare;
10.30 pm; closed Sun D.*

Eight Over Eight SW3 £56 3 3 4
392 King's Rd 020 7349 9934 6–3B
*"Delicious southeast Asian food and a fun vibe"
draws a lively crowd to Will Ricker's clubby Chelsea
hang-out: nowadays the best known of his small
group, and "always consistent". / SW3 5UZ;
www.rickerrestaurants.com/eight-over-eight; 11 pm, Sun
10.30 pm.*

Electric Diner W11 £49 2 2 3
191 Portobello Rd 020 7908 9696 7–1B
*Brunch with the trustafarian crowd at this "fun"
Notting hill hangout (nowadays part of Soho
House), whose plush interior – homage à the US
diner – sits at the base of one of London's oldest
cinemas (a landmark of Portobello). / W11 2ED;
www.electricdiner.com; @ElectricDiner; 11 pm, Fri &
Sat midnight, Sun 10 pm.*

No.11 Cadogan Gardens SW3 £64
11 Cadogan Gardens 020 7730 7000 6–2D
*"A hidden gem in the heart of Chelsea" – this
swish boutique hotel (formerly operated on a club
basis) has been taken over by the team behind
Chewton Glen and Cliveden, and its ground-floor
restaurant serving a brasserie-style menu is now
open to the public. Too little feedback for a rating
so far, but its afternoon tea, complete with edible
flowers, has already had the thumbs up. / SW3 2RJ;
www.11cadogangardens.com.*

Ella Canta W1
InterContinental London Park Lane, Park Lane
020 7318 8715 3–4A
*World's 50 Best chef, Martha Ortiz, of Mexico
City's Dulce Patria, opened her first London venture
alongside Theo Randall at The Intercontinental Park
Lane's second restaurant. The new dining room,
designed by David Collins Studio, serves the chef's
take on Mexican cuisine. The name by the way
means 'She Sings'. / W1J 7QY; www.ellacanta.com; @
ellacantalondon.*

Elliot's Café SE1 £55 3 3 3
12 Stoney St 020 7403 7436 10–4C
*Limited but all-round positive feedback on Brett
Redman's bare-brick café, whose tapas-style dishes
and all-natural list of wines are a staple of Borough
Market. / SE1 9AD; www.elliotscafe.com; @elliotscafe;
10 pm; closed Sun.*

Ellory, Netil House E8   **£59**   **3**|**5**|**3**
1 Westgate St   020 3095 9455   14–2B
"A fab place run by fab people!" – "passionate staff" breath lots of like into Matthew Young's "hipster hangout" in London Fields (part of a set of creative studios) which has a strong wine offering, and where on most (if not quite all) accounts "the food has bags of flavour too". "When full, all the high ceilings and hard surfaces can make it deafening". / E8 3RL; www.ellorylondon.com; @ellorylondon; 11 pm, Sun 9 pm; booking max 6 may apply.

Elystan Street SW3   **£98**   **4**|**4**|**2**
43 Elystan St   020 7628 5005   6–2C
"A vast improvement over the late and not-lamented Restaurant Tom Aikens that previously occupied this space" – Phil Howard's Chelsea yearling (in partnership with restaurateur Rebecca Mascarenhas) has proved one of the better openings of the year, with a "mature reinvention" of his style at The Square: a seasonal, 'Flexitarian' approach that's "bang-up-to-date, light, fresh, modern and exciting!" Feedback is not totally free of quibbles though – in particular even for the area it's "pricey" (especially given the more fuss-free style) – and the interior is a tad "sexless". / SW3 3NT; www.elystanstreet.com; @elystanstreet; set weekday L £69 (FP), set Sun L £78 (FP).

Ember Yard W1   **£53**   **2**|**3**|**3**
60 Berwick St   020 7439 8057   3–1D
"Very accomplished" small plates, cooked over charcoal (hence the name), have carved a reputation for this stylish Soho sibling to Salt Yard. But, as with a number of Salt Yard properties this year, marks are down this year, especially for food, amid the odd report of a "shameful decline from early acclaim". / W1F 8SU; www.emberyard.co.uk; @emberyard; 11 pm, Sat midnight, Sun 10 pm; booking max 13 may apply.

Emilia's Crafted Pasta E1 **NEW**   **£44**   **4**|**3**|**3**
Unit C3 Ivory House, St Katharine Docks
020 7481 2004   10–3D
"A table outside overlooking the dock is perfect, and I haven't even mentioned the delicious pasta!" – this St Katharine's Dock newcomer does what it says on the tin, and early reports are full of praise for its "authentic homemade dishes at a great price". E1W 1AT; www.emiliaspasta.com; @emiliaspasta.

The Empress E9   **£49**   **4**|**3**|**4**
130 Lauriston Rd   020 8533 5123   14–2B
"This ideal local" – "a sort of bistro-pub hybrid" beside Victoria Park that was one of east London's first dining destinations – still "never disappoints". "There's an interesting and always spot-on seasonal menu, good beer and a varied and lively crowd". /

E9 7LH; www.empresse9.co.uk; @elliottlidstone; 10 pm, Sun 9 pm; closed Mon L; No Amex.

Encant WC2   **£55**   **4**|**2**|**3**
16 Maiden Ln   020 7836 5635   5–4D
Victor Garvey's Covent Garden two-year-old serves "innovative and most importantly delicious modern Spanish food" ("sometimes overly fussy, but the flavours are strong"). It's "fun" (if "noisy") too, and "warmly welcoming", but "ridiculously small – they put four people on a table which seemed just OK for two!". / WC2E 7NJ; www.encantlondon.com; @encantlondon; 11.30 pm.

Eneko at One Aldwych, One Aldwych Hotel WC2   **£76**   **3**|**3**|**2**
1 Aldwych   020 7300 0300   2–2D
Fans of this year-old régime of a much-fêted Spanish chef, hail this Aldwych basement as an "undiscovered gem" with "inventive Basque food" that's "very modern, but not over-complex". However, even though "they've evidently spent a lot of money on refurbishing the old Axis site" (RIP), the venture can still seem "rather let down by its unconventional and rather uncongenial space", and even many supporters have concerns about "inflated prices" and food that's "a mix of the incredible and the rather boring". / WC2B 4BZ; www.eneko.london; @OneAldwych; 11 pm, Sun 10 pm; set pre theatre £54 (FP).

Enoteca Turi SW1   **£74**   **3**|**4**|**3**
87 Pimlico Rd   020 7730 3663   6–2D
"If you like Italian wine there is nowhere better in London" than Giuseppi and Pamela Turi's Pimlico venture which – having lost their SW15 premises of decades standing due to a rent review – "has magnificently managed the tumultuous move from Putney to near Sloane Square", and offers Sig. Turi's "wonderful wine list, embellished by his own personal remarks". Its new home is more "elegant" than its last, but it's the "family touch that elevates the place above the norm" and "preserves what was good about its original incarnation, while becoming smarter". The "trusty northern Italian menu augmented by seasonal daily specials" has also transplanted well, although some old regulars note that "overall it seems more expensive now, making it more of a special occasion than a regular treat". / SW1W 8PH; www.enotecaturi.com; @EnotecaTuri; 10.30 pm, Fri & Sat 11 pm; closed Sun; booking max 8 may apply; set weekday L £48 (FP).

The Enterprise SW3   **£54**   **3**|**3**|**5**
35 Walton St   020 7584 3148   6–2C
Where the 'Made in Chelsea' crowd go when they become older singles! – this chichi stalwart in a gorgeous enclave near Knightsbridge is a cosy rendezvous with very dependable cooking. / SW3 2HU; www.theenterprise.co.uk; 10.30 pm, Sun 10 pm.

L'Escargot W1 £70 444
48 Greek St 020 7439 7474 5–2A
"Everything is quite perfect" at this "civilised" but also "quirky" Gallic classic that has notched up 90 years in the heart of Soho (nowadays under owner Brian Clivaz). Though not as high profile as once it was, it remains by all accounts "a very special destination", with "brilliant, non-intrusive service", a "wonderful" and "romantic" room, and "excellent" French cuisine. / W1D 4EF; www.lescargot.co.uk; @LEscargotSoho; 11.30 pm; closed Sun D; set weekday L & pre-theatre £42 (FP).

Essenza W11 £68 343
210 Kensington Park Rd 020 7792 1066 7–1A
This "reliable Italian with good wine and friendly staff" is a smartly turned-out Notting Hill fixture, with a solid menu of classic dishes. Many of the ingredients used are imported from Italy – including the black and white truffles which are a house speciality. / W11 1NR; www.essenza.co.uk; 11.30 pm; set weekday L £43 (FP).

Est India SE1 £39 333
73-75 Union Street, Flat Iron Square
020 7407 2004 10–4B
"New age Indian" dishes in a "fun underground space" in the Flat Iron Square development. / SE1 1SG; www.estindia.co.uk; @EstIndiaLondon; 11 pm, Sun 10.30 pm.

Estiatorio Milos SW1 £122 324
1 Regent St 020 7839 2080 4–4D
"The setting is impressive and dramatic… as are some of the prices" at Costas Spiladis's glamourous West End yearling, where the centrepiece is "a terrific display and choice of Mediterranean fish flown in daily" ("you choose your fish and pay by weight"). All the many reports it inspires are of "masterfully prepared and sensational" dishes using "sublimely fresh" ingredients, and – leaving aside the "eyewatering expense" – the consensus is that it's "worth a visit" and emerging as one of London's top addresses for fish and seafood. / SW1Y 4NR; www.milos.ca/restaurants/london; 11 pm; set weekday L £62 (FP), set pre-theatre £85 (FP).

Ethos W1 £54 333
48 Eastcastle St 020 3581 1538 3–1C
"I'm not vegetarian but the wide-ranging offerings here could (almost) make me one!" – limited but positive feedback on this self-service veggie near Oxford Circus. "Food is charged by weight (not yours thankfully!)". / W1W 8DX; www.ethosfoods.com; @ethosfoods; 10 pm, Sat 9.30 pm, Sun 4 pm; May need 6+ to book.

L'Etranger SW7 £70 332
36 Gloucester Rd 020 7584 1118 6–1B
This French restaurant with Japanese influences is most acclaimed for its extremely impressive wine list and represents a "good option in an otherwise difficult part of town", near the Royal Albert Hall. Top Tip – "the under-advertised set pre-theatre menu is excellent value for the area". / SW7 4QT; www.etranger.co.uk; @letrangerSW7; 11 pm; credit card required to book; set weekday L £46 (FP).

Everest Inn SE3 £43 323
41 Montpelier Vale 020 8852 7872 1–4D
"Great-tasting gurkha curries" and good tandoor-oven specials ensure that this Blackheath Nepalese is "better than the average curry house". Even some fans however concede that "it's a little bit expensive". / SE3 0TJ; www.everestinnblackheath.co.uk; 11.30 pm, Fri & Sat midnight.

Eyre Brothers EC2 £67 433
70 Leonard St 020 7613 5346 13–1B
Don't be deceived by its English name – "posh tapas", and other "top-notch" Spanish and Portuguese dishes are matched with "very good wine" from the Iberian peninsula at this still-stylish Shoreditch joint, which has been around for yonks but can still seem like a "surprise find". / EC2A 4QX; www.eyrebrothers.co.uk; @eyrebrothers2; 10.30 pm, Sat 11 pm; closed Sat L & Sun.

Faanoos £31 332
472 Chiswick High Rd, W4
020 8994 4217 8–2A
11 Bond St, W5 020 8810 0505 1–3A
481 Richmond Rd, SW14
020 8878 5738 1–4A
"One of the best local cheap eats" – this pair of Persian kitchens in Chiswick and East Sheen are "not to be missed if in the locale". / SW14 11 pm; W4 11 pm; Fri & Sat midnight.

Fairuz W1 £45 332
3 Blandford St 020 7486 8108 2–1A
No fireworks at this "favourite" Mayfair Lebanese – just solidly rated and affordable mezze, plus more substantial fare. / W1H 3DA; www.fairuz.uk.com; 11 pm, Sun 10.30 pm.

Falafel King W10 £8 332
274 Portobello Rd 020 8964 2279 7–1A
It's "worth going out of your way for the best freshly cooked falafel" at this simple and popular Notting Hill pit stop. / W10 5TE; 7 pm; L & early evening only; Cash only; no booking.

La Famiglia SW10 £63 223
7 Langton St 020 7351 0761 6–3B
"Always fun and typically Italian" is how many long-term fans still regard this long-standing Chelsea favourite, renowned for its family-friendly style ("it's full of groups with kids at the weekend"), and "delightful" back garden. It's always been "inclined to be rather expensive" though, and – now long in the tooth – the odd former fan feels it's becoming "a shadow of what it was in its heyday". / SW10

0JL; www.lafamiglia.co.uk; @lafamiglia_sw10; 11 pm,
Sun 9 pm.

Fancy Crab W1 NEW
92 Wigmore St   020 3096 9484   3–1A
Although the name suggests the opposite, this
all-day Marylebone restaurant promises 'accessibly
priced' seafood – with Red King Crab as the star
dish. Have this North Pacific Ocean crustacean cold
on ice with dipping sauce and pickle; grilled with
butter, thyme and hollandaise sauce; tempura-
style crab claws; crab salad; Singaporean chilli
crab or as a Fancy Crab Burger! / W1U 3RD;
www.fancycrab.co.uk; @fancycrabuk.

Farang N5   £37   4 4 3
72 Highbury Park 0207 226 1609 9–1D
"Terrific food" – "zesty" and "unusual" dishes "from
a relatively short menu" – have won instant acclaim
for Seb Holmes's "very buzzy"Thai pop-up, near
Arsenal. In what is a slightly "weird set up", "they've
kept the Italian decor from the previous restaurant"
(the much loved San Daniele RIP) but it only "adds
to the charm". / N5 2XE; www.faranglondon.co.uk;
@farangLDN; 10.30 pm, Sun 5 pm; closed Mon &
Sun D.

Farmacy W2   £57   3 3 4
74 Westbourne Grove   020 7221 0705   7–1B
Camilla Al Fayed's health-conscious yearling,
complete with pharmacist-inspired decor, wins
strong (if not quite universal) support for its "very
imaginative" vegan cuisine. Its "really buzzy"
atmosphere also wins particular praise, even before
its recent introduction of 'High' tea – afternoon tea
that not only avoids refined sugars, but uses hemp
leaf infusions! / W2 5SH; www.farmacylondon.com;
@farmacyuk; 11 pm, Sun 7 pm.

Fenchurch Restaurant, Sky Garden
EC3   £91   3 2 3
20 Fenchurch St   033 3772 0020   10–3D
"The view is great (well it should be at these
prices!)", perched on top of the City's 'Walkie-Talkie'
tower. Sceptics say the food is "overpriced for what it
is", but harsh critiques are notable by their absence,
and fans by contrast are enthusiastic, saying the
cuisine (overseen since April 2017 by ex Square
head chef, Dan Fletcher) is "superlative, creative,
and well-judged". / EC3M 3BY; skygarden.london/
fenchurch-restaurant; @SG_Fenchurch; 10.15 pm;
booking max 7 may apply; set weekday L £69 (FP).

FERA AT CLARIDGE'S, CLARIDGE'S
HOTEL W1   £108
49 Brook St   020 7107 8888   3–2B
"Here's hoping it sustains its magic post Simon
Rogan" – In April 2017, the L'Enclume chef
terminated his tenure at this "beautiful Art Deco
chamber", leaving his head chef Matt Starling
to maintain the "exotic and quixotic" dishes

("delicately balanced between being intriguing
and not daunting") that have placed this famously
elegant hotel's dining room firmly in London's
first rank. Claridge's had a good record of running
this restaurant prior to any celebrity involvement,
and – though there may be some bumps after
his departure – we'd wager this "superb" all-
rounder will maintain its appeal. / W1K 4HR;
www.feraatclaridges.co.uk; @FeraAtClaridges; 10 pm;
set weekday L £73 (FP).

Ferdi W1 NEW   £78   1 1 2
30 Shepherd Market   073 7553 8309   3–4B
"There's nothing wrong with this place… other than
its ridiculous small size, average food and crazy
prices!" Paris comes to London – not in a good
way – at this new Shepherd Market spin-off from
an über-trendy 1er arrondissement brasserie (Kim
Kardashian's go-to spot when in the City of Light).
"It's terrible and they're still snotty"… "I'd rather
be a sardine than be packed in here". / W1J 7QN;
www.ferdi-restaurant.com; @ferdi.london; 11.30 pm.

La Ferme London EC1   £45   3 3 3
102-104 Farringdon Rd   020 7837 5293   10–1A
"Possibly the Frenchest restaurant ever" – this
"cosy", rustique-style deli/restaurant near Exmouth
Market has a small but enthusiastic fan club
for its fairly ambitious Gallic cuisine. / EC1R 3EA;
www.lafermelondon.com; @lafermelondon; 10 pm.

Fernandez & Wells   £54   3 3 3
43 Lexington St, W1   020 7734 1546   4–2C
55 Duke St, W1   020 7042 2774   3–2A NEW
1-3 Denmark St, WC2
020 3302 9799   5–1A NEW
Somerset Hs, Strand, WC2
020 7420 9408   2–2D
8 Exhibition Rd, SW7   020 7589 7473   6–2C
Although they boast pre-date the 'hipster', these
high-quality, funky little cafés, with their "superb
coffee, great tapas, freshly squeezed juices, breads,
cakes and toasties" hold their own well against
newer competitors. "The best F&W is at Somerset
House, where on a sunny day you can sit outside
and look at the beautiful architecture and fountains,
just a minute from the Courtauld and the Strand".
/ www.fernandezandwells.com; 11 pm, Sun 6 pm; St
Anne's Court closed Sun.

Fez Mangal W11   £26   5 4 3
104 Ladbroke Grove   020 7229 3010   7–1A
"Top notch meat and super-tasty salads and dips",
plus the chance to BYO "makes for a cheap but
great dinner" at this "exceptional"Turkish kebab
house in Ladbroke Grove. It's "small and very
crammed": "the queues out of the door speak
volumes…" / W11 1PY; www.fezmangal.com;
@FezMangal; 11.30 pm; No Amex.

Fifteen N1 £69 2️⃣2️⃣2️⃣
15 Westland Place 020 3375 1515 13–1A
If it were not for Jamie Oliver's celebrity, it would be hard to justify a listing nowadays for this once-famous Hoxton Italian, which seems increasingly ignored by reporters, and which continues to inspire deeply mixed opinions. / N1 7LP; www.fifteen.net; @JamiesFifteen; 10.30 pm, Sun 9.30 pm; booking max 12 may apply.

Fischer's W1 £64 2️⃣3️⃣4️⃣
50 Marylebone High St 020 7466 5501 2–1A
"You feel like you are in a grand coffee shop in Vienna", at Corbin & King's "beautiful, wood-panelled" Marylebone venture, whose "buzzy" (quite "noisy") quarters are particularly "ideal for a winter meal". The food splits opinion – to fans its schnitzel and wurst are "a stodgy, warm embrace", but there's also quite a feeling that "while it's fun for a change, at the price, it needs more polish". / W1U 5HN; www.fischers.co.uk; @FischersLondon; 11 pm, Sun 10 pm.

Fish Central EC1 £32 3️⃣2️⃣2️⃣
149-155 Central St 020 7253 4970 13–1A
"Freshly fried fish", "the warmest of welcomes" and "great value for money" all strike the right note at this "reliable" Clerkenwell chippie. There's "some creativity in the specials" – "the fish of the day is always interesting and beautifully cooked". / EC1V 8AP; www.fishcentral.co.uk; @fishcentral1968; 10.30 pm, Fri 11 pm; closed Sun.

Fish in a Tie SW11 £36 3️⃣3️⃣3️⃣
105 Falcon Rd 020 7924 1913 11–1C
A "good-value" and "varied selection" of Mediterranean dishes is on the menu at this slightly "kitsch" local bistro near Clapham Junction station, where service is "cheerful" and the "atmosphere is always great". / SW11 2PF; www.fishinatie.com; midnight, Sun 11 pm.

Fish Market EC2 £57 3️⃣3️⃣2️⃣
16a New St 020 3503 0790 10–2D
"Reasonably priced fresh fish cooked perfectly" is the promise of this lesser-known D&D London warehouse conversion, near Bishopsgate. Even those who feel "the room itself is nothing special" say "the fish is excellent". / EC2M 4TR; www.fishmarket-restaurant.co.uk; @FishMarketNS; 10.30 pm; closed Sun.

fish! SE1 £54 3️⃣2️⃣2️⃣
Cathedral St 020 7407 3803 10–4C
"Still going strong in its atmospheric Borough Market location" – this "noisy, echoey and crammed-in" glazed shed is arguably a bit touristy and pricey, but generally lives up to its name with "fresh fish, simply and deliciously cooked". / SE1 9AL; www.fishkitchen.com; @fishborough; 11 pm, Sun 10.30 pm.

Fishworks £62 3️⃣2️⃣3️⃣
7-9 Swallow St, W1 020 7734 5813 4–4C
89 Marylebone High St, W1
020 7935 9796 2–1A
"An excellent selection of very fresh, simply cooked fish" inspires very consistent satisfaction with these straightforward bistros in Marylebone and near Piccadilly Circus (survivors of what was once a medium-sized chain); "a mixed West End crowd makes for a jolly atmosphere". / www.fishworks.co.uk; W1B 10.30 pm, Fri & Sat 11 pm; W1U 10.30 pm.

Fiume SW8 NEW
Circus West Village, Sopwith Way awaiting tel 11–1C
Hot on the heels of opening Radici, Francesco Mazzei and D&D London are set to open this modern Italian, in the revamped Battersea Power Station site, in autumn 2017. That's the headline anyway, but the man actually in the kitchen day-to-day is Francesco Chiarelli (who worked with Mazzei at L'Anima). / SW8 4NN; www.danddlondon.com/restaurant/fiume.

THE FIVE FIELDS SW3 £89 5️⃣5️⃣4️⃣
8-9 Blacklands Ter 020 7838 1082 6–2D
"The Elysian Fields?" – Taylor Bonnyman's "graceful and intimate dining room", tucked away in Chelsea offers an "exemplary experience", which for all-round quality and consistency has few rivals in the capital. "Phenomenal cooking" – from either the prix fixe or tasting menu – is delivered by "faultless, thoroughly attentive yet unpretentious" staff and "a contented buzz in the room ensures the ambience is never hushed". / SW3 2SP; www.fivefieldsrestaurant.com; @The5Fields; 10 pm; D only, closed Mon & Sun; No trainers.

Five Guys £19 3️⃣2️⃣2️⃣
1-3 Long Acre, WC2 020 7240 2657 5–3C
71 Upper St, N1 020 7226 7577 9–3D
"A guilty pleasure" that's "a real step up in fast food" ("no table service") – this US-based chain may look "Spartan", but serves "the juiciest, most delicious burgers" ("it must be the peanut oil they fry them in"), alongside "yummy fries in huge portions" and "top shakes". Also, "it's ideal for fussy people as you build your own (with multiple free topping choices)". "Sure, it's expensive, but leagues ahead of McDonald's and Burger King; but with none of the pretence of Byron". / 11 pm, Thu-Sat midnight.

500 N19 £52 3️⃣3️⃣2️⃣
782 Holloway Rd 020 7272 3406 9–1C
"Beautifully cooked Italian and Sicilian dishes" at this "excellent" little local near Archway make it "so much better than the generic pizza and pasta joints in the Holloway area": "a real find, and well worth a

journey to visit". / N19 3JH; www.500restaurant.co.uk; @500restaurant; 10.30 pm, Sun 9.30 pm; Mon-Thu D only, Fri-Sun open L & D.

500 Degrees SE24   £24   3 3 2
Herne Hill, 153a Dulwich Rd
020 7274 8200   11–2D
Above-average wood-fired pizza wins consistent ratings for this straightforward Herne Hill yearling (a business with family connections back to a famous Naples pizzeria). / SE24; www.500degrees.co; @500degreesuk; 11 pm, Sun 10 pm.

Flat Iron   £32   4 4 3
17 Beak St, W1   020 3019 2353   4–2B
17 Henrietta St, WC2   020 3019 4212   5–3C
9 Denmark St, WC2   no tel   5–1A
46 Golborne Rd, W10 7–1A NEW
77 Curtain Rd, EC2   no tel   13–1B
"If you are only going to do one thing, do it well ...and they do!" Charlie Carroll's small chain offers "a limited menu but a great piece of steak" (plus a veggie alternative), which is "simply and perfectly cooked" and "free homemade ice cream is a lovely surprise" to finish. "You don't go for an intimate meal, but service is straightforward and effective". (Expect more expansion, as he just raised £10m from Piper private equity to grow the brand.) / www.flatironsteak.co.uk; midnight, Sun 11.30pm; EC2 11 pm; W1F 11 pm, Thu 11.30 pm, Fri & Sat midnight, Sun 10.30 pm; no bookings.

Flat Three W11   £88   4 4 3
120-122 Holland Park Ave
020 7792 8987   7–2A
With its funky six-course tasting menus of experimental Japanese and Nordic fusion food – with a 100% vegan option – this good-looking, Holland Park haunt deserves to be better discovered and, though feedback is limited, fans "love it". 'Cook like Pavel' masterclasses are a feature – a 90-minute demo, followed by lunch. / W11 4UA; www.flatthree.london; @infoflat3; 9.30 pm; set weekday L £60 (FP).

Flavour Bastard W1 NEW £54
63-64 Frith St   020 7734 4545   5–2A
Yes, they really called it that! So what's in a name – it seems that chef-patron Pratap Chahal is keen to use a fusion of flavours – gleaned from his time at Claridge's, Chez Bruce, Cinnamon Club and Galvin Bistrot – to create an international menu with 'no attempt at authenticity'. It opens in September 2017, taking over the former site of Arbutus in Soho. / W1D 3JW; www.flavourbastard.com; @flavourbastard; 10.30 pm, Fri & Sat 11 pm, Sun 10 pm.

Flesh and Buns WC2   £53   4 3 3
41 Earlham St   020 7632 9500   5–2C
"A taste sensation" – this "party vibe" Japanese izakaya in a Soho basement (part of the Bone Daddies group) wins consistently rave reviews for its steamed buns, loaded with "high quality meat". Top Tip – "Sunday brunch is a firm favourite": "an amazing amount of food and drink for the price". / WC2H 9LX; www.bonedaddies.com/restaurant/flesh-and-buns; @FleshandBuns; 10 pm, Wed-Sat 11 pm, Sun 9.30 pm; booking max 8 may apply.

Flora Indica SW5   £47   3 2 3
242 Old Brompton Rd   020 7370 4450   6–2A
"Sophisticated Indian cuisine at the right price point" makes this yearling an appealing option on the two-floor (ground and basement) Earl's Court site that some oldies still remember as Mr Wing (now long RIP). / SW5 0DE; www.flora-indica.com; @Flora_Indica; 1 am.

Flotsam and Jetsam SW17   £26   3 4 4
4 Bellevue Parade   020 8672 7639   11–2C
"It's a little too popular with the yummy mummies of Wandsworth Common", but that's the worst folk have to say about this "lovely buzzing cafe" towards its edge, whose "generally speedy service" and "well-prepared fresh food" make it a "great local coffee shop". / SW17 7EQ; www.flotsamandjetsamcafe.co.uk; @_flotsam_jetsam; 5 pm; L only; no booking.

FM Mangal SE5   £32   3 3 2
54 Camberwell Church St
020 7701 6677   1–4D
A "proper old-style grill bar" – this Camberwell Turk delivers "magnificent grilled onions, spiced flat breads and meaty treats", and "carnivores should look no further for food that's well-cooked and inexpensive". / SE5 8QZ; midnight; No Amex; no booking.

Foley's W1   £44   4 4 4
23 Foley St   020 3137 1302   2–1B
"Buzzing with energy and wonderful, eclectic food" – that's the dominant view on ex-Palomar chef Mitz Vora's Fitzrovia venue, which serves "an enticing, really interesting and unusual menu" combining myriad influences, and where there's the option of eating at the counter by the open kitchen. Ratings would be even higher, were it not for a couple of disappointing reports. / W1W 6DU; www.foleysrestaurant.co.uk; @foleyslondon.

Fortnum & Mason, The Diamond Jubilee Tea Salon W1   £67   3 3 3
181 Piccadilly   020 7734 8040   3–3D
For "a quintessential afternoon tea" in the heart of the West End, the "delightfully traditional" third-floor chamber of Piccadilly's world-famous grocer slugs it out with the nearby Ritz (and to a lesser extent The Wolseley) as London's best-known destination. Naturally "it's a tourist trap, but not overwhelmingly so", and – although some reporters feel "there is

better elsewhere for a fraction of the cost" – the majority view remains that the "non-stop sandwiches and delicious cakes-with-a-twist" are "still special" here (there are also "lots of savoury and dairy free options"). "The choice of teas is extensive too, and you can sample different ones throughout the afternoon". "You will not need an evening meal…". Top Tip – "the scones are a piece of heaven: fresh, fluffy and warm with a dusting of sugar alongside their own dream-come-true jams". / W1A 1ER; www.fortnumandmason.com; @fortnumandmason; 7 pm, Sun 6 pm; L & afternoon tea only.

45 Jermyn Street SW1   £66   3 4 4
45 Jermyn Street, St. James's
020 7205 4545   3–3D
Fortnum & Mason's "very positive" relaunch of the all-day eatery at the rear of the store, whose "chic" looks are in stark contrast to its former traditional style (as the long-running Fountain, RIP). No longer consigned to maiden aunts and their godchildren, "the cocktail chaps shake up an irresistible storm" at the bar, and it offers a "consistently interesting menu and service to match". Top Tip – some traditions have been maintained – breakfast here goes down a treat. / SW1Y 6DN; www.45jermynst.com; @Fortnums; 11 pm, Sun 6 pm; closed Sun D.

40 Maltby Street SE1   £54   4 4 3
40 Maltby St   020 7237 9247   10–4D
"The cooks work miracles in a tiny kitchen" tucked under the railway arches at this wine warehouse in one of Southwark's foodiest of enclaves near London Bridge. Chef Steve Williams uses "imaginative combinations of seasonal ingredients" in the daily menu he chalks up on a blackboard. Ironically, "while certainly interesting, the natural wines are arguably the least enjoyable aspect of the offer" (they can be "very challenging!"). / SE1 3PA; www.40maltbystreet.com; @40maltbystreet; 9.30 pm; closed Mon, Tue, Wed L, Thu L, Sat D & Sun; No Amex; no booking.

The Four Seasons   £46   4 1 1
12 Gerrard St, W1   020 7494 0870   5–3A
23 Wardour St, W1   020 7287 9995   5–3A
84 Queensway, W2   020 7229 4320   7–2C
"Succulent and not too fatty" – the "excellent roast duck" lining the window of these "dingy", "shabby", "shouty" canteens in Chinatown and Bayswater is some "the tastiest in town". There are "absolutely no frills" and "rude service is part of the traditional charm" but even so you'll "leave with a smile on your face". Top Menu Tip – the crispy pork belly here also rates mention. / www.fs-restaurants.co.uk; 11pm-midnight.

The Fox & Hounds SW11 £48   4 3 4
66-68 Latchmere Rd   020 7924 5483   11–1C
"This atmospheric old corner pub in Battersea" is a "buzzy, friendly, traditional spot" serving "a Med-

inspired menu that never disappoints". "Cosy and warm in winter, with stunning Christmas decorations, it also has a fabulous rose-clad garden in summer". / SW11 2JU; www.thefoxandhoundspub.co.uk; @thefoxbattersea; 10 pm; Mon-Thu D only, Fri-Sun open L & D.

The Fox and Anchor EC1 £53   3 3 4
115 Charterhouse St   020 7250 1300   10–1B
A "great Smithfield institution" – this imposing Victorian tavern is one of a handful in London to be licensed from the early hours to serve workers in the nearby meat market, and is known for its traditional, hearty cooked breakfast washed down with a pint – "a wonderful way to start a day". It's moved with the times, too: "they do a great avocado on toast!" / EC1M 6AA; www.foxandanchor.com; @foxanchor; 9.30 pm, Sun 6 pm.

Foxlow   £50   2 2 2
Lower James St, W1
020 7680 2710   4–3C NEW
11 Barley Mow Pas, W4   020 7680 2702   8–2A
15-19 Bedford Hill, SW12
020 7680 2700   11–2C
St John St, EC1   020 7014 8070   10–2A
For a "cheap 'n' cheerful" steak, most reporters do commend these Hawksmoor-lite spin-offs as a "fun" and affordable option (including for brunch). But while "it's a decent standard of food, nothing is out-of-the-ordinary". / www.foxlow.co.uk; 10 pm, Fri & Sat 10.30 pm, Sun 9 pm; EC1 10.30 pm, Sun 3.30 pm ; EC1 closed Sun D; SRA-Food Made Good – 2 stars.

Franco Manca   £27   3 3 2
"If this is what passes for chain-pizza these days, we are indeed living in fine times!" From humble Brixton Market origins, these "frenetic" and "rather basic" cafés have embarked on "a mammoth roll-out" and even if ratings don't equal the early days, most reporters marvel at how steady quality has remained. It's the sourdough bases – "crispy on the outside with a fine, chewy taste towards the centre" – that make dishes "so much better than bog standard", along with "bold" toppings ("away from the run-of-the-mill") all at "keen prices". / www.francomanca.co.uk; 10 pm, Wed-Sat 11 pm; no bookings.

Franco's SW1   £74   3 3 3
61 Jermyn St   020 7499 2211   3–3C
A "smart" interior where white linen abounds, and "very good" and courteous service are the badges of distinction at this St James's institution (one of London's oldest Italians, est 1946). "It's very pleasant, even if the lack of space between tables is not ideal" and a major favourite amongst local pinstripes. "Perfect for a working breakfast too… unless you find the whole concept abhorrent!" / SW1Y 6LX; www.francoslondon.com; @francoslondon; 10.30 pm; closed Sun.

Franklins SE22 £56 🎦🎦🎦
157 Lordship Ln   020 8299 9598   1–4D
"The trad British menu, brilliantly done – if
sometimes a leap of faith" has put this pub
conversion (with a farm shop opposite) on the south
London map. "East Dulwich is lucky to have such a
great local". / SE22 8HX; www.franklinsrestaurant.com;
@frankinsse22; 10.30 pm, Sun 10 pm; No Amex; set
brunch £32 (FP).

Frantoio SW10 £61 🎦🎦🎦
397 King's Rd   020 7352 4146   6–3B
The owner Bucci "makes the place, he couldn't be
more welcoming" at this World's End "gem", which
inspires a small but passionate fan club. "Standards
are high" and results from the menu (enhanced
by blackboard specials) are delivered in "huge
portions". "We've been going for years and the
whole family feel at home here – young and old". /
SW10 0LR; www.frantoio.co.uk; 11 pm.

Frederick's N1 £64 🎦🎦🎦
106 Camden Passage   020 7359 2888   9–3D
"An old favourite" that "never disappoints" – this
Islington veteran with a "lovely conservatory" and
cocktail bar is run with high "professionalism" and
has a "great buzz". The "unexciting but safe food"
has been "resting on its laurels" for at least a couple
of decades now. / N1 8EG; www.fredericks.co.uk;
@fredericks_n1; 11 pm; closed Sun; set weekday L &
pre-theatre £39 (FP).

Frenchie WC2 £79 🎦🎦🎦
18 Henrietta St   020 7836 4422   5–3C
"Interesting but ungimmicky" modern French
cuisine has helped win a big following for
Grégory Marchand's Parisian import – a "chilled"
Gallic yearling on the Covent Garden site that
was for aeons Porters: nowadays an "informal"
contemporary bistro, with ground floor dining
room, plus basement (the latter complete
with open kitchen). Service can lapse however,
and the interior is "very noisy". / WC2E 8QH;
www.frenchiecoventgarden.com; @frenchiecoventgarden;
10.30 pm; set weekday L £57 (FP).

The Frog £49 🎦🎦🎦
35 Southampton St, WC2
020 7199 8370   5–3D 🆕
2 Ely's Yard, Old Truman Brewery, Hanbury St, E1
020 3813 9832   13–2C
"Bold British tapas, with interesting combinations,
textures and flavours" goes down a storm at Adam
Handling's "superb newcomer" – an "echoey", rather
"Spartan" operation in Brick Lane's Truman Brewery,
where "you observe the fierce concentration of the
chefs, who also serve you"; and which achieved top
marks for food in spite of significant grumbling even
from fans over its "unbelievably high bills". He must
be doing something right, as in September 2017
he's already opened branch number two, in Covent

Garden. Top Menu Tip – "the best mac 'n' cheese in
London". / www.thefrogrestaurant.com.

La Fromagerie £45 🎦🎦🎦
2-6 Moxon St, W1   020 7935 0341   3–1A
52 Lamb's Conduit St, WC1 awaiting tel
2–1D 🆕
30 Highbury Park, N5   020 7359 7440   9–2D
Superior café for light bites (soups, sandwiches,
salads) and brunches attached to one of London's
foremost cheese stores in Marylebone. A Bloomsbury
branch opened in September 2017 with its most
ambitious food operation yet, incorporating a
seafood bar. / www.lafromagerie.co.uk.

The Frontline Club W2 £54 🎦🎦🎦
13 Norfolk Pl   020 7479 8960   7–1D
"Useful in the culinary desert that is Paddington",
this "stylish" and "buzzy" venue is part of a club
for war reporters (with pics on the walls providing
"reminders of the big news events from the start
of the Cold War to the fall of the Berlin Wall").
Most reports praise its "well-prepared classic food",
but there's also a feeling that "erratic cooking can
let down an otherwise sensible option in an area
that needs it". / W2 1QJ; www.frontlineclub.com;
@frontlineclub; 11 pm; closed Sat L & Sun; booking
max 6 may apply.

Fucina W1 🆕 £47 🎦🎦🎦
26 Paddington St   020 7058 4444   2–1A
"Overwhelming design, underwhelming food" seems
to be the diagnosis at Kurt Zdesar's "buzzy and
really cool-looking" Marylebone newcomer, whose
organic Italian cooking is too often "disappointing"
and "average-tasting". / W1U 5QY; fucina.co.uk.

Fumo WC2 £61 🎦🎦🎦
37 St Martin's Lane   020 3778 0430   5–4C
This "attractive", year-old, all-day Italian in Covent
Garden, near the ENO (part of the national San
Carlo group) wins pretty consistent praise for its
"good value". Service is a bit hit-and-miss, though,
with different reporters complaining of either
"interminable waits" or of food arriving "too quickly".
/ WC2N 4JS; www.sancarlofumo.co.uk/fumo-london/; @
sancarlo_fumo.

Gabeto Cantina NW1 🆕
Chalk Farm Rd   020 7424 0692   9–3B
On the first floor of Camden Stables, this new
Camden Town brasserie, which includes a
weatherproof roof terrace, opened in July 2017,
complete with an ex-Chiltern Firehouse chef,
and self-confessed 'design swagger'. / NW1 8AH;
www.gabeto.co.uk; booking max 8 may apply.

Gaby's WC2 £36 🎦🎦🎦
30 Charing Cross Rd   020 7836 4233   5–3B
"Ignore the unappealing, grot hole façade" – this
"cramped and rather tatty" theatreland relic by

Leicester Square tube is "an institution you need to try", serving authentic Jewish and Middle Eastern specials, including "the best falafels in the West End" (possibly a first when it opened in 1965) and perfect for "salt beef, latkes and a pickle with retsina before a show". Apparently Jeremy Corbyn's favourite pit stop, it won major kudos for thwarting its aristocratic landlord's efforts to redevelop in 2011. / WC2H 0DE; midnight, Sun 10 pm; No Amex.

Galley N1   **£56**   🄳🄶🄳
105-106 Upper St   020 3670 0740   9–3D
An "interesting menu" of modern European dishes, "especially seafood", makes this a "welcome and upmarket addition" to Upper Street in Islington – although "it's not cheap". There's an impressive sharing platter of hot seafood, crab and fish, and they also deliver a superior "fish 'n' chip fix". / N1 1QN; www.galleylondon.co.uk; @Galleylondon; 11 pm; set weekday L £36 (FP).

Gallipoli   **£32**   🄴🄶🄱
102 Upper St, N1   020 7359 0630   9–3D
107 Upper St, N1   020 7226 5333   9–3D
120 Upper St, N1   020 7226 8099   9–3D
"Real old Upper Street favourites", these Ottoman-themed Turkish cafés are "buzzy, bustling and loud – so you have to be in the right mood". Arguably the cheap scoff is a tad "routine" nowadays, but on most accounts, you still get "plentiful food at reasonable prices" and a fair dose of "fun". / www.cafegallipoli.com; 11 pm, Fri & Sat midnight.

Galvin at the Athenaeum
W1   **£65**   🄳🄸🄴
Athenaeum Hotel, 116 Piccadilly
020 7640 3333   3–4B
Plusses and minuses for the Galvin Bros new more "casual" and "café-style" regime at this hitherto rather overlooked dining room (whose 2016 relaunch is part of a programme to boost the profile of this Art Deco hotel, facing Green Park). To its credit, it does inspire much more feedback nowadays, with praise for its "friendly staff and bistro cooking". On the downside though, "much of its previously characterful atmosphere was lost in the massive refurb" leaving the space feeling "humdrum and hotel-y". Top Tip – "fab value lunchtime menu". / W1J 7BJ; www.athenaeumhotel.com; @galvinathenaeum; 10.30 pm.

Galvin at Windows, Park Lane
London Hilton Hotel W1 £111   🄴🄴🄵
22 Park Ln   020 7208 4021   3–4A
"The view would melt anyone's heart" at this 28th-floor eyrie, overlooking Buckingham Palace's gardens and Hyde Park. But whereas many fans see it as a "fantastic all-rounder", particularly for business or romance, refuseniks rail at food that's "somewhat pedestrian" and service that's surprisingly "hit 'n'

miss". Top Tip – the neighbouring bar actually has a better outlook! / W1K 1BE; www.galvinatwindows.com; @GalvinatWindows; 10 pm, Thu-Sat 10.30 pm, Sun 3 pm; closed Sat L & Sun D; No trainers; booking max 5 may apply; set weekday L £61 (FP), set Sun L £84 (FP).

Galvin Bistrot de Luxe
W1   **£69**   🄴🄴🄴
66 Baker St   020 7935 4007   2–1A
"It never lets you down", say fans of this "staple favourite" south of Baker Street tube – the Galvin brothers first venture, known for its "sophisticated and well-presented" bistro cuisine and "bustling, business-like and atmospheric" style. Top Tip – "the set menu is an absolute steal". / W1U 7DJ; www.galvinbistrotdeluxe.com; @bistrotdeluxe; 10.30 pm, Thu-Sat 10.45 pm, Sun 9.30 pm; set weekday L £33 (FP), set pre-theatre £37 (FP), set Sun L £48 (FP).

Galvin HOP E1   **£57**   🄴🄴🄴
35 Spital Sq   020 7299 0404   13–2B
"Not so much has changed since Café à Vin was converted into a pub", but views differ as to whether that's a good thing for this "busy bar". For fans the Galvin Bros' posh gastro-fare ("a decent steak" in particular) is "brilliantly adaptable", but it can also be "hit 'n' miss" and critics "are not sure the overall concept works: it's not really a bistro, not really a gastropub either". / E1 6DY; www.galvinrestaurants.com/section/621/galvinhop; @Galvin_brothers; 10.30 pm, Sun 9.30 pm; booking max 5 may apply; set pre theatre £38 (FP).

GALVIN LA CHAPELLE
E1   **£85**   🄴🄴🄴
35 Spital Sq   020 7299 0400   13–2B
"A sumptuous and dramatic setting" – the "elegant" conversion of a Victorian school chapel – provides "one of the best dining rooms in London" at the Galvin's celebrated Spitalfields fixture. At its best it's still a "fabulous all-rounder" for business or pleasure, with "superb French food, served with flair". Its ratings have slipped in the last couple of years however – "disjointed service" is the biggest bugbear. / E1 6DY; www.galvinlachapelle.com; @galvin_brothers; 10.30 pm, Sun 9.30 pm; No trainers; booking max 8 may apply; set weekday L, pre-theatre & Sun L £54 (FP).

The Game Bird at The Stafford
London SW1   **£70**   🄴🄴🄴
16-18 St James's Place   020 7518 1234   3–4C
"Very comfortable, discreet luxury hotel, hidden away in St James's" that's always been curiously off the radar from a culinary standpoint. Under chef James Durrant, it's "light, airy and opulent, marbled dining room around a large bar" was relaunched in 2017 aiming to showcase UK produce, with a particular focus on game, and wins solid support, particularly from business diners, thanks to its "fabulous" cuisine and "professional and

dependable" standards. Top Menu Tip – "chicken Kiev with 150g of truffle butter… what more could you want?" / SW1A 1NJ; thestaffordlondon.com/the-game-bird; @TheGameBirdLON; 10 pm.

Ganapati SE15 £45 5⃞4⃞3⃞
38 Holly Grove   020 7277 2928   1–4C
"South India comes to South London" at this "friendly and cosy" Peckham "perennial" – the area's longest serving foodie hotspot – which is "untypical, as you sit at long wooden tables and are served by female, non-Asian staff" (it's run by Brit Claire Fisher who was inspired to open it after her return from travelling). "Fabulous spicing, good quality ingredients, and a regularly changing menu ensure fresh surprises at each visit!" / SE15 5DF; www.ganapatirestaurant.com; 10.30 pm, Sun 10 pm; closed Mon; No Amex.

The Garden Cafe at the Garden Museum SE1 NEW
5 Lambeth Palace Rd   020 7401 8865   2–4D
Lambeth's very civilised Garden Museum, highly favoured by ladies who lunch, is converted from one of London's oldest churches, by Lambeth Palace, and its café re-opened in summer 2017, with a new copper-and-glass pavilion building as its home. Chefs Harry Kaufman (St John Bread & Wine) and George Ryle (Padella, Primeur) present a menu of seasonal British fare – initial press feedback is very upbeat. / SE1 7LB; www.gardenmuseum.org.uk; @GardenMuseumLDN; 5 pm, Sat 3.30 pm; L only.

Le Garrick WC2 £54 2⃞3⃞4⃞
10-12 Garrick St   020 7240 7649   5–3C
"Warm and welcoming staff" and an inviting interior ("improved after a recent refit") add to the appeal of this "reliable old favourite" in Covent Garden. "The menu comprises the usual French suspects and even if the cooking won't rock your world, the pre-theatre menu is good value for money". / WC2E 9BH; www.legarrick.co.uk; @le_garrick; 10.30 pm, Sun 5pm; closed Sun; set pre theatre £34 (FP).

The Garrison SE1 £51 3⃞3⃞3⃞
99 Bermondsey St   020 7089 9355   10–4D
This "very enjoyable and busy, buzzy ex-pub" was one of the first gastro-destinations in Bermondsey, and "remains a favourite", thanks in no small part to its "ever-changing seasonal menu". / SE1 3XB; www.thegarrison.co.uk; @TheGarrisonSE1; 10 pm, Fri & Sat 10.30 pm, Sun 9 pm.

Gastronhome SW11 £71 4⃞4⃞2⃞
59 Lavender Hill, London
020 3417 5639   11–2C
"Brilliantly done!" Damien Fremont's contemporary take on classic French cuisine has built a small but enthusiastic following at the venue he founded on Lavender Hill with Christopher Nespoux. But while fans say its "five-course 'surprise' tasting menu is

a sublime lesson in elegant simplicity", the odd reporter has the opposite reservation: "too chefy looking – everything looks pretty, with smears and flower sprinkles, but it detracts from the food". / SW11; www.gastronhome.co.uk; @gastronhome1; 10:15 pm; closed Mon & Sun; No jeans.

The Gate £52 4⃞3⃞3⃞
22-24 Seymour Place, W1
020 7724 6656   2–2A NEW
51 Queen Caroline St, W6
020 8748 6932   8–2C
370 St John St, EC1   020 7278 5483   9–3D
"I'm not a veggie but this was one of the best meals I've had in the last year" – typical praise for these "ingenious" veggies, which offer "an unmatched range of such accomplished dishes, beautifully sourced and expertly presented". From the "lovely hidden-gem original in Hammersmith" (behind the Hammy-O), they added a similarly "top notch" branch in trendy Seymour Place this year. Islington is probably the weakest performer of the three – "it's let down by a noisy environment" – but even so it's "decent and very handy for Sadlers Wells". / www.thegaterestaurants.com; 10.30 pm; W1 Sun 9.45 pm; W6 Sun 9.30 pm; SRA-Food Made Good – 3 stars.

Gaucho £82 2⃞2⃞2⃞
As "a place to impress", especially on business, these well-known Argentinian steak houses are still well-recommended by some reporters for their "fine steaks" and "fabulous South American wines". Even fans can find the bill "noticeably painful" however, particularly given the "indifferent" service, and critics feel the overall offering is "bland" and "outrageously overpriced". / www.gauchorestaurants.co.uk; 11 pm, Thu-Sat midnight ; EC3 & EC1 closed Sat & Sun, WC2 & EC2 closed Sat L & Sun.

GAUTHIER SOHO W1 £79 5⃞5⃞4⃞
21 Romilly St   020 7494 3111   5–3A
"The charming necessity to ring the doorbell to get in" helps "to whisk you miles from Soho" at this "intimate" and "elegant" townhouse, whose "calm and quiet atmosphere is amazing for somewhere just one street away from Shaftesbury Avenue". Alexis Gauthier's "mind-blowingly fantastic" seasonal cuisine is "some of the best French cooking in London" – "classic, but never old fashioned" – and backed up by an "unusual and interesting wine selection"; while "uncloying" service is of the "nothing-is-too-much-trouble" variety. "The absence of a Michelin Star since 2012 is baffling" and starkly calls into question the judgement of the tyre men. Top Tip – "lunch is a real snip". / W1D 5AF; www.gauthiersoho.co.uk; @GauthierSoho; 9.30 pm, Fri & Sat 10.30 pm; closed Mon & Sun; booking max 7 may apply.

LE GAVROCHE W1 £134 [4][5][4]
43 Upper Brook St   020 7408 0881   3–2A
"A well-oiled, old-school machine that still delivers!"
The Roux dynasty's Mayfair icon "never goes
out of fashion" to its army of fans for whom it's
"simply the best". Founded in Chelsea in 1967, it
moved to its current "cosy" site round the corner
from the American Embassy in 1982, and even
if the occasional reporter "wishes it wasn't in a
basement" the general effect "oozes class and
charm". Michel Roux Jr succeeded his father at the
helm in 1991, and "the regular presence of the
great man himself adds value; he takes time with
his customers and actually talks!" (Currently his
daughter Emily is being primed as next in line.) The
Gallic cuisine – under head chef Rachel Humphrey
– is "rich and sumptuous", while the "polished but
un-condescending" service under Emanuel Landré
is "almost other-worldly good". "A hefty chunk out
of the wallet" is of course de rigueur, but even so
gripes about "arm-and-a-leg" bills increased this year,
contributing to the food grade missing a 5/5 for the
first time in a few years. Top Tip – "The fixed price
lunch menu is still the best deal in London!" / W1K
7QR; www.le-gavroche.co.uk; @michelrouxjr; 10 pm;
closed Sat L & Sun; Jacket required; booking essential;
set weekday L £101 (FP).

Gay Hussar W1 £51 [1][2][4]
2 Greek St   020 7437 0973   5–2A
*"Another year of hearty Hungarian fare" has passed
by at this venerable Soho institution – "a haven on
a cold winter's day" with lashings of "old fashioned
atmosphere" and decades of Labour Party legend
on the side. For some reporters, the "tasty goulash"
never fails to delight, but it's really not a culinary
hotspot: "the quality of the caricatures on the walls
is far higher than the dishes on the table". / W1D
4NB; www.gayhussar.co.uk; @GayhussarsSoho; 10.45
pm; closed Sun.*

Gaylord W1 £60 [4][4][3]
79-81 Mortimer St   020 7580 3615   2–1B
*Half a century and counting, and this stately
and "impeccably run" Fitzrovia veteran is "still
always enjoyable" according to reports. Praise too
for "new menu additions with a modern twist",
such as "Golgappa street-food shots – a food
journey transporting you straight to the lanes of
Old Delhi or beaches of Chowpatty!" / W1W 7SJ;
www.gaylordlondon.com; @gaylord_london; 10.45 pm,
Sun 10.30 pm.*

Gazette £47 [2][2][3]
79 Sherwood Ct, Chatfield Rd, SW11
020 7223 0999   11–1C
100 Balham High St, SW12
020 8772 1232   11–2C
147 Upper Richmond Rd, SW15
020 8789 6996   11–2B
"Trying and largely succeeding" is a fair view on

these jolly Gallic "neighbourhood bistros" in Balham,
Clapham and Putney, particularly praised for their
"excellent value set price deals". Disasters are not
un-known here though, and it's also true to say
that they can be "middling and inconsistent" ("I
will return… but only with friends who know it!)". /
www.gazettebrasserie.co.uk; 11 pm.

GBR SW1 NEW £70
St James's St   020 7491 4840   3–4D
*Launched in May 2017 simultaneously in Duke's
London (St James's) and Duke's Dubai (Jumeirah
Palm), GBR – Great British Restaurant – is an
all-day homage to British scoff, open from breakfast
time through lunch to afternoon tea and dinner.
/ SW1A 1NA; www.gbrrestaurantslondon.com; @
gbr_london.*

Geales £56 [2][2][2]
1 Cale St, SW3   020 7965 0555   6–2C
2 Farmer St, W8   020 7727 7528   7–2B
*This fish 'n' chip veteran (est 1939) just off Notting
Hill Gate (with a more recent spin-off in Chelsea)
still has a few fans, but dwindling feedback can
make it seem surprisingly obscure nowadays. /
www.geales.com; 10.30 pm, Sun 4 pm; W8 closed Mon;
SW3 closed Sun & Mon.*

Gelupo W1 £8 [5][2][2]
7 Archer St   020 7287 5555   4–3D
*"The best ice cream in London, simple as that",
say addicts of Jacob Kenedy's little Soho gelateria
(opposite his Bocca di Lupo) where the selection
is "not quite your traditional Italian flavours"
but rather a series of "adventurous (but not
actually bonkers) flavour combos". / W1D 7AU;
www.gelupo.com; @GelupoGelato; 11 pm, Fri & Sat
midnight; No Amex; no booking.*

Gem N1 £32 [3][4][2]
265 Upper St   020 7359 0405   9–2D
*"It's not flash", but "unusually good value" enthuses
reports on this "no-frills" Turkish-Kurdish local near
Angel, which offers "lovely mezze" in "generous
portions", and whose "super staff make families
very welcome". "BYO if you ask". / N1 2UQ;
www.gemrestaurant.org.uk; @Gem_restaurant; 11 pm,
Sun 10 pm; No Amex.*

George in the Strand WC2
213 Strand   020 7353 9638   2–2D
*Too few reports for a rating for the traditionalist-
looking, first-floor restaurant (with open kitchen)
of this revamped, black and white, half-timbered
pub opposite the Royal Courts of Justice, but
one early report suggests the chef is helping its
gastropub menu punch well above its weight,
as do many initial online reviews. / WC2R 1AP;
www.georgeinthestrand.com; @thegeorgestrand; 10pm,
Fri & Sat 10.30pm, Sun 9pm.*

German Gymnasium N1 £72 ②②③
1 King's Boulevard   020 7287 8000   9–3C
"What a stunner!" A former Victorian gymnasium right next to King's Cross station was converted two years ago into this "impressive and unique" D&D London venue, and, especially given its unusual Teutonic formula, it has all the elements for a smash hit… except the execution: too often the "solid German fare" feels "average and significantly overpriced", which – not helped by "slow" service – can create "a let-down given all the hype". Still, there's always solace in the "joy" of a wine list – being focused on Germany and Austria "forces you to veer away from the standard and what discoveries that brings". / N1C 4BU; www.germangymnasium.com; @TheGermanGym; 11 pm, Sun 9 pm; set weekday L & pre-theatre £48 (FP).

Giacomo's NW2 £40 ③③②
428 Finchley Rd   020 7794 3603   1–1B
For a "cheap 'n' cheerful" nosh up Child's HIII way, bear in mind this cosy, consistently well-rated, family-run Italian of over fifteen year's standing. / NW2 2HY; www.giacomos.co.uk; 10 pm.

Gifto's Lahore Karahi UB1 £25 ③②②
162-164 The Broadway   020 8813 8669   1–3A
This large, well-known Pakistani canteen on one of Southall town centre's main roads offers "great value" – "especially for its grills". / UB1 1NN; www.gifto.com; 11.30 pm, Sat & Sun midnight; booking weekdays only.

The Gilbert Scott NW1 £74 ②③④
Euston Rd   020 7278 3888   9–3C
"Even the splendour of the dining room does not explain the bill" at Marcus Wareing's "airy" and "atmospheric" venue, near the Eurostar Platforms – even those who feel the British cuisine is good can find prices "excessive", and its worst critics feel the mismatch is "ridiculous". / NW1 2AR; www.thegilbertscott.co.uk; @Thegilbertscott; 11 pm, Sun 9 pm; booking max 7 may apply.

Ginger & White £13 ③④③
2 England's Ln, NW3   020 7722 9944   9–2A
4a-5a, Perrins Ct, NW3   020 7431 9098   9–2A
"Top-quality coffee", "great breakfasts" and "excellent cakes" are the winning formula for these "casual" Antipodean-style caffeine stops off Hampstead High Street and Belsize Park. They can be "cramped and busy", but "you feel somebody is making food you like, just for you". / www.gingerandwhite.com; 5.30 pm; W1 closed Sun.

Ginza Onodera SW1 NEW £86 ④⑤②
15 Bury St   020 7839 1101   3–3D
"Recently refurbished and renamed from Matsuri" (RIP after 23 years but same owners) – this ambitious fixture (part of an international chain) in a large basement near Piccadilly Circus recently emerged from a £2.5m renovation, and the 128-seat space continues to provide a wide array of eating options (from sushi to teppan and robata, from private rooms to the Chef's Table). Even if it has been overlooked in recent years, this has always been a top quality, traditional Japanese and early reports suggest it's on fine form: "gobsmackingly expensive, but equally gobsmackingly delicious". / SW1Y 6AL; onodera-group.com/uk/#menu; @Onodera_London; 10 pm.

Giraffe £40 ②②②
"The free giraffe-shaped drinks stirrers are always a winner" for amusing youngsters at these supremely family-friendly diners, where "staff are happy to work around balloons and colouring". Its world food menu offers "great choice" but divides views – a sizeable minority feel results are plain "dispiriting" nowadays, but parents in particular still say it's "good value and fun". / www.giraffe.net; 11 pm, Sun 10.30 pm; no booking; Sat & Sun 9 am-5 pm.

The Glasshouse TW9 £82 ⑤④③
14 Station Pde   020 8940 6777   1–3A
"Interesting cuisine in the style of sister establishments, Chez Bruce and La Trompette" help distinguish this bright, contemporary ("slightly bland") dining room by Kew Gardens as "a real treat of a local". Ratings recovered this year, thanks to consistent praise for its "discreet and polite service" and "food that's always bang on". / TW9 3PZ; www.glasshouserestaurant.co.uk; @The__Glasshouse; 10.30 pm, Sun 10 pm; booking max 8 may apply.

Globe Tavern SE1 £51 ③③③
8 Bedale St   020 7407 0043   10–4C
Bridget Jones's Diary was filmed above this Borough Market boozer – an atmospheric spot in the heart of the area, with dishes sourced from the market traders. / SE1 9AL; www.theglobeboroughmarket.com; @TheGlobeSE1.

Go-Viet SW7 NEW £57 ④③③
53 Old Brompton Rd   020 7589 6432   6–2C
"Fun and casual" spin-off from Jeff Tan's Soho Viet Food – "the food tastes great and looks magic too" at this a 60-cover café near South Kensington tube. / SW7 3JS; vietnamfood.co.uk/go-viet; 10 pm, Fri & Sat 10.30 pm.

Goddards At Greenwich SE10 £15 ③④④
22 King William Walk   020 8305 9612   1–3D
"There's a good selection, but why would you want anything other than the most traditional pie, mash and liquor, plus a mug of tea?", if you visit this Greenwich veteran (est 1890) – one of London's dying breed of traditional pie 'n' mash shops. / SE10 9HU; www.goddardsatgreenwich.co.uk; @GoddardsPieMash; 7.30 pm, Fri & Sat 8 pm; L & early evening only.

Gogi W2 £40 3️⃣3️⃣3️⃣
451 Edgware Rd   020 7724 3018   9–4A
Moody, "slightly clubby" decor adds to the atmosphere of this consistently well-rated Korean BBQ, well positioned near the canal in Little Venice. / W2 1TH; www.gogi-restaurant.com; 10.30 pm, Sun 10 pm.

Gökyüzü N4 £33 3️⃣3️⃣3️⃣
26-27 Grand Pde, Green Lanes
020 8211 8406   1–1C
The "super-fresh ingredients", "tip-top grilled meats", "vast portions and terrific prices" at this "very slick operation" on Harringay's Grand Parade "set the Turkish standard". "You can feed the whole family for less than £40". / N4 1LG; www.gokyuzurestaurant.co.uk; @Gokyuzulondon; midnight, Fri & Sat 1 am.

Gold Mine W2 £38 4️⃣2️⃣2️⃣
102 Queensway   020 7792 8331   7–2C
"Nobody does it better" say fans of the "top crispy roast duck" at this Bayswater Cantonese, which they claim vies with the more famous Four Seasons next door. "Don't expect fab service or elegant ambience, but foodwise you won't be disappointed". / W2 3RR; 11 pm.

Golden Chippy SE10 £14 3️⃣4️⃣2️⃣
62 Greenwich High Rd   020 8692 4333   1–3D
You definitely get the "best fish 'n' chips in the area" at Chris Kanizi's Greenwich chippy. We mean it no disrespect when we say that TripAdvisor's November 2016 ranking of '#1 out of 17,372 Restaurants in London' was over-egging it a tad. / SE10 8LF; www.thegoldenchippy.com; 11 pm.

Golden Dragon W1 £31 4️⃣2️⃣2️⃣
28-29 Gerrard St   020 7734 1073   5–3A
"If in doubt in Chinatown, you won't go far wrong" if you choose this busy staple which is "worth the ten minute wait for dim sum and decent noodles" (and there's also "a very interesting menu in Chinese"). "I took some fussy Chinese friends there and they were pleasantly surprised!". STOP PRESS: A Collindale outpost opened summer 2017 (see Bang Bang Oriental). / W1 6JW; goldendragonlondon.com; 11.30 pm, Fri-Sun midnight; no booking.

Golden Hind W1 £36 3️⃣3️⃣2️⃣
73 Marylebone Ln   020 7486 3644   2–1A
"You won't find fresher fish or better (greaseless) chips anywhere else in London", say fans of this well-loved Marylebone institution, founded in 1914. But while on most accounts it's "still a classic", ratings slipped a tad this year, and some regulars still "miss the previous owner" ("under the new management you can no longer BYO, which was one of its best features!)". / W1U 2PN; www.goldenhindrestaurant.com; 10 pm; closed Sat L & Sun.

Good Earth £63 2️⃣2️⃣2️⃣
233 Brompton Rd, SW3   020 7584 3658   6–2C
143-145 The Broadway, NW7
020 8959 7011   1–1B
11 Bellevue Rd, SW17   020 8682 9230   11–2C
"A very old friend that continues to please" is how many long-term fans still see these "comfortable" Chinese stalwarts in Balham, Knightsbridge and Mill Hill, where the prix/qualité verdict has traditionally been that they're "slightly overpriced, but worth it". Ratings overall remain on the wane however, and – even if harsh critiques are rare – there's a feeling that they're "not as good as they used to be". / www.goodeathgroup.co.uk; Mon-Sat 10.45 pm, Sun 10 pm; NW7 11.15 pm, Sun 10.45 pm.

The Good Egg N16 £53 4️⃣4️⃣3️⃣
93 Church St   020 7682 2120   1–1C
"It's worth braving the queues", in particular at brunch, for this white-brick-walled Stokey deli. The odd dish can seem "strange", but the Middle Eastern/American cooking is "exceptional quality", and service is from "genuine staff who clearly love the place". STOP PRESS: A Soho outfit is slated to open November 2017. / N16 0AS; www.thegoodeggn16.com; @TheGoodEgg_; 10.30 pm, Sun 3.30 pm; no booking; SRA-Food Made Good – 3 stars.

Goodman £93 4️⃣4️⃣2️⃣
24-26 Maddox St, W1   020 7499 3776   3–2C
3 South Quay, E14   020 7531 0300   12–1C
11 Old Jewry, EC2   020 7600 8220   10–2C
"Every cut is served exactly the way it should be" at these testosterone-heavy, NYC-style steakhouses, which – amongst the multiples (including Hawksmoor) – serve "the best steak in London full stop", and are naturally "ideal for business". "Staff are personable which keeps the atmosphere buzzing", and "while they are far from cheap, the meat is top quality, ranging from UK, US and further afield; matched with an excellent, varied wine list, with US bottles very well represented". / www.goodmanrestaurants.com; 10.30 pm; W1 closed Sun, EC2 closed Sat & Sun, E14 closed Sat L & Sun.

Gordon Ramsay SW3 £157 2️⃣2️⃣2️⃣
68-69 Royal Hospital Rd
020 7352 4441   6–3D
"The old standard of cooking is long gone, yet the bill defies gravity…" – that's the overall verdict on the TV chef's "chic" (but some would say "surprisingly small and claustrophobic") Chelsea flagship, whose long overdue turnaround would provide great material for one of his TV shows. On the plus-side, there are many loyal fans who say Matt Abe's cuisine can be "fabulous" and who continue to laud Jean-Claude Breton's "impeccable" service. Criticisms that the place is "stuck up", "down a notch on previously" or just "quite underwhelming overall" are far too prevalent however, which

given the "shocking prices" can lead to a sense of "crushing disappointment". Mr Michelin Man wake up – this is not a three star performance. / SW3 4HP; www.gordonramsay.com; @GordonRamsay; 10.15 pm; closed Sat & Sun; No jeans; booking max 9 may apply; set weekday L £106 (FP).

Gordon's Wine Bar WC2 £38 ②②⑤
47 Villiers St 020 7930 1408 5–4D
"Dark cave-like cellars" create a superb atmosphere at this epic old wine bar (dating from 1890) by Embankment Gardens, which also boasts one of central London's nicest outside terraces (with BBQ in summer). The "excellent choice of wine and sherries" is another reason the world and his dog flock to the place – the self-service pies, cold cuts, cheeses and salads are certainly no incentive to hurry along. / WC2N 6NE; www.gordonswinebar.com; @GordonsWineBar; 11 pm, Sun 10 pm.

Gourmet Burger Kitchen £28 ③②②
"Hard to beat, even with all the new competition" – this "always reliable" stalwart (the first of the upmarket burger chains to hit the capital) still "does what it says on the tin": "the burgers here are great, and as a venue for a no-fuss meal when the family are hungry and in a hurry" it's "good value" and "very tasty". / www.gbkinfo.com; most branches close 10.30 pm; no booking.

Gourmet Goat SE1 £12 ④④②
Borough Market, Unit 27a Rochester Walk
020 8050 1973 10–4C
Sustainable kid goat, rose veal and mutton are cooked Greek-Cypriot style by Nadia and Nick Stokes at this Borough Market specialist, which again earned consistently high grades from reporters. / SE1 9AH; www.gourmetgoat.co.uk; @gourmet_goat; no booking; SRA-Food Made Good – 3 stars.

The Gowlett Arms SE15 £37 ④③④
62 Gowlett Rd 020 7635 7048 1–4D
"Decent pizzas in a back-street boozer" is an accurate but understated description of a combination that's gone down a treat for many years at this wood-panelled Peckham hotspot, also serving meats home-smoked in the cellar. / SE15 4HY; www.thegowlett.com; @theGowlettArms; 10.30 pm, Sun 9 pm; Cash only.

Goya SW1 £46 ③③②
34 Lupus St 020 7976 5309 2–4C
"Genuine, tasty tapas" and "friendly" service ensure this family-run Pimlico Spaniard is "always busy", even though "the tables are too tight". Try to sit upstairs ("the basement dining room is less charming"). / SW1V 3EB; www.goyarestaurant.co.uk; midnight, Sun 11.30 pm.

The Grand Imperial, Guoman Grosvenor Hotel SW1 £62 ③②②
101 Buckingham Palace Rd
020 7821 8898 2–4B
"A surprising location for a quiet and spacious Chinese" – this hotel dining room by Victoria station does "superb dim sum", and some other "very good" Cantonese fare. "While the food remains above average, it's now very expensive for what it is though, and service sometimes struggles". / SW1W 0SJ; www.grandimperiallondon.com; 10.30 pm; set weekday L £39 (FP).

Grand Trunk Road E18 £59 ④④③
219 High St 020 8505 1965 1–1D
"The depth of flavour of the dishes is incredible" say fans of this comparatively elegant high street Indian yearling in Woodford: brainchild of Rajesh Suri and Dayashankar Sharma, the ex-manager and ex-head chef of Mayfair's Tamarind. / E18 2PB; www.gtrrestaurant.co.uk; @GT_Road; 10.30pm; closed Mon & Sun D.

Granger & Co £53 ③③③
237-239 Pavilion Rd, SW1
020 3848 1060 6–2D **NEW**
175 Westbourne Grove, W11
020 7229 9111 7–1B
Stanley Building, St Pancras Sq, N1
020 3058 2567 9–3C
The Buckley Building, 50 Sekforde St, EC1
020 7251 9032 10–1A
"Friends have returned from Australia full of the joys of Bill Granger, now we can get the real thing!" – so say fans of these "cool and airy", "posh-brunch heavens" who are prepared to endure the savage queues and "sometimes indifferent service" for his "brilliant and very different breakfasts", and other "healthy and innovative food (although a menu which requires a dictionary might be seen as a bit pretentious!)". However, at the W11 original in particular, there are critics who say: "it's not worth the wait given plenty of alternatives nearby". / Mon-Sat 10 pm, Sun 5pm.

The Grazing Goat W1 £60 ②③③
6 New Quebec St 020 7724 7243 2–2A
The "lovely venue" can outshine the other elements of the experience at this extremely popular dining pub (in fact with no space for drinking only any more), a short walk from Marble Arch. / W1H 7RQ; www.thegrazinggoat.co.uk; @TheGrazingGoat; 10 pm, Sun 9.30 pm.

Great Nepalese NW1 £38 ③④③
48 Eversholt St 020 7388 6737 9–3C
"A valiant survivor (I've been going here for 50 years!)" – this veteran "no frills" curry house on a grotty Euston side street serves "some very unusual dishes", with plenty of choice for veggies. Some long term fans however fear it's "not quite so special as

it was before". / NW1 1DA; www.great-nepalese.co.uk; 11.30 pm, Sun 10 pm.

Great Queen Street WC2 £54   3|2|2
32 Great Queen St   020 7242 0622   5–1D
Seasonal British cooking that's "unusual and always interesting" has won a big foodie following for this Covent Garden gastropub. A 'Curate's Egg' quality to reports has emerged in recent times however: "borderline good, but lacking the punchiness of the past"… "great food, but complacent on the service". / WC2B 5AA; www.greatqueenstreetrestaurant.co.uk; @greatqueenstreet; 10.30 pm, Sun 3.30 pm; closed Sun D; No Amex.

The Greek Larder, Arthouse
N1   £58   3|2|2
1 York Way   020 3780 2999   9–3C
In ever-more-"arty" King's Cross, Theodore Kyriakou's "fun and trendy" two-year-old offers his "modern take on Greek cuisine" and is "smaller than some of its more impersonal and noisy competitors nearby". Upbeat feedback is sometimes tinged with "inconsistencies" of both food and service, but "when you can eat in the sun, it's a welcome reminder of Aegean island life". / N1C 4AS; www.thegreeklarder.co.uk; @thegreeklarder; 10.30 pm, Sun 5 pm; set weekday L £38 (FP).

The Green EC1   £48
29 Clerkenwell Grn   020 7490 8010   10–1A
Prominently-sited on a corner of Clerkenwell Green, this attractive new pub shares the superior design DNA of its sibling The Culpeper, and a similar setup with ground floor bar and first floor restaurant. / EC1R 0DU; www.thegreenclerkenwell.com; 10 pm, Sun 6 pm.

Green Cottage NW3   £38   3|2|2
9 New College Pde   020 7722 5305   9–2A
This longstanding "neighbourhood Chinese" in a parade of shops in Swiss Cottage endures thanks to its "reliably good" and "inexpensive" chow – expect neither a cheery welcome nor a scintillating atmosphere. / NW3 5EP; 11 pm; No Amex.

The Green Room, The National
Theatre SE1   £46   2|2|2
101 Upper Ground   020 7452 3630   2–3D
Decorated with props and scenery from prior productions, the NT's ("very noisy") 'neighbourhood diner' is an airy space (surrounded by a sustainable garden). Some reports are lukewarm at best, but most consider the food "decent", certainly for a pre-show bite. / SE1 9PP; www.greenroom.london; @greenroomSE1; 10.30 pm, Sun 7 pm.

Greenberry Café NW1   £54   3|3|3
101 Regents Park Rd   020 7483 3765   9–2B
"Good daily specials and a reasonable, weekday prix fixe menu" along with "popular breakfasts

and weekend brunch" help keep things busy at this all-day Primrose Hill local ("always crowded with babies and dog-owners"). It's "not entirely cheap, but there's an excellent price/quality ratio", and it's "run very graciously and effectively". / NW1 8UR; greenberrycafe.co.uk; @Greenberry_Cafe; 10 pm; closed Mon D & Sun D; No Amex; set weekday L £33 (FP).

The Greenhouse W1   £110   4|4|4
27a Hays Mews   020 7499 3331   3–3B
Marlon Abela's "serene oasis tucked away in the midst of bustling Mayfair is a delight", and was one of London's highest-rated all-rounders this year. Arnaud Bignon's "terrific cuisine" has "the hallmarks of impressive refinement and precision", but even so risks being eclipsed by arguably "the biggest and most-in-depth wine list in the country". Service is "exceptional", in particular the "charming and knowledgeable sommelier", and "a well-spaced interior that ought be be very corporate is actually lovely and memorable". "The only downer is the eye-popping prices" but on practically all accounts they are worth it. / W1J 5NY; www.greenhouserestaurant.co.uk; @greenhouse27a; 10.30 pm; closed Sat L & Sun; booking max 12 may apply; set weekday L £45 (FP).

Greenwood SW1   NEW   £49
170 Victoria St   020 3058 1000   2–4B
Another new opening (alongside Aviary) for the ETM Group, this time in the Nova mega-development in Victoria – a split level venue with a sports lounge upstairs, all-day dining on the ground floor, and (possibly a first for us) an in-house barber and brow 'n' lashes bar for those can't-wait grooming needs. / SW1E 5LB; www.greenwoodlondon.com.

Gremio de Brixton, St Matthew's
Church SW2   £44   3|3|3
Effra Rd   020 7924 0660   11–2D
Fun, "friendly" tapas haunt in the atmospheric crypt under Brixton's St Matthew's Church, fuelled by cocktails and a decent wine selection; DJs at the weekend. / SW2 1JF; www.gremiodebrixton.com; @gremiobrixton; 10.30 pm, Sat 11 pm, Sun 10 pm.

The Grill at McQueen
EC2   £70   3|4|3
59-61 Tabernacle St   020 7036 9229   13–1A
All things Steve McQueen provide the theme for this comfortable and plushly decked out Shoreditch grill, which has "upped its game since a revamp last October", serving very decent steaks and "killer cocktails". Top Tip – BYO free on Tuesdays. / EC2A 4AA; www.thegrillmcqueen.co.uk; @TheGrillMcQueen; No shorts.

Ground Coffee Society
SW15 £30 **3** **4** **3**
79 Lower Richmond Rd 0845 862 9994 11–1B
"The coffee's fantastic" at this Antipodean
outfit, also with cakes and light bites, but even
in sedate Putney "there can be long queues" ("I
can no longer even get a table!"). / SW15 1ET;
www.groundcoffeesociety.com; @groundcoffeesociety; 6
pm; L only; no booking.

Guglee
£38 **3** **2** **2**
7 New College Pde, NW3
020 7722 8478 9–2A
279 West End Ln, NW6 020 7317 8555 1–1B
"Original", street food-influenced cooking wins
solid praise for this modern Indian duo in West
Hampstead and Swiss Cottage. / www.guglee.co.uk;
11 am.

The Guildford Arms
SE10 £51 **3** **4** **3**
55 Guildford Grove 020 8691 6293 1–3D
"A hidden gem we hope stays hidden" – this three-
storey Georgian pub in Greenwich offers "great
cooking and attentive but not intrusive service" in
the upstairs dining room. Chef-director Guy Awford
previously ran "the wonderful Inside" (RIP, long
considered "the best in Greenwich"). / SE10 8JY;
www.theguildfordarms.co.uk; @GuildfordArms_; 10 pm,
Sun 9 pm; closed Mon.

The Guinea Grill W1
£75 **4** **4** **4**
30 Bruton Pl 020 7409 1728 3–3B
"Suddenly fashionable despite its old school
ambience" – this "surprising" grill room, behind a
pub in a picturesque Mayfair mews, provides some
of London's best steaks and pies (albeit at "very
expensive" prices) in a well-preserved, traditional
setting. / W1J 6NL; www.theguinea.co.uk; @guineagrill;
closed Sat L & Sun; booking max 8 may apply.

Gul and Sepoy E1 NEW
65 Commercial St 020 7247 1407 13–2C
The latest Indian restaurant from Harneet and
Devina Baweja, the duo behind the flavoursome
Gunpowder and Madame D's (also located
on Commercial Street), arrives in the City in
October 2017. / E1 6BD; www.gulandsepoy.com; @
GulandSepoy.

The Gun E14
£65 **3** **3** **4**
27 Coldharbour 020 7515 5222 12–1C
This historic Docklands tavern has "a wonderful
atmosphere right on the Thames" and views directly
across the O2. "Long established as a riverside
gastropub", it serves "imaginative, distinctive food"
in the "classy dining room" or al fresco on a heated
terrace. / E14 9NS; www.thegundocklands.com;
@thegundocklands; 10 pm, Sun 7.30 pm.

Gunpowder E1
£44 **4** **3** **3**
11 Whites Row 020 7426 0542 13–2C
"Surprising" flavours help "put a great spin on
Indian food" at this "tiny" Spitalfields yearling, whose
"fantastic tapas-style dishes" seem "completely
authentic, based on family recipes". Top Tips –
"venison doughnut" and "wild rabbit pulao – a thing
of beauty". / E1 7NF; www.gunpowderlondon.com;
@gunpowder_ldn; 10.30 pm.

Gustoso Ristorante & Enoteca
SW1 £47 **3** **4** **3**
33 Willow Pl 020 7834 5778 2–4B
"Continuing to enchant…" – this "wonderful Italian"
is "a jolly place, really hidden away in Pimlico, but
with a very local feel to it as it's off-the-beaten-
track". Staff are "exceptionally friendly" and
"the food is good and doesn't cost an arm and a
leg" ("after a hiccough in recent times, it's had a
definite return to form"). "And they adore kids…
it's very Italian". / SW1P 1JH; ristorantegustoso.co.uk;
@GustosoRist; 10.30 pm, Fri & Sat 11 pm, Sun 9.30
pm.

GYMKHANA W1
£61 **4** **4** **4**
42 Albemarle St 020 3011 5900 3–3C
"Absolutely the bee's knees" – the Sethi family's
"classy" Mayfair five-year-old near the Ritz
remains London's best-known nouvelle Indian by
dint of mixing "terrifically-spiced" cuisine ("whose
refinement doesn't detract from powerful punchy
flavours") and "heroic wine pairings", with a
good pinch of "old-colonial glamour" ("very in
keeping with the India I grew up in"). There's
also a superb cocktail bar in the basement. Top
Tip – "goat brains are a must try!" / W1S 4JH;
www.gymkhanalondon.com; @GymkhanaLondon; 10.30
pm; closed Sun.

Haché
£38 **3** **4** **4**
95-97 High Holborn, WC1
020 7242 4580 2–1D NEW
329-331 Fulham Rd, SW10
020 7823 3515 6–3B
24 Inverness St, NW1 020 7485 9100 9–3B
37 Bedford Hill, SW12 020 8772 9772 11–2C
153 Clapham High St, SW4
020 7738 8760 11–2D
147-149 Curtain Rd, EC2
020 7739 8396 13–1B
Amongst the elite of the posh burger groups – this
"cheerful" small group "never lets you down" with
its "great variety" ("awesome by itself, or go mad
with the toppings"). and yummy sides (including
"the best sweet potato fries ever"). "And a focus on
quality enables them to serve the real thing" (it's
one of the few chains that will do burgers medium
rare). / www.hacheburgers.com; 10.30 pm, Fri-Sat 11
pm, Sun 10 pm; WC1 9 pm; WC1 Sat & Sun.

Hai Cenato SW1 🆕 **£55** 3️⃣3️⃣2️⃣
2 Sir Simon Milton Square, 150 Victoria St
020 3816 9320   2–4B
"Fantastic sourdough pizzas-with-a-twist" are the main event at Jason Atherton's much-heralded newcomer, and they "almost make up for the dreadful ambience of the soulless new Nova development". Overall, its ratings are middling though, and sceptics feel that "notwithstanding the well-presented food, Hai Cenato commits the crime of just not being very interesting". Maybe try the bar upstairs first. / SW1H 0HW; haicenato.co.uk; @haicenato; 10 pm, Sun 9.30 pm; booking max 6 may apply; set pre theatre £37 (FP).

Hakkasan **£96** 3️⃣2️⃣4️⃣
17 Bruton St, W1   020 7907 1888   3–2C
8 Hanway Pl, W1   020 7927 7000   5–1A
"Fast paced, seductive, club-like" – these "wonderfully vibey" operations may be "so busy and very noisy" but have founded a global brand on the strength of their "feel-good" ambience and "brilliantly executed Chinese/pan-Asian cuisine". However, even some fans concede that they can also seem "hideously expensive" and "brusque" service ("we were kept waiting, only then to be hassled to order or risk being kicked off the table at the end or our 2-hour slot") is a perennial gripe. Top Tip – "Their Dim Sum Sunday is exquisite". / www.hakkasan.com; 12.30 am, Sun 11.15 pm; W1 12.30 am, Thu-Sat 12.45 am, Sun midnight; no trainers, no sportswear.

Ham Yard Restaurant, Ham Yard Hotel W1 **£67** 2️⃣3️⃣5️⃣
1 Ham Yd   020 3642 1007   4–3D
"Sit outside in the quiet courtyard and enjoy a civilised lunch away from the bustle of Soho" at this "lovely" Firmdale hotel ("the set deal is fab value"), which provides an amazingly tranquil "haven" for the West End, and particularly comes into its own for a "fun, delicious and affordable" afternoon tea. In the evenings (including pre-theatre) feedback is less positive, with accusations of "style with no substance" ("very beautiful, but nothing that earnt the price demanded"). / W1D 7DT; www.firmdalehotels.com; @Ham_Yard; 11.30 pm, Sun 10.30 pm; set pre theatre £43 (FP).

The Hampshire Hog W6 **£51** 3️⃣2️⃣4️⃣
227 King St   020 8748 3391   8–2B
Unusually attractive, "always busy" gastropub, on a grotty bit of highway near Hammersmith Town Hall, which also benefits from a large garden. It inspired the odd critique this year, but overall is well-rated for its decent level of cooking. / W6 9JT; www.thehampshirehog.com; @TheHampshireHog; 10 pm, Sun 4 pm; closed Sun D.

Hanger SW6 **£50** 3️⃣4️⃣3️⃣
461-465 North End Rd   020 7386 9739   6–4A
"A great steak formula – specialising in this undervalued cut of beef, cooked rare with triple-cooked chips, plus a glass of Malbec – for under £30 its a steal!" Top Tip – 'bottomless' basement brunch. / SW6 1NZ; www.hangersteak.co.uk; @hanger_sw6; 10 pm, Sun 9 pm.

The Harcourt W1 **£58** 4️⃣3️⃣4️⃣
32 Harcourt St   020 3771 8660   7–1D
"Only a gastropub by dint of its decor, as the cuisine is restaurant quality" – this excellent Marylebone yearling provides "terrific Scandi food" and while the cooking is distinctive "it makes a welcome change from over-inventive eclectic menus you see elsewhere". One gripe – "the music can be deafening!" / W1H 4HX; www.theharcourt.com; @the_harcourt; 11 pm, Fri & Sat 11.30 pm, Sun 10 pm.

Hard Rock Café W1 **£64** 3️⃣3️⃣4️⃣
150 Old Park Ln   020 7514 1700   3–4B
Drugs and nuclear weapons are still forbidden (as they have been since 1971) at this aging rocker, near Hyde Park Corner – the cradle of the global franchise – where the noise level and queue still show no sign of abating. Perhaps surprisingly the burgers here are pretty decent – "huge and a real mouthful". / W1K 1QZ; www.hardrock.com/london; @HardRockLondon; 12.30 am, Fri & Sat 1 am, Sun 10.30 pm; May need 20+ to book.

Hardy's Brasserie W1 **£59** 3️⃣3️⃣3️⃣
53 Dorset St   020 7935 5929   2–1A
"I go there whenever I'm in the neighbourhood – I love it!" – this old-school, independent wine bar and brasserie is tucked away in Marylebone, and though it's never going to set the world on fire its welcoming charm and modest prices maintain a loyal fan club. / W1U 7NH; www.hardysbrasserie.com; @hardys_W1; 10 pm; closed Sat & Sun.

Hare & Tortoise **£42** 3️⃣2️⃣2️⃣
11-13 The Brunswick, WC1
020 7278 9799   2–1D
373 Kensington High St, W14
020 7603 8887   8–1D
156 Chiswick High Rd, W4
020 8747 5966   8–2A
38 Haven Grn, W5   020 8810 7066   1–2A
296-298 Upper Richmond Rd, SW15
020 8394 7666   11–2B
90 New Bridge St, EC4   020 7651 0266   10–2A
"A regular when the fridge is empty" – this "casual" pan-Asian chain is a "cheap 'n' cheerful" staple thanks to its "diverse range of dishes from quality, fresh ingredients" and "buzzy" ("loud") atmosphere. Ratings slipped a little this year though on a couple of disappointing reports. /

www.hareandtortoise-restaurants.co.uk; 11 pm; EC4 10.30, Fri 11 pm; EC4 closed Sun;W14 no bookings.

Harry Morgan's NW8 £43 2️⃣2️⃣2️⃣
29-31 St John's Wood High St
020 7722 1869 9–3A
This "friendly and cheerful" kosher institution in St John's Wood keeps its many fans happy with Jewish deli classics, including "chicken soup just like Mum used to make", latkes and salt beef. Perennially there are gripes however that it's "going downhill". / NW8 7NH; www.harryms.co.uk; @morgan_hm; 10 pm.

Harwood Arms SW6 £68 4️⃣3️⃣3️⃣
Walham Grove 020 7386 1847 6–3A
"Worth a taxi-ride from central London!" – this "good old-fashioned pub" in a quiet Fulham backstreet has won renown (including from the tyre men) for its "adventurous" British cooking, particularly of game (culinary oversight comes from Brett Graham of The Ledbury and Mike Robinson of Berkshire's Pot Kiln). Top Tip "go for the venison and try one of the Scotch eggs". / SW6 1QP; www.harwoodarms.com; 9.30 pm, Sun 9 pm; closed Mon L; credit card required to book.

Hashi SW20 £37 3️⃣4️⃣2️⃣
54 Durham Rd 020 8944 1888 11–2A
This "reliable and friendly local Korean/Japanese" joint in suburban Raynes Park is "a gem, despite the look from outside", delivering "really good sushi and other Japanese fare", and "good value for money". Top Tip – option to BYO £4 corkage. / SW20 0TW; 10.30 pm; closed Mon; No Amex.

Hatchetts W1 £56 2️⃣3️⃣2️⃣
5 White Horse St 020 7409 0567 3–4B
Set over two floors near lovely Shepherd Market, this year-old bar/restaurant with regular live music still only generates limited feedback, but even those who feel it draws "an uninspiring crowd" rate it well for its "great food and great value". / W1J 7LQ; www.hatchetts.london; @hatchettslondon; 10 pm; set weekday L £35 (FP).

The Havelock Tavern W14 £51 3️⃣2️⃣3️⃣
57 Masbro Rd 020 7603 5374 8–1C
"One of the top gastropubs around" – this backstreet Olympia hotspot is "past its best" according to some age old aficionados, but "the crowds don't seem to have noticed" as its "buzzing every evening and for Sunday lunch"; "steak is a highlight" of an "interesting" menu. / W14 0LS; www.havelocktavern.com; @HavelockTavern; 10 pm, Sun 9.30 pm.

Haven Bistro N20 £49 2️⃣3️⃣2️⃣
1363 High Rd 020 8445 7419 1–1B
Fans of this Whetstone "oasis" vaunt it for its "well presented and interesting food" and say "there's nowhere like it in the area". Sceptics though say

it's over popular: "the grub's not bad, but it suffers from a lack of local competition". / N20 9LN; www.haven-bistro.co.uk; 10.30 pm, Sun 10 pm; No shorts.

Hawksmoor £79 3️⃣3️⃣3️⃣
5a Air St,W1 020 7406 3980 4–4C
11 Langley St,WC2 020 7420 9390 5–2C
3 Yeoman's Row, SW3 020 7590 9290 6–2C
16 Winchester Walk, SE1
020 7234 9940 10–4C **NEW**
157 Commercial St, E1 020 7426 4850 13–2B
10-12 Basinghall St, EC2
020 7397 8120 10–2C
Huw Gott and Will Beckett's zeitgeisty steakhouse chain still hits just the right vibe for many savvy Londoners with their "casual but professional" service of "sublime" British-bred meat and "superb" cocktails, and for cooler business-types in particular "they never fail to impress". Some "whopping price tags" give rise to complaints, but even though ratings have ebbed a little over the years with the roll-out of branch after branch (the latest in spring 2017 was a new "hipster" branch near Borough Market) the brand's legions of fans remain very loyal: "It costs an arm and a leg, but you can rest assured that the arm and leg will be perfectly cooked!" / www.thehawksmoor; 10.30 pm;W1 & WC2 Fri & Sat 11 pm, Sun 9pm-10 pm; EC2 closed Sat & Sun; SRA-Food Made Good – 2 stars.

Haz £45 2️⃣2️⃣2️⃣
9 Cutler St, E1 020 7929 7923 10–2D
34 Foster Ln, EC2 020 7600 4172 10–2B
64 Bishopsgate, EC2
020 7628 4522 10–2D **NEW**
112 Houndsditch, EC3 020 7623 8180 10–2D
6 Mincing Ln, EC3 020 7929 3173 10–2D
"Still a decent option in the City" for a cheapo bite – these "functional" Turkish operations offer "tasty grills" and "a wide selection of mezze". They are "aimed at the business crowd and perhaps tourists" – particularly the "lovely, large venue at St Paul's". / www.hazrestaurant.co.uk; 11.30 pm; EC3 closed Sun.

Heddon Street Kitchen W1 £62 1️⃣1️⃣2️⃣
3-9 Heddon St 020 7592 1212 4–3B
It's potentially a "lovely big space" just off Regent Street, but Gordon Ramsay's West End operation is another one of his very own Kitchen Nightmares. There are fans for whom it's "quick, cheerful, buzzy and does what it sets out to do", but there are also too many critics who say to "avoid at all costs": "it feels like a conveyor belt", with "indifferent and chaotic service" and "laughably bad food". / W1B 4BE; www.gordonramsayrestaurants.com/heddon-street-kitc; @heddonstkitchen; 11 pm, Sun 9 pm; set pre theatre £41 (FP).

Hedone W4 £118 **3** **3** **2**
301-303 Chiswick High Rd
020 8747 0377 8–2A
"You either 'get' this restaurant or you don't",
and views on Mikael Jonsson's "innocuous" and
"homely"-looking Chiswick project remain somewhat
divided. For a strong majority, "the best ingredients
in the UK, coupled with sophisticated cooking
technique" provides a "thought-provoking" and
"most exciting" tasting menu experience that's
"just about perfect... not too heavy, not too showy,
very well balanced, surprising… from a master
just riffing in his open kitchen and passing you
something like he's just thought it up, which always
tastes great". Ratings are undercut however, by a
vociferous minority, who just "don't see it", or who
feel a meal is "30-50% overpriced". / W4 4HH;
www.hedonerestaurant.com; @HedoneLondon; 9.30
pm; closed Mon, Tue L, Wed L & Sun; booking max 7
may apply; set weekday L £73 (FP).

Heirloom N8 £53 **3** **3** **3**
35 Park Rd 020 8348 3565 9–1C
"Love the ethos! (as much produce as possible from
their own farm in Bucks) and the cooking lives up to
it", say fans of this field-to-fork operation, in Crouch
End. / N8 8TE; www.heirloomn8.co.uk; @HeirloomN8;
11 pm, Sun 7 pm.

**Hélène Darroze, The Connaught
Hotel W1** £136 **3** **4** **4**
Carlos Pl 020 3147 7200 3–3B
With its "laser-like precision", Hélène Darroze's
Gallic cuisine is "simply stunning" in this plush
and "stylish" Mayfair chamber, whose "perfectly
attentive" service adds a lot to the experience.
Just one gripe – it's "unbelievably expensive"
– but fans say "those who complain about
the prices are missing the point!" / W1K 2AL;
www.the-connaught.co.uk; @TheConnaught; 10 pm,
Sun 9 pm; closed Mon & Sun; No trainers; set weekday
L £87 (FP).

Heliot Steak House WC2 £64 **4** **4** **4**
Cranbourn St 020 7769 8844 5–3B
For a surprisingly high quality steak at a very good
price, check out this glitzily glam' grill – in the
circle of the original theatre – which nowadays has
a birds-eye view over the gambling tables of the
UK's biggest casino (right over Leicester Square
tube). Top Tip – great 2-course, pre-theatre deal at
£14.95. / WC2H 7AJ; www.hippodromecasino.com;
@HippodromeLDN; midnight, Sat 1 am, Sun 11 pm; set
pre theatre £37 (FP).

Henrietta WC2 **NEW**
Henrietta St 020 3794 5314 5–3C
This late spring 2017 dining room opening from
the Experimental Group (who own this plush, new
hotel – sibling to Grand Pigalle in Paris) is most
notable for the consultancy of Ollie Dabbous in the

kitchen. It opened too late for survey feedback on
his trademark exotic small plates – press reviews
report the odd miss, but mostly hits. / WC2E 8NA;
www.henriettahotel.com.

Hereford Road W2 £48 **4** **4** **3**
3 Hereford Rd 020 7727 1144 7–1B
Chef/Patron Tom Pemberton's "hearty, fresh,
seasonal British cooking" is "very reasonably priced
for London" and maintains his "elegant and low key"
Bayswater venture as "a fabulous neighbourhood
restaurant" (but one which draws fans from across
town). Top Tip – "the good value lunch menu, which
cuts no corners". / W2 4AB; www.herefordroad.org;
@3HerefordRoad; 10.30 pm, Sun 10 pm.

High Road Brasserie W4 £59 **2** **2** **2**
162-166 Chiswick High Rd
020 8742 7474 8–2A
Fans of this slightly self-conscious all-day hang-out
in Chiswick (part of a boutique hotel in the Soho
House group) laud it as a "handy local", especially
for a see-and-be-seen brunch on its prominent
terrace, but it's always seemed a bit "pretentious
and overpriced for food that's nothing special". / W4
1PR; highroadbrasserie.co.uk; @HRBrasserie; 11 pm, Fri
& Sat midnight, Sun 10 pm; booking max 8 may apply;
set weekday L £34 (FP).

High Timber EC4 £68 **3** **5** **3**
8 High Timber St 020 7248 1777 10–3B
This "relaxed" "wine-dining" spot beside the Wobbly
Bridge is an "oasis of joy in the City", with a
"fantastic view of the Thames" and across the river
to Tate Modern. A "big part of the fun" is "the ability
to mooch around the wine cellar and cheese room"
(the "excellent wine list" has a focus on South Africa,
thanks to the ownership by a Stellenbosch vineyard).
/ EC4V 3PA; www.hightimber.com; @HTimber; 10 pm;
closed Sat & Sun; set weekday L £43 (FP).

Hill & Szrok E8 £55 **4** **4** **4**
60 Broadway Mkt 0207 254 8805 14–2B
Very positive all-round, if limited feedback this year
on this vibey Broadway Market butchers, which
transforms at night into a counter-style diner,
selling grills, with a small number of sides, plus
a small but high quality array of wines. / E8 4QJ;
www.hillandszrok.co.uk; @hillandszrok; Mon - Sat
11pm, Sun 9pm; No Amex; no booking.

Hilliard EC4 £25 **4** **4** **4**
26a Tudor St 020 7353 8150 10–3A
"Sandwiches above the usual cut" and "especially
good salads and tarts (savoury as well as sweet)"
meet the brief at this "well executed" coffeehouse,
ensuring it is always "full of lawyers from the local
legal scene". / EC4Y 0AY; www.hilliardfood.co.uk;
@hilliardcafe; 5.30 pm; L only, closed Sat & Sun; no
booking.

Hispania EC3 £66 3 2 2
72-74 Lombard St   020 7621 0338   10–3D
This Spanish two-year-old, over two floors right opposite the Bank of England, "caters for all types of business wining and dining", "be it private dining, a formal meal, tapas or bar snacks over wine". It's "just informal enough to feel relaxed", but it can get very busy. / EC3V 9AY; www.hispanialondon.com; @hispanialondon; 10pm, Mon 9.30 pm; closed Sat & Sun.

Hix W1 £64 1 2 3
66-70 Brewer St   020 7292 3518   4–3C
Mark Hix's flagship Soho venture inspires limited feedback nowadays, and continues to disappoint as much as it delights, although "it's not so much bad as underwhelming". Top Tip – "there's a great buzz about the basement bar". / W1F 9UP; www.hixrestaurants.co.uk/restaurant/hix-soho/; @HixRestaurants; 11.30 pm, Sun 10.30 pm.

Hix Oyster & Chop House EC1 £62 2 2 2
36-37 Greenhill Rents, Cowcross St
020 7017 1930   10–1A
Mark Hix's original solo operation, near Smithfield, excels at "the simple things" – specifically "everyday and special-occasion steaks (sometimes with a Hixian twist)". On the debit side, "some of the specials don't work too well", "the waiting staff are pleasant but inefficient", and it's a bit "pricey". / EC1M 6BN; www.hixrestaurants.co.uk/restaurant/hix-oyster-cho; @hixchophouse; 11 pm, Sun 9 pm; closed Sat L; set pre theatre £38 (FP).

HKK EC2 £74 5 5 3
88 Worship St, Broadgate Quarter
020 3535 1888   13–2B
"Probably the best Chinese food in London" (not least "the best Peking Duck this side of Beijing") inspires a hymn of praise to this "calm and relaxed" Hakkasan-cousin, north of Liverpool Street. Despite some "whopping" prices, no quibbles are raised – "it's just fantastic". Top Tip – "the amazing and excellent value Duck and Bubbles lunch". / EC2A 2BE; www.hkklondon.com; @HKKlondon; 10 pm; closed Sun.

Hoi Polloi, Ace Hotel E1 £62 3 2 3
100 Shoreditch High St   020 8880 6100   13–1B
For the "best brunch my miles..", fans tip this trendy hangout in a hip Shoreditch hotel, also a useful all-day option hereabouts (including for afternoon tea). / E1 6JQ; hoi-polloi.co.uk; @wearehoipolloi; midnight, Thu-Sat 1 am.

Holborn Dining Room WC1 £70 3 3 4
252 High Holborn   020 3747 8633   2–1D
This "lovely, grand dining room" on the edge of the City is designed to impress, and provides "a great buzz", and "classic staple dishes" to a largely business clientele, including first thing when it's "an excellent breakfast venue". Sartorially speaking, views divide on the "amusing trousers" which are standard issue for the waiting staff. STOP PRESS: In autumn 2017 a dedicated pie hatch is due to open. / WC1V 7EN; www.holborndiningroom.com; @HolbornDining; 11.15 pm, Sun 10.15 pm; set pre theatre £46 (FP).

Homeslice £34 4 4 4
52 Wells St, W1   020 3151 7488   2–1B
13 Neal's Yd, WC2   020 7836 4604   5–2C
Television Centre, W12 awaiting tel 8–1C **NEW**
374-378 Old St, EC1   020 3151 1121   13–1B
Bloomberg Arcade, Queen Victoria St, EC4 awaiting tel 10–2C **NEW**
"Excellent, enormous pizzas with a decent variety of toppings" wins a major fanbase for these buzzy and cheery pit stops. "It's quick and dirty with paper plates and plastic cutlery – lingering is not encouraged". (Fascinating fact: it's owned by the late Terry Wogan's sons!) / www.homeslicepizza.co.uk; 11 pm, EC1 & W1 Sun 10 pm; no booking.

Honest Burgers £28 3 3 3
"The best and most distinctive of the upmarket burger chains": they "dare to serve them medium-rare as standard", alongside those "deliciously moreish rosemary fries, which deserve mention as a stand out simple side"; all this plus "warm and welcoming staff and a cool vibe"… "what more can a girl want?" / www.honestburgers.co.uk; 10 pm-11 pm; SW9 closed Mon D; EC3 closed Sat & Sun; no booking.

Honey & Co W1 £46 3 3 2
25a Warren St   020 7388 6175   2–1B
"Food straight from the streets and markets of the Middle East" – "absolutely divine, regularly changing Israeli-inspired recipes with surprising twists on very simple dishes" (and, in particular, marvellous cakes) – has won impressive fame for this "delightfully friendly" Warren Street "hideaway". Even some fans now admit however that "it's on the expensive side considering that it's more of a café than a restaurant" (and a mightily "cramped" one at that). Top Tip – "the breakfast mezze is enough for the whole day". / W1T 5JZ; www.honeyandco.co.uk; @Honeyandco; 10.30 pm; closed Sun; No Amex.

Honey & Smoke W1 **NEW** £49 5 4 2
216 Great Portland St   020 7388 6175   2–1B
"Whoa, brilliant!" – "Honey & Co's bigger sibling" opened to rightful acclaim in late 2016, south of Great Portland Street tube. A modern take on a Middle Eastern grill house, it serves a "seemingly endless array" of "spectacular but completely honest" mezze ("you rediscover dishes you thought you knew like hummus or falafel, and you marvel at simple raw veg which feels re-invented"). On the

downside, the site is "a bit lacking in ambience", but given its "upbeat" and "enthusiastic" staff most reporters don't quibble . Top Menu Tip – "I'd run a marathon just for the cheesecake!" / W1W 5QW; www.honeyandco.co.uk/smoke; @Honeyandco; 11.30 pm; closed Mon & Sun.

Hood SW2 **£50** 4 3 2
67 Streatham Hill   020 3601 3320   11–2D
"A great find in the heart of Streatham", this "fantastic" two-year-old bases its "regularly changing" menu around "locally sourced produce and fabulous English wine", with "increasingly exciting flavours" as the kitchen develops. "We went as a family of 11 and sampled most of the menu between us – we were all thrilled!" / SW2 4TX; www.hoodrestaurants.com; @HoodStreatham; 11 pm.

Hoppers **£49** 5 4 3
49 Frith St, W1   no tel   5–2A
77 Wigmore St, W1
020 3319 8110   3–1A **NEW**
"I went over 15 times last year. I can't get enough!" The Sethi family's "tiny", "fun" Soho two-year-old punches well above its weight with its "ultra-tasty" Sri Lankan and Tamil street food – "perfectly spiced bites" (majoring in rice pancake 'hoppers') that "burst with flavour and texture" ("I was born in Sri Lanka, and this place is pretty authentic"). Given the no-bookings policy, "it's a disaster to get into, but damn it, it's worth it!" In mid-September 2017, they opened a much-anticipated spin-off in Marylebone which, thankfully, does take bookings..

The Horseshoe NW3 **£53** 3 3 4
28 Heath St   020 7431 7206   9–2A
This atmospheric gastro-boozer is "rather more buzzy than most Hampstead restaurants or pubs". The menu comprises Mediterranean-influenced classics, while the bar stocks the entire range of the Camden Town Brewery – founded on-site before moving down the road. / NW3 6TE; www.thehorseshoehampstead.com; @TheHorseShoeCTB; 10 pm, Fri & Sat 10.30pm, Sun 9.30 pm.

Hot Pot W1 **NEW** **£39**
Wardour St   020 7287 8881   4–2D
Authentic communal Asian dining comes to Chinatown, thanks to Taechaubol Group, owners of 148 hot pot or 'huo guo' restaurants in Bangkok; the new, two-floor, 148-seat Wardour Street branch is the upmarket version, using British free-range ingredients where possible. / W1F 8ZP; www.hotpotrestaurants.co.uk; @HotPotLondon_; 12.30 am, Sat 1.30 am, Sun midnight.

Hot Stuff SW8 **£23** 3 5 3
19-23 Wilcox Rd   020 7720 1480   11–1D
"You're treated as a friend" at this "old favourite" curry house in the 'Little Portugal' stretch near

Vauxhall (immortalised in the film, My Beautiful Laundrette). It's been scoring well for its "really well spiced fresh food" for years; and the "terrific value" is increased if you BYO. / SW8 2XA; www.welovehotstuff.com; 10 pm; closed Mon; No Amex.

The Hour Glass SW3 **£53** 3 4 2
279-283 Brompton Rd   020 7581 2497   6–2C
"Top-quality bar dishes" and "efficient young staff" inspire warm vibes for this "bright and cheerful old pub" in South Ken, run for the past year by the duo behind Brompton Food Market. / SW3 2DY; hourglasspub.co.uk; @TheHourGlassSK; 10 pm, Sun 4 pm; closed Sun D.

House of Ho W1 **£60** 3 3 3
1 Percy St   020 7323 9130   2–1C
This modern Vietnamese/Japanese mashup occupies the decadent and vibey Fitzrovia townhouse vacated by Bam-Bou (RIP), and though feedback is still quite limited, its enthusiastic small fanclub says it's beginning to live up both to its predecessor and to the extensive hype at launch. Top Tip – "Saturday bottomless brunch, with a high-end Vietnamese twist". / W1T 1DB; www.houseofho.co.uk; @HouseOfHo; 11 pm.

House Restaurant, National Theatre SE1 **£52** 2 3 2
National Theatre, South Bank
020 7452 3600   2–3D
"Useful before or after a performance", the National Theatre's in-house venue is a bit of a "glorified cafeteria" but benefits from "quick and efficient service", which means "you're out in time for the show without being rushed or pushed to the wire". The food perhaps does rely on its "captive audience", but most feel it's "a good option". / SE1 9PX; house.nationaltheatre.org.uk; @NT_House; 11 pm; D only (L served on matinee days), closed Sun.

Hubbard & Bell, Hoxton Hotel WC1 **£57** 3 2 3
199-206 High Holborn   020 7661 3030   2–1D
"Dude food plus" ("great pancakes"; "classic burgers") and "a very cool vibe" win a food thumbs up for this "canteen-type eatery in a trendy and expensive hotel" (from Soho House) which despite its name is actually in Holborn. "Whatever your thoughts on the clientele, which can make it feel a bit dystopian and/or like an Apple advert, the food is really rather good". / WC1V 7BD; www.hubbardandbell.com; @HubbardandBell; midnight, Sun 11 pm.

Humble Grape **£49** 3 4 4
Theberton St, N1   020 3904 4480   9–3D **NEW**
2 Battersea Rise, SW11
020 3620 2202   11–2C
1 Saint Bride's Passage, EC4
020 7583 0688   10–2A

A "great selection of interesting small-batch wines" is served by the glass, bottle or case at this popular yearling – an offshoot of a Battersea wine bar in the lovely crypt of St Bride's, Fleet Street (with a new Islington branch, which opened in summer 2017). "The simple food and platters complement the vino nicely". Top Tip – "go on a Monday, and you can drink at retail prices". / www.humblegrape.co.uk.

Hunan SW1　　　　　**£93**　⑤②①
51 Pimlico Rd　020 7730 5712　6–2D
"The food keeps on coming until you stay 'stop'!" – "a seemingly never-ending stream of perfectly judged dishes" – at this Pimlico veteran, where "Mr Peng decides what you'll eat, and my goodness he is right!" It's "Russian roulette but fantastic if you're not a fussy eater" and regularly scores as "the best Chinese in London (if not the planet)". The room itself is "slightly odd" and "minor language problems" can impede the service, but overall it's "a genius way to have a social meal". "The wine list is pretty amazing too!" – "thoughtfully matched, with lots of Germanic and other aromatic whites, including a number of excellent mature Rieslings". / SW1W 8NE; www.hunanlondon.com; 11 pm; closed Sun; set weekday L £66 (FP).

Hush　　　　　　　**£81**　②②❸
8 Lancashire Ct, W1　020 7659 1500　3–2B
95-97 High Holborn, WC1
020 7242 4580　2–1D
A "magical location" (a cute courtyard just off Bond Street) creates "a little oasis in the middle of the London mêlée" for this all-day Mayfair brasserie, which – "refreshed after a recent refurb" – is "great for business or fun in the West End". But the setting outstrips the food, with reports on the latter ranging from "first class" to merely "average". Limited feedback on its handily-located sibling, by Holborn tube. / www.hush.co.uk; W1 11 pm, Sat 10 pm, Sun 9 pm; WC1 11 pm; WC1 closed Sun.

Hutong, The Shard SE1　**£88**　①②⑤
31 St Thomas St　020 3011 1257　10–4C
"Try to get a window seat at dusk and watch the sun go down over London: it's magic", at this "lush" and "romantic" 33rd floor eyrie. It helps to be starry eyed though – "you don't go for the Chinese food", which critics feel come at utterly "outrageous" prices for such an "ordinary" standard ("I've had better at M&S!"), nor the "patchy" and "brusque" service. STOP PRESS: in July 2017 Sifu Fei Wang was appointed as the new head chef – perhaps he can at last take the cooking here to real heights… / SE1 9RY; www.hutong.co.uk; @HutongShard; 10 pm; No shorts; set weekday L £62 (FP).

Iberia N1　　　　　　**£36**　❸❸②
294-296 Caledonian Rd
020 7700 7750　9–2D
The 'Iberia' in question is Georgia not Spain (who

knew!), and this simply decorated Islingtonian is a low key but pleasant way to discover a cuisine that's "quite a cultural melting pot and not as heavy as might be feared". / N1 1BA; www.iberiarestaurant.co.uk; 11 pm, Sun 9 pm; closed Mon, Tue-Fri D only, Sat & Sun open L & D.

Ibérica　　　　　　　**£53**　②②❸
Zig Zag Building, 70 Victoria St, SW1
020 7636 8650　2–4B
195 Great Portland St, W1
020 7636 8650　2–1B
12 Cabot Sq, E14　020 7636 8650　12–1C
89 Turnmill St, EC1　020 7636 8650　10–1A
"I don't know if they're really all that special, but they're terrifically enjoyable" – so say fans of these "vibrant", contemporary Spanish operations, whose City and Canary Wharf branches are "good for business". / 11pm, SW1 Sun 10.30 pm; W1 closed Sun D.

Ikoyi SW1　🆕
1 St James's Market　020 3583 4660　4–4D
West African-influenced cuisine – a modern take on traditional Nigerian, Ghanaian and Senegalese flavours, without particular reference to indigenous dishes – comes to St James's, thanks to (Canadian-Chinese) chef Jeremy Chan (who has previously worked at Dinner by Heston Blumenthal, Noma and Hibiscus) and native Nigerian, Iré Hassan-Odukale (born in Ikoyi, Lagos's most affluent suburb). The venture – part of the extensive redevelopment of St James's Market, and by far London's swankiest African-inspired venture to-date – follows a successful pop-up career (including at Carousel). / SW1Y 4AH; www.ikoyilondon.com.

Il Guscio N5　　　　　**£50**　❸④❸
231 Blackstock Rd　020 7354 1400　9–1D
"We're lucky to have such a great local!" – so say fans of this "courteous", three-year-old Highbury haunt. "The interior is a little cramped, but all their authentic Sardinian food is excellent (pizza is particularly good)". / N5 2LL; www.ilgusciohighbury.co.uk; 10.30 pm, Fri & Sat 11 pm.

India Club, Strand Continental Hotel WC2　　　　**£28**　②②①
143 Strand　020 7836 4880　2–2D
This veteran near the Indian High Commission in the Strand "has been around for more than 50 years" and "hardly changes". "So basic it's almost a parody", it is reached via an "unappealing entrance and up two flights of stairs", but "very good value and authentic" scoff still justifies the trip. "A miracle it has survived in redeveloping London – if it ever goes, we will miss it!". BYO, or buy beer from the hotel bar. STOP PRESS: Redevelopment is now threatened here with news that the lease is expiring in 2019, and plans to modernise the site have been submitted. Join the online petition to save the

place! / WC2R IJA; www.strand-continental.co.uk;
@hostelstrandcon; 10.50 pm; Cash only; booking max
6 may apply.

Indian Accent W1 NEW
16 Albemarle St awaiting tel 3–3C
On the former site of Chor Bizarre (RIP, but from
the same owner, Old World Hospitality) – another
nouvelle Indian restaurant with sibling venues in
New York and New Delhi. The New Delhi original
is on the World's 50 Best List. / W1S 4HW;
www.indianaccent.com/indianaccent/london/; @
indianaccentlon.

Indian Moment SW11   £42   3 3 2
47 Northcote Rd   020 7223 6575   /
020 7223 1818   11–2C
The "delicious and varied menu" at this "friendly"
Indian, on the 'Nappy Valley' main drag near
Clapham Junction station, means "you can always
find something you want, whatever your mood"
(and it's "not designed to blow your head off"
either). / SW11 1NZ; www.indianmoment.co.uk;
@indianmoment; 11.30 pm, Fri & Sat midnight.

Indian Ocean SW17   £36   3 3 2
214 Trinity Rd   020 8672 7740   11–2C
"Unusual spicing takes the food a cut above the
average", according to the big local fanclub of this
"old-school Indian" near Wandsworth Common,
which is "reliable, friendly and great value". / SW17
7HP; www.indianoceanrestaurant.com; 11.30 pm, Sat
11.45 pm, Sun 11 pm.

Indian Rasoi N2   £36   3 3 2
7 Denmark Terrace   020 8883 9093   1–1B
This "tiny local Indian" in Muswell Hill specialises in
Mughal-era cuisine, producing "unusual dishes, that
are always delicious". "Looks like nothing from the
outside, but don't be fooled – it's great". / N2 9HG;
www.indian-rasoi.co.uk; 10.30 pm; No Amex.

Indian Zing W6   £53   4 4 2
236 King St   020 8748 5959   8–2B
"It's well worth the tube ride" to Manoj Vasaikar's
well-known, "wonderful" little Indian, a short
walk from Ravenscourt Park. "It's still right up
there as one of the best Indians in West London"
with "consistently superb", "non-mainstream"
cuisine all "at a reasonable price point", delivered
by "willing and thoughtful staff". / W6 0RS;
www.indian-zing.co.uk; @IndianZing; 11 pm, Sun 10
pm.

Indigo, One Aldwych
WC2   £65   3 4 3
1 Aldwych   020 7300 0400   2–2D
This hotel mezzanine boasts a "brilliantly
convenient" West End location – "get a table
overlooking the Lobby Bar for atmosphere and fun"
– and "makes a great place for meetings" of many

kinds. "It's especially a joy to be able to take people
who are coeliac or can't eat dairy to a decent
restaurant" – the "clever" menu is entirely dairy-free
and gluten-free. / WC2B 4BZ; www.onealdwych.com;
@OneAldwych; 10.15 pm.

Ippudo London   £43   3 2 2
1 Crossrail Pl, E14   020 3326 9485   12–1C
"Decent ramen and one of the better food options
on the Wharf" – twin selling points of this global,
Japan-based noodle outfit (whose unit in WC2's
Central St Giles Piazza doesn't incite any feedback).
/ WC2 10.30 pm; E14 9.30 pm, Sun 8.30 pm; no
bookings.

Isabel W1 NEW
26 Albemarle St   020 3096 9292   3–3C
On the Mayfair site that was Sumosan (RIP), Juan
Santa Cruz opened this sibling to Notting Hill's
eurotrash favourite, Casa Cruz in late spring 2017.
It serves a long, modern Mediterranean menu of
meat and fish plates plus accompaniments in very
glam surroundings, all day from breakfast to late
night. / W1S 4HQ; isabelw1.london.

Isarn N1   £46   4 4 2
119 Upper St   020 7424 5153   9–3D
The "pretty authentic food" and attentive staff
win consistent praise for this Islington fixture. The
"modern decor is a cut above the normal high street
Thai", making the best of what could be a tricky
narrow space. / N1 1QP; www.isarn.co.uk; 11 pm, Sat
& Sun 10 pm.

Ishtar W1   £51   3 4 2
10-12 Crawford St   020 7224 2446   2–1A
"Excellent Anatolian food – a level above the
usual local Turkish" – has won this Marylebone
fixture "a big local following". Top Tip – "the
fixed-price set lunch and early evening dinner is
unbeatable for quality and value". / W1U 6AZ;
www.ishtarrestaurant.com; 11.30 pm, Sun 10.30 pm;
set weekday L £29 (FP).

The Ivy WC2   £69   3 4 5
1-5 West St   020 7836 4751   5–3B
"When you step through the doors, it's reassuring
to know you'll be well-fed and treated like a king"
at Richard Caring's "sophisticated" Theatreland
legend, whose revamp a year ago stemmed years
of decline, and where "so long as you don't expect
to be challenged by the grown-up comfort food, the
old favourite dishes don't disappoint". True, the celeb
crowd primarily frequent the neighbouring Ivy Club
nowadays, and true, it's no longer in the survey's Top
40 Most Mentioned restaurants, and true, this is
now the flagship for a fast-expanding chain of spin-
offs, so it's no surprise a few reporters now dismiss
it as "just a chain restaurant for out-of-towners",
but actually catty comments are most notable
by their absence. / WC2H 9NQ; www.the-ivy.co.uk;

FSA

@TheIvyWestSt; 11.30pm, Thu-Sat midnight, Sun 10.30 pm; No shorts; booking max 6 may apply.

The Ivy Café £57 1️⃣2️⃣3️⃣
96 Marylebone Ln, W1   020 3301 0400   2–1A
120 St John's Wood High St, NW8
020 3096 9444   9–3A
75 High St, SW19   020 3096 9333   11–2B
9 Hill St, TW9   020 3146 7733   1–4A NEW
Bistro fare that's "deeply average at best",
particularly at the newest St John's Wood branch (on
the site of Megan's, RIP) of these still-young spin-offs
from the legendary original – plus "snobbish and
unhelpful service" – do not bode well for Richard
Caring's rapid roll-out of (ie shameless cashing-in
on) this celebrated brand, of which these The 'Ivy
Cafés' are the sub-sub-brand (compared with the
slightly more upmarket sub-brand 'The Ivy Grills &
Brasseries'). The West End outlets are better, and
fans do say their atmosphere generally "lifts them
out of the ordinary", but "with this caché surely they
can afford better chefs?" / 11 pm, Fri & Sat 11.30
pm, Sun 10.30 pm; SW19 11 pm, Sun 10.30 pm;
midnight.

Ivy Grills & Brasseries £58 2️⃣2️⃣3️⃣
26-28 Broadwick St, W1
020 3301 1166   4–1C NEW
1 Henrietta St, WC2   020 3301 0200   5–3D
197 King's Rd, SW3   020 3301 0300   6–3C
96 Kensington High St, W8
020 3301 0500   6–1A
One Tower Bridge, 1 Tower Bridge, SE1
020 3146 7722   10–4D
Dashwood House, 69 Old Broad St,, EC2
020 3146 7744   10–2C NEW
The vote remains fairly equally split on Richard
Caring's burgeoning bevy of Ivy spin-offs which are
popping up like mushrooms 'in carefully selected
locations' across the country. (These – the 'Grills &
Brasseries' are not to be confused with the mere
'Cafés', and aim for a more faithful reproduction
of the original's magic). For 'The Ayes', they make
"a great local addition" providing "great British
food in a buzzy setting" ("I keep expecting to be
disappointed, and I'm not!"). For 'The Nays', "hugely
underwhelming food" and "uneven" standards
generally make it "feel like they are trying to milk
the franchise, but are destroying it in the process".
The most popular is the "ladies-who-lunch" favourite
on the King's Road, whose "garden is to die for"
(although "it's an uphill struggle actually being
seated in it") – a "super, bustling and tastefully
decorated venue with fabulous people watching
opportunities" (and where the Top Tip is "its great
breakfast: it's much quieter so service is spot on!)". /
ivycollection.com.

J Sheekey Atlantic Bar WC2 £68 3️⃣4️⃣4️⃣
28-34 St Martin's Ct   020 7240 2565   5–3B
"A sense of excitement and glamour" has long
given Sheekey's adjacent bar a distinct identity
from the restaurant – hence its relaunch last year
under the new 'Atlantic' brand. Its performance is
not quite as stellar as a few years ago when it felt
less discovered, but "its tasty fish tapas is lovely for
sharing pre-theatre" and still "delivered with style
and panache in a wonderful old-fashioned room".
"Fresh oysters and champagne on the doorstep of
Covent Garden – what more could you ask for?"
/ WC2N 4AL; www.j-sheekey.co.uk; @JSheekeyRest;
11.30 pm, Sun 10.30 pm; booking max 3 may apply.

Jackson & Rye £56 1️⃣2️⃣2️⃣
56 Wardour St, W1   020 7437 8338   4–2D
219-221 Chiswick High Rd, W4
020 8747 1156   8–2A
Hotham House, 1 Heron Sq, TW9
020 8948 6951   1–4A
"Decent brunch options" are the best bet at these
well-resourced American-style diners, and the
riverside branch at Richmond makes good use of
its "great location". But, more generally, too many
punters report "uninteresting food" leaving them
"most disappointed". / www.jacksonrye.com; 11 pm,
Sun 10.30 pm; EC2 closed Sat & Sun.

Jaffna House SW17 £23 5️⃣2️⃣2️⃣
90 Tooting High St   020 8672 7786   11–2C
"Mind-bogglingly hot Sri Lankan and South Indian
curries", all at "bargain prices" make this family-run
outfit in Tooting a must-visit. "Cafeteria-style by
day and licensed restaurant (which resembles a
suburban dining-room) by night". Top Tip – "the
lunchtime deal is astonishing value: a selection of
vegetarian or non-veggie dishes and a soft drink for
a fiver". / SW17 0RN; 11.30 pm.

Jamavar W1 £88 5️⃣4️⃣4️⃣
8 Mount St   020 7499 1800   3–3B
Leela Palace's "stunning" newcomer in Mayfair's
most fashionable restaurant row has immediately
established itself as "the best Indian restaurant
in town, indeed it's amongst the best restaurants
of any cuisine". Ex Gymkhana chef, Rohit Ghai's
"expert" and "exquisite" dishes are "genuinely top
class" (while "still remaining properly authentic
to the flavours you might find in New Delhi or
Mumbai") and the interior (modelled, apparently,
on the Viceroy's House of New Delhi) is a picture
of "elegance and sophistication". STOP PRESS: In
December 2017 a sequel, Dabbawala, is due to open at
29 Maddox Street (formerly Hibiscus, RIP). / W1K
3NF; www.jamavarrestaurants.com; @JamavarLondon.

James Cochran £53 5️⃣1️⃣2️⃣
21 Parkfield St, N1   020 3489 2090   9–3D NEW
19 Bevis Marks, Liverpool St, EC3

020 3302 0310 10–2D **NEW**
"Superb cooking is in evidence" at ex-Ledbury chef, James Cochran's newcomer, a couple of minutes from Liverpool Street, where his British small plates are "the stuff of dreams" and "at prices seldom seen for food of this quality in the City". There are negatives – too often "it is let down by very amateur service", and "the decor is not terribly inspiring", but all-in-all it's still highly recommended. In July 2017, he announced a second 60-seater at Angel Central.

Jamie's Italian £49 111
"Jamie get out!" – "you can do better" than this "dreadful, truly dreadful" Italian chain that "used to be enjoyable, but has gone downhill badly" and is "not much better, perhaps no better than school dinners" nowadays. / www.jamiesitalian.com; 11.30 pm, Sun 10.30 pm; booking: min 6.

JAN SW11 £37
78 Northcote Rd 0207 525 9446 11–2C
"A new addition to Northcote Road offering Caspian cuisine that replaces the missed Lola Rojo (RIP)" – limited but positive feedback so far on this funkily and expensively decorated year-old corner-site. / SW11 6QL; www.myjan.co.uk; @jan_restaurant; 9.30 pm.

Japan Centre Food Hall SW1 **NEW**
35b Panton St 020 3405 1246 5–4A
Since 1976, Tak Tokumine's Japanese cultural centre, complete with food hall and canteen, has occupied a variety of sites near Piccadilly Circus. This latest 6,000 sq ft incarnation is planned to open in September 2017, with 100-seater dining hall, surrounded by open kitchens. / SW1Y 4EA; www.japancentre.com; @JapanCentre.

Jar Kitchen WC2 £50 253
Drury Ln 020 7405 4255 5–1C
At its best (although mis-fires are not unknown), this sweet (if somewhat "done on the cheap") two-year-old café in Covent Garden supplies "lovely" farm-to-fork cooking, "even lovelier service and a warm, friendly atmosphere". "Don't worry, the jars are just the lighting decor, which works well… you get your food on plates!". / WC2B 5QF; www.jarkitchen.com; @JarKitchen; 9 pm; booking max 6 may apply.

Jashan N8 £32 442
19 Turnpike Ln 020 8340 9880 1–1C
This "lovely local Indian" attracts fans from across London to unlovely Turnpike Lane for another fix of its "awesome food". Lamb chops are a particular crowd favourite, but there are also many "excellent" dishes not found on menus elsewhere. / N8 0EP; www.jashan.co.uk; 10.15 pm, Fri & Sat 10.30 pm; D only; No Amex; May need 6+ to book.

Jean-Georges at The Connaught W1 **NEW**
The Connaught, Carlos Place
020 7107 8861 3–3B
No-one comes to The Connaught to save money, but early press reviews on this summer 2017 revamp of the hotel's 'second' restaurant (the slightly less informal one) under star Jean-Georges Vongerichten, are slightly guarded when it comes to the NYC chef's haute-comfort food here: not because it's bad, but because £25-£30 is a lot for a pizza or burger, even if the former has truffle on it. (The launch PR also insists that you can now order pizza take-out from The Connaught – go on we dare you…) / W1K 2AL; w.the-connaught.co.uk/mayfair-restaurants/jean-georges; @TheConnaught; 11 pm.

Jikoni W1 £64 334
21 Blandford St 020 70341988 2–1A
"Marina's review was spot on: this clubbable and laid-back newcomer is a triumphant, kick-you-in-the-crotch winner where diners spontaneously rave to neighbours about their meals!" – so say fans of food writer Ravinder Bhogal's "cosy" Marylebone debutante, which mashes up flavours from East Africa, the Middle East, Asia and the Britain. A big minority though are nonplussed – they say that "when you read the menu is looks adventurous" but claim the end result is "overhyped" and "bland". / W1U 3DJ; www.jikonilondon.com; @JikoniLondon.

Jin Kichi NW3 £46 543
73 Heath St   020 7794 6158 9–1A
"This cosy, cramped little Japanese stalwart in Hampstead is absolutely great" ("I always leave feeling the world is a better place"). "The seats upstairs near the grill are best", and there's a wide-ranging menu incorporating "top quality sushi and tempura", which are arguably "the best in north London". "Service is very fast (almost too fast)". / NW3 6UG; www.jinkichi.com; 11 pm, Sun 10 pm; closed Mon L.

Jinjuu W1 £61 334
16 Kingly St 0208 1818887 4–2B
Fom Korean-American TV chef Judy Joo, this "buzzy" Korean bar (with DJ some nights) and basement restaurant off Regent Street, "instantly wipes away the cares of a busy work week". "Great Korean fried chicken and prawn lollipops" are the standout items on a menu which is "that little bit different". / W1B 5PS; www.jinjuu.com; @JinjuuSoho; 11.30 pm, Thu-Sat 1 am, Sun 9.30 pm.

Joanna's SE19 £47 354
56 Westow Hill 020 8670 4052 1–4D
"Just the sort of place you want on your doorstep", this family-owned Crystal Palace institution celebrates its 40th anniversary next year. It serves American-style food and cocktails, kicking off every

morning with a "great casual breakfast". / SE19
1RX; www.joannas.uk.com; @JoannasRest; 10.45 pm,
Sun 10.15 pm.

Joe Allen WC2 £53 1️⃣2️⃣4️⃣
2 Burleigh St 020 7836 0651 5–3D
In September 2017, this "always buzzing" 40-year-old "West End institution" (no longer co-owned with its NYC cousin) moved to a new site just 25m from the original, to accommodate Robert de Niro's new Wellington hotel (opening in 2018). They've taken everything with them from the panelling to the posters and piano, and we've rated it assuming nothing changes, that is: "you go for the bustle and the showbiz feel" and by-and-large "forget the food" ("little better than an upmarket TGI fridays"). Top Menu Tip – "the favourite staple is the off-menu burger that's always available". / WC2E 7PX; www.joeallen.co.uk; @JoeAllenWC2; 11.30 pm, Fri & Sat 12.30 am, Sun 10 pm; set weekday L & pre-theatre £34 (FP).

Joe Public SW4 £17 4️⃣3️⃣3️⃣
4 The Pavement 020 7622 4676 11–2D
A former WC by Clapham Common (geddit?), is the spot for this hip, year-old pizza-by-the-slice operation – "it might be only a tiny, essentially takeaway or eat outside joint, but you'll go a long way to get a better piece of pizza!". / SW4 7AA; www.joepublicpizza.com; @JoepublicSW4; midnight, Sun 11pm; no booking.

The Joint SW9 £28 3️⃣3️⃣3️⃣
87 Brixton Village, Coldharbour Ln 07717
642812 11–2D
"There's a long queue but it's worth it" insist fans of this Brixton Market BBQ, known for its "gorgeous pulled pork and brisket". Service can be "brusque" though, and the odd reporter felt very short-changed here: "maybe they'd run out, because we were passed off with rubbish". / SW9 8PS; www.the-joint.co/; @thefoodjoint; 10 pm.

Jolly Gardeners SW18 £52 3️⃣3️⃣3️⃣
214 Garratt Ln 020 8870 8417 11–2B
"Such a good spot – but no-one really knows its there!"; a "nice, airy room at the back" of an Earlsfield gastropub, where "former MasterChef winner Dhruv Baker puts his skills to good use", with an "interesting menu" that "gets rather more elaborate later in the week". / SW18 4EA; www.thejollygardeners.com; @Jollygardensw15; 9.30 pm.

Jones & Sons N16 £51 4️⃣4️⃣4️⃣
Stamford Works, 3 Gillett St
020 7241 1211 14–1A
It's "worth crossing London for the beautiful steaks, excellent flavours and great atmosphere" at this "utterly brilliant" venture, which recently moved into "fabulous" new open-plan premises in Dalston. "A constantly changing menu keeps me coming back but I often end up ordering the sharing rib-eye – Hawksmoor at half the price!" / N16 8JH; www.jonesandsonsdalston.com; @JonesSons; 10 pm, Fri & Sat 11 pm, Sun 7 pm; booking max 7 may apply.

The Jones Family Project EC2 £58 4️⃣4️⃣4️⃣
78 Great Eastern St 020 7739 1740 13–1B
"Heartily recommended" – this Shoreditch basement beneath a cocktail bar is renowned for "excellent steak (sourced from the Ginger Pig)" and "a diverse wine list served by knowledgeable staff". / EC2A 3JL; www.jonesfamilyproject.co.uk; @JonesShoreditch; 10.30 pm, Sun 6 pm; set weekday L & Sun L £33 (FP).

José SE1 £48 5️⃣4️⃣5️⃣
104 Bermondsey St 020 7403 4902 10–4D
"I'd travel here from Spain for the pluma Iberica!" – José Pizarro's original Bermondsey tapas bar "somehow has the edge over the competition" serving some of "the best tapas you will find"… "if you can get in (it's always heaving)". / SE1 3UB; www.josepizarro.com; @Jose_Pizarro; 10.15 pm, Sun 5.15 pm; closed Sun D; no booking.

José Pizarro EC2 £59 3️⃣3️⃣2️⃣
Broadgate Circle 020 7256 5333 13–2B
Tapas king, José P's "quick and easy" two-year-old is "well-located in the revamped Broadgate Circle", and can become extremely busy ("it was too loud to hear one another talk"). But while fans do extol its "excellent food", overall feedback is a little middling and muted for such a hallowed name. / EC2M 2QS; www.josepizarro.com/jose-pizarro-broadgate; @JP_Broadgate; 10.45 pm, Sat 9.45 pm; closed Sun; set pre theatre £39 (FP).

Joy King Lau WC2 £37 3️⃣2️⃣2️⃣
3 Leicester St 020 7437 1132 5–3A
"Very much better than the average for Chinatown" – this "old school", three-floor operation just north of Leicester Square delivers just what you hope for in the area (but is so often hard to find) with its "no frills and great value". Top billing goes to its "fantastic dim sum" but "evening hits the spot too, with plenty for the adventurous diner: sea cucumber, ducks' beaks, drunken chicken feet, curry whelks…" / WC2H 7BL; www.joykinglau.com; 11.30 pm, Sun 10.30 pm.

Jugemu W1 🆕 £42 5️⃣2️⃣3️⃣
3 Winnett St 020 7734 0518 4–2D
A diminutive new 'Japanese tapas bar' in Soho – there are a few tables but the Top Tip is to sit up at the bar and watch chef Yuya Kikuchi (previously at Kirazu) in action. "The authentic (slightly bewildering), Japanese food's quite an adventure… and I thought I was a Japanese restaurant pro"; but it's brilliantly "well made" ("the sushi rivaled the best I've ever had"!). / W1D 6JY; jugemu-uk.crayonsite.com.

The Jugged Hare EC1   £63   3|2|3
49 Chiswell St   020 7614 0134   13–2A
"A meat-eater's delight" – this "quirky" City-fringe gastropub serves "proper British food" and "they know their game here" (as the "animals hanging in the window" hint). It's "always busy" and "noisy" and as a result service can be "perfunctory". / EC1Y 4SA; www.thejuggedhare.com; @juggedhare; 11 pm, Thu-Sat midnight, Sun 10.30 pm.

Jules SW15 NEW   £42
5 Lacy Rd   020 8780 3033   11–2B
Straightforward new all-day brasserie in Putney aiming to deliver a neighbourhood-y cocktails and tapas formula. (It's the first business venture of George Herbert, heir to Downton Abbey, aka Highclere). / SW15 1NH; julesputney.co.uk.

Julie's W11   £61
135 Portland Rd   020 7229 8331   7–2A
For the third year, this seductive 48-year-old – a lush, subterranean warren in a gorgeous Holland Park street that was an A-lister magnet in the '70s and '80s – remains closed, with its website promising a forthcoming re-launch for which the date is perennially pushed-out (currently it reads 'we hope to open in September 2017'). We don't know the backstory here, but hopefully it will re-appear one day as promised. / W11 4LW; www.juliesrestaurant.com; 11 pm.

Jun Ming Xuan NW9   £44   2|3|2
28 Heritage Ave   020 8205 6987   1–1A
"Very strong dim sum" still justifies the trip for some fans of this Cantonese, in a "strange, rather soulless new development" in Colindale – hailed in The Times a couple of years ago as the UK's best. There is also a school of thought though which says "don't bother!" / NW9 5GE; www.junming.co.uk; @jun_ming_xuan; 11 pm.

The Junction Tavern NW5   £49   3|3|3
101 Fortess Rd   020 7485 9400   9–2B
Limited but all-round upbeat feedback on this popular gastropub on the Tufnell Park/Kentish Town borders, complete with conservatory and small garden. / NW5 1AG; www.junctiontavern.co.uk; @JunctionTavern; 11 pm, Fri & Sat midnight, Sun 11 pm; Mon-Thu D only, Fri-Sun open L & D; No Amex.

Juniper Tree NW3 NEW   £58   3|2|2
72 Belsize Lane   020 3019 7303   9–2A
Organic British cooking (of some ambition) is the self-appointed mission of this Belsize Park newcomer, decorated in pleasant if slightly anodyne modern style – early reports on culinary results vary from "just OK" to "fantastic". / NW3 5BJ; www.junipertree.london; @JuniperTreeLDN; 10 pm; closed Mon.

K10   £35   3|4|2
3 Appold St, EC2   020 7539 9209   13–2B
Minster Ct, Mincing Ln, EC3
020 3019 2510   10–3D
"The sushi's always fresh, and the hot food's worth a look too" as it circulate on the conveyor belt of these handy city operations. The Copthall Avenue original copped it this year at the hands of the developers, but the remaining branches are "a good option for a quick lunch". / www.k10.com; 3 pm; Appold 9 pm; Closed D, closed Sat & Sun; no booking at L.

Kaffeine   £13   3|5|4
15 Eastcastle St, W1   020 7580 6755   3–1D
66 Great Titchfield St, W1
020 7580 6755   3–1C
"Consistently incredible coffee" (and "superb salads and sarnies" too) give this incredibly "welcoming" Aussie/Kiwi-owned duo a serious claim to being "London's top independent coffee houses". "Both branches are fabulous; the Eastcastle one is a bit more relaxed". / kaffeine.co.uk/Eastcastle/; 6 pm, Sun 5 pm; no bookings.

Kai Mayfair W1   £108   3|2|2
65 South Audley St   020 7493 8988   3–3A
"A very modern take on Chinese cuisine" excites devotees of Bernard Yeoh's "stylish and contemporary" Mayfair fixture, one of London's top Asian venues. "I'm not sure it is genuine Chinese rather than influenced by China, but presentation is artistic and there are really interesting menu choices". "Eyewatering" prices "befit the location" however, as does the heavyweight wine list which features many famous French names. / W1K 2QU; www.kaimayfair.co.uk; @kaimayfair; 10.45 pm, Sun 10.15 pm.

Kaifeng NW4   £69   3|3|3
51 Church Rd   020 8203 7888   1–1B
"Good Kosher Chinese" is the USP of this Hendon stalwart. There's the odd gripe that it's "overpriced", but on most accounts its "high standards continue to be maintained" with food that's "excellent and authentic". / NW4 4DU; www.kaifeng.co.uk; 10 pm; closed Fri & Sat.

Kanada-Ya   £29   5|2|2
3 Panton St, SW1   020 7930 3511   5–4A
64 St Giles High St, WC2
020 7240 0232   5–1B
"Delicious ramen, unsurpassed in London" ("the broth is clearly a labour of love, so rich and silky") is the verdict on these "authentic" outposts of a noodle chain, based in Japan: "no wonder there's always a queue out the door!". Top Tip – "the eggs are also amazing – order an extra one to add to your bowl". / 10.30 pm; WC2 no bookings.

Kaosarn   £28   **4**|**3**|**3**
110 St Johns Hill, SW11
020 7223 7888   11–2C
Brixton Village, Coldharbour Ln, SW9
020 7095 8922   11–2D
*"Fresh spicy flavours" ("they're not afraid of
chillies") ensure this "rustic", "family-run Thai group"
in southwest London is "still firing on all cylinders".
"Good value" and with a "busy", "studenty" feel,
they're always hopping". And they're "BYO to boot".
/ SW9 10 pm, Sun 9 pm; SW11 closed Mon L.*

Kappacasein SE16   £8   **5**|**3**|**2**
1 Voyager Industrial Estate 07837 756852 12–2A
*"Elevating melted cheese into high art" – this
wizard Borough Market stall uses a mix of cheeses,
leek, onions, shallots and sourdough bread to
create "the best cheese toastie in the world, bar
none!!". Expect to queue at busy times. / SE16 4RP;
www.kappacasein.com; @kappacasein; 2pm; Sat L only;
Cash only; no booking.*

Karma W14   £44   **4**|**3**|**1**
44 Blythe Rd   020 7602 9333   8–1D
*"Never-failing" curries at this Indian local, tucked
away behind Olympia, help it consistently exceed
expectations; less so the atmosphere, which more
rarely takes flight. / W14 0HA; www.k-a-r-m-a.co.uk;
@KarmaKensington; 11 pm; No Amex.*

Kashmir SW15   £42   **4**|**3**|**3**
18-20 Lacy Rd 07477 533 888 11–2B
*"On the site of longstanding Samratt" (RIP),
on a side street off Putney High Street, this
"extremely hospitable" yearling "has raised the
bar for Indian cuisine in SW15". "A short but
interesting and carefully prepared menu, and a
calm atmosphere makes for a good combination,
albeit at the pricier end of the range". / SW15 1NL;
www.kashmirrestaurants.co.uk; @KashmirRestUK;
10.30 pm, Fri & Sat 11 pm.*

**Kaspar's Seafood and Grill, The
Savoy Hotel WC2**   £88   **3**|**3**|**4**
100 The Strand   020 7836 4343   5–3D
*"Lovely fish served in a beautiful room" – in prior
decades known as The Savoy's River Restaurant –
has won a renewed following and consistent high
praise for this convenient Thames-side chamber.
Top Tip – "ideal for a pre/post theatre set deal"
and lunch too. / WC2R 0EU; www.kaspars.co.uk;
@KasparsLondon; 11 pm; set pre theatre £58 (FP).*

Kateh W9   £66   **3**|**2**|**3**
5 Warwick Pl   020 7289 3393   9–4A
*"The well executed dishes are just delicious" at this
jolly modern Iranian joint in Little Venice, where you
squish in cheek-by-jowl. Top Tip – "the upstairs dining
room is preferable to the basement". / W9 2PX;
www.katehrestaurant.co.uk; @RestaurantKateh; 11 pm,
Sun 9.30 pm; closed weekday L.*

Kazan   £44   **3**|**3**|**3**
77 Wilton Rd, SW1   020 7233 8298   2–4B
93-94 Wilton Rd, SW1   020 7233 7100   2–4B
*"A long-standing, beautifully run Pimlico gem" – this
Turkish café (and its offshoot across the road)
provides "reliably good value" at a "handy address
close to Victoria station". "Comfortable, with always
cheerful service… it's popular for good reason". /
www.kazan-restaurant.com; 10 pm, Fri & Sat 10.30 pm,
Sun 9.30 pm.*

**The Keeper's House, Royal
Academy W1**   £66   **2**|**2**|**2**
Royal Academy of Arts, Burlington House,
020 7300 5881   3–3D
*"OK post-culture", but "could do better" remains a
fair assessment of this popular operation, hidden
in the vaults of the Royal Academy (which is
reserved at lunchtime for RA members and their
guests). "It's a useful location" (if a slightly "gloomy"
one), but while fans say it's "lovely" it disappoints
too often to be a totally recommendable one. /
W1J 0BD; www.royalacademy.org.uk/keepers-house;
@KHRestaurant; closed Sun.*

Ken Lo's Memories SW1   £60   **3**|**3**|**2**
65-69 Ebury St   020 7730 7734   2–4B
*Ken Lo's traditional Belgravia operation not far
from Victoria Station "doesn't change much: but
if it ain't broke, why fix it?" The odd reporter does
feel "it has gone down over the years", but more
commonly there's praise for "consistently good food
in a very convivial atmosphere". / SW1W 0NZ;
www.memoriesofchina.co.uk; 11 pm, Sun 10.30 pm.*

**Kennington Tandoori
SE11**   £54   **4**|**4**|**4**
313 Kennington Rd   020 7735 9247   1–3C
*"The mix of locals, politicians, and a convivial
owner and staff ensure a happy evening" at "this
most magical of restaurants" – a Kennington curry
house notoriously popular with MPs from nearby
Westminster. Expect "high quality Indian fare, with
not too many fussy frills but large doses of flavour,
a warm atmosphere and low lighting!" / SE11 4QE;
www.kenningtontandoori.com; @TheKTLondon; No
Amex.*

Kensington Place W8   £62   **3**|**2**|**2**
201-209 Kensington Church St
020 7727 3184   7–2B
*This "glass-fronted bastion" – in its day, a seminal
icon of the 1990s restaurant scene near Notting
Hill – nowadays, under D&D London, specialises in
fish with its own fishmonger next door. "Not as slick
or smart as it was" in its heyday – and "not cheap"
– but the food is "fresh and well-cooked". (Avoid the
place if you don't like "distracting acoustics" – it can
get far "too noisy".) / W8 7LX;*

www.kensingtonplace-restaurant.co.uk;
@KPRestaurantW8; 10 pm, Fri & Sat 10.30 pm; closed
Mon L & Sun D.

Kensington Square Kitchen
W8 £37 3️⃣4️⃣3️⃣
9 Kensington Sq   020 7938 2598   6–1A
"Perfect breakfasts", "brilliant brunch", and "really
good coffee" ensure that this cute, little two-
storey café in one of Kensington's oldest squares
has a "regular and loyal clientele". "If you're not
into a Full English there are masses of other
yummy things on the menu", along with "great-
value fresh and seasonal lunches". / W8 5EP;
www.kensingtonsquarekitchen.co.uk; @KSKRestaurant;
4.30 pm, Sun 4 pm; L only; No Amex.

The Kensington Wine Rooms
W8 £56 2️⃣3️⃣3️⃣
127-129 Kensington Church St
020 7727 8142   7–2B
This modern wine bar (with branches in Fulham
and Hammersmith) gives you the chance to
sample an "excellent range" of more than 40
"high-end wines by the glass". The food is a bit of a
supporting act, but even those who feel it's "slightly
uninventive" find it "perfectly satisfactory". / W8
7LP; www.greatwinesbytheglass.com; @wine_rooms;
11.30 pm.

Kerbisher & Malt £24 3️⃣3️⃣2️⃣
53 New Broadway, W5   020 8840 4418   1–2A
164 Shepherd's Bush Rd, W6
020 3556 0228   8–1C
170 Upper Richmond Road West, SW14
020 8876 3404   1–4A
50 Abbeville Rd, SW4   020 3417 4350   11–2D
This "hipsters' take on the urban chippy", founded
six years ago in Brook Green, now also boasts
branches in East Sheen and Clapham (Ealing and
Islington are no more). They're "unpretentious, the
fresh fish is superb, and the chips aren't half bad
either". / www.kerbisher.co.uk; 10-10.30 pm, Sun &
Mon 9-9.30 pm; W6 closed Mon; no booking.

Khan's W2 £23 3️⃣2️⃣2️⃣
13-15 Westbourne Grove
020 7727 5420   7–1C
"Rather down-to-earth, but always excellent" sums
up the Khan family's popular and fast-paced Indian
canteen in Bayswater, founded in 1977 (which, for
the past 18 years, has been alcohol-free). / W2
4UA; www.khansrestaurant.com; @KhansRestaurant;
11.30 pm.

Kiku W1 £62 3️⃣3️⃣2️⃣
17 Half Moon St   020 7499 4208   3–4B
"Very enjoyable (if slightly expensive) dishes" are the
hallmark of this veteran Japanese in Mayfair, served
in traditionally austere and formal surroundings. /
W1J 7BE; www.kikurestaurant.co.uk; 10.15 pm, Sun
9.45 pm; closed Sun L.

Kikuchi W1 £76 4️⃣3️⃣2️⃣
14 Hanway St   020 7637 7720   5–1A
This little izakaya in the backstreets near Tottenham
Court Road tube attracts a small but dedicated fan
club, who say: "don't look at the bill whatever you do,
but prepare to be amazed by the food!" / W1T 1UD;
10.30 pm, Sat 9.30 pm; closed Sun; no booking.

Killer Tomato W12 £24 4️⃣3️⃣2️⃣
18 Goldhawk Rd   020 8743 0082   8–1C
"East London comes to the Goldhawk Road" with
this street food yearling in Shepherds Bush, whose
tacos and burritos deliver "fresh Mexican flavours
from a short, focused menu", and whose "mezcal
margaritas alone are worth a visit". Coming soon
– a second branch on Portobello Road. / W12 8DH;
killertomato.co.uk; @eatkillertomato; 9.30 pm, Thu-Sat
10 pm, Sun 9 pm; no booking.

Kiln W1 £33 5️⃣4️⃣4️⃣
58 Brewer St   no tel   4–3C
"A rare London venture that feels genuinely
different" – Ben Chapman's "vibey", "little" Soho
haunt is "the best casual opening of the year" and
its "inspired", "palate-searing" small plates ("taking
a bite is like travelling abroad") are "made totally
unique by dint of their incredible sourcing, ballsy
spicing and cooking everything over charcoal". "No
reservations + very popular = annoyingly large wait
times though". / W1F 9TL; www.kilnsoho.com.

Kintan WC1 £42 3️⃣2️⃣3️⃣
34-36 High Holborn   020 7242 8076   10–2A
This Japanese/Korean tabletop BBQ near Holborn
wins consistent praise for its yakiniku (grilled meat)
dishes. / WC1V 6AE; www.kintan.uk; @kintanuk; 10.30
pm, Sun 9.30 pm.

Kipferl N1 £46 3️⃣2️⃣3️⃣
20 Camden Passage 020 77041 555 9–3D
"Great strudel, and the best sachertorte north of
Vienna!" help score fans for this modern Austrian
coffee house in Islington (with a new branch in
Ladbroke Grove), and there's also a "small, unusual
menu" of more substantial dishes like Viennese
sausages, dumplings and schnitzels. / N1 8ED;
www.kipferl.co.uk; @KipferlCafe; 9.25 pm; closed Mon;
booking weekdays only.

Kiraku W5 £37 4️⃣4️⃣2️⃣
8 Station Pde   020 8992 2848   1–3A
This low-key café near Ealing Common tube station
– heavily patronised by west London's Japanese
expat community – doesn't win the raves it once
did, but is still praised for top-value dishes.
/ W5 3LD; www.kiraku.co.uk; @kirakulondon; 10 pm;
closed Mon; No Amex.

Kiru SW3 £52 **443**
2 Elystan St   020 7584 9999   6–2D
"In the ever-growing range of Asian fusion restaurants", this year-old, neighbourhood Japanese on Chelsea Green "is a great new addition". The prices raise the odd complaint however – "it's good, but for these prices it would have to be the best in London..." / SW3; www.kirurestaurant.com; @KiruRestaurant; 10 pm, Fri & Sat 10.30 pm.

Kitchen W8 W8 £71 **443**
11-13 Abingdon Rd   020 7937 0120   6–1A
"The cuisine has recently gone up another notch: it was always top quality, but is even subtler now", at this unexpectedly fine neighbourhood restaurant, just off Kensington's main drag, where Phil Howard's consultancy helps yield a "very slick and professional" approach. Ambience-wise, it generally rates well, but even fans can find it "a little empty emotionally". / W8 6AH; www.kitchenw8.com; @KitchenW8; 10.30 pm, Sun 9.30 pm; booking max 6 may apply; set weekday L £46 (FP), set pre-theatre £49 (FP).

Kitty Fisher's W1 £75 **333**
10 Shepherd Mkt   020 3302 1661   3–4B
No-one disputes that this "gorgeous quirky restaurant" in cute Shepherd Market provides "lovely" British dishes and an "intimate" ("squashed") setting. But having been the place about which Le Tout Londres raved non-stop a couple of years ago, even many fans now feel that "while it's perfectly good, it's not as exceptional as some reviews might lead you to believe". / W1J 7QF; www.kittyfishers.com; @kittyfishers; 9.30 pm; closed Sun.

Knife SW4 **NEW** £57 **544**
160 Clapham Park Rd   020 7627 6505   11–2D
"Elegantly cooked steaks, beautifully presented with deep umami flavours" make Matt-'The Dairy'-Wells's new "small but perfectly formed" 'neighbourhood steak restaurant' an "absolutely fantastic" addition to SW4. The first part of a planned local chain – all the meat is British, from the Lakes – and there's Cornish fish and seafood too. / SW4 7DE; kniferestaurant.co.uk; @KnifeLondon; 10 pm, Sun 4 pm; closed Mon, Tue & Sun D.

Koba W1 £44 **433**
11 Rathbone St   020 7580 8825   2–1C
"New Malden may boast the highest concentration of Korean BBQs, but Koba in Fitzrovia is the chicest – it offers delicious, authentic tabletop cooking in an elegant room and a pure Seoul vibe!" Staff are "welcoming" and the experience "reasonably priced". / W1T 1NA; kobalondon.com; @kobalondon; 10.45 pm; closed Sun L.

Koji SW6 £80 **444**
58 New King's Rd   020 7731 2520   11–1B
"Sushi, ceviche and a robata grill" earn high marks for Pat & Mark Barnett's smart modern Japanese fusion joint in Parsons Green (which for ages, they ran as Mao Tai, long RIP), whose "cocktails are a great motor-starter!" / SW6 4LS; www.koji.restaurant; @koji_restaurant; D only, Sun open L & D.

Kolossi Grill EC1 £32 **333**
56-60 Rosebery Ave   020 7278 5758   10–1A
This "tiny, welcoming Greek" off Exmouth Market "hasn't changed in 40 years". The "real taverna feel" makes it an eternal "great favourite" for regulars, even if, in contemporary culinary terms, it is arguably no more than "hanging in there". / EC1R 4RR; www.kolossigrill.com; 10.30 pm; closed Sat L & Sun.

Koya £32 **333**
50 Frith St, W1   020 7434 4463   5–2A
Bloomberg Arcade, Queen Victoria St, EC2   no tel   10–2C **NEW**
"Excellent udon noodles, just like in Japan", are "worth the wait" – there's no booking at this Soho destination (with a City outpost opening in late 2017), so be prepared to queue at busy times. There are also "nice additional starters like the pork belly or tempura – all delicious, simple food done well and served by friendly staff". / www.koyabar.co.uk; W1 10.30 pm, Thu-Sat 11 pm, Sun 10 pm; no booking; SRA-Food Made Good – 1 star.

Kricket W1 £47 **544**
12 Denman St   020 7734 5612   4–3C
"Living up to all the rave reviews… and then some!" Rik Campbell and Will Bowlby's "fun dive, off increasingly gaudy Shaftesbury Avenue" (the Soho successor to the wildly popular Brixton prototype in a shipping container) is "a whole new ball game!" offering "a great experience, even if it's mad and rushed". The "design is simple but sophisticated", with much of the seating on stools at a long counter; and the "profoundly original dishes" – "derived largely from Mumbai street food but either elevated a notch or transformed imaginatively" – is "spicy without being overpowering" and "quite exceptional". / W1D 7HH; www.kricket.co.uk; @kricketlondon; 10 pm.

Kulu Kulu £34 **321**
76 Brewer St, W1   020 7734 7316   4–3C
51-53 Shelton St, WC2   020 7240 5687   5–2C
39 Thurloe Pl, SW7   020 7589 2225   6–2C
"My go-to for cheap, reliable Japanese food" – these "unchanging" (read dated and drab) conveyor-belt sushi dives (Kulu Kulu means 'sushi-go-round') "feel authentic" and "won't break the bank". / 10 pm, SW7 10.30 pm; closed Sun; no Amex; no booking.

Kurobuta £63 **3**|**2**|**2**
312 King's Rd, SW3   020 7920 6442   6–3C
17-20 Kendal St, W2   020 7920 6444   7–1D
"A great punky Australian/Asian mashup"
characterises the menu at these "fun" izakaya-
style venues, where "stunning grill dishes" are the
highlights of the "funky" fare. On the downside
they're "not all that cheap" and "loud". In July 2017
(post survey) founder Scott Hallsworth sold out
to his business partners, so change may be afoot.
/ www.kurobuta-london.com; 10.30 pm; SW3 closed
Mon-Thu L.

The Ladbroke Arms W11£53 **3**|**3**|**3**
54 Ladbroke Rd   020 7727 6648   7–2B
This attractive and atmospheric "gourmet pub", at
the Holland Park end of Ladbroke Grove, "definitely
requires a reservation, especially on weekends",
but it's "worth the aggravation" for the "delicious
food" and "great local beer". Top Tip – "the real
draw is the terrace on a nice day". / W11 3NW;
www.ladbrokearms.com; @ladbrokearms; 10 pm, Sat
10.30 pm, Sun 9 pm; no booking after 8 pm.

Lady Mildmay N1 **NEW** £40 **3**|**4**|**3**
92 Mildmay Park   020 7241 6238   1–1C
"A great addition to local eateries" – this handsome,
"recently refurbished pub" on the corner of
Newington Green was relaunched in February 2016
and provides "excellent food" from an open kitchen
at good prices. / N1 4PR; www.ladymildmay.com;
@theladymildmaypub; 10 pm, Sun 9 pm; May need
6+ to book.

Lahore Karahi SW17 £26 **4**|**2**|**2**
1 Tooting High Street, London
020 8767 2477   11–2C
"Fabulous Pakistani cooking at ridiculously
inexpensive prices" makes this "quirky" BYO
canteen one of the best in Tooting. "Expect
to have to wait for a table." / SW17 0SN;
www.lahorekarahirestaurant.co.uk; 11.45 pm; No Amex.

Lahore Kebab House £25 **4**|**3**|**2**
668 Streatham High Rd, SW16
020 8765 0771   11–2D
2-10 Umberston St, E1   020 7481 9737   12–1A
"Still dishing up exceptional value Punjabi cuisine
after all these years (despite the various changes in
setup and clientele)"; this "cheap and no-nonsense"
Whitechapel dive is a legend for its "amazing
curries" and lamb chops, and – "despite a swathe
of competitors now" – for fans "it's still the winner".
That said, the "cavernous" upstairs has "all the
ambience of a school canteen rented out to a stag
do operator" – "if you get a table downstairs it's
a bit calmer". Meanwhile, its Streatham cousin
inspires only a tiny amount of feedback, but it's just
as upbeat: "fantastic, fresh dishes – efficient and
friendly service – and nicer than the E1 aircraft
hangar". / midnight.

Lamberts SW12 £55 **4**|**5**|**3**
2 Station Parade   020 8675 2233   11–2C
"Superb in every respect" and "extremely good
value" – Joe Lambert's "Balham gem" is renowned
locally for its "informal-but-not-sloppy service" and
a "very high standard of seasonal cooking" that, for
its most ardent fans, "classes it as a competitor to
Chez Bruce". A couple of regulars reported a "loss of
mojo" here this year however – "it was disappointing,
but we hope this let-down was a one off". / SW12
9AZ; www.lambertsrestaurant.com; @lamberts_balham;
10 pm, Sun 5 pm; closed Mon & Sun D; No Amex.

The Landmark, Winter Garden
NW1 £77 **2**|**4**|**5**
222 Marylebone Rd   020 7631 8000   9–4A
The "very beautiful surroundings" of this romantic,
light-filled Marylebone atrium make it a "top-
notch" choice for Sunday brunch or afternoon
tea treats, when the "sheer volume and amazing
range" of the food impress. "Service is excellent",
with waiters who "keep the Champagne flowing"
(it's 'all-you-can-drink' at brunch). / NW1 6JQ;
www.landmarklondon.co.uk; @landmarklondon; 10.15
pm; No trainers; booking max 12 may apply.

Langan's Brasserie W1 £67 **2**|**3**|**4**
Stratton St   020 7491 8822   3–3C
"Like an old pair of slippers, you just feel
comfortable with!" – this famous and "fun" brasserie
near The Ritz, celebrating its 40th year, remains, for
its older fan club, "something magical, steeped in
gastronomic history, and never failing to impress".
The less rose-tinted view is that it looks "tired"
and serves "nursery food gone wrong". / W1J 8LB;
www.langansrestaurants.co.uk; @langanslondon; 11 pm,
Fri & Sat 11.30 pm; closed Sun.

Palm Court, The Langham
W1 £75 **3**|**3**|**4**
1c Portland Place   020 7965 0195   2–1B
The "quintessentially English" afternoon tea in
the civilised lounge of this well-known hotel is "so
beautifully crafted you feel it's a shame to bite in!",
with "portions so generous you might need a doggy
bag". "Super location and staff and a great cocktail
menu make it a winner for meeting up with friends"
at other times too. / W1B 1JA; www.palm-court.co.uk;
@Langham_London; 10.30 pm; No trainers.

Lantana Cafe £43 **3**|**3**|**3**
13-14 Charlotte Pl, W1   020 7323 6601   2–1C
45 Middle Yd, Camden Lock Pl, NW1
020 7428 0421   9–2B
Ground Floor West, 44-46 Southwark St, SE1
no tel   10–4C
Unit 2, 1 Oliver's Yd, 55 City Rd, EC1
020 7253 5273   13–1A
"One of the first to do an Aussie brunch and
still one of the best" – these "funky" Antipodean
hangouts also serve an "interesting" and "super-

tasty" choice of "bistro-style food" at lunchtime. / lantanacafe.co.uk; EC1 9.30 pm, Sat & Sun 3 pm; W1 3.30 pm, Sat & Sun 5 pm; NW1 5.30 pm; NW1 closed Sun; W1 no booking Sat & Sun.

Lao Cafe WC2 NEW £38 3 3 2
60 Chandos Place   020 3740 4748   5–4C
In another successful transition from pop-up to permanent, Saiphin Moore's (of Rosa's Thai) dim-lit café just off the Strand, follows the popularity of a temporary home in Victoria last year. "Whether this is really Lao or northern Thai/Isarn food is an open question, and the menu is small, but the dishes are delicious and at the right spice level." / WC2N 4HG; laocafe.co.uk; May need 8+ to book.

Lahpet E8 NEW £42 3 3 3
5 Helmsley Place   020 3883 5629   14–2B
"A great chance to try an underrepresented cuisine" – this new Burmese communal canteen in Hackney (previously a Maltby Street stall) is well-rated in reports: "traditional dishes like the tea salad are the best options". / E8 3SB; www.lahpet.co.uk; @Lahpet; 10.30 pm, Sun 5 pm.

Lardo £50 3 3 2
158 Sandringham Rd, E8
020 3021 0747   14–1B
197-201 Richmond Rd, E8
020 8533 8229   14–1B
"A short list of properly made thin-crust pizzas" pack in the hip crowd at this Italian in the Arthaus building near London Fields – a "must-visit before the Hackney Empire". Good, if limited, feedback on the second branch, Bebè, nearby. / 10.30 pm, Sun 9.30 pm.

LASSCO Bar & DIning
SE1 NEW £50
Ropewalk, 37 Maltby St
020 7394 8061   10–4D
From one overcrowded hipster market to another – bar manager Jerome Slesinski and chef James Knox Boothman worked together at The Royal Oak in Columbia Road's Flower Market, and now they have teamed up again to run the restaurant and bar at LASSCO's (London Architectural Salvage and Supply Company) Ropewalk warehouse, in the heart of über-trendy Maltby St Market. It's a not-dissimilar idea to LASSCO's well-established operation at Brunswick House. / SE1 3PA; www.lasscobar.co.uk; @lassco_bar; 10 pm; closed Mon-Wed D & Sun D.

Latium W1 £58 3 3 2
21 Berners St   020 7323 9123   3–1D
"A solid choice if you are seeking a classic Italian" – this "tranquil" and "white-table-clothed" Fitzrovia fixture has "lost a bit of wow-factor since the change of personnel" a couple of years ago, but with its "subtle dishes, and unobtrusive service" it's still seen by most reporters as "a stalwart of very good Italian cuisine"; and the fact that it's "blessedly

un-noisy at lunchtime" makes it "perfect for business discussions". / W1T 3LP; www.latiumrestaurant.com; @LatiumLondon; 10.30 pm, Sat 11 pm, Sun 9.30 pm; closed Sat L & Sun L; set weekday L £37 (FP).

Laughing Gravy SE1 £56 3 4 3
154 Blackfriars Rd   020 7998 1707   10–4A
Billing itself as 'London's best-kept secret' – this tucked-away bar/restaurant in Southwark can be "a lovely find" despite its "unexceptional location", thanks to its "top cocktails" and consistently good cooking – in particular "stand out steak" and "stunning puddings". / SE1 8EN; www.thelaughinggravy.co.uk; @laughinggravyuk; 10 pm, Fri & Sat 10.30 pm, Sun 4.30 pm; closed Sun D; no booking.

The Laughing Heart
E2 NEW £64 3 2 3
277 Hackney Rd   020 7686 9535   14–2A
"It's been a favourite with the critics" and fans find it "bangin' on all fronts", but the overall view is more nuanced when it comes to Charlie Mellor's "dark and moodily-lit" new Hackney wine bar and off-licence. True, nearly all reports do acknowledge the "interesting food" and "inventive wine list" (featuring many top biodynamic wines), but even fans can feel that "the price and pretensions are not that laughable", given the "expensive and small" dishes. / E2 8NA; thelaughingheartlondon.com.

Launceston Place W8 £73 3 4 4
1a Launceston Pl   020 7937 6912   6–1B
This "lovely townhouse tucked away in the back streets of Kensington" has "had several recent changes of chef/patron under D&D group", of which the latest is Ben Murphy, who arrived from The Woodford in early 2017. Fans say his "modern, inventive and delicious cuisine is taking them back into Michelin territory" but there are also those who feel "it's now more expensive and impressive rather than compelling". Top Tip – "excellent value early bird menu". / W8 5RL; www.launcestonplace-restaurant.co.uk; @LauncestonPlace; 10 pm, Sun 9.30 pm; closed Mon & Tue L.

THE LEDBURY W11 £142 5 5 4
127 Ledbury Rd   020 7792 9090   7–1B
"Wow! I didn't think this place could possibly live up to the hype, but it did… and easily!" Brett Graham's "sophisticated" Notting Hill HQ delivers a pitch-perfect performance and again topped the survey's nominations for offering London's best meal of the year. But for all his "stunningly well-crafted" cuisine ("so many dishes that were so memorable") and "perfectly matched wines", it's the "unpretentious, customer-first attitude that makes a meal here that much more enjoyable": "everyone's relaxed and having a great time!" / W11 2AQ; www.theledbury.com; @theledbury; 9.45 pm; closed

Mon L & Tue L; booking max 6 may apply; set weekday L £97 (FP).

Legs E9 £50 **3** **4** **4**
120 Morning Lane   020 3441 8765   14–1B
This hip yearling from Aussie chef Magnus Reid (founder of Shoreditch coffeehouse C.R.E.A.M.) "never disappoints", with "great" modern dishes and a "relaxing" boho atmosphere. Diners perch facing the window looking across to the new Hackney Walk fashion hub, and there's an interesting list of small producer wines (the name, 'Legs', is wine lingo). / E9 6LH; www.legsrestaurant.com; @legsrestaurant; 11 pm; D only, Sat L & D, Sun L only, closed Mon & Tue; no booking L.

Lemonia NW1 £49 **1** **3** **4**
89 Regent's Park Rd   020 7586 7454   9–3B
This "vast Greek taverna" has become a landmark after 40 years on Primrose Hill, and is "extraordinarily busy" due to the "unique experience and family atmosphere" it offers. But the cooking "is average at best, and less-than-average of late"; "I've been coming here for 25 years and the food is nothing like it used to be, which is very sad because it's a fun place". / NW1 8UY; www.lemonia.co.uk; @Lemonia_Greek; 11 pm; closed Sun D; No Amex.

The Lido Café, Brockwell Lido
SE24 £43 **2** **2** **4**
Dulwich Rd   020 7737 8183   11–2D
"Great for a brunch watching the swimmers" – getting wet is not compulsory if you visit this all-day café attached to Brixton's wonderfully characterful and lovingly preserved Lido. / SE24 0PA; www.thelidocafe.co.uk; @thelidocafe; 4 pm; closed Sun D; No Amex; booking max 8 may apply.

The Light House SW19 £54 **3** **3** **2**
75-77 Ridgway   020 8944 6338   11–2B
"What a neighbourhood restaurant should strive to be", this long-running, bare-walled (hence "noisy") Wimbledon indie has a "slightly quirky menu" with "seasonal produce to share". Fans feel it's "seemingly underrated", but there's also always been a "hit 'n' miss" element to reports here. / SW19 4ST; www.lighthousewimbledon.com; 10.30 pm; closed Sun D; set weekday L £35 (FP).

The Lighterman N1 £59 **3** **4** **4**
3 Granary Square   020 3846 3400   9–3C
"A terrific location at Granary Square" – with "stunning views overlooking the canal", "a sunny terrace with lots of outside space" and attractive first-floor dining room – win massive popularity for this "very atmospheric" King's Cross yearling. And it's "well-run" too – staff are "surprisingly efficient and personable" and its "typical British dishes" are "well-executed and tasty" with impressive consistency. / N1C 4BH; www.thelighterman.co.uk; @TheLightermanKX; 10.30 pm, Sun 9.30 pm.

Lima Fitzrovia £70 **3** **2** **2**
31 Rathbone Pl, W1   020 3002 2640   2–1C
14 Garrick St, WC2   020 7240 5778   5–3C
"Very pretty and delicious food in a fun setting" is the promise of these modern Peruvians, in Fitzrovia and Covent Garden ('Lima Floral'). On the downside, they can feel "understaffed" or "a little basic given the price", and sceptics feel that "the food looks like a picture, but can taste a little underwhelming". / www.limalondongroup.com/fitzrovia; 10.30 pm, Sun 9.30 pm; Mon L closed.

Lisboa Pâtisserie W10 £8 **3** **3** **4**
57 Golborne Rd   020 8968 5242   7–1A
"Simply the best pastéis de nata in London, and excellent coffee too" make it worth adding this "truly unpretentious" and "good value" Portuguese café into a trip down Portobello way, although NB "it's very crowded most of the time". / W10 5NR; 7 pm; L & early evening only; no booking.

The Little Bay NW6 £33 **2** **3** **4**
228 Belsize Rd   020 7372 4699   1–2B
"An intimate and romantic interior and low prices" have long sustained this theatre-themed bistro, "hidden" off Kilburn High Road, complete with little balconies for couples. / NW6 4BT; www.littlebaykilburn.co.uk; midnight, Sun 11pm.

Little Bird £58 **2** **2** **4**
1 Station Parade, W4   020 3145 0894   1–3A
1 Battersea Rise, SW11
020 7324 7714   11–2C **NEW**
Lorraine Angliss's (Annie's, Rock & Rose) latest exercise in neighbourhood glam combines eclectic, exotic decor, with "excellent cocktails" and a (slightly rootless) Asian/European menu. Good vibes from locals to the first branch, "in a quiet backwater, right by Chiswick Station" – there's now also a second in the heart of Battersea.

Little Georgia Cafe £40 **3** **2** **3**
14 Barnsbury Rd, N1   020 7278 6100   9–3D
87 Goldsmiths Row, E2   020 7739 8154   14–2B
"Interesting wines and lots of garlic" enliven the "reliable" hearty fodder at this duo of Georgian cafés, in Islington and Hackney, which inspire limited but positive feedback. / www.littlegeorgia.co.uk; N1 11 pm, Sun 10 pm; E2 11 pm, Mon 5 pm; N1 closed Mon, E2 closed Mon D.

Little Social W1 £79 **2** **2** **2**
5 Pollen St   020 7870 3730   3–2C
Across the road from Pollen Street, Jason Atherton's more informal second 'Social' is "enjoyable, but nowhere near as good as over the road", "with some interesting dishes but all-in-all a bit expensive". / W1S 1NE; www.littlesocial.co.uk; @_littlesocial; 10.30 pm; closed Sun; booking max 6 may apply; set pre theatre £51 (FP).

Little Taperia SW17   £42   3|3|3
143 Tooting High St   020 8682 3303   11–2C
"A Tooting find", this "fun and buzzy" Spanish two-year-old provides "plate after plate of fresh tapas, all served with friendly advice" ("it's so good, you just keep on ordering!") / SW17; www.thelittletaperia.co.uk; @littletaperia; 10 pm, Fri & Sat 11 pm, Sun 9.30 pm; May need 6+ to book.

Lluna N10   £43   3|3|3
462 Muswell Hill Broadway
020 8442 2662   3–3B
Right on the Broadway in Muswell Hill, this bright, modern Spanish bar/restaurant serves a "very varied menu" from breakfast onwards, including "delicious tapas". "It can get very loud at the front when it's busy." / N10 1BS; lalluna.co.uk; @lallunalondon; 9 pm.

LOBOS Meat & Tapas SE1   £50   4|4|2
14 Borough High St   020 7407 5361   10–4C
"Outstanding and inventive, meat-based tapas" – "served with attitude" (in a good way) – make it well worth seeking out this "hard-to-find" two-year-old "squashed under a rail viaduct" at Borough Market. Set up by alumni of nearby Brindisa, whose "passion shines through", it is "chaotic and busy" – but "somehow it works". / SE1 9QG; www.lobostapas.co.uk; @LobosTapas; 11 pm, Sun 10 pm; booking max 8 may apply.

Locanda Locatelli, Hyatt Regency W1   £85   4|3|3
8 Seymour St   020 7935 9088   2–2A
"Classic food is beautifully presented and served with an understated aura of luxury" in Giorgio Locatelli's "dim-lit" (slightly '90s) Marylebone HQ – one of London's most "polished" Italian dining rooms ("at its best, nowhere else matches it"). Service is "slick" but some prefer to "hit the wrong note. / W1H 7JZ; www.locandalocatelli.com; 11 pm, Thu-Sat 11.30 pm, Sun 10.15 pm; booking max 8 may apply.

Locanda Ottomezzo W8   £67   3|3|3
2-4 Thackeray St   020 7937 2200   6–1B
"Excellent, genuine Italian cuisine" helps makes this an "atmospheric" local in a backstreet near Kensington Square Garden. "Everything is homemade from the grissini to the pasta", and they also do a "great breakfast and top pizzas". / W8 5ET; www.locandaottoemezzo.co.uk; 10.30 pm; closed Mon L, Sat L & Sun.

Loch Fyne   £43   2|3|3
"A good variety of nicely cooked fish" is a perhaps lukewarm but fair estimation of this "dependable" national chain, liked also for its well-appointed branches and "polite" service. / www.lochfyne-restaurants.com; 10 pm, WC2 Mon-Sat 10.30 pm.

Lockhouse W2 NEW   £38   3|2|3
3 Merchant Square   020 7706 4253   7–1D
"Newly opened in Paddington Quay" – and with "a great ambience from being by the canal's waterside" – this large operation offers "a fine range of trendy ales and lagers" and a menu headlining with 'award winning Lockhouse Loaded burgers'. The odd early report says it's "excellent value". / W2 1AZ; www.lockhouselondon.co.uk; @Lockhouselondon; 23.30, Sat 5pm.

London House SW11   £60   2|2|2
7-9 Battersea Sq   020 7592 8545   11–1C
Gordon Ramsay's Battersea venue wins some praise for "decent food and cocktails", but its ratings have suffered as a result of an apparent identity crisis: "It doesn't know if it's a restaurant or a pub, which made it feel like it was neither…"; "Bring back the white tablecloths! It's much less special than when it first opened. What went wrong?" / SW11 3RA; www.gordonramsayrestaurants.com/london-house; @londonhouse; 11 pm, Sun 9 pm.

London Shell Co. W2 NEW   £66   4|5|5
Sheldon Square 07818 666005 7–1C
"A highly original dining experience!" – a converted wide beam canal boat ('The Prince Regent') moored in the Paddington Central development, offering a simple, "very seasonal and carefully sourced menu of amazingly fresh and perfectly cooked fish". "It's fun and they're very friendly." / W2 6EP; www.londonshellco.com; @LondonShellCo; dinner cruises depart at 7.30 pm; closed Mon, Sun & Sat L.

Lorne SW1 NEW   £60   4|5|3
76 Wilton Rd   020 3327 0210   2–4B
"A triumph from the River Café/Chez Bruce/ The Square's Katie Exton and Peter Hall" – this "confident, new modern British kid on ever-more-interesting Pimlico culinary block" (on the same street as A Wong) is yet another reason to brave the "grimy streets surrounding Victoria station". "The seasonal menu is expertly created and cooked" and matched with a "concise but astonishingly tempting wine list" in a "light", simple space. / SW1V 1DE; www.lornerestaurant.co.uk; 9.30 pm; closed Sun.

Louie Louie SE17 NEW   £43   3|3|3
347 Walworth Rd   020 7450 3223   1–3C
"Exponentially raising the attractiveness of SE17 as a culinary destination!" – this white-walled, all-day café opened as a result of a successful 2016 crowdfund by the owners of nearby Fowlds, and transforms (four nights a week) into a hip restaurant with guest chefs and DJ nights. / SE17 2AL; louielouie.london; @LouieLouie_Ldn; closed Mon D & Sun D.

Luardos EC1 £9 **5 4**
Pitch 39, Whitecross St Market   no tel   13–1A
"You don't go for ambience, but those burritos are the stuff of dreams" – so say addicted fans of this 10-year-old Mexican food truck biz, who have added a KERB Camden stall to the original Whitecross Street pitch, where they still sell from their first Citroën H van, 'Jesus'. / EC1Y 8JL; luardos. co.uk.

Luca EC1 NEW £73 **3 4 4**
88 St John St   020 3859 3000   10–1A
"It's not the Clove Club: get over it!" – this new Clerkenwell sibling to Shoreditch's legendary foodie temple takes a totally different culinary tack, delivering a menu of "high quality, refined Italian dishes" using the best British produce. Not everyone loves it (especially those burdened by Clove Club expectations), but most reports are of "outstanding" cooking, "extremely accommodating staff" and a "beautiful" and "romantic" interior (the rambling site once known as Portal (long RIP), with a cosy bar at the front and conservatory and private rooms towards the rear). Top Menu Tip – "the Parmesan fries are truly the work of angels (addictively moreish!)". / EC1M 4EH; luca.restaurant; @LucaRestaurant.

Luce e Limoni WC1 £59 **4 4 3**
91-93 Gray's Inn Rd   020 7242 3382   10–1A
"Service with passion and a smile" from "great host" Fabrizio matched with "fantastic, freshly cooked Sicilian food and wine" is a winning combination at this Bloomsbury Italian: "it's not very near anywhere, but worth a trip". / WC1X 8TX; www.luceelimoni.com; @Luce_e_Limoni; 10 pm, Fri & Sat 11 pm.

Luciano's SE12 £52 **3 3 3**
131 Burnt Ash Rd   020 8852 3186   1–4D
This "fabulous family-run (and family-friendly) pizza and pasta joint in Lee is always full". Arguably "it's nothing more than a friendly neighbourhood place" but the worst anyone has to say about the food is that it's "OK". / SE12; www.lucianoslondon.co.uk; @LucianosLondon; 10.30 pm, Sun 10 pm.

Lucio SW3 £75 **3 4 3**
257 Fulham Rd   020 7823 3007   6–3B
A "family-owned" Chelsea trattoria "run with real professionalism", and with "a calm and relaxing" style. Pasta dishes are particularly good. Top Tip – go for the "amazing value set lunch". / SW3 6HY; www.luciorestaurant.com; 10.45 pm.

Lupins SE1 NEW £48
66 Union St   020 3617 8819   10–4B
Chefs Lucy Pedder and Natasha Cooke met working at Medlar and set up a catering collective together; this is their first permanent restaurant venture, which opened in mid 2017 in Flat Iron Square food hub, a short walk from Borough Market, with

a menu full of 'seasonal British produce with a splash of sunshine' (on which early press reviews are upbeat). / SE1 1TD; www.lupinslondon.com; 10.30 pm; closed Mon D & Sun D.

Lupita £46 **3 2 2**
13-15 Villiers St, WC2   020 7930 5355   5–1C
7 Kensington High St, W8
020 3696 2930   6–1A
60-62 Commercial Street, Spitalfields, E1
020 3141 6000   13–2C
This "fun", budget dive is "a cut above most Mexicans" serving "authentic" dishes ("excellent guacamole") just where you expect them least – on the grotty street, right next to Charing Cross station. Very limited but positive feedback on its City-fringe and Kensington branches too.

Lure NW5 £37 **3 5 3**
56 Chetwynd Rd   020 7267 0163   9–1B
"How all fish 'n' chip shops ought to be!", say fans of Aussie Philip Kendall's Dartmouth Park three-year-old – "a lovely neighbourhood restaurant" with "friendly and humorous service" producing "a simple menu of good-quality fresh produce, well cooked and served". "Smell-free too – no fears about eating in!" / NW5 1DJ; www.lurefishkitchen.co.uk; @Lurefishkitchen; 10 pm, Sun 9.30 pm; booking weekends only.

Lurra W1 £55 **3 3 3**
9 Seymour Place   020 7724 4545   2–2A
"A mouthful of Galician aged beef, or unbelievably tender and succulent, grilled octopus" represent "Basque grills at their best" to the many fans of this stylish "slice of San Sebastian in London", near Marble Arch, whose "outstanding steak" is amongst the best in town. Ratings have slipped since it opened a couple of years ago however, with growing fears that it risks seeming "over-rated" and "not justifying its prices". / W1H 5BA; www.lurra.co.uk; @LurraW1; 10.30 pm, Sun 3.30 pm; closed Mon L & Sun D.

Lutyens EC4 £78 **2 2 2**
85 Fleet St   020 7583 8385   10–2A
Sir Terence Conran's business-centric brasserie off Fleet Street is a "solid" performer focused on a City-based market: even fans admit "the ambience is decidedly corporate" – there's "nothing wrong here, except the daft prices" (and the "slightly dull room"). / EC4Y 1AE; www.lutyens-restaurant.com; 9.45 pm; closed Sat & Sun.

Lyle's E1 £78 **4 2 2**
The Tea Building, 56 Shoreditch High St
020 3011 5911   13–1B
"A pioneer in the new world of London restaurants and the UK scene generally" – James Lowe's "so-very-trendy Shoreditch fixture" is much more than a "casual" hipster haven, and for most reporters his

"always surprising, frequently stunning" cuisine, "with incredible intensity of flavours" makes it a "five-star all-round experience". Ratings here came off the boil a tad this year however, with reservations creeping in regarding "off-hand service", the "very, very stark setting" and some meals that were "clever, but lacked wow-factor". / E1 6JJ; www.lyleslondon.com; @lyleslondon; 10 pm; closed Sat L & Sun.

M Restaurants £89 ②②②
Zig Zag Building, Victoria St, SW1
020 3327 7776 2–4B
Brewery Wharf, London Rd, TW1
020 3327 7776 1–4A NEW
2-3 Threadneedle Walk, EC2
020 3327 7770 10–2C
"When you want to impress your companions" many reporters do recommend these "swanky and shiny", Vegas-style operations in the City and Victoria (and very recently opened in Twickenham, too), applauding the "superb" steaks, and "innovative and original wine list". To their critics however, it's "massively a case of style over substance", with "food that's designed to sound fancy and exotic" but which seems "mediocre at the inflated prices": "I went on a deal, which brought the cost for the albeit good meal down from outrageous to merely expensive". / midnight; EC2 closed Sat L & Sun, SW1 closed Sun.

Ma Goa SW15 £41 ④④③
242-244 Upper Richmond Rd
020 8780 1767 11–2B
"Still producing exceptional cooking" after all these years – this "excellent" family-run Goan delights its Putney regulars who consider themselves "lucky to have this as a local", with food that's "consistently fresh, aromatic and spicy without being OTT". Now the family have opened a wine shop next door, they also offer one of "the best affordable wine lists of any local Indian". / SW15 6TG; www.ma-goa.com; @magoarestaurant; 10.30 pm, Fri & Sat 11 pm, Sun 10pm.

Ma La Sichuan SW1 £58 ④③①
37 Monck St 020 7222 2218 2–4C
"The level and authenticity of the spicy Sichuanese cooking are entirely unexpected" (and "you can have the degree of spice and heat altered to taste") at this Westminster venture, which serves an array of "unusual, non-routine dishes, not usually found in Chinese restaurants". Notwithstanding the "rather bland" decor and "unlikely location", reports say it "deserves more recognition". / SW1P 2BL; malasichuan.co.uk; 11 pm, Sun 10.30 pm.

Mac & Wild £52 ④③④
65 Great Titchfield St, W1
020 7637 0510 3–1C
9a Devonshire Square, EC2
020 7637 0510 10–2D NEW

"Really good venison" is the star turn at this Fitzrovia two-year-old specialising in Scottish game (much of it from the family estate of owner Andy Waugh), delivering "very tasty, gamey flavours for not terribly high prices". Having started out as a street stall, the venture now has a second branch at Devonshire Square, near Liverpool Street.

Macellaio RC £56 ③②③
84 Old Brompton Rd, SW7
020 7589 5834 6–2B
Arch 24, 229 Union St, SE1 07467 307682
10–4B
124 Northcote Rd, SW11
020 3848 4800 11–2C NEW
38-40 Exmouth Market, EC1
020 3696 8220 10–1A
"A wacky way of issuing cutlery (plunging the steak knives into the table!)" adds a further frisson to these "memorable venues" – "an interesting concept where the butcher's counter sits in the middle of the restaurant". "Steak or tuna, that's your only choice", but the former in particular is "superb", "melt-in-the-mouth" Piemontese Fassone meat matched with "delicious Italian wines". There are two 'flies in the ointment' – "prices are now approaching 'rip off' levels", and hit unlucky and service can be "rude, arrogant and slow". / 11 pm.

Machiya SW1 NEW £45
5 Panton St 020 7925 0333 5–4A
Positive early reports on this "yummy new Japanese from the folks behind Kanada-Ya" (just down the street). Upstairs it's a neutrally decorated café with a to-the-point short menu – downstairs a bar serves a wide range of sakes and whiskys. / SW1Y 4DL; machi-ya.co.uk; @MachiyaLondon; 10.30 pm, Fri & Sat 11 pm, Sun 10 pm.

Madame D's E1 NEW £34
76 Commercial St awaiting tel 13–2C
"Original Himalayan sharing plates, most with a great chilli kick" feature in one early report on this "small dining den" (from the founders of Gunpowder) – a room above a pub, near Spitalfields. / E1 6LY; madame-d.com; @madame_d_london.

Made in Italy £40 ③②③
50 James St, W1 020 7224 0182 3–1A
249 King's Rd, SW3 020 7352 1880 6–3C
141 The Broadway, SW19
020 8540 4330 11–2B
"Great elongated pizza" (sold by the metre) make it worth remembering these crowded cafés in Chelsea and Wimbledon. / www.madeinitalygroup.co.uk; SW3 11.30 pm; W1 11.30 pm, Sun 10.30 pm; SW19 11 pm; SW3 closed Mon L.

Made of Dough
SE15 `NEW` **£33**
182 Bellenden Rd   020 7064 5288   1–4D
Pop Brixton's buzzing Made of Dough pizzeria
grew permanent roots with this bright new café
which opened in Peckham in June 2017.The dough
in question is fermented for over 60 hours before
being zapped in a wood fire oven. / SE15 4BW;
www.madeofdough.co.uk; @MadeOfDoughLDN; 10.30
pm, Sun 9 pm; no booking.

Madhu's UB1
£42 `4` `4` `3`
39 South Rd   020 8574 1897   1–3A
Sanjay Anand's legendary Southall curry house is
"simply the best", say fans of its Kenyan-influenced
Punjabi cooking. It is now the flagship of a catering
empire that takes in Harrods and Harvey Nichols,
among others. / UB1 1SW; www.madhus.co.uk; 11.30
pm, Fri-Sun midnight; closed Tue, Sat L & Sun L; no
booking.

The Magazine Restaurant, Serpentine Gallery W2
£59 `3` `3` `4`
Kensington Gdns   020 7298 7552   7–2D
This Zaha Hadid-designed gallery restaurant in
Hyde Park "deserves more recognition" according
to reporters, who think it "a great space", with
"interesting food" (maybe only being open for
lunch and afternoon tea is what keeps it under
the radar). Perhaps a new team, scheduled to
take over its management in late 2017, will
finally put it properly on the map? / W2 2AR;
www.magazine-restaurant.co.uk; @TheMagazineLDN;
10.45 pm,Tue & Sun 6 pm; closed Mon,Tue D & Sun
D.

Maggie Jones's W8
£61 `2` `2` `5`
6 Old Court Pl   020 7937 6462   6–1A
"You can hide in the booths and hold hands" at
this eccentric, extremely "romantic", rustic-style
operation near Kensington Palace (named after the
pseudonym Princess Margaret once used here).The
dated Gallic cooking is "average for the price", but
only those with the hardest hearts "are surprised
there are really so many first dates looking for
novelty decor and uneven staircases?" / W8 4PL;
www.maggie-jones.co.uk; 11 pm, Sun 10.30 pm.

Magpie W1 `NEW`
10 Heddon St   020 7254 8311   4–3B
Co-founders of Hackney's stellar Pidgin (James
Ramsden and Sam Herlihy) have headed West, just
off Regent Street, for their latest newcomer, opened
in July 2017.The revolutionary concept is British dim
sum, with diners choosing plates (and cocktails!)
straight off circulating trolleys. / W1B 4BX; www.
magpie-london.com.

Maguro W9
£57 `3` `4` `2`
5 Lanark Pl   020 7289 4353   9–4A
"Tiny" Japanese outfit near Little Venice where

"lovely" service helps offset the "cramped and
uncomfortable" interior. "There is better sushi
in London, but the price, selection and relaxed
style ensure this is a top pick". / W9 1BT;
www.maguro-restaurant.com; 10.30 pm, Sun 10 pm;
No Amex.

Maison Bertaux W1
£8 `3` `4` `4`
28 Greek St   020 7437 6007   5–2A
"Still unique" – this 'Patisserie Francaise' in Soho,
opened in 1871, and, run (slightly "eccentrically")
by sisters Michelle and Tania Wade since the late
1980s, seems ever-more precious in a world of
ubiquitous Starbucks and Costa Coffees. "I'm
always a bit shocked at the prices, but the quality
is top notch", and it's "surprisingly good for quiet
conversation". / W1D 5DQ; www.maisonbertaux.com;
@Maison_Bertaux; 10.15 pm, Sun 8.45 pm.

Malabar W8
£47 `5` `4` `3`
27 Uxbridge St   020 7727 8800   7–2B
"Amazing Indian food" – "still inventive and fresh",
"even after well over 30 years" – maintains
this distinctive (it looks more like an Italian
restaurant) and distinguished curry house off
Notting Hill Gate as "a real gem". "Staff are
nearly as lovely as the delicious menu." / W8 7TQ;
www.malabar-restaurant.co.uk; 11 pm.

Malabar Junction WC1
£41 `3` `3` `2`
107 Gt Russell St   020 7580 5230   2–1C
"Ignore the unpromising exterior: it belies an
airy atrium within" at this "easygoing" Indian,
"handy for the British Museum nearby". "Modern
decor combines with southern Indian cuisine",
provided by "very charming staff." / WC1B 3NA;
www.malabarjunction.com; 11 pm.

MAM W11 `NEW`
16 All Saints Rd awaiting tel 7–1B
Colin Tu, owner of Salvation in Noodles, opened this
street-food-inspired Vietnamese BBQ in the second
half of 2017; expect skewers cooked on a robata
grill, pho and fish sauce wings. MAM is pronounced
'mum' and means fermentation in Vietnamese. /
W11 1HH; mamlondon.com.

Mamma Dough
£39 `3` `3` `4`
179 Queen's Rd, SE15   020 7635 3470   1–4D
76-78 Honor Oak Pk, SE23
020 8699 5196   1–4D
354 Coldharbour Ln, SW9
020 7095 1491   11–2D
Despite all the competition in the pizza market,
this small South London group (Brixton, Peckham
and Honor Oak Park) won very high ratings this
year.The interiors are all stripped-down wood and
brickwork, and the main event is complemented
by local craft beer, coffee roasted in Shoreditch,
and ginger beer brewed on site.Top Tip – half-sized
plates available for kids. / www.mammadough.co.uk;

SE23 10 pm, SW9 11 pm, SE15 10.30 pm; Mon-Thu closed L.

Mandarin Kitchen W2 £41 [4][2][1]
14-16 Queensway   020 7727 9012   7–2C
"It's always full (the sign of a great place)", but don't go to this crowded Bayswater Chinese expecting much in the way of ambience. Stick to the "consistently outstanding" seafood dishes – "the best lobster noodles in the world" are the "must-try" signature dish – but "in truth, the Peking duck is a bit less good". / W2 3RX; 11.15 pm.

Mangal 1 E8 £28 [5][4][2]
10 Arcola St   020 7275 8981   14–1A
"Absolutely the best kebabs this side of Istanbul" have turned this Turkish grill into a "Dalston institution" over 20 years. "Exceptional meat from the barbecue" is backed up by "good salads and BYO (keeping the price down)". "Despite the proliferation of Mangal offshoots, the Arcola street original is still the best!" / E8 2DJ; www.mangal1.com; @Mangalone; midnight, Sat & Sun 1 am; Cash only; no booking.

Manicomio £68 [2][3][3]
85 Duke of York Sq, SW3
020 7730 3366   6–2D
6 Gutter Ln, EC2   020 7726 5010   10–2B
Although their prime locations – next to the Saatchi Gallery off Sloane Square in Chelsea and in the City – mean they are "not cheap", these "good-natured" Italians provide a "solid" level of cooking and a "fun" atmosphere. Top Tip – lovely outside terrace in SW3. / www.manicomio.co.uk; SW3 10 pm, Sun 4 pm; EC2 10 pm; EC2 closed Sat & Sun.

Manna NW3 £56 [2][2][2]
4 Erskine Rd   020 7722 8028   9–3B
From "exceptional" to "slightly off the boil" – the UK's oldest veggie (Primrose Hill, 1968) perennially attracts inconsistent and fairly middling feedback. If you like meat-free food and are in north London give it a try, but it's not a certain bet. / NW3 3AJ; www.mannav.com; @mannacuisine; 10 pm, Sun 7.30 pm; closed Mon.

The Manor SW4 £58 [3][3][3]
148 Clapham Manor St   020 7720 4662   11–2D
"Weird… in a good way!", say fans of Robin Gill's "buzzy, bare and loud" venture in a Clapham backstreet (a sibling to the nearby Dairy), who extol its "truly memorable modern British cooking". To its detractors, though, it's simply "too hyped" – "so hipster it hurts, with too many misses for the price". / SW4 6BS; www.themanorclapham.co.uk; 10 pm, Sun 4 pm.

Manuka Kitchen SW6 £53 [3][4][3]
510 Fulham Rd   020 7736 7588   6–4A
"Cosy", "little" New Zealand-inspired bistro near

Fulham Broadway with a "great open kitchen, good food and nice atmosphere" – probably best for "brunch rather than a full meal, but most enjoyable" (and with a downstairs gin bar). / SW6 5NJ; www.manukakitchen.com; @manukakitchen; 10 pm, Tue-Sat 11 pm, Sun 4 pm; closed Sun D; booking max 8 may apply.

Mar I Terra SE1 £43 [3][4][3]
14 Gambia St   020 7928 7628   10–4A
"Tapas that's a cut above-the-norm" helps makes this "slightly cramped" former boozer in a Southwark backstreet a favourite pre-theatre pit stop, and "great after-work place". / SE1 0XH; www.mariterra.co.uk; 11 pm; closed Sat L & Sun.

Marcus, The Berkeley SW1 £122 [3][2][3]
Wilton Pl   020 7235 1200   6–1D
Marcus Wareing's "spacious" and "peaceful" Belgravia chamber is "the epitome of what a special restaurant should be" for its very many admirers, not least when it comes to the "incredible" cooking with "maximum flavours to the fore", be it from the à la carte, or 5- and 8-course tasting options. However, its ratings are dragged down by a vociferous minority who diss the "disengaged" service and an experience where "everything is fine but nothing is great": is that second Michelin star just boosting expectations too high? / SW1X 7RL; www.marcusrestaurant.com; @marcusbelgravia; 10 pm; closed Sun; No trainers; booking max 6 may apply; set weekday L £88 (FP).

Mare Street Market E8 NEW
89-115 Mare St awaiting tel   14–2B
Star ex-Viajante, Chiltern Firehouse, etc chef Nuno Mendes teams up with Barworks to launch a new neighbourhood venue in Hackney's Keltan House, incorporating a bar, restaurant, deli and café. / E8 4RU.

Margot WC2 £56 [4][5][5]
45 Great Queen St   020 3409 4777   5–2D
"An instant classic, bravo!" This "very elegant Italian on the edge of Covent Garden" proved one of the best arrivals of 2016 and although the odd report complains it's been "hyped" the vast majority say it's plain "stunning". "Quality and service are in abundance" – the comfortable interior feels enjoyably "superior", and "staff make the meal into an occasion – they make you feel very special". "Most of the menu is of traditional dishes with a twist" and it's "damned good too". Top Menu Tip – "the best ever Osso Buco". / WC2B 5AA; www.margotrestaurant.com; @MargotLDN; 10.45 pm, Sun 9.30 pm.

Mari Vanna SW1 £79 [3][3][4]
116 Knightsbridge   020 7225 3122   6–1D
This "romantic" and luxurious Knightsbridge

fixture attracted few reports this year, but all of them highly upbeat regarding its simple Russian cooking (and huge range of vodkas). / SW1X 7PJ; www.marivanna.co.uk; @marivannalondon; 11.30 pm.

Marianne W2 £128 544

104 Chepstow Rd   020 3675 7750   7–1B
"Marianne Lumb nails it, spot on, time and time again" at her "very special, petite restaurant" (just 14 covers) in Bayswater. La patronne herself "is not only a brilliant chef, but also a charming and welcoming host" and the "tiny but lovely" set-up is "perfect for a romantic evening" (if "without a lot of buzz"). "The set menu is chosen with good taste rather than extravagance, and the cooking is peerless perfection" ("it is rare that a tasting menu is all hits but this place manages it"). Finally, "the wine list is a real draw too – a terrific selection at prices that are actually affordable". / W2 5QS; www.mariannerestaurant.com; @Marianne_W2; 10 pm; closed Mon; booking max 6 may apply; set weekday L £71 (FP).

The Marksman E2 £62 434

254 Hackney Rd   020 7739 7393   14–2A
"Ignore the hipster-beards!" – this "relaxed East End boozer serving top notch nosh" is "too good to be written-off as just-another-hangout-of-the-terminally-trendy!" "Impeccably cooked, thoroughly modern British dishes" are "cheerfully and efficiently served" and while "it's always crowded", "it's got a good buzz, still feels like a pub (almost)" and "it's great that its old character and charm still thrive". / E2 7SJ; www.marksmanpublichouse.com; @marksman_pub; 10 pm, Sun 8 pm; closed weekday L & Sun D.

Maroush £52 322

I) 21 Edgware Rd, W2   020 7723 0773   7–1D
II) 38 Beauchamp Pl, SW3
020 7581 5434   6–1C
V) 3-4 Vere St, W1   020 7493 5050   3–1B
VI) 68 Edgware Rd, W2   020 7224 9339   7–1D
'Garden') 1 Connaught St, W2
020 7262 0222   7–1D
"It's the starters and mezze that hold centre stage" (although the mains are "tasty" too) at this successful Lebanese chain, whose café sections with excellent menus of wraps (part of I and II) are better known than the adjoining more formal (rather "stiff and impersonal") restaurants. Head to the Marble Arch original for regular music and belly dancing. / www.maroush.com; most branches close between 12.30 am-5 am.

Masala Zone £37 334

"We always go for the Grand Thali and it's a knockout!" – These "ever-buzzing" contemporary Indians make a very "handy backstop", with WC2 in particular "an excellent pre-theatre option" for a "fast and delicious" meal. "We thought it

might be chain-bland, but the food was good and quite authentic… and good value too!" / www.realindianfood.com; 11 pm, Sun 10.30 pm; W1U 9 pm, Sun 4 pm; booking: min 8.

MASH Steakhouse W1 £81 222

77 Brewer St   020 7734 2608   4–3C
This Danish-owned, American-style steakhouse, occupying a "massive basement" near Piccadilly Circus, divides opinion. To fans, it's an "awesome" place full of "old-fashioned" qualities. Critics, though, complain of "very disappointing beef, cooked merely adequately", "highly overpriced wine" and "dire surroundings". / W1F 9ZN; www.mashsteak.co.uk; @mashsteaklondon; 11.30 pm; closed Sun L; set pre-theatre £47 (FP), set weekday L £51 (FP).

Massimo, Corinthia Hotel WC2 £80 223

10 Northumberland Ave
020 7321 3156   2–3D
Few restaurants can match the truly "special", "sumptuous", "spacious" decor of this "simply stunning" Italian dining room (designed by David Collins) in a luxury hotel off Trafalgar Square. It's never really caught on however, and though it has a few fans and avoids harsh criticism is still sometimes "empty". / WC2N 5AE; www.massimo-restaurant.co.uk; @massimorest; 10.45 pm; closed Sun.

Masters Super Fish SE1 £24 322

191 Waterloo Rd   020 7928 6924   10–4A
"Being full of black cab drivers adds to the atmosphere of this traditional chippie", which is both handy for Waterloo, and also serves "fish and chips that are really VERY good", "in generous portions, with crispy batter", all "at reasonable prices". "If you like napiery, etc this isn't for you: it's basic Formica". Top Tip – BYO (£4.50 corkage). / SE1 8UX; masterssuperfish.com; 10.30 pm; closed Sun; No Amex; no booking, Fri D.

Matsuba TW9 £46 342

10 Red Lion St   020 8605 3513   1–4A
"Very good sashimi" and sushi head the "varied menu" at this "tiny" Korean-run Japanese joint in Richmond town centre. The location and setting may not be perfect, but it's a "much-appreciated attraction" in the area. / TW9 1RW; www.matsuba-restaurant.com; @matsuba; 10.30 pm; closed Sun.

Max's Sandwich Shop N4 £32 443

19 Crouch Hill   no tel   1–1C
"Epic sarnies" – home-baked focaccia stuffed with hot fillings – make "legend" Max Halley's Crouch Hill sandwich shop an entertaining destination, whose "great value" door-stops are accompanied by "good beers and nice grooves on the jukebox". (Now also at Birthdays in Stoke Newington.) / N4 4AP;

www.maxssandwichshop.com; @lunchluncheon; 11 pm,
Fri & Sat midnight, Sun 6 pm; closed Sun D; No Amex;
no booking.

May The Fifteenth SW4 **£57** 3️⃣4️⃣2️⃣
47 Abbeville Rd   020 8772 1110   11–2D
This "solid" Clapham operation (formerly Abbeville
Kitchen) is "excellent for breakfast, brunch, lunch,
dinner…" – it's the sort of place locals "love to have
on the doorstep". / SW4 9JX; www.maythe15th.com;
11 pm, Sun 9.30 pm.

Mayfair Garden W1 NEW **£62** 4️⃣3️⃣2️⃣
8-10 North Audley St   020 7493 3223   3–2A
"On the site of the Princess Garden… it's hard to
tell if anything has actually changed other than the
name" at this elegant Chinese stalwart in Mayfair
– "the cooking's good, the duck exceptional, but
beyond that the service and atmosphere aren't
such as to get too excited about". / W1K 6ZD;
www.mayfairgarden.co.uk; 11.30 pm, Sun 11 pm.

**Mayfair Pizza Company
W1** **£52** 3️⃣4️⃣3️⃣
4 Lancashire Ct   020 7629 2889   3–2B
A "great location off the beaten track" is one reason
to truffle out this bright and airy pizzeria, hidden
in a cute courtyard off Bond Street – others are
friendly service and sensible prices. / W1S 1EY;
www.mayfairpizza.com; @mayfairpizzaco; 11 pm,
Sun 10 pm.

maze W1 **£85** 2️⃣2️⃣1️⃣
10-13 Grosvenor Sq   020 7107 0000   3–2A
Gordon Ramsay's Mayfair outfit was a star of the
London gastronomic scene a decade ago, under
founding chef Jason Atherton (who is now long
gone), but "has lost its way" bigtime in recent years.
True, some fans do say it's "simply amazing", but
even they can find it "eye-wateringly expensive" –
and too many critics complain of a "below average"
or even "awful" experience, in "an unsympathetic
room that could be an airport restaurant". /
W1K 6JP; www.gordonramsayrestaurants.com;
@mazerestaurant; 11 pm; No trainers; booking max 9
may apply.

maze Grill W1 **£77** 1️⃣2️⃣2️⃣
10-13 Grosvenor Sq   020 7495 2211   3–2A
"Very disappointing… not great flavours…
came out hungry and went for something to eat
afterwards!" – Gordon Ramsay's Mayfair grill is
not without its fans, but yet again incites too many
harsh criticisms to justify a recommendation. / W1K
6JP; www.gordonramsay.com; @mazegrill; 11 pm; No
shorts.

maze Grill SW10 **£54** 2️⃣2️⃣2️⃣
11 Park Wk   020 7255 9299   6–3B
The most eloquent comment on Gordon Ramsay's
two-year-old in the Chelsea street where he made
his name is how little feedback is received. Have

people finally lost interest in him? It doesn't help
that of the few reporters who did care to opine, the
majority were unimpressed: "dreadful service…",
"what a disappointment… won't be returning". /
SW10 0AJ; www.gordonramsay.com/mazegrill/park-walk;
@GordonRamsayGRP; 11 pm.

Mazi W8 **£64** 3️⃣3️⃣3️⃣
12-14 Hillgate St   020 7229 3794   7–2B
"Exciting" dishes still win fans for this "classy" and
"highly creative modern Greek", on the site of
successive Notting Hill tavernas for almost 70 years.
Scores dropped across the board this year though
– it's becoming "very expensive" and some diners
felt 'processed' ("we were served so fast we were
finished in 45 minutes"). / W8 7SR; www.mazi.co.uk;
@mazinottinghill; 10.30 pm; closed Mon L & Tue L.

MEATliquor **£37** 3️⃣2️⃣4️⃣
74 Welbeck St, W1   020 7224 4239   3–1B
6 St Chad's Place, WC1
020 7837 0444   9–3C NEW
17 Queensway, W2   020 7229 0172   7–2C NEW
133b Upper St, N1   020 3711 0104   9–3D
37 Lordship Lane, SE22   020 3066 0008   1–4D
If and when you have "beer, bondage and burgers
fantasies", these "outlandish" grunge-fests are
unparalleled with their "wild (and LOUD) interiors"
and "street food with attitude" – "legendary dirty
burgers" ("the Dead Hippie is a Big Mac on
steroids")… wings… chili cheese fries. / meatliquor.
com; W1 midnight (Fri & Sat 2 am), N1 11 pm, SE22
midnight, Sun 10.30 pm-11.30 pm; booking: min 6.

MEATmarket WC2 **£28** 3️⃣3️⃣2️⃣
Jubilee Market Hall, 1 Tavistock Ct
020 7836 2139   5–3D
This West End outpost of the wilfully grungy
MEATliquor franchise is "quick and tasty, fun
and cheap" – "just what you want from a burger
joint"… "and in Covent Garden, too". / WC2E 8BD;
www.themeatmarket.co.uk; @MEATmarketUK; 11 pm,
Fri & Sat midnight, Sun 10 pm; No Amex; no booking.

MEATmission N1 **£32** 3️⃣3️⃣4️⃣
14-15 Hoxton Market   020 7739 8212   13–1B
If you like "dirty burgers and great cocktails", you'll
"love this place". Hoxton Square's MEATliquor
outpost has all the group's signature flavours,
including Dead Hippie sauce and chili cheese fries.
/ N1 6HG; www.meatmission.com; @MEATmission; 11
pm, Sun 10 pm.

MeatUp SW18 **£55** 3️⃣2️⃣2️⃣
350 Old York Rd   020 8425 0017   11–2B
Wandsworth Town yearling that manages to live
up to its name – a "fun place to meet up with
a good choice of BBQ-type dishes", and also a
decent range of cocktail, beers and wine make it
"a useful addition to the local scene". / SW18 1SS;
www.meatupgrill.com; @meatupuk.

Mediterraneo W11 £65 3️⃣2️⃣3️⃣
37 Kensington Park Rd 020 7792 3131 7–1A
This "classic Italian with great food and service" has been a Notting Hill "favourite" for the best part of two decades. "It never changes… which is a good thing!" / W11 2EU; www.mediterraneo-restaurant.co.uk; 11.30 pm, Sun 10.30 pm; booking max 10 may apply.

Medlar SW10 £76 4️⃣4️⃣2️⃣
438 King's Rd 020 7349 1900 6–3B
"Joe Mercer-Nairne should have a Michelin star" and why the tyre men took it away is bonkers given the "faultless, complex cuisine with modern flair" and "slick and pleasant service" at this well-known and extremely popular "hidden gem", at the 'wrong' end of the King's Road. At best the slightly awkward interior feels "classy" and "convivial", but it can also appear "staid" and "strangely low key". / SW10 0LJ; www.medlarrestaurant.co.uk; @MedlarChelsea; 10.30 pm, sun 9.30pm.

Megan's £42 2️⃣3️⃣3️⃣
571 Kings Rd, SW6 020 7371 7837 6–4A
Unit B, 57-69 Parsons Green Lane, SW6
020 7348 7139 11–1B NEW
A "lovely outdoor space, which is covered in the winter" is the special draw to this atmospheric all-day King's Road café, praised for its "wholesome" fare, particularly for brunch; a new branch opened in Parsons Green in September 2017.

Mei Ume EC3 NEW £88
10 Trinity Square 020 3297 3799 10–3D
Open alongside La Dame de Pic inside the City's new Four Seasons hotel, this Chinese and Japanese fusion café opened too late for survey feedback. The team of chefs hail from Royal China, Sake no Hana and Yauatcha, and – in keeping with the swish setting – ambitions are high. / EC3N 4AJ; www.meiume.com; @FSTenTrinity; 10 pm.

Melange N8 £50 3️⃣2️⃣2️⃣
45 Topsfield Parade, Tottenham Lane
020 8341 1681 9–1C
This "excellent value local" in Crouch End mixes dishes of French and Italian inspiration. "Service is smooth and friendly, and the food consistent and comforting after a hard day at work". / N8 8PT; www.melangerestaurant.co.uk; @malange_malange; 10.30 pm, Fri-Sun 11 pm.

Mele e Pere W1 £54 3️⃣4️⃣3️⃣
46 Brewer St 020 7096 2096 4–3C
"Straightforward, well-prepared Italian cooking" wins praise from this central trattoria, which is "great fun too, with very reasonable prices for Soho". "Its bar is a super hang-out", featuring "an excellent range of Vermouth cocktails that are quite delicious". / W1F 9TF; www.meleepere.co.uk; @meleEpere; 11 pm, Sun 10 pm; set weekday L £33 (FP).

Melody at St Paul's W14 £58 2️⃣3️⃣3️⃣
153 Hammersmith Rd 020 8846 9119 8–2C
Limited but positive feedback (as a business destination) for this calm, very grandly situated dining room – part of a hotel set in a grand Gothic Victorian building at the south end of Brook Green that formed part of the original St Paul's Boys' School. / W14 0QL; www.themelodyrestaurant.co.uk; 10 pm; set weekday L £35 (FP).

Menier Chocolate Factory SE1 £54 2️⃣2️⃣3️⃣
51-53 Southwark St 020 7234 9610 10–4B
"The meal deal tickets combining show and dinner are good value (if hard to book)" at this theatre café in a Victorian former chocolate factory. If you can't get the package however maybe hold off – "with foodie Borough Market just over the road there are plenty of other nicer options nearby". / SE1 1RU; www.menierchocolatefactory.com; @MenChocFactory; 11 pm; closed Mon & Sun D.

Meraki W1
80-82 Gt Titchfield St 020 7305 7686 3–1C
Can the Waney family (the powerhouse behind Roka, Zuma and the Arts Club) bring their magic to contemporary Greek cuisine with this summer 2017 newcomer in Fitzrovia? A 100-cover venture boasting two al fresco terraces; the name is a Greek term that refers to the love and passion that someone puts into their work. / W1W 7QT; www.meraki-restaurant.com.

Mercato Metropolitano SE1 £25 3️⃣2️⃣5️⃣
42 Newington Causeway
020 7403 0930 1–3C
This year-old, 45,000 sq ft street food centre, just south of Elephant & Castle, makes "a fab hangout whatever the weather" – the food can be "hit and miss" and it's "slow when busy", but there's "so much choice" and it's "great for a chilled evening in a group". / SE1 6DR; www.mercatometropolitano.co.uk; @mercatometropol; 11pm, Sun 9pm.

The Mercer EC2 £62 2️⃣2️⃣2️⃣
34 Threadneedle St 020 7628 0001 10–2C
"Classic British dishes in a smart dining room" is the understated offer in this converted banking hall, "tucked away on Threadneedle Street". "It doesn't shout about its presence" and even fans can find it "a little boring", but it makes a "reliable choice for business lunches, without melting the credit card". / EC2R 8AY; www.themercer.co.uk; @TheMercerLondon; 9.30 pm; closed Sat & Sun.

Merchants Tavern EC2 £61 3️⃣2️⃣4️⃣
36 Charlotte Rd 020 7060 5335 13–1B
"A terrific bar at the right price-point, kitchen on display and live vinyl in the background" all contribute to the "terrific atmosphere" at Angela

Hartnett's stylish, big Shoreditch gastropub (the conversion of a former warehouse). Some feedback is mixed, but the overall verdict is of "lovely" food and solid value for money. / EC2A 3PG; www.merchantstavern.co.uk; @merchantstavern; 11 pm, Sun 9 pm.

Le Mercury N1 £34 [2][2][4]
154-155 Upper St 020 7354 4088 9–2D
"Terrific value" old, candle-lit bistro that's a "cheap 'n' cheerful" and "romantic" Islington classic, and also "handy for the Almeida Theatre opposite". "I'm not surprised it's always packed", but do "request a table downstairs to make the most of the evening". / N1 1QY; www.lemercury.co.uk; midnight, Sun 10 pm; Mon-Thu only, Fri-Sun open L & D.

Mere W1 £89 [3][5][3]
74 Charlotte St 020 7268 6565 2–1B
MasterChef: The Professionals judge, Monica Galetti's Fitzrovia newcomer opened shortly before our 2017 survey and gives the impression of still settling down. On the plus side, the service (overseen by husband, ex-Gavroche sommelier, David) is "exceptionally friendly and top notch" and the "comfortable" basement setting feels "classy" and "perfectly relaxed". A number of reports find the (primarily Gallic) cuisine "needing to improve" or "lacking in wow factor", but "excellent" meals are also noted and the fairest view is "this is one to watch and likely to get more polished with time". / W1T 4QH; www.mere-restaurant.com; @mererestaurant; Jacket & tie required; set weekday L £67 (FP).

Meson don Felipe SE1 £40 [2][2][3]
53 The Cut 020 7928 3237 10–4A
"Reminiscent of a holiday in Spain", this "fun" tapas-veteran, conveniently located for the Old and Young Vics, may have an "unprepossessing exterior, but inside it's buzzy, lively and nicely decorated" (if "a bit 1960s nowadays"), and you eat pretty well without spending a packet too. Top Tip – "avoid the evening when a guitarist blows you away". / SE1 8LF; www.mesondonfelipe.com; 10 pm; closed Sun; No Amex; no booking after 8 pm.

Messapica NW10 NEW £23
109 Chamberlayne Rd 020 8964 3200 1–2B
New to Kensal Rise from the owners of nearby Ostuni, an all-day 'café, deli, bombetteria and juice bar' (named for a town in Puglia) which is open daily for breakfast, lunch and dinner. An Italian charcoal grill produces the 'bombetta' – bite-sized meaty street food snacks – and stonebaked pizzas. / NW10 3NS; 10 pm, Thu-Sat 10.30 pm.

Mews of Mayfair W1 £70 [3][3][3]
10 Lancashire Court, New Bond St
020 7518 9388 3–2B
"Arrive early to get a table in the cobbled courtyard", which are the best seats during the

summer months at this versatile Mayfair charmer, owned by Roger Moore's son. Other attractions include "professional and enjoyable brasserie-style food", a well-stocked bar, and afternoon tea. / W1S 1EY; www.mewsofmayfair.com; @mewsofmayfair; 10.45 pm; closed Sun D.

Meza £37 [3][3][2]
34 Trinity Rd, SW17 07722 111299 11–2C
70 Mitcham Rd, SW17 020 8672 2131 11–2C
"Fresh and tasty mezze" at "good-value" prices have built a strong reputation for these two tiny cafés in Tooting. Softer ratings mirror reports of "some falling off in quality" but on most accounts they're still "reliably good". / www.mezarestaurant.co.uk; 11 pm, Fri & Sat 11.30 pm.

Michael Nadra £60 [4][3][2]
6-8 Elliott Rd, W4 020 8742 0766 8–2A
42 Gloucester Ave, NW1
020 7722 2800 9–3B
"Excellent modern French cuisine and a variable atmosphere" are the common themes which unite feedback on Michael Nadra's accomplished but disparate duo of ventures. Both occupy "difficult" sites – the Chiswick original is notably tightly packed, while Camden Town (right next to Regent's Canal) has an unusual lay-out. In more mainstream locations, he would enjoy a much higher profile. / www.restaurant-michaelnadra.co.uk; W4 10 pm, Fri-Sat 10.30 pm, NW1 10.30 pm, Sun 9 pm; NW1 closed Mon, W4 closed Sun D.

Mien Tay £37 [4][3][2]
180 Lavender Hill, SW11
020 7350 0721 11–1C
122 Kingsland Rd, E2 020 7729 3074 14–2A
"Goat and galangal – just love it!" The signature dish at this "great value" Vietnamese group in Battersea, Fulham and Shoreditch is a legend. "The place may look a bit rough and ready but the food's hard to resist!" and they're always "rammed". / 11 pm, Sun 10 pm; E2 Sun 10.30 pm.

Mildreds £46 [3][3][3]
45 Lexington St, W1 020 7494 1634 4–2C
200 Pentonville Rd, N1
020 7278 9422 9–3D NEW
9 Jamestown Rd, NW1
020 7482 4200 9–3B NEW
Ground floor Thomas Tower, Upper Dalston Sq, E8 020 8017 1815 14–1A NEW
That "it's always over-crowded, with never-a-free table" speaks volumes for this long-enduring veggie café in Soho, whose "simple and delicious recipes" have been packing 'em in for decades. All of a sudden they've decided to 'go for it' expansion-wise though: there is also one near King's Cross now, as well as Camden Town ("unlike the original, you can book, thus avoiding the horrendous waits!") and a Dalston branch opened in summer 2017.

Milk SW12 £21 **4 3 3**
20 Bedford Hill 020 8772 9085 11–2C
"The best breakfast in town", with "great staples
and specials that deliver on flavour", has earned
cult status for this Antipodean café in Balham, now
branching into evening service. "You have to pick
your times to get a seat", though – "my absolute
favourite place to be at 10.30am on a Saturday
morning; unfortunately, I'm not the only one...". A
cynical minority do loathe the place though: "it's
masquerading as some sort of high-end funky elite
dining experience" for "wannabe hipsters". / SW12
9RG; www.milk.london; @milkcoffeeldn; 10 pm; booking
D only.

**Min Jiang, The Royal Garden Hotel
W8** £81 **4 4 5**
2-24 Kensington High St 020 7361 1988 6–1A
"Never failing to impress my Chinese wife or
anyone we invite here" – this "very professional
and impressive" 8th-floor operation is not only one
of London's very best Chinese dining rooms, but –
"despite being in a hotel" – it also manages not to
be blighted by its "stunning views" ("go in daylight
to get the best of the panorama over Kensington
Gardens"). "If you want excellent dim sum or Peking
duck look no further": the food is "fresh and totally
engrossing" – particularly the wood-fired duck which
is "incredible" – and "given the quality and freshness
of the ingredients it is money well spent". / W8 4PT;
www.minjiang.co.uk; @minjianglondon; 10 pm.

Minnow SW4 **NEW** £54
21 The Pavement 020 7720 4105 11–2C
British food with an International twist is promised
at this new Clapham Common dining spot (literally
a little fish in a big pond, hence the name); chef
Jake Boyce formerly headed up the team at Jason
Atherton's Social Wine and Tapas. The all-day
restaurant runs a range of tricks to attract the local
hipsters – not just brunch and a Robata grill, but
also breakfast cocktails, 'pay-as-you-drink' wine by
the bottle, a walled garden and an honesty box. /
SW4 0HY; minnowclapham.co.uk; @minnowclapham;
10 pm.

Mint Leaf £69 **4 4 4**
Suffolk Pl, Haymarket, SW1
020 7930 9020 2–2C
Angel Ct, Lothbury, EC2
020 7600 0992 10–2C
The "wonderful and imaginative cuisine" matches
the snazzy contemporary décor at this Indian duo,
in a basement off Trafalgar Square and near Bank,
which scored well across the board this year. "Praise
was unanimous in our party of 30"; "we love this
place!" / www.mintleafrestaurant.com; 10.45 pm; SW1
closed Sat L & Sun D, EC2 closed Sat & Sun.

Mirch Masala SW17 £26 **4 2 1**
213 Upper Tooting Rd 020 8767 8638 11–2D
"Great flavours at very low prices" make it "well

worth travelling to Tooting" for this "no-nonsense"
Pakistani canteen, whose BYO policy, "bold
and chilli-hot flavours, and generous portions"
create "such great value". Top Tip – "weekends
(which can be busy) also offer some amazing
slow-cooked meat specials". / SW17 7TG;
www.mirchmasalarestaurant.co.uk; midnight; Cash only.

MNKY HSE W1 £86 **1 2 3**
10 Dover St 020 3870 4880 3–3C
"A great, happening vibe, and the food's not bad
either!" – so say fans of this large, "luxurious",
Latino dining and drinking den with resident DJ on
the Mayfair site that for decades was The Dover
Street Wine Bar (RIP). A significant minority find it
seriously disappointing however, particularly in the
food department. / W1S 4LQ; www.mnky-hse.com;
@mnky_hse; set weekday L £46 (FP).

The Modern Pantry £64 **2 2 2**
47-48 St Johns Sq, EC1 020 7553 9210 10–1A
The Alphabeta Bldg, 14 Finsbury Sq, EC2
020 3696 6565 13–2A
Aussie chef, Anna Hansen's "somewhat Spartan"
looking fusion ventures in Clerkenwell ("the better
of the two") and Finsbury Square are "great for
brunch", when options like "miso pancakes (who
knew?)" draw a major fan club. More generally
though her funky fusion dishes divide views – fans
praise "enjoyable combinations confounding any bias
against fusion fare", but critics disparage "over-fussy
straining with exotic ingredients doing nothing for
taste". / www.themodernpantry.co.uk; 10.30 pm, Sun
10 pm.

MOMMI SW4 £45 **3 4 3**
44 Clapham High St 020 3814 1818 11–2D
"Fun, buzzy local" in Clapham High Street offering
a "sensibly priced Asian-fusion menu and good
cocktails" – it seems to have bedded-in in its second
year, with improving scores for both food and service.
/ SW4 7UR; www.wearemommi.com; @wearemommi;
11 pm.

Momo W1 £72 **3 3 4**
25 Heddon St 020 7434 4040 4–3B
Twenty years on, the smart crowd have forgotten
it but the party's still going strong at Mourad
Mazouz's "chaotic but charming Moroccan" in
the Heddon Street foodie enclave off Regent
Street, whose couscous, tagines and other North
African dishes earn solid marks. / W1B 4BH;
www.momoresto.com; @momoresto; 11.30 pm, Sun 11
pm; credit card required to book.

Mon Plaisir WC2 £52 **2 3 5**
19-21 Monmouth St 020 7836 7243 5–2B
"I've been coming with friends since the '60s, and
though it's nothing too fancy (escargots, steak-frites,
excellent cheese) it never disappoints" – that's the
kind of loyalty which keeps this "very cosy", 70-year-
old bistro in business, and even if "maybe it's past its

best", "it's still hard not to fall in love with it". Much-extended over the years, "there are lots of small rooms, and although I can never decide if the food is as good as the decor, the eccentric layout is certainly all part of its charm". Top Tip – "pre-theatre it's a steal". / WC2H 9DD; www.monplaisir.co.uk; @MonPlaisir4; 11 pm; closed Sun.

Mona Lisa SW10　　　**£40**　　🇳🇿
417 King's Rd　020 7376 5447　6–3B
"Great value for money in Chelsea" is to be had at this veteran, Italian-run greasy spoon near World's End, which has "a super feel to it". Service starts at 7am with "the best old-fashioned classic English trucker's breakfast" and runs through to 11pm. Top Tip – miraculously for SW10, you can still get a "hearty" three-course evening meal for £10: no wonder it's "always packed". / SW10 0LR; monalisarestaurant.co.uk; 11 pm, Sun 5.30 pm; closed Sun D; No Amex.

Monkey Temple W12　　**£30**　　🇳🇿
92 Askew Rd　020 8743 4597　8–1B
"Delicious Nepali curries" make this newish cuzza a welcome addition on ever-more "happening Askew Road" (in deepest Shepherds Bush). They're "building a loyal local clientele" with their speciality dishes but also do the "usual suspects" of Indian cuisine, all at good prices. / W12 9BL; monkeytempleonline.co.uk; 10 pm, Fri & Sat 10.30 pm, Sun 9.30 pm.

Monmouth Coffee Company　　　**£7**　　🇳🇿
27 Monmouth St, WC2　020 7232 3010　5–2B
Arch 3 Spa North, btwn Dockley Rd & Spa Rd, SE16　020 7232 3010　12–2A
2 Park St, SE1　020 7232 3010　10–4C
"It's cramped, it's busy", but "you'll never get bored of the variety of coffee flavours on offer", at these epic caffeine-stops – the best-known of London's top tier coffee house chains – where "excellent recommendations" from the "really knowledgeable" staff ("who will let you sample and taste different growths") really add to the experience. Borough Market is the definitive branch, and – as well as the pastries offered elsewhere in the group – also has bread and jam on hand to soak up the brews. / www.monmouthcoffee.co.uk; WC2 6:30 pm; SE1 6 pm; SE16 Sat 1.30 pm; WC2 & SE1 closed Sun; no Amex; no booking.

Monty's Deli N1 NEW　　**£36**　🇳🇿
225-227 Hoxton St　020 7729 5737　14–2A
After many years in Bermondsey and a £50k crowdfund, Mark Ogus and Owen Barratt now have a stylish, boothed (if "noisy") Hoxton diner in which to serve their "great sandwiches and bagels" and other 'Jewish soul food'. / N1; montys-deli.com; @MontysDeli.

Morada Brindisa Asador W1　　　**£50**　🇳🇿
18-20 Rupert St　020 7478 8758　4–3D
"Excellent meat from the asador" – a Castilian-style wood-fire roasting oven – "is the main point" at this stylish, but slightly clinical two-year-old off Shaftesbury Avenue (from the Brindisa group), but its other "tasty" tapas dishes generally also get the thumbs up. / W1D 6DE; www.brindisatapaskitchens.com/morada; @Brindisa; 11 pm.

The Morgan Arms E3　　**£49**　🇳🇿
43 Morgan St　020 8980 6389　14–2C
This "high-end gastropub" in Mile End is "often rammed" and "a bit noisy due to lack of soft furnishings". But you usually (if not quite always) get "great food here" – "especially Sunday lunch". / E3 5AA; www.morganarmsbow.com; @TheMorganArms; 10 pm.

Morito　　　　**£44**　🇳🇿
195 Hackney Rd, E2　020 7613 0754　14–2A
32 Exmouth Mkt, EC1　020 7278 7007　10–1A
"Moro's little sister two doors down from Moro itself" nowadays also has a Hackney outpost, near Columbia Road Flower Market, and although the newer branch is "more roomy" and "less frenetic than the original", "pressure on tables is fierce" at both of these "crowded, small eateries". That said, they "run like clockwork" on the whole, and service is "incredibly helpful and knowledgeable". The draw? – "scrumptious" Spanish/North African tapas with "imaginative modern twists" at prices that are "terrific value". / EC1 11 pm, Sun 4 pm; E2 10.30 pm, Sun 9 pm; EC1 closed Sun D; no booking.

MORO EC1　　　　**£61**　🇳🇿
34-36 Exmouth Mkt　020 7833 8336　10–1A
"I've been going for 20 years but it still surprises me" – Samuel and Samantha Clark's epic Exmouth Market "institution" remains "a regular haunt" for hordes of reporters thanks to its "sunshine-filled" neo-Spanish and north African dishes, even if "the poor acoustics of this former supermarket make it hard to maintain a conversation when it's busy". By and large it "goes from strength to strength" – if ratings aren't quite as stratospheric as once they were maybe it's just "no longer so different from the competition as to be as remarkable as it was". / EC1R 4QE; www.moro.co.uk; 10.30 pm; closed Sun D.

Motcombs SW1　　　**£55**　🇳🇿
26 Motcomb St　020 7235 6382　6–1D
That it's "stuck somewhere in the '70s" is a good thing for most (if not quite all) who report on this "Belgravia stalwart", applauding its "always reliable" standards (both in the upstairs wine bar and downstairs restaurant). / SW1X 8JU; www.motcombs.co.uk; @Motcombs; 10 pm; closed Sun D.

Kricket W1

La Dame de Pic EC3

Minnow SW4

Mother SW11 `NEW`
2 Archers Lane   020 7622 4386   11–1C
From Copenhagen's meatpacking district – the first UK venture of this hugely popular pizza concept in Denmark, is one of the first outlets to have opened in Battersea Power Station's Circus West Village in July 2017, occupying a moodily, low-lit railway arch near Chelsea Bridge. The website promises 'Italian pizza without all the nonsense'… but still notes its 'signature sourdough', 'seawater' and 'manufacturing its own mozzarella'. / SW11 8AB; www.motherrestaurant.co.uk; @mother_ldn.

Mr Bao SE15   **£35**   **4**|**3**|**3**
293 Rye Ln   020 7635 0325   1–4D
"Cute and cool, with interesting cocktails" – this "small and friendly" Taiwanese inspires "absolute love" with its "great bao buns and sides" that are "cheap, filling and really, really delicious". / SE15 4UA; www.mrbao.co.uk; @MrBaoUK; 11 pm.

Mr Chow SW1   **£88**   2|2|2
151 Knightsbridge   020 7589 7347   6–1D
Scant reports this year at this datedly-glamorous A-lister of yesteryear near 1 Hyde Park, which built an international brand in the '60s with its formula of Chinese cuisine served by Italian waiters. In recent years its food has been consistently tolerable, but very pricey, so we have felt able to keep last year's rating, although feedback was too thin to rate it properly. / SW1X 7PA; www.mrchow.com; @mrchow; midnight; closed Mon L.

Murano W1   **£99**   **5**|**5**|**4**
20-22 Queen St   020 7495 1127   3–3B
As it enters its tenth year, Angela Hartnett's "understatedly brilliant" Mayfair haven is an unusual example of a swanky, celeb-backed restaurant just getting better and better as it approaches middle age. Though not enormously distinctive in design, "the dining room is beautifully set up – you don't feel crowded" – and the "charmingly kind staff" help "create a wonderful and romantic atmosphere". Head chef Pip Lacey's Italian-inspired cooking is taking the food quality here to new heights – "fantastically good" – and reporters "love that you can construct your own tasting menu", whereby you select any number of dishes from the menu's five sections in the order of your choosing. STOP PRESS: in July 2017, Pip Lacey left Murano, to be replaced by Oscar Holgado. Here's hoping he can keep up the good work. / W1J 5PP; www.muranolondon.com; @muranolondon; 11 pm; closed Sun; credit card required to book; set weekday L £57 (FP).

Mustard W6   **£44**   **3**|**3**|**3**
98-100 Shepherd's Bush Rd
020 3019 1175   8–1C
Smart brasserie decor (superior to the Café Rouge it replaced) and a professional attitude up the tone of this neighbourhood yearling north of Brook Green.
The affordable cuisine? – it's mostly decent, but can also be a little "comme ci, comme ça". / W6 7PD; www.mustardrestaurants.co.uk; @mustarddining; 10 pm, Sun 5 pm; closed Mon & Sun D.

My Neighbours The Dumplings E5   **£41**   **4**|2|2
165 Lower Clapton Rd   020 3327 1556   14–1B
"Excellent and innovative" Chinese dumplings win praise for this engaging if sometimes "chaotic" Clapton canteen – a year-old pop-up-turned-permanent, which in summer 2017 opened a large lantern-lit 'Hanging Garden' space. / E5 8EQ; www.myneighboursthedumplings.com; @my_neighbours; 10.30 pm, Fri & Sat 11 pm, Sun 9.30 pm; closed Mon.

Namaaste Kitchen NW1 £43   **3**|**3**|2
64 Parkway   020 7485 5977   9–3B
"Everything seems to be cooked from scratch" at this Camden Town curry house, "so be prepared to wait, especially if you don't have a starter!". "The cooking can miss its mark, but is often very good." / NW1 7AH; www.namaastekitchen.co.uk; @NamaasteKitchen; 11 pm.

Nanashi EC2 `NEW`   **£61**
14 Rivington St   020 7686 0010   13–2B
"Top notch sushi with some great accompaniments" feature in one early report on this 'environmentally conscious modern Japanese', newly opened in Shoreditch. / EC2A 3DU; www.nanashi.co.uk; 10 pm, Sat 11 pm.

Nanban SW9   **£44**   **4**|**3**|**3**
Coldharbour Ln   020 7346 0098   11–2D
"The food is so different!" – "very unusual combos that you don't think are going to work, but which they pull off" – at former MasterChef winner Tim Anderson's "thoroughly interesting Japanese-soul-food-fusion" venue beside Brixton market. "Staff are great and really work hard too, but there can be delays in getting attention". / SW9 8LF; www.nanban.co.uk; @NanbanLondon; 11 pm, Sun 10 pm.

The Narrow E14   **£57**   **3**|**3**|**4**
44 Narrow St   020 7592 7950   12–1B
*Is Gordon Ramsay's Limehouse pub finally, after all these years, starting to live up to its "lovely riverside setting"? Even a reporter who can't resist a swipe at the "****" food admits that "the building and location make it great for a family-and-friends lunch" and all other feedback this year praises "tasty food at quite reasonable prices". / E14 8DP; www.gordonramsayrestaurants.com/the-narrow; @thenarrow; 10.30 pm, Sun 8 pm.*

Native WC2   **£55**   **4**|**3**|2
3 Neal's Yd   020 3638 8214   5–2C
With an emphasis on game and foraging dishes, this "bijou" Covent Garden yearling is "right on trend".

There's a small upstairs, and larger basement whose "minimalist decor gives rise to poor acoustics", but "stick with it, as the unusual combinations work well and are full of flavour". / WC2H 9DP; www.eatnative.co.uk; @eatnativeuk; 10 pm.

Naughty Piglets SW2 £56 5 5 3
28 Brixton Water Ln   020 7274 7796   11–2D
That "every dish is a stand out, every time", plus the "really exciting natural wine list" has made a smash hit of this "personal and friendly" two-year-old, "tucked away in a Brixton side street" and "run by a charming husband-and-wife team", Margaux Aubry and Joe Sharratt. On the strength of this debut, Andrew Lloyd Webber recently scouted them to open 'The Other Naughty Piglets', see also. / SW2 1PE; www.naughtypiglets.co.uk; 10 pm, Sun 3 pm.

Nautilus NW6 £35 4 3 1
27-29 Fortune Green Rd
020 7435 2532   1–1B
"It has seen better days in terms of décor" (and we've been saying that for over 20 years), but no-one is put off at this classic West Hampstead chippy, where "plaice fried in matzo" is a highlight of the "excellent, fresh fish". Top Tip – "best for takeaway!" but eat in and you can BYO. / NW6 1DU; 10 pm; closed Sun; No Amex.

The Ned EC2 NEW
27 Poultry   020 3828 2000   10–2C
If Cecil B DeMille had designed a City food court, it might have looked something like Soho House & Co's and Sydell Group's gob-smacking refurbishment of the banking hall of the former, Lutyens-designed, Grade I, Midland Bank HQ, just next to the Bank of England. With 850 covers split between seven different operations, it is long on glamour, short on cosiness, and feels like the ginormous hotel foyer that it now is. The food offering mixes existing brands – like Cecconi's – with those created for the operation: Millie's Lounge (British), The Nickel Bar (American), Zobler's Delicatessen ('NYC'-Jewish), Malibu Kitchen (Californian), Kaia (Asian-Pacific) and Café Sou (French). Members bypass all that 'open air' eating for the cosier 'Lutyens Grill' (a steakhouse) or head for one of the two club bars, either in the roof, or the old bank vaults. / EC2R 8AJ; www.thened.com; @TheNedLondon.

Needoo E1 £25 4 3 2
87 New Rd   020 7247 0648   13–2D
"It's like eating a great curry in a school cafeteria", say fans of this East End Pakistani BYO (a rival to nearby Tayyab's) – "the food is awesome! Please pass the lamb chops…" / E1 1HH; www.needoogrill.co.uk; @NeedooGrill; 11.30 pm.

Neo Bistro W1 NEW £54
11 Woodstock St   0207 499 9427   3–1B
On paper, this summer 2017 newcomer near the

top of New Bond Street has a fine pedigree – Alex Harper was formerly head chef at The Harwood Arms and Mark Jarvis is chef-patron of Anglo. As the name hints, it's inspired by the modern bistros of Paris, offering a short à la carte plus, in the evening, a 6-course tasting menu. Early press reports on its creative modern European dishes wax lyrical. / W1C 2JF; www.neobistro.co.uk; @neo_bistro; 9.45 pm.

New World W1 £35 2 1 2
1 Gerrard Place   020 7734 0677   /
020 7734 0396   5–3A
"Dim sum still served from old-fashioned trolleys" ensure this massive fixture is still "fabulous fun!" – "in and out as quick as you like, with a little bit of theatre". "Otherwise the food is average for Chinatown." / W1D 5PA; www.newworldlondon.com; 10.30 pm, Sun 9.30 pm.

Niche EC1 £53 2 3 2
197-199 Rosebery Avenue
020 7837 5048   9–3D
"You wouldn't know it from the pastries" but this casual spot, "well-placed for Sadler's Wells and Angel" is 100% gluten free and Grade A certified by Coeliac UK, and "offers a good mix of choices from healthy (salads) to less so (pie and mash, burgers etc)". Most reports say it's "a great choice for a quick bite", but even a critic who claimed the fare was "absolutely tasteless" said: "my friend with strict dietary requirements loved having a choice of whatever she wanted". / EC1R 4TJ; www.nichefoodanddrink.com; @Nichefooddrink ; 9.45 pm, Fri & Sat 10.15 pm, Sun 3.30 pm.

The Ninth London W1 £68 4 3 3
22 Charlotte St   020 3019 0880   2–1C
Jun Tanaka's "consistently brilliant food – simple but immaculately presented, with amazing flavours" – wins rave reviews for his "shabby-chic-meets-modern-industrial" Fitzrovia yearling, also praised also for its "lovely" staff. Having said that, there is a minority who feel it has been hyped: "it was good, but after all the raves, I somehow expected more". / W1T 2NB; www.theninthlondon.com; @theninthlondon; 10 pm, Thu-Sat 10.30 pm; closed Sun.

Ninth Ward EC1 £32 2 3 4
99-101 Farringdon Rd   020 7833 2949   10–1A
"A very good range of craft beers and interesting decor" are perhaps the highlights of this dark and divey, southern US-themed hangout near Farringdon station, but its filling dude food can be "great value" too. / EC1R 3BN; www.ninthwardlondon.com; @9thWardLondon; 10 pm.

Nirvana Kitchen W1 £69 4 2 2
61 Upper Berkeley St   020 7958 3222   7–1D
There's relatively limited feedback so far – but all of it positive – for this glossy pan-Asian yearling adjoining a hotel near Marble Arch, which combines

cuisines stretching from India eastwards to Korea and Japan… sometimes within a single dish; service seems to be the weakest link. / W1H 7PP; www.nirvana.restaurant; @KitchensNirvana; 10.45 pm; closed Sun; set weekday L £42 (FP).

No 197 Chiswick Fire Station W4 £53 2|2|4
197-199 Chiswick High Rd
020 3857 4669 8–2A
A "re-invention of the old fire station in Chiswick" – from neighbourhood bar chain Darwin & Wallace – "an open airy space, successfully divided into various differing areas". Its Aussie-style menu generally produces "well thought-out" and "tasty" dishes, but although service is "friendly" its speed can be "very slack". / W4 2DR; www.no197chiswickfirestation.com; @No197Chiswick; midnight, Fri & Sat 1 am, Sun 11 pm; booking max 9 may apply.

Noble Rot WC1 £66 3|3|4
51 Lamb's Conduit St 020 7242 8963 2–1D
The "ridiculously comprehensive and thoughtful wine list" has established Mark Andrew and Daniel Keeling's "knockout" Bloomsbury yearling as London's No.1 destination for œnophiles. Housed in the "buzzy", "dark-wooded" premises which traded for decades as Vats, the variety of vintages is "fascinating", with "some exceptional rarities, many in per glass portions". "They take pride in the food too", but it's relatively "simple" and no criticism to say this is "more a wine bar than a restaurant". Top Menu Tip – fish dishes in oxidized white burgundy. / WC1N 3NB; www.noblerot.co.uk; @noblerotbar; 10 pm; set weekday L £42 (FP).

Nobu, Metropolitan Hotel W1 £99 3|2|1
19 Old Park Ln 020 7447 4747 3–4A
Celebrating its 20th anniversary this year – this once-trailblazing Japanese fusion icon, overlooking Hyde Park, "doesn't pull the crowds the way it used to" ("go if you like loud groups of celebratory thirtysomethings, or watching people taking endless selfies") but "the food can still sparkle" to the extent fans find "incredible". "There are IKEA salesrooms that look more luxurious than this place", however, "prices are eyewatering", and "it's insulting how staff's main aim seems to be turning tables faster than you can eat"… at least some things never change. / W1K 1LB; www.noburestaurants.com; @NobuOldParkLane; 10.15 pm, Fri & Sat 11 pm, Sun 10 pm; set weekday L £69 (FP).

Nobu Berkeley W1 £88 3|2|3
15 Berkeley St 020 7290 9222 3–3C
"It still has it on the fusion-food front", and this 'newer Nobu' in Mayfair inspires much more feedback and is rated considerably higher nowadays than the original Park Lane branch, particularly the ambience. The criticisms it attracts haven't

changed since day one – it's above "a pretentious bar", some tables are "cramped" and "canteen"-like, it can seem "grossly overpriced", and critics feel "it's one for the tasteless 'in' crowd". / W1J 8DY; www.noburestaurants.com; @NobuBerkeleyST; 11 pm, Thu-Sat midnight, Sun 9.45 pm; closed Sun L.

Nobu Shoreditch EC2 NEW
10-50 Willow St 020 3818 3790 13–1B
Inside the brand's newly opened (July 2017) Shoreditch hotel, the 240-seat restaurant incorporates a sushi counter, bar and outdoor courtyard, and occupies almost an entire floor of the building. It opened too late for survey feedback, but aside from the odd exclusive dish here, a repeat of the cooking at the other two London Nobus is our expectation. / EC2A 4BH; www.nobuhotelshoreditch.com; @NobuShoreditch.

Noizé W1 NEW
39 Whitfield St 2–1C
Opening in early October 2017, on the former site of Ollie Dabbous's "loft-style", industrial-chic restaurant, Dabbous, comes a rustic French bistro (quite a departure!) from former co-owner and manager of Pied à Terre, Mathieu Germond (and Pied à Terre owner, David Moore, is also involved). / W1T 2SF; @NoizeRestaurant.

Noor Jahan £43 3|3|3
2a Bina Gdns, SW5 020 7373 6522 2–2B
26 Sussex Pl, W2 020 7402 2332 7–1D
"A sure thing after over 20 years" – this "unfailing and very traditional" (and "sensibly priced") Earl's Court curry house is "the perfect Indian" for its well-heeled regular crowd, and is perpetually "buzzing" and "crowded". It has a lesser-known Bayswater spin-off, which is likewise a "cut above the norm". / W2 11.30 pm, Sun 11 pm; SW5 11.30 pm.

Nopi W1 £74 4|3|3
21-22 Warwick St 020 7494 9584 4–3B
"The flavours in the food just leap out and astound you" at Yotam Ottolenghi's "bustling and deservedly popular" (if "slightly clinical") Soho flagship, serving a "sensational" selection of the Middle Eastern/Mediterranean small plates that have made him a household name, with "lovely fresh ingredients and wonderful combinations of flavour, colourfully presented". / W1B 5NE; www.nopi-restaurant.com; @ottolenghi; 10.30 pm, Sun 4 pm; closed Sun D.

Nordic Bakery £13 3|2|3
14a Golden Sq, W1 020 3230 1077 4–3C
37b New Cavendish St, W1
020 7935 3590 2–1A
48 Dorset St, W1 020 7487 5877 2–1A
55 Neal Street, Seven Dials, WC2
020 7836 4996 5–3C
"You can't better the cinnamon buns, rye rolls and coffee" served at this quartet of Scandi cafés in

Soho, Marylebone and now also Covent Garden, which – leaving aside a hint of "design mag self-consciousness" – are "great for a sweet or savoury treat". / nordicbakery.com; Golden Square 8 pm, Sat & Sun 7 pm; Cavendish Street & Dorset Street 6.30 pm, Sun 6 pm.

The Norfolk Arms WC1 £46 🟥2️⃣2️⃣
28 Leigh St   020 7388 3937   9–4C
The Spanish-accented scoff is "surprisingly good" at this "noisy and unattractive pub" near King's Cross: "it can seem a bit disorganised", but "the quality of the food belies the absence of sophistication" and "makes it worth sticking it out". / WC1H 9EP; www.norfolkarms.co.uk; 11pm, Sun 10.30 pm; No Amex.

North China W3 £43 🟥4️⃣2️⃣
305 Uxbridge Rd   020 8992 9183   8–1A
"Whenever the itch comes for a Chinese", Acton folk head for this above-average neighbourhood stalwart – "the food's just right and the welcome is real". / W3 9QU; www.northchina.co.uk; 11 pm, Fri & Sat 11.30 pm.

North Sea Fish WC1 £44 🟥2️⃣2️⃣
7-8 Leigh St   020 7387 5892   9–4C
"One of London's better chippies" – this "traditional family-run" outfit in Bloomsbury remains hugely popular thanks to its big variety of "very fresh, totally reliable fish" (all deep-fried) in "large portions". It has "generally freshened itself up since the new generation took the reins", bringing a "slightly smarter ambience and decor". / WC1H 9EW; www.northseafishrestaurant.co.uk; 10 pm, Sun 9.30 pm; closed Sun D; No Amex.

The Northall, Corinthia Hotel WC2 £89 🟥3️⃣3️⃣
10a Northumberland Ave
020 7321 3100   2–3C
Given its "giant" and – to many tastes – "wonderful" interior, this plush five-star hotel dining room near Trafalgar Square is surprisingly "not on the radar", and especially "if you want somewhere with understated class in which to do business", and with "good-quality modern British cuisine", it can be ideal. On the debit side, "some dishes lack oomph", and, particularly when empty, it can "lack ambience" ("it felt like we were eating in a provincial railway station waiting room"). / WC2N 5AE; www.thenorthall.co.uk; @CorinthiaLondon; 10.45 pm; set pre-theatre £52 (FP), set weekday L £53 (FP).

Northbank EC4 £58 🟥2️⃣3️⃣
One Paul's Walk   020 7329 9299   10–3B
"Food with a view" across the Thames is a "real treat" at this 10-year-old City stalwart beside the Wobbly Bridge, directly opposite Tate Modern. After a wobble in last year's survey, marks for food have revived under new chef John Harrison. / EC4V 3QH; www.northbankrestaurant.co.uk; @NorthbankLondon; 10 pm; closed Sun.

Novikov (Asian restaurant) W1 £94 🟥2️⃣🟥
50a Berkeley St   020 7399 4330   3–3C
"Sod the bill!" – "The buzz is electric and the pan-Asian small plates delectable" at this "brassy" and "theatrical" Russian-owned scene near Berkeley Square, where the crowd's "always very glamorous". / W1J 8HA; www.novikovrestaurant.co.uk; @NovikovLondon; 11.15 pm; set weekday L £49 (FP).

Novikov (Italian restaurant) W1 £106 1️⃣2️⃣2️⃣
50a Berkeley St   020 7399 4330   3–3C
"Come to see and be seen" – "but not on an empty stomach, as you pay so much for the location not the food" – if you visit the Italian rear dining room of this glam, Russian-owned eurotrash-magnet in Mayfair, which serves "unexceptional Italian fare at exceptional prices". / W1J 8HA; www.novikovrestaurant.co.uk; @NovikovLondon; 11.45 pm.

Nukis Kitchen W13 £27 🟥2️⃣2️⃣
58 Northfield Avenue   020 8579 2113   1–3A
"You must book in advance for this local Thai yearling" – the best eating option in Northfields: "it's always packed" (but then it is tiny…) / W13 9RR; 10 pm.

Numero Uno SW11 £54 🟥4️⃣3️⃣
139 Northcote Rd   020 7978 5837   11–2C
"Consistently good over 20 years" – this Italian stalwart in Battersea's Nappy Valley has "very friendly staff who love children" and is "always packed". The food? "not in 'wow'-factor territory but more-than-competent". / SW11 6PX; 11.30 pm; No Amex.

Nuovi Sapori SW6 £49 🟥4️⃣3️⃣
295 New King's Rd   020 7736 3363   11–1B
Limited but upbeat feedback on this "friendly local Fulham trattoria" near Parsons Green – "always a pleasant experience with food that doesn't disappoint". / SW6 4RE; www.nuovisaporilondon.co.uk; 11 pm; closed Sun; booking max 6 may apply.

Nutbourne SW11 NEW £59 🟥3️⃣4️⃣
29 Ransomes Dock, 35-37 Parkgate Rd
020 7350 0555   6–4C
"A worthy successor to Ransome's Dock" (long RIP) – the Gladwin brothers' Battersea haunt has a very pleasant "backwater" location in docks by the Thames and provides "rather good, rustic" 'farm-to-table' British small plates alongside some "amazing English wine" (the restaurant is named for the family vineyard in Sussex). / SW11 4NP; www.nutbourne-restaurant.com; @NutbourneSW11; set weekday L £37 (FP).

O'ver SE1 £51 4 3 3
44-46 Southwark St   020 7378 9933   10–4C
Sea water is a key ingredient of the "perfect pizza" at Tommaso Mastromatteo's popular, new white-walled Neapolitan café in Southwark, which also serves other "really interesting" regional dishes. / SE1 1UN; www.overuk.com; 10.30 pm.

Oak £50 3 3 4
243 Goldhawk Rd, W12   020 8741 7700   8–1B
137 Westbourne Park Rd, W2
020 7221 3355   7–1B
"Delicious, light, crispy pizza" in a "retired pub" remains a "winning formula", both at the "lovely, cosy and very atmospheric" Notting Hill haunt, and its sizeable and "relaxing" Shepherd's Bush follow-up. / W12 10.30pm, Fri & Sat 11 pm Sun 9.30pm; W2 10.30pm, Fri & Sat 11 pm, Sun 10 pm.

Oak N4 N4 NEW £31
5-7 Wells Terrace 07710 761606 9–1D
You can select from 150 wines by the bottle to drink-in or take-away at this new indie wine store and tasting rooms. Limited feedback to-date say it's "a great addition to the area and presumably will find a larger audience once the developments at nearby Finsbury Park station have been completed". The "the simple nibbly platters" very much play second fiddle however. / N4 3JU; oakn4.co.uk; @oak_n4; 11 pm, Fri & Sat midnight; closed Mon.

Obicà £56 3 2 2
11 Charlotte St, W1   020 7637 7153   2–1C
19-20 Poland St, W1   020 3327 7070   4–1C
96 Draycott Ave, SW3   020 7581 5208   6–2C
1 West Wintergarden, 35 Bank St, E14
020 7719 1532   12–1C
4 Limeburners Lane, 1 Ludgate Hill, EC4
020 3327 0984   10–2A
This Rome-based chain is inspired by Japanese sushi-bars and serves "tasty small plates of Italian food". The five "efficiently run" London branches, from South Ken to Canary Wharf, provide a "surprisingly good experience… so long as you like mozzarella or burrata". / obica.com; 10 pm - 11 pm; E14 Sat 8 pm; E14 & EC4 Closed Sun.

Oblix SE1 £87 2 2 3
Level 32, The Shard, 31 St. Thomas St
020 7268 6700   10–4C
"Yes the views are amazing and that is what you go for" (including on business), but this 32-floor venue is "living off its location" – the food is "expensive and nothing to write home about" and service – though more amiable of late – still so so. / SE1 9RY; www.oblixrestaurant.com; @OblixRestaurant; 11 pm; booking max 6 may apply.

Odette's NW1 £68 4 3 4
130 Regents Park Rd   020 7586 8569   9–3B
Bryn Williams's "consistently excellent" cuisine is

"really good value for the quality" and ensures that this well-known venue maintains its held-long reputation as "the best in Primrose Hill". It's "a good place for a celebration", especially of the "romantic" variety; "book yourself in a corner and the atmosphere is lovely". / NW1 8XL; www.odettesprimrosehill.com; @Odettes_rest; 10 pm, Sat 10.30 pm, Sun 9.30 pm; closed Mon; No Amex; set weekday L £42 (FP).

Ognisko Restaurant SW7 £50 3 3 5
55 Prince's Gate, Exhibition Rd
020 7589 0101   6–1C
The "very beautiful time-warp setting" of an impressive old émigrés club, complete with "clubby" bar and "high-ceilinged dining room", helps create a "very relaxing" experience at Jan Woroniecki's South Kensington gem (whose "terrace at the rear is a hidden secret for outdoor summer dining"). The "Polish comfort food" is "lighter than you expect", and there's "a huge range of vodkas". / SW7 2PN; www.ogniskorestaurant.co.uk; @OgniskoRest; 11.15 pm, Sun 10.30 pm; closed Mon L; No trainers.

Oka £49 4 2 2
Kingly Court, 1 Kingly Court, W1
020 7734 3556   4–2B
251 King's Rd, SW3   020 7349 8725   6–3C
71 Regents Park Rd, NW1
020 7483 2072   9–3B
"Sushi that is inventive and spankingly fresh" along with "delicious" Asian fusion dishes deliver "great value for money" at these little Japanese outlets – "the only problem is that they're so small you often can't get in!". / www.okarestaurant.co.uk; 10.30 pm.

Oklava EC2 £56 4 2 3
74 Luke St   020 7729 3032   13–1B
Selin Kiazim showcases her "superb, generous, tasty and thought-through Turkish food" in this "small but elegant", tile-and-brick two-year-old, complete with open kitchen, in Shoreditch. / EC2A 4PY; www.oklava.co.uk; @oklava_ldn; 10.30 pm, Sun 4 pm; booking max 6 may apply.

Oldroyd N1 £51 4 3 2
344 Upper St   020 8617 9010   9–3D
That "it's a bit of a basic, tiny space" colours feedback on Tom Oldroyd's accomplished but "crushed" Islington yearling. On most accounts his "fabulously tasty, daily changing (if limited) menu" is full compensation, but there's a noticeable minority for whom "though it's undeniably good", the size hinders appreciation. / N1 0PD; www.oldroydlondon.com; @oldroydlondon; 10.30 pm, Fri 11 pm, Sun 9.30 pm; booking max 4 may apply.

Oliver Maki W1 £69 3 3 3
33 Dean St   020 7734 0408   5–2A
Mixed views on this two-floor Soho yearling – first London branch of a Gulf-based fusion chain: fans

say the *"sushi's delicious to eat and beautiful to look at"*, but doubters find the whole approach *"a bit too cookie cutter"*. / W1D 4PW; www.olivermaki.co.uk; @OliverMakiUK; 10.30 pm, Fri & Sat 11 pm, Sun 9.30 pm.

Oliveto SW1 £60 4 2 1
49 Elizabeth St   020 7730 0074   2–4A
"You can't go wrong", say fans of this *"very busy"* Sardinian, which provides pizza and pasta *"of a consistently high standard"* and which is *"good value for money"* too, at least by the standards of pricey Belgravia; it's also *"excellent for families with children"*. / SW1W 9PP; www.olivorestaurants.com/oliveto; 10.30 pm, Sun 10 pm; booking max 7 may apply.

Olivo SW1 £75 3 3 2
21 Eccleston St   020 7730 2505   2–4B
"The original of this Belgravia chain of Sardinian stalwarts" – this *"friendly and efficient"* fixture is a *"classic Italian"* which provides a *"failsafe choice, with excellent seasonal specials"*. *"A very welcome refurbishment means it's even now possible to hold a conversation while eating!"* / SW1W 9LX; www.olivorestaurants.com; 10.30 pm; closed Sat L & Sun L.

Olivocarne SW1 £64 3 3 2
61 Elizabeth St   020 7730 7997   2–4A
Part of the local Olivo, Oliveto, etc empire – this offbeat but upscale Belgravian continues in the good-but-pricey mould of Mauro Sanna's other venues – here the traditional Sardinian cuisine puts more of an emphasis on meat. / SW1W 9PP; www.olivorestaurants.com; 11 pm, Sun 10.30 pm.

Olivomare SW1 £69 3 2 2
10 Lower Belgrave St   020 7730 9022   2–4B
"Memorably succulent fish" is the acclaimed highlight of Mauro Sanna's *"cosmopolitan"* Sardinian in Belgravia, which on many accounts is an accomplished and *"enjoyably hustling and bustling"* all-rounder. To some tastes however, the idiosyncratic decor is more soulless than it is stylish, and the odd blip on service also hit ratings this year. / SW1W 0LJ; www.olivorestaurants.com; 11 pm, Sun 10.30 pm; booking max 10 may apply.

Olympic, Olympic Studios SW13 £50 2 2 3
117-123 Church Rd   020 8912 5161   11–1A
This *"lively"* all-day brasserie forms part of Barnes's indie cinema and members' club, in a former recording studio (famous amongst '60s/'70s rock anoraks for many iconic tracks). For the well-heeled locals *"it ticks all the boxes"* – *"great for breakfast/ brunch, both healthy and indulgent"*, and *"perfect before or after a film"*. It does run the risk of being *"complacent"* though, and *"the cooking is a bit ordinaire"*. / SW13 9HL; www.olympiccinema.co.uk;

@Olympic_Cinema; 11 pm, Fri & Sat midnight, Sun 10 pm.

Olympus Fish N3 £35 4 5 2
140-144 Ballards Ln   020 8371 8666   1–1B
"Outstanding fresh fish cooked on a charcoal grill" – and tablecloths! – ensure this *"delightful"* family-run fixture in Finchley is *"definitely the best fish 'n' chips in the area"*. / N3 2PA; www.olympusrestaurant.co.uk; @Olympus_London; 11 pm.

On The Bab £36 3 2 2
39 Marylebone Ln, W1   020 7935 2000   2–1A
36 Wellington St, WC2   020 7240 8825   5–3D
305 Old St, EC1   020 7683 0361   13–1B
9 Ludgate Broadway, EC4
020 7248 8777   10–2A
"Amazingly tasty bites" (*"very good chicken"* is the standout) keeps these *"fun, modern and minimalist"*, K-pop-styled street food joints *"crowded and bustling"*; expect *"lots of directional haircuts among fellow diners"*. / onthebab.co.uk; EC1 & WC2 10.30 pm, Sun 10 pm; W1 & EC4 4 pm; EC4 closed Sat & Sun; W1 closed Sun.

One Canada Square E14 £62 2 4 3
1 Canada Square   020 7559 5199   12–1C
In the lobby of Canary Wharf's most iconic building, it's no surprise that this modern European outfit is geared towards business dining – a function it generally performs well. On Friday and Saturday nights, it caters for post-office excess with a *"bottomless dinner"*. / E14 5AB; www.onecanadasquarerestaurant.com; @OneCanadaSquare; 10.45 pm; closed Sun.

108 Brasserie W1 £59 3 3 3
108 Marylebone Ln   020 7969 3900   2–1A
Attractive, spacious hotel dining room at the top end of Marylebone Lane, which wins praise as an *"efficient and useful option"* serving a wide variety of consistently well-rated brasserie fare, much of it from the Josper Grill. / W1U 2QE; www.108brasserie.com; @108Marylebone; 10.30pm.

108 Garage W10 NEW £60 5 4 5
108 Golborne Rd   020 8969 3769   7–1A
Just about *"the hottest newcomer of the year"*: *"chef Chris Denny is truly talented, and a name to remember!"*. This *"wacky, noisy and stimulating"*, *"NYC-vibe"* debutante is a *"laid-back"*, cooly grungy garage-conversion, on *"one of West London's most interesting streets"* (at the top end of Portobello Market). The food is *"to die for"* – *"light but satisfying cooking with brilliant use of herbs and greens"*. It's just *"a pity you can't get in any more"*. (In September 2017, they are set to open a second venture nearby: Southam Street.) / W10 5PS; www.108garage.com.

100 Wardour Street W1 £69 [2][2][3]
100 Wardour St   020 7314 4000   4–2D
Latest, year-old incarnation of this two-floor venue – once famous as the Marquee Club, and which since 1995 under D&D London has been multiply re-launched (as Mezzo, Floridita, Carom… maybe others we've forgotten). All the feedback we have for its latest, plus-ça-change mix of DJs, cocktails, Asian/European cuisine and dancing are OK, but given its massive central Soho site, what's most striking is how little interest it piques. / W1F 0TN; www.100wardourst.com; @100WardourSt.

1 Lombard Street EC3 £71 [2][2][3]
1 Lombard St   020 7929 6611   10–3C
"A great central location" – a former banking hall "right in the heart of the City" – is key to the success of Soren Jessen's well-known expense-accounter favourite. The jaundiced view is that it's "a boring place" for "City types who can't think of anywhere else": a more upbeat take is that while it's "overpriced", it's "decent and trusty". / EC3V 9AA; www.1lombardstreet.com; 10 pm; closed Sat & Sun; booking max 10 may apply.

One-O-One, Park Tower Knightsbridge SW1 £98 [4][3][1]
101 Knightsbridge   020 7290 7101   6–1D
"I want to get a petition going to get more people to eat here!". Pascal Proyart's cuisine "when it is on song, is majestic" at this Knightsbridge hotel dining room, known particularly for his "fabulous and beautifully presented fish and seafood". "Sadly the room can be empty" – it has "an awful ambience, akin to an airport lounge" – "which just drags down the mood". / SW1X 7RN; www.oneoonerestaurant.com; @OneOOneLondon; 10 pm; closed Mon & Sun; booking max 7 may apply; set weekday L £47 (FP).

Les 110 de Taillevent W1 £72 [4][4][3]
16 Cavendish Square   020 3141 6016   3–1B
"The wine is second to none" – a "fabulous selection" of 110 vintages "available by the glass and without melting your wallet" – at this London outpost of the famous Parisian venue, which occupies a "smart (without being overbearing)" converted banking hall on the square behind Oxford Street's John Lewis. "There's a very good kitchen here" too, producing "high quality", "classic" Gallic cuisine, while service is "delightful" and "prompt". / W1G 9DD; www.les-110-taillevent-london.com; @110London; 10.30 pm; closed Sat L & Sun; set weekday L & pre-theatre £45 (FP).

Opera Tavern WC2 £52 [4][4][3]
23 Catherine St   020 7836 3680   5–3D
"Exceptional tapas" tastes like "it's been beamed over straight from Spain", according to fans of the Salt Yard group's two-floor Covent Garden pub-conversion – an "always welcoming" venue that's "perfect for a light meal before or after the theatre".

/ WC2B 5JS; www.saltyardgroup.co.uk/opera-tavern; @saltyardgroup; 11.15 pm, Sun 9.45 pm.

Opso W1 £48 [3][3][3]
10 Paddington St   020 7487 5088   2–1A
Limited and uneven feedback on this casual Marylebone three-year-old. Fans are delighted with its modern Greek-with-a-twist dishes and cleanly designed interior, but its detractors rate it as average on both these counts. / W1U 5QL; www.opso.co.uk; @OPSO_london; 10:30pm, Sun 10 pm; closed Sun D.

The Orange SW1 £60 [3][3][4]
37 Pimlico Rd   020 7881 9844   6–2D
"In a pretty part of Pimlico", overlooking Orange Square, this attractive boozer can usually be relied upon to provide "good pub grub", including wood-fired pizza. / SW1W 8NE; www.theorange.co.uk; @theorangesw1; 10 pm, Sun 9.30 pm.

Orange Pekoe SW13 £35 [3][4][4]
3 White Hart Ln   020 8876 6070   11–1A
"The best tea shop in existence" may be stretching it, but this Barnes tea room is permanently rammed to overflowing onto the pavement. "It's my favourite place for a reasonably priced 'full English' tea", with excellent coffee and "mouthwatering cakes supported by unusual lunchtime salads". / SW13 0PX; www.orangepekoeteas.com; @OrangePekoeTeas; 5 pm; L only.

Orchard SE4 £55 [2][2][2]
5 Harefield Rd   020 8692 4756   1–4D
"A Brockley meeting place which copes with families, digital hipsters and friends without being defined by them" – this "convivial" gastropub is the best in these parts, although "some dishes missed their mark this past year". / SE4 1LW; www.thebrockleyorchard.com; @The_Orchard_; 11 pm, Sun 10.30 pm.

Orée £12 [3][2][3]
275-277 Fulham Rd, SW10
020 3813 9724   6–3B
65 King's Rd, SW3   020 3740 4588   6–3D **NEW**
147 Kensington High St, W8
020 3883 7568   6–1A **NEW**
"An on-site bakery ensures everything is super-fresh" at this "lovely, light and bright location" near the Chelsea & Westminster Hospital: "great coffees, cakes and French-styles brunches". They must be doing something right as in mid 2017 they launched new stores on the King's Road and in Kensington. / www.oree.co.uk.

Ormer Mayfair W1 £120 [4][3][3]
Half Moon St   020 7016 5601   3–4B
Star Channel Islands chef, Shaun Rankin "brings Jersey flavours to the heart of London" at this year-old venture: the new occupant of a classically smart, basement dining room of a Mayfair hotel. It's one

of the highest-rated openings of recent times: "the food looks fabulous but even better is its exceptional flavour". / W1J 7BH; www.ormermayfair.com; @ormermayfair; No shorts; set weekday L £93 (FP).

Oro Di Napoli W5 £34 ④③②
6 The Quadrant, Little Ealing Lane
020 3632 5580 1–3A
That it's "marginally better even than Santa Maria" is a claim sometimes made of this South Ealing Neapolitan, even if its "very good wood-fired pizza" isn't (yet) quite as highly rated as its famous local rival. / W5 4EE; www.lorodinapoli.co.uk; 11 pm.

Orrery W1 £90 ③③②
55 Marylebone High St 020 7616 8000 2–1A
"You can hear each other speak" in this "quiet" and "pleasant" first-floor dining room over Marylebone's Conran Shop, which makes "stylish" use of a slightly "odd" space, and is best-visited when the roof terrace is open in summer. Long renowned as "one of the better D&D establishments", its profile has lessened of late, but its modern French cuisine still wins reasonable support from reporters. A strong wine list is a feature. / W1U 5RB; www.orreryrestaurant.co.uk; @orrery; 10 pm, Fri & Sat 10.30 pm; booking max 8 may apply; set weekday L £53 (FP), set Sun L £56 (FP).

Oscar Wilde Bar at Cafe Royal W1 £82
68 Regent St 020 7406 3333 4–4C
Famous for its rococo decor, this truly dazzling room, a short hop from Piccadilly Circus, is one of London's most venerable restaurant spaces (dating from 1865), but – despite various reformattings by different owners – has sunk from view in recent times. More change may be on the cards in 2018, but for the time being it's mainly worth visiting for its award winning afternoon tea. / W1B; www.hotelcaferoyal.com/oscarwildebar; @HotelCafeRoyal; 6 pm; L & afternoon tea only.

Oslo Court NW8 £64 ④⑤⑤
Charlbert St 020 7722 8795 9–3A
"How restaurants used to be" – this "fun throwback to the 1970s", "quirkily located at the foot of a Regent's Park apartment block" perfectly preserves the plush pink style of the era; while its "wonderful happy atmosphere" is buoyed along by celebratory parties of septuagenarian north Londoners bantering with long-serving staff for whom "nothing is too much trouble". The generous dishes are "old-fashioned, but superb if you like the style" ("where else can you find a proper veal Holstein?") and "there's always a full house because it's such good value" ("it's booked well ahead by those who know it"). Be sure to leave space for Neil's dessert trolley. / NW8 7EN; www.oslocourtrestaurant.co.uk; 11 pm; closed Sun; No jeans.

Osteria, Barbican Centre EC2 £57 ②②③
Level 2 Silk St 020 7588 3008 10–1B
"Super views" make this "quiet and unobtrusive venue" at the Barbican Centre a "really handy and pleasant" option for theatre and concert-goers for whom there's a "reasonable set menu". Judged as a foodie destination however, "the food continues to disappoint" despite the arrival of chef Anthony Demetre (late of Soho's Arbutus, RIP) to boost the Italian cuisine provided by contract caterer Searcys. / EC2Y 8DS; osterialondon.co.uk; @osterialondon; 10.30 pm, Sat 11.30 pm; closed Sun; set weekday L £38 (FP).

Osteria Antica Bologna SW11 £47 ③②②
23 Northcote Rd 020 7978 4771 11–2C
A "friendly, long-established local near Clapham Junction", well-known in the area for its "competent North Italian cooking and pleasant ambience". "Wild boar ragu on black pepper spaghetti is one highlight from a menu of simple authenticity". / SW11 1NG; www.osteria.co.uk; @OsteriaAntica; 10.30 pm, Sun 10 pm.

Osteria Basilico W11 £63 ③③④
29 Kensington Park Rd 020 7727 9957 7–1A
An enduring pillar of the Notting Hill restaurant scene, this fun Italian isn't as high profile as once it was, but still knows how to please its clientele, with authentic pizzas, homemade pasta or more sophisticated specials. / W11 2EU; www.osteriabasilico.co.uk; 11.30 pm, Sun 10.30 pm; no booking, Sat L.

Osteria Dell'Angolo SW1 £59 ③③①
47 Marsham St 020 3268 1077 2–4C
"A good standby for politicos trapped in the Westminster bubble" – this "comfortable" Italian "just opposite the Home Office" can seem very "quiet" (although some reporters find it "romantic"). The "authentic" cooking is "very acceptable", and "as it never appears too busy, you get plenty of attention!" / SW1P 3DR; www.osteriadellangolo.co.uk; @Osteria_Angolo; 10 pm; closed Sat L & Sun.

Osteria Tufo N4 £48 ③③②
67 Fonthill Rd 020 7272 2911 9–1D
"Rich and interesting Neapolitan home cooking" makes this "delightful and idiosyncratic neighbourhood Italian" in Finsbury Park a "real find": an "all-female outfit" run by the owner, Paola, who shares with you her "enthusiasm and love of food". Just one request: "the savoury tomato-based sauces can all blend into one another – a tweak to differentiate them would unlock even more potential in the place". / N4 3HZ; www.osteriatufo.co.uk; @osteriatufo; 10.30 pm, Sun 9.30 pm; closed Mon & Sun L; No Amex.

Ostuni **£58** [2][3][3]
1 Hampstead Lane, N6   020 7624 8035   9–1B
43-45 Lonsdale Rd, NW6
020 7624 8035   1–2B
*This four-year-old Italian in Queen's Park – and its
more recent Highgate sibling – specialise in the
cuisine of Puglia in southern Italy. Service is "friendly"
and there's a "great atmosphere", but while fans
report "thoroughly enjoyable cooking on every visit"
critics are "not so impressed with all the dishes". /
10.30 pm; N6 closed Mon L; no booking at D.*

The Other Naughty Piglet
SW1 NEW **£60** [4][4][3]
12 Palace St   020 7592 0322   2–4B
*"What a great addition to the otherwise pretty
dreary dining scene around Victoria" – Andrew
Lloyd Webber's has teamed up to good effect with
Brixton's Naughty Piglets for the 'small plates'
restaurant on the first floor of his 'The Other Palace
Theatre' (formerly the St James's Theatre): "the
food's stunning and the staff charming" and even
if "the location and decor don't really match", the
interior's "been nicely refitted and it's great fun to
sit up at the kitchen counter and watch the chefs".
/ SW1E 5JA; www.theothernaughtypiglet.co.uk; booking
max 10 may apply.*

Otto's WC1 **£72** [4][5][4]
182 Gray's Inn Rd   020 7713 0107   2–1D
*"For a superb, Escoffier-style dining experience", this
"quirky", unpromising-looking fixture on a grungy,
out-of-the-way Bloomsbury street might seem an
improbable destination, but it's something of a
"dream restaurant". "Proper, old-school, luxurious
French gastronomic dishes" are "served with charm
and wit by Otto himself" in an "attractive and
old-fashioned" room ("where you can hear yourself
speak"). Top Menu Tip – "everyone should go here
for the pressed duck at least once in their lives".
/ WC1X 8EW; www.ottos-restaurant.com; 9.30 pm;
closed Mon, Sat L & Sun.*

Ottolenghi **£57** [4][3][2]
13 Motcomb St, SW1   020 7823 2707   6–1D
63 Ledbury Rd, W11   020 7727 1121   7–1B
287 Upper St, N1   020 7288 1454   9–2D
50 Artillery Pas, E1   020 7247 1999   10–2D
*"The salads on display as you enter get your gastric
juices moving!" at Yotam Ottolenghi's communal
cafés, whose "enterprising" Middle Eastern dishes
remain "fresh, delicious and interesting" ("cakes and
desserts are not to be missed" either). If there are
drawbacks, it's "variable service", "terrible acoustics"
and the wait to be seated. Nor is it cheap, but it's
worth it ("cook books are all very well, but the prep
takes hours!"). / www.ottolenghi.co.uk; N1 10.30 pm,
Sun 7 pm; W11 & SW1 8 pm, Sat 7 pm, Sun 6 pm;
E1 10.30 pm, Sun 6 pm; N1 closed Sun D; Holland St
takeaway only; W11 & SW1 no booking.*

Outlaw's at The Capital
SW3 **£91** [4][4][2]
22-24 Basil St   020 7591 1202   6–1D
*"A lot easier to get to than Cornwall!" – Nathan
Outlaw's "small and intimate dining room" near the
back of Harrods lives up to his renown as one of
the UK's top fish and seafood chefs with "superb
and superbly fresh dishes" delivering "delightful"
and "delicate" flavours. That it's a "quiet space (so
hard to find in central London)" is valued by some,
although others feel "atmosphere can be lacking".
Note, the hotel – a rare independent – was sold to
a small American group in January 2017. Top Tips –
value-wise "the lunchtime menu is hard to beat" and
"you can BYO with no corkage on Thursdays". / SW3
1AT; www.capitalhotel.co.uk; @OUTLAWSinLondon;
10 pm; closed Sun; credit card required to book; set
weekday L £59 (FP).*

Over Under SW5 NEW **£13** [4][4][2]
181a Earl's Court Rd 07944 494555 6–2A
*This "new Antipodean coffee shop" near Earl's Court
tube "feels different to others out there" – "a small
space run by a great young team producing familiar-
with-a-twist and yummy breakfast fare (bircher
muesli, porridge, avocado toast, generous granola
etc) and importantly, exceptional brews". / SW5 9RB;
www.overundercoffee.com; @overundercoffee.*

Oxo Tower, Restaurant
SE1 **£86** [1][1][2]
Barge House St   020 7803 3888   10–3A
*"A real tourist conveyor belt" on the South Bank,
where "prices, relative to the quality of the food,
are ridiculous". "How do they get away with it
year after year? The wonderful view!!" / SE1 9PH;
www.harveynichols.com/restaurant/the-oxo-tower;
@OxoTowerWharf; 11 pm, Sun 10 pm; booking max
8 may apply; set weekday L £57 (FP); SRA-Food Made
Good – 2 stars.*

Oxo Tower, Brasserie
SE1 **£75** [1][1][2]
Barge House St   020 7803 3888   10–3A
*"Great views" – ("among the best in London")
– tempt diners to this brasserie section of
the landmark South Bank tower. But, oh dear,
"everything else is not good" ("don't go, unless
you are compelled to as a guest"). / SE1 9PH;
www.harveynichols.com/restaurants/oxo-tower-london;
11 pm, Sun 10 pm; May need 2+ to book.*

**The Oystermen Seafood Kitchen &
Bar WC2** **£50**
32 Henrietta St   020 7240 4417   5–3D
*A June 2017 opening from former pop-up caterers,
The Oystermen; their new, simple, tightly packed
Covent Garden home features shellfish and seafood,
fresh from the boats, or pickled, smoked and cured
by the owners Matt Lovell and Rob Hampton. Top
Tip – 'Bubbles 'n' Oysters Happy Hour' (3pm-5pm*

every day; six oysters and a glass of fizz for £10). /
WC2E 8NA; oystermen.co.uk; @theoystermen.

Ozone Coffee Roasters
EC2   **£40** 4️⃣4️⃣4️⃣
11 Leonard St   020 7490 1039   13–1A
"Unbeatable… except for the queues in the
morning"; the habit-forming smell from the big
roasting machines in the basement is justification
enough for a trip to this superbly hip, Kiwi-owned
Shoreditch haunt, which provides exceptional
brews and does a "fab" brunch too. / EC2A 4AQ;
ozonecoffee.co.uk; @ozonecoffeeuk; 9 pm, Sat & Sun
4.30 pm; May need 8+ to book.

P Franco E5   **£48** 4️⃣3️⃣3️⃣
107 Lower Clapton Rd   020 8533 4660   14–1B
"Wonderful, innovative food cooked up on two hot
plates at the end of a communal table" makes this
in-the-know Clapton wine shop a really interesting
dining destination. The wine, from the people behind
Noble Fine Liquor on Broadway Market, is not your
standard plonk, either. / E5 0NP; www.pfranco.co.uk;
@pfranco_e5; Thu-Sat 10 pm, Sun 9 pm; closed Mon-
Wed, Thu-Sat D only, Sun L & D; No Amex; no booking.

Pachamama W1   **£65** 3️⃣2️⃣2️⃣
18 Thayer St   020 7935 9393   2–1A
"Innovative and delicious" Peruvian-inspired fusion
dishes combined with cocktails based on pisco and
mezcal to create a buzz at this Marylebone three-
year-old. / W1U 3JY; www.pachamamalondon.com;
@pachamama_ldn; 10.45 pm, Sun 10 pm; closed Mon
L; set brunch £38 (FP).

Padella SE1   **£28** 5️⃣4️⃣4️⃣
6 Southwark St   no tel   10–4C
"Oh wowza! pasta perfection!!!!!" – "the best in
town and so incredibly cheap" – "no wonder the
capital has gone mad for this gem of a Borough
Market yearling" from the team behind Trullo:
"a simple concept brilliantly executed". Staff are
"engaging" and "efficient" too but getting in is a
challenge: "queues are longer than an economy-
class check-in to Ibiza". / SE1 1TQ; www.padella.co;
@padella_pasta; 10 pm, Sun 5 pm; no booking.

The Painted Heron
SW10   **£57** 5️⃣4️⃣2️⃣
112 Cheyne Walk   020 7351 5232   6–3B
A "slightly awkward location" is no barrier to
enjoyment of this "out-of-the-way gem", just
off Chelsea Embankment. "Staff try to please"
and the Indian cuisine represents "exceptional
value" – "well-prepared with a light and individual
touch" and "with unusual layers of flavours and
spicing". / SW10 0DJ; www.thepaintedheron.com;
@thepaintedheron; 10.30 pm.

Palatino EC1 🆕   **£58** 4️⃣5️⃣3️⃣
71 Central St   020 3481 5300   10–1B
Stevie Parle's "hip, urban (and urbane) newcomer
in trendy Clerkenwell" is one of his best openings
yet. An "airy", warehouse-y corner-site that's part
of FORA (a 'pro-working' space) – "once you get
past the office-style reception", the "incredibly
friendly" service is "low key and efficient" and the
"straightforward", "authentically Roman" cooking
is "delicious" and "surprisingly good value" too ("I
thought the bill was wrong, it was so cheap!"). /
EC1V 8AB; palatino.london; @PalatinoLondon; 10 pm;
closed Sun.

The Palmerston SE22   **£56** 4️⃣3️⃣3️⃣
91 Lordship Ln   020 8693 1629   1–4D
This "East Dulwich gastropub consistently gets
things right" – a "fantastic old-fashioned boozer
with terrific beer", but also whose "adventurous"
food hints at "real talent in the kitchen" ("you
can take foodie friends with confidence that they
won't snark"). / SE22 8EP; www.thepalmerston.co.uk;
@thepalmerston; 10 pm, Sun 9.30 pm; No Amex; set
weekday L £33 (FP).

The Palomar W1   **£62** 4️⃣4️⃣3️⃣
34 Rupert St   020 7439 8777   4–3D
"The Israeli answer to Barrafina" – this "compact"
("squashed", "noisy" and sometimes "boiling") Tel
Aviv import is a "joyous" and "horizon-opening"
experience, where "the good humour of the
staff is infectious" and the "clever" (if sometimes
"miniscule") small plates dish up "whizz-bang"
flavours that "demand to be noticed". "Sitting at
the counter, interacting with the chefs" is the way
to go – you can only book for the much less funky
dining room. / W1D 6DN; www.thepalomar.co.uk;
@palomarsoho; 11 pm, Sun 9 pm; closed Sun L.

Pamban NW1 🆕
North Yard, Chalk Farm Rd   no tel   9–3B
A new all-day chai and coffee house in Camden
Market, owned by Mayhul Gondhea and Aruna
Sellahewa, opened in July 2017. The food offering
includes curry, stuffed pancakes and sweet buns.
/ NW1 8AH; www.camdenmarket.com/food-drink/
pamban.

Il Pampero SW1 🆕   **£75**
20 Chesham Place   020 3189 4850   6–1D
With an interior aiming to 'embody chic and
vintage glamour', this new hotel dining room in
Belgravia delivers a traditional Italian menu, under
chef Claudio Covino – only limited feedback so far,
but all positive. / SW1X 8HQ; www.ilpampero.com;
@ilPamperoLondon; 22.30pm.

The Pantechnicon SW1 🆕
18 Motcomb St 6–1D
This superb, neo-classical 1830 Grade II listed
building in Belgravia, owned by Grosvenor Estates,

is to take on a new lease of life in 2018 as a new 10,000 sq ft retail and restaurant space, the latter incorporating a basement café/bar, second floor restaurant and roof terrace. / SW1X 8LA; www.thepantechnicon.com; 9.30 pm, Sun 9 pm; booking max 12 may apply.

Pappa Ciccia £36 333
105 Munster Rd, SW6 020 7384 1884 11–1B
41 Fulham High St, SW6
020 7736 0900 11–1B
"Delicious crispy thin pizzas" and "particularly good antipasti" are "a substantial cut above average" at these stalwart Fulham and Putney cafés – and they're "well priced for southwest London". They also do good gluten-free pizza and pasta options, but "sadly they've stopped BYO at the weekends". / www.pappaciccia.com; SW6 5RQ 11 pm, Sat & Sun 11.30 pm; SW6 3JJ 11 pm.

Parabola, Design Museum
W8 £70 323
224-238 Kensington High St
020 7940 8795 6–1A
Off the airy foyer of the new design museum – and named for the curve of its roof – this minimalist yearling "serves interesting food in a part of Kensington that's a bit of a food desert", along with "an excellent selection of wine". However, it also expresses some of Prescott & Conran's less desirable restaurant DNA with its "variable service" and some prices that "are not really justified". Perhaps that will change for the good with the September 2017 appointment of well-known chef, Rowley Leigh as permanent chef – previously there was a roster of guest chefs (of which he had been one). Top Tip – "pick a window seat" for the best views of Holland Park. / W8 6AG; www.parabola.london; @ParabolaLondon; 9.45 pm.

Paradise by Way of Kensal Green
W10 £48 334
19 Kilburn Lane 020 8969 0098 1–2B
"A wonderful unexpected find in an offbeat location" – this huge, rambling shabby-chic tavern in Kensal Green has been a magnet for the local cool crowd for over 20 years, with gardens, roof-terraces and bars a go-go; and a large rear dining room that's very atmospheric. / W10 4AE; www.theparadise.co.uk; @weloveparadise; 10.30 pm, Fri & Sat 11 pm, Sun 9 pm; closed weekday L; No Amex.

Paradise Garage E2 £54 443
254 Paradise Row 020 7613 1502 14–2B
"Tucked under the arches in Bethnal Green" – this "fantastic" two-year-old from chef Robin Gill (of hip Clapham duo Manor and Dairy) has an "outstanding and inventive menu" packed with "unusual delights". / E2 9LE; www.paradise254.com; @ParadiseRow254; 10 pm; closed Mon, Tue L & Sun D; booking max 6 may apply.

Paradise Hampstead
NW3 £38 454
49 South End Rd 020 7794 6314 9–2A
This veteran Hampstead Heath curry house is now run by the founder's son, but has lost none of its legendary welcome: "they pretend to know you like an old friend!" "It looks a bit dated now" and the food may be very traditional, but it's "always delicious – with never a bad meal". / NW3 2QB; www.paradisehampstead.co.uk; 10.45 pm.

El Parador NW1 £40 323
245 Eversholt St 020 7387 2789 9–3C
"Rich and authentic tapas" in "generous portions" makes it worth discovering this "busy but friendly" Hispanic, near Mornington Crescent. Some sections of the "small" interior are "noisy", but there's a great garden for sunny days. / NW1 1BA; www.elparadorlondon.com; 11 pm, Fri & Sat 11.30 pm, Sun 9.30 pm; closed Sat L & Sun L; No Amex.

Park Chinois W1 £95 224
17 Berkeley St 020 3327 8888 3–3C
"The opulence is astonishing and so seductive", say fans of Alan Yau's ultra-"glamorous" homage to 1920's Shanghai, complete with live music, in Mayfair – "you could lose yourself here for hours". Even those who acknowledge a "wonderful experience" however, find it "shockingly expensive" given the unexceptional Chinese cuisine and to a few reporters the vibe is plain "horrible" – "like a brothel for billionaires". / W1S 4NF; www.parkchinois.com; 11 pm, Sun 10.15 pm; No jeans.

Parlez SE4 NEW
16 Coulgate St 020 8691 0202 1–4D
This new all-day restaurant is aiming to make Brockley the envy of all of its South London neighbours, with a mantra of 'local is gospel', seasonal menus and local artist involvement. / SE4 2RW; www.parlezlocal.com; @parlezlocal.

Parlour Kensal NW10 £49 454
5 Regent St 020 8969 2184 1–2B
"Chef Jesse Dunford Wood's food just goes from strength to strength" at this Kensal Rise pub conversion, which, as well as more typical options, goes further down serious dining options than most gastroboozers: "the Chef's Table overlooking the kitchen is an experience second to none". / NW10 5LG; www.parlourkensal.com; @ParlourUK; 10 pm; closed Mon.

Passione e Tradizione
N15 NEW £36 432
451 West Green Rd 020 8245 9491 1–1C
"Note-perfect Italian cooking and stylish presentation left us blown away – it was more reminiscent of a seasoned, high end establishment in Central London than a small, reasonably priced eatery around Turnpike Lane!" – Mustapha

Mouflih's "offshoot of Anima e Cuore" feels like an "overdue and hugely welcome arrival" in Haringey, serving "wonderful pizzas from a woodfired oven alongside many of the favourite dishes from the sister restaurant". / N15 3PL; spinach.london; 11 pm.

Pasta Remoli N4 £35 ☒☒☒

7 Clifton Terrace   020 7263 2948   9–1D
"A brilliant pasta café next door to the Park Theatre" – "everything's freshly cooked, and there are delicious sauces". / N4 3JP; www.pastaremoli.co.uk; @PastaRemoli; 11 pm, Sun 10.30 pm.

Pastaio W1 NEW

19 Ganton St awaiting tel 4–2B
The latest venture from chef/restaurateur Stevie Parle (Dock Kitchen, Rotorino, Craft, Palatino) – a freshly made pasta spot, on the former site of Alan Yau's Cha Cha Moon in Soho's Kingly Court, to open in autumn 2017. / W1F 7BU; www.pastaio.london; @pastaiolondon.

El Pastór SE1 £44 ☒☒☒

7a Stoney St   no tel   10–4C
"Just like being in Mexico" – the Hart Bros brick-lined new Borough Market taqueria delivers "stunning tacos" that are "up there with the best of the best" in conditions of "glorious managed chaos". No bookings, of course. / SE1 9AA; www.tacoselpastor.co.uk; @Tacos_El_Pastor; 11 pm; no booking.

Patara £60 ☒☒☒

15 Greek St, W1   020 7437 1071   5–2A
5 Berners St, W1   020 8874 6503   3–1A
7 Maddox St, W1   020 7499 6008   4–2A
181 Fulham Rd, SW3   020 7351 5692   6–2C
9 Beauchamp Pl, SW3   020 7581 8820   6–1C
82 Hampstead High St, NW3
020 7431 5902   9–2B NEW
18 High St, SW19   020 3931 6157   11–2B NEW
"Time and again we get fine Thai tastes!" This enduring chain is, in a low key way, one of London's most consistent performers, combining "well-above average food", with "very attentive service" and "beautiful decor". / www.pataralondon.com; 10.30 pm, Thu-Sat 11 pm; Greek St closed Sun L.

Paternoster Chop House EC4 £56 ☒☒☒

1 Warwick Court   020 7029 9400   10–2B
That its main claim to fame nowadays is as the location for TV show First Dates speaks volumes for the unimpressive performance of this modern steakhouse, by St Paul's, which has never really made the grade with its natural City business-dining constituency. "Of all the D&D London places, this is near the bottom, with impossibly slow service, tables too close, little ambience or magic to the room itself, and average food". (And in real-life, heart-throb maître d' Fred Sirieix doesn't work here, but at Galvin at Windows on Park Lane.) / EC4M

7DX; www.paternosterchophouse.co.uk; @paternoster1; 10.30 pm; closed Sat & Sun D; booking max 12 may apply.

Patogh W1 £13 ☒☒☒

8 Crawford Pl   020 7262 4015   7–1D
"Some might feel the decor is a bit basic" but don't let that put you off this "shabby but very friendly" Edgware Road BYO – a "cheap 'n' cheerful" classic thanks to its "simple Persian food, invariably perfectly cooked". / W1H 5NE; 11 pm; Cash only.

Patron NW5 £59 ☒☒☒

26 Fortess Rd   020 7813 2540   9–2C
"Frogs' legs, snails, pâté and duck confit – and how we've missed them…" makes this "buzzy" little Kentish Town two-year-old a nostalgic "trip down memory lane to what French restaurants used to be". But while fans applaud its "classic flavours" sceptics fear that a significant amount of its output is "not brilliantly cooked". / NW5 2HB; www.patronlondon.com; @PatronNW5; 11 pm, Sun 10 pm.

Patty and Bun £27 ☒☒☒

18 Old Compton St, W1   020 7287 1818   5–2A
54 James St, W1   020 7487 3188   3–1A
14 Pembridge Rd, W11
020 7229 2228   7–2B NEW
36 Redchurch St, E2   020 7613 3335   13–1C
2 Arthaus Building, 205 Richmond Rd, E8
020 8525 8250   14–1B NEW
22-23 Liverpool St, EC2
020 7621 1331   10–2D
Swingers Crazy Golf, 8 Brown's Buildings, Saint Mary Axe, EC3   020 3846 3222   10–2D NEW
"Be prepared to use loads of napkins, it gets too messy without a plate..." at these "quirky and cool cafés" whose "delicious-beyond-compare dirty burgers are just the right side of sloppy" and in contention for "London's best". / www.pattyandbun.co.uk; 10 pm-11.30 pm, Sun 9 pm-10pm.

Pavilion Cafe & Bakery E9 £14 ☒☒☒

Victoria Park, Old Ford Rd
020 8980 0030   14–2C
This quaint looking domed structure, "overlooking the boating lake at Victoria Park" is "a wonderful setting for a locally-sourced, full English, all-day breakfast, and serves superlative coffee too". / E9 7DE; www.pavilionbakery.com; @pavilionbakery; 3 pm; L only.

The Pear Tree W6 £48 ☒☒☒

14 Margravine Rd   020 7381 1787   8–2C
This cute, little Victorian free house (rare in London) is hidden away in Baron's Court, behind Charing Cross Hospital, and on most (if not quite all) accounts, is well worth remembering for its "fab" food from a short menu. / W6 8HJ;

www.thepeartreefulham.com; 9.30 pm, Fri-Sun 9 pm; Mon-Thu D only, Fri-Sun open L & D.

Pearl Liang W2 £46 🔳2️⃣2️⃣
8 Sheldon Square   020 7289 7000   7–1C
"Fabulous dim sum" has helped earn this big basement in Paddington Basin a reputation as one of London's top Cantonese spots. But marks have slipped this year across the board, perhaps because "the location has transformed from a wasteland to a happening destination, so service has suffered under the pressure". / W2 6EZ; www.pearlliang.co.uk; @PearlLiangUK; 11 pm.

Peckham Bazaar SE15 £51 🔳5️⃣3️⃣4️⃣
119 Consort Rd   020 7732 2525   1–4D
"Finally, some decent Greek food in London!", extol fans of this "fun" and brilliant Peckham venue serving dishes inspired by the eastern Med from the Balkans to the Middle East. There's "great chargrilled seafood and meat", "delivered to your table as it is cooked", and an "interesting wine list at fair prices", including hard-to-find bottles from the Greek islands. / SE15 3RU; www.peckhambazaar.com; @PeckhamBazaar; 10 pm, Sun 8 pm; closed Mon, Tue-Fri D only, Sat & Sun open L & D; No Amex.

**Peckham Refreshment Rooms
SE15** £50 🔳3️⃣3️⃣3️⃣
12-16 Blenheim Grove   020 7639 1106   1–4D
Behind Peckham Rye station, this chilled all-day café/bar is worth knowing about for coffee or a light bite – it attracts only limited feedback, but to the effect that it's an all-round good place. / SE15 4QL; www.peckhamrefreshment.com; @peckhamrefresh; midnight; closed Sun D.

Pedler SE15 £44 🔳3️⃣3️⃣4️⃣
58 Peckham Rye   020 3030 1515   1–4D
"Intimate and super-cool" Peckham two-year-old bistro, with "engaging food" and a "great bar"; its headline attraction is its "seriously interesting brunch, well worth lingering over". / SE15 4JR; www.thebeautifulpizzaboy.london; @pizzaboylondon1; 10.15 pm, Sun 8.30 pm; closed Mon, Tue L, Wed L, Thu L & Sun D; May need 6+ to book.

**Pellicano Restaurant
SW3** £58 🔳3️⃣4️⃣3️⃣
19-21 Elystan St   020 7589 3718   6–2C
"You're always assured a good welcome when going to this lively Italian" in a quiet Chelsea backwater, which serves a "limited, primarily Sardinian menu". "Gold star to them for making visits with children and/or grandparents so relaxed!" / SW3 3NT; www.pellicanorestaurant.co.uk; 11 pm, Sun 9.30 pm.

E Pellicci E2 £16 🔳3️⃣4️⃣5️⃣
332 Bethnal Green Rd   020 7739 4873   13–1D
"A piece of London history" – this Bethnal Green caff (the wood-panelled Art Deco interior is listed) has "not yet been captured by hipsters (who

probably think the coffee is awful) and attracts a real mix of locals". Fans say breakfast "is the best in town… and you'll never feel a stranger here". / E2 0AG; epellicci.com; 4 pm; L only, closed Sun; Cash only.

Pentolina W14 £51 🔳4️⃣5️⃣4️⃣
71 Blythe Rd   020 3010 0091   8–1C
"We love it!" – neighbourhood restaurants "don't come much better" than this "lovely" (and affordable) contemporary Italian in the backstreets of Olympia, where "Michele in the kitchen always delivers wonderful food, while Heidi is always charming as front of house". One gripe: "please could they vary their menu a bit more – we'd eat there far more if we hadn't already seen it all!" / W14 0HP; www.pentolinarestaurant.co.uk; 10 pm; closed Mon & Sun; No Amex.

The Pepper Tree SW4 £33 2️⃣3️⃣3️⃣
19 Clapham Common South Side
020 7622 1758   11–2D
For a "cheap 'n' cheerful" bite, long-term fans still tip this Thai canteen stalwart in Clapham; it's no longer the area's 'go-to' standby though. / SW4 7AB; www.thepeppertree.co.uk; @PepperTreeSW4; 10.45 pm, Sun & Mon 10.15 pm; no booking.

Percy & Founders W1 £57 🔳3️⃣3️⃣3️⃣
1 Pearson Square, Fitzroy Place
020 3761 0200   2–1B
"Tables are well-spaced for business", at this "smart, urban dining pub" – a large "bustling" space with kitchen on view occupying the ground floor of a Fitzrovia development on the site of the old Middlesex Hospital; in particular "breakfast is always very good". / W1W 7EY; www.percyandfounders.co.uk; @PercyFounders; 10.30 pm, Sun 9.30 pm; closed Sun D.

Perilla N16 £62 🔳4️⃣4️⃣3️⃣
1-3 Green Lanes   07467 067393   1–1C
"A youthful team in the kitchen is pulling out all the stops" at Ben Marks and Matt Emerson's new permanent venture near Newington Green – "one of the least stuffy upmarket restaurants ever", which "makes the most of a slightly odd L-shaped room". "Beautiful, fresh ingredients are 'zhooshed up' to great heights" – with the options of "a small but carefully calibrated menu" or an "amazing" 10-course taster menu plus matching wines – and "although not every dish is 100% successful, each is interesting and well-priced enough that all can be forgiven." "Thoughtful and intelligent service" completes an impressive debut. / N16 9BS; www.perilladining.co.uk; @perilladining; 10.30 pm, Sun 8.30 pm.

The Perry Vale SE23 £58 🔳3️⃣4️⃣3️⃣
31 Perry Vale   020 8291 0432   1–4D
Limited but positive feedback on this sibling to Camberwell's Crooked Well in up-and-coming Forest Hill – "someone in the kitchen really knows and

loves their food, and the service is also excellent!" /
SE23 2AR; www.theperryvale.com; @theperryvale.

Persepolis SE15   £23   4 3 2
28-30 Peckham High St   020 7639 8007   1–4D
"Quirky, a bit shabby, maybe not for everyone…
but the food is top notch!" – cookery book author
Sally Butcher's well-known, eccentric corner shop
in Peckham delivers zesty, eclectic, Persian, African
and Middle Eastern-influenced dishes and a lot of
personality in its in-store café 'Snackistan'. / SE15
5DT; www.foratasteofpersia.co.uk; @PersiainPeckham;
9 pm.

Pescatori W1   £75   2 4 3
57 Charlotte St   020 7580 3289   2–1C
Especially by the standards of West End Italians,
this traditional-ish, fish-focussed Fitzrovian is a
favourite for a good number of fans, inspiring
consistent feedback across the board. / W1T 4PD;
www.pescatori.co.uk; 10.30 pm; closed Sat L & Sun; set
weekday L £49 (FP).

The Petersham WC2 NEW
Floral Court, off Floral St
020 8940 5230   5–3C
The Boglione family, owners of Richmond's
Petersham Nurseries, venture into central London,
with this newcomer in the courtyard of the 'Floral
Court' new CapCo property development between
Floral Street and King Street. The menu is primarily
Italian-led and when it's warm you can eat alfresco.
They are also opening a deli, and adjoining bar and
small plates restaurant, 'La Goccia'. / WC2E 9DJ;
petershamnurseries.com; midnight.

Petersham Hotel TW10   £65   3 3 4
Nightingale Lane   020 8939 1084   1–4A
"A window table for lunch is one of the nicest
spots in London", at this old-fashioned Richmond
hotel, with "incredible views over the Thames", and
whose "rather formal" style suits its older clientele.
"The food is good by hotel standards, especially the
Sunday lunch, but it's advisable to book." / TW10
6UZ; petershamhotel.co.uk/restaurant; @thepetersham;
9.45 pm.

Petersham Nurseries Cafe
TW10   £77   2 1 5
Church Lane (signposted 'St Peter's Church'), off
Petersham Rd   020 8940 5230   1–4A
"It looks so magical", and there's "genuinely
nowhere else like" this "secret-garden-style" venue
near Richmond Park – a "truly enchanting" candle-
lit greenhouse, within a garden centre – and the
fact that "you can take a riverside stroll before
or after your meal is heaven!". "On a dull day
however, the wobbly tables and chairs, untrained
waiters, and ridiculous queues for the toilets make
you feel that at these prices, you're being ripped
off", especially as when it comes to the ambitious

cuisine nowadays, while "the ingredients are
interesting, their realisation is only fair". / TW10 7AB;
www.petershamnurseries.com; 2 pm, Sat & Sun 3.30
pm; L only, closed Mon; SRA-Food Made Good – 3 stars.

Petit Ma Cuisine TW9   £50   2 2 3
8 Station Approach   020 8332 1923   1–3A
This "proper little French bistro" with a "nice
local feel" is "tucked away in a side street near
Kew Gardens station". Fans still say "they really
know their way around a cassoulet" or "wonderful
boudin blanc", but ratings have dipped due to
views that – since they moved in 2016 to the
smaller neighbouring site – "prices have moved
up, while the quality has gone down". / TW9 3QB;
www.macuisinebistrot.co.uk; 10 pm, Fri & Sat 10.30 pm;
No Amex; set weekday L £32 (FP).

Petit Pois Bistro N1   £53   3 3 2
9 Hoxton Square   020 7613 3689   13–1B
"Small and quite crowded, but friendly" year-
old bistro (with terrace) in hip Hoxton Square
offering a "short menu, well cooked to order" of
"decent Gallic fare" (steak-frites, etc). / N1 6NU;
www.petitpoisbistro.com; @petitpoisbistro; 10.30 pm,
Sun 9 pm.

The Petite Coree NW6   £41   4 4 2
98 West End Lane   020 7624 9209   1–1B
'Modern bistro with a Korean twist' characterises
the distinctive cuisine at this husband-and-wife outfit
in West Hampstead, and results in "delicious and
interesting dishes" and at "very low prices" too. Top
Tip – the evening set menu (not Friday or Saturday)
is brilliant value. / NW6 2LU; www.thepetitecoree.com;
@thepetitecoree; 9.30 pm; booking max 6 may apply.

La Petite Maison W1   £90   4 3 3
54 Brook's Mews   020 7495 4774   3–2B
"Stunning French (but not stereotypically French)
sharing plates" that really "taste of their ingredients"
help induce a happy, if "noisy" buzz at this little
piece of the Côte d'Azur, just around the corner
from Claridges. "It caters to a Mayfair clientele, who
obviously love it (and can afford it)", and "whilst it's
ridiculously expensive, it's always enjoyable". / W1K
4EG; www.lpmlondon.co.uk; @lpmlondon; 10.45 pm,
Sun 9.45 pm.

Pétrus SW1   £118   3 3 2
1 Kinnerton St   020 7592 1609   6–1D
Gordon Ramsay's "luxurious and well-spaced"
Belgravian – whose centrepiece is a circular, glass-
walled wine vault – is arguably his best London
restaurant nowadays, winning consistent praise for
its "faultless" cuisine and "efficient but unobtrusive"
service. "The dining room is very pleasant and
comfortable – just not quite as spectacular as some
others at this price level". Top Tip – "excellent lunch
deal". / SW1X 8EA;

www.gordonramsayrestaurants.com; @petrus; 10 pm; closed Sun; No trainers; set weekday L £65 (FP).

Peyote W1 £82 3 3 2
13 Cork St 020 7409 1300 4–4A
Arjun Waney's fashionably located Latino, just off Bond Street; it continues to attract surprisingly little feedback to the effect that although the quality is OK "the menu needs an overhaul – it needs to figure out if it's a restaurant or a club". / W1S 3NS; www.peyoterestaurant.com; @peyotelondon; 1 am, Fri & Sat 2 am; closed Sat L & Sun; set weekday L & pre-theatre £47 (FP).

Peyotito W11 £56 2 2 2
31 Kensington Park Rd 020 7043 1400 7–1A
Uneven reviews for this Mexican yearling in Notting Hill, featuring mezcal cocktails and sharing plates: all reports find something to praise and something to criticise (different in each case). / W11 2EU; www.peyotitorestaurant.com; @peyotitolondon; midnight, Fri & Sat 1 am, Sun 10.30 pm.

PF Chang's Asian Table WC2 NEW
10 Great Newport St 01923 555161 5–3B
Already a household name in the States, this pan-Asian powerhouse brings its popular dumplings and Dynamite shrimp to the heart of the West End. Ex-Nobu chef Deepak Kotian heads up the kitchen. / WC2H 7JA; www.pfchangs.co.uk; @PFChangs.

Pham Sushi EC1 £39 4 3 2
159 Whitecross St 020 7251 6336 13–2A
"Excellent value and authenticity" make this Japanese duo near the Barbican and Silicon Roundabout well worth knowing about. "It's not about the ambience, but the sushi and fresh sashimi remain really good quality." / EC1Y 8JL; www.phamsushi.com; @phamsushi; 10 pm; closed Sat L & Sun.

Pharmacy 2, Newport Street Gallery SE11 £62 2 3 3
Newport St 020 3141 9333 2–4D
Mark Hix's wilfully "sterile" dining room in Damien Hirst's Vauxhall art gallery splits reporters – sometimes in the same sentence! "Tiny portions make for a disappointing and overpriced experience – but the food is lovely and the room is amazing" is one example. Another is: "this could be a disastrous concept, but in fact it seems to work quite well". / SE11 6AJ; www.pharmacyrestaurant.com; @Ph2restaurant; midnight, Sun 6 pm; credit card required to book.

Pho £38 2 2 2
"Very passable pho" and other "generous and healthy dishes" maintain the appeal of these Vietnamese street-food outlets, which, even if they're "not as good as they were" when the chain was younger, are still "OK as a pit stop". / www.phocafe.co.uk; 10 pm-11pm, Sun 6.30 pm-10 pm; EC1 closed Sun L & Sun; no booking.

Pho & Bun W1 £46 4 3 2
76 Shaftesbury Ave 020 7287 3528 5–3A
"Fabulous pho" or Vietnamese steamed bun burgers make for a "great, cheap 'n' cheerful snack" at this simple café in the heart of Theatreland. / W1D 6ND; vieteat.co.uk/pho-bun; @phoandbun; 10.30 pm, Sat 11 pm, Sun 9.30 pm; booking max 8 may apply.

Phoenix Palace NW1 £56 3 2 2
5-9 Glentworth St 020 7486 3515 2–1A
This well-established Cantonese near Baker Street is something of a dim sum Mecca, and although it's arguably "rather dated" and has seen "erratic swings in quality over the years", it wins nothing but praise this year for "food that's always good". "Brusque" service "is a reminder you're in a Chinese venue" but "staff are patient with kids". / NW1 5PG; www.phoenixpalace.co.uk; 11.30 pm, Sun 10.30 pm.

Picture £67 3 3 2
110 Great Portland St, W1
020 7637 7892 2–1B
19 New Cavendish St, W1
020 7935 0058 2–1A
"Together with The Portland, this group has made local dining worthwhile!" – So say Fitzrovia foodies, who applaud the "brilliant selection of small plates, good choice of wine and very friendly service" at these low-key but accomplished ventures, near Broadcasting House and in Marylebone. Even supporters concede that they are "a bit pricey" however, and that "the stripped back interiors and rather hard chairs will not be to everyone's taste". / 10.30 pm; closed Sun.

Pidgin E8 £66 5 4 3
52 Wilton Way 020 7254 8311 14–1B
"What a fascinating dining experience – if it wasn't so hyped, I would probably have enjoyed it even more!" This "tiny" Hackney yearling has instantly won gigantic acclaim for "heavenly, delicate and inventive" cuisine, bringing a "substantial Asian influence onto modern British ideas". "Space is very tight" and though "you get to know your fellow diners intimately" the end result seems "so special, cosy and romantic" to most reporters – "it's like eating in your friend's front room, it just turns out your friend is a top chef!". Founding chef Elizabeth Allen moved on in February 2017 to open Shibui (see also), but early reports say "nothing has been lost from the cooking here during the change". See also Magpie. / E8 1BG; www.pidginlondon.com; @PidginLondon; 11 pm; closed Mon & Tue, Wed & Thu D only, Fri-Sun L & D.

Piebury Corner £20 3 4 3
3 Caledonian Rd, N1
020 7700 5441 9–3C NEW
209-211 Holloway Rd, N7
020 7700 5441 9–2D
"Food and service really warm the cockles of your heart!", at this popular 'pie deli' near The Emirates,

providing well-stuffed pies (with weird, Arsenal-related names) and craft beers to Gunners fans and foodies alike. The formula has now also spread to King's Cross with a slightly grander, but still bare-brick 'n' tiles spin-off. / www.pieburycorner.com; N7 9 pm; N1 11 pm; N7 closed Mon-Wed & Sun D, N1 closed Sun D.

Pied à Terre W1 £112 **4** **4** **3**
34 Charlotte St 020 7636 1178 2–1C
"David Moore runs a tight ship to maintain standards" and his "comfortable" Fitzrovia townhouse represents "perfection" for its many fans on account of its "unfailingly impressive" cuisine, "awesome" wines, and "good but not overly solicitous service". There's an undertow on ratings however, from sceptics who are slightly less wowed – they say "it's not a bad place, but for these prices perhaps a bit, well… beige". The griping is from a small minority though – overall this remains one of London's highest-achieving foodie temples. (There has been a lot of change afoot here post-survey. Popular sommelier and co-owner Mathieu Germond announced he was to leave to establish nearby Noize, and in September 2017 chef Andy McFadden moved on, with Asimakis Chaniotis moving up within the ranks.) / W1T 2NH; www.pied-a-terre.co.uk; @PiedaTerreUK; 10.45 pm; closed Sat L & Sun; booking max 7 may apply; set weekday L £64 (FP), set pre-theatre £66 (FP).

Pig & Butcher N1 £52 **4** **5** **4**
80 Liverpool Rd 020 7226 8304 9–3D
"Mighty meaty matey!" – this "lovely spacious and airy Islington gastropub on the corner of one of the area's nicest streets" is "brilliant for carnivores", serving "generous portions of lovingly sourced meat" (which they butcher on-site), but "veggie options are superb" too, and there's a good selection of craft beer. Top Tip – "it's worth it just for the beef dripping and bread!" / N1 0QD; www.thepigandbutcher.co.uk; @pigandbutcher; 10 pm, Sun 9 pm; Mon-Thu D only, Fri-Sun open L & D.

Pilpel £11 **4** **3** **2**
38 Brushfield Street, London, E1
020 7247 0146 13–2B
60 Alie St, E1 0207 952 2139 10–2D **NEW**
Old Spitalfields Mkt, E1 020 7375 2282 13–2B
146 Fleet St, EC4 020 7583 2030 10–2A
Paternoster Sq, EC4 020 7248 9281 10–2B
"Brilliantly fresh and zingy falafel wraps and salads are the point" at these "bright and busy" Middle Eastern cafés, whose "efficient and friendly staff seem to really want you to enjoy the food". / www.pilpel.co.uk; EC4 4 pm; E1 6 pm; Brushfield St & Alie St 9pm, Fri 4pm, Sun 6pm; Paternoster Sq 9 pm, Fri 4 pm; EC4 branches closed Sat & Sun; no booking.

Pique Nique SE1 £58
32 Tanner St 020 7403 9549 10–4D
This proper, French rotisserie from the backers of Bermondsey's little Parisian bistro Casse-Croute opened just as the survey concluded in May 2017. Just across the road from its sister restaurant, this 40-seater café in Tanner Street Park revolves around spit-roast chicken (geddit), specialising in designer breed Poulet de Bresse. / SE1 3LD; pique-nique.co.uk; @piquenique32.

El Pirata W1 £42 **3** **3** **4**
5-6 Down St 020 7491 3810 3–4B
"Classic tapas served well" and at "extremely reasonable prices for the location" make this busy old Hispanic haunt a good option in Mayfair, especially for lunch. There's a "great atmosphere" and "lovely waiters". Top Tip – "try to get a table upstairs". / W1J 7AQ; www.elpirata.co.uk; @elpirataw1; 11.30 pm; closed Sat L & Sun.

Pisqu W1 **NEW** £54
23 Rathbone Place 020 7436 6123 5–1A
"A small, casual newcomer near Charlotte Street" dedicated to Peruvian cuisine – limited feedback so far, but one early report endorses its "unique and excellent food and cocktails!" / W1T 1HZ; www.pisqulondon.com; @PisquLondon; set weekday L & pre-theatre £32 (FP).

Pitt Cue Co EC2 £58 **4** **3** **3**
1 The Ave, Devonshire Sq
020 7324 7770 10–2D
Designed "for hearty appetites", Tom Adams's American-style BBQ remains a big hit in its "newish, large and glamorous" premises near Liverpool Street (although "everyone in suits at lunchtime doesn't feel 100% right for this sort of food"). The menu is "unusual but worth grappling with" and excels through "the quality of the ingredients and the subtle simplicity of the cooking, which delivers special results". / EC2; www.pittcue.co.uk; @PittCueCo; 10.30 pm.

Pizarro SE1 £60 **3** **3** **3**
194 Bermondsey St 020 7256 5333 10–4D
"In the creative quarter that is Bermondsey St", Sr. P's busy sibling to his nearby José "is a far cry from the tapas bar down the road, with more substantial dishes and a very modern design". On most accounts it delivers "extremely flavoursome Spanish dishes to a very high level", but a hint of resistance is creeping into its prices and a perceived "sense of entitlement, as it's so busy and popular". Top Tip – "The Presa Iberica was superb and so tender". / SE1 3TQ; www.josepizarro.com; @Jose_Pizarro; 10.45 pm, Sun 9.45 pm.

Pizza East £52 **3** **2** **4**
310 Portobello Rd, W10 020 8969 4500 7–1A
79 Highgate Rd, NW5 020 3310 2000 9–1B

56 Shoreditch High St, E1
020 7729 1888   13–1B
"If you can tolerate the noise and the hipsters"
(particularly at the "cavernous and noisy" Shoreditch
original), these "slick" Soho House-owned haunts
provide "decent pizza" with "interesting toppings
and flavours" and "have a good vibe as well". /
www.pizzaeast.com; E1 midnight, .

Pizza Metro Pizza   **£40**   3⃞3⃞3⃞
147-149 Notting Hill Gate, W11
020 7727 8877   7–2B
64 Battersea Rise, SW11
020 7228 3812   11–2C
There's "always a great night out" at this Battersea
Neapolitan (now with a Notting Hill sibling), which
pioneered rectangular pizza in London, selling it 'al
metro'. Recommended for groups, "it's fun having a
whole metre-long pizza to share". / pizzametropizza.
com/battersea/; 11 pm, Fri & Sat midnight.

Pizza Pilgrims   **£37**   4⃞3⃞3⃞
102 Berwick St, W1 0778 066 7258 4–1D
11-12 Dean St, W1   020 7287 8964   4–1D
Kingly Ct, Carnaby St, W1
020 7287 2200   4–2B
23 Garrick St, WC2   020 3019 1881   5–3C
12 Hertsmere Rd, E14
020 3019 8020   12–1C **NEW**
136 Shoreditch High St, E1
020 3019 7620   13–1B **NEW**
15 Exmouth Mkt, EC1   020 7287 8964   10–1A
Swingers Crazy Golf, 8 Brown's Buildings, Saint
Mary Axe, EC3   no tel   10–2D **NEW**
"Believe the hype!" – "If you have a craving for
pizza", the Elliot brothers' "no-nonsense" pit stops
are some of the capital's best antidotes: "the menu
is simple but they use top quality ingredients" and
"what a hit – YUM!" / pizzapilgrims.co.uk; 10.30pm,
Sun 9.30 pm; WC2 11 pm, Sun 10 pm; Dean St
booking: min 8.

PizzaExpress   **£46**   2⃞2⃞2⃞
For the first 20 years of this guide, this famous
pizza chain with its "surprisingly distinctive
branches" was – with tedious regularity – the
survey's most mentioned group: constantly re-
inventing itself to remain everyone's favourite
standby, especially with kids in tow. Competition is
sharper nowadays however, and since its ownership
changed a couple of years ago (to Hony Capital)
ratings and the volume of feedback have slipped
well below their historical average. Yes, it is still
much-mentioned, and still "as reliable as ever"
to armies of loyal supporters, but harsher critics
"are stunned by the complacency and staleness
of the brand: even the ubiquitous, good value
voucher deals are starting to lose their shine". /
www.pizzaexpress.co.uk; 11.30 pm - midnight; most
City branches closed all or part of weekend; no booking
at most branches.

Pizzastorm SW18 **NEW**   **£27**   3⃞3⃞1⃞
Southside Shopping Centre, 4 Garratt Lane
020 8877 0697   11–2B
"First pizza choice for anyone who's fussy about
their toppings" – you select pick 'n' mix style at
this efficient shopping centre fast-food outlet:
"bases are thin and crispy, the toppings super
fresh and everything is done to order". / SW18 4TF;
www.pizzastorm.pizza; @PizzaStormUK; 10 pm, Thu-
Sat 11 pm, Sun 9 pm.

Pizzeria Pappagone N4   **£35**   3⃞4⃞4⃞
131 Stroud Green Rd   020 7263 2114   9–1D
This "traditional Italian trattoria" in Finsbury Park
"is a proper neighbourhood favourite". Locals
love "the lively atmosphere, reliable food from
a vast menu, and a nice mixed crowd". "Super-
speedy service makes it an easy family choice
– despite having no kids' menu, they're happy to
make half-portions or plain pizzas". / N4 3PX;
www.pizzeriapappagone.co.uk; @pizza_pappagone;
midnight.

Pizzeria Rustica TW9   **£40**   3⃞2⃞2⃞
32 The Quadrant   020 8332 6262   1–4A
"It may look cheap 'n' cheerful, but the pizzas are
very good" at this convenient outlet in Richmond
town centre, next to the station. / TW9 1DN;
www.pizzeriarustica.co.uk; @RusticaPizzeria; 11 pm,
Sun 10 pm; No Amex.

Pizzicotto W8   **£50**   4⃞4⃞3⃞
267 Kensington High St   020 7602 6777   6–1A
Directly opposite the new Design Museum in
Kensington High Street, this more casual offshoot of
the venerable, family-run Il Portico five doors away is
two years old. The "fantastic young and enthusiastic
staff" "exude Italian hospitality", and there's a
"short but interesting menu", majoring in "excellent
wood-fired pizza". / W8 6NA; www.pizzicotto.co.uk;
@pizzicottow8; 10.30 pm, Sun 9.30 pm.

Plaquemine Lock N1 **NEW**
139 Graham St   020 7688 1488   9–3D
Despite the very English-looking exterior overlooking
Regent's Canal, Jacob Kenedy's (Bocca di Lupo,
Gelupo) pub-newcomer, which opened in June 2017,
aims to serve up authentic Cajun and Creole dishes
in a fairly sparse, jazzily muralled interior; very
encouraging press reviews so far. / N1 8LB; plaqlock.
com.

Plateau E14   **£73**   2⃞3⃞3⃞
4th Floor, Canada Sq   020 7715 7100   12–1C
Spectacular cityscape views have always established
this D&D London operation as one of the "go-to
business lunch venues in Canary Wharf". It still
take occasional knocks for being "overpriced", but
Chef Jeremy Trehout's "great French cooking" won
consistent praise this year. / E14 5ER;

www.plateau-restaurant.co.uk; @plateaulondon; 10.30 pm; closed Sat L & Sun.

Platform1 SE22 **£49** 3 3 3
71 Lordship Lane 020 3609 2050 1–4D
"A great little (read: very tiny) joint in East Dulwich run by two amazing women who do a few months at a time, so the menu is always fresh." / SE22 8EP; www.platform1.london; @Platform_1ldn; 10.30 pm; D only, closed Sun-Wed.

Plot SW17 NEW **£39** 3 3 3
Unit 70-72 Broadway Market, Tooting High St
020 8767 2639 11–2C
"You can eat at narrow tables with benches or perched at the bar" at this 'British Kitchen' in Tooting's Broadway Market. "Market life goes on around you, which is amusing if not particularly comfortable" – the key draw is the consistently well-rated selection of small plates. / SW17 0RL; plotkitchen.com; @plot_kitchen.

The Plough SW14 **£44** 3 3 5
42 Christ Church Rd 020 8876 7833 11–2A
"Always busy with good vibes" – this attractive hostelry (with large terrace) occupies a picturesque corner of East Sheen and is perfect after a yomp with your dog through neighbouring Richmond Park. "It does many traditional pub staples, as well as 'smarter' dishes, and the food is restaurant quality." / SW14; www.theplough.com; 9.30 pm, Fri & Sat 10 pm, Sun 9 pm; 12 – 3pm and 6.30pm – 9.30pm, Fri - Sat - 12 – 5pm and 6.30pm – 10pm, Sun - 12 – 9pm.

Plum + Spilt Milk, Great Northern Hotel N1 **£73** 2 2 3
King's Cross St Pancras Station, Pancras Rd
020 3388 0818 9–3C
Right by King's Cross, this "well-located" hotel brasserie (named for the livery of the 'Flying Scotsman') is attractively "slightly out-of-the-ordinary" and has a good atmosphere. At best it's a "professional" spot with "decent food", but inevitably "it trades on its location" a bit: it can seem "reasonable but pricey" or merely "pleasant enough". / N1C 4TB; plumandspiltmilk.com; @PlumSpiltMilk; 11 pm, Sun 10 pm.

POLLEN STREET SOCIAL W1 **£101** 3 2 3
8-10 Pollen St 020 7290 7600 3–2C
"Slick" and "always buzzing" – Jason Atherton's first Mayfair building block of his expanding restaurant empire mixes "serious" cuisine ("exquisitely presented dishes on a different level to most you encounter") with a "relaxing but smart" atmosphere that lives up to its 'Social' branding. Mind you, even

fans note that "it can be very expensive", but – on most accounts the pain is "worth it for that special occasion". / W1S 1NQ; www.pollenstreetsocial.com; @PollenStSocial; 10.30 pm; closed Sun; booking max 7 may apply; set weekday L £66 (FP).

Polpetto W1 **£48** 3 3 3
11 Berwick St 020 7439 8627 4–2D
Surprisingly limited feedback this year for Russell Norman's little heart-of-Soho 'bacaro' behind what used to be called Raymond's Revue Bar, although such as there is continues to laud its "delicious small plates". / W1F 0PL; www.polpetto.co.uk; @polpettoW1; 11 pm, Sun 10.30 pm; booking L only.

Polpo **£50** 2 2 2
41 Beak St, W1 020 7734 4479 4–2B
142 Shaftesbury Ave, WC2
020 7836 3119 5–2B
6 Maiden Ln, WC2 020 7836 8448 5–3D
Duke Of York Sq, SW3 020 7730 8900 6–2D
126-128 Notting Hill Gate, W11
020 7229 3283 7–2B
2-3 Cowcross St, EC1 020 7250 0034 10–1A
"Delicious Venetian-style tapas" is still applauded by the big fanclub of Russell Norman's "rammed-and-noisy or buzzy (you take your pick)" cicchetti cafés, which can still offer "a fun time" without breaking the bank. However there's also a significant sceptical minority, who nowadays view their performance as "a bit tired" or even "oh-so-disappointing". / www.polpo.co.uk; 10 pm-11.30 pm, EC1 Sun 4 pm; EC1 closed D Sun; no bookings.

Pomaio E1 NEW **£42** 3 4 3
224 Brick Lane 020 3222 0031 13–2C
Bravissimo! Named after their winery Podere di Pomaio in Arezzo, brothers Marco & Lacopo Rossi opened this Brick Lane enoteca in late 2016. Feedback is thin but effusive regarding its "top wine list – from new wave to Tuscan classics – a real find at great prices too", soaked up with authentic Tuscan tapas. / E1 6SA; www.enotecapomaio.com; @pomaiobrickln; 11 pm, Fri midnight, Sun 7 pm; closed Mon & Sun D.

Pomona's W2 NEW **£68** 3 3 3
47 Hereford Rd 020 7229 1503 7–1B
"Bright LA-style newcomer" occupying a converted Notting Hill pub once known as The Commander, complete with garden. The zingy fare 'with an emphasis on fresh veg', grains and charcoal grills is "surprisingly good". / W2 5AH; www.pomonas.co.uk; @PomonasLondon; 10 pm, Fri & Sat 10.30 pm, Sun 9 pm.

Le Pont de la Tour SE1 **£78** 2 2 3
36d Shad Thames 020 7403 8403 10–4D
"It's wonderful if you get a table outside in good weather" at this smart D&D London Thames-sider, named for its superb views of Tower Bridge. When

it was first opened by Sir Terence Conran it was the hottest ticket in town, but – despite a major refurb last year – only a dwindling number of fans still see it as "a special place for special occasions", and increasingly it is viewed as "overpriced and coasting along on its past reputation". / SE1 2YE; www.lepontdelatour.co.uk; @lepontdelatour; 10.30 pm, Sun 9.30 pm; No trainers.

Pop Brixton SW9   £14   5|4|3
49 Brixton Station Rd 07725 230995 11–1D
Over 50 traders help transform this formerly disused plot in Brixton into a funky community space with numerous street-food options (a partnership with Lambeth Council currently planned to run till August 2018). Survey favourites include Baba G's Bhangra Burger ("a well thought out Indian take on burgers", with "phenomenal mango chips and lamb jalfrezi burger"), Duck Duck Goose ("simple but excellent duck, rice and greens"… "if nothing else, come and marvel at how 3 not-small blokes manage in a kitchen that size in a sea container"), Donostia Social Club and Koi Ramen. See also Smoke & Salt. / SW9 8PQ; www.popbrixton.org; 10 pm.

Popeseye   £51   3|2|2
108 Blythe Rd, W14   020 7610 4578   8–1C
36 Highgate Hill, N19   020 3601 3830   9–1B
277 Upper Richmond Rd, SW15
020 8788 7733   11–2A
"You can keep your Hawksmoors and Goodmans: this is the real deal for me": so say fans of this "time-warp" Olympia steak-bistro (the 1994 original branch), whose Highgate spin-off (the newest, opened in 2015), also inspires a fair amount of (more up-and-down) feedback. All deliver a "no pretensions" formula combining a short selection of cuts supported by a well-chosen list of affordable reds. / www.popeseye.com; W14 11.30 pm; SW15 11 pm; N19 10.30 pm, Sun 9 pm; W14 & SW15 closed Sun; N19 closed Mon.

Popolo EC2 NEW   £52   5|4|3
26 Rivington St   020 7729 4299   13–1B
"Precious moments" are created by Jonathan Lawson's superb small plates ("pasta is especially wonderful") at this artfully worn-looking and laid back newcomer in Shoreditch (where else?), comprising a compact ground floor bar area, and "nice but slightly cramped" upstairs room. / EC2A 3DU; popoloshoreditch.com; @popolo_EC2; no booking.

Poppies   £40   3|2|3
59 Old Compton St, W1
020 7482 2977   4–2D
30 Hawley Cr, NW1   020 7267 0440   9–2B
6-8 Hanbury St, E1   020 7247 0892   13–2C
"Excellent, fresh-cooked fish 'n' chips" is served with lashings of nostalgia, provided by the post-war memorabilia on the walls at these "great fun" venues in Spitalfields, Camden Town and Soho. East

Ender Pat "Pops" Newland, the founder, entered the trade aged 11 in 1952, and he has created "a great vibe". / 11 pm, Fri & Sat 11.30 pm, Sun 10.30 pm.

La Porchetta Pizzeria   £41   2|3|2
33 Boswell St, WC1   020 7242 2434   2–1D
141-142 Upper St, N1   020 7288 2488   9–2D
147 Stroud Green Rd, N4
020 7281 2892   9–1D
74-77 Chalk Farm Rd, NW1
020 7267 6822   9–2B
84-86 Rosebery Ave, EC1
020 7837 6060   10–1A
After 27 years and with five branches across north London, these old school, family-owned pizza cafés have built a fan base on "large and delicious portions" and "exceptionally family-friendly" staff. "In an area now drowning in pizzerias, Porchetta is still ace!" / www.laporchetta.net; N1, NW1 & EC1 11pm, Fri & Sat midnight, Sun 10 pm; N4 11 pm, Sun 10 pm; WC1 11 pm, Fri midnight; WC1 closed Sat & Sun; NW1, N1 & N4 closed Mon-Fri L; EC1 closed Sat L; no Amex.

La Porte des Indes W1   £75   3|2|4
32 Bryanston St   020 7224 0055   2–2A
Rather "a fascinating place" – this Tardis-like, converted underground Edwardian ballroom near Marble Arch serves "fresh and original, French influenced" Indian cuisine in a "tropical and lush", foliage-filled interior. At times "service could be sharper" though, and even many fans would concede that eating here costs a "lotta loot". / W1H 7EG; www.laportedesindes.com/london/; @LaPorteDesIndes; 11.30 pm, Sun 10.30 pm; No Amex; set weekday L £45 (FP).

Il Portico W8   £60   3|5|4
277 Kensington High St   020 7602 6262   8–1D
"Very few restaurants can claim the staying power" of this "busy and noisy" family-run trattoria in Kensington. Its "honest", "traditional" Italian dishes come in "huge portions", "but it's the wonderful and caring service that is really outstanding". / W8 6NA; www.ilportico.co.uk; 11 pm; closed Sun.

Portland W1   £84   4|4|3
113 Great Portland St   020 7436 3261   2–1B
"An unpretentious Michelin winner" – this Fitzrovia two-year-old offers "modern, informal dining at its very best" and "although it looks a little sparse from the outside, inside the welcome is warm". "Polite and eloquent" staff offer dishes "combining creativity with attention to detail, plus brilliantly chosen wines" ("ask for the specials list for some well priced fun"). "Success has bred a bit more cockiness with the pricing" however, so it's no longer quite the ace bargain it debuted as. / W1W 6QQ; www.portlandrestaurant.co.uk; 9.45 pm; closed Sun.

Portobello Ristorante Pizzeria W11 £52 3️⃣4️⃣4️⃣
7 Ladbroke Rd 020 7221 1373 7–2B
"Very friendly, and full of Italians"— this "good value" neighbourhood spot with an outside terrace, just off Notting Hill Gate, remains "on good form", serving more than just pizza and pasta. "A favourite with families", it can be "very noisy". / W11 3PA; www.portobellolondon.co.uk; 10 pm, Fri & Sat 11 pm, Sun 10 pm.

The Portrait, National Portrait Gallery WC2 £67 2️⃣2️⃣3️⃣
St Martin's Place 020 7306 0055 5–4B
"Views over the rooftops lend a very spacy and special ambience" to this top-floor dining room above the gallery and "justify the trip alone". "You pay a premium" for "mainstream" cooking, but it's "not bad" and "great for guests from out of town". / WC2H 0HE; www.npg.org.uk/visit/shop-eat-drink/restaurant.php; @NPGLondon; 8.30 pm; Sun-Wed closed D; set pre theatre £44 (FP).

Potli W6 £43 4️⃣4️⃣3️⃣
319-321 King St 020 8741 4328 8–2B
"The menu changes regularly and is really worth exploring" at this "fun and busy Indian" on the 'restaurant row' near Ravenscourt Park — its "well judged" and "unusual" street food dishes deliver "vibrant" tastes that fans find "quite unbelievable". "I've taken at least 50 friends there in the last 12 months and all have returned to eat there!". Top Menu Tip – "black daal that's cooked for 24 hours". / W6 9NH; www.potli.co.uk; @Potlirestaurant; 10.15 pm, Fri & Sat 10:30 pm, Sun 10 pm; booking essential.

La Poule au Pot SW1 £62 2️⃣2️⃣5️⃣
231 Ebury St 020 7730 7763 6–2D
"The deliciously dark and candle-lit interior is romance personified", at this "sensual French delight" in Pimlico, whose intimate nooks and crannies have made it a famed trysting spot for as long as anyone can remember. The food "has come off the boil" in recent times: "just in case you notice it, it's old fashioned, bistro fare, and not particularly cheap, but no-one cares". Service meanwhile is very Gallic – "they respond more favourably to Francophones!" Top Tip – "fab outside space in summer". / SW1W 8UT; www.pouleaupot.co.uk; 10 pm.

Prawn on the Lawn N1 £58 4️⃣4️⃣3️⃣
292-294 St Paul's Rd 020 3302 8668 9–2D
This "small but perfectly formed" Highbury Corner outfit "can't make up its mind whether it's a fish shop, wine bar or restaurant". But "don't be put off"— the tapas-style fish and platters of Cornish crab, lobster and fruits de mer on ice are "delicious, fresh and moreish". / N1 2LY; prawnonthelawn.com; @PrawnOnTheLawn; 11 pm; closed Mon & Sun; No Amex.

Primeur N5 £55 4️⃣4️⃣4️⃣
116 Petherton Rd 020 7226 5271 1–1C
"Busy" (sometimes "overcrowded") Highbury local that offers "a daily changing menu with good combinations of well-executed food" and an "esoteric, if expensive wine list". Sharing plates are selected from a blackboard: "we ordered everything on the menu… and loved it all!" / N5 2RT; www.primeurN5.co.uk; @Primeurs1; 10.30 pm, Sun 5 pm; closed Mon, Tue L, Wed L, Thu L & Sun D; booking max 7 may apply.

Princess of Shoreditch EC2 £55 3️⃣2️⃣2️⃣
76 Paul St 020 7729 9270 13–1B
One of the first gastropubs on the City's Shoreditch border, this place takes old-timers "back to the early '00s!". What they do, "they do well", whether you're eating in the bar or on the upstairs mezzanine. / EC2A 4NE; www.theprincessofshoreditch.com; @princessofs; 10.30 pm, Sun 9 pm; No Amex; booking D only.

Princi W1 £37 3️⃣2️⃣3️⃣
135 Wardour St 020 7478 8888 4–1D
Smart Soho outlet of a Milanese bakery, whose self-service and restaurant-service areas both get "extremely busy". Breakfast/brunch is "joy", at other times pizza is more to the fore. "Grab a seat by the window, and it's great for people-watching". / W1F 0UT; www.princi.com; 11 pm, Sun 10 pm; no booking.

Prix Fixe W1 £45 3️⃣3️⃣2️⃣
39 Dean St 020 7734 5976 5–2A
"For the price, it is hard to find anything better in central London" than this "always reliable" venue "in the heart of Soho", whose "classic French bistro dishes" represent "extraordinarily good value". / W1D 4PU; www.prixfixe.net; @prixfixelondon; 11.30 pm.

The Promenade at The Dorchester W1 £124 2️⃣4️⃣4️⃣
The Dorchester Hotel, 53 Park Lane
020 7629 8888 3–3A
"For a fantastic afternoon tea in plush surroundings", it's worth trying the swagged, padded and cushioned environs of this opulent Mayfair hotel lounge, which provides "superb service and an endless amount of sandwiches and sweet treats!" / W1K 1QA; www.dorchestercollection.com/en/london/the-dorchester/restaurant-bars/afternoon-tea; @TheDorchester; 10.30 pm; No shorts.

Provender E11 £42 3️⃣4️⃣4️⃣
17 High St 020 8530 3050 1–1D
"Yes, it is worth the trek!", say fans of this latest venture from veteran restaurateur Max Renzland – an "authentic" bistro, whose "old style French cuisine" makes it "a safe and happy choice for those out and about in Wanstead and Snaresbrook". Top Tip – "good value set menu". / E11 2AA;

www.provenderlondon.co.uk; @ProvenderBistro; 10 pm,
Fri & Sat 10.30 pm, Sun 9 pm; booking max 10 may
apply.

The Providores and Tapa Room
W1 £73 4️⃣3️⃣2️⃣
109 Marylebone High St 020 7935 6175 2–1A
"The menu knocks your socks off!" – "Peter Gordon
continues to excel", at the renowned Kiwi chef's
Pacific fusion venue in Marylebone; still serving
"beautiful, inventive and original dishes" well into
its second decade, with marks for its food riding
higher than ever. "The tables are too close together
and it's pricey, but I keep going back..." / W1U 4RX;
www.theprovidores.co.uk; @theprovidores; 10 pm, Sun
9.45 pm; SRA-Food Made Good – 2 stars.

Prufrock Coffee EC1 £13 3️⃣2️⃣4️⃣
23-25 Leather Ln 07852 243470 10–2A
"Leading the pack in coffee (and its new
stoneground oolong tea is amazing!)" – this caffeine
haven near Chancery Lane offers "a great value
brunch for a City location, but it's always packed so
arrive early". / EC1N 7TE; www.prufrockcoffee.com;
@PrufrockCoffee; L only; No Amex.

Pulia SE1 £34 3️⃣4️⃣3️⃣
36 Stoney St 020 7407 8766 10–4C
"Really interesting and different Italian food" and
"knowledgeable staff" win praise for this "friendly,
buzzing and modern" deli/café "on the borders
of Borough Market" (the first outside Italy for a
Puglian-based group). / SE1 9AD; www.pulia.com;
@Puliauk; 10.30 pm, Sun 8.30 pm.

The Punchbowl W1 £61 3️⃣4️⃣3️⃣
41 Farm St 020 7493 6841 3–3A
Once owned by film director Guy Ritchie, Madonna's
ex, this atmospheric 18th-century Mayfair boozer
has dropped out of sight a little since he sold up, but
it's a good all-rounder in this pricey 'hood. / W1J 5RP;
www.punchbowllondon.com; @ThePunchBowlLDN; 11
pm, Sun 10.30 pm; closed Sun D.

Punjab WC2 £35 3️⃣2️⃣3️⃣
80 Neal St 020 7836 9787 5–2C
"Good food at good prices… but then they rush
you out"; "especially considering its location", this
long-lived Covent Garden curry house avoids (most
of) the pitfalls of its tourist trap potential and is
resolutely "free of the gimmicks that plague more
modern Indians!" / WC2H 9PA; www.punjab.co.uk; 11
pm, Sun 10 pm; booking max 8 may apply.

Pure Indian Cooking
SW6 £50 4️⃣3️⃣2️⃣
67 Fulham High St 020 7736 2521 11–1B
A "hidden gem" behind a little shopfront north
of Putney Bridge – this "slightly austere" three-
year-old is a first venture as boss for chef Shilpa
Dandekar, who used to work for Raymond Blanc,

and her contemporary dishes are consistently
"interesting and well presented". / SW6 3JJ;
www.pureindiancooking.com; @PureCooking.

QP LDN W1 £102 3️⃣3️⃣3️⃣
34 Dover St 020 3096 1444 3–3C
The "subdued and romantic" Mayfair showcase for
Amalfitan chef Antonio Mellino's cooking offers a
"top dining experience", with "wonderful Italian
cuisine" presented by "staff who go the extra mile".
It inspires only limited feedback however, perhaps
something to do with its not-inconsiderable prices. /
W1S 4NG; www.quattropassi.co.uk; @quattropassiuk;
10.30 pm; closed Sun D; set pre theatre £60 (FP).

Quaglino's SW1 £74 1️⃣2️⃣3️⃣
16 Bury St 020 7930 6767 3–3D
This vast and "plush" St James's basement – an
age-old venue (est 1929) that became an icon of
the '90s restaurant boom when it was relaunched
by Sir Terence Conran in 1993 – can still seem
like a "smashing environment" for an occasion.
"It could aim higher in the food department"
though – the cuisine is "acceptable but no more"
and comes at intimidating prices – and while
fans love the music and entertainment, it can be
so loud as "to kill the conversation". / SW1Y 6AJ;
www.quaglinos-restaurant.co.uk; @quaglinos; 10.30 pm,
Fri & Sat 11 pm; closed Sun; No trainers.

The Quality Chop House
EC1 £64 3️⃣3️⃣3️⃣
94 Farringdon Rd 020 7278 1452 10–1A
"If you can tolerate the discomfort" of the "terrible",
bum-numbing benches, the "authentic Victorian
wooden booths lend charm" to this restored Grade
II listed 'Working Class Caterer', which in the '90s
helped establish the environs of Exmouth Market
as the foodie hotspot it has become. Nowadays
with Shaun Searley at the stoves, it continues in the
oft-"excellent" but sometimes "variable" vein that it
has under its predecessors, offering a meaty menu
"clearly influenced by Henderson and St John"
and a wine list "full of interesting gems (some on
Coravin)." / EC1R 3EA; www.thequalitychophouse.com;
@QualityChop; 10.30 pm; closed Sun.

Quantus W4 £56 4️⃣5️⃣3️⃣
38 Devonshire Rd 020 8994 0488 8–2A
"Passionate and exceptional service from Leo
Pacarada and his team" lifts the experience at this
little venture in a Chiswick side street – a "favourite"
amongst its small fan club thanks to its "excellent"
Latin-influenced modern European cooking. / W4
2HD; www.quantus-london.com; 10 pm; closed Mon L,
Tue L & Sun.

Quartieri NW6 NEW £37 4️⃣3️⃣3️⃣
300 Kilburn High Rd 020 7625 8822 1–2B
"A great addition to the neighbourhood" – this
new, small but stylish Kilburn pizza-stop is owned

by Neapolitans and it shows: despite the odd report that it was "shambolic in its early days", all agree that "the pizza is amazing". / NW6 2DB; www.quartieri.co.uk; @quartierilondon; 11 pm.

Le Querce SE23   £42   **4****4****3**
66-68 Brockley Rise   020 8690 3761   1–4D
"Customers are welcomed like old friends" at this family-run neighbourhood Italian in Brockley, which is "only improved by being Sardinian, with great specials, fish and burrata". (For years, it won some of southeast London's highest ratings – nowadays its scores are very respectable but not quite as earth shattering.) / SE23 1LN; www.lequerce.co.uk; 9.30 pm, Sun 8.15 pm; closed Mon & Tue L.

Quilon SW1   £71   **5****4****3**
41 Buckingham Gate   020 7821 1899   2–4B
Sriram Aylur's "glorious, creative, original take on Keralan cuisine, with great integrity to its origins, but enough latitude to feel very unusual and special" has long established Taj Group's luxurious venue near Buckingham Palace as one of London's top subcontinentals ("My Indian colleagues swear by it when they're in the UK"). Staff "go out of their way to be polite and helpful too", and the only reservation is that the "spacious" interior can seem "a bit sterile". / SW1E 6AF; www.quilon.co.uk; @thequilon; 11 pm, Sun 10.30 pm; SRA-Food Made Good – 2 stars.

Quirinale SW1   £64   **4****3****2**
North Ct, 1 Gt Peter St   020 7222 7080   2–4C
"Precise and elegant" Italian cuisine, "lovely wine", "exemplary discreet service" and "a rarity – a quiet interior", make this "airy" ("but dull") basement a perfect venue for entertaining MPs or senior civil servants from nearby Westminster; hence "it's great for parliamentarian-spotting". / SW1P 3LL; www.quirinale.co.uk; @quirinaleresto; 10.30 pm; closed Sat & Sun.

Quo Vadis W1   £60   **4****5****5**
26-29 Dean St   020 7437 9585   4–1D
"Benefitting from its reduction in size to accommodate Barrafina's move from Frith Street, QV is now more intimate" than it was before, and the ground floor of the Hart Bros' Soho classic also feels even more "relaxed and convivial", aided by its "sublimely attentive, yet also informal staff". Appreciation for Jeremy Lee's cuisine has stepped up a notch too – "sensational British food using the best seasonal produce". / W1D 3LL; www.quovadissoho.co.uk; @QuoVadisSoho; 11 pm; closed Sun.

Rabbit SW3   £46   **3****3****2**
172 King's Rd   020 3750 0172   6–3C
"You squeeze in on wobbly chairs, next to cramped wobbly tables" at the Gladwin brothers (Shed, Nutbourne) quirky Chelsea venture, serving distinctive, farm-to-table British tapas. Critics

(more numerous this year) say "the novelty of eating expensive, tiny bits of food wears off pretty quickly", but most reporters still applaud its "interesting small dishes concept". / SW3 4UP; www.rabbit-restaurant.com; @RabbitResto; midnight, Mon 11 pm, Sun 6 pm; closed Mon L & Sun D.

Rabot 1745 SE1   £63   **2****2****2**
2-4 Bedale St   020 7378 8226   10–4C
"The huge vat of melted chocolate is the big draw" at this "curious concept" in Borough Market: "a cafe styled like a St Lucian cocoa plantation". There are cakes for afternoon tea, "chocolate fusion cuisine", and "a proper bar at night in case you fancy a cocoa-infused beer or gin". The only unqualified success, however, is the "wonderful hot chocolate!" / SE1 9AL; www.rabot1745.com; @rabot1745; 9.30 pm, closed Mon & Sun.

Radici N1 **NEW**   £61   **2****2****3**
30 Almeida St   020 7354 4777   9–3D
"Newly rooted near the Almeida Theatre", this rustically-themed, south Italian newcomer – D&D London's replacement for The Almeida (RIP) – has made a tepid debut, despite the much-hyped involvement of Francesco Mazzei, and although its "competent cooking" isn't terribly rated, Islingtonians in particular preferred its fairly middling predecessor: "I really wanted to like this place and I love the chef, but this looks like a chain using a famous name without being prepared to source quality ingredients or cook them with real love". End result – "too expensive for a casual local, but not good enough for a special occasion". / N1 1AD; www.radici.uk; @radici_n1.

Ragam W1   £28   **4****2****1**
57 Cleveland St   020 7636 9098   2–1B
"Spectacularly good South Indian meals" at a "wonderfully cheap" price won renewed acclaim this year for this grungy Keralan stalwart, near the Telecom Tower. Especially since its recent makeover it can seem even more "drab and harshly-lit", but on all accounts it's still "a tremendous recommendation". / W1T 4JN; www.ragam.co.uk; 11 pm.

Rail House Café SW1   £60   **2****2****2**
Sir Simon Milton Sq   020 3906 7950   2–4B
The task of feeding 300-plus diners over two floors of Victoria's new Nova development was never going to be a doddle, and Adam White's year-old venue has yet to make a consistent go of it: there are fans, but too many critics feel "it doesn't live up to its sibling Riding House Café, on any front" – "the food is all over the place, and service is either too keen or just disappears!" / SW1H 0HW; www.railhouse.cafe; @railhouse_cafe.

Rainforest Café W1   £61   **2****3****3**
20-24 Shaftesbury Ave   020 7434 3111   4–3D
"I'm a parent get me out of here!… but I admit

they cater for large groups including children very well…"; this lavish Piccadilly Circus venue – complete with animatronic animals and indoor rain storms – isn't a foodie choice, but it is a very kid-friendly one. / W1V 7EU; www.therainforestcafe.co.uk; @RainforestCafe; 9.30 pm, Sat 10 pm; credit card required to book.

Rambla W1 NEW
64 Dean St awaiting tel 5–2A
Named for Barcelona's famous restaurant strip, this third opening from Victor 'Encant' Garvey is set to open in October 2017, promising a Catalan menu in a larger (60 cover) space than his openings to date. / W1D 4QG; @ramblasoho.

Randall & Aubin W1   £60   3|3|4
14-16 Brewer St   020 7287 4447   4–2D
"The epitome of a Soho lifestyle" is to be found at this "fun" classic, near The Box Soho, where "great people watching" helps whet the appetite for some "brilliant fruits de mer and fabulous fish", enjoyed while nattering and perched on high bar stools. "Service is warm, friendly and, occasionally, quirky in a good way". "Be prepared to queue but it's worth the wait". / W1F 0SG; www.randallandaubin.com; @randallandaubin; 11 pm, Fri & Sat 11.30 pm, Sun 9.30 pm; booking L only.

Randy's Wing Bar E15   £34   4|3|3
28 East Bay Lane, The Press Centre, Here East, Queen Elizabeth Olympic Park
020 8555 5971   14–1C
Olympic Park outlet doling out a variety of catchily-named burgers and wings with funky flavourings and lashings of fun attitude – limited reports as yet, but all of them positive. / E15 2GW; www.randyswingbar.co.uk; @randyswingbar; 11 pm, Thu-Sat 11.30 pm, Sunday 6 pm; closed Sun D.

Rani N3   £34   4|2|2
7 Long Lane 020 8349 4386/2636 1–1B
The "outstanding buffet" is a decades-old feature and continues to inspire enthusiastic (if limited) feedback for 'London's oldest Gujarati' in Finchley. / N3 2PR; www.raniuk.com; 10.30 pm.

Raoul's Café   £44   3|2|3
105-107 Talbot Rd, W11   020 7229 2400   7–1B
13 Clifton Rd, W9   020 7289 7313   9–4A
"Still the best eggs in the world", with "the most amazing deep-yellow yolks", are the signature attraction at these "very busy" brunch hangouts in Maida Vale and Notting Hill. / www.raoulsgourmet.com; W9 10.15 pm, W11 10 pm; booking after 5 pm only.

Rasa   £35   3|3|3
6 Dering St, W1   020 7629 1346   3–2B
Holiday Inn Hotel, 1 Kings Cross, WC1
020 7833 9787   9–3D
55 Stoke Newington Church St, N16
020 7249 0344   1–1C
56 Stoke Newington Church St, N16
020 7249 1340   1–1C
"Enough to make a believer of the most ardent meat-eater": these "rather basic" and primarily veggie Keralans are so good, especially the Stoke Newington original, that "it's hard not to overeat". But while they remain "great value" there's a feeling amongst long-term fans that "a little extra would be needed to regain full marks" – "it's still good, but the menu never changes, and doesn't excite me like it did". / www.rasarestaurants.com; N16 & Travancore N16 10.45 pm, Fri & Sat 11.30 pm, W1 11 pm, Sun 9 pm; WC1 closed L, Sun L&D, N16 closed Mon-Fri L, Travancore closed L.

Ravi Shankar NW1   £30   3|2|2
132-135 Drummond St   020 7388 6458   9–4C
"Really tasty food at amazing prices" makes this vegetarian stalwart one of the stars of the Little India curry zone near Euston station. Value is best – and dishes tastiest – at the lunchtime and weekend buffet, "when staff add items from the à la carte menu". The surroundings are definitely "bargain basement". / NW1 2HL; www.ravishankarbhelpoori.com; 10.30 pm.

Red Fort W1   £72   4|3|2
77 Dean St   020 7437 2525   4–1D
"Still excelling after all this time", say fans of this long-established Soho North Indian, whose contemporary looks postdate a fire a few years ago. But while it's consistently well-rated, the volume of feedback it attracts is quite low these days. / W1D 3SH; redfort.co.uk; @redfortlondon; 10.30 pm; closed Sat L & Sun L; No shorts; set pre theatre £45 (FP).

The Red Lion & Sun N6   £52   3|2|3
25 North Rd   020 8340 1780   9–1B
"An unpretentious country pub in a leafy part of London" – Highgate locals say it's "just what a gastropub should be", with "reasonably priced" food "consistent with the character of the environment, but very well cooked". / N6; www.theredlionandsun.com; @redlionandsun; 10 pm.

The Red Pepper W9   £50   3|2|2
8 Formosa St   020 7266 2708   9–4A
Cramped café in Maida Vale, consistently well-rated for its wood-fired pizza. / W9 1EE; www.theredpepperrestaurant.co.uk; 10.30 pm, Fri & Sat 11 pm, Sun 10 pm; closed weekday L; No Amex.

Red Rooster EC2 NEW   £69
45 Curtain Rd   020 3146 4545   13–1B
Ethiopian-Swedish chef, Marcus Samuelsson brings his southern-soul-food-via-Scandinavia cuisine to the eclectically decorated basement of an oh-so-hip Shoreditch boutique hotel and members club. It opened in mid 2017 – early press feedback is positive. / EC2A 4PJ;

www.thecurtain.com; @RoosterHarlem; midnight, Wed 1 am, Thu-Sat 2 am, Sun 5 pm; closed Sun D.

Le Relais de Venise L'Entrecôte £47 **3** **2** **2**
120 Marylebone Ln, W1   020 7486 0878   2–1A
50 Dean St, W1   020 3475 4202   5–3A **NEW**
18-20 Mackenzie Walk, E14
020 3475 3331   12–1C
5 Throgmorton St, EC2   020 7638 6325   10–2C
"You know what you are getting" at this Gallic steakhouse chain whose "unique formula" delivers "excellence through simplicity" – the only menu option is "tasty" steak-frites (with unlimited seconds), garnished with their "to-die-for secret sauce". / www.relaisdevenise.com; 10.45 pm-11 pm, Sun 9 pm-10.30 pm; EC2 closed Sat & Sun; no booking.

Restaurant Ours SW3 £78 **1** **2** **3**
264 Brompton Rd   020 7100 2200   6–2C
It's "amusingly eurotrashy" – if you like that kind of thing – but this "buzzing and vibrant" South Kensington yearling "doesn't quite hit the mark" (and it's no huge surprise that über-chef Tom Sellers decided to move on just a year after its much-hyped launch). True to the form of predecessors on this site, the design-values may be "inspirational", but even fans say "it's not one to go to on a budget" and given "food that doesn't always match up" it too often seems "dire". / SW3 2AS; www.restaurant-ours.com; @restaurant_ours; midnight, Fri & Sat 1.30 am; closed Mon & Sun.

Reubens W1 £57 **2** **2** **2**
79 Baker St   020 7486 0035   2–1A
"Salt beef is still excellent" at this long-running kosher deli-diner in Marylebone, while other dishes vary from merely "OK" to "good". "The downstairs restaurant a bit of a squeeze." / W1U 6RG; www.reubensrestaurant.co.uk; 10 pm; closed Fri D & Sat; No Amex.

The Rib Man E1 £12 **5** **4**
Brick Lane, Brick Lane Market   no tel   13–2C
"The best rib rolls in London", made by the legendary Mark Gevaux, are "just extraordinarily good street food" – and, for aficionados, "the only reason to go to Brick Lane on a Sunday". You'll have to get there early, because his "perfect" pulled pork always sells out. The rest of the week, fans make do with one of his trademark condiments, led by Holy F**k hot sauce. "You cannot fault this guy: he loves what he produces and it shows". / E1 6HR; www.theribman.co.uk; @theribman; Cash only; no booking.

Rib Room, Jumeirah Carlton Tower Hotel SW1 £100
Cadogan Pl   020 7858 7250   6–1D
This luxurious Sloane Street address, long known as a temple to roast beef and steak – will reopen in late 2017 as the new London vehicle for Marlow's 'Hand & Flowers' chef, Tom Kerridge. What we know from the PR so far: it will keep the name, it will evoke the spirit of Knightsbridge in the swinging '60s (groovy baby), and it will aim to be good value (not something the site has achieved hitherto). / SW1X 9PY; www.theribroom.co.uk; @RibRoomSW1; 9.30 pm, Sat 10 pm; set weekday L, dinner & pre-theatre £65 (FP).

Riccardo's SW3 £47 **2** **2** **3**
126 Fulham Rd   020 7370 6656   6–3B
A "reliable if not exciting" Chelsea local which offers a "great choice of genuine Italian food and wine in an informal environment". While nowadays it may not seem as notable as it once was, "it provides value for money" in a posh part of town. / SW3 6HU; www.riccardos.it; @ricardoslondon; 11.30 pm, Sun 10.30 pm.

Rick Stein SW14 **NEW** £67 **3** **2** **5**
Tideway Yard, 125 Mortlake High St
020 8878 9462   11–1A
"Little changed in decor since its days as The Depot" (now RIP) – the Stein empire's new (and first) foray into the capital inhabits a well-known neighbourhood spot, near Barnes Bridge, never known for its gastronomy. Sceptics feel that "confused if well-meaning service" is one plus-ça-change reminder of the old days, as is the fact that "you get a substantial bill for what amounts to enthusiastic brasserie fare" but the more positive (and also oft-expressed view) is that it produces "wonderful fish that finally lives up to this terrific riverside location". / SW14 8SN; www.rickstein.com/eat-with-us/barnes; @SteinBarnes; 9.30 pm.

Riding House Café W1 £58 **2** **2** **4**
43-51 Great Titchfield St
020 7927 0840   3–1C
"Cool" Fitzrovia haunt, exuding all the right design pheromones, whose "interesting breakfast choices (both healthy and less so)" and "informal vibe" make it "spot on for weekend brunch". Fans do recommend it at other times too, but service is "uneven" and the overall food offering can seem "rather uninspiring". A sibling, Rail House Café, opened in Nova Victoria in early 2017. / W1W 7PQ; www.ridinghousecafe.co.uk; 10.30 pm, Fri & Sat 11 pm, Sun 9.30 pm.

Rigo' SW6 **NEW**
277 New King's Rd   020 7751 3293   11–1B
New ambitious modern Italian which opened its doors post-survey in Fulham in July 2017; chef Gonzalo Luzarraga and Francesco Ferretti are the owners – Luzarraga trained with Alain DuCasse and has cooked all over the world. / SW6 4RD; rigolondon.com.

The Rising Sun NW7 £58 3️⃣2️⃣3️⃣
137 Marsh Ln 020 8959 1357 1–1B
"A local pub in Mill Hill, run by a very friendly Italian family" ("they know all about entertaining children"): sounds a good formula, and, though "sometimes it's too busy for their own good" fans from across north London say it's "definitely a winner", with "very good quality Italian cooking". / NW7 4EY; www.therisingsunmillhill.com; @therisingsunpub; 10 pm, Fri & Sat 11 pm, Sun 8.30 pm; closed Mon L.

Ristorante Frescobaldi
W1 **£82** 3️⃣3️⃣2️⃣
15 New Burlington Pl 020 3693 3435 4–2A
This pricey two-year-old Mayfair Tuscan has yet to make waves, but on (practically) all accounts is "most enjoyable", with a "nice interior and friendly service". Its top feature is a wine list reflecting its ownership by a 700-year-old Florentine wine and banking dynasty, for whom this is a first UK venture. / W1S 5HX; www.frescobaldirestaurants.com; @frescobaldi_uk; 11 pm.

The Ritz W1 £132 3️⃣4️⃣5️⃣
150 Piccadilly 020 7493 8181 3–4C
"The most beautiful dining room on the planet" – this "stunning" Louis XVI chamber is "a wonderful place for a celebratory experience", especially a romantic one. The "glorious classical cuisine" has "stepped up a notch" in recent years, and "even though it's eye-wateringly expensive it's always impressive", and delivered by "knowledgeable and passionate staff". Top Tip – "the latest incarnation of its weekend dinner dance is also excellent". / W1J 9BR; www.theritzlondon.com; @theritzlondon; 10 pm; Jacket & tie required; booking essential; set weekday L £101 (FP); SRA-Food Made Good – 3 stars.

The Ritz, Palm Court
W1 **£87** 2️⃣4️⃣5️⃣
150 Piccadilly 020 7493 8181 3–4C
Even those who find this famous afternoon tea experience "a bit cheesy", feel "it has to be done" given its status as the benchmark that has for so long epitomised the occasion, and it's "possibly the best of its type in grand surroundings". Yes, it's "expensive – but if you're going to do it, do it in style". Top Tip – "you'll need to book months ahead for that special event". / W1J 9BR; www.theritzlondon.com; Jacket & tie required.

Riva SW13 £64 3️⃣3️⃣2️⃣
169 Church Rd 020 8748 0434 11–1A
Andreas Riva's enduring destination in out-of-the-way Barnes is known as a very "understated" stalwart, whose "simple, seasonal north Italian cooking" has long made it a clandestine Mecca for in-the-know foodies, and bizarrely means the venue can be "great for spotting celebs" (but only the kind you might hear on Radio 4). But while it's a genuine "favourite" for many habitués, occasional visitors can

feel "let down" by "snooty" service (it can feel like "the owner spends all his efforts on regulars"), or perceive it as "overpriced". / SW13 9HR; 10.30 pm; Sun 9 pm; closed Sat L.

Rivea, Bulgari Hotel
SW7 **£80** 3️⃣4️⃣3️⃣
171 Knightsbridge 020 7151 1025 6–1C
Alain Ducasse's luxe Knightsbridge dining room offers "exceptionally skilful" and "exquisitely presented" Italian-French small plates, with "the smooth and charming service you would expect" of the French superchef. "Not everyone likes the hotel decor and basement setting" (with "lots of cold chrome and heavily lacquered wood") but some do "love it". / SW7 1DW; www.bulgarihotels.com; @bulgarihotels; 10.30 pm; booking max 7 may apply.

THE RIVER CAFÉ W6 £97 3️⃣3️⃣3️⃣
Thames Wharf, Rainville Rd
020 7386 4200 8–2C
"The sheer genius and simplicity of always-exciting Tuscan food prepared from ingredients of unparalleled quality" have won global renown for this "unique", "off-the-beaten-track Italian, in the obscure backstreets of Hammersmith. Its prices, however, are "daylight robbery" – and while its army of fans say that "if you believe it's overpriced, you don't get its concept of provenance, care and integrity", an equally large band of sceptics "appreciate the top-quality sourcing, but still think charges are absurd for rustic dishes (it might be cheaper to fly to Italy for the day, dine and fly back...").And the atmosphere? "On a summer evening you could not ask for a better location" than its Thames-side terrace, but when it comes to eating inside first-timers can be surprised at how "hectic and noisy" its canteen-like set-up can be; service meanwhile veers from "charming" to "indifferent". Still, it's always full, so you can't blame them" and "if I was a billionaire I'd go every week!" / W6 9HA; www.rivercafe.co.uk; @RiverCafeLondon; 9 pm, Sat 9.15 pm; closed Sun D; set weekday L £59 (FP).

Rivington Grill SE10 £54 2️⃣2️⃣2️⃣
178 Greenwich High Rd 020 8293 9270 1–3D
Ironically this Greenwich grill is now the sole bearer of the 'Rivington' brand as the Rivington Street original in Shoreditch shut up shop in August 2017. Critics see this straightforward British restaurant as a tad "mundane", but as "there's just about nowhere really decent to eat in SE10", its supporters boost it as arguably "the best option in the area" – "go for the grilled meats and excellent selection of gins". / SE10 8NN; www.rivingtongrill.co.uk; 11 pm, Sun 10 pm; closed Mon, Tue L & Wed L.

Roast SE1 £68 2️⃣2️⃣3️⃣
Stoney St 0845 034 7300 10–4C
"The marvellous space is exhilarating" – and ideal for business – at this potentially brilliant fixture over

Borough Market (partially constructed from a glazed Victorian structure that was originally a portico of the Royal Opera House's Floral Hall).When it comes to the traditional British meat dishes, however, "the food's OK, but nothing special for the hefty price tag" with enjoyment often "dependent on whether you make a good menu choice" ("some dishes show good promise, others are simply no more than the sum of their ingredients"), and "service can be slow".Top Tip – "magnificent Full English breakfast – there's no need to eat again that day!" / SE1 1TL; www.roast-restaurant.com; @roastrestaurant; 10.45 pm; closed Sun D.

Rocca Di Papa £38 [3][3][4]
73 Old Brompton Rd, SW7
020 7225 3413 6–2B
75-79 Dulwich Village, SE21
020 8299 6333 1–4D
These "cosy, busy and good-value" local Italians in South Kensington and Dulwich do the simple things well:"handmade pasta, great pizzas and lovely service". "Perfect for families – kids are well-treated" (so "it can be a bit of a creche if you go at the wrong time"). / www.roccarestaurants.com; SW7 11.30 pm; SE21 11 pm.

Rochelle Canteen E2 £59 [3][3][4]
Rochelle School, Arnold Circus
020 7729 5677 13–1C
"A hidden treat" in Spitalfields – this offbeat (and on a sunny day "amazing"), venue from Melanie Arnold and Margot Henderson – wife of St John's Fergus – occupies the converted bike sheds of a former school ("just lovely on a summer's day sitting outside in what was the playground, now a walled courtyard") and offers "simple, well-cooked food for those in-the-know" (NB it's no longer BYO, they now have a license). In September 2017, a new 'Rochelle' was announced taking over the bar/ café at the ICA on the Mall – spiritually speaking, the two locations seem poles apart. / E2 7ES; www.arnoldandhenderson.com; 4.30 pm, Thu-Sat 9 pm; L only, Thu-Sat L & D; No Amex.

Rök £53 [4][2][2]
149 Upper St, N1 no tel 9–3D
26 Curtain Rd, EC2 020 7377 2152 13–2B
"Lovely combinations of Scandinavian food", much of it brined or smoked, is the calling card at this "great little bar" in Shoreditch, now with an Islington offshoot. "It's un-glossy and unpretentious, but don't be fooled by appearances." / N1 midnight, EC2 11 pm, Fri & Sat 1 am; EC2 closed Sun.

Roka £80 [4][3][3]
30 North Audley St, W1 020 7305 5644 3–2A
37 Charlotte St, W1 020 7580 6464 2–1C
Aldwych House, 71-91 Aldwych, WC2
020 7294 7636 2–2D
Unit 4, Park Pavilion, 40 Canada Sq, E14

020 7636 5228 12–1C
"Some of the best fusion fare that will pass your lips" – these "always buzzy" and "vibey" Japanese-inspired operations dazzle with their "beauteous robata dishes", "amazing black cod", sushi and other "superb Asian dishes", and even if "the prices are as incredible as the food" it's "money well spent". That they are perennially ignored by Michelin is incomprehensible. / www.rokarestaurant.com; 11.30 pm, Sun 10.30 pm; E14 11pm, Sun 8.30 pm; WC2 11 pm, Sun 8 pm; booking: max 5 online.

Rola Wala E1 [NEW]
36 Brushfield St 13–2B
After a long residency at Street Feast, this spicy street food concept (already rooted in Leeds since 2014) is adding a permanent London branch in Spitalfields, with a menu including low-calorie, low-carb and gluten-free options. / E1 6AT; www.rolawala.com; @RolaWala.

Romulo Café W8 £58 [3][3][3]
343 Kensington High St 020 3141 6390 6–1A
Limited reports to-date on this year-old venture – one of London's few Filipino restaurants – decorated with portraits of the owner's ancestors, but all feedback says it's a "great new arrival". / W8 6NW; www.romulocafe.co.uk; @romulolondon; 10 pm.

Rosa's £42 [2][2][2]
5 Gillingham St, SW1 020 3813 6773 2–4C
23a Ganton St, W1 020 7287 9617 4–2B
48 Dean St, W1 020 7494 1638 5–3A
246 Fulham Rd, SW10 020 7583 9021 6–3B
6 Theberton St, N1
020 3393 2482 9–3D [NEW]
152a West End Lane, NW6
020 3773 1568 1–1B [NEW]
36 Atlantic Rd, SW9 020 3393 8562 11–2D
Westfield Stratford City, E15
020 8519 1302 14–1D
12 Hanbury St, E1 020 7247 1093 13–2C
This "hectic" and "cheerful" Thai café chain has grown apace over the years. Compared with the early days (when "the original E1 branch set the standards for the roll-out") its spicy fare is probably "nothing to write home about", but most reports still say it's "tasty and fresh" and "really well priced". / rosasthaicafe.com; 10.30 pm, Fri & Sat 11 pm; E15 9 pm, Sat 10 pm, Sun 9 pm; W1F & W1D Sun 10 pm; ; E1, SW1 & SW9 6+ to book, W1 4+ to book.

The Rosendale SE21 £52 [3][4][3]
65 Rosendale Rd 020 8761 9008 1–4D
Handsome Victorian coaching inn (with a large garden) in West Dulwich, consistently well-rated for its quality gastropub cooking. / SE21 8EZ; www.therosendale.co.uk; @threecheerspubs; 10 pm, Sat 9.30 pm, Sun 9 pm; No Amex.

Rossopomodoro £45 3️⃣2️⃣2️⃣
John Lewis, 300 Oxford St, W1
020 7495 8409 3–1B
50-52 Monmouth St, WC2
020 7240 9095 5–3B
214 Fulham Rd, SW10 020 7352 7677 6–3B
1 Rufus St, N1 020 7739 1899 13–1B
10 Jamestown Rd, NW1 020 7424 9900 9–3B
46 Garrett Ln, SW18 020 8877 9903 11–2B
"They know how to make a decent pizza" (wood-fired) – as indeed they should! – at this "affordable" global chain, which is based in Naples, and where many of the ingredients (and staff and customers) are imported from Italy. / www.rossopomodoro.co.uk; 11 pm, Fri & Sat 11.30 pm, Sun 10 pm.

Roti Chai W1 £46 4️⃣3️⃣4️⃣
3 Portman Mews South 020 7408 0101 3–1A
The "spicy" dishes are "damned good" at this "original and interesting" Indian operation near Selfridges, serving street-hawker-style small plates on the "more casual", "grab-and-go" ground floor and tandoori grills plus regional specialities in the "more formal" basement. Both options are "very good value for central London". / W1H 6HS; www.rotichai.com; @rotichai; 10.30 pm; booking D only.

Roti King, Ian Hamilton House NW1 £22 5️⃣2️⃣1️⃣
40 Doric Way 020 7387 2518 9–3C
"Fabulous rotis" – "the best in town" – and "really good Malaysian street food at bargain prices" mean this "crowded basement dive" in Euston is one of the few places "worth queuing for". Don't let "the location put you off", and come prepared to share a table with the "students and Malaysians" who flock here. / NW1 1LH; www.rotiking.in; no booking.

Rotorino E8 £49 2️⃣4️⃣2️⃣
434 Kingsland Rd 020 7249 9081 14–1A
Stevie Parle's Italian-inspired outfit in Dalston can still impress, but all feedback this year (which was quite limited) was shot through with pluses and minuses: "great local eatery, maybe losing its shine", was typical; "it felt technically great but could do with some more soul" was another. / E8 4AA; www.rotorino.com; @Rotorino; 10 pm.

Rotunda Bar & Restaurant, Kings Place N1 £55 3️⃣4️⃣4️⃣
90 York Way 020 7014 2840 9–3C
"Especially on a sunny day, overlooking the canal" (by which it has a large terrace), this "buzzy" arts centre brasserie provides a "beautiful setting". Some dishes can seem "run-of-the-mill", but, Top Tip – "they serve wonderful meat" from their own Northumberland farm (and it's "very good for Sunday lunch"). / N1 9AG; www.rotundabarandrestaurant.co.uk; @rotundalondon; 10.30 pm, Sun 6.30 pm; closed Sun.

Roux at Parliament Square, RICS SW1 £91 5️⃣5️⃣3️⃣
12 Great George St 020 7334 3737 2–3C
"Perfection!" – "I enjoyed every single mouthful!" – "wonderful food and service in the Roux tradition" is the consistent accolade for this formal Parliament Square venue, where the kitchen is run by MasterChef winner Steve Groves. "It's a bit quiet and sedate… but that's not a criticism." / SW1P 3AD; www.rouxatparliamentsquare.co.uk; @RouxAPS; 9 pm; closed Sat & Sun; No trainers; set weekday L £71 (FP).

Roux at the Landau, The Langham W1 £101 2️⃣3️⃣3️⃣
1c Portland Pl 020 7965 0165 2–1B
Fans of the Roux's management of this "calm and elegant" chamber truly adore its "quiet" and "romantic" style, while also praising its "polite and seriously attentive service" and "superb French cuisine". Its ratings have waned in the last couple of years however, as a small but vociferous minority give it flak for "unadventurous" food they consider "average for the price". / W1B 1JA; www.rouxatthelandau.com; @Langham_Hotel; 10.30 pm; closed Sat & Sun; No trainers; set brunch £61 (FP), set weekday L, dinner & pre-theatre £63 (FP).

Rowley's SW1 £70 3️⃣3️⃣3️⃣
113 Jermyn St 020 7930 2707 4–4D
"The (unlimited!) fries are a treat" at this venerable St James's steakhouse, set in the original Wall's sausages and ice cream premises. Though dogged in the past by inconsistent standards, all feedback this year says it's a "reliable" option that's "great for Chateaubriand". / SW1Y 6HJ; www.rowleys.co.uk; @rowleys_steak; 10.30 pm.

Rox Burger SE13 £32 4️⃣3️⃣3️⃣
82 Lee High Rd 020 3372 4631 1–4D
"Top burgers" washed down with craft beers win rave reviews from far and wide for this popular little outfit in Lewisham. Don't despair if you can't get a seat: "they do takeaway…" / SE13 5PT; www.roxburger.com; @RoxburgerUK; 10 pm, Fri & Sat 11 pm.

Royal China £54 3️⃣1️⃣2️⃣
24-26 Baker St, W1 020 7487 4688 2–1A
805 Fulham Rd, SW6 020 7731 0081 11–1B
13 Queensway, W2 020 7221 2535 7–2C
30 Westferry Circus, E14
020 7719 0888 12–1B
"My Chinese friend will not go anywhere else!"; these "garish black and gold" Cantonese stalwarts (particularly the Baker Street and Bayswater branches) remain many Londoners 'go-to' choice for "particularly authentic and economical dim sum" ("never had a bad dish in 20 years!"), although the full menu is less of an attraction. "Expect a queue at the weekend" and prepare for "abrupt" service and

a setting that's "lively without being very convivial". / www.royalchinagroup.co.uk; 11 pm, Sun 10 pm; W1 Fri & Sat 11.30 pm; no booking Sat & Sun L.

Royal China Club W1   £68   4️⃣2️⃣2️⃣

40-42 Baker St   020 7486 3898   2–1A

"Delectable dim sum" that's "comparable to the best in HK" ensures the accomplished Marylebone flagship of the China Club group is "always packed". Especially given "an interior that could be improved" however, even fans can find it "overpriced". / W1U 7AJ; www.royalchinagroup.co.uk; 11 pm, Sun 10.30 pm; booking weekdays only.

The Royal Exchange Grand Café, The Royal Exchange EC3 £51   2️⃣3️⃣4️⃣

The Royal Exchange Bank
020 7618 2480   10–2C

For an informal business bite (including a "top quality breakfast") it's worth remembering the café in the "very handsome" covered courtyard of this Victorian pile, right at the heart of the City of London. / EC3V 3LR; www.royalexchange-grandcafe.co.uk; @rexlondon; 10 pm; closed Sat & Sun; credit card required to book.

Rucoletta EC2   £48   2️⃣2️⃣2️⃣

6 Foster Lane   020 7600 7776   10–2C

"Simple, well-prepared Italian food in a City backstreet" near St Paul's makes this a useful lunch spot in a busy part of town. But reporters are split over the quality of the offer, with comments ranging from "great" to "totally careless". / EC2V 6HH; www.rucoletta.co.uk; @RucolettaLondon; 9.30 pm, Thu & Fri 10 pm; closed Sat D & Sun; No Amex.

Rugoletta   £41   3️⃣3️⃣2️⃣

308 Ballards Ln, N12   020 8445 6742   1–1B
59 Church Ln, N2   020 8815 1743   1–1B

These "cramped Italian" local favourites in Barnet and East Finchley are "well worth knowing" and "excellent value" for their traditional dishes, especially the pasta. / www.la-rugoletta.com; 10.30 pm; N12 Fri & Sat 11 pm; N2 closed Sun.

Rules WC2   £78   2️⃣3️⃣5️⃣

35 Maiden Ln   020 7836 5314   5–3D

"Step into London's history" on entering the capital's oldest restaurant (established 1798), whose "stunning" panelled premises near Covent Garden have a "timeless feel – Victorian diners wouldn't look out of place, nor modern, open-collared business folk". For "so-traditional British fare" ("wonderful game" and "top steak puddings") it can still deliver "old-school perfection", and though "foreign visitors love it", it's still "an absolute favourite" for many locals. That said, they need to watch the ever-more "inflated prices" here: "step this way and empty your wallet!" / WC2E 7LB; www.rules.co.uk; 11.45 pm, Sun 10.45 pm; No shorts.

Sabor W1   NEW

35 Heddon St awaiting tel   4–3A

Nieves Barragán Mohacho and José Etura, who met working at Barrafina (where the former was the executive head chef), have unsurprisingly chosen a Spanish style for their autumn newcomer, which – with additional bar and asador (wood-fired oven), will open in Heddon Street. The ground-floor will feature a fresh seafood counter and an open kitchen producing regional dishes from across Spain, while the upstairs restaurant will focus on the cuisine of Galicia and Castile. / W1B 4BP; @NievesBarragan1.

Le Sacré-Coeur N1   £39   2️⃣2️⃣2️⃣

18 Theberton St   020 7354 2618   9–3D

Mixed views this year on this Gallic veteran, north of Angel. Supporters continue to hail it as a "lovely bistro" with "reasonably priced" fare, but sceptics feel "it's lost some of its old charm" of late, and become "very average". / N1 0QX; www.lesacrecoeur.co.uk; @LeSacreCoeurUK; 11 pm, Fri & Sat 11.30 pm, Sun 10.30 pm.

Sacro Cuore   £37   5️⃣4️⃣2️⃣

10 Crouch End Hill, N8   020 8348 8487   1–1C
45 Chamberlayne Rd, NW10
020 8960 8558   1–2B

"Authentic" Neapolitan-style pizza is the single main course offered at this Kensal Rise pizzeria (now with a Crouch End branch). But what a pizza it is: "brilliant" – "one of the best outside Italy". "The only con is that you can't eat anything else" – although there is a short and tasty menu of starters and desserts.

Sagar   £35   3️⃣2️⃣1️⃣

17a Percy St, W1   020 7631 3319   3–2B
31 Catherine St, WC2   020 7836 6377   5–3D
157 King St, W6   020 8741 8563   8–2C

"Fresh South Indian vegetarian food", including "monster-sized dosas", all at low prices wins a sizeable fan club this small chain (Covent Garden, Tottenham Court Road, Hammersmith and Harrow) despite its incredibly "ordinary" decor. / www.sagarveg.co.uk; W1 10.45 pm-11pm, Sun 10 pm.

Sagardi EC2   £62   2️⃣2️⃣2️⃣

Cordy House, 95 Curtain Rd
020 3802 0478   13–1B

"The meat is delicious", say fans of this Basque yearling in Shoreditch (part of an international chain specialising in Galician Txuleton beef cooked on a charcoal grill). The problem here can be the price: "while the food and wine selection was very good, the small-plates concept meant costs soared very quickly". / EC2A 3AH; www.sagardi.co.uk; @Sagardi_UK; 11 pm.

FSA

Sager + Wilde £62 2**4**4
193 Hackney Rd, E2 020 8127 7330 14–2A
250 Paradise Row, E2 020 7613 0478 14–2B
A "funky wine selection" is a feature of both these
Hackney haunts, although only the Paradise Row
venue – set in a hip railway arch, and with "a lovely
outside space" – serves substantial food (it's just
tiny bites in Hackney Road). Chris Leach (formerly
of Kitty Fisher's) took over the stoves in February
2017, and reports (mostly) say the cooking is also
an attraction in itself.

Saigon Saigon W6 £36 2**3**3
313-317 King St 020 8748 6887 8–2B
"Always crowded", long-serving Hammersmith
Vietnamese with atmospheric, if faded, decor
and serving "a huge menu" of flavoursome
dishes – if you're flummoxed by the choice, "just
order appetizers and a bowl of pho". / W6 9NH;
www.saigon-saigon.co.uk; @saigonsaigonuk; 10.30 pm,
Fri & Sun 11 pm.

Sail Loft SE10 £51 2**3**4
11 Victoria Parade 020 8222 9310 1–3C
"Lovely views across the Thames to Canary Wharf"
are the highlight at this Fullers pub in Greenwich.
No surprises on the pub grub, but it's dependably
well-rated. / SE10 9FR; www.sailloftgreenwich.co.uk;
@SailLoftLondon; 11 pm, Sun 10.30 pm.

St John Bread & Wine E1 £62 3**3**2
94-96 Commercial St 020 7251 0848 13–2C
"It looks basic, but that's because every single
dish speaks for itself, or should that be SHOUTS!"
– the accepted view on this engaging, if slightly
"bleak" Spitalfields canteen – "younger sibling
to the Smithfield veteran", whose "lip smacking"
menu of offal-centric British "delights" has long
made it "a real favourite". Several meals this
year however "didn't live up to its reputation",
and ratings have dipped as a result. / E1 6LZ;
www.stjohngroup.uk.com/spitalfields; @StJBW; 10.30
pm, Mon 8 pm.

St Johns N19 £52 3**4**5
91 Junction Rd 020 7272 1587 9–1C
"Unrivalled in this neck of the woods"; this "genuine
gastropub" has a particularly "convivial" atmosphere,
both in the "more formal rear dining room" – a
lovely, striking space built as a ballroom, and serving
"hearty modern British cooking" – and in the bar,
where there are "excellent tapas-style options". /
N19 5QU; www.stjohnstavern.com; @stjohnstavern; 10
pm, Tue-Sat 11 pm, Sun 9 pm; Mon-Thu D only, Fri-Sun
open L & D; No Amex; booking max 12 may apply.

**Saint Luke's Kitchen, Library
WC2** £59 3**3**3
112 Saint Martin's Lane 020 3302 7912 5–4C
Limited reports on this boutique-guesthouse near
the Coliseum, which launched in 2016 (and which

took on new head chef, Daniel Petitta in spring
2017): fans though "love the quality, presentation
and awesome surroundings". / WC2N 4BD;
www.lib-rary.com; @LibraryLondon; midnight; No
trainers; booking essential.

St Moritz W1 £55 3**3**4
161 Wardour St 020 7734 3324 4–1C
A "hilarious evening of kitsch" ("the cow bells are
too tempting not to ring") is guaranteed at this
long-running tribute to all things Swiss, set in a
chalet-style interior in the heart of Soho. "Cheese
fondue is great", although the odd reporter
feels the accompanying dishes are "stuck in the
1970s" (ie, pretty genuine). "It would probably
treble profits in Fulham full of folk just back from
'Verbs', but it's a fun time nonetheless". / W1F 8WJ;
www.stmoritz-restaurant.co.uk; 11.30 pm, Sun 10.30
pm.

**Saiphin's Thai Kitchen
E8** NEW £35
381 Railway Arches, Mentmore Terrace
020 3603 9968 14–1B
Saiphin and Alex Moore are at it again: their Rosa's
Thai Cafe group is now ten-strong, with further
openings expected for 2018; Lao Cafe opened
in December 2016, and they launched this new
proto-chain in London Fields in late spring 2017,
featuring a similar menu to Rosa's. No reports as
yet. / E8 3PH; www.saiphinsthaikitchen.com; 10 pm, Fri
& Sat 10.30 pm.

Sakagura W1 £58 4**4**3
8 Heddon St 020 3405 7230 4–3B
"Excellent, authentic Japanese food with a modern
twist" inspires numerous enthusiastic reports for
this year-old operation (where the sake collection
is a feature) just off Regent Street, from the group
behind Shoryu Ramen and the Japan Centre.
Wagyu beef is made quite a highlight, but equally
there's a dedicated vegetarian menu. / W1B 4BU;
www.sakaguralondon.com; @sakaguraldn; 10.30 pm,
Thu-Sat 11.30 pm, Sun 10 pm.

Sake No Hana SW1 £62 4**3**3
23 St James's St 020 7925 8988 3–4C
Though part of the can't-put-a-step-wrong
Hakkasan Group, this wackily impressive modern
Japanese, in a deeply 1960s St James's building
next to The Economist, has divided opinion in
the past, not helped by the fact that its "closely
packed" interior "can lack ambience when empty".
Still, its "delicate", "melt-in-the-mouth" cuisine
wins over all reporters this year. / SW1A 1HA;
www.sakenohana.com; @sakenohana; 11 pm, Fri & Sat
11.30 pm; closed Sun.

Sakonis HA0 £24 5**2**1
127-129 Ealing Rd 020 8903 9601 1–1A
"You don't go to impress!" when you visit this

grungy veggie canteen in Wembley, but "the food is top notch from the fresh and large-ranging menu" (including some Chinese and Hakka dishes). / HA0 4BP; www.sakonis.co.uk; @sakonis; 9.30 pm; No Amex.

Salaam Namaste WC1 £47 🗓🗓🗓
68 Millman St   020 7405 3697   2–1D
This "good-quality mid-range Indian offering intelligent cooking" is handily central (but "off the beaten track") in Bloomsbury. Reasonable prices too for somewhere so conveniently located. / WC1N 3EF; www.salaam-namaste.co.uk; @SalaamNamasteUK; 11.30 pm, Sun 11 pm.

Sale e Pepe SW1 £67 🗓🗓🗓
9-15 Pavilion Rd   020 7235 0098   6–1D
"Such fun, and unchanged in 30 years" – this "lively" veteran trattoria near Harrods thrives on its "very friendly" service ("we were welcomed like long lost friends on our first visit!"), and it's also "not bad value for money in this busy neighbourhood". Any negatives? – can be "noisy" and "a bit cramped". / SW1X 0HD; www.saleepepe.co.uk.

Salloos SW1 £55 🗓🗓🗓
62-64 Kinnerton St   020 7235 4444   6–1D
"Divine Pakistani food" has maintained the popularity of this dated (and eternally pricey) veteran, hidden in a Belgravia mews venue, for decades. Top Tip – classic lamb chops. / SW1X 8ER; www.salloos.co.uk; 11 pm; closed Sun; May need 5+ to book.

Salon Brixton SW9 £53 🗓🗓🗓
18 Market Row   020 7501 9152   11–2D
Hip-ly located upstairs at Brixton Market (with a new ground floor bar), this crammed-in café wins limited but all-round very upbeat feedback for its seasonal British grub, nowadays primarily veg-focussed, but with meat and fish accompaniments also available. / SW9 8LD; www.salonbrixton.co.uk; @Salon_Brixton; 10 pm.

Le Salon Privé TW1 £52 🗓🗓🗓
43 Crown Rd   020 8892 0602   1–4A
"Perfectly pitched" St Margaret's bistro – "relaxed yet smart, attentive yet discreet, understated yet amicable"; its "classic French cooking" helps make it "delightful for a cosy romantic meal or for a special occasion". / TW1 3EJ; lesalonprive.net; @lesalon_tweet; 10.30 pm.

Salt & Honey W2 £53 🗓🗓🗓
28 Sussex Pl   020 7706 7900   7–1D
This tiny and "inventive" two-year-old near Paddington station does a good job of "spicing up French bistro standards" (it's run by the Kiwi couple behind Fulham's popular Manuka Kitchen). / W2 2TH; www.saltandhoneybistro.com; @SaltHoneyBistro; 10 pm, Sun 9 pm; closed Mon; booking max 8 may apply; set weekday L £31 (FP).

Salt Yard W1 £52 🗓🗓🗓
54 Goodge St   020 7637 0657   2–1B
"Tapas slightly outside the normal offerings (courgette flowers and squid croquettes are especially good)" have made a big name for Simon Mullins's "always packed and squeezed in" Fitzrovia "favourite" (the original member of his group). It's no longer a 'wow' nowadays though, and some fear "the bill's always a bit bigger than expected". / W1T 4NA; www.saltyard.co.uk; @SaltYardGroup; 10.45 pm, Sun 9.45 pm; booking max 8 may apply.

Salut N1 £61 🗓🗓🗓
412 Essex Rd   020 3441 8808   9–3D
"Worth the trip to the fringes of Islington", says (a Hammersmith-based) fan of this quite ambitious yearling, at the wrong end of the Essex Road – "the people couldn't be nicer", it has a "great vibe" and its Nordic-influenced modern cuisine is consistently highly rated. / N1 3PJ; www.salut-london.co.uk; @Salut_London; 11 pm, Sun 10 pm.

Salvation in Noodles £38 🗓🗓🗓
122 Balls Pond Rd, N1   020 7254 4534   14–1A
2 Blackstock Rd, N4   020 7254 4534   9–1D
"Authentic tasting pho" wins limited but positive feedback for these modern Vietnamese noodle cafés, in Dalston and Finsbury Park. / www.salvationinnoodles.co.uk; 10.30 pm; closed Mon-Fri L.

San Carlo Cicchetti £56 🗓🗓🗓
215 Piccadilly, W1   020 7494 9435   4–4C
30 Wellington St, WC2   020 7240 6339   5–3D
"You feel like you're in a smart Venetian brasserie" at these "classy and sassy" – if "hectic and noisy" – Italians (part of a national chain) which successfully create "a brilliant vibe in tourist hellhole locations", particularly the "buzzy, buzzy, buzzy" branch a few feet from Piccadilly Circus. Service is "on the ball" and you get "proper" cooking from "an interesting selection of Italianate tapas-style dishes". / www.sancarlocicchetti.co.uk/; W1 11.30 pm; WC2 midnight; M1 11 pm, Sun 10 pm.

The Sands End SW6 £51 🗓🗓🗓
135 Stephendale Rd   020 7731 7823   11–1B
One of Prince Harry's favourites (and owned by one of his greatest pals) – this "very busy" backstreet gastroboozer attracts the young Fulham set and wins consistently high ratings for its "well-sourced" British scoff. / SW6 2PR; www.thesandsend.co.uk; @thesandsend; 10 pm, Sun 9 pm.

Santa Maria £37 🗓🗓🗓
"The best pizza in London" – "similar to what you'd get in Naples" – ensures these "basic but cool" cafés are "always busy whatever the time of day". The 14-seat Ealing original has just "had a great expansion into the pub next door – now it's easier to get in!" / 10.30 pm; W5 no booking.

Santini SW1 £72 [2][3][3]
29 Ebury St 020 7730 4094 2–4B
*This swanky Belgravia stalwart was a big-hitter
in the 80s, but attracts mixed praise these days.
"Competent Italian food with good professional
service and some style" is the majority view, but even
fans can find it "surprisingly pricey for what it offers"
and to critics "what used to be justified by fine
cooking and a sense of verve, now seem expensive
for something that's slapdash and fraying at the
edges". / SW1W 0NZ; www.santini-restaurant.com;
@santinirest; 10 pm, Sat 11 pm.*

Santo Remedio SE1 [NEW]
152 Tooley St 10–4D
*Husband and wife team, Edson and Natalie
Diaz-Fuentes are back with their trendy Mexican
street-food spot following a successful Kickstarter
campaign. The new Bermondsey location features
a tequila and mezcal bar, a new charcoal grill and
Mexican wines. There will even be reservations!
Santo Remedio's original (queue-tastic)
Shoreditch site closed in August 2016. / SE1 2TU;
www.santoremedio.co.uk; @santoremediouk; 10 pm,
Sat 11 pm.*

Santore EC1 £51 [4][3][3]
59-61 Exmouth Mkt 020 7812 1488 10–1A
*'Traditional wood-fired pizza al metro' (plus
some pasta) is the proposition at this agreeable
Neapolitan – a handy, fairly "cheap 'n' cheerful"
option in trendy Exmouth Market. / EC1R 4QL;
www.santorerestaurant.london; @Santore_london; 11
pm.*

Sapori Sardi SW6 £56 [3][3][3]
786 Fulham Rd 020 7731 0755 11–1B
*Fulham neighbourhood Italian run by a husband-
and-wife team, whose Sardinian cooking is highly
rated by a small but enthusiastic fan club. / SW6
5SL; @saporisardi; 10.30 pm; No Amex.*

Saravanaa Bhavan HA0 £32 [5][2][1]
531-533 High Rd 020 8900 8526 1–1A
*"Top dosas" are a highlight at this "exceptional
cheap 'n' cheerful" veggie, mixing north and south
Indian dishes – one of the better bets in Wembley.
/ HA0 2DJ; www.saravanabhavanuk.com; Mon - Thurs
10.30pm, Fri-Sun 11pm.*

Sardine N1 £57 [3][2][2]
15 Micawber St 020 7490 0144 13–1A
*"A short but interesting menu inspired by the south
of France" realised by Alex Jackson generated
gushing press reviews for the opening of this "slightly
hard-to-find eatery, just off City Road" (part of
Stevie Parle's empire), but while reporters generally
judge it to be "authentic and delicious" they can
also find it "something of a let down after all the
publicity". The naming of the venture is all too apt,
and even fans can find this "small, high-ceilinged
space" to be "too crowded" and "very noisy with all
the hard surfaces". / N1 7TB; www.sardine.london;
@sardinelondon; 10 pm.*

Sardo W1 £58 [3][3][2]
45 Grafton Way 020 7387 2521 2–1B
*"Sardinian regional cooking with an excellent list of
Sardinian wines" have carved a foodie reputation
for this "well established" Fitzrovia venue, and it's
consistently well-rated for its "unfussy, well-cooked
fare". / W1T 5DQ; www.sardo-restaurant.com; 11 pm;
closed Sat L & Sun.*

Sarracino NW6 £45 [4][3][2]
186 Broadhurst Gdns 020 7372 5889 1–1B
*A West Hampstead stalwart, this rustic-style
Neapolitan trattoria (best known for its pizza) has
scored consistently well for its food over a number of
years. There's a sibling, Sole d'Oro, in Palmers Green.
/ NW6 3AY; www.sarracinorestaurant.com; closed
weekday L.*

Sartoria W1 £76 [3][3][3]
20 Savile Row 020 7534 7000 4–3A
*"When you need quiet to have a good business
conversation", this "very comfortable and well-
spaced" Mayfair Italian, with its "very refined
Calabrian cucina", "very smart" decor and
"particularly professional" service is just the ticket.
All this comes at a price naturally, and while the
overall offer escapes any serious criticisms, and
draws a good degree of praise, the overall verdict
value-wise is really quite mixed, especially measured
by Francesco Mazzei's involvement and its much-
publicised revamp two years ago. / W1S 3PR;
www.sartoria-restaurant.co.uk; @SartoriaRest; 10.45
pm; closed Sat L & Sun.*

Satay House W2 £35 [3][3][3]
13 Sale Pl 020 7723 6763 7–1D
*For a dependable meal, not of the cutting edge
variety, fans continue to recommend this Malaysian
stalwart (est 1973), just off Edgware Road. / W2
1PX; www.satay-house.co.uk; 11 pm; booking max 9
may apply.*

**Sauterelle, Royal Exchange
EC3** £62 [3][3][4]
Bank 020 7618 2483 10–2C
*The marvellous backdrop of the Royal Exchange's
internal courtyard sets the tone at this business-
friendly mezzanine, "whose good acoustic
means you don't have to bellow, and whose
well-spaced tables mean you needn't fear
being overheard". A D&D London operation, its
food wins consistently solid ratings. / EC3V 3LR;
www.sauterelle-restaurant.co.uk; 9.30 pm; closed Sat &
Sun; No trainers.*

Savini at Criterion W1 £87 ②②⑤
224 Piccadilly 020 7930 1459 4–4D
Too often branded "a disappointment… and an expensive disappointment at that" – this incredible, gilded neo-Byzantine chamber on Piccadilly Circus has been through a succession of owners, of which this year-old Milanese régime is the latest. By-and-large ignored by Londoners nowadays, such feedback as there is talks of "bland food, poorly presented". / W1J 9HP; www.saviniatcriterion.co.uk; @SaviniMilano; midnight; set weekday L £59 (FP), set pre-theatre £62 (FP).

Savoir Faire WC1 £45 ⑧④⑧
42 New Oxford St 020 7436 0707 5–1C
Long-established Gallic bistro near the British Museum (plastered with posters from West End shows) which "never disappoints". Even those who say the food's "never exciting", see it as "an efficient and good value staple" and more commonly there's praise for its "generous portions and keenly priced wines". / WC1A 1EP; www.savoir.co.uk; 10 pm.

The Savoy Hotel, Savoy Grill WC2 £94 ②⑧⑧
Strand 020 7592 1600 5–3D
"Discretion is assured" in this "smooth" and "comfortable" panelled chamber, whose "well-spaced tables" and "formal" styling have made it a power-dining favourite since time immemorial. Run by Gordon Ramsay for nearly 15 years now, the celeb chef's operation puts in a middling performance: the traditional British fare is arguably "too expensive", and can be "uninspired", but is generally "competently cooked" and of "high quality". / WC2R 0EU; www.gordonramsayrestaurants.com; @savoygrill; 11 pm, Sun 10.30 pm; set weekday L & pre-theatre £56 (FP).

Savoy Thames Foyer WC2 £97 ②③④
The Savoy, The Strand 020 7420 2111 5–3D
The "sensational" setting beneath a glass dome, with a pianist tickling the ivories while you eat, complements the "exquisitely prepared and presented" afternoon tea at this grand London landmark. The staff are "very welcoming", and make "extra effort to accommodate dietary requests". / WC2R; www.fairmont.com/savoy-london; @fairmonthotels; 11 pm.

Scalini SW3 £76 ⑧⑧⑧
1-3 Walton St 020 7225 2301 6–2C
"I love Scalini's!" – this "buzzy" (perennially "noisy") stalwart on the fringes of Knightsbridge is "a great, traditional Italian": "it's not the best food in the world" ("respectable but at stratospheric prices") "but the staff are super, the atmosphere is fun, and it's not pretentious or showy". / SW3 2JD; www.scalinilondon.co.uk; 11 pm; No shorts.

Scandinavian Kitchen W1 £17 ⑧④②
61 Great Titchfield St 020 7580 7161 2–1B
"As a Dane, I go when I'm homesick for my local food". This "charming" Nordic café/grocer is a handy destination in Fitzrovia, serving "attractive open sandwiches" and other smorgasbord offerings. "With 'Abba Nice Day' on the T-shirts it's strong on Scandi-Blanc humour too." / W1W 7PP; www.scandikitchen.co.uk; @scanditwitchen; 7 pm, Sat 6 pm, Sun 3 pm; L only; no booking.

SCOTT'S W1 £85 ④④⑤
20 Mount St 020 7495 7309 3–3A
"Possibly the best all-round dining experience in London" – James Bond's favourite lunch-spot remains, under Richard Caring's ownership, a "sophisticated" Mayfair institution that's "worth it if you can afford it" thanks to its "classic" seafood (it's "a paradise for fish lovers"), "exemplary" service and "perfect atmosphere". Its "effortless" style suits all occasions, but in particular it's a "power-brokers' favourite". / W1K 2HE; www.scotts-restaurant.com; 10.30 pm, Sun 10 pm; booking max 6 may apply.

Sea Containers, Mondrian London SE1 £68 ②②②
20 Upper Ground 020 3747 1063 10–3A
"Top-floor prices with a ground-floor view" makes for an often unhappy combination in the "trying-to-be-über-cool" dining room of this Thames-side, US-owned hotel, near Blackfriars Bridge. The odd fan does applaud its "fabulous Eurofusion fare", but the whole "bizarre sharing concept" seems like "too much style-over-substance" and "hugely overpriced: even with someone else paying it seemed like a rip off". / SE1 9PD; www.seacontainersrestaurant.com; @MondrianLDN; 11 pm.

Seafresh SW1 £45 ⑧⑧②
80-81 Wilton Rd 020 7828 0747 2–4B
"Not to be compared with Sheekey or Scott's, but the fish 'n' chips are better!". This age-old Pimlico veteran has "become quite upmarket" nowadays, "serving lobster, oysters, and very fresh plaice alongside its excellent fish 'n' chips". The interior though remains fairly "basic". / SW1V 1DL; www.seafresh-dining.com; @SeafreshLondon; 10.30 pm; closed Sun.

The Sea Shell NW1 £49 ⑧②②
49 Lisson Grove 020 7224 9000 9–4A
"If you just want good old fashioned fish 'n' chips", what is probably London's most famous chippie (certainly one of its oldest) "is the place to come to introduce the national dish to your foreign guest". Top Tip – "it's best for take-away – the restaurant area is good, but somehow the food's not quite the same". / NW1 6UH; www.seashellrestaurant.co.uk; @SeashellRestaur; 10.30 pm; closed Sun.

Season Kitchen N4 £49 🔢🔢🔢
53 Stroud Green Rd 020 7263 5500 9–1D
A "neighbourhood gem" in Finsbury Park, where
"food is cooked with expertise and love" and
served "with charm" from a small menu. A flat
cash mark-up is charged on wine instead of the
traditional percentage (it's not every restaurant
where you can enjoy Saint-Emilion Grand Cru at
£36) – "excellent, should be the norm!" / N4 3EF;
www.seasonkitchen.co.uk; @seasonkitchen; 10.30 pm,
Sun 8 pm; D only.

Señor Ceviche W1 £48 🔢🔢🔢
Kingly Ct 020 7842 8540 4–2B
A "fun" Peruvian street-food hang-out in Soho's
Kingly Court gastro hub that's generally well-
rated. As well as the eponymous raw fish, it
serves Peruvian-Japanese BBQ dishes and pisco
cocktails. / W1B 5PW; www.senor-ceviche.com;
@SenorCevicheLDN; 11.30 pm, Sat midnight, Sun
10.30 pm; booking max 6 may apply.

Seven Park Place SW1 £103 🔢🔢🔢
7-8 Park Pl 020 7316 1615 3–4C
"The food actually reduced my husband to tears
(in a good way!)…" The "quirky but cosy" dining
room of this luxurious St James's hotel deserves
a much higher profile – "staff take real pride in
their work and take such good care of you", and
William Drabble's "consistently reliable and refined"
cooking is "too delicious for words". / SW1A 1LS;
www.stjameshotelandclub.com; @SevenParkPlace; 10
pm; closed Mon & Sun; set weekday L £59 (FP).

Sexy Fish W1 £91 🔢🔢🔢
1-4 Berkeley Sq 020 3764 2000 3–3B
"It's certainly an experience", and no-one disputes
that Richard Caring's "flashy and brassy" Mayfair
venture is "good for people-watching". But while
for fans the "amazing" interior and "sublime and
sexy" sushi, robata and Asian seafood, all justify the
monumental expense, there are too many critics
for whom it's "the most overpriced, over-rated
restaurant in London" – "a trashy, vulgar hellhole
filled to the brim with people dressed for cameos
in a cheap US cable-TV soap opera, and not for
anyone with the slightest disinclination for being
fleeced rotten!" Maybe the best advice is "go
once, get it out of your system, then leave it to
those where money isn't an issue..." / W1J 6BR;
www.sexyfish.com; @sexyfishlondon; 11 pm, Sun 10.30
pm; booking max 6 may apply.

Shackfuyu W1 £48 🔢🔢🔢
14a, Old Compton St 020 7734 7492 5–2A
"Genuinely fantastic", westernised-Japanese joint
in Soho – "a busy, bright, well-staffed sister to the
wonderful Bone Daddies", offering "a great all-round
experience". Top Menu Tip – "that dessert! Kinako
French Toast with the Matcha soft serve! Got me
into green tea!" / W1D 4TH;

www.bonedaddies.com; @shackfuyu; 11 pm, Mon & Tue
10 pm, Sun 9 pm; no booking.

Shake Shack £29 🔢🔢🔢
Nova, Nova, Victoria St, SW1 awaiting tel 2–4B
80 New Oxford St, WC1 01925 555171 5–1B
24 The Market, WC2 020 3598 1360 5–3D
The Street, Westfield Stratford, E20 01923
555167 14–1D
"Top burgers for texture and taste" ("with potato
rolls flown specially in from the US!") win numerous
fans for Danny Meyer's "no fuss no fancy" burger
operations. Even supporters can find them "bloody
pricey" however, and critics gripe about "anaemic"
portions, and "long waits". / WC2 & E14 11 pm, Sun
9 pm-10.30 pm; E20 9.30 pm, Fri & Sat 11 pm.

Shampers W1 £47 🔢🔢🔢
4 Kingly St 020 7437 1692 4–2B
A perfectly preserved, "proper" 1970s wine bar in
Soho, where the atmosphere always fizzes "with
a good buzz of conversation" and you'll always
find a "warm welcome". Great for "not-too-serious
business", it has a "sensibly priced wine list
that's a pleasure to work your way through" and
"classic, albeit old-school food" that's "pretty good".
"Been coming here for well nigh 30 years, and
it's home from home: Simon and his team always
deliver. Bravo!" / W1B 5PE; www.shampers.net;
@shampers_soho; 11 pm; closed Sun.

The Shed W8 £55 🔢🔢🔢
122 Palace Gardens Ter 020 7229 4024 7–2B
"Bonkers, quirky but delicious" – the Gladwin
family's "oddball" farm-to-table venture in Notting
Hill has won many converts to its seasonal British
small plates, aided by its "charming" staff and
"attractive" (if "slightly uncomfortable") rustic-style
interior. / W8 4RT; www.theshed-restaurant.com;
@theshed_resto; 11 pm; closed Mon L & Sun; SRA-
Food Made Good – 3 stars.

J SHEEKEY WC2 £81 🔢🔢🔢
28-34 St Martin's Ct 020 7240 2565 5–3B
"Well deserving its status as a West End Institution",
Richard Caring's "very classy" Theatreland Icon
(est 1896) offers "plenty of star gazing after the
theatre", and remains both the survey's most
talked-about destination, and its No. 1 tip for fish
(eclipsing its stablemate Scott's for nominations
as London's best). Sitting in a narrow, Dickensian
alleyway off St Martin's Lane, you pass its doorman
and etched-glass façade to enter a series of snug
("poky") panelled chambers, where "white-aproned
waiters deliver whip-sharp service and a menu that
sings of the sea: from shellfish platters and superior
classics (eg lobster thermidor) to creamy, comforting
fish pie". "Nothing is experimental or over fussy":
"it's without fripperies, foams and smears – just
perfectly sourced and cooked seafood". The ongoing
drive to expand the business (including here the

September 2016 rebranding of the bar into the 'Atlantic Bar') seemed to put some pressure on ratings this year however, with a tiny but tangible proportion of reports saying "expansion has hit standards a bit" (hence a slight dip in grades). The general verdict however? "Always magical!" / WC2N 4AL; www.j-sheekey.co.uk; @JSheekeyRest; 11.30 pm, Sun 10 pm; booking max 6 may apply; set weekday L £53 (FP).

Shepherd's SW1 £56 **3** **4** **4**
Marsham Ct, Marsham St
020 7834 9552 2–4C
This traditional British stalwart – resurrected a couple of years ago after a period of closure – is something of a "Westminster favourite", on account of its "well spaced tables, calm atmosphere and good comfort food", all of which make it "ideal for a business lunch" (particularly of a politico nature). / SW1P 4LA; www.shepherdsrestaurant.co.uk; @shepherdsLondon; 10.30 pm; closed Sat & Sun.

Shikumen, Dorsett Hotel
W12 £56 **4** **3** **2**
58 Shepherd's Bush Grn 020 8749 9978 8–1C
In the unusual setting of an upmarket new hotel by grungy Shepherd's Bush Green, this contemporary dining room has won something of a name as "one of London's better Chinese restaurants". More downbeat reports say it's "vibeless, not bad but not that good, and not cheap", but more commonly it's praised for "unexpectedly authentic cooking" – in particular "dim sum that comprehensively beats much more expensive places". / W12 5AA; www.shikumen.co.uk; @ShikumenUK; 10.30 pm, Sun 10 pm.

Shilpa W6 £31 **5** **2** **1**
206 King St 020 8741 3127 8–2B
"Lip-smackingly delicious Keralan food" at "unbelievably low prices" ("incredible for food of this quality") is the surprise find at this "very basic" South Indian, easily missed in an anonymous row of shops in Hammersmith. "Staff mean well, but don't expect too much in the way of service." / W6 0RA; www.shilparestaurant.co.uk; 11 pm, Thu-Sat midnight.

Shoryu Ramen £48 **3** **2** **2**
9 Regent St, SW1 no tel 4–4D
3 Denman St, W1 no tel 4–3C
5 Kingly Ct, W1 no tel 4–2B
Broadgate Circle, EC2 no tel 13–2B
"Super-tasty ramen soups and moreish meat-filled buns" still win praise for these "very cramped" Japanese pit stops. Fans say "they put pretenders like Wagamama to shame", but overall ratings here are not as stratospheric as once they were. / 11 pm-midnight, Sun 9.30 pm-10 pm; E14 9 pm, Sun 6 pm; no booking (except Kingly Ct).

Sibarita WC2 NEW £45
7 Maiden Lane 020 7497 0999 5–3D
Even with Rambla (opening later this year) still in the pipeline, Encant's Victor Garvey found time to open this cosy, closely packed, small (26 seats) wine, cheese, and tapas bar almost next door (with his dad!) in July 2017; early press reviews are very upbeat. / WC2E 7NA; www.sibaritalondon.com; @sibaritalondon; Jacket required.

The Sichuan EC1 £57 **4** **3** **3**
14 City Rd 020 7588 5489 13–2A
"A real find", near the Honourable Artillery Company, this "cracking" yearling serves "palate-blasting" Sichuan dishes from chef Zhang Xiao Zhong that "really hit the spot", and prices are "great" for food of this quality. / EC1Y 2AA; www.thesichuan.co.uk; 11 pm.

Sichuan Folk E1 £45 **3** **3** **2**
32 Hanbury St 020 7247 4735 13–2C
"The very good traditional Sichuan food" at this Brick Lane canteen makes a trip "way better than a visit to Chinatown". Conditions are "pretty basic", but staff are "very helpful to newcomers to the cuisine". / E1 6QR; www.sichuan-folk.co.uk; 10.30 pm; No Amex.

Signor Sassi SW1 £76 **3** **3** **3**
14 Knightsbridge Green 020 7584 2277 6–1D
That it "can be noisy" is all part of the charm of this classic trattoria near Harrods, which continues to do what it does with a fair amount of pizzazz. / SW1X 7QL; www.signorsassi.co.uk; @SignorSassi; 11.30 pm.

Silk Road SE5 £23 **5** **2** **2**
49 Camberwell Church St
020 7703 4832 1–3C
"Awesome food from the northwest frontier province of Xinjiang" at this "noisy and ridiculously good-value" canteen in Camberwell presents a "whole new take on Chinese cuisine". It's "spicy and fiery", "closer to the sub-continent than typical Chinese", and "the homemade noodles are silky and chewy and incredible". Top Tips: "amazing offal", "melt-in-the-mouth lamb", and "the chicken plate is one of the best dishes in London!". / SE5 8TR; 10.30 pm; closed Sat L & Sun L; Cash only.

Simpson's in the Strand WC2 £76
100 Strand 020 7420 2111 5–3D
After too many years in the wilderness, this "tired war horse of British cuisine" underwent a 10-week revamp in summer 2017 in a bid to restore its "faded elegance". Having been consigned in recent decades to tourists and breakfasting businessmen, it remains to be seen whether its legendary trolley-service of roasts will cease to "trade on its historic reputation". / WC2R 0EW; www.simpsonsinthestrand.co.uk; @simpsons1828; No trainers.

Simpson's Tavern EC3   £35   2|3|4

38 1/2 Ball Ct, Cornhill   020 7626 9985   10–2C
"I imagine Billy Bunter would have enjoyed
Simpson's!". This "City institution" dating back to
1757 is tucked down a Dickensian alleyway and
has "barely changed for a century", making it well
worth a visit, even if the food – "simple British
stodge" – "is not really the point". / EC3V 9DR;
www.simpsonstavern.co.uk; @SimpsonsTavern; 3.30 pm;
L only, closed Sat & Sun.

Sinabro SW11   £59   3|4|3

28 Battersea Rise   020 3302 3120   11–2C
"Cosy" (under 30 seats), husband-and-wife team,
Battersea bistro, whose local fan club applauds
"delicious Asian-French fusion fare executed with
great care", plus "attentive service and a pleasing
ambience". On Friday and Saturday evenings, only
the most ambitious tasting menu is available. /
SW11 1EE; www.sinabro.co.uk; @SinabroLondon; 10
pm, Fri & Sat 10.30 pm.

Singapore Garden NW6   £48   3|3|2

83a Fairfax Rd   020 7624 8233   9–2A
The very definition of "a solid performer" – this
"reliable" and "reasonably priced" Asian in a tucked-
away Swiss Cottage parade of shops has long
been a big north London favourite (including with
Giles Coren). It offers a mix of Chinese, Malaysian
and Singaporean dishes – "be adventurous in
ordering to get the most benefit". / NW6 4DY;
www.singaporegarden.co.uk; @SingaporeGarden.

Six Portland Road W11   £57   4|4|3

6 Portland Rd   020 7229 3130   7–2A
"Clever without being pretentious" (with
"something always tempting on the specials
board") characterises the somewhat "unusual"
Gallic-influenced modern cuisine at this "classy"
(if "cramped and noisy") neighbourhood spot in
Holland Park, where supporting attractions include
"well-chosen wine and a warm welcome". / W11
4LA; www.sixportlandroad.com; @SixPortlandRoad; 10
pm; closed Mon & Sun D; set weekday L £35 (FP).

Sketch, Lecture Room W1   £147   4|4|5

9 Conduit St   020 7659 4500   4–2A
"Take your sense of humour and embrace the
place", say fans of this "crazy, wonderful" chamber
– "a stunning" space on the first floor of a huge
Mayfair palazzo. That it's "shockingly expensive"
occasions less outrage nowadays, and when it comes
to the tasting menus (overseen by Pierre Gagnaire),
while "there may be a few more components in
each dish too many" there are "some nice marriages
of flavours" and results can be "remarkable".
"It's not everyone's cup of tea, but the trick is to
admire the quality and meticulousness, while not
taking the ponciness too seriously." / W1S 2XG;
www.sketch.uk.com; @sketchlondon; 10.30 pm; closed

Mon, Sat L & Sun; No trainers; booking max 6 may
apply; set weekday L £65 (FP).

Sketch, Gallery W1   £85   1|2|3

9 Conduit St   020 7659 4500   4–2A
"Everything from the David Shrigley sketches
covering the candy-pink walls to the teacups are
witty and whimsical" at this Mayfair fashionista
favourite – and the famous egg-shaped pods in
the "space-age loos" are "worth the queue" too.
Was there something else? Ah yes, the food…
"also completely OTT, and not in a good way, and
eye-wateringly expensive with no reason to be". Top
Tip – the "fun-filled" afternoon tea. / W1S 2XG;
www.sketch.uk.com; @sketchlondon; booking max 6
may apply.

Skewd Kitchen EN4 NEW   £47   3|3|3

12 Cockfosters Parade   020 8449 7771   1–1C
"Fantastic kebabs" win praise for this attempt
to modernise the Turkish grill experience in
Cockfosters. / EN4 0BX; www.skewdkitchen.com;
@SkewdKitchen; 11 pm.

Skylon, South Bank Centre SE1   £75   2|2|2

Belvedere Rd   020 7654 7800   2–3D
"Terrific views of the Thames", particularly from the
window tables, are the star feature of this striking
and "spacious" chamber within the Southbank
Centre, earning it nominations for both business
and romance. "You shouldn't just have to pay for
the vista" though, so it's a shame about the "boring
food, mediocre service and sky high prices". See also
Skylon Grill. / SE1 8XX; www.skylon-restaurant.co.uk;
@skylonsouthbank; closed Sun D; No trainers; set Sun
L £49 (FP).

Skylon Grill SE1   £69   2|2|3

Belvedere Rd   020 7654 7800   2–3D
Like its more expensive adjacent sibling, this D&D
London venue should be "the perfect venue to take
visitors to London", given its amazing views. But
even more enthusiastic reports concede that "it
doesn't justify the price tag" however, and too often
it serves food that's "very poor for the price". / SE1
8XX; www.skylon-restaurant.co.uk; @skylonsouthbank;
11 pm; closed Sun D.

Smith & Wollensky WC2   £102   2|1|2

The Adelphi Building, 1-11 John Adam St
020 7321 6007   5–4D
"A little bit of NYC in London… but at what a
frightening price". This "huge", two-year-old outpost
of the famous US brand in the ground floor of the
Adelphi has a slight feel of the "white elephant" to
it, and to a surprising extent has wholly failed to
gain traction as a business-dining mecca. Yes, the
meat is top quality and there's "an amazing US
wine list", but the menu can seem "predictable",
service is "very poor quality" for this level, and

"there are better places in town to go to for a good steak". / WC2N 6HT; www.smithandwollensky.co.uk; @sandwollenskyuk; 10.30 pm, Fri & Sat 11 pm; booking max 12 may apply; set weekday L & pre-theatre £50 (FP).

Smith's Wapping E1 £71 4️⃣4️⃣4️⃣
22 Wapping High St   020 7488 3456   12–1A
"The view of Tower Bridge and The Shard is stunning" from this Wapping brasserie (offshoot from the long-established Ongar original), which has a "wonderful location by the Thames". "They do serve meat, but the fish or seafood is the way to go" – "it's exceptional, very fresh and well-presented". / E1W 1NJ; www.smithsrestaurants.com; @smithswapping; 10 pm; closed Sun D; No trainers; set weekday L £44 (FP), set dinner £48 (FP).

Smiths of Smithfield, Top Floor
EC1 £77 3️⃣3️⃣4️⃣
67-77 Charterhouse St   020 7251 7950   10–1A
The "wonderful rooftop location", with "old London lit up all around and visible from all parts of the restaurant", makes this an "excellent night-time venue". "The food is first-class", too, with a focus on rare-breed British beef, appropriate for the meat-market setting, while service is "attentive without being overbearing". "With a little more care this has the potential to be really outstanding! / EC1M 6HJ; www.smithsofsmithfield.co.uk; @thisissmiths; 10.45 pm; closed Sat L & Sun; booking max 10 may apply; set weekday L & pre-theatre £45 (FP).

Smiths of Smithfield, Dining Room
EC1 £69 2️⃣2️⃣2️⃣
67-77 Charterhouse St   020 7251 7950   10–1A
"The steaks are OK (if nothing to write home about)" at this first-floor dining room by Smithfield meat market. It's "quite pricey for what's on offer" though, not helped by the challenging acoustics of the space which can make it very noisy. / EC1M 6HJ; www.smithsofsmithfield.co.uk; @thisissmiths; 10.45 pm; closed Sat L & Sun; booking max 12 may apply; set weekday L & pre-theatre £39 (FP).

Smiths of Smithfield, Ground Floor
EC1 £32 2️⃣2️⃣3️⃣
67-77 Charterhouse St   020 7251 7950   10–1A
This big and once-famous brunch destination across the road from Smithfield Market is still a "favourite breakfast spot" for some, thanks to its all-day breakfasts and 'bottomless' brunch. / EC1M 6HJ; www.smithsofsmithfield.co.uk; @thisissmiths; 5 pm; L only; no booking.

Smokehouse Chiswick
W4 £51 3️⃣2️⃣3️⃣
12 Sutton Lane North   020 3819 6066   8–2A
"The meat is right on the money" – "beautifully cooked" – at this "relaxed" two-year-old Chiswick outpost of Islington's Smokehouse, in a

converted pub with very cute garden. It's "dog-friendly", too, although your poor canine may drool with envy in this environment! / W4 4LD; www.smokehousechiswick.co.uk; @smokehouseN1; 10 pm, Sun 9 pm; Mon-Thu D only, Fri-Sun open L & D.

Smokehouse Islington
N1 £55 3️⃣3️⃣2️⃣
63-69 Canonbury Rd   020 7354 1144   9–2D
"A carnivore's heaven"; this Canonbury gastro-boozer serves "brilliant meat", smoked or roasted, backed up by a "great wine list". There is a sister branch in Chiswick. / N1 2RG; www.smokehouseislington.co.uk; @smokehouseN1; 10 pm, Sun 9 pm; closed weekday L.

Smokestak E1 £48 5️⃣3️⃣3️⃣
35 Sclater St   020 3873 1733   13–1C
David Carter's "super-on-trend" yearling has left its street food origins behind, "taking smoked meats to a more civilised level" at the 2m wide charcoal grill of this "well-designed and stripped-back" site, just off Brick Lane. "The smokey room adds to the atmosphere" and although "it's so much more expensive now that it's gone permanent" the "very imaginative BBQ" served tapas-style makes it "arguably the best smokehouse in London" right now. Just one thing: "the interior's extremely dark (your camera phone lights may be needed to read the menu!)". Top Menu Tips – the brisket ("like butter"), and the crispy pig tail ("taking pork scratchings to supreme heights!"). / E1 6LB; www.smokestak.co.uk.

Smoking Goat £47 4️⃣3️⃣2️⃣
7 Denmark St, WC2   no tel   5–1B
64 Shoreditch High St, E1   no tel   13–1B 🆕
"Small plates maybe, but with big, big flavours": Ben Chapman's "zingy" Thai-inspired BBQ delivers "some real standout dishes" in a "dark and atmospheric" – if "hipster-infested" – Soho setting, where "they also serve decent beers on tap". "Now and again they miss, but when they get it right they really nail it". 'Smoking Goat 2.0' opens in its spiritual home of Shoreditch in October 2017; the new place will be bigger, and the menu will focus on serving just a couple of signature Thai dishes each day. Top Menu Tip – "fiery chicken wings and scallop with chilli". / www.smokinggoatsoho.com.

Snaps & Rye W10 £59 3️⃣4️⃣3️⃣
93 Golborne Rd   020 8964 3004   7–1A
"Unique, fresh combos of Scandi flavours, particularly fish" score well at this "highly commendable" Danish diner in North Kensington; also "great for breakfast or brunch" ("really good coffee"), "informal lunch", and the "weekly set four-course dinner", with "an extensive selection of akvavit". / W10 5NL; www.snapsandrye.com; @snapsandrye; 10 pm; L only, Fri open L & D, closed Mon.

Social Eating House W1 **£72** **5 5 4**
58-59 Poland St   020 7993 3251   4–1C
*"Living up to its name" – Jason Atherton's Soho
'Social' provides "one of the most enjoyable dining
experiences" in town, with its "rare combination"
of "exceptional value" dishes ("such modern,
interesting yet 'familiar' food, focussed on flavour and
pure pleasure") delivered by "really attentive yet un-
pushy staff" in "a casual and buzzy setting". / W1F
7NR; www.socialeatinghouse.com; @socialeathouse; 10
pm; closed Sun; set weekday L £46 (FP).*

Social Wine & Tapas W1 **£53** **3 4 4**
39 James St   020 7993 3257   3–1A
*An "extensive and great value wine list" presided
over by a "fantastic sommelier" is perhaps the
biggest attraction at Jason Atherton's Marylebone
two-year-old – "buzzy upstairs, cosier downstairs" –
but it scored extremely strongly all-round this year,
including for its "really top small plates". / W1U
1EB; www.socialwineandtapas.com; @socialwinetapas;
10.30 pm; closed Sun; credit card required to book; set
weekday L £32 (FP).*

Soif SW11 **£59** **3 4 3**
27 Battersea Rise   020 7223 1112   11–2C
*A sibling of the better-known Terroirs, this
"enterprising", "noisy and buzzy" Battersea bistro
offers the same "amazing organic wine list" ("tread
carefully"), "plus a mix of small tasting plates". It's
"not the place to go if you are dieting – the food is
extremely rich... but just so good!" / SW11 1HG;
www.soif.co; @Soif_SW11; 10 pm, Sun 4 pm; closed
Mon L & Sun D.*

Som Saa E1 **£51** **5 4 4**
43a Commercial St   020 7324 7790   13–2C
*"Your eyes water and it feels like steam is fizzing
out of your ears, but with tons of amazing, aromatic
flavours that make your taste buds literally zing" at
this "terrific" Thai yearling in Spitalfields – "possibly
London's best, with many dishes not often seen
outside Thailand". "Friendly service too" in "a hip
East End space" with "a great vibrant buzz". / E1
6BD; www.somsaa.com; @somsaa_london; 11.30 pm,
Sat midnight, Sun 10.30 pm; May need 4+ to book.*

Sông Quê E2 **£32** **3 3 2**
134 Kingsland Rd   020 7613 3222   14–2A
*"Very keen pricing" ensures that this "long-
standing Vietnamese" canteen on a busy stretch
of Shoreditch's Kingsland Road is always hopping,
its sharing tables crammed with customers
wolfing down pho and other Viet dishes. / E2 8DY;
www.songque.co.uk; 11 pm, Sun 10.30 pm; No Amex.*

Sonny's Kitchen SW13 **£56** **2 2 2**
94 Church Rd   020 8748 0393   11–1A
*Rebecca Mascarenhas's long-serving Barnes local
retains a devoted following for whom it has always
been "a great neighbourhood restaurant". It's not*

the stand-out it once was however, and views differ
on whether partnership with Phil Howard (who lives
nearby and is now a part-owner) has put it back
on track: cynics still "prefer the Olympic across the
way" but optimists feel that "after some years in
the wilderness, it's much improved". / SW13 0DQ;
www.sonnyskitchen.co.uk; @sonnyskitchen; 10 pm, Fri
& Sat 10.30 pm, Sun 9 pm; booking max 5 may apply.*

Sophie's Steakhouse **£65** **2 3 3**
42-44 Great Windmill St, W1 awaiting tel
4–3D **NEW**
311-313 Fulham Rd, SW10
020 7352 0088   6–3B
*A new 120-cover Soho opening – in the renovated
Moulin Theatre – looks set to raise the profile of
this long-running steakhouse brand (which closed
its Covent Garden branch this year). Founded in
Fulham over 10 years ago, it serves decent steaks,
but wins higher ratings for its "enthusiastic" service.
/ www.sophiessteakhouse.com; SW10 11.45 pm, Sun
10.45 pm; WC2 12.45 am, Sun 10.45 pm; no booking.*

**Sosharu, Turnmill Building
EC1** **£79** **3 3 3**
63 Clerkenwell Rd   020 3805 2304   10–1A
*"One of the best places in London to sit at the
counter and watch the chefs at work" is how fans
see Jason Atherton's izakaya-themed Japanese
in Clerkenwell, whose formerly lacklustre ratings
improved this year. It's still an "almost, but not
quite" for some reporters however, and in August
2017, Atherton announced he is looking to shift the
concept to a new location (like Mayfair or Soho)
in the coming months, acknowledging that it is not
really working out in its original form. / EC1M 5NP;
www.sosharulondon.com; @SocialCompany; 10 pm, Fri
& Sat 10.30 pm; set weekday L £52 (FP).*

Southam Street W10 **NEW**
36 Golborne Rd awaiting tel 7–1A
*The co-founders of Notting-Hill's awesome 108
Garage are to launch a second venture nearby, on
the former site of Victorian boozer West Thirty Six
(RIP) in late 2017; the new place will cover three
storeys and include a Japanese robata grill, a private
BBQ area, a raw bar serving Nikkei (Peruvian-
Japanese fusion) cuisine and a private member's
champagne bar. / W10 5PR.*

Sparrow SE13 **NEW** **£54**
Rennell St   020 8318 6941   1–4D
*Is this Lewisham's first proper neighbourhood spot?
Close to the station, it opened in late spring 2017,
too late to garner survey feedback, but early media
reviews of its seasonal small plates with Sri Lankan
influences are upbeat. / SE13 7HD; sparrowlondon.
co.uk; @sparrowlondon.*

The Spencer SW15 £51 3 4 3
237 Lower Richmond Rd
020 8788 0640   11–1A
A huge outside area across the road, with picnic tables on Putney Common (where you can order food), is a hard-to-beat summer feature of this "great South London gastropub", which serves very dependable scoff to all-and-sundry (including dog-lovers). / SW15 1HJ; www.thespencerpub.co.uk; 10 pm, Sun 9 pm.

Spinach SE22 NEW £53 3 3 3
161 Lordship Lane   020 8299 3344   1–4D
"A lively and ambitious spot that outshines many of its more established local rivals" – this "pleasant", bright, white-walled Dulwich café offers enjoyable cooking of the "I could cook this at home but I'll eat out tonight" variety, with an emphasis on veg. / SE22 8HD; spinach.london; 11 pm; closed Mon D & Sun D; set weekday L £32 (FP).

Spring Restaurant WC2 £85 3 3 4
New Wing, Lancaster Pl   020 3011 0115   2–2D
"The most beautiful interior (is it the prettiest in London?)", sets up a "very elegant and refined" atmosphere – ideal for romance or business entertaining – at this "bright" and serene chamber in Somerset House, and most feedback applauds Skye Gyngell's "light and delicate" cuisine too. "You do pay for it though", and some reporters diagnose "style over substance", or find the cooking a tad "poncy" or "pedestrian". / WC2R 1LA; www.springrestaurant.co.uk; @Spring_Rest; 10.30 pm; closed Sun D; credit card required to book; set pre-theatre £41 (FP), set weekday L £54 (FP).

Spuntino W1 £45 3 3 3
61 Rupert St   020 7734 4479   4–2D
Grab a stool at Russell Norman's industrial chic bar in Soho, which makes a "very welcoming spot for a solo luncher" (there are only about 30 seats), and serves Italian-American bites. / W1D 7PW; www.spuntino.co.uk; @Spuntino; 11.30 pm, Sun 10.30 pm; no booking.

The Square W1 £140 3 3 1
6-10 Bruton St   020 7495 7100   3–2C
"New owners and chef have a lot to do to reclaim the plaudits of old!" at this "grown up" foodie temple in Mayfair, where owner Marlon Abela took over a year ago from Phil Howard and Nigel Platts Martin: post-sale sceptics felt you "paid two star prices for nothing food that wasn't star quality", and felt the switch had done nothing for the "sterile" ambience (never exactly a riot here). It seems that Abela has 'smelt the coffee' because replacement chef Yu Sigimoto left in August 2017 as the restaurant closed for a total revamp to re-open in October 2017 with 'a new concept [that] will reflect an energetic, urban and contemporary attitude underpinned by elegant and luxurious style'. [Did he really write that? Ed] / W1J 6PU; www.squarerestaurant.com; @square_rest; 9.45 pm, Sat 10.15 pm, Sun 9.30 pm; closed Sun L; booking max 8 may apply; set weekday L £66 (FP).

Sree Krishna SW17 £32 4 3 2
192-194 Tooting High St
020 8672 4250   11–2C
The "best dosas in London" are menu highlights at this "consistently good, long-established Keralan on Tooting's main drag of curry houses" which offers "extremely good South Indian classics for the prices". "Unlike many of its competitors, it is spacious and comfortable enough for an evening out as opposed to a quick bite". / SW17 0SF; www.sreekrishna.co.uk; @SreeKrishnaUk; 10.45 pm, Thu 12.45 am, Fri & Sat 11.30 pm.

St John Smithfield EC1 £64 5 4 3
26 St John St   020 7251 0848   10–1B
"You either love or hate the austerity of the dining room, and the uncompromising nature of the 'nose to tail' offal-heavy approach" that's made this "stark", white-walled ex-smokehouse in Smithfield "the high altar" of challenging British cuisine. "The extraordinary longevity of the place suggests that most people do get it" and "Fergus Henderson and his team continue to turn the humdrum off-cuts into something magical" – "it's hard to better such straightforward heavenly food" – with "something that's always new or different to tempt regulars back and to intrigue the uninitiated." Top Menu Tips – game in season, "brilliant suckling pig", bone marrow salad ("dem bones, dem bones…"), and the Eccles cakes. / EC1M 4AY; www.stjohngroup.uk.com; @SJRestaurant; 11 pm, Sun 4 pm; closed Sat L & Sun D.

The Stable £37 2 2 3
Unit 12, 8 Kew Bridge Rd, TW8
020 8568 8667   1–3A
16-18 Whitechapel Rd, E1
020 7377 1133   13–2D
Expanding, 17-strong national chain, with recent openings in Whitechapel and in the new riverside development right by Kew Bridge. Fans like the "beautifully crafted thin bases and wide variety of craft ciders and beers", but there's some concern "quality is dropping now the roll-out to the capital has begun".

Stagolee's SW6 NEW £34
453 North End Rd   020 3092 1766   6–4A
A new southern-US style 'hot chicken and liquor joint', near Fulham Broadway – a stripped-back café also serving cornmeal-battered fried fish alongside various finger-lickin' sides. / SW6 1NZ; stagolees. co.uk; @stagoleesldn.

Star of India SW5 £55 **4** **3** **3**
154 Old Brompton Rd   020 7373 2901   6–2B
This "old favourite" – one of London's first curry houses – on the Earl's Court-Kensington border, is an unflagging provider of "good value, great quality and interesting flavours", serving "modern, evolved Indian food including game". "Service has improved, but some of the decor is looking tired." / SW5 0BE; www.starofindia.eu; 11.45 pm, Sun 11.15 pm.

Stecca SW10 **NEW**
14 Hollywood Rd   020 7460 2322   6–3B
A new Chelsea Italian from Stefano Stecca (Toto's, Baglioni, Zafferano) on cute Hollywood Road, near the Chelsea & Westminster Hospital; a small rear garden adds charm. / SW10 9HY; www.stecca.co.uk; 10 pm.

Stick & Bowl W8 £24 **5** **3** **1**
31 Kensington High St   020 7937 2778   6–1A
This "unreconstructed noodle bar" – whose "pretty tatty" looks are in sharp contrast to ever-more chichi High Street Ken – is "the real thing, for when you're tired of Wagamama" (which it predates by decades). "Service is fast", providing "a large choice of delicious Chinese chow to take away or eat in, at bargain prices". / W8 5NP; 10.45 pm; Cash only; no booking.

Sticks'n'Sushi £52 **4** **2** **2**
3 Sir Simon Milton Sq, Victoria St, SW1
020 3141 8810   2–4B **NEW**
11 Henrietta St, WC2   020 3141 8810   5–3D
Nelson Rd, SE10   020 3141 8220   1–3D
58 Wimbledon Hill Rd, SW19
020 3141 8800   11–2B
Crossrail Pl, E14   020 3141 8230   12–1C
"They come from Denmark (of all places!)" and these large Scandi-Asian-fusion venues serve a "winning combination" of "delicious sushi, beautifully tender sticks of meat, and enjoyable cocktails" to create an "innovative" and "really fun" concept. Even those who say it's "a bit of a gimmick" and "doesn't justify the price tag" concede the food's "quite good". / www.sticksnsushi.com; 10 pm, Wed-Sat 11 pm.

Sticky Mango at RSJ
SE1 **NEW** £46
33 Coin St   020 7803 9733   10–4A
The "unchanging" style of this South Bank stalwart has – for over 30 years – made it a "comforting" refuge near the National Theatre. But now "this longtime favourite has gone down the fusion route" (in partnership with a former chef), with an updated look, and "serving South East Asian cuisine in the place of the traditional Franco/modern British grub". There's very little feedback on its latest direction, hence we've left it unrated, but Nigel Wilkinson remains a partner in the business, and his "unbeatable" Loire wine list ("the most extensive in the UK") remains a headline attraction. / SE1 9NR;
www.stickymango.co.uk; @stickymangoldn; 10.30 pm; closed Sat L & Sun.

The Stoke House
SW1 **NEW** £49
81 Buckingham Palace Rd
020 7324 7744   2–4B
Will Ricker (of Bodega Negra, E&O, Eight over Eight) brings this new American BBQ venture to Victoria's gigantic Nova development; customers can choose their cut of meat at the counter and pay according to its weight; also offering breakfast, brunch and Sunday roasts. / SW1W 0AJ; www.thestokehouse.com; @stokehouseuk; 11 pm, Sat & Sun 9 pm.

STORY SE1 £154 **4** **3** **3**
199 Tooley St   020 7183 2117   10–4D
"I preferred it to The Fat Duck!" – Tom Sellers's "edgy, modernist culinary temple", quirkily situated near Tower Bridge, delivers some of "the most interesting meals ever", and although its ratings fell just outside London's Top 5 last year, they picked up considerably again this year (perhaps due to the ending of his Ours consultancy?), and he's once more "making a decent bid to be the capital's best restaurant". "Allow plenty of time for the show" ("as the name hints, everything has a story") – 12 courses of "experimental" cuisine, "staggeringly executed" and delivered with "real panache". "It's not the cosiest of settings, but they do give you a little footstool to put your handbag on." / SE1 2UE; www.restaurantstory.co.uk; @Rest_Story; 9.15 pm; closed Mon & Sun; set weekday L £69 (FP).

Strangers Dining Room, House of Commons SW1 **NEW** £99 **2** **3** **5**
St Margarets St   no tel   2–4D
The House of Commons now opens this august chamber (created in 1867) to the public, and bookings must be made on the website (max 8) – expect rigorous security checks! "It's a wonderful day out" and even if elements of the experience are a bit "clunky", it's worth it for the chance to dine in the hallowed halls of Westminster. Only a set menu formula (currently £75pp) is available; bookings currently only open up 90 days in advance. / SW1A 0AA; www.parliament.uk/dining; booking essential; set weekday L £71 (FP).

Street XO W1 **NEW** £98 **1** **1** **2**
15 Old Burlington St   020 3096 7555   4–3A
"The most exciting newcomer in years" or "a totally confused, fusion concept" – views split sharply on David Muñoz's nightclubby, open-kitchen Mayfair launch (a spin-off from his Madrid Michelin 3-star, Diver XO). Even some who hail the "beyond original" small plates ("meat-centric with Asian and Hispanic twists") as "genius" note "they seem double the price charged in Spain". Critics, meanwhile, find prices plain "obnoxious" for "horrible, flashy, irritatingly wacky" tapas-style creations served by

"patronising staff" in a "classic hipster venue with limited substance" (and "music so thumpingly loud, you could neither hear the waiters, nor focus properly on the interesting-looking food"). / W1X 1RL; www.streetxo.com; @StreetXO_London; Mon - Fri 11pm, Sat 12, Sun 9.30; set weekday L £53 (FP).

Stuzzico W2 £68 3️⃣3️⃣3️⃣
24 Kendal St 020 7262 9122 7–1D
Luca Riccio's well-established and "friendly" Italian in Bayswater's 'Connaught Village' provides classic cuisine in a simple, stylish setting. / W2 2AW; www.stuzzico.co.uk; @StuzzicoLondon; 10.15 pm.

Suda WC2 £45 3️⃣3️⃣3️⃣
23 Slingsby Place, St Martin's Court
020 7240 8010 5–2C
"A fusion of delicious Asian flavours" secures votes for the fuss-free dining at this "contemporary Thai", in the St Martin's Courtyard development. / WC2E 9AB; www.suda-thai.com; 10 pm, Thu-Sat 10.30 pm; booking max 10 may apply.

Sukho Fine Thai Cuisine
SW6 £52 5️⃣4️⃣3️⃣
855 Fulham Rd 020 7371 7600 11–1B
"Exceptional Thai cuisine" – among the best in London – justifies the "very crowded" conditions at this attractive shop conversion in deepest Fulham. Staff are full of "charm" too, and although "service is sometimes a little slow", it holds up impressively well given the perpetually full house. / SW6 5HJ; www.sukhogroups.com; 11 pm.

Suksan SW10 £43 4️⃣3️⃣2️⃣
7 Park Walk 020 7351 9881 6–3B
The "fantastic food" at this Chelsea corner café inspires consistently upbeat feedback from reporters – it's the more casual sibling of the epic Sukho Fine Thai Cuisine in Fulham. / SW10 0AJ; www.sukhogroups.com; 10.45 pm, Sun 9.45 pm.

The Summerhouse W9 £62 2️⃣2️⃣5️⃣
60 Blomfield Rd 020 7286 6752 9–4A
"A favourite spot due to its beautiful setting and decor" – this Little Venice fixture enjoys a "great canal-side location" and "on a sunny summer's evening you might imagine you were in the South of France eating fish straight from the sea". / W9 2PA; www.thesummerhouse.co; @FRGSummerhouse; No Amex.

Summers NW6 NEW £57
264-266 Kilburn High Rd
020 7693 5443 1–2B
"Newly opened in an area crying out for good quality food" – initial vibes are good for the "small (and, when busy, noisy)" dining room above the Sir Colin Campbell pub, where chef Ruairidh Summers (formerly of St John Bread and Wine) himself delivers food to the table: "the Irish-slanted menu changes weekly and is great value for

money". / NW6 2BY; www.summersdining.co.uk; @summersdining; 10.30 pm, Sun 7.30 pm; booking max 8 may apply.

Sumosan Twiga SW1 NEW
165 Sloane St 020 7495 5999 6–1D
Re-located from Mayfair to the Sloane Street site old-timers will recall as Monte's and Pengelley (long RIP), this fusion Japanese – part of a Russian-owned chain also operating in Moscow, Monte Carlo and Dubai – now serves Italian cuisine alongside its hallmark sushi, black cod and other Nobu-esque fare. It was formerly quite well-known, but since it reopened here in November 2016, it seems to have fallen into the international, Gucci-clad black hole that is central Belgravia, attracting zero survey feedback and few press reviews. / SW1X 9QB; www.sumosan.com; @sumosantwiga.

Sunday N1 £43 4️⃣2️⃣3️⃣
169 Hemingford Rd 020 7607 3868 9–2D
"Fantastic brekkies and brunches are adaptable and tailored to each customer", says a fan from SE13, who crosses town for this "understandably busy and welcoming café", on the fringes of Islington: "get there early if you don't want to queue". / N1 1DA; @sundaybarnsbury; 10.30 pm; closed Mon, Tue D, Wed D & Sun D; No Amex.

Super Tuscan E1 £51 4️⃣4️⃣3️⃣
8a Artillery Passage 020 7247 8717 13–2B
"A great find!" – this "small", little-known "hidden gem", down an alley on the edge of the City, is a haven of "authentic Italian food cooked with skill and passion" from "a really interesting, ever-changing menu", plus "a great wine list". "Great welcome from the staff too, who include the two owner brothers". Top Tip – "limited seating space" and "no email to book – you have to ring and re-confirm your table". / E1 7LJ; www.supertuscan.co.uk; 10 pm; closed Sat & Sun.

Sushi Bar Makoto W4 £46 4️⃣3️⃣2️⃣
57 Turnham Green Terrace
020 8987 3180 8–2A
A "tiny neighbourhood Japanese café" in the strip near Turnham Green tube (recently relocated from nearby) – "the specials are good value and interesting, but the highlight is the sublime sushi, with excellent well-flavoured rice and beautiful fish". / W4 1RP; www.sushibarmakoto.co.uk; 10 pm, Sun 9 pm.

Sushi Masa NW2 £43
33b Walm Lane 020 8459 2971 1–1A
Feedback is still very limited on this Willesden Green Japanese, but such as there is says: "it's managing to do a very difficult thing well – to succeed Sushi Say!" (the wonderful, authentic family-run stalwart which shut up shop two years ago, RIP). / NW2 5SH; 10 pm.

F S A

Sushi Tetsu EC1   **£89**   🔳🔳🔳
12 Jerusalem Pas   020 3217 0090   10–1A
"Less hyped than Araki, with great food at one-
seventh the price!" – "Toru Takahashi entertains
both your taste buds and your eyes" at his
"charming" Clerkenwell 7-seater: "a showcase
for his uncompromising attention to detail and
illusionist-like skills". "It feels like a stellar, very
special experience" – "as close as you can get
to authentic Japanese dining in London" – and
delivers "astonishingly good sushi, yet without an
absurd price tag". The catch? – "it's a nightmare
getting a seat". / EC1V 4JP; www.sushitetsu.co.uk;
@SushiTetsuUK; 7.45 pm, Thu-Fri 8 pm, Sat 7 pm;
closed Mon & Sun; booking essential.

Sushisamba   **£96**   🔳🔳🔳
The Piazza, WC2 awaiting tel 5–3D
Heron Tower, 110 Bishopsgate, EC2
020 3640 7330   10–2D
"It's high up and happening" ("even the lift to get
up there is brilliant!") and "you can't knock the
breathtaking view, or for that matter the food" on
the "impressive" 39th floor of the Heron Tower,
which "shouts romance" and has "a beautiful roof
balcony" to boot. Even so, whether you can justify
the "astronomical" prices is debatable, and while
the "bold" Japanese/South American fusion bites
are "exquisitely tangy and fresh", it can seem like
"there's even more emphasis on how they look than
how they taste". A sibling Sushisamba is to open in
Covent Garden Market's Opera Terrace as we go to
press. / 1.30 am, Wed-Sat 2 am.

Sutton and Sons   **£35**   🔳🔳🔳
90 Stoke Newington High St, N16
020 7249 6444   1–1C
356 Essex Rd, N1   020 7359 1210   14–1A
240 Graham Rd, E8   020 3643 2017   14–1B
"Fabulous fish 'n' chips" at "decent value" prices
are delivered "without pretension" at these
"brilliant" venues in Stokey and Hackney Central. /
www.suttonandsons.co.uk; 10 pm, Fri & Sat 10.30 pm;
E8 Fri 10 pm; no bookings.

The Swan W4   **£52**   🔳🔳🔳
1 Evershed Walk, 119 Acton Ln
020 8994 8262   8–1A
Fans hail "the best pub garden in London"
("loads of tables set amongst leafy trees") at this
hidden-away Chiswick-fringe gastropub, but its
panelled, cosy interior is lovely too. "Charming"
staff and "consistently delicious, keenly priced"
food make it an impressive all-rounder. / W4 5HH;
www.theswanchiswick.co.uk; @SwanPubChiswick; 9 pm,
Fri & Sat 10 pm, Sun 9 pm; closed weekday L.

**The Swan at the Globe
SE1**   **£60**   🔳🔳🔳
21 New Globe Walk   020 7928 9444   10–3B
"Wonderful river and City views" are the obvious

draw to this mock-historic tavern attached to
Shakespeare's Globe theatre. The food has had its
ups and downs in recent years, but the hiring of
chef Allan Pickett (after the demise of Piquet, RIP)
seems to be improving matters, with reports of
"some deceptively good cooking going on here". Top
Tip – "arrive after theatregoers have gone in!" / SE1
9DT; www.swanlondon.co.uk; @swanabout; 10.30 pm,
Sun 9 pm.

Sweet Thursday N1   **£42**   🔳🔳🔳
95 Southgate Rd   020 7226 1727   14–1A
This "popular" and kid-friendly local pizzeria in
De Beauvoir provides "reliable" food, and has
an unusually "good drinks list" as it doubles as
a wine shop. / N1 3JS; www.sweetthursday.co.uk;
@Pizza_and_Wine; 10 pm, Fri & Sat 10 pm, Sun 9
pm.

Sweetings EC4   **£76**   🔳🔳🔳
39 Queen Victoria St   020 7248 3062   10–3B
For "old school cooking in a traditional setting"
few London restaurants can genuinely live up to
this "unfailingly beguiling" Victorian time warp,
which has served "expensive but gorgeous" fish
and seafood, English puds, tankards of beer and
exclusively French wines to pinstriped City gents
for more than a century. "I take all my most
important clients here – it's a treat!" / EC4N 4SA;
www.sweetingsrestaurant.co.uk; 3 pm; L only, closed Sat
& Sun; no booking.

Taberna do Mercado E1   **£44**   🔳🔳🔳
Spitalfields Mkt   020 7375 0649   13–2B
"Full marks for originality" to star chef Nuno
Mendes' taberna, where fans extol the "inspired"
petiscos from his Portuguese homeland, and
overlook the "modest" interior of his two-year-old
unit in Spitalfields Market. That some dishes are
"challenging" and "not for everyone" has always
been part of its authentic appeal, but ratings
slipped this year generally, with the occasional
fear that it's become too "hyped". / E1 6EW;
www.tabernamercado.co.uk; @tabernamercado; 9.30
pm, Sun 7.30 pm.

Taberna Etrusca EC4   **£58**   🔳🔳🔳
9 -11 Bow Churchyard   020 7248 5552   10–2C
On a sunny day in particular, this central City
fixture, with its tucked-away location off Bow
Churchyard is just the job, thanks to its quiet setting
and al fresco patio; limited but positive feedback
too on its traditional Italian fare. / EC4M 9DQ;
www.etruscarestaurants.com; 9.30 pm; closed Sat &
Sun.

The Table SE1   **£39**   🔳🔳🔳
83 Southwark St   020 7401 2760   10–4B
This communal canteen to the south of Bankside is
"a useful venue close to Tate Modern", and does a
good line in quality breakfast and lunch dishes. / SE1

0HX; www.thetablecafe.com; @thetablecafe; 10.30 pm; closed Mon D, Sat D & Sun D; booking weekdays only.

Table Du Marche
N2 NEW **£54** 🖪🖪🖪
111 High Rd   020 8883 5750   1–1B
"A great addition to East Finchley" – this "solidly French" bar/bistro yearling "brings some welcome culinary ambition to a high street packed with cafés and quick eats", exciting the locals with its "fantastic" food and "informal" style. / N2 8AG; www.tabledumarche.co.uk; @TableDuMarche; 11 pm.

Taiwan Village SW6
£38 🖪🖪🖪
85 Lillie Rd   020 7381 2900   6–3A
"Home Taiwanese cooking at its best" is found at this "slightly quirky, family-run restaurant" lurking unobtrusively near crossroads between Lillie Road and the North End Road, whose dedicated small fanclub has long rated it as one of London's better Chinese kitchens. Top Tip – "always take the 'leave it to the chef' option for a fantastic feast". / SW6 1UD; www.taiwanvillage.com; 11 pm, Sun 10.30 pm; closed weekday L; booking max 20 may apply.

TAKA W1 NEW
18 Shepherd Market awaiting tel 3–4B
High-end Japanese food at affordable prices. In Mayfair's Shepherd Market? That's the promise of the pre-launch PR regarding this split-level restaurant and sake bar from restaurateur Andrey Datsenko and his sister Anastasi, due to open as we go to press. / W1J 7QH; www.takalondon.com; @takamayfair.

Takahashi SW19
£44 🖪🖪🖪
228 Merton Rd   020 8540 3041   11–2B
"I don't really want to tell people about it!" – The "tiny" yearling from an ex-Nobu chef in a parade near South WImbledon station is "not the easiest to get to if you don't live in SW19", and has "no decor" to speak of, but the food is "just heavenly": "amazing, contemporary Japanese cuisine", "as good as anything in the West End". / SW19; www.takahashi-restaurant.co.uk; @takahashi_sw19; 10 pm, Fri & Sat 11 pm, Sun 9 pm.

Talli Joe WC2
£38 🖪🖪🖪
152-156 Shaftesbury Avenue
020 7836 5400   5–2B
Queue at Dishoom too large? Maybe take your chances at this heart-of-Theatreland yearling from ex-Benares chef Sameer Taneja, which – though not yet quite as highly rated – likewise provides a highly popular and consistently well-rated combo of "cleverly constructed" tapas "packing a good clout flavour-wise", and a "fun" and "really lively" setting. / WC2H 8HL; www.tallijoe.com; @tallijoe; 11 pm.

Tamarind W1
£69 🖪🖪🖪
20 Queen St   020 7629 3561   3–3B

The "subtle and fully-flavoured" modern cuisine of this "flamboyantly decorated" Mayfair basement has returned to "exceptional" form – "it hits a perfect balance between being authentically Indian, with Western modernisations" and "even standard dishes are a revelation". "Caring staff" ("it's like they arrive by magic carpet") further add to the experience. / W1J 5PR; www.tamarindrestaurant.com; @TamarindMayfair; 10.45 pm, Sun 10.30 pm; closed Sat L; No trainers.

Tamarind Kitchen
W1 NEW **£47** 🖪🖪🖪
167-169 Wardour St   020 7287 4243   4–2D
On the big Soho site of Imli Street (RIP), this "semi-casual" spin-off from posh Mayfair Indian, Tamarind, lives up to its parent's stylish looks. On limited early reports, one diner had a couple of mixed trips, but all other feedback is upbeat about the cooking's "sophisticated Asian flavours". / W1F 8WR; tamarindcollection.com.

Tamp Coffee W4
£46 🖪🖪🖪
1 Devonshire Rd   no tel   8–2A
From brewing some of the "best coffee in West London" by day, this Chiswick spot transmogrifies into a "great tapas bar" serving Spanish cured ham and Argentinian empanadas by night, along with wines from the two countries. / W4; www.tampcoffee.co.uk; @tampcoffee; 6 pm; L only; booking max 6 may apply.

Tandoor Chop House
WC2 NEW **£49** 🖪🖪🖪
Adelaide St   020 3096 0359   5–4C
"Succulent and delicious tandoori dishes, offering a different experience of Indian cooking", win fans for this "approachable" newcomer near Trafalgar Square, whose evocative panelled decor seems to owe a fair amount of inspiration to Dishoom. ("A good place for sure, but I suspect the swooning and gushing comes from people who've never visited the classics of Tooting and Commercial Road".) / WC2N 4HW; tandoorchophouse.com; @tandoorchop; 10 pm, Sun 9 pm; booking max 6 may apply.

Tangerine Dream, Chelsea Physic Garden SW3
£30 🖪🖪🖪
66 Royal Hospital Rd   020 7352 5646   6–3D
"Salads are a forte" while the fruit tarts can be "sublime" at this airy, rather retro tea room, whose location amidst stunning gardens makes this "a wonderful choice on a sunny day". But, oh dear, "it's all a bit disorganised and out of control", with "very slow queues on busy days". And "prices are fairly stratospheric, even by Chelsea standards". / SW3 4HS; www.chelseaphysicgarden.co.uk; @TangerineDCafe; 5 pm, Sun 6 pm; closed Mon & Sat.

Tapas Brindisa
£50 🖪🖪🖪
18-20 Rupert St, W1   020 7478 8758   4–3D

46 Broadwick St, W1   020 7534 1690   4–2B
18-20 Southwark St, SE1
020 7357 8880   10–4C
*The "insanely busy" Borough Market original, and
also its "incredibly noisy" Soho spin-off, inspire high
loyalty with their authentic approach (from a top
firm of Spanish food importers) to "sound and
unpretentious tapas". "It's no Barrafina" however
– some of the dishes are distinctly "unmemorable" –
and arguably it's "just too popular to be that good".
/ www.brindisakitchens.com; 11 pm-11.30 pm, EC2
12.30 am, Morada Sun 4 pm; Morada closed Sun D;
SE1 no booking.*

Taqueria W11   **£40**   4 4 3
141-145 Westbourne Grove
020 7229 4734   7–1B
*"Really fresh food with a genuine Mexican taste"
ensures a packed crowd at this "friendly" cantina
on the Notting Hill/Bayswater border. The menu is
dominated by tacos, cocktails and beer. / W11 2RS;
www.taqueria.co.uk; @TaqueriaUK; 11 pm, Fri & Sat
11.30 pm, Sun 10.30 pm; No Amex.*

Taro   **£36**   3 2 2
10 Old Compton St, W1   020 7439 2275   5–2B
61 Brewer St, W1   020 7734 5826   4–3C
193 Balham High Rd, SW12
020 8675 5187   11–2C **NEW**
44a Cannon St, EC4   020 7236 0399   10–3B
*"Service is brusque and the venues fairly basic", but
these "canteen-style" eateries (the originals in Soho
are best-known) still deliver a "simple formula of
good Japanese nosh and excellent value" (mostly
"cheap and cheerful noodle soups and sushi"). /
www.tarorestaurants.co.uk; W1F 10.30 pm, Fri & Sat
11 pm, Sun 9.30 pm; W1D 10.30 pm, Fri & Sat 10.45
pm, Sun 9.30 pm, Mon 10 pm; no Amex; Brewer St only
small bookings.*

Tas   **£43**   2 2 2
*Leave aside the fact that "they used to be better"
– these "handy" and "down-to-earth refuelling
stops" are "reliable for a cheap 'n' cheerful meal"
especially pre-theatre, serving "unpolished" Turkish
mezze and (on the Southbank) pide (like pizza). /
www.tasrestaurant.com; 11.30 pm, Sun 10.30 pm; EC4
Sat 5 pm; 72 Borough High St 6 pm, Sat & Sun 4 pm;
EC4 closed Sat D & Sun, cafe SE1 closed D.*

Tas Pide SE1   **£37**   2 3 3
20-22 New Globe Walk
020 7928 3300   10–3B
*An "ideal location", right by Shakespeare's Globe
makes this "unpolished but good-value" branch of
the Turkish chain a useful option beside the Thames
in Southwark. The pide (Turkish pizza) are "worth
trying", and the menu "nicely varied". / SE1 9DR;*

*www.tasrestaurants.co.uk; @TasRestaurants; 11.30 pm,
Sun 10.30 pm.*

**Tate Britain, Whistler Restaurant
SW1**   **£60**   2 2 5
Millbank   020 7887 8825   2–4C
*"The room and the wine dominate" as always, when
it comes to this "delightful" museum café, where
"the restored Whistler murals look fantastic". The
"conventional" British food "is well done, but not
over-exciting" – gastronomically the main event is
Hamish Anderson's scorcher of a list with "very well
chosen vintages, plus beer and ciders, from all over
the world, all at relatively low markups". / SW1 4RG;
www.tate.org.uk/visit/tate-britain/rex-whistler-restaurant;
@Tate; 3 pm, Sat & Sun 5 pm; L & afternoon tea only;
booking L only.*

**Tate Modern Restaurant
SE1**   **£63**   2 3 4
Level 9, Blavatnik Building (formerly Switch
House), Bankside   020 7401 5108   10–3B
*Limited but positive feedback on Tate Modern's 9th-
floor restaurant in the swish new Blavatnik Building
(fka the Switch House). It is now the gallery's main
eatery, having somewhat supplanted the operation
on Level 6 of the main building (Boiler House, now
re-christened a 'kitchen & bar'). NB no river views
here – just skyline – and they're best from the
non-window tables (as the genius architects put the
windows at shoulder height). / SE1 9TG; www.tate.org.
uk/visit/tate-modern/restaurant.*

**Tate Modern, Restaurant, Level 6
SE1**   **£58**   3 2 4
Bankside   020 7887 8888   10–3B
*"Keep it simple with the food, and you won't be
disappointed" is good advice at this stark showcase
for British produce and drink on an upper floor
of the famous gallery – "it's really all about that
amazing view over the Thames". / SE1 9TG;
www.tate.org.uk; @TateFood; 9 pm; Sun-Thu L only, Fri
& Sat open L & D.*

Taylor St Baristas   **£11**   2 3 3
*"Baristas who seem to have studied caffeine to
degree level or higher" help win high popularity for
these hip operations serving "great artisan coffee"
alongside "a limited but good quality lunch/snack
offering". / www.taylor-st.com; most branches close 5
pm-5.30 pm, WC2 7 pm, Wed-Fri 9 pm; Old Broad ST,
Clifton St, W1, E14 closed Sat & Sun; New St closed Sat;
TW9 closed Sun.*

Tayyabs E1   **£28**   4 1 2
83 Fieldgate St   020 7247 6400   10–2D
*"Brilliant as ever, despite the chaos" – this 500-seat,
"noisy and rambunctious" Whitechapel "scrum" ("full
of smoke and smells") is "the king of the East End"
for fans of its "incredibly good value" meat platters
and curries, and "is worth the trip just for the
lamb chops alone". Even if you've booked however,*

getting a table can be an "ordeal"."It's BYO, shop for beer up the street at the Tesco Metro." / E1 1JU; www.tayyabs.co.uk; @1tayyabs; 11.30 pm.

temper £37 ③④⑤
25 Broadwick St, W1 020 3879 3834 4–1C
Angel Court, EC2 020 3004 6984 10–2C **NEW**
"A place of worship for all carnivores!" – Neil Rankin's "underground BBQ and fire pit yearling" in Soho "is like a descent into Dante's dark and confusing world full of smoke" and "if you can sit at the bar, clustered around the firepit, you get the full-on smoke experience" – "a theatrical and fascinating evening leaving you with an understanding of the hard work that goes into flawless carnivorous cooking" (although "you may be smelling it in your clothes for days"). Most of the many reports say that "if you like flesh, it's a must" – "simply cooked smoked meats; beef, lamb, goat served on a perfectly puffed flatbread or tacos, with a range of exceptional tapas and sides, delivering a truly multi-sensory event, with beautifully complimentary flavours". Ratings are undercut however, by a disgruntled minority who just don't 'get it': "for me, it just didn't live up to the hype and the bill really stung!". In July 2017, branch two opened in the City, in Bank's Angel Court development, with more Indian/curry influences (rather than Mexican ones, as in Soho). / temperrestaurant.com.

Temple & Sons EC2 **NEW** £67 ③③②
22 Old Broad St 0207 877 7710 10–2C
"Jason does it again!", say fans of Atherton's "carnivore's delight" – an "interestingly shaped" (awkward?) space near Tower 42 where "quirky starters and sides complement the meat (and fish) grills, with some unusual cocktails too" – "City friendly food but with a higher degree of quality compared to a lot of City venues". / EC2N 1HQ; templeandsons.co.uk; @templeandsons; 10 pm; closed Sun.

The 10 Cases WC2 £53 ②③③
16 Endell St 020 7836 6801 5–2C
"An unexpected variety of affordable vintages" from "an interesting and frequently changing wine list" ("talk to them to get the best choices") is the reason to visit this "quirky", extremely popular bar near the Donmar Theatre. The "limited menu" of "simple food" plays second fiddle but inspires no complaints. / WC2H 9BD; www.the10cases.co.uk; @10cases; 11 pm; closed Sun.

10 Greek Street W1 £57 ④④③
10 Greek St 020 7734 4677 5–2A
"No pretensions, just a pure celebration of real food" is the vibe at this simple modern wine bar in the heart of Soho, which provides "wonderful, brilliantly executed dishes, full of big flavours on every visit", plus "a dozen or so house wines available by the glass at very modest markups". "Tables are

squashed in, so you have to talk to your neighbours, but it works!" / W1D 4DH; www.10greekstreet.com; @10GreekStreet; 10 pm; closed Sun; booking L only.

Tendido Cero SW5 £52 ③③③
174 Old Brompton Rd 020 7370 3685 6–2B
Consistently delicious "designer tapas", and an "amazing wine list" make this "buzzing" venue an ongoing hit with "a sleek crowd of South Kensington thirty-somethings" but there is a catch… it's "very expensive!" But "it's also one of the most authentic Spanish bars in London… and I say this as someone who grew up in Spain!" / SW5 0BA; www.cambiodetercio.co.uk; @CambiodTercio; 11 pm.

Tendido Cuatro SW6 £52 ③③③
108-110 New King's Rd
020 7371 5147 11–1B
This authentic if pricey Parsons Green tapas bar (sibling to Earl's Court's Cambio de Tercio) improved its scores across the board this year – fans say it's "perfect for all occasions no matter how hungry you are!" / SW6 4LY; www.cambiodetercio.co.uk; @CambiodTercio; 10.30 pm, Tue-Fri 11 pm, Sun 10.30 pm.

Terroirs WC2 £52 ③②③
5 William IV St 020 7036 0660 5–4C
"It's hard to navigate the wine lists, but they're always exciting and full of interest" at this "handy pit stop near Charing Cross" which feels "French through and through"; and whose "really interesting, if simple, meaty and cheesy Gallic plates, and knowledgeable and friendly staff ensure it's always buzzing". (That it lacks the massive profile it once enjoyed has more to do with how far London has improved since it opened in 2009, than anything that's much changed in itself.) / WC2N 4DW; www.terroirswinebar.com; @TerroirsWineBar; 11 pm; closed Sun; set weekday L £30 (FP).

Test Kitchen W1 **NEW** £65
54 Frith St 020 7734 8487 5–2A
Chef Adam Simmonds (Le Gavroche, Le Manoir) has opened up a year-long 'test' (some might say 'pop-up') kitchen in the Soho premises that until recently were Barrafina's legendary first site; seating is still counter-style, so you can report your thoughts directly as you eat. It opened in May 2017 – too late for survey feedback: whether it's worth the (fairly steep) prices for the honour of being chef's guinea pig remains to be seen. / W1D 4SL; www.thetestkitchen.uk.

Texture W1 £112 ④③③
34 Portman St 020 7224 0028 2–2A
"Packed with clean Icelandic flavours and textures and presented as works of art" – Aggi Sverrisson's "Scandi-inspired" dishes, married to a list of "fabulous New World wines" have won a major reputation for this "smart" and "well-spaced" (if

somewhat "low key") ten-year-old, off the foyer of a hotel near Selfridges (but with its own dedicated entrance). / W1H 7BY; www.texture-restaurant.co.uk; @TextureLondon; 10.30 pm; closed Mon & Sun; set weekday L £60 (FP).

Thali SW5 £48 4 4 3
166 Old Brompton Rd   020 7373 2626   6–2B
"A welcome change from the average Indian" – this "intimate" South Kensington café follows family recipes creating a "very original menu that's far from run-of-the-mill, and beautifully prepared". Bollywood posters and "very attentive service" add further character. It's not as famous as its nearby Indian rivals, and fans feel it "seems to fly under the radar", but "knocks its more illustrious neighbours into a cocked hat". / SW5 0BA; @ThaliLondon; 11.30 pm, Sun 10.30 pm.

Theo Randall W1 £91 3 3 2
InterContinental Hotel, 1 Hamilton Pl
020 7318 8747   3–4A
"Fabulous Italian cuisine in hearty portions" and "friendly" service delight fans of this ex-River Café chef's "calm and quiet" HQ, off the foyer of a luxury hotel by Hyde Park Corner. As ever, there are gripes that "it feels very much like a brightly-lit 'hotel' restaurant", but the consensus is that "the refurbishment to the room a couple of years ago is a definite improvement". / W1J 7QY; www.theorandall.com; @theorandall; 11 pm, Sun 10.30 pm; closed Sat L & Sun; set weekday L £60 (FP).

Theo's SE5 £39 3 4 3
2 Grove Ln   020 3026 4224   1–3C
"Delicious pizzas" – with a "amazing, thin sourdough base" and "super toppings (not too overloaded)" – go down a storm at this "relaxed" Camberwell spot, and numerous reports also applaud the "friendly" staff. / SE5; www.theospizzeria.com; @theospizzaldn; 10.30 pm, Fri & Sat 11 pm, Sun 10 pm; No Amex; May need 6+ to book.

Theo's Simple Italian SW5 £69 3 2 3
34 - 44 Barkston Gardens, Kensington
020 7370 9130   6–2A
The harshest critic of acclaimed chef Theo Randall's casual snacks-and-dining sideline, in a fairly anodyne Earl's Court hotel, says "the food's pretty good", but thinks the overall venture "feels like an afterthought rather than anyone's focus". Other reports though are more upbeat. / SW5 0EW; www.theossimpleitalian.co.uk; @TRSimpleItalian; 10.30 pm.

34 Mayfair W1 £79 3 3 4
34 Grosvenor Sq   020 3350 3434   3–3A
"Very large portions of first-class and well-cooked meat at very large prices" characterises the straightforward ("quite basic"), plutocratic "posh nosh" at Richard Caring's upscale grill, near the old US Embassy. Inevitably it's quite a hit with expense accounters, and does a good breakfast too. / W1K 2HD; www.34-restaurant.co.uk; @34_restaurant; 11 pm, Sun 10 pm; set weekday L & dinner £48 (FP).

The Thomas Cubitt SW1 £63 3 4 4
44 Elizabeth St   020 7730 6060   2–4A
"The bright and airy upstairs dining room is more refined; the downstairs bar is bustling" (and "very noisy"), at this "crazy busy" Belgravia pub, where "good hearty fayre" is provided by "smiley" service throughout. / SW1W 9PA; www.thethomascubitt.co.uk; 10 pm, Sun 9.30 pm.

Thyme and Lemon N1 £43 3 3 4
139 Upper St   020 7704 6855   9–3D
"The kind of place it can be hard to find amidst the hurly burly of Upper Street" – a cheerful venture with "very decent, imaginative tapas and great cocktails": "all the usual suspects are on the menu but each dish is made with real care and attention to detail." / N1 1QP; www.thymeandlemon.co.uk; @thymeandlemon; 11.30 pm, Fri & Sat midnight, Sun 11 pm.

tibits £35 3 2 3
12-14 Heddon St, W1   020 7758 4110   4–3B
124 Southwark St, SE1   10–4B NEW
"Healthy and reasonably priced!!" This Swiss cafeteria chain's attractive, veggie-vegan self-service buffet concept – wherein you help yourself and pay per 100g – is "a handy West End option" ("initially I thought it was pricey, but given it's off Regent Street, I think it's worth it!"). A new branch opened in June 2017 near Tate Modern. / www.tibits.co.uk.

Timmy Green SW1 NEW £64 2 3 3
Unit 18, Nova Victoria, 11 Sir Simon Milton Square   020 3019 7404   2–4B
Mixed views on this big Nova Victoria newcomer – one of the more ambitious outlets of the 'Daisy Green' Aussie brasserie chain, with much of its more substantial fare produced on a Josper grill. Critics feel that "while the marketing blurb leads you to expect a personal experience, the actual restaurant is depressingly chain-y", but fans applaud its health-conscious dishes for coffee or brunch. / SW1E 5BH; www.daisygreenfood.com/venues/timmy-green; 11 pm, Sun 10 pm.

TING SE1 £98 3 3 4
Level 35, 31 St Thomas St
020 7234 8000   10–4C
"You can choose between traditional and really different Asian afternoon teas" while enjoying "stunning views of London" on this plush perch on the 35th floor of the Shard, and its "quiet and spacious" quarters are also "an ideal location for business". Of course it's decidedly "not cheap",

and the odd report on those paying their own way at dinner here suggests "the electronic loos can be more memorable than the cuisine". / SE1 9RY; www.ting-shangri-la.com; @ShangriLaShard; 11 pm; No trainers; credit card required to book; set weekday L £64 (FP).

Toff's N10 £40 [3][3][2]
38 Muswell Hill Broadway
020 8883 8656 1–1B
Fans still cross north London for this "crowded and noisy" Muswell Hill stalwart – "a high calibre, Greek Cypriot-run fish 'n' chips restaurant" whose "notable Greek salad and homemade tartare sauce" are a foil to the "finest fish 'n' chips". / N10 3RT; www.toffsfish.co.uk; @toffsfish; 10 pm; closed Sun.

Tokimeite W1 £104 [4][3][3]
23 Conduit St 020 3826 4411 3–2C
"Layers of flavour and umami" reveal the magic of kaiseki cuisine at renowned Japanese chef Yoshihiro Murata's Mayfair yearling (backed by Japan's largest agricultural co-op), which, for its disciples, delivers dishes that are "beyond fresh, and raise the pure essence of simple ingredients like yuzu and matcha to the divine". Natch, it's "very pricey", which perhaps is why it still hasn't built a huge fanbase. / W1S 2XS; www.tokimeite.com; @tokimeitelondon; 10.30 pm.

Tokyo Diner WC2 £24 [3][3][3]
2 Newport Place 020 7287 8777 5–3B
"Just like the kind of Japanese restaurants you find in Japan" – this "bargain" diner, on the fringe of Chinatown, is "really small, but comfy and welcoming". "Delicious noodles and tasty sushi keep cost-conscious fans coming, and the no-tips policy also helps keep the bill down." / WC2H 7JJ; www.tokyodiner.com; 11.30 pm; No Amex.

Tom Simmons SE1 [NEW] £60
2 Still Walk 020 3848 2100 10–4D
Pembrokeshire-born chef Tom Simmons, who appeared on MasterChef: The Professionals, opened in the One Tower Bridge development in July 2017, with an emphasis on the use of top Welsh ingredients. By the standards of the area, it's one of the more foodie options. / SE1 2UP; tom-simmons. co.uk; @TomSimmons_TB; 11 pm, Sun 6 pm; closed Sun D.

Tom's Kitchen £65 [2][2][2]
Somerset House, 150 Strand, WC2
020 7845 4646 2–2D
27 Cale St, SW3 020 7349 0202 6–2C
11 Westferry Circus, E14
020 3011 1555 12–1C
1 Commodity Quay, E1
020 3011 5433 10–3D
Erstwhile haute cuisine star Tom Aikens has switched his focus to these casual diners in recent years. Fans

(the majority) praise their "lively" staff and "good bistro cooking at friendly prices", but ratings are still dragged down by numerous reports of "slapdash" results. / www.tomskitchen.co.uk; SW3 10.30 pm, Sun 9.30 pm; WC2 10 pm; E14 9.30 pm; E1 10.30 pm; SE1 6 pm; B1 10.30 pm, Sun 5 pm; WC2, E14, B1 & E1 closed Sun D.

Tommi's Burger Joint £29 [3][3][3]
30 Thayer St, W1 020 7224 3828 3–1A
37 Berwick St, W1 020 7494 9086 4–2D
342 Kings Rd, SW3 020 7349 0691 6–3C
Icelander Tomas Andres Tomason's three cool self-service venues offer "delish burgers at a good price", complemented by "fantastic sweet potato fries"; "now licensed for wine and beer". / www.burgerjoint.co.uk; 10.30 pm, Sun 9 pm; booking: min 5.

The Tommy Tucker SW6 £55 [3][3][3]
22 Waterford Rd 0207 736 1023 6–4A
A short walk from Fulham Broadway, this attractive gastropub provides "an interesting variety of good dishes" thanks to the involvement of the team from Parson's Green's Claude's Kitchen. / SW6 2DR; www.thetommytucker.com; @tommytuckerpub; 10 pm, Sun 9 pm.

Tomoe SW15 £41 [4][2][2]
292 Upper Richmond Rd
020 3730 7884 11–2B
This "underrated" Putney Japanese sits behind the "shabby exterior" inherited from its predecessor on the site, Cho-San, and although the personnel have changed, the "authentic" ethos remains the same. "The owner works the sushi bar himself", results are above-par ("proper sushi, udon and many classic dishes"), and "you know it's a good place when you always see Japanese there". / SW15; 9.30 pm.

Tonkotsu £41 [3][2][3]
Selfridges, 400 Oxford St, W1
020 7437 0071 3–1A
63 Dean St, W1 020 7437 0071 5–2A
7 Blenheim Cr, W11 020 7221 8300 7–1A
4 Canvey St, SE1 020 7928 2228 10–4B
382 Mare St, E8 020 8533 1840 14–1B
Arch 334, 1a Dunston St, E8
020 7254 2478 14–2A
Fans still hail "the most amazing ramen outside Japan!" at these cramped noodle stops, but for doubters they "were so good, but are more average now". A fair middle view is they are "quick and cheap, with a nice ambience". / www.tonkotsu.co.uk; 10 pm-11 pm; Selfridges 30 mins before store closing; no bookings.

Tosa W6 £36 [3][3][2]
332 King St 020 8748 0002 8–2B
This "good local Japanese" in Stamford Brook is "well worth a look", especially for the "fine sashimi"

and yakitori (charcoal-grilled chicken skewers), the house speciality. / W6 0RR; 10.30 pm, Sun 10 pm.

Tozi SW1 £50 3️⃣3️⃣2️⃣
8 Gillingham St 020 7769 9771 2–4B
This "big, bustling, Italian small-plates place" attached to a hotel "works surprisingly well" and is a "great standby given the dearth of quality dining spots near Victoria". The Venetian-inspired dishes are "robustly flavoured", and staff create a "friendly atmosphere". / SW1V 1HN; www.tozirestaurant.co.uk; @ToziRestaurant; 10 pm.

The Tramshed EC2 £58 3️⃣3️⃣4️⃣
32 Rivington St 020 7749 0478 13–1B
Surprisingly limited, but consistently upbeat feedback nowadays on Mark Hix's "buzzy" converted Victorian tramshed in Shoreditch, where art from Damien Hirst et al sets the tone ("the cow in formaldehyde is stunning and really adds to the place!"). The focus is "great steaks and whole roasted chicken" (the latter served dramatically, claws poking up). / EC2A 3LX; www.hixrestaurants.co.uk/restaurant/tramshed/; @the_tramshed; 11 pm, Wed-Sat midnight, Sun 9.30 pm.

Trangallan N16 £45 4️⃣4️⃣3️⃣
61 Newington Grn 020 7359 4988 1–1C
"Authentic Spanish cooking" from a "very interesting menu" draws a steady crowd to this "rather cramped" and "slightly eccentric" Hispanic by Newington Green. Even fans can find it "a little too pricey" however. / N16 9PX; www.trangallan.com; @trangallan_n16; 10.30 pm; closed Mon; No Amex; No trainers.

Tratra E2 🆕 £64
2-4 Boundary St 020 7729 1051 13–1B
Spacious and stylish Shoreditch hotel basement, formerly home to Conran's The Boundary Restaurant (RIP), which now hosts this Gallic newcomer from Parisian chef and cookery writer Stéphane Reynaud – his first venture outside France. Reynaud grew up on a pig farm in the Ardèche, and the menu majors on regional classics, with lots of pork. See also Boundary Rooftop. / E2 7DD; boundary.london.

Trawler Trash N1 🆕 £46
205 Upper St 020 3637 7619 9–2D
From the company behind Fitzrovia's Firedog comes a new type of fish 'n' chip restaurant – fittingly on a Canonbury site that's been serving up Britain's favourite takeaway for over 50 years (Seafish, RIP). The 'trash' part of the name refers to the fact that they serve the less popular types of fish – pilchards, coley, sprat and grey mullet, for example – and only ever fish caught that day. / N1 1RQ; www.trawler-trash.com; @TrawlerTrashN1.

Tredwell's WC2 £60 2️⃣2️⃣2️⃣
4 Upper St Martin's Ln 020 3764 0840 5–3B
Views divide sharply on Marcus Wareing's Theatreland diner, which has yet to fully find its mojo. It does have a growing profile, and fans for whom its "clever-but-not-too-clever (fairly robust and rich) cooking" makes for "a very enjoyable night out". Even those who like its "nice buzzy feel" can feel the food is only "decent enough", however, especially as it ain't cheap, and there are still too many reports of some plain "dismal" meals. / WC2H 9NY; www.tredwells.com; @tredwells; 10 pm, Fri & Sat 11 pm.

Treves & Hyde E1 🆕 £54
15-17 Leman St 020 3621 8900 10–2D
With a coffee shop and terrace downstairs, and a restaurant and bar upstairs, this new operation near Aldgate East tube – part of a boutique Aparthotel complex – covers all the bases – even brunch at weekends. No survey feedback yet, but positive press reports on its small plates from chef George Tannock. / E1 8EN; trevesandhyde.com; @trevesandhyde; 10.30 pm, Sun 3 pm.

Tried & True SW15 £25 3️⃣3️⃣3️⃣
279 Upper Richmond Rd
020 8789 0410 11–2A
"Great breakfasts in massive portions" plus a mean cup of coffee have established this Kiwi outfit on the Putney café scene. Welcoming to dogs and children – "it can be trying when Torquil and Samantha are running around expressing themselves and your quiet moment is lost". / SW15; www.triedandtruecafe.co.uk; @tried_true_cafe; 4 pm, Sat & Sun 4.30 pm; L only.

Trinity SW4 £75 5️⃣5️⃣3️⃣
4 The Polygon 020 7622 1199 11–2D
"We are privileged to have it as our local!" – Adam Byatt's Clapham landmark "goes from strength to strength", and "at last has a well deserved Michelin star" (though we're not sure what took them so long). "The whole team are so knowledgeable and committed to providing a memorable meal", and results are "exceptional" from an à la carte menu that's more "conventional" than its former multi-course tasting format. "They've greatly improved the decor since refurbishing a couple of years ago too, but it can still lack buzz." See also Upstairs at Trinity. / SW4 0JG; www.trinityrestaurant.co.uk; @TrinityLondon; 10 pm, Sun 9 pm; closed Mon L & Sun D.

Trinity Upstairs SW4 £47 5️⃣4️⃣4️⃣
4 The Polygon 020 3745 7227 11–2D
"Far much more casual than downstairs, but the food is AMAZING!!" – "Adam Byatt's cracking foil to the main outlet", relatively recently opened above his Clapham HQ, serves a small-plates menu "full of lip smacking choices", and "there's more buzz than below with raised counters, no white tablecloths, and quaffable rosé on a pump". "Be prepared

to sit on stools all evening though!" / SW4 0JG; www.trinityrestaurant.co.uk; @trinityupstairs ; 10 pm.

Trishna W1 £83 5️⃣3️⃣3️⃣
15-17 Blandford St   020 7935 5624   2–1A
"Even better than its slightly more glamorous sibling Gymkhana"; the Sethi family's "exceptional" Mumbai import delivers "memorably gorgeous" cuisine (most famously fish) with "lovely subtle flavours and a deft touch to the spicing". Only the food is a stand-out however: in other respects "it looks and feels like an easygoing Marylebone restaurant". / W1U 3DG; www.trishnalondon.com; @TrishnaLondon; 10.30 pm, Sun 9.45 pm.

LA TROMPETTE W4 £82 5️⃣4️⃣3️⃣
5-7 Devonshire Rd   020 8747 1836   8–2A
"A consistent class act, year-in-year-out" – this "perfect local" ("people of Chiswick, do you know how lucky you are?") is "pretty much on a par with Chez Bruce", its stablemate. "The sublime cooking manages to be classic, yet with exciting elements popping up in each dish", staff are "first rate" and – though "relaxed" – its "elegant" styling would not be out of place in the West End. / W4 2EU; www.latrompette.co.uk; @LaTrompetteUK; 10.30 pm, Sun 9.30 pm.

Trullo N1 £59 4️⃣4️⃣3️⃣
300-302 St Paul's Rd   020 7226 2733   9–2D
"Terrific food is simply but superbly realised (from a daily menu reflecting the freshest of ingredients)" at Tim Siadatan and Jordan Frieda's "top drawer Italian" – "an unexpected find in this part of Islington" ("just off Highbury Corner") – and it helps that "staff look like they enjoy their work". "Downstairs is dark and sexy, especially the booths; upstairs is light and airy and great in the summer." / N1 2LH; www.trullorestaurant.com; @Trullo_LDN; 10.15 pm; closed Sun D; No Amex.

The Truscott Arms W9 NEW
55 Shirland Rd   020 7266 9198   1–2B
Back with a bang! – this Maida Vale gastropub is also back from the dead as Henry Harris (formerly of Knightsbridge's Racine, long RIP) takes over the kitchen. It closed in August last year after a lengthy legal battle over rent increases, and is set to re-open in late 2017. / W9 2JD; www.thetruscottarms.com; @TheTruscottArms; 10 pm, Sat & Sun 11 pm.

Tsunami SW4 £48 4️⃣2️⃣3️⃣
5-7 Voltaire Rd   020 7978 1610   11–1D
"Far superior to Nobu and a fraction of the price!"; this fusion Japanese is a long-running fixture on the Clapham scene thanks to its "complex menu" of "consistently delicious" fusion fare and "fabulous" cocktails. Drawbacks? – service can be "clueless" and the interior "noisy". Note, the West End branch (in Charlotte Street) is now closed, although the team has opened Yama Momo in East Dulwich. /

SW4 6DQ; www.tsunamirestaurant.co.uk; 11 pm, Fri-Sun midnight; closed Sat L & Sun; No Amex.

Tulse Hill Hotel SE24 £50 3️⃣3️⃣3️⃣
150 Norwood Rd   020 8671 7499   1–4D
"Who'd expect such a hip hangout on the South Circular!?" – "the food is good and the vibe is great" at this trendy gastropub with a fantastic garden, between Brixton and Dulwich. / SE24 9AY; www.tulsehillhotel.com; @TulseHillHotel; 10 pm, Sun 9 pm.

Tuyo E2 NEW
129a Pritchard's Rd   020 7739 2540   14–2B
Sitting alongside the canal by Hackney's foodie Broadway Market, a new Mediterranean tapas joint serving a selection of pinchos and small bites mixing Levantine, Spanish and other influences. The backing comes from the owners of Islington perennial Gallipoli, while former Salt Yard group chef Ricardo Pimentel heads up the kitchen. / E2 9AP; www.tuyo.london; @Tuyocafebistro; 10 pm, Fri-Sun 11 pm.

28 Church Row NW3 £52 4️⃣4️⃣3️⃣
28 Church Row   020 7993 2062   9–2A
"A real addition to the desert of Hampstead!" This no-reservations, "very buzzy" ("it can get very full") new tapas bar – a townhouse cellar in a super-cute street – breathes a bit of much-needed life into NW3's dining options, serving "typical Spanish staples (boquerones, patatas fritas, chorizo) alongside enticing and original specials on the board". "Service is borne of a genuine enthusiasm for the place and its customers." / NW3 6UP; www.28churchrow.com; @28churchrow; 10.30 pm, Sun 9.30 pm.

28-50 £57 2️⃣4️⃣3️⃣
15-17 Marylebone Ln, W1
020 7486 7922   3–1A
17-19 Maddox St, W1   020 7495 1505   4–2A
140 Fetter Ln, EC4   020 7242 8877   10–2A
"Fantastic wines at fantastic prices" (in a variety of glass sizes) underlies the high ongoing popularity of these "lively" bar/bistros – to accompany, "simple" fare (like burgers) that's "enjoyable, if basic". / www.2850.co.uk; 9.30 pm-10.30 pm; EC4 closed Sat & Sun, W1S closed Sun.

Twist W1 £63 4️⃣4️⃣4️⃣
42 Crawford St   020 7723 3377   2–1A
"Each tapas-style dish is a delight – with crisp distinctive flavours, and fabulous for sharing", say fans of Eduardo Tuccillo's Italo-Spanish "fusion-tapas" cuisine at this Spartan but "charming" Marylebone two-year-old (on the site that was for many years Garbos, long RIP). / W1H 1JW; www.twistkitchen.co.uk; @twistkitchen; closed Sun; SRA-Food Made Good – 2 stars.

Two Brothers N3 £34 3 2 2
297-303 Regent's Park Rd
020 8346 0469 1–1B
"Consistently high quality, fresh fish" continues to win a near-universal thumbs-up for this traditional Finsbury chippy: a long-standing major favourite in the area. / N3 1DP; www.twobrothers.co.uk; 10 pm; closed Mon.

2 Veneti W1 £54 3 4 3
10 Wigmore St 020 7637 0789 3–1B
Steering clear of standard Italian cuisine, this well regarded outfit near the Wigmore Hall impresses reporters with the quality of its service and its "imaginative Venetian food". There's also a strong list of Italian wines and grappas. / W1U 2RD; www.2veneti.com; @2Veneti; 10.30 pm, Sat 11 pm; closed Sat L & Sun.

Typing Room, Town Hall Hotel E2 £95 5 5 3
Patriot Square 020 7871 0461 14–2B
Lee Westcott's "delicate but unfussy cooking, with strong flavours, and beautiful presentation" is matched with "perfectly judged" service from the open kitchen at this "unpretentious" but "pleasantly buzzing" green-walled dining room – the corner of Bethnal Green's monolithic old town hall that's nowadays a trendy boutique hotel (and which first found fame as Viajante, long RIP). "How this place doesn't have a Michelin star is beyond belief!" / E2 9NF; www.typingroom.com; @TypingRoom; 10 pm; closed Mon & Tue L; booking max 4 may apply; set weekday L £56 (FP).

Uchi E5 £41 4 2 2
144 Clarence Rd 020 3302 4670 14–1B
"Not much to look at from the outside and still a bit surprising to find even though the area is very up and coming" – this "tucked away" Japanese café is esteemed by its small fan club for "utterly delicious" sushi: "you won't even notice that you're perched on a wooden stool". / E5 8DY; www.uchihackney.com; @uchihackney; 11 pm, Sun 10 pm.

Uli W11 £46 3 3 3
5 Ladbroke Rd 020 3141 5878 7–2B
"It is great to have Uli back in a new location after an absence of a few years!" – so say numerous loyal fans of this resurrected Notting Hill pan-Asian, where "host Michael Lim is as hospitable as ever in the new flashier surroundings". It's still finding its stride however: "while the food's great, it could use more work – at times it's patchy and lacking the flair of the original". / W11 3PA; www.ulilondon.com; @ulilondon; 11.45 pm; D only, closed Sun.

Umu W1 £120 3 4 3
14-16 Bruton Pl 020 7499 8881 3–2C
The doors slide back Star Trek-style at this bijou Japanese restaurant "tucked away discreetly" in

a cute Mayfair mews – one of London's leading providers of "sublime and sophisticated" Kyoto-style kaiseki cuisine… but "ye gods, the prices!" Chef Yoshinori Ishii is "the ultimate Renaissance man – he makes the pottery, does the flowers and calligraphy, teaches fisherman how to treat the catch and takes cooking to another level!" / W1J 6LX; 10.30 pm; closed Sat L & Sun; No trainers; booking max 14 may apply.

Union Street Café SE1 £62 2 2 3
47-51 Great Suffolk St 020 7592 7977 10–4B
Gordon Ramsay's "busy and bustling" casual Italian in Borough attracts a wide spectrum of very mixed views. For fans, it's "a gastronomic find" and "very special", but its worst foes say "never again" having experienced "some of the most dire food ever". Top Tip – "the lunch menu is good value". / SE1 0BS; www.gordonramsayrestaurants.com/union-street-cafe; @unionstreetcafe; 10.45 pm; closed Sun D.

Le Vacherin W4 £64 3 3 2
76-77 South Parade 020 8742 2121 8–1A
Malcolm John's "reliable local brasserie" by Acton Green feels like it's been airlifted from provincial France, and, at its best, its traditional Gallic fare can really hit the heights. Top Tip – "good value lunch". / W4 5LF; www.levacherin.co.uk; @Le_Vacherin; 10.30 pm, Sun 9 pm; closed Mon L; set weekday L & pre-theatre £41 (FP).

Vagabond Wines £32 3 3 4
Unit 77, Nova Building, 77 Buckingham Palace Rd, SW1 020 7630 7693 2–4B
25 Charlotte St, W1 020 3441 9210 2–1C
18-22 Vanston Place, SW6 020 7381 1717 6–4A
4 Northcote Rd, SW11 020 7738 0540 11–2C
67 Brushfield St, E1 020 3674 5670 13–2C
"A very cool concept" – a 5-store chain providing "an excellent way to while away a few hours", whereby you "top up an Oyster-style card and then you're able to make your way around the room, grabbing yourself samples or large glasses from a vast array of wines". "Nibble on charcuterie and cheeses and other sharing plates as you go" but "while the food is good, it's really all about the vino".

Vanilla Black EC4 £63 2 2 2
17-18 Tooks Ct 020 7242 2622 10–2A
This ambitious and upmarket veggie operation near Chancery Lane has divided opinion this year, with its food scores falling dramatically. For fans, it still serves "vegetarian food lifted to the level of fine dining" – "imaginative, bursting with taste and barely a lentil in sight". But there was much unaccustomed bitter disappointment too: "fell really short…" "landfill…", "they must hate veggies to treat us like this!" / EC4A 1LB; www.vanillablack.co.uk; @vanillablack1; 10 pm; closed Sun; No Amex.

Vasco & Piero's Pavilion W1 £60 **3**|**4**|**3**
15 Poland St 020 7437 8774 4–1C
A "hidden gem" in the heart of Soho – this "cramped" old-world Italian "ristorante" run by three generations of the same family specialises in Umbrian cuisine. It's "not yet quite vintage but in something of a timewarp, and offers surprisingly and genuinely good food with well managed service". / W1F 8QE; www.vascosfood.com; @Vasco_and_Piero; 9.30 pm; closed Sat L & Sun.

Veeraswamy W1 £78 **4**|**4**|**3**
Victory Hs, 99-101 Regent St
020 7734 1401 4–4B
You would never guess from its "beautiful and relaxed" interior that this first-floor Indian veteran, near Piccadilly Circus, is London's oldest (est 1926). Service is "professional" and the "delicate and expertly prepared" cuisine has fully moved with the times – "it shows just how the amazing flavours of subcontinental cooking can be elevated!" / W1B 4RS; www.veeraswamy.com; @theveeraswamy; 10.45 pm, Sun 10:15 pm; booking max 12 may apply.

Veneta SW1 £50 **3**|**3**|**2**
3 Norris St 020 3874 9100 4–4D
"Choices from the fish bar are a highlight" at this year-old Salt Yard Group venture, whose "Italian-style" small plates formula here is "mainly focussed on Venetian dishes". Occupying a unit in the new St James's Market development, all the "glass, flash and tourists" of this "big, chimney-like space" are at odds with the cosy style of its stablemates. / SW1Y 4RJ; www.saltyardgroup.co.uk/veneta; @venetastjames.

Verdi's E1 £45 **3**|**4**|**3**
237 Mile End Rd 020 7423 9563 14–2B
"Just how a neighbourhood restaurant should be", this "authentic, family-run trattoria serving cuisine from Emilia Romagna" is "surprising for Stepney" and "fantastic every time". "Prices are a little higher than average for the area, but not excessive for such thoughtful, well-executed cooking". / E1 4AA; www.gverdi.uk; @verdislondon.

Il Vicolo SW1 £54 **3**|**4**|**2**
3-4 Crown Passage 020 7839 3960 3–4D
"Surprisingly affordable" for St James's – this family-run Italian is tucked down an "out-of-the-way" alley. Run with "efficiency and charm" by "the patron and his daughters", "service is miraculous even when busy" – which is often. Recommended for both business lunchers, and family dinners. / SW1Y 6PP; www.ilvicolorestaurant.co.uk; 10 pm; closed Sat L & Sun.

The Victoria SW14 £53
10 West Temple Sheen 020 8876 4238 11–2A
A favourite refuelling stop after walks in Richmond Park, Paul Merrett's "attractive gastropub" – complete with large dining conservatory and "good facilities for children outside" – is a popular destination, serving a "very accessible" menu. Feedback was "uneven" this year, but in August 2017 they announced an impending facelift which seems likely to pep the place back up to form again. / SW14 7RT; victoriasheen.co.uk; @TheVictoria_Pub; 10 pm, Sun 9 pm; No Amex.

Viet Food W1 £32 **3**|**3**|**3**
34-36 Wardour St 020 7494 4555 5–3A
"Fresh and flavourful Vietnamese food" is the hallmark of former Hakkasan chef, Jeff Tan's Chinatown operation: "it's rare to find quality cooking, at a decent price, in the centre of London". / W1D 6QT; www.vietnamfood.co.uk; 10.30 pm, Fri & Sat 11 pm.

Viet Grill E2 £45 **3**|**2**|**2**
58 Kingsland Rd 020 7739 6686 14–2A
"Clear fresh flavours" and "charming service" enable this studenty-looking Vietnamese café to stand out among stiff competition on Kingsland Road's 'pho mile'. / E2 8DP; www.vietnamesekitchen.co.uk; @CayTreVietGrill; 11 pm, Fri & Sat 11.30 pm, Sun 10.30 pm.

Vijay NW6 £35 **3**|**3**|**1**
49 Willesden Ln 020 7328 1087 1–1B
"Food good, decor awful": a report that could have been written any time in the last 40 years on this "perennial Kilburn curry house favourite" – opened in 1964 and seemingly "frozen in time", yet "consistently delivering delicious, south Indian grub" (to a surprisingly well-heeled crowd). Top Tip – option to BYO £2.50 corkage. / NW6 7RF; www.vijayrestaurant.co.uk; 10.45 pm, Fri & Sat 11.45 pm; no booking.

Villa Bianca NW3 £60 **2**|**2**|**2**
1 Perrins Ct 020 7435 3131 9–2A
This stalwart Hampstead Italian is "a reassuring time warp" for fans, bowled over by its hyper-cute village location and '70s-style glamour. A fair assessment is that "it's not bad, not brilliant – just a nice place to be". / NW3 1QS; www.villabiancanw3.com; @VillaBiancaNW3; 11.30 pm, Sun 10.30 pm.

Villa Di Geggiano W4 £63 **3**|**3**|**4**
66-68 Chiswick High Rd 020 3384 9442 8–2B
"Authentic Tuscan fodder in charming surroundings" highlights this ambitious (somewhat "pricey") three-year-old "a definite cut above the standard Italian experience" ("given so many chains in Chiswick, it really stands out"). "It's a brave venture too, in a large space where others have failed", and with a big summer terrace. / W4 1SY; www.villadigeggiano.co.uk; @villadigeggiano; 10 pm; closed Mon.

Villandry £61 ❶❶❸
11-12 Waterloo Pl, SW1   020 7930 3305   2–3C
170 Gt Portland St, W1   020 7631 3131   2–1B
"Great ambience" and "good locations" in St
James's and Marylebone may keep these rather
grand-looking cafés ticking over, but they incite
complaints of "pretensions of grandeur above their
station", taking flak for food and service that often
seem "complacent", "formulaic" and "ordinary". /
www.villandry.com/; W1 & SW1 10.30 pm, Sun 6 pm;
W1 & SW1 closed Sun D.

The Vincent E8 NEW £31
3 Atkins Sq, Dalston Lane
020 8510 0423   14–1B
The trio who previously ran Bethnal Green
boozer The Sebright Arms together opened this
airy all-day Hackney spot in May 2017. Local
beers, coffee, Sunday brunches and roasts aim
to make it a linchpin of the local scene. / E8 1FN;
www.thevincent-e8.com; @thevincente8; 10 pm, Sat 3
pm, Sun 5 pm; May need 6+ to book.

The Vincent Rooms, Westminster
Kingsway College SW1 £37 ❸❹❸
76 Vincent Sq   020 7802 8391   2–4C
"It's so enjoyable to chat with the enthusiastic
trainees" at this catering college dining room in a
quiet corner of Westminster, staffed by the students.
Not only that, but "the set lunch menu is a steal" for
"witty and beautifully presented food" delivered by
"well-meaning if haphazard" servers. / SW1P 2PD;
www.westking.ac.uk/about-us/vincent-rooms-restaurant/;
@thevincentrooms; 7 pm; closed Mon D, Tue D, Fri D,
Sat & Sun; No Amex.

Vineet Bhatia London
SW3 £146 ❸❸❷
10 Lincoln St   020 7225 1881   6–2D
"Amid increasing competition, still London's top
fine-dining Indian!" – so say most reports on
Vineet Bhatia's "superbly re-invented cuisine" at
this "impeccably run" Chelsea townhouse, which
is "unique amongst upmarket Indians in aiming
to be quiet and intimate rather than buzzy and
fashionable". Formery Rasoi, it relaunched one
year ago, and fans are "extremely happy that
this wonderful place is just as refined as before,
but with a slightly different focus (perhaps less
led by luxury ingredients)". Even supporters give
"a word of warning however – don't even think
about the prices" – and there is the odd critic
who says "are they kidding? Just go to Gymkhana,
Trishna or Jamavar for £50 less!" / SW3 2TS;
www.vineetbhatia.london; @VineetBhatiaLDN; 10.15
pm.

Vinoteca £55 ❸❸❹
15 Seymour Pl, W1   020 7724 7288   2–2A
55 Beak St, W1   020 3544 7411   4–2B
18 Devonshire Rd, W4   020 3701 8822   8–2A

One Pancras Sq, N1   020 3793 7210   9–3C
7 St John St, EC1   020 7253 8786   10–1B
Considering that the "simple" fare is "incidental" to
the "terrific selection of wines at reasonable prices",
the cooking is "surprisingly good" and "reasonably
priced" at these "bustling" and extremely popular
modern watering holes. / www.vinoteca.co.uk; 11 pm;
W1H & W4 Sun 4 pm; W1F 10.45 pm, Sun 9.30 pm;
EC1 closed Sun; W1H & W4 closed Sun D.

Vivat Bacchus £60 ❸❹❷
4 Hay's Ln, SE1   020 7234 0891   10–4C
47 Farringdon St, EC4   020 7353 2648   10–2A
A "fantastic range of mainly South African vintages"
helps provide the justification for consuming the
"perfectly cooked steaks" at this wine bar duo
with branches in Farringdon and Bankside. Top
Tip – don't miss the 'Cheese Room Experience'. /
www.vivatbacchus.co.uk; 10.30 pm; closed Sun.

VIVI WC1 NEW
Centre Point awaiting tel 5–1A
As part of the renovation of the entire, iconic Centre
Point complex, London restaurateurs rhubarb (Sky
Garden, Saatchi Gallery, Royal Albert Hall) will open
this new flagship restaurant as part of the bridge
link overlooking the new square in late 2017. /
WC1A 1DD; www.rhubarb.co.uk.

VQ £44 ❷❹❸
St Giles Hotel, Great Russell St, WC1
020 7636 5888   5–1A
325 Fulham Rd, SW10   020 7376 7224   6–3B
24 Pembridge Rd, W11   020 3745 7224   7–2B
9 Aldgate High St, EC3
020 3301 7224   10–2D NEW
"Very handy for early hours refuelling" – particularly
the venerable SW10 original of these late night
diners, which has provided "great all-day breakfasts"
(and all night ones) and "service with a smile" since
the '80s. / www.vingtquatre.co.uk; open 24 hours,
W11 1 am, Thu-Sat 3 am, Sun midnight; booking: max
6 online.

Vrisaki N22 £35 ❸❸❸
73 Middleton Rd   020 8889 8760   1–1C
"The facelift hasn't spoilt it!" – this venerable
Bounds Green Greek has updated its old taverna-
style decor in recent times, but the food (most
famously the humongous mezze special) is "still
really good". / N22 8LZ; @vrisakiuk; 11.30 pm, Sun 9
pm; closed Mon; No Amex.

Wagamama £44 ❷❸❷
"You know what to expect" and "you still get what
you pay for" at these "good staple" Asian canteens,
which "epitomise cheap and cheerful dining" and
whose "reliable and reasonably healthy" noodles and
curries are "great for a speedy, fresh-cooked meal",
particularly with kids in tow. / www.wagamama.com;

10 pm - 11.30 pm; EC2 Sat 9 pm; EC4 closed Sat & Sun; EC2 closed Sun; no booking.

Wahaca £37 3️⃣3️⃣3️⃣
"Fun and lighthearted" style – and providing "zingy" dishes at "great-value" prices, "fab cocktails" and "friendly service" – Thomasina Miers's feisty street-food chain *"shows no sign of decline, despite its expansion".* It's *"streets ahead of other Mexican groups"* and *"always a solid standby when you want a quick meal".* / www.wahaca.com; 11 pm, Sun 10.30 pm; W12, Charlotte St, SW19 Sun 10 pm; no booking or need 6+ to book.

Waka EC3 NEW
39a Eastcheap no tel 10–3D
'Nikkei' cuisine – Japanese meets Peruvian – features at this City newcomer, which opened in the shadow of the Walkie Talkie in September 2017. Upstairs is 'grab and go' and there's to be a 60-cover basement dining area. / EC3M 1DT; www.waka-uk.com; @WakaLdn; 6pm; No bookings.

The Wallace, The Wallace Collection W1 £51 2️⃣1️⃣5️⃣
Hertford Hs, Manchester Sq
020 7563 9505 3–1A
The "gorgeous setting" of the Wallace Collection's café, in the glass-covered atrium of one of London's most interesting smaller museums, "is delightful, especially on a bright day" – enough to transform a *"teatime treat" into a "fairytale experience".* But *"the food and service are not much more than so-so"* – *"I hope it's changed since the demise of Peyton & Byrne"* (the caterers who went into administration in October 2016). / W1U 3BN; www.peytonandbyrne.co.uk; 9.30 pm; Sun-Thu closed D; No Amex; booking max 10 may apply.

Walnut N4 NEW
The Arts Building, Morris Place
020 7263 5289 9–1D
This crowdfunded new neighbourhood restaurant in Finsbury Park's John Jones Arts Building opened in May 2017. Chef Emma Duggan is an Angela Hartnett protégée, and according to early reviews combines affordable scoff with a pleasing polished-concrete aesthetic. / N4 3JG; walnutdining.co.uk; @Walnut_Dining.

Waterloo Bar & Kitchen SE1 £55 2️⃣2️⃣2️⃣
131 Waterloo Rd 020 7928 5086 10–4A
"Handy for the Old Vic and Waterloo station", this busy brasserie provides *"good portions and friendly service".* Some say *"the food is OK rather than great",* but it's *"reasonably priced".* / SE1 8UR; www.barandkitchen.co.uk; @BarKitchen; 10.30 pm.

The Waterway W9 £52 2️⃣2️⃣2️⃣
54 Formosa St 020 7266 3557 9–4A
"The best time to go is in the summer when you can sit outside" on the big terrace of this tranquil hangout – a converted 20th century pub, attractively set on the water in Little Venice, where the food offering is "limited" but "reliable". / W9 2JU; www.thewaterway.co.uk; @thewaterway_; 11 pm, Sun 10.30 pm.

The Wells NW3 £55 2️⃣2️⃣3️⃣
30 Well Walk 020 7794 3785 9–1A
"Lovely after a walk on the Heath" – Hampstead's most popular pub (owned by Fay Maschler's sister, Beth Coventry) has a prime location and is *"a wonderful local, full of character and charm".* You can eat either in the *"very civilised" upstairs room or the downstairs bar – "the food is pricey, but in fairness I always end up enjoying it".* / NW3 1BX; thewellshampstead.london; @WellsHampstead; 10 pm, Sun 9.30 pm.

Westerns Laundry N5 NEW £57
34 Drayton Park 020 7700 3700 9–2D
Primeur owners David Gingell (chef) and Jérémie Cometto-Lingenheim (manager) have opened a second restaurant, in a modishly understated, converted 1950s former laundry (hence the name) in the shadow of the Emirates Stadium in Holloway. Early press reviews are ecstatic (Grace Dent food 5/5, ambience 5/5) regarding its simply prepared seasonal small plates – 'focusing on produce from the sea' – and educated selection of natural wines. / N5 1PB; www.westernslaundry.com; @WesternsLaundry; 10.30 pm, Sun 5 pm.

The Wet Fish Café NW6 £50 3️⃣3️⃣4️⃣
242 West End Lane 020 7443 9222 1–1B
A "high-quality café/bistro in the heart of West Hampstead" (named after the Art Deco-tiled fishmongers premises it inherited) that's *"always busy" thanks to its "relaxed" style and "good value".* Top Tip – *"great for brunch",* especially on Sunday, when it's very popular. / NW6 1LG; www.thewetfishcafe.co.uk; @thewetfishcafe; 10 pm; No Amex; booking D only; set weekday L £32 (FP).

White Bear EC1 £33 3️⃣3️⃣3️⃣
57 St. John St 020 7490 3535 10–1A
"What was until last year a depressing, down-at-heel pub (although with a good fringe theatre attached) has been enlarged by Young's". *"The theatre still thrives after its move upstairs",* while *"at the rear there's a pleasant, light dining area".* *"It's not gastro', but above average for pub food".* / EC1M 4AN; www.thewhitebearojs.co.uk; 11.30 pm, Fri midnight.

The White Onion SW19 £65 3️⃣3️⃣2️⃣
67 High St 020 8947 8278 11–2B
"To have a consistently good restaurant in Wimbledon" is a major boon, and this high quality two-year-old enchants its very large local fan club with "classic French cuisine" and "casual" style.

The worst thing anyone says about the place is that "while very good, it's not as good as its Surbiton sibling, The French Table". / SW19 5EE; www.thewhiteonion.co.uk; @thewhiteonionSW; 10.30 pm; closed Mon, Tue L, Wed L & Thu L; set weekday L £41 (FP).

The White Swan EC4   £62 🟦🟦🟦

108 Fetter Ln   020 7242 9696   10–2A
"Great bar snacks" and casual pub dishes can be had in this smart and often loud boozer, off Fleet Street. Or head upstairs for a more ambitious menu in the "much quieter" dining room. / EC4A 1ES; www.thewhiteswanlondon.com; @thewhiteswanEC4; 10 pm; closed Sat & Sun.

The Wigmore, The Langham
W1 [NEW]   £48

1c Portland Pl   020 7965 0198   2–1B
Michel Roux Jr oversees the 'quintessential British pub fare' (yes, you read that right) at this 're-imagining of the Great British pub', which opened in The Langham in July 2017. / W1B 1JA; www.the-wigmore.co.uk; @Langham_London; Mon-Wed midnight, The-Sat 1 am.

Wild Honey W1   £79 🟦🟦🟦

12 St George St   020 7758 9160   3–2C
Anthony Demetre's agreeably "restrained" (and business-friendly) Mayfair venture has won renown for its "intelligent and accomplished" cooking and "extensive and not outrageously priced wine list, with most available in 250ml carafes, so you can have two or three in the course of a meal". Top Tip – "very good lunch menu of British fare at reasonable prices" ("things you wouldn't necessarily choose but all well cooked and worth it if you are prepared to experiment"). / W1S 2FB; www.wildhoneyrestaurant.co.uk; @whrestaurant; 10.30 pm; closed Sun.

Wilmington EC1   £52 🟦🟦🟦

69 Rosebery Avenue   020 7837 1384   10–1A
Limited feedback on this handsome corner pub in Clerkenwell, but such reports as we have particularly recommend its "very good pre-Sadler's Wells deals on food". / EC1R 4RL; www.wilmingtonclerkenwell.com; @wilmingtonec1; 10pm, Fri & Sat 10.30pm , Sun 9pm.

Wiltons SW1   £95 🟦🟦🟦

55 Jermyn St   020 7629 9955   3–3C
"The courtesy and class is evident from the moment you make the reservation" at this "stalwart of St James" (est 1742, here since 1984): "a perfect and unchanging haven" for "the very best of British classics" – in particular "fabulous" fish and seafood (and also game). "Make sure there is plenty of money available on your credit card, as it is powerfully expensive, but it's "an ideal location for serious business discussions" ("I'd sign anything you put in front of me in this place, and then apologise

for having the wrong sort of pen!"). / SW1Y 6LX; www.wiltons.co.uk; @wiltons1742; 10.15 pm; closed Sat L & Sun; Jacket required; set weekday L £64 (FP).

The Windmill W1   £49 🟦🟦🟦

6-8 Mill St   020 7491 8050   4–2A
Looking for "great pies"? – You'll find 'em at this traditional Mayfair boozer where they headline the bill of "good old-fashioned British fare" at "reasonable prices" and in "huge portions"; cask beer, "excellent chips" and Sunday roasts are all tipped here too. / W1S 2AZ; www.windmillmayfair.co.uk; @tweetiepie_w1; 10 pm Sun 5 pm; closed Sat D & Sun.

The Wine Library EC3   £40 🟦🟦🟦

43 Trinity Sq   020 7481 0415   10–3D
"A huge choice of wines with only a modest corkage charge" is the irresistible draw to this ancient cellar bar near Tower Hill. "The food is casual party fare – pâtés, breads, cheeses, all very fresh". "Only go if you're not intending to do much work for the rest of the day." / EC3N 4DJ; www.winelibrary.co.uk; 7.30 pm; closed Mon D, Sat & Sun.

Winemakers Deptford SE8 [NEW]

209 Deptford High St   020 8305 6852   1–3D
It opened too late for survey feedback this year, but press reports suggest this casual wine bar from Winemakers Club, a Farringdon wine importers, is an important step in the gentrification of Deptford, providing accomplished cooking and a superior list of biodynamic wines. / SE8 3NT; thewinemakersclub. co.uk; 11 pm, Fri & Sat midnight, Sun 6 pm; closed Mon, Tue-Thu D only, Fri-Sat L & D, Sun L only.

THE WOLSELEY W1   £62 🟦🟦🟦

160 Piccadilly   020 7499 6996   3–3C
"Always bustling" and "a real occasion" – Corbin & King's "large, continental and sophisticated" Grand Café near The Ritz is "a marvellous, metropolitan meeting point" not least for the capital's movers 'n' shakers (it's "great for subtle star-spotting!") for whom the "courteous and very professional service" helps make it the town's No. 1 choice for business. The "brasserie comfort food is unambitious but well done", and it's as "a go-to venue for breakfast" (it's "THE place in London") that it particularly shines. Another Top Tip – "afternoon tea to die for". / W1J 9EB; www.thewolseley.com; @TheWolseleyRest; midnight, Sun 11 pm.

Wong Kei W1   £33 🟦🟦🟦

41-43 Wardour St   020 7437 8408   5–3A
"Service atrocious, ambience zero… but you can't beat their steaming bowls with change from £10 in central London!" This famous – and famously rude – multi-storey canteen in Chinatown "goes from strength to strength" thanks to its "ultra-cheap", and "incredibly reliable" chow. Abuse from the staff is so institutionalised "you can even buy a T-shirt with

'upstairs, downstairs' which is what they bark at you when you enter", but in recent years some regulars claim the treatment here is "more polite than in the past". / W1D 6PY; www.wongkeilondon.com; 11.15 pm, Sun 10.30 pm; Cash only.

Wright Brothers £66 4️⃣3️⃣3️⃣
13 Kingly St, W1   020 7434 3611   4–2B
56 Old Brompton Rd, SW7
020 7581 0131   6–2B
11 Stoney St, SE1   020 7403 9554   10–4C
Battersea Power Station, 188 Kirtling St, SW11
awaiting tel 11–1C NEW
8 Lamb St, E1   020 7377 8706   10–2D
"A haven for top notch oysters and shellfish" (they have their own Cornish farm and wholesalers) – these "bustling" bistros have grown from their Borough Market origins on the back of their "sparklingly fresh and delicious" dishes, plus "good wines by the glass". "That they're cramped is all part of the charm". Battersea is the latest addition to the family, and in SW7 fans tip "the little gem of a Mermaid Bar, like a luxurious grotto with elegant cocktails". / SE1 10 pm, Sat 11 pm; W1 11 pm, Sun 10 pm; E1 10.30 pm, Sun 9 pm; SW7 10.30 pm, Sun 9.30 pm; booking: max 8.

Xi'an Impression N7 £31 4️⃣2️⃣2️⃣
117 Benwell Rd   020 3441 0191   9–2D
Some of "the best authentic, lip-tingling Shaanxi food in the UK" can be found at this basic, Formica-tabled "little gem in the back streets of Holloway" – "bizarrely located across the road from the Emirates Stadium". "Their noodles are very fresh, incredibly tasty, beautifully cooked and so verrrry long!" / N7; www.xianimpression.co.uk; @xianimpression; 10 pm.

XU W1 NEW £60
30 Rupert St   020 3319 8147   4–3D
Backed by JKS Restaurants and the brains behind the hugely successful Bao chain; an elegant, wood-panelled, two-floor café serving traditional Taiwanese cooking and teas. Xu (named for co-founder and chef Erchen Chang's late grandfather) opened in Chinatown in early summer 2017 (too late for survey feedback). / W1D 6DL; xulondon.com; @XU_london; 11 pm.

Yalla Yalla £39 3️⃣2️⃣2️⃣
1 Green's Ct, W1   020 7287 7663   4–2D
12 Winsley St, W1   020 7637 4748   3–1C
Greenwich Peninsula Sq, SE10 0772 584 1372
9–3C
Tiny, "cheap 'n' cheerful" Lebanese street food cafés, whose "interesting" choice of "fresh and zingy" mezze and other dishes "never fails to deliver". / www.yalla-yalla.co.uk; Green's Court 11 pm, Sun 10 pm; Winsley Street 11.30 pm, Sat 11 pm; W1 closed Sun; booking min 10.

Yama Momo SE22 £53 4️⃣2️⃣3️⃣
72 Lordship Ln   020 8299 1007   1–4D
"Consistently delicious sushi" and inventive cocktails create the buzz at this "atmospheric local" in East Dulwich. It's an offshoot of Clapham's long-running Tsunami, bringing Pacific fusion elements to Japanese cuisine in a contemporary, clubby setting. / SE22 8HF; www.yamamomo.co.uk; @YamamomoRest; 10 pm, Fri & Sat 10.30 pm, Sun 9.30 pm; closed weekday L.

Yard Sale Pizza £35 4️⃣3️⃣2️⃣
54 Blackstock Rd, N4   020 7226 2651   9–1D
Hoe St, E17   020 8509 0888   1–1D NEW
105 Lower Clapton Rd, E5
020 3602 9090   14–1B
"Delicious, freshly made pizza with unusual toppings" attract raves for these hip pizzerias in Clapton, Walthamstow and Finsbury Park. They're "friendly", but "pretty basic" – "not a place to hang around". / 11 pm, Sun 10 pm; closed Mon-Thu L.

Yashin W8 £86 4️⃣3️⃣2️⃣
1a Argyll Rd   020 7938 1536   6–1A
This modern Japanese in Kensington inspired only a few reports this year: all of them, though, were highly complimentary regarding its ambitious cuisine. (Its lesser-known 'Ocean' branch, on the Old Brompton Road, continues to inspire this but more feedback to the effect that "prices are nuts, there's no real atmosphere, and the whole set-up is a bit weird".) / W8 7DB; www.yashinsushi.com; @Yashinsushi; 10 pm; booking max 7 may apply.

Yauatcha Soho £81 4️⃣3️⃣3️⃣
Broadwick Hs, 15-17 Broadwick St, W1
020 7494 8888   4–1C
Broadgate Circle, EC2   020 3817 9888   13–2B
"Fabulously tasty dim sum with a modern twist" and "slick" styling fuel the fun at this incredibly popular and vibey, Chinese-fusion duo, with the more moody Soho original still outscoring its big and "bright" Broadgate Circle spin-off. Service is the weakest link – it can be "somewhat haphazard". / W1 10 pm, Fri & Sat 10.30 pm; EC2 11.30 pm; EC2 closed Sun.

The Yellow House SE16 £45 3️⃣3️⃣3️⃣
126 Lower Rd   020 7231 8777   12–2A
"Reliably yummy" wood-fired pizza and charcoal grills are the menu mainstays at this "friendly" neighbourhood indie, right next to Surrey Quays station. / SE16 2UE; www.theyellowhouse.eu; @theyellowhousejazz; 10 pm, Sun 8 pm; closed Mon, Tue-Sat D only, Sun open L & D.

Yipin China N1 £45 4️⃣3️⃣2️⃣
70-72 Liverpool Rd   020 7354 3388   9–3D
An "unglamorous, cash-only" operation serving "spectacular Sichuan and Hunanese food" near Angel. "It's not fancy" – "decor is functional"

– "but that's part of the charm!" / N1 0QD; www.yipinchina.co.uk; 11 pm.

Yming W1   £45   [3][5][2]
35-36 Greek St   020 7734 2721   5–2A
This "reliable stalwart of the Soho Chinese food scene" provides "an oasis of calm" just a 1-minute walk from Chinatown. "Managed by the awesome William and Christine", its "serene" and "welcoming" style suits its older fanbase, as do the "interesting if un-challenging" dishes. Potentially under threat (like the nearby Soho Curzon) from demolition for Crossrail 2 – we hope they don't retire: "it would be the end of an institution… and some very good food!" / W1D 5DL; www.yminglondon.com; 11.45 pm.

Yolk EC2 NEW   £10
Container 4, Finsbury Avenue Sq   no tel   13–2B
A shipping container by Liverpool Street is the pop-up to more permanent home of this street food venture, where they know their way around an egg. / EC2M 2PA; www.yolklondon.com; @YolkLondon; 4 pm; L only, closed Sat & Sun.

York & Albany NW1   £59   [2][2][3]
127-129 Parkway   020 7592 1227   9–3B
Gordon Ramsay's Georgian tavern by Regent's Park is a large and handsome venue, with bags of potential, but while not totally lacking fans, its middling scores continue to confirm its performance as "nothing special". / NW1 7PS; www.gordonramsayrestaurants.com/york-and-a; @yorkandalbany; 10.30 pm, Sun 10 pm; booking essential.

Yoshi Sushi W6   £39   [3][3][2]
210 King St   020 8748 5058   8–2B
This nondescript-looking Korean/Japanese stalwart near Ravenscourt Park tube is worth discovering for its "reasonably priced" and dependable classic dishes. / W6 0RA; www.yoshisushi.co.uk; 11 pm, Sun 10.30 pm; closed Sun L.

Yoshino W1   £44   [4][4][2]
3 Piccadilly Pl   020 7287 6622   4–4C
Hiding in a side alley, this "favourite Japanese" is an "oasis of calm of the highest quality in Piccadilly". "The welcome is always amazing" ("I feel like a treasured friend"), and the food (which has had its ups and downs over the years) "very fresh and simple" but "artfully produced". There's quite a contrast in style between the ground floor counter and small upstairs space. / W1J 0DB; www.yoshino.net; @Yoshino_London; closed Sun.

Yosma W1   £51   [3][3][2]
50 Baker St   020 3019 6282   2–1A
It can be "off puttingly noisy" – at night, the background beats are sometimes "club-level loud" – but most reporters are "loving this new

Turkish-inspired venue on Baker Street", whose "beautifully spiced" dishes "beat the old skool Turkish joints" and are "sensibly priced" too. / W1U 7BT; www.yosma.london; @Yosma_London; 11 pm, Thu-Sat midnight; set weekday L £32 (FP).

Zafferano SW1   £90   [2][2][2]
15 Lowndes St   020 7235 5800   6–1D
"A lovely top-class Italian" is the verdict of most reporters on this "old-fashioned" (and business-friendly) Belgravian, which in the noughties was regularly fêted as London's best and which, on most accounts, "still produces really wonderful dishes, especially fresh pasta and fish". Its ratings continue to be hampered, though, by a disgruntled minority who think "it used to be fantastic, but has become stodgy". / SW1X 9EY; www.zafferanorestaurant.com; 10.30 pm, Sun 10 pm; set weekday L £60 (FP).

Zaffrani N1   £48   [3][2][2]
47 Cross St   020 7226 5522   9–3D
This "excellent and above-average local Indian" off Islington's main drag boasts an "unusual and well-executed menu". / N1 2BB; www.zaffrani.co.uk; 10.30 pm.

Zaibatsu SE10   £35   [4][3][2]
96 Trafalgar Rd   020 8858 9317   1–3D
"Very good Japanese food" and "cheapish" prices mean you should make the effort to "book in advance" at this Greenwich café. It's "hectic, basic and BYO, but all the nosh is prepared excellently". / SE10 9UW; www.zaibatsufusion.co.uk; @ong_teck; 11 pm; closed Mon; Cash only.

Zaika of Kensington W8 £65   [3][2][3]
1 Kensington High St   020 7795 6533   6–1A
"Exquisite flavours" have won renown for this spacious (somewhat "cavernous") banking hall conversion by Kensington Gardens Hotel as "one of the better Indians around". But marks fell a little this year, due to gripes about "hit-and-miss service" and the odd report of food that was "not as refined as in the past". / W8 5NP; www.zaikaofkensington.com; @ZaikaLondon; 10.45 pm, Sun 9.45 pm; closed Mon L; credit card required to book; set weekday L & pre-theatre £43 (FP).

Zelman Meats   £58   [5][4][4]
Harvey Nichols, Fifth Floor, 109-125 Knightsbridge, SW1   020 7201 8625   6–1D
2 St Anne's Ct, W1   020 7437 0566   4–1D
"The 'dirty' steak is just something else" at Misha Zelman's (of Goodman's fame) genius brainchild – a cutely tucked-away, industrial cool unit (with an offshoot in residence at Harvey Nicks), where, he has reinvented "steak as a fastish-food concept", providing "really superior steaks to share with generous side portions". There's also a "varied and not too expensive beer and wine list", which helps fuel the fun atmosphere. / W1 10.30 pm, Sun 8 pm;

SW1 10 pm, Sun 7 pm; N4 midnight; W1 closed Mon L, N4 closed Mon-Fri L.

Zeret SE5 £29 **4 5 3**
216-218 Camberwell Rd 020 7701 8587 1–3C
"Despite the bleak location, the food is anything but!" at this Camberwell café – *"a great find"* thanks to its *"very good value"* and unusual, traditional Ethiopian dishes, and a commitment to cater for meat-eaters and vegans alike. It helps that *"the people running it are incredibly nice"*. / SE5 0ED; www.zeretkitchen.com; 11 pm.

Zero Degrees SE3 £45 **3 3 4**
29-31 Montpelier Vale 020 8852 5619 1–4D
"You can't go wrong with pizza and a beer brewed in-house (and the moules frites are decent too)" at this popular Blackheath microbrewery – *"it's dead cheap too and has an amazing atmosphere!"* / SE3 0TJ; www.zerodegrees.co.uk; @Zerodegreesbeer; midnight, Sun 11.30 pm.

Zest, JW3 NW3 £60 **3 3 2**
341-351 Finchley Rd 020 7433 8955 1–1B
"Surprising and very satisfying" Middle Eastern cooking has won converts for this modern Israeli restaurant/café/bar in West Hampstead. *"It may not be quite as good"* (or as famous) *"as the Honeys, but ingredients are always fresh and excellent"*. / NW3 6ET; www.zestatjw3.co.uk; @ZESTatJW3; 9.45 pm; closed Fri & Sat L.

Zheng SW3 NEW £61
4 Sydney St 020 7352 9890 6–2C
On the 'revolving doors' Chelsea site most lately occupied by Brasserie Gustave (RIP), this swish, black-walled newcomer – sibling to the renowned Oxford Chinese/Malaysian operation – opened too late for survey feedback but to excellent reviews in late spring 2017: perhaps it will finally provide a formula that 'sticks' here. / SW3 6PP; www.zhengchelsea.co.uk; 11.30 pm, Sun 10 pm.

Zia Lucia N7 £35 **4 3 3**
157 Holloway Rd 020 7700 3708 9–2D
"The best thing to happen around Holloway Road for some time!" – this *"mega-busy"* yearling, built around a *"Dante-esque, wood fired oven"*, takes *"pizza into the realm of fine dining"* with its *"unique choice of vegetarian and easy-to-digest, 48-hour fermented doughs"* and *"perfect toppings"*. *"Remember to book, otherwise it's hopeless"*. / N7 8LX; www.zialucia.com; @zialuciapizza; 10.30 pm.

Ziani's SW3 £62 **2 3 2**
45 Radnor Walk 020 7351 5297 6–3C
"The tables are squashed together and it's hard to manoeuvre" at this *"friendly and welcoming"* trattoria just off the King's Road. *"Great fun"*, with lots of *"buzz, but not much privacy"* – *"it's full of locals"*, here for the *"good food and large portions"*.

/ SW3 4BP; www.ziani.co.uk; 11 pm, Sun 10 pm; set Sun L £40 (FP).

Zima W1 £44 **3 2 3**
45 Frith St 020 7494 9111 5–2A
"Russian street food" served in a speakeasy-style venue next door to Ronnie Scott's jazz club makes Russki celeb chef, Alexei Zimin's Soho yearling *"fun and something a bit different"*. / W1D 4SD; www.zima.bar; @ZimaLondon; 11.30 pm, Sun 8.30 pm; closed Mon; set weekday L £26 (FP).

Zoilo W1 £59 **4 3 3**
9 Duke St 020 7486 9699 3–1A
"I adore this place!" – this Argentinian bar between Selfridges and the Wallace Collection dazzles its small and varied fanclub with its *"frequently changing menu"* of *"very good tapas"*, complemented by an all-Argentinian wine list. / W1U 3EG; www.zoilo.co.uk; @Zoilo_London; 10.30 pm; closed Sun.

Zuma SW7 £82 **5 3 3**
5 Raphael St 020 7584 1010 6–1C
"Exceptional" Japanese-fusion cuisine still wins very consistent praise for this svelte, *"very buzzy"* Knightsbridge haunt, whose appeal – in its fifteenth year – still stacks up well. OK, there's some *"tossing around of black credit cards"* by its eurotrashy following, but this can make for *"awesome people-watching"*, and even though *"it's very expensive, it's worth it"*. / SW7 1DL; www.zumarestaurant.com; 10.45 pm, Sun 10.15 pm; booking max 8 may apply.

Tom Simmons SE1

The Wigmore W1

Temper City EC2

An asterisk (*) after an entry indicates exceptional or very good cooking

AMERICAN

Central
The Avenue *(SW1)*
Balthazar *(WC2)*
Big Easy *(WC2)*
Bodean's *(W1)*
Breakfast Club *(W1)*
The Chiltern Firehouse *(W1)*
Christopher's *(WC2)*
Colony Grill Room, Beaumont Hotel *(W1)*
Hai Cenato *(SW1)*
Hard Rock Café *(W1)*
Hubbard & Bell, Hoxton Hotel *(WC1)*
Jackson & Rye *(W1)*
Joe Allen *(WC2)*
Rainforest Café *(W1)*
Shake Shack *(WC1,WC2)*
Spuntino *(W1)*

West
Big Easy *(SW3)*
Bodean's *(SW6)*
Electric Diner *(W11)*
Jackson & Rye Chiswick *(W4)*
Pomona's *(W2)*
Stagolee's *(SW6)*

North
Breakfast Club Hoxton *(N1)*
Delisserie *(NW8)*
Frederick's *(N1)*

South
Bodean's *(SW17, SW4)*
Counter Vauxhall Arches *(SW8)**
Jackson & Rye Richmond, Hotham House *(TW9)*
The Joint *(SW9)*

East
Big Easy *(E14)*
Bodean's *(EC1, EC3)*
Breakfast Club *(E1)*
Pitt Cue Co *(EC2)**
Shake Shack *(E20)*

AUSTRALIAN

Central
Bronte *(WC2)*
Granger & Co *(SW1)*
Lantana Café *(W1)*
Timmy Green *(SW1)*

West
Granger & Co *(W11)*

North
Granger & Co *(N1)*
Lantana Cafe *(NW1)*

Sunday *(N1)**

South
Flotsam and Jetsam *(SW17)*
Lantana London Bridge *(SE1)*

East
Granger & Co, The Buckley Building *(EC1)*
Lantana Café *(EC1)*

BRITISH, MODERN

Central
The Alfred Tennyson *(SW1)*
Alyn Williams, Westbury Hotel *(W1)*
Andrew Edmunds *(W1)*
Aster Restaurant *(SW1)*
Aurora *(W1)*
Balthazar *(WC2)*
Barbecoa Piccadilly *(W1)*
Bellamy's *(W1)*
The Berners Tavern *(W1)*
Bob Bob Ricard *(W1)*
Bonhams Restaurant, Bonhams Auction House *(W1)**
The Botanist *(SW1)*
Cambridge Street Kitchen *(SW1)*
Le Caprice *(SW1)*
Caxton Grill *(SW1)*
Clipstone *(W1)**
The Collins Room *(SW1)*
Comptoir Café & Wine *(W1)*
Coopers Restaurant & Bar *(WC2)*
Daylesford Organic *(SW1,W1)*
Dean Street Townhouse *(W1)*
Dorchester Grill, Dorchester Hotel *(W1)*
Duck & Waffle Local *(SW1)*
Ducksoup *(W1)*
Ebury Restaurant & Wine Bar *(SW1)*
Fera at Claridge's, Claridge's Hotel *(W1)*
45 Jermyn Street *(SW1)*
The Frog *(WC2)**
Galvin at the Athenaeum *(W1)*
George in the Strand *(WC2)*
Gordon's Wine Bar *(WC2)*
The Grazing Goat *(W1)*
Great Queen Street *(WC2)*
Greenwood *(SW1)*
Ham Yard Restaurant, Ham Yard Hotel *(W1)*
Hardy's Brasserie *(W1)*
Hatchetts *(W1)*
Heddon Street Kitchen *(W1)*
Heliot Steak House *(WC2)**
Hix *(W1)*
Hush *(W1,WC1)*
Indigo, One Aldwych *(WC2)*
The Ivy *(WC2)*
The Ivy Café *(W1)*
The Ivy Market Grill *(WC2)*
Jar Kitchen *(WC2)*

The Keeper's House, Royal Academy *(W1)*
Kitty Fisher's *(W1)*
Langan's Brasserie *(W1)*
Little Social *(W1)*
Lorne *(SW1)**
Magpie *(W1)*
Marcus, The Berkeley *(SW1)*
Mews of Mayfair *(W1)*
Native *(WC2)**
Noble Rot *(WC1)*
The Norfolk Arms *(WC1)*
The Northall, Corinthia Hotel *(WC2)*
108 Brasserie *(W1)*
The Orange *(SW1)*
Ormer Mayfair *(W1)**
The Other Naughty Piglet *(SW1)**
The Pantechnicon *(SW1)*
Percy & Founders *(W1)*
The Petersham *(WC2)*
Picture *(W1)*
Pollen Street Social *(W1)*
Polpo at Ape & Bird *(WC2)*
Portland *(W1)**
The Portrait, National Portrait Gallery *(WC2)*
The Punchbowl *(W1)*
Quaglino's *(SW1)*
Quo Vadis *(W1)**
Rail House Café *(SW1)*
Roux at Parliament Square, RICS *(SW1)**
Roux at the Landau, The Langham *(W1)*
Saint Luke's Kitchen, Library *(WC2)*
Savoy Thames Foyer *(WC2)*
Seven Park Place *(SW1)**
Shampers *(W1)*
Social Eating House *(W1)**
Spring Restaurant *(WC2)*
Tate Britain, Whistler Restaurant *(SW1)*
10 Greek Street *(W1)**
Terroirs *(WC2)*
The Thomas Cubitt *(SW1)*
Tom's Kitchen, Somerset House *(WC2)*
Tredwell's *(WC2)*
Villandry *(W1)*
The Vincent Rooms, Westminster Kingsway College *(SW1)*
Vinoteca Seymour Place *(W1)*
VIVI *(WC1)*
VQ, St Giles Hotel *(WC1)*
Wild Honey *(W1)*
The Wolseley *(W1)*

West
The Abingdon *(W8)*
The Anglesea Arms *(W6)**
Babylon, Kensington Roof Gardens *(W8)*
Blue Boat *(W6)*

Bluebird *(SW3)*
The Brackenbury *(W6)**
Brackenbury Wine Rooms *(W6)*
Brinkley's *(SW10)*
The Builders Arms *(SW3)*
Charlotte's Place *(W5)*
Charlotte's W4 *(W4)*
Charlotte's W5, Dickens Yard *(W5)*
City Barge *(W4)*
Clarke's *(W8)**
Claude's Kitchen, Amuse
    Bouche *(SW6)**
The Colton Arms *(W14)*
Core by Clare Smyth *(W11)*
The Cross Keys *(SW3)*
The Dartmouth Castle *(W6)*
Daylesford Organic *(W11)*
The Dock Kitchen, Portobello
    Dock *(W10)*
The Dove *(W6)*
Duke of Sussex *(W4)*
Ealing Park Tavern *(W5)*
Elystan Street *(SW3)**
The Enterprise *(SW3)*
The Five Fields *(SW3)**
The Frontline Club *(W2)*
Harwood Arms *(SW6)**
The Havelock Tavern *(W14)*
Hedone *(W4)*
High Road Brasserie *(W4)*
The Hour Glass *(SW3)*
The Ivy Chelsea Garden *(SW3)*
The Ivy Kensington Brasserie *(W8)*
Julie's *(W11)*
Kensington Place *(W8)*
Kensington Square Kitchen *(W8)*
Kitchen W8 *(W8)**
The Ladbroke Arms *(W11)*
Launceston Place *(W8)*
The Ledbury *(W11)**
The Magazine Restaurant,
    Serpentine Gallery *(W2)*
Manuka Kitchen *(SW6)*
Marianne *(W2)**
maze Grill *(SW10)*
Medlar *(SW10)**
Megan's Delicatessen *(SW6)*
Mustard *(W6)*
No 197 Chiswick Fire Station *(W4)*
Parabola, Design Museum *(W8)*
Paradise by Way of Kensal
    Green *(W10)*
The Pear Tree *(W6)*
Rabbit *(SW3)*
Restaurant Ours *(SW3)*
Salt & Honey *(W2)*
The Sands End *(SW6)*
The Shed *(W8)**
Six Portland Road *(W11)**
Tangerine Dream, Chelsea Physic
    Garden *(SW3)*
Tom's Kitchen *(SW3)*
The Tommy Tucker *(SW6)*

The Truscott Arms *(W9)*
Vinoteca *(W4)*
VQ *(SW10, W11)*
The Waterway *(W9)*

North
The Booking Office, St Pancras
    Renaissance Hotel *(NW1)*
Bradley's *(NW3)*
The Bull *(N6)*
Caravan King's Cross *(N1)*
Chriskitch *(N1, N10)**
The Clifton *(NW8)*
Dandy *(N16)**
Dartmouth Arms *(NW5)*
The Drapers Arms *(N1)*
Fifteen *(N1)*
Frederick's *(N1)*
Gabeto Cantina *(NW1)*
The Good Egg *(N16)**
Haven Bistro *(N20)*
Heirloom *(N8)*
The Horseshoe *(NW3)*
Humble Grape *(N1)*
The Ivy Café *(NW8)*
James Cochran N1 *(N1)**
The Junction Tavern *(NW5)*
Juniper Tree *(NW3)*
The Landmark, Winter Garden *(NW1)*
The Lighterman *(N1)*
Oak N4 *(N4)*
Odette's *(NW1)**
Oldroyd *(N1)**
Parlour Kensal *(NW10)**
Pig & Butcher *(N1)**
Plum + Spilt Milk, Great Northern
    Hotel *(N1)*
The Red Lion & Sun *(N6)*
Rotunda Bar & Restaurant, Kings
    Place *(N1)*
Season Kitchen *(N4)*
Walnut *(N4)*
The Wells *(NW3)*
Westerns Laundry *(N5)*
The Wet Fish Café *(NW6)*

South
Albion *(SE1)*
Aqua Shard *(SE1)*
The Avalon *(SW12)*
Babette *(SE15)*
The Bingham *(TW10)**
Bistro Union *(SW4)*
Black Prince *(SE11)*
Blueprint Café *(SE1)*
La Bonne Bouffe *(SE22)*
The Brown Dog *(SW13)*
Brunswick House Café *(SW8)*
The Camberwell Arms *(SE5)**
Cannizaro House, Hotel du
    Vin *(SW19)*
Caravan Bankside *(SE1)*
Catford Constitutional Club *(SE6)*
Chez Bruce *(SW17)**

Counter Culture *(SW4)**
Craft London *(SE10)**
The Crooked Well *(SE5)*
The Dairy *(SW4)**
Duckroad *(SW8)*
The Dysart Petersham *(TW10)*
Earl Spencer *(SW18)*
Edwins *(SE1)*
Elliot's Café *(SE1)*
40 Maltby Street *(SE1)**
Franklins *(SE22)*
The Garden Cafe at the Garden
    Museum *(SE1)*
The Garrison *(SE1)*
The Glasshouse *(TW9)**
Globe Tavern *(SE1)*
The Green Room, The National
    Theatre *(SE1)*
The Guildford Arms *(SE10)*
Hood *(SW2)**
House Restaurant, National
    Theatre *(SE1)*
Humble Grape *(SW11)*
The Ivy Café *(SW19, TW9)*
The Ivy Tower Bridge *(SE1)*
Jules *(SW15)*
Lamberts *(SW12)**
LASSCO Bar & DIning *(SE1)*
Laughing Gravy *(SE1)*
The Lido Café, Brockwell
    Lido *(SE24)*
Louie Louie *(SE17)*
Lupins *(SE1)*
The Manor *(SW4)*
May The Fifteenth *(SW4)*
Menier Chocolate Factory *(SE1)*
Minnow *(SW4)*
Nutbourne *(SW11)*
Oblix *(SE1)*
Olympic, Olympic Studios *(SW13)*
Orchard *(SE4)*
Oxo Tower, Restaurant *(SE1)*
Oxo Tower, Brasserie *(SE1)*
The Palmerston *(SE22)**
Parlez *(SE4)*
Peckham Refreshment Rooms *(SE15)*
The Perry Vale *(SE23)*
Petersham Hotel *(TW10)*
Petersham Nurseries Cafe *(TW10)*
Pharmacy 2, Newport Street
    Gallery *(SE11)*
Plot *(SW17)*
The Plough *(SW14)*
Le Pont de la Tour *(SE1)*
Rivington Grill *(SE10)*
The Rosendale *(SE21)*
Salon Brixton *(SW9)**
Sea Containers, Mondrian
    London *(SE1)*
Skylon, South Bank Centre *(SE1)*
Skylon Grill *(SE1)*
Soif *(SW11)*
Sonny's Kitchen *(SW13)*

Sparrow (SE13)
The Spencer (SW15)
Story (SE1)*
The Swan at the Globe (SE1)
The Table (SE1)
Tate Modern Restaurant (SE1)
Tate Modern, Restaurant,
Level 6 (SE1)
Tom Simmons (SE1)
Tried & True (SW15)
Trinity (SW4)*
Trinity Upstairs (SW4)*
Tulse Hill Hotel (SE24)
Union Street Café (SE1)
The Victoria (SW14)
Waterloo Bar & Kitchen (SE1)
Winemakers Deptford (SE8)

East
Anglo (EC1)*
The Anthologist (EC2)
Bird of Smithfield (EC1)
Bistrotheque (E2)
Bob Bob Cité (EC3)
Bokan (E14)
The Botanist (EC2)
The Bothy (E14)
Bread Street Kitchen (EC4)
Café Below (EC2)
Cafe Football, Westfield
Stratford (E20)
Caravan (EC1, EC2)
Chiswell Street Dining Rooms (EC1)
City Social (EC2)
The Clove Club (EC1)*
The Culpeper (E1)
Darwin Brasserie (EC3)
The Don (EC4)
The Don Bistro and Bar (EC4)
Duck & Waffle (EC2)
Eat 17 (E17)
Ellory, Netil House (E8)
The Empress (E9)*
Fenchurch Restaurant, Sky
Garden (EC3)
The Frog (E1)*
Galvin HOP (E1)
The Green (EC1)
The Gun (E14)
High Timber (EC4)
Hilliard (EC4)*
Hoi Polloi, Ace Hotel (E1)
Humble Grape (EC4)
James Cochran EC3 (EC3)*
Jones & Sons (N16)*
The Jugged Hare (EC1)
Legs (E9)
Luca (EC1)
Lyle's (E1)*
Mare Street Market (E8)
The Mercer (EC2)
Merchants Tavern (EC2)

The Modern Pantry (EC1, EC2)
The Morgan Arms (E3)
The Narrow (E14)
Northbank (EC4)
One Canada Square (E14)
1 Lombard Street (EC3)
P Franco (E5)*
Paradise Garage (E2)*
Pidgin (E8)*
Princess of Shoreditch (EC2)
Rochelle Canteen (E2)
Rök (EC2)*
Sager + Wilde (E2)
St John Bread & Wine (E1)
Smith's Wapping (E1)*
Smiths of Smithfield, Top Floor (EC1)
Smiths of Smithfield, Ground
Floor (EC1)
Tom's Kitchen (E1, E14)
Treves & Hyde (E1)
The Vincent (E8)
Vinoteca (EC1)
VQ (EC3)
The White Swan (EC4)
Wilmington (EC1)
Yolk (EC2)

BRITISH, TRADITIONAL
Central
Boisdale of Belgravia (SW1)
Brown's Hotel, The English Tea
Room (W1)
Brown's Hotel, HIX Mayfair (W1)
Butler's Restaurant, The
Chesterfield Mayfair (W1)
Corrigan's Mayfair (W1)
Dinner, Mandarin Oriental (SW1)
The Game Bird at The Stafford
London (SW1)
GBR (SW1)
George in the Strand (WC2)
The Dining Room, The Goring
Hotel (SW1)
The Guinea Grill (W1)*
Hardy's Brasserie (W1)
Holborn Dining Room (WC1)
Rib Room, Jumeirah Carlton
Tower Hotel (SW1)
The Ritz (W1)
Rules (WC2)
The Savoy Hotel, Savoy Grill (WC2)
Scott's (W1)*
Shepherd's (SW1)
Simpson's in the Strand (WC2)
Strangers Dining Room, House
of Commons (SW1)
Tate Britain, Whistler Restaurant
(SW1)
The Wigmore, The Langham (W1)
Wiltons (SW1)
The Windmill (W1)

West
Bumpkin (SW3, SW7)
Maggie Jones's (W8)

North
The Gilbert Scott (NW1)
Piebury Corner (N1, N7)
St Johns (N19)
York & Albany (NW1)

South
The Anchor & Hope (SE1)*
Butlers Wharf Chop House (SE1)
Canton Arms (SW8)*
Goddards At Greenwich (SE10)
Jolly Gardeners (SW18)
Roast (SE1)
The Swan at the Globe (SE1)

East
Albion (E2)
Albion Clerkenwell (EC1)
Boisdale of Bishopsgate (EC2)
Bumpkin, Westfield Stratford
City (E20)
The Fox and Anchor (EC1)
Hix Oyster & Chop House (EC1)
The Marksman (E2)*
Paternoster Chop House (EC4)
E Pellicci (E2)
The Quality Chop House (EC1)
St John Bread & Wine (E1)
St John Smithfield (EC1)*
Simpson's Tavern (EC3)
Sweetings (EC4)
White Bear (EC1)
Wilmington (EC1)

DANISH
Central
Sticks'n'Sushi (WC2)*
West
Snaps & Rye (W10)
South
Sticks'n'Sushi (SE10, SW19)*
East
Sticks'n'Sushi (E14)*

EAST & CENT. EUROPEAN
Central
The Delaunay (WC2)
Fischer's (W1)
Gay Hussar (W1)
The Harcourt (W1)*
The Wolseley (W1)
West
Belvedere Restaurant (W8)
North
Bellanger (N1)
German Gymnasium (N1)
Kipferl (N1)

FISH & SEAFOOD
Central
Barbecoa Piccadilly *(W1)*
Bellamy's *(W1)*
Bentley's *(W1)*
Black Roe *(W1)*
Blandford Comptoir *(W1)*
Bonnie Gull *(W1)**
Bonnie Gull Seafood Shack *(W1)**
Burger & Lobster, Harvey Nichols *(SW1,W1)*
Estiatorio Milos *(SW1)*
Fancy Crab *(W1)*
Fishworks *(W1)*
Hix *(W1)*
J Sheekey Atlantic Bar *(WC2)*
Kaspar's Seafood and Grill, The Savoy Hotel *(WC2)*
Olivomare *(SW1)*
One-O-One, Park Tower Knightsbridge *(SW1)**
Ormer Mayfair *(W1)**
The Oystermen Seafood Kitchen & Bar *(WC2)*
Pescatori *(W1)*
Quaglino's *(SW1)*
Randall & Aubin *(W1)*
Rib Room, Jumeirah Carlton Tower Hotel *(SW1)*
Royal China Club *(W1)**
Scott's *(W1)**
Sexy Fish *(W1)*
J Sheekey *(WC2)*
Wiltons *(SW1)*
Wright Brothers *(W1)**

West
Bibendum Oyster Bar *(SW3)*
Big Easy *(SW3)*
The Chipping Forecast *(W11)*
The Cow *(W2)*
Geales *(W8)*
Kensington Place *(W8)*
London Shell Co. *(W2)**
Mandarin Kitchen *(W2)**
Outlaw's at The Capital *(SW3)**
The Summerhouse *(W9)*
Wright Brothers *(SW7)**

North
Bradley's *(NW3)*
Carob Tree *(NW5)*
Galley *(N1)*
Lure *(NW5)*
Olympus Fish *(N3)**
Prawn on the Lawn *(N1)**
Toff's *(N10)*
Two Brothers *(N3)*

South
Applebee's Fish *(SE1)**
fish! *(SE1)*
Le Querce *(SE23)**
Rick Stein *(SW14)*

Sea Containers, Mondrian London *(SE1)*
Wright Brothers *(SE1, SW11)**

East
Angler, South Place Hotel *(EC2)*
Burger & Lobster *(EC1, EC4)*
Fish Central *(EC1)*
Fish Market *(EC2)*
Hix Oyster & Chop House *(EC1)*
The Royal Exchange Grand Café, The Royal Exchange *(EC3)*
Smith's Wapping *(E1)**
Sweetings *(EC4)*
Wright Brothers *(E1)**

FRENCH
Central
Alain Ducasse at The Dorchester *(W1)*
Antidote Wine Bar *(W1)*
L'Artiste Musclé *(W1)*
L'Atelier de Joel Robuchon *(WC2)*
The Balcon, Sofitel St James *(SW1)*
Bar Boulud, Mandarin Oriental *(SW1)*
Bellamy's *(W1)*
Blanchette *(W1)**
Blandford Comptoir *(W1)*
Bon Vivant *(WC1)*
Boudin Blanc *(W1)*
Boulestin *(SW1)*
Brasserie Zédel *(W1)*
Café Monico *(W1)*
Céleste, The Lanesborough *(SW1)*
Cigalon *(WC2)*
Clarette *(W1)*
Clos Maggiore *(WC2)*
Colbert *(SW1)*
L'Escargot *(W1)**
Ferdi *(W1)*
Frenchie *(WC2)**
Galvin at Windows, Park Lane London Hilton Hotel *(W1)*
Galvin Bistrot de Luxe *(W1)*
Le Garrick *(WC2)*
Gauthier Soho *(W1)**
Le Gavroche *(W1)**
The Greenhouse *(W1)*
Hélène Darroze, The Connaught Hotel *(W1)*
Henrietta *(WC2)*
maze *(W1)*
Mon Plaisir *(WC2)*
Neo Bistro *(W1)*
The Ninth London *(W1)**
Noizé *(W1)*
Les 110 de Taillevent *(W1)**
Orrery *(W1)*
Otto's *(WC1)**
La Petite Maison *(W1)**
Pétrus *(SW1)*
Pied à Terre *(W1)**

La Poule au Pot *(SW1)*
Prix Fixe *(W1)*
Relais de Venise L'Entrecôte *(W1)*
Savoir Faire *(WC1)*
The Savoy Hotel, Savoy Grill *(WC2)*
Seven Park Place *(SW1)**
Sketch, Lecture Room *(W1)**
Sketch, Gallery *(W1)*
The Square *(W1)*
Terroirs *(WC2)*
28-50 *(W1)*
Villandry *(W1)*
Villandry St James's *(SW1)*
The Wallace, The Wallace Collection *(W1)*

West
Albertine *(W12)*
Angelus *(W2)*
Bandol *(SW10)*
Bel Canto, Corus Hotel Hyde Park *(W2)*
Belvedere Restaurant *(W8)*
Bibendum *(SW3)*
Bibendum Oyster Bar *(SW3)*
Cepages *(W2)*
Cheyne Walk Brasserie *(SW3)*
Le Colombier *(SW3)*
L'Etranger *(SW7)*
Gordon Ramsay *(SW3)*
Michael Nadra *(W4)**
Orée *(SW10, SW3)*
Quantus *(W4)**
La Trompette *(W4)**
Le Vacherin *(W4)*

North
L'Absinthe *(NW1)*
L'Aventure *(NW8)*
Bistro Aix *(N8)**
Bradley's *(NW3)*
La Cage Imaginaire *(NW3)*
Melange *(N8)*
Le Mercury *(N1)*
Michael Nadra *(NW1)**
Oslo Court *(NW8)**
Patron *(NW5)*
Petit Pois Bistro *(N1)*
Le Sacré-Coeur *(N1)*
Table Du Marche *(N2)*
The Wells *(NW3)*

South
Augustine Kitchen *(SW11)*
Boro Bistro *(SE1)*
Brasserie Toulouse-Lautrec *(SE11)*
La Buvette *(TW9)*
Casse-Croute *(SE1)**
Counter Vauxhall Arches *(SW8)**
Gastronhome *(SW11)**
Gazette *(SW11, SW12, SW15)*
Petit Ma Cuisine *(TW9)*
Pique Nique *(SE1)*
Le Salon Privé *(TW1)**

Sinabro *(SW1)*
Soif *(SW1)*
The White Onion *(SW19)*

East

Le Bar *(EC1)*
Blanchette East *(E1)**
Bleeding Heart Restaurant *(EC1)*
Cabotte *(EC2)**
Café du Marché *(EC1)*
Club Gascon *(EC1)*
Comptoir Gascon *(EC1)*
Coq d'Argent *(EC2)*
La Dame de Pic London *(EC3)*
The Don *(EC4)*
La Ferme London *(EC1)*
Galvin La Chapelle *(E1)*
James Cochran EC3 *(EC3)**
Lutyens *(EC4)*
Plateau *(E14)*
Provender *(E11)*
Relais de Venise L'Entrecôte
   (E14, EC2)
The Royal Exchange Grand
   Café, The Royal Exchange *(EC3)*
Sauterelle, Royal Exchange *(EC3)*
Tratra *(E2)*
28-50 *(EC4)*

FUSION

Central

Asia de Cuba, St Martin's Lane
   Hotel *(WC2)*
Bubbledogs, Kitchen Table *(W1)**
Carousel *(W1)**
La Porte des Indes *(W1)*
The Providores and Tapa Room *(W1)**
Twist *(W1)**

West

E&O *(W11)*
Eight Over Eight *(SW3)*
L'Etranger *(SW7)*
108 Garage *(W10)**
Romulo Café *(W8)*

North

Caravan *(N1)*
The Good Egg *(N16)**
The Petite Coree *(NW6)**

South

Caravan *(SE1)*
Tsunami *(SW4)**

East

Caravan *(EC1)*

GAME

Central

Bocca Di Lupo *(W1)**
Boisdale of Belgravia *(SW1)*
Mac & Wild *(W1)**

Rules *(WC2)*
Wiltons *(SW1)*

West

Harwood Arms *(SW6)**

South

The Anchor & Hope *(SE1)**

East

Boisdale of Bishopsgate *(EC2)*
The Jugged Hare *(EC1)*
Mac & Wild *(EC2)**

GREEK

Central

Estiatorio Milos *(SW1)*
Meraki *(W1)*
Opso *(W1)*

West

Mazi *(W8)*

North

Carob Tree *(NW5)*
The Greek Larder, Arthouse *(N1)*
Lemonia *(NW1)*
Vrisaki *(N22)*

South

Peckham Bazaar *(SE15)**

East

Kolossi Grill *(EC1)*

HUNGARIAN

Central

Gay Hussar *(W1)*

INTERNATIONAL

Central

Boulestin *(SW1)*
Colony Grill Room, Beaumont
   Hotel *(W1)*
Cork & Bottle *(WC2)*
Flavour Bastard *(W1)*
Foley's *(W1)**
La Fromagerie Bloomsbury *(WC1)*
La Fromagerie Café *(W1)*
Gordon's Wine Bar *(WC2)*
Isabel *(W1)*
Jikoni *(W1)*
Mere *(W1)*
Motcombs *(SW1)*
The 10 Cases *(WC2)*
Test Kitchen *(W1)*

West

The Admiral Codrington *(SW3)*
The Andover Arms *(W6)*
Annie's *(W4)*
No.11 Cadogan Gardens *(SW3)*
The Kensington Wine Rooms *(W8)*
Melody at St Paul's *(W14)*
Mona Lisa *(SW10)*
Rivea, Bulgari Hotel *(SW7)*

North

Andi's *(N16)*
Banners *(N8)*
Bull & Last *(NW5)*
8 Hoxton Square *(N1)*
La Fromagerie *(N5)*
Haven Bistro *(N20)*
Primeur *(N5)**
Salut *(N1)**

South

Annie's *(SW13)*
Arthur Hooper's *(SE1)*
Brookmill *(SE8)*
Joanna's *(SE19)*
The Light House *(SW19)*
London House *(SW11)*
Minnow *(SW4)*
Pedler *(SE15)*
Platform1 *(SE22)*
Rabot 1745 *(SE1)*
Sparrow *(SE13)*
Spinach *(SE22)*
Tulse Hill Hotel *(SE24)*
Vivat Bacchus *(SE1)*
The Yellow House *(SE16)*

East

Blixen *(E1)*
Bokan *(E14)*
Dokke *(E1)*
Eat 17 *(E9)*
The Laughing Heart *(E2)*
Niche *(EC1)*
Sager + Wilde Restaurant *(E2)*
Typing Room, Town Hall Hotel *(E2)**
Vivat Bacchus *(EC4)*
The Wine Library *(EC3)*

IRISH

West

The Cow *(W2)*
The Sands End *(SW6)*

North

Summers *(NW6)*

ITALIAN

Central

Al Duca *(SW1)*
Assunta Madre *(W1)*
Bar Italia *(W1)*
Bar Termini *(W1)*
Il Baretto *(W1)*
Bernardi's *(W1)*
Bocca Di Lupo *(W1)**
Bocconcino *(W1)*
Briciole *(W1)*
C London *(W1)*
Cacio & Pepe *(SW1)*
Café Murano *(SW1)*
Café Murano Pastificio *(WC2)*
Caffè Caldesi *(W1)*

Caraffini *(SW1)*
Cecconi's *(W1)*
Chucs *(W1)*
Ciao Bella *(WC1)*
Como Lario *(SW1)*
Il Convivio *(SW1)**
Da Mario *(WC2)*
Dehesa *(W1)*
Delfino *(W1)**
Enoteca Turi *(SW1)*
Franco's *(SW1)*
Fucina *(W1)*
Fumo *(WC2)*
Gustoso Ristorante & Enoteca *(SW1)*
Hai Cenato *(SW1)*
Latium *(W1)*
Locanda Locatelli, HyattRegency *(W1)**
Luce e Limoni *(WC1)**
Made in Italy James St *(W1)*
Margot *(WC2)**
Mele e Pere *(W1)*
Murano *(W1)**
Novikov (Italian restaurant) *(W1)*
Obicà *(W1)*
Oliveto *(SW1)**
Olivo *(SW1)*
Olivocarne *(SW1)*
Olivomare *(SW1)*
Opera Tavern *(WC2)**
Osteria Dell'Angolo *(SW1)*
Il Pampero *(SW1)*
Pastaio *(W1)*
Pescatori *(W1)*
Polpetto *(W1)*
Polpo *(W1,WC2)*
La Porchetta Pizzeria *(WC1)*
Princi *(W1)*
QP LDN *(W1)*
Quirinale *(SW1)**
Ristorante Frescobaldi *(W1)*
Rossopomodoro, John Lewis *(W1,WC2)*
Sale e Pepe *(SW1)*
Salt Yard *(W1)*
San Carlo Cicchetti *(W1,WC2)*
Santini *(SW1)*
Sardo *(W1)*
Sartoria *(W1)*
Savini at Criterion *(W1)*
Signor Sassi *(SW1)*
Theo Randall *(W1)*
Tozi *(SW1)*
2 Veneti *(W1)*
Vasco & Piero's Pavilion *(W1)*
Veneta *(SW1)*
Il Vicolo *(SW1)*
Zafferano *(SW1)*

West

Aglio e Olio *(SW10)*
L'Amorosa *(W6)**
Assaggi *(W2)**
Assaggi Bar & Pizzeria *(W2)**

The Bird in Hand *(W14)*
Buona Sera *(SW3)*
Chelsea Cellar *(SW10)**
Chucs *(W11)*
Cibo *(W14)**
Da Mario *(SW7)*
Daphne's *(SW3)*
La Delizia Limbara *(SW3)*
Edera *(W11)*
Essenza *(W11)*
La Famiglia *(SW10)*
Frantoio *(SW10)*
Locanda Ottomezzo *(W8)*
Lucio *(SW3)*
Made in Italy *(SW3)*
Manicomio *(SW3)*
Mediterraneo *(W11)*
Mona Lisa *(SW10)*
Nuovi Sapori *(SW6)*
The Oak W12 *(W12,W2)*
Obicà *(SW3)*
Osteria Basilico *(W11)*
Pappa Ciccia *(SW6)*
Pellicano Restaurant *(SW3)*
Pentolina *(W14)**
Polpo *(SW3,W11)*
Il Portico *(W8)*
Portobello Ristorante Pizzeria *(W11)*
The Red Pepper *(W9)*
Riccardo's *(SW3)*
Rigo' *(SW6)*
The River Café *(W6)*
Rossopomodoro *(SW10)*
Sapori Sardi *(SW6)*
Scalini *(SW3)*
Stecca *(SW10)*
Stuzzico *(W2)*
Theo's Simple Italian *(SW5)*
Villa Di Geggiano *(W4)*
Ziani's *(SW3)*

North

Anima e Cuore *(NW1)**
Artigiano *(NW3)*
L'Artista *(NW11)*
La Collina *(NW1)*
500 *(N19)*
Giacomo's *(NW2)*
Il Guscio *(N5)*
Melange *(N8)*
Messapica *(NW10)*
Osteria Tufo *(N4)*
Ostuni *(N6, NW6)*
Passione e Tradizione *(N15)**
Pasta Remoli *(N4)*
Pizzeria Pappagone *(N4)*
La Porchetta Pizzeria *(N1, N4, NW1)*
Quartieri *(NW6)**
Radici *(N1)*
The Rising Sun *(NW7)*
Rugoletta *(N12, N2)*
Sarracino *(NW6)**
Trullo *(N1)**

Villa Bianca *(NW3)*

South

A Cena *(TW1)*
Al Forno *(SW15, SW19)*
Artusi *(SE15)**
Bacco *(TW9)*
Belpassi Bros *(SW17)*
Al Boccon di'vino *(TW9)*
Buona Sera *(SW11)*
Capricci *(SE1)**
Fiume *(SW8)*
Luciano's *(SE12)*
Macellaio RC *(SE1)*
Made in Italy *(SW19)*
Mercato Metropolitano *(SE1)*
Numero Uno *(SW11)*
O'ver *(SE1)**
Osteria Antica Bologna *(SW11)*
Padella *(SE1)**
Pizza Metro *(SW11)*
Pizzeria Rustica *(TW9)*
Pulia *(SE1)*
Le Querce *(SE23)**
Riva *(SW13)*
The Table *(SE1)*

East

L'Anima *(EC2)**
L'Anima Café *(EC2)*
Apulia *(EC1)*
Bombetta *(E11)*
Il Bordello *(E1)*
Campania & Jones *(E2)*
Canto Corvino *(E1)**
Caravaggio *(EC3)*
Emilia's Crafted Pasta *(E1)**
Lardo Bebè *(E8)*
Luca *(EC1)*
Macellaio RC *(EC1)*
Manicomio *(EC2)*
The Ned *(EC2)*
Obicà *(E14, EC4)*
Osteria, Barbican Centre *(EC2)*
Palatino *(EC1)**
E Pellicci *(E2)*
Polpo *(EC1)*
Pomaio *(E1)*
Popolo *(EC2)**
La Porchetta Pizzeria *(EC1)*
Rotorino *(E8)*
Rucoletta *(EC2)*
Santore *(EC1)**
Super Tuscan *(E1)**
Taberna Etrusca *(EC4)*
Verdi's *(E1)*

MEDITERRANEAN

Central

About Thyme *(SW1)*
Blandford Comptoir *(W1)*
Massimo, Corinthia Hotel *(WC2)*
The Ninth London *(W1)**

Nopi *(W1)**
The Norfolk Arms *(WC1)*
100 Wardour Street *(W1)*
Opso *(W1)*
Riding House Café *(W1)*
Vagabond Wines *(SW1,W1)*

West
Adams Café *(W12)*
The Atlas *(SW6)**
Ceru *(SW7)**
Cumberland Arms *(W14)**
Locanda Ottomezzo *(W8)*
Made in Italy *(SW3)*
Mediterraneo *(W11)*
The Oak W12 *(W12)*
Raoul's Café *(W9)*
Raoul's Café & Deli *(W11)*
The Swan *(W4)*
Vagabond Wines *(SW6)*

North
Alcedo *(N7)*
Lady Mildmay *(N1)*
The Little Bay *(NW6)*
Sardine *(N1)*
Vinoteca *(N1)*

South
Bean & Hop *(SW18)*
The Bobbin *(SW4)**
Fish in a Tie *(SW11)*
The Fox & Hounds *(SW11)**
Gourmet Goat *(SE1)**
Peckham Bazaar *(SE15)**
Sail Loft *(SE10)*
Vagabond Wines *(SW11)*

East
Brawn *(E2)**
The Eagle *(EC1)**
Morito *(EC1)**
Tuyo *(E2)*
Vagabond Wines *(E1)*
Vinoteca *(EC1)*

ORGANIC
Central
Daylesford Organic *(SW1,W1)*
West
Daylesford Organic *(W11)*
North
Juniper Tree *(NW3)*
East
Smiths of Smithfield, Dining Room *(EC1)*

POLISH
West
Daquise *(SW7)*
Ognisko Restaurant *(SW7)*

South
Baltic *(SE1)**

PORTUGUESE
West
Lisboa Pâtisserie *(W10)*
South
Bar Douro *(SE1)**
East
Corner Room *(E2)*
Eyre Brothers *(EC2)**
Taberna do Mercado *(E1)*

RUSSIAN
Central
Bob Bob Ricard *(W1)*
Mari Vanna *(SW1)*
Zima *(W1)*

SCANDINAVIAN
Central
Aquavit *(SW1)*
Bageriet *(WC2)**
The Harcourt *(W1)**
Nordic Bakery *(W1)*
Nordic Bakery *(WC2)*
Scandinavian Kitchen *(W1)*
Texture *(W1)**
West
Flat Three *(W11)**
North
Rök *(N1)**

SCOTTISH
Central
Boisdale of Belgravia *(SW1)*
Boisdale of Mayfair *(W1)*
Mac & Wild *(W1)**
East
Boisdale of Bishopsgate *(EC2)*
Boisdale of Canary Wharf *(E14)*
Mac & Wild *(EC2)**

SPANISH
Central
About Thyme *(SW1)*
Ametsa with Arzak Instruction, Halkin Hotel *(SW1)*
Aqua Nueva *(W1)*
Barrafina *(W1,WC2)**
Barrica *(W1)*
Cigala *(WC1)*
Dehesa *(W1)*
Donostia *(W1)**
Drakes Tabanco *(W1)*
Ember Yard *(W1)*
Encant *(WC2)**

Eneko at One Aldwych, One Aldwych Hotel *(WC2)*
Goya *(SW1)*
Ibérica, Zig Zag Building *(SW1,W1)*
Kitty Fisher's *(W1)*
Lurra *(W1)*
Morada Brindisa Asador *(W1)*
Opera Tavern *(WC2)**
El Pirata *(W1)*
Rambla *(W1)*
Sabor *(W1)*
Salt Yard *(W1)*
Sibarita *(WC2)*
Social Wine & Tapas *(W1)*
Street XO *(W1)*

West
Cambio de Tercio *(SW5)*
Capote Y Toros *(SW5)*
Casa Brindisa *(SW7)*
Duke of Sussex *(W4)*
Tendido Cero *(SW5)*
Tendido Cuatro *(SW6)*

North
Bar Esteban *(N8)**
Café del Parc *(N19)**
Camino King's Cross *(N1)*
Lluna *(N10)*
El Parador *(NW1)*
Thyme and Lemon *(N1)*
Trangallan *(N16)**
28 Church Row *(NW3)**

South
Boqueria *(SW2, SW8)**
Brindisa Food Rooms *(SW9)*
Camino Bankside *(SE1)*
Gremio de Brixton, St Matthew's Church *(SW2)*
José *(SE1)**
Little Taperia *(SW17)*
LOBOS Meat & Tapas *(SE1)**
Mar I Terra *(SE1)*
Meson don Felipe *(SE1)*
Pizarro *(SE1)*
Tapas Brindisa *(SE1)*

East
Bravas *(E1)*
Camino Blackfriars *(EC4)*
Camino Monument *(EC3)*
Eyre Brothers *(EC2)**
Hispania *(EC3)*
Ibérica *(E14, EC1)*
José Pizarro *(EC2)*
Morito *(E2, EC1)**
Moro *(EC1)**
Sagardi *(EC2)*

STEAKS & GRILLS
Central
Barbecoa, Nova *(SW1)*
Barbecoa Piccadilly *(W1)*

Beast *(W1)*
Bentley's *(W1)*
Black Roe *(W1)*
Blacklock *(W1)**
Bodean's *(W1)*
Boisdale of Mayfair *(W1)*
Bukowski Grill *(W1)*
Christopher's *(WC2)*
Cut, 45 Park Lane *(W1)*
Flat Iron *(W1,WC2)**
Foxlow *(W1)*
Goodman *(W1)**
The Guinea Grill *(W1)**
Hawksmoor *(W1,WC2)*
Heliot Steak House *(WC2)**
M Restaurant Victoria Street,
   Zig Zag Building *(SW1)*
MASH Steakhouse *(W1)*
maze Grill *(W1)*
Le Relais de Venise L'Entrecôte *(W1)*
Rib Room, Jumeirah Carlton Tower
   Hotel *(SW1)*
Rowley's *(SW1)*
Smith & Wollensky *(WC2)*
Sophie's Steakhouse *(W1)*
34 Mayfair *(W1)*
Zelman Meats *(SW1,W1)**
Zoilo *(W1)**

West
Bodean's *(SW6)*
Flat Iron *(W10)**
Foxlow *(W4)*
Haché *(SW10)*
Hanger *(SW6)*
Hawksmoor Knightsbridge *(SW3)*
Lockhouse *(W2)*
Macellaio RC *(SW7)*
Megan's Delicatessen *(SW6)*
No 197 Chiswick Fire Station *(W4)*
Popeseye *(W14)*
Smokehouse Chiswick *(W4)*
Sophie's Steakhouse *(SW10)*

North
Haché *(NW1)*
Popeseye *(N19)*
Smokehouse Islington *(N1)*

South
Arlo's *(SW12)*
Bodean's *(SW4)*
Bukowski Grill, Brixton Market *(SW9)*
Cau *(SE3, SW19)*
Coal Rooms *(SE15)*
The Coal Shed *(SE1)*
Counter Vauxhall Arches *(SW8)**
Foxlow *(SW12)*
Hawksmoor *(SE1)*
Knife *(SW4)**
M Bar & Grill Twickenham *(TW1)*
Macellaio RC *(SW11)*
Naughty Piglets *(SW2)**
Oblix *(SE1)*

Popeseye *(SW15)*

East
Aviary *(EC2)*
Barbecoa *(EC4)*
Bodean's *(EC1, EC3)*
Buen Ayre *(E8)*
Bukowski Grill, Boxpark *(E1)*
Cau *(E1)*
Flat Iron *(EC2)**
Foxlow *(EC1)*
Goodman *(E14)**
Goodman City *(EC2)**
The Grill at McQueen *(EC2)*
Hawksmoor *(E1, EC2)*
Hill & Szrok *(E8)**
Hix Oyster & Chop House *(EC1)*
Jones & Sons *(N16)**
The Jones Family Project *(EC2)**
M Restaurant Threadneedle
   Street *(EC2)*
Paternoster Chop House *(EC4)*
Relais de Venise L'Entrecôte *(E14, EC2)*
Simpson's Tavern *(EC3)*
Smith's Wapping *(E1)**
Smiths of Smithfield, Top Floor *(EC1)*
Smiths of Smithfield, Dining
   Room *(EC1)*
Smiths of Smithfield, Ground
   Floor *(EC1)*
Temple & Sons *(EC2)*
The Tramshed *(EC2)*

SWISS
Central
St Moritz *(W1)*

VEGETARIAN
Central
by Chloe *(WC2)*
Chettinad *(W1)**
Ethos *(W1)*
Galvin at the Athenaeum *(W1)*
The Gate *(W1)**
Malabar Junction *(WC1)*
Mildreds *(W1)*
Ormer Mayfair *(W1)**
Ragam *(W1)**
Rasa *(W1)*
Rasa Maricham, Holiday Inn
   Hotel *(WC1)*
Sagar *(W1)*
The Square *(W1)*
Texture *(W1)**
tibits *(W1)*

West
Farmacy *(W2)*
The Gate *(W6)**
Sagar *(W6)*

North
Chutneys *(NW1)*

Diwana Bhel-Poori House *(NW1)*
Jashan *(N8)**
Manna *(NW3)*
Mildreds *(N1, NW1)*
Rani *(N3)**
Rasa *(N16)*
Sakonis *(HA0)**
Vijay *(NW6)*

South
Ganapati *(SE15)**
Le Pont de la Tour *(SE1)*
Skylon, South Bank Centre *(SE1)*
Spinach *(SE22)*
Sree Krishna *(SW17)**
Tas Pide *(SE1)*
tibits *(SE1)*

East
The Gate *(EC1)**
Mildreds *(E8)*
Vanilla Black *(EC4)*

AFTERNOON TEA
Central
Brown's Hotel, The English Tea
   Room *(W1)*
Butler's Restaurant, The
   Chesterfield Mayfair *(W1)*
Dalloway Terrace, Bloomsbury
   Hotel *(WC1)*
The Collins Room, Berkeley
   Hotel *(SW1)*
The Delaunay *(WC2)*
Fortnum & Mason, The Diamond
   Jubilee Tea Salon *(W1)*
La Fromagerie Café *(W1)*
Galvin at the Athenaeum *(W1)*
The Game Bird at The Stafford
   London *(SW1)*
The Goring Hotel *(SW1)*
Ham Yard, Ham Hotel *(W1)*
Palm Court, The Langham *(W1)*
Maison Bertaux *(W1)*
Oscar Wilde Bar at Cafe Royal *(W1)*
The Promenade at The
   Dorchester *(W1)*
The Ritz, Palm Court *(W1)*
Savoy Thames Foyer *(WC2)*
Sketch, Gallery *(W1)*
Villandry *(W1, SW1)*
The Wallace, The Wallace
   Collection *(W1)*
The Wolseley *(W1)*
Yauatcha *(W1)**

West
Farmacy *(W2)*
No.11 Cadogan Gardens *(SW3)*

North
The Booking Office, St Pancras
   Renaissance Hotel *(NW1)*

181

Brew House Café, Kenwood
  House *(NW3)*
The Landmark, Winter Garden *(NW1)*

South

Cannizaro House,
  Hotel du Vin *(SW19)*
House Restaurant, National
  Theatre *(SE1)*
Oxo Tower, Brasserie *(SE1)*
Petersham Hotel *(TW10)*
Petersham Nurseries Cafe *(TW10)*
Rabot *(SE1)*
TING *(SE1)*

East

Hoi Polloi, Ace Hotel *(E1)*

BURGERS, ETC

Central

Bar Boulud, Mandarin Oriental *(SW1)*
Bleecker Burger *(SW1)**
Bobo Social *(W1)*
Bodean's *(W1)*
Burger & Lobster, Harvey
  Nichols *(SW1,W1,WC1)*
Five Guys *(WC2)*
Goodman *(W1)**
Haché *(WC1)*
Hard Rock Café *(W1)*
Hawksmoor *(W1,WC2)*
Joe Allen *(WC2)*
MEATLiquor *(W1)*
MEATliquor *(WC1)*
MEATmarket *(WC2)*
Opera Tavern *(WC2)**
Patty and Bun *(W1)**
Rainforest Café *(W1)*
Shake Shack *(SW1,WC1,WC2)*
Tommi's Burger Joint *(W1)*
Zoilo *(W1)**

West

The Admiral Codrington *(SW3)*
Big Easy *(SW3)*
Bodean's *(SW6)*
Electric Diner *(W11)*
Haché *(SW10)*
Lockhouse *(W2)*
MEATliquor *(W2)*
Patty and Bun *(W11)**
Tommi's Burger Joint *(SW3)*

North

Dirty Burger *(NW5)*
Duke's Brew & Que *(N1)**
Five Guys Islington *(N1)*
Haché *(NW1)*
Harry Morgan's *(NW8)*
MEATLiquor Islington *(N1)*
MEATmission *(N1)*

South

Bodean's *(SW4)*
Dip & Flip *(SW11, SW17, SW19, SW9)*
Dirty Burger *(SW8)*
Haché *(SW12, SW4)*
MEATliquor ED *(SE22)*
Pop Brixton *(SW9)**
Rivington Grill *(SE10)*
Rox Burger *(SE13)**
Sonny's Kitchen *(SW13)*

East

Bleecker Burger *(E1, EC4)**
Bodean's *(EC1, EC3)*
Burger & Lobster *(E14, EC1, EC4)*
Chicken Shop & Dirty Burger *(E1)*
Comptoir Gascon *(EC1)*
Dirty Burger *(E1)*
Goodman *(E14)*
Goodman City *(EC2)**
Haché *(EC2)*
Hawksmoor *(E1, EC2)*
Ninth Ward *(EC1)*
Patty and Bun *(E2, E8, EC2, EC3)**
The Rib Man *(E1)**
Shake Shack *(E20)*
Smiths of Smithfield, Dining
  Room *(EC1)*

FISH & CHIPS

Central

Golden Hind *(W1)*
North Sea Fish *(WC1)*
Poppies *(W1)*
Seafresh *(SW1)*

West

The Chipping Forecast *(W11)*
Geales *(W8)*
Geales Chelsea Green *(SW3)*
Kerbisher & Malt *(W5,W6)*

North

Cannons *(N8)**
Nautilus *(NW6)**
Olympus Fish *(N3)**
Poppies Camden *(NW1)*
The Sea Shell *(NW1)*
Sutton and Sons *(N1, N16)**
Toff's *(N10)*
Trawler Trash *(N1)*

South

Brady's *(SW18)*
fish! *(SE1)*
Golden Chippy *(SE10)*
Kerbisher & Malt *(SW14, SW4)*
Masters Super Fish *(SE1)*

East

Ark Fish *(E18)*
Poppies *(E1)*
Sutton and Sons *(E8)**

ICE CREAM

Central

Chin Chin Club *(W1)*
Gelupo *(W1)**

West

Bears Ice Cream *(W12)*

PIZZA

Central

Il Baretto *(W1)*
Delfino *(W1)**
Fucina *(W1)*
Homeslice *(W1,WC2)**
Mayfair Pizza Company *(W1)*
Oliveto *(SW1)**
The Orange *(SW1)*
Pizza Pilgrims *(W1,WC2)**
La Porchetta Pizzeria *(WC1)*
Princi *(W1)*
Rossopomodoro *(WC2)*

West

The Bird in Hand *(W14)*
Buona Sera *(SW3)*
Da Mario *(SW7)*
La Delizia Limbara *(SW3)*
Homeslice *(W12)**
Made in Italy *(SW3)*
The Oak W12 *(W12,W2)*
Oro Di Napoli *(W5)**
Osteria Basilico *(W11)*
Pappa Ciccia *(SW6)*
Pizza East Portobello *(W10)*
Pizza Metro *(W11)*
Pizzicotto *(W8)**
Portobello Ristorante Pizzeria *(W11)*
The Red Pepper *(W9)*
Rocca Di Papa *(SW7)*
Rossopomodoro *(SW10)*
Santa Maria *(SW6,W5)**

North

L' Antica Pizzeria *(NW3)**
L'Antica Pizzeria da Michele *(N16)*
Passione e Tradizione *(N15)**
Pizza East *(NW5)*
Pizzeria Pappagone *(N4)*
La Porchetta Pizzeria *(N1, N4, NW1)*
Rossopomodoro *(N1, NW1)*
Sacro Cuore *(N8, NW10)**
Sweet Thursday *(N1)*
Yard Sale Pizza *(N4)**
Zia Lucia *(N7)**

South

Addomme *(SW2)**
Al Forno *(SW15, SW19)*
Bean & Hop *(SW18)*
Buona Sera *(SW11)*
Dynamo *(SW15)*
Eco *(SW4)*

500 Degrees *(SE24)*
The Gowlett Arms *(SE15)**
Joe Public *(SW4)**
Made of Dough *(SE15)*
Mamma Dough *(SE15, SE23, SW9)*
Mother *(SW11)*
Numero Uno *(SW11)*
Pedler *(SE15)*
Pizza Metro *(SW11)*
Pizzastorm *(SW18)*
Pizzeria Rustica *(TW9)*
Rocca Di Papa *(SE21)*
Rossopomodoro *(SW18)*
The Stable *(TW8)*
Theo's *(SE5)*
The Yellow House *(SE16)*
Zero Degrees *(SE3)*

East

Il Bordello *(E1)*
Corner Kitchen *(E7)*
Crate Brewery and Pizzeria *(E9)*
Homeslice *(EC1, EC4)**
Pizza East *(E1)*
Pizza Pilgrims *(E1, E14, EC1, EC3)**
La Porchetta Pizzeria *(EC1)*
The Stable *(E1)*
Yard Sale Pizza *(E17, E5)**

SANDWICHES, CAKES, ETC

Central

Bageriet *(WC2)**
Bea's Cake Boutique *(WC1)*
Daylesford Organic *(W1)*
Dean & DeLuca *(W1)*
Dominique Ansel Bakery
London *(SW1)**
Fernandez & Wells *(W1, WC2)*
Kaffeine *(W1)*
Maison Bertaux *(W1)*
Monmouth Coffee Company *(WC2)**
Nordic Bakery *(W1)*
Nordic Bakery *(WC2)*
Scandinavian Kitchen *(W1)*
Workshop Coffee *(W1)*

West

Angie's Little Food Shop *(W4)*
Fernandez & Wells *(SW7)*
Lisboa Pâtisserie *(W10)*
Oree *(W8)*
Orée *(SW3)*
Over Under *(SW5)**
Tamp Coffee *(W4)*

North

Brew House Café, Kenwood
House *(NW3)*
Doppio *(NW1)*
Ginger & White *(NW3)*
Greenberry Café *(NW1)*
Max's Sandwich Shop *(N4)**
Monty's Deli *(N1)*

South

Cut The Mustard *(SW16)*
Ground Coffee Society *(SW15)*
Kappacasein *(SE16)**
Milk *(SW12)**
Monmouth Coffee
Company *(SE1, SE16)**
Orange Pekoe *(SW13)*

East

Brick Lane Beigel Bake *(E1)**
Department of Coffee, and Social
Affairs *(EC1)*
Ozone Coffee Roasters *(EC2)**
Pavilion Cafe & Bakery *(E9)*
Prufrock Coffee *(EC1)*
Rola Wala *(E1)*
Treves & Hyde *(E1)*
Workshop Coffee Holborn *(EC1)*

CHICKEN

Central

Bao *(W1)**
Chick 'n' Sours *(WC2)*
Chicken Shop *(WC1)*
Chik'n *(W1)*
Randall & Aubin *(W1)*

West

Chicken Shop *(W5)*
Cocotte *(W2)**
Stagolee's *(SW6)*

North

Chicken Shop *(N7, N8, NW5, NW8)*

South

Chicken Shop *(SW17, SW9)*
Chicken Shop & Dirty Burger
Balham *(SW12)*
Pique Nique *(SE1)*

East

Chick 'n' Sours *(E8)*
Chicken Shop & Dirty Burger *(E1)*
Randy's Wing Bar *(E15)**
Red Rooster *(EC2)*
The Tramshed *(EC2)*

BBQ

Central

Bodean's *(WC2)*
The Stoke House *(SW1)*
temper Soho *(W1)*

West

MAM *(W11)*

North

Bodean's *(N10)*
CôBa *(N7)**
Smokehouse Islington *(N1)*

South

MeatUp *(SW18)*

East

Blacklock *(EC3)**
Smokestak *(E1)**
temper City *(EC2)*

ARGENTINIAN

Central

Zoilo *(W1)**

West

Quantus *(W4)**

East

Buen Ayre *(E8)**

BRAZILIAN

East

Sushisamba *(EC2)*

CAJUN/CREOLE

North

Plaquemine Lock *(N1)*

MEXICAN/TEXMEX

Central

La Bodega Negra Cafe *(W1)*
Cantina Laredo *(WC2)*
Corazón *(W1)*
Ella Canta *(W1)*
Lupita *(WC2)*
Peyote *(W1)*

West

Killer Tomato *(W12)**
Lupita West *(W8)*
Peyotito *(W11)*
Taqueria *(W11)**

South

Cartel *(SW11)*
El Pastór *(SE1)**
Santo Remedio *(SE1)*

East

Breddos Tacos *(EC1)**
Luardos *(EC1)**
Lupita *(E1)*

PERUVIAN

Central

Casita Andina *(W1)**
Ceviche Soho *(W1)**
Coya *(W1)**
Lima *(W1)*
Lima Floral *(WC2)*
Pachamama *(W1)*
Pisqu *(W1)*
Señor Ceviche *(W1)*

West

Chicama *(SW10)*
Southam Street *(W10)*

South
MOMMI *(SW4)*

East
Andina *(E2)**
Ceviche Old St *(EC1)**
Sushisamba *(EC2)*
Waka *(EC3)*

SOUTH AMERICAN

Central
MNKY HSE *(W1)*

West
Casa Cruz *(W11)*
Quantus *(W4)**

South
MOMMI *(SW4)*

AFRO-CARIBBEAN

North
Messapica *(NW10)*

ETHIOPIAN

South
Zeret *(SE5)**

MOROCCAN

Central
Momo *(W1)*

West
Adams Café *(W12)*

NORTH AFRICAN

Central
The Barbary *(WC2)**
Momo *(W1)*

SOUTH AFRICAN

Central
Bbar *(SW1)*

TUNISIAN

West
Adams Café *(W12)*

WEST AFRICAN

Central
Ikoyi *(SW1)*

EGYPTIAN

North
Ali Baba *(NW1)*

ISRAELI

Central
The Barbary *(WC2)*
Gaby's *(WC2)*
Honey & Co *(W1)*
Honey & Smoke *(W1)**
Ottolenghi *(SW1)**
The Palomar *(W1)**

West
Ottolenghi *(W11)**

North
Ottolenghi *(N1)**

East
Ottolenghi *(E1)**

KOSHER

Central
Reubens *(W1)*

North
Kaifeng *(NW4)*
Zest, JW3 *(NW3)*

East
Brick Lane Beigel Bake *(E1)**

LEBANESE

Central
Fairuz *(W1)*
Maroush *(W1)*
Yalla Yalla *(W1)*

West
The Cedar Restaurant *(W9)*
Chez Abir *(W14)*
Maroush *(SW3)*
Maroush Gardens *(W2)*

North
The Cedar Restaurant *(NW6, NW8)*
Crocker's Folly *(NW8)*

South
Arabica Bar and Kitchen *(SE1)*
Meza Trinity Road *(SW17)*
Yalla Yalla *(SE10)*

MIDDLE EASTERN

Central
The Barbary *(WC2)**
Honey & Co *(W1)*
Honey & Smoke *(W1)**
The Palomar *(W1)**
Patogh *(W1)**

West
Falafel King *(W10)*

North
The Good Egg *(N16)**

South
Bala Baya *(SE1)*
Gourmet Goat *(SE1)**

JAN *(SW11)*

East
Berber & Q *(E8)**
Berber & Q Shawarma Bar *(EC1)**
Morito *(EC1)**
Pilpel *(E1, EC4)**

PERSIAN

Central
Patogh *(W1)**

West
Alounak *(W14,W2)*
Faanoos *(W4,W5)*
Kateh *(W9)*

South
Faanoos *(SW14)*
Persepolis *(SE15)**

SYRIAN

West
Abu Zaad *(W12)*

TURKISH

Central
Le Bab *(W1)**
Babaji Pide *(W1)*
Cyprus Mangal *(SW1)*
Ishtar *(W1)*
Kazan (Café) *(SW1)*
Yosma *(W1)*

West
Best Mangal *(SW6,W14)**
Fez Mangal *(W11)**

North
Black Axe Mangal *(N1)**
Diyarbakir Kitchen *(N4)*
Gallipoli *(N1)*
Gem *(N1)*
G.kyüzü *(N4)*
Skewd Kitchen *(EN4)*

South
FM Mangal *(SE5)*
Tas Pide *(SE1)*

East
Haz *(E1, EC2, EC3)*
Mangal 1 *(E8)**
Oklava *(EC2)**

AFGHANI

North
Afghan Kitchen *(N1)**
Ariana II *(NW6)*

BURMESE

East
Laphet *(E8)*

CHINESE
Central
AWong *(SW1)**
Baozi Inn *(WC2)*
Barshu *(W1)**
The Bright Courtyard *(W1)**
Chilli Cool *(WC1)**
China Tang, Dorchester Hotel *(W1)**
The Duck & Rice *(W1)*
The Four Seasons *(W1)**
Golden Dragon *(W1)**
The Grand Imperial *(SW1)*
Hakkasan *(W1)*
Hunan *(SW1)**
Joy King Lau *(WC2)*
Kai Mayfair *(W1)*
Ken Lo's Memories *(SW1)*
Ma La Sichuan *(SW1)**
Mayfair Garden *(W1)**
Mr Chow *(SW1)*
New World *(W1)*
Park Chinois *(W1)*
Royal China *(W1)*
Royal China Club *(W1)**
Wong Kei *(W1)*
Yauatcha *(W1)**
Yming *(W1)*

West
Dragon Palace *(SW5)**
The Four Seasons *(W2)**
Gold Mine *(W2)**
Good Earth *(SW3)*
Mandarin Kitchen *(W2)**
Min Jiang *(W8)**
North China *(W3)*
Pearl Liang *(W2)*
Royal China *(SW6,W2)*
Shikumen, Dorsett Hotel *(W12)**
Stick & Bowl *(W8)**
Taiwan Village *(SW6)**
Uli *(W11)*
Zheng *(SW3)*

North
Good Earth *(NW7)*
Green Cottage *(NW3)*
Kaifeng *(NW4)*
Phoenix Palace *(NW1)*
Sakonis *(HA0)**
Singapore Garden *(NW6)*
Xi'an Impression *(N7)**
Yipin China *(N1)**

South
Dragon Castle *(SE17)**
Good Earth *(SW17)*
Hutong, The Shard *(SE1)*
Silk Road *(SE5)**

East
HKK *(EC2)**
Mei Ume *(EC3)*
Royal China *(E14)*
The Sichuan *(EC1)**

Sichuan Folk *(E1)*
Yauatcha City *(EC2)**

CHINESE, DIM SUM
Central
Beijing Dumpling *(WC2)**
The Bright Courtyard *(W1)**
Golden Dragon *(W1)**
The Grand Imperial *(SW1)*
Hakkasan *(W1)*
Joy King Lau *(WC2)*
New World *(W1)*
Novikov (Asian restaurant) *(W1)*
Royal China *(W1)*
Royal China Club *(W1)**
Yauatcha *(W1)**

West
Min Jiang *(W8)**
Pearl Liang *(W2)*
Royal China *(SW6,W2)*
Shikumen, Dorsett Hotel *(W12)**

North
Jun Ming Xuan *(NW9)*
Phoenix Palace *(NW1)*

South
Dragon Castle *(SE17)**
Duddell's *(SE1)*

East
My Neighbours The Dumplings *(E5)**
Royal China *(E14)*
Yauatcha City *(EC2)**

FILIPINO
West
Romulo Café *(W8)*

GEORGIAN
North
Iberia *(N1)*
Little Georgia Café *(N1)*

East
Little Georgia Café *(E2)*

INDIAN
Central
Amaya *(SW1)**
Benares *(W1)*
Chettinad *(W1)**
Chutney Mary *(SW1)**
Cinnamon Bazaar *(WC2)*
The Cinnamon Club *(SW1)*
Cinnamon Soho *(W1)*
Darjeeling Express *(W1)**
Dishoom *(W1,WC2)**
Dum Biryani *(W1)**
Gaylord *(W1)**
Gymkhana *(W1)**
India Club *(WC2)*

Indian Accent *(W1)*
Jamavar *(W1)**
Kricket *(W1)**
Malabar Junction *(WC1)*
Mint Leaf *(SW1)**
La Porte des Indes *(W1)*
Punjab *(WC2)*
Ragam *(W1)**
Red Fort *(W1)**
Roti Chai *(W1)**
Sagar *(W1,WC2)*
Salaam Namaste *(WC1)*
Salloos *(SW1)**
Talli Joe *(WC2)*
Tamarind *(W1)**
Tamarind Kitchen *(W1)*
Tandoor Chop House *(WC2)**
Trishna *(W1)**
Veeraswamy *(W1)**

West
Anarkali *(W6)*
Bombay Brasserie *(SW7)*
Bombay Palace *(W2)**
Brilliant *(UB2)**
Chakra *(W8)*
Dishoom *(W8)**
Flora Indica *(SW5)*
Gifto's Lahore Karahi *(UB1)*
Indian Zing *(W6)**
Karma *(W14)**
Khan's *(W2)*
Madhu's *(UB1)**
Malabar *(W8)*
Monkey Temple *(W12)*
Noor Jahan *(SW5,W2)*
The Painted Heron *(SW10)**
Potli *(W6)**
Pure Indian Cooking *(SW6)**
Sagar *(W6)*
Star of India *(SW5)**
Thali *(SW5)**
Vineet Bhatia London *(SW3)*

North
Bonoo *(NW2)**
Chai Thali *(NW1)*
Chutneys *(NW1)*
Delhi Grill *(N1)*
Dishoom *(N1)**
Diwana Bhel-Poori House *(NW1)*
Great Nepalese *(NW1)*
Guglee *(NW3, NW6)*
Indian Rasoi *(N2)*
Jashan *(N8)**
Namaaste Kitchen *(NW1)*
Paradise Hampstead *(NW3)**
Rani *(N3)**
Ravi Shankar *(NW1)*
Sakonis *(HA0)**
Saravanaa Bhavan *(HA0)**
Vijay *(NW6)*
Zaffrani *(N1)*

South

Babur (SE23)*
Baluchi, Lalit Hotel London (SE1)
Bistro Vadouvan (SW15)
Chit Chaat Chai (SW18)*
Dastaan (KT19)*
Est India (SE1)
Everest Inn (SE3)
Ganapati (SE15)*
Hot Stuff (SW8)
Indian Moment (SW11)
Indian Ocean (SW17)
Kashmir (SW15)*
Kennington Tandoori (SE11)*
Lahore Karahi (SW17)*
Lahore Kebab House (SW16)*
Ma Goa (SW15)*
Mirch Masala (SW17)*
Sree Krishna (SW17)*

East

Bangalore Express (EC3)
Brigadiers (EC2)
Café Spice Namaste (E1)*
Cinnamon Kitchen (EC2)*
Darbaar (EC2)*
Dishoom (E2)*
Grand Trunk Road (E18)*
Gul and Sepoy (E1)
Gunpowder (E1)*
Lahore Kebab House (E1)*
Madame D's (E1)
Mint Leaf Lounge (EC2)*
Needoo (E1)*
Rola Wala (E1)
Tayyabs (E1)*
temper City (EC2)

INDIAN, SOUTHERN

Central

Hoppers (W1)*
India Club, Strand Continental
   Hotel (WC2)
Malabar Junction (WC1)
Quilon (SW1)*
Ragam (W1)*
Rasa (W1)
Rasa Maricham, Holiday Inn
   Hotel (WC1)
Sagar (W1,WC2)

West

Sagar (W6)
Shilpa (W6)*
Zaika of Kensington (W8)

North

Chutneys (NW1)
Rani (N3)*
Rasa (N16)
Vijay (NW6)

South

Ganapati (SE15)*
Jaffna House (SW17)*
Sree Krishna (SW17)*

JAPANESE

Central

Anzu (SW1)
The Araki (W1)*
Atari-Ya (W1)*
Bone Daddies, Nova (SW1,W1)*
Chisou (W1)*
Chotto Matte (W1)*
Defune (W1)
Dinings (W1)*
Dozo (W1)
Eat Tokyo (W1,WC1,WC2)*
Flesh and Buns (WC2)*
Ginza Onodera (SW1)*
Japan Centre Food Hall (SW1)
Jugemu (W1)*
Kanada-Ya (SW1,WC2)*
Kiku (W1)
Kikuchi (W1)*
Kintan (WC1)
Koya-Bar (W1)
Kulu Kulu (W1,WC2)
Machiya (SW1)
Nobu, Metropolitan Hotel (W1)
Nobu Berkeley (W1)
Oka, Kingly Court (W1)*
Oliver Maki (W1)
Roka (W1,WC2)*
Sakagura (W1)*
Sake No Hana (SW1)*
Shoryu Ramen (SW1,W1)
Sticks'n'Sushi (SW1,WC2)*
Sumosan Twiga (SW1)
Sushisamba (WC2)
TAKA (W1)
Taro (W1)
Tokimeite (W1)*
Tokyo Diner (WC2)
Tonkotsu, Selfridges (W1)
Umu (W1)
Vasco & Piero's Pavilion (W1)
Yoshino (W1)*

West

Atari-Ya (W3,W5)*
Bone Daddies, Whole Foods (W8)*
Chisou (SW3)*
Dinings (SW3)*
Eat Tokyo (W6,W8)*
Flat Three (W11)*
Kiraku (W5)*
Kiru (SW3)*
Koji (SW6)*
Kulu Kulu (SW7)
Kurobuta (SW3,W2)
Maguro (W9)
Oka (SW3)*

South

Southam Street (W10)
Sushi Bar Makoto (W4)*
Tonkotsu (W11)
Tosa (W6)
Yashin (W8)*
Yoshi Sushi (W6)
Zuma (SW7)*

North

Asakusa (NW1)*
Atari-Ya (N12, NW6)*
Dotori (N4)*
Eat Tokyo (NW11)*
Jin Kichi (NW3)*
Oka (NW1)*
Sushi Masa (NW2)

South

Hashi (SW20)
Matsuba (TW9)
MOMMI (SW4)
Nanban (SW9)*
Sticks'n'Sushi (SE10, SW19)*
Takahashi (SW19)*
Taro (SW12)
Tomoe (SW15)*
Tonkotsu Bankside (SE1)
Tsunami (SW4)*
Yama Momo (SE22)*
Zaibatsu (SE10)*

East

Bone Daddies, The Bower (EC1)*
Ippudo London (E14)
K10, Appold Street (EC2, EC3)
Koya (EC2)
Mei Ume (EC3)
Nanashi (EC2)
Nobu Shoreditch (EC2)
Pham Sushi (EC1)*
Roka (E14)*
Shoryu Ramen (EC2)
Sosharu, Turnmill Building (EC1)
Sticks'n'Sushi (E14)*
Sushisamba (EC2)
Sushi Tetsu (EC1)*
Taro (EC4)
Tonkotsu (E8)
Uchi (E5)*
Waka (EC3)

KOREAN

Central

Bibimbap Soho (W1)
Bó Drake (W1)
Jinjuu (W1)
Kintan (WC1)
Koba (W1)*
On The Bab (WC2)
On The Bab Express (W1)

West

Gogi (W2)
Yoshi Sushi (W6)

North
Dotori (N4)*
The Petite Coree (NW6)*

South
Cah-Chi (SW18, SW20)
Matsuba (TW9)

East
Bibimbap (EC3)
On The Bab (EC1, EC4)

MALAYSIAN

Central
C&R Café (W1)*

West
C&R Café (W2)*
Satay House (W2)

North
Roti King (NW1)*
Singapore Garden (NW6)

South
Champor-Champor (SE1)*

PAKISTANI

Central
Salloos (SW1)*

South
Lahore Karahi (SW17)*
Lahore Kebab House (SW16)*
Mirch Masala (SW17)*

East
Lahore Kebab House (E1)*
Needoo (E1)*
Tayyabs (E1)*

PAN-ASIAN

Central
Hare & Tortoise (WC1)
Hot Pot (W1)
Jean-Georges at The
   Connaught (W1)
Nirvana Kitchen (W1)*
Nopi (W1)*
Novikov (Asian restaurant) (W1)
PF Chang's Asian Table (WC2)

West
E&O (W11)
Eight Over Eight (SW3)
Hare & Tortoise (W14,W4,W5)
Little Bird Chiswick (W4)
Uli (W11)
Zheng (SW3)

North
Bang Bang Oriental (NW9)
Pamban (NW1)

South
Hare & Tortoise (SW15)
Little Bird Battersea (SW11)
Sticky Mango at RSJ (SE1)

East
Hare & Tortoise (EC4)

THAI

Central
Crazy Bear Fitzrovia (W1)
Kiln (W1)*
Lao Cafe (WC2)
Patara Mayfair (W1)*
Rosa's (SW1)
Rosa's Soho (W1)
Smoking Goat (WC2)*
Suda (WC2)

West
Addie's Thai Café (SW5)
Nukis Kitchen (W13)
Patara (SW3)*
Rosa's Fulham (SW10)
Sukho Fine Thai Cuisine (SW6)*
Suksan (SW10)*
Uli (W11)

North
Farang (N5)*
Isarn (N1)*
Patara (NW3)*
Rosa's (N1, NW6)

South
Awesome Thai (SW13)
The Begging Bowl (SE15)*
Champor-Champor (SE1)*
Kaosarn (SW11, SW9)*
Patara (SW19)*
The Pepper Tree (SW4)
Rosa's (SW9)

East
Rosa's (E1, E15)
Saiphin's Thai Kitchen (E8)
Smoking Goat (E1)*
Som Saa (E1)*

VIETNAMESE

Central
Cây Tre (W1)
House of Ho (W1)
Pho & Bun (W1)*
Viet Food (W1)

West
Go-Viet (SW7)*
MAM (W11)
Saigon Saigon (W6)

North
CôBa (N7)*
Salvation In Noodles (N1, N4)
Singapore Garden (NW6)

South
Bánh Bánh (SE15)
Café East (SE16)*
Mien Tay (SW11)*

East
Cây Tre (EC1)
City Càphê (EC2)
Mien Tay (E2)*
Sông Quê (E2)
Viet Grill (E2)

TAIWANESE

Central
Bao Fitzrovia (W1)*
XU (W1)

West
Taiwan Village (SW6)*

South
Mr Bao (SE15)*

East
Bao Bar (E8)*

Nobu Shoreditch EC2

Plot SW17

Radici N1

Red Rooster EC2

CENTRAL

Soho, Covent Garden & Bloomsbury (Parts of W1, all WC2 and WC1)

£110+	L'Atelier de Joel Robuchon	French	2	1	2
£100+	Smith & Wollensky	Steaks & grills	2	1	2
£90+	Savoy Thames Foyer	British, Modern	2	3	4
	The Savoy Hotel, Savoy Grill	British, Traditional	2	3	3
	Sushisamba	Japanese	3	2	5
£80+	Bob Bob Ricard	British, Modern	3	4	5
	Hush	"	2	2	3
	The Northall	"	3	3	3
	Spring Restaurant	"	3	3	4
	Kaspar's Seafood and Grill	Fish & seafood	3	3	4
	J Sheekey	"	3	3	4
	Asia de Cuba	Fusion	2	2	3
	Massimo, Corinthia Hotel	Mediterranean	2	2	3
	MASH Steakhouse	Steaks & grills	2	2	2
	Oscar Wilde Bar	Afternoon tea	–	–	–
	Yauatcha	Chinese	4	3	3
	Roka, Aldwych House	Japanese	4	3	3
£70+	Christopher's	American	2	2	3
	Balthazar	British, Modern	2	2	4
	Social Eating House	"	5	5	4
	Holborn Dining Room	British, Traditional	3	3	4
	Rules	"	2	3	5
	Simpson's in the Strand	"	–	–	–
	Clos Maggiore	French	3	4	5
	L'Escargot	"	4	4	4
	Frenchie	"	4	2	2
	Gauthier Soho	"	5	5	4
	Otto's	"	4	5	4
	Nopi	Mediterranean	4	3	3
	Eneko	Spanish	3	3	2
	Hawksmoor	Steaks & grills	3	3	3
	Lima Floral	Peruvian	3	2	2
	Red Fort	Indian	4	3	2
£60+	Bronte	Australian	2	3	4
	Dean Street Townhouse	British, Modern	2	2	4
	Ducksoup	"	3	3	4
	Ham Yard Restaurant	"	2	3	5
	Heliot Steak House	"	4	4	4
	Hix	"	1	2	3
	Indigo, One Aldwych	"	3	4	3
	The Ivy	"	3	4	5

Noble Rot	"		3 3 4
The Portrait	"		2 2 3
Quo Vadis	"		4 5 5
Tom's Kitchen	"		2 2 2
Tredwell's	"		2 2 2
J Sheekey Atlantic Bar	Fish & seafood		3 4 4
Randall & Aubin	"		3 3 4
Wright Brothers	"		4 3 3
Café Monico	French		2 2 4
Test Kitchen	International		– – –
Bocca Di Lupo	Italian		4 4 3
Café Murano Pastificio	"		3 2 3
Fumo	"		3 2 3
Vasco & Piero's Pavilion	"		3 4 3
100 Wardour Street	Mediterranean		2 2 3
Aqua Nueva	Spanish		2 2 3
Sophie's Steakhouse	Steaks & grills		2 3 3
Rainforest Café	Burgers, etc		2 3 3
The Palomar	Middle Eastern		4 4 3
Chotto Matte	Japanese		4 3 5
Oliver Maki	"		3 3 3
Jinjuu	Korean		3 3 4
Patara Soho	Thai		4 4 4
XU	Taiwanese		– – –
£50+ Big Easy	American		2 2 3
Bodean's	"		2 2 2
Hubbard & Bell	"		3 2 3
Jackson & Rye	"		1 2 2
Joe Allen	"		1 2 4
Andrew Edmunds	British, Modern		3 4 5
Aurora	"		3 4 4
Great Queen Street	"		3 2 2
The Ivy Market Grill	"		2 2 3
Jar Kitchen	"		2 5 3
Native	"		4 3 2
Polpo at Ape & Bird	"		2 2 2
Saint Luke's Kitchen, Library	"		3 3 3
10 Greek Street	"		4 4 3
Terroirs	"		3 2 3
Vinoteca	"		3 3 4
The Ivy Soho Brasserie	British, Traditional		2 2 3
The Delaunay	Central European		2 4 5
Bonnie Gull Seafood Shack	Fish & seafood		5 3 3
Oystermen	"		– – –
Antidote Wine Bar	French		2 2 3
Blanchette	"		4 3 4
Bon Vivant	"		3 3 3
Cigalon	"		3 4 4
Le Garrick	"		2 3 4

Name	Cuisine			
Mon Plaisir	"	2	3	5
Gay Hussar	Hungarian	1	2	4
Cork & Bottle	International	2	3	5
Flavour Bastard	"	–	–	–
The 10 Cases	"	2	3	3
Da Mario	Italian	3	4	3
Dehesa	"	3	2	3
Luce e Limoni	"	4	4	3
Margot	"	4	5	5
Mele e Pere	"	3	4	3
Obicà	"	3	2	2
Polpo	"	2	2	2
San Carlo Cicchetti	"	3	3	4
Ember Yard	Spanish	2	3	3
Encant	"	4	2	3
Morada Brindisa Asador	"	2	2	2
Opera Tavern	"	4	4	3
Foxlow	Steaks & grills	2	2	2
Zelman Meats	"	5	4	4
St Moritz	Swiss	3	3	4
Dalloway Terrace	Afternoon tea	3	2	4
Burger & Lobster	Burgers, etc	3	2	3
Fernandez & Wells	Sandwiches, cakes, etc	3	3	3
Bodean's	BBQ	2	2	2
Cantina Laredo	Mexican/TexMex	3	2	3
Ceviche Soho	Peruvian	4	3	3
Barshu	Chinese	4	2	2
The Duck & Rice	"	3	3	4
Dum Biryani	Indian	4	4	3
Flesh and Buns	Japanese	4	3	3
Sticks'n'Sushi	"	4	2	2
Bó Drake	Korean	2	2	3
£40+				
Breakfast Club	American	3	3	3
Spuntino	"	3	3	3
Coopers Restaurant & Bar	British, Modern	2	3	3
The Frog	"	5	3	2
The Norfolk Arms	"	3	2	2
Shampers	"	2	4	5
VQ, St Giles Hotel	"	2	4	3
Brasserie Zédel	French	1	3	5
Prix Fixe	"	3	3	2
Relais de Venise L'Entrecôte	"	3	2	2
Savoir Faire	"	3	4	3
La Fromagerie Bloomsbury	International	3	2	2
Ciao Bella	Italian	2	3	4
Polpetto	"	3	3	3
La Porchetta Pizzeria	"	2	3	2
Zima	Russian	3	2	3
Barrafina	Spanish	5	5	5

	Cigala	"	3	3	3
	Sibarita	"	–	–	–
	Mildreds	Vegetarian	3	3	3
	North Sea Fish	Fish & chips	3	2	2
	Poppies	"	3	2	3
	Rossopomodoro	Pizza	3	2	2
	Chick 'n' Sours	Chicken	3	3	3
	La Bodega Negra Cafe	Mexican/TexMex	3	2	4
	Corazón	"	3	4	3
	Lupita	"	3	2	2
	Señor Ceviche	Peruvian	3	2	4
	The Barbary	North African	5	5	4
	Le Bab	Turkish	5	4	3
	Babaji Pide	"	3	2	2
	The Four Seasons	Chinese	4	1	1
	Yming	"	3	5	2
	Cinnamon Bazaar	Indian	2	3	3
	Cinnamon Soho	"	3	2	2
	Darjeeling Express	"	4	3	3
	Dishoom	"	4	4	5
	Kricket	"	5	4	4
	Malabar Junction	"	3	3	2
	Salaam Namaste	"	3	3	2
	Tamarind Kitchen	"	3	3	4
	Tandoor Chop House	"	4	3	3
	Hoppers	Indian, Southern	5	4	3
	Bone Daddies	Japanese	4	3	3
	Dozo	"	3	3	3
	Jugemu	"	5	2	3
	Kintan	"	3	2	3
	Oka, Kingly Court	"	4	2	2
	Shoryu Ramen	"	3	2	2
	Tonkotsu	"	3	2	3
	Hare & Tortoise	Pan-Asian	3	2	2
	Rosa's Soho	Thai	2	2	2
	Smoking Goat	"	4	3	2
	Suda	"	3	3	3
	Cây Tre	Vietnamese	3	3	2
	Pho & Bun	"	4	3	2
£35+	Gordon's Wine Bar	International	2	2	5
	Bar Termini	Italian	3	3	5
	Princi	"	3	2	3
	Blacklock	Steaks & grills	4	4	4
	Bukowski Grill	"	3	3	2
	Haché	Burgers, etc	3	4	4
	MEATliquor	"	3	2	4
	Pizza Pilgrims	Pizza	4	3	3
	Bea's Cake Boutique	Sandwiches, cakes, etc	3	3	3
	temper Soho	BBQ	3	4	5

	Casita Andina	Peruvian	4	3	4
	Gaby's	Israeli	3	2	2
	Yalla Yalla	Lebanese	3	2	2
	Joy King Lau	Chinese	3	2	2
	NewWorld	"	2	1	2
	Punjab	Indian	3	2	3
	Sagar	"	3	2	1
	Talli Joe	"	3	3	4
	Rasa Maricham	Indian, Southern	3	3	3
	Taro	Japanese	3	2	2
	On The Bab	Korean	3	2	2
	Hot Pot	Pan-Asian	–	–	–
	Lao Cafe	Thai	3	3	2
£30+	Café in the Crypt	British, Traditional	2	1	4
	Bar Italia	Italian	2	3	5
	Flat Iron	Steaks & grills	4	4	3
	Homeslice	Pizza	4	4	4
	Chicken Shop	Chicken	3	3	3
	Chilli Cool	Chinese	5	2	1
	Golden Dragon	"	4	2	2
	Wong Kei	"	3	2	1
	Beijing Dumpling	Chinese, Dim sum	4	2	2
	Koya-Bar	Japanese	3	3	3
	Kulu Kulu	"	3	2	1
	C&R Café	Malaysian	4	2	2
	Kiln	Thai	5	4	4
	Viet Food	Vietnamese	3	3	3
£25+	MEATmarket	Burgers, etc	3	3	2
	Patty and Bun Soho	"	4	3	3
	Shake Shack	"	2	2	2
	Tommi's Burger Joint	"	3	3	3
	India Club	Indian	2	2	1
	Eat Tokyo	Japanese	4	3	2
	Kanada-Ya	"	5	2	2
	Bibimbap Soho	Korean	3	2	2
	Bao	Taiwanese	4	3	2
£20+	Baozi Inn	Chinese			
	Tokyo Diner	Japanese	3	3	3
£15+	Five Guys	Burgers, etc	3	2	2
£10+	Nordic Bakery	Scandinavian	3	2	3
	Bageriet	Sandwiches, cakes, etc	4	4	3
£5+	Maison Bertaux	Afternoon tea	3	4	4
	Gelupo	Ice cream	5	2	2
	Monmouth Coffee Company	Sandwiches, cakes, etc	4	5	4

Mayfair & St James's (Parts of WI and SWI)

£380+	The Araki	Japanese	5 5 3
£140+	Sketch, Lecture Room	French	4 4 5
	The Square	"	3 3 1
£130+	The Ritz	British, Traditional	3 4 5
	Alain Ducasse	French	2 2 2
	Le Gavroche	"	4 5 4
	Hélène Darroze	"	3 4 4
£120+	Ormer Mayfair	British, Modern	4 3 3
	Estiatorio Milos	Greek	3 2 4
	The Promenade	International	2 4 4
	Cut, 45 Park Lane	Steaks & grills	2 2 2
	Umu	Japanese	3 4 3
£110+	Galvin at Windows	French	2 2 5
	The Greenhouse	"	4 4 4
£100+	Dorchester Grill	British, Modern	3 4 4
	Fera at Claridge's	"	– – –
	Pollen Street Social	"	3 2 3
	Seven Park Place	French	4 5 4
	Assunta Madre	Italian	3 3 3
	Novikov (Italian restaurant)	"	1 2 2
	QP LDN	"	3 3 3
	Kai Mayfair	Chinese	3 2 2
	Benares	Indian	2 2 2
	Tokimeite	Japanese	4 3 3
£90+	Alyn Williams	British, Modern	3 3 2
	Corrigan's Mayfair	British, Traditional	3 4 3
	Wiltons	"	3 4 5
	Sexy Fish	Fish & seafood	1 1 3
	La Petite Maison	French	4 3 3
	C London	Italian	1 1 3
	Murano	"	5 5 4
	Theo Randall	"	3 3 2
	Street XO	Spanish	1 1 2
	Goodman	Steaks & grills	4 4 2
	Hakkasan Mayfair	Chinese	3 2 4
	Park Chinois	"	2 2 4
	Nobu, Metropolitan Hotel	Japanese	3 2 1
	Novikov (Asian restaurant)	Pan-Asian	3 2 3
£80+	Le Caprice	British, Modern	2 4 4
	Hush	"	2 2 3

Butler's Restaurant	British, Traditional	2	4	3
Bentley's	Fish & seafood	3	4	4
Scott's	"	4	4	5
maze	French	2	2	1
Sketch, Gallery	"	1	2	3
Bocconcino	Italian	3	3	3
Chucs	"	3	3	3
Ristorante Frescobaldi	"	3	3	2
Savini at Criterion	"	2	2	5
The Ritz, Palm Court	Afternoon tea	2	4	5
Peyote	Mexican/TexMex	3	3	2
Coya	Peruvian	4	3	5
MNKY HSE South	American	1	2	3
China Tang	Chinese	4	3	3
Chutney Mary	Indian	4	4	4
Jamavar	"	5	4	4
Ginza Onodera	Japanese	4	5	2
Nobu Berkeley	"	3	2	3
Roka	"	4	3	3

£70+				
Colony Grill Room	American	3	3	3
Bonhams Restaurant	British, Modern	4	5	2
Kitty Fisher's	"	3	3	3
Little Social	"	2	2	2
Mews of Mayfair	"	3	3	3
Quaglino's	"	1	2	3
Wild Honey	"	3	4	3
Brown's, English Tea Room	British, Traditional	3	4	4
The Game Bird	"	3	4	4
GBR	"	–	–	–
Boulestin	French	3	3	2
Ferdi	"	1	1	2
Cecconi's	Italian	2	2	3
Franco's	"	3	3	3
Sartoria	"	3	3	3
Aquavit	Scandinavian	3	3	3
Boisdale of Mayfair	Scottish	3	3	3
Barbecoa Piccadilly	Steaks & grills	2	2	2
The Guinea Grill	"	4	4	4
Hawksmoor	"	3	3	3
maze Grill	"	1	2	2
Rowley's	"	3	3	3
34 Mayfair	"	3	3	4
Momo	Moroccan	3	3	4
Veeraswamy	Indian	4	4	3

£60+				
The Avenue	American	2	4	3
Hard Rock Café	"	3	3	4
Bellamy's	British, Modern	3	4	3
Galvin at the Athenaeum	"	3	4	2

	Heddon Street Kitchen	"	**1**	**1**	**2**
	The Keeper's House	"	**2**	**2**	**2**
	Langan's Brasserie	"	**2**	**3**	**4**
	The Punchbowl	"	**3**	**4**	**3**
	The Wolseley	"	**3**	**4**	**5**
	Brown's Hotel, HIX Mayfair	British, Traditional	**2**	**2**	**3**
	Black Roe	Fish & seafood	**3**	**2**	**2**
	Fishworks	"	**3**	**2**	**3**
	The Balcon, Sofitel St James	French	**2**	**2**	**2**
	Villandry St James's	"	**1**	**1**	**3**
	Café Murano	Italian	**3**	**2**	**3**
	Fortnum, Diamond Jubilee	Afternoon tea	**3**	**3**	**3**
	Mayfair Garden	Chinese	**4**	**3**	**2**
	Gymkhana	Indian	**4**	**4**	**4**
	Mint Leaf	"	**4**	**4**	**4**
	Tamarind	"	**5**	**4**	**3**
	Kiku	Japanese	**3**	**3**	**2**
	Sake No Hana	"	**4**	**3**	**3**
	Patara Mayfair	Thai	**4**	**4**	**4**
£50+	Comptoir Café & Wine	British, Modern	–	–	–
	Duck & Waffle Local	"	–	–	–
	Hatchetts	"	**2**	**3**	**2**
	The American Bar	British, Traditional	–	–	–
	Boudin Blanc	French	**3**	**3**	**4**
	Neo Bistro	"	–	–	–
	28-50	"	**2**	**4**	**3**
	Al Duca	Italian	**3**	**3**	**2**
	Veneta	"	**3**	**3**	**2**
	Il Vicolo	"	**3**	**4**	**2**
	Burger & Lobster	Burgers, etc	**3**	**2**	**3**
	Delfino	Pizza	**4**	**3**	**2**
	Mayfair Pizza Company	"	**3**	**4**	**3**
	Fernandez & Wells	Sandwiches, cakes, etc	**3**	**3**	**3**
	Chisou	Japanese	**4**	**3**	**2**
	Sakagura	"	**4**	**4**	**3**
£40+	The Windmill	British, Traditional	**3**	**3**	**3**
	L'Artiste Musclé	French	**2**	**2**	**5**
	El Pirata	Spanish	**3**	**3**	**4**
	Anzu	Japanese	–	–	–
	Shoryu Ramen	"	**3**	**2**	**2**
	Yoshino	"	**4**	**4**	**2**
£35+	tibits	Vegetarian	**3**	**2**	**3**
	Rasa	Indian, Southern	**3**	**3**	**3**

Fitzrovia & Marylebone (Part of W1)

£130+	Bubbledogs, Kitchen Table	*Fusion*	5 3 4
£110+	Pied à Terre	*French*	4 4 3
	Texture	*Scandinavian*	4 3 3
	Beast	*Steaks & grills*	1 2 2
£100+	Roux at the Landau	*British, Modern*	2 3 3
£90+	The Chiltern Firehouse	*American*	1 1 3
	Orrery	*French*	3 3 2
	Hakkasan	*Chinese*	3 2 4
£80+	Portland	*British, Modern*	4 4 3
	Clarette	*French*	– – –
	Mere	*International*	3 5 3
	Locanda Locatelli	*Italian*	4 3 3
	Trishna	*Indian*	5 3 3
	Roka	*Japanese*	4 3 3
£70+	The Berners Tavern	*British, Modern*	2 3 5
	Pescatori	*Fish & seafood*	2 4 3
	Les 110 de Taillevent	*French*	4 4 3
	The Providores	*Fusion*	4 3 2
	Il Baretto	*Italian*	2 2 2
	Palm Court, The Langham	*Afternoon tea*	3 3 4
	Lima	*Peruvian*	3 2 2
	La Porte des Indes	*Indian*	3 2 4
	Defune	*Japanese*	3 2 1
	Kikuchi	"	4 3 2
	Crazy Bear Fitzrovia	*Thai*	3 3 4
£60+	Clipstone	*British, Modern*	4 4 3
	The Grazing Goat	"	2 3 3
	Picture	"	3 3 2
	Fischer's	*Central European*	2 3 4
	Fishworks	*Fish & seafood*	3 2 3
	Galvin Bistrot de Luxe	*French*	3 3 3
	Villandry	"	1 1 3
	Twist	*Fusion*	4 4 4
	Jikoni	*International*	3 3 4
	Caffè Caldesi	*Italian*	2 3 3
	Blandford Comptoir	*Mediterranean*	3 3 3
	The Ninth London	"	4 3 3
	Pachamama	*Peruvian*	3 2 2
	The Bright Courtyard	*Chinese*	4 2 2
	Royal China Club	"	4 2 2
	Gaylord	*Indian*	4 4 3

	Dinings	*Japanese*	5	4	2
	Nirvana Kitchen	*Pan-Asian*	4	2	2
	Patara Fitzrovia	*Thai*	4	4	4
	House of Ho	*Vietnamese*	3	3	3
£50+	Daylesford Organic	*British, Modern*	3	2	3
	Hardy's Brasserie	"	3	3	3
	The Ivy Café	"	1	2	3
	108 Brasserie	"	3	3	3
	Percy & Founders	"	3	3	3
	Vinoteca Seymour Place	"	3	3	4
	Bonnie Gull	*Fish & seafood*	4	3	3
	28-50	*French*	2	4	3
	The Wallace	"	2	1	5
	Carousel	*Fusion*	5	4	4
	Bernardi's	*Italian*	3	3	4
	Briciole	"	3	4	3
	Latium	"	3	3	2
	Obicà	"	3	2	2
	Sardo	"	3	3	2
	2 Veneti	"	3	4	3
	Riding House Café	*Mediterranean*	2	2	4
	The Harcourt	*Scandinavian*	4	3	4
	Mac & Wild	*Scottish*	4	3	4
	Barrica4	*Spanish*	3	2	2
	Donostia	"	4	4	4
	Ibérica	"	2	2	3
	Lurra	"	3	3	3
	Salt Yard	"	3	3	2
	Social Wine & Tapas	"	3	4	4
	Ethos	*Vegetarian*	3	3	3
	The Gate	"	4	3	3
	Burger & Lobster	*Burgers, etc*	3	2	3
	Daylesford Organic	*Sandwiches, cakes, etc*	3	2	3
	Zoilo	*Argentinian*	4	3	3
	Pisqu	*Peruvian*	–	–	–
	Reubens	*Kosher*	2	2	2
	Maroush	*Lebanese*	3	2	2
	Ishtar	*Turkish*	3	4	2
	Yosma	"	3	3	2
	Royal China	*Chinese*	3	1	2
£40+	Lantana Café	*Australian*	3	3	3
	The Wigmore, The Langham	*British, Traditional*	–	–	–
	Opso	*Greek*	3	3	3
	Foley's	*International*	4	4	4
	La Fromagerie Café	"	3	2	2
	Fucina	*Italian*	1	2	4
	Made in Italy James St	"	3	2	3
	Rossopomodoro, John Lewis	"	3	2	2

	Drakes Tabanco	Spanish	3	2	2
	Le Relais de Venise	Steaks & grills	3	2	2
	Bobo Social	Burgers, etc	3	3	3
	Fairuz	Lebanese	3	3	2
	Honey & Co	Middle Eastern	3	3	2
	Honey & Smoke	"	5	4	2
	Chettinad	Indian	4	3	3
	Roti Chai	"	4	3	4
	Hoppers	Indian, Southern	5	4	3
	Bone Daddies	Japanese	4	3	3
	Tonkotsu, Selfridges	"	3	2	3
	Koba	Korean	4	3	3
£35+	MEATLiquor	Burgers, etc	3	2	4
	Golden Hind	Fish & chips	3	3	2
	Workshop Coffee	Sandwiches, cakes, etc	3	4	4
	Yalla Yalla	Lebanese	3	2	2
	Sagar	Indian	3	2	1
	On The Bab Express	Korean	3	2	2
£30+	Vagabond Wines	Mediterranean	3	3	4
	Homeslice	Pizza	4	4	4
	Atari-Ya	Japanese	4	2	1
£25+	Patty and Bun	Burgers, etc	4	3	3
	Tommi's Burger Joint	"	3	3	3
	Ragam	Indian	4	2	1
	Bibimbap Soho	Korean	3	2	2
	Bao Fitzrovia	Taiwanese	4	3	2
£15+	Scandinavian Kitchen	Scandinavian	3	4	2
	Chik'n	Chicken	–	–	–
£10+	Nordic Bakery	Scandinavian	3	2	3
	Kaffeine	Sandwiches, cakes, etc	3	5	4
	Patogh	Middle Eastern	4	3	2

Belgravia, Pimlico, Victoria & Westminster (SW1, except St James's)

£120+	Marcus, The Berkeley	British, Modern	3	2	3
£110+	Dinner, Mandarin Oriental	British, Traditional	2	3	2
	Pétrus	French	3	3	2
£100+	Céleste, The Lanesborough	French	2	3	5
	Rib Room, Jumeirah Carlton Tower Hotel	Steaks & grills	–	–	–

£90+	The Collins Room	*British, Modern*	2 4 5
	Goring Hotel	"	3 4 4
	Roux at Parliament Square	"	5 5 3
	Strangers Dining Room,	*British, Traditional*	2 3 5
	One-O-One	*Fish & seafood*	4 3 1
	Zafferano	*Italian*	2 2 2
	Ametsa	*Spanish*	3 3 2
	Hunan	*Chinese*	5 2 1
£80+	M Restaurant	*Steaks & grills*	2 2 2
	Mr Chow	*Chinese*	2 2 2
	Amaya	*Indian*	4 2 3
	The Cinnamon Club	"	3 3 4
£70+	Caxton Grill	*British, Modern*	2 3 3
	Como Lario	*Italian*	2 3 2
	Il Convivio	"	4 3 4
	Enoteca Turi	"	3 4 3
	Olivo	"	3 3 2
	Il Pampero	"	– – –
	Santini	"	2 3 3
	Signor Sassi	"	3 3 3
	Mari Vanna	*Russian*	3 3 4
	Barbecoa, Nova	*Steaks & grills*	2 2 2
	Quilon	*Indian, Southern*	5 4 3
£60+	Timmy Green	*Australian*	2 3 3
	The Alfred Tennyson	*British, Modern*	3 3 4
	The Botanist	"	2 2 2
	45 Jermyn Street	"	3 4 4
	Lorne	"	4 5 3
	The Orange	"	3 3 4
	The Other Naughty Piglet	"	4 4 3
	Rail House Café	"	2 2 2
	Tate Britain	"	2 2 5
	The Thomas Cubitt	"	3 4 4
	Olivomare	*Fish & seafood*	3 2 2
	Bar Boulud	*French*	3 4 4
	Colbert	"	2 2 3
	La Poule au Pot	"	2 2 5
	Caraffini	*Italian*	3 5 3
	Olivocarne	"	3 3 2
	Quirinale	"	4 3 2
	Sale e Pepe	"	3 4 4
	Boisdale of Belgravia	*Scottish*	3 2 4
	Oliveto	*Pizza*	4 2 1
	The Grand Imperial	*Chinese*	3 2 2
	Ken Lo's Memories	"	3 3 2

£50+	Granger & Co	Australian	3	3	3
	Aster Restaurant	British, Modern	3	3	3
	Cambridge Street Kitchen	"	3	4	4
	Daylesford Organic	"	3	2	3
	Ebury	"	2	2	3
	Shepherd's	British, Traditional	3	4	4
	Motcombs	International	2	2	3
	Cacio & Pepe	Italian	3	2	2
	Hai Cenato	"	3	3	2
	Osteria Dell'Angolo	"	3	3	1
	Ottolenghi	"	4	3	2
	Tozi	"	3	3	2
	About Thyme	Spanish	2	3	3
	Ibérica, Zig Zag Building	"	2	2	3
	Zelman Meats	Steaks & grills	5	4	4
	Burger & Lobster	Burgers, etc	3	2	3
	Bbar South	African	3	4	3
	Ma La Sichuan	Chinese	4	3	1
	Sticks'n'Sushi	Japanese	4	2	2
	Salloos	Pakistani	4	2	2
£40+	Greenwood	British, Modern	–	–	–
	Gustoso	Italian	3	4	3
	Goya	Spanish	3	3	2
	Seafresh	Fish & chips	3	3	2
	The Stoke House	BBQ	–	–	–
	Kazan (Café)	Turkish	3	3	3
	A Wong	Chinese	5	5	3
	Bone Daddies, Nova	Japanese	4	3	3
	Machiya	"	–	–	–
	Rosa's	Thai	2	2	2
£35+	The Vincent Rooms	British, Modern	3	4	3
	Cyprus Mangal	Turkish	3	2	2
£30+	Vagabond Wines	Mediterranean	3	3	4
£25+	Shake Shack	Burgers, etc	2	2	2
	Kanada-Ya	Japanese	5	2	2
£20+	Bleecker Burger	Burgers, etc	5	2	2
	Dominique Ansel Baker	Sandwiches, cakes, etc	5	4	3

WEST

Chelsea, South Kensington, Kensington, Earl's Court & Fulham (SW3, SW5, SW6, SW7, SW10 & W8)

£150+	Gordon Ramsay	*French*	2	2	2
£140+	Vineet Bhatia London	*Indian*	3	3	2
£100+	Bibendum	*French*	2	2	3
£90+	Elystan Street	*British, Modern*	4	4	2
	Outlaw's at The Capital	*Fish & seafood*	4	4	2
£80+	The Five Fields	*British, Modern*	5	5	4
	Rivea, Bulgari Hotel	*International*	3	4	3
	Daphne's	*Italian*	2	2	2
	Min Jiang	*Chinese*	4	4	5
	Koji	*Japanese*	4	4	4
	Yashin	"	4	3	2
	Zuma	"	5	3	3
£70+	Babylon	*British, Modern*	2	2	4
	Bluebird	"	3	3	3
	Clarke's	"	5	5	4
	Kitchen W8	"	4	4	3
	Launceston Place	"	3	4	4
	Medlar	"	4	4	2
	Parabola, Design Museum	"	3	2	3
	Restaurant Ours	"	1	2	3
	Cheyne Walk Brasserie	*French*	2	2	3
	L'Etranger	"	3	3	2
	Lucio	*Italian*	3	4	3
	Scalini	"	3	3	3
	Cambio de Tercio	*Spanish*	3	3	2
	Hawksmoor Knightsbridge	*Steaks & grills*	3	3	3
£60+	The Abingdon	*British, Modern*	3	3	4
	Brinkley's	"	2	2	3
	Harwood Arms	"	4	3	3
	Kensington Place	"	3	2	2
	Tom's Kitchen	"	2	2	2
	Maggie Jones's	*British, Traditional*	2	2	5
	Wright Brothers	*Fish & seafood*	4	3	3
	Bandol	*French*	3	3	3
	Belvedere Restaurant	"	2	3	4
	Le Colombier	"	3	5	4
	Mazi	*Greek*	3	3	3
	No.11 Cadogan Gardens	*International*	–	–	–
	La Famiglia	*Italian*	2	2	3

	Frantoio	"		3	3	4
	Manicomio	"		2	3	3
	Il Portico	"		3	5	4
	Theo's Simple Italian	"		3	2	3
	Ziani's	"		2	3	2
	Locanda Ottomezzo	*Mediterranean*		3	3	3
	Sophie's Steakhouse	*Steaks & grills*		2	3	3
	Good Earth	*Chinese*		2	2	2
	Zheng	"		–	–	–
	Bombay Brasserie	*Indian*		3	4	3
	Zaika of Kensington	*Indian, Southern*		3	2	3
	Dinings	*Japanese*		5	4	2
	Kurobuta	"		3	2	2
	Patara	*Thai*		4	4	4
£50+	Big Easy	*American*		2	2	3
	Bodean's	"		2	2	2
	The Builders Arms	*British, Modern*		2	2	3
	Claude's Kitchen	"		4	4	4
	The Cross Keys	"		3	4	4
	The Enterprise	"		3	3	5
	The Hour Glass	"		3	4	2
	The Ivy Chelsea Garden	"		2	2	3
	Manuka Kitchen	"		3	4	3
	maze Grill	"		2	2	2
	The Sands End	"		3	3	3
	The Shed	"		4	4	4
	The Tommy Tucker	"		3	3	3
	Bumpkin	*British, Traditional*		2	2	2
	Bibendum Oyster Bar	*Fish & seafood*		3	2	3
	The Admiral Codrington	*International*		2	3	4
	Kensington Wine Rooms	"		2	3	3
	Obicà	*Italian*		3	2	2
	Pellicano Restaurant	"		3	4	3
	Polpo	"		2	2	2
	Sapori Sardi	"		3	3	3
	The Atlas	*Mediterranean*		4	4	4
	Ognisko Restaurant	*Polish*		3	3	5
	Capote Y Toros	*Spanish*		3	4	4
	Tendido Cero	"		3	3	3
	Tendido Cuatro	"		3	3	3
	Hanger	*Steaks & grills*		3	4	3
	Macellaio RC	"		3	2	3
	Geales Chelsea Green	*Fish & chips*		2	2	2
	Pizzicotto	*Pizza*		4	4	3
	Fernandez & Wells	*Sandwiches, cakes, etc*		3	3	3
	Chicama	*Peruvian*		2	2	3
	Maroush	*Lebanese*		3	2	2
	Royal China	*Chinese*		3	1	2
	Romulo Café	*Filipino*		3	3	3

	Chakra	*Indian*	3	3	3
	The Painted Heron	"	5	4	2
	Pure Indian Cooking	"	4	3	2
	Star of India	"	4	3	3
	Chisou	*Japanese*	4	3	2
	Kiru	"	4	4	3
	Eight Over Eight	*Pan-Asian*	3	3	4
	Sukho Fine Thai Cuisine	*Thai*	5	4	3
	Go-Viet	*Vietnamese*	4	3	3
£40+	Megan's Delicatessen	*British, Modern*	2	3	3
	Rabbit	"	3	3	2
	VQ	"	2	4	3
	Mona Lisa	*International*	3	4	2
	Aglio e Olio	*Italian*	3	3	3
	Buona Sera	"	3	3	3
	Chelsea Cellar	"	4	4	3
	Da Mario	"	3	3	4
	Made in Italy	"	3	2	3
	Nuovi Sapori	"	3	4	3
	Riccardo's	"	2	2	3
	Daquise	*Polish*	2	3	2
	Casa Brindisa	*Spanish*	2	2	2
	La Delizia Limbara	*Pizza*	3	3	3
	Rossopomodoro	"	3	2	2
	Lupita West	*Mexican/TexMex*	3	2	2
	Best Mangal	*Turkish*	4	3	3
	Dragon Palace	*Chinese*	4	2	2
	Dishoom	*Indian*	4	4	5
	Flora Indica	"	3	2	3
	Malabar	"	5	4	3
	Noor Jahan	"	3	3	3
	Thali	"	4	4	3
	Bone Daddies, Whole Foods	*Japanese*	4	3	3
	Oka	"	4	2	2
	Rosa's Fulham	*Thai*	2	2	2
	Suksan	"	4	3	2
£35+	Kensington Square Kitchen	*British, Modern*	3	4	3
	Churchill Arms	*British, Traditional*	3	2	5
	Pappa Ciccia	*Italian*	3	3	3
	Ceru	*Mediterranean*	4	3	2
	Haché	*Steaks & grills*	3	4	4
	Rocca Di Papa	*Pizza*	3	3	4
	Santa Maria	"	5	3	3
	Taiwan Village	*Taiwanese*	4	5	3
£30+	Tangerine Dream	*British, Modern*	3	1	3
	Vagabond Wines	*Mediterranean*	3	3	4
	Stagolee's	*Chicken*	–	–	–

	Kulu Kulu	Japanese	**3**	**2**	**1**
	Addie's Thai Café	Thai	**3**	**2**	**2**
£25+	Tommi's Burger Joint	Burgers, etc	**3**	**3**	**3**
	Eat Tokyo	Japanese	**4**	**3**	**2**
£20+	Stick & Bowl	Chinese	**5**	**3**	**1**
£10+	Orée	French	**3**	**2**	**3**
	Orée	Sandwiches, cakes, etc	**3**	**2**	**3**
	Over Under	"	**4**	**4**	**2**

Notting Hill, Holland Park, Bayswater, North Kensington & Maida Vale (W2, W9, W10, W11)

£140+	The Ledbury	British, Modern	**5**	**5**	**4**
£120+	Marianne	British, Modern	**5**	**4**	**4**
£90+	Bel Canto	French	**2**	**3**	**3**
£80+	Chucs	Italian	**3**	**3**	**3**
	Casa Cruz South	American	**2**	**3**	**4**
	Flat Three	Japanese	**4**	**4**	**3**
£70+	Angelus	French	**3**	**5**	**3**
	Assaggi	Italian	**4**	**5**	**2**
£60+	Pomona's	American	**3**	**3**	**3**
	The Dock Kitchen	British, Modern	**2**	**2**	**3**
	Julie's	"	–	–	–
	London Shell Co.	Fish & seafood	**4**	**5**	**5**
	The Summerhouse	"	**2**	**2**	**5**
	108 Garage	Fusion	**5**	**4**	**5**
	Edera	Italian	**3**	**4**	**3**
	Essenza	"	**3**	**4**	**3**
	Mediterraneo	"	**3**	**2**	**3**
	Osteria Basilico	"	**3**	**3**	**4**
	Stuzzico	"	**3**	**3**	**3**
	Kateh	Persian	**3**	**2**	**3**
	Kurobuta	Japanese	**3**	**2**	**2**
£50+	Granger & Co	Australian	**3**	**3**	**3**
	Daylesford Organic	British, Modern	**3**	**2**	**3**
	The Frontline Club	"	**2**	**2**	**4**
	The Ladbroke Arms	"	**3**	**3**	**3**
	The Magazine Restaurant	"	**3**	**3**	**4**
	Salt & Honey	"	**3**	**3**	**2**
	Six Portland Road	"	**4**	**4**	**3**

The Waterway	"		2 2 2
Snaps & Rye	Danish		3 4 3
Cepages	French		3 3 3
The Cow	Irish		3 3 4
Assaggi Bar & Pizzeria	Italian		4 3 2
The Oak	"		3 3 4
Ottolenghi	"		4 3 2
Polpo	"		2 2 2
Portobello Ristorante	"		3 4 4
Farmacy	Vegetarian		3 3 4
Pizza East Portobello	Pizza		3 2 4
The Red Pepper	"		3 2 2
Peyotito	Mexican/TexMex		2 2 2
Maroush Gardens	Lebanese		3 2 2
Royal China	Chinese		3 1 2
Maguro	Japanese		3 4 2
E&O	Pan-Asian		3 3 3
£40+	Electric Diner	American	2 2 3
	Paradise	British, Modern	3 3 4
	VQ	"	2 4 3
	Hereford Road	British, Traditional	4 4 3
	The Chipping Forecast	Fish & seafood	3 3 3
	Raoul's Café & Deli	Mediterranean	3 2 3
	Pizza Metro	Pizza	3 3 3
	Cocotte	Chicken	4 3 4
	Taqueria	Mexican/TexMex	4 4 3
	The Cedar Restaurant	Lebanese	3 3 3
	The Four Seasons	Chinese	4 1 1
	Mandarin Kitchen	"	4 2 1
	Pearl Liang	"	3 2 2
	Bombay Palace	Indian	4 4 2
	Noor Jahan	"	3 3 3
	Tonkotsu	Japanese	3 2 3
	Gogi	Korean	3 3 3
	Uli	Pan-Asian	3 3 3
£35+	Lockhouse	Burgers, etc	3 2 3
	MEATliquor	"	3 2 4
	Gold Mine	Chinese	4 2 2
	Satay House	Malaysian	3 3 3
£30+	Flat Iron	Steaks & grills	4 4 3
	C&R Café	Malaysian	4 2 2
£25+	Patty and Bun	Burgers, etc	4 3 3
	Alounak	Persian	3 2 3
	Fez Mangal	Turkish	5 4 3

£20+	Khan's	Indian	3 2 2

£5+	Lisboa Pâtisserie	Sandwiches, cakes, etc	3 3 4
	Falafel King	Middle Eastern	3 3 2

Hammersmith, Shepherd's Bush, Olympia, Chiswick, Brentford & Ealing (W4,W5,W6,W12,W13,W14,TW8)

£110+	Hedone	British, Modern	3 3 2

£90+	The River Café	Italian	3 3 3

£80+	La Trompette	French	5 4 3

£60+	Michael Nadra	French	4 3 2
	Le Vacherin	"	3 3 2
	Villa Di Geggiano	Italian	3 3 4

£50+	Jackson & Rye Chiswick	American	1 2 2
	The Anglesea Arms	British, Modern	4 4 4
	Blue Boat	"	2 2 3
	The Brackenbury	"	4 4 3
	Brackenbury Wine Rooms	"	3 3 4
	Charlotte's Place	"	3 3 4
	Charlotte's W4	"	3 4 3
	City Barge	"	3 2 3
	The Dove	"	3 3 4
	Ealing Park Tavern	"	3 4 3
	The Havelock Tavern	"	3 2 3
	High Road Brasserie	"	2 2 2
	No 197 Chiswick Fire Stn	"	2 2 4
	Vinoteca	"	3 3 4
	The Hampshire Hog	British, Traditional	3 2 4
	Albertine	French	3 3 4
	The Andover Arms	International	3 5 4
	Melody at St Paul's	"	2 3 3
	Cibo	Italian	4 5 3
	The Oak W12	"	3 3 4
	Pentolina	"	4 5 4
	The Swan	Mediterranean	3 4 4
	Foxlow	Steaks & grills	2 2 2
	Popeseye	"	3 2 2
	Smokehouse Chiswick	"	3 2 3
	The Gate	Vegetarian	4 3 3
	Quantus South	American	4 5 3
	Shikumen, Dorsett Hotel	Chinese	4 3 2
	Indian Zing	Indian	4 4 2
	Little Bird Chiswick	Pan-Asian	2 2 4

£40+	The Colton Arms	British, Modern	2 3 4
	The Dartmouth Castle	"	3 4 4
	Duke of Sussex	"	2 3 4
	Mustard	"	3 3 3
	The Pear Tree	"	3 3 4
	Annie's	International	2 3 4
	L'Amorosa	Italian	4 4 3
	Cumberland Arms	Mediterranean	4 4 3
	The Bird in Hand	Pizza	3 3 4
	Tamp Coffee	Sandwiches, cakes, etc	3 3 4
	Best Mangal	Turkish	4 3 3
	North China	Chinese	3 4 2
	Brilliant	Indian	4 4 3
	Karma	"	4 3 1
	Madhu's	"	4 4 3
	Potli	"	4 4 3
	Sushi Bar Makoto	Japanese	4 3 2
	Hare & Tortoise	Pan-Asian	3 2 2
£35+	Santa Maria	Pizza	5 3 3
	Chez Abir	Lebanese	3 3 2
	Anarkali	Indian	– – –
	Sagar	"	3 2 1
	Kiraku	Japanese	4 4 2
	Tosa	"	3 3 2
	Yoshi Sushi	"	3 3 2
	Saigon Saigon	Vietnamese	2 3 3
£30+	Homeslice	Pizza	4 4 4
	Oro Di Napoli	"	4 3 2
	Angie's Little Food Shop	Sandwiches, cakes, etc	3 3 3
	Chicken Shop	Chicken	3 3 3
	Adams Café	Moroccan	3 5 3
	Faanoos	Persian	3 3 2
	Monkey Temple	Indian	3 4 3
	Shilpa	Indian, Southern	5 2 1
	Atari-Ya	Japanese	4 2 1
£25+	Alounak	Persian	3 2 3
	Gifto's Lahore Karahi	Indian	3 2 2
	Eat Tokyo	Japanese	4 3 2
	Nukis Kitchen	Thai	3 2 2
£20+	Kerbisher & Malt	Fish & chips	3 3 2
	Killer Tomato	Mexican/TexMex	4 3 2
	Abu Zaad	Syrian	3 3 2
£5+	Bears Ice cream	Ice cream	3 3 3

NORTH

Hampstead, West Hampstead, St John's Wood, Regent's Park, Kilburn & Camden Town (NW postcodes)

| £70+ | The Landmark | British, Modern | 2 4 5 |
| | The Gilbert Scott | British, Traditional | 2 3 4 |

£60+	The Booking Office	British, Modern	2 2 4
	Bradley's	"	3 2 2
	Odette's	"	4 3 4
	L'Aventure	French	3 4 4
	Michael Nadra	"	4 3 2
	Oslo Court	"	4 5 5
	Bull & Last	International	3 3 3
	Villa Bianca	Italian	2 2 2
	Zest, JW3	Kosher	3 3 2
	Crocker's Folly	Lebanese	2 2 4
	Good Earth	Chinese	2 2 2
	Kaifeng	"	3 3 3
	Patara	Thai	4 4 4

£50+	The Horseshoe	British, Modern	3 3 4
	The Ivy Café	"	1 2 3
	Juniper Tree	"	3 2 2
	The Wells	"	2 2 3
	The Wet Fish Café	"	3 3 4
	York & Albany	British, Traditional	2 2 3
	Patron	French	2 3 3
	Summers	Irish	– – –
	Artigiano	Italian	3 2 2
	La Collina	"	3 4 3
	Ostuni	"	2 3 3
	The Rising Sun	"	3 2 3
	28 Church Row	Spanish	4 4 3
	Manna	Vegetarian	2 2 2
	Pizza East	Pizza	3 2 4
	Greenberry Café	Sandwiches, cakes, etc	3 3 3
	Phoenix Palace	Chinese	3 2 2

£40+	Delisserie	American	3 2 2
	Lantana Cafe	Australian	3 3 3
	The Junction Tavern	British, Modern	3 3 3
	Parlour Kensal	"	4 5 4
	L'Absinthe	French	2 4 3
	La Cage Imaginaire	"	2 2 3
	Lemonia	Greek	1 3 4
	Anima e Cuore	Italian	5 4 1
	L'Artista	"	3 4 4
	Giacomo's	"	3 3 2

	La Porchetta Pizzeria	"	2	3	2
	Sarracino	"	4	3	2
	El Parador	*Spanish*	3	2	3
	Mildreds	*Vegetarian*	3	3	3
	Harry Morgan's	*Burgers, etc*	2	2	2
	Poppies Camden	*Fish & chips*	3	2	3
	The Sea Shell	"	3	2	2
	L' Antica Pizzeria	*Pizza*	4	4	3
	Rossopomodoro	"	3	2	2
	The Cedar Restaurant	*Lebanese*	3	3	3
	Skewd Kitchen	*Turkish*	3	3	3
	Jun Ming Xuan	*Chinese, Dim sum*	2	3	2
	Bonoo	*Indian*	5	4	3
	Namaaste Kitchen	"	3	3	2
	Jin Kichi	*Japanese*	5	4	3
	Oka	"	4	2	2
	Sushi Masa	"	–	–	–
	The Petite Coree	*Korean*	4	4	2
	Singapore Garden	*Malaysian*	3	3	2
	Rosa's	*Thai*	2	2	2
£35+	Lure	*Fish & seafood*	3	5	3
	Carob Tree	*Greek*	3	4	3
	Quartieri	*Italian*	4	3	3
	Haché	*Steaks & grills*	3	4	4
	Nautilus	*Fish & chips*	4	3	1
	Sacro Cuore	*Pizza*	5	4	2
	Green Cottage	*Chinese*	3	2	2
	Great Nepalese	*Indian*	3	4	3
	Guglee	"	3	2	2
	Paradise Hampstead	"	4	5	4
	Vijay	"	3	3	1
	Asakusa	*Japanese*	5	2	2
	Bang Bang Oriental	*Pan-Asian*	–	–	–
£30+	The Little Bay	*Mediterranean*	2	3	4
	Dirty Burger	*Burgers, etc*	3	2	2
	Brew House Café	*Sandwiches, cakes, etc*	2	2	3
	Chicken Shop	*Chicken*	3	3	3
	Chai Thali	*Indian*	3	3	4
	Ravi Shankar	"	3	2	2
	Saravanaa Bhavan	"	5	2	1
	Atari-Ya	*Japanese*	4	2	1
£25+	Ali Baba	*Egyptian*	3	2	2
	Ariana II	*Afghani*	3	2	2
	Chutneys	*Indian*	3	2	2
	Diwana Bhel-Poori House	"	3	2	1
	Eat Tokyo	*Japanese*	4	3	2

£20+	Messapica	*Italian*	– – –
	Sakonis	*Indian*	**5** 2 1
	Roti King	*Malaysian*	**5** 2 1
£10+	Ginger & White	*Sandwiches, cakes, etc*	**3 4 3**
£5+	Doppio	*Sandwiches, cakes, etc*	**3 3 3**

Hoxton, Islington, Highgate, Crouch End, Stoke Newington, Finsbury Park, Muswell Hill & Finchley (N postcodes)

£70+	Plum + Spilt Milk	*British, Modern*	2 2 **3**
	German Gymnasium	*Central European*	2 2 **3**
£60+	Fifteen	*British, Modern*	2 2 2
	Frederick's	"	**3 4 4**
	Perilla	*Central European*	**4 4 3**
	Salut	*International*	**4 4 4**
	Radici	*Italian*	2 2 **3**
£50+	Granger & Co	*Australian*	**3 3 3**
	The Bull	*British, Modern*	**3 4 4**
	Caravan King's Cross	"	**3 3 4**
	Chriskitch	"	**4 3 3**
	Dandy	"	**4 4 3**
	The Drapers Arms	"	**3** 2 **3**
	Heirloom	"	**3 3 3**
	James Cochran N1	"	**5** 1 2
	The Lighterman	"	**3 4 4**
	Oldroyd	"	**4 3** 2
	Pig & Butcher	"	**4 5 4**
	The Red Lion & Sun	"	**3** 2 **3**
	Rotunda	"	**3 4 4**
	Westerns Laundry	"	– – –
	St Johns	*British, Traditional*	**3 4 5**
	Bellanger	*Central European*	2 **3 3**
	Galley	*Fish & seafood*	**3** 2 **3**
	Prawn on the Lawn	"	**4 4 3**
	Bistro Aix	*French*	**4 3 4**
	Petit Pois Bistro	"	**3 3** 2
	Table Du Marche	"	**3 3 3**
	The Good Egg	*Fusion*	**4 4 3**
	The Greek Larder, Arthouse	*Greek*	**3** 2 2
	8 Hoxton Square	*International*	**3 3 3**
	Primeur	"	**4 4 4**
	500	*Italian*	**3 3** 2
	Il Guscio	"	**3 4 3**
	Melange	"	**3** 2 2
	Ostuni	"	2 **3 3**
	Ottolenghi	"	**4 3** 2

	Trullo	"	4 4 3
	Sardine	*Mediterranean*	3 2 2
	Vinoteca	"	3 3 4
	Rök	*Scandinavian*	4 2 2
	Camino King's Cross	*Spanish*	3 3 2
	Popeseye	*Steaks & grills*	3 2 2
	Smokehouse Islington	"	3 3 2
	Duke's Brew & Que	*Burgers, etc*	4 3 4
	Bodean's	*BBQ*	2 2 2
£40+	Breakfast Club Hoxton	*American*	3 3 3
	Sunday	*Australian*	4 2 3
	Haven Bistro	*British, Modern*	2 3 2
	Humble Grape	"	3 4 4
	Season Kitchen	"	3 3 2
	Kipferl	*Central European*	3 2 3
	Andi's	*International*	3 4 4
	Banners	"	3 4 5
	La Fromagerie	"	3 2 2
	Osteria Tufo	*Italian*	3 3 2
	La Porchetta Pizzeria	"	2 3 2
	Rugoletta	"	3 3 2
	Alcedo	*Mediterranean*	3 4 3
	Lady Mildmay	"	3 4 3
	Bar Esteban	*Spanish*	4 4 4
	Café del Parc	"	4 5 3
	Lluna	"	3 3 3
	Thyme and Lemon	"	3 3 4
	Trangallan	"	4 4 3
	Mildreds	*Vegetarian*	3 3 3
	Toff's	*Fish & chips*	3 3 2
	Trawler Trash		– – –
	Rossopomodoro	*Pizza*	3 2 2
	Sweet Thursday	"	3 2 2
	Black Axe Mangal	*Turkish*	5 4 2
	Yipin China	*Chinese*	4 3 2
	Little Georgia Café	*Georgian*	3 2 3
	Dishoom	*Indian*	4 4 5
	Zaffrani	"	3 2 2
	Isarn	*Thai*	4 4 2
	Rosa's	"	2 2 2
	CôBa	*Vietnamese*	4 4 3
£35+	Le Sacré-Coeur	*French*	2 2 2
	Vrisaki	*Greek*	3 3 3
	Passione e Tradizione	*Italian*	4 3 2
	Pasta Remoli	"	3 2 2
	Pizzeria Pappagone	"	3 4 4
	MEATLiquor Islington	*Burgers, etc*	3 2 4
	Cannons	*Fish & chips*	4 4 2

Olympus Fish	"	**4** **5** **2**		
Sutton and Sons	"	**4** **4** **2**		
Sacro Cuore	Pizza	**5** **4** **2**		
Yard Sale Pizza	"	**4** **3** **2**		
Zia Lucia	"	**4** **3** **3**		
Monty's Deli	Sandwiches, cakes, etc	**3** **4** **4**		
Diyarbakir Kitchen	Turkish	**3** **3** **3**		
Iberia	Georgian	**3** **3** **2**		
Indian Rasoi	Indian	**3** **3** **2**		
Rasa	Indian, Southern	**3** **3** **3**		
Farang	Thai	**4** **4** **3**		
Salvation In Noodles	Vietnamese	**3** **2** **2**		
£30+ Oak N4	British, Modern	– – –		
Two Brothers	Fish & seafood	**3** **2** **2**		
Le Mercury	French	**2** **2** **4**		
MEATmission	Burgers, etc	**3** **3** **4**		
Max's Sandwich Shop	Sandwiches, cakes, etc	**4** **4** **3**		
Chicken Shop	Chicken	**3** **3** **3**		
Gallipoli	Turkish	**2** **3** **4**		
Gem	"	**3** **4** **2**		
G.kyüzü	"	**3** **3** **3**		
Xi'an Impression	Chinese	**4** **2** **2**		
Jashan	Indian	**4** **4** **2**		
Rani	"	**4** **2** **2**		
Atari-Ya	Japanese	**4** **2** **1**		
Dotori	Korean	**4** **3** **2**		
£25+ Afghan Kitchen	Afghani	**4** **3** **2**		
Delhi Grill	Indian	**3** **2** **2**		
£20+ Piebury Corner	British, Traditional	**3** **4** **3**		
L'Antica Pizzeria da Michele	Pizza	**3** **4** **3**		
£15+ Five Guys Islington	Burgers, etc	**3** **2** **2**		

SOUTH

South Bank (SE1)

£150+	Story	British, Modern	4 3 3
£100+	Aqua Shard	British, Modern	1 1 2
£90+	TING	International	3 3 4
£80+	Oblix	British, Modern	2 2 3
	Oxo Tower, Restaurant	"	1 1 2
	Hutong, The Shard	Chinese	1 2 5
£70+	Oxo Tower, Brasserie	British, Modern	1 1 2
	Le Pont de la Tour	"	2 2 3
	Skylon, South Bank Centre	"	2 2 2
	Hawksmoor	Steaks & grills	3 3 3
	Baluchi, Lalit Hotel London	Indian	– – –
£60+	Sea Containers	British, Modern	2 2 2
	Skylon Grill	"	2 2 3
	The Swan at the Globe	"	3 2 3
	Tate Modern Restaurant	"	2 3 4
	Tom Simmons	"	– – –
	Union Street Café	"	2 2 3
	Butlers Wharf Chop House	British, Traditional	2 2 3
	Roast	"	2 2 3
	Applebee's Fish	Fish & seafood	4 3 2
	Wright Brothers	"	4 3 3
	Arthur Hooper's	International	– – –
	Rabot 1745	"	2 2 2
	Vivat Bacchus	"	3 4 2
	Pizarro	Spanish	3 3 3
	Bala Baya	Middle Eastern	3 2 3
£50+	Albion	British, Modern	2 2 2
	Caravan Bankside	"	3 3 4
	Edwins	"	3 4 4
	Elliot's Café	"	3 3 3
	40 Maltby Street	"	4 4 3
	The Garrison	"	3 3 3
	Globe Tavern	"	3 3 3
	House Restaurant	"	2 3 2
	The Ivy Tower Bridge	"	2 2 3
	LASSCO Bar & DIning	"	– – –
	Laughing Gravy	"	3 4 3
	Menier Chocolate Factory	"	2 2 3
	Tate Modern, Restaurant	"	3 2 4

	Waterloo Bar & Kitchen	"	2	2	2
	The Anchor & Hope	British, Traditional	4	2	2
	fish!	Fish & seafood	3	2	2
	Casse-Croute	French	4	3	4
	Capricci	Italian	4	4	3
	Macellaio RC	"	3	2	3
	O'ver	"	4	3	3
	Baltic	Polish	4	4	4
	Bar Douro	Portuguese	4	3	3
	Camino Bankside	Spanish	3	3	2
	LOBOS Meat & Tapas	"	4	4	2
	Tapas Brindisa	"	2	2	2
	Pique Nique	Chicken	–	–	–
	Arabica Bar and Kitchen	Lebanese	3	2	3
	Champor-Champor	Thai	4	4	4
£40+	Lantana London Bridge	Australian	3	3	3
	Blueprint Café	British, Modern	2	2	4
	The Green Room	"	2	2	2
	Lupins	"	–	–	–
	Boro Bistro	French	3	4	3
	José	Spanish	5	4	5
	Mar I Terra	"	3	4	3
	Meson don Felipe	"	2	2	3
	El Pastór	Mexican/TexMex	4	3	4
	Tonkotsu Bankside	Japanese	3	2	3
	Sticky Mango at RSJ	Pan-Asian	–	–	–
£35+	The Table	British, Modern	3	2	2
	tibits	Vegetarian	3	2	3
	Tas Pide	Turkish	2	3	3
	Est India	Indian	3	3	3
£30+	Pulia	Italian	3	4	3
£25+	Mercato Metropolitano	Italian	3	2	5
	Padella	"	5	4	4
£20+	Masters Super Fish	Fish & chips	3	2	2
£10+	Gourmet Goat	Middle Eastern	4	4	2
£5+	Monmouth Coffee Company	Sandwiches, cakes, etc	4	5	4

Greenwich, Lewisham, Dulwich & Blackheath
(All SE postcodes, except SE1)

£60+	Craft London	British, Modern	4	4	2
	Pharmacy 2	"	2	3	3
£50+	La Bonne Bouffe	British, Modern	3	2	3
	The Camberwell Arms	"	4	3	3
	Franklins	"	3	3	2
	The Guildford Arms	"	3	4	3
	Orchard	"	2	2	2
	The Palmerston	"	4	3	3
	Peckham Refresh' Rooms	"	3	3	3
	The Perry Vale	"	3	4	3
	Rivington Grill	"	2	2	2
	The Rosendale	"	3	4	3
	Sparrow	"	–	–	–
	Brasserie Toulouse-Lautrec	French	3	3	3
	Peckham Bazaar	Greek	5	3	4
	Brookmill	International	3	3	3
	Tulse Hill Hotel	"	3	3	3
	Luciano's	Italian	3	3	3
	Sail Loft	Mediterranean	2	3	4
	Cau	Steaks & grills	2	2	2
	Spinach	Vegetarian	3	3	3
	Babur	Indian	5	5	4
	Kennington Tandoori	"	4	4	4
	Sticks'n'Sushi	Japanese	4	2	2
	Yama Momo	"	4	2	3
£40+	The Crooked Well	British, Modern	3	2	3
	Brockwell Lido Café	"	2	2	4
	Louie Louie	"	3	3	3
	Joanna's	International	3	5	4
	Platform1	"	3	3	3
	The Yellow House	"	3	3	3
	Artusi	Italian	4	4	3
	Le Querce	"	4	4	3
	Pedler	Pizza	3	3	4
	Zero Degrees	"	3	3	4
	Dragon Castle	Chinese	4	3	3
	Everest Inn	Indian	3	2	3
	Ganapati	"	5	4	3
	The Begging Bowl	Thai	4	3	2
£35+	Babette	British, Modern	3	3	4
	Black Prince	"	3	3	3
	Catford Constitutional Club	"	3	4	4
	MEATliquor ED	Burgers, etc	3	2	4
	The Gowlett Arms	Pizza	4	3	4

	Mamma Dough	"		3 3 4
	Rocca Di Papa	"		3 3 4
	Theo's	"		3 4 3
	Yalla Yalla	Lebanese		3 2 2
	Zaibatsu	Japanese		4 3 2
	Bánh Bánh	Vietnamese		3 4 3
	Mr Bao	Taiwanese		4 3 3
£30+	Rox Burger	Burgers, etc		4 3 3
	Made of Dough	Pizza		– – –
	FM Mangal	Turkish		3 3 2
£25+	Zeret	Ethiopian		4 5 3
£20+	500 Degrees	Pizza		3 3 2
	Persepolis	Persian		4 3 2
	Silk Road	Chinese		5 2 2
	Café East	Vietnamese		5 2 2
£15+	Goddards At Greenwich	British, Traditional		3 4 4
£10+	Golden Chippy	Fish & chips		3 4 2
£5+	Kappacasein	Sandwiches, cakes, etc		5 3 2
	Monmouth Coffee Company	"		4 5 4

Battersea, Brixton, Clapham, Wandsworth
Barnes, Putney & Wimbledon (All SW postcodes south of the river)

£80+	Chez Bruce	British, Modern		5 5 4
£70+	Trinity	British, Modern		5 5 3
	Gastronhome	French		4 4 2
£60+	Rick Stein	Fish & seafood		3 2 5
	Wright Brothers	"		4 3 3
	The White Onion	French		3 3 2
	London House	International		2 2 2
	Riva	Italian		3 3 2
	Good Earth	Chinese		2 2 2
	Patara	Thai		4 4 4
£50+	Bodean's	American		2 2 2
	Counter Vauxhall Arches	"		4 3 4
	Bistro Union	British, Modern		3 3 3
	Brunswick House Café	"		3 3 5
	Cannizaro House	"		1 2 3
	Counter Culture	"		4 3 3
	Hood	"		4 3 2

The Ivy Café	"	1	2	3
Lamberts	"	4	5	3
The Manor	"	3	3	3
May The Fifteenth	"	3	4	2
Minnow	"	–	–	–
Nutbourne	"	3	3	4
Olympic, Olympic Studios	"	2	2	3
Salon Brixton	"	3	3	3
Sonny's Kitchen	"	2	2	2
The Spencer	"	3	4	3
The Victoria	"	–	–	–
Canton Arms	British, Traditional	4	2	4
Jolly Gardeners	"	3	3	3
Augustine Kitchen	French	3	4	2
Sinabro	"	3	4	3
Soif	"	3	4	3
The Light House	International	3	3	2
Numero Uno	Italian	3	4	3
The Bobbin	Mediterranean	4	4	4
Brindisa Food Rooms	Spanish	2	2	2
Cau	Steaks & grills	2	2	2
Foxlow	"	2	2	2
Knife	"	5	4	4
Macellaio RC	"	3	2	3
Naughty Piglets	"	5	5	3
Popeseye	"	3	2	2
MeatUp	BBQ	3	2	2
Bistro Vadouvan	Indian	–	–	–
Sticks'n'Sushi	Japanese	4	2	2
Little Bird Battersea	Pan-Asian	2	2	4
£40+ The Avalon	British, Modern	2	2	3
The Brown Dog	"	3	3	3
The Dairy	"	4	4	4
Earl Spencer	"	3	2	4
Humble Grape	"	3	4	4
Jules	"	–	–	–
The Plough	"	3	3	5
Trinity Upstairs	"	5	4	4
Gazette	French	2	2	3
Annie's	International	2	3	4
Belpassi Bros	Italian	3	3	3
Buona Sera	"	3	3	3
Made in Italy	"	3	2	3
Osteria Antica Bologna	"	3	2	2
Pizza Metro	"	3	3	3
The Fox & Hounds	Mediterranean	4	3	4
Boqueria	Spanish	4	4	4
Gremio de Brixton	"	3	3	3
Little Taperia	"	3	3	3

	Arlo's	Steaks & grills	2	3	2
	Addomme	Pizza	4	3	2
	Al Forno	"	2	4	4
	Dynamo	"	3	3	3
	Rossopomodoro	"	3	2	2
	MOMMI	Peruvian	3	4	3
	Chit Chaat Chai	Indian	4	3	2
	Indian Moment	"	3	3	2
	Kashmir	"	4	3	3
	Ma Goa	"	4	4	3
	Nanban	Japanese	4	3	3
	Takahashi	"	5	4	3
	Tomoe	"	4	2	2
	Tsunami	"	4	2	3
	Hare & Tortoise	Pan-Asian	3	2	2
	Rosa's	Thai	2	2	2
£35+	Plot	British, Modern	3	3	3
	Fish in a Tie	Mediterranean	3	3	3
	Bukowski Grill	Steaks & grills	3	3	2
	Haché	Burgers, etc	3	4	4
	Brady's	Fish & chips	3	3	3
	Eco	Pizza	3	3	3
	Mamma Dough	"	3	3	4
	Orange Pekoe	Sandwiches, cakes, etc	3	4	4
	Cartel	Mexican/TexMex	–	–	–
	Meza Trinity Road	Lebanese	3	3	2
	JAN	Middle Eastern	–	–	–
	Indian Ocean	Indian	3	3	2
	Hashi	Japanese	3	4	2
	Taro	"	3	2	2
	Cah-Chi	Korean	3	4	3
	Mien Tay	Vietnamese	4	3	2
£30+	Vagabond Wines	Mediterranean	3	3	4
	Dip & Flip	Burgers, etc	3	3	3
	Dirty Burger	"	3	2	2
	Ground Coffee Society	Sandwiches, cakes, etc	3	4	3
	Faanoos	Persian	3	3	2
	Sree Krishna	Indian	4	3	2
	The Pepper Tree	Thai	2	3	3
£25+	The Joint	American	3	3	3
	Flotsam and Jetsam	Australian	3	4	4
	Tried & True	British, Modern	3	3	3
	Pizzastorm	Pizza	3	3	1
	Lahore Karahi	Pakistani	4	2	2
	Lahore Kebab House	"	4	3	2
	Mirch Masala	"	4	2	1

	Awesome Thai	*Thai*	3	4	3
	Kaosarn	"	4	3	3
£20+	Kerbisher & Malt	*Fish & chips*	3	3	2
	Cut The Mustard	*Sandwiches, cakes, etc*	3	2	3
	Milk	"	4	3	3
	Hot Stuff	*Indian*	3	5	3
	Jaffna House	*Indian, Southern*	5	2	2
£15+	Joe Public	*Pizza*	4	3	3
£10+	Bean & Hop	*Mediterranean*	3	3	2
	Pop Brixton	*Burgers, etc*	5	4	3

Outer west: Kew, Richmond, Twickenham, Teddington

£80+	The Glasshouse	*British, Modern*	5	4	3
	M Bar & Grill Twickenham	*Steaks & grills*	2	2	2
£70+	The Dysart Petersham	*British, Modern*	3	4	4
	Petersham Nurseries Cafe	"	2	1	5
£60+	The Bingham	*British, Modern*	4	5	4
	Petersham Hotel	"	3	3	4
	Al Boccon di'vino	*Italian*	3	4	5
£50+	Jackson & Rye	*American*	1	2	2
	The Ivy Café	*British, Modern*	1	2	3
	Petit Ma Cuisine	*French*	2	2	3
	Le Salon Privé	"	4	3	4
	A Cena	*Italian*	3	4	4
	Bacco	"	3	2	2
£40+	La Buvette	*French*	3	3	3
	Pizzeria Rustica	*Pizza*	3	2	2
	Matsuba	*Japanese*	3	4	2
£35+	The Stable	*Pizza*	2	2	3
	Dastaan	*Indian*	5	4	3

EAST

Smithfield & Farringdon (EC1)

Price	Restaurant	Cuisine			
£100+	The Clove Club	British, Modern	5	4	4
£90+	Club Gascon	French	–	–	–
£80+	Sushi Tetsu	Japanese	5	5	4
£70+	Luca	Italian	3	4	4
	Smiths, Top Floor	Steaks & grills	3	3	4
	Sosharu, Turnmill Building	Japanese	3	3	3
£60+	Anglo	British, Modern	5	4	2
	Chiswell St Dining Rooms	"	2	2	2
	The Jugged Hare	"	3	2	3
	The Modern Pantry	"	2	2	2
	The Quality Chop House	British, Traditional	3	3	3
	St John Smithfield	"	5	4	3
	Bleeding Heart Restaurant	French	3	3	5
	Moro	Spanish	4	3	3
	Hix Oyster & Chop House	Steaks & grills	2	2	2
	Smiths, Dining Room	"	2	2	2
£50+	Bodean's	American	2	2	2
	Granger & Co,	Australian	3	3	3
	Bird of Smithfield	British, Modern	2	2	2
	Caravan	"	3	3	4
	Vinoteca	"	3	3	4
	Wilmington	"	3	4	3
	Albion Clerkenwell	British, Traditional	2	2	2
	The Fox and Anchor	"	3	3	4
	Café du Marché	French	3	3	5
	Comptoir Gascon	"	3	3	2
	Niche	International	2	3	2
	Apulia	Italian	3	3	3
	Macellaio RC	"	3	2	3
	Palatino	"	4	5	3
	Polpo	"	2	2	2
	Santore	"	4	3	3
	Ibérica	Spanish	2	2	3
	Foxlow	Steaks & grills	2	2	2
	The Gate	Vegetarian	4	3	3
	Burger & Lobster	Burgers, etc	3	2	3
	Ceviche Old St	Peruvian	4	3	3
	The Sichuan	Chinese	4	3	3

£40+					
Lantana Café	Australian	3	3	3
The Green	British, Modern	–	–	–
La Ferme London	French	3	3	3
La Porchetta Pizzeria	Italian	2	3	2
Morito	Spanish	4	4	4
Breddos Tacos	Mexican/TexMex	4	4	4
Berber & Q Shawarma Bar	Middle Eastern	4	3	3
Bone Daddies, The Bower	Japanese	4	3	3
Cây Tre	Vietnamese	3	3	2

£35+					
The Eagle	Mediterranean	4	2	5
Pizza Pilgrims	Pizza	4	3	3
Workshop Coffee Holborn	Sandwiches, cakes, etc	3	4	4
Pham Sushi	Japanese	4	3	2
On The Bab	Korean	3	2	2

£30+					
Smiths, Ground Floor	British, Modern	2	2	3
White Bear	British, Traditional	3	3	3
Fish Central	Fish & seafood	3	2	2
Kolossi Grill	Greek	3	3	3
Ninth Ward	Burgers, etc	2	3	4
Homeslice	Pizza	4	4	4

£10+					
Department of Coffee	Sandwiches, cakes, etc	3	4	4
Prufrock Coffee	"	3	2	4

£5+					
Luardos	Mexican/TexMex	5	4	–

The City (EC2, EC3, EC4)

£100+					
La Dame de Pic London	French	3	3	2

£90+					
Fenchurch Restaurant	British, Modern	3	2	3
Angler, South Place Hotel	Fish & seafood	3	2	2
Goodman City	Steaks & grills	4	4	2
Sushisamba	Japanese	3	2	5

£80+					
City Social	British, Modern	2	3	5
Coq d'Argent	French	2	2	3
M Restaurant	Steaks & grills	2	2	2
Yauatcha City	Chinese	4	3	3
Mei Ume	Japanese	–	–	–

£70+					
Duck & Waffle	British, Modern	2	2	5
1 Lombard Street	"	2	2	3
Sweetings	Fish & seafood	3	2	4
Lutyens	French	2	2	2
L'Anima	Italian	4	4	3
Boisdale of Bishopsgate	Scottish	3	2	3

	Barbecoa	Steaks & grills	2 2 2	
	The Grill at McQueen	"	3 4 3	
	Hawksmoor	"	3 3 3	
	HKK	Chinese	5 5 3	
£60+	The Botanist	British, Modern	2 2 2	
	Bread Street Kitchen	"	2 2 2	
	Darwin Brasserie	"	2 3 4	
	The Don	"	3 3 2	
	High Timber	"	3 5 3	
	The Mercer	"	2 2 2	
	Merchants Tavern	"	3 2 4	
	The Modern Pantry	"	2 2 2	
	The White Swan	"	3 3 2	
	Cabotte	French	4 5 4	
	Sauterelle, Royal Exchange	"	3 3 4	
	Vivat Bacchus	International	3 4 2	
	Caravaggio	Italian	3 2 2	
	Manicomio	"	2 3 3	
	Eyre Brothers	Spanish	4 3 3	
	Hispania	"	3 2 2	
	Sagardi	"	2 2 2	
	Temple & Sons	Steaks & grills	3 3 2	
	Vanilla Black	Vegetarian	2 2 2	
	Red Rooster	Chicken	– – –	
	Darbaar	Indian	4 3 2	
	Mint Leaf Lounge		4 4 4	
	Nanashi	Japanese	– – –	
£50+	Bodean's	American	2 2 2	
	Pitt Cue Co	"	4 3 3	
	The Anthologist	British, Modern	2 2 3	
	Caravan	"	3 3 4	
	The Don Bistro and Bar	"	3 3 4	
	James Cochran EC3	"	5 1 2	
	Northbank	"	3 2 3	
	Princess of Shoreditch	"	3 2 2	
	Rök	"	4 2 2	
	Paternoster Chop House	British, Traditional	2 1 2	
	Fish Market	Fish & seafood	3 3 2	
	Royal Exchange Grand Café,	French	2 3 4	
	28-50	"	2 4 3	
	L'Anima Café	Italian	3 3 2	
	Obicà	"	3 2 2	
	Osteria, Barbican Centre	"	2 2 3	
	Popolo	"	5 4 3	
	Taberna Etrusca	"	2 3 3	
	Mac & Wild	Scottish	4 3 4	
	Camino Monument	Spanish	3 3 2	
	José Pizarro	"	3 3 2	

	Aviary	*Steaks & grills*	–	–	–
	The Jones Family Project	"	4	4	4
	The Tramshed	"	3	3	4
	Burger & Lobster	*Burgers, etc*	3	2	3
	Oklava	*Turkish*	4	2	3
	Cinnamon Kitchen	*Indian*	4	3	3
£40+	Café Below	*British, Modern*	3	2	3
	Humble Grape	"	3	4	4
	VQ	"	2	4	3
	The Wine Library	*International*	1	3	5
	Rucoletta	*Italian*	2	2	2
	Relais de Venise L'Entrecôte	*Steaks & grills*	3	2	2
	Ozone Coffee Roasters	*Sandwiches, cakes, etc*	4	4	4
	Haz	*Turkish*	2	2	2
	Shoryu Ramen	*Japanese*	3	2	2
	Hare & Tortoise	*Pan-Asian*	3	2	2
£35+	Simpson's Tavern	*British, Traditional*	2	3	4
	Haché	*Burgers, etc*	3	4	4
	Pizza Pilgrims	*Pizza*	4	3	3
	Blacklock	*BBQ*	4	4	4
	temper City	"	3	4	5
	Bangalore Express	*Indian*	3	3	3
	K10, Appold Street	*Japanese*	3	4	2
	Taro	"	3	2	2
	On The Bab	*Korean*	3	2	2
£30+	Flat Iron	*Steaks & grills*	4	4	3
	Homeslice	*Pizza*	4	4	4
	Koya	*Japanese*	3	3	3
£25+	Hilliard	*British, Modern*	4	4	4
	Patty and Bun	*Burgers, etc*	4	3	3
	Bibimbap	*Korean*	3	2	2
£20+	Bleecker Burger	*Burgers, etc*	5	2	2
£15+	City Càphê	*Vietnamese*	3	3	2
£10+	Yolk	*British, Modern*	–	–	–
	Pilpel	*Middle Eastern*	4	3	2

East End & Docklands (All E postcodes)

Price	Restaurant	Cuisine			
£90+	Typing Room	International	5	5	3
	Goodman	Steaks & grills	4	4	2
£80+	Galvin La Chapelle	French	3	2	4
	Roka	Japanese	4	3	3
£70+	Lyle's	British, Modern	4	2	2
	Smith's Wapping	"	4	4	4
	Plateau	French	2	3	3
	Bokan	International	–	–	–
	Hawksmoor	Steaks & grills	3	3	3
£60+	The Gun	British, Modern	3	3	4
	Hoi Polloi, Ace Hotel	"	3	2	3
	One Canada Square	"	2	4	3
	Pidgin	"	5	4	3
	Sager + Wilde	"	2	4	4
	Tom's Kitchen	"	2	2	2
	The Marksman	British, Traditional	4	3	4
	St John Bread & Wine	"	3	3	2
	Wright Brothers	Fish & seafood	4	3	3
	Tratra	French	–	–	–
	The Laughing Heart	International	3	2	3
	Sager + Wilde Restaurant	"	2	4	4
	Canto Corvino	Italian	4	3	3
	Brawn	Mediterranean	4	3	3
	Boisdale of Canary Wharf	Scottish	3	3	4
	Buen Ayre	Argentinian	4	4	2
£50+	Big Easy	American	2	2	3
	Bistrotheque	British, Modern	3	2	4
	The Bothy	"	–	–	–
	The Culpeper	"	2	2	3
	Ellory, Netil House	"	3	5	3
	Galvin HOP	"	2	3	3
	Jones & Sons	"	4	4	4
	Legs	"	3	4	4
	The Narrow	"	3	3	4
	Paradise Garage	"	4	4	3
	Rochelle Canteen	"	3	3	4
	Treves & Hyde	"	–	–	–
	Albion	British, Traditional	2	2	2
	Bumpkin	"	2	2	2
	Blanchette East	French	4	3	4
	Bombetta	Italian	3	4	2
	Il Bordello	"	3	3	4
	Lardo Bebè	"	3	3	2
	Obicà	"	3	2	2

	Super Tuscan	"	4	4	3
	Corner Room	*Portuguese*	3	4	4
	Ibérica	*Spanish*	2	2	3
	Cau	*Steaks & grills*	2	2	2
	Hill & Szrok	"	4	4	4
	Burger & Lobster	*Burgers, etc*	3	2	3
	Pizza East	*Pizza*	3	2	4
	Andina	*Peruvian*	4	3	3
	Ottolenghi	*Israeli*	4	3	2
	Royal China	*Chinese*	3	1	2
	Café Spice Namaste	*Indian*	5	5	3
	Grand Trunk Road	"	4	4	3
	Sticks'n'Sushi	*Japanese*	4	2	2
	Som Saa	*Thai*	5	4	4

£40+	Breakfast Club	*American*	3	3	3
	Cafe Football	*British, Modern*	2	2	2
	Eat 17	"	3	4	3
	The Empress	"	4	3	4
	The Frog	"	5	3	2
	The Morgan Arms	"	3	2	3
	P Franco	"	4	3	3
	Provender	*French*	3	4	4
	Blixen	*International*	3	3	3
	Dokke	"	–	–	–
	Eat 17	"	3	4	3
	Emilia's Crafted Pasta	*Italian*	4	3	3
	Pomaio	"	3	4	3
	Rotorino	"	2	4	2
	Verdi's	"	3	4	3
	Taberna do Mercado	*Portuguese*	3	3	2
	Bravas	*Spanish*	3	4	3
	Morito	"	4	4	4
	Relais de Venise L'Entrecôte	*Steaks & grills*	3	2	2
	Mildreds	*Vegetarian*	3	3	3
	Poppies	*Fish & chips*	3	2	3
	Corner Kitchen	*Pizza*	3	3	3
	Chick 'n' Sours	*Chicken*	3	3	3
	Smokestak	*BBQ*	5	3	3
	Lupita	*Mexican/TexMex*	3	2	2
	Berber & Q	*Middle Eastern*	5	2	5
	Haz	*Turkish*	2	2	2
	Laphet	*Burmese*	3	3	3
	Sichuan Folk	*Chinese*	3	3	2
	My Neighbours The Dumplings	*Chinese Dim su*	4	2	2
	Little Georgia Café	*Georgian*	3	2	3
	Dishoom	*Indian*	4	4	5
	Gunpowder	"	4	3	3
	Ippudo London	*Japanese*	3	2	2
	Tonkotsu	"	3	2	3

Price	Name	Cuisine	Rating		
	Uchi	"	4	2	2
	Rosa's	Thai	2	2	2
	Smoking Goat	"	4	3	2
	Viet Grill	Vietnamese	3	2	2
£35+	Bukowski Grill, Boxpark	Steaks & grills	3	3	2
	Ark Fish	Fish & chips	3	3	2
	Sutton and Sons	"	4	4	2
	Pizza Pilgrims	Pizza	4	3	3
	The Stable	"	2	2	3
	Yard Sale Pizza	"	4	3	2
	Saiphin's Thai Kitchen	Thai	–	–	–
	Mien Tay	Vietnamese	4	3	2
£30+	The Vincent	British, Modern	–	–	–
	Vagabond Wines	Mediterranean	3	3	4
	Dirty Burger	Burgers, etc	3	2	2
	Chicken Shop	Chicken	3	3	3
	Randy's Wing Bar	"	4	3	3
	Madame D's	Indian	–	–	–
	Sông Quê	Vietnamese	3	3	2
£25+	Patty and Bun	Burgers, etc	4	3	3
	Shake Shack	"	2	2	2
	Crate Brewery and Pizzeria	Pizza	3	2	4
	Mangal 1	Turkish	5	4	2
	Lahore Kebab House	Pakistani	4	3	2
	Needoo	"	4	3	2
	Tayyabs	"	4	1	2
	Bao Bar	Taiwanese	4	3	2
£20+	Bleecker Burger	Burgers, etc	5	2	2
£15+	E Pellicci	Italian	3	4	5
£10+	The Rib Man	Burgers, etc	5	4	–
	Pavilion Cafe & Bakery	Sandwiches, cakes, etc	3	2	4
	Pilpel	Middle Eastern	4	3	2
£5+	Brick Lane Beigel Bake	Sandwiches, cakes, etc	4	1	1

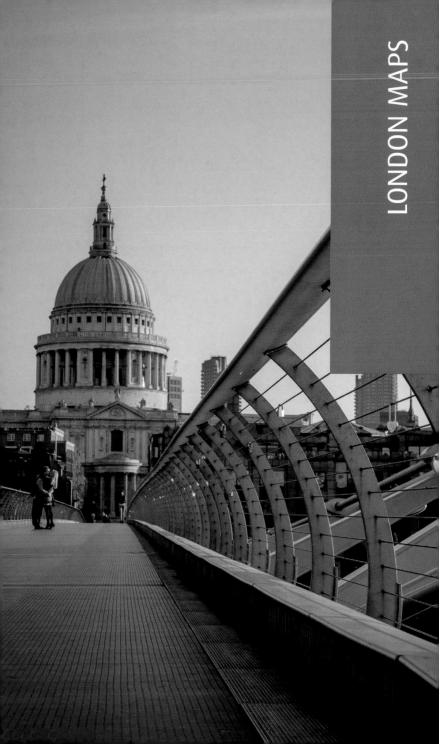

MAP **1** – LONDON OVERVIEW

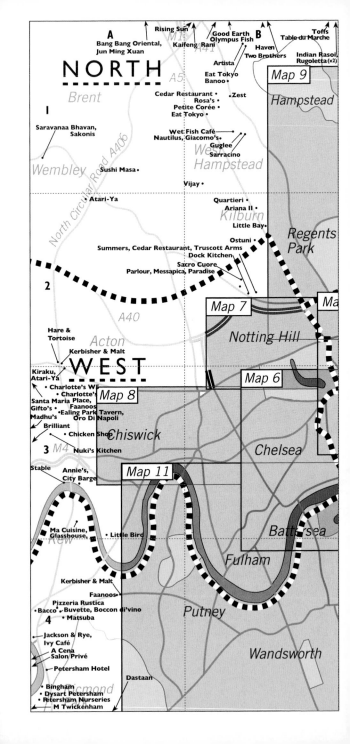

NORTH

A
Bang Bang Oriental,
Jun Ming Xuan

Rising Sun
Kaifeng Rani

Good Earth
Olympus Fish

B
Toffs
Table du Marche

Haven
Two Brothers

Indian Rasoi,
Rugoletta (x2)

Artista

Brent

A41

A5

Eat Tokyo
Banoo

Map 9

Cedar Restaurant •
Rosa's •
Petite Corée •
Eat Tokyo

• Zest

Hampstead

I

Saravanaa Bhavan,
Sakonis

Wet Fish Café
Nautilus, Giacomo's•

West

Guglee

Wembley

Sushi Masa •

Hampstead

Sarracino

Vijay •

Quartieri •
Ariana II •

Kilburn

• Atari-Ya

Little Bay•

*Regents
Park*

Ostuni •

Summers, Cedar Restaurant, Truscott Arms
Dock Kitchen
Sacro Cuore

Parlour, Messapica, Paradise •

Map 7

Ma

A40

Hare &
Tortoise

Acton

Kerbisher & Malt

Notting Hill

WEST

Kiraku,
Atari-Ya

Map 6

• Charlotte's W
• Charlotte's
Santa Maria Place,
Gifto's •
•Faanoos
Madhu's •Ealing Park Tavern,
Oro Di Napoli

Map 8

Chiswick

Chelsea

Brilliant

• Chicken Shop

3 *M4* • Nuki's Kitchen

Stable

Annie's,
City Barge

Map 11

Ma Cuisine,
Glasshouse,

• Little Bird

Battersea

Kew

Fulham

Kerbisher & Malt

Faanoos•

Pizzeria Rustica
•Bacco •Buvette, Boccon di'vino
4 • Matsuba

Putney

Jackson & Rye,
Ivy Café
A Cena
Salon Privé

Petersham Hotel

Wandsworth

• Bingham
• Dysart Petersham
• Petersham Nurseries
• M Twickenham

Dastaan

Richmond

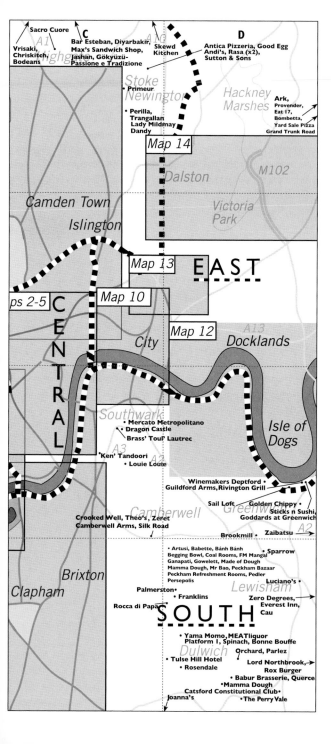

MAP **1** – LONDON OVERVIEW

Sacro Cuore

C

Vrisaki, Chriskitch, Bodeans

Bar Esteban, Diyarbakir, Max's Sandwich Shop, Jashan, Gökyüzü-Passione e Tradizione

Skewd Kitchen

D

Antica Pizzeria, Good Egg Andi's, Rasa (x2), Sutton & Sons

Stoke Newington
• **Primeur**

Hackney Marshes

Ark, Provender, Eat 17, Bombetta, Yard Sale Pizza Grand Trunk Road

• **Perilla, Trangallan Lady Mildmay Dandy**

Map 14

Dalston

M102

Camden Town

Islington

Victoria Park

Map 13

E A S T

ps 2-5

C

Map 10

E N T R A L

Map 12

City

Docklands

A13

Southwark

• **Mercato Metropolitano**
• **Dragon Castle**
Brass' Tou' Lautrec

Isle of Dogs

•**'Ken' Tandoori**
• **Louie Louie**

Winemakers Deptford • Guildford Arms, Rivington Grill

Sail Loft — Golden Chippy •
Sticks n Sushi, Goddards at Greenwich

Camberwell

Greenwich

Crooked Well, Theo's, Zeret Camberwell Arms, Silk Road

Brookmill •

Zaibatsu

A2

• Artusi, Babette, Bánh Bánh Begging Bowl, Coal Rooms, FM Mangal Ganapati, Gowelett, Made of Dough Mamma Dough, Mr Bao, Peckham Bazaar Peckham Refreshment Rooms, Pedler Persepolis

• Sparrow

Brixton

Clapham

Palmerston•

• **Franklins**

Rocca di Papa•

Lewisham

Luciano's •

Zero Degrees, Everest Inn, Cau

S O U T H

• Yama Momo, MEATliquor Platform 1, Spinach, Bonne Bouffe

Dulwich

Orchard, Parlez

• **Tulse Hill Hotel**
• **Rosendale**

Lord Northbrook,→ Rox Burger

• Babur Brasserie, Querce
•**Mamma Dough**
Catsford Constitutional Club•

Joanna's•

•The Perry Vale

MAP 2 – WEST END OVERVIEW

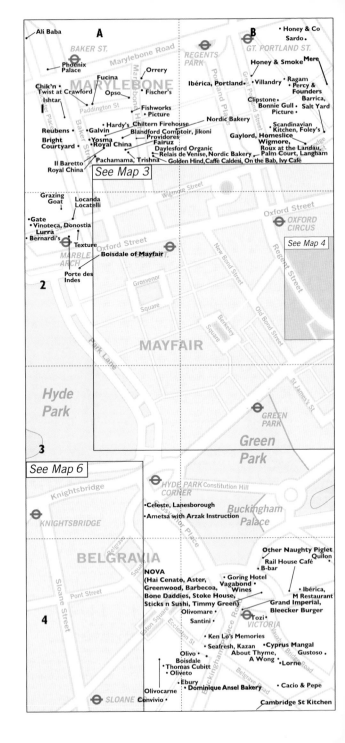

Ali Baba

A

BAKER ST.

Marylebone Road

REGENTS PARK

GT. PORTLAND ST.

B

• Honey & Co
Sardo •

Phoenix Palace

Fucina
Orrery

Honey & Smoke

Mere

MARYLEBONE

Ibérica, Portland •

• Villandry

• Ragam
• Percy & Founders

Chik'n •
Twist at Crawford

Opso

• Fischer's

Clipstone •
Bonnie Gull •

Barrica,
• Salt Yard

Ishtar

Paddington St

Fishworks
• Picture

Picture •

Hardy's Chiltern Firehouse

Nordic Bakery

Scandinavian
Kitchen, Foley's

Reubens •

Galvin

Blandford Comptoir, Jikoni
Providores

Gaylord, Homeslice

Bright
Courtyard •

• Yosma
• Royal China

Fairuz
Daylesford Organic

Wigmore,
Roux at the Landau,
Palm Court, Langham

Il Baretto
Royal China

Relais de Venise, Nordic Bakery
Pachamama, Trishna

Golden Hind, Caffè Caldesi, On the Bab, Ivy Café

See Map 3

Wigmore Street

Grazing
Goat

Locanda
Locatelli

Oxford Street

OXFORD CIRCUS

• Gate
• Vinoteca, Donostia
Lurra
• Bernardi's

Texture

Oxford Street

See Map 4

MARBLE ARCH

Boisdale of Mayfair

New Bond Street

Regent Street

2

Porte des Indes

Grosvenor

Old Bond Street

Grosvenor
Square

Berkeley
Square

MAYFAIR

Park Lane

St James's St

Hyde
Park

GREEN PARK

3

Green
Park

See Map 6

HYDE PARK CORNER

Constitution Hill

Knightsbridge

• Celeste, Lanesborough

Buckingham
Palace

KNIGHTSBRIDGE

• Ametsa with Arzak Instruction

Belgrave

Other Naughty Piglet
Quilon

BELGRAVIA

Rail House Café
• B-bar

Sloane Street

Pont Street

NOVA
(Hai Cenato, Aster,
Greenwood, Barbecoa,
Bone Daddies, Stoke House,
Sticks n Sushi, Timmy Green)

• Goring Hotel
Vagabond •
Wines

• Ibérica,
M Restaurant
Grand Imperial,
Bleecker Burger

Olivomare •

Tozi •

Santini •

VICTORIA

4

• Ken Lo's Memories

Eaton Square

Eccleston St

• Seafresh, Kazan

Olivo •

• Cyprus Mangal

About Thyme,

Gustoso •

Boisdale
• Thomas Cubitt
• Oliveto

A Wong •

• Lorne

• Ebury

• Cacio & Pepe

Olivocarne

• Dominique Ansel Bakery

SLOANE

Convivio •

Cambridge St Kitchen

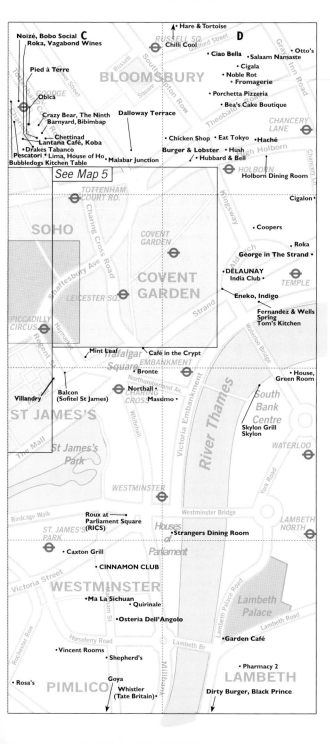

MAP 2 – WEST END OVERVIEW

C

Noizé, Bobo Social
Roka, Vagabond Wines

Pied à Terre

Obica

Crazy Bear, The Ninth
Barnyard, Bibimbap
Chettinad
Lantana Café, Koba
Drakes Tabanco
Pescatori • Lima, House of Ho
Bubbledogs Kitchen Table • Malabar Junction

Dalloway Terrace

BLOOMSBURY

D

Hare & Tortoise
Chilli Cool

Ciao Bella
Otto's
Salaam Namaste
Cigala
Noble Rot
Fromagerie
Porchetta Pizzeria
Bea's Cake Boutique

CHANCERY
LANE

Chicken Shop • Eat Tokyo • Haché
Burger & Lobster • Hush
Hubbard & Bell

HOLBORN
Holborn Dining Room

See Map 5

SOHO

COVENT
GARDEN

COVENT
GARDEN

LEICESTER SQ.

PICCADILLY
CIRCUS

Cigalon •

Coopers

Roka
George in The Strand •

DELAUNAY
India Club •

Eneko, Indigo

TEMPLE

Fernandez & Wells
Spring
Tom's Kitchen

Mint Leaf
Café in the Crypt
Bronte
Northall •
Massimo •

House,
Green Room

South
Bank
Centre
Skylon Grill
Skylon

WATERLOO

Balcon
(Sofitel St James)

Villandry

ST JAMES'S

St James's
Park

WESTMINSTER

River Thames

Birdcage Walk

ST. JAMES'S
PARK

Roux at
Parliament Square
(RICS)

Houses
of
Parliament

Westminster Bridge

Strangers Dining Room

LAMBETH
NORTH

Caxton Grill

CINNAMON CLUB

WESTMINSTER

Victoria Street

Ma La Sichuan
Quirinale •
Osteria Dell'Angolo •

Lambeth
Palace

Lambeth Road

Vincent Rooms
Shepherd's

Garden Café

Horseferry Road

Rosa's

PIMLICO

Goya
Whistler
(Tate Britain) •

Pharmacy 2

LAMBETH

Dirty Burger, Black Prince

MAP 3 – MAYFAIR, ST. JAMES'S & WEST SOHO

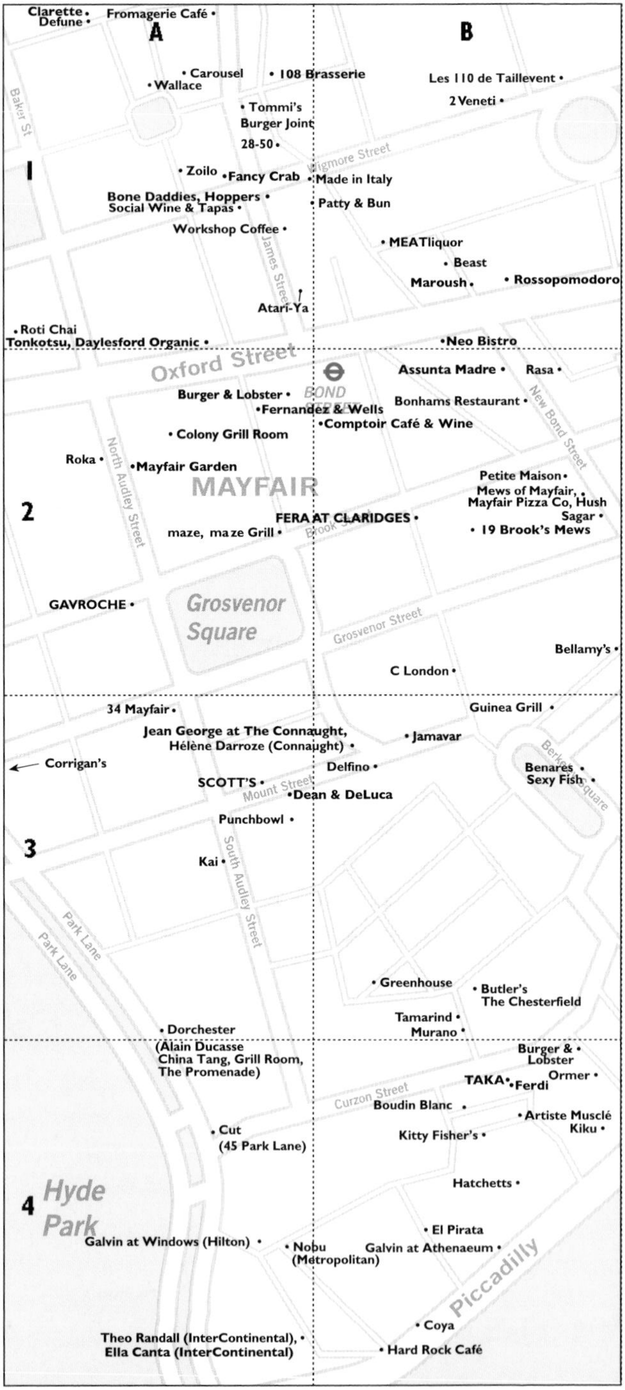

A
B
1
2
3
4
Clarette
Defune
Fromagerie Café
Carousel
Wallace
108 Brasserie
Les 110 de Taillevent
2 Veneti
Baker St
Tommi's Burger Joint
28-50
Wigmore Street
Zoilo
Fancy Crab
Made in Italy
Bone Daddies, Hoppers
Social Wine & Tapas
Patty & Bun
Workshop Coffee
MEATliquor
Beast
James Street
Maroush
Rossopomodoro
Atari-Ya
Roti Chai
Tonkotsu, Daylesford Organic
Neo Bistro
Oxford Street
BOND STREET
Assunta Madre
Rasa
Burger & Lobster
Fernandez & Wells
Bonhams Restaurant
New Bond Street
Comptoir Café & Wine
Colony Grill Room
Roka
North Audley Street
Mayfair Garden
MAYFAIR
Petite Maison
Mews of Mayfair,
Mayfair Pizza Co, Hush
FERA AT CLARIDGES
Sagar
maze, maze Grill
Brook Street
19 Brook's Mews
GAVROCHE
Grosvenor Square
Grosvenor Street
Bellamy's
C London
34 Mayfair
Guinea Grill
Jean George at The Connaught,
Hélène Darroze (Connaught)
Jamavar
Corrigan's
Delfino
Berkeley Square
Benares
Sexy Fish
SCOTT'S
Mount Street
Dean & DeLuca
Punchbowl
Kai
South Audley Street
Park Lane
Park Lane
Greenhouse
Butler's
The Chesterfield
Tamarind
Murano
Dorchester
(Alain Ducasse
China Tang, Grill Room,
The Promenade)
Burger & Lobster
Ormer
TAKA
Ferdi
Curzon Street
Boudin Blanc
Artiste Musclé
Kiku
Cut
(45 Park Lane)
Kitty Fisher's
Hatchetts
Hyde Park
El Pirata
Galvin at Windows (Hilton)
Nobu
(Metropolitan)
Galvin at Athenaeum
Piccadilly
Coya
Theo Randall (InterContinental),
Ella Canta (InterContinental)
Hard Rock Café

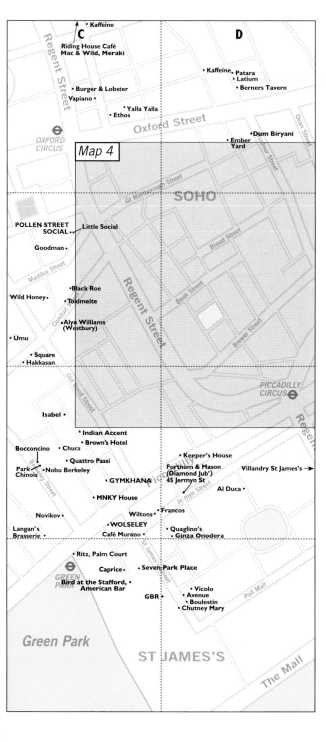

MAP **3** – MAYFAIR, ST. JAMES'S & WEST SOHO

C

D

• Kaffeine

Riding House Café
Mac & Wild, Meraki

• Kaffeine, Patara
• Latium
• Berners Tavern

• Burger & Lobster
Vapiano •

• Yalla Yalla
• Ethos

Oxford Street

•Dum Biryani
• Ember
Yard

OXFORD
CIRCUS

Map 4

Regent Street

Gt Marlborough Street

SOHO

POLLEN STREET
SOCIAL •• Little Social

Broad Street

Goodman •

Maddox Street

•Black Roe
•Tokimeite

Beak Street

Wild Honey•

Regent Street

Conduit

•Alyn Williams
(Westbury)

Brewer Street

• Umu

• Square
• Hakkasan

Old Bond Street

PICCADILLY
CIRCUS

Isabel •

• Indian Accent
• Brown's Hotel

Bocconcino • Chucs
• Quattro Passi

Park
Chinois •Nobu Berkeley

• GYMKHANA

• MNKY House

• Keeper's House

Fortnum & Mason
(Diamond Jub')
45 Jermyn St

Villandry St James's →

Al Duca •

Novikov •

Wiltons • •Francos

Langan's
Brasserie •

•WOLSELEY
Café Murano •

Je myn Street

• Quaglino's
• Ginza Onodera

• Ritz, Palm Court

Caprice •

GREEN
PARK

Bird at the Stafford, •
American Bar

• Seven Park Place

GBR •

• Vicolo
• Avenue
• Boulestin
• Chutney Mary

Pall Mall

Green Park

ST JAMES'S

The Mall

MAP **4** – WEST SOHO & PICCADILLY

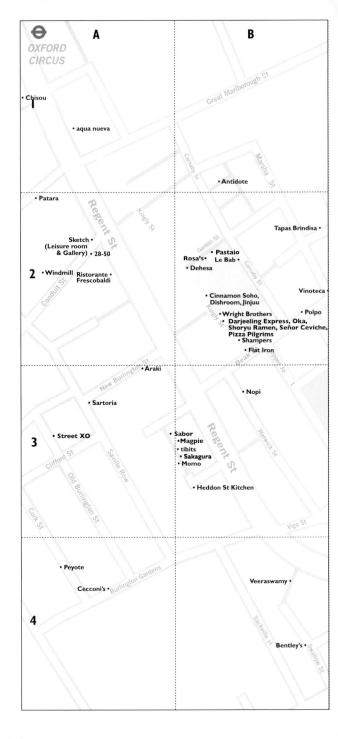

OXFORD CIRCUS

A

B

• Chisou

1

• aqua nueva

Great Marlborough St

Carnaby St

Marsha St

• Antidote

• Patara

Regent St

Kingly St

Tapas Brindisa •

Sketch •
(Leisure room
& Gallery) • 28-50

Ganton St

Rosa's•   • Pastaio
           Le Bab •

Carnaby St

2 • Windmill   Ristorante •
                  Frescobaldi

• Dehesa

Vinoteca •

Conduit St

• Cinnamon Soho,
  Dishroom, Jinjuu

Kingly St

• Polpo

• Wright Brothers
• Darjeeling Express, Oka,
  Shoryu Ramen, Señor Ceviche,
  Pizza Pilgrims
• Shampers

Beak St

Upper Jo

• Flat Iron

New Burlington St

• Araki

• Nopi

• Sartoria

Regent St

Warwick St

3 • Street XO

• Sabor
• Magpie
• tibits
• Sakagura
• Momo

Clifford St

Old Burlington St

Saville Row

Cork St

• Heddon St Kitchen

Vigo St

• Peyote

Burlington Gardens

Cecconi's •

Veeraswamy •

4

Sackville St

Bentley's •

Swallow St

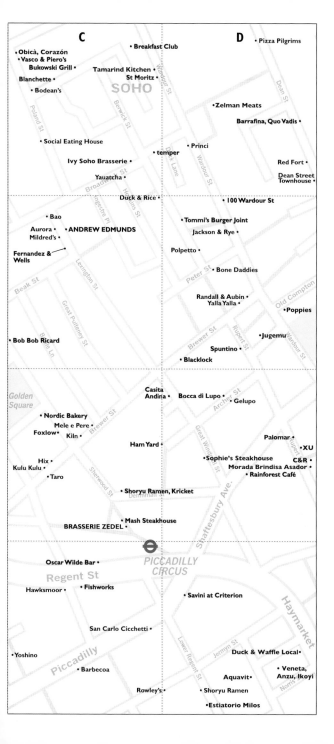

MAP 4 – WEST SOHO & PICCADILLY

C

D

• Pizza Pilgrims

• Breakfast Club

• Obicà, Corazón
• Vasco & Piero's
Bukowski Grill •

Tamarind Kitchen •
St Moritz •

Blanchette •

• Bodean's

SOHO

• Zelman Meats

Barrafina, Quo Vadis •

• Social Eating House

• Princi

• temper

Ivy Soho Brasserie •

Red Fort •

Yauatcha •

Dean Street
Townhouse •

Duck & Rice •

• 100 Wardour St

• Bao

• Tommi's Burger Joint

Aurora •   • ANDREW EDMUNDS
Mildred's •

Jackson & Rye •

Fernandez &
Wells

Polpetto •

• Bone Daddies

Randall & Aubin •
Yalla Yalla •

• Poppies

• Bob Bob Ricard

• Jugemu

Spuntino •

• Blacklock

Casita
Andina •   • Bocca di Lupo •
• Gelupo

• Nordic Bakery
Mele e Pere •
Foxlow •   Kiln •

Palomar •
• XU

Ham Yard •

•Sophie's Steakhouse   C&R •
Morada Brindisa Asador •
• Rainforest Café

Hix •
Kulu Kulu •
• Taro

• Shoryu Ramen, Kricket

• Mash Steakhouse
BRASSERIE ZEDEL •

PICCADILLY
CIRCUS

Oscar Wilde Bar •

Regent St

Hawksmoor •   • Fishworks

• Savini at Criterion

San Carlo Cicchetti •

• Yoshino

Duck & Waffle Local•

Piccadilly

• Veneta,
Anzu, Ikoyi

• Barbecoa

Aquavit•

Rowley's •   • Shoryu Ramen

•Estiatorio Milos

MAP **5** – EAST SOHO, CHINATOWN & COVENT GARDEN

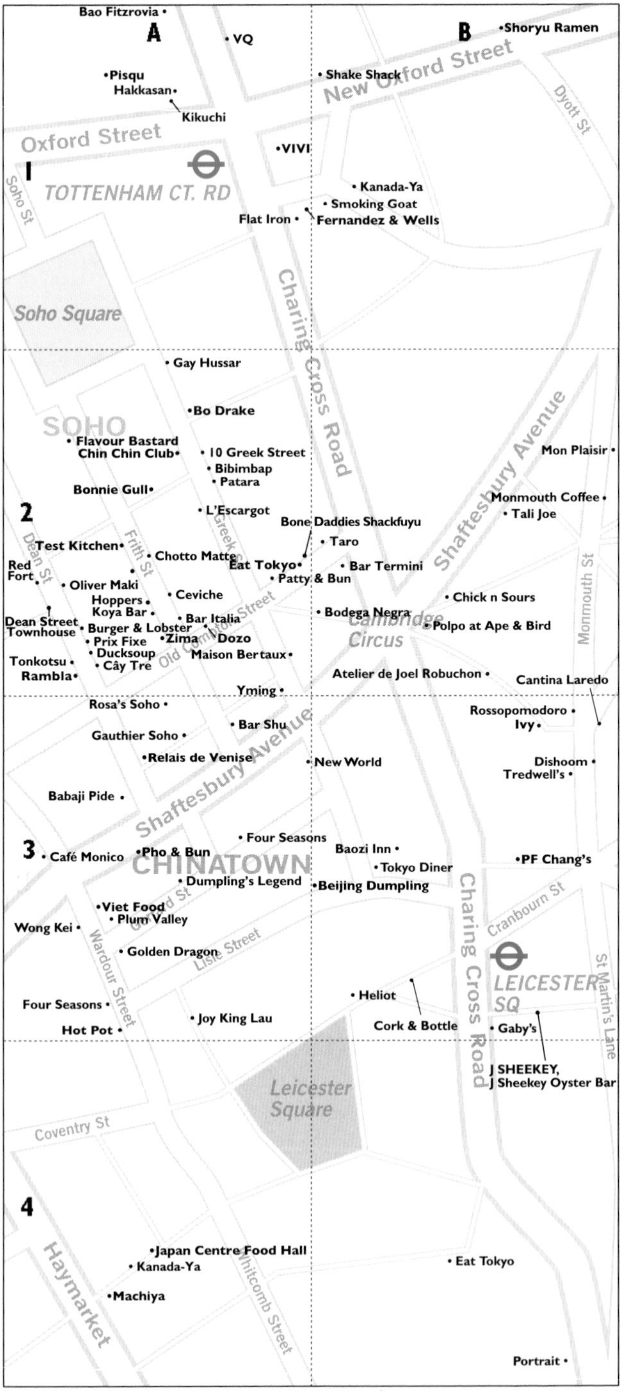

A

B

Bao Fitzrovia •

• VQ

• Shoryu Ramen

New Oxford Street

• Shake Shack

• Pisqu
Hakkasan•

Kikuchi

Dyott St

Oxford Street

Soho St

1

TOTTENHAM CT. RD

• VIVI

• Kanada-Ya
• Smoking Goat
Flat Iron • Fernandez & Wells

Soho Square

Charing Cross Road

• Gay Hussar

• Bo Drake

SOHO

Shaftesbury Avenue

• Flavour Bastard
Chin Chin Club• • 10 Greek Street
• Bibimbap
• Patara

Mon Plaisir •

Bonnie Gull•

Monmouth Coffee •
• Tali Joe

Greek Street

2

• L'Escargot

Bone Daddies Shackfuyu

Dean St

Frith St

• Taro

Monmouth St

Test Kitchen•
Red
Fort

• Chotto Matte

Eat Tokyo• • Bar Termini
• Patty & Bun

• Chick n Sours

• Oliver Maki
Hoppers • • Ceviche
Koya Bar •
Dean Street Burger & Lobster • • Bar Italia
Townhouse • Prix Fixe •Zima •Dozo
• Ducksoup Maison Bertaux •
Tonkotsu •
Rambla• • Cây Tre

• Bodega Negra
Cambridge
Circus

•Polpo at Ape & Bird

Old Compton Street

• Atelier de Joel Robuchon

• Cantina Laredo

• Yming

Rosa's Soho •

• Bar Shu

Rossopomodoro •
Ivy •

Gauthier Soho •

Shaftesbury Avenue

•Relais de Venise

• New World

Dishoom •
Tredwell's •

Babaji Pide •

3 • Café Monico •Pho & Bun
CHINATOWN

• Four Seasons

Baozi Inn •

• PF Chang's

•Dumpling's Legend

• Tokyo Diner
•Beijing Dumpling

Charing Cross Road

•Viet Food
• Plum Valley

Cranbourn St

Wong Kei •

LEICESTER
SQ

Wardour Street

Lisle Street

• Golden Dragon

St Martin's Lane

Four Seasons •

• Heliot

Hot Pot •

• Joy King Lau

Cork & Bottle

• Gaby's

J SHEEKEY,
J Sheekey Oyster Bar

Leicester
Square

Coventry St

4

Haymarket

•Japan Centre Food Hall
• Kanada-Ya

Whitcomb Street

• Eat Tokyo

•Machiya

Portrait •

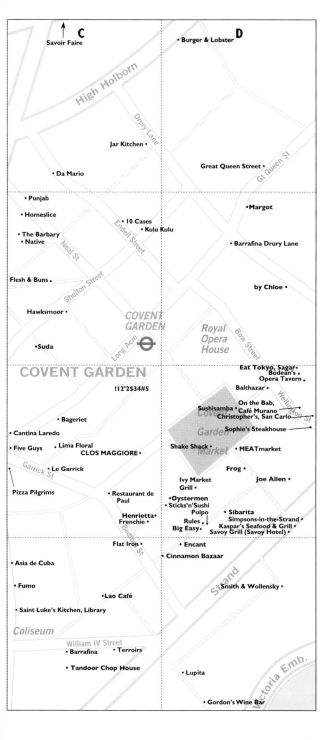

MAP **5** – EAST SOHO, CHINATOWN & COVENT GARDEN

C

D

• Savoir Faire

• Burger & Lobster

High Holborn

Drury Lane

• Jar Kitchen

• Great Queen Street

Gt. Queen St

• Da Mario

• Punjab

• Margot

• Homeslice

• 10 Cases

Endell Street

• Kulu Kulu

• The Barbary

• Native

Neal St

• Barrafina Drury Lane

Flesh & Buns •

Shelton Street

by Chloe •

Hawksmoor •

COVENT
GARDEN

Royal
Opera
House

Bow Street

•Suda

Long Acre

COVENT GARDEN

Eat Tokyo, Sagar•
Bodean's •
Opera Tavern •

!12'2$34#5

Balthazar •

Wellington St

On the Bab,
Sushisamba • Café Murano
Christopher's, San Carlo

• Bageriet

Cove

• Cantina Laredo

Garden

Sophie's Steakhouse

• Five Guys • Lima Floral

Market

Shake Shack •

• MEATmarket

CLOS MAGGIORE •

Garrick St • Le Garrick

Frog •

Joe Allen •

Pizza Pilgrims

Ivy Market
Grill •

• Restaurant de
Paul

•Oystermen
• Sticks'n'Sushi
Polpo   • Sibarita

Henrietta•
Frenchie •

Rules ,↓ Simpsons-in-the-Strand •
Kaspar's Seafood & Grill •

Big Easy• Savoy Grill (Savoy Hotel) •

Bedford St

Flat Iron •

• Encant

• Asia de Cuba

• Cinnamon Bazaar

Strand

• Fumo

•Smith & Wollensky •

•Lao Café

• Saint Luke's Kitchen, Library

Coliseum

William IV Street

• Barrafina   • Terroirs

• Tandoor Chop House

• Lupita

Victoria Emb.

• Gordon's Wine Bar

MAP **6** – KNIGHTSBRIDGE, CHELSEA & SOUTH KENSINGTON

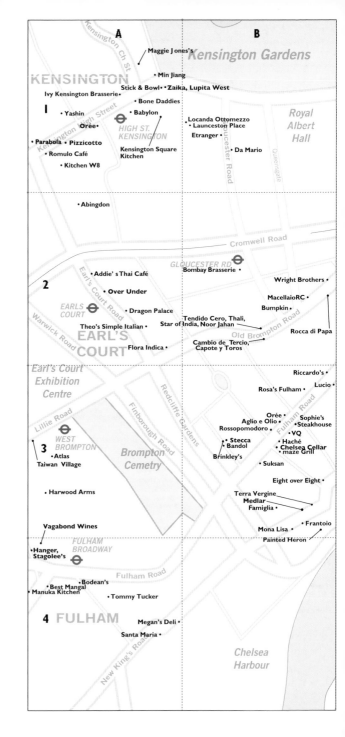

A

B

Kensington Ch St.

• Maggie Jones's

Kensington Gardens

KENSINGTON

• Min Jiang

Stick & Bowl • • Zaika, Lupita West

Ivy Kensington Brasserie •

• Bone Daddies

1

• Yashin

• Babylon

Orée •

*HIGH ST.
KENSINGTON*

*Royal
Albert
Hall*

• Locanda Ottomezzo
• Launceston Place

• Parabola   • Pizzicotto

• Romulo Café

Etranger •

• Da Mario

• Kitchen W8

Kensington Square
Kitchen

Gloucester Road

Queensgate

• Abingdon

Cromwell Road

GLOUCESTER RD

Bombay Brasserie •

• Addie's Thai Café

Wright Brothers •

2

Earl's Court Road

• Over Under

MacellaioRC •

*EARLS
COURT*

• Dragon Palace

Bumpkin •

Warwick Road

Theo's Simple Italian •

Tendido Cero, Thali,
Star of India, Noor Jahan

Old Brompton Road

Fulham Road

Rocca di Papa •

**EARL'S
COURT**

• Flora Indica

Cambio de Tercio,
Capote y Toros

*Earl's Court
Exhibition
Centre*

Redcliffe Gardens

Riccardo's •

Rosa's Fulham •

Lucio •

Finborough Road

Orée •
Aglio e Olio •
Rossopomodoro •

Sophie's
• Steakhouse

Lillie Road

*WEST
BROMPTON*

• VQ

• Haché

• Stecca
• Bandol

3

*Brompton
Cemetery*

• Atlas

Taiwan Village

Brinkley's

• Chelsea Cellar
• maze Grill

• Suksan

Eight over Eight •

• Harwood Arms

Terra Vergine
Medlar
Famiglia •

Vagabond Wines

• Frantoio

Mona Lisa •

Painted Heron

*FULHAM
BROADWAY*

• Hanger,
Stagolee's

Fulham Road

• Bodean's

• Best Mangal

• Manuka Kitchen

• Tommy Tucker

4 **FULHAM**

Megan's Deli •

Santa Maria •

New King's Road

*Chelsea
Harbour*

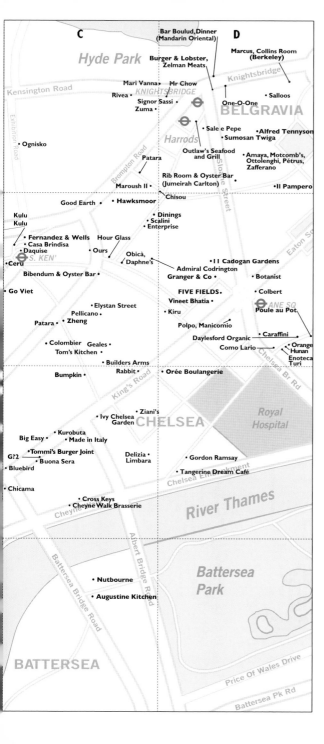

MAP 6 – KNIGHTSBRIDGE, CHELSEA & SOUTH KENSINGTON

C

D

Hyde Park

Bar Boulud, Dinner
(Mandarin Oriental)

Burger & Lobster,
Zelman Meats

Marcus, Collins Room
(Berkeley)

Knightsbridge

Kensington Road

Mari Vanna •

Rivea • KNIGHTSBRIDGE

Signor Sassi •
Zuma •

Mr Chow

• Salloos

One-O-One

BELGRAVIA

• Ognisko

Harrods

• Sale e Pepe
• Sumosan Twiga

• Alfred Tennyson

Patara •

Outlaw's Seafood
and Grill

• Amaya, Motcomb's,
Ottolenghi, Pétrus,
Zafferano

Maroush II •

Rib Room & Oyster Bar
(Jumeirah Carlton)

•Il Pampero

Good Earth • • Hawksmoor

Chisou

Kulu
Kulu

• Dinings
• Scalini
• Enterprise

• Fernandez & Wells
• Casa Brindisa
• Daquise

Hour Glass

•Ceru

• Ours

Obicà,
Daphne's

•11 Cadogan Gardens

Bibendum & Oyster Bar •

Admiral Codrington
Granger & Co •

• Botanist

• Go Viet

FIVE FIELDS•

• Colbert

• Elystan Street

Vineet Bhatia •

SLOANE SQ

Pellicano •

• Kiru

Poule au Pot

Patara • • Zheng

Polpo, Manicomio

• Colombier
Tom's Kitchen •

Geales •

Daylesford Organic •

• Caraffini

Como Lario

•Orange
Hunan
Enoteca
Turi

Bumpkin •

• Builders Arms

Rabbit •

• Orée Boulangerie

King's Road

• Ziani's

• Ivy Chelsea
Garden

CHELSEA

*Royal
Hospital*

Big Easy •

• Kurobuta
• Made in Italy

G?2

•Tommi's Burger Joint
• Buona Sera

Delizia •
Limbara

• Gordon Ramsay

• Bluebird

• Tangerine Dream Café

• Chicama

Chelsea Embankment

• Cross Keys
• Cheyne Walk Brasserie

Cheyne

River Thames

• Nutbourne

• Augustine Kitchen

Battersea Bridge Road

Albert Bridge Road

*Battersea
Park*

BATTERSEA

Price Of Wales Drive

Battersea Pk Rd

MAP **7** – NOTTING HILL & BAYSWATER

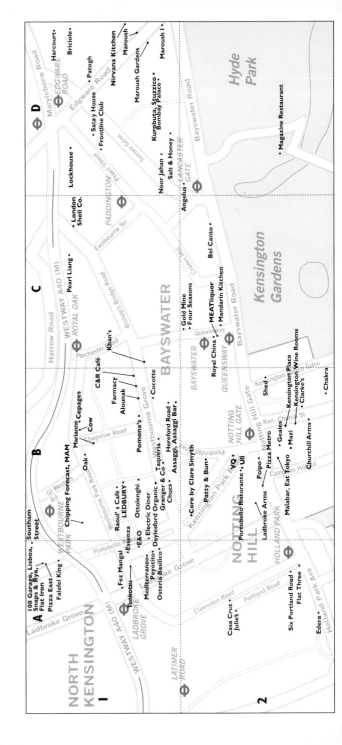

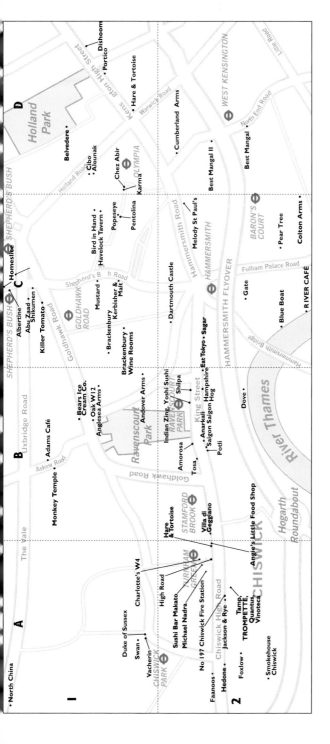

MAP **8** – HAMMERSMITH & CHISWICK

MAP 9 – HAMPSTEAD, CAMDEN TOWN & ISLINGTON

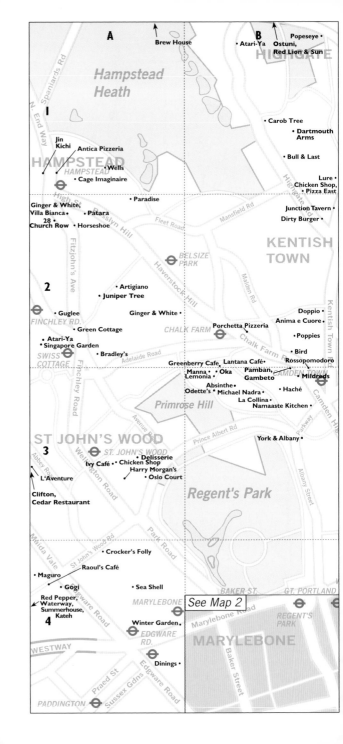

A

Brew House

B
· Atari-Ya   Popeseye ·
Ostuni,
Red Lion & Sun

HIGHGATE

Hampstead
Heath

Spaniards Rd

N. End Way

1

· Carob Tree
· Dartmouth
Arms

· Bull & Last

Jin
Kichi
· Antica Pizzeria

HAMPSTEAD
HAMPSTEAD   ·Wells
· Cage Imaginaire

Lure ·
Chicken Shop,
· Pizza East

High St.

· Paradise

Ginger & White,
Villa Bianca ·   · Patara
28 ·
Church Row   · Horseshoe

Rosslyn Hill

Fleet Road

Mansfield Rd

Junction Tavern ·

Dirty Burger ·

KENTISH
TOWN

Fitzjohn's Ave

BELSIZE
PARK

Haverstock Hill

Maiden Rd

2

· Artigiano
· Juniper Tree

· Guglee

FINCHLEY RD.

Ginger & White ·

CHALK FARM

Porchetta Pizzeria

Chalk Farm Rd

Kentish Town Rd

Doppio ·
Anima e Cuore ·

· Poppies

· Green Cottage

· Atari-Ya
· Singapore Garden

SWISS
COTTAGE   · Bradley's

Finchley Road

Adelaide Road

· Bird
Rossopomodoro

Greenberry Cafe   Lantana Café ·

Manna · · Oka   Pamban,
Lemonia ·   Gambeto

· Mildreds

CAMDEN

Absinthe ·   · Haché
Odette's · Michael Nadra ·
La Collina ·
Namaaste Kitchen ·

Camden Hi

Primrose Hill

ST JOHN'S WOOD

Avenue Rd

Prince Albert Rd

York & Albany ·

3

ST. JOHN'S WOOD
· Delisserie
Ivy Café · · Chicken Shop
Harry Morgan's
· Oslo Court

Wellington Road

Parkway

Albany Street

L'Aventure

Abbey Road

Clifton,
Cedar Restaurant

Regent's Park

Park Road

Maida Vale

St John's Wood Rd

· Crocker's Folly

Raoul's Café

· Maguro

· Gogi

Red Pepper,
Waterway,
Summerhouse,
Kateh

Edgware Road

· Sea Shell

BAKER ST.   GT. PORTLAND

MARYLEBONE   See Map 2

REGENT'S
PARK

Baker Street

4

Winter Garden.

EDGWARE
RD.

Marylebone Rd

MARYLEBONE

WESTWAY

Dinings ·

PADDINGTON   Praed St   Sussex Gdns   Edgware Road

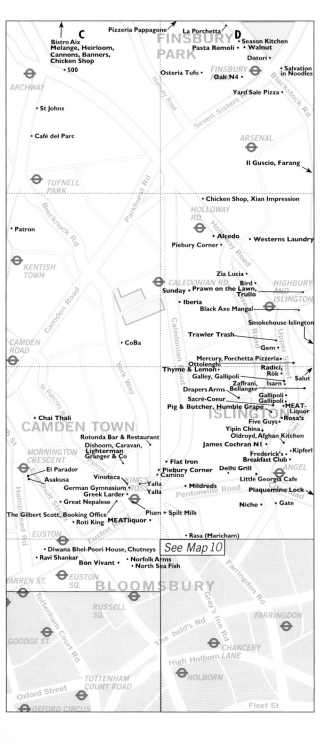

MAP **9** – HAMPSTEAD, CAMDEN TOWN & ISLINGTON

C
Pizzeria Pappagone · La Porchetta ·
Bistro Aix
Melange, Heirloom,
Cannons, Banners,
Chicken Shop
· 500
FINSBURY PARK
D
· Season Kitchen
Pasta Remoli · Walnut
Dotori ·
· Salvation in Noodles
Osteria Tufo · FINSBURY
Oak N4 ·
Yard Sale Pizza ·
Hornsey Road
Seven Sisters
Blackstock Rd

ARCHWAY

· St Johns

· Café del Parc

ARSENAL

Il Guscio, Farang

TUFNELL PARK

Parkhurst Rd

· Chicken Shop, Xian Impression
HOLLOWAY RD.

· Patron

Brecknock Rd

· Alcedo
Piebury Corner ·
· Westerns Laundry

KENTISH TOWN

CALEDONIAN RD.
Zia Lucia ·
Bird ·
Sunday · Prawn on the Lawn, Trullo
· Iberia
Black Axe Mangal
HIGHBURY AND ISLINGTON

Camden Road

· CoBa
CAMDEN ROAD
Smokehouse Islington

Trawler Trash
Gem ·

Caledonian Road

York Way

St Pancras Rd

Mercury, Porchetta Pizzeria·
Ottolenghi·   Radici·
Thyme & Lemon·   Rök ·
Galley, Gallipoli·   Salut
Zaffrani,   Isarn ·
Drapers Arms· Bellanger
Sacré-Coeur·   Gallipoli
Gallipoli
Pig & Butcher, Humble Grape ·MEAT-
Liquor
·Rosa's
Yipin China·   Five Guys ·
Oldroyd, Afghan Kitchen
James Cochran N1 ·
Frederick's · ·Kipferl
Breakfast Club ·
· Chai Thali
CAMDEN TOWN
Rotunda Bar & Restaurant
Dishoom, Caravan,
Lighterman
Granger & Co
MORNINGTON CRESCENT
· El Parador
Asakusa
German Gymnasium·
Greek Larder ·
· Great Nepalese
The Gilbert Scott, Booking Office
· Roti King MEATliquor ·
· Flat Iron
· Piebury Corner Delhi Grill
· Camino
Vinoteca
·Yalla
KING'S Yalla
CROSS
· Mildreds
Pentonville Road
Plum + Spilt Milk
ISLINGTON
Little Georgia Cafe
Plaquemine Lock
Niche ·   · Gate
ANGEL

Hampstead Rd

EUSTON

· Rasa (Maricham)

See Map 10

WARREN ST.
EUSTON SQ.
· Diwana Bhel-Poori House, Chutneys
· Ravi Shankar
Bon Vivant ·   · Norfolk Arms
· North Sea Fish
BLOOMSBURY
Farringdon Rd

RUSSELL SQ.

GOODGE ST.
Tottenham Court Rd
The bald's Rd
Gray's Inn Rd
FARRINGDON

CHANCERY LANE

High Holborn LANE
HOLBORN

Oxford Street
TOTTENHAM COURT ROAD
OXFORD CIRCUS
Fleet St

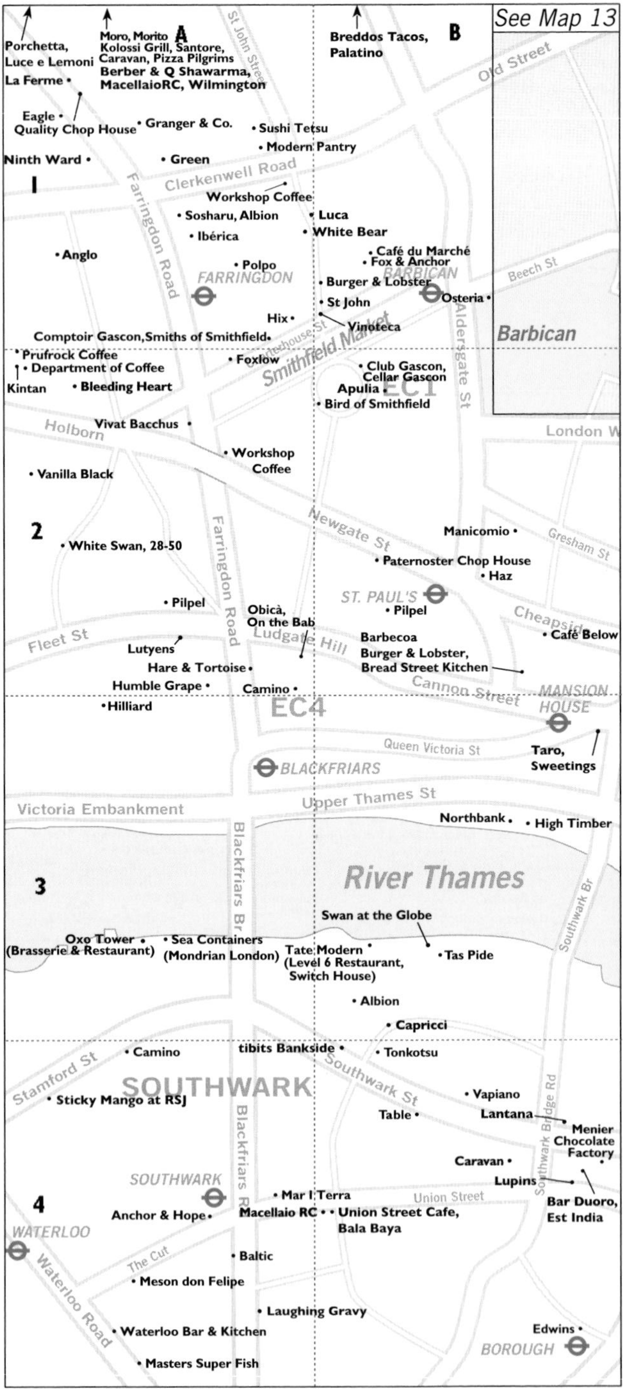

MAP **10** – THE CITY

See Map 13

A

B

Porchetta,
Luce e Lemoni
La Ferme •

Moro, Morito
Kolossi Grill, Santore,
Caravan, Pizza Pilgrims
Berber & Q Shawarma,
MacellaioRC, Wilmington

Breddos Tacos,
Palatino

St John St

Old Street

Eagle •
Quality Chop House •

• Granger & Co.

• Sushi Tetsu

• Modern Pantry

Ninth Ward •

• Green

Clerkenwell Road

I

Workshop Coffee

Farringdon Road

• Luca

• Sosharu, Albion

• White Bear

• Café du Marché

• Ibérica

• Fox & Anchor

BARBICAN

Beech St

• Anglo

• Polpo

FARRINGDON

• Burger & Lobster

Osteria •

Aldersgate St

Barbican

Charterhouse St

• St John

Vinoteca

Hix •

Smithfield Market

Comptoir Gascon, Smiths of Smithfield •

• Prufrock Coffee

• Foxlow

• Club Gascon,
Cellar Gascon

↑ • Department of Coffee

EC1

Kintan • • Bleeding Heart

Apulia •

• Bird of Smithfield

London W

Vivat Bacchus •

Holborn

• Workshop
Coffee

• Vanilla Black

2

• White Swan, 28-50

Newgate St

Gresham St

Manicomio •

• Paternoster Chop House

Farringdon Road

• Haz

ST. PAUL'S

Cheapside

• Pilpel

• Pilpel

• Café Below

Obicà,
On the Bab

Fleet St

Ludgate Hill

Barbecoa

Lutyens

Burger & Lobster,
Bread Street Kitchen

Hare & Tortoise •

Cannon Street

MANSION

Humble Grape •

Camino •

HOUSE

EC4

• Hilliard

Queen Victoria St

Taro,
Sweetings

BLACKFRIARS

Upper Thames St

Victoria Embankment

Northbank •

• High Timber

Blackfriars Br

River Thames

3

Southwark Br

Swan at the Globe

Oxo Tower •
(Brasserie & Restaurant)

• Sea Containers
(Mondrian London)

Tate Modern •
(Level 6 Restaurant,
Switch House)

• Tas Pide

• Albion

• Capricci

• Camino

tibits Bankside •

• Tonkotsu

Stamford St

SOUTHWARK

Southwark St

• Vapiano

• Sticky Mango at RSJ

Blackfriars Rd

Table •

Lantana

Southwark Bridge Rd

Menier
Chocolate
Factory

Caravan •

SOUTHWARK

Lupins •

4

• Mar I Terra

Union Street

Bar Duoro,
Est India

Anchor & Hope •

Macellaio RC • • Union Street Cafe,
Bala Baya

WATERLOO

• Baltic

Waterloo Road

The Cut

• Meson don Felipe

• Laughing Gravy

Edwins •

• Waterloo Bar & Kitchen

BOROUGH

• Masters Super Fish

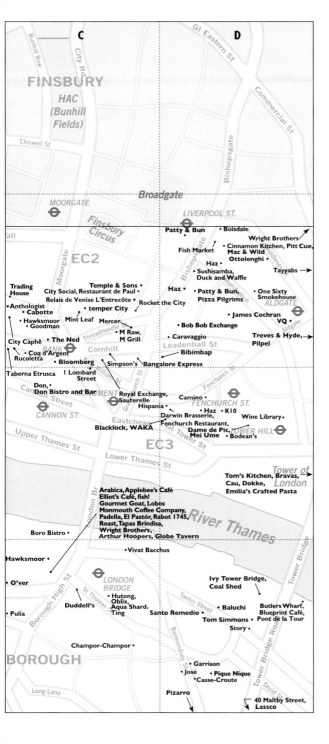

MAP 10 – THE CITY

C **D**

Gt Eastern St

Bunhill Row

City Rd

FINSBURY

*HAC
(Bunhill
Fields)*

Commercial St

Chiswell St

Bishopsgate

Broadgate

all

MOORGATE

LIVERPOOL ST.

*Finsbury
Circus*

Patty & Bun • Boisdale

Wright Brothers

EC2

Moorgate

Fish Market • Cinnamon Kitchen, Pitt Cue,
Mac & Wild
Ottolenghi •

Bishopsgate

Haz •

Tayyabs →

• Sushisamba,
Duck and Waffle

**Trading
House**

Temple & Sons •
City Social, Restaurant de Paul •
Relais de Venise L'Entrecôte •

Haz •

• Patty & Bun,
Pizza Pilgrims

• One Sixty
Smokehouse

•Anthologist
• Cabotte

• temper City

Rocket the City

ALDGATE

• James Cochran

VQ •

Aldgate

• Hawksmoor
• Goodman

Mint Leaf   Mercer •

Threadneedle St

• M Raw,
M Grill

• Bob Bob Exchange

Treves & Hyde, →
Pilpel

City Càphê • The Ned

BANK

• Caravaggio

Cornhill

Leadenhall St

• Coq d'Argent
Rucoletta

• **Bloomberg**

Bibimbap

Taberna Etrusca

I Lombard
Street

Simpson's Bangalore Express

William St

Fenchurch St

Don, •
Don Bistro and Bar

MENT

Royal Exchange,
Sauterelle

Camino •

FENCHURCH ST.

Cannon Street

CANNON ST.

Hispania •

• Haz • **K10**

Wine Library •

Eastcheap

Darwin Brasserie,
Fenchurch Restaurant,
Dame de Pic, **TOWER HILL**
Mei Ume • Bodean's

Upper Thames St

Blacklock, WAKA

EC3

Gt Tower St

Lower Thames St

*Tower of
London*

Tom's Kitchen, Bravas, →
Cau, Dokke,
Emilia's Crafted Pasta

Arabica, Applebee's Café
Elliot's Café, fish!
Gourmet Goat, Lobos
Monmouth Coffee Company,
Padella, El Pastór, Rabot 1745,
Roast, Tapas Brindisa,
Wright Brothers,
Arthur Hoopers, Globe Tavern

London Br

River Thames

Boro Bistro •

Tower Bridge

• **Vivat Bacchus**

Hawksmoor •

**LONDON
BRIDGE**

**Ivy Tower Bridge,
Coal Shed**

• **O'ver**

St Thomas St

Tooley Street

**Butlers Wharf,
Blueprint Café,
Pont de la Tour**

Borough High St

• Hutong,
Oblix,
Aqua Shard,
Ting

• Baluchi

• **Pulia**

Duddell's

Santo Remedio •

Tom Simmons •

Bermondsey St

Story •

Tower Bridge Road

Champor-Champor •

BOROUGH

• **Garrison**

• **José** • **Pique Nique**
•**Casse-Croute**

Druid St

Long Lane

Pizarro
↓

↙ **40 Maltby Street,
Lassco**

MAP 11 – SOUTH LONDON (& FULHAM)

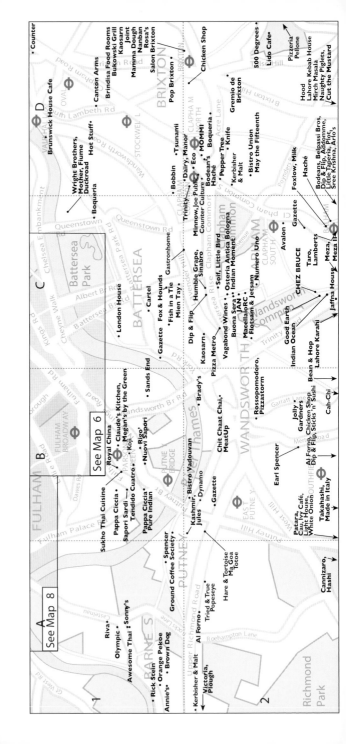

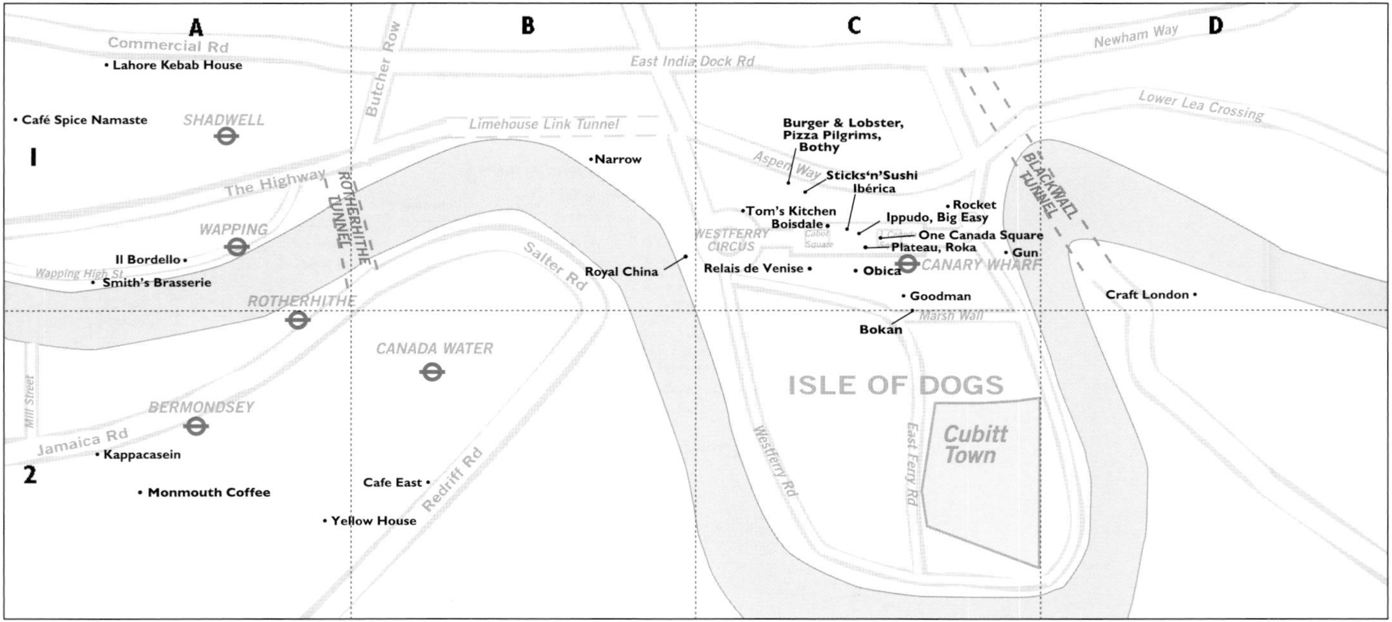

MAP **12** – EAST END & DOCKLANDS

A **B** **C** **D**

1

Commercial Rd
• Lahore Kebab House

• Café Spice Namaste

SHADWELL Φ

Butcher Row

The Highway

Wapping High St
Il Bordello •
• Smith's Brasserie

WAPPING Φ

ROTHERHITHE
TUNNEL

Limehouse Link Tunnel

East India Dock Rd

• Narrow

BLACKWALL
TUNNEL

Newham Way

Lower Lea Crossing

Craft London •

Burger & Lobster,
Pizza Pilgrims,
Bothy

Aspen Way   Sticks'n'Sushi
Ibérica
• Tom's Kitchen
Boisdale •
ASPEN
Square

• Rocket
• One Canada Square
Ippudo, Big Easy

Plateau, Roka
• Obicà   CANARY WHARF Φ

• Goodman
Bokan

• Gun

WESTFERRY
CIRCUS
Relais de Venise •

Royal China •

Salter Rd

ISLE OF DOGS

Cubitt
Town

East Ferry Rd

Marsh Wall

Westferry Rd

2

ROTHERHITHE Φ

CANADA WATER Φ

Redriff Rd

Cafe East •
• Yellow House

BERMONDSEY Φ

Jamaica Rd

• Monmouth Coffee

• Kappacasein

Mill Street

MAP 13 – SHOREDITCH & BETHNAL GREEN

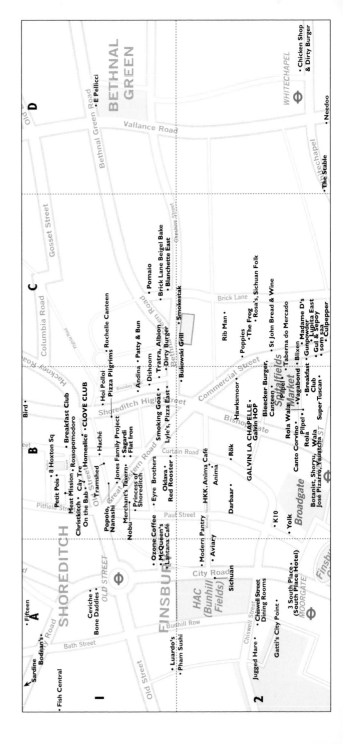

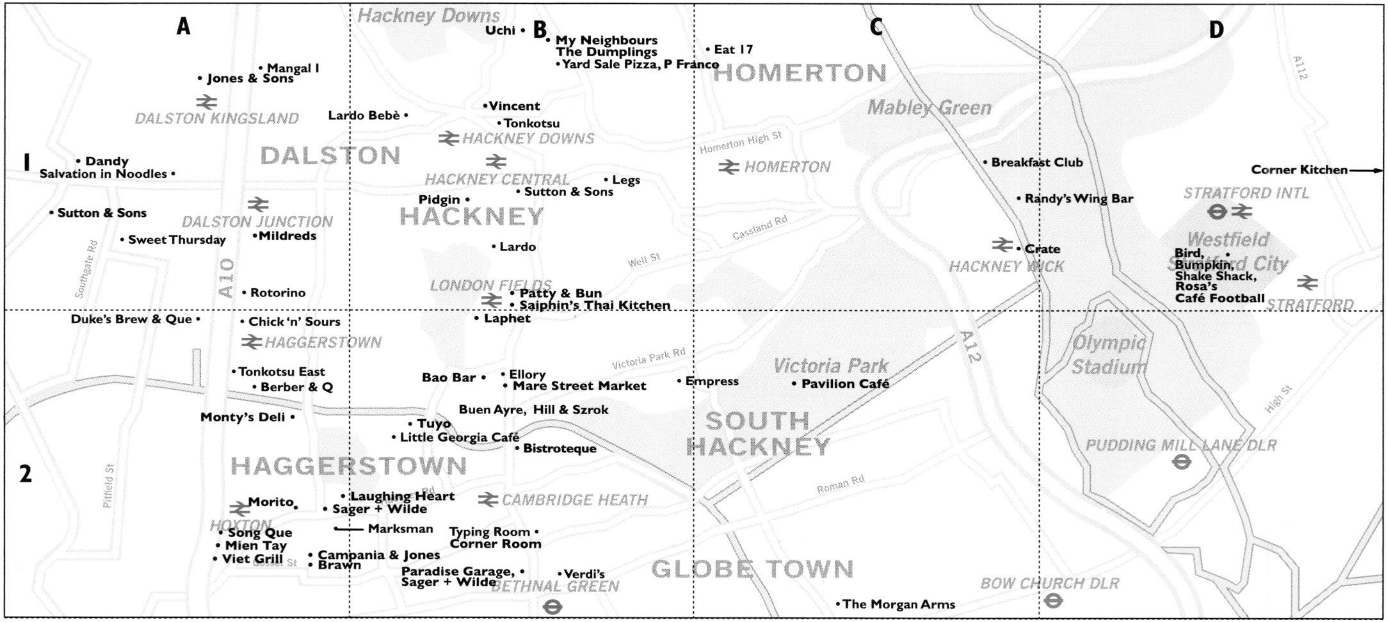

MAP **14** – EAST LONDON

A   B   C   D

Hackney Downs

A112

Corner Kitchen →

STRATFORD INTL

Uchi • **B** • My Neighbours
The Dumplings • P Franco
Yard Sale Pizza,

• Eat 17

HOMERTON

Mabley Green

STRATFORD

Westfield
Bird,
Bumpkin, City
Shake Shack,
Rosa's
Café Football

1

• Dandy
Salvation in Noodles •

• Jones & Sons
• Mangal I

Lardo Bebè •

DALSTON KINGSLAND

DALSTON

Vincent
Tonkotsu

Pidgin •
HACKNEY CENTRAL

• Legs
• Sutton & Sons

HACKNEY

• Lardo

HACKNEY DOWNS

• Breakfast Club

• Randy's Wing Bar

*Olympic
Stadium*

HACKNEY WICK

• Crate

PUDDING MILL LANE DLR

Homerton High St

HOMERTON

Casland Rd

Well St

Victoria Park Rd

Victoria Park
• Pavilion Café

*SOUTH
HACKNEY*

• Empress

Roman Rd

BOW CHURCH DLR

• Sutton & Sons
• Sweet Thursday

• Rotorino

DALSTON JUNCTION

• Mildreds

LONDON FIELDS

• Patty & Bun
Salpin's Thai Kitchen

• Laphet

Bao Bar • • Ellory
• Mare Street Market

Buen Ayre, Hill & Szrok

• Tuyo
• Little Georgia Café
• Bistroteque

CAMBRIDGE HEATH

ETHNAL GREEN

GLOBE TOWN

• The Morgan Arms

Duke's Brew & Que •

• Chick 'n' Sours

HAGGERSTOWN

• Tonkotsu East
• Berber & Q

Monty's Deli •

A10

HAGGERSTOWN

• Laughing Heart
• Sager + Wilde

• Marksman

Typing Room •
Corner Room

Paradise Garage, •
• Verdi's
Sager + Wilde

HOXTON
• Song Que
• Mien Tay
• Viet Grill

• Morito,

• Campania & Jones
• Brawn

Hackney Rd

Pitfield St

Southgate Rd

A112

A12

2

Artichoke, Amersham

The Oxford Blue, Old Windsor

THE OXFORD BLUE

The Shore, Penzance

Sir Charles Napier, Chinnor

These are the restaurants outside London that were mentioned most frequently by reporters (last year's position is shown in brackets). For a list of London's most mentioned restaurants, see page 29.

1   **Manoir aux Quat' Saisons** (1)
   Great Milton, Oxon
2   **Waterside Inn** (2)
   Bray, Berks
3   **Sportsman** (5)
   Whitstable, Kent
4   **Midsummer House** (6)
   Cambridge, Cambs
5   **Hand & Flowers** (8)
   Marlow, Bucks

Manoir aux Quat' Saisons

6   **L'Enclume** (4)
   Cartmel, Cumbria
7   **Fat Duck** (11)
   Bray, Berks
8   **Restaurant Nathan Outlaw** (9)
   Port Isaac, Cornwall
9=   **Artichoke** (7)
   Amersham, Bucks
9=   **Hambleton Hall** (14)
   Hambleton, Rutland

L'Enclume

11   **Black Swan** (-)
   Oldstead, North Yorkshire
12=   **Northcote** (13)
   Langho, Lancs
12=   **Magpie** (17=)
   Whitby, N Yorks
14   **Restaurant Sat Bains** (12)
   Nottingham, Notts
15   **French Table** (-)
   Surbiton, Surrey

Restaurant Sat Bains

16=   **Great House** (-)
   Lavenham, Suffolk
16=   **Gidleigh Park** (10)
   Chagford, Devon
18=   **Adams** (15=)
   Birmingham, West Midlands
18=   **Restaurant Martin Wishart** (-)
   Edinburgh, City of Edinburgh
18=   **Maison Bleue** (-)
   Bury St Edmunds, Suffolk

Great House

All restaurants whose food rating is 🔳 *plus restaurants whose price is £60+*
with a food rating of 🔳

£340	The Fat Duck *(Bray)*	4 4 3
£190	Belmond Le Manoir aux Quat' Saisons *(Great Milton)*	5 5 5
£170	Waterside Inn *(Bray)*	5 5 5
	L'Enclume *(Cartmel)*	5 5 4
£160	Gidleigh Park *(Chagford)*	5 5 5
£150	Restaurant Nathan Outlaw *(Port Isaac)*	5 4 5
£140	Andrew Fairlie, Gleneagles Hotel *(Auchterarder)*	5 4 4
	Midsummer House *(Cambridge)*	5 4 4
£130	Gareth Ward at Ynyshir *(Eglwys Fach)*	5 5 4
	The Latymer, Pennyhill Park Hotel *(Bagshot)*	5 4 4
	Restaurant Sat Bains *(Nottingham)*	5 4 3
	Raby Hunt *(Summerhouse)*	5 3 3
£120	Casamia, The General *(Bristol)*	5 4 5
	Black Swan *(Oldstead)*	5 5 4
	Paris House *(Woburn)*	4 3 5
£110	Restaurant Martin Wishart *(Edinburgh)*	5 4 4
	Yorke Arms *(Ramsgill-in-Nidderdale)*	5 4 4
	Fraiche *(Oxton)*	5 5 3
	Lucknam Park, Luckham Park Hotel *(Colerne)*	4 4 5
	The Man Behind The Curtain *(Leeds)*	4 3 3
	The Pass Restaurant, South Lodge Hotel *(Lower Beeding)*	4 3 3
£100	Where The Light Gets In *(Stockport)*	5 5 4
	Bybrook Restaurant, Manor House Hotel *(Castle Combe)*	5 4 4
	Rabbit in the Moon *(Manchester)*	5 3 4
	The Kitchin *(Edinburgh)*	5 3 4
	Winteringham Fields *(Winteringham)*	4 5 4
	Fischers at Baslow Hall *(Baslow)*	4 4 4
	Number One, Balmoral Hotel *(Edinburgh)*	4 4 4
	The Samling *(Windermere)*	4 4 4
	Llangoed Hall *(Llyswen)*	4 3 4
£90	Buckland Manor *(Buckland)*	5 4 5
	The Feathered Nest Inn *(Nether Westcote)*	5 4 5
	The Three Chimneys *(Dunvegan)*	5 4 5
	Tyddyn Llan *(Llandrillo)*	5 4 5
	House of Tides *(Newcastle upon Tyne)*	5 3 5
	Adam's *(Birmingham)*	5 5 4
	Bohemia, The Club Hotel & Spa *(Jersey)*	5 5 4
	Hambleton Hall *(Hambleton)*	5 5 4

TOP SCORERS

Lumière (Cheltenham)		5 5 4
Moor Hall (Aughton)		5 5 4
Northcote (Langho)		5 5 4
The Box Tree (Ilkley)		5 5 4
Morston Hall (Morston)		5 4 4
Roger Hickman's (Norwich)		5 4 4
The Orangery, Rockliffe Hall (Darlington)		5 4 4
Checkers (Montgomery)		5 3 3
Le Champignon Sauvage (Cheltenham)		5 5 2
The Art School (Liverpool)		4 5 5
Longueville Manor (Jersey)		4 4 5
Sharrow Bay (Ullswater)		4 4 5
Purnells (Birmingham)		4 5 4
21212 (Edinburgh)		4 4 4
Manchester House (Manchester)		4 4 4
Gilpin Hotel (Windermere)		4 4 3
The Vineyard at Stockcross (Stockcross)		4 3 3

£80	The Forest Side (Grasmere)	5 5 5
	Pale Hall Hotel Restaurant (Bala)	5 4 5
	The Neptune (Old Hunstanton)	5 5 4
	The Torridon Restaurant (Annat)	5 5 4
	Coombeshead Farm (Lewannick)	5 4 4
	Lympstone Manor (Exmouth)	5 4 4
	Monachyle Mhor (Balquhidder)	5 4 4
	Lake Road Kitchen (Ambleside)	5 5 3
	Cotto (Cambridge)	5 4 3
	The Whitebrook, Restaurant with Rooms (Whitebrook)	5 4 3
	The Clock House (Formerly Drakes) (Ripley)	5 3 3
	Harry's Place (Great Gonerby)	5 5 2
	Wilks (Bristol)	5 5 2
	Samuel's, Swinton Park Hotel & Spa (Masham)	4 5 5
	Summer Lodge, Summer Lodge Country House (Evershot)	4 4 5
	Driftwood Hotel (Rosevine)	4 4 4
	The Kitchen at Chewton Glen (New Milton)	4 4 4
	Yorebridge House (Bainbridge)	4 4 4
	Carters of Moseley (Birmingham)	4 4 3

£70	Paul Ainsworth at No. 6 (Padstow)	5 4 5
	Artichoke (Amersham)	5 5 4
	Braidwoods (Dalry)	5 5 4
	Little Barwick House (Barwick)	5 5 4
	Stovell's (Chobham)	5 5 4
	The Harrow at Little Bedwyn (Marlborough)	5 5 4
	Freemasons at Wiswell (Wiswell)	5 4 4
	Le Cochon Aveugle (York)	5 4 4

Ox *(Belfast)*		5 4 4
The Albannach *(Lochinver)*		5 4 4
The Cellar *(Anstruther)*		5 4 4
The Seahorse *(Dartmouth)*		5 4 4
The Woodspeen *(Newbury)*		5 4 4
Restaurant James Sommerin *(Penarth)*		5 3 4
Little Fish Market *(Brighton)*		5 5 3
5 North Street *(Winchcombe)*		5 4 3
Horto Restaurant at Rudding Park *(Follifoot)*		5 4 3
John's House *(Mountsorrel)*		5 4 3
Stark *(Broadstairs)*		5 4 3
The Olive Tree, Queensberry Hotel *(Bath)*		5 4 3
Thompsons *(Newport)*		5 4 3
Whites *(Beverley)*		5 4 3
Hooked *(Windermere)*		5 3 2
The Sir Charles Napier *(Chinnor)*		4 3 5
Hipping Hall *(Kirkby Lonsdale)*		4 4 4
Old Downton Lodge *(Ludlow)*		4 4 4
Peace & Loaf *(Newcastle upon Tyne)*		4 4 4
Restaurant 56 *(Faringdon)*		4 4 4
The Star Inn *(Harome)*		4 4 4
The Tudor Room, Great Fosters Hotel *(Egham)*		4 4 4
Clock Tower, Rudding Park *(Harrogate)*		4 3 4
Dan Moon at The Gainsborough *(Bath)*		4 3 4
Ondine *(Edinburgh)*		4 3 4
Sindhu *(Marlow)*		4 3 4
Terravina, Hotel Terravina *(Woodlands)*		4 5 3
Vero Gusto *(Sheffield)*		4 5 3
Cheal's of Henley *(Henley in Arden)*		4 4 3
Fishmore Hall *(Ludlow)*		4 4 3
The Cross at Kenilworth *(Kenilworth)*		4 4 3
Pike + Pine *(Brighton)*		4 3 3
Thompson *(St Albans)*		4 3 3
Timberyard *(Edinburgh)*		4 3 3
The Flitch of Bacon *(Dunmow)*		4 2 3
£60 Kentisbury Grange Hotel *(Kentisbury)*		5 4 4
Orwells *(Shiplake)*		5 4 4
Pierhouse Hotel *(Port Appin)*		5 4 4
Sosban And The Old Butchers *(Menai Bridge)*		5 4 4
The Peat Inn *(Cupar)*		5 4 4
The Pony & Trap *(Chew Magna)*		5 4 4
The West House *(Biddenden)*		5 4 4
Aizle *(Edinburgh)*		5 5 3
The French Table *(Surbiton)*		5 5 3

TOP SCORERS

The Old Inn *(Drewsteignton)*	5	5	3
Adelina Yard *(Bristol)*	5	4	3
Cail Bruich *(Glasgow)*	5	4	3
Joro *(Sheffield)*	5	4	3
Menu Gordon Jones *(Bath)*	5	4	3
Norn *(Edinburgh)*	5	4	3
Old Stamp House *(Ambleside)*	5	4	3
Restaurant Tristan *(Horsham)*	5	4	3
St Enodoc Restaurant *(Rock)*	5	4	3
Verveine Fishmarket Restaurant *(Milford-on-Sea)*	5	4	3
The Oyster Box *(Jersey)*	5	3	3
The Vanilla Pod *(Marlow)*	5	3	3
The Walnut Tree *(Llandewi Skirrid)*	5	3	3
Apicius *(Cranbrook)*	5	4	2
Lasan *(Birmingham)*	5	4	2
Rick Stein *(Sandbanks)*	4	5	5
The Pipe & Glass Inn *(South Dalton)*	4	5	5
Fairyhill *(Reynoldston)*	4	4	5
The Jetty *(Christchurch)*	4	4	5
Killiecrankie Hotel *(Killiecrankie)*	4	5	4
Rafters *(Sheffield)*	4	5	4
Swan *(Long Melford)*	4	5	4
Chez Roux, Greywalls Hotel *(Gullane)*	4	4	4
Coast *(Saundersfoot)*	4	4	4
Darleys *(Derby)*	4	4	4
Lickfold Inn *(Lickfold)*	4	4	4
Mash Inn *(Radnage)*	4	4	4
Northcote Manor *(Umberleigh)*	4	4	4
Pebble Beach *(Barton-on-Sea)*	4	4	4
Restaurant 27 *(Southsea)*	4	4	4
Riverside *(Bridport)*	4	4	4
The Bay Horse *(Hurworth)*	4	4	4
The Black Rat *(Winchester)*	4	4	4
The Castle Bow Restaurant *(Taunton)*	4	4	4
The Hind's Head *(Bray)*	4	4	4
The Pheasant Hotel *(Harome)*	4	4	4
The Salt Room *(Brighton)*	4	4	4
The Wee Restaurant *(Edinburgh)*	4	4	4
Toi Et Moi *(Abbey Dore)*	4	4	4
Two Fat Ladies at The Buttery *(Glasgow)*	4	4	4
Anchor *(Ripley)*	4	3	4
Crab & Lobster *(Asenby)*	4	3	4
Eckington Manor *(Pershore)*	4	3	4
Stravaigin *(Glasgow)*	4	3	4
Whitstable Oyster Fishery Co. *(Whitstable)*	4	3	4

Drakes of Brighton (Brighton)	4	5	3
Sebastian's (Oswestry)	4	5	3
The Westwood Restaurant (Beverley)	4	5	3
Wedgwood (Edinburgh)	4	5	3
Beehive (White Waltham)	4	4	3
Eat on the Green (Ellon)	4	4	3
Eric's (Huddersfield)	4	4	3
Gamba (Glasgow)	4	4	3
Hawksmoor (Manchester)	4	4	3
La Chouette (Dinton)	4	4	3
La Rock (Sandiacre)	4	4	3
Lawns Restaurant, Thornton Hall Hotel & Spa (Thornton Hough)	4	4	3
Purslane (Cheltenham)	4	4	3
The Butcher's Arms (Eldersfield)	4	4	3
The Fox And Hounds Inn (Goldsborough)	4	4	3
The Leconfield (Petworth)	4	4	3
The Lighthouse Restaurant (Ashbourne)	4	4	3
The Old Passage Inn (Arlingham)	4	4	3
The Patricia (Jesmond)	4	4	3
The Sundial (Herstmonceux)	4	4	3
Kota (Porthleven)	4	3	3
Tanroagan (Douglas)	4	3	3
The Mason's Arms (Knowstone)	4	2	3
Haywards Restaurant (Epping)	4	4	2
The Oxford Kitchen (Oxford)	4	4	2
Dining Room (Rock)	4	3	2
Chino Latino, Park Plaza Hotel (Nottingham)	4	2	2
The Cartford Inn (Little Eccleston)	4	2	2

£50	The Sportsman (Seasalter)	5	5	5
	Orchid (Harrogate)	5	5	4
	Pea Porridge (Bury St Edmunds)	5	5	4
	Yalbury Cottage (Lower Bockhampton)	5	5	4
	Castle Dairy (Kendal)	5	4	4
	Inver Restaurant (Strachur)	5	4	4
	Kilberry Inn (Argyll)	5	4	4
	Loch Bay Restaurant (Stein)	5	4	4
	Maison Bleue (Bury St Edmunds)	5	4	4
	Prithvi (Cheltenham)	5	4	4
	The Great House Hotel & Restaurant, Lavenham (Lavenham)	5	4	4
	White Post (Yeovil)	5	4	4
	Yu And You (Copster Green)	5	4	4
	Bull & Ram (Ballynahinch)	5	3	4
	Sugo (Altrincham)	5	3	4
	Lanterna (Scarborough)	5	5	3

TOP SCORERS

The Hare Inn Restaurant *(Scawton)*		5 5 3
1921 Angel Hill *(Bury St Edmunds)*		5 4 3
64 Degrees *(Brighton)*		5 4 3
Ben's Cornish Kitchen *(Marazion)*		5 4 3
Bosquet *(Kenilworth)*		5 4 3
Henry's Restaurant *(Bath)*		5 4 3
Prevost *(Peterborough)*		5 4 3
Terre à Terre *(Brighton)*		5 4 3
The Ambrette *(Margate)*		5 4 3
The Rabbit Hole *(Edinburgh)*		5 4 3
The Wildebeest Arms *(Stoke Holy Cross)*		5 4 3
Crabshakk *(Glasgow)*		5 3 3
Ee-Usk *(Seafood Restaurant) (Oban)*		5 3 3
Benedicts *(Norwich)*		5 3 2
£40 Bia Bistrot *(Edinburgh)*		5 5 4
The Parkers Arms *(Newton-in-Bowland)*		5 5 4
Wheelers Oyster Bar *(Whitstable)*		5 5 4
Arbequina *(Oxford)*		5 4 4
Baratxuri *(Ramsbottom)*		5 4 4
Cafe Fish Tobermory *(Tobermory)*		5 4 4
Crab House Café *(Weymouth)*		5 4 4
Crab Shack *(Teignmouth)*		5 4 4
Harborne Kitchen *(Birmingham)*		5 4 4
Paco Tapas, The General *(Bristol)*		5 4 4
Pascal At The Old Vicarage *(Burton On Trent)*		5 4 4
Pysgoty *(Aberystwyth)*		5 4 4
The Coach *(Marlow)*		5 4 4
The Wheel House *(Falmouth)*		5 4 4
Wallfish Bistro *(Bristol)*		5 4 4
Butley Orford Oysterage *(Orford)*		5 4 3
Indian Zest *(Sunbury on Thames)*		5 4 3
Shillingfords *(Sudbury)*		5 4 3
Skosh *(York)*		5 4 3
White Swan at Fence *(Fence)*		5 4 3
Acorn Vegetarian Kitchen *(Bath)*		5 3 3
Indique *(Manchester)*		5 3 3
The Chilli Pickle *(Brighton)*		5 3 3
The Marram Grass *(Newborough)*		5 3 3
Umezushi *(Manchester)*		5 3 3
Yuzu *(Manchester)*		5 3 3
Seafood Shack *(Ullapool)*		5 4 2
Ebi Sushi *(Derby)*		5 3 2
Sojo *(Oxford)*		5 3 2
Yang Sing *(Manchester)*		5 3 2

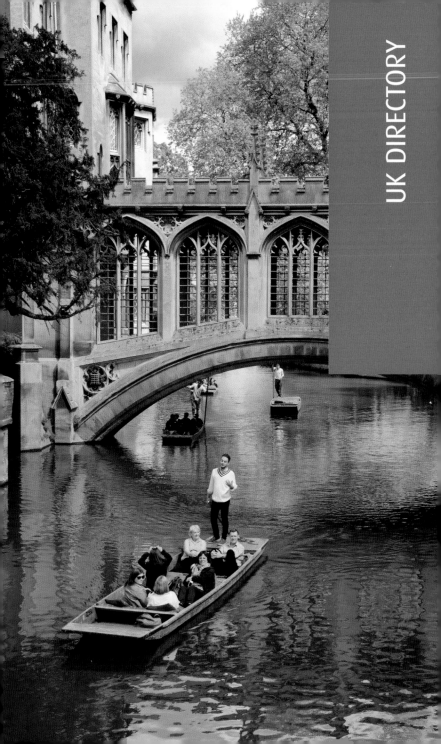

ABBEY DORE, HEREFORDSHIRE	2–1A

Toi Et Moi £65 444
Holling Grange HR2 0JJ 01981 240244
Cédric Lherbier's "small French restaurant in the lovely Herefordshire countryside" is a bit of a "hidden gem", pairing "wonderful" locally sourced food and "perfect hosts". Sample praise: "every single element was spot-on", "our favourite place for a long, lazy lunch". / Details: www.toietmoi.co.uk; 9 pm.

ABERAERON, CEREDIGION	4–3C

Harbourmaster £53 323
2 Quay Pde SA46 0BT 01545 570755
"Both bar and restaurant are equally good" at this harbourside hotel – a "very busy" spot with a "great buzz", where fish receives top billing; "amazing breakfasts" too. / Details: www.harbour-master.com; @hmaberaeron; 9 pm; No Amex. / Accommodation: 13 rooms, from £110

ABERDEEN, ABERDEENSHIRE	9–2D

Silver Darling £63
North Pier House, Pocra Quay AB11 5DQ 01224 576229
In an "awesome location watching the boats come and go", this converted former harbour control building has long been the "culinary star of Aberdeen", known for its "very good seafood" and "exemplary service". But having recently celebrated its 30th year, owner Didier Dejean retired in October 2017, selling to the McGinty's group – hence we've left it un-rated for the time being. / Details: www.thesilverdarling.co.uk; 9.30 pm; closed Sat L & Sun; children: +16 after 8 pm.

ABERDOUR, FIFE	9–4C

Room With A View, Forth View Hotel £47 444
Forth View Hotel, Hawkcraig Point KY3 0TZ 01383 860 402
"Brilliant fish and seafood" (with special "variations") is the lure to this "well-established" waterside haunt overlooking the Forth estuary; its "husband-and-wife team ensure that each customer is treated as a special guest" – one reason for its "loyal clientele". / Details: 9 pm, Sun 2 pm; closed Mon, Tue & Sun D.

ABERGAVENNY, MONMOUTHSHIRE	2–1A

The Angel Hotel £54 333
15 Cross St NP7 5EN 01873 857121
Handy for Abergavenny Castle, a polished and "superior hotel" with a stately dining room and also incorporating a "fabulous" "Foxhunters' dining bar. "High quality ingredients" star in the "always consistent" meals, while afternoon tea here is something of a legend. / Details: www.angelabergavenny.com/dining; @lovetheangel; 10 pm. / Accommodation: 35 rooms, from £101

The Hardwick £62 322
Old Raglan Rd NP7 9AA 01873 854220
Mixed feedback again this year on Stephen Terry's rural gastropub-with-rooms: one of Wales's best known culinary destinations. For the majority of reviewers, its "well-sourced and accurately cooked dishes" make it "the top choice in the area"; but for a sizeable minority it's "such a disappointment", having waited for ages to make a special trip". / Details: www.thehardwick.co.uk; @The_Hardwick; 10 pm, Sun 9 pm; No Amex. / Accommodation: 8 rooms, from £150

ABERTHIN, VALE OF GLAMORGAN	2–2A

Hare & Hounds £48 443
CF71 7LG 01446 774892
"A chef who formerly worked in a Michelin starred kitchen has left the froths and foams in London behind and has rejuvenated this pub with no-nonsense quality cooking": so say fans of Tom Watts-Jones notably accomplished food at this hostelry on the outskirts of Cowbridge. / Details: www.hareandhoundsaberthin.com; @Hare__Hounds.

ABERYSTWYTH, POWYS	4–3C

Pysgoty £46 544
The Harbour, South Promenade SY23 1JY 01970 624611
"Situated on the harbour front and directly facing a beautiful sea vista", this "small and intimate" gem is "amusingly located in a converted Art Deco public toilet but the ambience is more that of a Californian beach shack – especially in summer when you eat outside on a sail-covered deck". To eat: "essentially fish and seafood that's simply but beautifully cooked". / Details: pysgoty.co.uk/home/; @Pysgoty.

Ultracomida £36 443
31 Pier St SY23 2LN 01970 630686
A relaxed Spaniard of some renown for its "well-prepared, tasty tapas", and whose owners are also "working to bring an imaginative range of Spanish wines (especially reds) onto its list". Downside? The

back-of-deli seating – high stools or a communal table – can make it feel "a bit cramped". / Details: www.ultracomida.com; @ultracomida; 9 pm; Mon-Thu & Sat L only, Fri open L & D, closed Sun.

ALBOURNE, WEST SUSSEX   3–4B

The Ginger Fox   £52   3️⃣4️⃣4️⃣
Muddleswood Road BN6 9EA 01273 857888
This "very relaxing" country outpost by Brighton foodie icons the Gingerman Group has a "lovely" thatched pub setting on the edge of the South Downs; add in "delicious and unusual food" and it's a winner all-round. / Details: thegingerfox.com/; @GingerfoxDish; 9 pm, Fri & Sat 10 pm.

ALDEBURGH, SUFFOLK   3–1D

Aldeburgh Fish And Chips   £16   3️⃣2️⃣1️⃣
226 High St IP15 5DB 01728 454685
"The beach is your dining room" ("fighting off the gulls whilst eating adds to the experience") and the fish 'n' chips are "very fresh" at this veteran family-run fixture. / Details: www.aldeburghfishandchips.co.uk; @aldefishnchips; Tue & Wed 2 pm, Thu & Sat 8 pm, Fri 9 pm, Sun 2.30; closed Mon, Tue D, Wed D & Sun D; Cash only.

The Lighthouse   £45   3️⃣4️⃣4️⃣
77 High Street IP15 5AU 01728 453377
"Aldeburgh is one of those lovely Suffolk coastal towns that punches way above its weight for restaurants, and the Lighthouse on the High Street, near the cinema, is the best for food (especially fresh fish)". Leaving the "reliably competent" cooking aside though, it's "the welcome that's really the big thing here", led by the "very friendly front of house" Sam. / Details: www.lighthouserestaurant.co.uk; @AldeLighthouse; 10 pm.

Regatta   £46   3️⃣2️⃣2️⃣
171 High Street IP15 5AN 01728 452011
"A very popular and trusted old fish stalwart", where "the catch is always fresh daily, and comes directly from the fisherman based within 500 yards of the restaurant". On the downside "the space is a bit rectangular" and it can get "noisy", but the cooking's "consistently good" (and staff are family friendly too). / Details: www.regattaaldeburgh.com; @AldeburghR; 10 pm.

Sea Spice, The White Lion Hotel   £59   3️⃣2️⃣4️⃣
Market Cross Place IP15 5BU 01728 451800
This upmarket Indian (inside an hotel) has had a warm welcome, considering it's in the most traditional of Suffolk seaside towns, winning

consistently high ratings. / Details: seaspice.co.uk; @SeaSpiceAlde; 10 pm; closed Mon.

ALDERLEY EDGE, CHESHIRE   5–2B

The Alderley, Alderley Edge Hotel   £69   3️⃣4️⃣4️⃣
Macclesfield Rd SK9 7BJ 01625 583033
A "great location" in an upmarket 1850 mansion sets the (WAG-friendly) tone at Chris Holland's fine dining spot; NB a three-month refurb to add a new bar/lounge and restaurant area was due to begin in September 2017, with a limited menu served in the bar in the interim. / Details: www.alderleyedgehotel.com; @AlderleyHotel; 9.45 pm, Sun 4 pm; closed Sun.

Yu Alderley   £59   3️⃣3️⃣4️⃣
London Road SK9 7QD 01625 569922
That its bar is "a well-known hangout for WAGs" leads to some accusations that this "stylish" Asian in chichi Alderley Edge is pricey and "too pretentious even by Cheshire standards", but even critics say the "high quality" Chinese cuisine here is good, and for fans it's "the best ever". / Details: yualderleyedge. com; @Yu_Alderleyedge; 10.30 pm, Sun 10 pm; Booking max 12 may apply.

ALDFORD, CHESHIRE   5–3A

The Grosvenor Arms   £42   3️⃣4️⃣4️⃣
Chester Rd CH3 6HJ 01244 620228
A "comfortable and very characterful" outpost of the Brunning & Price chain in a "large and traditional" ducal pub near one of the gates to the Duke of Westminster's estates (complete with lovely garden in summer). All reports praise "really good food from a versatile menu to suit all tastes; an impressive selection of wines, cask beers and spirits; and friendly service". / Details: www.grosvenorarms-aldford.co.uk; @GrosArmsAldford; 6m S of Chester on B5130; 10 pm, Sun 9 pm.

ALKHAM, KENT   3–3D

The Marquis   £54   2️⃣2️⃣3️⃣
Alkham Valley Rd CT15 7DF 01304 873410
This gentrified village boozer nowadays classifies itself as a 'Luxury Hotel with a Fine Dining Restaurant' and reviewers are split on the change. Critics say the "all-too-common revamp has 'bland-ified' a previously characterful old pub..." ("I hear millions were spent on this historic building but, that doesn't buy you a quality restaurant"). On a more positive note, fans hail "beautifully crafted" dishes "conjuring distinctive flavours" in "comfortable surroundings". / Details:

www.themarquisatalkham.co.uk; @marquisalkham;
9.30 pm, Sun 8.30 pm; children: 8+ at D. /
Accommodation: *10 rooms, from £95*

ALNWICK, NORTHUMBERLAND   8–1B

**Treehouse, Alnwick
Castle**   **£46**   3̄3̄5̄
The Alnwick Garden NE66 1YU
01665 511350
*"A dream for big kids" – a "hobbit-like restaurant
in a treehouse", next to the castle's gardens; add
in "competent cooking" (though perhaps not
quite on par with the "fabulous, magical setting")
and it's a recipe for "a great day" out. /* **Details:**
*www.alnwickgarden.com; @AlnwickGarden; Mon-Wed
3 pm, Thu-Sun 9.15 pm; closed Mon D, Tue D & Wed D.*

ALRESFORD, HAMPSHIRE   2–3D

Caracoli   **£21**   3̄4̄4̄
15 Broad St SO24 9AR   01962 738730
*"Really excellent coffee… delicious Portuguese
custard tarts, and other stunning pastries to
accompany it" – this packed city-centre branch of
the cookware chain "has reproduced the excellence
of the original Alresford store" and "it's brilliant for a
'pop-in' brew or lunch". /* **Details:** *www.caracoli.co.uk;
@Caracolistore; L only; No Amex; No bookings.*

Pulpo Negro   **£40**   3̄3̄4̄
28 Broad Street SO24 9AQ   01962 732262
*Andres & Marie-Lou Alemany's "fabulous" (but no-
frills) follow-up to the nearby Purefoy Arms, praised
for delivering "delicious tapas in a lovely room with
a cosy bar downstairs". /* **Details:** *pulponegro.co.uk;
@pulpo__negro; 10.30 pm; closed Mon & Sun.*

ALSTONEFIELD, DERBYSHIRE   5–3C

The George   **£50**   3̄2̄4̄
DE6 2FX   01335 310205
*"Tuck yourself into The George, a quintessential
English pub in the Peak District... and tuck into one
of their amazing pies or a spot-on roast"; first-timers
are "very pleasantly surprised" by the quality of the
cooking. /* **Details:** *www.thegeorgeatalstonefield.com;
Mon-Sat 11 pm, Sun 9.30 pm.*

ALTRINCHAM, GREATER MANCHESTER 5–2B

The Con Club   **£52**
48 Greenwood St WA14 1RZ   0161 696 6870
*In autumn 2016 this former Working Men's
Conservative Club in Altrincham was transformed
into a stylishly tricked-out brasserie and*

---

*microbrewery, serving up charcoal grilled meats,
sushi and sashimi. The owner, David Vanderhook, is
also behind The George Charles pub in Didsbury
and Lime bar at Salford Quays. Too limited
feedback for a rating, but one early report praises
"very convivial surroundings and an excellent
addition to Altrincham's dining scene". /* **Details:**
www.conclubuk.com; @ConClubAlty.

**Honest Crust, Market
House**   **£12**   4̄3̄4̄
26 Market Street WA14 1PF   no tel
*"In the busy and buzzing Altrincham market
hall", this funky outfit "stacks up very well against
Manchester's various pizza offerings, both old and
new", featuring "excellent quality" options with
"sourdough bases, finished off in a wood-fired oven".
In September 2017, the same team behind Alti's
hit revamp helped relaunch Mackie Mayor market,
in the Northern Quarter. /* **Details:** *@Honest_Crust;
9.30 pm; closed Mon & Sun D.*

Sugo   **£51**   5̄3̄4̄
22 Shaw's Rd, Altrincham WA14 1QU
0161 929 7706
*"A very busy, buzzy place" – this "inviting and
casual" (albeit "small") two-year-old Italian, handy
for Altrincham Market, wins raves for its "honest
food prepared with skill and passion" and delivering
"strong flavours with flair" from a menu majoring in
"authentic pasta dishes". Following the launch of a
next door deli/sandwich shop in 2016, a new sibling
will join Ancoats' growing foodie scene in early 2018.
/* **Details:** *www.sugopastakitchen.co.uk; @Sugo_Pasta.*

ALVESTON, WARWICKSHIRE   2–1C

Baraset Barn   **£49**   3̄4̄3̄
Pimlico Lane CV37 7RJ   01789 295510
*This popular and "well-run" 200-year-old country
pub and grill remains of note for its lunch, but
the victuals – including daily seafood specials
– are "most enjoyable" at any time. /* **Details:**
www.barasetbarn.co.uk.

AMBERLEY, WEST SUSSEX   3–4A

Amberley Castle   **£98**   3̄4̄5̄
BN18 9LT   01798 831992
*"It's so romantic" eating in this historic venue,
complete with peacocks, ruined ramparts and
working portcullis! Inevitably it's not the best
option for a cheap date and opinions are mixed
as to the value it delivers – for critics the cuisine is
"not special enough" and the dining room "lacks
ambience despite its evident history", but more
typical is a reviewer who feels "it's a bit overpriced"
but still finds it "a lovely experience". /* **Details:**

---

www.amberleycastle.co.uk; @amberleycastle; N of
Arundel on B2139; No jeans; Booking max 6 may apply;
children: 8.

AMBLE, NORTHUMBERLAND   8–1B

The Old Boat House
Amble   **£49**   4 4 3
Leazes Street NE65 0AA   01665 711 232
"In a quayside location that's easily missed", this
"small" venue provides "caring service" and "a
wonderful choice of fresh fish". It's "excellent
value" too. / **Details:** boathousefoodgroup.co.uk/
theoldboathouse-amble.html; @TOBHFoodGroup; Mon-
Thu 9 pm, Fri & Sat 9.30 pm, Sun 9 pm.

AMBLESIDE, CUMBRIA   7–3D

Drunken Duck   **£59**   4 4 5
Barngates LA22 0NG   01539 436347
"A remote, cosy inn (and microbrewery) in the
Lakeland Fells" that owes its high popularity
to its cooking with "amazing attention to
detail" and "exemplary service". / **Details:**
www.drunkenduckinn.co.uk; @DrunkenDuckInn; 3m
from Ambleside, towards Hawkshead; 9 pm; No Amex;
Booking evening only. / **Accommodation:** 17 rooms,
from £105

Fellini's   **£44**   3 4 3
Church St LA22 0BT   01539 432487
A "brilliant vegetarian restaurant attached to a
cinema"; the "usually enterprising Italian dishes" are
"very tasty" and the "menu changes regularly" too.
/ **Details:** www.fellinisambleside.com; 10 pm; D only;
No Amex.

Lake Road Kitchen   **£83**   5 5 3
3 Sussex House, Lake Road LA22 0AD
015394 22012
"Startlingly good food, brilliantly explained" is a
recipe for ongoing rapturous reviews concerning
ex-Noma chef James Cross and his partner's
"fantastic and cosy" Scandi-style venture, decorated
with much use of wood, and with the kitchen
partially on view: "a special destination run with
tremendous enthusiasm by two of the most
passionate people in the game", producing "some of
the best ever food, and a splendid experience that
could be enjoyed over and over again". / **Details:**
www.lakeroadkitchen.co.uk; @LakeRoadKitchen; 9 pm;
closed Mon & Tue.

Old Stamp House   **£63**   5 4 3
Church St LA22 0BU   015394 32775
"Chef Ryan Blackburn will no doubt go from
strength to strength" at this three-year-old, which
already offers the "best food in Ambleside" –
"yes, the basement is a little bland and sparsely

decorated", but the "brilliantly imaginative"
cooking "shines like a beacon". / **Details:**
www.oldstamphouse.com; 9 pm; closed Mon & Sun.

Zeffirelli's   **£36**   3 3 3
Compston Rd LA22 9AD   01539 433845
"Just an absolute joy" – a "superior vegetarian
restaurant in a spacious and interesting room under
the cinema of the same name" (and where, like
its nearby sibling Fellini's, there are "great deals"
to be had if you opt to combine food and a film).
/ **Details:** www.zeffirellis.com; @ZeffsFellinis; 10 pm;
No Amex.

AMERSHAM, BUCKINGHAMSHIRE   3–2A

Artichoke   **£77**   5 5 4
9 Market Sq HP7 0DF   01494 726611
"Perfect, perfect, perfect!" – "It's such a surprise
to find this gem nestled in Old Amersham", and
this "magnificent" establishment on a picturesque
Georgian street would enjoy a much higher profile
if it were not bizarrely overlooked by Michelin
year-on-year. Chef/Patron Laurie Gear's "complex
cooking comes with a very deft touch": "beautifully
crafted, rich, with gorgeous accompanying wine,
and delivered by staff who make you feel a million
dollars". "It is incomprehensible that it doesn't have
a star" – in fact some say "it's worthy of two" – yet
a number of fans feel that "the fact that it lacks
recognition almost improves it": "please let them
keep missing out, because it keeps the place just
about affordable, and we can get a table when
we want!" / **Details:** www.artichokerestaurant.co.uk;
@ArtichokeChef; 9.15 pm, lunch 1.45pm; closed Mon
& Sun; No shorts.

Gilbey's   **£60**   3 4 4
1 Market Sq HP7 0DF   01494 727242
"No complaints at all" about this "consistently good
all-rounder", fusing a "lovely" interior ("understated,
tasteful and relaxing") and "wine from the owners'
vineyard", with "food that's always well-prepared". /
Details: www.gilbeygroup.com/restaurants/gilbeys-old;
@GilbeysAmersham; 9.30 pm, Sat 9.45 pm, Sun
8.45 pm.

The Grocer at 91   **£12**   3 3 3
91 High Street, Amersham, Buckinghamshire,
HP7 0DT   01494 724581
A winning indie café, community shop, greengrocer
and deli with two local branches – set just a few
minutes' apart from one another along the High
Street – and a nice line in sandwiches, cakes and
bacon sarnies. / **Details:** www.thegrocershops.co.uk;
@thegrocershops; No bookings.

Hawkyns, The Crown Inn **£71**   1 2 3
16 High Street HP7 0DH   01494 721541
"After much fanfare it's so average!" This timber-

framed Elizabethan coaching inn starred in 'Four Weddings and a Funeral', and is once again drawing attention thanks to Atul Kochhar (of Benares fame) making it the home of his latest restaurant in January 2017. But for far too many reporters, his Indian twist on British favourites is "dismal", with "dreary food" and "friendly but hopelessly amateur service". / Details: www.hawkynsrestaurant.co.uk; @Hawkynsamersham; Mon-Thu 9.30 pm, Fri & Sat 10 pm, Sun 9 pm.

ANNAT, WESTER ROSS　　9–2B

The Torridon Restaurant £85 5️⃣5️⃣4️⃣
The Torridon IV22 2EY　01445 791242
"It's a long journey to get there, but worth it!" – an imposing country hotel, at the end of a loch, whose restaurant provides "an excellent ambience, great food – especially the seven-course tasting menu – and fine wines". Stop Press – Ross Stovold, ex-of the acclaimed Isle of Eriska hotel, took over chef duties in summer 2017. / Details: www.thetorridon.com/restaurant; @thetorridon.

ANSTRUTHER, FIFE　　9–4D

Anstruther Fish Bar £27 5️⃣4️⃣3️⃣
42-44 Shore St KY10 3AQ　01333 310518
"The best fish 'n' chips in bonny Scotland!" ("and also the best cup of tea around") plus a "lovely harbour setting" continue to make this "diner"-style venture a "very popular" destination; "it would cost at least double elsewhere!" / Details: www.anstrutherfishbar.co.uk; 9.30 pm; No Amex; No bookings.

The Cellar £73 5️⃣4️⃣4️⃣
24 East Green KY10 3AA　01333 310378
"Run by a local lad" (Billy Boyter) who "returned home and earned a Michelin star and 3 rosettes within 18 months of opening", this celebrated address is "going from strength to strength" with its "exquisitely flavoured" food (especially fish) based on Scottish produce; it "can be difficult to find but persevere". / Details: www.thecellaranstruther.co.uk; @The_Cellar_Fife; in the harbour area; Wed-Sun 9 pm; closed Mon, Tue & Wed L; No Amex.

APPLECROSS, HIGHLAND　　9–2B

Applecross Inn £42 4️⃣4️⃣4️⃣
Shore St IV54 8LR　01520 744262
A "stunning" Highlands peninsula setting adds a sense of drama to this "very busy but well-organised" restaurant-with-rooms; add in "consistently good" and "great value" food (local catch being the speciality) and it's easy to see why it has such a "loyal fanbase". / Details: www.applecross.uk.com/inn/; off A896, S of Shieldaig; 9 pm; No Amex; May need 6+ to book. / Accommodation: 7 rooms, from £90

APPLEDORE, DEVON　　1–2C

The Coffee Cabin £16 4️⃣4️⃣4️⃣
22 The Quay EX39 1QS　01237 475843
"Brilliant coffee and wonderful homemade cakes" have made the name of this cute three-year-old café, also reputed for its stellar crab sandwiches and estuary views; their menu and seating have expanded of late, but surely you can't get too much of a good thing? / Details: L only; No Amex; No bookings.

The Seagate £48 4️⃣4️⃣4️⃣
EX39 1QS　01237 472589
A "fabulous inn overlooking the Torridge Estuary" and quaint fishing village of Appledore, with "brilliant staff" and "very good pub food and accommodation". / Details: www.theseagate.co.uk; @TheSeagate68; 9 pm.

ARGYLL, ARGYLL AND BUTE　　9–3B

Kilberry Inn £57 5️⃣4️⃣4️⃣
Kilberry PA29 6YD　01880 770223
"A wonderful drive" up the single-track B8024, skirting the coast of the Knapdale peninsula, and with stunning views of the Inner Hebrides, leads to this "most welcoming inn", with a "lovely", laid back atmosphere; "truly fresh produce" informs the "beautifully cooked" fare (and especially "excellent seafood"). / Details: www.kilberryinn.com; @Kilberryinn; 9 pm; closed Mon, Tue L & Wed L; No Amex. / Accommodation: 5 rooms, from £210

ARLINGHAM, GLOUCESTERSHIRE　　2–2B

The Old Passage Inn £68 4️⃣4️⃣3️⃣
Passage Road GL2 7JR　01452 740547
A "great location overlooking the Severn" ("seemingly in the middle of nowhere, with fabulous views") is matched by "superb" and "elegantly plated" fish dishes at this "modern, bright and light" (but slightly "noisy") dining room. It's "best experienced in the summer", when the "terrace is a great delight". / Details: www.theoldpassage.com; @OldPassageInn; 9 pm; closed Mon & Sun D. / Accommodation: 2 rooms, from £80

ARUNDEL, WEST SUSSEX   3–4A

Motte And Bailey Cafe   £28   🅱🅳🅱
BN18 9AG   01903 883813
*Chef/owner Michael Etherington's "incredibly
friendly" corner venture is an unusual combination:
traditional tearoom by day, with "terrific English
breakfasts", lunch and cakes, and "great" Moroccan/
Spanish tapas haunt from Thursday to Saturday
night. / Details: 10.30 pm, Fri & Sat 11 pm.*

Parsons Table   £66
2 & 8 Castle Mews BN18 9DG   01903 883477
*Chef Lee Parsons – who honed his skills at
Raymond Blanc's Le Manoir et al – and wife Liz
have opened their first restaurant in this picturesque
town, showcasing West Sussex produce. / Details:
theparsonstable.co.uk/; @tpt_restaurant; 9.30 pm.*

The Town House   £51   🅴🅴🅴
65 High Street BN18 9AJ   01903 883847
*"The owner is an excellent host" at this "lovely"
restaurant-with-rooms, where the dining room's
talking point is a ceiling originating in late
16th century Florence. "The food remains
fabulous" too. / Details: www.thetownhouse.co.uk;
@thetownhousearundel; 9.30 pm; closed Mon & Sun. /
Accommodation: 4 rooms, from £95*

ASCOT, BERKSHIRE   3–3A

Restaurant Coworth Park   £100   🅱🅴🅴
Coworth Park, Blacknest Rd SL5 7SE
01344 876600
*"That it's reassuringly expensive, doesn't seem
to dampen the enthusiasm of the clientele" of
the Dorchester Collection's "delightful" country
pile, set in "beautiful gardens" just a short drive
outside the M25. Adam Smith's "brilliant" cooking
is available à la carte or from a 7-course tasting
menu and service has "an eye for detail". Top Tip
– "fabulous afternoon tea, with the most delicious
finger sandwiches!" / Details: www.coworthpark.com;
@CoworthParkUK; Mon & Tue 10.30am, Wed-Fri 9 pm,
Sat 10 pm; closed Sun D.*

ASENBY, NORTH YORKSHIRE   8–4C

Crab & Lobster   £68   🅴🅱🅴
Dishforth Rd YO7 3QL   01845 577286
*It's "worth a trip from Hull or York for the variety
and quality of fish alone" at this "wonderful quirky
place", just off the A1, crammed with bunting and
bric-a-brac. The "fabulous" plates (from the catch
delivered daily from Hartlepool) comes "in Yorkshire*

sizes"; if you overindulge, repair to the Crab Manor
hotel next door. / **Details:** www.crabandlobster.co.uk;
@crabandlobster; at junction of Asenby Rd & Topcliffe
Rd; 9 pm, Sat 9.30 pm. / **Accommodation:** 17 rooms,
from £160*

ASHBOURNE, DERBYSHIRE   5–3C

The Lighthouse Restaurant   £62   🅴🅴🅱
New Road, Boylestone DE6 5AA
01335 330658
*"Sitting at the back of the Rose and Crown pub in
the middle of nowhere", this "gem" of a restaurant is
a bit of a "revelation" in the local "culinary desert".
The young team ("all seemingly 30 or below")
"oozes slick professionalism in the kitchen" and
provide a "delightful experience at reasonable
prices" – the "seasonal and superb" nine-course
tasting menu just "gets better and better". / Details:
www.the-lighthouse-restaurant.co.uk/; midnight; closed
Sun-Tue.*

AUCHTERARDER, PERTH AND KINROSS 9–3C

Andrew Fairlie, Gleneagles Hotel   £146   🅵🅴🅴
PH3 1NF   01764 694267
*"Stratospheric prices are justified" at Andrew
Fairlie's "cocoon-like" dining room, whose position
deep within this famous Scottish bastion creates
"an intimate bubble" which "adds to the lovely
experience". "If you would like to have a once-in-
a-lifetime gastronomic blow-out this is an excellent
place to do so". The cuisine is "Scotland's best" – "a
truly remarkable adventure in fine dining" from
tasting menus with "outstanding" wine pairings that
provide a series of "incomparable and memorable
dishes". One former fan who has accused it of
"resting on its laurels" in recent surveys, found it
"back to its best" this year. Top Menu Tip – "the
lobster infused with whisky – if I was on death
row, this would be my final meal!" / Details:
www.andrewfairlie.co.uk; @AndrewFairlie1; 10 pm; L
only, closed Sun; children: 12+.*

Jon & Fernanda's   £52   🅴🅴🅱
34 High Street PH3 1DB   01764 662442
*"A great alternative to the nearby Gleneagles Hotel
restaurants" (where the owners used to work) –
this "delightful" venue provides "lovey light and
fresh cuisine" which in many reviewers' eyes bears
comparison with its starrier competitor, and eating
here is "much cheaper than up the hill". / Details:
www.jonandfernandas.co.uk; 9 pm; D only, closed Mon
& Sun; No Amex; children: 10+.*

AUGHTON, LANCASHIRE   5–2A

Moor Hall   **£93**   🄻🄻🄻
Prescot Rd L39 6RT 01695 572511
"A new star is born in the North West" at
ex-L'Enclume head chef, Mark Birchall's new
restaurant-with-rooms, which opened just prior to
our survey in March 2017 and instantly inspired a
good number of reports saying that "so far, it shows
amazing promise"; and, at a regional level, "is a
gamechanger for West Lancashire (with Liverpool
just 10 miles to the south)". The main building – a
Grade II-listed gentry house – is "already lovely" and
reviewers "can't wait to see new developments on
the site unfold" as "The Barn (a 65-seater, providing
more casual dining, as well as a small dairy,
bakery, curing room and mini-brewery) and the
planting of the large kitchen garden is completed".
"Service is full of care and love"; if "some of the
staff are recognisable from L'Enclume, so is the
faultless food", which is "delivered with the style
and panache" one would expect ("open only a few
weeks and already some the best food I have ever
eaten"). "The cheese room is a fun addition" too. "All
in all, it's an exceptional experience (and one more
relaxed than L'Enclume too)". STOP PRESS – at the
end of October 2017, The Barn opened. / **Details:**
www.moorhall.com; @restmoorhall.

AXMINSTER, DEVON   2–4A

River Cottage Canteen   **£51**   🄱🄱🄿
Trinity Square EX13 5AN 01297 631715
This branch of the TV chef's buzzing communal
dining rooms continues to put in a steady
performance: "a good place for lunch – especially
with children" (who can profit from the notably
virtuous kids' menu). / **Details:** www.rivercottage.net;
@axcanteen; Mon 4 pm, Tue-Sat 9 pm, Sun 6 pm;
closed Mon D & Sun D.

AYLESBURY, BUCKINGHAMSHIRE   3–2A

**Hartwell House, Hotel, Restaurant
and Spa**   **£74**   🄱🄲🄻
Oxford Road HP17 8NR 01296 747444
A visit to this "lovely" Relais & Châteaux country
house hotel "feels as if you're transported to
another era"; perhaps it's "not a place for the
young", but those with grown up tastes will enjoy
the "very good" afternoon tea – held in the
venue's "exquisitely grand and ornate" historic
lounges – and "set lunch is a great buy" too. /
Details: www.hartwell-house.com/wine-and-dine/;
@HartwellHouse; 2m W of Aylesbury on A418;
9.45 pm; No jeans; children: 4+. / **Accommodation:**
50 rooms, from £290

The King's Head   **£32**   🄱🄱🄱
Kings Head Passage, Market Square HP20 2RW
01296 718812
"The best pub in Aylesbury" might sounds like a
dubious honour, but not everywhere is owned by The
National Trust, and this ancient property – one of
the oldest taverns in the south of England – is a fine
Tudor building. The dining room – run by the Chiltern
Brewery – offers reliable pub grub but arguably
the greater attractions are the beers, plus wines
from the Rothschild estate (who originally owned
the pub). / **Details:** www.kingsheadaylesbury.co.uk;
@Kings_Head.

AYMESTREY, HEREFORDSHIRE   5–4A

Riverside Inn   **£48**   🄱🄲🄱
HR6 9ST 01568 708440
In a "lovely riverside setting in an out-of-the-way
corner of Herefordshire", this picturesque 16th
century inn was taken over by longtime chef
Andy Link in May 2016. An "elegant French-
style country chic" refurb' has added to its
charms, and his locally sourced food remains
"unassuming" but "mouthwatering". / **Details:**
www.riversideaymestrey.co.uk.

BAGSHOT, SURREY   3–3A

**The Latymer, Pennyhill Park
Hotel**   **£135**   🄱🄲🄲
London Road GU19 5EU 01276 486150
Teething problems after Michael Wignall's exodus
to Gidleigh Park are long forgotten at the ornate,
wood-panelled dining room of this famed country
house hotel. This year it garnered near-perfect
reports, with chef Matt Worswick (who joined in
March 2016) turning out "absolutely delicious"
tasting menus complemented by some "unusual"
wine flights – "very expensive but a real treat". /
Details: www.exclusive.co.uk; @PennyhillPark; 9 pm;
closed Mon, Tue L, Sat L & Sun; Booking max 8 may
apply; children: 12+. / **Accommodation:** 123 rooms,
from £315

BAINBRIDGE, NORTH YORKSHIRE   8–3A

Yorebridge House   **£85**   🄳🄳🄳
DL8 3EE 01969 652060
Nestled by two rivers on the North Yorks side of
the Dales, this plush boutique hotel occupies an
old Victorian schoolhouse, headmaster's house
and barn. Food that's "a delight for the eyes
and the taste buds" (with "lots of extras such as
canapés, amuse bouche, palate cleansers, pre-
desserts") won it high ratings this year. / **Details:**
www.yorebridgehouse.co.uk; @yorebridgehouse; 9 pm.

Piedaniels   £51   4 4 2
Bath St DE45 1BX   01629 812687
*"Tucked down a side-street and way better than
the mundane Bakewell coffee shop average, this
husband-and-wife restaurant has been going for
years, offering serious French traditional cooking
that never changes and doesn't chase trends but
which is amazing value… you might find the
decor a bit much but don't be put off." / Details:
www.piedaniels-restaurant.com; 10.30 pm, open on Sun
only 2 weekends per month; closed Mon & Sun D.*

**Pale Hall Hotel
Restaurant**   £84   5 4 5
LL23 7PS   01678 530 285
*Limited but ecstatic feedback on this "lovely"
Victorian pile, on the edge of Snowdonia (once
owned by the Duke of Westminster), where the
dining room was initially "under the aegis of
Michael Caines": Gareth Stevenson's cuisine is
"delicious and beautifully presented, and though
portions look small they prove fully satisfying: well
worth the journey to a remote location". / Details:
@palehallhotel; 9 pm.*

Bull & Ram   £58   5 3 4
1 Dromore Street BT24 8AG   028 9756 0908
*Situated in a beautiful Grade-I listed Edwardian
butcher's shop of an attractive market town, this
shrine to Northern Irish beef has won major
plaudits from local and national press for its prime
cuts, expertly cooked. Early feedback is of "amazing
quality meat at prices that are outrageous value".
In summer 2017 chef-patron Kelan McMichael
announced plans to open an outpost in Belfast. /
Details: www.bullandram.com; @bullandram.*

Monachyle Mhor   £82   5 4 4
FK19 8PQ   01877 384622
*"Just the perfect place for romance"; way out in
the Trossachs National Park, and "looking out on
snow-capped mountains", this "small farmstead"-
turned "pleasant, relaxing country hotel" is a "simply
magical" spot for "locally sourced", "quite classically
cooked" grub. "Exquisite. Not much more to say…
just go there". / Details: www.mhor.net; take the Kings
House turning off the A84; 9 pm. / Accommodation:
14 rooms, from £195*

The Potted Lobster   £50   3 3 3
3 Lucker Road NE69 7BS   01668 214088
*"Locally caught fish and shellfish handled with a
deft touch (langoustines to die for!)" win consistent
high praise for this snug, new fish bistro in a cute
coastal village, which provides "very acceptable
quality, in a very underserved area". / Details:
www.thepottedlobsterbamburgh.co.uk.*

Savoro   £47   3 2 2
206 High Street EN5 5SZ   020 8449 9888
*This hotel dining room, occupying a former
boathouse set back from the main street, has
built up a loyal local following for its "dependable
food" – grilled fish, steaks, risotto and so on – and
"reasonable prices" (especially the bargain set
menu). / Details: www.savoro.co.uk; Mon-Sat 10 pm,
Sun 9 pm; closed Sun D. / Accommodation: 9 rooms,
from £75*

The Village Pub   £48   3 2 3
GL7 5EF   01285 740 421
*"Best enjoyed in winter to cosy up by the roaring
log fires", but "well worth the detour" at any time,
this "incredibly friendly" gastroboozer gains plaudits
for hearty "pub food as it should be". / Details:
www.thevillagepub.co.uk; @The_Village_Pub; 9.30 pm,
Sun 9 pm. / Accommodation: 6 rooms, from £130*

**Montys Caribbean
Kitchen**   £30   5 4 3
19 Tuly Street EX31 1DH   01271 372985
*"Delicious and very reasonably priced" Caribbean
street food (plus great cocktails) are served at a
rapid pelt at this simple, happy-go-lucky two-year-
old outfit – operating from a van for a year before
that – run by an Anglo/Jamaican husband-and-wife
team. / Details: www.montyscaribbeankitchen.co.uk;
@montyskitchen; Fri & Sat 11 pm; No bookings.*

The Blacksmith's Arms   £65   3 3 3
2-4 Church Lane LE12 8PP   01509 413100
*Jill Townend and Mark Hammond's "pleasant,
welcoming and efficient" gastropub generated
all-round positive feedback for its reliable fare*

and agreeable interior, with attractive modern dining annex. / **Details:** www.blacksmiths1753.co.uk; @Blacksmiths1753; 9 pm.

BARTON-ON-SEA, HAMPSHIRE	2–4C

Pebble Beach £61 4 4 4
Marine Drive BH25 7DZ 01425 627777
"A stupendous backdrop" – "there are stunning views from the Isle of Wight to the Purbecks" both from the superb terrance and the interior – is matched by "amazing seafood" ("straightforward" but "staggering") at Pierre Chevillard's stalwart restaurant with rooms, where "you are made to feel very welcome". "What better place for lunch on a summer's day?" / **Details:** www.pebblebeach-uk.com; @pebblebeachUK; Mon-Fri 9.30 pm, Sat & Sun 10 pm. / **Accommodation:** 4 rooms, from £100

BARWICK, SOMERSET	2–3B

Little Barwick House £73 5 5 4
BA22 9TD 01935 423902
Handy for Barwick Park and its follies, Emma & Tim Ford's "incomparable" restaurant-with-rooms has a "lovely atmosphere" and "when full, the place sings". Tim's British food is "always fabulous" ("the cheeseboard is one of the best") and "Emma gives amazing wine advice" from an "excellent and varied wine list with prices that aren't greedy". / **Details:** www.littlebarwickhouse.co.uk; @LittleBarwick; take the A37 Yeovil to Dorchester road, turn left at the brown sign for Little Barwick House; 9 pm; closed Mon, Tue L & Sun; children: 5+. / **Accommodation:** 6 rooms, from £69

BASINGSTOKE, HAMPSHIRE	2–3D

Glasshouse Restaurant, Oakley Hall £59 2 2 3
Rectory Rd RG23 7EL 01256 783350
Afternoon tea is a highlight at this hotel and conference centre, set in impressive gardens. Limited feedback on more comprehensive dining: one reviewer reported "service not what you'd expect of this fine-looking establishment" and "expected more of the menu", yet still awarded good ratings overall. / **Details:** www.oakleyhall-park.com; @oakleyhall; 9.30 pm; No jeans.

BASLOW, DERBYSHIRE	5–2C

Fischers at Baslow Hall £105 4 4 4
Calver Rd DE45 1RR 01246 583259
"By far the best restaurant in Derbyshire / South Yorkshire" – Susan & Max Fischer's well-established

destination in an Edwardian house built in the style of a 17th-century manor has "maintained high standards over decades" and if anything "upped its game of late", with meals at the "exceptional Kitchen Tasting Bench" inspiring particularly enthusiastic reports. / **Details:** www.fischers-baslowhall.co.uk/; @FischersBaslow; on the A623; 8.30 pm; No trainers. / **Accommodation:** 11 rooms, from £180

Rowley's £56 3 3 2
Church Lane DE45 1RY 01246 583880
From the people behind Fischers of Baslow Hall, a "pleasant brasserie-style" venture, by the Chatsworth Estate, which in particular is "a great place for a family meal"; regulars say the food has "varied up and down as chefs have come and gone", but all reporters rate it good or better. / **Details:** www.rowleysrestaurant.co.uk; @RowleysBaslow; Mon-Fri 9 pm, Sat 9.30 pm, Sun 3 pm; closed Mon & Sun D; No Amex.

BASSENTHWAITE, CUMBRIA	7–3C

Bistro At The Distillery £51 3 2 2
Setmurthy CA13 9SJ 01768788850
"Part of the glamorous (whisky-oriented) Lakes Distillery complex outside Keswick", and set in a former Victorian cattle parlour – Terry Laybourne's two-year-old might sound like a tourist trap, but in fact it offers "good food in an area short of it". / **Details:** www.bistroatthedistillery.com; @BistroTLD; 9 pm.

BATH, SOMERSET	2–2B

Acorn Vegetarian Kitchen £48 5 3 3
2 North Parade Passage BA1 1NX 01225 446059
"The food has gone from strength to strength in recent years at this longstanding vegetarian destination (which used to be Demuths, long RIP)". Nowadays it offers "fine dining for veggies", with "delicious dishes that are surprisingly filling considering the elegant, colourful, but not over-large helpings" (examples include "exquisite cashew purée" and "cucumber three ways"). "Good choices of organic wines and beers" too. / **Details:** www.acornvegetariankitchen.co.uk; @AcornVegetarian; 9.30 pm, Sat 10 pm.

The Bath Priory £122 3 4 4
Weston Rd BA1 2XT 01225 331922
"The canapés were so good, we decided to try the tasting menu!" – this "very atmospheric" hotel dining room just outside the city provides an excellent all-round experience: "the taste, presentation, service

together with excellent wines make for a most enjoyable meal!" / **Details:** www.thebathpriory.co.uk; @Thebathpriory; No jeans; children: 5+ L, 12+ D.

Cafe Lucca £17 3|3|3
1-2 Bartlett Street BA1 2QZ 01225 938282
While it's "not haute cuisine", this popular café, oddly set in a concept shop, and handy for the "lovely old" antiques hub opposite, makes a "good bet for a shoppers' lunch" based on "excellent" salads, bruschettas and paninis (and "great cakes" for afters). / **Details:** www.cafelucca.co.uk; No bookings.

The Circus £51 4|4|3
34 Brock St BA1 2LN 01225 466020
"Still a great place to eat after many years on the scene" – this "buzzy" indie bistro, near the Royal Crescent, remains one of the most commented-on destinations in town thanks to its "excellent", "straightforward" cooking ("from a monthly changing menu of locally sourced seasonal ingredients, mixing modern tastes with old classics") and "enthusiastic service". / **Details:** www.thecircuscafeandrestaurant.co.uk; @CircusBath; 10.30 pm; closed Sun; No Amex; children: 7+ at D.

Clayton's Kitchen £58 4|2|3
15A, George St BA1 2EN 01225 585 100
"Every tourist city should have one"; set in stylish Georgian townhouse, Rob Clayton's "very pleasant" all-rounder turns out "vibrant" and "keenly priced" Med food. Try the basement Circo Bar for "great" cocktails pre- or post-. / **Details:** theporter.co.uk/ claytons-kitchen; @PorterBath.

Clifton Sausage
5 Bladud Buildings, The Paragon BA1 5LS 01225 433633
"A new output to the Bristol business, with great views" over the town, and serving its stablemate's trademark sausage-mad menu, alongside other staunch British classic dishes. / **Details:** www.cliftonsausage.co.uk/bath; @cliftonsausage.

Colonna & Smalls £11 3|3|4
6 Chapel Row BA1 1HN 07766 808067
"A treat for coffee aficionados" run by "award-winning genuine expert" (and three-time UK Barista Champion) Maxwell Colonna-Dashwood – a minimal-chic café, by Queen Square; OK cakes too, but it's really all about the brews. / **Details:** www.colonnaandsmalls.co.uk; @colonnaandsmalls; L only; No Amex; Booking max 6 may apply.

Corkage £38 3|4|3
132 Walcot St BA1 5BG 01225 422577
Open for a couple of years now, this "refreshing, buzzing place" is a real hit, combining wine bar, bottle shop and small plates. Co-owner Marty Grant "takes you on an educational journey of different

wines" and chef Richard Knighting's "food is well matched – a miracle given the small galley kitchen!" A second outpost opened on Chapel Row in August 2017. / **Details:** corkagebath.com; @corkagebath.

Dan Moon at The Gainsborough, The Gainsborough Hotel £70 4|3|4
Beau Street BA1 1QY 01225358888
The July 2017 renaming of the restaurant is a vote of confidence in head chef Dan Moon at this luxury 5-star in the heart of the city, whose dining room is praised in the survey for "faultless cooking that's utterly delicious and pretty as a picture on the plate... and good value for such excellence too!" If you need to entertain on business in the city, you'll struggle to find a better venue. / **Details:** @GainsBathSpa; 10 pm.

Hare & Hounds £49 3|3|4
Lansdown Road BA1 5TJ 01225 482682
In a "beautiful setting with great views over the countryside", this "friendly" gastropub (in The Bath Pub Company group) delivers "gorgeous, hearty food" (from "brilliant" meat to "original veggie dishes"). / **Details:** www.hareandhoundsbath.com; @HareHoundsBath; Mon-Sat 9 pm, Sun 8 pm; No Amex.

Henry's Restaurant £52 5|4|3
4 Saville Row BA1 2QP 01225 780055
"A great follow-on to the sadly departed Casanis" – this "pared-back" but "relatively upmarket" spot has a "tiny menu but with big flavours!" (the separate vegan menu is also "worth investigating"). Chef Henry Scott "experiments" with "novel" creations to "superb" effect, and – "nice touch" – "usually brings one of the courses to the table". "'Amazing' is an overused word in today's world, but it applies to Henry's food!" / **Details:** www.henrysrestaurantbath. com.

Indian Temptation £35 4|2|3
09-10 High Street (Cheap Street) BA1 5AQ 01225464631
"Indian vegetarian dishes never before seen and well worth exploring" again win praise for this first-floor subcontinental, in an attractive 18th-century room with views of Bath Abbey. / **Details:** www.indiantemptation.com/; 10.30 pm.

The Ivy Bath Brasserie £54
39 Milsom St BA1 1DS awaiting tel
In a 'roll-out' that would do McDonald's proud, this iconic brand has gone for it this year, opening virtually simultaneously in practically all of the UK's top restaurant cities. The ambition is impressive: let's hope standards hold up better than they did when, for example, 'Browns' tried to pull off a similar trick. / **Details:** theivybathbrasserie.com; @ivybathbrass.

Menu Gordon Jones £69 5️⃣4️⃣3️⃣
2 Wellsway BA2 3AQ 01225 480871
Don't expect a menu ("the chef decides what to cook when he sees what his suppliers deliver in the morning") but do expect a "great experience" at this small and unusual spot with an open kitchen, on the outskirts of town, benefitting from "lots of natural light", and notably creative multi-course tasting menus. / Details: www.menugordonjones.co.uk; @MenuGordonJones; 9 pm; closed Mon & Sun; No Amex.

The Mint Room £39 4️⃣3️⃣3️⃣
Longmead Gospel Hall, Lower Bristol Rd
BA2 3EB 01225 446656
"Upmarket and inventive Indian cooking" wins enthusiastic feedback for this "unexpectedly nice and buzzy venue" on a busy road out of the city. / Details: www.themintroom.co.uk; @themintroom; 11 pm, Fri & Sat 11.30 pm; No shorts.

The Olive Tree, Queensberry Hotel £71 5️⃣4️⃣3️⃣
Russell St BA1 2QF 01225447928
Chris Cleghorn's "hidden away" basement hotel haunt is "quite different to most top restaurants… there's a relaxed air yet it's not casual in the wrong way"; on the food front he "never fails" – turning out "innovative dishes combined with expert presentation and at a sensible price". / Details: www.thequeensberry.co.uk; @OliveTreeBath; 10 pm; Mon-Thu D only, Fri-Sun open L & D; No Amex; No shorts. / Accommodation: 29 rooms, from £125

The Pump Room £48 2️⃣2️⃣5️⃣
Stall St BA1 1LZ 01225 444477
With its "beautiful, airy setting", "the atmosphere is amazing" at this famous Georgian dining rooms (especially "with a classical quartet playing"); food isn't really the main event, although it can be "delicious", and the afternoon tea and "champagne tasting board" are a "real treat". / Details: www.searcys.co.uk; @searcysbars; L only; Booking weekdays only.

Rosarios £32 4️⃣4️⃣3️⃣
18 Northumberland Place BA1 5AR
01225 469590
A relaxed "Italian, family-run" establishment "serving exceptional coffee", in a Georgian building on one of Bath's best shopping streets (there's also a Bristol branch in Clifton Village). The food, running from all-day breakfasts to pasta and gluten-free fare, is "more than adequate" (particularly the "wonderful" pastries). / Details: www.rosarioscafe.co.uk/.

Scallop Shell £34 4️⃣3️⃣3️⃣
22 Monmouth Place BA1 2AY 01225 420928
"Fabulous", "good-value" seafood attracts acclaim for this "no-fuss" two-year-old with nautical decor; it "gets very busy now as it's so good", but as they've "just added an extra floor, the long waits (albeit in

the pub next door) should be a thing of the past". / Details: www.thescallopshell.co.uk; @thescallopshell; 9.30 pm; closed Sun; No bookings.

Sotto Sotto £50 3️⃣4️⃣5️⃣
10 North Pde BA2 4AL 01225 330236
Those who descend into the depths of this brick-vaulted, candlelit cellar for the first time are apt to report a "happy surprise" – locals would already attest to its excellent ambience and crowd-pleasing Italian classics. / Details: www.sottosotto.co.uk; @sottosottobath; 10 pm; Booking max 8 may apply.

BAUGHURST, HAMPSHIRE 2–3D

The Wellington Arms £60 4️⃣4️⃣4️⃣
Baughurst Rd RG26 5LP 0118 982 0110
"A lovely gastropub/restaurant, deep in the country and if the weather is warm it is brilliant to be outside in the beautiful garden". Thanks to the commitment of owners Jason King and Simon Page, "staff are incredibly friendly and helpful" and the cooking is "consistently very good in terms of quality and variety". / Details: www.thewellingtonarms.com; @WellingtonArms; 8.30 pm, Fri & Sat 9 pm; closed Sun D; No Amex. / Accommodation: 4 rooms, from £130

BEACONSFIELD, BUCKINGHAMSHIRE 3–3A

The Cape Grand Cafe & Restaurant £52 3️⃣3️⃣3️⃣
6a, Station Rd HP9 1NN 01494 681137
South African food and wines – and a top-notch brunch – bring something a bit different to the party at this "consistently great", eclectically decorated fixture, handy for the railway station. NB Open for dinner on Friday and Saturday only. / Details: www.thecapeonline.com; @capegrandcafe; 9.30 pm; closed Mon D, Tue D, Wed D, Thu D & Sun D; No Amex.

The Royal Standard of England £49 2️⃣3️⃣5️⃣
Forty Green HP9 1XT 01494 673382
"Just a proper pub that does food and doesn't try to be anything else" – although, to be fair, that does miss out the fact that it's the oldest freehouse in England; set down a country lane, it can "take a little time to find". / Details: www.rsoe.co.uk; @TheRSOEpub; Mon-Sat 10 pm, Sun 9 pm; No Amex.

BEAMINSTER, DORSET 2–4B

Brassica £45 4️⃣4️⃣3️⃣
4 The Square DT8 3AS 01308 538100
Cass Titcombe and Louise Chidgey lend "a real sense of passion in everything they do" at their "convivial" combination of café and retail operation, where fans

hail its "innovative food and delightful service". /
Details: www.brassicarestaurant.co.uk/Site/Home.html;
@brassica_food; 9.30 pm, Sun 2.30 pm; closed Mon,
Tue & Sun D.

BEARSTED, KENT	3–3C

Fish On The Green £60 4️⃣3️⃣2️⃣
Church Ln ME14 4EJ 01622 738300
"It is always a pleasure to enjoy a beautifully
prepared meal" at this "consistent" restaurant and
bar, occupying a converted stable on the village
green; the main event – fish – is particularly
"excellent". / **Details:** www.fishonthegreen.com;
9.30 pm, Fri & Sat 10 pm; closed Mon & Sun D; No
Amex.

BEAULIEU, HAMPSHIRE	2–4D

The Terrace, Montagu Arms Hotel £100 2️⃣3️⃣3️⃣
SO42 7ZL 01590 612324
This New Forest hotel has had its ups-and-downs in
recent times, with critical survey feedback echoing
the loss of its Michelin star in late 2016. Reviews
are seldom all gloom though – even a reporter
"very disappointed" generally said service was
"exceptional" – another read "lovely location but
overpriced for what it is… unless you like croquet,
in which case spend the afternoon in their garden
and then it's not overpriced at all!" Perhaps the
appointment of a new General Manager (Andrew
Nightingale) in August 2017 will get it firing on all
cylinders. / **Details:** www.montaguarmshotel.co.uk;
@themontaguarms; 9.30 pm; closed Mon & Tue L; No
jeans; children: 11+ D. / **Accommodation:** 22 rooms,
from £143

BEAUMARIS, ISLE OF ANGLESEY	4–1C

The Bull Beaumaris, Ye Olde Bull's Head £57 3️⃣3️⃣4️⃣
Castle Street LL58 8AP 01248 810329
Limited but positive feedback on the 'posh' upstairs
dining room of this characterful, very ancient inn on
the main street. There's also a cheaper, brasserie
conservatory annex at the back on the ground floor.
/ **Details:** www.bullsheadinn.co.uk; @bullsheadinn; on
the High Street; 9.30 pm; D only, closed Mon & Sun; No
jeans; children: 7+ at D. / **Accommodation:** 26 rooms,
from £105

BECKENHAM, KENT	3–3B

Chai Naasto £34 4️⃣3️⃣3️⃣
2-4 Fairfield Rd BR3 3LD 020 3750 0888
This "welcome addition to Beckenham" is "not your

everyday curry house", but a more "interesting"
and funky set-up that provides "exquisite" street
food combinations and "cocktails to die for". It
also now has a sibling in Hammersmith. / **Details:**
www.chai-naasto.co.uk/restaurant/beckenham;
@ChaiNaasto.

BEELEY, DERBYSHIRE	5–2C

Devonshire Arms at Beeley £52 2️⃣2️⃣3️⃣
Devonshire Square DE4 2NR 01629 733259
For fans of this "pleasant", old-school pub-with-
rooms on the Chatsworth Estate, "everything
is lovely, with the added bonus of rooms if you
fancy a tipple or two". It continues to receive
the odd downbeat report too however. / **Details:**
www.devonshirebeeley.co.uk; @DevArmsBeeley;
9.30 pm. / **Accommodation:** 14 rooms, from £125

BELFAST, COUNTY ANTRIM	10–1D

Hadskis £47 3️⃣4️⃣3️⃣
Commercial Ct BT1 2NB 028 9032 5444
A chic Cathedral Quarter two-year-old, set in a
former 1760s iron foundry, from James Street South
luminary Niall McKenna; the set lunch includes
some "great culinary delights", and is a bit of a steal.
/ **Details:** www.hadskis.co.uk; @hadskis_; 9.30 pm,
Thu-Sat 10 pm.

James Street South £59 4️⃣4️⃣4️⃣
21 James Street South BT2 7GA
028 9043 4310
"A contemporary twist to some great Irish classics"
keeps Niall McKenna's well-established destination
(celebrating 15 years this year) at the forefront of
the local dining scene. There's an à la carte menu,
but fans recommend the "divine tasting menu"
which provides a four-course and five-course option.
/ **Details:** www.jamesstreetsouth.co.uk; @jamesstsouth;
10.30 pm; closed Sun.

Jean-Christophe Novelli at City Quays
21 Clarendon Road BT1 3BG awaiting tel
Celebrity chef JC Novelli brings his name to the
restaurant at Belfast City Quay's new £25 million
Marriott Hotel, planned for early 2018. The site will
feature double-height windows with views across the
Lagan and a French-style brasserie menu.

Molly's Yard £54 4️⃣3️⃣4️⃣
1 College Green Mews, Botanic Ave BT7 1LW
028 90322600
"Small but with big ambitions" – this "tiny but
amazing" courtyard eatery in converted Victorian
stables turns "good locally-sourced produce into

solid, tasty cooking" ("goat's cheese pannacotta anyone?)". / **Details:** www.mollysyard.co.uk; 9.30 pm.

Mourne Seafood Bar £49 |4|4|4|
34 - 36 Bank Street BT1 1HL 028 9024 8544
The changing blackboard menu of fish dishes including shellfish sourced from the owners' own beds, plus "great service and a lovely atmosphere" ensure the ongoing popularity of this local landmark, situated in boozer-like premises (also hosting a fishmonger's and cookery school). "So good we went twice in the same weekend!" / **Details:** www.mourneseafood.com; @msbbelfast; 9.30 pm, Fri & Sat 10.30 pm, Sun 9 pm; No bookings at lunch.

Ox £74 |5|4|4|
1 Oxford St BT1 3LA 028 9031 4121
Launched in 2013 by local boy Stephen Toman (ex-of James Street South) and Brittany native Alain Kerloc'h, this acclaimed riverside venue is artfully "austere" in design, and the cooking is "exceptional" – "real haute cuisine with a sense of place". Try the Ox Cave next door for "a great wine experience" plus "wonderful" charcuterie and cheese. / **Details:** www.oxbelfast.com; @oxbelfast; 8.30 pm.

Saphyre £70 |3|4|5|
135 Lisburn Road BT9 7AG 028 9068 8606
"Renowned and inventive chef Joery Castel, who moved recently from the multi-award-winning Boathouse in Bangor" has set up Belfast's most "luxurious" new eatery, in a "beautiful old church" plushly converted by celeb designer Kris Turnbull. Enter through an interior design shop and be rewarded with "wonderful food, including a not-too-expensive tasting menu".

BEMBRIDGE, ISLE OF WIGHT 2–4D

The Crab And Lobster Inn £49 |3|4|3|
32 Forelands Field Rd PO35 5TR
01983 872244
"Wonderful fresh seafood of all types" stars on the menu of this "lovely", well-known inn set in a "super" clifftop setting overlooking Bembridge Ledge, whose "delicious" grub is "quite pricey, but great as a special treat". (It was recently taken over by IOW pub group Character Inns – hopefully it will continue to thrive despite chainification.) / **Details:** www.crabandlobsterinn.co.uk; @CrabLobsterIOW; 9 pm, Fri & Sat 9.30 pm; No Amex. / **Accommodation:** 5 rooms, from £80

BENDERLOCH, ARGYLL AND BUTE 9–3B

Eriska Hotel £70 |3|3|4|
PA37 1SD 01631 720371
"A lovely location", in a 19th century Scottish baronial mansion on a private island accessible by bridge, sets a romantic tone at this "very comfortable" Relais & Châteaux country house hotel, whose well-regarded restaurant turns out "competent and well-presented" fare. / **Details:** www.eriska-hotel.co.uk; @isleoferiska; 9 pm; D only; No shorts; children: 10. / **Accommodation:** 25 rooms, from £340

BERKHAMSTED, HERTFORDSHIRE 3–2A

The Gatsby £58 |3|3|3|
97 High St HP4 2DG 01442 870403
"Interesting, well-presented quality food and good staff" again win praise for this eatery in the foyer of an old '30s cinema; "good value pre-Rex cinema meals" too. / **Details:** www.thegatsby.net; @thegatsbyathome; 10 pm, Sun 9.30 pm; No Amex; Booking max 10 may apply.

Porters Restaurant £51 |3|3|3|
Unit 3, 300 High Street HP4 1ZZ
01442 876666
Solid all-round ratings for Richard Bradford's airy and well-appointed modern brasserie, with large outside dining space (featuring summer BBQs). / **Details:** www.porters.uk.com; @simonpiemaker; 10 pm.

BESSELS GREEN, KENT 3–3B

The Kings Head £46 |3|3|3|
2 Westerham Rd TN13 2QA 01732 452081
A large garden, popular roasts and lively contemporary interior are highpoints at this sizeable hostelry, serving a variety of modern pub grub dishes. / **Details:** www.kingsheadbesselsgreen.co.uk; @Kings_Head_BG.

BEVERLEY, EAST YORKSHIRE 6–2A

Ogino £50 |4|5|3|
1st floor Beaver House, Butcher row HU17 0AA 01482 679500
There's some "truly amazing Japanese cooking" on offer at Julian & Rieko Ogino-Stamford's sleek five-year-old hidden gem, tucked away up a staircase in an unpromising side alley. / **Details:** ogino.co.uk/; @oginojapanese; 9.30 pm.

The Pig & Whistle £40
Sow Hill Road HU17 8BG 01482 874083
Former Pétrus chef James Allcock quit the capital to open this pint-sized (25-cover) bistro and charcuterie bar in East Yorkshire in March 2017. He hopes to introduce a new dining concept to the area, serving only small plates of British-sourced

cured meats and cheeses in the hope visitors will drop in before or after eating elsewhere. / *Details:* pigandwhistlebeverley.co.uk; @ThePigBeverley; Mon-Sat 11 pm, Sun 10 pm.

The Westwood Restaurant £67 **4 5 3**
New Walk HU17 7AE 01482 881999
"Nothing is too much trouble" at Matt and Michelle Barker's modern brasserie in an old Georgian courthouse, where "service is exemplary without being condescending" and the "interesting, seasonally changing" menu "never fails to deliver". / *Details:* www.thewestwood.co.uk; @The_Westwood; 9.30 pm; closed Mon & Sun D; No Amex.

Whites £71 **5 4 3**
12-12a North Bar Without HU17 7AB 01482 866121
Chef John Robinson "is just exceptional" and his "passion shines through" at this "low-key" restaurant-with-rooms, where "every time you go he manages to create a menu that surprises the brain and taste buds". / *Details:* www.whitesrestaurant.co.uk; @Whitesbeverley; 9 pm; closed Mon & Sun D; No Amex. / *Accommodation:* 4 rooms, from £85

BIDBOROUGH, KENT 3–3B

Kentish Hare £46 **4 4 4**
95 Bidborough Ridge TN3 0XB 01892 525709
It "doesn't look promising from the outside" – that'll be the petrol station neighbour – but step through the doors of the Tanner bros'"lovely" rural operation, and you'll find an airy conservatory, terrace and garden, plus some "excellent pub food" – especially meat. / *Details:* www.thekentishhare.com; @TheKentishHare; 9.30 pm; closed Mon & Sun D.

BIDDENDEN, KENT 3–4C

The West House £64 **5 4 4**
28 High St TN27 8AH 01580 291341
"Everything is full flavoured, best-that-it-could-be good: fresh, seasonal, local ... all those overused words, but here they hold true!" Graham Garrett and his family's "absolutely winning" village restaurant is "a very special place" whose "easygoing atmosphere belies its quality". / *Details:* www.thewesthouserestaurant.co.uk; @grahamgarrett; 10 pm; closed Mon, Sat L & Sun D; No Amex; Booking max 6 may apply.

BIDDESTONE, WILTSHIRE 2–2B

Biddestone Arms
The Green SN14 7DG 01249 714377
This pretty whitewashed stone pub in a picturesque Wiltshire village has been enthusiastically reviewed by national and local press thanks to its 'proper pub grub', including signature homemade pies from chef-patron James Hedges, and good selection of beers on tap. / *Details:* www.biddestonearms.co.uk.

BIDFORD ON AVON, WARWICKSHIRE 2–1C

The Bridge £48 **4 3 4**
High St B50 4BG 01789 773700
"A treasure in this part of Warwickshire" – this "beautifully located" riverside eaterie on the banks of the Avon really comes into its own in summer on its two-tier outside terrace. It serves a wide variety of dishes, from lunchtime sarnies to steaks from the char-grill. / *Details:* www.thebridgeatbidford.com/; 9 pm, Fri & Sat 9.30 pm; closed Sun D; No Amex.

BIGBURY-ON-SEA, DEVON 1–4C

Burgh Island Hotel £96 **3 4 5**
TQ7 4BG 01548 810514
"Could you find a more romantic destination" than this "thrilling" Art Deco hotel, beloved of Agatha Christie, and offering "the chance to dress up" (if not to do away with your fellow guests!)? Reporters all "love the place" – though, to quibble, the food, albeit good, is not the equal of the "unique atmosphere" and "terrific" cocktails. / *Details:* www.burghisland.com; @burgh_island; 8.30 pm; D only, ex Sun open L & D; No Amex; Jacket & tie required; children: 12+ at D. / *Accommodation:* 25 rooms, from £400

The Oyster Shack £51 **4 2 4**
Millburn Orchard Farm, Stakes Hills TQ7 4BE 01548 810876
Albeit an "unassuming" and "basic" sort of place, this "quirky" hilltop eatery is a well-known "hidden gem" where "the shellfish is delicious, including of course the oysters", which are sourced from beds nearby. / *Details:* www.oystershack.co.uk; @theoystershack; 9 pm.

BILDESTON, SUFFOLK 3–1C

The Bildeston Crown £55 **3 2 3**
104 High St IP7 7EB 01449 740510
For "creative and sound cooking" that's "very good value" too, this genteel Suffolk coaching inn is just the ticket – especially since the return of original husband-and-wife team Chris & Hayley Lee after a

short break. / **Details:** www.thebildestoncrown.com;
@BildestonCrown; from the A14, take the B1115 to
Bildeston; 9.45 pm, Sun 9 pm. / **Accommodation:** 12
rooms, from £100

BILLERICAY, ESSEX	3–2C

The Magic Mushroom   **£58**   **4|3|3**
Barleylands Road   CM11 2UD   01268 289963
Just round the corner from Essex's leading
falconry centre (insert 'Birds of a Feather' pun?),
Darren Bennet's relaxed bistro is lauded as
one of the best bets in these parts. / **Details:**
www.magicmushroomrestaurant.co.uk; next to
Barleylands Farm; midnight; closed Mon & Sun D.

BINFIELD HEATH, BERKSHIRE	3–3A

Bottle and Glass Inn   **£54**   **3|4|3**
Bones Lane   RG9 4JT   01491 412 625
"The Harwood touch arrives in South Oxfordshire"
at this thatched pub just outside Henley run by two
alumni of the famous Fulham hostelry (with a menu
incorporating game from the Phillimore Estate) –
"newly opened and off to a very promising start". /
Details: www.bottleandglassinn.co.uk.

BIRMINGHAM, WEST MIDLANDS	5–4C

**Adam's, New Oxford
House**   **£91**   **5|5|4**
16 Waterloo St   B2 5UG   0121 643 3745
"If it was in France it would have its second star
already!" – Adam & Natasha Stokes's "smart,
elegant and well-spaced" venture in the city centre
delivers an "outstanding" all-round experience, and
is now firmly established not only as Brum's best,
but also as one of the UK's top dining destinations.
"Sensational and eclectic" dishes (from a 3-course
or more extensive 8-course taster menu) "never fail
to wow even for the most jaded palates" and service
is "immaculate". For "the pinnacle of fine dining"
fans recommend the 10-seater Chef's Table, "which
sits in full view of the vast kitchen where Adam
and his young team prepare their tiny creations
with military precision". When it comes to the wine:
"Trust in Lionel! (the sommelier) whose knowledge
but also personality will enhance your visit, with
recommendations delivered with insight, warmth
and humour!" / **Details:** www.adamsrestaurant.co.uk;
@RestaurantAdams; 9.30 pm; Booking max 10 may
apply.

Al Frash   **£27**   **3|3|2**
186 Ladypool Rd   B12 8JS   0121 753 3120
"Best balti and naan in Brum" is still the view fans
express of this Balti Triangle veteran, although it

attracted very limited feedback this year. BYO. /
Details: www.alfrash.com; @AlFrashBalti; 11 pm, Sun
10 pm.

Carters of Moseley   **£89**   **4|4|3**
2c Wake Green Rd   B13 9EZ   0121 449 8885
"Where others have moved downmarket Carters
continues to soar", and while some regulars feel
that "if they would just move back to having an à
la carte menu it would be perfect" its dedication
to a tasting formula generally pays off, with an
"ever-changing" array of dishes that are "tasty and
interesting and – while not particularly complex –
work well". / **Details:** www.cartersofmoseley.co.uk;
@cartersmoseley; 9 pm; closed Mon & Tue; children: 8+.

Edgbaston Hotel   **£45**   **3|3|5**
18 Highfield Road   B15 3DU   0121 454 5212
"Just WOW" – "set in a high-class 'burb of
Birmingham", this "fantastic" and opulent boutique
hotel is a "real find"; with three cocktail bars and no
formal dinner service, food isn't a focal point – with
one exception: the "stunning" afternoon tea, with
presentation straight "out of Hollywood". / **Details:**
www.theedgbaston.co.uk/; @theedgbaston

Harborne Kitchen   **£43**   **5|4|4**
175-179 High St   B17 9QE   0121 439 9150
A "new fine dining experience in Harborne, near
Michelin-starred Turners" – and also surprisingly
situated amid charity shops in a residential part of
town. As befits the ambition of chef/patron Jamie
Desogus, dinner options include three courses à
la carte or "delicious" six- or eight-course tasting
menus, with "amazing flavour combinations at
reasonable prices for the level of cooking". / **Details:**
www.harbornekitchen.com; @harbornekitchen; 11pm.

Jyoti's Vegetarian   **£24**   **4|2|1**
1045 Stratford Road   B28 8AS   0121 778 5501
A "buzzy family-run" Hall Green veggie that's
"still streets ahead of other South Indians at not
much more than half the price"; "what it lacks
in ambience ("pity about the strip lighting" and
Formica-topped tables) it makes up for in delicious
food… who needs meat with vegetarian cooking
this good?" / **Details:** www.jyotis.co.uk; 9 pm, Sun
8 pm; closed Mon & Tue; No Amex.

Lasan   **£63**   **5|4|2**
3-4 Dakota Buildings, James Street   B3 1SD
0121 212 3664
"A distinct cut above the normal Brummie Indian"
– Jabbar Khan's "upmarket" Jewellery Quarter
destination is the survey's most-commented-on curry
house in town, delivering "a twist on the usual fare"
with "challenging" and "really different" flavours.
Just before we went to press in autumn 2017 there
was big upheaval here: first the restaurant closed
for a major overhaul and nothing short of a 'rebirth'
was promised with a new interior and menu to

*match; then it was announced that the business's 'front man' Aktar Islam was to leave. / **Details:** www.lasan.co.uk; @lasan; Mon-Sat 11 pm, Sun 9 pm; closed Sat L; No trainers.*

Not Real Indian (NRI) £44
The Mailbox, 1 Commercial St B1 1RS
awaiting tel
*Chef and restaurateur Atul Kochhar opened his first UK restaurant under the Not Real Indian (NRI) brand in autumn 2017. The new 180-cover venture in Birmingham's Mailbox development serves Sri Lankan, Malaysian, and British-Indian inspired dishes. NRI's first site launched in Mumbai in 2016. / **Details:** www.nrirestaurant.com; @nribkc; 11.30 pm.*

Opus Restaurant £66 3 4 3
54 Cornwall Street B3 2DE 0121 200 2323
*Despite being on the roomy side, this Colmore Business District brasserie still retains a "great" atmosphere, and it's "very good value given the standard of the food". / **Details:** www.opusrestaurant.co.uk; @opuscornwallst; 9.15 pm; closed Sun D.*

Original Patty Men £29 5 3 2
9 Shaw's Passage B5 5JG 0121 643 2546
*"Birmingham's best burger!" (officially, according to survey ratings) and a tempting selection of beers from locals Siren Craft Brew are two compelling reasons to ignore the gratingly hip self-presentation of these 'Patty Pimps and Purveyors of Filth'. / **Details:** www.originalpattymen.com; @OriginalPattyM; No bookings.*

Plough £60 3 4 4
21 High St B17 9NT 0121 427 3678
*This "wonderfully relaxed" yet "really lively" local staple is particularly known as a "favourite brunch spot", delivering "big portions" of "good" grub and "a great variety of stone-baked pizzas". / **Details:** theploughharborne.co.uk/; @PloughHarbourne; Mon-Wed 11 pm, Thu-Sat midnight, Sun 10.30 pm.*

Purnells £97 4 5 4
55 Cornwall St B3 2DH 0121 212 9799
*"Stunning flavours, contrasting combinations and presentation… by the time you reach the dry ice, dried mint leaves and theatre of the final course, you're a convert!" – TV-chef Glynn Purnell creates an experience that's "special but not stuffy" at his "understatedly luxurious" (and "romantic") city-centre HQ, providing "great menu options that deliver on their promise and friendly but unobtrusive staff" who show "attention to detail at its best". The competition in this "much under-rated culinary city" is fierce nowadays, but for its fan club it's "the top choice in town". / **Details:** www.purnellsrestaurant.com; @purnellsrest; 9.30 pm; closed Mon, Sat L & Sun; children: 6+.*

Rofuto £62 2 3 4
160 Broad Street B15 1DT 0121 369 8888
*"Oh the view!" from the 16th-floor of the Park Regis (Brum's highest restaurant!), home to Des McDonald's year-old izakaya-themed venue. Some feedback gripes of "heavy handed, English-friendly Japanese food", but the opposing verdict is that it's "consistently excellent". / **Details:** www.rofuto.co.uk; @RofutoTweets; 10.30 pm, Fri & Sat 11.30 pm; closed Mon; Booking max 8 may apply.*

Sabai Sabai £40
268 High Street B17 9PT 0121 426 2688
*More reports please on Torquil and Juree Chidwick's stylish modern Harborne Thai: part of a local mini-chain of upmarket Thai restaurants founded in Moseley in 2003. / **Details:** www.sabaisabai-restaurant.co.uk/; @SabaiSabai1; 10.30 pm.*

San Carlo £54 3 3 3
4 Temple Street B2 5BN 0121 633 0251
*Launched in the 1990s, the original city-centre outpost of this WAG-happy northern chain is still a "lively authentic Italian", whose "extensive menu" usually has something to suit. / **Details:** sancarlo.co.uk/restaurants/birmingham/; @SanCarlo_Group; 11 pm.*

Simpsons £94 3 3 3
20 Highfield Road B15 3DU 0121 454 3434
*This Edwardian villa in Edgbaston continues to split views ever since its major makeover in mid-2015, which gave it more of a brasserie feel, and the changes can still come as "a bit of a shock: everything but the exterior was different, with an interior high on echo and to be honest not particularly comfortable". When it comes to the overall verdict doubters feel the transformation represents "a bizarre dumbing down", but – notwithstanding the change of approach – most reporters feel that the "high quality of its ingredients", "skillful cooking" and "innovative" style leads to a "beautiful" all-round gastronomic experience. / **Details:** www.simpsonsrestaurant.co.uk; @simpsons_rest; Mon-Thu 9 pm, Fri & Sat 9.30 pm, Sun 4.30 pm; closed Sun D. / **Accommodation:** 4 rooms, from £160*

Tom's Kitchen £59
53/57 Wharfside Street B1 1RE
0121 289 5111
Tom Aikens brought his 'Kitchen' chain to Birmingham in early 2017 with this brasserie, bar and deli located in The Mailbox in the city centre, his first UK foray for the brand outside of London.

The Wilderness £84 3 3 2
1 Dudley Street B5 4EG 0121 643 2673
Inside Birmingham Open Media, with just 24 covers, this modern British joint headed up by Alex

Claridge has caused quite a stir since its late 2016 launch. "The dining room is a bit make-shift and cluttered – like a pop-up waiting for a better venue to come along" – but the tasting menus focused on foraged and locally sourced ingredients that reflect the native 'outdoors, weather and landscape' are "great value". / *Details:* wearethewilderness.co.uk; @thewildernessb5; 8.30 pm.

BISHOPS TACHBROOK, WARWICKSHIRE 5–4C

Mallory Court £71 3️⃣2️⃣4️⃣
Harbury Lane CV33 9QB 01926 330214
This grand Relais & Châteaux outpost put in a strong performance this year, with reviews citing its "intensely flavourful" cuisine and "unpretentious" and "very quiet and appropriate country house hotel atmosphere". / *Details:* www.mallory.co.uk; @mallorycourt; 2m S of Leamington Spa, off B4087; 9.30 pm, Sun 3.30 pm; closed Sat L; No trainers. / *Accommodation:* 31 rooms, from £159

BLACKBURN, LANCASHIRE 5–1B

Café Northcote £27 4️⃣4️⃣3️⃣
Blackburn Cathedral, Cathedral Close BB1 1FB
01254 260520
Opened in summer 2016, "this newish offshoot of the Northcote empire" – famed for the nearby country house hotel – "is a cafe adjoining the Cathedral buildings" just subject to a £30m development. The "bright, modern" daytime spot can seem "appealing" or "sterile", but all agree on the "interesting, locally focussed menu" (overseen by Northcote's Ambassador Nigel Haworth). / *Details:* www.cafenorthcote.com; @CafeNorthcote; L only.

BLAIRGOWRIE, PERTH AND KINROSS 9–3C

Kinloch House £82 3️⃣4️⃣4️⃣
PH10 6SG 01250 884732
Limited but very positive feedback ("excellent every time") on this stately Relais & Châteaux property's dining room, offering traditional cuisine showcasing fine Scottish ingredients. / *Details:* www.kinlochhouse.com; past the Cottage Hospital, turn L, procede 3m along A923, (signposted Dunkeld Road); 8.30 pm; No Amex; Jacket required; children: 6 for dinner. / *Accommodation:* 15 rooms, from £230

BLAKENEY, NORFOLK 6–3C

The Moorings £46 4️⃣3️⃣3️⃣
High Street NR25 7NA 01263 740054
It "looks like a modest little cafe, tucked out of sight halfway up a street in this sleepy little town", but

this "great little" bistro is in fact "one of the best fish restaurants in Norfolk"; "how they cope with the numbers yet still serve fish so well is a mystery!" / *Details:* www.blakeney-moorings.co.uk; 10.30 pm; closed Mon & Sun; No Amex.

BODIAM, EAST SUSSEX 3–4C

The Curlew £60 3️⃣2️⃣4️⃣
Junction Rd TN32 5UY 01580 861394
With a change of regime, and new chef Gary Jarvis (ex-The Barn at Coworth Park) at the helm, this art-lined, remote coaching inn seems to be "back on track". Some reports are still critical, but more often it's credited with turning out "imaginative" food that's "worth paying a little more for". / *Details:* www.thecurlewrestaurant.co.uk; @thecurlewbodiam; 9.30 pm; closed Mon; Booking max 4 may apply.

BOLLINGTON, CHESHIRE 5–2B

The Lime Tree £41 3️⃣5️⃣4️⃣
18-20 High Street SK10 5PH 01625 578182
Not as famous as its Didsbury sibling, but – if on limited feedback – this relaxed destination also offers "an enjoyable experience" with food offering "solid reliability and value". / *Details:* www.limetreebollington.co.uk; @thelimetreeres; 10 pm, Fri & Sat 11 pm; closed Mon.

BOLNHURST, BEDFORDSHIRE 3–1A

The Plough at Bolnhurst £57 4️⃣4️⃣4️⃣
MK44 2EX 01234 376274
"A long way from anywhere but well worth the drive" – this "delightful" country pub has won a big local following due to its excellent all-round experience comprising a "relaxed atmosphere", "attentive service from an excellent team" and "perfectly cooked seasonal ingredients". / *Details:* www.bolnhurst.com; @atBolnhurst; 9.30 pm; closed Mon & Sun D; No Amex.

BOLTON ABBEY, NORTH YORKSHIRE 5–1B

Burlington, The Devonshire Arms £95 3️⃣3️⃣3️⃣
BD23 6AJ 01756 718111
This "wonderful small hotel in the stunning environs of Bolton Abbey", owned by the Duke of Devonshire, is a well-known luxury destination. The cuisine in its traditional dining room escaped criticisms this year, winning consistently high ratings, but the top draw here remains "the justly renowned wine cellar, with blue chip names (Pétrus etc.) alongside excellent French regional bottles". / *Details:*

www.thedevonshirearms.co.uk; 9.30 pm, Sat & Sun 10 pm; closed Mon; Jacket required; children: 7+. / Accommodation: 40 rooms, from £250

BOREHAMWOOD, HERTFORDSHIRE   3–2A

Kiyoto Sushi   **£33**   🄸🄸🄸
31 Shenley Road WD6 1AE   020 3489 6800
"In the otherwise desperate environs of Borehamwood, great sushi has at last arrived" at this simple venture near Elstree & Borehamwood Station. It now has a Mill Hill spin-off too. / Details: www.kiyotosushi.co.uk/; Mon-Fri 9.30 pm, Sat & Sun 10 pm.

BOUGHTON LEES, KENT   3–3C

The Manor Restaurant, Eastwell Manor   **£77**   🄸🄸🄸
Eastwell Pk TN25 4HR   01233 213000
One "for those special occasions" – a "gracious" dining room "in an Elizabethan manor house with lovely views over the countryside"; the food doesn't quite live up to it, but the arrival of a new chef has marked a "fine improvement" of late, and afternoon tea remains a favourite ("beautifully presented" and with an "excellent" choice). / Details: www.eastwellmanor.co.uk; @EastwellManor; 3m N of Ashford on A251; 9.30 pm; No jeans; Booking max 8 may apply. / Accommodation: 62 rooms, from £180

BOURNEMOUTH, DORSET   2–4C

Arbor Restaurant, The Green House Hotel   **£52**   🄸🄸🄸
4 Grove Rd BH1 3AX   01202 498900
"Very good, surprising food" makes this engaging hotel restaurant a destination worth remembering. But, if you're of an eco frame of mind, it's a must-visit, as you can enjoy your meal with a clear conscience: not only is there much focus on local artisan suppliers and ethical sourcing, but they sending waste cooking oil to be converted into biofuel, have bee hives on the roof, and use chairs made out of recycled Playstations! / Details: www.arbor-restaurant.co.uk; @arborrest.

Chez Fred   **£30**   🄸🄸🄸
10 Seamoor Rd BH4 9AN   01202 761023
"Excellent fish 'n' chips as always – plain but super fresh", with "crisp but tasty batter" (and "with refills of chips!") – helps inspire love for Fred Capel's famous chippie, which is "much better now that the restaurant has finally been expanded". / Details: www.chezfred.co.uk; @ChezFredUK; 9 pm, Sun 8.30 pm; closed Sun L; No Amex; No bookings.

WestBeach   **£55**   🄸🄸🄸
Pier Approach BH2 5AA   01202 587785
"Amazing views" are assured at this light-filled, airy restaurant with a deck right on the beach; the menu focuses on local seafood and steak, and the kids' version is also "very good". / Details: www.west-beach.co.uk; @WestBeachBmouth; 10 pm.

BOURTON ON HILL, GLOUCESTERSHIRE 2–1C

Horse & Groom   **£46**   🄸🄸🄸
GL56 9AQ   01386 700413
"What a find" – those who stumble across this Georgian gastropub, "in the heart of the Cotswolds", and with a large rear garden, proclaim it a "fantastic" spot with a "destination restaurant". It scooped GPG Pub of the Year in 2016 and "won worthily" by all accounts. / Details: www.horseandgroom.info; @thehorsengroom; Mon-Thu 9 pm, Fri & Sat 9.30 pm; closed Sun D; No Amex. / Accommodation: 5 rooms, from £120

BOVINGDON GREEN, BUCKINGHAMSHIRE 3–3A

The Royal Oak   **£47**   🄸🄸🄸
Frieth Road SL7 2JF   01628 488611
This "real country gem" is a "lovely place to go for all sorts of reasons": both "cosy" and "dog-friendly" (owners are "not ostracised and the dogs nearly always get treats"), it's "a go-to for a lady's lunch", a family celebration or a "great" Sunday roast. / Details: www.royaloakmarlow.co.uk; @royaloakSL7; Mon-Thu 9.30 pm, Fri & Sat 10 pm, Sun 9 pm.

BRACKLESHAM, WEST SUSSEX   3–4A

Billys On The Beach   **£49**   🄸🄸🄸
Bracklesham Lane PO20 8JH   01243 670373
Overlooking the Isle of Wight, this Billy's On the Road sibling is an "exceptional beachside restaurant (more of a large shack really)" combining "fantastic service and really good fresh food – mainly fish, as you'd expect". It's "the best place to pop into following a bracing seafront walk" – but you'll want to book. Good breakfasts too. / Details: www.billysonthebeach.co.uk; @BillysontheBeach.

BRADFORD, WEST YORKSHIRE   5–1C

Akbar's   **£31**   🄸🄸🄸
1276 Leeds Rd BD3 8LF   01274 773311
The big and bustling original branch of this northern chain – now almost as large an operation as its famous monster naans – wins high ratings from

all who report on it, particularly for its spicy scoff. /
Details: *www.akbars.co.uk; @OfficialAkbars; midnight, Sun 11.30 pm; D only.*

Mumtaz £30 4️⃣3️⃣3️⃣
386-410 Great Horton Rd BD7 3HS
01274 571861
Airy curry capital stalwart (on the site of the chain's original 1970s stall) that has won renown for its high quality Kashmiri fare; drinkers NB – they don't serve alcohol and you can't BYO. / **Details:**
www.mumtaz.com; @Mumtaz; midnight, Fri & Sat 1 am.

BRADWELL, DERBYSHIRE 5–2C

The Samuel Fox Country Inn £55 4️⃣4️⃣3️⃣
Stretfield Rd S33 9JT 01433 621562
"A real find"; at this intimate and polished country inn, James Duckett delivers some "brilliant cooking" from a "mouthwatering menu" spanning "homemade breads" and "gorgeous desserts". /
Details: *www.samuelfox.co.uk; @JamesEDuckett; 9 pm, Sun 8 pm.*

BRANCASTER STAITHE, NORFOLK 6–3B

The White Horse £52 3️⃣2️⃣4️⃣
Main Rd PE31 8BY 01485 210262
"Grand views of the marshes" from the newish dining conservatory mean "you can watch the fishermen come in while you delve into your pot of mussels" at this "excellent and busy" coastal pub. "There's a great feel about the place, and service is warm". / **Details:** *www.whitehorsebrancaster.co.uk; @whitehorsebranc; 9 pm; No Amex. /*
Accommodation: *15 rooms, from £94*

BRANCASTER, NORFOLK 6–3B

The Jolly Sailors £38 3️⃣3️⃣3️⃣
PE31 8BJ 01485 210314
"An oasis in Norfolk from soaring prices and dodgy quality elsewhere" – this relaxed pub just across the road from the harbour and beach wins praise for its "good straightforward fare", and serves some interesting ales too. Kids in tow? – it also has a big play ground.

BRAY, BERKSHIRE 3–3A

Caldesi in Campagna £77 3️⃣4️⃣4️⃣
Old Mill Ln SL6 2BG 01628 788500
"Transporting you to Italy" – Giancarlo Caldesi's "lovely"Thames-side venture is a huge local favourite, and even if some feel "it's the charm of

the place" that's perhaps central to its appeal, its "hearty Italian cuisine" is "reasonably priced (for Bray at least)" and on most accounts "excellent". It recently celebrated its 10th year with a major revamp, including an enlargement of its dining conservatory. / **Details:** *www.caldesi.com; @CaldesiCampagna; 9.30 pm; closed Mon & Sun D.*

Crown Inn £60 4️⃣3️⃣4️⃣
High St SL6 2AH 01628 621936
Heston's "outstanding old pub" (not that you'd instantly realise it was out of the ordinary) is a quaint, beamed local in the centre of the village. Less ambitious (and pricey) than his nearby Hind's Head, the food is consistently highly rated. / **Details:**
www.thecrownatbray.com; @thecrownatbray; 9.30 pm, Fri & Sat 10 pm, Sun 8 pm.

The Fat Duck £346 4️⃣4️⃣3️⃣
High St SL6 2AQ 01628 580333
"Inspiration, as much as food: a conversation-starting, memory-rousing tour de force!" – Heston Blumenthal's world-famous pub-conversion a short drive outside London delivers "a fairytale journey back to childhood" (they call you in advance to ask about your memories), and its "personalisation to the diner is a joyous and incredible added extra touch, showing staggering attention to detail". The resulting cuisine can be "sheer genius, with dishes, planned to the minutest item, executed to the highest standard, and with a focus on flavour sensations that are at once familiar yet often completely unique". There's the obvious catch – "it's crazy money" – and, although the outrage at the prices died down a little this year, they still inspire much more resistance than before The Fat Duck's relaunch a couple of years ago ("no matter how great an experience it is, it a meal for two with wine at what can easily be nigh on £1,000 is just too expensive!") Still, for most reporters "it was on my bucket list, and it was unbelievable!" / **Details:**
www.thefatduck.co.uk; 9 pm; closed Mon & Sun.

The Hind's Head £69 4️⃣4️⃣4️⃣
High Street SL6 2AB 01628 626151
"Retaining its old world feel, with wooden beams, uneven floors and walls and a roaring fireplace" – Heston's mega-popular gastropub next door to the Fat Duck "continues to offer an imaginative take on classic British dishes", "perfectly executed" and "packed with flavour" ("I challenge anyone to find better bar snacks than they do here!"). "The cocktails are just amazing" too. "When molecular gastronomy has gone the way of cassis, kale and the dodo, everyone will still want to eat the actually delicious food here". / **Details:**
www.hindsheadbray.com; closed Sun D.

FSA

Waterside Inn £175 5│5│5
Ferry Rd SL6 2AT 01628 620691
*A leading light in the UK's gastronomic constellation
since it first opened in 1972 – this famous
Thames-sider (a favourite of the Royal Family) is
run nowadays by Alain Roux (with father, Michel, still
sometimes popping up in the dining room). "Swans
are usually in view" in its "glorious" and "peaceful"
riverside location, and in particular the setting is
"unsurpassable on a warm evening in summer",
when a meal typically starts off with a glass of
champagne on the terrace, or even a jaunt in the
restaurant's private launch. The meal itself at any
time of year takes place in a plush conservatory
overlooking the river. Stylewise, you could be in rural
France, and to some tastes this classic temple of
Gallic gastronomy "feels a bit of a time warp" with
perennial calls in some quarters for "a bit more risk
and creativity" in the cuisine. For the vast majority
of reporters however, the overriding impression
is that "attention to detail is a way of life here",
with the kitchen's "classical French perfection"
judged "absolutely outstanding in every way", and
service likewise – overseen by long-term general
manager Diego Masciaga is "unmatched". / Details:
www.waterside-inn.co.uk; @rouxwaterside; off A308
between Windsor & Maidenhead; 9.30 pm; closed Mon
& Tue; No jeans; Booking max 10 may apply; children: 9.
/ Accommodation: 11 rooms, from £240*

BREARTON, NORTH YORKSHIRE 8–4B

The Malt Shovel £51 3│4│3
HG3 3BX 01423 862929
*There's "always a warm welcome at this lovely
country pub", whose "cosy interior" dates from
the 16th century; the "inspired, ever-changing
menu" is ably abetted by "super service". / Details:
www.themaltshovelbrearton.co.uk; @BleikerFamily; off
A61, 6m N of Harrogate; 10 pm, Sun 4 pm; closed Mon
& Sun D.*

BRECON, POWYS 2–1A

The Felin Fach Griffin £48 4│3│4
Felin Fach LD3 0UB 01874 620111
*"Walking in the Brecon Beacons and eating great
food – does life gets much better?" This "stupendous
value" gastropub for years been a linchpin of
the local dining scene: "the cooking's of a very good
standard" and "it's a tremendous venue for Sunday
lunch, brunch or just loafing about". / Details:
www.eatdrinksleep.ltd.uk; @felinfachgriff; 20 mins NW
of Abergavenny on A470; 9 pm, Fri & Sat 9.30 pm. /
Accommodation: 7 rooms, from £115*

BRENTWOOD, ESSEX 3–2B

Alec's £76 3│3│3
Navestock Side CM14 5SD 01277 375696
*"An oasis of fishy goodness" – this glitzy, "TOWIE"-
esque brasserie is "unsurprisingly always packed!"
thanks to its consistently high quality cooking. /
Details: www.alecsrestaurant.co.uk; @Alecsrestaurant;
10 pm, Sun 4.30 pm; closed Mon, Tue L, Wed L & Sun
D; No Amex; Credit card deposit required to book;
children: 12+.*

BRIDPORT, DORSET 2–4B

Riverside £61 4│4│4
West Bay DT6 4EZ 01308 422011
*"Despite its near-perfect location and fame,
it remains unpretentious" – Arthur Watson's
"unfaltering" destination set in TV's 'Broadchurch'
(West Bay) "offers the freshest of fish in simple
sauces" and is "always welcoming". / Details:
www.thefishrestaurant-westbay.co.uk; @RiversideWB;
8.30 pm; closed Mon & Sun D.*

BRIGHTON, EAST SUSSEX 3–4B

Basketmakers Arms £42 4│3│4
12 Gloucester Rd BN1 4AD 01273 689006
*"As ever, Brighton's best pub grub" (of the
comfort-food classic variety) garners praise
for this popular and cosy Victorian corner
boozer, handy for the North Laines. / Details:
www.basket-makers-brighton.co.uk/; 9 pm; No bookings.*

Bincho Yakitori £34 4│3│2
63 Preston Street BN1 2HE 01273 779021
*"This is where most Brighton chefs eat out on their
day off" – a Japanese izakaya-style venture which,
oddly, began life in London's OXO Tower, before
transferring to Brighton's 'restaurant row' two years
back. The stripped-back decor isn't much to look
at, but the "fantastic" charcoal grills are "superb". /
Details: www.binchoyakitori.com; @BinchoYakitori.*

Burger Brothers £13 5│4│2
97 North Rd BN1 1YE 01273 706980
*A "tiny, heaving shop" in North Laine – "sharpen
your elbows to get served" – delivering "amazing
burger after amazing burger" ("the essence of beefy
savouriness"); it "makes my mouth water just writing
about it". "The guys who run it are super-cool" and
"good at at making you feel at home". / Details:
@BurgerBrethren; 10 pm; No bookings.*

The Chilli Pickle £49 5│3│3
17 Jubilee St BN1 1GE 01273 900383
*"Still the best Indian for miles around" – this "ace"
and "far-from-bog-standard" venue with open*

FSA Ratings: from [1] (Poor) to [5] (Exceptional) **281**

kitchen in the Arts Quarter remains the most commented-on destination in town. "Noisy, brash and full of interest describes both the food and the decor" – "so many different flavours are on offer, and expertly turned out with cracking home made breads and chutneys – it's a winner every time!" / **Details:** www.thechillipickle.com; @TheChilliPickle; 10.30 pm, Sun 10 pm; closed Tue.

Chimney House £48 3 4 4
28 Upper Hamilton Rd BN1 5DF
01273 556708
Near Seven Dials, but slightly "out of the way", this unpretentious gastroboozer "produces modern cooking you'd be delighted with in an upmarket London restaurant" – and also ticks all those (by now mandatory) local/seasonal boxes. / **Details:** www.chimneyhousebrighton.co.uk; @chimneyhousebr.

La Choza £34 4 4 4
36 Gloucester Rd BN1 4AQ 01273 945926
"Fun, chaotic, loud, colourful and wipe-clean" North Laine street-food bar which provides "everything you need for messy Mexican food with lots of friends", including "lethal margaritas" and "superb" burritos and nachos. / **Details:** www.lachoza.co.uk; @Lachoza2; Mon 4 pm, Tue-Sun 10 pm; May need 10+ to book.

Cin Cin £42 4 3 3
13-16 Vine St BN1 4AG 01273 698813
"Sit on stools around the U-shaped bar and watch as the team slice, chop and cook simple and delicious rustic Italian food" at this "small and slightly industrial side street venue" (in a former garage) – a "very welcome change from the pile-it-high and sell-it-cheap pizza and pasta joints which are the norm locally". / **Details:** www.cincin.co.uk; @CinCinUK.

The Coal Shed £61 3 2 3
8 Boyces St BN1 1AN 01273 322998
"As well as top-quality steaks, they serve an excellent wagyu burger" (plus beef dripping chips and local fish and seafood) at this "always lovely" industrial-style bar/bistro that fans say is "everything a modern British venue should be". NB Mondays you can BYO wine for a small corkage fee. / **Details:** www.coalshed-restaurant.co.uk; @thecoalshed1; 10 pm, Fri & Sat 10.30 pm.

Coggings & Co £35 3 3 3
87-93 Dyke Rd BN1 3JE 01273 220220
Arguably the "best burgers in Brighton" are the draw to this three-year-old, by Andrew Coggings, ex-of local gastropub Preston Park Tavern; the local/sustainable ethos spans beef, beers, ciders and wines, and there's a suntrap garden alongside the gallery-style dining room. / **Details:** www.coggingsandco.com; @coggingsandco; 10 pm, Sun 6 pm.

Curry Leaf Cafe £40 3 4 3
60 Ship St BN1 1AE 01273 207070
"Very basic" but "buzzing" and "very friendly" Lanes café serving "a small range" of "proper spicy dishes", "with an emphasis on the slightly lighter side of Indian cooking, and good for veggies too". Also now with a 'Kemptown Kitchen' and kiosk at the station. / **Details:** www.curryleafcafe.com; @curryleafcaff; 10 pm, Fri & Sat 10.30 pm.

Donatello £32 2 2 3
1-3 Brighton Pl BN1 1HJ 01273 775477
"Donatello has become a kind of Brighton institution over the years"; "ideal for families (even with kids) and groups of friends with its hundreds of seats outside" ("don't expect much elbow room" inside, though), this Lanes spot provides "huge portions of home cooked food" that's "value for money". / **Details:** www.donatello.co.uk; @donatello__; 11 pm; No Amex.

Drakes of Brighton, Drakes Hotel £69 4 5 3
43 - 44 Marine Parade BN2 1PE
01273 696934
On the seafront, the smart dining room of this Kemptown boutique hotel continues to please – fans say "if it weren't in the basement it would be up there with Gingerman". In the meantime, a visit to the upstairs cocktail bar will provide the requisite views. / **Details:** drakesofbrighton.com/restaurant; @drakeshotel; 9.45 pm; children: 8. / **Accommodation:** 20 rooms, from £115

Edendum £43 3 4 2
69 East Street BN1 1HQ 01273 733800
Diego & Lorenza Cacciolatti's Lanes' Italian (plus food shop) has won fans since opening in 2016; the duo started out importing Piedmontese fare, which provides the backdrop to a menu spanning "authentic" mains and "great value pizza". / **Details:** www.edendum.co.uk/home/; @EdendumUK; 11pm.

English's £60 3 4 4
29-31 East St BN1 1HL 01273 327980
"Warm welcome, exceptional oysters from Falmouth, entertaining server keeping up parallel conversations with two regulars" – all par for the course at this "most convivial" Lanes veteran (est. 1890s). It has long been traditional reviewers' tip as the "best seafood in Brighton, particularly if you're sticking to classic dishes". / **Details:** www.englishs.co.uk; @englishsoB; 10 pm, Sun 9.30 pm.

Etch £66 3 2 3
216 Church Rd BN3 2DJ 01273 227485
A stone's throw from the Hove shoreline, this newcomer – the first solo effort of ex-Pass chef Steven Edwards – serves up four, five and eight-course seasonal tasting menus using local Sussex

produce. Fans hail *"a fantastic dining experience with real attention to detail"* and *"very accomplished cuisine"* – sceptics say that *"although professionally executed, the tasting menu simply doesn't justify its price tag". / Details: www.etchfood.co.uk; @EtchFood.*

Fatto A Mano £38 ③③③
77 London Rd BN1 4JF 01273 600621
For *"very authentic"* wood-fired pizzas *"like you get in Italy"*, this *"good value", "friendly"* Neapolitan-style two-year-old is just the ticket; it's also *"great to sit outside the Hove branch in summer"* (the latter benefitting from a more rangy terrace than its parent). / *Details: www.fattoamanopizza.com/; @fattoamanopizza; 10 pm, Sun 9.30 pm; May need 6+ to book.*

Food for Friends £42 ④③②
17-18 Prince Albert St BN1 1HF
01273 202310
"One of the must-try places if you're up for a guilt-free meal in this leftie-Mecca of a city" – this Lanes fixture *"has matured over the years into a sophisticated, not-to-be-missed veggie paradise"* serving food that's *"always interesting and challenging"*; and staff are *"welcoming and very chatty too"*. *"Trying to go there without making a reservation means you can write off most of your day: it's super busy and you'll need to wait for at least an hour!" / Details: @FoodforFriends; 10 pm, Fri & Sat 10.30 pm; no booking, Sat L & Sun L.*

The Ginger Dog £50 ④③③
12 College Pl BN2 1HN 01273 620990
This laid-back Kemptown link in the local Gingerman chain is *"simply one of the best places to let a lunch drift on through the afternoon"*, and equally *"lovely for a private celebration". / Details: www.gingermanrestaurants.com; @GingerDogDish; off Eastern Road near Brighton College; 10 pm.*

The Ginger Pig £55 ④③③
3 Hove St BN3 2TR 01273 736123
"I love this pub!" – The Gingerman group's Hove hostelry remains Brighton's most popular gastropub. *"Everything works: staff are very helpful, there are great roasts, perfectly cooked veg, rabbit or similar game that makes me so happy; and then there's the pies... I'm going weak at the knees... if there is a heaven..." / Details: www.thegingerpigpub.com; @gingerpigdish; 10 pm, Sun 9 pm; No trainers.*

Gingerman £57 ④⑤④
21a Norfolk Sq BN1 2PD 01273 326688
"An absolute stalwart gem, with many years serving Brighton" – the Gingerman group's flagship is turning twenty this year and this small, unpretentious dining room near the seafront is still a big favourite with locals and out-of-towners alike. The only drawback is that the room is *"rather cramped"* – the *"concept-free"* food is

"terrific" and the *"friendly, knowledgeable and diligent"* service particularly stands out. / *Details: www.gingermanrestaurant.com; @thegingerchef; 9.45 pm; closed Mon.*

Indian Summer £46 ④④③
69 East St BN1 1HQ 01273 711001
"Posh Indian" in the Lanes of the *"not-your-standard-curry-house"* variety, acclaimed for its *"lovely"* interior and *"fresh"* food that provides *"something a bit different". / Details: www.indiansummerbrighton.co.uk; @indiansummer108; 10.30 pm, Sun 10 pm; closed Mon L.*

Isaac@ £74
2 Gloucester Street BN1 4EW 07765 934740
Former pop-up-turned-permanent fine dining restaurant from chef-patron Isaac Bartlett-Copeland in North Laines with a stripped-back, Scandi-esque interior. Too little feedback for a rating, but one reporter is wowed: *"a really clever concept, staffed by passionate people serving extraordinary food and their commitment to keeping food miles really, really low is fantastic. They deserve to do well!" / Details: www.isaac-at.com; @Isaac_at.*

Iydea £21 ③③②
17 Kensington Gardens BN1 4AL
01273 667992
"Staff are great, the music's cool, and you always end up having a nice chat with fellow diners" – so say fans of this *"always busy", "cheap 'n' cheerful"* North Laine veggie cafeteria: *"the essence of Brighton". / Details: www.iydea.co.uk; @iydea; Mon-Thu 4.30 pm, Fri & Sat 5 pm, Sun 4.30 pm; No Amex.*

Little Fish Market £71 ⑤⑤③
10 Upper Market St BN3 1AS 01273 722213
"One of a number of restaurants bringing new energy into the Brighton restaurant scene in recent years" – this former fishmonger's (*"a tiny restaurant, where Duncan Ray operates in a very basic kitchen"*) delivers *"an incredible all-round dining experience"* wherein *"fabulous fish"* from the tasting menu is *"matched with wine and exceptional service from front of house Rob". / Details: www.thelittlefishmarket.co.uk; 10 pm; closed Mon, Tue L, Wed L, Thu L, Fri L & Sun.*

Market £48 ③③③
42 Western Rd BN3 1JD 01273 823707
A *"really well-executed"* two-year-old, on the former premises of Graze, and clad in verdant Victorian metro tiles; it combines a *"fun atmosphere"* and locally sourced small plates. / *Details: www.market-restaurantbar.co.uk/; @dineatmarket; 9.30 pm.*

F S A

Pascere
8 Duke St BN1 1AH   01273 917949
*A new Brighton Lanes restaurant from the food and drink editor of Platinum Business magazine, Amanda Menahem. Press reception of its modern British small plates and tasting menus, overseen by chef Johnny Stanford, has been adulatory. / **Details:** pascere.co.uk; @pascerebrighton.*

Pike + Pine   £79   **4 3 3**
1d St James's Street BN2 1RE   01273 686668
*"The vast glass door welcomes you in" at this evening-only dining spot from Matt Gillan (formerly of The Pass at the South Lodge Hotel near Horsham) located within the veteran Kemptown Red Roaster coffee shop and roastery. Six and eight course tasting menus emanate from the open kitchen ("where the team work remarkably calmly and well together") which is surrounded by a counter, for those who want to get even closer to the action. "Dishes are cleverly created" and the best are "out of this world". / **Details:** www.pikeandpine.co.uk; @PikeandPine_at.*

Plateau   £73   **3 3 2**
1 Bartholomews BN1 1HG   01273 733085
*"A great little independent (handy for The Lanes) that cooks up some proper tasty food" from a "really quirky" menu based on small plates and natural wines; "the guys who run the joint could not be lovelier chaps". / **Details:** www.plateaubrighton.co.uk; 10 pm.*

Polpo   £48   **2 3 3**
20 New Rd BN1 1UF   01273 697 361
*This "very busy" South Coast outpost of Russell Norman's affordable bàcaro chain is perhaps "better than its London siblings" but echoes their profile – "the small dishes could be a little more imaginative, but it's still a fun time". / **Details:** www.polpo.co.uk; @Polpo; 11 pm, Sun 10.30 pm; Booking lunch only.*

The Regency Restaurant £33   **3 3 3**
131 Kings Rd BN1 2HH   01273 325014
*This long-standing (est. 1930s) Brighton seafront haunt, with top views of the West Pier, still offers an "authentic fish 'n' chips experience" (plus a huge range of grilled catch, cold buffet etc.). / **Details:** www.theregencyrestaurant.co.uk; 10 pm. / **Accommodation:** 30 rooms, from £50*

Riddle & Finns   £56   **4 4 4**
12b Meeting House Ln BN1 1HB
01273 821218
*"Perhaps the freshest fish restaurant in Brighton" – this communal Lanes venture offers "a unique experience where you share a table" with "other random diners" (making "for fun evenings" for more than one reporter). "Food and wine are just delicious" and there's always a "great buzz". / **Details:** www.riddleandfinns.co.uk; @RiddleandFinns1; 10 pm, Fri & Sat 11 pm; No bookings.*

Riddle & Finns On The Beach   £54   **3 4 4**
139 Kings Road Arches BN1 2FN
01273 821218
*A "small" venue, with quite a local following, that's "well located on Brighton beach yet close to the town" and its elder Lanes sibling. "If you can get a window seat it's the perfect spot to watch the sun set" over "tip-top seafood", a "big range of catch of the day" or a "great value" lunch. / **Details:** www.riddleandfinns.co.uk; @riddleandfinns2; 10 pm.*

The Salt Room   £66   **4 4 4**
106 Kings Road BN1 2FA   01273 929488
*Overlooking the ruined West Pier, this "superb" and hugely popular seafood restaurant doesn't just have a "great location on the seafront" – with a "standout seaview terrace" and a "galleried interior" with "a nice bright atmosphere" – but provides a great all-round experience incorporating "excellent cooking" ("especially the shared whole fish for two"), together with "friendly and very easy going service". The talking point remains 'The Taste of the Pier': "the best dessert in town: not for the faint hearted but a dizzying array of nostalgic sweet treats!" / **Details:** www.saltroom-restaurant.co.uk; @TheSaltRoomUK; Mon-Thu 10 pm, Fri & Sat 10.30 pm, Sun 10 pm.*

Semolina   £47   **4 3 3**
BN1 4JN   01273 697259
*"Good quality and adventurous bistro cuisine" awaits at this diminutive husband-and-wife spot, "tucked away in the Brighton backstreets"; "the lunch offer is a steal". / **Details:** www.semolinabrighton.co.uk/; @SemolinaBistro; 9.45 pm.*

Set, Unique Hotel   £51   **4 3 3**
33 Regency Square BN1 2GG   01273 855572
*"Attached to a very hip hotel with a great cocktail bar" – this former pop-up is "up there amongst the top Brighton places". The food is "possibly a little over-elaborate", but even a reviewer who feels its style is "maybe a little bit too experimental for many Brightonians to fall completely in love with it" says "there's no doubting that it's a fabulous experience". / **Details:** www.thesetrestaurant.com; @theset_brighton; 9.30 pm; closed Mon & Sun.*

Silo   £32   **4 2 3**
39 Upper Gardner St, North Laine BN1 4AN
01273 674259
*"Full marks for the ecological ethos" at Dougie McMaster "waste-free 'concept' place", in North Laine. Despite the in-your-face composter, it's "not too far up itself" and "the food is top-notch". / **Details:** www.silobrighton.com; @silobrighton; 11 pm, Sun & Mon 4 pm; closed Mon D, Tue D, Wed D & Sun D.*

284   FSA Ratings: from [1] (Poor) to [5] (Exceptional)

FSA

64 Degrees £50 5️⃣4️⃣3️⃣
53 Meeting House Lane BN1 1HB
01273 770115
"All the hype is true!" – "fabulous food is served with a smile in uncomplicated surroundings" and it can be "a revelation (the simpler it sounded, the better it tasted!)" at Michael Bremner's "real Brighton star" in the Lanes, which "serves tapas-size dishes prepared in front of you in the open kitchen" (some fans prefer to sit up at the counter). "It's not often you go to a place that's truly doing things a bit differently and enjoying it so much" – "it's actually just a shame that it isn't larger!" / **Details:** www.64degrees.co.uk; @chef64degrees; 9.45 pm.

Small Batch Coffee £10 3️⃣4️⃣4️⃣
17 Jubilee St BN1 1GE 01273 697597
On the fringes of North Laine, the flagship of this popular local chain is the biggest of its now eight-strong roster, with a four-seater brew bar, indoor and outdoor seating. There's a good selection of cakes and pastries, but coffee is the star. / **Details:** www.smallbatchcoffee.co.uk; @SmallBatchCR; 7 pm, Sun 6 pm; L only; No bookings.

Terre à Terre £54 5️⃣4️⃣3️⃣
71 East St BN1 1HQ 01273 729051
"Still Mecca for vegetarians" – this "creative and superb" Lanes legend provides cooking that's "refreshingly different to the usual boring veggie dishes" and is arguably "the best non-meat cuisine in the country". "When I first heard about it, I wasn't particularly excited, but all aspects of our evening were amazing – I've eaten at the Connaught but our experience surpassed that!" / **Details:** www.terreaterre.co.uk; @TerreaTerre; 10.30 pm, Sat 11 pm, Sun 10 pm; Booking max 8 may apply.

Urchin £40 3️⃣4️⃣4️⃣
15-17 Belfast St BN3 3YS 01273 241881
"Shellfish cooked simply and with care" helps draw crowds to this "lively, friendly" three-year-old boozer, which boasts an "amazing variety" of craft beers, plus Brighton Gin (courtesy of the basement tenant). "It can get noisy, but there are tables outside". / **Details:** www.urchinpub.wordpress.com/; @urchinpub; 9.30 pm, Fri & Sat 10 pm.

BRILL, BUCKINGHAMSHIRE 2–1D

Pointer £68 3️⃣3️⃣4️⃣
27 Church St HP18 9RT 01844 238339
"Absolutely delicious food that's worth every penny and staff who couldn't be more helpful" inspire a string of glowing nominations for this "friendly and comfortable" gastropub – a lovely beamed building (still with a proper bar) in a cute Bucks village, where many of the ingredients come from the owner's farm. / **Details:** www.thepointerbrill.co.uk; 8.30 pm, Fri & Sat 9.30 pm.

BRISTOL, CITY OF BRISTOL 2–2B

Adelina Yard £62 5️⃣4️⃣3️⃣
Queen Quay, Welsh Back BS1 4SL
0117 911 2112
Jamie Randall and Olivia Barry have parlayed stints at leading London lights (Galvin Bistro Deluxe, Odette's, Corrigan's Mayfair) into this superlative two-year-old indie, tucked away near Queen's Square; its seasonal fare is "imaginative" and "superbly cooked" (with meats cured in-house) and staff are notably "engaging" too. / **Details:** www.adelinayard.com; @AdelinaYard; 9.30 pm.

Bell's Diner And Bar Rooms £52 4️⃣3️⃣3️⃣
1 York Rd BS6 5QB 0117 924 0357
The latest, four-year-old incarnation of this Montpelier veteran – once a greengrocer's, but a well-known, shabby-chic Bristol haunt since the '70s – "offers small, well-flavoured plates" but as big a draw is the "very well chosen wine list including some gems by the glass". / **Details:** www.bellsdiner.com; 10 pm; closed Mon L & Sun.

Bellita £37 4️⃣3️⃣3️⃣
34 Cotham Hill BS6 6LA 0117 923 8755
The jolly baby sister to Montpelier's Bell's Diner manages to outshine it with its "inventive" baby-Bell's menu nodding to Spain and north Africa. Numerous reports this year honed in on the "interesting lesser known wines" resulting from their "an all-women winemakers" policy. / **Details:** www.bellita.co.uk; @BellitaBristol; 11 pm.

Birch £51 4️⃣4️⃣3️⃣
47 Raleigh Rd BS3 1QS 01179 028 326
After honing their talents in some of Bristol and London's top gastro-spots (St John, 40 Maltby Street) Sam Leach & Beccy Massy are now racking up praise for their own "fantastic neighbourhood restaurant", in Southville; the "exquisite" small plates – many of the ingredients sourced from their own field on the outskirts of town – are a "total bargain" and "well worth more than one visit". / **Details:** www.birchbristol.co; 10 pm; D only, closed Sun-Tue.

Bordeaux Quay £57 2️⃣3️⃣3️⃣
Canons Way BS1 5UH 0117 943 1200
A "lovely harbourside setting" is the backdrop to this "spacious, stylish, informal" venue (brasserie, deli, bakery and restaurant) located in an old warehouse; it offers a "good choice of food, including vegetarian", only don't read too much into the name – "the food was further from France than we actually were". / **Details:** www.bordeaux-quay.co.uk; @bordeauxquay; Mon-Sat 10.30 pm, Sun 9.30 pm.

FSA Ratings: from [1] (Poor) to [5] (Exceptional) **285**

Bosco Pizzeria £39 **3 3 3**

96 Whiteladies Rd BS8 2QX   0117 973 7978

A "superb, authentic" three-year-old Italian using "genuine Italian ingredients"; it's about "more than just pizza" – although its Neapolitan-style versions are the bedrock of its reputation – and the "very pleasant staff" cope admirably with the (sizeable) crowds. / **Details:** www.boscopizzeria.co.uk; @boscopizzeria; 10 pm; May need + to book.

Box-E £48 **4 5 4**

Unit 10, Cargo 1, Wapping Wharf BS1 6WP   no tel

Elliott Lidstone, ex-of The Empress in Hackney, has left the Big Smoke for this new solo venture on Bristol harbour. "Restaurants don't get much smaller than this" – a tiny 14-cover spot "tucked into a shipping container" like its retail park neighbours – but the "refined" and "robust" cooking is "exactly spot-on" (including some old Empress faves). "If you are lucky enough to get the chef's table you can see absolutely everything Elliott does". / **Details:** www.boxebristol.com; @boxebristol.

Bravas £38 **3 4 4**

7 Cotham Hill BS6 6LD   0117 329 6887

"Somehow they have managed to create a terrific atmosphere in an ordinary shopfront" at this "small, lively tapas bar" (and former pop-up) on Cotham Hill; on the food front, they "don't content themselves with blind imitation", resulting in "rustic" and "interesting" dishes, best chased with one of their "amazing gins". / **Details:** www.bravas.co.uk; @bravasbristol; 11 pm, Thu-Sat midnight; closed Mon & Sun.

Bulrush £51 **4 4 2**

21 Cotham Road South BS6 5TZ
0117 329 0990

"The latest reincarnation of this Kingsdown perennial" (an ex-greengrocer's that housed stalwarts Bistro 21 and Juniper) is a hit; George Livesey and Katherine Craughwell deliver "really top-class food" that "blends modern British and interesting Japanese and foraging influences" – and it's "amazing value" too. / **Details:** www.bulrushrestaurant.co.uk; @bulrushbs6.

Casamia, The General £129 **5 4 5**

Guinea St BS1 6SY   0117 959 2884

"Having moved to a new location and despite the loss of one of the Sanchez brothers, this fine dining eatery is still in the top tier" – the Sanchez-Iglesias family's "relaxed and stylish" dining room beneath central Bristol's old General Hospital wins formidable all-round support as a "magical experience" with "clever cuisine", "intriguing wine", "impeccable service" and yet "somehow still with a cosy and friendly feel about it". There is the odd caveat about prices that are becoming "extremely steep for Bristol" however, and even those who say it's "undeniably excellent" can find it becoming "absurdly expensive". / **Details:** www.casamiarestaurant.co.uk; @casamia_; 9.30 pm; closed Mon & Sun; No Amex.

The Cauldron £44

98 Mina Road BS2 9XW   0117 914 1321

Opened in 2016 by chef-patron Henry Eldon, this Montpelier venue has quickly picked up enthusiastic reviews and attention for its 'primordial' style and commitment to celebrating international cultures with locally sourced ingredients. Meals are cooked in cast-iron cauldrons over open fires. Limited feedback to-date – such as we have is middling to good. / **Details:** www.thecauldron.restaurant.

Clifton Sausage £54 **3 3 3**

7 Portland St BS8 4JA   0117 973 1192

"Despite the name, they do offer other, mainly British dishes, as well as a wide variety of sausages (which can all be served as toad in the hole)" at this straightforward contemporary café. / **Details:** www.cliftonsausage.co.uk; @cliftonsausage.

The Cowshed £51 **2 3 3**

44-46 Whiteladies Rd BS8 2NH
0117 973 3550

Lots of exposed stone cladding the walls helps promote a rustic style at this "consistently good" Clifton venture, majoring in West Country steaks (but also with a variety of fish and other offerings). / **Details:** www.thecowshedbristol.com; @Cowshedbristol; 10 pm, Fri & Sat 10.30 pm, Sun 9.30 pm.

Flour & Ash £38 **3 3 2**

230b Cheltenham Rd BS6 5QX
0117 908 3228

A high-profile pizza joint and ice cream pitstop, touted for its sourdough bases and "great use of local produce to create interesting toppings". It may be "a bit overrated by the trendies", but reports are solid in the main. In spring 2017 they surprisingly closed their recently-opened outpost (in Casamia's old Westbury-on-Trym home) to focus efforts on this their HQ. / **Details:** www.flourandash.co.uk.

Hari Krishnans Kitchen £33 **3 3 4**

31A Zetland Road BS6 7AH   01179 422 299

A "good South Indian restaurant offering different fare from the usual Bangladeshi restaurants" – ie "lovely authentic Keralan" cuisine – with "flavours that are always top notch". / **Details:** harikrishnanskitchen.info/zetland/; 11 pm, Sat & Sun midnight; closed Mon.

The Ivy Clifton Brasserie £53 **2 2 4**

42-44 Caledonia Place BS8 4DN
0117 203 4555

"The big new kid on the block in Bristol" – the London icon's West Country brasserie is clearly *"trying hard to impress", a task ably facilitated by its "splendid" ex-bank setting. For too many reporters however it's "disappointing after all the hype" – "the very impressive interior doesn't make up for the not-very-special, and expensive, fare". / Details: theivycliftonbrasserie.com; @ivycliftonbrass.*

The Jetty Restaurant £47
49/55 Corn Street BS1 1HT 0117 203 4456
Located in Bristol's historic financial quarter, this hotel dining room ensconced in a former banking hall boasts an outpost of Alex Aitken's famous Christchurch fish restaurant. Alongside a selection of seafood and steaks there is a full vegan and vegetarian menu. / Details: www.bristol-harbour-hotel.co.uk/; @BristolHHotel; Mon-Thu 10 pm, Fri & Sat 10.30 pm, Sun 9 pm.

Lido £55 345
Oakfield Pl BS8 2BJ 0117 933 9533
A "great place to take friends who are blown away by the first glimpse of the pool" – this "very unusual" and "very relaxing" Bristol icon is part of a restored and immensely characterful Victorian lido. Ex-Moro chef Freddie Bird's distinctive Mediterranean/ North African slanted cuisine is "equally good in the upstairs restaurant and poolside tapas bar". / Details: www.lidobristol.com; @lidobristol; 10.30 pm, Sun 10 pm; closed Sun D; No Amex.

Lockside £36 322
No.1 Brunel Lock Road BS1 6XS
0117 9255 800
A former transport café under a flyover in the Avon Gorge might not immediately conjure up visions of culinary greatness – but this "vibrant" spot (where Sid supped in 'Only Fools and Horses') continues to surprise with its fab brunch featuring "superb, freshly cooked ingredients". / Details: www.lockside.net.

The Mint Room £42 443
12-16 Clifton Rd BS8 1AF 01173 291 300
"Indian 'fine dining' with superb use of spices" and featuring "modernised versions of old-favourite dishes" as "artistic as they are succulent" wins consistent praise for this "high end Indian". / Details: www.themintroom.co.uk/bristol.

No Man's Grace £60 433
BS6 6PE 07436 588273
Ex-Casamia chef John Watson's relaxed three-year-old seems to be well and truly settled on foodie mecca Chandos Road and its contemporary local fare won consistent praise this year. / Details: www.nomansgrace.com; 10 pm.

Nutmeg £40 434
10 The Mall BS8 4DR 0117 360 0288
"A wonderful new addition to the burgeoning food scene in Clifton" – "no ordinary Indian", but a long,

narrow and vividly stencilled subcontinental "with a wide range of choices from all regions of India" and the "mix of interesting spices and cooking styles" this entails. / Details: www.nutmegbristol.com; @nutmegclifton; 11pm, Sun 9 pm.

Paco Tapas, The General £48 544
Lower Guinea St BS1 6SY 0117 959 2884
"The best tapas ever (especially having watched them make them by sitting at the bar) with superb flavours followed by desserts to die for" has made an instant smash hit of the Sanchez-Iglesias family's Spanish tapas and sherry bar, where "the ambience makes the best even better!" / Details: www.sanchez-brothers.co.uk; @PacoTapas_.

Pasta Loco £58 332
37A Cotham Hill BS6 6JY 0117 973 3000
"Fab homemade pasta" is unsurprisingly the star of this "lively" establishment – "another good addition to the Cotham Hill scene", which has made waves since opening in 2016. Owners Ben Harvey and Dominic Borel are slated to open a ravioli bar, in the city's banking district, in November 2017, with Ben's chef brother Joe (ex-of local icon Bellita) at the helm. / Details: www.pastaloco.co.uk; @pasta_loco/; 10 pm.

Pi Shop, The General £52 343
Guinea St BS1 6SY 0117 925 6872
Set next to its newly relocated parent in Bristol's handsome new waterside development The General, this is "Casamia's shot at a pizza joint – and it's a bullseye": "splendidly floury" sourdough and "first class ingredients make for top notch pizza and the bill is not as eye watering as one might imagine!" / Details: www.thepishop.co.uk/; @PiShop_; 10 pm.

Polpo £36 222
50 Whiteladies Road BS8 2NH 0117 973 3100
"Contributing little to Bristol's burgeoning quality restaurant scene" – this beyond-the-M25 branch of Russell Norman's trendy cicchetti chain does receive the odd "cheap 'n' cheerful" recommendation, but the majority of reviewers find it "disappointing after all the anticipation". / Details: www.polpo.co.uk; @Polpo; Mon-Wed 10 pm, Thu-Sat 11 pm, Sun 10 pm; Booking lunch only.

River Cottage Canteen £49 222
St Johns Ct, Whiteladies Rd BS8 2QY
0117 973 2458
Hugh Fearnley-Whittingstall's restored Victorian church looks good, but feedback on it remains limited and very patchy. One reviewer felt it has "upped its game of late" but there are still reports of the "utter fiasco… interminable waits… disorganised service… incredibly underwhelming" variety. / Details: www.rivercottage.net/canteens; @plymouthcanteen; 9.15 pm, Sun 4 pm.

FSA

riverstation £54 2️⃣2️⃣4️⃣
The Grove BS1 4RB 0117 914 4434
"Often overlooked as it has been here a while, and so isn't part of the über-trendy new Bristol foodie scene" – this striking-looking dockside feature (with downstairs bar and upstairs restaurant) was taken over by Young's in late 2016. The food is generally well-rated – the worst criticism of it, is that it can be a bit "meh" – and some of the decor "is looking a bit shabby" but it's a "buzzy" haunt, with a "delightful summer terrace", and "you can't go wrong here if you can get a table overlooking the floating harbour". / Details: www.riverstation.co.uk; @riverstation_; 10.30 pm, Fri & Sat 11 pm; closed Sun D; No Amex.

San Carlo £44 3️⃣3️⃣4️⃣
44 Corn Street BS1 1HQ 0117 922 6586
"Super dooper!"; you "can't go wrong at this Bristol stalwart" – one of the oldest members of the successful national chain – known for its "very glitzy" glamour and "reliable" (but pricey) cuisine. / Details: www.sancarlo.co.uk; @SanCarlo_Group; 11 pm.

Shop3 Bistro £56
3a Regent Street BS8 4HW 01173 822 235
This neighbourhood bistro opened quietly in Clifton late last year offering a small, daily changing menu of local, rustic and foraged fare – local press and bloggers love the place. / Details: www.shop3bistro.co.uk/; @shop3bistro.

Sky Kong Kong
2 Haymarket Walk BS1 3LN 0117 239 9528
An organic Korean restaurant in Bristol's Haymarket offering a simple set menu of inexpensive bento boxes. The BYO (with £1.50 corkage) policy helps make this an even more reasonable night out. / Details: skykongkong.co.uk; @SkyKongKongCafe; 8.30 pm.

Souk Kitchen £39 4️⃣2️⃣3️⃣
277 North St BS3 1JP 0117 966 6880
A good "cheap 'n' cheerful" pre- or post-theatre venue for The Tobacco Factory opposite – Darren & Ella Lovell's acclaimed street food spot offers an adventurous menu cherry-picking from the whole ex-Ottoman Empire (with "very good vegetarian" options in particular). A Clifton sibling, which also sells supplies, opened a few years back. / Details: www.soukitchen.co.uk; @soukkitchenbris; 8.30 pm.

Spiny Lobster £58 4️⃣4️⃣3️⃣
128-130 Whiteladies Road BS8 2RS
0117 973 7384
"The gastronomic equivalent of a warm bath"; Mitch Tonk's New England-style restaurant (FKA Rockfish Grill and sister to Dartmouth's The Seahorse) is an "utterly dependable" sort of spot combining "comfy booths" and "exceptional quality" fish. "The little shop attached is an added boon". /

Details: *www.thespinylobster.co.uk; @_SpinyLobster; 10 pm, Fri & Sat 10.30 pm; closed Mon & Sun.*

Spoke And Stringer £40 4️⃣3️⃣5️⃣
The Boat House, Unit 1 Gasworks Lane BS1 5AD 0117 925 9371
A favourite Bristol breakfast haunt enjoying a "super dockside location, with outdoor seating as well as a cosy interior" featuring "great cycling-themed decor" and adventure sports goods to buy; by day you can enjoy "fabulous brunch food", and there's "lovely tapas"Thursday to Saturday night. / Details: www.spokeandstringer.com; @Spoke_Stringer; 9.30 pm, Sun 3 pm.

The Thali Café £33 3️⃣3️⃣3️⃣
12 York Rd BS6 5QE 0117 942 6687
The original branch of this "authentic Indian street food" chain remains of note for its "quirky", "laid-back atmosphere" and "very reasonable prices", and is "particularly good for veggies" and teetotallers. Stop Press – their first non-Brizzle outpost landed on George Street, Oxford, in July 2017. / Details: www.thethalicafe.co.uk; @thethalicafe; 10 pm; closed weekday L; No Amex; SRA-Food Made Good – 3 stars.

Wallfish Bistro £45 5️⃣4️⃣4️⃣
112 Princess Victoria St BS8 4DB
01179 735435
"Seldon Curry and Liberty Wenham continue to excel and have created a large and loyal following" for this "little gem in Clifton". It gets "top marks for versatility, innovation and remarkable choice, coming out of a tiny kitchen" ("makes me want to move to Bristol and if I did I'd eat the amazing value lunch here everyday"). / Details: www.wallfishbistro.co.uk; @wallfishbristol; 10 pm, Sun 9 pm; closed Mon & Tue.

Wilks £82 5️⃣5️⃣2️⃣
1 Chandos Rd BS6 6PG 0117 973 7999
James Wilkins's "world class" food delights a committed fanclub of his backstreet Redland HQ, where "classical cuisine with imaginative flavouring" is "impeccably served, but in a manner that's in no way stuffy". If there's a reservation it's the "slightly dull room" – but in a better location this could rival Casamia as Bristol's most highly rated destination. / Details: www.wilksrestaurant.co.uk/; @wilksrestaurant; Wed-Sun 9 pm; closed Mon & Tue; No Amex.

Wilson's £50 4️⃣4️⃣3️⃣
24 Chandos Rd BS6 6PF 0117 973 4157
"Holding its own on a street shared with two Michelin winners" – Jan and Mary Ostle's "tiny" independent bistro in Redlands "contrives to be busy in this suburban area even on a weekday lunchtime". The draw – "exceptional food from the freshest ingredients" (many gathered, grown or hunted by the owners) from a focussed menu and service that's "so friendly". / Details: wilsonsrestaurant.co.uk; @JanWilsons; 9.30 pm.

Adam's, Birmingham

Cricketers, Cobham

Aizle, Edinburgh

BROADSTAIRS, KENT   3–3D

Stark   **£70**   5️⃣4️⃣3️⃣
1 Oscar Road CT10 1QJ   01843 579786
*Ben Crittenden (formerly head chef at West
House in Biddenden) and his wife Sophie opened
this 12-cover, prix-fixe restaurant in Broadstairs
just before Christmas 2016. Early reports from
locals and Londoners can't praise it enough: "in
a tiny space they conjure up superb food for a
six course tasting menu with a very modestly
priced but thoughtful wine flight". / Details:
www.starkfood.co.uk; 9.30 pm; closed Sun-Tue.*

Wyatt & Jones   **£55**   4️⃣4️⃣4️⃣
23-27 Harbour St CT10 1EU   01843 865126
*"Picturesque" and "stylish" harbourside restaurant
with "great views", by Broadstairs beach – a "great
place to savour fish", but there's "plenty more on the
inventive menu". / Details: www.wyattandjones.co.uk;
Wed & Thu 9 pm, Fri & Sat 10 pm, Sun 5 pm.*

BROADWAY, WORCESTERSHIRE   2–1C

Russell's of Broadway   **£62**   3️⃣3️⃣3️⃣
20 High Street WR12 7DT   01386 853555
*In a "lovely Cotswold location", an old restaurant-
with-rooms "with modern interior decor"; reports
on the food vary from "competent plus a few
interesting touches", to accounts of plates
"virtually licked clean by all"; for a simpler bite, the
owner also runs the chippy next door. / Details:
russellsofbroadway.co.uk/restaurant/; @russelsRandR;
Mon-Sat 9.15 pm, Sun 2.30 pm; closed Sun D. /
Accommodation: 7 rooms, from £110*

BROCKDISH, SUFFOLK   3–1D

Old Kings Head   **£39**   3️⃣3️⃣3️⃣
IP2 4JY   01379 668843
*A nicely renovated pub that "only specialises in
pizza and some pasta" but does what it does
very well (with "lots of interesting toppings and
beautifully light and crispy bases"). / Details:
www.kingsheadbrockdish.co.uk/; @OKHBrockdish;
10 pm, Fri & Sat 11pm, Sun 9 pm.*

BROCKENHURST, HAMPSHIRE   2–4D

Cambium, Careys Manor £70
Lyndhurst Rd SO42 7RH   01590 623551
*This New Forest-inspired restaurant boasts a menu
that is completely local, sourced and farmed in
surrounding Hampshire. Head chef Alistair Craig
promises to add a 'new dimension' to classic
ingredients and serve seasonal dishes inspired by
nature. Too limited feedback for a rating, but such as
we have is upbeat. / Details: www.careysmanor.com.*

The Pig   **£56**   3️⃣4️⃣4️⃣
Beaulieu Road SO42 7QL   01590 622354
*"Tucked away in the middle of the New Forest" –
the first of the 'Pig' chain (created by Hotel du Vin
founder, Robin Hutson) has "a glorious location",
and its artfully "shabby chic" interior carefully
"combines formal and casual English country house
styles" with "delicious" food to create "a relaxed yet
special atmosphere" ("fun, but sometimes spoilt by
the London luvvie set and a number of ill-behaved
children"). "Local ingredients (many sourced from
the garden)" is part of the ethos, and helps win
praise for its "fresh and well-presented" cooking,
although quite a few reporters feel the food is
"generally serviceable, but not exactly as distinctive
as it's hyped to be". / Details: www.thepighotel.com;
@The_Pig_Hotel; 9.30 pm. / Accommodation: 26
rooms, from £139*

BROMESWELL, SUFFOLK   3–1D

The Unruly Pig   **£49**   3️⃣2️⃣3️⃣
Orford Rd IP12 2PU   01394 460 310
*Views divide on this 16th-century inn "attractively
re-opened after a fire" a couple of years ago.
For fans "Brendan and his team have nailed
it" serving "adventurous" fare with "wit and
professional charm", but for foes the management
can seem "overbearing" and the food "priced
so as to leave you feeling fleeced". / Details:
www.theunrulypig.co.uk; @unrulypig; 9.30 pm, Fri & Sat
10 pm, Sun 8 pm; closed Sun.*

BROMLEY, GREATER LONDON   3–3B

Cinnamon Culture   **£59**   3️⃣3️⃣3️⃣
46 Plaistow Ln BR1 3PA   020 8289 0322
*"It's great to have such a local little star" – a
"spacious and airy" fine dining Indian, where
"fragrant" food is "served with flair" and "they
have a super cocktail and wine list, including some
lovely Indian wines". Top Tip – Indian BBQ Sundays
in summer. / Details: www.cinnamonculture.com;
@cinnamonculture; 10.30 pm, weekends 11 pm; closed
Mon; No Amex.*

BROSELEY, SHROPSHIRE   5–4B

King And Thai   **£41**   4️⃣3️⃣3️⃣
The Forester Arms, Avenue Road TF12 5DL
01952 882004
*Even those who say its "prices are more restaurant
than pub" hail this "Thai in an old inn" for its
"amazing quality and imaginative creative cooking".
"I have just one complaint: it's a 40 minute
drive away!" / Details: www.thekingandthai.co.uk;
@KingandThaiRest; 9 pm; closed Mon & Sun.*

BROUGHTON, LANCASHIRE	5–1A

Italian Orchard **£47** 🟦3🟦3🟦4
96 Whittingham Lane PR3 5DB 01772 861240
"The flagship of the Bragagnini family's small group
of restaurants in and around Preston continues
being all things to all people": "some have a pint,
a garlic bread and pizza and are out within 20
minutes", while others "pick their way through the
Britalian crowd-pleasers on the menu to find the
excellent charcuterie and pasta specials". "The scale
of the operation is mind-boggling", too! / **Details:**
www.italianorchard.com; 10.30 pm.

BROUGHTON, NORTH YORKSHIRE	8–4B

Bull at Broughton **£46** 🟦3🟦4🟦3
BD23 3AE 01756 792065
"Excellent pub food with plenty of choice for
everyone" and "dogs also welcome" – two of
the charms of this solidly performing, poshified
outpost of Ribble Valley Inns. / **Details:**
www.thebullatbroughton.com; @Bull_Broughton;
8.30 pm, Fri & Sat 9 pm; No bookings.

BRUTON, SOMERSET	2–3B

At the Chapel **£48** 🟦3🟦2🟦4
28 High St BA10 0AE 01749 814070
This minimal-chic chapel conversion (with eight luxe
bedrooms upstairs) is quite the local hangout, not
least for its wood-fired pizzas. Best "come when it's
empty at 9am and the croissants are just out of the
oven…as the sun shines through the huge windows
you can have a great breakfast, read the papers
and while away an hour without noticing". / **Details:**
www.atthechapel.co.uk; @at_the_chapel; 9.30 pm, Sun
8 pm. / **Accommodation:** 8 rooms, from £100

Roth Bar & Grill **£40** 🟦3🟦3🟦4
Durslade Farm, Dropping Ln BA10 0NL
01749 814060
"Full of fun, culture and atmosphere – and the food
is pretty special too!" Blue chip gallery Hauser &
Wirth's West Country seat is set on a working farm
and juxtaposes vaulted art galleries with a "quirky",
salvage-chic restaurant. "They can't always cope
at the weekend" but there's some "fantastic sharp
dishes", plus more straightforward fare ("excellent
brunches with bacon to die for", "fabulous steaks"
and "half a chicken with a delicious salad never fails
to be enjoyed"). / **Details:** www.rothbarandgrill.co.uk;
@rothbarandgrill; 9 pm.

BUCKFASTLEIGH, DEVON	1–3D

Riverford Field Kitchen **£51** 🟦4🟦3🟦3
Wash Barn, Buckfast Leigh TQ11 0JU
01803 762074
"Wonderful meals with an emphasis on veg"
(sourced from the farm) are what "make the
Field Kitchen special"; chance plays a role – you
eat what's fresh and, given the "sociable setting"
(communal tables, sharing platters etc) you have
to "hope that your neighbours aren't too greedy"
– but results are typically "just fantastic!" A stroll
around the farm completes the trip. / **Details:**
www.riverford.co.uk; @riverford; 8 pm; closed Sun D;
Booking lunch only.

BUCKLAND, WORCESTERSHIRE	2–1C

Buckland Manor **£99** 🟦5🟦4🟦5
WR12 7LY 01386 852626
"Each plate a mini work of art and ingredients
from local suppliers" (mainly in the neighbouring
Vale of Evesham) won stellar marks this year
for William Guthrie's cuisine at this "gorgeous",
small country house hotel – a Relais & Châteaux
property – where "standards have steadily improved
under Brownsword's ownership". / **Details:**
www.bucklandmanor.co.uk; @Buckland_Manor; 2m
SW of Broadway on B4632; Jacket & tie required;
Booking max 8 may apply; children: 12+.

BUNBURY, CHESHIRE	5–3B

The Dysart Arms **£51** 🟦3🟦3🟦4
Bowes Gate Road CW6 9PH 01829 260183
You'll be assured of a "friendly" welcome, "great
food and a wide choice menu" at this "nice old
pub" with "original features" – a "popular" spot
that's part of the Brunning & Price chain. / **Details:**
www.dysartarms-bunbury.co.uk; 9.30 pm, Sun 9 pm.

BURCOT, OXFORDSHIRE	2–2D

The Chequers **£42** 🟦3🟦3🟦3
Abingdon Road OX14 3DP 01865 407771
Above average pub cooking wins solid ratings for
this thatched inn, set in an attractive Thames-
side village. In August 2017, chef and owner
Steve Sanderson gave it a modish makeover,
complete with 'greige' interior and putting steak
centre-stage on the modernised menu. / **Details:**
www.thechequers-burcot.co.uk/The_Chequers/The_
Chequers_at_Burcot.html.

BURTON BRADSTOCK, DORSET	2–4B

Hive Beach Cafe £44 ▣▣▣
Beach Road DT6 4RF 01308 897070
"A longstanding favourite for no-frills, excellent food" – this seaside café is a "convivial if somewhat hectic spot" serving "fabulously fresh fish and shellfish" (and the "fish 'n' chips is very good as well"). / **Details:** www.hivebeachcafe.co.uk; @HiveBeachCafe; 8 pm July & August only; L only; No bookings. / **Accommodation:** 2 rooms, from £95

The Seaside Boarding House Hotel £56 ▢▣▣
Cliff Road DT6 4RB 01308 897205
London creatives have a new reason to visit Dorset's Jurassic Coast – a "tastefully refurbished" two-year-old clifftop hotel from the tastemakers behind the mythic Groucho; even those who feel that "the food (albeit decent) needs to go up a notch" say that "the location and sea view alone make this worth a visit". / **Details:** www.theseasideboardinghouse.com; @SeasideBH; 10 pm.

BURTON ON TRENT, STAFFORDSHIRE 5–3C

Pascal At The Old Vicarage £45 ▣▣▣
2 Main Street DE14 3EX 01283 533222
Launched by a husband-and-wife team in 1999, this redbrick villa's standards "would be the envy of any top-class restaurant" and it provides "fine dining at incredibly affordable prices" – "the setting is very comfortable, polite service is friendly and extremely efficient, and the exceptional cuisine is English with a French twist". / **Details:** www.pascalattheoldvicarage.co.uk/; @PascalArnoux; Mon-Thu 9 pm, Fri & Sat 10 pm.

BURY ST EDMUNDS, SUFFOLK	3–1C

Bourgee
7 The Traverse IP33 1BJ 01284 245008
Affordable luxury, steak and lobster is what's promised at this newcomer occupying Grade-I listed Cupola House in Bury St Edmunds, part of a small chain with sites in Chelmsford and Southend-on-Sea. / **Details:** www.bourgeerestaurants.com; @BourgeeUK

Maison Bleue £58 ▣▣▣
30-31 Churchgate St IP33 1RG 01284 760623
"Superior to many Michelin starred restaurants, and much better value" – Pascal and Karine Canavet's characterful Gallic restaurant sits near the cathedral of this picturesque town and "just gets better and better". The cuisine is "exceptional" and "beautifully presented too", service is "impeccable" and the "very fine looking dining room" is "just the place to go to for romance". / **Details:** www.maisonbleue.co.uk; @Maison_Bleue; 9 pm, Sat 9.30 pm; closed Mon & Sun.

1921 Angel Hill £54 ▣▣▣
19-21 Angel Hill IP33 1UZ 01284 704870
"Make sure you get some of the canapés to kick things off" at Zack Deakins's ambitious venture, which inhabits a "charming and ancient" building in the heart of the town. The "finely wrought" cooking here is characterised by "flourishes such as accompanying flowers and small pickles" but "along with the huge amount of detailing goes a huge amount of flavour". "After all the work involved the bill is not onerous and they deserve to do very well". / **Details:** nineteen-twentyone.co.uk; @1921ah; 9.30 pm; closed Sun; No bookings.

Northgate £52 ▢▢▣
Northgate Street P33 1HP 01284 339604
FKA Ounce House under longtime ex-owners the Potts, this Victorian pile has had a metro-chic makeover by East Anglia's Chestnut Group. "Despite being well renovated" however, its cooking divides opinion and sceptics feel it "doesn't know what it wants to be" ("guesthouse, cocktail bar or restaurant"). / **Details:** www.thenorthgate.com.

Pea Porridge £55 ▣▣▣
28-29 Cannon St IP33 1JR 01284 700200
"Interesting cuts and techniques" ("where else will you find a starter of hares' livers and kidneys?") characterises Justin Sharp's nose-to-tail approach at this "intimate and romantic" small restaurant, "tucked away in side street away from the centre of this glorious town", where his "unusual and exciting menu offerings" are "prepared with great flair". He runs it with his wife Jurge, and "they try very hard indeed" / **Details:** www.peaporridge.co.uk; @peaporridge; 9 pm, Fri & Sat 9.30 pm; closed Mon, Tue L & Sun; No Amex; No bookings.

Valley Connection £46 ▣▣▣
42 Churchgate St IP33 1RG 01284 753161
"Above-average Indian food, well cooked and presented in a modern setting" again wins praise for this town-centre Indian. / **Details:** www.valley-connection.com; 11.30 pm.

Voujon £36 ▣▣▣
29 Mustow St IP33 1XL 01284 488122
"The best for miles around" owing to its "well-prepared regular Indian fare"; okay, so there are "no surprises", but what you get is "nicely cooked". / **Details:** www.voujonburystedmunds.co.uk; 11.30 pm.

BUSHEY, HERTFORDSHIRE	3–2A

St James £51 3️⃣3️⃣2️⃣
30 High St WD23 3HL   020 8950 2480
"After 19 years, this high street modern European, presided over by the ever-smiling proprietor Alfonso, continues to provide an outpost of quality food in the underserved north London/Herts borders"; happily, the "vibrant" food still comes at "sound prices" too. / *Details: www.stjamesrestaurant.co.uk; opp St James Church; 9 pm, Sun 2 pm; closed Sun D; No Amex.*

CAMBER, EAST SUSSEX	3–4C

The Gallivant £54 3️⃣3️⃣3️⃣
New Lydd Rd TN31 7RB   01797 225 057
A converted old motel, across from the dunes, whose New England-chic dining room combines ultra-local-sourcing (within 15 miles) and a prohibition on tips and service charges, and serves "excellent food" (not least fish). / *Details: www.thegallivant.co.uk; @thegallivant; 9.30 pm; children: under 12s 8.30pm.* / *Accommodation: 20 rooms, from £115; SRA-Food Made Good – 3 stars.*

CAMBRIDGE, CAMBRIDGESHIRE	3–1B

Alimentum £94 3️⃣3️⃣1️⃣
152-154 Hills Rd CB2 8PB   01223 413000
Mark Poynton's "rather clinical" venue has always put in a Curate's Egg performance in our survey due to its location ("a bit off", near a major road junction), its decor ("not a lot of soul") and sometimes its service (on occasion "intrusive"). Michelin chose this year to strip the place of its star, but there's no support in our feedback for this decision as – despite all the above caveats – all reports this year noted that its ambitious cuisine (nowadays from chef Samira Effa) is "undoubtedly good" if not "excellent". Perhaps a planned refurb in early 2018 will finally put a tiger in its tank. / *Details: www.restaurantalimentum.co.uk; @alimentum1; Mon-Thu 9.30 pm, Sat 10 pm, Sun 9 pm.*

The Cambridge Chop House £57 3️⃣2️⃣3️⃣
1 Kings Parade CB2 1SJ   01223 359506
In a "brilliant location" opposite King's, this "convivial" staple serves "simply presented" carnivorous fare at a "solid" and "fairly priced" level (but "we're not talking about Smithfield's St John!"); "interesting cellars" an added boon. / *Details: www.cambscuisine.com; @cambscuisine; 10.30 pm, Sat 11 pm, Sun 9.30 pm.*

Cambridge Wine Merchants £35 3️⃣3️⃣4️⃣
32 Bridge St CB2 1UJ   01223 568989
"Amazing wine recommendations" and a stupefying selection of bottles from the indie owners' 900-strong range get top billing at this four-year-old wine bar, by Magdalene Bridge, and with views over the namesake college; there's also "nice food to go along with it" – of a cold deli platter, Scotch egg kind of bent.

Cotto, The Gonville Hotel £87 5️⃣4️⃣3️⃣
Gonville Place, CB1 1LY   01223 302010
After a decade in smallish premises near the Grafton Centre, Hans Schweitzer's superior Italian venture upped sticks to the plusher environs of the Gonville Hotel in January 2017. This smartly decorated spot now offers a better backdrop for his "high-style dining with superb attention to detail" (with "surprises even in old-favourite dishes"). / *Details: www.cottocambridge.co.uk; @cottocambridge; 9.15 pm; D only, Wed-Sat; No Amex; need + to book.*

Fitzbillies £38 3️⃣3️⃣2️⃣
51 - 52 Trumpington Street CB2 1RG
01223 352500
This Cambridge icon (est 1921) famous for its Chelsea buns has inspired mixed views since FT columnist Tim Hayward took the reins in 2011. For some long-term sceptics "this new trendy journalist owner has ruined the place (despite its friendly staff, they can't even get marmalade on toast right!)" but fans were more in evidence this year, boosting its "excellent brekkies" ("sourdough smash is just great"), "amazing cakes and good coffee too". / *Details: www.fitzbillies.com; Mon-Thu 6 pm, Fri & Sat 7 pm, Sun 6 pm; closed Mon D, Tue D, Wed D & Sun D.*

The Ivy Cambridge Brasserie £54
16 Trinity Street CB2 1TB   awaiting tel
In a 'roll-out' that would do McDonald's proud, this iconic brand has gone for it this year, opening virtually simultaneously in practically all of the UK's top restaurant cities. The ambition is impressive: let's hope standards hold up better than they did when, for example 'Browns' tried to pull off a similar trick. The Cambridge branch is due to open in Spring 2018. / *Details: www.theivycambridgebrasserie.com.*

Midsummer House £148 5️⃣4️⃣4️⃣
Midsummer Common CB4 1HA
01223 369299
Daniel Clifford's "haven of calm and delight" occupies a beautifully located Victorian villa bordering Midsummer Common and the banks of the Cam ("lovely river views from the lounge"), and continues to maintain its renown as one of the country's top culinary destinations. From a series of tasting options (including a vegetarian menu), results from the open kitchen are "adventurous without

being silly" and "the theatrical presentation which accompanies each course truly makes for a meal to remember", complemented well by a "brilliant choice of wines" and "exceptional service with a smile". "Excellence doesn't come cheap" however, and although major disappointments are rare here, mild panic on the arrival of the bill goes with the territory. / **Details:** www.midsummerhouse.co.uk; @Midsummerhouse; 9.30 pm; closed Mon, Tue L & Sun.

Millworks **£54** 2️⃣2️⃣4️⃣
Newnham Rd CB3 9EY 01223 367507
A "new restaurant in a lovely old watermill" ("with working wheel as part of the interior decor") from the "small local group" who run the city's well-known Chop House restaurants; the brasserie fare is of a "decent standard" but, bar the odd "unusual" dish, not quite of a par with the vibe and "very nice waterside location". / **Details:** 10 pm, Fri & Sat 10.30 pm, Sun 9.30 pm.

Navadhanya Cambridge £45 4️⃣4️⃣3️⃣
73 Newmarket Rd CB5 8EG 01223 300583
"Intense reduced sauces, perfectly cooked venison and an intriguing plate of pudding choices" exemplify the very "modern and refined" cuisine at this "interesting" three-year-old, where a seven course tasting menu features alongside the à la carte. It's quite an "ambient" space, but, in the upstairs room in particular, can seem a mite "clinical". / **Details:** www.navadhanya.co.uk; @navadhanyauk.

Oak Bistro **£56** 3️⃣4️⃣3️⃣
6 Lensfield Road CB2 1EG 01223 323361
With its "lovely and convenient setting with charming courtyard", plus "very good food" and "amazing hospitality" this indie neighbourhood bistro is, by all accounts, "one of the best places in Cambridge for an enjoyable laidback meal". / **Details:** www.theoakbistro.co.uk; @theoakbistro; 9.30 pm, Fri & Sat 9.45 pm; closed Sun; No bookings.

Old Bicycle Shop **£58** 3️⃣2️⃣3️⃣
CB2 1DP 01223 859909
It only opened in May 2016, but the Cambridge Brew House's sibling "feels like it's been there forever" (a claim more apt for the previous tenant, Howes Cycles, which had been trading for 173 years when it closed in 2013!) "It always seems to be rammed", and although "service can be a bit patchy", the food's "absolutely fine". / **Details:** www.oldbicycleshop.com; @oldbicycleshop; 11pm.

Parker's Tavern
1 Park Terrace CB1 1JH awaiting tel
This new restaurant in the revamped University Arms Hotel overlooking Parker's Piece was expected to open as this guide went to press in late 2017.

Chef Tristan Welch (who has trained with Gary Rhodes, Gordon Ramsay and Michel Roux Jr) heads-up the kitchen. / **Details:** www.universityarms.com.

Petersfield **£56** 3️⃣4️⃣4️⃣
2 Sturton Street CB1 2QA 01223 306306
Typical corner pub from the outside, and strikingly modern gastroboozer (with bottles inset into the ceiling) inside – this lavishly revamped pub (est. February 2017) is the latest addition to the local City Pub Company. Feedback is limited so far, but reporters praise its "superb Sunday lunch", and you can expect top beers from its sibling the Cambridge Brew House. / **Details:** www.thepetersfield.co.uk; @ThePetersfield; midnight, Sun 10.30 pm.

Pint Shop **£48** 3️⃣2️⃣3️⃣
10 Peas Hill CB2 3PN 01223 352293
"Fun, with decent food and a really good selection of beers" (and gins) – this gastropub three-year-old makes an excellent destination in a gaggle of mates. But when it's busy, don't expect top service – it can turn "manic, with everything seeming rushed and frantic". "The bar snacks are lovely though if you can't get a table" ("Scotch eggs to die for"). Cute garden too. / **Details:** www.pintshop.co.uk; @PintShop; 11 pm; No bookings.

**The St John's Chop
House** **£57** 3️⃣3️⃣3️⃣
21-24 Northampton St CB3 0AD
01223 353110
With its "good, solid and nicely presented" food (of carnivorous bent) this 19th century exposed-beam eatery is "an excellent venue for treating student members of the family"; refreshingly, it's "not overpriced for the area" (especially the "good value" set lunch). / **Details:** www.cambscuisine.com/st-johns-chop-house; @cambscuisine; 10.30 pm, Sun 9 pm.

Steak & Honour **£17** 4️⃣3️⃣2️⃣
4 Wheeler Street, Cambridge, CB2 3QB
CB2 3QB 07766 568430
As of January 2017, this highly rated mobile burger outfit has a fixed home by the Corn Exchange, on Wheeler St – order at the take-away counter downstairs and eat in the Lego-like upstairs. Their fleet of Citroen vans is still plying Cambridge's streets though. / **Details:** www.steakandhonour.co.uk; @steakandhonour; No bookings.

Trinity **£56** 4️⃣4️⃣3️⃣
15 Trinity Street CB2 1TB 01223 322130
The smart new sibling to Cambridge's Varsity Restaurant opened not far from the eponymous college in April 2017; one early days reporter hails the "great" fish- and meat-centric fare and says they're "excellent" at catering for those tricky dietary requirements. / **Details:** www.trinitycambridge.co.uk; 10 pm, Fri & Sat 10.30 pm, Sun 9.30 pm.

Restaurant 22 £58 4|4|4
22 Chesterton Road CB4 3AX 01223 351880
"Cambridge's best-kept secret!", say fans of this
elegant Victorian townhouse outside the centre, near
Victoria Avenue Bridge – whose dining room offers
a fixed-price monthly menu: "a continued delight",
which they hail as "wonderful in every way". /
Details: www.restaurant22.co.uk; 9 pm; D only, closed
Mon & Sun; children: 12+.

CANTERBURY, KENT 3–3D

The Ambrette
Canterbury £50 4|4|3
14 - 15 Beer Cart Lane CT1 2NY
01227 200777
"The younger sister of The Ambrette in Margate,
Dev Biswal's airy, converted pub delivers a wonderful
dining experience". The setting is "warm and inviting"
and the cooking – "not purely Indian, but very good
fusion-with-an-Indian-base" – provides "marvellous
flavours" ("every mouthful is a delight!"). / **Details:**
www.theambrette.co.uk; @The_Ambrette; Mon-Thu
9.30 pm, Fri-Sun 10 pm.

Café des Amis £44 3|3|4
95 St Dunstan's St CT2 8AD 01227 464390
"Still a favourite", this "buzzy" Westgate Mexican
is "always reliable and good value" ("been dining
here for over 25 years and the food, service and
ambience is as awesome as ever"). / **Details:**
www.cafedez.com; 10 pm, Fri & Sat 10.30 pm, Sun
9.30 pm; Booking max 6 may apply.

Cafe Mauresque £42 4|4|3
8 Butchery Ln CT1 2JR 01227 464300
This Moorish-styled city-centre venture is "the best
of its kind in Canterbury by a long way", thanks to
its "interesting and good north African dishes" (plus
Andalucian fare). / **Details:** www.cafemauresque.com;
@CafeMauresque; 10 pm, Fri & Sat 10.30 pm.

County Restaurant, ABode
Canterbury £63 3|3|3
High St CT1 2RX 01227 766266
The "attractive lunch menu" helps make this
smart venue a handy option in the city-centre,
and its cooking is consistently well rated. / **Details:**
www.abodecanterbury.co.uk; @ABodecanterbury;
10.30 pm; closed Sun D. / **Accommodation:** 72
rooms, from £125

Deeson's British
Restaurant £52 3|4|3
25-27 Sun St CT1 2HX 01227 767854
A family-run establishment, stumbling distance
from cathedral and theatre, that "does what it does
very well" – in particular straightforward British
cooking. / **Details:** www.deesonsrestaurant.co.uk;
@DeesonsBritish; 10 pm.

Goods Shed £48 3|2|5
Station Road West CT2 8AN 01227 459153
"Perched above the farmer's market which provides
the ingredients" – an "attractive" outfit, which is
especially "buzzing at lunch", and whose "ever-
changing menu offers tremendous value". NB roving
gastronauts – it's "only two minutes to the station
for metropolitan foodies exploring life away from
London!" / **Details:** www.thegoodsshed.co.uk; 9.30 pm;
closed Mon & Sun D.

CARBOST BEAG, HIGHLAND 9–2A

Oyster Shed £35 5|3|3
Carbost IV47 8SE 01478 640383
It's a "bit of a shed", as befits the name, and down
a one-road lane, but Paul McGlynn's humble venture
plays host to the most "wonderful fresh seafood"
on Skye – especially oysters, grown on his own beds
on Loch Harport (he recently launched tours of the
latter). / **Details:** www.skyeoysterman.co.uk; L only.

CARDIFF, CARDIFF 2–2A

Arbennig £47 3|3|4
6-10 Romilly Cr CF11 9NR 029 2034 1264
John & Ceri Cook's buzzy contemporary bistro in
Pontcanna garners praise for its "excellent food
and service" and "lovely atmosphere" too; however,
perhaps owing to the site's pedigree – it was for
many years Le Gallois (RIP) – the odd reporter was
"expecting a more interesting menu". / **Details:**
www.arbennig.co.uk; @ArbennigCardiff; 9.30 pm, Sat
10 pm, Sun 4 pm; closed Mon & Sun D.

Asador 44
14 - 15 Quay Street CF10 1EA 029 2002 0039
Limited but upbeat feedback on this ambitious,
spring 2017 Spanish venture in the city-centre –
new flagship of Tom and Owen Morgan's '44' group
– where dry-aged, old Galician beef cooked over
charcoal is a highlight (also Segovian suckling pig,
Welsh steaks and fish options), alongside a walk-in
wine cave showcasing 140 vintages, and a cheese
room. / **Details:** asador44.co.uk/; @asador44; 10 pm.

Bar 44 Cardiff £35 4|3|4
15-23 Westgate Street CF10 1DD
03333 444049
"A gem among the soulless, huge chain restaurants
in the centre of Cardiff." This latest two-year-
old outlet of a small indie group (with branches
in Cowbridge and Penarth) serves "very good
Spanish tapas (though the helpings are really like
the larger 'raciones')" and feels like "somewhere
with personality". / **Details:** www.bar44.co.uk;
@bar44cardiff; 11 pm, Fri & Sat midnight.

Cafe Citta £35 **3** **4** **3**
4 Church St CF10 1BG 029 2022 4040
A "family-run Italian", with a very narrow but
nonetheless very cosy city-centre dining room, that's very
well-known locally owing to its gimmick-free hit
parade of classics (pasta, pizza); "book, it's always
busy". / *Details: www.cafecitta.com.*

Casanova £49 **3** **4** **2**
13 Quay St CF10 1EA 029 2034 4044
"A rare stand-out in homogenised Cardiff" — a
"small" and "extremely accommodating" haunt
offering "obliging service" and food with a "true
taste of Italy". / *Details: www.casanovacardiff.com;*
@CasanovaCardiff; 10 pm; closed Sun.

Curado £41 **4** **3** **3**
2 Guildhall Pl CF10 1EB 029 2034 4336
Replacing the old Burger King on Westgate Street,
the "new venture from the team behind Ultracomida
in Narberth and Aberystwyth" is a two-floor bar,
restaurant and deli; "here they are serving up
pintxos and a great selection of Spanish drinks to
wash it down with" (including beer especially brewed
for the venue). / *Details: www.curadobar.com/; No
bookings.*

Deck £11 **4** **3** **4**
20 Harrowby St CF10 5GA 02921 150385
Away from the main Cardiff Bay sprawl, this
charismatic indie café and bakery is worth
seeking out for its "great hearty food in a really
friendly atmosphere"; cooked breakfasts and
moreish cakes are a particular forte. / *Details:
www.thedeckcoffeehouse.co.uk; No Amex; No bookings.*

I Giardino Di Sorrento £45 **3** **4** **4**
12 City Rd CF24 3DL 07703 429185
Since opening in 2016, this down-to-earth "family-
run Italian" has become a fast city favourite; it
"specialises in homemade pasta with a good choice
of specials daily", and dishes are mostly inspired
by Sorrento (hence the murals of Piazza Tasso on
the wall). / *Details: @i-giardinidisorrento; 10.30 pm;
closed Sun.*

Grazing Shed £19 **4** **3** **3**
1 Barrack Lane CF10 1AD 07599 882363
The name is a misnomer, but this bright, crate-lined
fast-food spot is a winner, turning out "top burgers"
with a "wonderful range of options" (including
"great combos of toppings for chips"). This, the HQ,
is handy for the St David's 2 complex, and there's
also a younger sibling on St Mary Street. / *Details:
www.thegrazingshed.com; @TheGrazingShed; 10 pm,
Fri & Sat 11pm, Sun 9 pm; No bookings.*

Mint and Mustard £30 **4** **4** **3**
134 Whitchurch Road CF14 3LZ
02920 620333
For the "best and most imaginative Indian food" in

town, try this "amazing, modern" outfit — certainly
"not your usual high street curry house", with its
exciting fusion fare ("especially the soft crab");
add in "fab customer service", and you're "never
disappointed". / *Details: www.mintandmustard.com;
@mintandmustard; 11 pm; No shorts.*

Moksh £39 **5** **4** **3**
Ocean Building, Bute Cr CF10 5AY
029 2049 8120
Rave views this year for this tangerine-coloured
quayside dining room, where chef Stephen Gomes
is hailed by fans as "India's answer to Heston
Blumenthal", delivering "mind blowing" creations
(mainly Goan, but nodding to China and Tibet) that
are "wonders to behold" and are "all served at
the table by the sous chef with pride". / *Details:
www.moksh.co.uk; @mokshcardiff; 10.30 pm, Fri & Sat
11.30 pm; closed Mon.*

The Potted Pig £55 **3** **2** **3**
27 High Street CF10 1PU 029 2022 4817
Located in a former bank vault, this central fixture
wins consistent praise for its modern British
dishes, and there's also a selection of aged Welsh
steaks, and gins. / *Details: www.thepottedpig.com;
@thepottedpig; 9 pm, Fri & Sat 9.30 pm; closed Mon
& Sun D.*

Purple Poppadom £48 **4** **4** **2**
185a, Cowbridge Road East CF11 9AJ
029 2022 0026
It's "not in a great location" (atop a shop on
Cowbridge Road East — even fans "wish it was a
nicer looking place"), but this haute-yet-trad curry
house has a "strong sense of place and origin" and
its "well executed, beautifully presented" fare is a
"must in Cardiff". / *Details: purplepoppadom.com;
@Purple_Poppadom; Mon-Sat 11 pm Sun 9 pm.*

Seafood Shack
5a High St CF10 1AW 07900 424644
A new proto-chain of American-style seafood
restaurants landed in Cardiff in June 2017 (with
eyes on other big cities including Leeds and
Manchester); designed to replicate the seafood
shacks of Florida and California, the concept has
been created by Irish hospitality entrepreneur
Darryl Kavanagh. The Cardiff branch features a
first-floor Champagne and oyster bar. / *Details:
@SeafoodShackCDF.*

Vegetarian Food Studio £24 **4** **4** **2**
115-117 Penarth Rd CF11 6JU 029 2023 8222
With its "very good value" veggie food, reporters are
"absolutely addicted" to this humbly decorated outfit,
by the Taff. / *Details: www.vegetarianfoodstudio.co.uk;
@VegFoodStudio; 9.30 pm, Sun 7 pm; closed Mon; No
Amex.*

Wallys **£26** 3️⃣4️⃣3️⃣
38-46 Royal Arcade CF10 1AE 029 2022 9265
A visit to this Viennese-style kaffeehaus and deli (est. 1981) in the Royal Arcade is "like stepping back in time"; it's "good for a lunch of cheese or cold meats" and there are "lots of coffees and cakes to tempt you" too. / Details: wallysdeli.co.uk; @wallysdeli.

CARLISLE, CUMBRIA 7–2D

Alexandros Greek Restaurant and Deli **£44** 3️⃣4️⃣2️⃣
68 Warwick Road CA1 1DR 01228 592227
A "well-established, buzzy local Greek" where "Aris and his family always go out of their way to give you a good meal" (based on fresh fish, Greek classics or weekly specials) and where there's a "great selection to take away from the deli" too. / Details: www.thegreek.co.uk; 9.45 pm; closed Mon L & Sun.

CARTMEL FELL, CUMBRIA 7–4D

The Masons Arms **£52** 3️⃣4️⃣5️⃣
Strawberry Bank LA11 6NW 01539 568486
"The lovely terrace has a great view of the Fell and on a sunny day this Lakeland pub is packed with walkers". "A trusted old favourite" it's worth the crush for its "good range of beers" and "imaginative" fare ("more pub food than the restaurant variety") – "keep to the smaller portions unless you have a huge appetite!" / Details: www.strawberrybank.com; @StrawberryBank/; W from Bowland Bridge, off A5074; 9 pm. / Accommodation: 7 rooms, from £75

CARTMEL, CUMBRIA 7–4D

L'Enclume **£172** 5️⃣5️⃣4️⃣
Cavendish St LA11 6PZ 01539 536362
"A mind-blowing experience!" – Simon Rogan's converted smithy in a gorgeous Lakeland village remains the north's pre-eminent foodie Mecca. A degree of "art and theatre" add to its appeal, but despite the potential to seem "show-off-y", the dominant theme running through most reports is the "exceptional" combination of "hard-to-beat innovation" – producing "light, clean dishes, packing huge flavours" – juxtaposed with a style that's "natural, and not at all pretentious for a restaurant of such high calibre". Enthusiasm too for a "delightfully simple and clean-lined setting that puts you instantly at ease, along with staff who were knowledgeable but approachable". / Details: www.lenclume.co.uk; @AulisSimonRogan; J36 from M6, down A590 towards Cartmel; closed Mon L & Tue L. / Accommodation: 16 rooms, from £119

Rogan & Co **£69** 3️⃣3️⃣2️⃣
Devonshire Square LA11 6QD 01539 535917
"Michelin star standards at bistro prices" inspires some hugely enthusiastic reviews for Simon Rogan's brasserie spin-off near the main HQ, with fans noting "excellent, balanced and indulgent small dishes with some remarkably bright flavours". It provoked descriptions of almost as many 'bad trips' though, with naysayers dissing a variety of shortcomings including "overbearing service (never mind 'too many cooks', this was definitely a case of 'too many waiters/waitresses)" and "poor execution". / Details: www.roganandcompany.co.uk; @simon_rogan; Mon-Sat 9 pm, Sun 5 pm; closed Sun; No Amex; Credit card deposit required to book.

CASTLE COMBE, WILTSHIRE 2–2B

Bybrook Restaurant, Manor House Hotel **£100** 5️⃣4️⃣4️⃣
SN14 7HR 01249 782206
Luxe manor house in a 'chocolate box' Cotswolds village, regularly acclaimed by gastronauts; (ex-Lucknam Park) chef Rob Potter has been at the stoves since early 2016, providing "excellent" seasonal cuisine ably matched by the "very knowledgeable" sommelier. / Details: www.exclusivehotels.co.uk; @themanorhouse; 9 pm, Fri & Sat 9.30 pm; closed Mon L & Tue L; No jeans; children: 11+. / Accommodation: 48 rooms, from £205

CAVENDISH, SUFFOLK 3–1C

The George **£46** 3️⃣3️⃣3️⃣
The Green CO10 8BA 01787 280248
"This old inn has a very warm charm about it, and is in the middle of a very pretty village"; "the food can always be relied on" (although it's not of a particularly gourmet persuasion) and the set menu in particular "is a steal". / Details: www.thecavendishgeorge.co.uk; @theGeorgecav; 9.30 pm, Sun 3 pm; closed Sun D. / Accommodation: 5 rooms, from £75

CHADDESLEY CORBETT, WORCESTERSHIRE 5–4B

Brockencote Hall **£66** 3️⃣3️⃣4️⃣
DY10 4PY 01562 777876
The Eden Collection's Victorian manor house hotel "is simply brilliant" by most (but not quite all) accounts; since August 2016, former sous chef Tim Jenkins has been at the helm, and his food is, for fans, "as good as gets". Top Tip – "For those wanting to sample the ambience and food quality try high tea...you'll be back for more, I guarantee". / Details:

www.brockencotehall.com; on A448, outside village;
9 pm; No trainers. / **Accommodation:** 21 rooms,
from £135

CHADWICK END, WEST MIDLANDS   5–4C

The Orange Tree   **£44**   3️⃣3️⃣
Warwick Rd B93 0BN   01564 785364
"A menu with wide variety" (including a good
selection of pizza) and "buzzy atmosphere"
help win good all-round marks for this relaxed,
contemporary-style country gastropub. / **Details:**
www.lovelypubs.co.uk/the-orange-tree; @LP_OrangeTree;
9.30 pm, Fri-Sat midnight, Sun 7 pm.

CHAGFORD, DEVON   1–3C

Chagford Inn   **£44**   3️⃣4️⃣2️⃣
7 Mill Street TQ13 8AW   01647 433109
"This former 'spit and sawdust' boozer has now
been transformed into a great village local with
upmarket pub food" (and rooms); "the USP is
the beef menu" – "the chef buys a whole animal
which he butchers and serves in trad and more
unusual dishes". / **Details:** www.thechagfordinn.com/;
@thechagfordinn.

Gidleigh Park   **£165**   5️⃣5️⃣5️⃣
TQ13 8HH   01647 432367
"Michael Wignall has perhaps even surpassed
Michael Caines" at this famous culinary Shangri-
La – a "special" Tudorbethan manor house in the
narrow back-lanes bordering Dartmoor ("if you'rw
looking for a special foodie break, then this is just
the place"). "The exceptional tasting menus top
anything the chef formerly produced at Pennyhill
Park, with a magnificent balance of tastes and
textures" ("sound absurd but marry perfectly"), and
"the intelligent sequencing of dishes" helps create "a
sensational gastronomic treat". There's "a marvellous
wine list" too and "top class service". "After a
meal you can sink into comfortable chairs in the
plush lounge for coffee and then wander around
the beautiful grounds: as an all-round experience,
it's hard to beat". / **Details:** www.gidleigh.co.uk;
@Gidleighhotel; from village, right at Lloyds TSB,
take right fork to end of lane; No jeans; children: 8. /
Accommodation: 24 rooms, from £350

CHANDLER'S CROSS, HERTFORDSHIRE   3–2A

Colette's, The Grove   **£93**   3️⃣3️⃣2️⃣
WD17 3NL   01923 296015
The swish main dining room of this 18th century
mansion, nowadays a luxe hotel, perennially garners
thin feedback and has never really established
itself as a foodie destination. Those who do review

it are impressed however – "if I won the lottery
I would make this my regular place". / **Details:**
www.thegrove.co.uk; @TheGroveHotel; 9.30 pm; D only,
closed Mon & Sun; children: 16+. / **Accommodation:**
227 rooms, from £310

**The Glasshouse, The
Grove**   **£69**   3️⃣3️⃣3️⃣
WD3 4TG   01923 296015
The "superb buffet" ("great for all the family"…
"our granddaughters loved it") with "a top mix
of everything" maintains the appeal of the
"always-buzzy" and "great-fun" second dining
room of this posh country house hotel. / **Details:**
www.thegrove.co.uk; @thegrovehotel; 9.30 pm, Sat
10 pm. / **Accommodation:** 227 rooms, from £310

**Prime Steak & Grill, The
Clarendon**   **£67**   3️⃣2️⃣3️⃣
Redhall Lane WD3 4LU   01923 264580
A converted pub in the leafy outer 'burbs can seem
like "an unlikely countrified location" for this "well
appointed" steak house. Some reporters find it
"hard to grade" ("variable…", "good but not the
best…", "only makes financial sense on a BYO
Monday") but there are no serious complaints and
fans say it's a "super venue" with "excellent" food. /
Details: www.primesteakandgrill.com/chandlers-cross;
@SteakPrime.

CHATTERTON VILLAGE, KENT   3–3B

Shampan Bromley   **£38**   3️⃣3️⃣3️⃣
38 Chatterton Road BR2 9QN   020 8460 7169
This well-established but recently refurbished
Indian of 40 years' standing has spawned
two other spin-offs nearby, and is one of the
best bets for a curry in these parts. / **Details:**
www.shampangroup.com/shampan-bromley.html;
@shampanbromley; Mon-Thu 10.30 pm, Fri & Sat
11 pm, Sun 10 pm.

CHEADLE, CHESHIRE   5–2B

Indian Tiffin Room   **£36**
2 Chapel Street SK8 1BR   0161 491 2020
"Original and forward-thinking but reasonably
priced" – the "fantastically well-flavoured" Indian
street food at this backstreet Cheadle venture has
won it many fans locally. It also has a spin-off in
Manchester's new First Street development: "easier
to get a table, but not sure we like the set-up
as much". / **Details:** www.indiantiffinroom.com;
@Indtiffinroom; 10 pm, Sun 9 pm.

CHEDDINGTON, BEDFORDSHIRE   3–2A

The Old Swan   £56   **3** **4** **4**
58 High St LU7 0RQ   01296 662171
Limited but very positive feedback on this lovingly restored, thatched traditional pub, not far from the Grand Union Canal, which wins all-round high scores for its superior pub grub. / Details: www.theoldswancheddington.co.uk; @theoldswan1; 9 pm; closed Sun D.

CHELTENHAM, GLOUCESTERSHIRE   2–1C

L'Artisan   £61   **3** **3** **3**
30 Clarence St GL50 3NX   01242 571257
Yves and Elisabeth Ogrodzki's decidedly Gallic four-year-old turns out traditional food with good attention to sourcing; ratings are consistently solid here and it's "not expensive". / Details: www.lartisan-restaurant.com.

Bhoomi   £55   **4** **3** **3**
52 Suffolk Rd GL50 2AQ   01242 222010
"Tasty, tasty, quality Indian food" – "with style" and "without compromising on flavour" – ensures the popularity of this "friendly and welcoming restaurant"; even those jaded by the proliferation of "dull and bland" Anglo-Indians found it "amazing, much to our surprise". / Details: www.bhoomi.co.uk; @bhoomichelt.

Le Champignon Sauvage £90   **5** **5** **2**
24-28 Suffolk Rd GL50 2AQ   01242 573449
"Husband and wife have yet to miss a service" at this "sophisticated" and pioneering 30-year-old near the town centre, long renowned as one of the UK's top culinary destinations. For its large fan club – foodies especially – it's a "yardstick by which all else is measured" thanks to the dedication of chef David Everitt Matthias and his "wildly inventive" cuisine (which, for example, included foraged ingredients long before the current vogue for them); plus the "always interesting wine list", about which his wife Helen is "exceptionally knowledgeable". The ambience of this "self effacing, restrained and quiet" venue can – especially at lunch time – be somewhat "iffy" though; and ratings here nearly slipped due to a couple of unusually duff experiences reported this year. / Details: www.lechampignonsauvage.co.uk; @lechampsauvage; 8.45 pm; closed Mon & Sun.

East India Cafe   £51   **3** **3** **2**
103 Promenade GL50 1NW   01242 300850
A "really good Indian" two-year-old that's "different to your standard" curry house, with cuisine "influenced by the British Raj"; "the cocktails and street food nibbles are super" and "the

tasting menus are excellent value" too. / Details: www.eastindiacafe.com; @eastindiacafe; 10 pm, Sun 9 pm; closed Mon.

The Ivy Montpellier Brasserie £54
Rotunda Terrace, Montpellier Street GL50 1SH
01242 894200
In a 'roll-out' that would do McDonald's proud, this iconic brand has gone for it this year, opening virtually simultaneously in practically all of the UK's top restaurant cities. The ambition is impressive: let's hope standards hold up better than they did when, for example 'Browns' tried to pull off a similar trick. Cheltenham's branch opens in early December 2017, inside the grade I listed Montpellier Rotunda. / Details: www.theivycheltenhambrasserie.com; @ivycheltenham.

Koj   £22
3 Regent Street GL50 1HE   01242 580455
MasterChef finalist Andrew Koj spent five years working towards opening his own restaurant; after crowdfunded investment, here it is – the eponymous, Asian café in Cheltenham draws on the chef's half-Japanese heritage and one early report praises "an excellent place to stop for a light meal". / Details: kojcheltenham.co.uk; @KojCheltenham.

Lumière   £91   **5** **5** **4**
Clarence Parade GL50 3PA   01242 222200
"A marriage made in heaven!" – "Helen overseeing the charming, friendly service and her husband Jon creating the beautiful presented dishes" – inspires stellar reviews of the Howe's "relaxing", "fine dining" venture. "Menus are tailored to individual tastes with advance notice and make good use of local ingredients". / Details: www.lumiere.cc; @LumiereChelt; 8.30 pm; closed Mon, Tue L, Wed L, Thu L & Sun; children: 8+ at D.

No 131   £70   **2** **1** **3**
131 Promenade GL50 1NW   01242 822939
Set on the Promenade in prime "Regency Cheltenham", this luxe Georgian townhouse hotel made quite a splash when it opened in 2013; but, while the "cool" vibe ("especially for Cheltenham") and "lovely" decor still impress, service is "slow", competing soundtracks between restaurant and bar can create a "cacophony", and the food is only "OK rather than great, and expensive for what it is". / Details: www.no131.com; @131TheProm; 9.30, Fri & Sat 10.30 pm.

Prithvi   £59   **5** **4** **4**
37 Bath Road GL53 7HG   01242 226229
"Everything is elegant" at this "stylish and modern take on Indian cuisine": the "setting oozes beautiful lighting and crystal clear glasses", staff "go the extra mile" and the "artistic and appealing cuisine"

delivers "excellent, refined flavours". / Details:
www.prithvirestaurant.com; @37Prithvi; 9.30 pm; closed
Mon & Tue L; No Amex.

Purslane   **£64**   4 4 3
16 Rodney Rd GL50 1JJ 01242 321639
Reporters just "love this restaurant" – a small but
"really special" backstreet venue where Gareth
Fulford turns out especially "wonderful fish dishes",
and where "the tasting menu is a particular
triumph". / Details: www.purslane-restaurant.co.uk;
@eatatpurslane; 9.30 pm; closed Mon & Sun.

The White Spoon   **£57**   4 3 3
Well Walk GL50 3JX 01242 228 555
"One of Cheltenham's star restaurants" – this
"excellent" yearling run by Chris White (ex Fat
Duck) and his partner Purdey Spooner "is making
a huge success of this new venue in the Minster
close" with cooking that's "very creative and
beautifully presented". Top Tip – "the set menus are
great value". / Details: www.thewhitespoon.co.uk;
@whitespoonchelt; 9 pm.

CHESTER, CHESHIRE   5–2A

La Brasserie, Chester
Grosvenor   **£69**   2 3 4
Eastgate CH1 1LT 01244 324024
A "good choice of dishes" and a "lovely atmosphere"
(not least since the recent-ish refurbishment) are
just two of the highlights at this buzzy brasserie, set
at pavement level next to the city's iconic clock. /
Details: www.chestergrosvenor.com; 10 pm, Sun 9 pm.
/ Accommodation: 80 rooms, from £230

Brewery Tap   **£28**   2 3 4
52-54 Lower Bridge Street CH1 1RU
01244 340999
From hometown brewery Spitting Feathers, this
favourite real-ale pub offers a stellar range of
cask ales, guest beers and hand-pulled ciders;
the food is never less than "solid" and it enjoys a
"unique" setting in a Jacobean great hall. / Details:
www.the-tap.co.uk.

The Chef's Table   **£55**   4 4 3
4 Music Hall Pas CH1 2EU 01244 403040
"An excellent recent arrival to the Chester dining
scene" – this two-year-old venture down one of the
city's cute city-centre passageways won very high
ratings this year for its "fabulous dishes… unusual
combinations that work really well". / Details:
www.chefstablechester.co.uk; @ChefsTableCH1; closed
Mon & Sun.

Hickorys Smokehouse   **£45**   3 4 4
Souters Lane CH1 1SH 01244 404000
The "best American-style restaurant outside of
the USA" is a claim too far for this riverside

venture – part of a carnivorous local chain; with
Yank competition thin in North Wales however,
it is, at any rate a "crowded" spot that's "tops for
families, with so much for kids to do". / Details:
www.hickorys.co.uk/chester/; @Hickorys_; 11 pm.

Jaunty Goat   **£11**   3 3 3
57 Bridge Street CH1 1NG 01244 421492
A hip, minimal and "slightly off-the-wall" café and
coffee supplier, which moved just a few doors down
from its original location a couple of years back;
the "quite intense" baristas turn out "perfect latte
art", accompanied by "reasonable sandwiches",
cakes and a concise breakfast menu. / Details:
www.jauntygoatcoffee.co.uk/; L only.

Joseph Benjamin   **£54**   3 3 4
140 Northgate Street CH1 2HT
01244 344295
"Lovely people, fantastic food and good prices" are a
winning trio at this "gem" of a deli-restaurant, close
to the city walls. It's "one not to be missed" – but
just remember to "book at lunchtime". / Details:
www.josephbenjamin.co.uk; @joseph_benjamin; Tue &
Wed 3 pm, Thu-Sat 9.30 pm, Sun 4 pm; closed Mon, Tue
D, Wed D & Sun D.

Moules A Go Go   **£53**   3 2 2
39 Watergate Row CH1 2LE 01244 348818
After nearly two decades on the medieval Rows, this
"always reliable" stalwart moved to a new address
(the old La Tasca site) in summer 2016, but all "is
much as previously", from the eponymous molluscs
to rotisserie fare and a "well-priced fixed lunch". /
Details: www.moulesagogo.co.uk; @MoulesaGoGo;
10 pm, Sun 9 pm.

La P'tite France   **£46**   3 3 3
63 Bridge Street CH1 1NG 01244 401635
In the city-centre, a "small French bistro run by
a French husband-and-wife" team; "cheerful and
affable Frédéric Lolliot looks after the front of the
house", while Pantxika Goyhetche produces "good
Gallic country cooking" in her tiny kitchen. / Details:
www.laptitefrance.co.uk/; 9 pm; closed Sun-Tue.

Simon Radley, The Chester
Grosvenor   **£106**   3 4 3
56-58 Eastgate Street CH1 1LT 01244 324024
The "quiet and unhurried" ("slightly stuffy") dining
room in the bowels of the Duke of Westminster's
grand city-centre hotel is "not the cheapest",
but "for an occasion that you want to cherish",
Simon Radley's "superior" cuisine (introduced by
a particularly "delicious" bread trolley) has long
been of note, and is matched with "excellent
accompanying wines" from the huge cellar. /
Details: www.chestergrosvenor.com; @TheGrosvenor;
9 pm; D only, closed Mon & Sun; No trainers; children:
12+. / Accommodation: 80 rooms, from £230

Sticky Walnut £53 ４５４
11 Charles St CH2 3AZ 01244 400400
If there was an award for self-publicity, owner Gary Usher would take first prize, and his force of personality has helped create a national reputation for this cute, small venture in Hoole (just outside the city centre). Its popularity doesn't rest on hype alone though – it's a "perfect neighbourhood bistro", with a "very welcoming and comforting feel to the place", plus "switched on and engaged service", "simple and delicious food" (for example "chateaubriand cooked to juicy perfection") and "a well-priced wine list". / **Details:** *www.stickywalnut.com; @stickywalnut; 9 pm, Fri & Sat 10 pm; Credit card deposit required to book.*

Twenty2, Edgar House £41 ２３５
22 City Walls CH1 1SB 01244 347007
Located on the city's amazing medieval walls, and with "excellent town-house ambience and a location overlooking the river", all agree this small hotel couldn't be better situated. Foodwise highs and lows were reported this year – more feedback please. / **Details:** *www.restauranttwenty2.co.uk; 9 pm, Sun 7 pm.*

Upstairs at the Grill £57 ４４３
70 Watergate St CH1 2LA 01244 344883
Limited, but all-good feedback this year on this split-level steakhouse and bar, which has a big name locally. / **Details:** *www.upstairsatthegrill.co.uk; @UpstairsGrill; 10.30 pm, Sun 9.30 pm; closed Mon L, Tue L & Wed L.*

CHEW MAGNA, SOMERSET 2–2B

The Pony & Trap £60 ５４４
BS40 8TQ 01275 332627
"Truly first-class cooking" ("local ingredients cooked incredibly well") maintains the appeal of Josh Eggleton's "wonderful" country gastropub which has a lovely rural outlook. It's not snooty about it either ("it's the first Michelin-starred restaurant that's let me bring the dog!"). / **Details:** *www.theponyandtrap.co.uk; @theponyandtrap; 8.45 pm; closed Mon; No Amex.*

CHICHESTER, WEST SUSSEX 3–4A

Field & Fork £42 ３２２
4 Guildhall St PO19 1NJ 01243 789915
Sam & Janet Mahoney's "pleasant" three-year-old follow-up to their outpost at the Pallant House Gallery offers "fine-ish dining" – "imaginative and very well-executed" dishes, which are "unfussily presented". Service? – "friendly if a little disinterested at times". / **Details:** *www.fieldandfork.co.uk; @samsfork; 10 pm; L only, closed Mon.*

Pallant Restaurant and Cafe £52 ３２３
East Pallant PO19 1TJ 01243 770827
"After visiting the fine exhibitions of Modernist Art" try this "surprisingly good gallery restaurant" – "a smartly run operation in a relatively small space that matches the quality of the gallery". / **Details:** *www.pallantrestaurantandcafe.co.uk; @EatAtPallant.*

The Richmond Arms £52 ３４３
Mill Road, West Ashling PO18 8EA
01243 572046
"Set in the West Sussex countryside beside a large duck pond, you are always assured of a lovely meal" at this "unpretentious" Goodwood Estate gastroboozer. / **Details:** *www.therichmondarms.co.uk; 9 pm; closed Mon, Tue & Sun D.*

CHINNOR, OXFORDSHIRE 2–2D

The Sir Charles Napier £74 ４３５
Spriggs Alley OX39 4BX 01494 483011
"Off the beaten track in the Chilterns but well worth the journey", Julie Griffith's "quirky but atmospheric" stalwart – a smartly converted pub decorated "with some outstanding original sculptures" – is "perfect for a lunch-stop off the M40" (once you've found the place!), or a day-trip out of the smoke, especially in summer when you can eat in the "exquisite gardens". "Portions seem to have slimmed a little as prices have risen over the years", and service can sometimes seem "distracted", but when it's firing on all cylinders this place is "exceptional on all fronts"; not least its "consistently high quality cooking, over so many years". / **Details:** *www.sircharlesnapier.co.uk; @SirCNapier; 9.30 pm, Sat 10 pm; closed Mon & Sun D.*

CHIPPING CAMPDEN, GLOUCESTERSHIRE 2–1C

The Ebrington Arms £53 ３３３
GL55 6NH 01386 593 223
This quintessential village pub (now with rooms) has kept locals in their cups since the 1640s; currently under the same owners as Killingsworth Castle, it delivers "good, honest pub food cooked with some flair", plus "excellent ales" from the owners' micro-brewery. / **Details:** *www.theebringtonarms.co.uk; @theebrington; 9 pm; No Amex. /* **Accommodation:** *5 rooms, from £110*

CHIPPING NORTON, OXFORDSHIRE 2–1C

Wild Thyme £55 ３４３
10 New St OX7 5LJ 01608 645060
"Just off the main strip in Chipping Norton",

Sally & Nick Pullen's "delightful" restaurant-with-rooms has "some seriously good cooking going on" (with "faultless preparation and presentation" and "respect for seasonality"). / *Details:* www.wildthymerestaurant.co.uk; @wtrestaurant; 9 pm, Fri & Sat 9.30 pm; closed Mon & Sun. / *Accommodation:* 3 rooms, from £75

CHOBHAM, SURREY   3–3A

Stovell's   £73   5 5 4
125 Windsor Road GU24 8QS   01276 858000
"Vaux le détour" – Fernando & Kristy Stovell's beamed farmhouse just outside Chobham deserves some recognition from the Michelin man, for its consistently "assured" and "sublime" cuisine. If there's a quibble it's that "the long and impressive wine list is a tad pricey". / *Details:* www.stovells.com; @Stovells; 10 pm; closed Mon, Sat L & Sun D.

CHOLMONDELEY, CHESHIRE   5–3A

Cholmondeley Arms   £45   3 3 3
Wrenbury Road SY14 8HN   01829 720 300
"In a quirky but interesting old school house" on the Cholmondeley Castle Estate, this boozer-with-rooms is a "bit full of the Cheshire set" on account of its "good, well-cooked gastropub food" ("the pies are a hit") and "amazing" gin. / *Details:* www.cholmondeleyarms.co.uk; @cholmarms; on A49, 6m N of Whitchurch; 10.30 pm; No Amex. / *Accommodation:* 6 rooms, from £80

CHRISTCHURCH, DORSET   2–4C

The Jetty, Christchurch Harbour Hotel & Spa   £62   4 4 5
95 Mudeford BH23 3NT   01202 400950
"Stunning views across Christchurch Harbour add to the exceptional dining experience" at Alex Aitken's "gorgeous and romantic", waterside structure ("there are not many restaurants with a better outlook so don't go in the dark!"). Prices strike some reporters as a little "extortionate" but it's a formidable all-rounder, with skillful cuisine – in particular "seafood is always amazing" – which is "complemented by attentive but unobtrusive service". / *Details:* www.thejetty.co.uk; @alexatthejetty; 9.45 pm, Sun 7.45 pm.

CIRENCESTER, GLOUCESTERSHIRE   2–2C

Jesses Bistro   £53   4 3 3
The Stableyard, Black Jack Street GL7 2AA
01285 641497
"Romantically located behind the main road"

down an alleyway, this cosy town-centre bistro is "part of the adjacent family butchers" – "meat dishes are king" but all the locally sourced fare here is consistently highly rated. / *Details:* www.jessesbistro.co.uk; @jessesbistro; 9.30 pm; closed Mon D & Sun.

Made By Bob, The Cornhall   £51   3 3 3
The Cornhall 26 Market Pl GL7 2NY
01285 641818
A "stylish bar/restaurant/deli that's open for lunch, plus tapas on Friday and Saturday evenings"; it's generally oversubscribed, but this leads to a pleasingly lively vibe. / *Details:* www.foodmadebybob.com; @MadeByBob; 9.30 pm; closed Mon D, Tue D, Wed D, Sat D & Sun D.

CLACHAN, ARGYLL AND BUTE   9–3B

Loch Fyne Restaurant and Oyster Bar   £54   4 4 3
Loch Fyne PA26 8BL   01499 600264
"The freshest seafood is served by friendly staff in a beautiful location" at this famous, out-of-the-way loch-side deli, restaurant, and in-house smoker – the original, 1970s-born inspiration for (but no longer connected to) the now 37-strong national chain. / *Details:* www.lochfyne.com; @lochfyneoysters; 10m E of Inveraray on A83; L only.

CLAUGHTON, LANCASHIRE   5–1A

The Fenwick Arms   £43   3 3 3
Lancaster Rd LA2 9LA   01524 221250
"The Lune Valley now has some excellent gastropubs," but this link in the Seafood Pub Company chain is a real "favourite" for numerous reporters thanks to its "splendid, good-value" fish. While the site, "hard up against the A road", has "long struggled" (under the old regime it "appeared on one of Big Sweary's failing restaurant TV programmes") even sceptics now find it a "useful" spot – "close enough to junction 34 of the M6 to be an attractive stopover". / *Details:* www.fenwickarms.co.uk; 10 pm.

CLAVERING, ESSEX   3–2B

The Cricketers   £47   2 2 3
Wicken Rd CB11 4QT   01799 550442
By the village green, this popular North Essex boozer-with-rooms – owned by Jamie Oliver Snr – continues to turn out "good food with attractive specials" and is solidly well-rated. Quibbles? Perhaps "the menu is a little settled". / *Details:* www.thecricketers.co.uk; @CricketersThe; on B1038

*between Newport & Buntingford; 9.30 pm, Sun 8 pm; No Amex. / **Accommodation:** 14 rooms, from £95*

CLAYGATE, SURREY   3–3A

The Swan Inn   £58 **3**|**3**|**3**
2 Hare Lane KT10 9BS 01372 462 582
*"Overlooking the village green", this year-old pub-with-rooms close to Esher Common wins attention thanks largely to its ownership by star chef Claude Bosi and brother Cedric. Reviews are a little up-and-down but even the least enthusiastic stresses that "the ingredients and cooking are good". / **Details:** www.theswanesher.co.uk; @theswan_esher; 9.30 pm, Sun 8.30 pm.*

CLIFTON, CUMBRIA   8–3A

George & Dragon   £50
CA10 2ER 01768 865381
*"A beautifully renovated pub just outside Penrith" (under the same ownership as Askham Hall) that was "a worthy winner of the Good Pub Guide 2017's best Cumbria's dining pub"; with its "varied and interesting food" it "makes you want to move to Clifton!" / **Details:** www.georgeanddragonclifton.co.uk; @GeorgeDragonCli; on the A6 in the village of Clifton; 9 pm; No bookings. / **Accommodation:** 12 rooms, from £95*

CLIMPING, WEST SUSSEX   3–4A

Bailiffscourt Hotel   £75 **3**|**4**|**5**
Climping St BN17 5RW 01903 723511
*Handy for Arundel Castle, this posh country house and spa sprawls across numerous cottages and houses on a 30-acre plot leading to Climping beach; by all accounts its medieval dining room – mullioned windows, tapestry-clad walls – is also "a great treat". / **Details:** www.hshotels.co.uk; 9.30 pm; Booking max 8 may apply; children: 7+. / **Accommodation:** 39 rooms, from £205*

CLIPSHAM, RUTLAND   6–4A

The Olive Branch   £55 **4**|**4**|**4**
Main St LE15 7SH 01780 410355
This "delightful country pub set in pretty Rutland" is not only "a convenient stopover just off the A1" but "an unexpectedly good gastroboozer", providing not only a "warm and friendly, traditional setting" but also "a very good range of set and à la carte options" featuring "wonderful", "hearty and seasonal" fare. It was at the vanguard of the rural gastropub revolution when it opened over a decade ago and locals say it's "upped its game

*again significantly in recent times". Top Tip – "stay the night in their adjacent Beech House". / **Details:** www.theolivebranchpub.com; @theolivebranch; 2m E from A1 on B664; 9.30 pm, Sun 9 pm; No Amex. / **Accommodation:** 6 rooms, from £135*

CLITHEROE, LANCASHIRE   5–1B

The Assheton Arms   £47 **4**|**4**|**5**
BB7 4BJ 01200 441227
*"In the delightful village of Downham with views of Pendle Hill", "what is probably the flagship of the ever-growing Seafood Pub Company chain" is "such a charming pub in such a charming setting". "There's always lovely fish dishes on offer, sometimes with a quirk added", but – when it comes to the added embellishments – there is a school of thought that "it would be better if they had the confidence to let the fish speak for itself". / **Details:** seafoodpubcompany.com/the-assheton-arms/; @SeafoodPubCo; 9 pm, Fri & Sat 10 pm, Sun 8 pm.*

The Inn at Whitewell   £56 **3**|**3**|**5**
Forest of Bowland BB7 3AT 01200 448222
*"In a beautiful location, by a river in the Forest of Bowland, this ancient inn has 'olde worlde' charm" in abundance, and "has kept an excellent atmosphere despite growing rapidly over the last few years". It is also renowned for "classic food of a very high standard" and a notable cellar, but expansion has taken a little bit of the gloss off standards over the years, and those who know it by its old reputation can feel "it's overhyped, and fine but nothing special" nowadays; whereas to those judging it without the baggage of its recent history it produces "superb local dishes, well-prepared and well-executed". / **Details:** www.innatwhitewell.com/; @innatwhitewell; 9.30 pm.*

CLYTHA LLANVIHANGEL GOBION,
MONMOUTHSHIRE   2–2A

**The Court Dining Room,
Llansantffraed Court
Hotel**   £58 **2**|**3**|**4**
NP7 9BA 01873 840678
*Gorgeously located in rural Monmouthshire, this attractive country house hotel just outside Abergavenny has been run by the same family for 20 years. Reviews in the 2018 survey repeated the some-for-some-against style of recent years, for sceptics "not as expected", for fans "all-round exceptional". / **Details:** www.llch.co.uk; @LLCHotel; 9 pm; No Amex.*

COBHAM, SURREY	3–3B

The Cricketers   **£49**   🗌🗌🗌
Downside Common   KT11 3NX
01932 862105
Solid marks again this year for this 17th-century
Cobham inn – nowadays part of Raymond Blanc's
growing White Brasserie Company. / **Details:**
www.cricketerscobham.com; @thecricketers1; 10 pm,
Fri & Sat 10.30 pm, Sun 9 pm.

The Ivy Cobham Brasserie   **£54**
48 High St   KT11 3EF   01932 901777
In a 'roll-out' that would do McDonald's proud,
this iconic brand has gone for it this year, opening
virtually simultaneously in practically all of the UK's
top restaurant cities. The ambition is impressive:
let's hope standards hold up better than they
did when, for example 'Browns' tried to pull off a
similar trick. / **Details:** theivycobhambrasserie.com;
@IvyCobhamBrass.

The Plough Inn   **£57**   🗌🗌🗌
Plough Lane   KT11 3LT   01932 589790
"A must-go any day of the week" say local fans of
this swish contemporary gastropub in the Plough
Corner Conservation Area near Cobham: the
passion project of four Surrey locals. "I used to
come here from Fulham regularly with my mother
in a wheelchair and a dog in tow and they always
looked after us so well. Thank you!" / **Details:**
www.theploughinncobham.co.uk; @PloughInnCobham;
Mon-Thu 9.30 pm, Fri & Sat 10 pm, Sun 6.30 pm.

COLERNE, WILTSHIRE	2–2B

**Lucknam Park, Luckham Park
Hotel**   **£114**   🗌🗌🗌
SN14 8AZ   01225 742777
With its "beautiful" setting, "fantastic" wines and
"consistently excellent" food from Hywel Jones, this
Palladian country house pile is "pretty well
perfect" by most accounts – be it for a special
occasion dinner or not-so-humble Sunday lunch. /
Details: www.lucknampark.co.uk; @LucknamPark;
6m NE of Bath; 10 pm; closed Mon, Tue-Sat D only,
closed Sun D; Jacket required; children: 5+ D & Sun L. /
Accommodation: 42 rooms, from £360

**Lucknam Park
(Brasserie)**   **£56**   🗌🗌🗌
SN14 8AZ   01225 742777
A "fabulous all-round experience" awaits at this
famed country pile's second restaurant – a relatively
relaxed brasserie, whose set lunch "must be one of
the best value meals out there"; reporters also liked
its "range of healthy alternatives", and being

"attached to the spa is an added bonus" for
virtuous types. / **Details:** www.lucknampark.co.uk;
@lucknampark; 6m NE of Bath; 10 pm; closed Mon
& Sun D.

COLNE ENGAINE, ESSEX	3–2C

Five Bells   **£46**   🗌🗌🗌
7 Mill Ln   CO6 2HY   01787 224166
Limited but upbeat feedback on this pub and
restaurant in a village overlooking the Colne Valley,
on the Essex/Suffolk borders, which wins praise as
an all-round good-value destination; lovely garden in
summer. / **Details:** www.fivebells.net; @The_FiveBells;
9.30 pm, Sun 8.30 pm.

COLNE, LANCASHIRE	5–1B

Banny's Restaurant   **£28**   🗌🗌🗌
1 Vivary Way   BB8 9NW   01282 856220
"Great fish 'n' chips" – "always well-cooked and hot"
("don't forget the mushy peas"!) are the lure to this
"child-friendly" venue, in a former Harry Ramsden's
at the Boundary Mill outlet. The interior itself is
pleasant enough but "a bit like sitting in a service
station café if you face the motorway!" / **Details:**
www.bannys.co.uk; @Bannys; 8.45 pm; No Amex.

COLWELL BAY, ISLE OF WIGHT	2–4D

The Hut   **£52**   🗌🗌🗌
Colwell Chine Road   PO40 9NP   01983 898637
A self-proclaimed, summer-only "easy-going beach
restaurant" (but hut in name only) right by the sand,
and with a rangy terrace to maximise its spectacular
views across the Solent; its fishy fare usually garners
decent feedback, though not everyone is keen
on the "loud yachties" in its clientele. / **Details:**
www.thehutcolwell.co.uk; 9 pm.

CONGLETON, CHESHIRE	5–2B

Pecks   **£73**   🗌🗌🗌
Newcastle Rd   CW12 4SB   01260 275161
It's "astonishing how they maintain service and
quality year after year" at this family-run stalwart, of
nearly three decades' standing; "some slightly more
adventurous items keep the menu contemporary
without sacrificing its core strengths" – and "there
is still nothing like Pecks' ("theatrical" 7-course)
'Dinner at 8'". / **Details:** www.pecksrest.co.uk;
@pecksrest; off A34; 8 pm; closed Mon & Sun D.

COOKHAM, BERKSHIRE	3–3A

Maliks £42 **4 3 4**
High St SL6 9SF 01628 520085
Very solid all-round marks again for this well-known
fixture on the high street, whose deft and refined
Indian cooking is in pleasant contrast to the very
traditional old cottage that it inhabits. / **Details:**
www.maliks.co.uk/; from the M4, Junction 7 for A4 for
Maidenhead; 11.30 pm, Sun 10.30 pm.

The White Oak £45 **3 4 3**
The Pound SL6 9QE 01628 523043
"A consistently high standard of cooking and
ingredients" means it's "always a pleasure" to visit
this "lovely, welcoming and reliable gastro-pub,
which has a beautiful garden for a good summer's
day". "Next day we travelled First Class on British
Airways to Johannesburg, and we both agreed
that our £17.95 lunch at the White Oak was the
better meal!" / **Details:** www.thewhiteoak.co.uk;
@thewhiteoakcoo; 9.30 pm, Sun 8.30 pm; No Amex.

COPSTER GREEN, LANCASHIRE	5–1B

Yu And You £54 **5 4 4**
500 Longsight Rd BB1 9EU 01254 247111
"An unremarkable building on the A59 between
Preston and Clitheroe houses this remarkable
Chinese-inspired restaurant", where the food – "a
westernised style" of Cantonese cuisine "like no
other" – is "not heavy or greasy", with "higher quality
ingredients than you'll find in many Chinatown
based operations". Service is "impeccable" too,
and even if "the decor is slightly dated" there's a
"buzzing" atmosphere. / **Details:** www.yuandyou.com;
@yuandyou; off the A59 7 miles towards Clitheroe;
11 pm; D only, closed Mon.

CORSE LAWN, GLOUCESTERSHIRE	2–1B

Corse Lawn Hotel £55 **3 4 4**
GL19 4LZ 01452 780771
"Excellent in every respect" – the Hine's
"comfortable" country house hotel occupies "a
beautiful, peaceful rural setting"; split between
"better value", "more convivial" bistro and formal
dining room, it serves "classic French food with
some original twists" – and "it's lovely to see (jolly
hostess) Baba out front chatting to guests". /
Details: www.corselawn.com; @corselawn; 5m SW of
Tewkesbury on B4211; 9.30 pm. / **Accommodation:**
18 rooms, from £120

CRANBROOK, KENT	3–4C

Apicius £65 **5 4 2**
23 Stone St TN17 3HF 01580 714666
Closed since October 2015, this remote village
restaurant is back with a bang since August 2016
with the same team at the helm (chef Tim Johnson
and his wife Faith Hawkins). Good news for Kent say
reporters, thanks to its "fantastic food, and the great
idea of being able to have a dish as either starter or
main!" / **Details:** www.restaurant-apicius.co.uk; 9 pm;
closed Mon, Tue, Sat L & Sun D; No Amex; children: 8+.

CRASTER, NORTHUMBERLAND	8–1B

Jolly Fisherman £47 **3 3 5**
Haven Hill NE66 3TR 01665 576461
This low-beamed pub has been a feature of
this fishing village since 1847, but is even more
"superb" after a refurb' several years back added
an airier, sea-view conservatory and outdoor
terrace; the main event – the likes of "great kippers
and crab sandwiches" but "good luck getting a
table!" / **Details:** www.thejollyfishermancraster.co.uk;
@TheJollyCraster; near Dunstanburgh Castle; Mon-Sat
8.30 pm, Sun 7 pm; No Amex; No bookings.

CRATHORNE, NORTH YORKSHIRE	8–3C

Crathorne Arms £51 **3 4 4**
TS15 0BA 01642 961402
"Now in its fourth year and still getting better",
Eugene & Barbara (ex-Cleveland Tontine) McCoy
"certainly have something special here" – namely
"just what a good pub serving quality food should
be". The menu spans "classic and more adventurous
dishes to tempt any taste" and "Eugene certainly
knows his wines". / **Details:** thecrathornearms.co.uk;
11 pm, Sun 7 pm; No bookings.

CREDITON, DEVON	1–2D

The Ring Of Bells £44 **4 4 4**
The Hayes, Cheriton Fitapaine EX17 4JG
01363 860111
This thatched pub is a "delightful Devon village
venue offering a warm friendly welcome, pleasant
garden with beer, cider (and with a lovely B+B
cottage too"). Good marks (if on limited reports) for
its "consistently reliable" fare, from a short menu
focussed mostly on traditional-ish British dishes. /
Details: www.theringofbells.com; 9.30 pm; closed Mon
& Sun D.

CROMARTY, HIGHLAND	9–2C

Sutor Creek £42 4️⃣4️⃣3️⃣
21 Bank St IV11 8YE 01381 600855
"A convivial room with lovely views of the harbour" repays investigation of this *"outstanding"* if humble-looking spot, which specialises in seafood and pizza – both earn recommendations, and *"friendly and efficient service is a bonus"*. / **Details:** www.sutorcreek.co.uk; 9 pm; closed Mon & Tue; No Amex.

CROMER, NORFOLK	6–3C

No1 £35 3️⃣3️⃣3️⃣
1 New St NR27 9HP 01263 512316
"Lovely fresh fish" – *"including (local star) crab of course"* – marks out Galton Blackiston's three-year-old seaside spot; downstairs is a *"frantically busy"* but *"child-friendly"* chippie, upstairs a restaurant with seasonal dishes plus *"wonderful views"* of the Pier and North Sea. Make sure to *"get a window seat"*. / **Details:** www.no1cromer.com; @no1cromer; 9 pm, Sun 7 pm.

CROWLE, WORCESTERSHIRE	5–4B

The Chequers at Crowle
Crowle Green WR7 4AA 01905 381772
This 120 seater pub is part of Warwickshire-based CD Pub Co, and relaunched after a major refurb in March 2016, featuring the group's menu, majoring in steaks from well-known Coventry-based butcher Aubrey Allen. / **Details:** www.thechequersatcrowle.com; @chequerscrowle.

CROYDON, SURREY	3–3B

Karnavar £41 4️⃣4️⃣3️⃣
62 Southend CR0 1DP 020 8686 2436
"Fantastic every time!" – this gourmet curry house inspires nothing but high praise for its *"stunning and elegant contemporary Indian cuisine"*: *"as good as central London but at local prices"*. / **Details:** Karnavar.com; @karnavarlondon; 10.30 pm, Sun 9 pm; closed Mon; No shorts.

McDermotts Fish & Chips £30 5️⃣4️⃣2️⃣
5-7 The Forestdale Shopping Centre Featherbed Ln CR0 9AS 020 8651 1440
"McDermott's is a Croydon phenomenon": albeit one *"set in a dull, suburban shopping centre"*, it *"consistently serves the best fish 'n' chips"*. The ambience – or lack of – has *"improved no end"*

after a recent revamp, and if anything the always *"brilliant"* staff *"seem to have doubled their efforts"* too. / **Details:** www.mcdermottsfishandchips.co.uk; 9.30 pm, Sat 9 pm; closed Mon & Sun.

CRUDWELL, WILTSHIRE	2–2C

The Potting Shed £47 3️⃣2️⃣4️⃣
The St SN16 9EW 01666 577833
"Warm and welcoming…like a big hug" – this *"great local gastropub"* continues to do a swift trade under newish management, serving food that's *"full of flavour"* (*"all I remember are the pig's head croquettes which were divine!"*) / **Details:** www.thepottingshedpub.com; @pottingshedpub; 11 pm; No Amex; No bookings. / **Accommodation:** 12 rooms, from £95

CRUNDALE, KENT	3–3D

The Compasses Inn £53 4️⃣3️⃣4️⃣
Sole St CT4 7ES 01227 700300
"Original and always excellent" – this country pub out in the sticks between Canterbury and Ashford makes a top destination on account of its refined gastropub cuisine and cosy interior. (In September 2017, it won Food Pub of the Year, in John Smith's Great British Pub Awards). / **Details:** www.thecompassescrundale.co.uk; @compasses_inn; 9.30 pm.

CUCKFIELD, WEST SUSSEX	3–4B

Ockenden Manor £96 3️⃣3️⃣3️⃣
Ockenden Ln RH17 5LD 01444 416111
In beautiful Sussex countryside, this *"superb"* Elizabethan country house hotel makes a *"romantic"* retreat from 'the smoke', *"with a wonderful dining room and rooms that are to die for"*. One former fan had a poor visit here this year, but the majority of feedback lauds Steve Crane's accomplished cuisine (there's an à la carte, or choice of six- and seven-course tasting menus). / **Details:** www.hshotels.co.uk/ockenden-manor-hotel-and-spa/; @OckendenManor; 9 pm; No trainers. / **Accommodation:** 28 rooms, from £190

Rose and Crown £51 4️⃣3️⃣3️⃣
London Road, RH17 5BS 01444 414217
Limited but upbeat feedback on this West Sussex pub run by father-and-son team, Mark and Simon Dennis since 2014. Dishes are imaginative rather than being unduly fancy, and wine-match suggestions are a feature on the range of menus. / **Details:** www.roseandcrowncuckfield.co.uk; 9.30 pm, Sat 10 pm, Sun 3.30; closed Mon & Sun D; No bookings.

CUPAR, FIFE 9–3D

The Peat Inn £67 **5 4 4**
KY15 5LH 01334 840206
"A winner on so many levels!" This well-known
country inn a short drive outside of St Andrews
has been a culinary destination for decades, and
run by Geoffrey and Katherine Smeddle since
2006. It had a contemporary refurb a couple of
years ago, and nowadays offers a "relaxed" yet
"first class experience that is hard to surpass"
with classically-rooted, ingredient-led cuisine that's
"exceptional". "We moved to Fife from London last
summer – this is as good as anything we had in
town with none of the pretentiousness: we count
ourselves very lucky to live so close!" / **Details:**
www.thepeatinn.co.uk; @thepeatinn; at junction of
B940 & B941, SW of St Andrews; 9 pm; closed Mon &
Sun. / **Accommodation:** 8 rooms, from £195

DALRY, NORTH AYRSHIRE 9–4B

Braidwoods £74 **5 5 4**
Drumastle Mill Cottage KA24 4LN
01294 833544
"There are very few restaurants that have 17
unbroken years with a Michelin star" but, by all
accounts, Keith & Nicola Braidwood's "unexpected"
venue – cross a cattle grid to get to the isolated
cottage – "always delivers outstandingly on all
fronts" and "no one can make you feel more at
home". / **Details:** www.braidwoods.co.uk; 9 pm; closed
Mon, Tue L & Sun D (open Sun L Oct-April); children:
12+ at D.

DANEHILL, EAST SUSSEX 3–4B

Coach And Horses £47 **3 3 3**
School Ln RH17 7JF 01825 740369
Attractive gardens and above-average pub fare
has ensured that this traditional gastroboozer, split
between a stone-walled dining room and cosy bar,
has remained "a favourite for many years"; it now
offers sparkling wines from the vineyard just up the
road. / **Details:** www.coachandhorses.co; off A275;
10 pm; closed Sun D.

DARLINGTON, COUNTY DURHAM 8–3B

**The Orangery, Rockliffe
Hall** £94 **5 4 4**
DL2 2DU 01325 729999
"A gem set in a fantastic hotel, golf club and
spa" – this striking glass-roofed chamber is part
of a luxurious five-star not far from Scotch Corner.
Reports on Richard Allen's cuisine are not numerous
but couldn't be more complimentary (and in

September 2017, the AA upgraded the restaurant
to being one of the limited number in the country
with four rosettes). / **Details:** www.rockliffehall.com;
@rockliffehall; 9.30 pm; Jacket required.

DARSHAM, SUFFOLK 6–4D

Darsham Nurseries £44 **3 3 4**
Main Rd IP17 3PW 01728 667022
A "quirky" converted-barn cafe in a nursery, where
chef Lola Demille's Middle Eastern-inspired small
plates attest to an "imaginative use of mainly
homegrown produce". Previously lunch-only, as
of April 2017 it now does dinner on Friday and
Saturday. / **Details:** www.darshamnurseries.co.uk;
@DarshamNurserie; closed Mon D, Tue D, Wed D, Thu
D, Sat D & Sun D.

DARTMOUTH, DEVON 1–4D

Rockfish £41 **3 2 3**
8 South Embankment TQ6 9BH 01803 832800
"Even better now they take bookings!" – Mitch
Tonk's "buzzy" original riverside chippie offers
"nothing fancy, but super-fresh fish, beautifully
cooked". Also it's "good to see less common fish
being used such as gurnard or sprats". / **Details:**
www.rockfishdevon.co.uk/index.php; @RockFishDart;
9.30 pm.

The Seahorse £74 **5 4 4**
5 South Embankment TQ6 9BH 01803 835147
"Incredible, fresh grilled fish, stunning in its
simplicity" – "including some never heard of
before!" – "served with real charm" wins huge
praise for Mitch Tonks's "small and welcoming"
dining room right by the seafront: one of the UK's
top destinations for fish and seafood. / **Details:**
www.seahorserestaurant.co.uk; @SeahorseDevon;
9.30 pm; closed Mon & Sun.

DATCHWORTH, HERTFORDSHIRE 3–2B

The Tilbury £57 **3 3 4**
Watton Rd SG3 6TB 01438 815550
"Always on top form" – James & Tom Bainbridge's
village gastroboozer is "more than a pub, and
deserves its popularity" owing to its "lovely" food. /
Details: www.thetilbury.co.uk; @the_tilbury; 9 pm, Fri
& Sat 9.30 pm; closed Mon & Sun D; No bookings.

DAVENTRY, NORTHAMPTONSHIRE 2–1D

Fawsley Hall £62 **2 2 4**
Fawsley NN11 3BA 01327 892000
"In the splendid baronial hall for an afternoon tea
with style and character" it's hard to improve on

this luxurious, countryside hotel. When it comes to the dining room however doubts creep in: despite being "a cramped space in small sections" it "should be a fabulous medieval venue" but instead can suffer from "staff who can't cope" and food that's "expensive for the quality". / **Details:** www.fawsleyhall.com; @FawsleyHall; on A361 between Daventry & Banbury; 9.30 pm. / **Accommodation:** 107 rooms, from £175

Fox & Hounds £52 3️⃣3️⃣3️⃣
Banbury Road, Charwelton NN11 3YY
01327 260611
"Taken over by new people and a huge improvement" – what is nowadays a community-owned gastropub re-opened in 2016 and wins praise for its "well-cooked menu" of superior pub grub. The manager is an ex-sommelier, and there's an interesting selection of craft beers, ciders and hand-pulled real ales. / **Details:** www.foxandhoundscharwelton.co.uk; @Charweltonfox; Mon-Thu 9 pm, Fri & Sat 10 pm, Sun 4 pm.

DEAL, KENT 3–3D

Frog & Scot £47 3️⃣3️⃣3️⃣
86 High Street CT14 6EG 01304 379444
"Already a much-loved Deal institution", despite its relative youth – this "charming, contemporary" pub turns out "perfectly cooked French-influenced dishes which let the quality of the ingredients ("fish direct from the boats on the beach", say) shine through". The owners also run wine bar Le Pinadier, up the road. / **Details:** www.frogandscot.co.uk; No bookings.

DEDHAM, ESSEX 3–2C

Milsoms £49 3️⃣2️⃣3️⃣
Stratford Rd CO7 6HW 01206 322795
On two floors of this Constable Country hotel, a "great pub-style restaurant" serving staples "with a twist"; it has tended to split opinion in the past, but reports – albeit limited – were good this year, praising the "entertaining" staff, "nice accommodation" and "great outdoor patio area for summer lunch". "Only issue: you can't book so have to take pot luck and wait in the bar". / **Details:** www.milsomhotels.com; @milsomhotels; 9.30 pm, Fri & Sat 10 pm; No bookings. / **Accommodation:** 15 rooms, from £120

The Sun Inn £49 3️⃣3️⃣3️⃣
High St CO7 6DF 01206 564325
Perennially a "great place to stop off if visiting Constable Country" – not least for its "lengthy and interesting wines from all round the world" (thanks to the list's curator, Tate wine guru, Hamish Anderson); it's a "place you come to

for lunch and don't leave for hours". / **Details:** www.thesuninndedham.com; @SunInnDedham; 9.30 pm, Fri & Sat 10 pm; No Amex. / **Accommodation:** 7 rooms, from £110

Le Talbooth £78 3️⃣4️⃣5️⃣
Gun Hill CO7 6HP 01206 323150
"What a setting!" – This half-timbered building on the banks of the Stour occupies the very definition of a picturesque setting (it features in Constable's paintings), and "a table here next to the river is especially romantic". But while fans say it "offers 5-star silver service with a smile", critics repeat age-old gripes that "it relies on its name and location" and "though good, needs to up its game". / **Details:** www.milsomhotels.com; @milsomhotels; 5m N of Colchester on A12, take B1029; 9 pm; closed Sun D; No jeans.

DEGANWY, CONWY 4–1D

Paysanne £47 3️⃣3️⃣2️⃣
147 Station Road LL31 9EJ 01492 582079
The Ross clan's longtime neighbourhood staple, a former favourite of Sir Roger Moore (RIP), combines "French bistro style" with prime Welsh ingredients to "excellent" effect (and the fish selection in particular is "superb"). / **Details:** www.paysannedeganwy.co.uk; @PaysanneDeganwy; 9 pm; No shorts.

DENHAM, BUCKINGHAMSHIRE 3–3A

The Swan Inn £52 3️⃣2️⃣3️⃣
Village Road UB9 5BH 01895 832085
"Very easy to get to from London, and nice to walk around the pretty village afterwards" – no wonder this gastroboozer (near the A40/M25 intersection), equipped with a pleasant garden, is so "popular and crowded" ("especially for Sunday lunch"); this year there were particular bouquets for the "delicious soufflés both savoury and sweet". / **Details:** www.swaninndenham.co.uk; @swaninnub9.

DERBY, DERBYSHIRE 5–3C

Darleys £64 4️⃣4️⃣4️⃣
Darley Abbey Mill DE22 1DZ 01332 364987
In a World Heritage-listed old mill, this "welcoming" fixture is still a "favourite place for a special occasion", offering "amazing value for money" and food that's "reliable and sometimes really good". It's "best on a sunny day when the new terrace beckons", with its views of the "spectacular weir" and "kayaks slaloming". / **Details:** www.darleys.com; @DarleysDerby; 9 pm; closed Sun D; No Amex; children: 10+ Sat eve.

Ebi Sushi £41 5 3 2
59 Abbey St DE22 3SJ 01332 265656
"A tiny café serving a range of lovingly presented Japanese dishes, including, of course, sushi. You will need to book quite a way in advance as it is always full of Japanese clients; Toyota is just down the road (literally) and the East Midlands has had nothing like it before…but, then again, nor will you". / ***Details:*** *10 pm; D only, closed Mon & Sun; No Amex.*

DINTON, BUCKINGHAMSHIRE 2–3C

La Chouette £63 4 4 3
Westlington Grn HP17 8UW 01296 747422
A visit to eccentric owner Freddie's Belgian-accented venture is quite an experience; but while not all respond well to his singular hosting style (he "never went to charm school") even sensitive types are duty bound to concede that "he can cook!" (And he has a good nose for interesting vintages too.) / ***Details:*** *www.lachouette.co.uk; off A418 between Aylesbury & Thame; 9 pm; closed Sat L & Sun; No Amex.*

DONHEAD ST ANDREW, WILTSHIRE 2–3C

The Forester Inn £49 3 4 4
Lower Street SP7 9EE 01747 828038
Head along "muddy lanes to nowhere" and with luck you'll end up at this "warm, welcoming, large and gorgeous" gastroboozer; "fish is a surprise speciality this far from the sea, and is very good to eat – but so is everything else". / ***Details:*** *www.theforesterdonheadstandrew.co.uk; @ForesterNews; off A30; 9 pm; closed Sun D.*

DORCHESTER, DORSET 2–4B

Sienna £52 4 4 3
36 High West Street DT1 1UP 01305 250022
MasterChef finalist Marcus Wilcox, who took up the baton here in May 2015, seems to be an able replacement for former owners Russell & Elena Brown at this tiny 16-seat dining room, turning out "well-crafted" and "tasty" British food that's "unlike anything else in Dorset". / ***Details:*** *www.siennadorchester.co.uk; @siennadorset; 9 pm, Sun 2 pm; closed Mon, Tue L & Sun; No Amex; children: 12+.*

DORKING, SURREY 3–3A

Sorrel
77 South Street RH4 2JU 01306 889414
In October 2017, Steve Drake (who established nearby Drakes, now re-named The Clock House) opened his new, 40-cover fine dining venture, with open kitchen, of which the highlight is a 9-course taster menu (but there is a 5-course alternative), showcasing British cuisine. "Obviously there will be a few similarities [with Drakes] but I want to move it on". / ***Details:*** *www.sorrelrestaurant.co.uk; @SteveDrakeFood.*

DORNOCH, HIGHLAND 9–2C

Dornoch Castle Whisky Bar and Bistro £52 3 3 3
Castle Street IV25 3SD 01862 810216
Family-owned hotel in a picture-book castle building that's been a hotel since the 1940s. The dining room is "not ostentatious" and features a modern bistro menu incorporating steaks and Scottish seafood alongside more international dishes. / ***Details:*** *www.dornochcastlehotel.com/dining/; @dornochcastle; Booking evening only.*

DOUGLAS, ISLE OF MAN 7–4B

Tanroagan £67 4 3 3
9 Ridgeway St IM1 1EW 01624 612355
This "small and intimate restaurant close to the harbour" – less unassuming since a recent-ish revamp – gets, for its many local fans, an "equal first for best fish and seafood" on the Isle of Man. / ***Details:*** *tanroagan.co.uk/; 9.30 pm.*

DREWSTEIGNTON, DEVON 1–3C

The Old Inn £68 5 5 3
EX6 6QR 01647 281276
"Wonderfully tasty food is served impeccably in a homely atmosphere" at Duncan Walker (ex-Gidleigh Park) and Anthea Christmas's restaurant-with-rooms, on the edge of Dartmoor. For one reviewer, the "personal service" starters with an "ideal" reception by "two friendly golden retrievers" – though "with just three tables in a small room" (and 17 covers total) you can't help but snoop on fellow diners. / ***Details:*** *www.old-inn.co.uk; @duncansoldinn; 9 pm; closed Sun-Tue, Wed L, Thu L; No Amex; children: 12+.* ***Accommodation:*** *3 rooms, from £90*

DUNBLANE, PERTH AND KINROSS 9–4C

Cromlix House £59 3 3 4
Kinbuck FK15 9JT 01786 825450
Sir Andy Murray's new Perthshire mansion is a "truly wonderful place", and according to most (if not quite all) reports offers a "fine blend of classic hotel and contemporary cooking" in its glass-walled conservatory restaurant (created in consultation with Albert Roux). / ***Details:*** *www.cromlix.com; @CromlixHotel.*

DUNMOW, ESSEX	3–2C

The Flitch of Bacon £75 4️⃣2️⃣3️⃣
The St CM6 3HT 01371 821660
"Multiple courses of deliciousness… but a long way from Daniel Clifford's original 'pub' mission statement". This two-year-old gastropub from the Midsummer House chef has gradually metamorphosed away from its original egalitarian aims and its relaunch in April 2017 confirmed its new fine dining mission. On most (if not quite all) accounts the experience is "expensive but worth it". / Details: www.flitchofbacon.co.uk; @flitchofbaconld; 9 pm, Sun 6.30 pm; Booking max 6 may apply.

DUNVEGAN, HIGHLAND	9–2A

The Three Chimneys £91 5️⃣4️⃣5️⃣
Colbost IV55 8ZT 01470 511258
"A long way to go, but boy is it worth it". This "most magical and mystical location" – a "remote" old crofter's cottage "with a little river running past" and "the most amazing views" – is often completed in reports by "some of the best food I've ever eaten". "The colourful food is beautifully presented and tastes fantastic" and experiences at the Chef's Table are particularly memorable. / Details: www.threechimneys.co.uk; @3_chimneys; 5m from Dunvegan Castle on B884 to Glendale; 9.30 pm ; children: 8+. / Accommodation: 6 rooms, from £345

DURHAM, CO DURHAM	8–3B

Crook Hall £33 3️⃣3️⃣5️⃣
Frankland Ln, Sidegate DH1 5SZ
0191 384 8028
"Five minutes from the centre of Durham", a "lovely house with gardens" whose "period room is gorgeous to eat in"; the garden café is "much less posh and expensive" than the hall itself but the food (at least tea) "seems to be the same", with "super scones and homemade cakes" a feature. / Details: www.crookhallgardens.co.uk; @CrookHall.

The Garden House Inn £47 3️⃣3️⃣3️⃣
Framwellgate, Peth DH1 4NQ 0191 386 3395
"A welcome addition to the offer in Durham"; Ruari MacKay, head chef at Terry Laybourne's now shuttered local foodie beacon Bistro 21, has decamped to this country-style low-ceilinged pub. His "imaginative" cuisine ranges all over the place – lobster sandwiches "to die for", Korean pork belly, Thai soup – but the results are "very good" and "excellent value" too. / Details: www.gardenhouseinn.com; @gardenhouseinn; 9.30 pm, Sun 6 pm.

DYFED, PEMBROKESHIRE	4–4B

The Grove - Narberth £89 3️⃣3️⃣4️⃣
Molleston SA67 8BX 01834 860915
"Just such a pleasant experience overall" – a plush country bolthole, overlooking the Preseli Hills; chef Allister Barsby, ex-of the famed Gidleigh Park, joined in early 2016 and supervises the ultra-locally sourced food. There was the odd off-report this year – hopefully just a blip. / Details: www.thegrove-narberth.co.uk/; @GroveNarbeth; 9.30 pm.

EARLS COLNE, ESSEX	3–2C

The Lion £52
High Street CO6 2PA 01787 226823
Traditional country pub inspiring limited but enthusiastic feedback. Most of the cooking takes place in a wood-fired oven, which delivers a variety of pizzas, plus a 'flagship Bavette Steak'. / Details: www.lionearlscolne.co.uk; @Lion_EarlsColne; 9.30 pm; No bookings.

EAST CHILTINGTON, EAST SUSSEX	3–4B

Jolly Sportsman £50 4️⃣4️⃣4️⃣
Chapel Ln BN7 3BA 01273 890400
"In the middle of nowhere" – sat nav will be a necessary evil – Bruce Wass's "cracking", "charmingly located" gastropub continues to impress with its "lack of pretense" and "excellent" cooking (not to mention its superior outdoor playground). / Details: www.thejollysportsman.com; @JollySportsman1; NW of Lewes; 9.30 pm, Fri & Sat 10 pm; closed Mon & Sun D; No Amex.

EAST CHISENBURY, WILTSHIRE	2–3C

Red Lion Freehouse £61 3️⃣4️⃣3️⃣
SN9 6AQ 01980 671124
"After taking over a somewhat dingy old man's pub, Zoe, Patrick and team have created a destination gastroboozer", where "the focus is on food rather than fussiness – the epitome of excellent, casual dining". / Details: www.redlionfreehouse.com; @redlionfreehse; Mon-Sat 9 pm, Sun 8 pm; No Amex; No bookings. / Accommodation: 5 rooms, from £130

EAST GRINSTEAD, WEST SUSSEX	3–4B

Gravetye Manor £105 3️⃣3️⃣5️⃣
Vowels Lane RH19 4LJ 01342 810567
"George Blogg's culinary touch is light, subtle and glorious" at this "beautiful old Elizabethan manor

house hotel with lovely old furniture". Without downplaying his contribution however, for many reporters "the highlight of a visit here remains the wonderful and extensive grounds" (which also contribute produce for the kitchen) – a "perfect setting" (which in the early 20th century was one of the most famous gardens in England). Stop Press: In November 2017, the hotel announced a four-month closure in early 2018 for the construction of a new restaurant, featuring a glass wall with views onto the gardens. / Details: www.gravetyemanor.co.uk; @GravetyeManor; 2m outside Turner's Hill; 9.30 pm; Booking max 8 may apply; children: 7+. / Accommodation: 17 rooms, from £250

EAST MOLESEY, SURREY   3–3A

Mezzet   **£36**   4️⃣4️⃣4️⃣
43 Bridge Rd KT8 9ER   020 8979 4088
"Authentic Lebanese food, a warm welcome and always a buzzing atmosphere" are the hallmarks of this polished venture; there's a younger Spanish-slanted sibling, Mezzet Dar, down the road. / Details: www.mezzet.co.uk; @Mezzet; 10 pm, Sun 9 pm.

EASTBOURNE, EAST SUSSEX   3–4B

The Mirabelle, The Grand Hotel   **£69**   2️⃣3️⃣3️⃣
King Edwards Parade BN21 4EQ
01323 412345
"A reminder of a more gilded age!" – this grand hotel-restaurant has long been a haven of old-school values, not least its "charming" service. Some doubts crept in this year however, and though it still wins many endorsements for its "superb cuisine" and "extensive wine list" it also took flak for some "bland" meals, or for seeming too "old fashioned and stuffy" generally. / Details: www.grandeastbourne.com; @Grandeastbourne; 10 pm; closed Mon & Sun; Jacket required. / Accommodation: 152 rooms, from £199

Wish Tower Restaurant
Wish Tower, South Downs Way BN21 4BY
awaiting tel
A £2m government-funded scheme to regenerate Eastbourne's shorefront after fire devastated its 146-year-old pier includes this £1.2m restaurant housed within the town's Wish Tower set to open spring 2018. Rick Stein's company was at one point rumoured to be favourite to head up the new venture, however the plum site will in fact house an outpost of French bistro chain Bistrot Pierre.

EASTON GREY, WILTSHIRE   2–2C

The Dining Room, Whatley Manor   **£131**   3️⃣3️⃣3️⃣
SN16 0RB   01666 822888
"A new chef has brought new ideas" – many of them imported from Japan and Korea – to this luxurious hotel dining room, where the start turn is the "real indulgence" of its 12-course tasting menu, which won very solid (if not absolutely stellar) ratings this year. Martin Bruge – who departed in December 2016 – had been at the stoves for 13 years and won it two Michelin Stars, and youngster 26-year-old Niall Keating, his successor will doubtless breathe a sigh of relief that in October 2017 he achieved one of the tyre men's gongs after less than a year at the stoves. / Details: www.whatleymanor.com; 8 miles from J17 on the M4, follow A429 towards Cirencester to Malmesbury on the B4040; 9.30 pm; D only, closed Mon-Tue; No jeans; children: 12+. / Accommodation: 23 rooms, from £305

EDINBURGH, CITY OF EDINBURGH   9–4C

Aizle   **£68**   5️⃣5️⃣3️⃣
107-109 St. Leonard's Street EH8 9QY
0131 662 9349
A three-year-old neo-bistro "with no fixed menu but a larder of seasonal ingredients that the chef plays with each night"; notwithstanding one bad trip reported, all other feedback on this five-course experience is of the 'rave review' variety. / Details: www.aizle.co.uk; @Aizle_Edinburgh; 9 pm.

Angels With Bagpipes   **£55**   3️⃣3️⃣4️⃣
343 High St, Royal Mile EH1 1PW
0131 220 1111
The "sumptuous surroundings" of an ancient building on the Royal Mile lend character to the Valvona & Crolla clan's two-floor operation (downstairs is Chanters, and upstairs the more intimate Halo). The "modern Scottish cuisine" contributes to a "lovely romantic evening", and one that's "surprising good given the tourist-trap location". / Details: www.angelswithbagpipes.co.uk; @angelsfood; 9.45 pm.

Beer Kitchen   **£40**   3️⃣3️⃣3️⃣
81-83 Lothian Road EH3 9AW   0131 228 6392
As per the name, it's the "amazing selection of craft beers from Innis and Gunn (who run it) and other brewers" that star at this industrial-styled bar/kitchen, handy for Usher Hall; wash it down with "good gastropub food at a reasonable price". / Details: www.thebeerkitchen.co.uk/bars/edinburgh/.

Bell's Diner £32 **3** **3** **3**
7 St Stephen St EH3 5EN 0131 225 8116
"Nothing fancy – just decent burgers, friendly
service and a laid-back ambience" is the deal
at this no-nonsense diner, which has been a
Stockbridge standby since 1972: "it seems like it's
been here forever! But it's totally reliable". / **Details:**
www.bellsdineredinburgh.co.uk; 10 pm, Mon 9 pm, Sun
9.30 pm; closed weekday L & Sun L; No Amex.

Bia Bistrot £42 **5** **5** **4**
19 Colinton Rd EH10 5DP 0131 452 8453
"What a find!" – a tucked-away and affordable
Morningside bistro where the local/seasonal food
(from an "interesting and unusual menu") is "always
exceptionally good". Add in "friendly, professional
service" and it's several reporters' "restaurant of
choice". / **Details:** www.biabistrot.co.uk; 10 pm.

Café Marlayne £47 **2** **3** **3**
1 Thistle Street EH2 1EN 0131 226 2230
This "friendly and fun" bistro has a "proper French
atmosphere" and "offers good value" for money by
the city's standards; same goes for the Antigua Street
sibling. / **Details:** www.cafemarlayne.com/thistle-street;
10 pm; No Amex.

The Café Royal Bar £59 **2** **3** **5**
19 West Register St EH2 2AA 0131 556 1884
A "great 19th century location ("smart but not
stuffy") with tiled walls", spectacular mosaic
windows and acres of Victorian mahogany; slightly
less superlatively, the "fish-dominated menu"
is merely "competently executed". (NB "there's
demarcation between the bar and restaurant
menus"). / **Details:** www.caferoyaledinburgh.co.uk/;
9.30 pm; children: 5.

Café St-Honoré £54 **3** **3** **4**
34 NW Thistle Street Ln EH2 1EA
0131 226 2211
"Perfect for that romantic occasion", but also a
"reliable choice" for a "great value lunch" or
"consistently good evening meal" – Neil Forbes's
"small" and "intimate" New Town brasserie ticks all
the boxes of a "classic French restaurant". / **Details:**
www.cafesthonore.com; @CafeStHonore; 10 pm;
SRA-Food Made Good – 3 stars.

The Castle Terrace £95 **3** **3** **3**
33-35 Castle Ter EH1 2EL 0131 229 1222
This high profile castle-side dining room, run with
the involvement of Tom Kitchin, elicited mixed
reviews this year. Fans accord it the highest ratings,
praising chef/patron Dominic Jack's "awesome"
cuisine, but quite a number of reviewers this year
found it "overpriced and underwhelming". / **Details:**
www.castleterracerestaurant.com; @dominicjack;
10 pm; closed Mon & Sun.

Chaophraya £52 **3** **4** **4**
33 Castle St EH2 3DN 01312 267614
"Views out over Edinburgh Castle" are a bonus
at this "really welcoming" contemporary Thai,
praised for its "lovely staff" and "a wide choice
of dishes all presented wonderfully". / **Details:**
www.chaophraya.co.uk; @ChaophrayaThai; On the 4th
Floor ; 10 pm.

Chop Chop £37
248 Morrison St EH3 8DT 0131 221 1155
Haymarket Chinese whose claim to fame is the
introduction of the dumpling to Edinburgh. Too
limited feedback for a rating, but one early reporter
notes: "service can be hit 'n' miss, the décor is
basic, the room can be draughty, but, on a good
day, dumplings, noodles and (interestingly) many of
their salads must be amongst the tastiest and most
authentic around!" / **Details:** www.chop-chop.co.uk;
10 pm; closed Mon; No Amex; No bookings.

The Dining Room £37 **4** **4** **5**
28 Queen St EH2 1JX 0131 220 2044
This year-old relaunch of The Scotch Malt Whisky
Society's dining room on the first floor of its
Georgian townhouse HQ was named AA Scottish
Restaurant of the Year in September 2017. Our
survey feedback is limited but extremely positive
praising "consistently imaginative tasty food and
great value for money". There's a short à la carte
here of which the most impressive feature is the
cheeseboard, or a £75 taster menu (including a
wine or whisky match at each stage). / **Details:**
www.thediningroomedinburgh.co.uk/booking;
@TheDiningRoomEd; 11.30 pm.

Dishoom Edinburgh £36 **4** **4** **4**
3a St Andrew Square EH2 2BD 01312 026 406
"Love it!" Folk of Edinburgh have rejoiced at the
"excellent all-round experience" offered by their
very own branch of this smash-hit Mumbai-style
import, which opened in St Andrew Square late last
year, with its "different" Indian dishes and "capable"
service. As in London, fans just "wish they took
bookings". / **Details:** www.dishoom.com; @Dishoom;
Mon-Wed 11 pm, Thu-Sat midnight; Sun 11 pm.

The Dogs £41 **3** **3** **3**
110 Hanover St EH2 1DR 0131 220 1208
"A great alternative to stuffy dining" – this "quirky
and fun" city-centre gastropub ("tasty with attitude")
has built up quite a local following for its "cheap and
cheerful cuisine". / **Details:** www.thedogsonline.co.uk;
@thedogsedin; 10 pm.

Educated Flea £44 **3** **4** **2**
32b Broughton St EH1 3SB 01315 568092
The "friendly and reasonably priced" new sibling
to Three Birds and Apiary is a dinky spot (with a
self-proclaimed "wee" wine list to match); pickling,
smoking and preserving is all done in-house, and

the menu picks and mixes from all over the place – South Africa, Scandinavia, the Middle East – to "interesting" effect. / *Details:* educatedflea.co.uk/; @edfleaedinburgh; 10 pm, Sun-Mon 9 pm.

El Cartel £25 4|3|4
64 Thistle St EH2 1EN 0131 226 7171
Despite a rough start – months after its November 2016 opening it closed following a fire – this small, dark New Town joint is doing a swift trade in "absolutely great Mexican" grub; join the queue for the "best tacos" around, frozen margaritas, mezcals etc ("I dream of the guacamole"). / *Details:* www.elcartelmexicana.co.uk; @elcartelmexican; Sun-Thu 10 pm, Fri & Sat midnight; No bookings.

L'Escargot Bleu £53 3|3|4
56 Broughton St EH1 3SA 0131 557 1600
In the West End, this "very French" spot, with clean, modern decor and a "lovely atmosphere", continues to please with "simple" bistro fare that's "very enjoyable". / *Details:* www.lescargotbleu.co.uk; @Lescargot_B; 10 pm, Fri & Sat 10.30 pm; closed Sun (except Festival); No Amex.

Favorita £43 4|4|4
325 Leith Walk EH6 8SA 0131 554 2430
"Do you like pizzas? Do you like proper Italian pizzas?" – the Crolla clan's "family favourite", on Leith Walk, turns out some "superb" wood-fired examples, plus homemade ice-cream, sharing platters and pasta. / *Details:* www.la-favorita.com; 11 pm.

Field £42 3|3|3
41 West Nicolson St EH8 9DB 01316 677010
"Lovely" if "tiny dining room" in the old town that wins outsized praise for its "fantastic food at a great price". / *Details:* www.fieldrestaurant.co.uk; @Field_Edinburgh; 9 pm; closed Mon.

Fishers Bistro £54 3|3|4
1 The Shore EH6 6QW 0131 554 5666
The original Fishers occupies a 17th century Leith watchtower, and has been a go-to for enjoyable fish and seafood for over two decades; consistently high ratings this year. / *Details:* www.fishersrestaurants.co.uk; @FishersLeith; 10.30 pm.

Fishers in the City £52 3|2|3
58 Thistle St EH2 1EN 0131 225 5109
"Smack in the city-centre" near the National Gallery, this well-established fish bistro is "always a pleasure" thanks to its "calm" style and "wide range of fish dishes" that are "reliable" and well-priced. / *Details:* www.fishersrestaurants.co.uk; @FishersLeith.

Galvin Brasserie de Luxe, The Caledonian £51
Princes St EH1 2AB 0131 222 8988
Good but surprisingly limited feedback this year for the Galvin brothers's smart hotel brasserie,

which is celebrating its fifth year. / *Details:* www.galvinbrasseriedeluxe.com; @galvinbrasserie; 10 pm, Sun 9.30 pm; Booking max 8 may apply. / *Accommodation:* 245 rooms, from £325

Gardener's Cottage £50 4|4|4
1 Royal Terrace Gardens, London Road EH7 5DX 0131 558 1221
"Completely original, full of life, soul and glorious seasonal food" – "You have to share tables (which is not for everyone)" at Dale Mailley and Edward Murray's "intimate" and "friendly" sustainably-minded venture ("enhanced by the turntable playing vinyls plucked from the stack"), in a small, stone building in the middle of Royal Terrace Gardens. In mid 2017, they opened a new spin-off, Quay Commons – a Leith bakery. / *Details:* www.thegardenerscottage.co; @gardenersctg; 10 pm; closed Tue & Wed.

La Garrigue £57 3|3|3
31 Jeffrey St EH1 1DH 0131 557 3032
"Dozens of wines (particularly from Languedoc) that you don't see anywhere else", plus "an outstanding menu of dishes from south-west France" ("basic French peasant food done very well") wins enthusiastic praise for Jean-Michel Gauffre's Old Town stalwart, behind Waverley Station. / *Details:* www.lagarrigue.co.uk; @lagarrigue; 9.30 pm.

Grain Store £68 3|2|4
30 Victoria St EH1 2JW 0131 225 7635
A reliable and "quirky", many-chambered fixture occupying a former storeroom on a touristy street in the Old Town, whose essentially classic Scottish cuisine is consistently well rated. / *Details:* www.grainstore-restaurant.co.uk; @grainstoreedin; Mon-Sat 9.45 pm, Sun 9.30 pm; closed Sun L.

Hendersons The Salad Table £38 2|2|2
94 Hanover St EH2 1DR 0131 225 2131
"For vegetarians seeking good food", Scotland's oldest veggie (est. 1962) has long been of note, and even if it's style is not cutting edge – "what vegetarian food was like in the 80's: if you're used to the quality and inventiveness of Terre à Terre – or even Food for Friends in Brighton – this will take you back to your student days" – provisions are nevertheless "plentiful, healthy and tasty". Its old New Town crypt branch is sadly now long RIP – additions include a vegan on Thistle Street and Henderson's Holyrood, but this branch, below the original deli/shop, is "increasingly pleasant" and sometimes with entertainment ("the atmosphere was – surprisingly! – improved by a gypsy swing trio…)" / *Details:* www.hendersonsofedinburgh.co.uk; @HendersonsofEdi; Mon-Thu 9 pm, Fri & Sat 10 pm, Sun 4 pm; closed Sun; No Amex.

The Honours £70 3️⃣3️⃣3️⃣
58a, North Castle Street EH2 3LU
0131 220 2513
"Maintaining high standards under the new head chef" – Martin Wishart's New Town brasserie spin-off is almost invariably praised for its "delicious food" (particularly its "great steak"). However, in the same breath, reports almost invariably caution that "it's expensive for what it is". / Details: www.thehonours.co.uk; @TheHonours; 10 pm; closed Mon & Sun.

The Ivy on the Square £54
6 St Andrew Square EH2 2BD 0131 526 4777
In a 'roll-out' that would do McDonald's proud, this iconic brand has gone for it this year, opening virtually simultaneously in practically all of the UK's top restaurant cities. The ambition is impressive: let's hope standards hold up better than they did when, for example 'Browns' tried to pull off a similar trick. / Details: theivyedinburgh.com; @ivyedinburgh.

Kanpai £36 4️⃣4️⃣3️⃣
8 - 10 Grindlay Street EH3 9AS
0131 228 1602
Handy for the Lyceum Theatre, this offshoot of local fixture Sushiya is a nicely minimal spot, with a calming, woody interior; less noodle-heavy than its parent, it focuses on "good, carefully prepared" sushi and sashimi. / Details: www.kanpaisushiedinburgh.co.uk/; 10.15 pm, Fri & Sat 10.30 pm; closed Mon.

The Kitchin £106 5️⃣3️⃣4️⃣
78 Commercial Street EH6 6LX
0131 555 1755
"They clearly value great produce and know just what to do with it" at Tom and Michaela Kitchin's Leith warehouse-conversion (expanded a year or two ago), which inspires many passionate reports of "outstanding meals every time" from its array of à la carte, set and tasting menus. The odd critic feels "the place thinks it is Michelin 3-star and charges accordingly", but for the vast majority of reporters it delivers "high end dining without all the pretentiousness". / Details: www.thekitchin.com; @TomKitchin; 10 pm, Fri & Sat 10.30 pm; closed Mon & Sun; Booking max 7 may apply; children: 5+.

Kyloe £57 4️⃣3️⃣2️⃣
1-3 Rutland Street EH1 2AE 01312 293402
"A great location for a business lunch – in the centre of town, with a great outlook and view of the castle" – is not the sole attraction of 'Edinburgh's leading gourmet steak restaurant' (on the first floor of a hotel) – the "brilliantly sourced steaks" (pedigree Aberdeen Angus) are "an excellent treat!" / Details: www.kyloerestaurant.com; @Kyloe_Edin; 10.30 pm.

Mimis Bakehouse £28 4️⃣4️⃣4️⃣
63 Shore EH6 6RA 0131 555 5908
The Leith original of this kitsch bakery café is a top destination for an "amazing afternoon tea" in "gorgeous surroundings" (or, for early-birds, their "'Before Noon tea' is well worth a visit" too). Also with a compact Royal Mile branch and Corstorphine yearling. / Details: mimisbakehouse.com; Online only.

Mother India's Cafe £35 5️⃣4️⃣3️⃣
3-5 Infirmary St EH1 1LT 0131 524 9801
With "Indian tapas that are almost too good to share", and mains that are "lovely and light", this Glasgow import has risen high in Auld Reekie's rankings over the past decade thanks to its "authentic and delicious" cooking. / Details: www.motherindiaglasgow.co.uk; @official_mindia; 10.30 pm, Fri & Sat 11 pm, Sun 10 pm; No Amex.

Navadhanya Edinburgh £51 4️⃣3️⃣3️⃣
88 Haymarket Terrace EH12 5LQ
0131 281 7187
"My new favourite in town!" – "With a range including authentic South Indian food (good dosas) and a cheery buzz about the place, plus very friendly staff", this shop-conversion near Haymarket Station offers very good, ambitious 'nouvelle Indian' cuisine. / Details: www.navadhanya-scotland.co.uk; @Navadhanya_Edin; 10.30 pm, Sun 9.30 pm.

New Chapter £65 3️⃣4️⃣3️⃣
18 Eyre Pl. EH3 5EP 0131 556 0006
"An exceptional value set lunch" is a key feature at this popular fixture between New Town and Canonmills, whose "well-cooked and thought-out" local food, by Maciek Szymij, ex-of Harvey Nichol's Fourth Floor restaurant, is "more than expected for the simple bistro ambience". It has just opened a sibling in the West End too (Otro, 22 Coates Crescent, EH3). / Details: newchapterrestaurant.co.uk; @newchapter18; 10 pm, Sun 9 pm.

Noks Kitchen £38 4️⃣3️⃣3️⃣
8 Gloucester St EH3 6EG 0131 225 4804
"Although newly opened in Stockbridge", this cosy family-run Thai stands on the site of a former such business (Songkran, RIP); limited feedback so far, with praise for its "brilliant" and "authentic" cooking. / Details: www.nokskitchen.co.uk; 10.30 pm.

Norn £62 5️⃣4️⃣3️⃣
50-54 Henderson Street EH6 6DE
0131 629 2525
"Amazing playful inventive food" – "an exquisite and mind-unravelling experience" – from chef Scott Smith and his team have made his "truly brilliant" Leith yearling (on the site of The Plumed Horse, RIP) a very "refreshing arrival on the Edinburgh scene". "It's strictly informal, with small tables, no cloths or flim-flam, and friendly, very well-informed staff who explain about ingredients, provenance

and technique". "Each dish is brought to the table and explained by the chef who had cooked it" and "it's worth hearing about them: local suppliers are heavily championed, as is seasonal produce and heritage techniques and ideas". Did Michelin only press their nose to the window this year? / *Details: www.nornrestaurant.com; @Nornrestaurant; 9 pm.*

Number One, Balmoral Hotel £107 🄸🄸🄸
1 Princes Street EH2 2EQ 0131 557 6727
"An absolute triumph from start to finish!" The plush basement of this famous luxury hotel continues to do justice to its name, and the "fantastic quality and presentation" of Jeff Bland's "extraordinary" cuisine matched with "faultless service" means it arguably deserves an even higher reputation than it already enjoys. "I would fly to Edinburgh again just to eat here!" / Details: www.thebalmoralhotel.com; 10 pm; D only; No jeans; Booking max 5 may apply. / Accommodation: 188 rooms, from £360

Ondine £74 🄸🄸🄸
2 George IV Bridge EH1 1AD 0131 226 1888
"Fresh and delicious fish and seafood" is served in a "classy" yet "friendly and informal" environment at this extremely popular "stylish modern venue", in an office block, "with great views over busy city streets in the centre of Edinburgh". Top Tip – "the extra bonus of 'Oyster Happy Hour' every day from 5:30-6:30: oysters for a pound at the best fish restaurant in town!" / Details: www.ondinerestaurant.co.uk; @OndineEdin; 10 pm; closed Sun; Booking max 6 may apply.

The Outsider £48 🄸🄸🄸
15 - 16 George IV Bridge EH1 1EE
0131 226 3131
"Extra marks for the ambience if you can get one of the tables with unbeatable views over the castle" at this "fun and lively" (but "very noisy") fixture – a "reliable" destination for "great tasting" Scottish food. / Details: www.theoutsiderrestaurant.com/; 11 pm; No Amex; Booking max 12 may apply.

The Pompadour by Galvin, The Caledonian £91 🄸🄸🄸
Princes Street EH1 2AB 0131 222 8975
The fame of this elegant chamber has never seemingly been matched by a huge fan club, and after six years of the Galvin Bros' tenancy, survey feedback on it remains surprisingly limited. Is it because "the menu shows considerable innovation but may be too fancy for the local market"? The overall verdict though remains: "expensive but well worth a visit". / Details: www.thepompadourbygalvin.com; @Galvin_Brothers; 10 pm; D only, closed Mon & Tue.

The Rabbit Hole £50 🄸🄸🄸
11 Roseneath St EH9 1JH 0131 229 7953
From a Sicilian owner, a "delightful" bistro which "opened recently in an unglamorous area of Edinburgh" (although being "next door to the renowned Eddie's fishmonger gives it direct access to the best and most unusual fish in town"). "The food combines Mediterranean and Scottish" influences leading to some "stunning and surprising" dishes. / Details: www.therabbitholerestaurant.com; 10 pm; closed Sun & Mon.

Restaurant Mark Greenaway £76 🄸🄸🄸
67 North Castle St EH2 3LJ 0131 557 0952
All agree the TV chef's Georgian house in New Town has potential. But while fans praise its "delicious" cuisine, the odd sceptic feels that "the end result did not warrant the evident effort that was put in". / Details: markgreenaway.com; @markgreenaway; 10 pm; Booking max 6 may apply.

Restaurant Martin Wishart £115 🄸🄸🄸
54 The Shore EH6 6RA 0131 553 3557
"Still remarkable in innovation and surprise after all this time" – Martin Wishart's Leith venture remains a haven of "culinary wizardry", with "wonderfully imaginative" but essentially classical cuisine, "superbly served" in a room that's "been attractively updated" in recent times. Top Tip – "go for the bargain lunch to eat some of the best food in Britain". / Details: www.martin-wishart.co.uk; @RMWLeith; 9.30 pm; closed Mon & Sun; No trainers.

Rhubarb, Prestonfield Hotel £71 🄸🄸🄸
Priestfield Rd EH16 5UT 0131 225 1333
"A fab experience from start to finish"; "so plush and warming" ("both genteel and relaxed") and with log fires crackling in its "highly decorated and historic rooms", this Georgian country pile certainly enjoys "memorable surroundings". Food is, mercifully, also "excellent" – not least an afternoon tea that "surpasses all others" (haggis bonbons, anyone?). / Details: www.prestonfield.com; @PrestonfieldHH; 10 pm; Booking max 8 may apply; children: 12+ at D, none after 7pm. / Accommodation: 23 rooms, from £295

Le Roi Fou £70
Forth Street EH1 3LE 0131 557 9346
First solo venture for French-Swiss chef Jérôme Henry (who previously headed-up Anton Mosimann's Belgravia dining club); Scottish ingredients and produce are used to create classic French dishes at this New Town venue which opened in April 2017. / Details: www.leroifou.com; @LeRoiFouEdin; 10.30 pm, Sun 4.30 pm.

Scran & Scallie £53 **4 4 4**
1 Comely Bank Rd EH4 1DT 0131 332 6281
"If you want to see and be seen in Stockbridge, this is the place for you", and Tom Kitchin's gastropub spin-off "lives up to the hype" with practically all reports saying it's "spot-on on every level" – "staff couldn't be nicer" and the "classic and high quality gastropub cuisine" is "brilliant". / Details: scranandscallie.com/; @ScranandScallie; 10 pm.

Soderberg £34 **4 3 3**
1 Lister Square EH3 9GL 0131 228 1905
Set below their bakery in Foster & Partners' glass-walled North Pavilion building, the Quartermile flagship of this Swedish-run enterprise is a "chilled" Scandi-style space; the "coffee's very good but not as good as the amazing Scandi buns" (or, arguably, the Swedish pizzas). / Details: www.soderberg.uk; 10 pm.

The Stockbridge £58 **4 4 4**
54 St Stephen's St EH3 5AL 0131 226 6766
"Classy and traditional" basement fixture, which is consistently praised for its "interesting" and "very delicious" Scottish cuisine. / Details: www.thestockbridgerestaurant.co.uk; @StockbridgeRest; 9.30 pm; D only, closed Mon; children: 18+ after 8 pm.

Timberyard £76 **4 3 3**
10 Lady Lawson St EH3 9DS 01312 211222
A "top spot for Edinburgh" – this "large and barn-like", "warehouse-style" venue is run by the younger generation of local restaurant impresarios, the Radford family. It gives rise to the odd niggle ("a bit too much hype"… "possibly takes itself a bit seriously"…) but for the most part wins high praise for its "warm modern style", and "innovative cuisine with the emphasis on foraging and sustainability". / Details: www.timberyard.co; @timberyard10; 9.30 pm; closed Mon & Sun; Booking max 5 may apply.

21212 £95 **4 4 4**
3 Royal Ter EH7 5AB 0845 222 1212
"An exceptional use of a variety of ingredients without overloading dishes" creates food that's "divine but not heavy" at Paul Kitching's offbeat but comfortable and "secluded" Georgian townhouse, where "attentive but relaxed and friendly service" adds to the experience. / Details: www.21212restaurant.co.uk; @paulk21212; 9.30 pm; closed Mon & Sun; children: 5+. / Accommodation: 4 rooms, from £95

Valvona & Crolla £41 **2 3 3**
19 Elm Row EH7 4AA 0131 556 6066
The large size of the dining annexe attached to this famous 80-year-old deli and wine importer, at the start of the road to Leith, can come as a surprise, and is something of an Edinburgh institution. Service can lag though, the food is often not as special as

one might expect, and the only thing consistently recommended here this year was the coffee! / **Details:** www.valvonacrolla.com; Mon-Thu 6 pm, Fri & Sat 6.30 pm Sun 5pm.

Wedgwood £62 **4 5 3**
267 Canongate EH8 8BQ 0131 558 8737
"Halfway down the Royal Mile – a charming little restaurant" (much of it in the cellar), which is many locals "go-to destination for a celebration meal" thanks to its "charming" style, "faultless service" and "excellent value and original Scottish fare": "it's so hard deciding what NOT to have for dinner!" / Details: www.wedgwoodtherestaurant.co.uk; @chefwedgwood; 10 pm.

The Wee Restaurant £63 **4 4 4**
61 Frederick Street EH2 1LH 0131 225 7983
Craig & Vikki Wood's yearling (a follow-up to the decade-old original of the same name), is "a real gem of an addition to the New Town" (and "saves a trip across the Forth to North Queensferry" to their other gaff). Between the "first-class food and service" (the former from ex-El Celler de Can Roca chef Michael Innes) it's "difficult to fault". / Details: www.theweerestaurant.co.uk/edinburgh; @weerestaurant; 9 pm, Fri & Sat 10 pm.

The Witchery by the Castle £73 **2 3 5**
Castlehill, The Royal Mile EH1 2NF
0131 225 5613
"Unique, delicious, atmospheric, amazing!"; though the food choice at this gothic dining room near the castle is "limited" (and tends to play second fiddle to the "extensive" wines), reporters don't much seem to mind – doubtless owing to the "dazzling" setting. The adjoining candle-lit Secret Garden, also simply "glows with romance". / Details: www.thewitchery.com; @thewitchery; 11.30 pm. / Accommodation: 8 rooms, from £325

EGHAM, SURREY 3–3A

The Tudor Room, Great Fosters Hotel £70 **4 4 4**
Stroude Rd TW20 9UR 01784 433822
"The setting is superb" at this "attractive Elizabethan manor in lovely gardens" and "you really feel you are being spoilt from the moment you arrive". "The Tudor Room is their fine dining option" (there is also the more affordable 'Estate Grill') and – though it's "expensive" – "chef, Douglas Balish, does not disappoint... every course is brilliant". Afternoon tea here is actually its most reported-on feature – it's relatively "affordable", "generous and elegant" (complete "with comfy seating and roaring log fire!") / Details: www.greatfosters.co.uk/Dining/TheTudorRoom.

EGLWYS FACH, POWYS   4–3D

Gareth Ward at Ynyshir £139 5️⃣5️⃣4️⃣
SY20 8TA 01654 781209
"It's highly recommended that you take the long drive to the west of Wales" to visit this small hotel – a "gorgeous" house once owned by Queen Victoria as a retreat next to the RSPB reserve of the same name. "The level of originality and innovation on show in Gareth Ward's kitchen is absolutely phenomenal" and – in the year where Ward and his partner Amelia Eiriksson took a stake in the business (and dropped 'Hall' from the name) – scores here have headed into the stratosphere, with numerous reporters "blown away" by "an experience like no other"… "the best meal ever"… "the next star on the World's 50-best". The 17-course tasting menu is a slow-food journey, and one reviewer describes the "indecently tasty" results as reminiscent of "the good old days of The Fat Duck". "Interesting, sometimes unusual, ingredients and flavour combinations are in perfect harmony using elaborate cooking processes explained by sous chefs brimming with enthusiasm. Staff are professional but relaxed, approachable and unpretentious. It's worth every penny!" / Details: www.ynyshir.co.uk; @ynyshirrest; signposted from A487; Credit card deposit required to book; children: 9+.

ELDERSFIELD, GLOUCESTERSHIRE 2–1B

The Butcher's Arms £66 4️⃣4️⃣3️⃣
Lime St GL19 4NX 01452 840 381
"Consistently wonderful food" wins very high ratings for James & Elizabeth Winter's rural pub – a well-known foodie destination, where the cooking is considerably fancier than the cosy interior. "Be sure and book". / Details: www.thebutchersarms.net; 9 pm; closed Mon, Tue L, Wed L, Thu L & Sun D; children: 10+.

ELLEL, LANCASHIRE 5–1A

The Bay Horse £48 4️⃣3️⃣3️⃣
Bay Horse Ln LA2 0HR 01524 791204
"If you're coming along the M6 and need a bite don't stop at Forton Services, why not stop at Craig WIlkinson's old pub in the eponymous hamlet?" "The menu is gastropub-meets-bistro, centring around traditional, familiar dishes, but done very well": eg "epic pies" or "mouth-wateringly magnificent steak". "It's a bit noisy, because it's crowded and the decor has hard surfaces" ("but is soon to be expanded we hear"). / Details: www.bayhorseinn.com; @bayhorseinn; 9 pm, Sun 8 pm; closed Mon; No Amex.

ELLON, ABERDEENSHIRE 9–2D

Eat on the Green £65 4️⃣4️⃣3️⃣
Udny Grn AB41 7RS 01651 842337
Self-proclaimed 'kilted chef' Chris Wilkinson's fine dining fixture, occupying a former post office, is a "top-class" affair – delivering a "consistently wonderful food experience" from satisfyingly local produce. / Details: www.eatonthegreen.co.uk; @EatOnTheGreen1; 9 pm, Sun 8 pm; closed Mon & Tue.

EMSWORTH, HAMPSHIRE 2–4D

Fat Olives £55 4️⃣5️⃣3️⃣
30 South St PO10 7EH 01243 377914
"A lovely little cottage" up the hill from the quay, which has won an extremely loyal fan club over the years thanks to "exceptional cooking by Lawrence (the chef/proprietor) who uses lots of local ingredients, and excellent service from Julia his wife and her team". The "small and intimate" premises help make it a sweet place, but even some fans "wish it was a bit bigger". / Details: www.fatolives.co.uk; @fat_olives; 9.15 pm; closed Mon & Sun; No Amex; children: 8+, except Sat L.

36 on the Quay £76 2️⃣2️⃣3️⃣
47 South St PO10 7EG 01243 375592
This cosy quayside restaurant-with-rooms has quite a pedigree (including holding a Michelin star for 18 years until 2015). For a long time now, however, reports have been patchy, not helped by "stuffy" or "slow" service and a sense the end-result is "very overpriced". Perhaps Gary & Martina Pearce, who are now overseeing the kitchen in partnership with longtime owners the Farthings, can sort things out? / Details: www.36onthequay.co.uk; off A27 between Portsmouth & Chichester; 9 pm; closed Mon & Sun; No Amex. / Accommodation: 5 rooms, from £100

EPPING, ESSEX 3–2B

Haywards Restaurant £64 4️⃣4️⃣2️⃣
111 Bell Common CM16 4DZ 01992 577350
"A real find where you'd least expect it", say fans of Jahdre and Amanda Hayward's four-year-old venture within the grounds of a family-run freehouse (The Forest Gate Inn). If there's a concern it's that it's "trying too hard", but most reports are of "impressive" cuisine from a "small but ambitious" menu and "very precise and polite service". / Details: www.haywardsrestaurant.co.uk; @HaywardsRestaur; Wed & Thu 9.30 pm, Fri & Sat 10 pm; Credit card deposit required to book; children: 10.

ESHER, SURREY   3–3A

Good Earth   £58 **3****4****4**
14 - 18 High Street KT10 9RT 01372 462489
*"Consistently good top end Chinese food, a really
friendly team and a lovely buzz" remains the
winning formula of this "top notch" Asian – the most
outer London member of the relatively posh family-
owned chain. / Details: www.goodearthgroup.co.uk;
Mon-Sat 11.15 pm, Sun 10.45 pm; Booking max 12
may apply.*

ETON, BERKSHIRE   3–3A

Gilbey's   £52 **2****4****3**
82 - 83 High Street SL4 6AF 01753 854921
*In an old butcher's, a High Street stalwart wine
bar with a "lovely cosy front eating area" and "nice
conservatory at the back, often filled with Etonians
and their parents celebrating rites of passage".
"The standard fare is of a perfectly acceptable
level, if not especially memorable". / Details:
www.gilbeygroup.com; @GilbeysEton; 5 min walk from
Windsor Castle; Mon-Thu 9.45 pm, Fri & Sat 10 pm,
Sun 9.45 pm.*

EVERSHOT, DORSET   2–4B

The Acorn Inn   £54 **3****3****3**
28 Fore St DT2 0JW 01935 83228
*Strong all-round marks from local fans of this
beautiful old 16th-century coaching inn, known
also for the very high quality of its accommodation.
/ Details: www.acorn-inn.co.uk; @Acorn_Inn;
One mile off A37 Yeovil - Dorchester Road; 9 pm. /
Accommodation: 9 rooms, from £135*

Summer Lodge, Summer Lodge
Country House   £86 **4****4****5**
DT2 0JR 01935 482000
*"Fine dining at its best in the most relaxing
environment" – this "grand" Relais & Châteaux
country house hotel inspires nothing but enthusiasm
for its romantic dining conservatory, and even
if the food can seem rather "elaborate" it's
"beautifully cooked and presented". / Details:
www.summerlodgehotel.co.uk; @Summer_Lodge;
12m NW of Dorchester on A37; 9.30 pm; No jeans. /
Accommodation: 24 rooms, from £235*

EXETER, DEVON   1–3D

Rendezvous Wine Bar   £46 **3****3****4**
38-40 Southernhay East EX1 1PE
01392 270222
*"A popular haunt for the business and legal classes
in Exeter"; this Southernhay basement wine bar is*

a "great place" where staff are "very obliging" and
the food is consistently well-rated (though arguably
it plays second fiddle to the wine). / **Details:**
www.winebar10.co.uk; @RendezvousWBar; 9.15 pm;
closed Sun.

EXMOUTH, DEVON   1–3D

Lympstone Manor   £83 **5****4****4**
Courtlands Lane EX8 3NZ 01395 202040
*With its "to-die for-views" over the Exe estuary,
Michael Caines "stunning" new venture (his solo
project after over 20 years at Gidleigh Park) "lives
up to expectations" for the fair number of reviewers
who have already made the pilgrimage to this
converted Georgian country pile (once owned by
the Baring family). "Furnished to compliment and
comfort" in style that's more "grand" and traditional
than it is funky or boutique-y, its "classic, top class
cooking" ("exquisite, balanced and satisfying")
plus "you-want-for-nothing" service all add up to
an experience that's "exceptional in every way".
In October 2017, Michelin speedily stepped up
to award it a first star – two next year? / Details:
www.lympstonemanor.co.uk; @Lympstone_Manor; No
shorts; children: 5.*

River Exe Cafe   £56 **4****3****5**
River Exe Estuary EX8 1XA 07761 116 103
*This "inventive" seasonal barge, in an "amazing
location in the middle of an estuary", has found the
perfect "recipe for success": "arrive by water taxi, sit
on the open deck, take in the views and enjoy some
simply cooked, very fresh, locally caught fish" ("and
plenty of alternatives for meat-eaters and veggies").
/ Details: @riverexecafe; Mon-Sat 10.30 pm, Sun
8.30 pm.*

Rockfish Exmouth   £50 **3****3****4**
Pier Head EX8 1DU 01395 272100
*"Lovely views of Dawlish Warren across the
estuary, if you are lucky enough to bag a table
overlooking the sea" feature in early reports
on this late 2016 new outpost of Mitch Tonks's
growing chain of upscale chippies, praised in
(still limited) early feedback for "beautifully
cooked fish that's as fresh as a daisy". / Details:
www.therockfish.co.uk/restaurants/exeter/.*

EXTON, HAMPSHIRE   2–3D

Shoe Inn   £43 **3****4****4**
Shoe Ln SO32 3NT 01489 877526
*"More open and lighter" since its recent refurb, this
stream-side pub offers "well-executed" food and
makes a handy stop for South Downs Way walkers. /
Details: www.theshoeexton.co.uk; 9 pm, Sun 8.30 pm.*

EXTON, RUTLAND   5–3D

The Fox and Hounds Hotel   £52 3 4 4
19 The Green LE15 8AP 01572812403
In a "pretty village setting in Rutland", this vine-covered 17th century coaching inn has been "delightfully refurbished with foxes everywhere" (and four luxe boutique rooms); "tables are set well apart for privacy" and "food is always excellent" in the dining room, though it's also "simply a great pub" with its own, more snacky menu. / **Details:** www.afoxinexton.co.uk; @afoxinexton.

FAIRSTEAD, ESSEX   3–2C

The Square and Compasses   £46 3 2 3
Fuller Street CM3 2BB 01245 361477
Upbeat all-round feedback on this converted 17th-century pub 10 minutes' drive from Chelmsford, where game in season is a feature of a traditional menu, whose ambitions run higher than standard pub-grub. / **Details:** www.thesquareandcompasses.co.uk; @SCFullerStreet; 9.30 pm.

FALMOUTH, CORNWALL   1–4B

The Cove Restaurant & Bar   £44 4 4 4
Maenporth Beach TR11 5HN 01326 251136
In a "stunning location" overlooking Maenporth Beach, this atmospheric, spot with large outside terrace is "as good as ever", offering "fresh flavoursome" fare spanning fishy tapas and "amazing seafood" mains. / **Details:** www.thecovemaenporth.co.uk; @covemaenporth; 9.30 pm; closed Sun D.

Oliver's   £50 4 4 3
33 High St TR11 2AD 01326 218138
Husband and wife team, Ken & Wendy provide "very good and varied food at this cramped and unpretentious restaurant" on the high street. "The quantities are larger than I need, but apparently locals demand it! – but the quality is there". / **Details:** www.oliversfalmouth.com; @oliversfalmouth; 9 pm; closed Mon & Sun; No Amex.

Rick Stein's Fish & Chips £42 3 3 2
Discovery Quay TR11 3XA 01841 532700
The TV chef's "big barn of a place" near the Maritime Museum offers on most (if not quite all) account a "great fish 'n' chip experience" – "flaky", "well-battered" and served in "generous portions". / **Details:** www.rickstein.com; @TheSeafood; 9 pm; No Amex; No bookings.

The Wheel House   £46 5 4 4
Upton Slip TR11 3DQ 01326 318050
"Seafood doesn't get better than this" says a fan of this tucked-away, diminutive joint, where the open kitchen turns out dishes that are "perfect every time" (and what's fresh right then is advertised on the chalkboard above them). NB Open Wednesday to Saturday only. / **Details:** 9 pm; D only, closed Sun-Tue.

FARINGDON, OXFORDSHIRE   2–2C

Magnolia Brasserie, Sudbury House   £44 3 3 3
56 London Street SN7 7AA 01367 241272
Limited but all-round upbeat feedback on the cheaper of the two dining options at Sudbury House Hotel, which features an open kitchen which majors in wood-fired pizza and char-grilled steaks. / **Details:** www.sudburyhouse.co.uk; @TheSudburyHouse; Mon-Thu 9 pm, Fri-Sun 9.30 pm; No shorts; children: 1.

Restaurant 56, Sudbury House   £79 4 4 4
56 London Street SN7 7AA 01367 245389
You can choose from a variety of set menus (from a two-course option, to a nine-course option) at this elegant dining room within the Georgian home that's the centrepiece of this rural hotel. Limited feedback on Andrew Scott's and Nick Bennett's cuisine, but such as there is says it's "exceptional". / **Details:** www.restaurant56.co.uk; @56_restaurant; 9 pm; closed Mon & Sun; Jacket required; Booking evening only.

FARNBOROUGH, HAMPSHIRE   3–3A

Aviator   £58 4 3 4
55 Farnborough Rd GU14 6EL 01252 555890
"In a culinary desert", this mid-century hotel-brasserie "has style and a spectacular location on the edge of the airfield"; while "possibly aimed at the business community", the food is "great" and the "cocktails are sublime" (particularly when taken in the glam Sky Bar). "worth checking out If flying in… or just in the area". / **Details:** www.aviatorbytag.com; 10 pm, Fri & Sat 10.30 pm, Sun 9.30 pm.

FAVERSHAM, KENT   3–3C

Read's   £83 3 4 4
Macknade Manor, Canterbury Rd ME13 8XE 01795 535344
"It's not trendy nor cutting edge and does not attempt to be, but consistently maintains excellent standards" – David and Rona Pitchford's "slightly old-fashioned" venture occupies "a delightful

Georgian manor" (with "a lovely garden for a pre lunch drink") and serves "classic" cuisine. *Top Tip* – "lunch is a special bargain". / **Details:** www.reads.com; @readsrest; 9.30 pm; closed Mon & Sun. / **Accommodation:** 6 rooms, from £165

Yard £14 🟦3️⃣4️⃣3️⃣

10 Jacob Yd, Preston St ME13 8NY
01795 538265
The "best café for miles around" is also the "newest of the many Italian eateries in town" and "more upmarket than the rest as pizza and pasta hardly figure"; instead, there's a "great" range of breakfasts, salads and sandwiches to peruse plus a "fantastic" value prix fixe with wine flights. / **Details:** @YardFaversham; L only, closed Sun; No bookings.

FELTON, NORTHUMBERLAND 8–2B

The Northumberland Arms £53

The Perth, West Thirston NE65 9EE
01670 787370
"An above normal standard of pub food" from a wide-ranging menu (from lunchtime sarnies and toasties to steaks and more 'serious' fare) wins praise for this "old village hostelry" by the River Coquet, in an attractive coaching inn about a mile from the A1. / **Details:** www.northumberlandarms-felton.co.uk; @thenlandarms; 9 pm.

FENCE, LANCASHIRE 5–1B

White Swan at Fence £42 5️⃣4️⃣3️⃣

300 Wheatley Lane Rd BB12 9QA
01282 611773
"Really fine, adventurous cooking from a small kitchen in unlikely pub premises" ("a lot more pubby than many gastropubs") again wins high praise for Tom Parker at this extremely popular destination. There have been shifts in recent times between à la carte and "keenly-priced" prix-fixe menus, and all agree the set menus are the way to go value-wise if you have the choice. "The wine list is nothing special, but fortunately there is a full selection of superb Timothy Taylor ales on tap: this being the only TT tied pub this side of the Pennines!" / **Details:** www.whiteswanatfence.co.uk; 8.30 pm, Fri & Sat 9 pm, Sun 7 pm; closed Mon.

FERRENSBY, NORTH YORKSHIRE 8–4B

General Tarleton £55 3️⃣4️⃣3️⃣

Boroughbridge Rd HG5 0PZ 01423 340284
Handy for the A1, "a special dining pub" – albeit one with "little hint of being a pub" these days, owing to its stylish and "comfortable" conversion (replete

with chi-chi cocktail bar). The "excellent" grub includes "some unusual dishes that deserve notice". / **Details:** www.generaltarleton.co.uk; @generaltarleton; 2m from A1, J48 towards Knaresborough; 9.15 pm. / **Accommodation:** 14 rooms, from £129

FLAUNDEN, HERTFORDSHIRE 3–2A

The Bricklayers Arms £59 4️⃣3️⃣3️⃣

Hogpits Bottom HP3 0PH 01442 833322
"All you want from country-pub fine dining"; it may be a "tricky place to find", but this ever-popular rural boozer is well "worth the effort" by all accounts thanks to its "lovely location" and "amazing food". / **Details:** www.bricklayersarms.com; @bricklayerspub; J18 off the M25, past Chorleywood; 9.30 pm, Sun 8.30 pm.

FLETCHING, EAST SUSSEX 3–4B

The Griffin Inn £47 3️⃣2️⃣3️⃣

TN22 3SS 01825 722890
A 400-year-old country pub-restaurant whose "wonderful garden" comes with "superb views" of the rolling countryside; longtime owners the Pullan family have ties to London's River Café, which are also (somewhat) reflected in the well-rated Mediterranean-influenced menu. / **Details:** www.thegriffininn.co.uk; @GriffinInnPub; off A272; 9.30 pm, Sun 9 pm. / **Accommodation:** 13 rooms, from £85

FOLKESTONE, KENT 3–4D

Rocksalt £55 4️⃣4️⃣5️⃣

4-5 Fishmarket CT19 6AA 01303 212070
"A lovely position with uninterrupted views of the most picturesque part of Folkestone Harbour and out to sea" is the crown jewel feature of Mark Sargeant's "beautifully located" venture ("make sure you book a window table"). Its fish and seafood cuisine is far from incidental though, and most reports record "fantastic" results. / **Details:** www.rocksaltfolkestone.co.uk; @rocksalt_kent; 10 pm; closed Sun D. / **Accommodation:** 4 rooms, from £85

FOLLIFOOT, NORTH YORKSHIRE 5–1C

Horto Restaurant at Rudding Park £73 5️⃣4️⃣3️⃣

HG3 1JH 01423 871350
"A pop-up that was so amazing" it has now found a permanent home in this classy hotel's ultra-lavish new £9.5m spa development, opened in May 2017. Chef Murray Wilson's "food is a little experimental" – à la carte, plus seven or nine-course

tasting menus – but the results are "stunning" (and sometimes "fun" too):"top marks". / **Details:** www.ruddingpark.co.uk; @ruddingpark; 10.30 pm; closed Mon.

FONTHILL GIFFORD, WILTSHIRE   2–3C

Beckford Arms   **£47**   🄷🄷🄷
SP3 6PX   01747 870 385
A "delightful posh pub", which "draws diners from miles around" with its "short and precise menu sourced from local ingredients and suppliers". It's an "accommodating" place (including to children), but strikes a couple of reporters as "a bit self-conscious in its tweedy smartness – the 'county' set comes here!" / **Details:** www.thebeckfordarms.co.uk; @beckfordarms; 9.30 pm, Sun 9 pm; No Amex. / **Accommodation:** 10 rooms, from £95

FORT WILLIAM, HIGHLAND   9–3B

Crannog   **£57**   🄴🄷🄷
Town Centre Pier   PH33 6DB   01397 705589
A well-situated institution, on a pier overlooking Loch Linnhe, which therefore "has the feeling of a sea-to-table" joint; it's "particularly good value if you get the cruise (from the same harbour the restaurant sits on) and lunch deal!" / **Details:** www.crannog.net; @CrannogHighland; 9 pm; No Amex.

FOWEY, CORNWALL   1–4B

The Q Restaurant, The Old Quay House   **£59**   🄷🄷🄵
28 Fore Street   PL23 1AQ   01726 833302
"A lovely situation overlooking river" with a terrace right by the water is the 'crown jewel' feature of this converted old house, but – on limited feedback – the locally sourced food from a short, to-the-point menu is exceptional too. / **Details:** theoldquayhouse. com; @theoldquayhouse; 9 pm; children: 8+ at D. / **Accommodation:** 11 rooms, from £190

FRESSINGFIELD, SUFFOLK   3–1D

The Fox & Goose   **£50**   🄷🄷🄷
Church Rd   IP21 5PB   01379 586247
"One of the best restaurants in East Anglia, which has maintained high standards for several years" – Paul Yaxley's "ever-reliable gastro-pub" in "an ancient and lovely building" puts in a "good-all-round" performance, not least its "ambitious (for the area)" cooking:"quality local ingredients cooked with care". / **Details:** www.foxandgoose.net; @Foxygossip; off A143; 8.30 pm, Sun 8.15 pm; closed Mon; children: 9+ at D.

FRILSHAM, BERKSHIRE   2–2D

The Pot Kiln   **£58**   🄸🄷🄷
RG18 0XX   01635 201366
A "lovely restaurant and pub in the middle of lovely nowhere in West Berkshire" with "cows just over the wall" (yet "very close to the M4"). Owner Mike Robinson – creator of shoot-and-cook DVDs, saviour of London's acclaimed Harwood Arms – oversees "lots of game options" which will "satisfy your meat urges for a long time". "Great garden for lunch on a sunny day" (though only a quite limited bar menu is available there). / **Details:** www.potkiln.org; between J12 and J13 of the M4; 9 pm, Sun 8 pm.

FRITHSDEN, HERTFORDSHIRE   3–2A

The Alford Arms   **£50**   🄷🄷🄷
HP1 3DD   01442 864480
A "proper country pub" in a "lovely setting" that's "back to its best after being closed due to fire" for six months in 2016;"the foods interesting without overdoing the inventiveness" and there's a "buzzy atmosphere" ("best in the bar area"). / **Details:** www.alfordarmsfrithsden.co.uk; @alfordarmshp1; near Ashridge College and vineyard; 9.30 pm, Fri & Sat 10 pm, Sun 9 pm; Booking max 12 may apply.

FROXFIELD, WILTSHIRE   2–2C

The Palm   **£39**   🄷🄷🄷
Bath Rd   SN8 3HT   01672 871818
Some "exceptional dishes" with seafood specialities win plaudits for this south Indian venture, located on the A4, in a swanky contemporary building. / **Details:** www.thepalmindian.com; 11.30 pm.

FYFIELD, OXFORDSHIRE   2–2D

White Hart   **£52**   🄷🄷🄷
Main Road   OX13 5LW   01865 390585
"An ancient converted chantry" that's "worth going out of your way to find". It "serves up everything you really want from a country pub" – "a cut above the norm" and "reasonably priced" too. / **Details:** www.whitehart-fyfield.com; @the_whitehart; off A420; 9.30 pm, Sun 3 pm; closed Sun D.

GATESHEAD, TYNE AND WEAR   8–2B

Eslington Villa Hotel   **£49**   🄷🄷🄸
8 Station Rd   NE9 6DR   0191 487 6017
"Convenient for Team Valley and Newcastle", the "discrete" dining room of this stately Victorian hotel is a notably consistent sort of spot and "the set

F S A

lunch menu is particularly good value". / **Details:**
www.eslingtonvilla.co.uk; @Eslingtonvilla; A1 exit for
Team Valley Trading Estate, then left off Eastern Avenue;
9.30 pm; closed Sat L & Sun D. / **Accommodation:**
75 rooms, from £90

Raval Luxury Indian Restaurant & Bar £36 ▨▨▨
Church Street, Gateshead Quays NE8 2AT
0191 477 1700
Limited reports this year on this Gateshead Quays
Indian with open kitchen, but feedback is all-round
very good when it comes to its sophisticated cuisine
and luxurious contemporary decor. / **Details:**
www.ravalrestaurant.com; @ravalrestaurant; 11 pm; D
only, closed Sun; No shorts.

Six, Baltic Centre for Contemporary Arts £61 ▨▨▨
Baltic (Sixth Floor), South Shore Road
NE8 3BA 0191 440 4948
"Super views" are the key draw to this sixth-floor
dining room "looking down the Tyne and across to
Newcastle on the other side of the river"; there's a
"Conran-ish focus on everything looking good and
making you feel great, but the underlying food is
average", bar the odd "interesting" dish, and some
"very slow in arriving". / **Details:** www.sixbaltic.com;
@six_baltic; Mon-Sat 9.30 pm, Sun 4 pm; closed Sun D.

GERRARDS CROSS, BUCKINGHAMSHIRE 3–3A

Maliks £42 ▨▨▨
14 Oak End Way SL9 8BR 01753 889634
The swish little sister of Cookham's top Indian
continues to rival its sibling – and has recently had
a considerable makeover, with a "very nice new
interior"; the odd sceptic feels that the food "isn't
as good as it used to be" – but that's not reflected
in the very solid marks. / **Details:** www.maliks.co.uk;
10.45 pm.

Three Oaks £42 ▨▨▨
Austenwood Ln SL9 8NL 01753 899 016
"The place to be in these parts" – this "top notch
gastropub" provides cuisine that "can go a level
above, into gourmet territory". There's the odd
fear that it's "trying too hard", but most reviews
say it's "terrific value and deservedly well-
patronised". / **Details:** www.thethreeoaksgx.co.uk;
@TheThreeOaksGX; 9.15 pm.

GISBURN, LANCASHIRE 5–1B

La Locanda £48 ▨▨▨
Main Street BB7 4HH 01200 445303
A quaint converted building in the Ribble Valley
provides the location for Maurizio and Cinzia
Bocchi's fixture of fifteen years' standing, which

takes pride in its local sourcing of Italian dishes. /
Details: www.lalocanda.co.uk; @LaLocandaCinzia;
9 pm.

GLASGOW, CITY OF GLASGOW 9–4C

Babu £28 ▨▨▨
186 W Regent St G2 4RU 0141 204 4042
"Just great Indian (street) food with attitude" – the
premise of this "really honest" and "tasty" 3-table
café, bringing a dose of Mumbai to the city-centre. /
Details: www.babu-kitchen.com; @babukitchen; 9 pm,
Mon 4 pm; closed Mon D & Sun.

The Bistro at One Devonshire Gardens £70 ▨▨▨
One Devonshire Gdns G12 0UX
0141 339 2001
The plush dining room of this West End boutique
hotel – nowadays part of the Hotel du Vin group
– has long been one of the City's top 'push-the-
boat-out' destinations. Its cuisine nowadays isn't
quite as famous as in past eras (under the likes
of Andrew Fairlie and Gordon Ramsay) but can
still "excite", as can the "exceptional wine list". /
Details: www.hotelduvin.com.

Black Dove £37 ▨▨▨
67 Kilmarnock Road G41 3YR 0141 231 1021
An array of "good quality small plates" has won
local foodie fame for this "upper-end bistro" in the
Southside of Glasgow, available à la carte, or from
the 5-course and 7-course tasting menus. / **Details:**
www.blackdovedining.com; @BlackDoveDining.

Bread Meats Bread £24 ▨▨▨
G2 5UB 0141 249 9898
A "fab cool burger joint" offering "big portions of
tasty food" (not least "exceptional" patties and
buns); just remember to "get in early to avoid the
queues". / **Details:** www.breadmeatsbread.com.

Café Gandolfi £47 ▨▨▨
64 Albion St G1 1NY 0141 552 6813
"Great, solid" Scottish food ("locally sourced, where
possible") has long been the calling card of this
Merchant City old-timer – now with numerous spin-
offs; despite being born in a pivotal year for punk
(1979) its woody interior is imbued with a more
bohemian vibe. / **Details:** www.cafegandolfi.com;
@cafegandolfi; 11.30 pm; Booking weekdays only.

Cail Bruich £63 ▨▨▨
725 Great Western Rd G12 8QX
01413 346265
When it comes to "Scottish contemporary cooking
at its best!", some cognoscenti tip brothers Paul &
Chris Charalambous's West End venture as "the
best fine-dining currently on offer in Glasgow". "It's
not on one of the most prepossessing stretches

322 FSA Ratings: from [1] (Poor) to [5] (Exceptional)

of road (if you weren't going here, you'd probably hurry past), but at night there's a subdued warm glow from the dim-lit interior, which has a vaguely French brasserie-cum-bistro feel: a bit old-fashioned, but nice and comfortable, dimly lit and cosy". The cuisine is "always inventive and majors on fresh local ingredients", from a variety of set menus, including a tasting option. / **Details:** www.cailbruich.co.uk; @CailBruich; closed Mon; children: 5.

Crabshakk £55 5|3|3
Finnestone G3 8TD 0141 334 6127
A tiny Finnieston classic offering the "best seafood in the area" in a stylish if cramped setting; the menu covers pretty much everything under the sea (all "fab") but it's the daily specials, chalked up on the board, that are "really special – try them!" / **Details:** www.crabshakk.com; @crabshakk; closed Mon; No Amex.

The Dhabba £40 3|3|3
44 Candleriggs G1 1LE 0141 553 1249
"Glasgow has many Indian restaurants, but The Dhabba is very different", offering tastebuds a "real exploration beyond the staple korma or tikka". The "contemporary interior", can seem "a little clinical" but most reviewers find it very atmospheric. / **Details:** www.thedhabba.com; @thedhabba; 11.30 pm.

Eusebi Deli £45 4|4|3
152 Park Road G4 9HB 01416 489999
Successor to an East End deli with a 40-year history, this "tiny"West End two-year old "a few minutes walk from Kelvinbridge station" is permanently "packed" and "buzzy" (in part thanks to Marina O'Loughlin regularly "singing its praises" before she left The Guardian). Its "innovative and delightful" dishes live up to the hype – "very light, packed full of flavour" – with a highlight being "superb" sweets ("the likes of which I've not seen outside Italy"). / **Details:** eusebideli.com/; @eusebi_deli; 10 pm.

The Fish People Cafe £49 4|3|3
350 Scotland Street G5 8QF 0141 429 8787
"Fantastic fresh fish cooked to perfection" is the hallmark of this "small friendly restaurant"; one reporter asks "what not to like?" – the response, if one were to be ungenerous, the slightly unglamorous location opposite Shields Road subway station. / **Details:** www.thefishpeoplecafe.co.uk/; 9 pm, Fri & Sat 10 pm, Sun 8 pm; closed Mon.

Gamba £67 4|4|3
225a West George St G2 2ND 0141 572 0899
Celebrating 20 years this year, Derek Marshall's city-centre basement has earned a very solid reputation over the last couple of decades as one of the city's top culinary destinations, on account of its unfailingly "excellent" preparation of "high quality" fish dishes and "efficient and pleasant service". / **Details:** www.gamba.co.uk; @Gamba_Glasgow; 9 pm, Sun 8.30 pm; closed Sun L; Booking max 6 may apply.

Gandolfi Fish £47 4|3|2
84 - 86 Albion Street G1 1NY 0141 552 9475
Café Gandolfi's nearby spin-off delivers "lovely and fresh fish" enjoyed against the backdrop of "Art Deco-style decor". / **Details:** www.cafegandolfi.com; @cafegandolfi; Mon-Sat 10.30 pm, Sun 9 pm.

The Gannet £53 4|3|4
1155 Argyle St G3 8TB 0141 2042081
At its best, this vibey Finnieston two-year-old is the epitome of "relaxed dining with great cooking, and a wine and beer selection that hits the mark". The experience can suffer though from "inconsistent service" and a feeling the albeit good food is "overpriced". / **Details:** www.thegannetgla.com/; @TheGannetGla; 9.30 pm, Sun 7.30 pm; closed Mon.

Hanoi Bike Shop £31 3|3|2
8 Ruthven Ln G12 9BG 0141 334 7165
"The tables are rickety", and the two-floor premises "quite uncomfortable", at this "quirky" and "buzzy" West End café, but its Vietnamese street food is "well worth it". / **Details:** www.hanoibikeshop.co.uk; @hanoibikeshop; 11 pm, Fri & Sat 12.30 am.

Mother India £39 4|4|3
28 Westminster Ter G3 8AD 0141 339 9145
"It's always busy so be prepared to queue" at this well-known West End Indian, for many years one of the most popular destinations in town thanks to its "unusual (but thankfully not fancy)" tapas dishes at "excellent value" prices and "helpful" staff. / Details: www.motherindiaglasgow.co.uk; @Official_Mindia; 10.30 pm, Fri & Sat 11 pm, Sun 10 pm; Mon-Thu D only, Fri-Sun open L & D.

Nippon Kitchen £54 3|3|3
91 W George Street G2 1PB 0141 328 3113
This "modern and fun" outfit – "a traditionally British wood-panelled dining room with oriental furniture" – serves "an interesting take on Japanese food" washed down with cocktails, plus "an extensive list of wines and Japanese beers". / **Details:** www.nipponrestaurant.co.uk; L only.

Ox and Finch £47 4|3|3
920 Sauchiehall St G3 7TF 0141 339 8627
This converted Finnieston pub is "a trendy, high-ceilinged venue with a casual vibe", whose Scottish take on tapas "offers creative, contemporary, relaxed sharing dining, with food that's innovative, more-ish and well worth a visit". In autumn 2017, they announced an Edinburgh spin-off called Baba to open in the New Town. / **Details:** www.oxandfinch.com; @OxAndFinch; 10 pm.

Paesano Pizza £34 5|3|3
G1 1DT 0141 258 5565
"Paesano does just one thing – pizza – but they do it very well", turning out "easily the best pizza in Glasgow" in a trendy, tiled and "very

laid back" setting. The "queues can be annoying on weekends" – and, alas, the same goes for its equally popular West End sibling, newly launched on Great Western Road. / **Details:** *paesanopizza. co.uk; @paesano_pizza.*

Porter And Rye   **£59**   4 4 4
1131 Argyle Street   G3 8ND   0141 572 1212
In buzzing Finnieston, a NYC-style two-year-old that "specialises in local farm-bred, air-dried beef steaks" full of "fantastic flavour and texture", and "accompanied by an interesting menu of locally sourced produce". / **Details:** *www.porterandrye.com; @PorterAndRye; 10.30 pm.*

Ranjits Kitchen   **£20**   3 2 2
607 Pollokshaws Road   G41 2QG
0141 423 8222
"Fantastic homemade Punjabi cooking is served by lovely people" at this alcohol-free veggie deli and restaurant (with an early dinner curfew). "There is always a queue, but it's worth the wait – and watching other people being served will get your appetite going". / **Details:** *8.30 pm.*

Rogano   **£59**   3 3 3
11 Exchange Place   G1 3AN   0141 248 4055
"Such an old-fashioned Glasgow institution" – this city-centre icon is famous for its prime Art Deco interiors by the same craftsmen who fitted out The Queen Mary. Its seafood isn't inexpensive but generally "served and cooked perfectly". / **Details:** *www.roganoglasgow.com; @roganoglagow; 10.30 pm.*

Shish Mahal   **£41**   4 4 2
60-68 Park Road   G4 9JF   0141 334 7899
"A Glasgow tradition for over 25 years" acclaimed for its "fantastic" scoff (including the chicken tikka masala, which it claims to have invented); "Mr Ali may not be around nowadays, but the legend lives on and can't be bettered". / **Details:** *www.shishmahal.co.uk; Mon-Thu 11 pm, Fri & Sat 11.30 pm, Sun 10 pm; closed Sun L; No bookings.*

Singl End   **£25**   4 3 3
265 Renfrew Street   G3 6TT   0141 353 1277
"If you are thinking about breakfast, brunch or lunch, climb the hill towards Glasgow Art School, turn left and be rewarded with the best bloomin' food you can think of" at this "quirky" and "welcoming" café/ bakehouse. Bread (ranging from "sourdough to Altamira, nut, olive and many, many others") is a highlight, and the full Scottish is "delicious" too.

Stravaigin   **£61**   4 3 4
28 Gibson St   G12 8NX   0141 334 2665
Colin Clydesdale's "unique" venue is a stalwart of the West End, particularly the upstairs bar that's "always full of a genuine crowd who want to soak up the ambience", and enjoy "local favourites from neeps and haggis to fish and chips" – all of

which can also be taken "more formally" in the downstairs restaurant. / **Details:** *www.stravaigin.co.uk; @straivaiging12; 11 pm; No Amex.*

Tuk Tuk   **£36**
426 Sauchiehall Street   G2 3JD   0141 332 2126
Sibling to Edinburgh's Indian street food joint, this stripped-back venue serving inexpensive snacks, curries and tandoor-cooked meats near the Glasgow School of Art opened in early 2017. / **Details:** *www.tuktukonline.com; @tuktukstreetuk.*

Two Fat Ladies at The Buttery   **£62**   4 4 4
652 Argyle St   G3 8UF   0141 221 8188
Ryan James's dark, tartan-clad Scots seafood operation (part of a small local chain) occupies a historic, wood-panelled site near the SECC, and won acclaim for some "fabulous" meals this year "efficient and friendly" service too. / **Details:** *www.twofatladiesrestaurant.com; 10 pm, Sun 9 pm.*

Ubiquitous Chip   **£60**   3 4 5
12 Ashton Ln   G12 8SJ   0141 334 5007
"After a few years of stooping from its previous heights the chip is back to its best!" This famous Glaswegian veteran (est. 1971) put in a strong showing in this year's survey, with general agreement that "it's still a top eating place" with a superbly "atmospheric" interior, "relaxed and knowledgeable staff" and "expensive but stunningly good", modern Scottish cuisine; with a particular highlight being the "fantastic wine and amazing malt whisky list". / **Details:** *www.ubiquitouschip.co.uk; @UbiquitousChip; 11 pm, Sun-Wed 10 pm.*

GLINTON, RUTLAND   6–4A

The Blue Bell   **£51**   4 3 3
10 High Street   PE6 7LS   01733 252285
"An excellent range of food at low prices that's all well presented and tasty" wins high praise for Will Frankgate's cosy village pub – "a great favourite with walkers". / **Details:** *www.thebluebellglinton.co.uk; @bluebellglinton; 9 pm, Sun 4.30 pm.*

GOLDSBOROUGH, NORTH YORKSHIRE 8–3D

The Fox And Hounds Inn £61   4 4 3
YO21 3RX   01947 893372
"Just uncomplicated tasty food" – the simple-but-hit formula at Jason Davies's unpretentious pub, set in rolling Yorks countryside, and with a distinct local slant. / **Details:** *www.foxandhoundsgoldsborough.co.uk; 8.30 pm; D only, closed Sun-Tue; No Amex.*

The Miller of Mansfield £59 🖻🖻🖻
High St RG8 9AW 01491 872829
In 2014 Mary & Nick Galer followed stints at Heston's Fat Duck Group by taking over this "friendly" 18th century (but contemporary style) pub-with-rooms in a picturesque village handy for the Berkshire Downs and Chilterns, praised by reviewers for its "lovely, well balanced dishes". / **Details:** *www.millerofmansfield.com; 0.*

Rossini at The Leatherne Bottel £64 🖻🖻🖻
Bridle Way RG8 0HS 01491 872667
In a "very romantic" riverside spot, this Thames Valley classic certainly has "lots of feel-good factor", not least on the terrace. Since its 2014 Italian revamp and rebrand, feedback has been more limited but it was consistently rated "an all-round enjoyable experience" this year. / **Details:** *www.leathernebottel.co.uk; @leathernebottel; 10.30 pm, Sun 3 pm; closed Mon & Sun D; children: 10+ for D.*

The Forest Side £83 🖻🖻🖻
LA22 9RN 01539 435250
"They sure know how to look after you" at this "lovely forest-themed dining room" whose "gorgeous" Scandi-esque looks contrast with the rest of this "beautifully renovated" Victorian building, which enjoys a "brilliant Lakeland setting" near Grasmere village (part of a year-old hotel within Andrew Wildsmith's small collection of boutique properties). Chef Kevin Tickle moved here from L'Enclume to open the restaurant, and "there is a similarity to the cuisine at Cartmel" in his ambitious multi-course menu here, which comes with "unusual drink pairings – not just wine" and with many 'biodynamique' vintages. Results are "absolutely delectable and impeccably prepared, showing the right balance between interesting contrasts and subtlety of flavours", while "staff are seamless and judge their interactions perfectly". "It's a wonderful experience from beginning to end" and "although it's definitely not cheap, I don't think anyone could argue that it's not good value". / **Details:** *www.theforestside.com; @TheForestSide; 9.30 pm.*

The Jumble Room £50 🖻🖻🖻
Langdale Road LA22 9SU 01539 435188
A "quirky", "fun" and "delightfully relaxed" stalwart, whose "enjoyable" food is "more adventurous than most Lakes bistros". / **Details:** *www.thejumbleroom.co.uk; 9.30 pm; closed Mon & Tue. /* **Accommodation:** *3 rooms, from £180*

Harry's Place £87 🖻🖻🖻
17 High Street NG31 8JS 01476 561780
Harry & Caroline Hallam's quaint 10-seater feels like you're dining in their front room – you are! – with Harry at the stoves presenting you with a small, hand-written menu with a couple of choices for each course, and Caroline front of House. Their venture was founded long before the term pop-up had acquired its current meaning: they are about to enter their 30th year in business! Reports are not as numerous as once they were, but their small, loyal fan club are as ecstatic as ever regarding the exceptional cuisine and genuine welcome. / **Details:** *on B1174 1m N of Grantham; 8.30 pm; closed Mon & Sun; No Amex; children: 5+.*

The New Inn £48 🖻🖻🖻
2 High St DN37 8JL 01469 569998
"The best steaks and the most delicious fish 'n' chips" grace the "unusual menu" (with produce from the local Brocklesby Estate) of this "calm and delightful" three-year-old – a former village pub taken over by Ian Matfin (ex-of Gordon Ramsay etc.) and his wife. / **Details:** *www.thenewinngreatlimber.co.uk; @tnigreatlimber; 9 pm, Sun 6 pm.*

Belmond Le Manoir aux Quat' Saisons £198 🖻🖻🖻
Church Road OX44 7PD 01844 278881
"I couldn't take any risks for my wife's 50th birthday weekend... so I placed my trust in Raymond's impeccable hotel and restaurant... result: perfection!" M Blanc's "magnificent" converted Elizabethan manor boasts a "dream location" in a picture-book village south of Oxford and, "if you want to spoil someone with luxury", an overnight stay here is "the ultimate 'because-you're-worth-it' experience". "Any visit must include a walk through the gardens", which not not only cap off "the perfect setting", but also help supply the restaurant and "would make any kitchen gardener green with envy". "Special praise also goes to the service: that all-too-rare combination of humanity, wonderful politeness and efficiency" that "sets a standard others only aspire to". Last but not least, when it comes to the cooking – "essentially French haute cuisine, but not so rich" – it is occasionally said to be a tad "safe", but more commonly it is described as "exquisite, with supreme attention for detail" (and – unusually for such a high profile restaurant – provokes vanishingly

few 'contrarian' negative reports). One unavoidable downside: "a visit is unfortunately hugely expensive"; but on most accounts "this is not just a meal, but a spa for the soul and the senses, generating a deep sense of well-being, and – viewed as such – is a good-value prescription!" / **Details:** www.manoir.com; @lemanoir; from M40, J7 take A329 towards Wallingford; 9.30 pm; Booking max 12 may apply. / **Accommodation:** 32 rooms, from £555; SRA-Food Made Good – 3 stars.

GREAT WALTHAM, ESSEX	3–2C

Galvin Green Man   **£40**   ②❸❸
Howe St CM3 1BG 01245 408820
Fans of the Galvins "very buzzy" (and "noisy") new country pub – dating from the 14th century and set in 1.5 acres – hail it as a "fabulous Essex restaurant, with fantastic interior design and clever food" – "like a superior London spot, but retaining the warmth and character of a really welcoming local". But there are a fair number of critics too, who say "the brothers can do better than this", and who feel it's "very pricey". / **Details:** www.galvinrestaurants.com; @Galvin_brothers.

GREETHAM, RUTLAND	5–3D

The Wheatsheaf   **£48**   ❸❸②
Stretton Rd LE15 7NP 01572 812325
This "cosseting" pub again wins a strong thumbs up – "yes, the decor can't compete with some of the local gastropubs, and yes, the small kitchen can mean slow service, but the welcome is always warm, and the food top-notch". / **Details:** www.wheatsheaf-greetham.co.uk; 9 pm; closed Mon & Sun D; No Amex.

GRESFORD, WREXHAM	5–3A

Pant-yr-Ochain   **£52**   ❸❸❺
Old Wrexham Road LL12 8TY 01978 853525
An "archetypal Brunning & Price gastropub", featuring a "characterful building and super location" (a lakeside manor with a "cracking garden"), "usually reliable dishes" and "great beers". / **Details:** www.brunningandprice.co.uk/pantyrochain; 1m N of Wrexham; 9.30 pm, Sun 9 pm.

GUERNSEY, CHANNEL ISLANDS	–

Le Nautique   **£68**   ❸❸❹
GY1 2LE 01481 721714
"On the St Peter Port Seafront", and with a "superb harbour view", this chic, modern venue has "been in Guernsey for years", but remains a

pillar of consistency, offering "high quality seafood" based on "imaginative local produce". / **Details:** lenautiquerestaurant.co.uk/; 10.30 pm.

La Reunion   **£53**   ❹❸❹
Cobo Coast Road GY5 7HB 01481 255600
"Marvellous sea views" are a draw to this light, stylishly decorated restaurant, right above local haunt The Rockmount, and with a terrace overlooking scenic Cobo Bay; the "great value" menu "focuses on local produce" and "not surprisingly it has fantastic fish and shellfish". / **Details:** www.lareunion.gg/; 9.30 pm; closed Mon & Sun D.

GUILDFORD, SURREY	3–3A

The Ivy Castle View   **£54**
Tunsgate Square, 98-100 High Street GU1 3HE
awaiting tel
In a 'roll-out' that would do McDonald's proud, this iconic brand has gone for it this year, opening virtually simultaneously in practically all of the UK's top restaurant cities. The ambition is impressive: let's hope standards hold up better than they did when, for example 'Browns' tried to pull off a similar trick. / **Details:** www.theivyguildford.com.

March Hare   **£44**   ❸❹❸
2-4 South Hill GU1 3SY 01483 401530
Launched in 2015, this "renovated inn" ("sort of pubby and restaurant-y at the same time") is part of Raymond Blanc's White Pub Company chain – a "really pleasant" spot, combining stylish decor, Guildford Castle views and a "strong French-themed menu that's well presented and delivered". / **Details:** www.marchhareguildford.com/; @MHguildford; 10 pm, Fri & Sat 10.30 pm, Sun 9 pm.

Rumwong   **£44**   ❹❸❸
18-20 London Rd GU1 2AF 01483 536092
The "best Thai around" is a "popular, bustling, pleasant" sort of place, which – even after 40 years – retains the locals' favour owing to its "good cuisine". / **Details:** www.rumwong.co.uk; 10.30 pm; closed Mon; No Amex.

The Thai Terrace   **£43**   ②❸❸
Castle Car Pk, Sydenham Rd GU1 3RW
01483 503350
Fans praise the "to-die-for Thai" food and "fabulous views" at this "very noisy" venture, in a bizarre setting atop a multi-storey car park; for critics, however, "in many ways it's a pretty standard" operation… although even they even add "but what a view!" / **Details:** thaiterrace.co.uk/; 10.30 pm; closed Sun; No Amex.

GULLANE, EAST LOTHIAN   9–4D

Chez Roux, Greywalls Hotel   **£65** 4 4 4
EH31 2EG   01620 842144
"Brilliant, friendly, personal service and excellent cuisine" help the dining room of this posh Lutyens-designed country house hotel do justice to the Roux brand. It's a favourite afternoon tea spot too: "expensive but worth it… and you get to play croquet!" / **Details:** www.greywalls.co.uk; @Greywalls_Hotel; 10 pm; Jacket required. / **Accommodation:** 23 rooms, from £260

GULWORTHY, DEVON   1–3C

The Horn of Plenty, Country House Hotel & Restaurant   **£72** 3 2 4
Country House Hotel & Restaurant PL19 8JD 01822 832528
"Super views from the terrace" and window tables of the Tamar Valley are a constant at this long-established, "quiet and lovely" venture, in "a beautiful location". But while fans hail "wonderful confident cooking with great flavours", critics feel the cuisine is "too fussy" or rail at "haphazard service". / **Details:** www.thehornofplenty.co.uk; @Hornofplenty1; 3m W of Tavistock on A390; 9 pm; No jeans. / **Accommodation:** 10 rooms, from £95

HAMBLETON, RUTLAND   5–4D

Finch's Arms   **£47** 2 2 4
Oakham Rd LE15 8TL   01572 756575
A "terrace overlooking Rutland Water" – "a delight on a summer evening" – sets the scene at this atmospheric pub in a super-cute hamlet. When it comes to eating here "it's ever the curate's egg" – "service has improved but can still be hit and miss" ("particularly in the busy tourist season"), and the food can be "excellent"… but can also be "overdone" or "feature slightly odd ingredient combinations". / **Details:** www.finchsarms.co.uk; 9.30 pm, Sun 8 pm.

Hambleton Hall   **£95** 5 5 4
LE15 8TH   01572 756991
"You arrive to the sound of gravel crunching beneath your tyres, the aroma of log burning fires, and views across Rutland Water" at Tim Hart's "beautiful" East Midlands retreat, and "if you are looking for the truly typical country house experience, Hambleton has it in spades". The style is "somewhat formal, but none the worse for that" and it's "the charm of the old-fashioned atmosphere that helps set it apart", as enhanced by the "faultless service". Aaron Patterson has been at the stoves since 1992, and he remains at the top of his

game, delivering a "true, classic British fine dining experience" wherein contemporary ideas enliven a fundamentally textbook approach. "The wine list is exceptional too, with some excellent good value bottles as well as the famous names" and sommelier Dominique Baduel is "a past master of finding little gems". / **Details:** www.hambletonhall.com; @hambleton_hall; near Rutland Water; 9.30 pm; children: 5+. / **Accommodation:** 17 rooms, from £265

HARDWICK, CAMBRIDGESHIRE   3–1B

The Blue Lion   **£49** 3 4 4
74 Main Street CB23 7QU   01954 210328
A cosy 18th-century village pub with quaint decor and a lovely garden; it offers an "imaginative menu" of "well-cooked" classics and more adventurous dishes – including some ingredients produced on the premises (they also rear their own rare-breed sheep). / **Details:** www.bluelionhardwick.co.uk; @bluelionhardwick; Mon-Fri 9 pm, Sat 9.30, Sun 8 pm; No Amex.

HAROME, NORTH YORKSHIRE   8–4C

The Pheasant Hotel   **£68** 4 4 4
YO62 5JG   01439 771241
It's not as famous as The Star Inn, but Andrew Pern's 'other' establishment is favoured by some reviewers over its better known sibling: "a lovely traditional and very civilised setting" ("like being wrapped in a warm, woollen blanket") serving "top class cuisine". / **Details:** www.thepheasanthotel.com; 9 pm; No Amex. / **Accommodation:** 15 rooms, from £155

The Star Inn   **£70** 4 4 4
Harome YO62 5JE   01439 770397
"One of the nicest pubs in one of the nicest villages, with some of the best pub food in England!" – Andrew Pern's famous "olde worlde" 14th-century thatched inn "was in the vanguard of the gastropub revolution" despite its "in-the-middle-of-nowhere" location north east of York. Nowadays the cooking remains "fabulous without being overly pretentious" – "very seasonal and local (with lots of game)". / **Details:** www.thestaratharome.co.uk; @TheStaratHarome; 3m SE of Helmsley off A170; Mon-Sat 9.30 pm, Sun 6 pm; closed Mon L & Sun D; No Amex. / **Accommodation:** 8 rooms, from £150

HARPENDEN, HERTFORDSHIRE   3–2A

Lussmanns   **£42** 2 3 3
20a Leyton Road AL5 2HU   01582 965393
"Ever-popular Harpenden branch of this local chain, that's busy and buzzy with folk of all ages enjoying themselves". Fans say it's "unfailingly good in all

areas", but to critics it's no more than a "pleasant enough local". / *Details: www.lussmanns.com/ restaurants/harpenden-restaurants/; @lussmanns; 9 pm; SRA-Food Made Good – 3 stars.*

HARROGATE, NORTH YORKSHIRE   5–1C

Bettys   £46   3 4 5
1 Parliament Street HG1 2QU   01423 814070
"Proper cakes, proper teas, silver service" and "outstanding Yorkshire hospitality" combine to make this legendary spot "the quintessential English tearoom that never fails to please"; indeed, "once you have got through the vast queues" it's "the most civilised place you'll ever spend an afternoon". / *Details: www.bettysandtaylors.co.uk; 9 pm; No Amex; No bookings.*

Bettys Garden Café, RHS Gardens Harlow Carr   £37   4 4 4
Crag Lane, Beckwithshaw HG3 1QB
01423 505604
Offering "all the favourites from the café in town (cakes, sandwiches, pastries) without the excessive queues" – and with "wonderful views over Harlow Carr gardens" to boot, this branch of the celebrated tearooms "never ever lets you down". / *Details: www.bettys.co.uk; @Bettys1919; 9 pm.*

Cardamon Black   £35   3 3 4
Cheltenham Parade HG1 1BX   01423 313136
Occupying a local landmark (built as The Empire Theatre) – Nick Rahman's "very busy" five-year-old juggles dramatic red-and-black decor and "consistently good", high-end Pan-Asian cuisine. / *Details: @Cardamom_Black.*

Clock Tower, Rudding Park   £78   4 3 4
Follifoot HG3 1JH   01423 871350
An "extremely enjoyable" spot – a posh hotel with a formal fine dining venue and more relaxed conservatory bar/restaurant, whose cuisine has a dedicated local fan club; afternoon tea in the latter location is "always great" here. / *Details: www.ruddingpark.com; @RuddingPark; 10 pm. / Accommodation: 49 rooms, from £170*

Drum & Monkey   £50   4 3 4
5 Montpellier Gdns HG1 2TF   01423 502650
"On top form" – this "timeless" and "beautifully civilised" Montpellier stalwart was taken over by the Carter family five years back, but "thankfully it never changes"; if anything it has actually "reached new heights" of late, with "delicious" seafood factoring into the "excellence on all fronts". / *Details: www.drumandmonkey.co.uk; @DrumAndMonkey; 9 pm; closed Sun; No Amex; Booking max 10 may apply.*

Graveley's Fish & Chip Restaurant   £46   4 3 2
8-12 Cheltenham Parade HG1 1DB
01423 507093
"Superbly fresh fish 'n' chips" remain the hallmark of this "bright and welcoming restaurant" – part of a well-established northern chain. / *Details: www.graveleysofharrogate.com; @graveleys; Mon-Thu 9 pm, Fri & Sat 10 pm, Sun 8-9 pm.*

The Ivy Harrogate   £54
7-9 Parliament Street HG1 2QU
01423 787100
In a 'roll-out' that would do McDonald's proud, this iconic brand has gone for it this year, opening virtually simultaneously in practically all of the UK's top restaurant cities. The ambition is impressive: let's hope standards hold up better than they did when, for example 'Browns' tried to pull off a similar trick. / *Details: www.theivyharrogate.com; @ivyharrogate.*

Norse   £34   5 4 3
22 Oxford St HG1 1PU   01423 202363
After three years sharing digs with Baltzersen's café, this "unique" fine dining spot ("managing to be both Scandinavian in approach as well as firmly rooted in Yorkshire") upped sticks to its own venue, on Swan Road, in April 2017. With its moss wall and handsome Nordic-style fittings, the crowdfunded space certainly looks the part; as we went to press, they were offering both à la carte and tasting menus – and, for the first time, Saturday lunch. We've maintained ratings in the expectation it will continue to deliver an "absolutely amazing experience" led by "clean-tasting and healthy" dishes using "locally sourced and foraged food". / *Details: www.norserestaurant.co.uk; @EatNorse; 9 pm.*

Orchid   £51   5 5 4
28 Swan Road HG1 2SE   01423 560425
"Stunning" Pan-Asian food with "very fresh oriental flavours" has carved a formidable reputation for Harrogate's best known dining destination – a contemporary space within The Studley Hotel – which has been "consistently excellent for many years". Top Tip – "the Sunday brunch buffet is especially good value and always popular". / *Details: www.orchidrestaurant.co.uk; @orchidnstudley; 10 pm; closed Sat L. / Accommodation: 28 rooms, from £115*

Sasso   £48   4 3 3
8-10 Princes Square HG1 1LX   01423 508833
This famous, much-loved basement local "sets high standards and maintains them", with dishes focussing on the Emilia Romagna region. / *Details: www.sassorestaurant.co.uk; @sassorestaurant; 9.30 pm, Fri & Sat 10 pm; closed Sun.*

Stuzzi **£47** 4 4 4
46B Kings Road HG1 5JW 01423 705852
With its "tatty school furniture" and "deli items on sale", this Italian hotel-brasserie is "a most unexpected type of restaurant in Harrogate", being "more typical of the trendier E London scruffy chic ascetic". Add in "absolutely super authentic small plates" and it's "very busy" indeed ("'twas packed on a Friday night – booking essential"). / Details: @stuzziharrogate; 10 pm.

Sukhothai **£44** 3 4 3
17-19 Cheltenham Pde HG1 1DD
01423 500869
"A real taste of Thailand" is to be had at this "atmospheric" branch of the Leeds-based indie chain, consistently praised for its "good quality Thai dishes" and high quality of service. / Details: sukhothai.co.uk; @Sukhothai_; 11 pm; Mon-Thu D only, Fri-Sun open L & D.

HARROW WEALD, MIDDLESEX 3–3A

The Hare **£51** 3 3 2
Old Redding HA3 6SD 020 8954 4949
This smart three-year-old acquisition of Raymond Blanc's ever-growing White Brasserie Co. gastropub chain turns out "good and interesting food" (British classics with a Gallic infusion) and is "popular with locals and walkers"; the nice garden is another boon. / Details: www.hareoldredding.com; @THOldredding; 10 pm, Fri & Sat 10.30 pm, Sun 9 pm .

HARROW, GREATER LONDON 3–3A

Incanto, The Old Post Office **£54** 3 3 3
41 High Street HA1 3HT 020 8426 6767
A "stylish" suburban Italian, with a deli/café up front, and a restaurant out back. Reporters divide between those who feel the food is "no longer special" nowadays, and others who say it's "well above average for the location". / Details: www.incanto.co.uk; @incantoharrow; 10.30 pm, Sun 3 pm; closed Mon & Sun D.

HASTINGS, EAST SUSSEX 3–4C

Maggie's **£25** 4 3 2
Rock-a-Nore Road TN34 3DW
01424 430 205
The "perfect place to go on a day trip to the seaside" – a top spot for "super fresh fish 'n' chips", "located in and amongst the black wooden fishing sheds". "Try and reserve a table by the window". /

Details: www.towncitycards.com/locations/hastings/ma; 9 pm; closed Mon D, Tue D, Wed D, Thu D & Sun; Cash only.

Rock a Nore Kitchen **£33** 4 3 3
23a Rock-A-Nore Rd TN34 3DW
01424 445425
"Just off the beach and close by the fishing boats", this informal eatery nestled between the fish market and traditional old fishing huts serves "great fresh seafood in generous portions, to say the least!" / Details: No bookings.

Webbe's Rock-a-Nore **£48** 3 3 3
1 Rock-a-Nore Road TN34 3DW
01424 721650
Opposite the Jerwood Gallery – host to another notch in the local Paul Webbe empire – this contemporary venue remains of note for its seafood platters, sourced from the fishermen on the beach, barely a minute from the kitchen; great views of the Old Town, sea and Eastbourne too. / Details: www.webbesrestaurants.co.uk; @WebbesRockaNore; 9.30 pm.

HATCH END, GREATER LONDON 1–1A

Sea Pebbles **£36** 3 2 3
348-352 Uxbridge Rd HA5 4HR
020 8428 0203
Expanded and appealingly refurbed, this veteran chippie is now a "clean and bright" space in which to enjoy "good fresh fish properly cooked" (plus "a fair selection of non-fish" for vegans et al); unusually for such an operation, Mondays are gluten-free. / Details: www.seapebbles.co.uk; 9.45 pm; closed Sun; May need 8+ to book.

HATFIELD PEVEREL, ESSEX 3–2C

The Blue Strawberry **£49** 3 3 3
The Street CM3 2DW 01245 381333
"Quality ingredients, quality staff, quality service… and all at a very reasonable price" still earn praise for this well-regarded village fixture, although it receives much less feedback nowadays than it did when it was the undisputed star of the county. / Details: www.bluestrawberrybistrot.co.uk; @thebluestrawb; 3m E of Chelmsford; Mon-Sat 10 pm, Sun 4 pm; closed Sun D; No Amex.

HAYWARDS HEATH, WEST SUSSEX 3–4B

The Crown **£44** 4 3 3
The Green, Horsted Keynes RH17 7AW
01825 791609
"After a change of management, the food is

now pretty good to excellent and the service is friendly (if not always slick)" at this 16th century gastropub with rooms, which since November 2016 has been run by Simon and Mark Dennis, owners of Cuckfield's Rose & Crown. / **Details:** www.thecrown-horstedkeynes.co.uk; 9 pm, Fri & Sat 9.30 pm.

Jeremy's at Borde Hill   £59   4 4 4
Borde Hill, Borde Hill Gardens RH16 1XP
01444 441102
"Dining on the terrace is something to look forward to" when the sun is shining at Jeremy and Vera Ashpool's "charming" and very well-known venture, in the "lovely" heart of Borde Hill Garden (200 acres of famous landscape gardens). "A favourite over many years", it continues to win consistent praise for its "excellent" cuisine (some of "the best in Sussex") and "friendly" style. / **Details:** www.jeremysrestaurant.com; @Jeremysrest; Exit 10A from the A23; 10 pm; closed Mon & Sun D.

HEDLEY ON THE HILL, NORTHUMBERLAND 8–2B

The Feathers Inn   £48   4 3 2
NE43 7SW   01661 843 607
"Fresh Northumbrian cooking with local produce is very difficult to find", and makes it "worth the effort" to truffle out this "out-of-the-way" but extremely popular village pub, serving "excellent locally sourced food with game in season". / **Details:** www.thefeathers.net; @thefeathersinn; 8.30 pm, Sun 4.30 pm; closed Mon, Tue & Sun D; No Amex.

HELMSLEY, NORTH YORKSHIRE   8–4C

Black Swan   £69   2 2 2
Market Pl YO62 5BJ   01439 770466
A "lovely old hotel", whose "gorgeous traditional afternoon tea served with a modern twist" is "absolutely outstanding". Reports on more serious cuisine here attracted mixed reports this year however – what is "totally delicious" to fans is to others "very average and at high prices". / **Details:** www.blackswan-helmsley.co.uk; 9.30 pm. / **Accommodation:** 45 rooms, from £130

HEMEL HEMPSTEAD, HERTFORDSHIRE 3–2A

Galvin at Centurion Club   £50   3 2 2
Centurion Club, Hemel Hempstead Road HP3 8LA   01442 510520
With its "lovely setting on a golf course", the Galvin's new opening is seen by many locals as "the great, high quality addition to the area that we really

needed", with a "fabulous bar" and "above average" cooking. What is a "tasteful modern interior" to some reviewers is "reminiscent of a Holiday Inn" to others however, and "amateurish service" can also be an issue. These were early reports though, and on most accounts it "comes up trumps". / **Details:** www.centurionclub.co.uk; 10.15 pm, Sun 7 pm.

HEMINGFORD GREY, CAMBRIDGESHIRE 3–1B

The Cock   £50   2 3 3
47 High St PE28 9BJ   01480 463609
A "great interior" adds charm to this popular pub-restaurant, in a classic English village near the Great River Ouse. Reports on the food were a little mixed though this year: to fans "top notch", but to critics "a little disappointing". / **Details:** www.cambscuisine.com/the-cock-hemingford; @cambscuisine; off the A14; follow signs to the river; 9 pm, Fri & Sat 9.30 pm, Sun 8.30 pm; children: 5+ at D.

HENLEY IN ARDEN, WARWICKSHIRE 5–4C

Cheal's of Henley   £75   4 4 3
64 High St B95 5BX   01564 793 856
Ex Simpsons chef Matt Cheal heads the stoves at this old house on a picturesque high street, which is owned by his parents Julie & Tony. The odd disappointment was recorded, but most reports here could not be more glowing for its ambitious cuisine (with the option of a nine-course tasting menu as well as the à la carte). / **Details:** www.chealsofhenley.co.uk; @Chealshenley.

HENLEY, WEST SUSSEX   3–4A

The Duke Of Cumberland   £54   4 3 5
GU27 3HQ   01428 652280
"Dining al fresco on a summers day is heavenly" at this extremely popular "old pub set in marvellous scenery" – "with stunning views" over the South Downs – and "serving wonderful food in an unpretentious manner". / **Details:** www.thedukeofcumberland.com; @theduke_Henley; 9 pm.

HENLEY-ON-THAMES, OXFORDSHIRE 3–3A

The Greyhound   £54   3 3 3
Gallowstree Rd, Peppard Common RG9 5HT
0118 972 2227
Antony and Jay Worrall-Thompson describe their pub and restaurant near Henley-on-Thames as 'the perfect local'. Well they would, wouldn't they? But it

turns out reporters are also enthusiastic about its "helpful staff" and "surprisingly extensive choice of delicious food". / Details: www.awtgreyhound.com/; @TheGreyhoundAWT; Wed-Thu 9.30 pm, Fri & Sat 10 pm, Sun 4 pm.

Luscombes at the Golden Ball £53 🖫🖪🖫

The Golden Ball, Lower Assendon RG9 6AH
01491 574157

"A charming old converted Chilterns pub" with a "tremendous garden", "very cosy upstairs" and "buzzy" downstairs; "the owners know what they're doing and serve diverse but unfussy food cooked with assurance time after time". / Details: www.luscombes.co.uk; 10 pm; No Amex.

Shaun Dickens at The Boathouse, The Boathouse £64 🖪🖫🖪

The Boathouse RG9 1AZ 01491 577937
Views divided this year on Shaun Dickens's contemporary-style venture, in "beautiful surroundings overlooking the Thames in Henley". To fans it serves "exceptional" and "original" dishes with service that's "so friendly and knowledgeable", but to its critics it is "overhyped, overpriced and pretentious". / Details: www.shaundickens.co.uk; @henleyboathouse; Wed-Sun 9.15 pm; closed Mon & Tue.

Villa Marina £48 🖫🖪🖫

18 Thameside RG9 1BH 01491 575262
This "reliable" riverside sibling to Marlow's Villa D'Este provides some "excellent Italian" cuisine, and even an old-school pudding trolley. / Details: www.villamarina-henley.com; @Villa_Marina_; opp Angel pub, nr Bridge; 10.30 pm, Sun 9 pm.

HEREFORD, HEREFORDSHIRE 2–1B

Beefy Boys £20 🖫🖪🖫

HR4 9HU 01432 359209
Opened by four local friends, this hip, two-floor outfit – a former pop-up – has caused big waves locally since its launch just after Christmas 2015; the main event is superlative – "best burger I've ever had" – and it has a handy location in a city-centre development. / Details: www.thebeefyboys.com.

Castle House Restaurant, Castle House Hotel £63 🖪🖫🖪

Castle St HR1 2NW 01432 356321
Swish Georgian townhouse hotel, "in a splendid riverside setting" overlooking gardens designed by Capability Brown. Food "cooked with care and sometimes flair" sometimes earns it a tip as "the best in Hereford" – doubters though find it "pricey" and feel it "rather fancies itself". / Details: www.castlehse.co.uk; @castlehsehotel; 9.30 pm, Sun 7 pm. / Accommodation: 24 rooms, from £150

HERNE BAY, KENT 3–3D

A Casa Mia £37 🖫🖪🖫

160 High Street CT6 5AJ 01227 372 947
"Fantastic pizza traditionally cooked in a clay oven" is the draw to Gennaro Esposito's "proper Neopolitan", improbably located "in that well-known suburb of Naples, Herne Bay!". Fun fact: it's one of only two UK pizzerias accredited by Naples' Associazione Verace Pizza. / Details: www.acasamia.co.uk; @AcasamiaHB; 11 pm, Fri & Sat 11.30 pm, Sun 10 pm.

Le Petit Poisson £44 🖪🖫🖫

Pier Approach, Central Parade CT6 5JN
01227 361199
"Very fresh, well-cooked fish" is, unsurprisingly, the highlight of the "small (but regularly changing) menu" at this brick-walled seafront spot, also tipped for its wallet-friendly prices and stellar views. / Details: www.lepetitpoisson.co.uk; Tue-Wed 4.30 pm, Thu-Sat 9 pm, Sun 4 pm; closed Mon & Sun D; No Amex.

HERSTMONCEUX, EAST SUSSEX 3–4B

The Sundial £65 🖪🖫🖪

Gardner St BN27 4LA 01323 832217
"A wonderful surprise in the Sussex countryside" – a chic, beamed Gallic venture, overlooking the South Downs, and delivering very "good" food and presentation; the worst complaint this year? – "too much food!". / Details: www.sundialrestaurant.co.uk; centre of village; 9.30 pm, Sat 10 pm; closed Mon & Sun D.

HESWALL, MERSEYSIDE 5–2A

Burnt Truffle £48 🖪🖫🖪

104-106 Telegraph Road CH60 0AQ
0151 342 1111
"You feel at home instantly" at Gary Usher's acclaimed crowdfunded bistro – his first follow-up to Sticky Walnut, "in a pretty cottage in the centre of this village on the Wirral". All feedback on the grub is upbeat: "novel, inventive, well-prepared and VERY tasty". / Details: www.burnttruffle.net; @BuRntTruffle; Mon-Thu 9 pm, Fri & Sat 10 pm, Sun 9 pm.

HETHE, OXFORDSHIRE 2–1D

The Muddy Duck £57 🖪🖫🖪

Main St OX27 8ES 01869 278099
Reporters enjoyed some "really lovely" meals this year at this remote village pub (handy for Bicester Village's shops and the M40); the "tasty

fare" goes down a treat, and in summer you can eat in the large and attractive garden. / Details: www.themuddyduckpub.co.uk; 9 pm, Sun 4 pm; closed Sun D.

HETTON, NORTH YORKSHIRE   5–1B

The Angel Inn   **£55**   3|3|3
BD23 6LT   01756 730263
In a tiny, picture-perfect Dales hamlet, this "lovely old" vine-covered inn helped pioneer the gastropub genre. The market may have caught up with it somewhat nowadays, but it remains a "very welcoming" spot for "excellent, unpretentious" grub and an "enormous" wine list curated by Pascal Watkins (son of Denis and Juliet who made the place famous). The "fun" bar may be preferred to the "reserved" restaurant. / Details: www.angelhetton.co.uk; @angelinnhetton; 5m N of Skipton off B6265 at Rylstone; 9 pm, Fri & Sat 9.30 pm; D only, ex Sun open L only.

HEXHAM, NORTHUMBERLAND   8–2A

Battlesteads   **£45**   3|4|3
Wark on Tyne   NE48 3LS   01434 230 209
An "old inn in a beautiful country setting" where "the food (including tasting menus) is clever" and whose "eco-ideals are carried through in a practical way" by "very hands-on owners Richard and Dee Slade" (who grow much of their own produce). "In the summer the garden at the back is one of the most peaceful hangouts anywhere". / Details: www.battlesteads.com; @Battlesteads.

Bouchon Bistrot   **£48**   3|3|3
4-6 Gilesgate   NE46 3NJ   01434 609943
"Like a small part of France" – this popular Gallic "relaxed venture in the centre of Hexham" is a key destination locally providing "good cooking of a bistro standard and a very Gallic welcome". "It's the kind of place everyone would love to have just around the corner from home". / Details: www.bouchonbistrot.co.uk; @bouchonhexham; 9.30 pm; closed Sun; No Amex.

The Rat Inn   **£42**   3|3|3
Anick   NE46 4LN   014 3460 2814
"The blackboard menu makes the most of local fresh produce" at this charming pub between Hexham and Hadrian's wall, which has "a lovely rural location overlooking the Tyne", "an excellent range of local ales" and "good choice of wine". / Details: www.theratinn.com; @ratales; closed Sun D.

HILDENBOROUGH, KENT   3–3C

Cafe 1809   **£13**   3|3|3
152-154 Tonbridge Rd   TN11 9HW
01732 667500
Dame Kelly Holmes' café is a "beautiful" spot that "caters to cyclists and casual passers-by alike", and offers "high-quality" food (plus lifestyle products) with a health-conscious bent. In the '80s, Dame Kelly was a paper girl for the sweet shop that stood on-site – "you occasionally see her in there now… serving!" / Details: www.cafe1809.co.uk; @Cafe1809; No bookings.

HINTLESHAM, SUFFOLK   3–1D

Hintlesham Hall   **£70**   2|2|3
Hintlesham   IP8 3NS   01473 652334
There are big plans afoot for this landmark country retreat – owned by Robert Carrier and Ruth Watson in its glory years – spanning a new herb garden and lots of hi-tech innovations; in the meantime the 700-year-old venue is "looking good", and remains a "real treat", with the table d'hôte and afternoon tea both recommended this year. / Details: hintleshamhall.co.uk/; @hintlesham_hall; 4m W of Ipswich on A1071; 9 pm; Jacket required; children: 12+. / Accommodation: 33 rooms, from £99

HINTON-ST-GEORGE, SOMERSET   2–3A

Lord Poulett Arms   **£49**   3|2|3
TA17 8SE   01460 73149
Quintessential Somerset inn with a "lovely traditional feeling"; it provoked the odd grumbling report this year, with "disjointed service" the main gripe, but on most accounts the cooking was well-rated. / Details: www.lordpoulettarms.com; @LordPoulettArms; 9 pm; No Amex. / Accommodation: 4 rooms, from £85

HITCHIN, HERTFORDSHIRE   3–2B

Hermitage Rd   **£55**   3|3|3
20-21 Hermitage Road   SG5 1BT
01462 433603
"You climb steep stairs, and it's a bit noisy, but it's worth a visit" to this impressive space with open kitchen, which occupies a lofty former ballroom, and serves a "delicious" menu majoring in char-grilled steaks, ribs and burgers, but with lots of choice for non meat-eaters. (Reporters "love the coffee shop" downstairs, too; barista "Magda is a star" and the fancy Faema E71 makes "by far the best coffee around"). / Details: www.hermitagerd.co.uk; @HermitageRd; Mon-Sat 10 pm, Sun 7 pm; No Amex.

Redcoats Farmhouse Hotel
Redcoats Green SG4 7JR 01438 729500
Limited but very upbeat feedback on this family-run hotel, set in the Hertfordshire countryside. In mid 2017 it was acquired by the local group Anglian Country Inns, who have announced a two-year upgrading programme and the introduction of a more field-to-fork culinary approach. / **Details:** *www.redcoats.co.uk; @redcoats; 9.30 pm. /* **Accommodation:** *13 rooms, from £90*

HOLKHAM, NORFOLK   6–3C

The Victoria at Holkham £53   🟦3🟦2🟦4
. NR23 1RG 01328 711008
"A firm favourite when visiting the North Norfolk coast" – a Holkham Estate coastal hotel-pub known for featuring unusual cuts of meat on its menu. / **Details:** *www.holkham.co.uk; @VictoriaHolkham; on the main coast road, between Wells-next-the Sea and Burnham Overy Staithe; 9 pm; No Amex. /* **Accommodation:** *10 rooms, from £140*

HOLT, NORFOLK   6–3C

Wiveton Hall Cafe   £45   🟦3🟦3🟦3
1 Marsh Lane NR25 7TE 01263 740515
Overlooking the marshes and sea, this "quirky" fruit farm café has a "super location" and a "great venue for all ages" (with "lots for children to eat and look at", plus "plenty of space to run around"). / **Details:** *www.wivetonhall.co.uk/restaurant-cafe/; @WivetonHall; closed Mon D, Tue D, Wed D, Thu D & Sun D; Booking lunch only.*

HONITON, DEVON   2–4A

The Pig, Combe House   £67   🟦3🟦3🟦3
Gittisham EX14 3AD 01404 540400
Opened in April 2016, this dramatic new outpost of the rural-chic Pig group enjoys a "wonderful (Elizabethan-era) location" – formerly Combe House Hotel – with a conservatory-style dining room delivering the "beautifully presented" local fare that's the hallmark of the brand. / **Details:** *www.combehousedevon.com; @CombeHouseDevon; on the outskirts of Honiton; not far from the A30, A375, 303; 9.30 pm; No Amex. /* **Accommodation:** *15 rooms, from £215*

The Holt   £49   🟦3🟦3🟦2
178 High Street EX14 1LA 01404 47707
"Still a pub at heart despite the rather upscale menu" – this "easy-going" spot (run by sons of the acclaimed Otter brewery) at the bottom of the main street is "well worth searching out" for its

---

"well-priced and interesting British tapas". / **Details:** *www.theholt-honiton.com; 9 pm, Fri & Sat 9.30 pm; closed Mon & Sun.*

HORDLE, HAMPSHIRE   2–4C

The Mill at Gordleton   £52   🟦3🟦4🟦5
Silver Street SO41 6DJ 01590 682219
A "simply beautiful setting" – an old mill on the banks of the Avon – and equally "beautiful food" conspire to create a "simply perfect" experience at this ivy-clad boutique hotel; even the most sceptical report allowed that the food is "not bad" and the "service is brilliant". / **Details:** *www.themillatgordleton.co.uk; on the A337, off the M27; Mon-Sat 9.15 pm, Sun 8.15 pm; No Amex. /* **Accommodation:** *8 rooms, from £150*

HORNDON ON THE HILL, ESSEX   3–3C

The Bell Inn   £49   🟦4🟦3🟦5
High Rd SS17 8LD 01375 642463
"The ambience is quintessential olde-worlde country pub, with a cosy bar area and roaring fire" at this 600-year-old, timber-framed coaching inn, which provides "a great mix of traditional pub atmosphere and fine dining" (the latter in "the adjacent dining room which is full of charm"). "Excellent food comes in generous portions and at very reasonable prices" and "caring" service from "staff who are friendly and helpful without being pushy" was often complimented in this year's feedback. / **Details:** *www.bell-inn.co.uk; @Bellhorndon; signposted off B1007, off A13; 9.45 pm; Booking max 12 may apply. /* **Accommodation:** *15 rooms, from £50*

HORSHAM, WEST SUSSEX   3–4A

Restaurant Tristan   £67   🟦5🟦4🟦3
3 Stans Way RH12 1HU 01403 255688
"In a very old building in the centre of Horsham", Tristan & Candy Mason's "always friendly" spot is "an ideal place for that special night out". Tristan's "almost faultless" food comes at "remarkably reasonable prices", while his "partner ensures the service is very good". / **Details:** *www.restauranttristan.co.uk; @tristanshorsham; 9.30 pm; closed Mon & Sun.*

WABI   £55   🟦4🟦4🟦3
38 East St RH12 1HL 01403 788 140
This upmarket Japanese emerged phoenix-like from a huge fire in 2014; now under Paul & Verity Craig, of Brighton's Bohemia (the original owners bowed out after launching an ill-fated London sibling), it seems to be back at its best, with "fantastic food on

every visit" (so "glad it came back after being burnt down!"). / **Details:** *www.wabi.co.uk; @WabiHorsham; 10.45 pm; closed Mon & Sun.*

HOWDEN, EAST YORKSHIRE   5–1D

Kitchen   **£25**   🟩3🟩3🟩3
38 Bridgegate   DN14 7AB   01430 430600
"A great spot for coffee and cake" (or "an excellent full English") – this simple tearoom is well worth remembering in the locale. / **Details:** *www.kitchensnaith.co.uk; @KitchenSnaith; L only; closed Sun.*

HOYLAKE, MERSEYSIDE   5–2A

Lino's   **£40**   🟩3🟩4🟩3
122 Market Street   CH47 3BH   0151 632 1408
This "Italian-influenced restaurant of long standing" is a "real old favourite" with an impressive pedigree (33 years and counting) – "I always enjoy a trip!" / **Details:** *www.linosrestaurant.co.uk; 3m from M53, J2; 10 pm; D only, closed Mon & Sun; No Amex.*

HUDDERSFIELD, WEST YORKSHIRE   5–1C

Eric's   **£65**   🟥4🟥4🟥3
73-75 Lidget St   HD3 3JP   01484 646416
"In a town with almost no restaurants of note, Eric's is the shining exception to the rule" – a "small and friendly" suburban all-rounder where "the lunches in particular are top-class". A sibling to the chef's hit local burger spin-off, PAX, was set to take over the old Yorkshire Building Society, in Mirfield, in early 2018. / **Details:** *www.ericsrestaurant.co.uk; @ericrestaurant; 10 pm, Sun 4pm; closed Mon, Sat L & Sun D; No Amex.*

HULL, EAST YORKSHIRE   6–2A

1884 Dock Street Kitchen   **£55**   🟩3🟩3🟩4
Humber Dock Street, Marina   HU1 1TB
01482 222260
"Lovely views over the Hull Marina and River Humber" accompany a visit to this "well-restored Victorian dockside building" which is approaching its fifth year in operation. "It's been a splendid addition to the Hull scene", and first-timers often find "the food far exceeds expectations". / **Details:** *www.1884dockstreetkitchen.co.uk/index.html; 9 pm; closed Mon & Sun D; Booking max 8 may apply.*

Old House A Pub By Shoot The Bull   **£75**   🟥3🟥4🟥4
5 Scale Lane   HU1 1LA   01482 210253
"The City of Culture at its best!" – "the first pub operated by the award-winning (street food outfit) Shoot The Bull" is a hipster destination set in Hull's "pretty old town" (in its oldest domestic dwelling). Chef Chris Harrison (ex-Fat Duck and 1884 Dock Street Kitchen) has "years of experience", resulting in a menu of "surprising creativity" spanning 'street food' ("burgers bursting with flavour with truffle chips to die for") to more "exciting taste combinations". / **Details:** *www.shootthebull.co.uk/the-old-house-1/; @shootthebulluk; 9.30 pm.*

HUNSDON, HERTFORDSHIRE   3–2B

The Fox And Hounds Restaurant & Bar   **£40**   🟩3🟩4🟩3
2 High Street   SG12 8NH   01279 843 999
A "lovely" decade-old country gastroboozer with a "great outdoor area and play stuff for the kids"; the menu includes a "variety of steak cuts from rare breed cattle including English Longhorn and Galloway, all grilled on a charcoal oven". / **Details:** *www.foxandhounds-hunsdon.co.uk; @thefoxhunsdon; off the A414, 10 min from Hertford; 9.30 pm; closed Mon; No Amex.*

HUNTINGDON, CAMBRIDGESHIRE   3–1B

Old Bridge Hotel   **£56**   🟦2🟩3🟩3
1 High St   PE29 3TQ   01480 424300
John Hoskins MW's ivy-clad hotel and wine shop is a "comfortable" spot that's also "handy to the town"; the food is a tad "variable" – "passable" enough if you want a "relaxing dinner with no cheffy surprises" – but it's the "fantastic" wine list which hogs the limelight. (Post recent refurb', the main dining room – often overlooked for the smaller one – is "more attractive than it was"). / **Details:** *www.huntsbridge.com; @oldbridgehotel; off A1, off A14; 10 pm.* / **Accommodation:** *24 rooms, from £160*

HURLEY, BERKSHIRE   3–3A

Hurley House Hotel   **£67**   🟩3🟩3🟩3
Henley Road   SL6 5LH   01628 568 500
"A relatively new eating house (plus swish boutique hotel) on the site of an 18th century inn called The Red Lion" – but built from scratch in 2016; "the restaurant, bar and more relaxed summer dining room offer daily set menus at reasonable prices", while ex-Petrus chef Michael Chapman's food is "always good". / **Details:** *www.hurleyhouse.co.uk; @HurleyHouseH.*

HURWORTH, COUNTY DURHAM   8–3B

The Bay Horse   £62   🔳🔳🔳
45 The Grn DL2 2AA   01325 720 663
"Imaginative cuisine that's really well presented"
("and excellent choice, including game in season")
wins a number of enthusiastic gastronomic
endorsements for this "great, renovated village
inn". "It can be noisy, for which the only solution is
to avoid it on busy nights (ie Thu-Sat)". / Details:
www.thebayhorsehurworth.com; @thebayhorse_;
9.30 pm, Sun 8 pm.

HYTHE, KENT   3–4D

Hythe Bay Seafood
Restaurant   £48   🔳🔳🔳
Marine Parade CT21 6AW   01303 233844
"In a brand new but sympathetic development",
this "large seafront space" is "the place for well-
presented, unfussy fish"; best book for a prime
window seat…the "view across the harbour should
have a webcam". "They must be good because they
have opened two more" (first Dover, then Deal). /
Details: www.hythebay.co.uk; 9.30 pm.

ILKLEY, WEST YORKSHIRE   5–1C

Bettys   £49   🔳🔳🔳
32 The Grove LS29 9EE   01943 608029
A "great place for a treat"; this branch of the
much-celebrated tearooms continues to "set the
standard for afternoon tea in Yorkshire", and offers
"consistently good food" at other times, too. /
Details: www.bettys.co.uk/tea-rooms/locations/ilkle; L
only; No Amex; No bookings.

The Box Tree   £90   🔳🔳🔳
35-37 Church St LS29 9DR   01943 608484
This "bastion of textbook gastronomy" (opened
in 1962 and nowadays run by Simon and Rena
Gueller) "continues its stately progress, with classic
food (though in a lighter idiom), old-fashioned,
besuited service, padded tablecloths, bespoke details,
and so on". "There is a consistency, attention to
detail and perfection that few restaurants achieve"
and although there is a 'Menu Gourmand'"there
is no suggestion that diners will want the tasting
menu: portion sizes are very good and the food
quality is sublime" with "flavours that are subtle and
balanced but identifiable". Didier the sommelier is
"excellent and knowledgeable too" and the wine
list is "very well chosen, not just featuring the most
expensive or the most obvious options". Naturally all
this doesn't come cheap, but "in Yorkshire, we always
believe you get what you pay for, and here this
totally applies!" / Details: www.theboxtree.co.uk;

@boxtreeilkley; on A65 near town centre; 9.30 pm;
closed Mon, Tue L, Wed L, Thu L & Sun D; No jeans;
children: 10+.

ILMINGTON, WARWICKSHIRE   2–1C

The Howard Arms   £48   🔳🔳🔳
Lower Green CV36 4LT   01608 682226
On the edge of the Cotswolds, this lovely old inn
(with spacious rooms) in a picturesque village won
high praise (if on limited feedback) for its high
quality pub grub. / Details: www.howardarms.com;
@thehowardarms; 8m SW of Stratford-upon-Avon
off A4300; Mon-Sat 9.30 pm, Sun 8 pm; No Amex. /
Accommodation: 8 rooms, from £110

IPSWICH, SUFFOLK   3–1D

Aqua Eight   £45   🔳🔳🔳
8 Lion St IP1 1DB   01473 218989
"Top quality fusion cuisine", wins high praise for
this pan-Asian venture (owned by a family who
originated in Hong Kong) which offers a wide
range of menus, including vegetarian and gluten-
free selections. / Details: www.aquaeight.com;
@aquaeight8; 11 pm, Fri & Sat 9 pm, Sun 10 pm;
practically no walk-ins – you must boo.

Mariners at Il Punto   £50   🔳🔳🔳
Neptune Quay IP4 1AX   01473 289748
"A great experience" – a very "romantic" floating
restaurant, on a century-old Belgian gunboat;
since being requisitioned by the Crépy family
back in 1994, its Gallic cuisine has received
very solid support year upon year. / Details:
www.marinersipswich.co.uk; @MarinersIpswich;
9.30 pm; closed Mon & Sun; No Amex.

Trongs   £35   🔳🔳🔳
23 St Nicholas St IP1 1TW   01473 256833
"Trongs never disappoints!" – not only are staff
"exceptional", but it's "a constant source of
amazement that Ipswich has such a good Chinese"
(with a "Vietnamese take on many dishes"). /
Details: www.trongs.co.uk; 10.30 pm; closed Sun.

IRBY, MERSEYSIDE   5–2A

Da Piero   £50   🔳🔳🔳
5-7 Mill Hill Rd CH61 4UB   0151 648 7373
Dawn & Piero Di Bella's "intimate" (though slightly
extended these days) venture has built up quite a
name on the Wirral. One or two reporters feel it's
a little "overrated" but mostly there's praise for its
"authentic" and "interesting" Italian/Sicilian food. /
Details: www.dapiero.co.uk; 9 pm; D only, closed Mon
& Sun; No Amex.

Bohemia, The Club Hotel & Spa   £92   5 5 4
Green St, St Helier JE2 4UH 01534 876500
"Steve Smith just gets better and better" – providing "stunning" flavour combinations that are "so light and clean" – at this acclaimed dining room: one of only 15 in the UK and Channel Islands to have five AA rosettes. There's a good range of eating options, including "tasting menus to die for", "memorable breakfasts", "the most beautiful afternoon teas, with scones and Jersey Black Butter"; plus a "varied and interesting wine list". / **Details:** www.bohemiajersey.com; 10 pm; No trainers. / **Accommodation:** 46 rooms, from £185

Longueville Manor   £93   4 4 5
Longueville Rd, St Saviour JE2 7WF
01534 725501
Real raves of late for this "totally beautiful" and "romantic" Relais & Châteaux manor house, with its "adorable bar and gorgeous garden". All reporters are wowed by "the most wonderful food" ("divine fish", an "exquisite cheese chariot"… "the list is endless") and "an outstanding wine list". / **Details:** www.longuevillemanor.com; @longuevillemanor; head from St. Helier on the A3 towards Gorey; less than 1 mile from St. Helier; 10 pm; No jeans. / **Accommodation:** 31 rooms, from £170

Mark Jordan at the Beach   £58   3 4 3
La Plage, La Route de la Haule, St Peter
JE3 7YD 01534 780180
An all-glass building in St Aubin's Bay houses this "very relaxed" beachside restaurant – a "fantastic" spot which fans say is "better than local rivals (fish especially)". / **Details:** www.markjordanatthebeach.com; 9.30 pm; closed Mon.

The Oyster Box   £60   5 3 3
St Brelade's Bay JE3 8EF 01534 850 888
"Beautiful fresh seafood and an amazing view on the edge of one of Jersey's most picturesque bays" (St Brelade's) contribute to the "always buzzy" ambience at this stellar New England-style bistro. / **Details:** www.oysterbox.co.uk; @jerzypottery; Mon-Thu 9 pm, Fri & Sat 9.30 pm, Sun 9 pm; closed Mon L & Sun D; No Amex.

The Spice House   £39   3 3 3
Le Neuve Route, St Aubin JE3 8BS
01534 746600
This spacious Indian by the waterfront – part of the Boat House Group – wins all-round praise for its quality cooking and attractive interior. / **Details:** www.theboathousegroup.com/our-restaurants/t; @boathousegroup; 10 pm.

The Patricia   £62   4 4 3
139 Jesmond Road NE2 1JY 0191 2814443
"A wonderful addition to the Newcastle foodie scene!" Chef-patron Nick Grieve (previously of The River Café and Fera at Claridge's) brought his skills to leafy Jesmond, in late-2016 with this bistro named after his grandmother; "interesting" cuisine and a "stylish" setting – "we loved it!" / **Details:** @thepatriciancl.

The Milestone   £48   4 3 3
84 Green Lane At Ball Street S3 8SE
0114 272 8327
After a lightning-fast closure and revamp following a fire in May 2017, this high performing Victorian gastroboozer is "back to form", offering locally sourced food (don't miss the "great brunch") that's "worth the search to find it" amid dilapidated old mills in an industrial stretch of town. / **Details:** www.the-milestone.co.uk; @TheMilestone; 10 pm; No Amex.

Castle Dairy   £56   5 4 4
26 Wildman St LA9 6EN 01539 733946
"The ambience is just unlike anywhere else – a building that's a quirky delight with lots of little nooks and crannies, it's like stepping back in time… but there is nothing dated about the food" at this Grade I-listed property staffed by Kendal College apprentices, which provides an excellent experience in the 'fine dining' mould. It's now reopened with the help of the council and English Heritage after Storm Desmond: "I don't know how I lived without this place when it was closed!" / **Details:** www.castledairy.co.uk; @castle_dairy; 9 pm.

Bosquet   £58   5 4 3
97a Warwick Rd CV8 1HP 01926 852463
"The range of choice now may sometimes be more limited than in the past, as Bernard concentrates more on his classics", "but the quality is as excellent as ever" at the Lignier's "superb" Gallic stalwart. It has been excelling for nearly 30 years now – "here's hoping Bernard and Jane can go on forever!" / **Details:** www.restaurantbosquet.co.uk; 9.15 pm; closed Mon, Sat L & Sun; closed 2 weeks in Aug.

The Cross at Kenilworth £73 [4][4][3]
16 New St CV8 2EZ 01926 853840
"For my local hostelry to have Adam Bennett as chef producing food of such quality, prepared with such flair and skill is a real privilege (and must be adding untold thousands to my property!)" – this "relaxed" venture complete with "smiling and helpful" staff successfully provides "precise cuisine" of a level of ambition you might not anticipate from its "well-presented pub interior". Lovely garden in summer. / **Details:** www.thecrosskenilworth.co.uk; @TheCrossKen; 10 pm; closed Sun L.

KENTISBURY, DEVON   1–2C

Kentisbury Grange
Hotel   £67 [5][4][4]
EX31 4NL 01271 882 295
For "a super degustation meal", it's hard to beat this 17th-century coaching house, on the grounds of a plush boutique retreat, which received consistently impressive marks in this year's survey. / **Details:** www.kentisburygrange.com/; @KentisburyG; 10 pm.

KESWICK, CUMBRIA   7–3D

Lingholm Kitchen   £38
Portinscale CA12 5TZ 01768 771206
Charming Lake District estate greenhouse café overlooking a reconstruction of the original, hexagonal kitchen garden (the inspiration for Mr McGregor's garden in Beatrix Potter's The Tale of Peter Rabbit). One initial early report praises "an impressive new facility on the estate with good food from a limited menu". / **Details:** thelingholmkitchen.co.uk.

Lyzzick Hall Country House
Hotel   £59 [3][3][3]
Underskiddaw CA12 4PY 017687 72277
"This lovely hotel tucked away in the north-western Lake District ticks all the boxes"; "the food is exceptional" – now including oft-changing tasting menus – and "the wine list (long the star asset) remains a real treat for Iberian fans". Just "make sure you exercise before dinner!" / **Details:** www.lyzzickhall.co.uk; @LyzzixkHall; 9 pm; No Amex. /
Accommodation: 30 rooms, from £148

KETTLESHULME, CHESHIRE   5–2B

The Swan Inn   £47 [4][3][3]
Macclesfield Rd SK23 7QU 01663 732943
"Tucked away in the beautiful High Peak countryside, this pub boasts a newly added dining-conservatory where seafood is a speciality" – and where the carnivorous choices also benefit from

being cooked in the Josper oven on proud display in the open kitchen. / **Details:** 8.30 pm, Thu-Sat 7 pm, Sun 4 pm; closed Mon; No Amex.

KEYSTON, CAMBRIDGESHIRE   3–1A

The Pheasant at
Keyston   £53 [3][2][2]
Loop Rd PE28 0RE 01832 710241
This "charming old" thatched pub (sibling and lookalike to the Old Bridge, Huntingdon) is "worth going to and worth going back to"; despite inspiring MOR scores, the overall experiences is more than the sum of its parts, with food that's "at the 'good' end of the standard pub range". / **Details:** www.thepheasant-keyston.co.uk; @pheasantkeyston; 1m S of A14 between Huntingdon & Kettering, J15; 9.30 pm, Sun 7.30 pm; closed Mon & Sun D; No Amex.

KIBWORTH , LEICESTERSHIRE   5–4D

The Lighthouse   £48 [4][4][4]
No 9 Station Street LE8 0LN 0116 2796260
The Boboli family's "friendly and unfussy" establishment – a more democratic, English follow-up to their popular Italian, Firenze – is "always a great choice for good fish and seafood" (and at "fair prices" too). / **Details:** www.lighthousekibworth.co.uk; @ourlighthouse; 9.30 pm; D only, closed Mon & Sun; No Amex.

KILLIECRANKIE, PERTHSHIRE   9–3C

Killiecrankie Hotel   £64 [4][5][4]
PH16 5LG 01796 473220
"Fantastic quality food, an excellent atmosphere and first class staff" win approval – if on limited feedback – for this small country house hotel, run with the personal touch by owner Henrietta Fergusson; the wine cellar here has something of a reputation. / **Details:** www.killiecrankiehotel.co.uk; @KilliecrankieHH; 8.30 pm; No Amex; No shorts. /
Accommodation: 10 rooms, from £150

KING'S LYNN, NORFOLK   6–4B

Market Bistro   £53 [4][4][4]
11 Saturday Market Pl PE30 5DQ
01553 771483
"Lucy at front of house and husband, Richard, chef, provide an excellent experience" – complete with "the personal touch" – at the Goldings' town-centre bistro, where the cooking is "always good and sometimes exceptional from produce that's local and delicious". In late 2017 their empire is

*expanding with the addition of a relaunched nearby pub, 'Goldings'. / **Details:** www.marketbistro.co.uk; @Market_Bistro; 8.30 pm, Fri & Sat 9 pm.*

KINGHAM, GLOUCESTERSHIRE   2–1C

Daylesford Café   **£42**   3 2 4
Daylesford near Kingham GL56 0YG
01608 731700
*Lady Bamford's ultra-chichi farmshop café wins most praise as a "great healthy brunch venue" (although fans say "the supper nights are amazing" too). Quality-wise "you get what you pay for here… even if you do pay a lot for it". / **Details:** www.daylesfordorganic.com; 7.30 pm; L only; I; SRA-Food Made Good – 3 stars.*

KINGHAM, OXFORDSHIRE   2–1C

The Kingham Plough   **£62**   3 3 3
The Green OX7 6YD   01608 658327
*"A brilliant pub with exquisite food and superb atmosphere" is still the mainstream view on this well-known Cotswolds destination, where the ambitious kitchen ("humble local gastropub it isn't") is headed by chef Emily Watkins; but reports overall were more up-and-down this year ("somewhat variable", "good, but not up to the hype", …). / **Details:** www.thekinghamplough.co.uk; @kinghamplough; 9 pm, Sun 8 pm; closed Sun D; No Amex. / **Accommodation:** 7 rooms, from £95*

The Wild Rabbit   **£73**   3 2 5
Church St OX7 6YA   01608 658389
*"Successfully transformed with no expense spared" – Lady Bamford's "stunning" and "very stylish" country pub is not just "a lovey place to stay", but also massively popular as "a really delightful and enjoyable dining experience", with a high level of ambition. On the downside, even numerous fans gripe about "slow" service, and – perhaps predictably – "they hit you with a big bill". / **Details:** www.thewildrabbit.co.uk; 9 pm.*

KINGSTON UPON THAMES, SURREY   3–3A

The Canbury Arms   **£51**   3 3 3
49 Canbury Park Road KT2 6LQ
020 8255 9129
*"Whatever the occasion the Canbury is always a firm favourite", whose "eclectic menu" is "of a quality that set it apart from the rest of Kingston's pubs". It's so "hard to find independent and really affordable places like this". / **Details:** www.thecanburyarms.com; @thecanburyarms; Mon-Sat 10 pm, Sun 8.30 pm.*

Jin Go Gae   **£42**   4 2 2
270- 272 Burlington Road KT3 4NL
020 8949 2506
*"Fantastic authentic Korean food" – not least bargain-friendly BBQ fare – warrants the journey to this simply furnished and somewhat off-the-beaten-track venue, which continues to be one of the top picks locally. / **Details:** jingogae.wordpress.com/menus/; 11 pm.*

Roz ana   **£49**   3 2 2
4-8 Kingston Hill KT2 7NH   020 8546 6388
*In Norbiton, a "cut-above Indian" – casual downstairs and with a posher colonial-tinged upstairs – whose "delicately spiced" dishes are full of "imagination and flavour". / **Details:** www.roz-ana.com; @Rozana; 10.30 pm, Fri & Sat 11 pm, Sun 10 pm; No Amex.*

KINGUSSIE, HIGHLAND   9–2C

The Cross   **£77**   3 3 4
Tweed Mill Brae, Ardbroilach Rd PH21 1LB
01540 661166
*Being set in the Cairngorms National Park, this 18th-century inn (formerly a watermill) is an admittedly "remote retreat", but David Skiggs' "excellent food and wine" (not least the six-course tasting menus) continue to justify a visit for all who comment on it. / **Details:** www.thecross.co.uk; @CrossRelax; 8.30 pm; children: 9+. / **Accommodation:** 8 rooms, from £100*

KIRKBY LONSDALE, CUMBRIA   7–4D

Hipping Hall   **£77**   4 4 4
Cowan Bridge LA6 2JJ   01524 271187
*"I never knew you could get so many different flavours and textures out of a simple Apple. Well done Oli Martin!" The flagship of the Wildsmith Hotels chain has a "sensational position" in the Lune valley and makes "a lovely place to stay and dine". / **Details:** www.hippinghall.com; @hippinghall; 9.30 pm; closed weekday L; No Amex; No trainers; children: 12+. / **Accommodation:** 10 rooms, from £239*

KIRKBY STEPHEN, CUMBRIA   8–3A

The Black Swan
Fell Road CA17 4NS   015396 23204
*Limited but highly positive feedback on Scott Fairweather's cuisine at this comfortable, traditional hotel, which has an attractive position in a Lakeland farming village (plus sizeable garden). / **Details:** www.blackswanhotel.com.*

KIRKCUDBRIGHT, DUMFRIES & GALLOWAY
7–2B

The Selkirk Arms Bar, Bistro and Restaurant £40 🟥🟥🟥
High Street DG6 4JG 01557 330402
"Some lovely and well-executed pub classics but a few more refined dishes too" win praise for this townhouse hotel, near the town's harbour; attractive garden in summer. / **Details:** *www.selkirkarmshotel.co.uk; @selkirkarms; 9 pm.*

KNOWSTONE, DEVON 1–2D

The Mason's Arms £68 🟧🟥🟥
South Molton EX36 4RY 01398 341231
"Quite a find miles from anywhere" – this "lovely and laidback" thatched inn is certainly "unique"… and that's just the Italianate hand-painted ceiling in the dining area. The food, by Mark Dodson (ex-Waterside Inn), is "always fantastic here and reasonably priced for what you get". / **Details:** *www.masonsarmsdevon.co.uk; @masonsknowstone; 9 pm; closed Mon & Sun D; Booking max 4 may apply; children: 5+ after 6pm.*

KNUTSFORD, CHESHIRE 5–2B

Belle Époque £56 🟦🟥🟧
60 King St WA16 6DT 01565 633060
Near the train station, this landmark hotel, whose gorgeous Art Nouveau interiors ensure a steady wedding trade, still has the capacity to delight some reporters – though the food has "steadily trundled downhill" over the years, and doubters warn you'll pay "high prices for very average victuals". / **Details:** *www.thebelleepoque.com; @TheBelleEpoque; 1.5m from M6, J19; 9.30 pm; closed Sun D; Booking max 6 may apply. /* **Accommodation:** *7 rooms, from £110*

KYLESKU, HIGHLAND 9–1B

Kylesku Hotel £52 🟧🟥🟥
IV27 4HW 01971 502231
This "remote" hotel dining room enjoys "fantastic views" of the neighbouring loch and rolling Highlands landscape, and the super local food (including seafood landed nearby) is "brilliant" too. / **Details:** *www.kyleskuhotel.co.uk; on A894, S of Scourie, N of loch inver; 9 pm. /* **Accommodation:** *8 rooms, from £55*

LANCASTER, LANCASHIRE 5–1A

Quite Simply French £61 🟥🟥🟥
27a St Georges Quay LA1 1RD 01524 843199
A "warm and welcoming" spot, well-known locally, combining a "lovely eating environment" with some "consistently excellent" food. Top Tip – "for great value, try their (two-course meal and wine deal) 'Simply Squiffy' early on a Sunday night". / **Details:** *quitesimplyfrench.co.uk/; @QSFLancaster; 9.30 pm, Sun & Mon 9 pm; D only, ex Sun open L & D; No Amex.*

LANGAR, NOTTINGHAMSHIRE 5–3D

Langar Hall £50 🟥🟧🟧
Church Ln NG13 9HG 01949 860559
Owner Imogen Skirving, who passed away in June 2016, "was most definitely a warm and very talented creator and chatelaine" and is "sadly missed" at the charming old-school country house hotel that she created in her grand family home. Arguably the venue "needs to re-establish itself" somewhat under granddaughter Lila, who has taken the reins here, but fans still find it a "memorable" spot. / **Details:** *www.langarhall.com; @Langarhallhotel; off A52 between Nottingham & Grantham; 9.30 pm; No Amex; No trainers. /* **Accommodation:** *12 rooms, from £100*

LANGHO, LANCASHIRE 5–1B

Northcote £98 🟩🟥🟧
Northcote Rd BB6 8BE 01254 240555
"A jewel 'up north!" The North West's best-known country house hotel "bears comparison with the Gavroches and Watersides of the world (certainly when it comes to the bill!") – and "even if it's not yet reached the effortless heights of some of its most famous competitors, the whole approach is so polished, it's nonetheless a remarkable experience". Set on the edge of the Ribble Valley, in a much-converted and extended old manor house, the management's high ambitions inspired a major upgrade a few years ago ("since, usefully toned down somewhat") and its combination of "sublime cooking" (led by executive head chef Lisa Goodwin-Allen), "passion for wine" ("reflected by MD Craig Bancroft and all his team") with "true, warm, friendly and totally unstuffy Lancastrian hospitality" means "they truly deserve the many awards they receive". But are they "pushing too hard for a second Michelin Star"? – there's the odd gripe about "weird combinations" ("nice to see new ideas, but not a huge success"), or the view that "aiming for technical perfection doesn't always make for a fun meal". (In October 2017, after 30 years, Chef/Patron Nigel Haworth announced he

*is to step back somewhat, taking on a new role as Northcote 'Ambassador', with a 50-day per annum commitment to the business). / **Details:** www.northcote.com; @NorthcoteUK; M6, J31 then A59; 10 pm, Sun 9 pm; No trainers. / **Accommodation:** 18 rooms, from £280*

LANGLAND, SWANSEA	1–1C

Britannia Inn
Llanmadoc SA3 1DB 01792 386624
*"A lovely pub on the Gower Peninsula" (whose sizeable garden has fine views). Its attractive menu wins praise for its "fresh preparation" and reporters "can't fault it". / **Details:** www.britanniainngower.co.uk.*

LAVENHAM, SUFFOLK	3–1C

**The Great House Hotel &
Restaurant, Lavenham** **£59** **5 4 4**
Market Pl CO10 9QZ 01787 247431
*"People will drive many many miles to eat at the Great House – one of the finest French Restaurants in Britain, in a stylish 14th Century old inn on the market square of the perfectly preserved half-timbered medieval village of Lavenham". "Classically French by cuisine, it's also classically French-run by owners the Crepy family (Regis and Martine) complete with old fashioned heavy eating irons, and pure white tablecloths" and "flexible and charming staff". "Much of the food is locally sourced, all ingredients of the highest quality" and results are "impeccable" down to "the most extravagantly rich cheese trolley anywhere!" / **Details:** www.greathouse.co.uk; @GreatHouseHotel; follow directions to Guildhall; 9.30 pm; closed Mon & Sun D; closed Jan; No Amex. / **Accommodation:** 5 rooms, from £95*

Lavenham Greyhound **£49** **3 3 3**
97 High Street CO10 9PZ 01787 249553
*As of spring 2017, the "fun" sibling to the Long Melford Swan has had an impressive refurb', and reporters "love the extension" into a barn area overlooking a "fabulous new garden for outside dining in the Great British sun". The "intriguing" new-look menu spans small plates to larger dishes and even a waffle section. / **Details:** www.lavenhamgreyhound.com; @LavenhamGH/; 10 pm.*

Number Ten **£40** **3 3 3**
10 Lady St CO10 9RA 01787 249438
*"Everyone loves Number Ten!"; situated in a 15th century house, this "small and welcoming" local bistro wins praise for its "home cooking with a twist"; or you can just drink in the adjoining wine bar. / **Details:** www.ten-lavenham.co.uk; 9 pm.*

Swan Hotel **£62** **3 4 5**
High St CO10 9QA 01787 247477
*"From the welcome to the farewell, simply fabulous in every respect" – that's the general verdict on this "romantic" 15th century inn: "an amazing setting, with centuries of history in every wooden beam". The dining room is "a solid hotel restaurant serving interesting locally inspired food" – sweets are particularly "fine" and "afternoon tea is a delight". "With the spa, bar and decent bistro you don't actually have to leave the building during a weekend away!" / **Details:** www.theswanatlavenham.co.uk; @SwanLavenham; 9 pm; No jeans; children: 12+ at D. / **Accommodation:** 45 rooms, from £195*

LEAMINGTON SPA, WARWICKSHIRE	5–4C

La Coppola **£49** **3 4 3**
86 Regent St CV32 4NS 01926 888 873
*"A warm and professional welcome" helps make this quirkily decorated Italian – with two popular local café siblings – a hit for its fans: "ticks all boxes for a ladies lunch", and "a first choice for a special meal". / **Details:** www.lacoppola.co.uk; 10 pm, Sun 9 pm; No Amex.*

Oscars French Bistro **£57** **3 4 4**
39 Chandos Street CV32 4RL 01926 452807
*"Bustling service and atmosphere bolster an authentic French bistro experience" at this "immensely popular" local, whose MO is "largely traditional, comforting fare"; "it's the kind of restaurant everyone would like within easy reach!" / **Details:** www.oscarsfrenchbistro.co.uk; @oscars_bistro; 9.30 pm; closed Mon & Sun.*

Restaurant 23 **£72** **3 4 3**
34 Hamilton Ter CV32 4LY 01926 422422
*"Against the trend for more basic surroundings, this is gorgeous restaurant", say fans of this suburban Victorian pile, which "continues to make its clients feel special and feed them memorable food". / **Details:** www.restaurant23.co.uk/#!; @Restaurant23; 9.30 pm; closed Mon & Sun; children: 12+.*

Tame Hare **£71**
97 Warwick Street CV32 4RJ 01926 316191
*Enthusiasm among food critics and bloggers has been high for the local produce-driven menus at this Leamington Spa newcomer, which also sources organic, biodynamic wines and small brewery beers. / **Details:** www.thetamehare.co.uk/; @thetamehare; 9 pm, Fri & Sat 9.30 pm, Sun 3pm.*

LECHLADE, GLOUCESTERSHIRE	2–2C

The Five Alls **£50** **4 3 4**
Filkins GL7 3JQ 01367 860875
Sebastian Snow's 18th century village pub-

*with-rooms (following his London haunt Snows on the Green and a stint at the famed Swan at Southrop) is on the up and up, winning very positive ratings across the board this year. / **Details:** www.thefiveallsfilkins.co.uk; @fiveallsfilkins; 9.30 pm, Fri & Sat 10 pm; closed Sun D; No Amex.*

LEEDS, WEST YORKSHIRE	5–1C

Aagrah £36 **3 4 3**
Aberford Rd LS25 2HF 0113 245 5667
*This well-placed branch of the hit northern Kashmiri chain is a "reliable and consistently performing spot" with "sensible" prices. Its most ardent fans love it bigtime – "worth the trip from London to Yorkshire to eat here!" / **Details:** www.aagrah.com; @Aagrahgroup; from A1 take A642 Aberford Rd to Garforth; 11.30 pm, Sun 10.30 pm; D only.*

Aagrah £36 **4 4 3**
St Peter's Sq LS9 8AH 0113 245 5667
*"Well-established, and completely on top of its game" – this city-centre outpost of the well-known Yorkshire chain delivers "no surprise" but "ticks all the boxes for Indian cuisine" and is "always a delight". / **Details:** www.aagrah.com; midnight, Sun 10.30 pm.*

Akbar's £35 **4 3 3**
16 Greek St LS1 5RU 0113 242 5426
*A continued strong showing in survey feedback for the stylishly decorated Leeds branch of this popular and ever-expanding Bradford-based Indian chain. / **Details:** www.akbars.co.uk; midnight; D only.*

Art's £45 **3 3 3**
42 Call Lane LS1 6DT 0113 243 8243
*"If in Leeds go to Art's café" – a wood-floored 1990s stalwart, near the Corn Exchange, where "you can be guaranteed good food and a relaxed atmosphere" (plus regular exhibitions by up-and-coming artists). / **Details:** www.artscafebar.com; @artscafeleeds; Mon-Thu 10 pm, Fri & Sat 10.30, Sun 10 pm.*

Bundobust £30 **5 3 3**
6 Mill Hill LS1 5DQ 0113 243 1248
*"The best Indian street food and top beers to boot" – plus a "special mention for the mango lassi" – mark this three-year-old collaboration between craft ale purveyors The Sparrow and local restaurant Prashad; albeit "very basic" in style (the veggie dishes are "served in paper bowls") it's "lots of fun and very tasty". / **Details:** www.bundobust.com; @Bundobust; Mon-Thu 9.30 pm, Fri, Sat 10 pm, Sun 8 pm; Booking weekdays only.*

Crafthouse, Trinity Leeds £64
Level 5 LS1 6HW 0113 897 0444
D&D London are onto a winner with their

*"sophisticated city-centre yearling" on top of a new shopping development. There's a wide variety of menus and eating options – including Orkney Island steaks from the Josper Grill – and even if perhaps "nothing is madly outstanding", overall it offers a "very buzzy" rendezvous and "a slightly pricey but fab experience". / **Details:** www.crafthouse-restaurant.com; @CrafthouseLeeds; 9.45 pm, Fri & Sat 10.30 pm; Booking max 8 may apply.*

Fuji Hiro £27 **4 3 2**
45 Wade Ln LS2 8NJ 0113 243 9184
*Some of the "best noodles ever" ensure the continuing popularity of this "bare and crowded" but "great traditional family Japanese", in the city-centre. / **Details:** 10 pm, Fri & Sat 11 pm; May need 5+ to book.*

Hansa's £33 **5 3 2**
72-74 North St LS2 7PN 0113 244 4408
*"Vegetarian heaven" rewards souls who make the trek to Mrs Hansa Dabhi's city-centre stalwart – a smart restaurant and cookery school turning out Gujarati food "at its best", from curries to special thalis. / **Details:** www.hansasrestaurant.com; 10 pm, Sat 11 pm; D only, ex Sun L only.*

Iberica £27 **3 4 4**
Hepper House, 17a East Parade LS1 2BH 01134 037007
*The seventh link in the London-centric tapas chain's empire – since followed by Glasgow, and with an Edinburgh sibling due in late 2017; the food is "generally OK" but is not as highly rated as the "spectacular" premises (which incorporate a "great cocktail bar and also a deli downstairs" too). / **Details:** www.ibericarestaurants.com/restaurants/iberica-leeds/; Mon-Sat 11 pm, Sun 4 pm.*

Issho £62
Victoria Gate, George St LS27 7AU 0113 426 5000
*D&D Group's third Leeds venture, a Japanese/Pan-Asian restaurant, with Ben Orpwood (previously of Sexy Fish) at the helm; at the top of the new Victoria Gate development, it shares a roof terrace with its stablemate 59th Street. / **Details:** www.issho-restaurant.com; 11 pm.*

Kendells Bistro £45 **3 4 4**
St Peters Square LS9 8AH 0113 243 6553
*A visit to this "buzzing", candlelit French outfit is "like walking into a Parisian bistro"; it combines "friendly service" with a "good choice of dishes, some of them excellent". / **Details:** www.kendellsbistro.co.uk; @KendellsBistro; 9 pm, Fri & Sat 10 pm; D only, closed Mon & Sun; No Amex.*

FSA

The Man Behind The Curtain £119 **4 3 3**
Top Floor Flannels, 68-78 Vicar Ln LS1 7JH
0113 243 2376
"The novelty of entering through Flannels menswear shop provides amusement on both the way in and out" of Michael O'Hare's "avant garde" city-centre venture – an "airy" rooftop space over a store (and bizarrely approached through it). Its fame has spread nowadays as a "never-had-anything-like-it" experience ("if you can actually get a table") – featuring "food as theatre" from "truly memorable" 10-course or 14-course tasting menus, all in a style that's "gastronomic but not pompous". "The wine-pairing is excellent too; intelligently done, and very good value". It's not for everyone. Even fans concede that "the food can be a bit of an assault on the senses", and while they say that's "in a brilliant way", there are a few sceptics to whom it "feels a bit like Emperor's New Clothes: too rich and with too little variation". More commonly though, it's judged "totally inspiring". / **Details:** www.themanbehindthecurtain.co.uk; @hairmetalchef; 9.30 pm; closed Mon, Tue & Sun.

Mustard Pot £36 **3 3 2**
20 Stainbeck Ln LS7 3QY 0113 269 5699
A "really good" redbrick Chapel Allerton gastropub with "nice real ales and friendly staff"; a "new chef has improved the quality of the offering" of late, with "especially good pies" and burgers. / **Details:** themustardpot.com/; @Mustardpot; Sun-Wed 11 pm, Thu 12 am, Fri & Sat 1 am.

Ox Club £57 **4 4 4**
19a The Headrow LS1 6PU 07470 359961
From the team behind Belgrave Music Hall, this "innovative" venture incorporates a fancy Grillworks grill, responsible for its funky charred and smoked (but "clean"-tasting) fare. An "amazing ice cream selection" is another draw – and "being part of Headrow House you can continue your evening in the beer hall, on the roof terrace, or checking out a live band". / **Details:** www.oxclub.co.uk; 10 pm.

Patty Smiths, Belgrave Music Hall £25 **4 4 3**
1 Cross Belgrave St LS2 8JP 0113 234 6160
One of two ground-floor eateries in this "trendy" multi-tasking "grunge music venue", this former pop-up is now a local staple known for its "very tasty" and "very messy" burgers plus "great dressed fries". "The location adds to the vibe, especially if there is a band playing" – and don't miss the excellent roof terrace. / **Details:** www.belgravemusichall.com; 10 pm.

Pintura £41 **4 4 3**
LS1 6AP 0113 4300 915
A vast, buzzy three-floor operation offering "delicious little regional dishes from all over Spain, but specialising in Basque cuisine"; there's also a gin bar and a "great selection of wines". / **Details:** www.pinturakitchen.co.uk.

Prashad £46 **4 3 2**
137 Whitehall Rd BD11 1AT 0113 285 2037
There's no let-up in the praise for the "exceptional" and "fresh" veggie cuisine offered by this stalwart Gujarati (a former Ramsay's Best Restaurant finalist); "shame about the relocation out of Bradford" a while back, but by all accounts the roomier venue is worth the schlep. / **Details:** www.prashad.co.uk; @prashad_veggie/; 10 pm, 9 pm; closed Mon, Tue L, Wed L & Thu L; No Amex.

Red Chilli £42 **4 4 3**
6 Great George Street LS1 3DW
01132 429688
"Good spicy" cuisine – not least the popular Sichuanese options, which it specialises in – ensure the popularity of this northern mini-chain's city-centre basement outpost, complete with 1920s Shanghai-esque decor. / **Details:** redchillirestaurant. co.uk/leeds/; Mon-Thu 10.30 pm, Fri & Sat 11.30 pm, Sun 10.30; closed Mon.

The Reliance £40 **3 4 4**
76-78 North St LS2 7PN 0113 295 6060
"What a surprise" – "buzzing" bar below, "perfect pub dining" upstairs, with a "varied menu" ("combinations I would not have thought possible"), incorporating home-cured charcuterie as a highlight. "All this and a pint of Beavertown Neck Oil and you cannot possibly go wrong". / **Details:** www.the-reliance.co.uk; @The_Reliance; 10 pm, Thu-Sat 10.30 pm, Sun 8.30 pm; No bookings.

Rola Wala £18 **3 3 2**
Trinity Kitchen, Albion St LS1 5AY
0113 244 4589
The first bricks and mortar site of Aussie Mark Wright's foodie-fave chain delivers "fab" and "good value Indian street food in the Trinity Centre"; following a second HQ at London's Spitalfields, a third opened in Oxford's Westgate shopping hub in October 2017. / **Details:** www.rolawala.com; @RolaWala.

Salvo's £47 **4 4 3**
115 & 107 Otley Road LS6 3PX
0113 275 2752
"Pizza, pasta, gelato!" – when it comes to "good Italian fodder" in a "great atmosphere" this Headingley stalwart can't be beat, and their new café/deli a few doors down is also a "super spot for lunch". Love or loathe the TV chef, "Gordon Ramsay

was right... this 'f-Word' winner is flippin' good!" /
*Details: www.salvos.co.uk; @salvosleeds; Mon-Thu
10 pm, Fri & Sat 10.30 pm, Sun 9 pm; No bookings
at diner.*

Sous le Nez en Ville £55 🗟🗟🗵
Quebec Hs, Quebec St LS1 2HA
0113 244 0108
A "great venue for a boozy business lunch or
dinner" – this "extremely busy" and "noisy"
basement stalwart boasts "many satisfied repeat
diners" thanks to its "highly dependable", French
regional cooking and bibulous possibilities ("if you
want to, it is possible to spend a lot on its very
good wine list"). Top Tip – "the early-bird menu is a
particular attraction". / *Details: www.souslenez.com;
@SousLeNezLeeds; 9.45 pm, Sat 10.30 pm; closed
Sun.*

Sukhothai £35 🗟🗃🗟
15 South Parade LS1 5QS 0113 242 2795
This five-year-old city-centre branch of the Thai
mini-chain (founded in Chapel Allerton) wins limited
but very positive feedback for its stylish, themed
interior and its dependable cuisine; lunchtime set
deals are a feature. / *Details: www.sukhothai.co.uk;
@Sukhothai_.*

Sukhothai £43 🗃🗃🗟
8 Regent St LS7 4PE 0113 237 0141
"Watch the cooks behind the glass" in the kitchen,
at the original Chapel Allerton branch of this Thai
chain – now fifteen years old – which is nowadays
expanding beyond its Yorkshire origins. Limited
feedback this year, but fans say it's "the best Thai in
Leeds". / *Details: www.sukhothai.co.uk; @Sukhothai_;
10.45pm; Mon-Thu D only, Fri-Sun open L & D; No
Amex.*

Tharavadu £39 🗟🗃🗟
7- 8 Mill Hill LS1 5DQ 0113 244 0500
"Really a breath of fresh air" – this "very popular"
Indian continues to take Leeds by storm, with
the "pure and excellent tastes" of its Keralan
cooking ("wonderful fish and dosas"). "Packed on
a Monday night in February: says it all!" / *Details:
www.tharavadurestaurants.com; @TharavaduRestau;
10 pm, Fri & Sat 10.30 pm; closed Sun.*

Zaap £29 🗟🗟🗟
16 Grand Arcade LS1 6PG 0113 243 2586
"A really busy and bustling venue reminiscent of
eating on the side of a Bangkok backstreet" (but in
reality set in the Grand Arcade in the city-centre);
it's "great fun" its Thai street food is "yummy",
prices are "cheap" and "it's always an experience". /
*Details: www.zaapthai.co.uk/zaap-leeds; @ZaapThai;
11 pm; No bookings.*

Zucco £45 🗃🗟🗟
603 Meanwood Road LS6 4AY 01132 249679
A "relentlessly excellent out-of-town Italian tapas"
joint turning out "delicious little regional dishes
from all over the country" ("although mostly
northern Italian", reflecting the owners'Venetian
roots); the "informal and friendly" spot has a "great
selection of Italian wines," too (including some "you
don't normally find in restaurants"). / *Details:
www.zucco.co.uk; @Zuccouk; 10 pm, Fri & Sat
10.30 pm, Sun 8.30 pm.*

LEICESTER, LEICESTERSHIRE 5–4D

Bobby's £25 🗟🗵🗐
154-156 Belgrave Rd LE4 5AT 0116 266 0106
Part restaurant, part take-away, part sweet shop,
this canteen institution has been a feature of the
Golden Mile since 1976; the Gujarati fare (ranging
from breakfast to buffets) is both bargainous and
entirely veggie. / *Details: www.eatatbobbys.com;
@bobbysleicester; 10 pm; No Amex.*

The Fish & The Chip, Hotel
Maiyengo £53
13-21 St Nicholas Place LE1 4LD
0116 251 8898
It's all change at this swish boutique hotel – a bit
of a pioneer when it opened a decade back – with
former owner Aatin Anadkat opting to focus solely
on the ground-floor restaurant; in August 2017,
replacing the fine dining spot of old, he launched
this new, more populist Union Jack-strewn concept
venue, serving comfort food classics (sausage 'n'
chips, surf 'n' turf burgers etc.) and, as of yore,
superior cocktails. / *Details: www.maiyengo.com;
@HotelMaiyango; Mon-Sat 9.30 pm, Sun 9 pm; closed
Mon L & Sun L. / **Accommodation:** 14 rooms, from
£90*

Kayal £37 🗃🗟🗟
153 Granby St LE1 6FE 0116 255 4667
"Not your ordinary curry" – a "brilliant" Keralan
venue "reflecting the origins of the family who own
it"; compared to your standard Bangladeshi, the
food is "less oily and makes more use of vegetables
and coconut". / *Details: www.kayalrestaurant.com/;
@kayalrestaurant; 11 pm, Sun 10 pm.*

LEWANNICK, CORNWALL 1–3C

Coombeshead Farm £85 🗟🗃🗃
Coombeshead Farm PL15 7QQ
01566 782 009
"If only all B&Bs cooked food this tasty!" – this rural
Cornish guesthouse on a working dairy farm is the
"clearly-on-trend" brainchild of April Bloomfield of
NYC's acclaimed Spotted Pig and Tom Adams of

Pitt Cue Co.The communal eating set-up (you are one of 14 diners enjoying a seasonal five-course set menu) means "you have to be ready to spend time with a range of people" but all reports applaud the "amazing food and great company". / Details: www.coombesheadfarm.co.uk.

LEYBURN, NORTH YORKSHIRE   8–4B

The Blue Lion   **£52** 3️⃣2️⃣3️⃣
East Whitton DL8 4SN 01969 624273
"The food is good mainstream" ("excellent grouse in season") at this "very-British-as-it-used-to-be" coaching inn, with a "lovely open-fired bar". / Details: www.thebluelion.co.uk; @blueloninn.

LICHFIELD, STAFFORDSHIRE   5–4C

McKenzie's   **£37** 3️⃣4️⃣4️⃣
The Corn Exchange, Conduit Street WS13 6JU 01543 417371
The town's converted Victorian corn exchange provides an "amazing" location for this 'bar lounge and restaurant' which serves a wide menu with a good variety of dishes for 'Non Red Meat Lovers' balancing an array of steaks and burgers. / Details: mckenziesrestaurant.com; @Mck_Lichfield; 9 pm, Fri & Sat 10 pm, Sun 8 pm.

LICKFOLD, WEST SUSSEX   3–4A

Lickfold Inn   **£62** 4️⃣4️⃣4️⃣
Highstead Ln GU28 9EY 01798 861285
"Enjoy the bluebells on the way to this rather tucked away pub" – a "well-restored country inn" bought a few years ago by London über-chef Tom Sellers from its former owner, DJ Chris Evans, which "serves food in both the bar (with open fire) and, more formally, upstairs". One reviewer found it "trying way too hard for a Michelin star", but most of the many reports we received this year were full of praise for its "seriously high standard of cooking" and "enchanting staff". / Details: www.thelickfoldinn.co.uk; @LickfoldInn; 3m N of A272 between Midhurst & Petworth; 9.30 pm, Sun 4 pm; closed Mon & Sun D; No Amex.

LIFTON, DEVON   1–3C

The Arundell Arms Hotel   **£63** 3️⃣2️⃣3️⃣
PL16 0AA 01566 784666
Famed for its angling associations – it houses one of the country's leading angling schools, with 20 miles of private fishing rights – this "welcoming and good value", family-run hotel is "worth a detour off the

A30" for the "well-balanced and tasty cooking" of its rather grand dining room (there's also a bar doing pub grub). / **Details:** www.arundellarms.com; 0.5m off A30, Lifton Down exit; 9.30 pm; No Amex; No jeans. / **Accommodation:** 21 rooms, from £179*

LINCOLN, LINCOLNSHIRE   6–3A

Bronze Pig   **£60** 4️⃣3️⃣3️⃣
4 Burton Road LN1 3LB 01522 524817
"Set up by a Masterchef semi-finalist" (Irishman Eamon Hunt) and Sicilian FOH Pompeo Siracusa, this "fabulous restaurant" with rooms has made waves in the city since opening in 2013.Two years back it moved to this bigger location, "in uphill Lincoln, in the shadow of the Castle", and wins praise for its "first-class food" that "changes with the seasons". Concerns? – it's not inexpensive, and the odd service glitch is reported. / Details: www.thebronzepig.co.uk; @thebronzepig; 10 pm, Sun 2 pm.

Jew's House Restaurant £55 3️⃣3️⃣4️⃣
15 The Strait LN2 1JD 01522 524851
Location, location, and location is a key strength of this "romantic" veteran venue in a low-beamed, 12th century building – one of England's earliest surviving townhouses.The cooking doesn't let the side down though, with much praise and no complaints this year. / Details: www.jewshouserestaurant.co.uk; @JewsHouselincs; 9.30 pm; closed Mon,Tue L & Sun; No Amex.

The Old Bakery   **£59** 4️⃣4️⃣4️⃣
26-28 Burton Road LN1 3LB 01522 576057
A "very romantic" restaurant-with-rooms that's "well worth making a detour to sample"; while some "miss the eclectic welcome" formerly provided by chef Ivano de Serio's padre, the food "gets better and better" ("always different, always adventurous"). / Details: www.theold-bakery.co.uk; @theoldbakeryrestaurant; 8.30 pm, Sun 1.30 pm; closed Mon; No jeans. / Accommodation: 4 rooms, from £65

Ole Ole   **£31** 3️⃣4️⃣4️⃣
33 Bailgate LN1 3AP 01522 534222
In a city underserved by good restaurants, this "marvellous place" is a bit of a beacon; it's "only small but the menu is large", and "when the sun's out, there's nothing nicer than sitting at a table in the garden" while you enjoy some "authentic" tapas. / Details: www.oleolelincoln.co.uk; 10 pm, Fri & Sat 10.30 pm.

FSA

LINLITHGOW, WEST LOTHIAN 9–4C

Champany Inn £81 ③③④
EH49 7LU 01506 834532
*"In a beautiful rural setting near The House of
Binns and Linlithgow Palace", this long-established
inn is known as "a good steak house" with a "very
varied wine selection", and on all accounts creates
the "special experience" for which is is renowned.
The prices though can seem "crazy – more than
you'd pay in London!" /* **Details:** *www.champany.com;
2m NE of Linlithgow on junction of A904 & A803;
10 pm; closed Sat L & Sun; No jeans; children: 8+. /*
Accommodation: *16 rooms, from £125*

LITTLE ECCLESTON, LANCASHIRE 5–1A

The Cartford Inn £63 ④②②
Cartford Lane PR3 0YP 01995 670 166
*"Brilliantly conceived" dishes "using local Lancashire
produce" won a major thumbs-up this year for this
"quirky" pub, whose "unique decor" (sceptics say "it
looks a bit like the designer was high on mushrooms
at the time") "includes charming artwork by
local artists", and which is "set in a beautiful part
of countryside next to the winding river Wyre".
"Service can be a bit quaintly local at times, but it's
always friendly". /* **Details:** *www.thecartfordinn.co.uk;
@Cartfordinn; Mon-Thu 9 pm, Fri & Sat 10 pm, Sun
8.30 pm; closed Mon L.*

LITTLE PETHERICK, CORNWALL 1–3B

The Old Mill Bistro £45 ④④③
The Old Mill House, PL27 7QT
01841 540388
*In a 16th century former corn mill (replete with
waterwheel), a family-run B&B and bistro where
chef "Adrian Oliver continues to cook really well"
– "not in cheffy show-off style", but "simply" and
"based on good quality ingredients". /* **Details:**
www.oldmillbistro.co.uk; @OldMillPadstow; 11 pm. /
Accommodation: *7 rooms, from £80*

LITTLEFIELD GREEN, BERKSHIRE 3–3A

The Royal Oak £62 ③③④
Paley Street SL6 3JN 01628 620541
*Parkie – and son Nick's – country inn is an
"excellent gastropub" strong on convivial
atmosphere and with consistently highly-
rated cooking. It does attract the odd poor
review however: does that Michelin star
unnecessarily raise expectations? /* **Details:**
*www.theroyaloakpaleystreet.com; @royaloakpaleystreet;
Mon-Thu 9.30 pm, Fri & Sat 10 pm; closed Sun D;
Booking max 4 may apply; children: 3+.*

LITTLEHAMPTON, WEST SUSSEX 3–4A

East Beach Cafe £44 ③③③
Sea Road BN17 5GB 01903 731 903
*"In a perfect seafront position" – this Thomas
Heatherwick-designed cafe was modelled on a
piece of driftwood; the "comfort-food"-style menu
(not least fish) is generally "simple" and "well-
cooked" – and, "even on a winter's day, looking
at grey gloom, it is a nice place to be". /* **Details:**
*www.eastbeachcafe.co.uk; @EastBeachCafe; 8.30 pm;
closed Mon D, Tue D, Wed D & Sun D.*

LIVERPOOL, MERSEYSIDE 5–2A

The Art School £94 ④⑤⑤
Sugnall St L7 7DX 0151 230 8600
*"Paul Askew is constantly raising the bar" at his
ambitious, open-kitchen two-year-old near the
Liverpool Philharmonic – a contemporary space with
a large glazed roof, "artfully suspended lights, very
comfortable seating and sumptuous table linen".
From a variety of tasting menus (including a vegan
option) the results are "gorgeous, with very attractive
presentation" and "service is attentive but not
intrusive". /* **Details:** *www.theartschoolrestaurant.co.uk;
@ArtSchoolLpool; 9 pm; closed Mon & Sun.*

**The Bastion, The Shankly
Hotel** £52 ③③③
Millenium House, 60 Victoria Street L1 6JD
0151 541 9999
*"Memorabilia of Bill Shankly and Liverpool
FC" decorates the bar and restaurant of this
city-centre hotel "close to the Queensway
Tunnel". The setup is "ideal for families" and the
food receives a fair billing too (with a selection
of steaks headlining a straightforward hotel
brasserie menu). Afternoon tea is also a feature.
/* **Details:** *www.shanklyhotel.com/restaurants-bars/;
@shanklybastion.*

Bistro Franc £37 ③④④
1 Hanover Street L1 3DW 0151 708 9993
*"Solid bistro fare at amazing prices" encapsulates
the appeal of this branch of a fast-growing local
chain, whose set deals (at lunch, or on Sunday nights
when you 'Dine with Wine') win it may "cheap 'n'
cheerful" nominations. /* **Details:** *www.bistrofranc.com;
10.30 pm, Sun 10 pm.*

Buyers Club £40 ③④③
24 Hardman St L1 9AX 0151 709 2400
*Tucked down a narrow city-centre driveway, this hip,
exposed-brick two-year-old bar, kitchen and music
venue was launched by the team behind local foodie
icon Bold Street Coffee in 2015; "the bar does
excellently cooked and imaginative small*

plates", and while "the restaurant isn't open all the time, they also serve excellent food". / **Details:** www.buyers-club.co.uk.

Etsu £41 ⑤③②
25 The Strand, Off Brunswick Street L2 0XJ
0151 236 7530
"In an office block near the docks", and just off The Strand, this "warm and low-key" joint is a "little gem" offering a "fresh and approachable Japanese menu". / **Details:** www.etsu-restaurant.co.uk; @EtsuRestaurant; off Brunswick street; 9 pm, Fri & Sat 10 pm; closed Mon, Wed L & Sat L.

Fonseca's £37 ⑤③②
12 Stanley St L1 6AF 0151 255 0808
FKA Delifonseca – the deli part has now moved both literally and in name to its dockside sibling – this Stanley St spot is "still an old favourite, which manages to be both reliable and interesting". Upstairs is a booth-lined dining room; downstairs, the former deli is now a vintage-chic cocktail bar offering nibbles and takeaways. / **Details:** www.delifonseca.co.uk; @Delifonseca; 9 pm, Fri & Sat 10 pm; closed Mon & Sun.

Host £41 ⑤③②
31 Hope St L1 9XH 0151 708 5831
"Good and quick Asian fusion meals in a friendly informal atmosphere" – the draw to this 60 Hope Street spin-off near the Phil, offering a more interesting antidote to the chain gang of Wagamama and co. / **Details:** www.ho-st.co.uk; @HOST_Liverpool; 11 pm, Sun 10 pm.

The Italian Club Fish £49 ③②③
128 Bold St L1 4JA 0151 707 2110
This airy café – The Italian Club's younger sibling – is one of the better options in the city for "delicious seafood" and "excellent fresh fish, served in a traditional way". / **Details:** www.theitalianclubfish.co.uk; @italianclubnews; 10 pm, Sun 9 pm; No Amex.

The London Carriage Works, Hope Street Hotel £64 ②②②
40 Hope Street L1 9DA 0151 705 2222
Ever-polarised reports on this grand and trendsetting design hotel; the problem is that "dishes vary too much here…some can be excellent and others very disappointing" and, despite its reputation, there "isn't much of a buzz about the place". The hotel part must be doing better: an extension to add 12 rooms and 12 suites was green-lit in January 2017. / **Details:** www.thelondoncarriageworks.co.uk; @LdnCarriageWrks; 10 pm, Sun 9 pm; No shorts; Booking max 8 may apply. / **Accommodation:** 89 rooms, from £150

Lunya £47 ④③③
18-20 College Ln L1 3DS 0151 706 9770
"A superb tapas restaurant (with a fantastic deli)" – Peter and Elaine Kinsella's successful fixture in Liverpool One (opened in 2010) is one of the best-known options in the city: "it's a cut above, and there's real attention to detail from Spanish staff who seem interested to see justice done to their cuisine"! In October 2017, it moved to a new unit a short distance from the original, and is now all on one level (but we've maintained the rating). / **Details:** www.lunya.co.uk; @Lunya; 9 pm, Wed & Thu 9.30 pm, Fri 10 pm, Sat 10.30 pm.

Maray £46 ④③④
91 Bold Street L1 4HF 0151 709 5820
"Often-unusual combinations of ingredients in small dishes" (it's slightly "hard to define the cooking style", but it's somewhat Ottolenghi-esque) creates "a yearning to keep on returning" to this "lively", "truly unique and impressive" city-centre cocktail bar/tapas café. It has a new Allerton Street spin-off now too, "frequented by ladies-who-lunch". / **Details:** www.maray.co.uk; @marayliverpool; 10 pm, Fri & Sat 11 pm, Sun 9 pm.

Milo Lounge £36 ②②③
90 Lark Ln L17 8UU 0151 727 2285
This appealingly vivid, art-lined café, by Sefton Park, is a "lovely place for a long relaxing brunch or lunch", or "good all-day food and wine". Children, dogs and large groups are all "welcomed, accommodated and (except the mutt, perhaps) very well-fed". / **Details:** thelounges.co.uk/lounges/milo-lounge/; 11 pm.

Mowgli £32 ⑤③③
69 Bold St L1 4EZ 0151 708 9356
"Fresh, zingy 'street' food made from ingredients that you feel are doing you good" ("especially the A1 vegetarian section"), helps inspire excited reviews for ex-barrister and food writer/vlogger Nisha Katona's "totally different style of Indian", lauded for its "enthusiastic young staff" and "give-away prices". Since December 2016, it's also had a bigger Castle Street sibling (as well as openings in Manchester, Birmingham…) / **Details:** www.mowglistreetfood.com; @Mowglifood; 9.10 pm, Thu-Sat 10 pm.

Neighbourhood Cafe £71
261 woolton road L2 7LQ 0161 832 6334
Café outpost of Manchester's New York-inspired all-day brasserie on the former site of a Liverpool grocery store. The Spinningfields original underwent a £1m refurb in 2016 and a Leeds branch arrived in autumn 2017. / **Details:** www.neighbourhoodrestaurant.co.uk; @NBHDRestaurants/; 10 pm, Sat 10.30 pm.

Neon Jamon £51 3️⃣3️⃣2️⃣
Berry Street L1 9DF 0151 709 4286
This busy tapas joint "originally opened in Allerton some years ago and now has this branch on (increasingly foodie) Berry Street in the city-centre"; a "very popular" two-year-old, it offers "very good tapas" with "wonderful sherry" in a "modern industrial/canteen environment". / Details: www.neonjamon.com; @neonjamon; midnight.

Panoramic 34, West Tower £63 3️⃣4️⃣5️⃣
Brook Street L3 9PJ 0151 236 5534
"Breathtaking views over the River Mersey, the Royal Liver building plus many other landmarks" ensure that this 34th-floor operation is "perfect for a special occasion", and – though prices are not bargain basement – the venue was consistently well-rated this year for its "nothing-is-too-much-trouble" service and dependable cuisine. Afternoon tea here is another option and "always superb". / Details: www.panoramic34.com/; @Panoramic34; 9.30 pm, Sun 8 pm; closed Mon; No Amex; No trainers.

Pauls Place £32 3️⃣4️⃣1️⃣
550 Aigburth Rd L19 3QG 0151 427 6747
It may be a "tiny place" and a "bit like a café" in vibe, but no one seems to mind very much owing to the "great cooking" and especially "exceptional Sunday lunch" at this well-established Aigburth Road bistro. / Details: www.paulsplaceaigburth.co.uk/; 11pm, Sun 5pm.

Pen Factory £38 3️⃣4️⃣4️⃣
13 Hope St L1 9BQ 0151 709 7887
"Paddy Byrne and chef Tom Gill have worked magic at this converted factory" – a "casual and pleasant" haunt set within a stage-whisper of Byrne's legendary former venture, the Everyman, and benefitting from a not dissimilar formula of "cheap, tasty, Mediterranean-style" small plates and full meals. "The wine is drinkable and fairly priced, the ambience is cheerful – what's not to like?" / Details: www.pen-factory.co.uk/; @ThePenFactory; midnight; closed Mon & Sun.

Puschka £54 3️⃣2️⃣2️⃣
16 Rodney Street L1 2TE 0151 708 8698
This "slightly quirky" Georgian Quarter restaurant is praised for its "superbly cooked" fish, "excellent set menu for early diners" and "great selection of specials"; "tables are fairly compact but it is a small price to pay". / Details: www.puschka.co.uk; @Puschkapeople; 10 pm; D only.

Salt House £41 3️⃣3️⃣3️⃣
1 Hanover Street L1 3DW 0151 706 0092
Reporters "love this place" – a "very popular" and "noisy" charcuteria and tapas bar with two floors and striking industrial-chic decor; the food ranges from "interesting" to "exceptional". One

peccadillo: "charging customers for tap water (even if the proceeds are apparently going to charity)". / Details: www.salthousetapas.co.uk; @salthousetapas; 10.30 pm.

Salt House Bacaro £37 3️⃣3️⃣3️⃣
47 Castle St L2 9UB 0151 665 0047
"Not many places come close to Bacaro," say fans of the Salt House Tapas crew's "busy, modern" Italian joint, in the business district; "the (small plates-style) menu changes regularly" and is "more eclectic than the Venetian-style name would imply". / Details: www.salthousebacaro.co.uk/; @salthousebacaro; 10.30 pm.

San Carlo £59 3️⃣3️⃣3️⃣
41 Castle St L2 9SH 0151 236 0073
A "lovely", "always busy" business district Italian that's part of the ever-growing, glossily glam national chain; reporters this year couldn't get enough of it – "nothing is too much trouble for the staff"… "pricey but we didn't care!" / Details: www.sancarlo.co.uk; @SanCarlo_Group; 11 pm.

60 Hope Street £56 4️⃣4️⃣4️⃣
60 Hope St L1 9BZ 0151 707 6060
Liverpool's restaurant scene has come a long way in the past 15 years – but this agreeably understated fixture, in a Georgian townhouse near the Anglican cathedral, is still a bit of a beacon for its "consistently high standard of food and service". / Details: www.60hopestreet.com; @60HopeSt; 10 pm, Sun 8 pm.

Spire £50 4️⃣4️⃣2️⃣
1 Church Road L15 9EA 0151 734 5040
"Great flavourful fare, consistently high standards, and good value for money" enthuse fans of this Wavertree favourite, in an unpromising location off Penny Lane; if there's a negative, it's the "cramped tables". / Details: www.spirerestaurant.co.uk; @spirerestaurant; 9 pm, Fri & Sat 9.30 pm; closed Mon L, Sat L & Sun.

LLANARTHNE, CARMARTHENSHIRE 4–4C

Wrights Food Emporium £37 4️⃣4️⃣4️⃣
Golden Grove Arms SA32 8JU 01558 668929
"Breakfast, brunch… or just tea and a divine cake… what's not to like about Wrights relaxed and relaxing Emporium!" – ex-AA chief inspector and Y Polyn owner Simon Wright's seasonally minded two-year-old deli/café attracts nothing but praise, including for food that's "sooooo tasty". / Details: maryann@wrightsfood.co.uk; @WrightsFood; 11 pm; closed Mon D, Tue D, Wed D, Thu D & Sun D; No bookings.

| LLANDEWI SKIRRID, MONMOUTHSHIRE 2–1A | LLANWRTYD WELLS, POWYS 4–4D |

The Walnut Tree £69 5️⃣3️⃣3️⃣
Llanddewi Skirrid NP7 8AW 01873 852797
"Since Shaun Hill took over the Walnut Tree, its regime is returned to its glory days under Franco and Ann Taruschio" and this "fabulously located" rural pub – "so very charming in its simplicity and transparency" – "truly earns its plaudits and accolades, with homely but nuanced cooking, served without pretence, but full of panache". / Details: www.thewalnuttreeinn.com; @lovewalnuttree; 3m NE of Abergavenny on B4521; 9.30 pm; closed Mon & Sun. / Accommodation: 5 rooms, from £300

Carlton Riverside £55 3️⃣3️⃣3️⃣
Irfon Cr LD5 4SP 01591 610248
There's a consensus that, while the new regime is "trying hard" the cooking at this famed riverside mid-Wales inn has become "less adventurous" since the exit of Alan & Mary Ann Gilchrist ("maybe they think that's what the local market is looking for"); that said, their protégé Luke Roberts' food is "still exceptionally well-cooked" and it "remains a great stalwart in these parts". / Details: www.carltonriverside.com; 8.30 pm; closed Mon L & Sun; No Amex. / Accommodation: 4 rooms, from £60

| LLANDRILLO, DENBIGHSHIRE 4–2D | LLYSWEN, POWYS 2–1A |

Tyddyn Llan £93 5️⃣4️⃣5️⃣
LL21 0ST 01490 440264
"Bryan Webb continues to excel, producing outstanding cuisine" at his and wife Susan's "comfortable country hotel" – a former hunting lodge of the Duke of Westminster in a "tranquil location" near Bala. "Staff take the time to chat", and "it's laid back style, lack of fuss, relaxing nature and extensive grounds" make it "a great place for a foodie date!" The "interesting but not over priced wine list" is also a major gastronomic highlight. / Details: www.tyddynllan.co.uk; @BryanWWebb; on B4401 between Corwen and Bala; 9 pm; Mon-Thu L by prior arrangement only; Credit card deposit required to book. / Accommodation: 12 rooms, from £180

Llangoed Hall £100 4️⃣3️⃣4️⃣
LD3 0YP 01874 754525
It's "onwards and upwards" for this country house hotel, in a "lovely location, handy for the Hay Festival", and long of note for its "old-hall decadence"; Nick Brodie's "exquisite" cuisine won extremely consistent praise this year: "worth every penny!" / Details: www.llangoedhall.com; @TheLlangoedHall; 11m NW of Brecon on A470; 8.45 pm; No Amex; Jacket required. / Accommodation: 23 rooms, from £210

| LLANDUDNO, CONWY 4–1D | LOCH LOMOND, DUNBARTONSHIRE 9–4B |

Bodysgallen Hall, Dining Room £75 3️⃣3️⃣4️⃣
The Royal Welsh Way LL30 1RS 01492 584466
This Elizabethan manor house hotel, owned by the National Trust, is "a delight":"very atmospheric", and with "simple but memorable" food. / Details: www.bodysgallen.com; @BodysgallenHall; 2m off A55 on A470; 9.15 pm, Fri & Sat 9.30 pm; closed Mon; No trainers; children: 6+. / Accommodation: 31 rooms, from £179

Martin Wishart, Cameron House £107 3️⃣3️⃣4️⃣
Cameron House G83 8QZ 01389 722504
"Unbeatable views" of Loch Lomond set the scene at Martin Wishart's "absolutely superb" rural operation (within an acclaimed and luxurious country house) where the "exceptional" cuisine – "art on a plate with every course a delight" – is "exquisite". Check with your financial advisor before you go however:"you need a very healthy bank balance". / Details: www.mwlochlomond.co.uk; @RMWLeith; over Erskine Bridge to A82, follow signs to Loch Lomond; 9.30 pm; closed Mon & Tue. / Accommodation: 134 rooms, from £215

| LLANGOLLEN, DENBIGHSHIRE 5–3A | LOCHINVER, HIGHLAND 9–1B |

Corn Mill £49 3️⃣3️⃣5️⃣
Dee Ln LL20 8PN 01978 869555
A "lovely setting" ("hanging over the River Dee" and its rapids) "makes this an idyllic spot at any time of the year"; rounding out the usual Brunning & Price formula, the food can be "varied and delicious" too. / Details: www.cornmill-llangollen.co.uk; 9.30 pm, Sun 9 pm.

The Albannach £71 5️⃣4️⃣4️⃣
Baddidarroch IV27 4LP 01571 844407
"Candlelit meals in a red-painted, cosy dining room, with wonderful views to the harbour and mountains" win raves for this distant venue – an "exceptional" spot with a very highly rated five-course tasting menu, matched by a predominantly French wine list. "Such a wonderful place, and well worth

The Salutation, Sandwich

Northcote, Langho

Breda Murphy, Whalley

our drive of 550 miles to get there!" / Details: www.thealbannach.co.uk; 8 pm; D only, closed Mon & Tue; No Amex; children: 12+. / Accommodation: 5 rooms, from £295

LOCKSBOTTOM, KENT   3–3B

Chapter One   £61   3 3 2
Farnborough Common BR6 8NF
01689 854848
"An outstanding out-of-town restaurant, with West End standards" is how its large fan club still regard this highly popular destination – just outside London's city limits – praising its "very high order of cooking and very professional service". "The atmosphere is a bit sterile" though, and ebbing ratings support those who feel it's "going downhill". That might be about to change however, as in September 2017, Ken McLeish (exec chef of the group which formerly owned it) bought out the restaurant with the aim of "a new influx of energy" (including a more modern approach, and more emphasis on the brasserie side of the business). / Details: www.chaptersrestaurants.com; @chapter1kent; No trainers; Booking max 12 may apply.

LONG CRENDON, BUCKINGHAMSHIRE 2–2D

The Angel   £53   3 2 3
47 Bicester Rd HP18 9EE   01844 208268
On the Oxfordshire borders, this favourite 16th century country inn lacks pretensions ("doesn't try to be what it isn't") but still turns out "good" and sometimes "really good" food. / Details: www.angelrestaurant.co.uk; @theangeluk; 2m NW of Thames, off B4011; 9.30 pm; closed Sun D. / Accommodation: 4 rooms, from £110

The Mole & Chicken   £55   4 4 4
Easington Lane HP18 9EY   01844 208387
"A lovely country pub-with-rooms", handy for the M40, and offering "superb" grub (including an "excellent breakfast") that's "served with a smile"; repair to the terrace for "splendid views" of the Oxfordshire countryside. / Details: www.themoleandchicken.co.uk; @moleandchicken; follow signs from B4011 at Long Crendon; 9.30 pm, Sun 9 pm. / Accommodation: 5 rooms, from £110

LONG MELFORD, SUFFOLK   3–1C

Melford Valley Tandoori £32   4 3 3
Hall St CO10 9JT   01787 311518
This casual, partly beamed venue, on the main road through Long Melford, is the "best Indian for a long way" according to fans; on the one hand, it offers a slimmer-friendly 'waist watchers' menu,

---

on the other a diet-unfriendly Sunday buffet with some 100 dishes. / Details: www.melfordvalley.com; @MelfordValley; 11 pm, Fri & Sat 11.30 pm.

Swan   £64   4 5 4
Hall St CO10 9JQ   01787 464545
The "jewel in the crown of the growing Macmillan family empire", this "stunningly beautiful Tudor pub" in a picture-perfect village "continues its transformation to full-blown restaurant", replete with tasting menu and a list of "serious Bordeaux and Burgundies"; it has "now expanded to include a new garden room and private dining room", plus seven "wonderful" bedrooms. / Details: www.longmelfordswan.co.uk; Mon-Thu 9 pm, Fri & Sat 10 pm; 1.

LOUGHBOROUGH, LEICESTERSHIRE 5–3D

The Hammer & Pincers   £51   4 4 3
5 East Rd LE12 6ST   01509 880735
"Unpretentious fine dining at its best" is winning a growing foodie reputation for this "down-to-earth" beamed village gastropub, where reports become ever-more enthusiastic. / Details: www.hammerandpincers.co.uk; 9.30 pm, Sun 4 pm; closed Mon & Sun D; No Amex.

LOWER BEEDING, WEST SUSSEX   3–4A

The Pass Restaurant, South Lodge Hotel   £110   4 3 3
Brighton Road RH13 6PS   01403 891711
Ex-Samling hotshot Ian Swainson is off to an impressive start at this "stunning" country hotel's restaurant, formerly under Matt Gillan, where "the bonus (with the dramatic open kitchen set-up) is that you can see your food being perfectly prepared in front of you", and where fans lionise the "superb" tasting menus. There's the odd gripe that it's "overhyped", but the only generally felt niggle concerns service that can be "so slow". / Details: www.exclusive.co.uk/south-lodge/restaurants-bars/the-pass; @southlodgehotel; 8.30 pm; closed Mon & Tue; children: 12+. / Accommodation: 89 rooms, from £235

LOWER BOCKHAMPTON, DORSET   2–4B

Yalbury Cottage   £55   5 5 4
DT2 8PZ   01305 262382
"This is food to look forward to for weeks!" – "all the extras like the homemade bread create that homegrown touch, yet the dishes are top-quality gastronomy"; "add to that a great location" on the outskirts of town and charming service and this little cottage is nigh on "perfect in every way". / Details: www.yalburycottage.com; @YalburyDorset; 9 pm; Tue

to Sat L - booking only; No Amex; practically no walk-ins – you must boo. / **Accommodation:** 8 rooms, from £120

LOWER FROYLE, HAMPSHIRE   2–3D

The Anchor Inn   £46   3️⃣2️⃣3️⃣
GU34 4NA   01420 23261
A "cosy country pub with a lovely atmosphere, log fires in winter and a large terrace for sunny days". The odd sceptic dismisses it as "very average" but even they feel that, "having said all that, they are charming people and the regulars clearly love it". / **Details:** www.anchorinnatlowerfroyle.co.uk; @anchorinnfroyle; 9 pm, Fri & Sat 9.30 pm, sun 8 pm. / **Accommodation:** 5 rooms, from £120

LOWER SLAUGHTER, GLOUCESTERSHIRE
2–1C

The Slaughters Manor House   £96   3️⃣3️⃣3️⃣
Copsehill Rd GL54 2HP   01451 820456
Reopened in March 2016 after a "really excellent refurb'" (and minor name change), this Brownsword Hotel group outpost now has a ritzy country-chic interior to match its manor house setting, sweeping lawns and "gorgeous food". / **Details:** www.slaughtersmanor.co.uk; @SlaughtersManor; 2m from Burton-on-the-Water on A429; No jeans; children: 8.

LOWER SWELL, SOMERSET   2–3A

Langford Fivehead   £59   4️⃣4️⃣4️⃣
TA3 6PG   01460 282020
"Delicious, well thought-out food is served in very peaceful surroundings" at Olly & Rebecca Jackson's restaurant-with-rooms – a 15th century Plantagenet great hall "with beautiful gardens" (which provide the lion's share of what's on the plate in summer). / **Details:** www.langfordfivehead.co.uk; @thebiggroup; 8.30 pm; closed Sun & Mon.

LUDLOW, SHROPSHIRE   5–4A

The Charlton Arms, Charlton Arms Hotel   £45   3️⃣3️⃣4️⃣
Ludford Bridge SY8 1PJ   01584 872813
His brother Claude helped to put Ludlow on the culinary map with his famed haunt Hibiscus, and Cedric Bosi continues to indulge local foodies with this four-year-old gastropub-with-rooms; "the cooking is consistently good and the views from the dining room over the River Teme are hard to beat". / **Details:** www.thecharltonarms.co.uk; @Charlton_Ludlow.

Fishmore Hall   £79   4️⃣4️⃣3️⃣
Fishmore Rd SY8 3DP   01584 875148
In this foodie town, a laid back country house hotel, where chef Andrew Birch wins ecstatic praise from (nearly) all reporters for "perfectly executed, innovative and delicious" food – even if the surroundings strike some as "a bit ordinary", the "brilliant" victuals "more than make up for it". / **Details:** www.fishmorehall.co.uk; @fishmorehall; 9.30 pm. / **Accommodation:** 15 rooms, from £99

Golden Moments   £32   3️⃣4️⃣3️⃣
50 Broad Street SY8 1NH   01584 878488
"Everything is cooked to order" and "so fresh!" at this smart subcontinental, on the most famous street in this foodie town, and in operation since just after the millennium. / **Details:** www.goldenmomentsofludlow.co.uk/; 11pm.

Green Café, Ludlow Mill On The Green   £37   3️⃣5️⃣4️⃣
Dinham Millennium Green SY8 1EG
01584 879872
Clive Davis's "secret gem" by the River Teme is "just fabulous" on a sunny day, and the "beautiful setting is coupled with exquisite cuisine" – both "good coffee and cakes", and more substantial fare. "Services comes with a personal touch: they've even been known to provide hot water bottles" for chilly days! / **Details:** www.thegreencafe.co.uk; @greencafeludlow; closed Mon, L only Tue-Sun.

Mortimers   £63   3️⃣4️⃣4️⃣
17 Corve St SY8 1DA   01584 872 325
Claude Bosi-trained chef Wayne Smith's "relaxed" two-year-old is "trying hard and doing well" in the old location of foodie fave La Bécasse (RIP). Even a reviewer who feels "the food needs to raise its game to compete with its forebear" says "it's a promising work-in-progress", and supporters say its "exceptional cuisine makes it a star-in-the-making". / **Details:** www.mortimersludlow.co.uk; @MortimersLudlow.

Old Downton Lodge   £72   4️⃣4️⃣4️⃣
Downton on the Rock SY8 2HU
01568 771826
A short drive from Ludlow, this attractive hotel occupies ancient barns and an old cider mill, and its medieval hall-like dining room offers six- or nine-course menus from chef Karl Martin. All-in-all, it wins praise for "people who really care about what they do, and do it well". / **Details:** www.olddowntonlodge.com; @olddowntonlodge; children: 11.

LUTON, BEDFORDSHIRE   3–2A

Luton Hoo, Luton Hoo Hotel   £54   2️⃣3️⃣4️⃣
The Mansion House, Luton Hoo Estate
LU1 3TQ   01582 734437
"Traditional afternoon tea in a splendid setting" is the most commented-on feature of this plush country house hotel (incorporating spa and golf course) and even if it's "pricey" fans say it's "good value compared to central London". When it comes to the stately 'Wernher' restaurant, some do praise a "wonderful experience" here too, but similarly the price tag can raise eyebrows. / **Details:** www.lutonhoo.co.uk; @lutonhoo; 10 pm, Sat 10.30 pm; L only; Online only.

LYDGATE, GREATER MANCHESTER   5–2B

The White Hart   £55   4️⃣4️⃣3️⃣
51 Stockport Rd OL4 4JJ   01457 872566
"Brilliant for lunch or dinner, casual or more formal dining" – this "beautifully located" and recently refurbed hillside inn – overlooking Manchester and the Cheshire Plain – "never disappoints" with its "great rooms" and Mike Shaw's "fantastic cooking usual local ingredients". FOH Charles is also a "firm favourite with his clientele". / **Details:** www.thewhitehart.co.uk; @whitehartlydgte; 2m E of Oldham on A669, then A6050; 9.30 pm. / **Accommodation:** 12 rooms, from £120

LYME REGIS, DORSET   2–4A

Hix Oyster & Fish House £58   3️⃣3️⃣4️⃣
Cobb Rd DT7 3JP   01297 446910
"Amazing views of Lyme Bay" ("especially if there's a wild sea") help set an upbeat tone at Mark Hix's "beautiful" cliff-top venture, and "it feels like an occasion to dine here". Nowadays renowned as one of the best restaurants in the south west, the place can seem "a touch self-absorbed", or "expensive" but is "generally up-to-scratch," and a typical report describes "a wide range of fresh, locally caught fish, well cooked and served up beautifully". "I expected a lazy star name rip off, but came away thoroughly enjoying myself!" / **Details:** www.restaurantsetcltd.co.uk; @hixlymeregis; 10 pm.

LYMINGTON, HAMPSHIRE   2–4C

Elderflower   £60   4️⃣4️⃣4️⃣
Quay St SO41 3AS   01590 676908
Andrew & Marjolaine Bourg's restaurant-with-rooms provides "textbook destination dining", with its "top-drawer French cooking" and "very warm",

"slick" service; all with a "great location (opposite the Pier) for walking off the meal!" / **Details:** www.elderflowerrestaurant.co.uk; @TheElderflower1; Wed & Thu 9.30 pm, Fri & Sat 10 pm.

LYMM, CHESHIRE   5–2B

La Boheme   £52   4️⃣4️⃣3️⃣
3 Mill Lane WA13 9SD   01925 753657
With its "top-drawer classic French cuisine", this "brilliant", newly extended outfit "attracts an eclectic mix of customers from the grey-pound brigade to the well-heeled of Hale and Bowdon". Part of the appeal is also that it's "excellent value". / **Details:** laboheme.co.uk; Mon-Sat 10 pm, Sun 9 pm; closed Mon L & Sat L.

LYNDHURST, HAMPSHIRE   2–4C

Hartnett Holder & Co, Lime Wood Hotel   £74   3️⃣3️⃣3️⃣
Beaulieu Rd SO43 7FZ   02380 287177
"If you've come to a New Forest country house for lunch from a famous London chef, then this might be more casual and relaxed than you were hoping for", with Italian food that's "not too complicated". But "even if it's not exciting cuisine, dishes are well-balanced adn of superior quality", service is "attentive", and at the end of the day everyone "loves the informal atmosphere". / **Details:** www.limewoodhotel.co.uk/food/hh-and-co; @limewoodhotel; Booking max 4 may apply.

LYTH VALLEY, CUMBRIA   7–4D

The Punch Bowl Inn   £54   4️⃣5️⃣5️⃣
LA8 8HR   01539 568237
"One of the valiant good foods places in the Lake" – this pub/hotel in a tiny village is beautifully located and "especially pleasant outdoors in summer" on its summer terrace, and serves robust, refined-rustic dishes from chef Arthur Bridgeman Quin. There's a strong service ethos too – "led by the delectable Lorraine, she has the front of house running like a machine being drip-fed WD40!" / **Details:** www.the-punchbowl.co.uk; @PunchbowlInn; off A5074 towards Bowness, turn right after Lyth Hotel; 8.45 pm. / **Accommodation:** 9 rooms, from £105

LYTHAM, LANCASHIRE   5–1A

Novello   £57   4️⃣3️⃣2️⃣
FY8 5EP   01253 730278
While it has "been an Italian restaurant for ages", there are signs that this two-floor venue is "trying to break out" (confusingly, given "a section on the

menu for cicchetti") to a more ambitious and generic modern European style. "The owner's son can cook" and there's high praise for "light, delicate, excellently conceived and cooked dishes" with "amazing presentation". But one regular cautions: "some items can be overworked, over-embellished or over-thought – it's very refined cooking, at times it's almost too refined, to the point the flavour risks being refined out of the food!" / *Details:* www.thenovello.co.uk; @novello_lytham; 10 pm, Sun 9 pm.

MADINGLEY, CAMBRIDGESHIRE   3–1B

Three Horseshoes   **£57**   3⎢3⎢4
High St CB23 8AB   01954 210221
"Definitely improving after its return to the Huntsbridge Group" – this "very attractive thatched gastropub" (a varsity fave as it's a short hop outside Cambridge) was "very nicely refurbished, particularly the conservatory" in summer 2016, and the food ("with an Italian theme") is back on "delicious" form. / *Details:* www.threehorseshoesmadingley.co.uk; @3hs_restaurant; 2m W of Cambridge, off A14 or M11; 9.30 pm.

MAIDENHEAD, BERKSHIRE   3–3A

The Crown   **£51**   4⎢4⎢4
Burchetts Green SL6 6QZ   01628 824079
Family-run gastropub in Burchetts Green which fuses French and English cuisine to great acclaim (including from the French tyre company). Fans extol "classic English dishes executed to perfection" and "a lovely experience all-round", but it's not without its doubters: "the meal was… nice, not exciting or standout… fine… most disappointing for Michelin-starred food". / *Details:* thecrownburchettsgreen.com.

MAIDSTONE, KENT   3–3C

Frederic Bistro   **£42**   3⎢4⎢3
Market Buildings, Earl St ME14 1HP
01622 297414
This "original gem in Maidstone" is "always full and buzzy" owing to its "very reasonable prices" and "great authentic" French cuisine. New development: "Frederic has now extended into the two shops next door" for his wine and cheese bar, home to a vastly expanded (350+) library of French wines ("especially Bordeaux"). / *Details:* www.fredericbistro.com; midnight.

MALMESBURY, WILTSHIRE   2–2C

The Old Bell Hotel   **£61**   3⎢3⎢3
Abbey Row SN16 0AG   01666 822344
A "traditional", ivy-covered hotel with some areas dating all the way back to 1220 (hence its styling as the "world's oldest hotel"); on the menu, appealing afternoon teas and consistently well-rated, locally sourced grub. / *Details:* www.oldbellhotel.com; @oldesthotel; Mon-Thu 9 pm, Fri & Sat 9.30 pm, Sun 9 pm. / *Accommodation:* 33 rooms, from £115

MANCHESTER, GREATER MANCHESTER 5–2B

Adam Reid at The French , Midland Hotel   **£119**   2⎢4⎢3
Peter St M60 2DS   0161 235 4780
It would be too strong to call it a disastrous decline, but since Simon Rogan severed his ties with this famous but "hushed and slightly stilted" chamber, performance has gone from rocky to a-bit-more-rocky. Loyalists feel "Adam Reid's style adds a warmth to the presentation and stays true to good produce and clean cooking" within the scope of his 4-, 6- and 9-course tasting menus; and praise staff who are "friendly and not stuffy". The scepticism of former years persists however, with critics feeling the performance is "too expensive" ("boy those portions are small!") or "lacking finesse". / *Details:* www.the-french.co.uk; @thefrenchmcr; 9 pm; closed Mon, Tue L & Sun; No trainers; children: 9+. / *Accommodation:* 312 rooms, from £145

Akbar's   **£35**   5⎢3⎢3
73-83 Liverpool Rd M3 4NQ   0161 834 8444
"A Manchester institution" – "you have to queue", but once through the doors of this "pile-them-in" Pakistani, the reward is "delicious", "great value" food (not least "incredible naan breads") with "a bit of showmanship". / *Details:* www.akbars.co.uk; 11 pm, Fri & Sat 11.30 pm; D only; May need 10+ to book.

Albert Square Chop House   **£52**   3⎢4⎢4
The Memorial Hall, Albert Sq M2 5PF
0161 834 1866
From the people behind Sam's and Mr Thomas's, this "restored and very cosy basement" offers an "exceptional British dining experience in the heart of the city". The victuals comprise "posh pub grub favourites" ("bread and dripping is a must" with "fish 'n' chips for the less adventurous") and, despite the odd off-report, even a cynic admits that "when good, it's very good". / *Details:* www.albertsquarechophouse.com; @chophouseAlbert; 9.30 pm, Fri & Sat 10 pm, Sun 8.30 pm.

Albert's Shed £51 4|3|3
20 Castle St M3 4LZ 0161 839 9818
"A lively longstanding feature of the Manchester scene", by the canal, which "always has a buzz to it and, being 'off the beaten track', you know it has to be good"; it's particularly recommended as a "perfect lunch destination" for "excellent food keenly priced". / Details: www.albertsshed.com; @alberts_shed; 10 pm, Fri 10.30 pm, Sat 11 pm, Sun 9.30 pm; No Amex.

Allotment
24 Dale Street M1 1FY 0161 222 0580
One encouraging early report on Matthew Nutter's (no relation to Andrew Nutter of Rochdale's 'Nutters') "superb" veggie/vegan in Stockport's Old Town: "I am a carnivore but firstly a lover of food and this restaurant is off the scale good!" / Details: www.allotmentbar.co.uk.

Almost Famous £31 4|2|3
100-102 High St M4 1HP 0161 244 9422
The original branch of this four-strong NW burger chain continues to win credit for "top burgers served with the best attitude anywhere" – plus "amazing chicken waffle fries", in a hipster vibe setting (all graffiti and exposed-brick). / Details: www.almostfamousburgers.com; @AlmostFamousNQ; 10 pm, Fri & Sat 11 pm; No bookings.

Are Friends Electric, Stock Exchange Building
4 Norfolk Street M2 1DW awaiting tel
No opening date yet for this joint venture from chef Michael O'Hare and footballers Gary Neville and Ryan Giggs (one of three they are planning together). It will occupy the rooftop of the former Manchester Stock Exchange building, which the trio are hoping to convert into a boutique hotel. Plans have been delayed due to a conflict with Historic England. See also the Man Who Fell to Earth. / Details: @urbisrabbit.

Artisan Cafe Bar, Artisan Kitchen & Bar £43 3|4|4
Avenue North, 18-22 Bridge St M3 3BZ
0161 832 4181
This big (12,000 square feet) loft-style operation on the first floor of The Avenue North in Spinningfields, Manchester makes "a nice place to linger over a meal" thanks to its "interesting interior with a great atmosphere" and wins nothing but praise for its good-value pizza, grills and steaks. / Details: www.artisan.uk.com; @Artisan_MCR; 10.45pm .

Asha's £47 4|3|3
47 Peter Street M2 3NG 0161 832 5309
"Beautiful, original, fresh and innovative Indian cuisine" – and ties with Bollywood legend Asha Bhosle – have made the name of this posh city-centre branch of the UAE chain; a second

UK outpost opened in Manchester two years back, and the tireless 83-year-old star owner reportedly has big plans for expansion... / **Details:** www.ashasrestaurant.co.uk; @AshasManchester.

Australasia £70 3|4|5
1 The Avenue Spinningfields M3 3AP
0161 831 0288
"Cool but fun" – this atmospheric Living Ventures operation off Deansgate is "surprisingly airy" for somewhere underground, and all reporters "love the place" thanks to its "impressive fusion food" and "well-informed and helpful staff". / Details: www.australasia.uk.com; @AustralasiaMcr; 10.45 pm.

La Bandera £52 3|3|3
2 Ridgefield M2 6EQ 0161 833 9019
Basque maestro Josetxo Arrieta's funky looking three-year-old off Deansgate, lined with eye-catching yellow leather booths, again divides opinion – one former fan feels it's "lost the plot", but others vaunt the "excellent" Spanish cuisine (primarily "very good tapas"). / Details: www.labandera.co.uk; @labanderauk; midnight; No Amex.

Bar San Juan £33 4|3|4
56 Beech Rd M21 9EG 0161 881 9259
"Pound for pound one of the best nights out in Manchester"; "it really feels like you have stepped into Spain" at this "always bustling" and notably consistent Chorlton spot – where, refreshingly, "no matter how important you think you are, Juan and the team are fair" with table waits ("dream on you BBC lot!"). / Details: barsanjuan.com; 11.30 pm, Fri & Sat midnight, Sun 11 pm.

Bundobust £30 4|2|3
61 Piccadilly M1 2AQ 0161 359 6757
"Flavour-packed" Indian street food combined with "a great selection of ales (a million miles better than any other Indian's I've been in!)" is a winning formula for this "concept-that's-about-to-turn-into-a-chain". Service perhaps "needs some working out" ("the big queue can move very very slowly") but "if the cardboard crockery and bar service for drinks are good enough for Jay Rayner, it's good enough for me". / Details: www.bundobust.com; @BundobustMCR.

Chaophraya £50 3|3|4
19 Chapel Walks, Off Cross Street M2 1HN
0161 832 8342
This swanky, two-floor outpost of the UK-wide Thai Leisure Group has built up quite a name for its "always excellent" and "refined Thai cuisine" and an all-round "pleasant experience". / Details: www.chaophraya.co.uk; @ChaophrayaThai; Mon-Sat 10.30 pm, Sun 10 pm.

Croma £37 [3][4][4]
1-3 Clarence St M2 4DE 0161 237 9799
Born in 2000, near Albert Square, the "unfailing" original HQ of this chain (which has a handful of outposts 'up north and outlets in Odeon cinemas) features a stylish, modern setting by Pizza Express interiors guru Enzo Apicella. On the menu: "enjoyable" Italian food, and in particular "pizza that's better than other places in central Manchester". / **Details:** *www.cromapizza.co.uk; @cromapizza; 10 pm, Fri & Sat 11 pm.*

Evuna £44 [3][3][4]
277 – 279 Deansgate M3 4EW 0161 819 2752
"Fantastic tapas" boosts the appeal of this atmospheric Deansgate bar and wine importer, although some reviewers feel that "TBH, the great wine list overshadows the food". It also has a Northern Quarter sibling (which inspires little feedback). / **Details:** *www.evuna.com; @evunamanchester; Mon 9 pm, Tue-Sat 10 pm, Sun 8 pm.*

Fazenda £47 [3][4][2]
The Ave M3 3AP 0161 207 1183
"Incredibly succulent meats carved onto your plate are complemented by an amazing array of salads" at this outpost of the Brazilian 'rodizio' ('eat-as-much-as-you-want-buffet') chain; "normally the expectation would be vast quantities of indifferent food; but not here." Also with branches in Liverpool and Leeds. / **Details:** *www.fazenda.co.uk/manchester; @fazendamanc; 10 pm, Sun 9 pm.*

El Gato Negro £46 [4][3][5]
52 King Street M2 4LY 0161 694 8585
"The hype is justified!" – This "dazzling addition to the Manchester restaurant scene" (which moved into town last year) is THE destination in the city-centre right now and Manc's most commented-on venue in this year's survey. A three-floor operation incorporating bar and rooftop level, it serves Simon Shaw's "creative small plates, in Spanish style and with Moorish influences" and despite the odd quibble that "it's not as good as the smaller, tighter set-up it was in Ripponden" most reporters feel its tapas is "some of the best ever". All this popularity also brings a few negatives though – at peak times service can become "disorganised", you run the gauntlet of "inhospitable door nazis", and "some diners have a touch of the Harry Enfields about them: 'I am considerably richer than yow'!" / **Details:** *www.elgatonegrotapas.com; @ElGatoNegroFood; Mon-Thu 10 pm, Fri & Sat 11 pm, Sun 9.30 pm.*

Glamorous £41 [3][2][2]
Wing Yip Bus' Centre, Oldham Rd M4 5HU
0161 839 3312
"If you had your eyes closed and only opened them in the restaurant you would think you were in Hong Kong" – rather than atop the Wing Yip supermarket

– at this well-known, bustling Cantonese outfit. Dim sum is the real draw, and other dishes can strike reporters as "substandard". / **Details:** *www.glamorous-restaurant.co.uk; @glamorous_uk; 11.30 pm, Fri & Sat midnight, Sun 11 pm.*

Grafene £61 [2][1][2]
55 King St M2 4LQ 0161 696 9700
Opened in July 2016 by the team behind Peak District hotel Losehill House, this "battleship grey" yearling "has been welcomed with disdain by Manchester", not helped by service that's "the definition of average" and "hard industrial", semi-unfinished decor which can just seem "like a boiler room". More upbeat reporters "don't quite understand why the city has such a downer on it", but a fair middle-view is that "while the food is consistently good, there's nothing exceptional here, which, given the cost and market it's aiming at, it needs to be!" / **Details:** *www.grafene.co.uk; @grafene.*

Grand Pacific £60 [3][4][5]
50 Spring Gardens M2 1EN 0161 839 9365
Opulence reigns at Mancs' hottest new arrival – a Pan-Asian in the magnificent old King Street home of The Reform Gentlemen's Club (latterly the Reform bar, and Room restaurant). Living Ventures boss Tim Bacon, who snapped it up in 2015, didn't live to see the project come to fruition, nowadays a stunning colonial-style space (with Raffles Singapore tribute bar). / **Details:** *www.grandpacific.uk.com; @GrandPacificMCR; 10 pm.*

Great Kathmandu £38 [4][2][2]
140-144 Burton Rd M20 1JQ 0161 434 6413
"I have been a customer for 30 years, and it's as good now as ever!" – this veteran West Didsbury Indian continues to turn out "fantastic" fare that fans feel is far better than on the curry mile. / **Details:** *www.greatkathmandu.com; midnight.*

Grill on the Alley £57 [2][3][3]
5 Ridgefield M2 6EG 0161 833 3465
This slick city-centre joint, on the proverbial alley off Deansgate (and with a sibling on New York Street) remains a popular spot locally for steak, burgers and sharing cuts – plus cocktails and seafood. / **Details:** *www.blackhouse.uk.com; @GrillManc; 11 pm.*

Hawksmoor £63 [4][4][3]
184-186 Deansgate M3 3WB 0161 836 6980
"Classy like a Rolls Royce… and just as reassuringly expensive" – the "Hawksmoor formula has transferred solidly from London to Manchester" where it occupies "an impressive Victorian building" and has become "a well-established part of the Manchester scene", inspiring more reports than anywhere else in the city this year. "The steaks are succulent and perfectly cooked", "the chips are the best in the NW!", "service is brilliant", in fact it's just "a-ma-zing" – OK, some would argue "overpriced",

*but for most folks "oh, so worth it". / **Details:** www.thehawksmoor.com; @HawksmoorLondon; Mon-Thu 10 pm, Fri & Sat 10.30 pm, Sun 9.30 pm.*

Hispi Bistro £53 ▢4▢3▢3
1c School Lane M20 6RD 0161 445 3996
*"A good replacement for 'Jem and I' whose site it took over" – Gary Usher's crowd-funded newcomer is "a welcome addition to Didsbury", with "some really good plates like the 'feather blade' beef and a very good offer under £20 for 'early birds'". / **Details:** www.hispi.net/; @HispiBistro; Mon-Thu 9 pm, Fri & Sat 10 pm, Sun 9 pm.*

Home £40 ▢3▢3▢4
2 Tony Wilson Place M15 4FN 0161 212 3500
*"Handy for the Bridgewater" – the café of this two-year-old arts centre "has a real buzz" and delivers "imaginative pizza" and other "quality" fare, "over which you can discuss films" (if you've been visiting one of the five on-site cinemas). "Forget the wines, go for the ales" from local microbreweries. / **Details:** homemcr.org; @HOME_mcr; 10 pm, Sun 9 pm.*

Ibérica, Spinningfields £48 ▢3▢3▢4
14-15 The Avenue M3 3HF 0161 358 1350
*"Manchester is spoilt with good Spanish restaurants" of late, with this "vibrant" two-year-old – a spin-off from the expanding national chain – a notable addition to the party. Both food and service have a "curate's egg" quality to them, but the "more inventive" fare is generally a hit, and seems "heartier than when it first opened (presumably in reaction to Mancs moaning they had to stop for chips on the way home"). / **Details:** www.ibericarestaurants.com; Mon-Thu 11 pm, Fri & Sat 11.30 pm, Sun 11 pm.*

Indian Tiffin Room £36 ▢4▢2▢2
2 Isabella Banks Street, First Street, M15 4RL
0161 228 1000
*With its "delicious snack food" – "a sort of Indian tapas" – this "large" new city-centre spin-off from the popular Cheadle operation in a striking glass-fronted building makes "a very welcome addition to the scene" on happening First Street. / **Details:** www.indiantiffinroom.com/manchester-restaur; @Indtiffinroom; Mon-Sat 10 pm, Sun 9 pm.*

Indique £44 ▢5▢3▢3
110-112 Burton Road M20 1LP
0161 438 0241
*"The absolute opposite of a bog standard curry house", this "truly original" new subcontinental – the name fuses 'Indian' and unique – "has now established itself as the place to go for different but delicious Indian food in South Manchester" (be it "superbly crafted" pastries, or regional specials). / **Details:** www.indiquerestaurant.co.uk/; 10.30 pm, Fri & Sat 11 pm; closed Mon.*

James Martin £56 ▢4▢4▢3
2 Watson St M3 4LP 0161 828 0345
*"Despite its unusual location, the decor is elegant, service professional, and the food excellent throughout" at the TV chef's city-centre venture: "and once you are in, you would never know you are in a casino!" / **Details:** www.jamesmartinmanchester.co.uk; @JamesMartinMCR; Mon-Thu 10 pm, Fri & Sat 11 pm, Sun 5 pm.*

Katsouris Deli £15 ▢3▢3▢2
113 Deansgate M3 2BQ 0161 937 0010
*"Hearty portions of wholesome food" feature at this bustling and spacious city-centre destination, with the main feature – mixed mezze plates – representing "great value for money"; okay, so there are "no airs and graces about it, but no need" for them, either. / **Details:** www.katsourisdeli.co.uk; Mon-Fri 4.30 pm, Sat 5.30 pm, Sun 4 pm; L only; No Amex.*

The Lime Tree £47 ▢4▢5▢4
8 Lapwing Ln M20 2WS 0161 445 1217
*"Still, after all these years, our favourite restaurant in Manchester" – this "totally charming" Didsbury brasserie "never lets you down in any department". It's "a real institution in the city" and for a number of reporters "Manchester's best restaurant": "the food is consistently beautiful without being over-elaborate and the service could not be better, with a relaxed feel". / **Details:** www.thelimetreerestaurant.co.uk; @thelimetreeres; 10 pm; closed Mon L & Sat L.*

Lunya £46 ▢3▢3▢2
Barton Arcade, Deansgate M3 2BW
0161 413 3317
*"New outpost of the popular Liverpool venture" – a "buzzing and vibrant deli and tapas bar in an arcade off Deansgate". Most reports are of "a successful transfer" with "quality tapas" and "an interesting range of Spanish wines", but even fans say "it doesn't reach the giddy heights of El Gato Negro or Evuna" and – in this more competitive restaurant city – critics feel it "lacks any notion of finesse", or is "OK but nothing special". / **Details:** www.lunya.co.uk/manchester; @lunyaMCR.*

The Man Who Fell to Earth, Manchester Stock Exchange
Manchester Stock Exchange, 2-6 Norfolk Street
M2 1DW awaiting tel
No opening date yet for this joint venture from chef Michael O'Hare and footballers Gary Neville and Ryan Giggs (one of three they are planning together). It will be a 'Parisian ballroom-style' venue, occupying the dining room of the former Manchester Stock Exchange building, which the trio are hoping to convert into a boutique hotel. Plans have been delayed due to a conflict with Historic England. See also Are Friends Electric, the rooftop restaurant.

Manchester House £90 [4][4][4]
18-22 Bridge St M3 3BZ 0161 835 2557
"It's surprising Michelin have withheld a star" from this "fabulous" contemporary restaurant, on the 2nd-floor of a Manchester office block – a "lovely and open" space, whose "high ceilings, open ducting and industrial looks" are juxtaposed with some "very classy" and "innovative" cooking (from the 10-course and 14-course tasting menus, alongside which there's also an à la carte). But despite consistently "outstanding" cuisine and "superb" service it was not to be, and, in September 2017, just prior to this year's announcement of the stars, chef Aiden Byrne scaled back his involvement here (did he have a tip off?) promoting chef Nathaniel Tofan in the process. / Details: www.manchesterhouse.uk.com; @MCRHouse; 9.30 pm; closed Mon.

Marble Arch £37 [3][3][4]
73 Rochdale Rd M4 4HY 0161 832 5914
"A proper, proper pub" with a "really wide selection of real ales" and "quality" hearty scoff, including a "superb cheese menu" ("I'm desperate to take some French friends so I can disabuse them of their assertion that English cheese is only Cheddar"). "Super original pub fittings make it a stand-out in terms of atmosphere".

Mei Dim £12 [4][1][2]
45-47 Faulkner St M1 4EE 0161 236 6868
This bustling "old-school" basement canteen is "basic in terms of service and decor" and "a good example of a cheap 'n' cheerful Hong Kong, Cantonese style restaurant which cooks the standard repertoire well and gets lots of, apparently well-satisfied, Chinese customers". "Dim sum is what it's about here", including some "hardcore", authentic choices: "lacking the refinement of Yang Sing, but the reward for that bit of coarseness is extra bright flavours".

Mi And Pho £25 [4][3][3]
M22 4FZ 0161 312 3290
This unassuming but "amazing Vietnamese in an unexpected area of Manchester" – on a never-ending road in southern suburb Northenden – is much talked-about among local foodies, owing to its reliably good curries, spring rolls and eponymous soups. / Details: www.miandpho.com; @MiandPho; 9 pm, Fri & Sat 10 pm, Sun 9 pm.

Mr Cooper's, The Midland Hotel £61 [3][3][3]
Peter St M60 2DS 0161 235 4781
"The sister restaurant to the upmarket French at the Midland, provides similarly high quality food but at much lower prices", and with its "top soundtrack" and "delightful garden style interior" (complete with its own tree) it's both less buttoned-down and better-rated nowadays than its more famous neighbour. / Details: www.mrcoopers.co.uk; @MrCoopersHouse; 10 pm, Sun 8 pm.

Mughli £32 [4][3][3]
30 Wilmslow Rd M14 5TQ 0161 248 0900
"Head and shoulders above the usual Rusholme curry house" – this highly rated destination "feels a million miles away from its neighbours" (although "it could do with a bit of a revamp") and is arguably "the best place on the Curry Mile!" It serves "a gorgeous range of street food" and dishes from the charcoal pit ("go for the lamb chops"). / Details: www.mughli.com; @mughli; 11.45 pm, Fri 12.15 am, Sat 2.45 am, Sun 10.45 pm.

Pasta Factory £51 [3][3][3]
77 Shudehill M4 4AN 0161 222 9250
Founded by friends from Turin, this two-year-old pasta shop and restaurant is just a stone's throw from Ancoats, FKA Manchester's Little Italy. The main event is homemade and "excellent", and there are "top Italian beers" and wines to go with it…"what's not to like"? / Details: www.pastafactory.co.uk; @pastafactoryuk; Sun 10 pm, Fri & Sat 11 pm.

Rabbit in the Moon, National Football Museum £104 [5][3][4]
Urbis Building, Cathedral Gardens, Todd St, City Centre M4 3BG 0161 804 8560
"Stunning innovation and creativity" win raves in early reports for this first of three joint ventures planned by whiz-bang chef Michael O'Hare and retired footballers Gary Neville and Ryan Giggs. It opened in spring 2017 at the National Football Museum in Manchester – "a cool setting with a quality soundtrack" – offering "exciting" 'space-age Asian food', including an ambitious 17-course tasting menu. "It still needs time to develop, and is definitely for the funky crowd not the traditionalists" but all feedback says it's "an experience to be remembered!" / Details: www.therabbitinthemoon.com; @urbisrabbit; 11 pm.

Randall & Aubin
64 Bridge Street M3 3BN 0161 711 1007
Manchester follow-up to Soho's "fun-and-frisky" seafood specialist, whose "so-fresh" fruits de mer have been delighting our reporters for over a decade. The northern outpost opened on the site of a former Spinningfields furniture store in May 2017. / Details: www.randallandaubin.com; @randallandaubinmcr; Mon-Thu 11pm, Fri & Sat midnight, Sun 10 pm; Booking lunch only.

Red Chilli £41 ④③②
70-72 Portland Street M1 4GU
0161 236 2888
*"The hottest gong bao chicken this side of
Chengdu" and "delights such as pigs' intestines
and other anatomically more challenging bits"
star at this "excellent value" Sichuanese, which "is
one of the more authentic options in Chinatown".
"I have not had a better Chinese meal for some
time and it cost just under £20!" / **Details:**
www.redchillirestaurant.co.uk; 11pm, Fri & Sat midnight;
closed Mon.*

Refuge by Volta £37 ③③④
Oxford Street M60 7HA 0161 223 5151
*DJs Luke Cowdrey and Justin Crawford, owners
of West Didsbury's Volta, launched their second
Manchester venture in this grand, elegantly
refurbished Victorian building (formerly the Refuge
Assurance Company, now the Palace Hotel) in late-
2016. With its atrium ceiling and ornate cupolas, it's
"a fantastic (if noisy) space" that "brings the delights
of small-plates eating to the city-centre". / **Details:**
www.refugemcr.co.uk; @TheRefugeMcr; Mon-Thu
10 pm, Fri & Sat 10.30 pm, Sun 9 pm.*

Rosso £79 ③③④
43 Spring Gardens M2 2BG 0161 8321400
*It can seem "overpriced", but most feedback
remains all-round complimentary about Rio
Ferdinand's stylish Italian restaurant and cocktails
bar in a "wonderful", swishly decked-out grade II
listed building. / **Details:** www.rossorestaurants.com;
@rossorestaurants; 10 pm; closed Sun.*

Rudys Pizza £25 ⑤④③
9 Cotton Street, Ancoats, M4 5BF
07931 162059
*"I don't even like pizza and I think this place is
superb!!" Fans hail some of "the best pizza in the
UK" at this "most basic" of industrial-look venues
in "not the most fashionable of areas". "Lovely soft
Neapolitan pizza" ("great digestible properly cooked
bases and quality ingredients on top") is sold at a
"fantastic price" and it's single-handedly "helping
revitalise the Ancoats area of Manchester". "The
secret is out so expect a wait (although you can
go to a nearby pub and they'll call you)". / **Details:**
www.rudyspizza.co.uk; @RudysPizzaMcr; No bookings.*

Salvis £50 ③④③
Unit 22b, The Corn Exchange, Corporation St
M4 3TR 0161 222 8021
*"Built (almost literally) around a deli selling wine
and other Italian staples", this Mozzarella Bar
& Restaurant in the Corn Exchange (which has
spawned a number of spin-offs) offers "a high
standard of Italian hospitality" alongside a good
range of pizza and pasta. / **Details:** salvismanchester.
co.uk/.*

Sam's Chop House £48 ③③③
Back Pool Fold off Cross Street M2 1HN
0161 834 3210
*"A Best of British experience" – with a decidedly
northern slant (black pud', Barnsley Chop…)
– awaits at this family-friendly icon (est. 1872);
further incentive to visit is provided by the
"eclectic, interesting wine list" from sommelier
George Bergier. / **Details:** www.samschophouse.com;
@chophousesams; 9.30 pm, Sat 10.30 pm, Sun 8 pm.*

San Carlo £59 ③④⑤
40 King Street West M3 2WY 0161 834 6226
*"The glitterati come out at night" to this "vibrant",
"see-and-be-seen" Italian in the city-centre – by day
more of a "bustling" venue for working or shopping
lunches. The "quality" cooking "can be very good if
you pick the right dish", and staff – when they're
not looking after the celebs – can "display some
excellent old-school skills (eg perfectly filleting a
sole at the tableside)". / **Details:** www.sancarlo.co.uk;
@SanCarlo_Group; 11 pm.*

San Carlo Cicchetti £51 ③③③
42 King Street West M3 2QG 0161 839 2233
*Limited reports this year on this busy and breezy
city-centre branch of the glossy Italian chain, and
its Venetian cicchetti formula – such feedback as
there was however rated it well across the board. /
Details: www.sancarlocicchetti.co.uk; @SC_Cicchetti;
11 pm, Sun 10 pm; Booking evening only.*

The Sculpture Hall Cafe £17 ③③⑤
The Town Hall Manchester, Albert Square M2
5DB 0161 827 8767
*"An oasis in a bustling city"; in the "amazing"
setting of the town's Victorian Gothic town hall,
and lined with statues of local luminaries, this
ground-floor eatery is particularly of note for
its sumptuous afternoon tea. "Manchester-
themed" lunches are also on offer too. / **Details:**
www.thetownhallmcr.co.uk/sculpture-hall-cafe.*

Siam Smiles £30 ⑤②①
48a George St M1 4HF 0161 237 1555
*The "brilliant, authentic Thai food" comes "at a
great price" at this "unbelievable supermarket
caff". "Don't expect either fancy surroundings or
professional service" – it can seem chilly ("the
first time my husband and I ate dinner with our
coats on") and the chairs "aren't very comfy", but
most reporters will "certainly return". / **Details:**
www.facebook.com/SiamSmilesCafe; @SiamSmilesCafe;
7.30 pm, Fri & Sat 9.30 pm.*

63 Degrees £69 ③③③
20 Church St M4 1PN 0161 832 5438
*The Moreau family's "so very classical" Northern
Quarter outfit is a bit of a "Marmite restaurant"
– "over-ambitious" to some, pleasing to others. It
moved from nearby Church St in early 2016, and*

the jury is also out on the roomier new locale; initial reports suggest that it "needs to be full to work", or risks feeling "like a morgue". / *Details:* www.63degrees.co.uk; @63DegreesNQ; 11 pm, Fri & Sat midnight, Sun 9 pm; closed Mon & Sun.

Solita £44
37 Turner St M4 1DW 0161 839 2200
"Hefty burgers (some overblown, but mostly the combinations work) and even heftier social media" has won fame for this hipster Northern Quarter hang-out (which now also has spin-offs in Didsbury, Prestwick and Preston). "Great home brews" and "very good cocktails" complete the experience. / *Details:* www.solita.co.uk; @SolitaNQ; 10 pm, Fri & Sat 11 pm, Sun 9 pm.

Tai Pan £41 |4|3|3|
81-97 Upper Brook St M13 9TX
0161 273 2798
This shed-like operation continues to please, even after several decades in business; "lots of Chinese eat here, especially university students and café owners which must indicate its authenticity!" / *Details:* www.taipanmanchester.co.uk; 10.30 pm, Sun 9.30 pm.

Tampopo £37 |3|4|3|
16 Albert Sq M2 5PF 0161 819 1966
"Still tops for fast and cheap street food" – the original branch of this canteen-style Pan-Asian chain remains "much better than its newer offshoots" (three locally, and one in the Big Smoke). / *Details:* www.tampopo.co.uk; @TampopoEats; 11 pm, Sun 10 pm; May need 7+ to book.

Tattu £72 |2|3|4|
3 Hardman Sq, Gartside St M3 3EB
0161 819 2060
Where 'The Real Housewives of Cheshire' go to party – all agree this glam Asian has had a "very good fit-out" and even a reviewer who said "it's not aimed at me, as I much prefer more authentic Chinese places" felt that "while it caters to up-market British customers with a taste for creative crossover dishes, I can understand why it's popular, as it does what it sets out to do very well". It takes predictable flak for the size of the bill though: "in price it targets the likes of Hakkasan/Yauatcha etc and while it's ok, it's just nowhere near as good as that". / *Details:* www.tattu.co.uk; @tattumcr; midnight.

Thaikhun £54 |3|3|4|
Unit 17, 3 Hardmen St M3 3HF
0161 819 2065
This Spinningfields branch of a 10-strong national Thai chain is the most commented-on in the group, and wins consistent praise for its "buzzing" style and also (mostly) too for its "fantastic" street food dishes. / *Details:* www.thaikhun.co.uk/; @thaikhun; 10 pm.

This & That £24 |5|2|2|
3 Soap St M4 1EW 0161 832 4971
"Filling up for a fiver on the most deeply flavoursome food this side of the indian ocean" has made "a Manchester institution" of this "reigning cheap-eats champion" in the Northern Quarter. "A remodel has turned the space from a rather down-at-heel caff into a perfectly pleasant canteen", but while "the new Scandi vibe and improved toilets make it a more enjoyable experience", the "location remains a bit dodgy… but that's part of its character!" / *Details:* www.thisandthatcafe.co.uk; closed Mon D, Tue D, Wed D, Thu D & Sun D; Cash only.

TNQ Restaurant & Bar £59 |4|4|2|
108 High St M4 1HQ 0161 832 7115
"Very decent and interesting dishes" from local and British produce helps establish this Northern Quarter corner-site as one of Manchester's better culinary destinations. "Always welcoming staff" enliven a space which could otherwise seem "a bit basic". / *Details:* www.tnq.co.uk; @TNQrestaurant; 10.30 pm, Sun 7 pm.

Umezushi £44 |5|3|3|
Unit 4, Mirabel Street M3 1PJ 0871 811 8877
After paeans from Jay Rayner and co, the secret is firmly out on this "17-odd-cover restaurant in a railway arch" down below Manchester Victoria station. A minimal spot, it's "excellent in all aspects", from superior-yet-superb-value sushi and sashimi, to the fact that – unusually – they make their unagi (eel) from scratch. / *Details:* www.umezushi.co.uk; @Umezushi_M31PJ; Booking max 10 may apply.

Whitworth Art Gallery £30 |2|3|5|
The University of Manchester, Oxford Rd M15 6ER 0161 275 7511
With "very friendly service", decent tapas-style food and a "beautifully designed" glass room boasting park views, this addendum to the revamped Whitworth Gallery is something of a "model museum café/restaurant" – so much so that "you wouldn't think you were in the notorious Moss Side". / *Details:* www.whitworth.manchester.ac.uk; @WhitworthArt; Thu 9 pm; closed Mon D, Tue D & Wed D; Booking evening only.

Wing's £48 |4|5|4|
1 Lincoln Sq M2 5LN 0161 834 9000
Wing Shing Chu's well-known destination in a city-centre office block "attracts the celeb set with its well-executed Cantonese and extensive wine list". "Yes, it is more expensive than Chinatown, and if you happen to want the less salubrious bits of the various animals (which I do now and then) you do need to go elsewhere", but both the "crossover cooking" and service are "excellent". / *Details:* www.wingsrestaurant.co.uk; 11.30 pm, Sun 10.30 pm; closed Sat L; children: 11+ after 8 pm Mon-Fri.

Yang Sing £42 5️⃣3️⃣2️⃣
34 Princess Street M1 4JY 0161 236 2200
"Take your taste buds out of this world!", say fans of Harry & Bonnie Yeung's famous Chinatown landmark, which celebrated 40 years in business this year with a refurb to bring it "bang up to date" (well nearly...). In recent years, its longstanding claim as "the best Chinese outside London" has sometimes been disputed – most notoriously in the last year by Giles Coren at the end of 2016 – but none of our reporters agree with The Times critic's assessment that results here are "absolutely minging", and such doubts as were expressed this year ("rather flat and average") were swamped by a wave of positivity for its "utterly delicious dim sum and Beijing duck". The overall verdict remains: "if you want the most innovative and creative Chinese food in the north, go to 'Yang Sing'!" / Details: www.yang-sing.com; @yangsing; Mon-Thu 11.30 pm, Fri 11.45 pm, Sat 12.15 am, S.

Yuzu £41 5️⃣3️⃣3️⃣
39 Faulkner St M1 4EE 0161 236 4159
"This charming little venture on the edge of Chinatown continues to provide superb Japanese food (verging on the exquisite)", and also "continues to stick to its no-sushi guns (their policy forbids it, as they have no chefs with the requisite seven years training)". Prop up a seat at the counter for some of "the best rice in the north-west". / Details: www.yuzumanchester.co.uk; @yuzumanchester; 9.30 pm; closed Mon & Sun.

MANNINGTREE, ESSEX 3–2C

Lucca Enoteca £40 3️⃣4️⃣4️⃣
39-43 High St CO11 1AH 01206 390044
"Better than all the chains and more authentic" – this Mistley Thorn sibling offers "great" Neapolitan pizza, and other "high-quality food" based on prime Italian ingredients. / Details: www.luccafoods.co.uk; @LuccaEnoteca; 9 pm, Wed-Thu 9.30 pm, Fri & Sat 10 pm.

MARAZION, CORNWALL 1–4A

Ben's Cornish Kitchen £51 5️⃣4️⃣3️⃣
West End TR17 0EL 01736 719200
Ben Prior's bistro in a "stunning" seaside location "goes on to greater things and is at last being recognised"; from the "fresh ingredients bursting with flavour" to the "faultless service" and "fantastic value", it won real bouquets from reporters this year. / Details: www.benscornishkitchen.com; @cornishkitchen; 8.30 pm; closed Mon & Sun.

MARGATE, KENT 3–3D

The Ambrette £57 5️⃣4️⃣3️⃣
44 King St CT9 1QE 01843 231504
"Fine Indian food with a European twist, with some superb flavours and interesting combinations" consistently wins rave reviews for Div Biswal's "relaxed" and "surprisingly great" pub-conversion, which "while perhaps not quite in the same league as London's best Indians such as Quilon, offers fantastic value for money": "I've visited at least 50 times and never had a bad meal!" See also Ambrette Canterbury. / Details: www.theambrette.co.uk; @the_ambrette; 9.30 pm, Fri-Sun 10 pm.

Bay at Sands, Sands Hotel £56 3️⃣4️⃣4️⃣
CT9 1DH 01843 228228
"With an amazing view of the sea and magnificent sunset", this boutique hotel houses "the nicest place in town with the freshest fish" – plus other "inventive", locally sourced fare. One reviewer "never thought to find such a great restaurant here", but it's just "symbolic of Margate's continuing renaissance!" / Details: www.sandshotelmargate.co.uk.

GB Pizza £32 4️⃣4️⃣3️⃣
14a Marine Drive CT9 1DH 01843 297700
"Fab pizza, fun decor and a sea view – what's not to like?!" The 'Great British Pizza Co' serves "the best pizza ever" – with "delicious thin crusts at really affordable prices" with "minimal toppings" – according to both local and London reviewers of this "small but perfectly formed" outfit. (In October 2017 it 'went national' – well nearly – with the opening of a franchise in far-away Didsbury, Manchester.) / Details: www.greatbritishpizza.com; @gbPizzaCo; 9.30 pm; closed Sun D.

Hantverk & Found £44 4️⃣4️⃣3️⃣
18 King Street CT9 1DA 01843 280454
"Tiny, cramped, uncomfortable" – there's no debate about the limitations of this sardine-sized spot, but then again there's also practically none about its major asset: "delicious" food (with a "strong emphasis on seafood, with flavours influenced by the chef's travels") whose "freshness cannot be gainsaid". / Details: www.hantverk-found.co.uk; @Hantverk_found.

MARLBOROUGH, WILTSHIRE 2–2C

The Harrow at Little Bedwyn £76 5️⃣5️⃣4️⃣
Little Bedwyn SN8 3JP 01672 870871
"Sue and Roger Jones deliver amazing food" at their famous converted inn, set in the middle of nowhere, and "Roger's creative pairings with the

wine make for simply marvellous meals" (his cellar is famously well-stocked). Perhaps, though, "where it really has the edge is the pure enthusiasm of its staff: instead of feeling like an elitist gourmet restaurant, it feels like you are chatting with friends over an outstanding meal". / **Details:** www.theharrowatlittlebedwyn.co.uk; @littlebedwyn; 9 pm; closed Mon, Tue & Sun; No trainers; Credit card deposit required to book.

Rick Stein £61 **3 4 4**
Lloran House, 42a High Street SN8 1HQ
01672 233333
"Set over two floors in an old building with some cosy nooks and crannies", this new opening from the Stein Empire is "a great addition to the area", which lacked a destination restaurant. But while it succeeds as "a high end bistro" with "unfussy, well-cooked food" and "good-humoured service", numerous reports suggest that "for a top name the quality is somewhat mixed" ("good but not extraordinary") and that "it has some way to go to be a match for the Sandbanks restaurant". / **Details:** www.rickstein.com/eat-with-us/marlborough/; @TheSeafood.

MARLOW, BUCKINGHAMSHIRE 3–3A

The Coach £49 **5 4 4**
3 West Street SL7 2LS 01628 483013
"You can't book so getting a table is very hit 'n' miss" at Tom Kerridge's "amazing" two-year-old, which "is not the local pub that it might appear to be, and full and buzzing from dawn to dusk". "It knocks the Hand & Flowers, just down the road (where there is an infinite wait for a booking and it often ends up overcrowded and pretentious) into a cocked-hat", with "smallish plates of the most intense food, all of which are well-conceived and delicious", and delivered from the open kitchen ("sitting at the bar is like a chef's table, but without the extra cost!"). "Stylish surroundings too, a busy happy atmosphere and cracking wine list and good beer. What's not to like?" (Actually, there is one niggle aside from the "deep frustration at no reservations": "where you wait for a table is a bit small and jammed-in".) / **Details:** www.thecoachmarlow.co.uk; @TheCoachMarlow; 10.30 pm, Sun 9 pm; No bookings.

Hand & Flowers £95 **3 3 3**
West Street SL7 2BP 01628 482277
"A top notch gastropub… but one that's horribly over-hyped and certainly nowhere near two Michelin stars". Due to the (over) recognition of the French tyre company a few years back, Tom Kerridge's renowned boozer on the "busy" approach-road to the town centre has achieved a level of fame out of all proportion to its humble quarters and (admittedly accomplished) culinary

performance, and risks becoming a victim of its own success. All reports agree that it's a "lovely and cosy" (if "cramped") honest pub, which despite its celebrity (and that of its TV chef owner) has stayed "very relaxed"; and legions of its fans do feel its "exceptional and traditional cooking delivers an amazing and authentic experience", enhanced by staff "who couldn't be more friendly". But the growing volume of critical feedback rings alarm bells this year: the level of table turning can be "astonishing"; and too many reports of food that was "I hate to say it, but just, well, 'nice'" (and very salty) means it risks now becoming "a cliché of ordinary cooking at bloated prices… for which it takes months to book!". / **Details:** www.thehandandflowers.co.uk; closed Sun D. / **Accommodation:** 4 rooms, from £140

The Ivy Marlow Garden £54
66-68 High St SL7 1AH 01628 902777
In a 'roll-out' that would do McDonald's proud, this iconic brand has gone for it this year, opening virtually simultaneously in practically all of the UK's top restaurant cities. The ambition is impressive: let's hope standards hold up better than they did when, for example 'Browns' tried to pull off a similar trick. / **Details:** www.theivymarlowgarden.com; @iymarlowgarden.

Marlow Bar & Grill £55 **2 2 2**
92-94 High Street SL7 1AQ 01628 488544
This slick, booth-lined bar and steakhouse is a bit of a local fixture ("get a window seat at lunchtime and play at yuppy-spotting"); "nothing much changes", though, "just the prices increase" – and "watch out now The Ivy's come to town!" (the ritzy group's Ivy Marlow Garden brasserie having opened, just along the High Street, in May 2017). / **Details:** www.individualrestaurants.com; towards the river end of the High Street; 11 pm, Sun 10.30 pm.

Sindhu, Macdonald Compleat Angler Hotel £71 **4 3 4**
The Compleat Angler SL7 1RG
01628 405405
"Exquisite food, beautifully presented by staff who are attentive but not stuffy" win very high praise for Atul Kochhar's ongoing regime at this famous landmark, superbly located on the river and with gorgeous views. "You expect this quality in London: not in the Thames Valley!" / **Details:** www.sindhurestaurant.co.uk; @SindhuMarlow; 10.30 pm, Sun 10 pm.

The Vanilla Pod £68 **5 3 3**
31 West St SL7 2LS 01628 898101
"An under-appreciated jewel!" say fans of Michael Macdonald's highly-rated venture – "an intimate, timbered (and nicely extended but still very small and very cramped) dining room" with "enthusiastic" staff (in what was once TS Eliot's home). Michael Mcdonald's "consistently brilliant" food is

"immaculate, the flavours beautifully calculated, the wine list is wide-ranging and imaginative, and prices are a snip compared with its many famous local competitors which it ranks highly against: why it has no Michelin recognition is baffling". / Details: www.thevanillapod.co.uk; 10 pm; closed Mon & Sun.

MARY TAVY, DEVON   1–3C

Elephants Nest   **£45**   3 3 3
PL19 9NQ   01822 810273
"A real find on Dartmoor"; this "really lovely" 16th century inn offers "a totally delicious treat" in a "good value pub cooking" mould; change may be afoot however – new chef Richard Greenway (formerly of Le Manoir aux Quat' Saisons) apparently has ambitions to create fancier fare. / Details: www.elephantsnest.co.uk/; @theelephantsnest; 11.30 pm.

MASHAM, NORTH YORKSHIRE   8–4B

Samuel's, Swinton Park Hotel & Spa   **£81**   4 5 5
Swinton Park   HG4 4JH   01765 680900
Real raves for the "magnificent" dining room and "outstanding" staff of this grand country house hotel, and Stephen Bulmer's "exceptionally good value" tasting menu, which provides some "wonderful" flavours. (In the adjoining lounges "the best afternoon tea" is another reason to visit, and can be rounded off with "beautiful walks in the grounds"). / Details: www.swintonestate.com/eating; @SwintonPark; 9.30 pm; closed weekday L; No jeans; children: 8+ at D.

The Terrace, Swinton Park Hotel & Spa   **£50**
Swinton Rd   HG4 4JH   01765 680900
Chris McPhee, formerly head chef at Three Chimneys on the Isle of Skye, heads up this grand country house hotel's new upscale all-day café, which opened in summer 2017 and adds a more relaxed dining destination than the well-known Samuel's; the aim is to use as much produce from the estate as possible. / Details: www.swintonestate.com/eating; @SwintonPark; 9.30 pm.

MATLOCK, DERBYSHIRE   5–2C

Stones   **£53**   4 4 4
1C Dale Rd   DE4 3LT   01629 56061
"Well designed and laid out" and with a "lovely terrace by the river", the Stone family's popular local staple strikes reporters as a "fantastic find" combining "very pleasant" service

---

with "splendid" modern cooking. / Details: www.stones-restaurant.co.uk; @stonesmatlock; 8.30 pm; closed Mon, Tue L & Sun; No Amex; No shorts.

MELLS, SOMERSET   2–3B

The Talbot Inn   **£54**   3 3 4
Selwood St   BA11 3PN   01373 812254
"Go for a walk across the fields or through the local woods then pop in for a meal here" – an upscale country inn with rooms, where you can either "sit by the fire" in the pub or opt to "eat in the grill"; all reviews laud the "enjoyable" cooking. / Details: www.talbotinn.com; @TheTalbotMells; 9.30 pm.

MENAI BRIDGE, GWYNEDD   4–1C

Dylan's Restaurant   **£49**   3 3 4
St George's Road   LL59 5EY   01248 716714
"Captivating views of the Menai straits" help underpin the appeal of this "jolly" waterfront operation: a "wine bar-style" outfit, but with some "tasty" cooking – particularly fish and seafood – which "tastes fab even on a rainy day in north Wales". / Details: www.dylansrestaurant.co.uk; @dylanspizzeria; 10 pm .

Sosban And The Old Butchers   **£65**   5 4 4
1 High St, Menai Bridge   LL59 5EE
01248 208131
"You don't know what you are going to get" at this "small" but stylish venue in an old butcher's, but the leap of faith is "well worth it" given the "really special" results: "every dish is perfectly prepared and follows on extremely well from the one before". By all accounts "they have deserved their recently awarded Michelin star". / Details: www.sosbanandtheoldbutchers.com; @The_oldbutchers; Thu-Sat midnight.

MILFORD-ON-SEA, HAMPSHIRE   2–4C

Verveine Fishmarket Restaurant   **£66**   5 4 3
98 High St   SO41 0QE   01590 642176
"David Wykes continues to impress, continuously developing and refining the menu with many a surprise on the plate" ("yet again a stunning, slightly crazy but absolutely delicious meal") at his small venture, behind a fishmongers. "Chefs are so friendly with their open plan kitchen and waiters are passionate and knowledgeable about the food". / Details: www.verveine.co.uk; @98verveine; 9.30 pm; closed Mon & Sun; No Amex.

MILTON ABBOT, DEVON	1–3C

Hotel Endsleigh £69 ②②❹
PL19 0PQ   01822 870000
*Channel 5's Hotel Inspector, Alex Polizzi, runs this "perfect venue" – a "deliciously cosy" grade I-listed shooting-and-fishing lodge in "beautiful" grounds with views of the Tamar between Dartmoor and Bodmin Moor. "Okay, the food isn't faultless" (a tad "simple" and "overpriced for what it is") but for the majority of reporters it's "still a great find worth revisiting". / **Details:** www.hotelendsleigh.com; @hotelendsleigh; 9.30 pm. / **Accommodation:** 16 rooms, from £180*

MILTON KEYNES VILLAGE, BEDFORDSHIRE	
3–2A	

The Swan Inn £59 ❸❹❹
Broughton Road   MK10 9AH   01908 665240
*Originating in the 13th century, this thatched country pub sits "at the heart of this market town" (the original Milton Keynes) – "a great experience, with food that's good-value, well-presented and well-cooked". / **Details:** theswan-mkvillage.co.uk; @swan_mk; Mon-Thu 9.30 pm, Fri-Sat 10 pm, Sun 8 pm.*

MILTON UNDER WYCHWOOD,	
OXFORDSHIRE	2–1C

Hare £49 ❸❺❹
3 High Street   OX7 6LA   01993 835763
*Back with a bang after a six years – this picturesque stone pub in a Cotswold village was rescued by publican Sue Hawkins in 2016 (the tenth hostelry she has taken over and turned around) and wins enthusiastic praise (if on still limited feedback) for its "lovely food" and "staff who have a good sense of humour". / **Details:** www.themiltonhare.co.uk; @themiltonhare; 9 pm, Fri & Sat 9.30 pm.*

MINSTER LOVELL, OXFORDSHIRE	2–1C

Old Swan & Minster Mill £59 ❸❸❹
Old Minster   OX29 0RN   01993 774441
*Very attractive, beamed and cosy country pub and hotel (part of the Brownsword group) "in a quaint Cotswold village". "The food is well presented and of the gastro' variety – no common pub grub here!" / **Details:** www.oldswanminstermill.co.uk; @OldSwanMinster; Mon-Thu 9 pm, Fri & Sat 9.30 pm, Sun 9 pm.*

MISTLEY, ESSEX	3–2D

The Mistley Thorn Restaurant & Rooms £47 ❸❸❸
High St   CO11 1HE   01206 392821
*Coastal gastropub with rooms backdropped by Stour Estuary views – an attractive spot turning out "always fresh and imaginative", seafood-centric fare. Besides "great 'fishy evenings' to entice the loyal and new customers", it "also has a cookery school" run by Californian chef-owner Sherri Singleton. / **Details:** www.mistleythorn.com; @mistleythorn; 9.30 pm. / **Accommodation:** 11 rooms, from £100*

MOIRA, COUNTY ARMAGH	10–2D

Wine and Brine £58 ❹❹❹
59 Main St   BT67 0LQ   028 9261 0500
*After 20 years working alongside leading London lights like Richard Corrigan, chef Chris McGowan and his wife returned home to open this spot on the main street of town, a couple of years ago – and locals feel "so fortunate" to have them. The food, with a focus on ageing, curing and brining, is very good, and has already helped the "fabulous local" rack up the awards. / **Details:** www.wineandbrine.co.uk; @wine_brine; 9 pm, Fri & Sat 9.30 pm.*

MONTGOMERY, POWYS	5–4A

Checkers £90 ❺❸❸
Broad St, Powys   SY15 6PN   01686 669822
*"Traditional and classic French cuisine with wonderful twists and flavour marriages" justify the pilgrimage to the Welsh outback for the many loyal fans of Stéphane Borie & Sarah Francis's 17th-century inn on the town square – a "peaceful and private" escape with five rooms. / **Details:** www.checkerswales.co.uk; @checkerswales; 9 pm; closed Mon, Tue L, Wed L, Thu L & Sun; No Amex; children: 8+ at D. / **Accommodation:** 5 rooms, from £125*

MORECAMBE, LANCASHIRE	5–1A

Midland Hotel £55 ❹❹❺
Marine Road west   LA4 4BU   01524 424000
*"It would be difficult to think of a better backdrop to a meal" than the "amazing views across Morecambe Bay to the Lake District" at this "iconic" and "very stylish" Art Deco hotel. Perhaps surprisingly, the food itself is also "lovely" and "not overpriced" – with the "quintessential English afternoon tea" a continuing highlight. / **Details:** www.englishlakes.co.uk; @englishlakes; 9.30 pm. / **Accommodation:** 44 rooms, from £94*

MORETON-IN-MARSH, GLOUCESTERSHIRE 2–1C	MOULTON, CAMBRIDGESHIRE 3–1C

The Fox Inn £44 3️⃣2️⃣3️⃣
Lower Oddington GL56 0UR 01451 870862
*This attractive Cotswold hamlet boasts a "perfect country pub" – an ivy-covered, flagstone-floored inn with rambling rooms, a lovely courtyard garden, real ales and superior gastro-fare. / **Details:** www.foxinn.net; @foxinn; on A436 near Stow-on-the-Wold; 9.30 pm; No Amex. / **Accommodation:** 3 rooms, from £85*

The White Hart Royal Hotel £46 2️⃣3️⃣3️⃣
High Street GL56 0BA 01608 650731
*Fine old Cotswolds coaching inn with attractive courtyard in the heart of this chocolate box town; it doesn't aim for culinary fireworks but serves "good, solid pub grub" in its restaurant and 'Snug Bar'. / **Details:** www.whitehartroyal.co.uk.*

MORSTON, NORFOLK 6–3C	

Morston Hall £98 5️⃣4️⃣4️⃣
Main Coast Rd NR25 7AA 01263 741041
*"A different tasting menu every day matched with wines" adds up to "culinary heaven" at Galton Blackiston's well-known country house hotel, near the coast, also praised for its "creative, seasonal approach" and "excellent execution". Aside from the odd niggle about the inevitably high price, feedback is uniformly upbeat. / **Details:** www.morstonhall.com; @MorstonHall; between Blakeney & Wells on A149; 8 pm; D only, eve Sun open L & D; practically no walk-ins – you must boo. / **Accommodation:** 13 rooms, from £330*

MOULSFORD, OXFORDSHIRE 2–2D	

The Beetle & Wedge Boathouse £54 2️⃣2️⃣4️⃣
Ferry Ln OX10 9JF 01491 651381
*"You go for the views and the relaxed atmosphere" at this former boathouse on the stretch of the Thames which inspired The Wind in the Willows. The "food can be a little over-complicated", but even those who feel that it's "not the standard it used to be" admit the place is "still a great location for a summer's afternoon". / **Details:** www.beetleandwedge.co.uk; on A329 between Streatley & Wallingford, take Ferry Lane at crossroads; 8.45 pm. / **Accommodation:** 3 rooms, from £90*

The Packhorse Inn £55 2️⃣3️⃣3️⃣
Bridge St CB8 8SP 01638 751818
*In a remote setting, this restaurant-with-rooms "pushes food out quickly with flavours that pack a punch". Some reports are qualified ("slipped a little, but is improving…", "prices more gastro than pub but lovely location…") but feedback is mostly upbeat. / **Details:** www.thepackhorseinn.com; @Moultopackhorse; 10 pm.*

MOUNTSORREL, LEICESTERSHIRE 5–4D	

John's House £70 5️⃣4️⃣3️⃣
139-141 Loughborough Road LE12 7AA 01509 415569
*"A real find: in a house next to a petting farm in an unprepossessing village" – John Duffin's "old farmhouse in suburbia" has found fame both locally and with Michelin in its three years of operation. His British cuisine is "exceptional" and "exquisitely presented" too. Top Tip – "lunch is remarkable value". / **Details:** www.johnshouse.co.uk; @JohnsHouseRest; 9 pm; closed Mon & Sun.*

MOUSEHOLE, CORNWALL 1–4A	

2 Fore Street Restaurant £46 4️⃣3️⃣3️⃣
2 Fore St TR19 6PF 01736 731164
*This "reliably good" bistro occupies a "whitewashed cottage near Mousehole harbour", with "simple, modern decor"; "you can't go wrong for seafood" in particular ("an exemplary staple like crab sandwich is elevated above the ordinary by excellent bread and well-judged seasoning"). / **Details:** www.2forestreet.co.uk; 9.30 pm. / **Accommodation:** 2 rooms, from £250*

MUDEFORD, DORSET 2–4C	

Beach House Café £46 4️⃣3️⃣2️⃣
The Spit BH23 3ND 01202 423474
*"Wonderful fresh fish and seafood" is "served pretty much on the beach itself" at this "cramped", nautically styled spot. / **Details:** www.beachhousecafe.co.uk.*

Noisy Lobster £58 4️⃣4️⃣4️⃣
BH23 4AN 01425 272162
*A "great find" in an "absolutely beautiful beachfront spot" ("especially if you catch a sunset over the water") – this "relaxed", red-brick restaurant and bakery wins warm applause for its "fresh delicious food" (as per the name, with the emphasis on seafood). / **Details:** avon-beach.noisylobster.co.uk/; @thenoisylobster.*

MURCOTT, OXFORDSHIRE	2–1D

The Nut Tree Inn £68
Main Street OX5 2RE 01865 331253
"Michael North's innovative cooking goes from strength to strength, while Imogen Young delivers the most calming front of house experience" at this thatched village pub, near Bicester ("a great stop-off if you are heading up the M40" and "well worth seeking out"). The result is a "relaxed yet elegant meal in beautiful Oxfordshire countryside", with "a highly recommended tasting menu for a special occasion" but where "you can still enjoy a pint at the bar with the locals". "They use lots of their own fantastic produce which is always a good sign" too, and there' a "well chosen wine list". Top Menu Tip – "exquisite soufflés". / Details: www.nuttreeinn.co.uk; 9 pm, Sun 3 pm; Booking max 4 may apply.

MUTHILL, PERTH AND KINROSS	9–3C

Barley Bree £64 3️⃣4️⃣3️⃣
6 Willoughby St PH5 2AB 01764 681451
"Fabrice and Alison Bouteloup provide an exceptional experience" at this appealingly rustic restaurant-with-rooms – an 18th century former coaching inn, near Gleneagles. The "French-style cooking is done very well", and makes top use of Scottish ingredients. / Details: www.barleybree.com; @barleybree6; 9 pm, Wed-Sat 7.30 pm; closed Mon & Tue; No Amex. / Accommodation: 6 rooms, from £110

NAILSWORTH, GLOUCESTERSHIRE	2–2B

Wild Garlic £51 3️⃣3️⃣2️⃣
3 Cossacks Sq GL6 0DB 01453 832615
It's "always enjoyable to eat" at Matthew Beardshall's "basic and modern" bistro-with-three-rooms, where the food "makes good use of local ingredients" and is "spot-on for flavour and balance, with inventive combinations you'd expect in a higher-end establishment". But, as it celebrates a decade in business, it is arguable that the "interesting cooking has now moved to (its new spin-off) Wilder, across the road" – a buzzy room dedicated to offering an eight-course blind tasting menus on Wednesday to Saturday nights. / Details: www.wild-garlic.co.uk; @TheWildGarlic; 9.30 pm, Tue 9 pm, Sun 2.30 pm; closed Mon, Tue & Sun D; No Amex. / Accommodation: 3 rooms, from £90

NANTGAREDIG, CARMARTHENSHIRE 4–4C

Y Polyn £58 4️⃣4️⃣4️⃣
Capel Dewi SA32 7LH 01267 290000
Albeit "quirky" and rather unassuming on the outside, this "unpretentious" ex-tollhouse ("run by owners who clearly love what they do") continues to satisfy its fan club with its "super and interesting" food (including an "amazing value" 'squeezed middle' lunch). It's just gained an upstairs room too. / Details: www.ypolyn.co.uk; @PolyNation; 9 pm; closed Mon & Sun D.

NETHER BURROW, CUMBRIA	7–4D

The Highwayman £54 4️⃣3️⃣3️⃣
Burrow LA6 2RJ 01524 273338
"Popular with families", this "nice, laidback" Ribble Valley Inn outpost is "always worth a visit" owing to its regularly changing seasonal menu, which achieved very strong ratings this year. / Details: www.highwaymaninn.co.uk; @highwayman_inn; Mon-Thu 9 pm, Fri & Sat 9.30 pm, Sun 9 pm.

NETHER WESTCOTE, OXFORDSHIRE 2–1C

The Feathered Nest Inn £96 5️⃣4️⃣5️⃣
OX7 6SD 01993 833030
"Scenes over rolling Cotswolds countryside" help set a "romantic" tone at this "historic pub, cleverly adapted with the addition of a comfortable dining room with country views" – "it has it all, with its beautiful surroundings, log fires in winter and summer al fresco". That goes for its "terrific fine dining" too – "exceptional food, time after time from a very talented brigade" led by Kuba Witkowski. "It's expensive, but never lets you down". / Details: www.thefeatherednestinn.co.uk; @FeatheredNestIn; 9.15 pm, Sun 3.15 pm; closed Mon & Sun D. / Accommodation: 4 rooms, from £150

NEW MILTON, HAMPSHIRE	2–4C

Chewton Glen £92 2️⃣2️⃣3️⃣
Chewton Glen Rd BH23 5QL 01425 282212
"One of the best luxury country hotels in the world in our opinion!" That's the kind of support that has for so long maintained this famous retreat: a much-extended old house set in 130 acres on the fringes of Bournemouth, which for its many (plutocratic) fans is "an old favourite that always delivers", particularly when it comes to its "exceptional wine list, with lots of interesting gems". That you really "pay the price for this experience" is a perennial issue however, as is a sense that culinary results can be a little "stolid". That said, the

majority of reporters "simply love it here". / **Details:** www.chewtonglen.com; @chewtonglen; on A337 between New Milton & Highcliffe; 10 pm; No trainers. / **Accommodation:** 70 rooms, from £325

The Kitchen at Chewton Glen £82 4|4|4
Chewton Farm Road BH23 5QL
01425 275341

A purpose-built cookery school opened at this famous country house hotel in spring 2017, and you can eat here, too, with wood-fired pizzas, burgers and superfood salads: early reports say it's "brilliant – an excellent casual additional to Chewton Glen", and one providing an affordable entrée into a luxury establishment not known for its bargain giveaways… / **Details:** www.chewtonglen.com/thekitchen/; @TheKitchenatCG.

NEWARK, NOTTINGHAMSHIRE	5–3D

Koinonia £36 3|4|3
19 St Marks Ln NG24 1XS 01636 706230

Ignore the "unlikely setting down an alley in a shopping precinct" – this is an "authentic South Indian local" that "makes the food of Kerala sing to jaded palates!". From the "exquisite" veggie dishes to other "lip-smackingly delicious" fare, it's "excellent all round". / **Details:** www.koinoniarestaurant.com; @Koinonia; 11 pm, Sat 11.30 pm, Sun 7.30 pm.

NEWBOROUGH, ISLE OF ANGLESEY	4–1C

The Marram Grass £48 5|3|3
White Lodge LL61 6RS 01248 440077

A "happy atmosphere" reigns at this cramped six-year-old venture, located in… a potting shed! "They seem to have everything right here and turn good local produce into great restaurant treats" (even the most critical reporter gives the food very good marks). / **Details:** www.themarramgrass.com; @TheMarramGrass; 9 pm.

NEWBURY, BERKSHIRE	2–2D

Chilis Restaurant £42 3|4|2
Station Approach RG14 5DG 01635 522577

Your best option for a curry in this cute market town is this unassuming-looking subcontinental, handy for the train station, with its "great selection of authentic Indian food" (from dosas to tandooris). / **Details:** www.chilisrestaurant.co.uk; @chilisfamily.

The Newbury £68 2|3|3
137 Bartholomew Street RG14 5HB 01635 49000

"Part of the West Berks eating and going out scene!" This five-year-old gastropub – complete with a cute garden and roof terrace – serves a good variety of fare, including pizza and steaks from the grill. / **Details:** www.thenewburypub.co.uk; @thenewburypub; Mon-Thu midnight, Sun 7pm.

The Woodspeen £72 5|4|4
Lambourn Rd RG20 8BN 01635 265070

"Exceptional cuisine from John Campbell and his team" ("their passion shines through") wins the highest praise for this modernised ex-pub "tucked-away a few miles from Newbury" and "certainly worth the drive". "Service is very effective and charming too – everyone smiles! – and the unique design of the building (with its striking high ceiling) and the surroundings make for a very elegant and pleasant experience". / **Details:** www.thewoodspeen.com; @thewoodspeen; 9.45 pm, Sun 5 pm; closed Mon.

NEWCASTLE UPON TYNE, TYNE AND WEAR	8–2B

Artisan, The Biscuit Factory £60 3|3|2
Stoddard St NE2 1AN 0191 260 5411

From "delightful tasting menus" to "excellent and generously proportioned Sunday lunches", the restaurant on the ground floor of this converted Victorian warehouse (nowadays the UK's largest arts and crafts gallery) wins praise for the "consistent quality" of Andrew Wilkinson's cuisine. / **Details:** www.artisannewcastle.com; 9.30 pm, Sun 4.30 pm; closed Sun D.

Blackfriars Restaurant £52 3|3|5
Friars St NE1 4XN 0191 261 5945

A superbly "atmospheric" 13th-century medieval friary houses Andy Hook's well-known local venue, which has a "low-key pub style" that draws "a proper local crowd". Most reviewers feel its "locally sourced food" ("traditional but interesting") really "goes the extra mile" (even if it arguably "stands in poor comparison with Dobson & Parnell" his new venue). In Spring 2017, there was a major makeover here, with expansion into the old parlour and library rooms, gaining extra seating, an open kitchen and surroundings cookery workshop. / **Details:** www.blackfriarsrestaurant.co.uk; @BlackfriarsRest; 10 pm; closed Sun D.

Broad Chare £45 3|3|4
25 Broad Chare NE1 3DQ 019 1211 2144

"A terrific bar, imaginative cooking, real ales and super daily specials – what more do you want?" So say fans of this "high class gastropub" on the

Quayside which "focuses on British fare" and goes well beyond the typical pub repertoire of pub dishes. / **Details:** www.thebroadchare.co.uk; @_thebroadchare; Mon-Sat, 5.30 pm-10 pm; closed Sun D; No Amex.

Café Royal £48 🟥🟥🟥
8 Nelson St NE1 5AW 0191 231 3000
"Stretching from light breakfasts to more elaborate lunchtime choices", this well-established grand café remains "a favourite in town". / **Details:** www.sjf.co.uk; @caferoyalsjf; L only; Booking weekdays only.

Caffé Vivo £44 🟦🟦🟦
29 Broad Chare NE1 3DQ 0191 232 1331
Terry Labourne's "great, buzzy" quayside ten-year-old has a solid local following thanks to its winning line in "tasty" peasant food. / **Details:** www.caffevivo.co.uk; @caffevivo; 10 pm; closed Sun.

Dabbawal £36 🟦🟥🟦
1 Brentwood Mews NE2 3DG 0191 281 3434
"They avoid the usual gloopy sauces" at this Jesmond spin-off from the city-centre original, which offers a similar on-trend Mumbai street food formula comprising some "fantastic, healthy Indian bites". / **Details:** www.dabbawal.com; @Dabbawal.

Dabbawal £38 🟦🟥🟦
69-75 High Bridge NE1 6BX 0191 232 5133
Funkily branded High Bridge street food kitchen, near the Theatre Royal (with a Jesmond sibling) celebrating ten years in business, which is consistently the city's most highly rated Indian option. "On my own, I love it. On a date night with my husband, we really love it. As a family of 4, we absolutely love it!" / **Details:** www.dabbawal.com; @dabbawal; 10 pm, Fri-Sun 10.30 pm; closed Sun.

Dobson And Parnell £57 🟦🟦🟦
21 Queen St NE1 3UG 0191 221 0904
On the old site of Pan Haggerty and Terry Labourne's acclaimed 21 Queen Street, this new arrival on the Quayside dining scene (est. late 2016) has a lot to live up to. By all accounts it's off to a promising start, with chef Troy Terrington (ex-of Blackfriars) praised for his "startlingly good" local cuisine in an elegant brasserie setting (the name stemming from the Victorian buildings architects). / **Details:** www.dobsonandparnell.co.uk; @DobsonParnell.

Francesca's £37 🟥🟥🟥
134 Manor House Rd NE2 2NE
0191 281 6586
A "cheap 'n' cheerful" Jesmond icon whose "fattening" Britalian fare (pizza, pasta and the "best garlic bread in town") is still "worth the queue"; "service can sometimes be a bit brusque, but that's

part of the ambience" (likewise the cheesy posters). / **Details:** www.francesca.com; 9.30 pm; closed Sun; No Amex; No bookings.

House of Tides £98 🟥🟥🟥
28-30 The Close NE1 3RN 0191 2303720
"Perched by the Tyne", this "former merchants house" on the Quayside is a "fascinating old building" that is nowadays "a blow-out destination" for Kenny Atkinson's "first-rate" tasting menus, which in particular "showcase the best of the North Sea catch (of special note are the Lindisfarne oysters)". There is the odd quibble – service is sometimes "variable" throughout a meal, and the dishes can sometimes seem "over-elaborate", but on most accounts it's "an absolute delight" delivering a "first rate gastronomic experience". / **Details:** www.houseoftides.co.uk; 9.30 pm, Sat 10 pm; closed Mon, Tue L & Sun; Booking max 4 may apply.

Jesmond Dene House £69 🟥🟦🟦
Jesmond Dene Rd NE2 2EY 0191 212 6066
Terry Laybourne's boutique hotel occupies "a lovely old house in a wooded 'dene'" in the city's most "salubrious suburb". It's one of the town's top gastronomic destinations thank to its high quality cuisine, including a selection of steaks ("in other top north eastern venues fish generally rules"). / **Details:** www.jesmonddenehouse.co.uk; @jesmonddenehous; 9.30 pm; Booking max 7 may apply. / **Accommodation:** 40 rooms, from £120

Nadon Thai £53 🟥🟦🟥
32-34 Mosley St NE1 1DF 0191 261 9768
"One of a small, three-strong chain of Thai restaurants in the North East"; admittedly there's "nothing unusual on the menu, but the food is very tasty"; "great service" too. / **Details:** www.nadonthai.co.uk; @nadonthai; 10.30 pm.

Pani's £33 🟥🟦🟥
61-65 High Bridge NE1 6BX 0191 232 4366
"A local institution which nearly always comes up trumps even when it is very busy"; staff "treat you like family", the "ambience is fab" and the bargainous Sardinian food is "always reliable" (homely classics being supported by "interesting and varied specials"). / **Details:** www.paniscafe.co.uk; @PanisCafe; 10 pm; closed Sun; No Amex; No bookings at lunch.

Paradiso £43 🟥🟦🟥
1 Market Ln NE1 6QQ 0191 221 1240
"Our own piece of Italy in the heart of the city" – this vivid, three-floor trattoria offers a supremely "warm welcome" and "consistently delicious food" ("Mediterranean" in style and with an "eclectic selection" of dishes). / **Details:** www.paradiso.co.uk; @ParadisoNE1; 10.30 pm, Fri & Sat 10.45 pm; closed Sun.

Peace & Loaf £75 ④④④
217 Jesmond Road NE2 1LA 0191 281 5222
"Set in a lovely space" – a split-level venue in
Jesmond – Dave Coulson's "very assured modern
british cooking" is "supported by attentive and
timely service" at this accomplished four-year-old,
which all reviewers see as "a class act". / *Details:*
www.peaceandloaf.co.uk; @peaceandloafjes; Mon-Sat
9.30 pm, Sun 3.30 pm; closed Sun D.

Sachins £40 ③③③
Forth Banks NE1 3SG 0191 261 9035
"All those eating here support the notion that
this is one of Newcastle's favourite curry houses"
– an Indian fixture, long run by Bob & Neeta
Arora, and handy for Central Station. / *Details:*
www.sachins.co.uk; @Sachins_NCL; 11 pm; closed
Sun L.

Smashburger
Grey's Quarter, Eldon Sq NE1 7JB
0191 261 4566
The third branch of this US burger chain – named
for the grilling method of 'smashing' a meatball
onto a hot, buttered grill – arrived in Newcastle
in early-2017. Further roll-out plans are in the
works for the brand, which is rapidly moving in on
our homegrown posh burger chains with sites in
Brighton, Milton Keynes, Bath, Glasgow, Wednesbury
and Dunfermline. / *Details:* www.smashburger.co.uk;
@smashburgeruk; 9 pm, Fri & Sat 11 pm.

Tapas Revolution £40
Greys Quarter, Intu Eldon Square NE1 7AP
0191 261 4948
The sixth branch of Spanish TV chef Omar Allibhoy's
growing UK tapas chain opened in Newcastle's
Eldon Square shopping centre in February 2017.
/ *Details:* www.tapasrevolution.com/newcastle/;
@tapasrevolution; 11 pm, Sun 10 pm.

A Taste of Persia £31 ④④②
14 Marlborough Cr NE1 4EE 0191 221 0088
One of the city's best-kept secrets for 17 years,
this brightly coloured, carpet-clad staple on the
outskirts continues to offer "something different"
– namely "good quality food" with an "authentic
Persian taste". A four-year-old Jesmond sibling is
also "excellent value for money and as good as the
original". / *Details:* www.atasteofpersia.com; 10 pm;
closed Sun.

21 £58 ④④④
Trinity Gdns NE1 2HH 0191 222 0755
"Terry Laybourne's original venture and his best" –
this "consistently excellent" city-centre all-rounder
remains the most commented-on venue in the City,
and many locals'"preferred choice for every special
occasion". It "reliably produces superb brasserie
food, while staff are outstanding and professional"
and "though it's a bit too rammed and noisy to
be a relaxing experience, if you like the buzz of a

crowded restaurant you won't be disappointed". /
Details: www.cafetwentyone.co.uk; @21Newcastle;
10.30 pm, Sun 8 pm.

Tyneside Coffee Rooms, Tyneside Cinema £32 ②④⑤
10 Pilgrim St NE1 6QG 0191 227 5520
"A piece of Art Deco history" – this "unique" spot
houses the UK's last full-time newsreel theatre. "I've
been coming here since I was a little girl in the early
1960s and it still feels the same"… this extends to
the "very simple and straightforward food (eg eggs
on toast)", but it's "a charming place to have a light
lunch or cuppa". / *Details:* www.tynesidecinema.co.uk;
9 pm; closed Sun D; No Amex.

Ury £33 ④④②
27 Queen Street NE1 3UG 0191 232 7799
"Just under the famous bridge", this "inexpensive
and very tasty" venture serves "outstanding Keralan
food, specialising in fish and vegetarian dishes"; it
"used to be (the well-regarded haunt) Rasa, but if
anything the South Indian dishes have improved". /
Details: www.uryrestaurants.com; @UryRestaurants;
10.30 pm, Sat 11pm.

Violets Cafe £14 ③③③
Quayside NE1 3JE 073 9151 2884
NE celeb chef Kenny Atkinson's wife Abigail, co-
owner of the acclaimed House of Tides round the
corner, has set up shop on the Quayside; reporters
say her venture is a "little gem" delivering gourmet
breakfasts, afternoon teas and sweet treats. /
Details: violetscafe.co.uk; @violetscafe.

NEWLYN, CORNWALL	1–4A

Mackerel Sky £37 ④④③
New Road TR18 5PZ no tel
"The freshest fish tapas" are to be found at this
"seasonal-only seafood bar" (closed November to
March), where the "speedy service" comes "with
a smile"; it's a "limited space" and "doesn't take
bookings, so getting in is often a lottery". / *Details:*
www.mackerelskycafe.co.uk; 9 pm.

NEWPORT ON TAY, FIFE	9–3D

Newport £51 ④④③
1 High Street DD6 8AA 01382 541449
Opened in March 2016, in a top setting overlooking
the Tay, MasterChef: The Professionals winner "Jamie
Scott's brilliant new venture succeeds at every
level". "Don't be put off by the fact that the venue
is shared by an old boozer!" (and a clinic, gallery
and hotel) – the Scottish small plate-oriented menu
is "delightful", "never losing sight of the quality of
the ingredients". / *Details:* www.thenewport.co.uk/;
9.30 pm.

NEWPORT, ISLE OF WIGHT	2–2A

Thompsons £71 5 4 3
11 Town Lane PO30 1JU   01983 526118
*"Worth a trip to the Isle of Wight!" Robert
Thompson's "year-old, concept restaurant" – a light,
café-like space where the top seats are downstairs
near the open kitchen – appears to be evolving on
a daily basis and is "probably the best meal on the
island": "very modern in style and presentation" with
"wonderful and varied flavours". "One to Watch!"*
Details: www.robertthompson.co.uk; @rthompsoniow;
10 pm.

NEWPORT, PEMBROKESHIRE	4–4B

Llys Meddyg £53 4 3 3
East Street SA42 0SY   01239 820008
*"Fairly local for us but we'd never been fearing
it was expensive… so glad we eventually gave it
a try as the food was very good!" This polished
restaurant-with-rooms is also strong on local-
sourcing credentials (with owners who run foraging,
butchery, smoking and curing courses).* / **Details:**
www.llysmeddyg.com; @llysmeddyg; 9 pm; D only,
closed Sun; No Amex. / **Accommodation:** 8 rooms,
from £100

NEWQUAY, CORNWALL	1–3B

Beached Lamb £28 3 4 4
TR7 1EY   01637 872297
*This "relaxed coffee bar with a funky surfer vibe"
is "absolutely the right place in the right location"
(midway between Fistral and Towan beaches) –
"always a pleasure for a shake and a cake".*

NEWTON LINFORD, LEICESTERSHIRE	5–4D

Grey Lady £41 3 3 2
Sharpley Hill LE6 0AH   01530 243558
*Near Bradgate Park, this comfortable restaurant
is a well-known local destination, where the food is
enjoyable and good-value rather than particularly
'gourmet', and where the top tip is the "very well
priced set lunch menu in the week". (Owners, the
Gibson family have also launched a nearby dining
and takeaway deli, suitable for a lighter bite).*
/ **Details:** www.the-grey-lady.co.uk; 9.30 pm, Sun
3.30 pm.

NEWTON ON OUSE, NORTH YORKSHIRE	
8–4C	

The Dawnay Arms £52 4 4 3
YO30 2BR   01347 848345
*"Unusual and fabulous, teasing dishes" sit
alongside "pub classics" (and everything comes
in Yorkshire portions) at this picturesque 18th
century inn with rugged stone floors, and gardens
leading down to the river. Chef Martel Smith,
trained with MPW, and all reports applaud the
"out-of-the-ordinary" performance here.* / **Details:**
www.thedawnayatnewton.co.uk; 9 pm; closed Mon &
Sun D.

NEWTON-IN-BOWLAND, LANCASHIRE	5–1B

The Parkers Arms £49 5 5 4
Hall Gate Hill BB7 3DY   01200 446236
*"Great folk behind the bar and evident genius in
the kitchen" makes it worth a fair-old schlep to this
"perfect pub run with love" – a "charming" old inn
("log fires in winter") in a "picturesque village" in
the Forest of Bowland. "Chef Stosie Madi continues
to provide some of the most heartfelt, most locally-
centred, most seasonal food in Lancashire. Pies
are a real highlight with unimprovable pastry and
delicious fillings, but the real treat comes when she
draws on her heritage to use the local produce in
Middle Eastern inspired dishes. The vegetarian and
vegan food here can be so attractive that it's worth
foregoing the meat (though maybe not in game
season…) – what she can do with a cauliflower,
cabbage or wild garlic is remarkable! Service is
led by Madi's business partner, Kathy Smith and
her brother AJ" and "there's always a personal and
friendly welcome" ("the best advice is just to go
with the flow and enjoy the way they do things").
"I'm glad I don't live any nearer or I'd be skint!"*
/ **Details:** www.parkersarms.co.uk; @parkersarms;
Wed-Fri 8.30 pm, Sat 9 pm; closed Mon & Tue. /
Accommodation: 4 rooms, from £77

NOMANSLAND, WILTSHIRE	2–3C

Les Mirabelles £53 4 5 4
Forest Edge Rd SP5 2BN   01794 390205
*"France in the New Forest" – this well-established
and well-known venture delivers a great all-round
formula of "outstanding Gallic cooking at terrific
value prices", married with an "an extensive wine
list which the very knowledgeable proprietor is
keen to advise on". 'Le Frog' – a cheaper bistro style
menu option – is a recent innovation.* / **Details:**
www.lesmirabelles.co.uk; off A36 between Southampton
& Salisbury; 10 pm; closed Mon & Sun; No Amex.

NORDEN, LANCASHIRE   5–1B

Nutter's   £57   4|4|3
Edenfield Road   OL12 7TT   01706 650167
"Andrew Nutter's indefatigable self-promoting social media could well put some people off" a visit to this "magnificent" manor house hotel dining room, but that would be a shame. OK "presentation is a bit 1980s", and even fans can feel "the cuisine is not as exceptional as the price", but "he can certainly cook", and all reports agree the "food is always good, and often very good". / Details: www.nuttersrestaurant.com; @nuttersofficial; between Edenfield & Norden on A680; 9 pm, Fri & Sat 9.30 pm; closed Mon.

NORTH SHIELDS, TYNE AND WEAR   8–2B

Staith House   £51   4|3|2
57 Low Lights   NE30 1JA   0191 270 8441
MasterChef finalist John Calton's upcycled, nautically styled pub, which arrived on the city's now booming fish quay three years ago, is "great for well-presented fish" (and also serves game in season). / Details: www.thestaithhouse.co.uk; @Thestaithhouse; 9 pm, Fri & Sat 9.30 pm, Sun 4 pm; Credit card deposit required to book.

NORTHLEACH, GLOUCESTERSHIRE   2–1C

Wheatsheaf Inn   £53   2|3|4
West End   GL54 3EZ   01451 860244
The Lucky Onion crew's "fabulously decorated" village outpost is "still one of the best gastropubs in the area" (and can be "rammed" and "noisy" as a result); "having a dedicated wine waiter is an unusually nice touch for a pub". / Details: www.cotswoldswheatsheaf.com; @wheatsheafgl54; 9 pm. / Accommodation: 14 rooms, from £140

NORWICH, NORFOLK   6–4C

Benedicts   £58   5|3|2
9 St Benedicts St   NR2 4PE   01603 926 080
Richard Bainbridge's "bistro-style" venue punches above its weight when it comes to the quality of his "wonderful" cooking, be it from the à la carte or the "incredibly enjoyable" 6-course and 8-course tasting menus (with meat dishes particularly well reviewed). Fans feel "it's unbelievable that it doesn't have a Michelin star" and it edged its local rival Hickman's in food ratings this year. / Details: www.restaurantbenedicts.com/home; @restbenedicts; just off the city centre (2 doors up from Pizza Express); 10 pm; closed Mon & Sun.

Farmyard   £44   3|4|3
23 St Benedicts St   NR2 4PF   01603 733188
Local boy Andrew Jones, who trained under Richard Corrigan and Claude Bosi, opened this "great new" swanky bistro in January 2017; early reports praise its "buzzy atmosphere" and "stylish modern British" (farm-to-fork) menu, though there is also view it "has potential, but needs to settle down". / Details: www.farmyardrestaurant.com; 9 pm, Fri & Sat 10 pm.

The Gunton Arms   £51   3|4|5
Cromer Rd, Thorpe Mkt   NR11 8TZ   01263 832010
"The views out over the deer park are lovely", at this quirkily styled country "pub with a difference". "It actually manages to remain a pub" ("still has a dart board, pool table and regulars drinking at the bar"), "despite the exquisite food", with much of the meat "cooked over an open fire". Good accommodation too. / Details: www.theguntonarms.co.uk; 10 pm. / Accommodation: 8 rooms, from £95

Last Wine Bar & Restaurant   £48   3|4|4
70 - 76 St Georges Street   NR3 1AB   01603 626 626
"A real Norwich institution" of decades standing, whose punning name references its Victorian shoe factory setting. While primarily known for its "excellent wine list with many, many wines by the glass or 250ml/500ml carafe", its cooking is "very consistent" too. / Details: www.thelastwinebar.co.uk; @LastWineBar; 10.30 pm; closed Sun.

Namaste Village   £41   3|3|2
131 Queens Road   NR1 3PN   01603 466466
Opened in summer 2016, a "lovely, friendly Indian veggie", in pleasantly vivid and airy surrounds, that's particularly "good at lunchtime"; the owners' cosier original, Namaste India – also a meat-free Gujarati – is on Opie Street. / Details: namasteindiannorwich.com/namastevillage/; @namaste_norwich; 10.30 pm, Fri & Sat 11 pm.

Roger Hickman's   £91   5|4|4
79 Upper St. Giles St   NR2 1AB   01603 633522
Roger Hickman's "quality, flavour and creativity" have only one serious rival in the town and it's a coin flip between this 'fine dining establishment' and the less buttoned-down Benedicts as to who takes the town's culinary crown. For a more august occasion, the plusher interior here would suit some tastes, and its matched with service that's "charming but formal enough". / Details: www.rogerhickmansrestaurant.com; @rogerhickmans; 10 pm; closed Mon & Sun.

NOSS MAYO, DEVON   1–4C

The Ship Inn   £49   3 4 4
PL8 1EW   01752 872387
A "lovely waterside pub" arrived at by meandering lanes and best prefaced by a "beautiful south-west coastal walk"; "good food" and "fantastic" service from hostess Lisa mean "booking is recommended". / **Details:** www.nossmayo.com; 9.30 pm.

NOTTINGHAM, NOTTINGHAMSHIRE 5–3D

Annie's Burger Shack   £18   3 2 3
5 Broadway NG1 1PR   0115 684 9920
"Great quirky burgers and an excellent selection of beers in a funky environment" still win numerous big thumbs-up for this "shabby chic burger bar for grown ups". Its ratings slipped this year though – some reviewers "don't get the hype" and one former fan returned to a "disappointing" experience. / **Details:** www.anniesburgershack.com; @original_annies.

Baresca   £35   3 3 3
9 Byard Ln NG1 2GJ   0115 948 3900
A "great addition to the (burgeoning) restaurant scene" on the outskirts of the city's hip Creative Quarter; this cosmopolitan sibling of Escabeche in West Bridgford continues to please with its "super tapas" and "exceptional value" lunches. / **Details:** www.baresca.co.uk; @barescanotts.

Cafe Roya   £41   3 4 3
130 Wollaton Rd NG9 2PE   0115 922 1902
"Roya is a wonder!" – a "vegetarian spot where you never miss the meat!"; the "delicious food combinations would rival any restaurant", and there's a "new menu every month". Reserve ahead – though rambling over two floors, it "gets booked up". / **Details:** @CafeRoya; 10 pm.

Chino Latino, Park Plaza Hotel   £61   4 2 2
41 Maid Marian Way NG1 6GD
0115 947 7444
"Somewhat experimental" Pan-Asian food has long compensated for the patchy service and odd setting – off the foyer of a bland business hotel – of this surprisingly funky dining room, though it's no longer quite the hotspot it once was. / **Details:** www.chinolatino.co.uk; @chinilatinoeu; 10.30 pm; closed Sun.

The Cumin   £41   4 5 2
62-64 Maid Marian Way NG1 6BQ
0115 941 9941
"Ten years of being at the top of the tree in Nottingham" – a curry strip Indian whose "excellent, authentic" and relatively light dishes ("best biryani ever"!) are "a little different to the usual"

subcontinental offerings. Another major plus is that it's "run by such a welcoming family". / **Details:** www.thecumin.co.uk; 11 pm, Fri & Sat 11.30 pm; D only, closed Sun.

French Living   £42   3 3 3
27 King St NG1 2AY   0115 958 5885
It's "nice to find French gastronomy in the heart of Nottingham" and a visit to this "authentic" bistro is "enriched by the hands-on approach of the ever-present owner": a "great venue for all occasions" – "be it an intimate evening à deux, or in a larger group". / **Details:** www.frenchliving.co.uk; 10 pm; closed Mon & Sun; No Amex.

Hart's   £66   3 4 3
Standard Hill, Park Row NG1 6GN
0115 988 1900
Tim Hart's "very polished" contemporary brasserie near the castle has been a linchpin of city-centre dining since the early '90s, and – outside of the 'fine dining' vein – remains the city's No. 1 destination, thanks to its combination of a "well-executed" modern menu produced "with some flair" and "very professional service". The setting provides "an excellent ambience for lunch meetings" – by night it can seem a little less atmospheric. / **Details:** www.hartsnottingham.co.uk; 10 pm, Sun 9 pm. / **Accommodation:** 32 rooms, from £125

Iberico   £42   4 4 4
The Shire Hall, High Pavement NG1 1HN
0115 941 0410
"Still miles ahead of competitors far and wide" – this "sophisticated" bar in a historic cellar on the Lace Market delivers a formidable package of "amazing tapas", "great sherry" and Iberian wines. "The quality wouldn't be out of place in central London". / **Details:** www.ibericotapas.com; @ibericotapas; 10 pm; closed Sun; children: 12+ D.

Masala Junction   £37   4 4 3
301-303 Mansfield Road, Carrington NG5 2DA
0115 962 2366
A "new addition receiving well-earned praise"; "from the previous owner of Memsahib" (well-known local restaurateur Nel Aziz), this "beautifully restored" old NatWest branch is now a top destination for some "truly excellent" contemporary Indian food. / **Details:** masalajunction.co.uk/; @masalajct; 10.30 pm, Sat 11.30 pm.

MemSaab   £44   4 4 4
12-14 Maid Marian Way NG1 6HS
0115 957 0009
This city-centre gem again elicits raves from reporters for its "outstanding" and "imaginative" food; "excellent service and atmosphere" too (owner "Anita gives her all to ensure everyone has a truly special time"). "We've been to Benares, Cinnamon Club and many others in and around London and this is easily the finest!" / **Details:**

www.mem-saab.co.uk; @MemSaabNotts; near Castle, opposite Park Plaza Hotel; 10.30 pm, Fri & Sat 11 pm, Sun 10 pm; D only; No shorts.

Merchants, Lace Market Hotel £57 🄷🄷🄸
29-31 High Pavement NG1 1HE
0115 958 9898
This trendy boutique hotel dining room on the Lace Market is something of an enigma. On the downside despite having an interior originally designed by the late David Collins, it never seems to generate a huge amount of buzz. On the plus side its "interesting" cooking is consistently well-rated and praised for its "good value". / Details: www.lacemarkethotel.co.uk; @LaceMarketHotel; 10 pm; closed Sat L. / Accommodation: 42 rooms, from £160

Restaurant Sat Bains £133 🄵🄸🄷
Lenton Lane NG7 2SA 0115 986 6566
"On the edge of an industrial estate, and under the A52 flyover might not sound the ideal place to take that special someone for dinner, but the experience makes up for it in spades" at Sat Bains's "wonderful oasis, between the pylons, concrete jungle roadways and nettles!" – one of the UK's most impressive restaurants (with rooms), on the outer-fringe of the city. "There is no other word than exceptional to describe his cuisine" (choose from a 7-course or 10-course menu) and "the unusual combinations are amazing without being different for the sake of it" ("horseradish ice cream sandwich was one of the nicest things I've ever tasted! and the chicken liver muesli was also a highlight!)". Have they been working on the service too? – "with just the right amount of friendliness and attentiveness" it scored particularly highly this year. 'Nucleus' is a further dining option here – a six-seater chef's table within the development kitchen, which couldn't be more rapturously rated by reviewers. / Details: www.restaurantsatbains.com; @satbains1; closed Mon & Sun; No Amex; children: 8+. / Accommodation: 8 rooms, from £129

The Ruddington Arms Pub Restaurant £48 🄸🄸🄷
NG11 6EQ 0115 984 1628
Terry Laybourne protégé Mark Anderson's "very pleasant" solo debut is a "class above many a gastropub", with "delicious" veggie fare and the "best full English in miles". (In August 2017 his Ruddy Good Pub Company chain added a second link: the lavishly refurbed White Lion, in Bingham). / Details: www.theruddingtonarms.com; @ruddingtonarms.

Shanghai Shanghai £31 🄵🄷🄸
15 Goose Gate NG1 1FE 0115 958 4688
A "run-of-the-mill setting" ("bit of a café atmosphere") doesn't seem to deter anyone from a visit to this Lace Market gem, beloved for its "incredible, authentic Sichuanese cooking"; it's "always well-frequented by Chinese

students – must be a good sign". / Details: www.shanghai-shanghai.co.uk; @ShanghaiShang; Mon-Thu 10 pm, Fri & Sat 11 pm, Sun 10 pm.

Table 8 £63 🄸🄸🄸
61 Wollaton Rd NG9 2NG 0115 922 9903
An appetising modern menu complete with a selection of steaks helps win consistently high marks for this jolly small bistro, in the 'burbs of Beeston. / Details: table-8.co.uk; 11pm.

Thea Caffea £21 🄸🄸🄸
Enfield Chambers, 14a Low Pavement NG1 7DL 0115 941 2110
"Tucked away from the city bustle", an idyllic tearoom with "brilliant decor" ("vintage china cups", chequered floors) and "unhurried service" – mightily "pleasant surroundings for an afternoon tea or light lunch". / Details: @TheaCaffea; L only.

200 Degrees £12 🄸🄷🄷
Heston Hs, Meadow Lane NG2 3HE no tel
"Coffee is served by real enthusiasts" at this "cool NYC vibe" venue, which has now spawned six spin-offs as far afield as Cardiff and Leeds. "The food is much better than your average coffee shop (an ever changing selection of really good sandwiches, and decent cakes too)". What's more, you actually get served at the table, which is lovely, not having to hang around at the counter while the baristas fanny about! / Details: www.200degs.com; @200degreescafe; 7pm, Sun 6 pm; No bookings.

Victoria Hotel £38 🄸🄸🄸
Dovecote Ln NG9 1JG 0115 925 4049
Stumbling distance from Beeston station, this red-brick Victorian freehouse is acclaimed for its "very wide range of food and drink" ("always something for everyone", including veggies). The worst report? – "always dependable, but never quite seems to excite". / Details: www.victoriabeeston.co.uk; @TheVicBeeston; 9.30 pm, Sun-Tue 9 pm; closed Mon for food; No Amex; children: 18+ after 8 pm.

The Wollaton £49 🄸🄸🄸
Lambourne Drive NG8 1GR 0115 928 8610
This Wollaton Park gastropub is consistently noted as being "very good for children", and "can be relied upon" for its "decent, locally sourced food" also. / Details: www.thewollaton.co.uk; 9 pm, Sun 5 pm; closed Sun D.

World Service £63 🄸🄷🄷
Newdigate Hs, Castlegate NG1 6AF 0115 847 5587
A very characterful and slightly offbeat restaurant profiting from the panelled interior of The Nottingham Club, whose building it shares, plus a "very romantic" courtyard garden come summer; its "very, very interesting food" doesn't always come off, but equally serious quibbles about it are

absent. / *Details: www.worldservicerestaurant.com;
@ws_restaurant; 10 pm; closed Sun D, except bank
holidays; children: 10+ at D.*

Zaap £34 🖪🖪🖪
Unit B, Bromley Place NG1 6JG
0115 947 0204
*"Great fun!" – "you could be in a street in Bangkok,
with tuk-tuks and authentic street signs, tin serving-
trays and cups" at this kitsch two-year-old, and the
street food-style cooking is "so reasonable" too. /
Details: www.zaapthai.co.uk; @ZaapNottingham;
11 pm.*

OARE, KENT 3–3C

The Three Mariners £43 🖪🖪🖪
2 Church Rd ME13 0QA 01795 533633
*"A textbook 'gastropub'" – a "remarkably
understated place" offering "quality food at
value-for-money prices". "Despite its rather remote
location, it's always well patronised – never had
a bad meal on numerous visits over the years". /
Details: www.thethreemarinersoare.co.uk; Mon-Thu
9 pm, Fri & Sat 9.30 pm, Sun 9 pm; No Amex.*

OBAN, ARGYLL AND BUTE 9–3B

**Ee-Usk (Seafood
Restaurant)** £51 🖪🖪🖪
North Pier PA34 5QD 01631 565666
*"With a super view on a sunny day" (of Oban
Bay) and a menu of top-flight fish and shellfish,
this bustling seafront café might just be the "best
restaurant in Oban". "It gave great pleasure to our
Parisian guests… what more needs to be said?!" /
Details: www.eeusk.com; @eeuskoban; 9-9.30 pm; No
Amex; children: 12+ at D.*

OFFCHURCH, WARWICKSHIRE 5–4C

The Stag At Offchurch £45 🖪🖪🖪
Welsh Road CV33 9AQ 01926 425801
*This "pleasant gastropub" (part of the CD Pub
Co) occupies a thatched property not far from
Leamington Spa, and serves a well-rated menu
rated from traditional pub grub to a selection of dry-
aged steaks. / Details: www.thestagatoffchurch.com;
@stagoffchurch; 9.30 pm; No trainers.*

OLD HUNSTANTON, NORFOLK 6–3B

The Neptune £83 🖪🖪🖪
85 Old Hunstanton Rd PE36 6HZ
01485 532122
Kevin Mangeolles's "exceptional and memorable"

cuisine – some of "the best in Norfolk" – is matched
with "perfectly pitched" service at this "very friendly
and approachable" old coaching inn, on the edge
of town, which he runs with wife Jacki. "We stayed
the night and the head chef doubled as a bellboy!" /
*Details: www.theneptune.co.uk; @NeptuneChef; 9 pm;
closed Mon, Tue-Sat D only, Sun open L & D; May need
+ to book; children: 10+. / Accommodation: 6 rooms,
from £120*

OLD WINDSOR, BERKSHIRE 3–3A

The Oxford Blue £90 🖪🖪🖪
10 Crimp Hill SL4 2QY 01753 861954
*Former Clare Smyth protégé, Steven Ellis, opened his
first solo venture in this 19th century inn (converted
from two game keepers' cottages) in Old Windsor
in late 2016. On initial feedback, its traditional,
British food 'with a twist' is consistently highly rated.
/ Details: www.oxfordbluepub.co.uk; @OxfordBluePub;
9.30 pm.*

OLDSTEAD, NORTH YORKSHIRE 5–1D

Black Swan £124 🖪🖪🖪
YO61 4BL 01347 868387
*"Well worth the long drive!". Twenty-eight-year-old
wünderkind, Tommy Banks "produces exceptional,
exciting – even mind-blowing – tastes and textures,
with subtlety, intensity, and integrity" at his family's
"sophisticated, elegant and welcoming" converted
drovers' inn, set in "a lovely location" down a
single-track lane, on the fringe of the North Yorks
Moors. Much of the produce is from the family
farm, and it's "the real sense of place that helps
mark the place out, as well as the warm and
friendly service" overseen by brother, James Banks.
"The wine list is superb too! Almost 100 wines
served by the glass using the Coravin method".
In October 2017, TripAdvisor crowned the place
'The Best Restaurant in the World'. That might
be overdoing it a fraction, but it's certainly one of
the top-20 highest rated destinations in our UK
survey. / Details: www.blackswanoldstead.co.uk;
@BlkSwanOldstead; 8.15 pm; closed weekday L; No
Amex. / Accommodation: 4 rooms, from £270*

OMBERSLEY, WORCESTERSHIRE 2–1B

Venture In £60 🖪🖪🖪
Main Road WR9 0EW 01905 620552
*"A real treat" – this very characterful timbered
15th-century house "can get a little crowded (and
"noisy") as it's quite a small venue", but by all
accounts the "wonderful" classical menu "makes up
for this". / Details: www.theventurein.co.uk; 9.30 pm.*

ONGAR, ESSEX	3–2B

Smith's Brasserie   £57   **4** **4** **3**
Fyfield Rd CM5 0AL 01277 365578
*"Fish dishes to die for, plus efficient, friendly staff"
power ongoing satisfaction with this "well-oiled
machine" of a restaurant, where "quality, no-
nonsense" food is served in a "bright and modern
dining room". / Details: www.smithsrestaurants.com;
@SmithsOfOngar; left off A414 towards Fyfield; Mon-Fri
10 pm, Sat 10.30 pm, Sun 10 pm; closed Mon L; No
trainers; children: 12+.*

ONICH, HIGHLAND	9–3B

Loch Leven Seafood Café £50   **4** **3** **3**
PH33 6SA 01855 821048
*"If you love seafood this is the best", say fans of
this no-nonsense café, perched by the eponymous
loch not far from Fort William; its "superb" grub
comes at "reasonable prices", and there's a
great fish shop on the premises too. / Details:
www.lochlevenseafoodcafe.co.uk; 9 pm; No Amex.*

ORFORD, SUFFOLK	3–1D

Butley Orford Oysterage£40   **5** **4** **3**
Market Hill IP12 2LH 01394 450277
*"A tradition that never disappoints" – the Pinney
family's "basic canteen-like room hardly ever
changes, but is still hard to beat in the area" and
"consistently does exactly what it knows it's good
at": "sublime seafood", including "oysters from their
own oyster beds" and "various smoked fish dishes".
"It's often noisy and can be chilly, but if that's the
price to pay it's still well worth the visit!" / Details:
www.butleyorfordoysterage.co.uk; @Pinneysoforford; on
the B1078, off the A12 from Ipswich; 9 pm; No Amex.*

The Crown & Castle   £58   **3** **3** **3**
IP12 2LJ 01394 450205
*This "very pleasant gastropub/restaurant-with-rooms
in a smart Suffolk village" has won a reputation
with its "always fresh, local food" and "efficient but
informal style of service". In October 2017, owners
of 18 years 'The Hotel Inspector' Ruth Watson and
her husband David sold up to local chain, the TA
Hotel Collection, but will apparently remain involved
with the management of the property. / Details:
www.crownandcastle.co.uk; @CrownandCOrford; on
main road to Orford, near Woodbridge; 8 pm, Fri & Sat
9 pm; No Amex; Booking max 10 may apply; children:
8+ at D. / Accommodation: 21 rooms, from £135*

ORPINGTON, KENT	3–3B

Xian   £39   **5** **3** **3**
324 High St BR6 0NG 01689 871881
*"Victor and his team produce top-notch Chinese
food" at this well-known but value-for-money High
Street staple – "so popular that you sometimes
can't even get a takeaway!". / Details: 11 pm; closed
Mon & Sun L.*

OSWESTRY, SHROPSHIRE	5–3A

Sebastian's   £64   **4** **5** **3**
45 Willow Street SY11 1AQ 01691 655444
*For "never-less-than-enticing, well-delivered and
delicious" fare, this "cosy" French-style restaurant-
with-rooms ticks all the boxes. Reflecting the
fact that the "kitchen supplies meals for the
Orient Express", it remains the very model of
consistency ("we've been visiting for 17 years
and have never had a poor meal"). / Details:
www.sebastians-hotel.co.uk; 9.30 pm; D only, closed
Mon & Sun; No Amex. / Accommodation: 5 rooms,
from £75*

OTTERSHAW, SURREY	3–3A

The Manor at Foxhills   £106   **3** **4** **5**
Stonehill Rd KT16 0EL 01932 872050
*"The best scones ever!" are part of a "lovely
afternoon tea with champagne à deux" that are
the most highly rated feature by reviewers of this
family-run hotel, golf club and spa, where the
centrepiece of the 400-acre estate is the "romantic"
19th-century manor house: "a beautiful setting,
full of old-style elegance". Good ratings too though
for a full meal from a straightforward modern
menu majoring in high quality protein. / Details:
www.foxhills.co.uk; @FoxhillsSurrey; J11 on M25, A320
to Ottershaw at 2nd roundabout turn right, turn right
again, then left; 10 pm; No jeans. / Accommodation:
36 rooms, from £135*

OXFORD, OXFORDSHIRE	2–2D

Al-Shami   £29   **4** **4** **3**
25 Walton Cr OX1 2JG 01865 310066
*"Al Shami is an Oxford institution: it has been here
for over three decades and has introduced many of
us to the delights of Lebanese cuisine" helped by its
embracing and welcoming style; the food "remains
excellent". / Details: www.al-shami.co.uk; midnight; No
Amex. / Accommodation: 12 rooms, from £60*

Arbequina   £40   **5** **4** **4**
74 Cowley Rd OX4 1JB 01865 792777
A "fantastic new find on the Cowley Road" from

Rufus Thurston, of hit local Oli's Thai; and Ben Whyles of east Oxford staple Door 74. The "fresh, minimalist" setting (a conversion of an old chemist) is an appealing backdrop to "yummy and authentic" tapas from a short, typed list showcasing "first-class ingredients". / *Details:* arbequina.co.uk; @arbequinaoxford.

Ashmolean Dining Room £54　②②④
Beaumont St OX1 2PH　01865 553823
"Sitting out in the centre of Oxford looking into the attic rooms of the Randolph and the rooftops of colleges" provides "a lovely setting for a sunny day" at this museum café. Mostly there's praise for the "tasty and well-priced" cooking, although it's pretty "unadventurous", but "tea is quite a bargain with good scones, sarnies and cakes", and you can stay entertained "watching the procession of tourists coming outside for selfies". / *Details:* www.ashmoleandiningroom.com; 10 pm; closed Mon, Tue D, Thu D & Sun D.

Atomic Burger　£31　③③③
92 Cowley Rd OX4 1JE　01865 790855
A "great bustling atmosphere and the best burgers" in these parts (plus top cocktails to sweeten the deal) continue to ensure loyalty to this fun indie joint. / *Details:* www.atomicburger.co.uk; @atomicburgers; 10.30 pm; No Amex.

Branca　£45　③③③
111 Walton St OX2 6AJ　01865 556111
A "spacious" Jericho Italian – long a varsity fixture, and with a "nice garden area" – which remains a "good standby" for its "interesting" stone-baked pizzas and "excellent lunch deal"; "lovely deli" on site, too. / *Details:* www.branca.co.uk; 11 pm; No Amex.

Brasserie Blanc　£54　②③③
71-72 Walton St OX2 6AG　01865 510999
"Reliable and very reasonable value for the main part" – fans of Raymond Blanc's original city-centre brasserie say it's "underrated compared to other chains in Oxford". Even these supporters tend to be fairly measured in their praise, but in this culinary "wasteland" of a city it's a venue that's worth remembering especially for "the splendid breakfast and first class Sunday lunch". / *Details:* www.brasserieblanc.com; @brasserieblanc; 10 pm, Sat 10.30 pm, Sun 9.30 pm.

Cherwell Boathouse　£47　③③⑤
Bardwell Road OX2 6ST　01865 552746
"Such a nice location, and the food is good… for Oxford": this "beautiful and calm", "old favourite" – "splendidly situated" on the river – is "especially lovely in good weather, when you can dine outside and gaze at each other, as well as at the assorted waterfowl that glide serenely past". Its top culinary feature is its "exceptional wine list, with a very good range from acceptably cheap to ridiculously expensive". / *Details:* www.cherwellboathouse.co.uk; @Cherwell_Boat; Mon-Thu 9 pm, Fri & Sat 9.30 pm, Sun 9 pm.

Chiang Mai　£47　③③③
Kemp Hall Passage, 130A High Street
OX1 4DH　01865 202233
"In a location more reminiscent of a Tudor tearoom" than one befitting its Thai menu, this "quirky" and "busy" ("cramped and noisy") staple in a medieval building down a passageway off the High "remains a delight". Its classics dishes may "have lost the epic qualities they had a few years back" ("nice but veering unpredictably from the bland to the very spicy"), but "it's still better than other Asians in the very centre of town". / *Details:* www.chiangmaikitchen.co.uk; 10.30 pm, Sun 10 pm; No Amex.

La Cucina　£39　③③③
39-40 St Clements OX4 1AB　01865 793811
A "regular 'turn to' restaurant for a tasty, enjoyable and relaxed Italian meal", where the "pizza and pasta staples are supplemented by a range of daily changing specials"; even those who visited in opening week a decade back "are yet to be disappointed". / *Details:* www.lacucinaoxford.co.uk; 10.30 pm.

Cuttlefish　£43　④④③
36-37 St Clement's St OX4 1AB
01865 243003
On the old site of Fishers (RIP), a "new, modern and chic addition to St Clements created by the experienced owners of La Cucina" next door. "A real discovery": "their slogan is 'Bringing the best seasonal sustainable fish to Oxford from the shore at the fairest of prices', and they largely live up to it". / *Details:* www.cuttlefishoxford.co.uk; @CuttlefishOx.

Gee's　£54　②②④
61 Banbury Rd OX2 6PE　01865 553540
This "very busy" long-established Victorian glasshouse in north Oxford makes "an exceptional venue for a meal" and, as ever, there's a strong theme in feedback: it's "a lovely environment but overpriced for what it is", with food that's "OK" (but "surely they could do better") and service that's "always friendly" but "occasionally slow". / *Details:* www.gees-restaurant.co.uk; @geesrestaurant; 10 pm, Fri & Sat 10.30 pm.

Jacob And Field　£41　④④④
15 Old High Street OX3 9HP　01865 766990
"Since they added a great extension and allowed booking" a couple of years back, this "beautiful" and "very friendly" Headington deli (part of a local mini-empire) is "really the place to come" – be it for "very tasty brunch", "good coffee", or "delicious" mains. / *Details:* jacobsandfield.com/.

Jolly Post Boy £47 [4][4][4]
22 Florence Park Road OX4 3PH
01865 777767
One of Oxford's best-known pubs is "newly refurbished and completely rejuvenated" since reopening its doors, under new management, in September 2016. "Whether you go for bar snacks or a small meal everything is spot-on" – and there are also 10 brews on tap, owing to a rare no-ties deal with the freeholders (Greene King). / Details: 11 pm, Sun 8 pm; closed Mon.

The Magdalen Arms £49 [3][2][3]
243 Iffley Road OX4 1SJ 01865 243159
This country sibling to London's famous Anchor & Hope is a little out of the town centre and specialises in the gutsy British scoff that's made the group's name. Fewer reports this year, but all feedback remains upbeat. / Details: www.magdalenarms.com; @magdalen_arms; Mon-Sat 10 pm, Sun 9 pm; closed Mon L; No Amex; No bookings.

My Sichuan £44 [4][2][2]
The Old School, Gloucester Grn OX1 2DA
01865 236899
"No gastronomical trip to Oxford should miss My Sichuan" – an "old-school building just by the bus station", whose food is "unashamedly what it says on the can" ("fiery" and "robust", with unusual meats like tripe and duck). As a result it "attracts a lot of Chinese diners" – others may "need help with the menu". / Details: www.mysichuan.co.uk; 11 pm.

Oli's Thai £32 [5][5][4]
38 Magdalen Rd OX4 1RB 01865 790223
"The warm peanut sauce is to die for… the silken super aubergine curry so yummy" – this "cramped and very informal" café serves "the best Thai food in Oxford by a mile" offering dishes with "just incredible tastes" and "their cult status hasn't gone to their heads". ("What sets Oli's Thai apart is the authentic home cooking found in Thailand: the massive flavours, the use of herbs and spices, and above all the consistency"). "If you can get a table (a BIG if!), it is well worth the time it takes to wait for one!" / Details: www.olisthai.com; 9 pm; closed Mon, Tue L & Sun.

The Oxford Kitchen £62 [4][4][2]
215 Banbury Rd OX2 7HQ 01865 511149
"It's nothing much to look at (from either the outside or the inside!) but the standard of cooking is remarkably good" (albeit somewhat "cheffy") at this modern British venue on Summertown's main drag. "There is no getting away from the fact that it is in a row of shops, with its ground floor windows onto the street" – "it's better to sit upstairs in the

front room, where the atmosphere is calmer and more relaxing". / Details: www.theoxfordkitchen.co.uk; @Kitchenoxford; 7 pm; L only.

The Perch £49 [4][3][4]
Binsey Ln OX2 0NG 01865 7228891
In a "wonderful setting in the tiny hamlet of Binsey" ("perfectly placed for a riverside walk"), a "justifiably popular" pub whose "delicious" cooking "draws North Oxford out to the country". "Eat by the open fire" or in the "ingenious" conservatory in winter, and profit from the "delightful" garden come summer. Veggie and Vegan options are particularly good here. / Details: www.the-perch.co.uk; @theperchinn; 10 pm, Sun 9 pm.

Pierre Victoire £45 [3][3][2]
Little Clarendon St OX1 2HP 01865 316616
"One of the few survivors from a nineties chain" – this "always-busting city-centre French Restaurant" delivers "such a good formula of a type that's increasingly hard to find" (and is one of the most commented-on venues in town as a result). Service is "very rapid" but "friendly" and offers "simple", "typical bistro fare" from a "wide range of classic dishes" that may be a tad "unexceptional", but which come at "amazingly cheap prices (including the wine)". / Details: www.pierrevictoire.co.uk; 11 pm, Sun 10 pm; No Amex.

Quod, Old Bank Hotel £51 [2][3][3]
92-94 High St OX1 4BJ 01865 202505
"Another ideal venue for treating student members of the family" – a "popular and busy but efficient" brasserie, on the High, that benefits from a "lovely rear garden for summer"; the food (including a "good breakfast") is generally on the "safe" side. / Details: www.oldbank-hotel.co.uk; @QuodBrasserie; 11 pm, Sun 10.30 pm; Booking max 10 may apply. / Accommodation: 42 rooms, from £140

Sojo £42 [5][3][2]
6-9 Hythe Bridge St OX1 2EW 01865 202888
"The best Chinese in Oxford" (some would say "by a margin") – this "always busy" venture "in the 'Little Asia' area close to the railway station" is "popular with both locals and Chinese/Hong Kong students and visitors" thanks to its "extensive and consistently excellent menu". "When they're swamped they will apologise for the delay in serving". / Details: www.sojooxford.co.uk; 11 pm, Sun 10 pm; No bookings.

Turl Street Kitchen £42 [3][2][3]
16 Turl St OX1 3DH 01865 264171
"The menu is limited, but the food is good" at this Spartan non-profit, with a local/seasonal schtick; nowadays there's the odd cynic, for whom it's "probably coming to the end of its time in the sun", but even they admit it's "still pretty good". / Details: www.turlstreetkitchen.co.uk; @turlstkitchen; 10 pm, Fri & Sat 10.30 pm.

The Vaults And Garden Cafe £21 [4][3][3]
University Church of St Mary the Virgin, Radcliffe Sq OX1 4AH 01865 279112
In the University's Old Congregation House, this "beautiful medieval room, brimming with students, churchy types and visitors", offers a "uniquely Oxford experience". A "very informal self-service" set-up, it revolves around "ample well-cooked dishesb using seasonal and organic ingredients". / **Details:** www.thevaultsandgarden.com; @VaultsandGarden; L only.

Zheng £38 [4][4][2]
82 Walton St OX2 6EA 01865 511188
"Giles Coren is a fan", and so are all who comment on this "very noisy" and "cramped" (yet "efficient") Pan-Asian "in Jericho, close to the Phoenix cinema", where the "Malaysian and Singaporean dishes are especially good", and the fare generally is "very reasonably priced". (See also its brand new, rather smarter Chelsea sibling.) / **Details:** www.zhengoxford.co.uk; 10.45 pm, Sun 10.15 pm; closed Tue L.

OXTON, CHESHIRE 5–2A

Fraiche £112 [5][5][3]
11 Rose Mount CH43 5SG 0151 652 2914
"There is nowhere better in the North West" than Marc Williamson's "very special" 12-seater on the fringe of Birkenhead. "Very much a labour of the chef"'s love, it is unique and hard to compare as his talent is invested into every conceivable aspect of the experience". "It's a fantastic effort all around, the music, the ambience; staff who are excellent, attentive, friendly and professional; but the best is the food, with exceptional taste and flavours". And it has "a brilliant wine list – exciting and well priced – for a small restaurant" too. / **Details:** www.restaurantfraiche.com; @marcatfraiche; 8.30 pm, Sun 7 pm; closed Mon, Tue, Wed L, Thu L, Fri L & Sat L; No Amex.

PADSTOW, CORNWALL 1–3B

Appletons at the Vineyard £67 [3][3][4]
Dark Lane PL27 7SE 01841 541413
"Head chef at Fifteen Watergate Bay for over nine years", Andy Appleton's new "refectory-style" venture enjoys "the most fabulous setting" just outside Padstow, and "in the heart of the vines on a working vineyard". "Lovely views" are assured – and there's well-received "Mediterranean-style food to match". / **Details:** www.trevibbanmill.com/appletons-at-the-vineyard/.

Paul Ainsworth at No. 6 £79 [5][4][5]
6 Middle St PL28 8AP 01841 532093
"WOW!" "The new-look No. 6 is better than ever. What an achievement!" Paul Ainsworth's tiny townhouse has "kept all the bits which were already fantastic" while undergoing an "urban-chic makeover" (and "adding a bar upstairs to make your pre-dinner drinks so much more comfortable"); and the "amazing" cooking, especially of fish, makes it "the very best choice for a foodie in Padstow" (despite all the local competition). / **Details:** www.number6inpadstow.co.uk; @no6padstow; 10 pm; closed Mon & Sun; No Amex; children: 4+.

Prawn on the Lawn £59 [4][3][3]
11 Duke Street PL28 8AB 01841 532223
A "great addition to the Padstow food scene" – this "quirky" two-year-old sibling to the Islington original is a great choice for "innovative and delicious" seafood; you can opt to enjoy it in the slightly "cramped" 24-cover dining room, or cart it away from the on-site fishmongers. / **Details:** prawnonthelawn.com; @PrawnOnTheLawn; midnight; closed Sun & Mon.

Rick Stein's Café £49 [2][3][2]
10 Middle Street PL28 8AP 01841 532700
Rick Stein's casual spin-off – one of his six ventures in the town – serves "a limited menu of well sourced and cooked items" (including a "rare treat" of a breakfast) that can be had "without breaking the bank". Some reporters prefer the "quieter" backroom. / **Details:** www.rickstein.com; 9.30 pm; closed Mon & Tue; No Amex; Booking evening only. / **Accommodation:** 3 rooms, from £100

Rojanos in the Square £51 [4][4][3]
9 Mill Sq PL28 8AE 01841 532796
"In a town dominated by Rick Stein places", former No. 6 Padstow chef Paul Ainsworth's "delightful" Italian offers some respite; the "really good food" – with "simply the best pizza" a highlight – is all "sourced locally". / **Details:** www.paul-ainsworth.co.uk/rojanos-in-the-square; @rojanos; 10 pm.

St Petroc's Hotel & Bistro £57 [3][2][2]
4 New Street PL28 8EA 01841 532700
Mixed feedback this year on the Stein empire's informal hotel-restaurant; fans find the "food can be very good" and a "hidden garden" adds to its charms, but the "poor table layout" continues to irk and "service could improve" – "come on Rick you could do better"! / **Details:** www.rickstein.com/eat-with-us/st-petrocs-bistro/; @TheSeafood; 10 pm; No Amex. / **Accommodation:** 10 rooms, from £150

Seafood Restaurant   £89   [3][3][4]
Riverside PL28 8BY 01841 532700
"The original and still the best! – well worth the trip
to Cornwall for the perfectly cooked fish, alongside
some seasonal specials like spider crabs, moules
and amazing seafood curries": that's the upbeat
and still probably the most commonplace view
on the Stein family's first and still-iconic venture
near the harbour – a "huge" room "squashed-
in" with tables so "it can accommodate a big
number of diners". On the downside, its profile
is nowhere near what it was, service "can be
slightly erratic" and it can seem "very expensive". /
Details: www.rickstein.com/eat-with-us/the-seafood-;
@TheSeafood; 9.45 pm; ; No Amex; Booking max 14
may apply; children: 3+. / **Accommodation:** 16 rooms,
from £150; SRA-Food Made Good – 1 star.

Stein's Fish & Chips   £41   [4][3][2]
South Quay PL28 8BL 01841 532700
Very high marks for the Stein empire's chippie
in its home town. For the best experience
though "you need to visit out of season". /
Details: www.rickstein.com/eat-with-us/steins-fish-;
@TheSeafood; 8 pm; No Amex; No bookings.

PEEBLES, SCOTTISH BORDERS   9–4C

Cringletie House   £55   [3][3][3]
Edinburgh Rd EH45 8PL 01721 725750
A "very relaxed country house hotel" – an old Scots
Baronial castle with medieval tourelles (mini-
turrets) – whose food, by all accounts, "matches the
ambience"; it's "a bit out of the way just for dinner"
(30 miles from Edinburgh) so "worth staying for
the full experience". / **Details:** www.cringletie.com;
@CringletieHouse; between Peebles and Eddleston on
A703, 20m S of Edinburgh; 9 pm; D only, ex Sun open
L & D; children: 4. / **Accommodation:** 15 rooms,
from £99

PENARTH, VALE OF GLAMORGAN   1–1D

Bar 44 Penarth   £35   [4][3][4]
Windsor Road CF64 1JH 033 3344 4049
"Authentic tapas y copas" win praise for this second
outlet of a local small indie group (with branches
in Cardiff and Cowbridge), which has now been a
feature of this seaside town for over five years. /
Details: bar44.co.uk; @bar44penarth; 11 pm, Fri &
Sat midnight; No Amex.

Restaurant James
Sommerin   £70   [5][3][4]
The Esplanade CF64 3AU 07722 216 727
"The position of the restaurant is superb" – a
Beach Cliff Edwardian building along from the pier,
whose large windows provide views over the Penarth

esplanade to the sea. "Excellent quality ingredients
are elevated to another level thanks to the talent of
chef James Sommerin" and his "friendly" family-led
team. / **Details:** www.jamessommerinrestaurant.co.uk;
@RestaurantJS; 9.30 pm; closed Mon.

PENN, BUCKINGHAMSHIRE   3–2A

The Old Queen's Head   £50   [4][2][5]
Hammersley Ln HP10 8EY 01494 813371
"For a pub, the ambience is exceptional due to
the layout with the old beams and nooks and
crannies" at this fine Tudor building in leafy Penn.
The "interesting and frequently changing menus"
are likewise "a very pleasant surprise", while the
"tireless staff" are "very friendly" (but, when
busy, service can be "pretty slow"). / **Details:**
www.oldqueensheadpenn.co.uk; @queensheadhp10;
9.30 pm, Fri & Sat 10 pm.

PENSFORD, SOMERSET   2–2B

The Pig, Hunstrete
House   £47   [3][5][5]
Hunstrete BS39 4NS 01761 490 490
The shabby-chic chain's "rather grand yet very
relaxed" Somerset outpost occupies a "wonderful"
Grade II-listed country house. Fans say they've
found the "perfect recipe for success": "great staff",
superior rooms and "brilliant locally sourced" food
plus wine that's "very reasonably priced" (not
forgetting a "classic" afternoon tea). / **Details:**
www.thepighotel.com/near-bath; @The_Pig_Hotel;
9.30 pm.

PENZANCE, CORNWALL   1–4A

The Shore   £52   [4][3][4]
13-14 Alverton Street TR18 2QP
01736 362444
"Tremendously skilled with all sorts of amazing
fish that's fresh off the boats" – Chef-patron Bruce
Rennie channels his lifelong love of the shoreline
into his cuisine and wows in all early reports
on this "tiny and friendly operation". / **Details:**
www.theshorerestaurant.uk/; @The_Shore_Pz; 9 pm;
closed Mon & Sun; No Amex.

Tolcarne Inn   £41   [4][3][3]
Tolcarne Pl TR18 5PR 01736 363074
"The combination of Ben Tunnicliffe and Newlyn
fish market" (barely 200m away round the corner)
"spells affordable magic!" to fans of the chef's
"nice, pubby" harbourside inn (even if there is the
odd reviewer however, who finds it "disappointing
after all the good write-ups"). / **Details:**
www.tolcarneinn.co.uk; 10 pm.

PERSHORE, WORCESTERSHIRE   2–1C

Eckington Manor   **£68** **4**|**3**|**4**
Hammock Road WR10 3BJ 01386 751600
"Former BBC MasterChef Professionals winner
Mark Stinchcombe is deeply talented" according
to fans of his and wife Sue's farm-to-table joint in
a medieval manor. The venue has attracted muted
praise in the past, but seemed to deliver on its
promise more consistently this year, with high praise
for its "absolutely delicious" cuisine and "top-class"
accommodation. / **Details:** @EckingtonManor; 9 pm,
Sun 3.30 pm. / **Accommodation:** 17 rooms, from
£169

PERTH, PERTH AND KINROSS   9–3C

Cafe Tabou   **£58** **3**|**3**|**2**
4 St John's Pl PH1 5SZ 01738 446698
"A little bit of France in Perth!"; while "the chef
is Polish and none of the staff would appear to
have any connection with 'la patrie'", that doesn't
dent the Gallic flair of this "very good value" bistro,
deemed "magnifique!" by fans; "go for breakfast, go
for lunch and try again in the evening!" / **Details:**
www.cafetabou.com; @CafeTabouPerth; 9.30 pm, Fri &
Sat 10 pm; closed Mon D & Sun; No Amex.

63 Tay Street   **£65** **3**|**3**|**2**
63 Tay St PH2 8NN 01738 441451
Graeme Pallister continues to turn out some "really
tasty food" at this elegant, elevated Tayside outfit,
which celebrated a decade in 2017. / **Details:**
www.63taystreet.com; @63TayStreet; on city side of
River Tay, 1m from Dundee Rd; 9 pm; D only, closed
Mon & Sun; No Amex.

PETERBOROUGH, PETERBOROUGH 6–4A

Prevost   **£52** **5**|**4**|**3**
20 Priestgate PE1 1JA 01733 313623
"Fine dining in Peterborough at last!"; reporters
"were treated to a marvellous gastronomic
experience by head chef and owner Lee Clarke"
at his bright, spacious new Priestgate restaurant,
opened in April 2016. "Overall it's very well worth
the effort, and money, to seek out", and "another
step up from his exploits at (former HQ) Clarke's".
/ **Details:** @foodleeclarke; No trainers; Credit card
deposit required to book.

PETERSFIELD, HAMPSHIRE   2–3D

JSW   **£76** **3**|**2**|**3**
20 Dragon Street GU31 4JJ 01730 262030
For the many fans of Jake Saul Watkin's well-
established destination in a former coaching inn, it
delivers "by far the best food in the area", with a
"clean-lined and simple interior" and "wonderful"
cuisine. Even some who consider it "excellent"
comment that "not everything hits the mark"
however, and there were a number of unenthusiastic
reports noting "inattentive" service or lacklustre
cuisine. / **Details:** www.jswrestaurant.com; on the old
A3; 8 min walk from the railway station; 9 pm; closed
Mon, Tue & Sun D; children: 5+ D. / **Accommodation:**
4 rooms, from £95

PETTS WOOD, KENT   3–3B

Indian Essence   **£48** **4**|**3**|**2**
176-178 Petts Wood Rd BR5 1LG
01689 838700
"Still fresh and exciting" – Atul Kochhar's
incongruously suburban venture "never lets you
down" according to the many reviewers who
comment on it, and "the amazing food is even
better considering it's in Petts Wood!" / **Details:**
www.indianessence.co.uk; @IndianEssence1; 10.45 pm,
Fri & Sat 11 pm; closed Mon L; No trainers.

PETWORTH, WEST SUSSEX   3–4A

The Leconfield   **£66** **4**|**4**|**3**
New Street GU28 0AS 01798 345111
In this pretty market town, a "traditional pub
transformed into a lovely restaurant upstairs", and a
downstairs that still "needs to work out its identity".
By all accounts it's a "very good place" – "much
better than some reports have indicated" – with
chef Mark Lawson (ex-of The Ritz) overseeing some
ambitious cuisine. / **Details:** www.theleconfield.co.uk;
@the_leconfield; 10.30 pm; closed Sun D, Mon & tue L.

The Noahs Ark Inn   **£55** **3**|**4**|**5**
Lurgashall GU28 9ET 01428 707346
This "quintessential English boozer" is a "favourite
for a (delicious) pub lunch" – perhaps "followed by a
pint or two watching the cricket on the neighbouring
village green" ("in summer it's nigh on perfect"). /
Details: www.noahsarkin.co.uk; @TheNoahsArkInn;
Mon-Sat 9.30 pm, Sun 3.15 pm; closed Sun D.

PICKERING, NORTH YORKSHIRE   8–4C

The White Swan   **£56** **3**|**3**|**3**
Market Pl YO18 7AA 01751 472288
"A classic hostelry to suit all tastes"; "though not
exceptional, the food is always reliable" and "lunch
here makes a very enjoyable break on the journey
to the Whitby area". / **Details:** www.white-swan.co.uk;
@wswanpickering; 9 pm. / **Accommodation:** 21
rooms, from £150

PINNER, GREATER LONDON 3–3A	PLYMOUTH, DEVON 1–3C

Friends £58 **3|3|4**
11 High St HA5 5PJ 020 8866 0286
"Long established and with a loyal clientele" – Terry
Farr's "intimate" half-timbered cottage is "the kind
of local you wouldn't want to lose". "Having eaten
here several times, I continue to be amazed by
the unusual quality of food in what is a deeply
suburban and unpromising context!" / *Details:*
www.friendsrestaurant.co.uk; 9.30 pm; closed Mon &
Sun D.

PLAYHATCH, BERKSHIRE 2–2D

The Crown £63 **3|3|4**
RG4 9QN 01189 472872
A large, well-equipped garden is just one highlight
of this stylishly refurbished ancient inn (with
accommodation), near Caversham Lakes (part of
the local Tailor Made Dining Company). Reviews
are still few, but praise its hearty gastropub fare,
majoring in steaks (and on Sundays there's a
carvery). / *Details:* www.tmdining.co.uk; @TMDining;
10 pm.

PLEASINGTON, LANCASHIRE 5–1B

Clog & Billycock £46 **2|2|2**
Billinge End Rd BB2 6QB 01254 201163
"Good honest grub" and "service with a smile" have
won a broad following for this well-known member
of the Ribble Valley Inns chain, "well-located" on
the 'Yellow Hills'. Its ratings were dragged down
this year however by a couple of disappointing
reports. / *Details:* www.theclogandbillycock.com;
@CloganBillycock; 9 pm, Fri & Sat 9.30 pm.

PLUMTREE, NOTTINGHAMSHIRE 5–3D

Perkins £59 **2|2|2**
Old Railway Station NG12 5NA
0115 937 3695
Very up-and-down feedback on this "quirky
restaurant" in an old Victorian train station in the
rolling countryside. Even a fan who cited it as a
"reliable and pleasant experience" cautioned
that the cooking "rarely rises to good and hardly
ever to exceptional", and a couple of former fans
related dismal experiences here this year. / *Details:*
www.perkinsrestaurant.co.uk; @PerkinsNotts; off A606
between Nottingham & Melton Mowbray; 9.30 pm;
closed Sun D.

Brown & Bean £52
68 Ebrington St PL4 9AA 01752 261671
Cosy neighbourhood hangout in an increasingly
foodie area of Plymouth with a focus on sustainable,
locally sourced produce. Initially launched with
MasterChef The Professionals winner Anton
Piotrowski at the helm in spring 2017, the kitchen
is now headed by Jimmy and Joe Cotton. / *Details:*
brownandbean.co.uk; @BrownAndBean16; 9 pm.

**Chloe's, Gill Akaster
House** £54 **3|3|3**
27 Princess St PL1 2EX 01752 201523
A smart, buzzing modern French bistro "conveniently
situated adjacent to Plymouth's Theatre Royal" and
still of note for its "good-value menus". / *Details:*
www.chloesrestaurant.co.uk; 9 pm; closed Sun.

Rock Salt £48 **4|3|3**
31 Stonehouse St PL1 3PE 01752 225522
A former scuzzy pub, in the former red-light district,
now plays host to this "affordable, friendly local
favourite"; "always a delight", it "continues to serve
beautiful dishes in a relaxed, informal setting" and
"they also do amazing roasts on Sunday". / *Details:*
www.rocksaltcafe.co.uk; @rocksaltcafeuk; 9.30 pm;
Booking max 6 may apply.

POLKERRIS, CORNWALL 1–3B

Sams on the Beach £48 **3|3|5**
PL24 2TL 01726 812255
A "unique setting right on the beach in a converted
lifeboat station" adds considerable wow-factor to
this "very relaxed" and "family-friendly" joint; foodwise, choose between a "limited fish menu simply
prepared" or "good, hearty" wood-fired pizzas. /
Details: www.samscornwall.co.uk; @samscornwall;
9 pm; No Amex.

POOLE, DORSET 2–4C

Branksome Beach £54 **3|3|4**
Pinecliff Rd BH13 6LP 01202 767235
"Right on the beach" and with "fabulous views" of
the surf, this converted Art Deco gastropub offers
"good food at a reasonable price"… especially
"considering this is practically Sandbanks". / *Details:*
www.branksomebeach.co.uk; @branksome_beach; L
only.

Guildhall Tavern £52 **4|4|4**
15 Market Street BH15 1NB 01202 671717
"A wonderful find tucked away in Poole" – a
well-established local favourite "on the harbour
seafront" where "a lovely French family

Tattu, Leeds

The Astor Grill,
Taplow

serve the most fantastic seafood". / **Details:**
www.guildhalltavern.co.uk; 10 pm; closed Mon & Sun;
No Amex.

POOLEY BRIDGE, CUMBRIA   7–3D

1863 Bar Bistro Rooms   £47   4 4 3
Elm House, High Street   CA10 2NH   017684
86334
This Lakeland bar-bistro with rooms is making
a name for itself as one of the better dining
options in the locale, and wins praise for its
"stunning food and impeccable service". / **Details:**
www.1863ullswater.co.uk; @1863Ullswater; 9 pm;
children: 10.

PORT APPIN, ARGYLL AND BUTE   9–3B

Airds Hotel   £76   3 3 3
PA38 4DF   01631 730236
"Very cosy in a rather olde-worlde way", and set
amidst "beautiful scenery" – this Relais & Châteaux
outpost in a former ferry inn is a "long way to travel
but worth it" by most accounts. Prices are high
however, leading to the odd accusation of "style
over substance". / **Details:** www.airds-hotel.com;
@AirdsHotel; 20m N of Oban; 9.30 pm; No jeans;
children: 8+ at D. / **Accommodation:** 11 rooms, from
£290

Pierhouse Hotel   £63   5 4 4
PA38 4DE   01631 730302
Set in the Pier Master's old house, and with epic
Loch Linnhe views, this "informal" family-run hotel
restaurant again won acclaim this year for its "fab
fresh seafood as always (but the menu is now
also enlivened by daily changing, more imaginative
specials)". / **Details:** www.pierhousehotel.co.uk;
@pierhousehotel; just off A828, follow signs for Port
Appin & Lismore Ferry; 9.30 pm. / **Accommodation:**
12 rooms, from £100

PORT ISAAC, CORNWALL   1–3B

Fresh From The Sea   £22   5 3 2
18 New Road   PL29 3SB   01208 880849
"This tiny converted fisherman's cottage stands
on the very harbour onto which the creels and
morning catch are unloaded from boats just in from
far out to sea". Primarily a retailer, there's a "cosy"
café where you can enjoy "what's essentially fish
tapas, with choice after choice of divine morsels,
with local wine and gin to match, and accompanied
by the sound of envious gulls..." / **Details:**
www.freshfromthesea.co.uk; L only; No bookings.

Outlaw's Fish Kitchen   £37   4 5 4
1 Middle St   PL29 3RH   01208 881138
"It's worth queueing outside in the rain for an
unbookable lunch table in this intimately cramped
room" – Nathan Outlaw's more affordable spin-off,
serving "fabulously tasty" fish tapas ("I always
wonder how they do this in such a tiny space but
they do"). But even fans acknowledge that "prices
are on the high side". / **Details:** www.outlaws.co.uk;
9 pm; closed Mon & Sun.

Port Gaverne Hotel   £56   3 4 3
PL29 3SQ   01208 880244
"A fascinating hotel, with lots of small rooms for
eating (easy to get lost!)" – this coastal gastropub-
with-rooms, complete with sea view, has "achieved
great popularity" thanks to its "unpretentious service
and a kitchen that delivers on all fronts". "Only
issue is the size of tables, which isn't generous". /
Details: www.portgavernehotel.co.uk; N of Port Isaac
on coast road (B3314); 8.30 pm; No Amex; children: 7+.
/ **Accommodation:** 15 rooms, from £53

Restaurant Nathan
Outlaw   £156   5 4 5
6 New Rd   PL29 3SB   01208 881 183
"The ne plus ultra of UK fish restaurants" – Nathan
Outlaw delivers "a masterclass in amazingly clean,
powerful yet pure fishy flavours – just the best I've
ever tasted" – and "the dishes feel so effortless"
too ("a nice balance of simplicity with panache"),
at his incredibly popular Cornish HQ, which moved
three years ago to the heart of this charming
fishing village from nearby Rock. "The terrific view
is almost as good as the food" – "a panorama
across the bay" that's "best enjoyed in daylight".
"It's wildly expensive but really worth it". / **Details:**
www.nathan-outlaw.com; @ResNathanOutlaw.

PORTHGAIN, PEMBROKESHIRE   4–4B

The Shed   £44   3 3 3
SA62 5BN   01348 831518
Reviewers disagree on the decor – "quirky"... "very
rustic"... "simple and unpretentious"... "dark, but
has character" – but all acclaim this harbourside
bistro for the "freshest possible" fish 'n' chips. /
Details: www.theshedporthgain.co.uk; @ShedPorthgain;
9 pm; No Amex.

PORTHLEVEN, CORNWALL   1–4A

Kota   £62   4 3 3
Harbour Head   TR13 9JA   01326 562407
New Zealander Jude and wife Jane Kereama's
restaurant with rooms is brilliantly located on the
harbour and has a growing reputation for its "lovely
and fresh" Cornish/Asian fusion cuisine. / **Details:**

www.kotarestaurant.co.uk; @KotaRestaurant; 9 pm; D only, closed Sun-Tue; No Amex. / **Accommodation:** 2 rooms, from £70

Kota Kai £43 3️⃣4️⃣3️⃣
Celtic House, Harbour Head TR13 9JY
01326 574411
This more "relaxed", café-style spin-off overlooking the harbour (with front lawn for dining out in good weather) also boasts "cheerful" service and funky Asian-influenced dishes. "It's not absolutely as good as Kota but well worth going to if Kota is full" (and a children's room here makes it the more kid-friendly option). / **Details:** www.kotakai.co.uk; @Kota_Kai; 9 pm.

Rick Steins Seafood Restaurant £89 3️⃣3️⃣4️⃣
Mount Pleasant TR13 9JS 01841 532700
Many fans do recommend the "fabulous" fish and seafood at this three-year-old spin-off from the Stein empire. "Ridiculous prices" are a turnoff for quite a few more sceptical reporters however, and the overall verdict is that the food is "well-prepared, but not a wow". / **Details:** www.rickstein.com; @TheSeafood; children: 3.

The Square at Porthleven £40 4️⃣4️⃣3️⃣
7 Fore Street TR13 9HQ 01326 573 911
"Despite the competition this café and restaurant holds its own in this small foodie haven" and it has "a beautiful location overlooking the harbour". "The emphasis is on local produce and it remains full even out of season" thanks to the "value for money" of its modern bistro/brasserie menu. / **Details:** www.thesquareatporthleven.co.uk; @thesquarepl; 9 pm.

PORTMAHOMACK, HIGHLAND 9–2C

The Oystercatcher £54 4️⃣3️⃣2️⃣
Main Street IV20 1YB 01862 871560
A favourite Highlands destination – this casual coastal bistro delivers "great seafood at very fair prices": "a must-visit!" / **Details:** www.the-oystercatcher.co.uk; Wed-Sat 10 pm, Sun 2.45 pm; closed Mon, Tue, Wed, Thu L & Sun D. / **Accommodation:** 3 rooms, from £82

PORTMEIRION, GWYNEDD 4–2C

Portmeirion Hotel £64 2️⃣2️⃣4️⃣
LL48 6ET 01766 772440
With its "lovely location", the estuary-view dining room at the heart of Sir Clough Williams-Ellis's whimsical Welsh tribute to Portofino has the "potential to be first rate". Reports have been more middling in recent years however, and though no disasters are recorded, gripes include "distant"

service and food that's "trying too hard". / **Details:** www.portmeirion-village.com/eat/the-hotel-dining-room/; off A487 at Minffordd; 9 pm. / **Accommodation:** 14 rooms, from £185

PORTRUSH, NORTHERN IREAND 10–1C

Portrush Deli Co £11 4️⃣4️⃣4️⃣
7 Bath Street BT56 8AN 028 7082 2871
A "tiny deli/café serving up tasty light lunches, and occasional degustation evenings, which are a gastronomic delight". / **Details:** www.portrushdeli.com.

PORTSCATHO, CORNWALL 1–4B

Hidden Hut £14 4️⃣3️⃣4️⃣
Portscatho Beach TR2 5EW no tel
"A remarkable place" – the "beautiful beach location with outdoor seating is special enough, but it is the food and the care" taken with it that's "outstanding" at this "lovely little open-air café" (essentially a shed with alfresco seating) "overlooking the sea and Southwest Coast Path", where "the chef creates a monthly changing menu of delicious and seasonal ingredients." Open daily for lunch, "as well as (thrice monthly) pop-up nights with a theme or guest chef". / **Details:** www.hiddenhut.co.uk; @TheHiddenHut; Cash only; No bookings.

PORTSMOUTH, HAMPSHIRE 2–4D

abarbistro £48 3️⃣3️⃣2️⃣
58 White Hart Rd PO1 2JA 02392 811585
In Old Portsmouth, and "well worth the effort to find it" – this cheerful bistro is "a regular haunt" handy for the IOW ferry and Gunwharf Quay. Above the restaurant they also run a wine business (Camber Wines). / **Details:** www.abarbistro.co.uk; @abarbistro; 10 pm.

PORTSTEWART, COUNTY LONDONDERRY 10–1D

Harry's Shack £38 4️⃣4️⃣4️⃣
118 Strand Road BT55 7PG 028 7083 1783
Reporters "love this simple restaurant on the beach" – "the menu is straightforward" (burgers and "properly cooked, well-priced fish 'n' chips") "but everything is fresh and delicious, especially the fish; no longer BYO, it now has a "small and pretty decent wine list". / **Details:** www.facebook.com/HarrysShack; @Harrys_Shack; 8 pm, Fri 8.30 pm, Sat & Sun 11.15 pm; closed Mon.

POULTON, GLOUCESTERSHIRE   2–2C

The Falcon Inn   £45   3|3|3
London Rd GL7 5HN   01285 850878
*Slap bang in a picture-perfect Cotswold village,
a charming destination for some "top-class pub
dining" (including a "very good" lunch) from a
"wide menu" full of local suppliers. / Details:
www.falconinnpoulton.co.uk; on A417 between
Cirencester and Fairford; 10 pm; closed Sun D; No
Amex.*

PRESTON BAGOT, WARWICKSHIRE   5–4C

The Crabmill   £48   3|2|2
B95 5EE   01926 843342
*A "reliable and buzzy (at times overly so!)
gastropub" with a handsome beamed interior and
"good set menu"; handy for the M40, too. / Details:
www.thecrabmill.co.uk; @lvlycrabmill; on main road
between Warwick & Henley-in-Arden; 9.30 pm, Sun
4 pm; closed Sun D; No Amex.*

PRESTON, LANCASHIRE   5–1A

Bukhara   £36   4|4|2
154 Preston New Rd PR5 0UP   01772 877710
*Fans "love the authentic food" at this alcohol-free
Indian/Pakistani venue, in a modern roadside
building. / Details: www.bukharasamlesbury.co.uk;
11 pm; closed weekday L.*

PURLEY, SURREY   3–3A

Dexter Burger   £30   4|4|3
10 High Street CR8 2AA   020 8660 9427
*"A great addition to the food wasteland that is
Purley" – this "great local burger restaurant" has
a definite Shoreditch vibe, with its school chairs,
industrial lights and local craft beers. The "beautiful
meat" stars, but the sides (homemade coleslaw and
"great rosemary fries and relish") are "fantastic"
too. A second branch took over The Pendleton pub
in St John's, near Redhill, in June 2017. / Details:
www.dexter-burger.com; 9.30 pm, Sun 8 pm.*

QUEENSBURY, MIDDLESEX   3–3A

Regency Club   £38   3|3|3
19-21 Queensbury Station Pde HA8 5NR
020 8952 6300
*"Delicious real Indian flavours" that are
"exceptional" for the environs of Edgware inspire
very consistent praise for this "buzzing and loud"
but "very good pub/club/curry house". / Details:*

*www.regencyclub.co.uk; @RegencuClubUK; 10.30 pm,
Fri & Sat 11 pm, Sun 10 pm; closed Mon L; children:
18+.*

RADNAGE, BUCKINGHAMSHIRE   3–2A

Mash Inn   £62   4|4|4
Horseshoe Rd, Bennett End HP14 4EB
01494 482 440
*After a rebrand and refurb', this 18th-century
inn is now a very promising pub-with-rooms, in a
"wonderful" setting in foodie country. OK, it's "so
hipster it hurts" (pro-foraging, and with grub "cooked
unusually over an open fire"), but they "really know
their food", with added praise for the service, too. /
Details: www.themashinn.com; 9.15 pm.*

RAMSBOTTOM, LANCASHIRE   5–1B

Baratxuri   £46   5|4|4
1 Smithy St BL0 9AT   01706 559090
*Whether you opt for a "kilo hunk of old Galician
cow" ("much cheaper than Hawksmoor and super
quality"), the marvellous mariscada (seafood
platter), or just churros and hot chocolate (not to
mention "top-notch" wines at "minimal markups")
all is bloomin' fantastic at this "beautiful" tiled spin-
off to elder sibling Levanter, just round the corner.
And it's just "so relaxed: you eat this pintxo. You have
a drink. Then another pintxo. Then try something off
the cooked-to-order menu. Have another drink," and
before long "you are pleasantly replete" and "have
not really spent that much". NB "Two small tables
in the window, the rest is bar stools or standing".
/ Details: www.levanterfinefoods.co.uk/baratxuri;
@BaratxuriBar; 9 pm.*

Eagle & Child   £50   3|3|3
3 Whalley Road BL0 0DL   01257 462297
*With investment from the Daniel Thwaites chain,
this recently refurbished 'food pub', with fine views,
is distinctive not only for its "great nosh", but also
its 'edible beer garden' (with outdoor kitchen,
polytunnels and children's area) plus "the added
benefit that they train young people as part of
their mission" (in supporting marginalised people
into work). / Details: www.ainscoughs.co.uk; M6, J27;
8.30 pm; No Amex.*

Levanter   £37   5|5|4
10 Square St BL0 9BE   01706 551530
*"A real taste of Spain in the hills north of
Manchester!" – Joe & Fiona Botham "ensure
Ramsbottom continues to figure prominently on the
foodie map" at this tiny joint (aided by its bar-like
sibling, Baratxuri, round the corner). The "bloody
good" grub is "generously priced", and all day long
"it buzzes with energy… and it's remarkable how a*

couple of backstreet tapas bars manage to attract such competent and friendly staff". "For Londoners, the 1kg txuleton steak available at weekends for a mere £45 will no doubt seem a bargain!" / **Details:** www.levanterfinefoods.co.uk; @levanterfoods; 10 pm, Sun 7.30 pm; closed Mon & Tue.

RAMSGATE, KENT   3–3D

The Empire Room, Royal Harbour Hotel   £43   4 4 4
10-12 Nelson Crescent CT11 9JF
01843 582511
"Freshly landed fish straight from boat to kitchen, is expertly prepared by chef Craig Mathers delicate touch" at this "hidden gem (in a poorly served area for decent restaurants) tucked away in the basement of the Royal Harbour Hotel (and with the ambience of a private dining club)". Top Tip – "excellent value set menu". / **Details:** theempireroom.co.uk/; @EmpRoom; Mon-Thu 9 pm, Fri 7 Sat 9.30 pm, Sun 3 pm.

Flavours By Kumar   £37   4 4 2
2 Effingham St CT11 9AT   01843 852631
"Don't be off put by being in a rather shabby former pub on a rather shabby side street in Ramsgate" – ex-Ambrette chef Anir Kumar's popular two-year-old serves "exceptional" food. / **Details:** 10.30 pm.

RAMSGILL-IN-NIDDERDALE, NORTH YORKSHIRE   8–4B

Yorke Arms   £115   5 4 4
HG3 5RL   01423 755243
Frances Atkins established herself as one of the UK's most accomplished chefs at this old coaching house made famous, and which she and husband Bill made famous, and which enjoys a "beautiful location", "overlooking the village green, out in the Dales". Its scores were as all-round impressive as ever this year thanks to her "inspirational" cooking (much of it from the kitchen garden) and "wonderfully relaxed" service, but post-survey in June 2017 she put the property on the market to allow Bill to retire, and so that she can potentially move onto a less all-consuming venture. (No announcement of a sale had been made by October 2017 however, and Michelin this year maintained their star for the property). / **Details:** www.yorke-arms.co.uk; @theyorkearms; 4m W of Pateley Bridge; 8.45 pm; closed Mon & Sun. / **Accommodation:** 16 rooms, from £200

READING, BERKSHIRE   2–2D

Forbury's   £68   3 3 2
1 Forbury Sq RG1 3BB   0118 957 4044
"Near the railway station", a hotel dining room that's particularly of note for its "intriguing" wine list (they also run regular wine nights); the ambience attracts the weakest ratings – "the decor and lighting can't quite decide if it's a wine bar or proper restaurant" – but all reviews agree the food is very "decent". / **Details:** www.forburys.co.uk; @forburys; 9.30 pm; closed Sun D.

London Street Brasserie £64   3 2 3
Riverside Oracle, 2 - 4 London Street RG1 4PN
0118 950 5036
"Our local go-to"; in a "nice location overlooking the canal in the centre of Reading", this is a "busy bistro that always delivers fresh seasonal delights" (of a "classic brasserie" bent). / **Details:** www.londonstbrasserie.co.uk; @lsb_reading; 10.30 pm, Fri & Sat 11 pm.

REIGATE, SURREY   3–3B

La Barbe   £66   3 3 3
71 Bell St RH2 7AN   01737 241966
"A little bit of the 10th arrondissement in Reigate" – Serge Tassi's "very jolly" Gallic venture (celebrating its 35th year of operation) serves "lovely French fare" and has "upped its game in recent times while retaining a brasserie feel". That the wines are "a bit pricey" is an occasional gripe. / **Details:** www.labarbe.co.uk; @LaBarbeReigate; 9.30 pm; closed Sat L & Sun D.

REYNOLDSTON, SWANSEA   1–1C

Fairyhill   £69   4 4 5
SA3 1BS   01792 390139
Owned by wedding specialists Oldwalls since November 2016, this small (but expanding) restaurant-with-rooms occupies a grade II manor house, beautifully set in a remote corner of the Gower peninsula. Feedback is limited, but very positive on its cuisine, which makes a feature of Welsh sourcing. / **Details:** www.fairyhill.net; @Fairyhill_Hotel; 20 mins from M4, J47 off B4295; 9 pm; No Amex; children: 8+ at D. / **Accommodation:** 8 rooms, from £180

RIBCHESTER, LANCASHIRE   5–1B

Angels   £60   3 3 4
Fleet Street Lane PR3 3ZA   01254 820212
A white baby grand helps set a glitzy and "romantic" tone at this cocktail bar and restaurant

in the Ribble Valley, praised by its local fan club for a good all-round experience. / *Details: www.angelsribchester.co.uk/; @AngelsRibchest.*

RICHMOND, SURREY   1–4A

Chez Lindsay   **£53**   **3 4 3**
11 Hill Rise TW10 6UQ   020 8948 7473
"Distinctively French" bistro and creperie, near Richmond Bridge, which arguably "under exploits its riverside setting". Breton dishes "are well executed from a simple menu" alongside a list of ciders and wine (and there are "good, cheap 2/3-course lunches"). "The dining room is a little lacklustre but there's plenty of room between tables so it's easy to chat and enjoy your space". / Details: www.chezlindsay.co.uk; @Chez_Lindsay; 11 pm; No Amex.

The Duke   **£49**   **2 3 3**
2 Duke St TW9 1HP   020 8940 4067
Just off Richmond Green, this Food & Fuel gastropub wins solid all-round ratings from fans across west London for its dependable dishes, including "fab steaks"; very popular for Sunday roast. / Details: www.thedukerichmond.co.uk; @TheDukePub; 10 pm, Sun 9 pm.

RIDGEWAY VILLAGE, SOUTH YORKSHIRE 5–2C

The Old Vicarage   **£80**   **3 3 3**
S12 3XW   0114 247 5814
Tessa Bramley's comfortable Victorian country house dining room has been an edge-of-town fixture for over 30 years – and, despite up-and-down reports on the service and cooking fronts in recent years, won consistent praise this year for "exceptional food in a lovely environment". It's had a recent makeover too. / Details: www.theoldvicarage.co.uk; 9.30 pm; closed Mon, Sat L & Sun; No Amex; children: call in advance.

RIPLEY, SURREY   3–3A

Anchor   **£67**   **4 3 4**
High St GU23 6AE   01483 211866
"It might be a pub setting, but its quality reflects the high standards imported from Drakes" just across the road, which proprietor Steve Drake used to run. "Thoughtful and beautifully prepared food" is "elegantly presented with thought and care" in a "very comfortable and cosy", "low-beamed" setting. / Details: www.ripleyanchor.co.uk; @RipleyAnchor; 11 pm, Sun 9 pm; closed Mon.

The Clock House (Formerly Drakes)   **£80**   **5 3 3**
The Clock Hs, High St GU23 6AQ
01483 224777
"Despite the departure of former chef proprietor Steve Drake and the change of name last year, this place goes from strength to strength, and it's better than ever!" Chef Fred Clapperton has helped regain a Michelin Star for Serina Drake's Georgian property, which changed its name from Drakes this year following her split from husband Steve (who owns the Anchor pub opposite, and has just opened Sorrel in Dorking). There's the odd grumble, but nearly all reports feel "the tradition of excellence continues here". / Details: www.theclockhouserestaurant.co.uk; @DrakesRipley; 9.30 pm; closed Mon, Tue L & Sun; No Amex.

Pinnocks   **£13**   **4 3 3**
High St GU23 6AF   01483 222419
"Excellent coffee" is the hallmark of this "laid back", "alternative" High Street café, which turns out "consistently good" grub (from cakes to lunch) in an "antique atmosphere" of bunting, beams and battered Chesterfields. / Details: www.pinnockscoffeehouse.com; @pinnockscoffee; L only.

ROCHDALE, LANCASHIRE   5–2B

Bird At Birtle   **£38**   **3 4 3**
239 Bury And Rochdale Old Road OL10 4BQ
01706 540500
Celeb chef Andrew Nutter's first gastropub, opened in summer 2016, is already a "very popular" spot, with "better-than-average" grub and "amazing cocktails"; the interior is "modern, bright and spacious", and the "exceptional wine list" at the original Nutters is "apparent", though more "slightly limited" here. / Details: www.thebirdatbirtle.co.uk.

ROCK, CORNWALL   1–3B

Dining Room   **£65**   **4 3 2**
Pavilion Buildings, Rock Rd PL27 6JS
01208 862622
"Husband and wife-team (chef and front of house) Fred and Donna continue to perform amazing culinary works at this unpretentious Rock restaurant", in a parade of shops. / Details: www.thediningroomrock.co.uk; @TheDiningRmRock; 9 pm; D only, closed Mon & Tue; No Amex; children: 10+.

Mariners   **£46**   **4 2 3**
PL27 6LD   01208 863679
This hook-up between celebrated chef Nathan Outlaw and Sharp's Brewery lives up to the billing,

with great Camel Estuary views from the terrace and balcony, alongside very solidly performing grub (not least locally sourced beef, and a "brilliant Sunday lunch"). / *Details: www.themarinersrock.com/; @TheMarinersRock; 9.30 pm Sun 4.30 pm.*

St Enodoc Restaurant, St Enodoc Hotel £68 5️⃣4️⃣3️⃣
Rock Road PL27 6LA   01208 863394
MasterChef winner "James Nathan's arrival on the banks of the River Camel (in early 2016) has heralded a new era for this hotel restaurant" – and some reporters "would always choose James" over "the more famous Nathan" (Outlaw) who used to cook here. Several constants in any case: "fabulous seafood and fish", a "bustling" vibe and "outstanding" estuary views. / Details: www.enodoc-hotel.co.uk/food.html; 9 pm.

ROCKBEARE, DEVON	1–3D

The Jack in the Green Inn £52 3️⃣3️⃣2️⃣
EX5 2EE   01404 822240
"Lovely pub food" continues to underpin the popularity of this very "lively", keenly priced and tardis-like roadside institution, which has racked up numerous awards during its quarter of a century in business. / Details: www.jackinthegreen.uk.com; @JackGreenInn; On the old A30, 3 miles east of junction 29 of M5; Mon-Thu 9 pm, Fri 9.30 pm; Sat 10 pm, Sun 9 pm; No Amex.

ROSEVINE, CORNWALL	1–4B

Driftwood Hotel £89 4️⃣4️⃣4️⃣
TR2 5EW   01872 580644
A "magical location" atop a cliff on the Roseland Peninsula is ably matched by Chris Eden's "exceptional" and "delicious" food at this acclaimed Cape Cod-style hotel and dining room, with views of Gull's Rock, and a private path down to its own secluded beach. / Details: www.driftwoodhotel.co.uk; @DriftwoodHotel; off the A30 to Truro, towards St Mawes; 9.30 pm; D only; children: 7. / Accommodation: 15 rooms, from £185

ROWSLEY, DERBYSHIRE	5–2C

The Peacock at Rowsley £78 3️⃣2️⃣3️⃣
Bakewell Rd DE4 2EB   01629 733518
A small, classy Peak District hotel where Tom Aikens protégé Dan Smith turns out some "excellent" dishes (and where even the most downbeat report noted the cooking's "clear potential"). There's also a cosy, more relaxed bar with its own menu. / Details: www.thepeacockatrowsley.com; @peacockrowsley;

9 pm, Sun 8.30 pm; Booking max 8 may apply; children: 10+ at D. / *Accommodation: 15 rooms, from £160*

ROYAL TUNBRIDGE WELLS, KENT	3–4B

The Beacon Kitchen £44 4️⃣4️⃣4️⃣
Tea Garden Lane TN3 9JH   01892 524252
An addition to Pete Cornwell's four-strong, memorably named 'I'll Be Mother' group three years ago – this relaunched country inn has made "an excellent addition to the local dining scene"; the rambling venue (set in 17 acres, with three lakes) offers "good food and service as well as an outstanding view from the terrace". / Details: www.the-beacon.co.uk; @Thebeacon_tw; Mon 5 pm, Tue-Sat 11.30 pm, Sun 6 pm. / Accommodation: 3 rooms, from £97

The Black Pig £46 3️⃣3️⃣3️⃣
18 Grove Hill Road TN1 1RZ   01892 523030
Launched a decade ago to inject some London gastropub style into the local market, this laidback joint – a nice bar at the front, and dining rooms to the rear – continues to please with its "generally good" Kent- and Sussex-sourced grub. / Details: www.theblackpig.net; @BlackPigTW; Mon-Thu 9.30 pm, Fri & Sat 10 pm, Sun 9 pm; No Amex.

Hotel du Vin & Bistro £55 2️⃣2️⃣3️⃣
Crescent Road TN1 2LY   01892 320749
A cute location in a Grade II-listed Georgian mansion adds to the appeal of this HdV branch – also boasting the chain's hallmark Gallic fare and quaffable wine list. / Details: www.hotelduvin.com/locations/tunbridge-wel; @HotelduVinBrand; Mon-Thu 10 pm, Fri & Sat 10.30 pm, Sun 9.30 pm; Booking max 10 may apply. / Accommodation: 34 rooms, from £120

The Ivy Royal Tunbridge Wells £54
46-50 High Street TN1 1XF   01892 240 700
In a 'roll-out' that would do McDonald's proud, this iconic brand has gone for it this year, opening virtually simultaneously in practically all of the UK's top restaurant cities. The ambition is impressive: let's hope standards hold up better than they did when, for example 'Browns' tried to pull off a similar trick. / Details: www.theivytunbridgewells.com; @ivytunbridge.

Sankey's The Old Fishmarket £49 3️⃣3️⃣4️⃣
19 The Upper Pantiles TN2 5TN
01892 511422
In the heart of the Pantiles, and set in the quaint Old Fishmarket building, a "small but perfectly formed" branch of a now four-strong local foodie empire; as befits the location, it majors in "great fish

well executed" (especially shellfish and oysters). /
Details: *www.sankeys.co.uk; @sankeysrtw; midnight; closed Mon D & Sun D.*

Thackeray's £79 323
85 London Rd TN1 1EA 01892 511921
"Superb flavours and complex dishes" still inspire many fans of this well-known culinary destination: a Regency villa near the town centre. Reports are a little up-and-down on numerous fronts however, although the most common theme is "service let it down, but the rest was amazing". / ***Details:*** *www.thackerays-restaurant.co.uk; @Thackeraysrest; 10.30 pm; closed Mon & Sun D.*

The Twenty Six £45 444
15a Church Road TN4 0RX 01892 544607
Simon Ulph's "imaginative food from an interesting menu" wins high praise for this "cosy" venture, named for the number of diners this 'test kitchen' – part of the 'I'll be Mother' group – can accommodate. / ***Details:*** *thetwenty-six.co.uk; @thetwenty_six; 9 pm.*

RUTHIN, DENBIGHSHIRE	4–1D

On The Hill £44 444
1 Upper Clwyd Street LL15 1HY
01824 707736
"A delightful restaurant on the hill in a delightful town". This beamed bistro in a 16th-century house only attracts limited feedback, but again wins strong praise for its "enormous portions" of excellent-value cooking and provides "such a welcome as well". "We'll be back, but with appetites prepared…" / ***Details:*** *onthehillrestaurant.co.uk/; 9 pm.*

RYDE, ISLE OF WIGHT	2–4D

Three Buoys £54 434
Appley Lane PO33 1ND 01983 811212
"Overlooking Appley Beach, with blankets provided for you to dine out on the terrace even if it's a little chilly", this "lovely restaurant" serves a "wide choice of food (plus a fantastic gin menu)". / ***Details:*** *www.threebuoys.co.uk; @Three_Buoys; 9 pm.*

RYE, EAST SUSSEX	3–4C

Landgate Bistro £47 422
5 - 6 Landgate TN31 7LH 01797 222829
"Impressive for such a small place" – this long-established bistro is "always worth a visit when in town", with local salt marsh lamb earning a particular thumbs up. / ***Details:*** *www.landgatebistro.co.uk; 9 pm, Sun 2.15 pm; closed Mon, Tue, Wed-Fri L & Sun D; No Amex.*

Tuscan Rye £39 443
8 Lion St TN31 7LB 01797 223269
Old owners Franco and Jen are now returned to this old favourite and it's "great to have them back"; with "wonderful Tuscan food" from him, and "great front-of-house attention from his lovely wife", it's "practically perfect in every way". "Don't let Franco give you too much grappa at the end of the evening". / ***Details:*** *www.tuscankitchenrye.co.uk; closed Mon, Tue, Wed L & Sat L.*

Webbe's at The Fish Cafe £49 322
17 Tower Street TN31 7AT 01797 222226
"From fish 'n' chips to lobsters are well-cooked and well-presented" at Paul and Rebecca Webbe's popular destination – a converted Edwardian 4-floor warehouse in the town centre incorporating a café, restaurant, banqueting suite and cookery school. / ***Details:*** *www.webbesrestaurants.co.uk/the-fish-cafe/; @webbesrye; 9.30 pm.*

SALCOMBE, DEVON	1–4C

Crab Shed £45 433
TQ8 8DU 01548 844280
A "great, small seafood restaurant perched on the water's edge close to their own factory where they produce 100% hand picked crab meat; they're provided with the best fresh seafood and shellfish daily from the factory and boats that operate out of the Fish Quay". / ***Details:*** *crabshed.com; @Crabshed; No Amex.*

South Sands Hotel £63 335
Bolt Head TQ8 8LL 01548 845900
This "super beachfront hotel restaurant" just outside Salcombe makes "a perfect place to relax with the family"; "the view is hard to match", but the classically oriented food can be "great", and there's an "interesting wine list" to go with it (plus regular special themed evenings). / ***Details:*** *www.southsands.com; @southsandshotel; 9 pm. /* ***Accommodation:*** *75 rooms, from £27*

SALISBURY, WILTSHIRE	2–3C

Anokaa £49 432
60 Fisherton St SP2 7RB 01722 414142
"Stylish fusion dishes" – "light, tempting, full of vegetables and a long way ahead of the usual birianis and tikkas" – helps this smart, contemporary spot "take Indian food to new heights" and presentation is "so imaginative" too. / ***Details:*** *www.anokaa.com; @eatatanokaa; 10.30 pm; No shorts.*

SALTAIRE, WEST YORKSHIRE   5–1C

Salts Diner, Salts Mill   £36   2️⃣3️⃣3️⃣
Victoria Road BD18 3LA   01274 530533
*For "good-quality food at a reasonable price in a
great location" you can't go wrong with this gallery
cafe in the UNESCO-listed surrounds of Salts Mill;
"as many reviewers have commented, the noise
level is intrusive" but there's consolation to be had in
those adorable David Hockney-designed (!) napkins.
/ Details: www.saltsmill.org.uk; 2m from Bradford on
A650; Mon-Fri 5 pm, Sat & Sun 5.30 pm; L & afternoon
tea only; No Amex; No bookings.*

SALTHOUSE, NORFOLK   6–3C

Dun Cow   £42   2️⃣3️⃣3️⃣
Purdy St NR25 7XA   01263 740467
*"Always good" classic country pub, with a charming,
beamed interior, airy views across the beach and
marshes, and solid gastro-style grub. / Details:
www.salthouseduncow.com; @salthouseduncow; 9 pm.*

SANDBANKS, DORSET   2–4C

Rick Stein   £63   4️⃣5️⃣5️⃣
10-14 Banks Rd BH13 7QB   01202 283000
*"A great improvement on the Padstow restaurant's
location!" – "the view across Poole Harbour is
superb, as is the food and service" at this Stein
empire yearling, which outscores all its stablemates
including the original Seafood Restaurant, and
which increasingly looks set to become the flagship
of the group. The following report (of the many
we received) nails the key points: "OK, so the Rick
Stein brand has been slightly diluted, so we were
prepared to be underwhelmed, but were very
impressed. It's a cool place, quite hushed, until about
10pm when the Sandbanks crowd let down their
hair (along with their pretensions). But, the main
point is, the fish is fabulous. Expensive compared
to other smart restaurants, down in Dorset and in
London, but good, very good. Second visit we took
our much-loved Australian in-laws, who know how
to eat well. They absolutely loved it!" / Details:
www.rickstein.com/eat-with-us/rick-stein-sandbanks;
@SteinSandbanks; 10 pm, Sun 9 pm; children: 3.*

SANDIACRE, NOTTINGHAMSHIRE   5–3D

La Rock   £69   4️⃣4️⃣3️⃣
4 Bridge Street NG10 5QT   0115 9399 833
*The location strikes some as "strange" – "near
a canal in a small unassuming town between
Nottingham and Derby" – but this "first-class"
venture pleases (nearly) all reviewers with its*
*"imaginative, tasty British cooking" and "excellent
service": "expensive but good value for money". /
Details: www.larockrestaurant.co.uk; @laRock_NG10;
Wed-Sat 8.30 pm, Sun 1.30 pm; closed Mon, Tue &
Wed L.*

SANDSEND, NORTH YORKSHIRE   8–3D

Estbek House   £57   4️⃣4️⃣4️⃣
East Row YO21 3SU   01947 893424
*In an imposing Georgian building on the
seafront, this restaurant-with-rooms offers "an
indulgent if expensive experience" with fish the
speciality. Even a reviewer who felt "the cooking
could be more adventurous" praised it for its
"excellent, well-sourced fresh seafood". / Details:
www.estbekhouse.co.uk; @estbekhouse; 9 pm; D only;
No Amex; No bookings at diner. / Accommodation: 5
rooms, from £125*

SANDWICH, KENT   3–3D

**The Salutation Hotel &
Restaurant**
Knightrider St CT13 9EW   01304 619919
*Boutique hotel in a Grade-I listed stately home
which, following a major refurb in 2016, boasts
17 bedrooms and three dining venues including
a tearoom, terrace, small plates and à la carte
restaurant with a Tasting Room which serves a blind
menu. The Faint Room, a drinking den, was set to
open in late 2017. / Details: www.the-salutation.com;
@Salut_Sandwich; 9 pm; May need + to book. /
Accommodation: 17 rooms, from £233*

SAPPERTON, GLOUCESTERSHIRE   2–2C

The Bell at Sapperton   £49   2️⃣2️⃣4️⃣
GL7 6LE   01285 760298
*"You can tether your horse at a rail in the car park"
of this country pub, which everyone agrees is a
"lovely" destination. Split views on the food remain
however – "improving" or "very good" to fans, but to
sceptics its "simple pub grub" is "very unremarkable"
and "amateur". / Details: www.bellsapperton.co.uk;
@bellsapperton; from Cirencester take the A419
towards Stroud, turn right to Sapperton; 9.30 pm, Sun
9 pm.*

SAUNDERSFOOT, PEMBROKESHIRE   4–4B

Coast   £68   4️⃣4️⃣4️⃣
Coppet Hall Beach SA69 9AJ   01834 810800
*"Breathtaking views" of the beach and
"accomplished" and "interesting" food make this a
"very special restaurant" indeed; patrons of chef/*

owner Will Holland's previous venues (L'Ortolan, La Bécasse) proclaim it even "better" than its predecessors! / **Details:** coastsaundersfoot.co.uk; 8.45 pm; closed Mon & Tue.

SCARBOROUGH, NORTH YORKSHIRE 8–4D

Lanterna £55 5️⃣5️⃣3️⃣
33 Queen Street YO11 1HQ 01723 363616
An "excellent, cosy" Italian that's also acclaimed as "the best fish restaurant in the area"; "the service is excellent and the all-round value is good". / **Details:** www.lanterna-ristorante.co.uk; 9.30 pm; D only, closed Sun; No Amex.

SCAWTON, NORTH YORKSHIRE 8–4C

The Hare Inn Restaurant £51 5️⃣5️⃣3️⃣
YO7 2HG 01845 597769
This 13th-century inn is "a little gem set on a hill overlooking the North Yorks Moors"; while Paul Jackson's cooking is "not what you would expect in these parts (Yorkshire food is not normally served up in seven small courses!)" – the results are "superb". / **Details:** www.thehare-inn.com; @harescawton; off A170; 9 pm, Sun 4 pm; closed Mon, Tue & Sun D; Credit card deposit required to book.

SCUNTHORPE, NORTH LINCOLNSHIRE 6–2A

San Pietro Restaurant £62 3️⃣3️⃣4️⃣
11 High Street East DN15 6UH
01724 277774
A converted four-storey windmill houses this restaurant-with-rooms, whose glam decor won it the AA's 'funkiest B&B' award a couple of years ago, and where the cuisine wins high ratings from reporters. / **Details:** www.sanpietro.uk.com/; @SanPietroNLincs; 11 pm. / **Accommodation:** 14 rooms, from £105

SEAHAM, COUNTY DURHAM 8–3C

Byron's Restaurant, Seaham Hall £71 3️⃣4️⃣5️⃣
Lord Byron's Walk SR7 7AG 0191 516 1400
"All gorgeous"… "simply fabulous" – the "romantic" and glam' dining room of this fine Georgian house won (almost) unanimous praise this year for its cuisine under Damian Broom, which offers a tasting option alongside a fairly conventional à la carte selection. / **Details:** www.seaham-hall.co.uk; @SeahamHallHotel; 9.30 pm; D only, ex Sun open L & D; No trainers; Booking max 8 may apply. / **Accommodation:** 20 rooms, from £300

SEASALTER, KENT 3–3C

The Sportsman £57 5️⃣5️⃣5️⃣
Faversham Road CT5 4BP 01227 273370
"If you want to discover what fine food is all about without the flummery head here!" Stephen Harris's famous seaside boozer on the marshes near Whitstable "is a surprise, as it looks scruffy, and the view from the back is of caravans and traffic cones". But "it represents a somewhat magical and cherished escape to discover this remote yet first-class place, characterised by its modestness and very down-to-earth yet dedicated staff". Key to the experience is the "out-of-this-world" food (from either the à la carte or tasting menu), "unfussily, yet superbly executed using fresh local produce" and its twinned with a wine list which, though less earth-shattering, represents "stunningly good value". And while it looks "very unprepossessing" outside, the dining room is beautifully "light and airy". "Fingers crossed they don't wreck it by expanding the building". Top Menu Tip – "the best ever homemade bread and butter" and "outstanding slip soles". / **Details:** www.thesportsmanseasalter.co.uk; @sportsmankent; 9 pm; closed Mon & Sun D; No Amex; children: 18+ in main bar.

SEAVIEW, ISLE OF WIGHT 2–4D

Seaview Hotel and Restaurant £17 3️⃣3️⃣4️⃣
The High Street PO34 5EX 01983 612711
For a holiday meal out, bear in mind the dining room of this popular coastal hotel: the food's not aiming for culinary pyrotechnics, but "high quality dishes are excellently cooked with lovely service". / **Details:** www.seaviewhotel.co.uk; @seaviewhotel?lang=en; 9.45 pm. / **Accommodation:** 17 rooms, from £70

SEER GREEN, BUCKINGHAMSHIRE 3–3A

The Jolly Cricketers £55 4️⃣3️⃣3️⃣
24 Chalfont Rd HP9 2YG 01494 676308
"Set in the most beautiful village of Seer Green", this "country gastropub" is a proper local with a buzzing vibe and bags of charm; fans say "the food is the best in the area by a long way". / **Details:** www.thejollycricketers.co.uk; @jollycricketers; 11.15 pm, Fri & Sat 11.30, Sun 10.30.

SEVENOAKS, KENT 3–3B

Little Garden £48 3️⃣3️⃣3️⃣
1-2 Well Court, Bank Street TN13 1UN
01732 469397
Opened in 2015 by Benjamin James, also

behind the George & Dragon in Chipstead, this "charming" two-floor spot (complete with decked courtyard) is apparently home to Sevenoaks' first Josper oven, which supplies much of the menu (which majors in burgers and steak). / *Details:* www.littlegardensevenoaks.com/; @Littlegarden7; Mon -Sat 10 pm, Sun 9 pm.

SHALDON, DEVON   1–3D

Ode   £59   4 4 3
21 Fore Street TQ14 0DE   01626 873977
This "small and intimate restaurant tucked away in the village" is part of a local foodie empire incorporating now a nearby pizzeria (Ode & Co: "not your normal pizza base or toppings… fantastic views from the sun terrace in the evenings") and café at Ness Cove. "Tim the owner prides himself on sourcing local produce" (most of it from a nearby farm). / *Details:* www.odetruefood.com; @odetruefood; 9 pm; D only, closed Sun-Thu; No Amex; children: 8+ after 8pm.

SHEFFIELD, SOUTH YORKSHIRE   5–2C

Joro   £65   5 4 3
294 Shalesmoor S3 8US 0114 299 1539
"What an amazing venture!" In an unexpected location (a shipping container), this Scandi-inspired fixture serving hyper-seasonal fare in a small plates, snacks and tasting menu format opened in early 2017. Early reports are adulatory: "the first restaurant in Sheffield that can be compared to the best in the UK" – "we literally spent the whole evening talking about the food as each flavour was exceptional". / *Details:* www.jororestaurant.co.uk; @JoroRestaurant; 9 pm; closed Sun-Tue.

Nonna's   £45   4 4 3
535 - 541 Eccleshall Road S11 8PR
0114 268 6166
A "classic Italian: noisy, busy, loud" – on all accounts Maurizio Mori's twenty-year-old Eccleshall staple remains "on song" and producing "food to savour". / *Details:* www.nonnas.co.uk; @NonnasCucina; Mon-Sat 11 pm, Sun 10.30 pm; No Amex.

Ottos   £53   4 4 3
344 Sharrow Vale Road S11 8ZP
0114 266 9147
Tucked off one of the city's main arteries, Otto Damahi's "always welcoming" local staple offers top Moroccan cuisine, including "gluten-free options", and very popular tagines. BYO for a small corkage fee. / *Details:* www.ottosrestaurant.co.uk; 11.30 pm.

Rafters   £65   4 5 4
220 Oakbrook Rd, Nether Grn S11 7ED
0114 230 4819

"Rafters has long been amongst the very best of restaurants in Sheffield and the surrounding area" and so this Nether Green fixture remains thanks to Tom Lawson's "superb cooking" and the "excellent wine list, with sound advice on the latter" from owner Alistair Myers. / *Details:* www.raftersrestaurant.co.uk; @rafterss11; 8.30 pm; D only, closed Tue & Sun; children: 8.

Silversmiths   £41   3 4 3
111 Arundel St S1 2NT   0114 270 6160
A "really cute dining room", well placed for the University and Lyceum Theatre, "with a menu that pays homage to its Yorkshire roots". / *Details:* www.silversmiths-restaurant.com; @Silversmiths; 9.30 pm, Fri & Sat 9.45; D only, closed Mon & Sun.

Street Food Chef   £12   3 2 2
90 Arundel St S1 4RE   0114 275 2390
For a "good, quick, Mexican" (free for those who triumph in their speed-eating 'El Bastardo' mega-burrito challenge) why not try this "cheap 'n' cheerful cantina"? "They have a takeaway outlet not too far away so you can get food on the go – but just remember the napkins: you'll need them!" / *Details:* www.streetfoodchef.co.uk; @streetfoodchef; 10 pm, Sun 9 pm; No Amex; No bookings.

Vero Gusto   £71   4 5 3
12 Norfolk Row S1 2PA   0114 276 0004
"An absolute gem in a back street near the Crucible" – this "sophisticated Italian could do with more space and better presentation to allow its imaginative and beautiful food to shine more". As great a draw is the "excellent Italian wine list" ("with rarity and exclusive prices at the top end") with very "helpful advice" provided. "It's tiny so booking is essential". / *Details:* www.verogusto.com; 10 pm; closed Mon & Sun.

SHEFFORD, BEDFORDSHIRE   3–1A

Black Horse at Ireland   £55   3 2 2
SG17 5QL   01462 811398
A "well-furnished" 17th-century pub-with-rooms whose "nice countryside location", in a small hamlet, makes it a "favourite", as does cooking that's "still very good". / *Details:* www.blackhorseireland.com; 9.30 pm, Fri & Sat 10 pm; closed Sun D. / *Accommodation:* 2 rooms, from £55

SHELLEY, WEST YORKSHIRE   5–2C

Three Acres   £66   3 4 4
Roydhouse HD8 8LR   01484 602606
"A windswept but lovely location" – high in the hills, near the Emley TV transmitter – sets the scene at this moor-top pub, which has been a well-known culinary destination for decades. It still provokes

the odd accusation of "living off its reputation", but most reports this year said it's "as good as ever" with "solid cooking in huge portions". / **Details:** www.3acres.com; @3AcresInn; 9.30 pm; No Amex. / **Accommodation:** 16 rooms, from £125

"based around local seasonal ingredients, beautifully dressed and presented". ("The owners and co-chefs live above their restaurant and also farm their own allotment, and are avid beekeepers too!"). Top Tip – "set lunch is a real bargain". / **Details:** www.orwellsatshiplake.co.uk; @Orwellshiplake; 9.30 pm; closed Mon, Tue & Sun D.

SHERBORNE, DORSET	2–3B

The Green **£60** 433
3 The Green DT9 3HY 01935 813821
This jewel of the local dining scene "never fails to please", with Russian chef/owner Sasha Matkevich's "imaginative, tasty food perfectly executed in the pleasant room". / **Details:** www.greenrestaurant.co.uk; @greensherborne; 9.30 pm; closed Mon & Sun.

SHERE, SURREY	3–3A

Kinghams **£58** 443
Gomshall Ln GU5 9HE 01483 202168
Paul Baker's stalwart – "a real country house restaurant in a super village setting" – provides a "lovely menu" full of "gorgeous local food" that's slickly delivered by "wonderful" staff. / **Details:** www.kinghams-restaurant.co.uk; @KinghamsShere; off A25 between Dorking & Guildford; 11 pm; closed Mon & Sun D.

SHINFIELD, BERKSHIRE	2–2D

L'Ortolan **£97** 333
Church Ln RG2 9BY 0118 988 8500
"Every mouthful of the beautifully presented food is a joy!", according to fans of this well-known posh destination – a converted manor in a village near the M4's Reading turn-off. Criticisms are sometimes levelled at it – of an atmosphere that's "boring" or food that "promises more than it delivers" – but on balance it's seen as "continuing an excellent tradition under chef Tom Clarke". / **Details:** www.lortolan.com; @lortolan; 8.30 pm; closed Mon & Sun.

SHIPLAKE, OXFORDSHIRE	2–2D

Orwells **£63** 544
Shiplake Row RG9 4DP 0118 940 3673
"In the middle of the woods between Reading and Henley", Ryan Simpson & Liam Trotman's converted pub – "a delightful spot with a secluded garden" – is firmly on the culinary map nowadays. "The interior has been done up smartly whilst retaining the character of a typical old beamy country inn, and is a good blend of ancient and modern". The food "is very definitely haute cuisine", and though the odd reporter "would prefer a bit more simplicity", most are wowed by its "seriously top end" cooking,

SHIPLEY, WEST YORKSHIRE	5–1C

Aagrah **£36** 332
4 Saltaire Rd BD18 3HN 01274 530880
The HQ of this northern Kashmiri chain remains of note for its "great buffet selection" upstairs; "the Indian sweets deserve a special mention" too – "save some space for them!" / **Details:** www.aagrah.com; @Aagrahgroup; 11.30 pm, Sun 10.30 pm; D only.

SHIPSTON-ON-STOUR, WARWICKSHIRE	2–1C

Bower House
Market Place CV36 4AG 01608 663333
Restaurant-with-rooms occupying a beautifully-restored Georgian townhouse, turning out 'modern British food with a French accent' from former West Stoke House chef Darren Brown. The spring 2017 launch was overseen by Henry Harris (of Racine fame) who is now linked to several new projects in London. / **Details:** thebowerhouseshipston.com; @The_Bower_House.

SHIRLEY, DERBYSHIRE	5–3C

The Saracen's Head **£42** 334
Church Lane DE6 3AS 01335 360330
A "reliable and pleasant" spot "in a lovely Derby Dale setting" (and opposite the village church) where the "great pub cooking" wins favour with all reporters. / **Details:** www.saracens-head-shirley.co.uk; 9 pm; No Amex.

SHREWSBURY, SHROPSHIRE	5–3A

Number Four **£38** 333
4 Butcher Row SY1 1UW 01743 366691
"Very busy but fantastically organised and well-run place that's ideal for brunch or lunch in the heart of Shrewsbury" – this "slightly cramped" café offers "very good value" light bites (not least "a huge array of delicious pies" and "the best eggs Benedict ever"). / **Details:** www.number-four.com; Mon-Tue 4pm, Wed-Thu 10 pm, Fri & Sat-11 pm; closed Mon D, Tue D & Wed D.

The Peach Tree £58

21 Abbey Foregate SY2 6AE 01743 355055

Not just one restaurant, but three – the Peach Tree (Mediterranean and British fusion), Cuban bar Havana Republic and Momo-No-Ki ramen bar – all overseen by chef Chris Burt from one kitchen. 'Somehow it works and it's lots of fun' is Jay Rayner's verdict on this Shrewsbury spot. / Details: www.thepeachtree.co.uk; @ThePeachTree1; 8.45 pm, Fri & Sat 9.45 pm.

SLEAT, HIGHLAND 9–2B

Kinloch Lodge £91 ③③③

Sleat IV43 8QY 01471 833333

Taken over by the Macdonald of Macdonalds – Lord Godfrey, 34th hereditary chief of the clan, and his food-writer wife Claire – in 1970, this "beautiful" island bastion is a "real gem" which has long enjoyed acclaim for its "very good" ("but very expensive") cuisine. / Details: www.kinloch-lodge.co.uk; @kinloch_lodge; 9 pm; No Amex. / Accommodation: 19 rooms, from £99

SNAPE, SUFFOLK 3–1D

The Crown Inn £42 ③③④

Bridge Rd IP17 1SL 01728 688324

"Who would have thought, in an out-of-the-way spot such as this, that such a high standard of cooking can be achieved?" – but, defying expectations, "the chef knows his onions" at this 15th-century smugglers' inn, and "they seem to pride themselves on sourcing as much local produce" as possible (down to the on-site pigs). / Details: www.snape-crown.co.uk; off A12 towards Aldeburgh; 9.30 pm, Sat 10 pm, Sun 9.30 pm; No Amex. / Accommodation: 2 rooms, from £90

The Plough and Sail £39 ③③②

Snape Bridge IP17 1SR 01728 688413

"Innovative menu choices, reasonably priced, friendly and satisfactory service": it's "all good" at Alex & Oliver Burnside's roomy pub – "especially considering the nice location on the edge of marshland adjacent to the concert hall and several arty shops" at Snape Maltings. / Details: www.theploughandsailsnape.com/; @PloughandSail; 10 pm.

SNETTISHAM, NORFOLK 6–4B

Rose & Crown £41 ③③③

Old Church Rd PE31 7LX 01485 541382

A packed north Norfolk fixture in moor land – a cosy 14th-century inn that turns out "some

excellent dishes including perfect fish 'n' chips". / Details: www.roseandcrownsnettisham.co.uk; @rosecrownsnetti; 9 pm, Fri & Sat 9.30 pm; No Amex. / Accommodation: 16 rooms, from £90*

SOLIHULL, WEST MIDLANDS 5–4C

Peel's, Hampton Manor £78 ③④⑤

Shadowbrook Lane B92 0EN 01675 446080

This very stately manor set in 45 acres on the outer fringes of Brum received a gong from the tyre men last year, but still inspires very few reviews. Such as came through are ecstatic however: "with a recently awarded star you expect the food to be of a high standard, but it is the innovative nature of the menu and the warm and welcoming service which makes Peel's a truly marvellous dining experience. (Oh! And take a good look at the silk hand embroidered wallpaper in the dining room)". / Details: hamptonmanor.com/; @HamptonManor; 9 pm.

SONNING-ON-THAMES, BERKSHIRE 2–2D

The French Horn £91 ③④⑤

RG4 6TN 0118 969 2204

"A stunning setting, overlooking beautifully manicured gardens and with the River Thames at the bottom of it (some guests arrive by boat)" sets a gorgeous tone at this well-known, long-established Thames-sider, whose old-school style carries through into "a carpeted and curtained dining room with gentle acoustics, very comfortable chairs and generously sized tables, starched linen tablecloths and napkins, and formal (but friendly) service to match". "Wonderful duck roasting in front of the fire in the small entrance lounge" is the famous highlight of the "classic Anglo/French fare", whose performance is – at the not inconsiderable price – somewhere between "patchy" and mostly good. / Details: www.thefrenchhorn.co.uk; @The_French_Horn; 9.30 pm, Sun 9 pm; Booking max 10 may apply. / Accommodation: 21 rooms, from £160

SOUTH DALTON, EAST YORKSHIRE 6–2A

The Pipe & Glass Inn £65 ④⑤⑤

West End HU17 7PN 01430 810246

"Situated in a beautiful East Yorkshire village", James and Kate Mackenzie's "delightful" pub has become one of the best-known in the country, never mind the county, thanks to its "stunning quality of cooking" and "friendly and assiduous staff for whom nothing is too much trouble". It also boasts "a small number of very chic luxurious rooms" – "we were so impressed we are travelling up to Yorkshire

*from the Midlands again this year to celebrate another birthday!" / **Details:** www.pipeandglass.co.uk; @pipeandglass; 9.30 pm, Sun 4 pm; closed Mon & Sun D.*

SOUTH FERRIBY, LINCOLNSHIRE	6–2A

Hope And Anchor   £48   3 4 3

Sluice Road   DN18 6JQ   01652 635334

*Right on the coast, five minutes from the Humber Bridge, and with wonderful views of the estuary, this "busy" large pub-with-rooms wins praise for its "welcoming" style, with "great steaks" (from the Lakes, and showcased in a MaturMeat cabinet) a culinary highlight (although vegan and veggie menus are also a feature). / **Details:** www.thehopeandanchorpub.co.uk; @hopeandanchorsf; 9 pm, Fri & Sat 10 pm, Sun 6 pm; closed Mon & Sun D.*

SOUTH MILTON SANDS, DEVON	1–4C

Beachhouse   £53   3 3 4

TQ7 3JY   01548 561144

*"Very good seafood is served in a rustic manner" at this "timbered shack on the cliffs" – "a crowded, communal place with bench seating a stone's throw from the beach in the beautiful South Hams" which at sunset in particular is "perfect". It's "not cheap" at all, but the "scrumptious", "simple" fare and "glorious" setting lead most reporters to conclude it's "gorgeous". / **Details:** www.beachhousedevon.com.*

SOUTH SHIELDS, TYNE AND WEAR	8–2B

Colmans   £35   5 5 4

182-186 Ocean Rd   NE33 2JQ   0191 456 1202

*"Take away if the sun is shining as the seafront is lovely" at this "always busy" family-run spot, famous for its "top-notch fish 'n' chips, and seafood". In May 2017 they brought their winning formula to iconic seafront building 'Gandhi's Temple', adding extra seafood dishes and a swish cocktail bar. / **Details:** www.colmansfishandchips.com; @ColmansSeafood; L only; No Amex; No bookings.*

SOUTHAMPTON, HAMPSHIRE	2–3D

Lakaz Maman   £25   4 3 3

22 Bedford Place   SO15 2DB   023 8063 9217

A "delightful, bustling Mauritian street food eatery from 2012 MasterChef winner Shelina Permalloo" – "a tiny place with beautiful decor that transports you to a tropical island", complete with "refreshingly different" cuisine that's "great value" too. Top Tip –

*"BYO for a small fee" (there's a "vast off-licence opposite"). / **Details:** www.lakazmaman.com; @lakazmaman; 10 pm, Sun 6 pm.*

---

7 Bone   £29   4 4 4

110 Portswood Road   SO17 2FW

023 8058 4607

*Reporters just "love" this stripped-back, NYC-style diner, turning out cocktails, BBQ fare and "quality" 'dirty' burgers; the owners brought their hit formula to Reading in early 2017, but it's this four-year-old Southampton branch that grabs the most attention. / **Details:** www.7bone.co.uk; 10 pm, Fri & Sat 11 pm, Sun 10 pm.*

SOUTHEND-ON-SEA, ESSEX	3–3C

The Pipe of Port   £52   3 3 3

84 High St   SS1 1JN   01702 614606

*Billing itself as a 'Wine Merchant & Dining Rooms', this ex-Davy's (run independently for over 30 years) is decently rated for its eclectic international fare (with pies and steaks the highlight) but the 150-strong wine list (selected by ex-wine-buyer and owner, Martin Day) is the prime attraction. / **Details:** www.pipeofport.co.uk; @ThePipeofPort; basement just off High Street; Mon-Sat 11 pm; closed Sun; No Amex; children: 16+.*

SOUTHPORT, MERSEYSIDE	5–1A

Bistrot Vérité   £50   3 4 3

7 Liverpool Road   PR8 4AR   01704 564 199

*"The ambience is that of a cosy French bistro, with low-level lighting and small tables" at this "welcoming and very professional" neighbourhood restaurant – a converted shop in Birkdale Village – which is "constantly busy with a local clientele" who "all seem to know each other". Fish soup and tarte tatin are the kind of classic dishes singled out for praise. / **Details:** www.bistrotverite.co.uk; Tue 5.30 pm, Wed-Sat 10 pm; closed Mon & Sun.*

The Vincent Hotel
V-Cafe   £50   3 4 3

98 Lord Street   PR8 1JR   0843 509 4586

*"Popular with Southport's 'glitterati'" – this "buzzy" ("echoey and hard-surfaced") hotel restaurant "overlooking Lord Street's gardens" unusually offers "sushi to die for", plus "consistently good" Italian grub. The food is surprisingly well rated – "even the fish 'n' chips are splendid". / **Details:** www.thevincenthotel.com; @vincenthotel; 10 pm. / **Accommodation:** 60 rooms, from £93*

SOUTHROP, GLOUCESTERSHIRE   2–2C

The Swan at Southrop   £55   3 4 3
GL7 3NU   01367 850205
Part of the sprawling Southrop Manor estate, with its boutique hotel, holiday cottages and cookery school – this plush, ivy-clad gastroboozer continues to garner solid marks for daily changing menus sourced from the kitchen garden. / Details: www.theswanatsouthrop.co.uk; @Thyme_England; Mon-Thu 9 pm, Fri & Sat 9.30 pm; closed Sun D; No Amex.

SOUTHSEA, HAMPSHIRE   2–4D

Restaurant 27   £65   4 4 4
27a Southsea Parade PO5 2JF   023 9287 6272
This smart and "consistent" venue is very much the place to be locally; already home to "excellent food and friendly service" (the tasting menu comes "with lots of little extras and treats") it now appears to be "striving for greater recognition". / Details: www.restaurant27.com; @R27_southsea; Sat 9.30 pm, Sun 2.30 pm; closed Mon, Tue, Wed-Sat L & Sun D.

SOUTHWOLD, SUFFOLK   3–1D

The Crown, Adnams Hotel   £56   1 2 4
90 High St IP18 6DP   01502 722275
"How the mighty have fallen!" at this Adnams inn, which was once a standard-bearer in this pukka seaside town. Its "always buzzy and friendly ambience" survives, but "the food varies alarmingly from inventive and tasty to heavy and uninspired from a menu that doesn't change often enough". / Details: www.adnams.co.uk/stay-with-us/the-crown; @CrownSouthwold; 9 pm; No Amex. / Accommodation: 14 rooms, from £160

Sole Bay Fish Company   £31   4 3 4
22e Blackshore IP18 6ND   01502 724241
"Do not be put off by the shack-like appearance" (it's "very quirky, but that's it's USP") – this "no-frills" restaurant and smokehouse is a "brilliant" place to visit for its "great cold seafood platters plus the option for super fresh fish dishes" by night. For good or ill, there's also now a "limited wine list" in lieu of BYO. / Details: www.solebayfishco.co.uk; closed Mon.

Sutherland House   £52   4 4 3
56 High St IP18 6DN   01502 724544
Reporters "love" the Bank family's medieval B&B, praising its "fabulous" fish-centric cooking. / Details: www.sutherlandhouse.co.uk; @SH_Southwold; 9.30 pm; closed Mon (winter). / Accommodation: 3 rooms, from £150

The Swan
The Market Pl IP18 6EG   01502 722186
This famous Adnams hotel dating back back to the 1600s re-opened in October 2017 (having been closed all year) following a 'once-in-a-generation' refit designed to bring it into the 21st century. Two new restaurants have been created (the more formal Still Room and all-day Tap Room) overseen by new exec head chef, Ross Bott. A re-boot here was past-due: here's hoping it re-establishes itself as the much-loved icon some still remember. / Details: www.adnams.co.uk/stay-with-us/the-swan; @swansouthwold; 9 pm; No Amex; No jeans; children: 5+ at D. / Accommodation: 42 rooms, from £185

SOWERBY BRIDGE, WEST YORKSHIRE   5–1C

Gimbals   £42   4 4 3
76 Wharf St HX6 2AF   01422 839329
In this quaint Yorkshire village, Janet & Simon Baker's eclectically decorated stalwart has long been a "go-to restaurant", owing to its "wonderful seasonal menu and amazing value for money". (In case you were wondering, "a gimbal is a stabiliser" used to keep compasses etc. horizontal in a moving vessel.) / Details: www.gimbals.co.uk; @gimbalsworld; 9.15 pm; D only, closed Sun; No Amex.

Syhiba   £26   5 4 2
HX6 2AF   01422 835959
"Better than the significant local competition"; it's "three times the size it used to be, but there's no change in the quality of the food" at this "consistently excellent", rather posh-looking and "always packed curry restaurant where you can BYO". / Details: www.syhibarestaurant.co.uk; 11.30 pm.

SPARKWELL, DEVON   1–3C

Treby Arms   £74
PL7 5DD   01752 837363
"Amusingly presented food, with fantastic flavours" won huge acclaim under Anton Piotrowski for this quality gastropub (originally built for workers on Brunel's Royal Albert Bridge). But he left just as our 2018 survey was getting underway, and one early report was very mixed, hence we've left it unrated until we receive more reviews on its cuisine under new chef Luke Fearon. / Details: www.thetrebyarms.co.uk; @thetrebyarms; 9 pm; closed Mon.

SPARSHOLT, HAMPSHIRE   2–3D

The Plough Inn   **£40**   **3**|**2**|**4**
Woodman Lane SO21 2NW   01962 776353
A "reliably good" rural gastroboozer with a "fantastic
choice of pub food and finer-dining food" – "it's
always packed" (and "often fully booked"). / **Details:**
www.ploughinnsparsholt.co.uk; 9 pm, Sun & Mon
8.30 pm, Fri & Sat 9.30 pm; No Amex.

ST ALBANS, HERTFORDSHIRE   3–2A

Barrissimo   **£12**   **3**|**4**|**3**
28 St Peters St AL1 3NA   01727 869999
"Everything is freshly prepared and served with a
smile" at this friendly indie, still thriving after the
departure of its popular former owners; it's "so good
to have such a high standard independent coffee
shop in the centre of town". / **Details:** @Barrissimo;
L only; Cash only.

The Cock Inn   **£40**   **2**|**3**|**4**
48 St Peters St AL1 3NF   01727 854816
A 17th-century pub with beamed ceilings, wooden
floors, log fire and garden, handily placed in the
city-centre; fans "have never been disappointed" by
the "very reasonably priced" food (especially lunch)
although cynics feel that it's "variable" at times. /
Details: www.thecockinnstalbans.co.uk; No Amex.

Dylans Kings Arms   **£48**   **3**|**4**|**4**
7 George Street AL3 4ER   01727 530332
This 15th-century boozer long lay dormant, but
is thriving since its revival two years ago by Sean
Hughes, of local light the Boot Inn, and Angela
Hartnett protégé Andrew Knight. It's essentially
a "bar with food, but the food is superb" – with
"unusual and tasty" snacks out front and à la carte
out back. / **Details:** www.dylanskingsarms.com.

Lussmanns   **£52**   **2**|**3**|**3**
Waxhouse Gate, High St AL3 4EW
01727 851941
"Reliable" is the word that crops up most often in
reviews of this "high quality" venture, right by the
cathedral: the original of a small Hertfordshire
chain nowadays backed by Luke Johnson. To fans
it's "the ideal local", and even those who say it's
"not especially remarkable" feel it's "perfectly
competent and worth a return visit". / **Details:**
www.lussmanns.com/restaurants/st-albans-restaurants/;
@lussmanns; 9.30 pm, Fri & Sat 10 pm, Sun 9 pm.

Prime Steak & Grill   **£65**   **3**|**4**|**3**
83 - 85 London Road AL1 1LN   01727 840309
"A shining light in the culinary desert that is St
Albans", this "noisy" city-centre spot services
"excellent steaks", chased with "great cocktails". /
Details: www.primesteakandgrill.com; Mon-Sat 11 pm,
Sun 10 pm.

Tabure   **£43**   **3**|**3**|**3**
AL3 5EG   01727 569068
"Family run and it shows" – a modern Turkish
three-year-old, where reporters are struck by the
"enthusiasm in all aspects"; the brasserie-style
room offers "inspired food with zest" and there's
"always something new to try" on the tapas-led
menu. / **Details:** www.tabure.co.uk/; @Tabure_Kitchen;
10.30 pm.

Thompson   **£73**   **4**|**3**|**3**
2 Hatfield Rd AL1 3RP   01727 730777
"The best restaurant in the area by a long
way" say fans of ex-Auberge du Lac chef Phil
Thompson's town-centre venue: "lovely for a
romantic meal for two" and "they do a great
tasting menu with fresh ingredients" too. / **Details:**
www.thompsonstalbans.co.uk; @ThompsonDining;
9 pm, Fri & Sat 9.30 pm.

ST ANDREWS, FIFE   9–3D

Seafood Restaurant   **£75**   **3**|**3**|**5**
The Scores, Bruce Embankment KY16 9AB
01334 479475
"Sunsets are awesome" at this glam, glass-walled
fish and seafood restaurant, brilliantly located "near
to The Old Course", and enjoying "beautiful views
over the West Sands"; "great scoff, with a panorama
to match". / **Details:** www.theseafoodrestaurant.com;
@seafoodrestau; 9.30 pm; children: 12+ at D.

Vine Leaf   **£46**   **4**|**4**|**3**
131 South Street KY16 9UN   01334 477497
Often tipped as "the best restaurant in St Andrews"
and "still going strong after 30 years"; Morag and
Ian Hamilton's popular favourite serves food that's
"always good quality (especially considering there is
a vast menu)". / **Details:** www.vineleafstandrews.co.uk;
9.15 pm; D only, closed Mon & Sun; Booking evening
only.

ST BRELADE, CHANNEL ISLANDS   –

**Ocean Restaurant, Atlantic
Hotel**   **£90**   **3**|**4**|**4**
Le Mont de la Pulente JE3 8HE   01534 744101
Mark Jordan produces some "superb food" (it's
"almost worth going for the Dauphinoise cappuccino
alone") in the swish dining room of this bayside
country hotel, which boasts fine views. It has kept
the tyre men's favour for a decade now – and even
the most sceptical report this year rated it as very
good all-round. / **Details:** www.theatlantichotel.com;
@atlanticjersey; 10 pm; No jeans. / **Accommodation:**
50 rooms, from £150

ST HELIER, CHANNEL ISLANDS	–

Ormer £78 3️⃣2️⃣3️⃣

7-11 Don Street JE2 4TQ 01534 725100

Shaun Rankin's highly accomplished cuisine from a variety of menus running up to a seven-course tasting option inspires some exceptional ratings for most (if not quite all) visitors to his slick restaurant, bar and deli. / **Details:** *www.ormerjersey.com; @OrmerJersey; 10 pm; closed Sun.*

ST IVES, CORNWALL	1–4A

The Black Rock £45 4️⃣3️⃣2️⃣

Market Pl TR26 1RZ 01736 791911

"Über-fresh fish and shellfish feature large" on the menu of this "small but stylish and tidy" town-centre bistro; "the head chef really knows his ingredients" and "shows them at their best" – though the "clinical" vibe "can't compete for ambience with the best of St Ives". / **Details:** *www.theblackrockstives.co.uk; @TheBlackRock10; 9 pm; D only, closed Sun; No Amex; max. table size 8 in summer.*

Porthgwidden Beach Café £41 2️⃣2️⃣4️⃣

Porthgwidden Beach TR26 1PL 01736 796791

"Facing east, so perfect for breakfast" – this café right on the beach has fine views. For more substantial fare however, it's not the fave rave it once was. / **Details:** *www.porthgwiddencafe.co.uk; 9.30 pm; No Amex; Booking max 10 may apply.*

Porthmeor Beach Cafe £41 4️⃣4️⃣5️⃣

Porthmeor Beach TR26 1JZ 01736 793366

"On a warm summer's evening, there is nowhere better in the UK" – the continuing verdict on this idyllic beachside café, near the Tate. It attracted less feedback than in previous years, but is usually lauded for its seafood tapas, 'build-your-own-breakfast' and mesmeric 'views of the rolling surf. / **Details:** *www.porthmeor-beach.co.uk; @PorthmeorStIves; 9 pm; D only, closed Nov-Mar; No Amex.*

Porthminster Café £64 2️⃣3️⃣5️⃣

Porthminster Beach TR26 2EB 01736 795352

"A beautiful location overlooking Porthminster Beach" remains the 'crown jewel' feature of this "fantastic beach restaurant". But while "it will always be a fantastic location in which to eat, over the years the food has definitely gone downhill", and while it can still deliver "a great, lazy, late Sunday lunch" or "fabulous breakfast overlooking the harbour", compared with yesteryear it's "resting on its laurels". / **Details:** *www.porthminstercafe.co.uk; @PorthBCafe; 9.30 pm; No Amex.*

ST LEONARDS-ON-SEA, EAST SUSSEX	3–4C

Half Man Half Burger £29 3️⃣3️⃣2️⃣

7 Marine Court TN38 0DX 01424 552332

Hip two-year-old burger joint, set in a fabulous seafront Art Deco complex designed to resemble the Queen Mary; it's lauded by all who comment on it for the "best hamburgers ever!" based on "good quality meat" (100% Sussex beef). The owners opened an Eastbourne sibling in December 2016. / **Details:** *www.halfmanhalfburger.com; @HalfManHalfBrgr; 10 pm, Sun 8 pm; No bookings.*

St Clement's £48 3️⃣3️⃣2️⃣

3 Mercatoria TN38 0EB 01424 200355

A "very friendly" backstreet neighbourhood stalwart hidden away from the seafront; with its "fantastic seafood" and "interesting menu" (plus "reasonably priced wines" and "unusual" sober options) reporters just "love visiting this place!" / **Details:** *www.stclementsrestaurant.co.uk; @StClementsRest; 9 pm, Sat 10 pm; closed Mon & Sun D.*

ST MARGARETS, SURREY	1–4A

The Crown £53 3️⃣3️⃣4️⃣

TW1 2NH 020 8892 5896

"The conversion from an old boozer has been superbly well done" at this "buzzy" Georgian tavern (part of a local chain) which has a "lovely garden area" too. With its "high standard of cooking" and "genuinely friendly and attentive staff", "it's clearly part of the Twickenham fabric" nowadays. / **Details:** *www.crowntwickenham.co.uk; @crowntwickenham; Booking max 7 may apply.*

ST MAWES, CORNWALL	1–4B

Hotel Tresanton £68 2️⃣3️⃣5️⃣

27 Lower Castle Road TR2 5DR 01326 270055

Transformed by 'The Hotel Inspector' Olga Polizzi two decades back, this luxe boutique hotel is a striking spot – all Mediterranean chic, and with stellar views over the bay to the Roseland Peninsula. Reports on its seafood-centric restaurant are more mixed, however, with those drawn by "glowing reviews" apt to leave "wondering what all the hype is about". / **Details:** *www.tresanton.com; @hoteltresanton; 9 pm; Booking max 10 may apply; children: 6+ at dinner.* / **Accommodation:** *40 rooms, from £250*

Watch House £60 4️⃣3️⃣3️⃣

1 The Square TR2 5DJ 01326 270038

"A welcoming café" ("great for children and dogs") with "no-nonsense decor" and a "fantastic" location

*"literally on the beach", in West Bay; the "very good food" includes wood-fired pizzas and "some splendid seafood". / **Details:** www.watchhousestmawes.co.uk.*

ST MERRYN, CORNWALL   1–3B

The Cornish Arms   £42   🟥2️⃣2️⃣
Churchtown PL28 8ND   01841 520288
*On the one hand, many regulars hail the Stein family's big, "bustling" inn as a "perfect neighbourhood spot", offering "real value for money" cooking in a still-pub-like setting ("good for a casual drink"), and a no-nonsense, 'welcome all comers' approach ("it's the first time we've seen nearly as many well-behaved dogs as guests for Sunday lunch"). On the downside, service can be "lacklustre" and "the slightly barn like interior detracts from the experience". / **Details:** www.rickstein.com; 8.30 pm; No Amex; Online only.*

ST PETER PORT, CHANNEL ISLANDS   –

Da Nello   £50   3️⃣3️⃣4️⃣
46, Le Pollet GY1 1WF   01481 721552
*"We come back, again and again whenever we're on the island" – this "helpful and friendly" Italian veteran in a 500-year-old building with pretty courtyard and atrium-topped restaurant continues to win a thumbs up. / **Details:** www.danello.gg; 10 pm.*

The Old Government House   £73   3️⃣4️⃣3️⃣
St Ann's Pl GY1 2NU   01481 724921
*"The Brasserie at the OGH does all you would expect from a top quality hotel: good food, well presented and impeccably served" (including a popular afternoon tea option). / **Details:** www.theoghhotel.com; @OGH_Guernsey; L only; Jacket required.*

Le Petit Bistro   £59   4️⃣2️⃣4️⃣
56 Lower Pollet GY1 1WF   01481 725055
*Romantic and very French establishment, tucked on a street corner by the harbour in St Peter Port; fish comes straight off the boat, while gourmet Gallic specialities like foie gras are sourced from the famed Rungis market outside Paris. / **Details:** www.petitbistro.co.uk; @PetitBistroGsy; 10 pm, Fri & Sat 10.30 pm; closed Sun.*

ST TUDY, CORNWALL   1–3B

St Tudy Inn   £52   3️⃣3️⃣3️⃣
Bodmin PL30 3NN   01208 850656
An "atmospheric old pub" in a "lovely village" taken over by "very talented" chef Emily Scott (ex-Harbour

*Inn, Port Isaac) two years back. Its "consistently excellent food (mainly seafood)" earns it a place "in the upper echelons of Cornish gastropubs". / **Details:** www.sttudyinn.com; @sttudyinn; 9 pm; closed Mon & Sun D; No Amex.*

STADHAMPTON, OXFORDSHIRE   2–2D

The Crazy Bear   £65   2️⃣3️⃣3️⃣
Bear Ln OX44 7UR   01865 890714
*Reports have been perennially up-and-down in recent years at this rural Anglo-Thai (each cuisine gets a dining room) and it continues to split opinion; fans hail its "reliably delicious" cooking, and the respectively "wonderfully over-the-top" (restaurant) or "quirky" (bar) decor, while critics feel the "OK but not spectacular" food comes at a cost that's "rather steep". / **Details:** www.crazybeargroup.co.uk; @CrazyBearGroup; 10 pm; children: 12+ at Fri & Sat D. / **Accommodation:** 16 rooms, from £169*

STAMFORD, LINCOLNSHIRE   6–4A

The George Hotel   £76   2️⃣2️⃣4️⃣
71 St Martins PE9 2LB   01780 750750
*"The panelled dining room is a wonderful place, almost untouched by time: all fine linen, gleaming cutlery and shining glass", at this huge, storybook coaching inn, at the centre of a marvellous Georgian town. "For traditional cuisine, including a dramatic beef trolley" with "classically fine" wines it does have many fans, although the experience can not-so-infrequently end up seeming "ludicrously expensive for indifferent food". NB Courtyard dining and a Garden Room bistro also feature on-site. / **Details:** www.georgehotelofstamford.com; @GeorgeStamford; 9.30 pm; Jacket required; children: 8+ at D. / **Accommodation:** 47 rooms, from £190*

Lambert's   £45   4️⃣4️⃣3️⃣
5 Cheyne Lane PE9 2AX   01780 767 063
*"Ex-Hambleton Hall chef Stephen Conway's deli-café" – soups and sandwiches by day, and fine dining on Thursday and Friday nights – wins praise for its "really good food and value". (It's named after celebrated fat man, Daniel Lambert, who 'exhibited himself for profit' in the 1800s.) / **Details:** www.lamberts-stamford.co.uk.*

STANHOE, NORFOLK   6–3B

The Duck Inn   £51   4️⃣4️⃣3️⃣
Burnham Rd PE31 8QD   01485 518 330
"Exceptional and high class cuisine, but with a real Norfolk smile… and the booze isn't bad either!" – that's the winning formula for this "relaxing and friendly gastropub with a good

range of local produce". "Definitely recommended if you find yourself in north Norfolk!" / **Details:** www.duckinn.co.uk; @duck_inn; 9 pm, Sun 7.45 pm.

STANTON, SUFFOLK 3–1C

Leaping Hare Vineyard £56 3️⃣3️⃣5️⃣
Wyken Vineyards IP31 2DW 01359 250287
"There's plenty to enthuse about" at this "gorgeous" oak-framed barn – the café of the acclaimed Wyken vineyard – "they do field to fork very well here" and "their own wines are always special". / **Details:** www.wykenvineyards.co.uk; 9m NE of Bury St Edmunds; follow tourist signs off A143; Fri & Sat 9 pm; L only, ex Fri & Sat open L & D.

STEIN, HIGHLAND 9–2A

Loch Bay Restaurant £55 5️⃣4️⃣4️⃣
1 Macleods Terrace IV55 8GA 01470 592235
"Michael Smith (formerly of foodie favourite The Three Chimneys) has taken dining in Skye to a new level of brilliance" according to fans of this small and "charming" venture (opened in spring 2016). The style here is "lovely" ("relaxed in a typical Skye way") and more informal than its other gourmet rivals in these parts, and he serves "beautiful" food (with the choice in the evening of a three-courser, or a five-course 'fruits de mer' menu). / **Details:** www.lochbay-seafood-restaurant.co.uk; @lochbayskye/; 22m from Portree via A87 and B886; 8m from Dunvegan; 8.45 pm, Sun 1.45 pm; closed Mon, Tue L, Wed L, Thu L, Fri L, Sat & Sun; No Amex; children: 8+ at D.

STOCKBRIDGE, HAMPSHIRE 2–3D

Clos du Marquis £56 3️⃣4️⃣3️⃣
London Rd SO20 6DE 01264 810738
In an out-of-the-way location, this former pub is now a "very characterful – and very French – restaurant" (run, somewhat unexpectedly, by a South African); all reports acclaim "classic cooking (in the best sense) with the flavours of good local ingredients shining through". / **Details:** www.closdumarquis.co.uk; 2m E on A30 from Stockbridge; 9 pm; closed Mon & Sun D.

Greyhound £63 3️⃣2️⃣4️⃣
31 High Street SO20 6EY 01264 810833
"As well as having outside seating on the River Test" this 1800s gastropub-with-rooms wins praise for its "lovely locally sourced foods, great ambience and good service" from (nearly) all reporters. / **Details:** www.thegreyhoundonthetest.co.uk; @GHStockbridge; 9.30 pm; Booking max 12 may apply. / **Accommodation:** 7 rooms, from £100

Thyme & Tides £33 3️⃣2️⃣2️⃣
The High St SO20 6HE 01264 810101
"Perfect for brunch", Friday fish 'n' chip nights or "excellent light meals" ("the deli sandwich is much more than it sounds") this posh café and fishmonger resides "in a Stockbridge deli – and in the garden behind, when the sun shines". / **Details:** www.thymeandtidesdeli.co.uk; @thymeandtides; closed Mon; No Amex; Booking weekends only.

STOCKCROSS, BERKSHIRE 2–2D

The Vineyard at Stockcross £95 4️⃣3️⃣3️⃣
RG20 8JU 01635 528770
"The cellar is the key point of the exercise", at Sir Peter Michael's "lovely" contemporary-style Relais & Châteaux property, built in part to showcase the vintages of his Sonoma county vineyard in California. But that is not to diss the accompanying cuisine from chef Robby Jenks, which was credited for a number of "sublime" meals here this year. Historically a rather pricey destination, the price/quality ratio seems to have moved in the customer's favour in recent times. / **Details:** www.the-vineyard.co.uk; @VineyardNewbury; from M4, J13 take A34 towards Hungerford; 9.30 pm; No jeans. / **Accommodation:** 49 rooms, from £194

STOCKPORT, CHESHIRE 5–2B

Easy Fish Company £58 3️⃣3️⃣3️⃣
117 Heaton Moor Road SK4 4HY
0161 442 0823
"Why aren't there more places like this?" – a "super" café-style space "at the back of a fishmonger and worth seeking out", for its "fabulous fresh fish cooked to order and a friendly and relaxed atmosphere". / **Details:** www.theeasyfishco.com; 11.30 pm.

Where The Light Gets In £105 5️⃣5️⃣4️⃣
7 Rostron Row SK1 1JY 0161 477 5744
"A thrilling new venture with great potential!" – Sam Buckley's new opening in a former coffee warehouse is proving an immediate hit, with its "blind tasting menu and open kitchen" and "excellent" Nordic (or maybe just 'nouvelle northern') cuisine (which press critic Marina O'Loughlin described as 'the most exciting food I've eaten in years'). / **Details:** wtlgi.co; @wtlgi; 9 pm.

STOKE HOLY CROSS, NORFOLK 6–4C

Stoke Mill £63 3️⃣2️⃣4️⃣
Mill Road NR14 8PA 01508 493337
Set in an attractively situated and converted old

mill – once home to the business that grew into Colman's Mustard – creates an atmospheric setting for Andy Rudd's contemporary-style country venture, where "the high standard of cooking" means "the restaurant regularly seems to be playing to a packed house". / **Details:** www.stokemill.co.uk; @StokeMill.

The Wildebeest Arms   £56   [5][4][3]
82-86 Norwich Rd NR14 8QJ 01508 492497
"A great favourite in earlier years", this wee village gastropub went through a minor lull "but is now in the hands of Daniel Smith of The Swan at Ingham (formerly Le Gavroche) and serving high quality fresh ingredients, well chosen and tastily cooked". / **Details:** thewildebeest.co.uk/; @wildebeestarms; from A140, turn left at Dunston Hall, left at T-junction; 9 pm.

STOKE ROW, OXFORDSHIRE   2–2D

The Crooked Billet   £58   [4][4][5]
Newlands Ln RG9 5PU 01491 681048
Paul Clerehugh "has really found the formula to please his customers" at this "tucked out-of-the-way" gastropub "down the narrow country lanes" of the Chiltern Hills, between Reading and Henley, where "there is always a friendly smile and something delicious on the menu". "I've been coming here roughly once a fortnight over 15 years, and it never fails to please!" / **Details:** www.thecrookedbillet.co.uk; @Crooked_Billet; off the A4130; 10 pm, Sat 10.30 pm.

STOKE-BY-NAYLAND, SUFFOLK   3–2C

The Crown   £50   [3][4][5]
Park Street CO6 4SE 01206 262001
"Wonderful pub food in lovely surroundings" wins (practically) unanimous praise for this "must-go-to" modern gastropub in Constable Country – an "always busy" but "well-run" operation offering "an extensive wine list and good beer too", plus attractive outside dining in summer (and accommodation). / **Details:** www.crowninn.net; @crowninnsuffolk; on B1068; Mon-Thu 9.30 pm, Fri & Sat 10 pm, Sun 9 pm. / **Accommodation:** 11 rooms, from £11

STOW ON THE WOLD, GLOUCESTERSHIRE
2–1C

The Old Butchers   £55   [4][4][3]
Park St GL54 1AQ 01451 831700
Launched in 2015, Peter & Louise Robinson's "fantastic little restaurant in the heart of the Cotswolds" is "as wonderful as always", and while this cosy spot espouses the nose-to-tail ethos, confusingly it actually specialises in "immaculate" seafood. / **Details:** www.theoldbutchers.com;

@Theoldbutchers; on the main road heading out of Stow on the Wold towards Oddington; 9.30 pm, Sat 10 pm; closed Mon & Sun; Booking max 12 may apply.

STRACHUR, ARGYLL AND BUTE   9–4B

Inver Restaurant   £55   [5][4][4]
Stracthlachlan PA27 8BU 01369 860537
On the Cowal Peninsula beside the shores of Loch Fyne, Pam Brunton and Rob Latimer's waterside dining room (once known as Inver Cottage) again inspires ecstatic feedback for its Nordic-style cuisine and "romantic" setting. / **Details:** www.inverrestaurant.co.uk; @inverrestaurant; 8.30 pm, Sun 3 pm; closed Mon & Tue & Sun D.

STRATFORD UPON AVON, WARWICKSHIRE
2–1C

The Fuzzy Duck   £51   [3][3][3]
Ilmington Rd CV37 8DD 01608 682635
"Worth the eight mile trip out of Stratford to find it!" This "contemporary-style restaurant with rooms" is "a great example of a reinvented country pub" ("good to see it still welcomes drinkers"), and with consistently well-rated cooking. "Staff are extremely efficient and helpful – down to the barmaid who called her uncle to taxi us back to town!" / **Details:** www.fuzzyduckarmscote.com/; 9 pm, Fri & Sat 9.30 pm, Sun 3 pm; closed Mon & Sun D.

Lambs   £50   [2][2][3]
12 Sheep Street CV37 6EF 01789 292554
"Ideal for pre-theatre" – the tenor of most reports on this "cheap and cheerful" outfit; the cosy, wood-beamed venue dates from the early 16th century, making it one of the oldest houses in town. / **Details:** www.lambsrestaurant.co.uk; @lambsrestaurant; 9 pm; closed Mon L; No Amex.

Loxleys   £53   [4][3][3]
3 Sheep St CV37 6EF 01789 292128
On two floors of a former city-centre clothes shop, this "very popular" five-year-old has an "ambience that varies depending on the room" and wins nothing but praise for its "lovely and reasonably priced food" from a large and versatile menu incorporating sharing plates and char-grilled steaks. / **Details:** loxleysrestaurant.co.uk/; @twitter.com/Loxleys; 11 pm, Sun 10.30 pm.

No. 9   £57   [3][3][2]
9 Church Street CV37 6HB 01789 415522
Wayne Thomson's quite ambitious venture is one of the town's best culinary destinations. The interior can seem a mite "bland", but his cooking wins (nearly) unanimous praise – not just the "excellent and reasonable pre-theatre menus" but also a tasting

option: "comforting regular dishes mixed with more innovative creations". / **Details:** *no9churchst.com; @dineno9; 9.30 pm.*

The Oppo £47 2️⃣2️⃣3️⃣
13 Sheep Street CV37 6EF 01789 269980
There's a "nice Tudor feel" to this stalwart bistro; some reviewers feel the food is a little "dull" or "just cruising", but more often it's felt to be "accurate, reliable and efficiently delivered". / **Details:** www.theoppo.co.uk; @OppoStratford; 9.30 pm, Fri & Sat 11 pm; closed Sun; No Amex; Booking max 12 may apply.

Rooftop Restaurant, Royal Shakespeare Theatre £44 3️⃣3️⃣4️⃣
Waterside CV37 6BB 01789 403449
"Make sure you have a table with a view" ("it's worth going just for the views of Stratford") if you stray up to the RSC's rooftop venue in the gods of the old theatre. It's not a foodie destination, but it's consistently well-rated. / **Details:** www.rsc.org.uk/eat; 9.45 pm; No Amex; Online only.

Sabai Sabai £41 3️⃣5️⃣4️⃣
19-20 Wood Street CV37 6JF 01789 508220
Limited but very positive feedback so far on this branch of a local mini-chain of upmarket Thai restaurants, which wins high marks all-round, especially for its "exceptional" service. / **Details:** sabaisabai-restaurant.co.uk; @sabaisabai1.

STUCKTON, HAMPSHIRE 2–3C

The Three Lions £62 3️⃣3️⃣2️⃣
Stuckton Rd SP6 2HF 01425 652489
"A bit of a time capsule but delightful nevertheless" – Mike & Jayne Womersley's "friendly and approachable" New Forest inn "never disappoints", not least owing to ex-Lucknam Park chef Mike's "unfussy" but "high quality" cooking. / **Details:** www.thethreelionsrestaurant.co.uk; off the A338; 9 pm, Fri & Sat 9.30 pm; closed Mon & Sun D; No Amex. / **Accommodation:** 7 rooms, from £105

STUDLAND, DORSET 2–4C

Pig on the Beach £54 3️⃣3️⃣5️⃣
Manor House, Manor Road BH19 3AU
01929 450288
"The house has a fairytale feel and the location looking out over Studland Bay is unbeatable" at this clifftop 'Pig' – "with views to die for". It expresses similar "well-heeled" but dressed down DNA to others in the chain, with similar pros and cons. There's a "cool", vibe in its restaurant conservatory, where "classic British dishes" ("sourced from both its own walled garden and from within 25 miles") are "served in generous portions" and where

"children are treated with charm and aplomb". On the downside, factor in "London prices" and the odd fear of "style over substance". / **Details:** www.thepighotel.com/on-the-beach/; 9.30 pm.

Shellbay £49 3️⃣4️⃣4️⃣
Ferry Road BH19 3BA 01929 450363
"A great location with sunset views over Poole harbour" guarantees a crowd at this "lovely", "relaxed" and "very romantic" restaurant; "the food is good also" – "very tasty fresh fish dishes, though erring on the side of pricey" ("not surprising as it seems to be full of very wealthy-looking Sandbanks types!") / **Details:** www.shellbay.net; near the Sandbanks to Swanage ferry; 9 pm.

SUDBURY, SUFFOLK 3–2C

Secret Garden £39 4️⃣4️⃣4️⃣
17 - 21 Friars Street CO10 2AA
01787 372030
In late 2016, a hit local café spawned this bold new offshoot – a wine bar and fine dining haunt (with prices to match) set in Buzzards Hall, the grand 400-year-old timbered building next door. The restaurant is open from Wednesday to Saturday for dinner (enjoy charcuterie and an artisanal cheese trolley in the bar); initial feedback is stellar, but devoid of detail. / **Details:** www.tsg.uk.net; 9 pm.

Shillingfords, The Quay Theatre £41 5️⃣4️⃣3️⃣
Quay Lane CO10 2AN 01787 374745
"A small, intimate restaurant at the top of the Quay theatre" which inspires effusive reports of Carl Shillingford's "star-quality dishes" from "fabulous ingredients" (for which he himself goes foraging), all "beautifully presented". NB this pop-up-style spot is open on Friday and Saturday nights only. / **Details:** www.quaysudbury.com/shillingfords-quay; @thequaytheatre; 11 pm.

SUMMERHOUSE, COUNTY DURHAM 8–3B

Raby Hunt £130 5️⃣3️⃣3️⃣
DL2 3UD 01325 374237
"I cried it was so good!"… "the single most satisfying food I've eaten in my 35 years on the planet!"… "James Close is one of the top, top chefs in the country and his incredible passion is shown in every detail" at this restaurant-with-rooms, "set in an unimposing, out-of-the-way village, in the Durham Dales". That said, since it was awarded two Michelin Stars its ratings actually declined a fraction this year as it took flak for a couple of disappointing experiences. Perhaps, though, it was the strain of preparing to have the builders in? (Towards the end of the survey, in May 2017,

the restaurant closed for a £400k extension and redevelopment, the building of a new restaurant entrance, and the installation of glass walls so diners can watch the chef and his team at work.) / **Details:** www.rabyhuntrestaurant.co.uk/; @therabyhunt; 9.30 pm; closed Mon, Tue & Sun. / **Accommodation:** 2 rooms, from £125

SUNBURY ON THAMES, SURREY   3–3A

Indian Zest £48   5 4 3
21 Thames Street TW16 5QF   01932 765000
"It may not have the cachet of a London address but it has a wow factor!" – Manoj Vasaikar's large, colonial-style villa out in the 'burbs delivers some "beautifully presented dishes" that are "tip top". Top Tips – "the lunch menu is particularly good" and they go "great take-out too". / **Details:** www.indianzest.co.uk; @Indian_Zest; midnight.

SUNNINGDALE, BERKSHIRE   3–3A

Bluebells £69   3 3 2
Shrubs Hill SL5 0LE   01344 622722
Deceptively humble-looking roadside feature offering "top-quality food with great service" (and at "very keen" prices too). While redevelopment into luxury flats is mooted, they were still taking bookings for Christmas 2017 ("we are hoping the new owners keep the place, as we would be lost without them!") / **Details:** www.bluebells-restaurant.com; 9.45 pm; closed Mon & Sun D.

SUNNINGHILL, BERKSHIRE   3–3A

Carpenter's Arms £57   3 3 4
78 Upper Village Rd SL5 7AQ   01344 622763
What was once a run-of-the-mill pub is now a "very Gallic" establishment that's "top for everyday simple dining". "Ignore any negative online reviews you see about the owners – they are great and just being French!" / **Details:** www.laclochepub.com; 10 pm.

SURBITON, SURREY   3–3A

The French Table £64   5 5 3
85 Maple Rd KT6 4AW   020 8399 2365
"Fully-booked, all night, even on a wet Thursday evening, in deepest Surbiton!!" – this well-discovered Gallic gem can, to first timers, seem like "an amazing find for somewhere hidden in a suburban shopping parade on a minor road". "Consistently excellent over many years, it's a fantastic achievement for the husband & wife proprietors", Sarah and Eric Guignard. "Seasonal produce is always centre-stage and unfussily marshalled into

unfailingly delicious dishes, while front-of-house staff make you feel very well looked after". "I feel genuinely blessed to have such a wonderful restaurant so close to where I live!" / **Details:** www.thefrenchtable.co.uk; @thefrenchtable; 10.30 pm; closed Mon & Sun.

No 97 £54   3 4 4
97 Maple Road KT6 4AW   020 3411 9797
"An unexpected treat in Surbiton" that "feels like London out of London" owing to the "buzz they have created" since opening in 2016; the downstairs gin bar offers an "amazing list" that's "served with style", and the "sophisticated food" has some "unique details and flourishes". Stop Press – rumours afoot that the team are set to take over the Retro Bistrot in Teddington. / **Details:** no-97.co.uk; @no_ninetyseven; 9 pm.

SUTTON GAULT, CAMBRIDGESHIRE   3–1B

The Anchor £49   3 2 3
Bury Ln CB6 2BD   01353 778537
"Next to the dyke for one of the fen drains" – the setting of this inn on the Great Ouse is "very, not slightly, bleak!" On the plus side there's "excellent" grub and guest beers and "it's been very reliable over the years". / **Details:** www.anchorsuttongault.co.uk; @TheanchorinnSG; 7m W of Ely, signposted off B1381 in Sutton; Mon-Fri 9 pm, Sat 9.30 pm, Sun 8.30 pm; No Amex. / **Accommodation:** 4 rooms, from £80

SWANSEA, SWANSEA   1–1C

Hanson At The Chelsea Restaurant £47   3 3 3
17 St Marys St SA1 3LH   01792 466200
Chef Andrew Hanson's staple remains a superior option locally ("better than most in central Swansea") thanks to its "good menu" and "proper dishes", often revolving around fish and seafood. Upstairs is preferred to the basement. / **Details:** www.hansonatthechelsea.co.uk; @hacolsa13l; 9.30 pm; No Amex.

Patricks With Rooms £58   3 3 3
638 Mumbles Rd SA3 4EA   01792 360199
Mumbles Bay restaurant-with-rooms benefiting from "agreeable service and a pleasant room overlooking Swansea bay"; it's "well worth seeking out, particularly at lunchtime", and overnighters laud the "lovely Welsh breakfast with cockles and laverbread". / **Details:** www.patrickswithrooms.com; @PatricksMumbles; in Mumbles, 1m before pier; 9.50 pm; closed Sun D. / **Accommodation:** 10 rooms, from £110

TADWORTH, SURREY	3–3B

The Blue Ball £44 🖪🖪🖪
Deans Lane, Walton on the Hill KT20 7UE
01737 819003
*The latest addition to the popular Whiting &
Hammond chain – this well-refurbished gastropub
with large garden wins high all-round ratings for its
decent cooking and inviting atmosphere. / Details:
www.theblueball.co.uk; @TheBlueBall_.*

TAPLOW, BERKSHIRE	3–3A

**The Astor Grill, Cliveden
Hotel** £72 🖪🖪🖪
Clivedon Road SL6 0JF 01628 607107
*Limited and mixed feedback on Cliveden's one-year-
old 'dressed down' option in the Stable Block. For
fans it's "a hidden gem", tipped for either a "family
lunch" or "business meal just off the M4", but for
foes "overpriced with rubbish service". / Details:
www.clivedenhouse.co.uk; @TheAstorGrill; 9.30 pm.*

**André Garrett At Cliveden,
Cliveden House** £105 🖪🖪🖪
Cliveden Rd SL6 0JF 01628 668561
*"The best view from a restaurant in Berkshire and
some of the very best food too from André Garrett"
create huge "romantic" appeal for the dining room
of this famous mansion and "though you take out
another mortgage, the place has 'between the
sheets' in its DNA". But while some reporters find
it "stuffy" others detect "a flicker on the naff-o-
meter" ("disparate groups of people having dinner
and spending the whole time on their mobile, or
as we saw in the summer, slightly mismatched
couples taking selfies on the terrace"). / Details:
www.clivedenhouse.co.uk; @Cliveden_House; 9.45 pm;
No trainers. / Accommodation: 48 rooms, from £445*

TATTENHALL, CHESHIRE	5–3A

Allium by Mark Ellis £65 🖪🖪🖪
Lynedale House, High Street CH3 9PX
01829 771477
*This "whitewashed former village shop has turned
gunmetal grey" with its transformation at the
hands of the ex-head chef of nearby Peckforton
Castle into an ambitious restaurant with rooms.
There's the odd mixed report on the service, but
most feedback suggests it's one to watch. / Details:
www.theallium.co.uk; @AlliumbyMark; Wed-Sat 9 pm,
Sun 6 pm.*

TAUNTON, SOMERSET	2–3A

Augustus £54 🖪🖪🖪
3 The Courtyard, St James St TA1 1JR
01823 324354
*"Still one of the only quality restaurants in Taunton's
culinary desert", this "lovely tucked-away venue" just
"gets better and better"; the ex-Castle Hotel team
serve up "consistent, inventive and wholesome food"
and it's "beautifully presented" to boot. / Details:
www.augustustaunton.co.uk; @augustustaunton;
9.30 pm; closed Mon & Sun; No Amex.*

**The Castle Bow
Restaurant** £61 🖪🖪🖪
Castle Bow TA1 1NF 01823 328328
*"Tasting menus can be risky: here it was terrific!"
Liam Finnegan's accomplished cuisine wins very
good all-round scores for this plush, traditional-
looking restaurant in the centre of the town (just
under the archway in Castle Bow). "Fabulous
afternoon teas" also rate mention. / Details:
www.castlebow.com; @CastleBow; 9.30 pm; children: 5.*

TEDDINGTON, MIDDLESEX	3–3A

Imperial China £42 🖪🖪🖪
196-198 Stanley Rd TW11 8UE
020 8977 8679
*"Terrific dim sum" is the main event at this large
and swanky suburban Chinese ("we are often
the only Europeans in there") but "they do other
dishes extremely well" too; "a real find, in that
it is not in the West End, but a heck of a lot
better than some Chinatown joints". / Details:
www.imperialchinalondon.co.uk; 11 pm, Fri & Sat
11.30 pm, Sun 10 pm.*

**The King's Head, The White
Brasserie Company** £42 🖪🖪🖪
123 High St TW11 8HG 020 3166 2900
*An "easy, relaxed local", from Raymond Blanc's
White Brasserie Company, set in a refurb'd Victorian
gastroboozer with snugs, log fires and a walled patio.
/ Details: kingsheadteddington.com/.*

TEIGNMOUTH, DEVON	1–3D

Crab Shack £44 🖪🖪🖪
3 Queen St TQ14 9HN 01626 777956
*"Unbelievably fresh seafood" ("an incredible treat
for crab lovers…", "tasty lobster roll", "fillets of
various fish") are "caught daily by local trawlers"
and "delivered straight from boat to plate in hours"
at this "funky waterfront location". "A lively shack
tucked away on the back beach", there's "nothing*

fancy about it", but service is "with a smile" and "the only problem is getting a table". / **Details:** www.crabshackonthebeach.co.uk/; 9 pm; closed Mon & Tue; No Amex.

TETBURY, GLOUCESTERSHIRE   2–2B

Gumstool Inn, Calcot Manor   **£52**   **3** **3** **4**
GL8 8YJ   01666 890391
Well-scrubbed-up, pub-style venue, incorporated within a swish, family-friendly Cotswolds country house hotel as its more relaxed dining option, and consistently highly rated for its quality cooking and "delightful" style. / **Details:** www.calcotmanor.co.uk; @Calcot_Manor; crossroads of A46 & A41345; 9.30 pm, Sun 9 pm; No jeans; No bookings; children: 12+ at dinner in Conservatory. / **Accommodation:** 35 rooms, from £240

THORNHAM, NORFOLK   6–3B

Eric's Fish & Chips   **£24**   **4** **3** **3**
Drove Orchard, Thornham Rd PE36 6LS
01485 472025
"A fish 'n' chip shop with a difference" – this industrial-chic venture run by Titchwell Manor chef Eric Snaith, is for its fans "a must-visit on the north Norfolk coast". / **Details:** www.ericsfishandchips.com; @ericsFandC; 9 pm; No bookings.

The Orange Tree   **£60**   **4** **4** **4**
High St PE36 6LY   01485 512213
In this pretty coastal village, this laidback and well-reputed dining pub-with-rooms is particularly known for its local seafood ("best moules marinières ever"). / **Details:** www.theorangetreethornham.co.uk; @OTThornham; 9.30 pm; No Amex. / **Accommodation:** 6 rooms, from £89

THORNTON CLEVELEYS, LANCASHIRE   5–1A

Twelve Restaurant & Lounge Bar   **£50**   **4** **4** **3**
Marsh Mill Village, Fleetwood Road North
FY5 4JZ   01253 821212
Opposite Europe's tallest working windmill, this "very consistent" husband-and-wife spot near Blackpool is praised by reporters for "17 years of top service and excellent food". Dishes are "clean-tasting" and "well prepared" and (post- a lorry crashing into it!) the new decor is appealing too, with booths and industrial-chic accents. / **Details:** www.twelve-restaurant.co.uk; closed Mon, Tue-Sat D only, closed Sun D.

THORNTON HOUGH, MERSEYSIDE   5–2A

Lawns Restaurant, Thornton Hall Hotel & Spa   **£66**   **4** **4** **3**
Neston Rd CH63 1JF   0151 336 3938
The new chef (Ben Mounsey) at this striking hotel dining room with a "stately home ambience" had a lot to live up to in predecessor Matt Worswick; even the odd reporter who initially found the style of cuisine "OTT" feels it's now "better suited to the venue", and all reviews still rate the cooking highly here. / **Details:** www.thorntonhallhotel.com; @thelawnsrest; 11 pm; Booking max 8 may apply.

The Red Fox   **£45**   **3** **3** **4**
Liverpool Road CH64 7TL   0151 353 2920
An "above average addition to the Brunning & Price chain"; this two-year-old acquisition, in a striking former country club, combines "friendly staff" and "always good pub food" (that's "good value" to boot). / **Details:** www.brunningandprice.co.uk/redfox; @redfoxpub; Mon-Sat 10 pm, Sun 9.30 pm.

TILLINGTON, WEST SUSSEX   3–4A

The Horse Guards Inn   **£44**   **4** **5** **5**
Upperton Rd GU28 9AF   01798 342 332
With "a beautiful garden for relaxing in Summer and such a cosy interior for cold winters" – this very popular, "upmarket dining pub" in "a gorgeous part of the country beneath the South Downs and on the edge of Petworth Park" is something of a rural idyll with "always welcoming and jovial staff" and "imaginative food from local produce". / **Details:** www.thehorseguardsinn.co.uk; 9 pm, Fri & Sat 9.30 pm; No Amex.

TITCHWELL, NORFOLK   6–3B

Titchwell Manor   **£60**   **4** **4** **3**
Titchwell Manor PE31 8BB   01485 210221
With its "wonderfully appointed" rooms, and "glorious walks nearby", the Snaith family's "beautiful", updated Victorian hotel is "the perfect place for recharging and restoring calm"; chef Chris Mann has come up with a "superb menu" that "pays great attention to its Norfolk coast setting". "Can't wait to go back!" / **Details:** www.titchwellmanor.com; @TitchwellManor; 9.30 pm.

TITLEY, HEREFORDSHIRE   2–1A

Stagg Inn   **£61**   **2** **3** **3**
HR5 3RL   01544 230221
"Locally sourced ingredients are always of the highest quality, and the wines (supplied by the excellent Tanners of Hereford) always do justice

to the food", say fans of this well-known pub, in a tiny village. But while it was the Good Pub Guide 2018's dining pub of the year for Herefordshire, our feedback this year was quite unsettled with a couple of "ghastly" visits reported. / **Details:** www.thestagg.co.uk; @TheStaggInn; on B4355, NE of Kington; 9 pm; closed Mon & Tue; Credit card deposit required to book. / **Accommodation:** 7 rooms, from £100

TOBERMORY, ARGYLL AND BUTE	9–3A

Cafe Fish Tobermory   £48   **5 4 4**
The Pier PA75 6NU   01688 301253
"This is seafood heaven" – a "wonderful, vibrant café" set "in the old ferry terminal building", on the edge of the harbour, where the "excellent fish meals" are "all landed just beyond the window". "Worth every hour of the journey to get there via sleeper and ferry!" / **Details:** www.thecafefish.com; 10 pm; closed Nov-Mar; No Amex; children: 14+ after 8 pm.

TONBRIDGE, KENT	3–3B

The Little Brown Jug   £48   **3 3 4**
Chiddingstone Causeway TN11 8JJ
01892 870318
"A favourite particularly in summer" – this Whiting & Hammond operation benefits from a vast garden, but also scores points for its all-round good performance, including well-prepared pub grub. / **Details:** www.thelittlebrownjug.co.uk; @LittleBrownJug1; Mon-Sat 9.30 pm, Sun 9 am; No Amex.

TORQUAY, DEVON	1–3D

Elephant Restaurant & Brasserie   £65   **3 3 3**
3-4 Beacon Ter, Harbourside TQ1 2BH
01803 200044
Simon Hulstone's "friendly" indie "continues to maintain high standards" – and this despite "the chef's frequent absences to do TV"; there's the odd sceptic for whom this restaurant in a Georgian terrace doesn't justify the tyre men's hype, but fans say that the tasting menus are "quite simply sublime". / **Details:** www.elephantrestaurant.co.uk; @elephantrest; 9 pm; closed Mon & Sun; children: 14+ at bar.

No 7 Fish Bistro   £50   **4 3 3**
7 Beacon Terrace TQ1 2BH   01803 295055
High marks again for this family-run harbour-view fish bistro, where the specials of the day are written up on a series of blackboards. / **Details:** www.no7-fish.com; @no7fishbistro; 9.45 pm.

TREBURLEY, CORNWALL	1–3C

Springer Spaniel   £61   **3 3 3**
The Springer Spaniel PL15 9NS   01579 370424
This relaxed, 18th-century inn earns feedback that's highly positive in the main. Most reviewers went for the taster menu, finding it "very competently executed throughout and fantastic value (if not quite on the same level as the best local places)". / **Details:** www.thespringerspaniel.co.uk; @SpringerThe; 4m S of Launceston on A388; 9 pm; No Amex.

TREEN, CORNWALL	1–4A

The Gurnard's Head   £51   **3 3 4**
TR26 3DE   01736 796928
"Well worth driving to the end of England for" – not least for the fabulous clifftop views – this bright-yellow-painted pillar of the local dining scene offers "restaurant-quality food in a friendly pub atmosphere"; from "kids' meals in two different sizes" to "very grown-up" puds, there's something to enjoy for all the family. / **Details:** www.gurnardshead.co.uk; @gurnardshead; on coastal road between Land's End & St Ives, near Zennor B3306; 9.15 pm; No Amex. / **Accommodation:** 7 rooms, from £7

TRURO, CORNWALL	1–4B

Hubbox   £32   **3 3 3**
116 Kenwyn Street TR1 3DJ   01872 240700
In an "interesting" old converted church, this happening Cornish chain turns out the "best burgers around" (plus hot dogs and craft beers); following branches in St Ives, Exeter, Plymouth and beyond, it took over the old Las Iguanas site, on Bristol's Whiteladies Road, in Spring 2017. / **Details:** www.hubbox.co.uk; @TheHubBox; 9 pm.

Tabb's   £55   **4 4 4**
85 Kenwyn St TR1 3BZ   01872 262110
Local luminary Nigel Tabb's "great, local fine dining" haunt is a "continued culinary delight", achieving a "great balance of flavours and textures" in a romantic, and surprisingly spacious, setting. / **Details:** www.tabbs.co.uk/; @Nigeltabb; 9 pm; closed Mon & Sun D; No Amex.

TUDDENHAM, SUFFOLK	3–1C

Tuddenham Mill, Tuddenham Mill Hotel   £59   **3 3 4**
High St IP28 6SQ   01638 713552
This "lovely boutique hotel in an old mill set on a river" near the A11 houses a "gorgeous dining room, and a bar and deck overlooking the water

*with swans to boot!" Notwithstanding a couple of downbeat reports, most reviews this year found its ambitious cuisine just "as good as ever". / **Details:** www.tuddenhammill.co.uk; @Tuddenham_Mill; 9 pm. / **Accommodation:** 15 rooms, from £205*

TWICKENHAM, SURREY	3–3A

Umi £26 5 5 3
30 York Street TW1 3LJ 020 8892 2976
*Opened in June 2016, this "fantastic sushi restaurant", which replaced another Japanese on the same site, is already a huge local favourite; reporters praise its "superb" gyoza, tempura, ramen, sushi et. al., and the "friendliest welcome" possible. / **Details:** 11 pm, Sun 10 pm.*

TYNEMOUTH, TYNE AND WEAR	8–2B

Longsands Fish Kitchen £42 4 4 4
27 Front Street NE30 4DZ 0191 272 8552
*"A great addition to Tynemouth's Front Street dining choice with its busy restaurant, as well as the best fish 'n' chips takeout around!" – this "buzzing" corner café is "consistently excellent" providing "unusual fish dishes with plenty of choice". / **Details:** www.longsandsfishkitchen.com; @LongsandsFish; 8 pm.*

Riley's Fish Shack £33 5 3 5
King Edward's Bay NE30 4BY 0191 257 1371
*"Occupying an iconic location on beautiful King Edward's Bay", this "utterly amazing hidden gem" – a "converted shipping container on the edge of the beach (just perfect at sundown)" – provides a "one-in-a-million" (well, nearly) experience combining "awesome" fish with "fantastic views out to sea". One prime caveat: it is "now massively popular", and you must "be prepared to queue, then wait more while the friendly but utterly overworked staff whip up your meal". "Hopefully the other people in the queue will be good company": "drinks orders are taken while you queue, there's great music" and most (if not quite all) reporters are just "on the beach and very happy". "The menu very much depends on the catch of the day, and can include the likes of cod, monkfish and lobster. Wraps are also served as well as mains cooked on a char grill or in a wood-fired oven". / **Details:** www.rileysfishshack.com; @rileysfishshack; 10pm, Sun & Mon 5.30 pm; closed Mon D, Tue & Sun D.*

TYTHERLEIGH, DEVON	2–4A

Tytherleigh Arms £51 4 4 3
EX13 7BE 01460 220214
*Not only a "good option in a place with few decent restaurants" – reviewers love this "well-established country pub" whose cuisine is "full of flair". "We proudly take our London friends here and they are always impressed!" / **Details:** www.tytherleigharms.com; @TytherleighArms; 9 pm, Fri & Sat 9.30 pm, Sun 8.30 pm; children: 5.*

ULLAPOOL, HIGHLAND	9–1B

Seafood Shack £45 5 4 2
West Argyle Street IV26 2TY 07876 142623
A "super little (seasonal) kiosk" – and BBC Food Awards winner – "selling freshly made and locally caught seafood: prawns, spinies, soups, crab" that's "cheerily cooked and served by the two lassies who run it". Handily "you can stroll a few yards down to the harbourside to devour it".

ULLSWATER, CUMBRIA	7–3D

Sharrow Bay £94 4 4 5
CA10 2LZ 01768 486301
*"We took our daughter as a treat and were given our own superb private alcove looking out onto the lake... the view was exceptional, food could not be better and the service wonderful!" – This landmark property overlooking Ullswater can lay claim to inventing the country house hotel genre, and though known for its very traditional style, "some features have been modernised" nowadays, and fans still see it as a natural choice "for a special occasion". It's "number one for afternoon tea" too. / **Details:** www.sharrowbay.co.uk; @sharrowbay; on Pooley Bridge Rd towards Howtown; 9 pm; No jeans; children: 8+. / **Accommodation:** 17 rooms, from £355*

UMBERLEIGH, DEVON	1–2C

Northcote Manor £67 4 4 4
Burrington EX37 9LZ 01769 560501
*"Very pleasant grounds for ambling around" set the scene at this "lovely" old manor house hotel in rural North Devon. Richie Herkes's accomplished cooking – including a 'gourmet' tasting option with wine matches – is of "super quality" (and the lunch option here is "a steal"). / **Details:** www.northcotemanor.co.uk; @NorthcoteDevon; 9 pm; No jeans. / **Accommodation:** 11 rooms, from £155*

UPPER SLAUGHTER, GLOUCESTERSHIRE	2–1C

Lords of the Manor £95 3 2 3
Stow-on-the-Wold GL54 2JD 01451 820243
This acclaimed Olde Englishe Cotswolds hotel has been in the wars; months after the exit of chef Richard Picard-Edwards in late 2016, it was revealed that, over several years, the former GM

had defrauded it to the tune of 170K. Perhaps new chef Charles Smith, ex-of Alyn Williams at The Westbury, can help get it back on track, although – notwithstanding the odd "underwhelming" report in this period – ratings have generally held up well. / *Details: www.lordsofthemanor.com; @CotswoldLords; 4m W of Stow on the Wold; 8.45 pm; D only, ex Sun open L & D; No jeans; children: 7+ at D in restaurant. / Accommodation: 26 rooms, from £199*

USK VALLEY, NEWPORT	2–2A

Cen, Celtic Manor Resort £56 2️⃣3️⃣3️⃣
NP18 1HQ   01633 410262
Slightly up-and-down reports this year on MasterChef finalist Larkin Cen's pan-Asian dishes at this huge resort in Newport, but feedback includes more hits than misses. / *Details: www.celtic-manor.com/cen; @TheCelticManor; 10 pm; Booking max 9 may apply.*

WADDESDON, BUCKINGHAMSHIRE	3–2A

The Five Arrows £55 3️⃣3️⃣3️⃣
High St HP18 0JE   01296 651727
At the gate of Waddesdon Manor, this former coaching inn is now a swish hotel (mixing neo-Tudor and neo-Elizabethan styles). While the "restaurant is rather plain compared to the rest of the building", reporters had some "wonderful" meals and wines here this year, best followed by a stroll around the Waddesdon Estate. / *Details: www.thefivearrows.co.uk; @WaddesdonManor; on A41; 9.15 pm. / Accommodation: 11 rooms, from £95*

WADDINGTON, LANCASHIRE	5–1B

The Higher Buck £49 4️⃣4️⃣3️⃣
The Square BB7 3HZ   01200 423226
In one of Lancashire's Best Kept Villages (officially), and part of the Thwaites chain, a "brilliant village pub with beautiful rooms"; chef-landlord Michael Heathcote's cooking is "reasonably priced, locally sourced" and "consistently good". / *Details: www.higherbuck.com; @thehigherbuck; Mon-Thu 9 pm, Fri & Sat 9.30 pm, Sun 8 pm.*

WADEBRIDGE, CORNWALL	1–3B

Bridge Bistro £45 3️⃣3️⃣2️⃣
4 Molesworth St PL27 7DA   01208 815342
"The great thing about the Bridge Bistro is how easy they make everything look": "delicious, thoughtful dishes" (check), fuss-free service (check) and "wonderfully relaxed atmosphere" (check – and

this despite doubling in size when they took over next door). / *Details: www.bridgebistro.co.uk/; @Bridge_Bistro; 9 pm; closed Sun D; No Amex.*

WALLINGFORD, OXFORDSHIRE	2–1D

Old Post Office £52 4️⃣3️⃣3️⃣
OX10 0AA   01491 836068
Part of a local chain, this newly, expensively refurbed spot is "based in the centre of this market town, in fact it is the centre of town!" The menu now offers "imaginative, tasty and huge" wood-fired pizzas (a staple in the venue's former Forno Vivo days), but other mains are "fabulous" too. / *Details: www.opowallingford.co.uk; @OPOWallingford.*

WARLINGHAM, SURREY	3–3B

Chez Vous £63 2️⃣2️⃣3️⃣
432 Limpsfield Rd CR6 9LA   01883 620451
This restaurant-with-rooms is worth knowing about in an area lacking culinary competition. Critics say "it doesn't always quite get its act together", but all feedback is positive regarding its "very tasty" cooking. / *Details: www.chezvous.co.uk; @ChezVousLtd; 9.30 pm, Fri & Sat 10 pm; closed Mon & Sun D.*

WARWICK, WARWICKSHIRE	5–4C

The Art Kitchen £49 3️⃣3️⃣2️⃣
7 Swan St CV34 4BJ   01926 494303
"Always a winner for exceptional Thai food in a warm, inviting atmosphere", a city-centre option acclaimed by most (but not quite all) reporters for its "consistently good" cuisine; "shame they have dropped the fixed-price lunch menu," though. / *Details: www.theartkitchen.com; @TheArtKitchen1; 10 pm.*

Tailors £57 4️⃣4️⃣3️⃣
22 Market place CV34 4SL   01926 410590
After former lives as a fishmonger, tailor's (hence the name), butcher and casino, this town-centre site now turns out "always excellent", ambitious food; given that it's a "small venue you'll need to book". / *Details: www.tailorsrestaurant.co.uk; 9 pm; closed Mon & Sun; No Amex; No bookings; children: 12+ for dinner.*

WATERGATE BAY, CORNWALL	1–3B

The Beach Hut, Watergate Bay Hotel £48 3️⃣3️⃣4️⃣
On The Beach TR8 4AA   01637 860543
Offering heady views of the surf below, this relaxed, woodsy beach hangout remains a useful address

that's welcoming to both four-legged friends and sand-strewn kids; the food (seafood, burgers and moules) is better than the location might suggest. / *Details:* www.watergatebay.co.uk; @WatergateBay; 9 pm; No Amex. / *Accommodation:* 69 rooms, from £105

Fifteen Cornwall, Watergate Bay Hotel £88 ☑️☑️☑️
TR8 4AA 01637 861000
"Try to arrive at sunset for one of the most romantic locations and one of the best views in England", if you visit Jamie Oliver's beachside destination, where you eat "watching the rolling waves of the Atlantic ocean". Staff are "so helpful and charming" and the "simple" food is "really great, too" (although it can seem "a bit pricey for what it is"). / *Details:* www.fifteencornwall.co.uk; @fifteencornwall; on the Atlantic coast between Padstow and Newquay; 9.15 pm; children: 4+ at D.

WATH-IN-NIDDERDALE, NORTH YORKSHIRE
8–4B

Sportsman's Arms £53 ☑️☑️☑️
The Sportsmans Arms HG3 5PP
01423 711306
In its gorgeous, remote setting, this country pub has been a consistent culinary destination for many-a-year now. Its old-fashioned style can seem "austere" (to more modern tastes "some pubs handle the 'pub-setting-but-posh-food' thing better than this") but all agree the food is "well-above-average". / *Details:* www.sportsmans-arms.co.uk; take Wath Road from Pateley Bridge; 9 pm; closed Sun D; No Amex. / *Accommodation:* 11 rooms, from £120

WEALD SEVENOAKS, KENT 3–3B

Giacomo £52 ☑️☑️☑️
Morleys Road TN14 6QR 01732 746200
An "old-fashioned" spot (think flambés and "excellent live entertainment") praised for its "real Italian cooking made with love". / *Details:* www.giacomos.uk.com; 9 pm.

WELLAND, WORCESTERSHIRE 2–1B

Inn at Welland £41 ☑️☑️☑️
Hook Bank, Drake St WR13 6LN
01684 592317
A stylish country inn with an "excellent restaurant" and views of the Malvern Hills; reports have been polarised in the past, but were uniformly solid this year. "The menu changes regularly, even for vegetarians and vegans". / *Details:* www.theinnatwelland.co.uk/; @innatwelland; 9.30 pm.

WELLING, KENT 3–3B

Shampan 3 £41 ☑️☑️☑️
8 Falconwood Parade, The Green DA16 2PL
020 8304 9569
"A good menu of very tasty food and great service" win praise for this representative of a local indie Indian chain. / *Details:* www.shampangroup.com; @ShampanGroup; Mon-Thu 10.30 pm, Fri & Sat 11 pm, Sun 10 pm.

WELLS NEXT THE SEA, NORFOLK 6–3C

Wells Crab House £48 ☑️☑️☑️
38 Freeman St NR23 1BA 013 2871 0456
"Opened in Easter 2016 with new owners", this "lovely restaurant near the quay" serves "the freshest and tastiest seafood" in town from a "varied" and "affordable" menu. "The service is wonderful, and the ambience classy – reminiscent of New England". / *Details:* wellscrabhouse.co.uk; @wellscrabhouse; 8.30 pm.

WELLS, SOMERSET 2–3B

Goodfellows £58 ☑️☑️☑️
5 - 5 B Sadler Street BA5 2RR 01749 673866
"For a restaurant this far inland", Adam Fellows's "quirky", intimate modern European turns out some "truly amazing" fish, and "friendly staff make the experience even better"; sample praise – "you could be in any simple brasserie in a French town". / *Details:* www.goodfellowswells.co.uk; @goodfellowswest; 9.30 pm, Fri & Sat 10 pm; closed Mon, Tue D & Sun.

WELWYN, HERTFORDSHIRE 3–2B

Auberge du Lac, Brocket Hall £90
AL8 7XG 01707 368888
Reports are still few and far between on this lakeside former hunting lodge on Lord Palmerston's erstwhile estate, which in years gone by was a major destination for a high quality romantic meal, especially in summer. Such as we have are upbeat, but we have held off on a rating till a clearer picture emerges. / *Details:* www.brocket-hall.co.uk; @AubergeBrocket; on B653 towards Harpenden; 9.30 pm; closed Mon & Sun L; No jeans; children: 12+. / *Accommodation:* 16 rooms, from £175

WEST BYFLEET, SURREY	3–3A

London House £58 4️⃣2️⃣3️⃣
30 Station Approach KT14 6NF   01932 482026
This well-established venture by MasterChef semi-finalist Ben Piette powers on in its new (as of April 2016) West Byfleet home; an "interesting restaurant in an area lacking good options", the slick, exposed-brick spot mixes "consistently excellent" grub with "thoughtful but somewhat quirky" presentation. / Details: www.londonhouseoldwoking.co.uk; 9.30 pm.

WEST CLANDON, SURREY	3–3A

The Onslow Arms £48 3️⃣3️⃣3️⃣
The St GU4 7TE   01483 222447
"Above-average pub grub" from a "very varied menu" makes it worth considering this "very popular" village boozer; "well done-up" garden come summer, too. / Details: onslowarmsclandon.co.uk; 9.30 pm, Fri & Sat 10 pm; children: 18+ after 7.30pm.

WEST HOATHLY, WEST SUSSEX	3–4B

The Cat Inn £52 4️⃣3️⃣3️⃣
North Lane RH19 4PP   01342 810369
"A great pint of Harveys, followed by very good local food" – two good reasons to justify a visit to this "excellent pub (with rooms) close to Wakehurst Place". / Details: www.catinn.co.uk; @TheCatInn; 9 pm, Fri & Sat 9.30 pm; closed Sun D; No Amex; children: 7+. / Accommodation: 4 rooms, from £110

WEST MALLING, KENT	3–3C

Frank's £46 3️⃣2️⃣4️⃣
53-57 High St ME19 6QH   01732 843247
'Mussels cooked 21 ways' is the mainstay of the menu at this Kent market town restaurant and mussel bar, housed in a beamed 16th-century former bakery. Initial feedback is limited but upbeat. / Details: www.franksrestaurantandmusselbar.com.

The Swan £54 3️⃣2️⃣2️⃣
35 Swan St ME19 6JU   01732 521910
With its "consistently good" cuisine and ever-"buzzing" vibe, this "smart conversion" of a 15th-century inn is "the best restaurant in West Malling" according to reviewers; breakfast is a highlight. / Details: www.theswanwestmalling.co.uk; @swanwm; 11 pm, Sun 7 pm.

WEST MERSEA, ESSEX	3–2C

The Company Shed £37 5️⃣2️⃣2️⃣
129 Coast Rd CO5 8PA   01206 382700
"Supplied by the boats landing just outside", this much-loved and descriptively named shack is "basic, but in an amusing, offbeat way to treasure".You queue, and also need to "bring your own bread and wine" so it's "therefore cheap". / Details: www.thecompanyshed.co; L only, closed Mon; No bookings.

West Mersea Oyster Bar £38 4️⃣3️⃣3️⃣
Coast Rd CO5 8LT   01206 381600
"What could be better than sitting on the waterfront at this casual but efficiently run seafood restaurant with its simple cuisine?"; while it's "a basic setting and you definitely need to book", food "doesn't come fresher!" – "Colchester native oysters at a fraction of London prices, top fish 'n' chips, delicious scallops and a variety of other choices". / Details: www.westmerseaoysterbar.co.uk; 8.30 pm; Sun-Thu closed D; No Amex; No shorts.

WEST WITTON, NORTH YORKSHIRE	8–4B

The Wensleydale Heifer £63 3️⃣2️⃣2️⃣
Main St DL8 4LS   01969 622322
"Excellent battered fish that's as light as a feather" stars at this foodie-friendly village pub-with-rooms, curiously known for its seafood, despite its decidedly non-coastal location: "that it has a daunting menu doesn't dilute the quality". / Details: www.wensleydaleheifer.co.uk; @wensleyheifer; 9.30 pm; Booking max 6 may apply. / Accommodation: 13 rooms, from £130

WESTERHAM, KENT	3–3B

Shampan 4 £48 3️⃣3️⃣4️⃣
The Spinning Wheel, Grays Road TN16 2HX   01959 572622
Nowadays the flagship of a local indie Indian chain, this large 'bar and lounge' on the Biggin Hill/Westerham borders provides a glossily glam setting for a night out, complete with above par cooking. / Details: www.shampangroup.com; @ShampanGroup; Sun 10 pm, Mon-Thu 10.30 pm, Fri & Sat 11pm.

WESTFIELD, EAST SUSSEX	3–4C

The Wild Mushroom £53 3️⃣3️⃣3️⃣
Woodgate House, Westfield Lane TN35 4SB   01424 751137
Paul Webbe's "consistent" converted farmhouse venture serves up a "fantastic dining experience" built on locally sourced ingredients (many foraged)

— reporters likewise "always enjoy the conservatory and garden". / Details: www.webbesrestaurants.co.uk; @WebbesGroup;Wed-Sat 9.30 pm, Sun 2 pm; closed Mon,Tue & Sun D.

WESTLETON, SUFFOLK	3–1D

The Westleton Crown £51 3️⃣2️⃣2️⃣
The St IP17 3AD 01728 648777
An old coaching inn turned smart hotel, bar and restaurant, the latter in a large rear conservatory; "each space has its own individual character" (the bar is "more informal"…"you can bring your dogs and have them made a fuss of") but both serve the same "lovely" menu. / Details: www.westletoncrown.co.uk; @Westleton_Crown; 9.30 pm.

WESTON SUPER MARE, SOMERSET	2–2A

Cove £45 2️⃣3️⃣4️⃣
Birnbeck Road BS23 2BX 01934 418217
"A lovely place in a town that for a long time was lacking in good eateries" – the food is dependable at this fish-centric ten-year-old, and "on a sunny day the setting by the sea is superb" with views to Steep Holm and Flat Holm. / Details: www.the-cove.co.uk; @CoveBarandRest; 9 pm, Sun 5 pm; closed Mon.

WESTWARD HO, DEVON	1–2C

Morans £39 4️⃣4️⃣3️⃣
EX39 1LH 01237 472070
An "eclectic mix of wonderful Thai" food is "served within sight of the sea" at this relaxed venue, right by the beach;"the evening menu is more interesting but it's always delicious whatever time you go" and "there are also English menu options in case" you have a violent craving for steak and chips. / Details: www.moransrestaurant.co.uk; @Moransbardevon; 11 pm, Fri & Sat midnight, Sun 5 pm.

The Pig on the Hill £55
EX39 5AH 01237 459222
Hilltop pub-with-rooms on the Devon coast (formerly a cowshed, apparently) serving local ales, traditional British grub and roasts on Sundays. / Details: pigonthehillwestwardho.co.uk; @PigontheHillND.

WETHERBY,WEST YORKSHIRE	5–1C

Piccolino £55 4️⃣4️⃣3️⃣
Wetherby Rd LS22 5AY 01937 579797
"Very definitely Italian-Italian (to the point of eccentricity)", this husband-and-wife-run venture is nominally part of the national chain, but very

much a one-off: a no-pizza, no-garlic bread sort of spot, whose "messianic" sourcing extends to Italian artisanal beers and even soft drinks. The slow food-style menu ("littered with DOPs") is "extraordinarily good", the "wine list is a joy" and "though prices are not low, portions are hearty". Top Tip – "the home made pasta dishes are rarely less than sublime". / Details: www.piccolinorestaurants.co.uk; 11 pm.

WEYBRIDGE, SURREY	3–3A

Meejana £44 3️⃣3️⃣3️⃣
49 Church St KT13 8DG 01932 830 444
Limited but positive feedback on this ten-year-old Lebanese (which also has a Kensington sibling), praising its high standards, including enjoyable mezze, lunchtime wraps and more substantial fare. / Details: www.meejana.co.uk; Mon-Sat 11 pm, Sun 4 pm .

WEYMOUTH, DORSET	2–4B

Crab House Café £49 5️⃣4️⃣4️⃣
Ferrymans Way, Portland Road DT4 9YU
01305 788867
"It's great fun cracking a whole crab with a hammer" or gargling down some of the other "amazing seafood" or "excellent fish" at this "relaxed beachside café" ("behind Chesil Beach and owned by local oyster farmers"):"on a relaxing sunny afternoon, the best place to be…" / Details: www.crabhousecafe.co.uk; @crabhousecafe; overlooking the Fleet Lagoon, on the road to Portland;Wed & Thu 8.30 pm, Fri & Sat 9 pm; closed Mon,Tue & Sun D; No Amex; 8+ deposit of £10 per head.

Al Molo £51 3️⃣3️⃣4️⃣
Pier Bandstand,The Esplanade DT4 7RN
01305 839888
In Weymouth's historic Pier Bandstand, this "beautifully decorated" contemporary Italian has fine views and "as you are sit overlooking the sea you feel like you are on a cruise ship sailing across the ocean!" Recommendations include the "thoughtful and stylishly presented" cooking and "top cocktails". / Details: www.almolo.co.uk; @AlMoloWeymouth; 9.30 pm, Fri & Sat 10 pm.

WHALLEY, LANCASHIRE	5–1B

Benedicts of Whalley £36 4️⃣4️⃣3️⃣
1 George St BB7 9TH 01254 824468
"The selection of cakes available to tempt you with your coffee has to be seen to be believed" at this "always busy" spot, which "also does a range of main meals";"unfortunately there is no booking", but they will call when a table is

ready – "giving you time to look around their deli or take in the delights of the village". / **Details:** www.benedictsofwhalley.co.uk; @BenedictsDeli; 7.30 pm, Sun 4 pm.

Breda Murphy Restaurant £50 4|4|4
41 Station Rd BB7 9RH 01254 823446
"Bijou outfit producing great food in a sophisticated setting, despite being located opposite the railway station". Originally a café/deli, this year it underwent a major refurb, creating more space and adding on 'Reilly's Gin Bar'; at dinner now, the British/Irish cuisine is firmly at 'restaurant' aspiration (with prices to match). Vegetarian and vegan menus are a feature. / **Details:** www.bredamurphy.co.uk/; @Breda_Murphy; 9.30 pm; closed Mon & Sun, Tue-Sat D.

The Three Fishes £49 3|3|3
Mitton Rd BB7 9PQ 01254 826888
"Well-appointed, and in a super part of the Lancashire countryside" – this "busy and atmospheric" conversion of an old village pub achieved local fame as the first of the Ribble Valley Inns chain. The odd "forgettable" meal is reported, but for the most part it's praised for its "lovely pub grub". / **Details:** www.thethreefishes.com; @the_threefishes; 9 pm, Fri & Sat 9.30 pm.

WHITBY, NORTH YORKSHIRE 8–3D

Magpie Café £38 5|4|3
14 Pier Rd YO21 3PU 01947 602058
"Bloody brilliant!" This "rightly famous" harbourside legend enjoys well-earned renown as "the UK's best chippy" ("there is a reason we wait in the cold North Sea air to get in here") and is "always a must-visit when in the area". "There's a huge menu, despite which everything is fantastically fresh" and dishes come in "Yorkshire portions"; and while "it can feel a bit cramped when full-to-bursting, it's worth it for a great lunch overlooking the sea". On May 1 2017, disaster struck when the upper floors of this 17th-century building were razed by fire, forcing the closure of the restaurant (but not the take-away). Re-opening is planned pre Christmas 2017. / **Details:** www.magpiecafe.co.uk; @themagpiecafe; 9 pm; No Amex; No bookings at lunch.

The Star Inn The Harbour
Langborne Road YO21 1YN 01947 821900
Andrew Pern (of The Star Inn at Harome) fulfilled his wish of having a restaurant in his hometown of Whitby in summer-2017. The harbour-side venture features Catch-of-the-Day fish specials and game from the North Yorkshire Moors. / **Details:** www.starinntheharbour.co.uk; @HarbourStarInn.

Trenchers £48 4|3|3
New Quay Rd YO21 1DH 01947 603212
A "good old-fashioned fish 'n' chippie at its best"; OK, so the "clean and efficient decor" can seem "a little clinical", but the food at this celebrated, booth-lined venue, a stone's throw from the quay, is "wholesome and enjoyable" and "some people go just to see the loos" (multi-award-winning and anything but bog-standard!) / **Details:** www.trenchersrestaurant.co.uk; 8.30 pm; May need 7+ to book.

WHITE WALTHAM, BERKSHIRE 3–3A

Beehive £61 4|4|3
Waltham Rd SL6 3SH 01628 822877
Since the arrival of "Michelin-recognised chef" Dom Chapman (ex-of Heston's Fat Duck, then local haunt The Royal Oak) a few years back, this former pub has had quite the turnaround; while there's still a bar area for locals, the relaxed seasonal food is now "very good indeed" and "the lunchtime special is a steal". / **Details:** www.thebeehivewhitewaltham.com; @thebeehivetweet; 9.30 pm.

WHITEBROOK, MONMOUTHSHIRE 2–2B

The Whitebrook £82 5|4|3
NP25 4TX 01600 860254
"In the middle of the lush Wye valley" ("no mobile reception here"), this long acclaimed "foodie gem" regained its star shortly after the arrival of chef/proprietor Chris Harrod in 2013 (and lost 'The Crown' from its name shortly after). Fans proclaim the "locally sourced and foraged" cuisine "unique" ("Noma in Britain!") with the "added benefit of eight comfy rooms to sleep it off". / **Details:** www.thewhitebrook.co.uk; @TheWhitebrook; 2m W of A466, 5m S of Monmouth; 9 pm; closed Mon; children: 12+ for D. / **Accommodation:** 8 rooms, from £145

WHITLEY BAY, TYNE AND WEAR 8–2B

Hinnies £35 4|4|3
10 East Parade NE26 1AP 0191 447 0500
"A great addition to the otherwise sparse dining in a resurgent town", set "on the changing seafront in Whitley Bay". This "offshoot of the longstanding Blackfriars Restaurant in nearby Newcastle" has "rapidly become a go-to place for locals enjoying imaginative seafood" and "Geordie specialities" (eg savaloy dip and singin hinnies – a type of griddle cake – for which it's named). / **Details:** www.hinnies.co.uk/; @hinniesrest; 11 pm, Sun 4 pm; closed Mon & Sun D.

WHITSTABLE, KENT   3–3C

Crab & Winkle   £52 **3** **3** **3**
South Quay, Whitstable Harbour CT5 1AB
01227 779377
"Amazing views of Whitstable Harbour through large windows, and an outside balcony for when the weather's good" help set this seaside café apart, but its highest rated feature is its fish-centric cuisine. / Details: www.crabandwinklerestaurant.co.uk; @Crab_Winkle; closed Mon & Sun D; No Amex; children: 6.

East Coast Dining Room £49 **4** **3** **2**
101 Tankerton Rd CT5 2AJ 01227 281180
A "small minimalist-style restaurant near the seafront at Tankerton", and offering "modern British cooking, well cooked and presented" (the latter drawing Londonites as well as locals). / Details: www.eastcoastdiningroom.co.uk; 9 pm, Fri & Sat 9.30 pm; closed Mon, Tue, Wed D & Sun D.

JoJo   £38 **3** **4** **4**
2 Herne Bay Rd CT5 2LQ 01227 274591
"Amazing views overlooking Whitstable and fantastic food" – with "wonderful combinations and flavours" – create an enthusiastic local following for this "brilliant tapas-type place" on Tankerton Slopes. Its "lively atmosphere" and "friendly staff" is good for when you have kids in tow too. / Details: www.jojosrestaurant.co.uk; @jojostankerton; 11pm; closed Mon, Tue, Wed L & Sun D; Cash only.

Krishna   £29 **4** **3** **2**
49 Old Bridge Road CT5 1RD 01227 282639
"Situated by Whitstable station, this Indian does not look special until you check out the refreshingly different menu"; and, "when the food arrives, it's delicious and well spiced" too. / Details: www.krishnarestaurant.co.uk; 10.30 pm; closed Mon.

The Lobster Shack
Restaurant   £24 **3** **2** **3**
East Quay CT5 1AB 01227 771923
There's "a great seaside experience" to be had at this "fun" joint, "right on the beach", and with ample outdoor tables to maximise the view; it "can get busy at peak times but it's worth the effort" for the "good range of reasonably priced seafood" (shellfish platters, fish 'n' chips and the headline crustacean – "yum"). / Details: www.eqvenue.com/restaurant; @brewerybarwhits; 9 pm.

Pearson's Arms   £54 **3** **2** **4**
The Horsebridge, Sea Wall CT5 1BT
01227 272005
Richard Phillips' pub and fine dining hybrid is an "atmospheric" spot with "superb views over the beach" and Thames Estuary from the upstairs restaurant. The kitchen turns out "excellent oysters and good fish generally" but, the lion's share of

praise singles out the "superb value set lunch". / Details: www.pearsonsarmsbyrichardphillips.co.uk; @pearsonsarms; 9 pm, Fri & Sat 9.30 pm, Sun 8.30 pm; closed Mon D.

Samphire   £47 **4** **3** **3**
4 High Street CT5 1BQ 01227 770075
A "lovely independent" bistro "in the town centre" with a "very quirky" atmosphere and "friendly owner and staff"; "the interesting menu uses locally sourced products" to "tasty, imaginative" effect and it's "always very busy". / Details: www.samphirewhitstable.co.uk; @samphirewhit; 9.30 pm; No Amex.

Wheelers Oyster Bar   £48 **5** **5** **4**
8 High Street CT5 1BQ 01227 273311
"Revamped but still maintaining the original eating parlour" – this "quirky, mildly eccentric, and very English" institution (est. 1856) has survived enlargement largely unscathed, and still provides "a bizarre environment – like eating in someone's front room" – that's "as cosy as a teapot". But "the modest frontage belies the superb cuisine inside", where "sublime" yet "unfussy" seafood dishes are served at "fair prices", and "BYO makes it a very good value experience" indeed. "I have had so much fun sitting in the 'shop' and falling into the most entertaining conversations with all types of people from a celebrated yet humble sax player, to a local plasterer, to a TV actor…" / Details: www.wheelersoysterbar.com; @WheelersOB; 9 pm, Fri 9.30 pm; closed Wed; Cash only.

Whitstable Oyster Fishery
Co.   £62 **4** **3** **4**
Royal Native Oyster Stores, Horsebridge
CT5 1BU 01227 276856
"Rustic decor adds to the fishy experience" at this well-known "slightly hidden away old warehouse" which has a "fantastic location on the beach". "You can't get fresher when it comes to oysters", and ("though quite pricey) it offers "very good food altogether". / Details: www.whitstableoystercompany.com; 8.45 pm, Fri 9.15 pm, Sat 9.45 pm, Sun 8.15 pm.

WILLIAN, HERTFORDSHIRE   3–2B

The Fox   £48 **3** **3** **3**
SG6 2AE 01462 480233
In a pretty location off the A1, this village gastroboozer with rooms (part of Anglia Country Inns group) inspires consistently upbeat reports for its high standard of cooking, both in the bar and slightly smarter restaurant. / Details: www.foxatwillian.co.uk; @FoxAtWillian; 1 mile from junction 9 off A1M; 9 pm; closed Sun D.

WINCHCOMBE, GLOUCESTERSHIRE   2–1C

5 North Street   **£76**   **5 4 3**
5 North St GL54 5LH   01242 604566
"Well worth a detour" – Marcus & Kate Ashenford's outfit in a "tiny", beamed former tea room in this picturesque Cotswold village; the pair make a "lovely team" (him at the pass, her out front), and the "wonderful freshness" and "intense flavours" of the cuisine make for a "special treat". / Details: www.5northstreetrestaurant.co.uk; 9 pm; closed Mon, Tue L & Sun D; No Amex.

WINCHESTER, HAMPSHIRE   2–3D

The Black Rat   **£63**   **4 4 4**
88 Chesil St SO23 0HX   01962 844465
Acclaimed chef Ollie Moore left for adventures new in July 2016, to be replaced by John Marsden-Jones; by most accounts the "change of chef has made little difference" to the "genuinely surprising and innovative" food on offer at this "very welcoming" edge-of-town pub. / Details: www.theblackrat.co.uk; @the_black_rat; 9.30 pm; closed weekday L; children: 18+ except weekend L.

The Chesil Rectory   **£54**   **3 3 5**
1 Chesil St S023 0HU   01962 851555
"For unique character it's hard to beat" this "attractive, exceptional and historic old building" which is "hands down the loveliest space to dine in, and perfect for special occasions" (especially of a romantic nature). The "delicious" food is hailed by fans as arguably Winchester's best ("though if visiting regularly the menu can become somewhat predictable"). / Details: www.chesilrectory.co.uk; @ChesilRectory; 9 pm, Fri & Sat 9.30 pm, Sun 8.30 pm; children: 12+ at D.

Gandhi Restaurant   **£33**   **4 4 4**
163-164 High St SO23 9BA   01962 863940
"The best Indian restaurant in the area with original dishes as well as excellent overall standards" – that's the uniform message of reports on this fixture near the cathedral, which is in contemporary style but has been run by the same family for over 30 years. / Details: www.gandhirestaurant.com/; 11.30 pm.

Hotel du Vin & Bistro   **£55**   **2 2 4**
Southgate Street SO23 9EF   01962 896329
The original HdV maintains its consistency… for inconsistency; while fans this year praised its "wonderful" rooms, "exemplary" wines and food "SO much better than expected", cynics felt the victuals "just didn't come up to standard", and service was also very "hit and miss". / Details: www.hotelduvin.com; @HdV_Winchester; Mon-Thu 10 pm, Fri & Sat 10.30 pm, Sun 9.30 am; Booking max 12 may apply. / Accommodation: 24 rooms, from £145

Kyoto Kitchen   **£41**   **4 5 3**
70 Parchment Street SO23 8AT   01962 890895
High scores again this year from fans who live far and wide of this authentic-style Japanese, in particular for its good value cuisine specialising in sushi and sashimi and charming service. / Details: www.kyotokitchen.co.uk; @Kyoto_Kitchen; 10.30 pm.

The Avenue, Lainston House Hotel   **£80**   **3 3 3**
Woodman Ln SO21 2LT   01962 776088
"A great summer afternoon cream tea, sitting outside on the patio, overlooking the rolling Hampshire countryside" is "probably the most affordable entry point" for sampling the cuisine of this plush country house hotel. When it comes to a full meal in the restaurant, Olly Rouse's cooking receives lots of nominations for top gastronomy, but there is also a lot of griping about how "extremely expensive" the experience can become. / Details: www.lainstonhouse.com; @lainstonhouse; 9.30 pm, Fri & Sat 10 pm. / Accommodation: 50 rooms, from £245

Palm Pan Asia   **£47**   **4 4 4**
166-167 High St SO23 9BA   01962 864040
"Well presented food that's excellent value (for Winchester!)" wins praise for this pan-Asian venture in the town centre. / Details: www.palmpanasia.co.uk/; @palm_panasia.

Rick Stein   **£62**   **3 3 2**
7 High Street SO23 9JX   01962 353535
"The seaside comes to Winchester" at this highly popular two-year-old, which on most accounts "carries on the Rick Stein tradition of good quality seafood without messing around". Even fans though acknowledge that the ambience can be "iffy", and there are a significant proportion of sceptics for whom the place is merely "fine" ("curiously just a little dull, with good but not outstanding food… impersonal… an upmarket price for almost a canteen experience"). / Details: www.rickstein.com; @SteinWinchester; 10 pm.

River Cottage Canteen   **£49**   **2 2 3**
Abbey Mill, Abbey Mill Gardens SO23 9GH   01962 457747
HFW's attractive but "noisy" mill conversion continues to be a "variable" spot; "the ingredients are normally excellent", but are ill-served by "sometimes strange" combinations, and "service needs improving" too. / Details: www.rivercottage.net/canteens/winchester; @WinCanteen; 9.15 pm, Sun 4 pm.

Wykeham Arms £56 2️⃣3️⃣5️⃣
75 Kingsgate St SO23 9PE 01962 853834
"The wonderful pub atmosphere outweighs the variable food" at this classic Victorian inn near the cathedral (nowadays managed by Fullers), where drinkers sit at old desks from the town's posh boys' school. / Details: www.wykehamarmswinchester.co.uk; @WykehmarmsLL; between Cathedral and College; 9.15 pm; children: 14+. / Accommodation: 14 rooms, from £139

WINDERMERE, CUMBRIA 7–3D

Cedar Manor
Ambleside Road LA23 1AX 015394 43192
"A short walk from Windermere", this attractive small hotel and restaurant wins praise for its "interesting and imaginative" cuisine. / Details: www.cedarmanor.co.uk; @CedarManorHotel.

Gilpin Hotel £91 4️⃣4️⃣3️⃣
Crook Rd LA23 3NE 01539 488818
Hrishikesh Desai's "creative genius makes every dish an adventure" in the restaurant of this Lakeland hotel, built in Georgian style in 1901, but significantly extended and boutique-ified over the years. "Fantastic Asian-fusion ideas" enliven the classic cuisine, providing "exciting" dishes, but with "wonderfully balanced flavours". / Details: www.thegilpin.co.uk; @chef_keller; 9.15 pm; No jeans; children: 7+. / Accommodation: 20 rooms, from £255

Holbeck Ghyll £94 3️⃣4️⃣4️⃣
Holbeck Lane LA23 1LU 01539 432375
This "romantic" Lakes destination occupies a luxurious old hunting lodge with epic Windermere views. There are sporadic critiques ("pleasant enough, but not worth the money") but no-one rates the quality of cuisine here as less than very good. / Details: www.holbeckghyll.com; @HolbeckGhyll; 3m N of Windermere, towards Troutbeck; 9.30 pm; No jeans; children: 7+ at D. / Accommodation: 33 rooms, from £190

Hooked £75 5️⃣3️⃣2️⃣
Ellerthwaite Square LA23 1DP 01539 448443
"Fresh fish cooked to perfection" is the simple but winning formula of this cosy venture; while no one debates the food quality, the setting can seem either unassuming or "average", and the Antipodean owner either charming or "overwhelming", depending on your perspective. / Details: www.hookedwindermere.co.uk/; 10.30 pm; D only, closed Mon; No Amex; Booking max 6 may apply.

Langdale Chase £67 2️⃣4️⃣5️⃣
Ambleside Road LA23 1LW 015394 32201
"The views of the gardens and Lake Windermere are stunning… even when it's raining!" at this "spectacularly located" Victorian mansion –

ideal in particular as an afternoon tea location. The hotel was sold mid-survey by the owners of the last 25 years to become part of the northerly Daniel Thwaites portfolio. / Details: www.langdalechase.co.uk/.

Linthwaite House £80
Crook Road LA23 3JA 015394 88600
Taken over by South Africa's Leeu Collection, who replaced longtime owner Mike Bevan, in April 2016, this "perfect hotel" in a fine Lakeland location is set to reopen in November 2017 after a £10 million, 5-month renovation set to add new interiors, including a more informal dining area with a terrace. / Details: www.linthwaite.com; @LinthwaiteHouse; near Windermere golf club; 9 pm; No jeans; children: 7+ at D. / Accommodation: 30 rooms, from £180

The Samling £107 4️⃣4️⃣4️⃣
Ambleside Road LA23 1LR 01539 431922
This stylish Windermere landmark recently reopened after major works adding a glass dining room extension, clutch of bedrooms and chef's table – and reporters are wowed by the "most impressive new surroundings". In October 2017 Peter Howarth (of the Latymer Restaurant at Pennyhill Park Hotel) was due to step in, following the departure of Nick Edgar after a very successful 20-month stint. Hopefully he can keep up the "stunning" standard. / Details: www.thesamlinghotel.co.uk; @theSamlingHotel; take A591 from town; 9.30 pm. / Accommodation: 11 rooms, from £300

WINDLESHAM, SURREY 3–3A

Brickmakers Arms £44 3️⃣3️⃣3️⃣
Churtsey Rd GU20 6HT 01276 472267
Locals hail this redbrick building with contemporary-style decor and a rangy garden as "the ultimate gastropub"; the "good range of interesting food" is "much better than your typical gastroboozer standards", and "you'll need to book". / Details: www.thebrickmakerswindlesham.co.uk; 9.45 pm.

WINDSOR, BERKSHIRE 3–3A

Al Fassia £44 4️⃣4️⃣3️⃣
27 St Leonards Rd SL4 3BP 01753 855370
This Moroccan shop-conversion is one of the few bright culinary sparks in this under-served town; following a recent refurb, "the food is still great and reliable" and the "service still welcoming and warm". / Details: www.alfassiarestaurant.com; @AlfassiaWindsor; 10 pm, Fri & Sat 10.30 pm, Sun 9 pm; closed Mon L.

WING, RUTLAND   5–4D

The Kings Arms Inn   £53   4 4 3
13 Top Street LE15 8SE   01572 737634
"A lovely original pub that serves everything but
ordinary pub food" – this traditional Rutland
hostelry offers "first class dishes served by
pleasant staff in a nicely renovated but homely
building". There's a "passion for provenance" and
options include in-house charcuterie from Jimmy's
Rutland Smokehouse, which is onsite. / **Details:**
www.thekingsarms-wing.co.uk/; @thekingsarmsinn. /
Accommodation: 8 rooms, from £90

WINSTON, COUNTY DURHAM   8–3B

Bridgewater Arms   £55   4 3 3
The Bridgewater Arms DL2 3RN
01325 730 302
Seemingly "aimed at visiting well-heeled Darlington
locals out for a good meal in t'country" – this
"charming one-time school" doesn't disappoint
thanks to a "very comprehensive menu (fresh fish
a speciality)" that's a "delight for the tastebuds". /
Details: www.thebridgewaterarms.com; 9 pm.

WINTERINGHAM, LINCOLNSHIRE   5–1D

Winteringham Fields   £107   4 5 4
1 Silver St DN15 9ND   01724 733096
Colin McGurran's "relaxing" restaurant with rooms
provides a comfortable destination, near the banks
of the Humber. There's the odd rumble, as there has
been for years, that it's "resting on its past laurels",
but for the most part his ambitious cooking is
praised as "first class". Its highest rated feature is its
service though – "so approachable, knowledgeable
and attentive without be overbearing" and "a credit
to the place". / **Details:** www.winteringhamfields.co.uk;
@winteringhamf; 4m SW of Humber Bridge; 9 pm;
closed Mon & Sun; No Amex; practically no walk-ins
– you must boo. / **Accommodation:** 11 rooms, from
£180

WISWELL, LANCASHIRE   5–1B

Freemasons at Wiswell   £75   5 4 4
8 Vicarage Fold Clitheroe BB7 9DF
01254 822218
"Unfairly overlooked by Michelin", this gourmet
village pub continues to produce "some of the finest
food in the Ribble Valley" and some locals "are
convinced that this place has made Northcote up
its game". "Steve Smith's cooking has a modern
idiom, but draws on classics and there's a heartiness
to many dishes that is both unexpected given its

contemporary style, but also keeps it rooted in
the building's heritage as a pub". All in all "it's fine
dining of a consistently high standard". But are
prices creeping up? In particular "the wine list takes
no prisoners (but fortunately there are some good
beers too)". / **Details:** www.freemasonswiswell.co.uk;
@Wiswellman; 9 pm, Fri & Sat 9.30 pm, Sun 6 pm;
closed Mon & Tue; No Amex; Booking max 6 may apply.

WIVETON, NORFOLK   6–3C

Wiveton Bell   £48   3 3 3
Blakeney Rd NR25 7TL   01263 740101
A "lovely" and "buzzy" gastroboozer, on the village
green, where the "wonderful gin and tonics and
delicious food (particularly the Sunday roast)"
continue to please. / **Details:** www.wivetonbell.co.uk;
@wivetonbell; 9 pm; No Amex. / **Accommodation:** 4
rooms, from £75

WOBURN, BUCKINGHAMSHIRE   3–2A

Birch   £51   3 2 2
20 Newport Rd MK17 9HX   01525 290295
This "well-run and reliable" venture – a bright,
spacious pub conversion – continues to score very
respectable marks for its "excellent" seasonal fare. /
Details: www.birchwoburn.com; between Woburn and
Woburn Sands on the Newport rd; 9.30 pm; closed
Sun D.

Paris House   £122   4 3 5
Woburn Park MK17 9QP   01525 290692
"In a beautiful setting and housed in an old Tudor
building on the Woburn Estate – the drive up to the
restaurant alone makes you feel you are somewhere
special", when you arrive at this well-known
ultra-"romantic" destination. It lost its Michelin
star a year ago, but the survey's feedback on Phil
Fanning's "professional yet unstuffy" dining room is
constantly full of praise and says that if anything it
has "raised its game" of late. In late spring 2017,
it also underwent a significant refurb. / **Details:**
www.parishouse.co.uk; @ParisHousechef; on A4012;
Wed & Thu 8.30 pm, Fri & Sat 9 pm; closed Mon, Tue
& Sun D.

WOKING, SURREY   3–3A

The Inn West End   £52   3 3 4
42 Guildford Rd GU24 9PW   01276 858652
"Now the place has had a makeover", this local
gastropub has morphed into an "upmarket pub
with an impressive menu, pleasant atmosphere and
helpful staff"; it makes a "perfect location for

a business lunch" where you're "looked after very well". / **Details:** www.the-inn.co.uk; @InnWestEnd; Mon-Sat 9.30 pm, Sun 9 pm; No trainers; children: 5+.

WOLLATON, NOTTINGHAMSHIRE   5–3D

Cods Scallops   £26   4 4 2
170 Bramcote Ln NG8 2QP 0115 985 4107
"Excellent fish 'n' chips" helps overcome the bland suburban locale at this booth-lined spot (also with wet fish counter). This is the original HQ, but a second outlet, in Sherwood, arrived in July 2016; and a third is coming soon in nearby Long Eaton. / **Details:** www.codsscallops.com; @TheCodsScallops; 9 pm, Fri & Sat 9.30 pm; closed Sun; No Amex; No bookings.

WOLVERCOTE, OXFORDSHIRE   2–2D

The Trout Inn   £49   2 2 4
195 Godstow Rd OX2 8PN 01865 510930
"An excellent location by the Thames" and "inviting Tardis-like interior" draws "crowds and busyness" to this mega-popular inn. The "unpretentious" pub grub can seem "ordinary", but most reporters find it "generous and affordable" (and if it all gets too much, "just close your eyes and think of Inspector Morse", whose favourite haunt this was). / **Details:** www.thetroutoxford.co.uk; @TheTroutOxford; 2m from junction of A40 & A44; 10 pm, Sat 10.30 pm, Sun 9 pm.

WOLVERHAMPTON, WEST MIDLANDS   5–4B

Bilash   £54   4 4 3
2 Cheapside WV1 1TU 01902 427762
Sitab Khan's acclaimed Cheapside stalwart, opposite the Civic, gained infamy when it played a starring role in the 'Curry House Conspiracy' that precipitated Tony Blair's downfall; over a decade on, and political intrigues aside, the "relaxing and sophisticated" spot retains its reputation for "unfailingly great" Indian nosh. / **Details:** www.thebilash.co.uk; @thebilash; 10.30 pm; closed Sun.

WOODBRIDGE, SUFFOLK   3–1D

The Table   £43   3 4 4
Quay St IP12 1BX 01394 382428
"Woodbridge's favourite meeting place" – this "buzzy" venue complete with courtyard garden is "the best in the area by far", with a "consistently high standard of cooking, and ever-helpful staff". / **Details:** www.thetablewoodbridge.co.uk; 9.30 pm, Sun 3 pm.

WOODLANDS, HAMPSHIRE   2–4C

Terravina, Hotel
Terravina   £70   4 5 3
174 Woodlands Rd, Netley Marsh, New Forest SO40 7GL 023 8029 3784
Acclaimed ex-Hotel du Vin guru Gerrard Bassett co-runs this "very friendly" New Forest inn with his wife Nina. There's a "fantastic wine list as expected, and coupled with decent brasserie food" it "makes for a good dining experience". Stay for the "lovely relaxed breakfast, newspapers included". / **Details:** www.hotelterravina.co.uk; @Hotel_TerraVina; 9.30 pm. / **Accommodation:** 11 rooms, from £165

WORTHING, WEST SUSSEX   3–4A

The Fish Factory   £44   4 4 2
51-53 Brighton Rd BN11 3EE 01903 207123
"It's all about the fish" (served trad-style with chips, or in popular fish mezze) at this laid-back spot – a "great choice" if you're in the mood for a "café experience". / **Details:** www.protorestaurantgroup.com; @loveproto; 10 pm.

WRINEHILL, CHESHIRE   5–2B

The Hand & Trumpet   £45   2 2 3
Main Rd CW3 9BJ 01270 820048
"One of the Brunning & Price pubs working to its successful formula": the interior is "interesting", "the beer maintains an excellent variety" and the food is consistently well rated. / **Details:** www.brunningandprice.co.uk/hand; 10 pm, Sun 9.30 pm.

WRINGTON, SOMERSET   2–2B

Ethicurean   £50   4 3 5
Barley Wood Walled Garden, Long Ln BS40 5SA 01934 863713
"Beautiful location, concept and food" – the verdict on this unusual ethical venue, which lies "adjacent to a working Victorian walled garden", making it "great for children in summer". / **Details:** www.theethicurean.com; @TheEthicurean; 8.30 pm, Sun 5 pm; closed Mon & Sun D.

WYE, KENT   3–3C

The Wife of Bath Restaurant, Rooms and Tapas Bar   £53   4 3 3
4 Upper Bridge St TN25 5AF 01233 812232
"This establishment which has been a restaurant for decades is now under new management and

you can see the improvements" at Mark Sargeant's quintessentially English Kent inn, which he's turned it into a restaurant inspired by northern Spanish cuisine: "really great tapas, staff and setting make it a great find". / **Details:** www.thewifeofbath.com; @TheWifeofBath2; off A28 between Ashford & Canterbury; 9 pm, Fri & Sat 9.30 pm, Sun 3 pm; closed Mon & Sun D; No Amex. / **Accommodation:** 5 rooms, from £95

WYKE REGIS, DORSET   2–4B

Billy Winters Bar & Diner
Ferry Bridge Boatyard, Portland Road, DT4 9JZ
01305 774954
A "wonderful situation with fantastic views" over Portland Harbour wins fans for this laid-back, basic-looking waterside operation in a jazzed-up pre-fab, serving a good variety of dude food and cocktails. (Billy Winters, by the way, is a reference to Weymouth Bay prawns). / **Details:** No bookings.

WYMONDHAM, LEICESTERSHIRE   5–3D

The Berkeley Arms   **£46**   🔳🔳🔳
59 Main St LE14 2AG   01572 787587
Neil & Louise Hitchen's "well run" and "lively" gastropub is "fast becoming a firm favourite and vying for best in the area status"; "of special mention is the extensive use of local game in season – all perfectly cooked". / **Details:** www.theberkeleyarms.co.uk; @TheBekeleyArms; 9 pm, Fri & Sat 9.30 pm, Sun 3 pm; closed Mon & Sun D; No Amex.

YEOVIL, DORSET   2–3B

White Post   **£54**   🔳🔳🔳
Rimpton Hill BA22 8AR   019 3585 1525
Brett & Kelly Sutton are "succeeding in spades" at their simply styled pub – now a restaurant-with-rooms; "Kelly always finds time to chat", and Brett turns out "top quality, local and fabulous" food, with the "B&B and 10-course tasting menu" being "a joy to eat and fantastic value too". Fact fans: the Somerset/Dorset border runs through the pub. / **Details:** thewhitepost.com; @thewhitepost; 9 pm.

YORK, NORTH YORKSHIRE   5–1D

Ambiente   **£28**   🔳🔳🔳
31 Fossgate YO1 9TA   01904 638252
A large and relatively recent outpost of this four-strong York-born chain (also in Leeds and Hull) with the "best atmosphere" of the hometown branches; its "lovely" tapas is praised for its "great value" by

fans – critics say it's "less exciting than it was" or attack some "ill-judged" combinations. / **Details:** www.ambiente-tapas.co.uk; 10 pm.

Bettys   **£44**   🔳🔳🔳
6-8 St Helen's Square YO1 8QP   01904 659142
"In a very pleasant timewarp" – a "splendid" room "with its Art Deco windows and mirrors", where a "pianist plays through the afternoon" – this institution continues to turn out "legendary" vanilla slices, "perfect sandwiches, cheese scones I'd travel miles for" and a "real treat" of a breakfast. Given the above, it's "worth every penny and every minute spent queuing up". / **Details:** www.bettys.co.uk/tea-rooms/locations/york; @Bettys1919; 9 pm; No Amex; Booking lunch only.

Cafe No. 8 Bistro   **£46**   🔳🔳🔳
8 Gillygate YO31 7EQ   01904 653074
"Amazing food from a tiny kitchen underneath the medieval walls" has won a culinary reputation for this "very cramped" bistro (with cute garden). "It now also has pop ups in the Art Gallery and the Merchant Adventurers Hall with excellent cake". / **Details:** www.cafeno8.co.uk; @cafeno8; 10 pm; No Amex.

Le Cochon Aveugle   **£79**   🔳🔳🔳
37 Walmgate YO1 9TX   01904 640222
"Sit back, relax and trust that you will eat a stupendously exciting meal" at Josh Overington's simple-looking, small venture – "a quirky outfit", whose "blind tasting menu" (you are served whatever the chefs decide to feed you) creates a sense of "pure theatre". "The food is full of surprises" and married with "some extraordinary wine pairings overseen by sommelier partner Vicky Roberts, from an entirely French wine list with something like 80-100 bins, and including some really unusual regions". "Staff are superb and it's entertaining to see them hard a work in the kitchen which is separated from the diners by a low wall". (They also run Cave du Cochon a few doors down – a natural wine bar, serving small plates, cheeses and charcuterie). / **Details:** www.lecochonaveugleyork.com; @lecochonaveugle; 9 pm; closed Mon & Sun.

Il Paradiso Del Cibo   **£38**   🔳🔳🔳
40 Walmgate YO1 9TJ   01904 611444
"Fabulous pizzas, fabulous fish and pasta, fabulous service…" – you "can't go wrong" at this "unique and quirky" Sardinian; "if you like watching Italian football on TV whilst eating" and if you don't mind the intimate setting, "you will truly be in paradise" (albeit one that's a "bit swamped by Tripadvisor devotees"). / **Details:** www.ilparadisodelciboyork.com; 10 pm; closed Mon D, Tue D, Wed D, Thu D & Fri D.

The Ivy St Helen's Square **£54**
2 Saint Helen's Square YO1 8QP awaiting tel
*In a 'roll-out' that would do McDonald's proud,
this iconic brand has gone for it this year, opening
virtually simultaneously in practically all of the UK's
top restaurant cities. The ambition is impressive: let's
hope standards hold up better than they did when,
for example 'Browns' tried to pull off a similar trick. /
Details: www.theivyyork.com; @theivyyork.*

Mannion & Co **£28** **3|3|3**
1 Blake St YO1 8QJ 01904 631030
*This city-centre deli-bakery "can be a bit cramped
and chaotic" but is "worth it for the food" – "tasty,
high quality produce" parlayed in sandwiches,
sharing platters and cakes (and "with interesting
specials") makes it "an excellent place for a bite". /
Details: www.mannionandco.co.uk; @MannionsofYork;
L only; No bookings.*

Melton's **£58** **4|4|3**
7 Scarcroft Rd YO23 1ND 01904 634341
*"In an old terraced house outside the main
city centre" (just beyond the city walls), this
"unpretentious" restaurant has long been a
mainstay of York's dining scene and, despite being
"away from the tourist traps", continues to be
one of the city's best-known destinations. There
are lunch and early evening deals as well as à
la carte and tasting options (5 courses for £50),
and there's "a great value wine list" too. The aim
is not for experimental cuisine, but "they keep
things up to date", and "there's a strong emphasis
on local produce". Results are "consistently
excellent" and "expertly presented". / Details:
www.meltonsrestaurant.co.uk; @meltons1; 9.30 pm;
closed Mon & Sun; No Amex.*

Middlethorpe Hall **£78** **3|3|4**
Bishopthorpe Road YO23 2GB 01904 641241
*This "lovely" country house with expansive gardens
and "elegant Georgian dining room" makes a
"special venue". Set lunch is "a bit of a bargain and
makes for a very civilised, good value day out", and
afternoon tea is also a key attraction. / Details:
www.middlethorpe.com; 9.30 pm; No shorts; children:
6+. / Accommodation: 29 rooms, from £199*

Mr Ps Curious Tavern **£39** **2|3|3**
71 Low Petergate YO1 7HY 01904 521177
*Yorkshire celeb chef, Andrew Pern's latest brainchild
is a self-consciously zany place, fitted out with fox's
tails and high stools, and offering "quirky small
sharing plates but with a Yorkshire twist" ("with
delights such as pressed mallard"). "Some dishes
are much better than others" though, but "it's
always buzzy". / Details: mrpscurioustavern.co.uk/;
@MrPsTavern; 9.30 pm.*

Mumbai Lounge **£35** **3|2|3**
47 Fossgate YO1 9TF 01904 654155
*A vibrant and "upmarket" Indian set apart by its
unusual flavour combinations (King Prawn Malibu,
anyone?); the service elicited schizophrenic feedback
this year – perfect for some tastes, tiresome to
others. / Details: www.mumbailoungeyork.co.uk;
11.30 pm, Fri & Sat midnight; closed Fri L.*

Rattle Owl **£50** **4|3|2**
104 Micklegate YO16 6JX 01904 658658
*Fans hail an "outstanding dining experience from
start to finish" at this diminutive joint – formerly
the Blake Head Bookshop and Vegetarian Café –
featuring "creative" local/seasonal food that's "spot
on". / Details: www.rattleowl.co.uk; @TheRattleOwl;
9.30 pm; closed Mon & Sun D.*

Skosh **£45** **5|4|3**
98 Micklegate YO1 6JX 01904 634849
*"I would be more cynical if it wasn't so brilliantly
executed!" – "Neil Bentnick has made his mark in
York in less than a year" with this "rather minimal,
up-market tapas newcomer", which comes
complete with "empathetic service and a relaxed
approach". Portions from the "small, ever-changing
and well-thought-out menu" may be "dainty" ("you
won't emerge feeling that full") but "such is the
inventiveness with flavours, textures and ingredients
you do leave feeling exhilarated that food can be so
interesting" ("only good manners stopped us licking
the plates clean!)". / Details: www.skoshyork.co.uk;
@skoshyork.*

Star Inn the City **£65** **1|1|3**
Lendal Engine House, Museum Street YO1 7DR
01904 619208
*"Try harder Andrew Pern!" His city cousin of the
Star Inn at Harome has a "beautiful setting" near
the river, but is far too "hit and miss". "Why the
food can't be better is a mystery" and although
some fans do hail its "deft British fare cooked with
passion", there are too many sceptics who feel
"it's not in the same class" with "real highs and
lows observed over a number of visits". / Details:
www.starinnthecity.co.uk; @Starinnthecity; 10 pm.*

The Whippet Inn **£42** **3|4|3**
15 North St YO1 6JD 01904 500660
*"A trendy steak restaurant in an old pub in a back
street" – this "comfortable and cosy spot" is "the
top place in town for a steak" and wins nothing but
praise for its locally sourced meat and "friendly"
service; eye-catching wallpaper too… / Details:
www.thewhippetinn.co.uk; @WhippetWhere.*

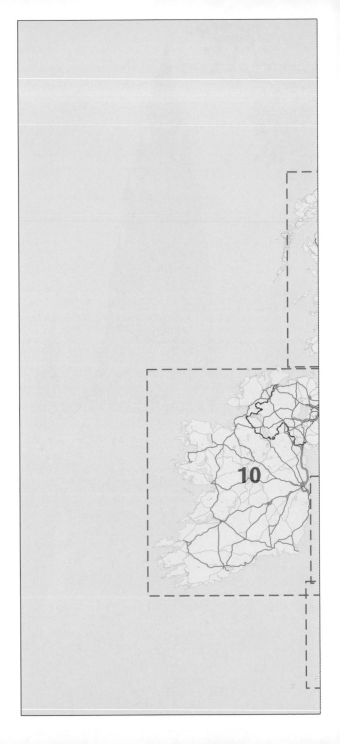

10

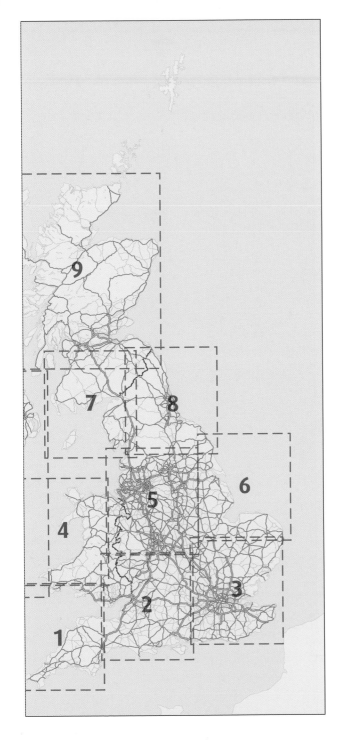

MAP 1

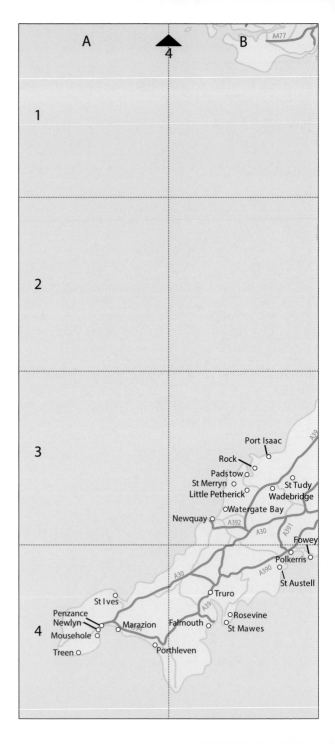

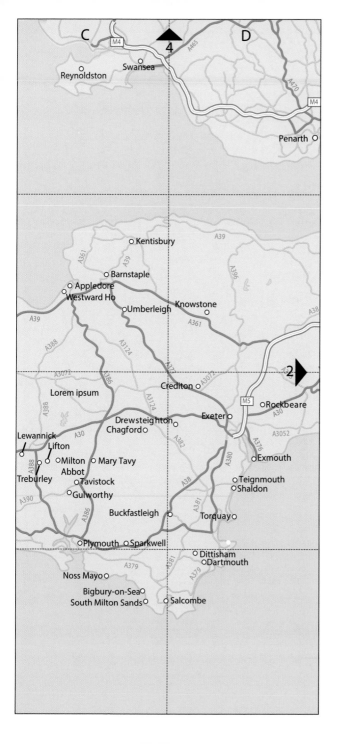

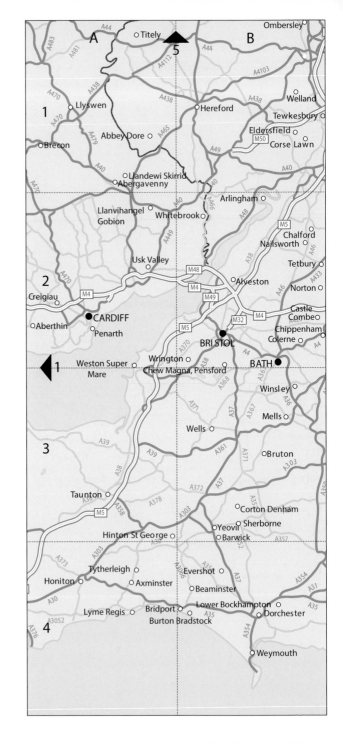

MAP 2

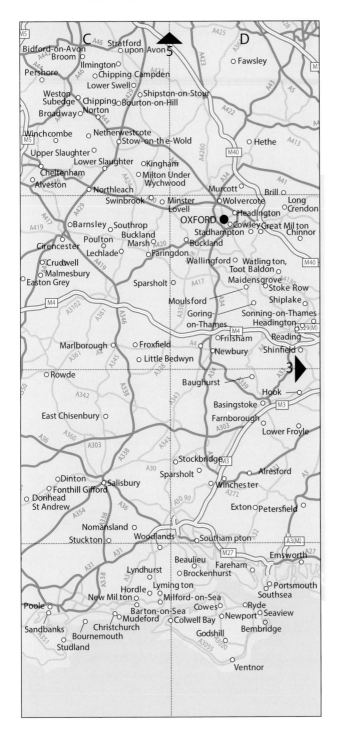

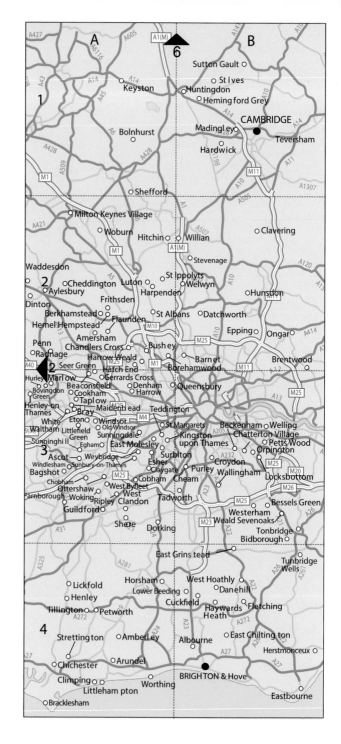

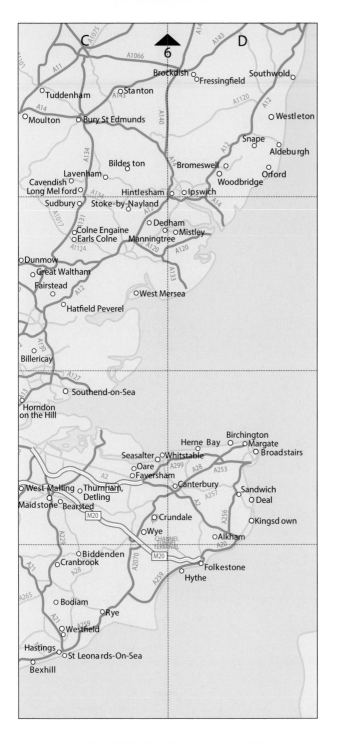

MAP 3

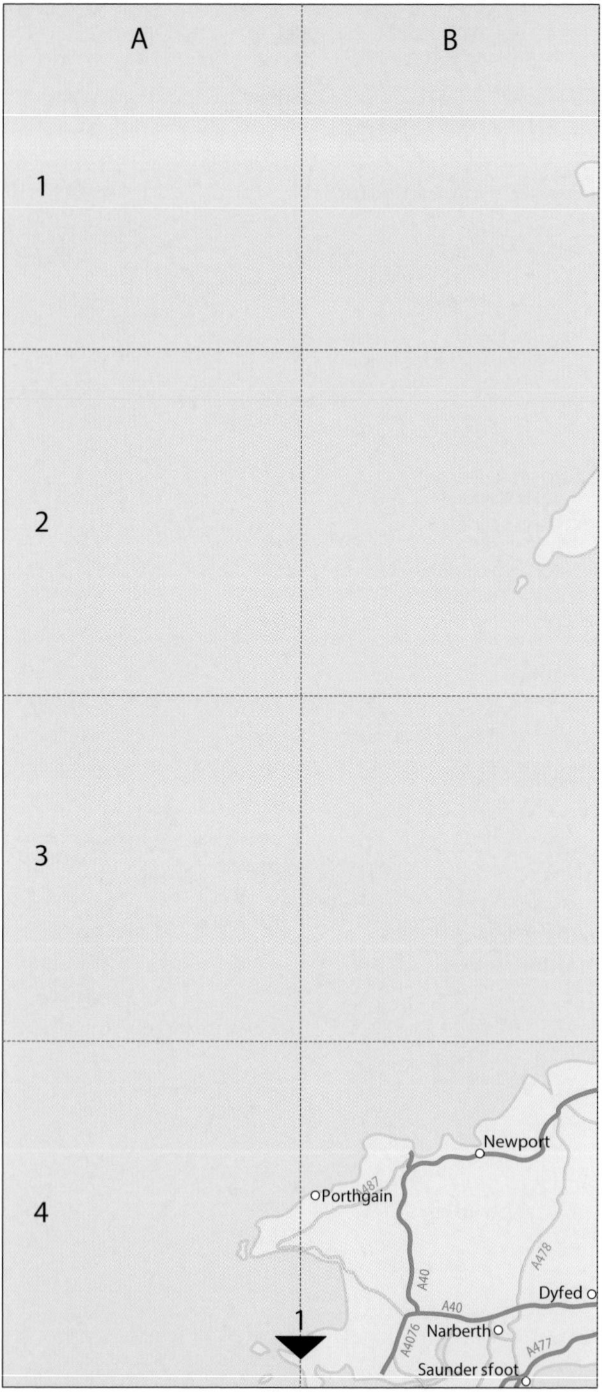

MAP 4

	A	B
1		
2		
3		
4		Newport ○Porthgain A487 A40 A4076 A40 Narberth○ Saunder sfoot ○ A478 Dyfed ○ A477

▼1

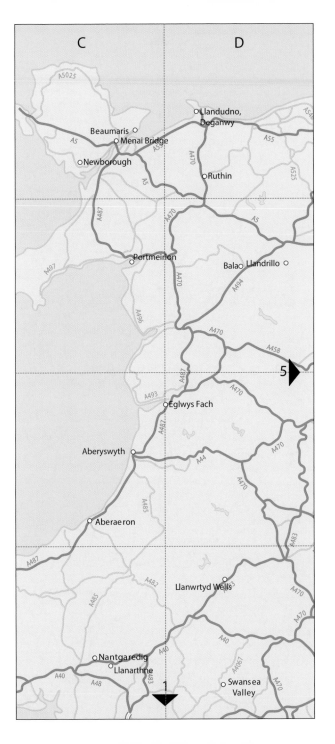

MAP 4

C | D

Llandudno,
Deganwy

Beaumaris ○
○ Menai Bridge

○ Newborough

○ Ruthin

Portmeirion ○

Bala ○ Llandrillo ○

5 ▶

○ Eglwys Fach

Aberyswyth ○

○ Aberaeron

Llanwrtyd Wells ○

○ Nantgaredig
○ Llanarthne

○ Swansea
Valley

1 ▼

MAP 5

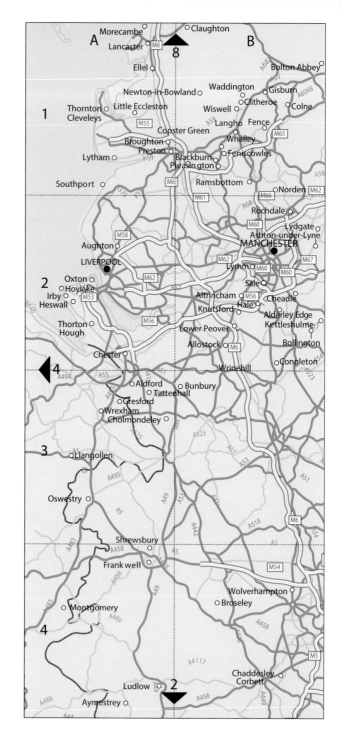

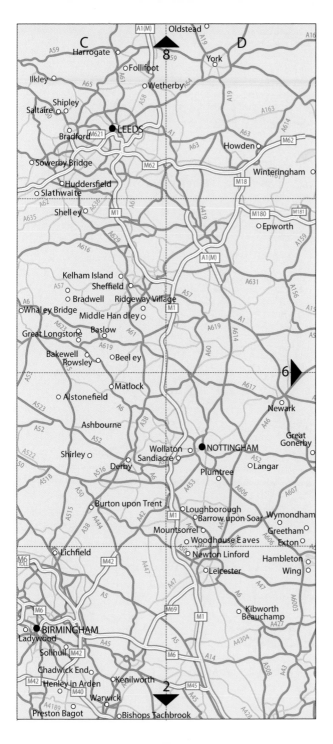

MAP 5

MAP 6

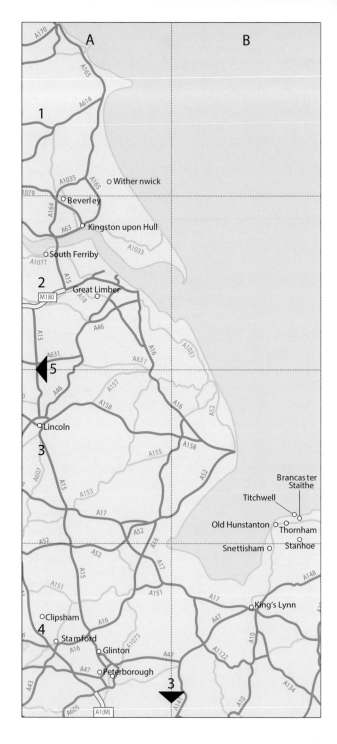

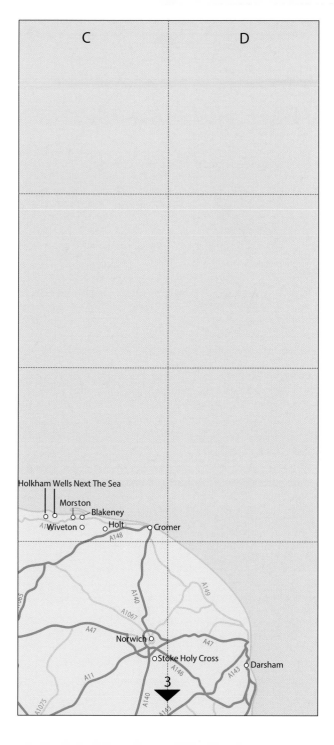

MAP 6

C

D

Holkham Wells Next The Sea

Morston

Blakeney

Wiveton O   Holt   O Cromer

A148

A140

A149

A1067

A47

A47

Norwich O

Stoke Holy Cross

A146   Darsham

A143

A11

3

A140

A1075

A143

MAP 7

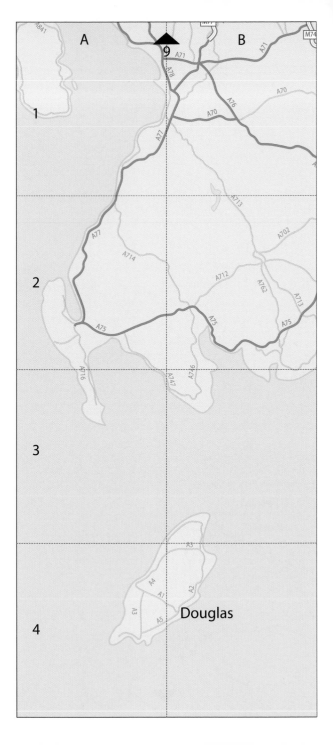

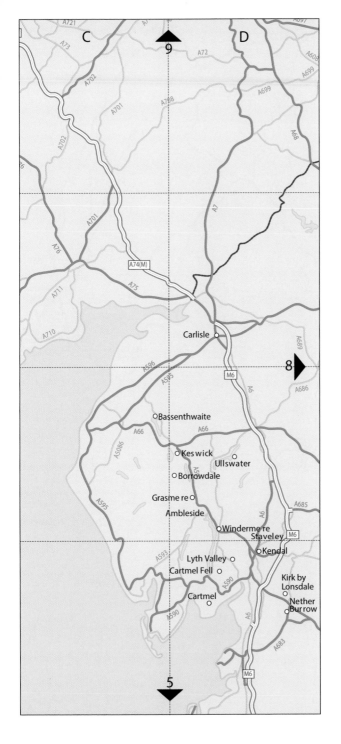

MAP 7

MAP 8

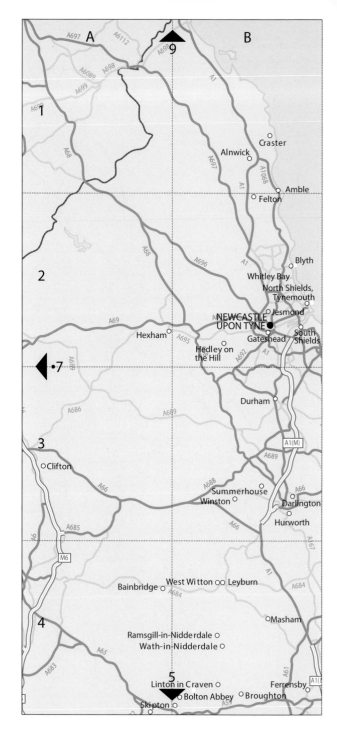

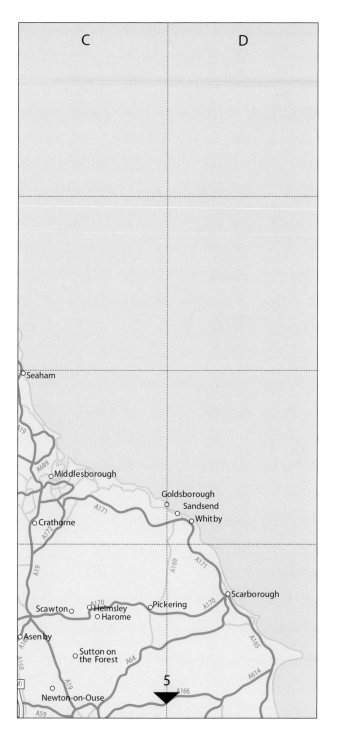

MAP 8

C

D

Seaham

A19

A689

Middlesborough

A171

Goldsborough

Sandsend

Crathorne

A172

Whitby

A19

A169

A171

Scarborough

A170

Scawton

Helmsley

Pickering

A170

Harome

Asenby

A165

Sutton on
the Forest

A64

A614

5

Newton-on-Ouse

A166

A59

MAP 9

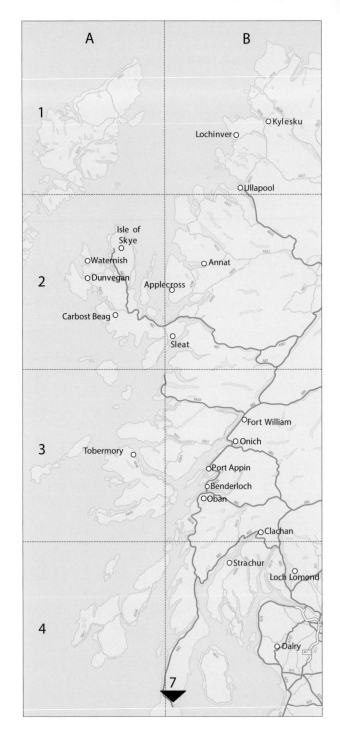

MAP 9

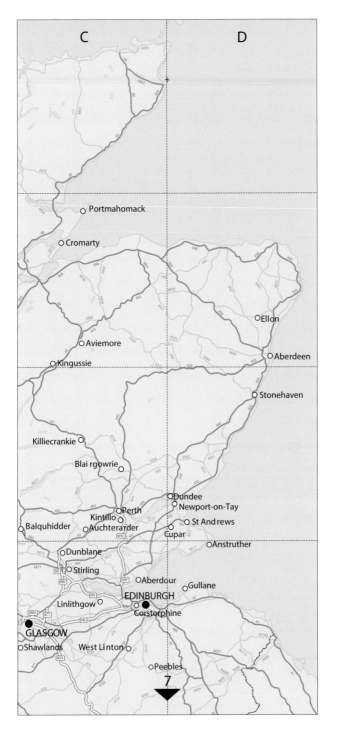

C

D

○ Portmahomack

○ Cromarty

○ Ellon

○ Aviemore

○ Kingussie

○ Aberdeen

○ Stonehaven

Killiecrankie ○

Blairgowrie ○

○ Dundee
○ Newport-on-Tay

○ Perth
Kintillo ○
○ Balquhidder   ○ Auchterarder
Cupar   ○ St Andrews

○ Anstruther

○ Dunblane
○ Stirling

○ Aberdour   ○ Gullane

EDINBURGH

Linlithgow ○
● Corstorphine

● GLASGOW
○ Shawlands   West Linton ○

○ Peebles

▼ 7

MAP **10**

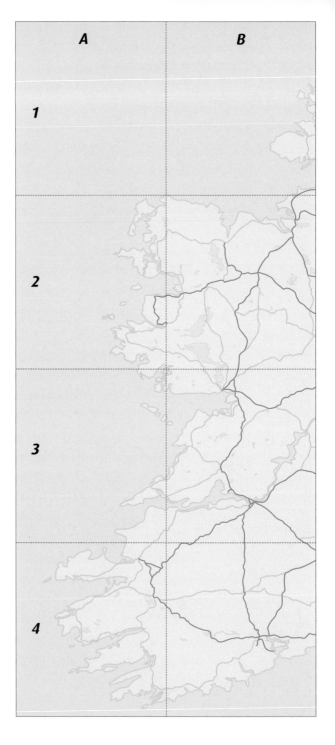

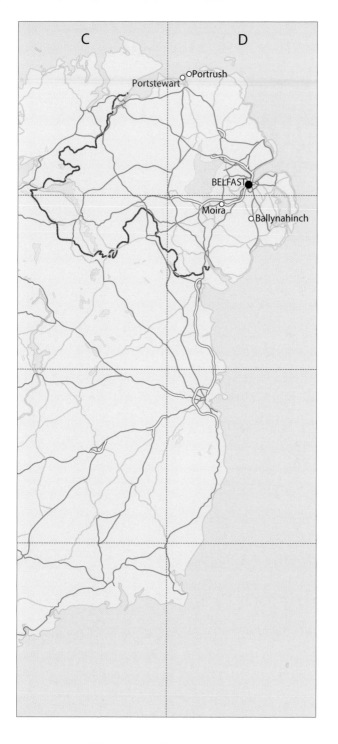

MAP **10**

ALPHABETICAL INDEX

ALPHABETICAL INDEX

ALPHABETICAL INDEX

ALPHABETICAL INDEX

ALPHABETICAL INDEX

ALPHABETICAL INDEX

ALPHABETICAL INDEX